Government and Not-For-Profit Accounting

Concepts and Practices

Government and Not-For-Profit Accounting

Concepts and Practices

Michael H. Granof
University of Texas, Austin

WILEY

JOHN WILEY & SONS, INC.
New York • Chichester • Weinheim • Brisbane • Singapore • Toronto

Acquisitions Editor	Rebecca Hope
Marketing Manager	Wendy Goldner
Production Editor	Edward Winkleman
Designer	Laura Boucher
Photo Editor	Hilary Newman
Illustration Coordinator	Anna Melhorn
Cover Photo	© Chad Ehlers/Tony Stone Images/New York, Inc.

This book was set 10/12 Janson by TC Systems Inc. and printed and bound by Donnelley/Willard. The cover was printed by Phoenix.

Portions of various GASB documents, copyright by the Governmental Accounting Standards Board, 401 Merritt 7, P.O. Box 5116, Norwalk, Connecticut 06856-5116, U.S.A. are reprinted with permission. Complete copies of these documents are available from the GASB.

FASB Concepts Statement No. 4, *Objectives of Financial Reporting by Nonbusiness Organizations*, and Statements No. 116, *Accounting for Contributions Received and Contributions Made*, and No. 117, *Financial Statements of Not-for-Profit Organizations*, are copyrighted by the Financial Accounting Standards Board, 401 Merritt 7, P.O. Box 5116, Norwalk, Connecticut 06856-5116, U.S.A. Portions are reprinted with permission. Complete copies of these documents are available from the FASB.

Materials from Uniform CPA Examinations and Unofficial Answers, Copyright © 1987–1994 by the American Institute of Certified Public Accountants, Inc. are reprinted (or adapted) with permission.

Library of Congress Cataloging-in-Publication Data
Granof, Michael H.
    Government and not-for-profit accounting : concepts and practices
/ Michael H. Granof.
      p.   cm.
    Includes index.
    ISBN 0-471-11588-6 (cloth : alk. paper)
    1. Finance, Public—United States—Accounting. 2. Finance,
Public—Accounting—Standards—United States. 3. Nonprofit
organizations—United States—Accounting. 4. Nonprofit
organizations—Accounting—Standards—United States. I. Title.
HJ9801.G7 1998
657'.835—dc21   97-28116
                                    CIP

Printed in the United States of America

10 9 8 7 6 5 4 3 2 1

In Memory of
My mother, Diana S. Granof (a teacher)
My father, David H. Granof (a CPA)

PREFACE

Governmental and not-for-profit accounting is perhaps the most intellectually demanding area of accounting. Business accounting focuses on profit, a relatively well-defined metric. By contrast, governmental and not-for-profit accounting is concerned with a wide variety of measures, most of which relate to the specific objectives of each individual organization. These objectives, however, are typically intangible and not readily specifiable, let alone quantifiable. Moreover, courses in governmental and not-for-profit accounting often encompass in a single course the functional areas of accounting, including external financial reporting, management accounting, and auditing, that are themselves the subject of individual courses.

Many of the problems and issues with which governmental and not-for-profit policy makers, managers, and practitioners must deal are conceptually and politically intractable. In this text, I strive to make the discipline not only comprehensible but also—at least to the extent feasible—enjoyable.

OBJECTIVES

This text aims to provide an understanding of the unique features of governmental and not-for-profit accounting. Now may be the best of times to be studying governmental accounting, as the Governmental Accounting Standards Board (GASB) is undertaking fundamental changes to the existing accounting and reporting models. By comparing current standards with those that are proposed and by assessing (and hopefully debating) their respective advantages and limitations, students have a unique opportunity to gain an understanding of the rationale for both the current standards and the proposed alternatives.

On the other hand, the changing governmental and not-for-profit environment creates special challenges. By having to become acquainted with both current and proposed practices, students can readily become confused between the two. Nevertheless, the accounting and reporting standards of five years from now may bear scant resemblance to those of today. For a text to present current accounting practices as if they will endure forever would be unconscionable. Students of today must be aware not only of what is, but also of what might be. Whereas some texts relegate proposed standards to either a separate chapter or to chapter appendices, this text **integrates them in the main body of applicable chapters.** It thereby emphasizes that a current accounting standard is generally only one of several possibilities. To minimize the risk of confusion, **it sets off the proposed practices in shaded type.**

Although the text addresses a range of subjects far broader than those covered on the CPA exam, it acknowledges the importance of that exam to many students. To help students prepare for the exam, **the end-of-chapter material includes most of the government-related questions that have appeared on the exams over the last decade**. All of these questions are answerable from the text itself.

The text strives to prepare students for, and encourages them to pursue, governmental and not-for-profit careers. Although it surely will furnish readers with skills and knowledge required in their first positions in accounting, its real goal is to prepare them for their last. Indeed, it seeks to lay the foundation for professional leadership—for students to become, for example, members of standard-settings boards, chief financial officers of governmental or not-for-profit organizations, or CPA firm partners specializing in governmental and not-for-profit entities.

The text also seeks to strengthen students' understanding of accounting in general, not merely governmental and not-for-profit accounting. As will be evident in the first few chapters, almost every issue in business accounting has a counterpart in governmental and not-for-profit accounting. Like business accounting, governmental and not-for-profit accounting is concerned with questions of revenue and expenditure recognition and of asset and liability valuation. Some issues are resolved similarly; some differently. **By approaching issues from a conceptual perspective and showing how issues of governmental and not-for-profit accounting are merely aspects of more global questions, this text will provide readers with greater insight into all aspects of the accounting discipline.**

Finally, and perhaps most significantly, the text is meant to expand students' minds and to enhance their abilities to read, write, and reason. To promote what is today termed *critical thinking*, it presents accounting issues so as to lead students to an understanding of the underlying concepts and to encourage them to draw their own conclusions as to how they should be resolved. The end-of-chapter material is challenging. Seldom will students be able to turn back to a comparable example in the text and simply replicate journal entries.

ORGANIZATION

The text differs organizationally from the typical text in governmental and not-for-profit accounting. Most other texts contain approximately twelve chapters pertaining to governmental accounting and then three or more chapters dealing with not-for-profits—one each for universities, hospitals, health and welfare organizations, and other types of entities. **This text, by contrast, integrates the material on not-for-profits with that on governments.** With its 1993 Statements No. 116, *Accounting for Contributions Received and Contributions Made* and No. 117, *Financial Statements of Not-for-Profit Organizations*, the FASB eliminated the key accounting and reporting differences among the various types of not-for-profit organizations. Now, therefore, the benefits of arranging the text around issues exceeds that of around organizations. The issue arrangement better facilitates comparisons between the FASB's and the GASB's approach to similar questions and enables students to fully appreciate the reasons why they might have resolved them differently. However, since the text clearly delineates the not-for-profit from the governmental materials, an instructor who prefers the traditional arrangement can easily identify the applicable sections and assign them as he or she deems most appropriate.

SPECIAL FEATURES

To enable students to obtain hands-on experience in reviewing and analyzing an actual comprehensive annual financial report (CAFR), **the text features a continuing problem.** In the first chapter, students are asked to obtain a CAFR and in subsequent chapters are required to answer specific questions about it. Recognizing the advantages of having all students work with the same CAFR, **the publisher has arranged** with the Metropolitan Government of Nashville and Davidson County to make available its annual report on a CD-ROM.

To enable students to take advantage of computer technology in another way, the author and publisher have provided a web page devoted to the text. This page will be characterized by two innovations. First, it will provide students with helpful hints to the text's end-of-chapter problems. Most of these will be in the form of leading questions that will point students in the direction toward a solution but not provide a specific answer. Second, it will keep students and instructors abreast of ongoing developments in the area of governmental and not-for-profit accounting and reporting. It will report on exposure drafts and official pronouncement, as well as on noteworthy news stories and emerging issues. Instructors can obtain information on both the CD-ROMs and the web site by contacting their Wiley representatives.

ACKNOWLEDGMENTS

In writing this text I have been fortunate to benefit from the sound guidance of academic and professional colleagues. Martin Ives, who has served as a member of both the GASB and the Federal Accounting Standards Advisory Board and has held positions at the local, state, and federal level, performed a thorough review of the text. His recommendations were always on target. Jay Fountain, a senior member of the GASB staff, and probably the world's expert on service efforts and accomplishments, reviewed Chapter 15, "Managing for Results." Robert Bramlett, a staff member of the Federal Accounting Standards Advisory Board, helped lead me through the maze of federal accounting and reporting.

Martin Ives and Allan R. Drebin (of Northwestern University) reviewed all of the end of chapter questions, exercises, and problems as well as the solutions that appear in an accompanying solutions manual. Owing to their help, the end of chapter materials and the solutions are both clearer and more correct than they would have been without it.

Gretchen Boyd was of extraordinary help in developing exercises, reviewing the manuscript, preparing the glossary, and performing a variety of administrative tasks. I am indebted also to Mark Holtzman and Susan Goodyear for their help in arranging the text for publication.

I am also extremely grateful for the helpful comments of the following manuscript reviewers: L. Charles Bokemeier (University of Michigan—Flint); Bruce Chase (Radford University); Lola Dudley (Eastern Illinois University); Carol A. Hilton (Ohio University); Jesse W. Hughes (Old Dominion University); Martin Ives (Pace University); Penny Marquette (University of Akron); Lucille Montondon (Southwest Texas State University); Marc A. Rubin (Miami University); Mary Alice Seville (Oregon State University); William T. Wrege (Ball State University); Alexander E.C. Yuen (San Francisco University).

M.H.G.
Austin, Texas

CONTENTS

CHAPTER 4

RECOGNIZING REVENUE IN GOVERNMENTAL FUNDS 127

CHAPTER 5

RECOGNIZING EXPENDITURES IN GOVERNMENTAL FUNDS 168

CHAPTER 6

REVENUES AND EXPENDITURES IN OTHER NOT-FOR-PROFIT ORGANIZATIONS 211

CHAPTER 10

CHAPTER 11

CHAPTER 12
....

ISSUES OF REPORTING, DISCLOSURE, AND FINANCIAL ANALYSIS   486

CHAPTER 13
....

USING COST INFORMATION TO MANAGE AND CONTROL   527

CHAPTER 14

CHAPTER 15

CHAPTER 16

The Government and Not-For-Profit Environment

Governments and not-for-profit organizations have much in common with businesses. However, colleges of business recognize that the differences between the two environments are sufficiently pronounced that they have established a separate course in governmental and not-for-profit accounting apart from the usual courses pertaining to accounting functions—financial accounting, managerial accounting, auditing, and information systems.

Every accounting issue or problem that affects governments and not-for-profits has its counterpart in the business sector. But the distinctions between the accounting for governments and not-for-profits and for businesses are so pronounced that the two disciplines warrant specialized textbooks, separate statements of concepts, and separate accounting principles and practices. As we shall see in this text, some of these differences may be justified by substantive distinctions in their operating environments, whereas others are the result of long-standing traditions or differences in the composition and perspective of standard-setting boards.

There is one accounting rule-making authority for governments—the **Governmental Accounting Standards Board (GASB).** There is another for all other types of enterprises—the **Financial Accounting Standards Board (FASB).** The FASB has issued several statements of accounting concepts for businesses and another for not-for-profits, but it has not issued a statement of concepts for any particular industry within the business environment.

This chapter is divided into five sections. The first addresses the ways in which governments and not-for-profits differ from businesses, and why they require unique accounting principles and practices. The second points out characteristics of governments and not-for-profits that might not distinguish them from businesses but nevertheless have significant implications for accounting and reporting. The third contrasts governments and not-for-profits, emphasizing that although they have much in common, they also differ significantly. The fourth provides an overview of financial reporting for governments and not-for-profits, highlighting key user groups, their information needs, and the resultant objectives of financial reporting. It also addresses the question of whether differences in accounting practices really matter. The fifth spotlights the GASB, the FASB, and other authorities responsible for establishing accounting and reporting standards.

In this text we have chosen the term *not-for-profit* rather than the equally acceptable *nonprofit*. *Not-for-profit* appears to be gaining in popularity, perhaps because it better differentiates entities that don't intend to earn a profit from those that simply fail to do so.

HOW DO GOVERNMENTS AND NOT-FOR-PROFITS COMPARE WITH BUSINESSES?

Governments and not-for-profits differ significantly from businesses in ways that have profound implications for financial reporting. For the most part, governments and not-for-profits provide services targeted to groups of constituents, advocating a political or social cause, or carrying out research or other activities for the betterment of society. The objectives of governments and not-for-profits cannot generally be expressed in dollars and cents, and they are often ambiguous and not easily quantifiable. Moreover, governments and not-for-profits have relationships with the parties providing their resources that are unlike those of businesses.

As implied by the designation *not-for-profits*, the goal of governments and similar organizations is something other than earning profit. A key objective of financial reporting is to provide information about an entity's performance during a period. The main objective of a typical business is to earn a profit—to assure that over the life of the enterprise, its owners are returned more cash than they contributed. Accordingly, financial statements that key on net income are in harmony with the entity's main objective. Specifically, an income statement is a report on how well the entity achieved its goals. To be sure, businesses may have objectives that go beyond "the bottom line." They may seek to promote the welfare of their executives and employees, improve the communities in which they are located, and produce goods that will enhance the quality of life. Financial accounting and reporting, however, are concerned almost exclusively with the goal of maximizing either profits or some variant of it, such as cash flows.

The financial reports of governments and not-for-profits can provide information as to an organization's inflows (revenues) and outflows (expenditures) of cash and other resources. As a general rule, an excess of expenditures over revenues, particularly for an extended period of time, signals financial distress or poor managerial performance. However, an excess of revenues over expenditures is not necessarily commendable. An excess of revenues over expenditures may be achieved, for example, merely by reducing the services provided to constituents—which may be at odds with the entity's objectives.

If the financial statements of a government or not-for-profit incorporate only monetary measures, such as dollars and cents, they cannot possibly provide the information necessary to assess the organization's performance. For an organization to report properly on its accomplishments, it must augment its financial statements to include nonfinancial data that relate to its objectives. A school, for example, might include statistics on student achievement, such as test scores or graduation rates. A center for the homeless, might present data on the number of people fed or adequately housed.

Governments and not-for-profits are governed by their budgets, not by the marketplace. Through the budget process, these organizations control or strongly influence both their revenues and expenditures. The revenues of a government may be determined by legislative fiat, and if they are, the government may not be subject to the forces of competition faced by businesses. Those of not-for-profits, while they cannot be established by legal mandate, may be obtained from contributions, dues, tuition, or user charges—none of which are comparable to the sales of a business.

Governments and many not-for-profits establish the level of services that they will provide, calculate their cost, and then set tax rates and other fees to generate the revenues required to pay for them. Colleges and universities, unlike businesses, do not set tuition charges at the highest level that the "market will bear." Instead, they calculate operating costs, estimate contributions, endowment revenues, and other sources of funds, and then set tuition charges at the rate necessary to cover the shortfall. Similarly, fraternities and sororities calculate their expenditures for housing, food, and social activities, and then set dues and other fees accordingly. In sum, expenditures drive revenues.

Although governments and not-for-profits do not participate in competitive markets, they cannot simply raise revenues without regard to their services or increase taxes without limit. Governments may be constrained by political forces. Universities

DIFFERENT MISSIONS

BUDGETS, NOT THE MARKETPLACE, GOVERN

EXPENDITURES MAY DRIVE REVENUES

may have to restrict tuition rates to approximately those of peer schools. Further, some not-for-profits such as the United Way or organizations that fund medical research base their expenditures exclusively on their revenues. The more funds they raise, the more they can spend.

THE BUDGET, NOT THE ANNUAL REPORT, IS THE MOST SIGNIFICANT FINANCIAL DOCUMENT

For businesses, the annual report is the most significant financial document. A major company's announcement of annual earnings (the preview of the annual report) makes front-page news. By contrast, its annual budget is nothing more than an internal document, seldom made available to investors or the general public.

A government or not-for-profit's release of its annual report is customarily ignored by both organizational insiders and outsiders. Seldom does the report contain surprises, for if revenues and expenditures were markedly different than what were initially budgeted, the entity probably was required to amend the budget during the year.

For governments and not-for-profits the budget takes center stage—properly so, because the budget is the culmination of the political process. It encapsulates most of the decisions of consequence made by the organization. It determines which constituents give to the entity and which receive; which activities are supported, which are assessed.

Because it is so important, the budget, unlike the annual report, is a source of constituent concern and controversy. Government budget hearings often draw standing-room-only crowds to the legislative chambers. The budget debates of church and synagogue members are frequently marked by fervor more intense than the congregants' worship services.

A government's budget may be backed by the force of law. Government officials are ordinarily prohibited from spending more than what was budgeted. Indeed, they can go to jail for severe violations of budgetary mandates. The budget is not a document to be taken lightly.

BUDGETS DRIVE ACCOUNTING AND FINANCIAL REPORTING

Constituents of an organization want information on the extent of adherence to the budget. They want assurance that the organization has not spent more than was authorized; they want to know whether revenue and expenditure estimates were reliable. The accounting system and the resultant financial reports must be designed to provide that information.

Also, managers need an accounting system that provides them with ongoing data as to whether they are on target to meet budget projections. Even more critically, they need a system that either prevents them from overspending or sets off warning signals when they are about to do so. The budget is a control device, but it requires the support of a complementary accounting and reporting system.

Finally, auditors and other parties concerned with the organization's performance require a basis on which to evaluate accomplishments. As will be discussed in subsequent chapters, state-of-the-art budgets establish that basis by indicating not only how much will be spent on a particular activity, but what the activity will achieve. A post-period assessment can then focus not only on whether the entity met its revenue and expenditure projections but, equally important, on whether it attained what was expected of it. Evaluators can then assess organizational efficiency by comparing *inputs* (such as dollar expenditures) with *outcomes* (results). The accounting system should be fashioned so as to facilitate this comparison, assuring that the organization reports and categorizes both revenues and expenditures in a way that is consistent with the budget. Currently, few governments and not-for-profits have established the budgetary and accounting systems to measure and report adequately on the nonmonetary aspects of their performance. However, accounting standard-setting authorities have recognized the importance of performance measures and are taking steps to assure that eventually they will be provided routinely.

Most governments are required by law, and most not-for-profits are expected by policy, to balance their operating budgets. Balanced operating budgets assure that in any particular period revenues cover expenditures and that, as a group, the entity's constituents pay for what they receive. If organizations fail to balance their budgets—and borrow to cover operating deficits—then the cost of benefits enjoyed by the citizens of today must be borne by those of tomorrow.

NEED TO ASSURE INTERPERIOD EQUITY

The concept that constituents pay for the services that they receive and do not shift the burdens to their children has traditionally been labeled **intergenerational equity.** In recent years, to emphasize that entities should not transfer the costs even to future years, to say nothing of future generations, the term **interperiod equity** has been accepted as more appropriate. Unfortunately, as will be discussed later in the text, some balanced budget laws are written so as to promote interperiod equity more in form than in economic substance.

To maintain interperiod equity, the accounting systems of governments and not-for-profits must provide information as to whether this objective is being attained. Table 1–1 compares fiscal practices that promote interperiod equity with those that do not.

The concept of interperiod equity does not suggest that governments should

---

TABLE 1–1
Fiscal Practices that Promote or Undermine Interperiod Equity

Promote	Undermine
1. Setting aside resources for employee pensions during the years in which the employees provide their services.	1. Paying the pensions of retired employees out of current operating funds.
2. Issuing conventional 30-year bonds to finance the purchase of a new building that is expected to have a useful life of 30 years; repaying the bonds, along with appropriate amounts of interest, over the 30-year period	2. Financing the purchase of the new building with 30-year zero-coupon bonds that permit the entire amount of principal and interest to be paid upon the maturity of the bonds; making no provision to set aside resources for payment of principal and interest on the bonds until the year they mature.
3. Paying the current-year costs of an administrative staff out of current operating funds.	3. Issuing 30-year bonds to finance the current-year operating costs of an administrative staff.
4. Charging payments of wages and salaries made in the first week of the current fiscal year to the previous fiscal year, that in which the employees actually provided their services.	4. Charging wages and salaries applicable to services provided in the last week of the current fiscal year in the following fiscal year, that in which the payments were made.
5. Charging the cost of supplies as expenditures in the year in which they were used rather than when they were purchased.	5. Charging the cost of supplies as expenditures in the year they were purchased irrespective of the year in which they were used.
6. Recognizing interest on investments in the year in which it is earned, irrespective of when it is received.	6. Recognizing interest in the year in which it is received, irrespective of when it is earned.
7. Setting aside funds each year to pay for an anticipated 20-year renovation of a college dormitory.	7. Paying for an anticipated 20-year renovation of a college dormitory out of current funds in the year the work is performed.

never borrow. The prohibition against debt applies only to operating, not capital, expenditures. A government-constructed highway or university-purchased lab equipment will produce benefits over more than one year. It is only fair, therefore, that they be paid for by incorporating debt service costs into the taxes or tuition charges of the citizens or students who will gain from them.

REVENUES NOT INDICATIVE OF DEMAND FOR GOODS OR SERVICES

For competitive businesses, revenues signal customer demand for goods and services. Holding prices constant, the greater the revenues, the greater the demand—an indication that the entity is satisfying a societal need.

In a government or not-for-profit, revenues may not be linked to constituent demand or satisfaction. An increase in tax revenues, for example, tells nothing about the amount or quality of service provided. Therefore, a conventional statement of revenues and expenditures cannot supply information on demand for services. Supplementary information is required.

NO DIRECT LINK BETWEEN REVENUES AND EXPENSES

Just as the revenues of governments and not-for-profits may not be directly linked to customer demand, so also may they be unrelated to expenditures. The revenues from donations of a not-for-profit entity may increase from one year to the next, but the change may be unaccompanied by a corresponding increase in the quantity, quality, or cost of services provided. Thus, the *matching concept*—financial accounting's central notion that expenditures must be paired with corresponding revenues—may have a different meaning for governments and not-for-profits than for businesses. Businesses attempt to match the costs of specific goods or services with the revenues that they generate. Governments and not-for-profits, however, can sometimes do no more than associate overall revenues with the broad categories of expenditures they are intended to cover.

CAPITAL ASSETS MAY NEITHER PRODUCE REVENUES NOR SAVE COSTS

Unlike businesses, both governments and not-for-profits make significant investments in assets that neither produce revenues nor reduce expenditures. Therefore, the conventional business practices used to value assets may not be applicable.

According to financial theory, the economic value of an asset is the present or discounted value of the cash inflows that it will generate or the cash outflows that it will enable the entity to avoid. Hence, conventional capital budgeting models specify that in evaluating a potential asset acquisition, the business should compare the present value of the asset's expected cash outflows with its inflows.

Many capital assets of governments and not-for-profits cannot be associated with revenues or savings. The highway or bridge being considered by a state or local government will not yield cash benefits—at least not directly to the government. The proposed college library may enrich the intellectual life of the community, but not the college's coffers. In fact, some government and not-for-profit "assets" may be more properly interpreted as liabilities. Inasmuch as they have to be maintained and serviced, they will consume rather than provide resources.

RESOURCES MAY BE RESTRICTED

In contrast to the resources of businesses, many of the assets of government and not-for-profit entities are restricted for particular activities or purposes. As shown in Figure 1-1, for example, a sizable share of one government's revenues may be from other governments, and, more than likely, restricted for specific purposes. For example, the federal government may give a state or local government a grant for construction of low-income housing. The award can be used only for low-income housing, not for any other purposes, irrespective of how worthy they might be.

Taxes and membership dues may also be restricted. A city's hotel tax may be ded-

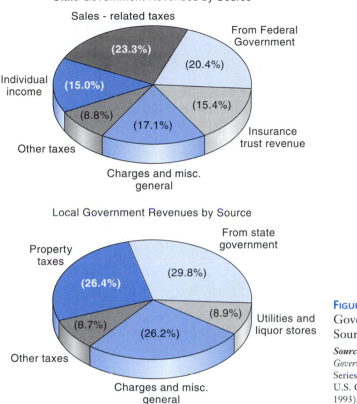

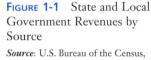

FIGURE 1-1   State and Local Government Revenues by Source

Source: U.S. Bureau of the Census, *Government Finances: 1990–1991*, Series GF/91-5. (Washington, D.C.: U.S. Government Printing Office, 1993).

icated to financing a local convention center or to promoting tourism. A state's gasoline tax may be targeted by law to highway construction and maintenance. A portion of a cemetery association's fees may have to be set aside for the acquisition of new land.

Both governments and not-for-profits need to assure the parties providing the restricted funds that the money is used properly. At the same time, they must show in their financial reports that the restricted resources are unavailable for purposes other than those specified. Therefore, the financial statements must either segregate the restricted from the unrestricted resources or disclose by some other means that some resources can be used only for specific purposes.

As with budgetary mandates, slip-ups regarding restrictions carry serious consequences. At the very least they may cause the organization to forfeit past and future awards. Therefore, as with budgets, the organization must engineer its accounting system so that management is prevented from inadvertently misspending restricted resources. To this end, governments and not-for-profits employ a system of accounting know as fund accounting. It will be described in Chapter 2.

NO DISTINCT OWNERSHIP INTERESTS

Neither governments nor not-for-profits have defined ownership interests like those of businesses. Typically, the entities cannot be sold or transferred. Should they be dissolved, there are no stockholders or bondholders who are entitled to receive residual resources.

The most obvious financial reporting implication of this distinction is that the mathematical difference between assets and liabilities cannot sensibly be termed *own-ers' equity*. Some other term is required.

More substantively, however, the distinction suggests that the financial statements of governments and not-for-profits must be prepared from the perspective of parties other than stockholders. The main groups of statement users will be identified later in this chapter.

Similarly, for certain entities the distinction implies that there may be less interest in the market values of their resources. Governments cannot typically sell their highways and sewers, and few statement users are interested in their market values. Libraries and museums may be able to sell their collections, but may have to use the funds to acquire similar assets. The market values may be of concern only if the entire institution were to be closed and its assets liquidated.

LESS DISTINCTION BETWEEN INTERNAL AND EXTERNAL ACCOUNTING AND REPORTING

In the government and not-for-profit arena, the line between external and internal accounting and reporting is less clear-cut than in the business sector. First, in the business sector, external reports focus on profits. Nevertheless, even in businesses, few organizational units are profit centers in which management controls all the key factors that affect profits. Therefore, internal reports present data on other measures of performance, such as total fixed costs or per-unit variable costs.

In the government and not-for-profit areas, profit is no more an appropriate measure of performance for external parties than it is for internal departments. The relevant performance measures must be drawn from the organizations' unique goals and objectives and are unlikely to be the same for all user groups.

Second, in business the budget is considered exclusively as an internal document, seldom made available to external parties. In governments and not-for-profits, it stands as the key fiscal document that is as important to taxpayers, bondholders, and other constituencies as it is to managers.

Third, the distinction between internal and external parties in governments and not-for-profits is more ambiguous than in business. Taxpayers and organizational members, for example, cannot neatly be categorized as either insiders or outsiders. Although they are not paid employees (and thus, not traditional "insiders") they may nevertheless have the ultimate say (through either direct vote or elected officers) as to organizational policies.

WHAT OTHER CHARACTERISTICS OF GOVERNMENTS AND NOT-FOR-PROFITS HAVE ACCOUNTING IMPLICATIONS?

Governments and not-for-profits have additional characteristics that do not necessarily distinguish them from businesses but have significant accounting and reporting implications.

MANY DIFFERENT TYPES OF GOVERNMENTS AND NOT-FOR-PROFITS

There are approximately 87,000 local governments in the United States (See Figure 1-2). In common usage a *municipality* is a village, town, or city. Government specialists, however, use the term to refer also to any other nonfederal government, including states, school districts, and public authorities.

The number of municipalities may be surprisingly large, but consider how many separate governments have jurisdiction over a typical neighborhood. The neighborhood may be part of a town, several of which comprise a township. The township may be part of a county, which, in turn, may be a subdivision of a state. Further, the neigh-

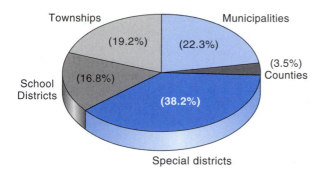

- The average number of local government units per state is 1,734, but Illinois has 6,809, whereas Hawaii has only 20.
- Nine states account for slightly less than half of all local government units in the nation.

FIGURE 1-2 Composition of the Local U.S. Government Units

Source: U.S. Bureau of the Census, *Government Finances: 1990–1991*, Series GF/91-5. (Washington, D.C.: U.S. Government Printing Office, 1993).

borhood school may be administered by an independent school district. The local hospital may be governed by a hospital district, the water and sewage system by a utility authority, and the bus system by a transportation authority. The community college may be financed by a community college district, and the nearby airport may be managed by an independent airport authority.

Each category of government will likely differ from others in the services provided, the type of assets it controls, its taxing and borrowing authority, and the parties to which it is accountable. Moreover, even governments in the same category may vary in the services they provide. New York and Dallas are among the nation's ten largest cities. But New York operates its own school system, whereas Dallas's schools are under the control of an independent school district. San Antonio—Texas's third largest city—provides electric service to its residents, whereas in Houston, the state's largest city, the citizens receive their power from a privately owned utility.

As shown in Table 1-2, not-for-profits are also many in number: there are close to a million in the United States. These constitute what is sometimes referred to as the *independent sector*.

This diversity limits the suitability of a common accounting model (i.e., set of ac-

---

TABLE 1–2
Dimensions of the Independent Sector

- There are approximately 983,000 not-for-profit organizations in the United States. These include:
  - schools
  - hospitals
  - social service organizations
  - advocacy organizations
  - civic, social, and fraternal organizations
  - religious organizations, such as churches, synagogues, and mosques
  - cultural organizations
  - foundations
- They create approximately 6.8 percent of total national income.
- They employ approximately 10.4 percent of the work force.

Source: Nonprofit Almanac 1992–1993: Dimensions of the Independent Sector (San Francisco: Jossey-Bass).

counting and reporting principles) to any individual, or even to any particular type of, government or not-for-profit entity. Assuming that comparability among entities is a desirable characteristic of financial reporting, standard-setting authorities face a policy question. To what extent should they adopt common standards for all governments and not-for-profits, as opposed to common standards only for entities of the same type? When entities are similar, common standards may promote comparability. When the entities are not, common standards may, like ill-fitting clothes, distort reality. As will be discussed in succeeding chapters, rule-making authorities are heading in the direction of one set of common principles for all not-for-profits and a separate set for all governments.

SHORT-TERM FOCUS OF MANAGERS

U.S. managers of both public and private enterprises have been accused of sacrificing the long-term welfare of their organizations for short-term benefits—sometimes for their organizations and other times only for themselves. This failing is said to be especially pronounced in government.

Government officials typically face election every two or four years. In the periods preceding an election, they have powerful incentives both to avoid unpopular measures, such as tax increases, and to make their government look fiscally sound. They can use budgetary and accounting techniques to make cosmetic improvements to their entity's budget or annual report. Many of these will be described throughout the text.

Standard-setting authorities, the accountants and auditors of individual organizations, and statement users need to be aware that officials may steer budgets and financial statements in a particular direction. They must resist and adjust for any biases. The difficulty they face, however, is that the motives for slanting budgets and statements vary from situation to situation. In some circumstances government officials may artificially *overestimate* revenues (or *underestimate* expenditures) so as to avoid cuts in services or increases in taxes. In others, however, they may do the opposite so they can take credit at year-end for managerial effectiveness by presenting better-than-anticipated results.

GOVERNMENTS AND NOT-FOR-PROFITS ENGAGE IN BUSINESS-TYPE ACTIVITIES

Many governments and not-for-profit organizations engage in business-type activities. Cities, for example, may operate electric utilities, trash collection services, and golf courses. Colleges and universities operate book stores, cafeterias, and computer repair services. Girl Scouts sell cookies.

Even if profit maximization is not their overriding objective, these enterprises may, and perhaps should, be managed as if it were. Therefore, both their managers and the parties to whom they are accountable need the same type of financial information as the owners and operators of businesses. The accounting and reporting practices that are appropriate for the business-type activities of governments and not-for-profits may differ from those that are most suitable for their nonbusiness activities. Thus, the challenge of developing accounting and reporting principles for governments and not-for-profits is made even more formidable by the potential need for more than one set of standards—even for a single organization.

HOW DO GOVERNMENTS COMPARE WITH NOT-FOR-PROFITS?

As explained earlier, governments and not-for-profits differ from businesses. But there are also important distinctions between governments and not-for-profits. Governments, unlike not-for-profits, have the authority to command resources. They have the power to tax, collect license and other fees, and impose charges. Should a government lack funds to satisfy its obligations or enhance services, it can obtain them by legislative action. From the perspective of an accountant or financial analyst, this ability suggests that the actual assets reported on a government's balance sheet may not represent all of the assets under its control. To obtain a comprehensive picture of a government's fiscal health, it may be necessary to consider not only the resources actually owned by the government, but also those that it has the power to summon.

Suppose, for example, that two towns each report an operating deficit and a high ratio of debt to financial assets. One is a wealthy community with high property values, prosperous industries, little unemployment, and a low tax rate. The other has low property values, little industry, high unemployment, and high tax rates. Clearly, the fiscal capacity of the first town exceeds that of the second. With greater fiscal effort—that is, by increasing tax rates—the first town can readily improve its economic circumstances, whereas the second cannot.

Governments are currently required to include in their annual reports substantial amounts of demographic and economic data about the jurisdictions that they serve. An ongoing issue, however, is how much disclosure is enough; what types of data are needed by statement users and to what extent are such disclosures within the purview of accounting and financial reporting.

Surprisingly, it is not always obvious whether an entity should be categorized as a government or as a not-for-profit, and there are no definitive criteria to distinguish between the two. The homeowners' association of a residential development, for example, may carry out activities similar to that of a government—constructing and maintaining roads, and providing utility and security services. Moreover, it may have the right to assess residents' annual fees. The following characteristics, in addition to the power to tax, are indicative of a government:

- *It has power to issue tax-exempt debt.* Section 103(a) of the Internal Revenue Code exempts the interest on the debt of states, territories, and their political subdivisions from federal taxation. Virtually all local governments qualify as subdivisions of states and territories. Not-for-profits, such as colleges, universities, and hospitals, do not have this power. However, they may be the beneficiaries of it, as governments are permitted to issue tax-exempt debt on their behalf.

- *Its governing bodies are either popularly elected or are appointed by another government.* The governing body of a typical government is elected by the citizens within its jurisdiction. The governing boards of other governments, particularly public authorities, may be appointed by the legislature or other public officials of another government.

- *Another government can unilaterally dissolve it and assume its assets* **without compensation.** Under our legal system, governments can arbitrarily seize the assets only of other governments within their jurisdiction—not those of not-for-profits or businesses.[1]

---

[1] These characteristics have been drawn from Martin Ives, "What is a Government?" *The Government Accountants Journal*, vol. XLIII (Spring 1994), 25–33. They are similar to those that have been agreed upon by the American Institute of Certified Public Accountants (AICPA) and the Governmental Accounting Standards Board (GASB).

WHAT IS THE PURPOSE OF FINANCIAL REPORTING?

Having considered the characteristics of government and not-for-profit entities, we shall now consider the general purposes that financial statements can serve and the groups most likely to use them. We can then address the need for specific objectives of financial reporting and can review the objectives as developed by both the GASB and the FASB.

The purposes to which external financial statements—those included in an annual report—are employed vary from user to user and facilitate a combination of functions.[2] For the most part, they should allow users to:

- *Assess financial condition.* Users need to analyze past results and current financial condition so as to determine the ability of the entity to meet its obligations and to continue to provide expected services. By establishing trends, users are better able to predict future fiscal developments and to foresee the need for changes in revenue sources, resources allocations, and capital requirements.

- *Compare actual results with the budget.* In light of the importance of the adopted budget, users want assurance that the entity adhered to it. Significant variations from the budget may signify either poor management or unforeseen circumstances that require an explanation.

- *Determine compliance with appropriate laws, regulations, and restrictions on the use the funds.* Users want evidence that the organization has complied with legal and contractual requirements, such as bond covenants, donor and grantor restrictions, taxing and debt limitations, and applicable laws. Violations can not only have serious financial repercussions, but could jeopardize the entity's viability.

- *Evaluate efficiency and effectiveness.* Users want to know whether the entity is achieving its objectives and if so, whether it is doing so efficiently and effectively. Hence, they need to compare accomplishments (outcomes) with service efforts and costs (resource inputs).

WHAT ARE THE USES OF FINANCIAL REPORTS?

The main users of the financial statements of governments and not-for-profits—like those of the financial statements of businesses—are the parties to whom the organizations are accountable. They include:

- governing boards
- investors and creditors
- taxpayers and citizens; organizational members

---

[2] These purposes are drawn from the Governmental Accounting Standards Board's Concepts Statement 1, *Objectives of Financial Reporting* (1987).

- donors and grantors
- regulatory and oversight agencies
- employees and other constituents

General purpose financial statements are targeted mainly at parties external to the organization. As is the case in corporate accounting, reports intended for external groups are inappropriate for many types of managerial decisions. Executives, agency heads, and other managers can, and should, rely on their organization's internal reporting system for the financial information they require. Nevertheless, there may be considerable overlap between the information needs of internal and external parties. Therefore, internal parties, though not intended as principal users of general purpose financial statements, may, in fact, rely on them for a considerable amount of necessary data.

This text focuses primarily on the information needs of external users and hence, is concerned largely with general purpose financial statements. Nonetheless, we also pay special attention to the interests of managers and other internal parties.

Just as the auditors' reports on the financial statements of corporations are generally addressed to their boards of directors, those of governments and not-for-profits are directed to their governing boards. That the governing boards are the prime recipients of the audit reports strongly implies that they are among the principal users of both the auditors' reports themselves and the accompanying financial statements.

GOVERNING BOARDS

A government's governing body would typically be either an elected or appointed legislature, such as a city council or a board of commissioners. A not-for-profit's governing body would usually be a board of trustees or a board of directors.

Governing boards cannot neatly be categorized as either internal or external users. Customarily they are composed of members from outside the management team. However, in almost all organizations, they approve budgets, major purchases, contracts, employment agreements with key executives and significant operating policies—thereby not only overseeing managers, but also getting involved, sometimes directly, in the decisions they make.

As noted earlier, neither governments nor not-for-profits have owners, and therefore, they do not issue shares of stock. Nevertheless, they look to the same financial markets as corporations to satisfy their capital requirements.

INVESTORS AND CREDITORS

As shown in Figure 1-3, in 1995 state and local governments had an estimated $1.3 billion of bonds outstanding. This compares to $1.7 billion outstanding for U.S. corporations. The amounts highlight the economic significance of the municipal bond segment. As indicated in Figure 1-4, the main purchasers of this debt are individual and institutional investors and insurance companies.

Both governments and not-for-profits issue bonds primarily to finance long-term assets. For governments these include buildings, parking garages, office buildings, roads, highways, and utility systems. For not-for-profits they include buildings, other facilities, and equipment.

Investors commonly acquire the bonds of governments and not-for-profits as part of an investment portfolio that also includes corporate securities. Their investment requirements are essentially the same as for similar corporate bonds. They want assurance that the issuing entity will meet its obligations to make scheduled interest and principal payments. In a sense, therefore, the same group of investors constitute the major users of business, government, and not-for-profit financial statements.

Outstanding Level of Public & Private Debt Securities
1980 – 1995E
($ Billions)

	Municipal	Treasury (1)	Agency Mortgage Backed (2)	U.S. Corporate
1980	365.4	616.4	110.9	471.5
1981	398.3	683.2	126.4	495.8
1982	451.3	824.4	176.3	527.5
1983	505.7	1,024.4	244.3	564.6
1984	564.4	1,176.6	289.4	627.3
1985	743.0	1,360.2	372.1	719.8
1986	789.6	1,564.3	534.4	860.9
1987	873.1	1,675.0	672.1	958.8
1988	939.4	1,821.3	749.9	1,071.1
1989	1,004.7	1,945.4	876.3	1,159.3
1990	1,184.4	2,195.8	1,024.4	1,231.9
1991	1,272.2	2,471.6	1,160.5	1,332.5
1992	1,302.8	2,754.1	1,273.5	1,430.6
1993	1,377.5	2,989.5	1,349.6	1,606.5
1994	1,348.2	3,126.0	1,441.9	1,656.6
1995E	1,300.0	3,352.2	1,515.4	1,792.5

Outstanding Level of Public & Private Debt Securities
1980 – 1995E

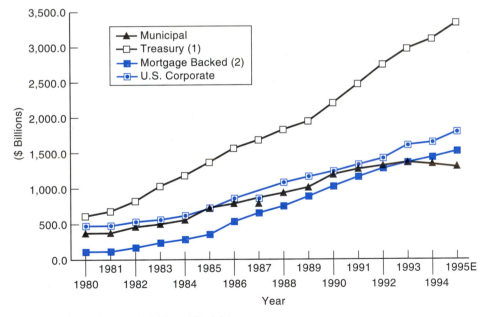

(1) Interest-bearing marketable public debt.
(2) Includes only GNMA, FNMA, and FHLMC mortgage-backed securities.

FIGURE 1-3   Outstanding Level of Public & Private Debt Securities

Source: U.S. Department of Treasury
Federal Reserve System
Federal National Mortgage Association
Government National Mortgage Association
Federal Home Loan Mortgage Corporation

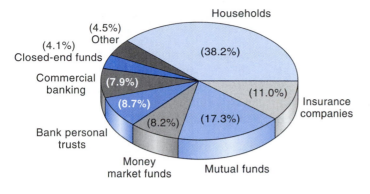

(4.5%)
Other

(4.1%)
Closed-end funds

Commercial
banking

Bank personal
trusts

Money
market funds

Mutual funds

Households

(38.2%)

(11.0%)
Insurance
companies

(17.3%)

(8.2%)

(8.7%)

(7.9%)

FIGURE 1-4   Holders of Tax-Exempt Debt, 1993
Source: Public Securities Association

Many—probably most—bondholders do not themselves evaluate the bonds they acquire. Instead, they rely on the assessments of bond-rating services and are thereby only indirect users of financial reports. The three best-known rating services are *Standard & Poor's*, *Moody's*, and *Fitch's Investor Service*. These services assign to publicly traded bonds a rating (e.g., AAA, AA, A, BBB) reflective of the securities' risk of default.

Governments and not-for-profits also borrow routinely from banks and other financial institutions. The loans may finance either new facilities or short-term imbalances between cash receipts and cash disbursements. The lenders and potential lenders use the financial statements of the governments and not-for-profits just as they would those of corporations—to help assess the credit-worthiness of the borrowers.

CITIZENS AND ORGANIZATIONAL MEMBERS

Citizens (or taxpayers) are invariably placed near the top of any list of government financial statement users. In reality, few citizens ever see the annual reports of the governments that have jurisdiction over them. Moreover, a government's release of its annual report is seldom newsworthy. The reports are ordinarily issued at least three months after the close of the government's fiscal year, and, as this text will show, current reporting practices are anything but user-friendly. As suggested by the following In Practice, most governments do not routinely send their reports to their local newspaper.

Do not minimize the significance of citizens as a primary user group. Citizens obtain financial data through a variety of "filters," including civic associations such as the League of Women Voters, political action groups, and newspapers, TV, and radio. Even if they don't pay attention to the annual report, they most definitely take notice, at any time of the year, of instances of fiscal mismanagement or other unforeseen circumstances that will cause unexpected revenue shortfalls or cost overruns.

The extent to which members of not-for-profit organizations are interested in either the statements themselves or data derived from them depends largely on the size of the organization and their involvement in it. A larger percentage of a country club's members can be expected to pay attention to their organization's fiscal affairs—mainly because it directly bears upon their dues and fees—than of broad-based organizations such as the National Geographic Society or the American Automobile Association.

DONORS AND GRANTORS

Few individuals—not even accountants—request financial statements each time they drop their coins into Salvation Army kettles or Muscular Dystrophy Association canisters. But major donors and grantors, such as the United Way, the Ford Foundation, and federal, state, and local governments, are more discriminating in how they part

IN PRACTICE

Members of the Hotel, Restaurant & Club Employees Union went on strike against New York's prestigious Harvard Club. Citing declining revenues, the club's president was particularly hard-nosed toward the strikers, demanding that the workers begin contributing to the cost of their health plan and "surrender the few extra dollars they were paid for doing so-called dirty jobs—unpleasant tasks like cleaning up after vomiting club members."

The union, however, was skeptical when they heard "the Harvard Club crying poverty." They pointed to a management-commissioned audit that had described the club as "relatively prosperous."

Source: Based on a *New York Times* (May 11, 1994) column, "Crimson Class" by Bob Herbert.

EMPLOYEES AS STATEMENT USERS

with their resources. They will not only request financial reports and other relevant fiscal information from supplicant associations, but will examine and analyze them with the same care as a banker making a loan.

In addition, individual donors can, and should, obtain financial information about a charity prior to contributing to it. They can inquire as to the organization's allocation of resources, the proportion of its resources directed to substantive programs as opposed to fundraising, and the salaries of the most highly paid executives. Such data will likely be available from the organization itself or from state or local regulatory authorities.

REGULATORY AGENCIES

Local governments are normally obligated to file financial reports with state agencies; charitable organizations may have to file with either state or local authorities; religious and fraternal associations may have to file with their umbrella organizations. The recipients of these reports use them to assure that the entities are spending and receiving resources in accordance with laws, regulations, or policies, to help assess management's performance, to allocate resources, and to exercise general oversight responsibility.

EMPLOYEES AND OTHER CONSTITUENTS

Few employees of governments or not-for-profits spend their off-hours poring over their organization's financial statements. But officers of their unions or employee associations may examine them, looking for ways to free up resources for salary increases or projects in which they have a special interest.

Other constituent or interest groups also use financial reports on an ad hoc basis. Almost certainly few readers of this text have ever seen the financial statements of the college or university they attend. However, students have been known to use budgets and annual reports to support claims that their college or university need not raise tuition, can afford a new student activities center, or should privatize a money-losing cafeteria or book store.

Although the groups just discussed constitute the main users of financial reports, a surprisingly small percentage of cities send their reports to members of these groups. Hence, it can be presumed that only a small percentage of the members actually use the statements. As noted in the following In Practice, for example, 9 percent of the cities do not send their annual reports even to members of their own councils.

A study of 178 U.S. cities with populations of more than 50,000 showed that the fol-lowing percentages of cities did *not* send their annual reports to the user groups that follow:

WHO RECEIVES ANNUAL REPORTS?

Local newspapers	60%
Insurance companies	58%
Municipal bond dealers	57%
Municipal underwriters	46%
Standard and Poor's bond rating service	31%
Moody's bond rating service	16%
City council members	9%

Source: Rubik Atamian and Gouranga Ganguli, "The Recipients of Municipal Annual Finan-cial Reports: A Nationwide Study," *The Government Accountants Journal*, vol. XXXX, no. 3 (Fall 1991), pp. 3–21.

These low percentages suggest that the reports may not be especially useful to these groups and, therefore, that the reports' form and content need be improved.

WHAT ARE THE OBJECTIVES OF FINANCIAL REPORTING?

The overall objective of financial reporting is to meet the information needs of statement users. But financial reports cannot possibly satisfy all requirements of all users. Therefore, both the Governmental Accounting Standards Board (GASB) and the Financial Accounting Standards Board (FASB) have established objectives that cir-cumscribe the functions of financial reports. These objectives lay the foundation for the standards they will subsequently establish. Having agreed on objectives at the out-set, the standard-setters should not have to determine the overall purpose of a pro-posed new standard each time they consider a specific accounting issue.

GASB'S OBJECTIVES

Taking into account the unique characteristics of governments and their environ-ment, the GASB established *accountability* as the cornerstone of financial reporting. "Accountability," it says, "requires governments to answer to the citizenry—to jus-tify the raising of public resources and the purposes for which they are used." It "is based on the belief that the citizenry has a 'right to know,' a right to receive openly declared facts that may lead to public debate by the citizens and their elected repre-sentatives."

The GASB divided the objective of accountability into three subobjectives:

- *Interperiod equity.* "Financial reporting should provide information to deter-mine whether current-year revenues were sufficient to pay for current-year services." It should show whether current-year citizens shifted part of the cost of services they received to future-year taxpayers.

- *Budgetary and fiscal compliance.* "Financial reporting should demonstrate whether resources were obtained and used in accordance with the entity's legally adopted budget; it should also demonstrate compliance with other finance-related legal or contractual requirements."

- *Service efforts, costs and accomplishments.* "Financial reporting should provide information to assist users in assessing the service efforts costs and accomplishments of the governmental entity." This information helps users assess the government's "economy, efficiency, and effectiveness" and "may help form a basis for voting or funding decisions."[3]

The GASB established two additional objectives, each also having three subobjectives. These are set forth in Table 1–3.

The GASB objectives, taken independently, are unquestionably reasonable. But taken together, do they establish the basis for resolving specific issues and establishing specific standards? Consider the following highly stylized example:

EXAMPLE   *Clash Among Reporting Objectives*

Voters approved the establishment of a county sanitation district and the county provided the new district with $10 million in start-up funds. During its first year of operations the district prepared a cash-based budget and engaged in the following summary transactions, all of which occurred without variance from the budget.

- It purchased sanitation vehicles and other equipment for $10 million cash. The anticipated economic lives of the assets were ten years.

- It billed residents for $9 million, but because bills for the last month of the year were not mailed until early the following year (as planned), it collected only $8.2 million.

- It incurred operating costs, all paid in cash, of $6 million.

Let us prepare a statement of revenues and expenses that would embody accounting standards consistent with the GASB objectives. The distinction between expenses and **expenditures,** a term commonly used in government accounting, will be drawn in a subsequently chapter. For now consider them to be the same.

Two problems are readily apparent:

- How should the district report the expense related to the equipment? Should it be the $10 million paid to purchase the equipment or $1 million, an amount representative of the one-tenth of the assets consumed during the period? The broader question is whether governments should be required to charge depreciation.

- How much revenue should the district recognize? Should it be the $9 million billed or the $8.2 million collected? More generally, should revenues be recognized on a cash or an accrual basis?

---

[3] See GASB Concepts Statement 1, *Objectives of Financial Reporting* (1987).

Inasmuch as the district prepared its budget on a cash basis, a statement of revenues and expenses that would fulfill the GASB's subobjective of reporting whether resources were obtained and used in accordance with the entity's legally adopted budget would also have to be on a cash basis. The district would recognize the revenue as the cash is collected; it would record the vehicle-related expense in the period in which the vehicles are acquired and paid for. Thus (in millions):

Revenues from customers		$ 8.2
Operating expenses	$ 6.0	
Vehicle-related costs	10.0	16.0
Excess of revenues over expenses		$(7.8)

As a consequence of preparing statements on a cash basis—the same basis as that on which the budget was prepared—the entire accounting burden of the cost of acquiring the long-term assets would fall on the taxpayers of the year of purchase. In the following nine years the district would report no further expenses related to the purchase or "consumption" of these particular vehicles. The financial statements would thereby allow management to appear far more efficient in those years than in the first year. Additionally, if tax rates were set so that revenues would cover expenses, taxpayers would enjoy a rate decrease. However, since the taxpayers of all ten years will benefit from the assets, the reporting objective of interperiod equity would not be served. On the other hand, the government would be credited with only $8.2 million in revenues, even though it provided $9.0 million in services—another, though opposite, violation of the interperiod equity concept.

By contrast, a statement that would fulfill the interperiod equity subobjective would recognize the $10 million in vehicle costs over the ten years in which they would be used and the $9.0 in revenues in the years in which the services were provided. Thus:

Revenues from customers		$ 9.0
Operating expenses	$ 6.0	
Vehicle-related costs	1.0	7.0
Excess of revenues over expenses		$ 2.0

But the statement, prepared on a full accrual basis, cannot readily be compared to the adopted budget and therefore cannot, without adjustment, be used to demonstrate budgetary compliance.

As will be apparent throughout this text, the conflict between the two objectives characterizes many of the issues that government accountants, and the GASB in particular, have to face in assuring that financial statements are informative and useful to the parties that rely upon them. In particular, the conflict casts doubt upon whether the objectives can be fulfilled within a single set of financial statements, or whether, as an alternative, two sets—one on a full accrual basis, the other on a budget or near budget basis—might be necessary.

FASB OBJECTIVES

FASB objectives for not-for-profit entities are, for the most part, similar to those of the GASB for governments. They are presented, in summary form, in Table 1–4.

FASB objectives refer only obliquely to budgetary compliance. They provide that information should be useful in "assessing how managers of a nonbusiness organiza-

TABLE 1–3
Governmental Accounting Standards Board's Additional Objectives of Financial Reporting

Financial reporting should assist users in evaluating the operating results of the governmental entity for the year.

a. Financial reporting should provide information about sources and uses of financial resources. Financial reporting should account for all outflows by function and purpose, all inflows by source and type, and the extent to which inflows met outflows. Financial reporting should identify material nonrecurring financial transactions.

b. Financial reporting should provide information about how the government entity financed its activities and met its cash requirements.

c. Financial reporting should provide information necessary to determine whether the entity's financial position improved or deteriorated as a result of the year's operations.

Financial reporting should assist users in assessing the level of services that can be provided by the governmental entity and its ability to meet its obligations as they become due.

a. Financial reporting should provide information about the financial position and condition of a governmental entity. Financial reporting should provide information about resources and obligations, both actual and contingent, current and noncurrent. The major financial resources of most governmental entities are derived from the ability to tax and issue debt. As a result, financial reporting should provide information about tax sources, tax limitations, tax burdens, and debt limitations.

b. Financial reporting should provide information about a governmental entity's physical and other nonfinancial resources having useful lives that extend beyond the current year, including information that can be used to assess the service potential of those resources. This information should be presented to help users assess long- and short-term capital needs.

c. Financial reporting should disclose legal or contractual restrictions on resources and risks of potential loss of resources.

Source: GASB Concepts Statement 1, *Objectives of Financial Reporting* (1987).

TABLE 1–4
Financial Accounting Standards Board's Objectives of Financial Reporting

- Financial reporting by nonbusiness organizations should provide information that is useful to present and potential resource providers and other users in making rational decisions about the allocation of resources to those organizations.

- Financial reporting should provide information to help present and potential resource providers and other users in assessing the services that a nonbusiness organization provides and its ability to continue to provide those services.

- Financial reporting should provide information that is useful to present and potential resource providers and other users in assessing how managers of a nonbusiness organization have discharged their stewardship responsibilities and about other aspects of their performance.

- Financial reporting should provide information about the economic resources, obligations, and net resources of an organization, and the effects of transactions, events, and circumstances that change resources and interests in those resources.

- Financial reporting should provide information about the performance of an organization during a period, periodic measurement of the changes in the amount and nature of the net resources of a nonbusiness organization, and information about the service efforts and accomplishments of an organization.

- Financial reporting should provide information about how an organization obtains and spends cash or other liquid resources, about its borrowing and repayment of borrowing, and about other factors that may affect an organization's liquidity.

- Financial reporting should include explanations and interpretations to help users understand financial information provided.

Source: FASB Statement of Financial Accounting Concepts 4, *Objectives of Financial Reporting by Nonbusiness Organizations* (1980).

tion have discharged their stewardship responsibilities." In elaborating upon this objective, the FASB stresses that external financial statements can "best meet that need by disclosing failure to comply with spending mandates [which presumably are expressed in budgets] that may impinge on an organization's financial performance or on its ability to provide a satisfactory level of services."

GASB and FASB objectives both endorse the notion that financial reporting encompasses information on service efforts and accomplishments. This information cannot easily be expressed in monetary units and has not traditionally been included in financial statements.

SERVICE EFFORTS AND ACCOMPLISHMENTS SEEN AS A LONG-TERM GOAL

Both boards emphasize that the ability to measure accomplishments is still undeveloped. Their discussions of their objectives relating to service efforts and accomplishments make it clear that they see this aspect of performance reporting as a long-term goal rather than an immediate imperative.

DO DIFFERENCES IN ACCOUNTING PRINCIPLES REALLY MATTER?

Financial statements demonstrate what happened to an entity in the past. But they present the evidence from the perspective of the accountant who prepared them. Other accountants may describe the events differently. The underlying accounting principles dictate how the evidence is presented. In this section, we address the issue of whether differences in accounting principles really affect the decisions made on the basis of financial statements.

Just as a witness's explanation of an accident cannot change what actually occurred, neither can an accountant's report on an entity's past transactions change what actually transpired. In the sanitation district example, the district paid $10 million in cash for vehicles, billed its customers $9 million for services, and paid $6 million in operating expenses. Whether the district's financial statements report revenues over expenditures of $2 million, expenditures over revenues of $7.8 million, or any amount in between is irrelevant to the actual event. Moreover, financial statements, no matter how prepared, do not directly impact the economic worth of an entity. At year-end the district's customers owed it $0.2 million, irrespective of whether the district would report a receivable of that amount (as it would under an accrual basis of accounting) or of zero (as it would under a cash basis of accounting).

Users of financial statements can be indifferent to how an entity's fiscal story is told, as long as they are given adequate information to reconfigure the statements to a preferred form. Research in the corporate sector provides compelling evidence that stockholders are able to see through differences in accounting practices and adjust financial statements to take the differences into account. Thus, if one firm reports higher earnings than another solely because it employs more liberal accounting principles, the total market value of its shares would be no greater.

USER ADJUSTMENTS

The "efficiency" of the municipal bond market—the extent to which it incorporates all public information in pricing securities—has been investigated much less than that of the corporate stock market. Nevertheless, the available evidence, albeit clearly inconclusive, suggests that investors in tax-exempt bonds, like their stock market counterparts, understand the impact of differences in accounting practices.

ECONOMIC CONSEQUENCES

Accounting principles can—and frequently do—have economic consequences. Important decisions and determinations are made on the basis of financial data as presented and without adjustment.

As suggested earlier, budgets are governments' paramount financial documents. Most jurisdictions must present balanced budgets (expenditures cannot exceed revenues) in accord with accounting principles that either they select themselves or that are imposed upon them by higher-order governments. The choice of accounting principles is critical. Whereas one set of accounting principles may result in a balanced budget, another, which includes identical revenue and expenditure proposals, may not. Most governments budget on a cash or near-cash basis. Were they required to budget on a full accrual basis, their balanced budgets might quickly become unbalanced.

Governments may face restrictions on the amount of debt they can incur. The use of one set of accounting principles in defining and measuring debt (for example, not counting a lease as an obligation), might enable them to satisfy the legal limits and thereby be permitted to issue additional bonds. The use of a different set (for example, counting the lease as a liability), might cause them to exceed the limits and be barred from further borrowing.

Other examples abound of how specific reporting practices have economic consequences. Many of these will be discussed again later in the text. To cite three:

- An alumnus makes a generous monetary gift to a university. He stipulates that the funds may be invested in stocks, bonds, and real estate, but only the income from the investment may be used to support university activities. If trading gains from the purchase and sale of the investments are accounted for as income, then the amount available to the university for expenditure would be significantly greater than if they were added to the original capital.

- A government agrees to keep its pension plan fully funded—that is, to make sufficient annual contributions to assure that the plan's assets equal or exceed the

IN PRACTICE

TESTING THE THEORY: DO INVESTORS ADJUST FOR DIFFERENCES IN ACCOUNTING PRINCIPLES?

In a study to test the efficiency of the municipal bond market, a researcher correlated the market prices of New York City bonds with two sets of accounting measures. The first were drawn from the financial statements as actually issued by New York during the years just prior to its 1975 fiscal crisis. The second were based on the same financial statements, but now adjusted to conform to generally accepted accounting principles (to which, at the time, the city did not adhere). The author found that the bond prices were far more sensitive to the measures based on the adjusted than the unadjusted statements. This indicates, she reasons, that bondholders were aware of New York's slide toward default, despite the misleading financial statements, and apparently based their investment decisions on other information.

Source: Virginia E. Soybel, "Municipal Financial Reporting and the General Obligation Bond Market: New York City, 1961–1975," *Journal of Accounting and Public Policy* (Fall 1992).

plan's actuarial liabilities. The way in which asset and liability values are established will determine its required annual payments.

- A city establishes a policy that it will contract-out for any services private vendors can provide for less than the city's own departments. The principles used to establish the cost of internal services will affect the decision to use internal departments or outside vendors.

Who Establishes Generally Accepted Accounting Principles?

Generally accepted accounting principles (GAAP) embrace the rules and conventions that guide the form and content of general-purpose financial statements. These principles are expressed mainly in pronouncements of officially designated rule-making authorities and should be consistent with the objectives that they established. However, in the absence of pronouncements by those authorities, the GAAP may also be derived from historical convention and widespread practice.

THE FUNCTION OF THE GASB, THE FASB, AND THE AICPA

For governments, excluding the federal government, the primary standard-setting authority is the Governmental Accounting Standards Board (GASB); for other not-for-profits it is the Financial Accounting Standards Board (FASB). Both of these organizations have been sanctioned by the **American Institute of Certified Public Accountants (AICPA)** to establish accounting principles pursuant to Rule 203 of its

IN PRACTICE

Assessing the Profitability of a Football Program

The president and other officials of a major university asserted that their school's football program is extremely "profitable." As evidence, they cite the program's budget and other financial reports that show impressive positive cash flows.

But would they be equally supportive of the program if "profitability" were calculated differently. For example, how much was the program charged for:

- the wages and salaries of campus police who work overtime on game days
- the costs of players' medical exams and care of injuries
- the marching band
- university overhead (it is a safe assumption that the university president devotes more time to the athletic department than the accounting department)
- the interest on the debt incurred to build or modernize the football stadium
- the "opportunity" cost of using the prime land on which the stadium is located for football rather than for an alternative purpose

On the other side of the journal, how much credit does the football program receive for the contributions of alumni and others attributable to the goodwill and publicity generated by the football team?

The program's "profitability," and hence all policies that affect it, may be no more objective than the team's ranking in the weekly polls.

Code of Professional Conduct. Rule 203 provides that an auditor should not express an unqualified opinion on financial statements that are in violation of the standards established by the designated authorities. In addition, the AICPA provides accounting guidance on issues not yet addressed by either the GASB or the FASB. Their guidance is incorporated into "industry audit guides" and "statements of position" (SOPs).

As illustrated in Figure 1-5, both the GASB and the FASB are financed and overseen by the Financial Accounting Foundation (FAF), a not-for-profit organization governed by trustees representing leading business and professional associations with an interest in financial reporting. Thus, standard-setting is carried out mainly in the private sector, not by any federal or state agency. Each organization is supported by an advisory council composed of representatives of constituent groups—the Governmental Accounting Standards Advisory Council (GASAC) for the GASB and the Financial Accounting Standards Advisory Council (FASAC) for the FASB. Both boards share facilities located in Norwalk, Connecticut. The GASB currently has a full-time chairman and six part-time members; the FASB has seven full-time members, including its chairman.

Established in 1984, the GASB succeeded the **National Council on Governmental Accounting (NCGA)** as the preeminent standard-setting body for state and local governments. The NCGA, which was sponsored by the Government Finance Officers Association, was thought to be too unwieldy (twenty-one volunteer members) and inadequately staffed to deal with the complexities of modern government finance.

The FASB, created in 1973, has directed its attention mainly to business enterprises, rather than not-for-profits. However, in 1979 it assumed responsibility for the not-for-profit and other specialized-industry accounting principles, with the exception of those pertaining to state and local governments, that had previously been addressed in the AICPA industry audit guides and SOPs.[4] The not-for-profit orga-

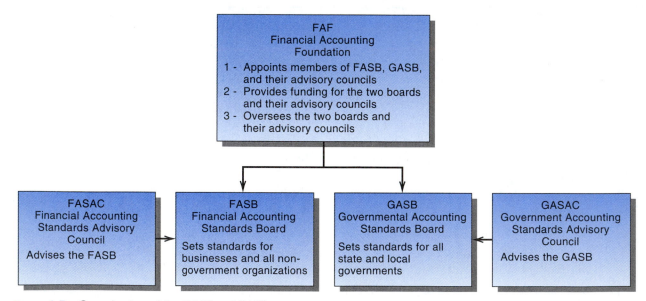

Figure 1-5 Organization of the GASB and FASB

---

[4] Financial Accounting Standards Board, *Statement of Financial Accounting Standards No. 32*, "Specialized Accounting and Reporting Principles and Practices in AICPA Statements of Position and Guides on Accounting and Auditing Matters," (Norwalk: Conn., 1979).

nizations dealt with in those AICPA pronouncements included universities, voluntary health and welfare organizations, and hospitals. Since then, the FASB has issued its previously discussed statement of objectives and standards dealing with the form and content of financial statements, depreciation, revenue recognition from contributions and valuation of investments.

Soon after the GASB was established, it and the FASB and their constituents faced a politically sensitive and potentially divisive issue: Which of the two should set standards for entities, such as colleges and universities, that are common to both the government and the not-for-profit sector? Some constituents of the two boards asserted that there are few conceptual or operational differences between same-type entities in the two sectors that justify different accounting standards and hence separate standard-setting authorities. Others, however, contended that governmental hospitals, utilities, and universities differ fundamentally from their not-for-profit counterparts in that they have different rights, responsibilities, and obligations. For example, they may have the ability to impose taxes and to issue tax-exempt debt and may be accountable to the citizenry at large rather than a board of trustees.

ENTITIES COMMON TO GOVERNMENT AND NOT-FOR-PROFIT SECTORS

The jurisdiction issue was made more complex by concerns over sovereignty. Some managers of the not-for-profit entities maintained that they had little in common with state and local governments and did not want to be within the authority of the GASB. Similarly, state and local government officials refused to yield standard-setting control over any of their component units to the FASB, a board mainly concerned with the private sector.

In 1989, the Financial Accounting Foundation and the constituents of the two boards agreed upon a jurisdictional formula that, in essence, reaffirmed the status quo: the GASB would have authority over all state and local government entities and the FASB would have authority over all other entities. Thus, government colleges and universities (such as The State University of New York) are now within the purview of the GASB; private colleges and universities (such as New York University) are within that of the FASB.

If the GASB or the FASB has not issued a pronouncement on a particular issue, then the organizations within each of their jurisdictions can look to other sources for guidance. These other sources are set forth in two "hierarchies" that were part of the jurisdiction agreement and were adopted by the AICPA in *Statement on Auditing Standards No. 23,* "The Meaning of Present Fairly in Conformity with Generally Accepted Accounting Principles in the Independent Auditor's Report." As shown in Table 1–5, in the column applicable to the GASB, a pronouncement of the FASB that has been specifically adopted by the GASB is of the same standing (the top category) as one issued by the GASB itself. However, a pronouncement of the FASB that has *not* been specifically adopted by the GASB ranks no higher than "other accounting literature" (the lowest category). The FASB hierarchy corresponds to, though is not a mirror image of, that of the GASB.

The influence of the FASB on the accounting practices of governments is greater than might appear from the hierarchies because governments engage in many business-type activities, such as operating utilities, parking garages, and hospitals. Governments have traditionally accounted for these activities in the same way as their private-sector counterparts and, with only a few exceptions, the GASB has permitted them to adhere to generally accepted accounting principles as established by the FASB.

TABLE 1–5
A Summary of The "Hierarchy" of Generally Accepted Accounting Principles

Governmental Entities	Nongovernmental Entities
a. GASB Statements and Interpretations; AICPA and FASB pronouncements specifically made applicable to state and local governments by the GASB	a. FASB Statements and Interpretations; AICPA Accounting Research Bulletins; Accounting Principles Board Opinions
b. GASB Technical Bulletins; AICPA Industry Audit Guides and Statements of Position if specifically made applicable to governments by the AICPA and cleared (not objected to) by the GASB	b. FASB Technical Bulletins; AICPA Industry Audit Guides and Statements of Position if cleared (not objected to) by the FASB
c. AICPA Practice Bulletins if specifically made applicable to governments by the AICPA; Consensus positions of a GASB Emerging Issues Task Force if and when established	c. AICPA Practice Bulletins if cleared by the FASB; Consensus positions of the FASB Emerging Issues Task Force
d. Implementation guides published by the GASB staff; practices that are widely recognized and prevalent in state and local government	d. Implementation guides published by the FASB staff; AICPA accounting interpretations and implementation guides; practices that are widely recognized and prevalent either generally or in the industry
e. Other accounting literature, including FASB pronouncements not specifically made applicable to state and local governments by the FASB	e. Other accounting literature, including GASB pronouncements

FASAB FOR THE FEDERAL GOVERNMENT

Although the U.S. government was constitutionally established in 1789, its accounting and financial reporting system is still in its infancy—a clear case of delayed development. It was not until the republic was more than two centuries old that Congress enacted the *Chief Financial Officers Act of 1990*. The act acknowledged that the federal government was losing billions of dollars each year through financial mismanagement and that its accounting system was incapable of issuing comprehensive financial statements that could earn the government an unqualified audit opinion. The measure took the first steps toward elevating the federal government to a level of fiscal proficiency taken for granted by businesses and other governments. The act:

- established a chief financial officer (CFO) for fiscal management, a new position housed within the Office of Management and Budget (OMB)
- created corresponding CFO positions in each of the federal departments and agencies
- mandated that the federal government develop accounting systems capable of providing complete, accurate, and timely financial information
- required that selected federal agencies prepare annual financial statements and make them subject to audits

The act also led the federal government's "big three" agencies concerned with financial reporting—the Department of the Treasury, the General Accounting Office (GAO), and the Office of Management and Budget (OMB)—to join forces to create the *Federal Accounting Standards Advisory Board* (FASAB). The function of this board is to recommend accounting standards for federal entities to the heads of the three agencies. It is up to three agencies to actually establish the standards. By limiting the FASAB's authority to what is technically an advisory role, the three agencies were able to sidestep the thorny question of which of them is legally empowered to specify accounting practices. Inasmuch as the GAO reports to Congress, whereas the other two agencies are accountable to the president, this issue involves fundamental constitutional questions as to whether federal standard-setting is within the purview of the government's executive or the legislative branch.

The FASAB, like the GASB and the FASB, has recommended a statement of objectives and a series of accounting standards and related pronouncements. As a result, there is now a reasonable degree of consistency among the reporting practices of federal agencies.

Because of the unique features of the federal government, federal accounting is addressed in Chapter 16, apart from that pertaining to other governments.

SUMMARY

Governments and not-for-profits need accounting principles and reporting mechanisms that differ from those of businesses. Most importantly, they have objectives other than profit maximization. Therefore, their performance cannot be assessed by the conventional "bottom-line" of businesses. Moreover, they are governed by their budgets rather than the competitive marketplace.

Other characteristics of governments and not-for-profits also have significant accounting and reporting implications. Governments and not-for-profits are extremely diverse and therefore one set of principles may not fit all entities. Managers tend to have a short-term focus of managers and may strive to delay recognition of expenditures and advance recognition of revenues. Business-type activities may be part of the organization and have to be accounted for differently than governmental activities. The distinction between internal accounting and external accounting is often blurred.

Governments, unlike not-for-profits, have the authority to command resources through taxes and other fees.

Therefore, a government's financial wherewithal cannot necessarily be assessed by examining only the resources directly tied to the government itself. Those of its constituents may also have to be taken into account.

The main users of government and not-for-profit financial reports include governing boards, investors and creditors, citizens and organizational members, donors and grantors, regulatory and oversight agencies, and other constituents. Each group may have different information needs.

The GASB and the FASB have developed objectives of financial reporting that stress the importance of providing information that enables users to assess interperiod equity and compliance with budget (or spending) mandates. Sometimes these objectives are in conflict in that a basis of accounting that satisfies one objective may not satisfy the other.

Choice of accounting principles has no direct effort on an entity's fiscal history or current status. It might, however, have significant economic consequences if decisions are based on the data as presented.

QUESTIONS FOR REVIEW AND DISCUSSION

1. What is the defining distinction between for-profit businesses and not-for-profit entities, including governments? What are the implications of this distinction for financial reporting?

2. Why is the budget a far more important document in both governments and not-for-profits than in businesses?

3. How and why might the importance of the budget affect generally accepted accounting principles for *external* (general purpose) reports?

4. What is meant by "interperiod equity," and what is its consequence for financial reporting?

5. Why may the "matching concept" be less relevant for governments and not-for-profits than for businesses?

6. What is the significance for financial reporting of the many restrictions that are placed upon a government's resources?

7. Why is it difficult to develop accounting principles that are appropriate for governments within the same category (e.g., cities, counties) and even more difficult to develop them for governments within different categories?

8. What is the significance for financial reporting of a

government's power to tax? How does it affect the government's overall fiscal strength?

9. Why has it proven especially difficult to establish accounting principles that enable governments to satisfy all three elements of GASB's first objective of financial reporting in a single statement of revenue and expenditures or balance sheet?

10. Why are measures of "service efforts and accomplishments" of more concern in government and not-for-profits than in businesses?

11. In what key ways does the FASB influence generally accepted accounting principles for governments?

12. Why is it more difficult to distinguish between internal and external users in governments than in businesses?

PROBLEMS

Continuing Problem

Obtain the financial statements (not a budget) of a city, town, or county with a population of 100,000 or more.

Financial statements can generally be obtained by writing to the government's controller or finance director. Whereas most institutions will provide the reports for free, some may charge a substantial amount.

These reports will form the basis of the "continuing problems" in the chapters that follow.

1-1

Budgeting practices that satisfy cash requirements may not promote interperiod equity.

The Burnet County Road Authority was established as a separate government to maintain county highways. The road authority was granted statutory power to impose property taxes on county residents to cover its costs but it is required to balance its budget, which must be prepared on a *cash basis*. In its first year of operations it engaged in the following transactions, all of which were consistent with its legally adopted, *cash-based*, budget:

- Purchased $10 million of equipment, all of which had an anticipated useful life of ten years. To finance the acquisition the authority issued $10 million in ten-year term bonds (i.e., bonds that mature in ten years)
- Incurred wages, salaries, and other operating costs, all paid in cash, of $6 million
- Paid interest of $0.5 million on the bonds
- Purchased $0.9 million of additional equipment, paying for it in cash. This equipment had a useful life of only three years

a. The authority's governing board levies property taxes at rates that will be just sufficient to balance the authority's budget. What is the amount of tax revenue that it will be required to collect?

b. Assume that in the authority's second year of operations, it incurs the same costs, except that it purchases no new equipment. What amount of tax revenue will it be required to collect?

c. Make the same assumption as to the tenth year, when it will have to repay the bonds. What amount of tax revenue will it be required to collect?

d. Comment on the extent to which the authority's budgeting and taxing policies promote interperiod equity. What changes would you recommend?

1-2

Financial statements of a government or not-for-profit organization may not provide sufficient information on which to make a loan decision.

Assume that you are a loan officer of a bank. A local church is seeking a $4 million, twenty-year loan to construct a new classroom building.

Church officers submit a comprehensive financial report that was audited by a reputable CPA firm. In summary form (the actual statement was broken down to show details), the church's statement of revenues and expenditures indicated the following (in millions):

Revenues from dues and contributions	$1.8
Revenues from other sources	0.2
Total revenues	$2.0
Total expenditures	2.0
Excess of revenues over expenditures	$ 0

The church prepared its financial statements on a near-cash basis, accounting for all fixed asset acquisitions as expenditures when acquired.

The church's balance sheet reported assets, mainly cash and investments (at market value) of $0.2 million. In addition, a note to the financial statements indicated that the current market value of its present buildings and equipment is approximately $3 million. The church has no outstanding debt.

a. Is there any information in the financial statements that would make you reluctant to approve the loan? If so, indicate and explain.

b. Is there any other financial information of the type likely to be reported in a conventional annual report that you would like to review prior to making a loan decision? If so, indicate and explain.

c. Is there any other information, of any type, that you would like to review prior to making a loan decision? If so, indicate and explain.

d. Comment on the inherent limitations of the financial statements of this church, or any comparable not-for-profit organization, as a basis for making loan decisions.

1-3

The dual objectives of assessing interperiod equity and assuring budgetary compliance may necessitate different accounting practices.

A city engages in the transactions described as follows. For each transaction indicate the amount of revenue or expenditure that it should report in 1997. Assume first that the main objective of the financial statements is to enable users to assess *budgetary compliance*. Then, assume alternatively that the main objective is to assess *interperiod equity*.

The city prepares its budget on a "modified" cash basis (that is, it expands the definition of cash to include short-term marketable securities) and its fiscal year ends on December 31.

a. Employees earned $128,000 in salaries and wages for the last five days in December 1997. They were paid on January 8, 1998.

b. A consulting actuary calculated that per an accepted actuarial cost method, the city should contribute $225,000 to its fire-fighters pension fund for 1997. However, the city contributed only $170,000, the amount budgeted at the start of the year.

c. The city acquired three police cars for $25,000 cash each. The vehicles are expected to last for three years.

d. On December 1, 1997, the city invested $99,000 in short-term commercial paper (promissory notes). The notes matured on January 1, 1998. The city received $100,000. The $1,000 difference between the two amounts represents the city's return (interest) on the investment.

e. On January 2, 1997, the city acquired a new $10 million office building, financing it with twenty-five-year serial bonds. The bonds are to be repaid evenly over the period they are outstanding—that is, $400,000 per year. The useful life of the building is twenty-five years.

f. On January 1, 1997, the City acquired another $10 million office building, financing this facility with twenty-five-year *term* bonds. These bonds will be repaid entirely when they mature on January 1, 2022. The useful life of this building is also twenty-five years.

g. City restaurants are required to pay a $1,200 annual license fee, the proceeds of which the city uses to fund its restaurant inspection program. The license covers the period July 1 through June 30. In 1997 the city collected $120,000 in fees for the license period beginning July 1, 1997.

h. The city borrowed $300,000 in November 1997 to cover a temporary shortage of cash. It expects to repay the loan in February 1998.

1-4

Do conventional financial statements satisfy the objectives of financial reporting?

The financial statements that follow were adapted from those of the University of Arizona. Both the statement of changes in fund balances and the notes to the statements have been omitted. Moreover, they show only the combined "totals" columns whereas the actual statements are multi-columned, indicating the various restrictions placed upon the university's resources. Also, a few of the line items have been aggregated.

The University of Arizona Balance Sheet, as of June 30 (in millions)

	1993	1992
Assets:		
Cash and investments	$ 145	$ 145
Donated land	3	3
Notes and accounts receivable (net of allowances for uncollectibles)	52	47
Inventories and supplies	8	8
Physical properties	995	945
Total assets	$1,203	$1,148
Liabilities and Fund Balances:		
Accounts payable	$ 16	$ 17
Accrued payroll	12	10
Deferred revenue and deposits	9	8
Funds held for others	11	8
Capitalized lease obligations	36	33
Bonds payable	241	243
Total liabilities	325	319
Fund balances	878	829
Total liabilities and fund balances	$1,203	$1,148

The University of Arizona Statement of Revenues, Expenditures, and Other Changes in Fund Balances For the Year Ending June 30 (in millions)

	1993	1992
Revenues:		
State appropriations	$245	$242
Tuition and fees	112	111
Federal grants and contracts	153	143

State grants and contracts	6	6
Local grants and contracts	1	1
Private gifts, grants, and contracts	48	44
Federal appropriations	5	5
Investment and endowment income	8	9
Sales and services of educational departments	8	6
Sales and services of auxiliary enterprises	69	66
Other	8	6
Total revenues	663	639

Expenditures and Transfers:

Education and general		
Instruction	182	181
Research	162	155
Public service	26	25
Academic support	51	52
Student services	13	15
Institutional support	36	37
Operation and maintenance of plant	36	34
Scholarships and fellowships	49	46
Total educational and general	555	545
Debt service and miscellaneous	23	14
Auxiliary enterprise expenditures	76	68
Total expenditures	654	627
Excess of revenues over expenditures	$ 9	$ 12

a. Based on the information included in the financial statements, respond as best you can to the following questions. If you believe the data in the financial statements are inadequate to answer the questions, then tell what additional information you would like and where you would most likely find it.

1. Were the accomplishments of the university greater or less in 1993 than in 1992?

2. Did the university achieve its goals more efficiently in 1993 than 1992?

3. Are the university's physical facilities adequate for the next two years? Ten years?

4. Did the university's long-term financial position improve or deteriorate between year-end 1992 and year-end 1993, taking account of the fiscal demands that will be placed upon it in the future?

5. Will the university be able to satisfy its short-term demands for cash?

b. Review the GASB and FASB objectives of financial reporting. Are any of the preceding questions inconsistent with those objectives? Comment on the extent to which conventional financial statements satisfy the GASB and FASB objectives and what additional types of information they will likely have to incorporate in order to satisfy these objectives.

1-5

The jurisdictional overlap among governments may have significant implications for financial reporting.

Suppose that you lived on a street adjoining the college in which you are taking this course.

a. List all the governments (e.g., state, county, town) that have jurisdiction over the residents or property of that street.

b. Indicate why it may be difficult to assess the financial wherewithal of one of those governments without taking into account the others. What are the implications for financial reporting of this jurisdictional overlap?

1-6

Choice of accounting principles may have significant economic consequences.

In preparing its budget proposals, a city's budget committee initially estimated that total revenues would be $120 million and total expenditures would be $123 million. In light of the balanced budget requirements that the city has to meet, the committee proposed several measures to either increase revenues or decrease expenditures. They included the following:

1. Delay the payment of $0.4 million of city bills from the last week of the fiscal year covered by the budget to the first week of the next fiscal year.

2. Change the way property taxes are accounted for in the budget. Currently, property taxes are counted as revenues only if they are expected to be collected during the budget year. New budgetary principles would permit the city to include as revenues all taxes expected to be collected within sixty days of the following fiscal year in addition to those collected during the year. The committee estimates that the change would have a net impact of $1.2 million.

3. Change the way that supplies are accounted for in the budget. Currently, supplies are recognized as expenditures at the time they are *ordered*. The proposal would delay recognition of the expenditure until they are actually *received*. The committee estimates a net effect of $0.8 million.

4. Defer indefinitely $1.5 million of maintenance on city roads.

Except as just noted with respect to supplies, the city currently prepares its budget on a *cash basis*, even though other bases are also legally permissible. It prepares its year-end financial statements, however, on an accrual basis.

a. Indicate the impact that each of the proposals would have on the city's (1) budget, (2) annual year-end financial statements, (3) "substantive" economic well-being. Be sure to distinguish between direct and indirect consequences.

b. It is sometimes said that choice of accounting principles doesn't matter in that they affect only the way the entity's fiscal "story" is told; they have no impact on the entity's actual fiscal history or current status. Do you agree? Explain.

1-7

Should there be differences in the accounting and reporting systems of governments and businesses that provide the same services?

A town "privatized" its sanitation department. It sold all its plant and equipment to a private corporation. The corporation agreed to hire most of the department's managers and other employees and was given an exclusive franchise, for a limited number of years, to offer the same service as previously provided by the town. While it operated the department, the town charged local residents fees based on the amount of trash collected. It set the scale of fees at a level intended to enable it to break even—to cover all its operating and capital costs, including interest on capital assets.

a. Do you believe that the objectives of financial accounting and *external* reporting of the private sanitation company should be any different than those of the town? Explain.

b. Do you see any differences in the information requirements of the *internal* managers now that they are employed by a private corporation rather than a government. If so, what are they?

1-8

Capital acquisition decisions may be far more complex in not-for-profit organizations than in businesses.

The Chicago Youth Association (CYA) and the Palmer Athletic Club (PAC) are each considering purchasing a van.

The CYA is a not-for-profit organization serving at-risk inner-city youth. It operates a center that provides after-school tutoring, counseling, and supervised athletic activities. It would use the van mainly to drive students from their schools to the center and from the center back to their homes. The CYA estimates that the van would enable it to increase by twenty the number of students it serves at any one time. The CYA is supported entirely by contributions from the United Way and other private sources.

The PAC is a private athletic facility serving the youth of a suburban community. It provides access to athletic facilities and instruction in several sports, including swimming, tennis, and gymnastics. It would use the van for the same purpose as the CYA—to transport students to and from the facility. The PAC estimates that the van would enable it to increase center capacity by twenty customers, each of whom pays weekly fees of $65.

Each organization estimates that the incremental cost of serving the additional twenty clients (including the operating costs of the van) would be $50 per client per week. Each operates fifty weeks per year.

The two vans would each cost $30,000 and have estimated useful lives of three years. Each organization estimates that its cost of capital is 10 percent.

a. Should the PAC acquire the van? Explain and show all computations.

b. Should the CYA acquire the van? Explain and show all computations.

c. Comment on any critical differences between capital budgeting in a business and a not-for-profit organization.

1-9

Financial information that is appropriate for some purposes may be inappropriate for others—just as in business.

A city operates a computer repair service department. The department maintains and repairs the computers of all other city departments, billing them for each job performed. The billing rates are established so as to cover the repair service's full cost of carrying out its function.

For the latest year available, the department reported the following (all amounts in millions):

Revenues from billing other departments		$8.9
Expenditures		
Wages and salaries	$4.0	
Supplies	2.6	
Other cash expenditures	1.3	
Overhead allocated from other departments	1.0	8.9
Excess of revenues over expenditures		$0.0

The allocated overhead consists mainly of city administrative costs, most of which would remain the same even if the department were to cease operations. However, it also includes $0.3 million in rent. Were the department to be eliminated, the city could move its legal department into the space now occupied by the computer repair service department. The move would save the city $0.2 million, the amount currently paid in rent by the legal department.

A private corporation has offered to provide the same repair service as the computer department for $8.5 million.

a. Based on the limited data provided, should the city accept the offer from the private corporation? Comment on the relevance for this decision of the $8.9 million in total cost—the measure used to establish billing rates.

b. Suppose, instead, that the city did not allocate overhead costs and hence total costs (and billing revenues) were only $7.9 million. Should the city accept the offer? Is the $7.9 million in unallocated costs any more relevant for this decision than the $8.9 million per the allocated statement?

1-10

Year-end financial accounting and reporting can reveal the economic substance of government actions taken mainly to balance the budget.

Public officials, it is often charged, promote measures intended to make the government "look good" in the short-term, but that may be deleterious in the long-term. Assume that the following actions, designed to increase a reported surplus, were approved by a city council:

1. It reduced the city's contributions to the employee "defined benefit" pension plan from the $10 million recommended by the city's actuary to $5 million. Under a defined benefit plan the employer promises employees specified benefits upon their retirement, and the level of benefits is independent of when and how much the employer contributes to the plan over the employees' years of service.

2. It reduced by $1 million the city's cash transfer to a "rainy day" reserve maintained to cover possible future reductions in tax collections attributable to a down-turn in the region's economy.

3. It sold securities that had been held as an investment. The securities had been purchased five-years earlier at a cost of $2 million. Market value at the time of sale was $5 million.

4. It delayed until the following year $10 million of maintenance on city highways.

Assume that the city's budget is on a cash or near-cash basis. Accordingly, each of these measures would, as the council intended, reduce budgetary expenditures or increase budgetary revenues.

a. Suppose that you were asked to propose accounting principles for external reporting that would capture the true economic nature of these measures—actions that, in substance, did not improve the city's fiscal performance or condition. For each measure, indicate how you would require that it be accounted for and reported.

b. Can you see any *disadvantages* to the principles that you propose?

Fund Accounting

In Chapter 1 we set forth some of the key characteristics that distinguish governments and not-for-profits from businesses. We also discussed their implications for accounting and reporting. In particular, we noted that governments and not-for-profits use fund accounting. In this chapter we explain the rationale for fund accounting, describe the main types of funds maintained, and examine the relationships among funds. In addition, inasmuch as the reporting structure of governments is currently under review, we also describe and discuss the ramifications of proposed changes.

WHAT IS A FUND?

Government and other not-for-profit organizations establish their accounting systems on a fund basis. In governmental and not-for-profit accounting, the term **fund** has a different meaning than in business accounting. In business accounting, funds typically refer either to working capital (current assets less current liabilities) or selected elements of working capital (such as cash and investments).

In governmental and not-for-profit accounting, a *fund* is a fiscal and accounting entity. Each fund has its own self-balancing set of accounts from which separate financial statements can be prepared. Governments and not-for-profits customarily use several funds to account for their resources and activities. For example, a church may use one fund to account for its general operating revenues and expenses, another to account for resources set aside to construct a new building, and a third to account for its religious school.

Governments and not-for-profits also maintain **account groups,** which, like funds, have self-balancing sets of accounts. However, they serve a different, albeit related, purpose than funds. The role of account groups and the connection between account groups and funds is almost always a source of confusion, yet it is necessary to an understanding of governmental accounting. Therefore, it will also be addressed in this chapter.

WHAT CHARACTERIZES FUNDS AND ACCOUNT GROUPS?

Each fund of a government or not-for-profit can be represented by a variation of the accounting equation that businesses use. Rather than

$$\text{assets} = \text{liabilities} + \text{owners' equity}$$

fund accounting uses the equation:

$$\text{assets} = \text{liabilities} + \text{fund balance}.$$

Remember, governments and not-for-profits may not have owners, so the term owners' equity is replaced by the term *fund balance*. Fund balance, like owners' equity, is a residual—the difference between the entity's assets and the claims against those assets. The fund balance is the amount left to the parties with rights to the assets after all other claims have been liquidated.

Because funds can be represented by the basic accounting equation used by businesses, they can also be accounted for by the same double-entry system of bookkeeping. Their current status and past performance can be summarized by financial statements similar to those of businesses. For example, the balance sheet of a fund can detail the specific assets, liabilities, and elements of fund balance that underlie the accounting equation as of any point in time. A statement of revenues, expenditures, and other changes in fund balance can explain the reasons for changes in fund balance during a specified period of time.[1] A statement of cash flows can reconcile the changes in cash between the beginning and the end of a period.

Governments and not-for-profits separate resources into funds for reasons that differ considerably from those for which businesses establish subsidiaries. Businesses generally establish subsidiaries to account for their activities by product or region, to isolate certain business risks, and to minimize their tax obligations.

USE OF MULTIPLE FUNDS TO ACCOUNT FOR AN ENTITY

Governments and not-for-profits, on the other hand, most commonly separate resources into funds to adhere to restrictions placed upon them by legislatures, grantors, donors or other outside parties. For example, were a university to receive a donation that may be used only for scholarships, then it would account for the resources received in a special scholarship fund. Fund accounting promotes both control and accountability over restricted resources.

To a lesser extent, governments and not-for-profits establish funds to account for certain activities, often those of a business type, that differ in nature from their usual activities. For example, a government might account for its golf course, which operates similarly to a privately owned course, in a fund separate from that used to account for its general operations. By accounting for these types of activities in their own accounting and fiscal entities, the government is better able to control their revenues and expenditures and to assess their overall performance.

RELATIONSHIPS AMONG FUNDS

To appreciate the relationship between the two or more funds used to account for a single entity, one must remember that each fund is a separate accounting entity. Thus, every transaction that affects a fund must be recorded by at least one debit and one credit. Any transaction that affects two or more funds must be accounted for as if it affected two or more independent businesses and must be recorded individually in each fund. Suppose, for example, that a city maintains two funds. A general fund accounts for its unrestricted resources and general operations. A utility fund accounts for its electric utility. The electric utility bills the other city departments, all of which are accounted for in the general operating fund, for $10,000. The following entries would be appropriate:

Utility fund

Accounts receivable (from general fund)	$10,000	
Revenue from sale of electricity		$10,000

To record the sale of electricity to general fund

General fund

Electricity expenditure	$10,000	
Accounts payable (to utility fund)		$10,000

To record the use of electricity

BASIS OF ACCOUNTING AND MEASUREMENT FOCUS

Basis of accounting determines *when* transactions and events are recognized. For instance, if an entity adopts the full accrual basis of accounting, a transaction is recognized when it has its substantive economic impact. If, on the other hand, it adopts the cash basis, the transaction is recognized only when cash related to the transaction is received or paid.

---

[1] As will be addressed later in the text, in government accounting *expenditures* are distinguished from *expenses*. For now, suffice it to note that "expenditures" is used in connection with funds that are accounted for on a modified accrual basis, whereas "expenses" is used in connection with those accounted for on a full accrual basis.

The **measurement focus** of an entity determines what is being reported upon—which assets and liabilities will be given accounting recognition and reporting on the balance sheet. The two concepts obviously are closely related; the selection of one implies the selection of the other. For example, if an entity adopts a cash basis of accounting, then its measurement focus will necessarily be upon cash. Only cash will be reported on its balance sheet. Correspondingly, measurement focus also determines whether net profit (the net increase in all economic resources) or merely selected resource flows (such as the net increase in current financial resources) is being reported upon.

If an entity adopts a full accrual basis of accounting, which is required of businesses, then its measurement focus will automatically be upon all economic resources, and its balance sheet will report on all assets and liabilities, both current and noncurrent. Increases or decreases in net fixed assets and long-term obligations are recognized as revenues or expenses. Suppose, for example, an organization purchases a vehicle for $25,000 by giving a note for the entire amount. The following entry (quite familiar to anyone who has studied conventional business accounting) would be appropriate:

Vehicles	$25,000	
Notes payable		$25,000

To record the acquisition of a vehicle

Inasmuch as governments and not-for-profits may be primarily concerned with the assets needed to satisfy current year obligations, they may adopt a **modified accrual basis** of accounting and a measurement focus on mainly short-term financial assets and liabilities. Therefore, long-lived assets and long-term liabilities would be excluded from the balance sheet and net changes in short-term financial assets and liabilities would be recognized as revenues or expenses or their equivalent. For example, if a government borrows $25,000 (issuing a long-term note) to purchase a vehicle, the following entries would be proper:

Cash	$25,000	
Proceeds from borrowing		$25,000

To record the issuance of a long-term note

Expenditure for vehicles	$25,000	
Cash		$25,000

To record the purchase of the vehicle

The government would report neither the vehicle nor the long-term note on its balance sheet. Instead, it would record both the increase and subsequent decrease in a financial asset (cash) on its statement of revenues and expenditures or a comparable statement that explains the changes in net financial resources. From an accounting standpoint, neither the vehicle nor the related liability would be recognized. The vehicle, in effect, would be written off (expensed) at the time acquired. The proceeds from the note would be recorded as proceeds from borrowing, an increase in fund balance that (like a revenue) would be closed to fund balance.

ACCOUNT GROUPS

To mitigate the disadvantages of using a basis of accounting that fails to recognize fixed assets and long-term debts, governments and not-for-profits establish account groups. Account groups, like funds, are self-balancing accounting entities. They are used almost exclusively to account for fixed assets and long-term obligations. Account groups are needed when governments and not-for-profits use a basis of accounting other than the full accrual basis and adopt a measurement focus that excludes long-lived assets and liabilities (e.g., that focuses only on cash or current assets and liabilities).

Account groups can be thought of as off-the-balance-sheet lists of either assets or liabilities that have been denied the accounting recognition they warrant. Thus, a **general fixed assets account group** (GFAAG) is a list of entity-owned fixed assets that are excluded from funds because the funds are accounted for by a basis of accounting that writes them off when they are acquired. A **general long-term debt account group** (GLTDAG) is a list of long-term obligations that, for the same reason, have also not been recorded.

But simple lists are not enough; accountants have been inculcated in the virtues of *double*-entry bookkeeping. Therefore, every item on a list must be counterbalanced by another. Accordingly, account group lists are offset by "artificial" counter-accounts. For assets, the counter-account is conventionally investment in general fixed assets. For liabilities it is some variant of amounts to be provided from general government resources or amount available in the debt service fund to retire debt (accounts that will be explained shortly).

Like funds, account groups are *accounting* entities, but unlike funds they are not *fiscal* entities. They have no cash or other resources with which to pay bills.

Reconsider the example in which the entity issued a $25,000 long-term note, using the proceeds to acquire a vehicle. The following two additional entries would be appropriate in a general fixed asset account group and a general long-term debt account group.

General long-term debt account group

Amounts to be provided from general government resources	$25,000	
Notes payable		$25,000

To record the issuance of a long-term note

General fixed assets account group

Vehicles	$25,000	
Investment in general fixed assets		$25,000

To record the acquisition of a vehicle

The term *account group* is most often associated with governments rather than not-for-profits. However, not-for-profits maintain comparable accounting entities. Usually lists of assets and related obligations are combined into a single account group. We will reencounter account groups in Chapters 8 and 9 pertaining to fixed assets and long-term debt.

In the remaining sections of this chapter, we will study the financial reports of governments and not-for-profit organizations to observe how they use funds and account groups to report their activities. We shall address the specific funds and account groups, noting the information they provide. To reinforce the purposes of fund accounting and the relationships among funds and account groups, we present a simple, highly stylized example of a fund accounting system used by a newly established university social club that provides its student-members with eating and living facilities. In particular note that:

- each fund is, in essence, a separate accounting and fiscal entity
- because the entity is not on a full accrual basis, some economic resources and obligations are not recognized as fund assets and liabilities

EXAMPLE *Fund Accounting at a University Social Club*

A newly formed university social club accounts for its activities on a cash basis (used for simplicity; this method is *not* generally accepted for external reporting). It maintains three funds and two account groups:

- *A dining fund.* This fund accounts for member fees that are restricted to maintaining dining facilities and providing meals.

- *A debt service fund.* This fund accounts for resources that will be set aside monthly to cover required year-end payments of interest and principal on its long-term debt. It may be viewed as a savings account (or **sinking fund**) for resources restricted by club policy to service the club's long-term debt. (Note that this fund is *not* to be used to record the long-term debt itself.)

- *A general operating fund.* This fund accounts for dues and other unrestricted resources.

- *A fixed assets account group.* This account group lists the club's long-lived assets.

- *A long-term debt account group.* This account group lists the club's long-term obligations.

During its first month, it engaged in the six transactions that follow:

1. It purchased a fully furnished house for $800,000, giving in exchange a twenty-year, 10 percent mortgage note. The note is to be repaid in twenty annual installments of $93,968.

    Because the club is on a cash basis of accounting and this transaction involves neither an inflow nor outflow of cash, it has no significance for any of the club's funds. Still, the club wants to maintain a record of its long-lived assets and obligations. Hence, the following two entries would be appropriate.

Fixed assets account group		
House	$800,000	
Investment in general fixed assets		$800,000
To record acquisition of house		

Long-term debt account group		
Amount to be provided to repay mortgage	$800,000	
Mortgage note payable		$800,000
To record mortgage note		

2. It collected $30,000 in membership dues.

    These dues are *unrestricted.* They are not legally or contractually designated for any specific purpose. Therefore, the club should record them in its general operating fund.

General operating fund		
Cash	$30,000	
Revenue from dues		$30,000
To record collection of member dues		

3. It incurred and paid $15,000 in general operating costs.

The club will pay these costs with unrestricted funds and should record them, like the unrestricted revenues, in its general operating fund.

General operating fund

Operating expenditures	$15,000	
Cash		$15,000

To record operating expenditures (In practice of course, the expenditures should be broken down into more specific accounts.)

4. It collected $9,000 in dining fees.

By agreement among members, these fees are restricted to maintaining dining facilities and providing meals. Therefore, the club should record them in its fund restricted for those purposes.

Dining fund

Cash	$9,000	
Revenue from dining fees		$9,000

To record collection of dining fees

5. It incurred cash costs of $6,000 related to the dining facilities.

These expenditures are to be made from resources restricted for dining-related activities and thus should also be recorded in the dining fund.

Dining fund

Dining-related expenditures	$6,000	
Cash		$6,000

To record dining-related expenditures

6. It transferred $7,831 from the general operating fund to the debt service fund as one-month's share of the annual required mortgage payment. These resources will be added to each month and retained in the debt service fund until year-end, when the mortgage payment is due. Of this amount, $1,164 is for repayment of principal; the remaining $6,667 is for interest.

This is a complex transaction, potentially confusing if not broken down into its components. The club records the transfer out of its general operating fund with a straightforward entry in the general operating fund:

General operating fund

Transfer to debt service fund	$7,831	
Cash		$7,831

To record transfer to debt service fund

Similarly, it records the transfer into the debt service fund with an equally simple entry in the debt service fund.

Debt service fund

Cash	$7,831	
Transfer from general operating fund		$7,831

To record transfer from general operating fund

There remains one additional adjustment, albeit one with relatively little accounting significance. The initial entry to the long-term debt account group indicated that $800,000 had to be provided to repay the mortgage. With the transfer from the operating fund, $1,164 (the principal portion of the payment) is now available to repay the obligation; only $798,836 must still be provided. Accordingly, the club should reclassify $1,164 from "to be provided" to "available"

Long-term debt account group
Amount available (in debt service fund) to
   repay mortgage $1,164
     Amount to be provided to repay mortgage $1,164
To note that $1,164 has been set aside in the debt service fund to repay the principal of the mortgage

The entries for these six transactions are intended to emphasize that:

- transactions between funds should be recorded in each fund as if they were with independent outside parties (just as if the transactions occurred between independent businesses)

- account groups provide a means to keep track of long-term assets and liabilities not recorded in their associated funds because the funds' basis of accounting precludes their recognition

Tables 2–1 and 2–2 summarize the transactions into balance sheets and statements of revenues and expenditures for the three funds. Balance sheets are the only statements prepared for the two account groups, since they are, in essence, lists and therefore do not have revenues or expenditures. For convenience, the statements are presented in columnar form. To emphasize that each fund is a separate accounting and reporting entity, combined totals are deliberately omitted. To stress that for reporting purposes other forms of presentation (such as consolidating all of the funds and account groups into a single column) are all possible—perhaps even desirable—an alternative balance sheet is also illustrated in Table 2–3. At this stage in the text, however, we wish to emphasize that each fund is, by itself, an accounting and fiscal entity.

TABLE 2–1
University Social Club Balance Sheet

	Funds			Account Groups	
	General	Dining	Debt Service	Fixed Assets	Long-term Debt
Assets and Other Debits:					
Cash	$7,169	$3,000	$7,831		
House				$800,000	
Amount Available (in Debt Service Fund) to Repay Mortgage					$ 1,164
Amount to Be Provided to Repay Mortgage					798,836
Totals	$7,169	$3,000	$7,831	$800,000	$800,000
Liabilities, Fund Balances and Other Credits:					
Mortgage Note Payable					$800,000
Investment in Fixed Assets				$800,000	
Fund Balances	$7,169	$3,000	$7,831		
Totals	$7,169	$3,000	$7,831	$800,000	$800,000

TABLE 2–2
University Social Club Statement of Revenues, Expenditures, and Other Changes in Fund Balances

| | Funds | | |
	General	Dining	Debt Service
Revenues From Dues and Fees	$30,000	$9,000	
Expenditures	15,000	6,000	
Excess of Revenues Over Expenditures	15,000	3,000	
Transfers-in			$7,831
Transfers-out	(7,831)		
Additions to Fund Balances	$ 7,169	$3,000	$7,831

HOW ARE GOVERNMENTS' FUNDS STRUCTURED?

OVERVIEW OF GOVERNMENT FUNDS

In this section we introduce the specific funds governments use to summarize and report upon their activities. First we present a brief overview of the funds structure; then we examine each type of fund in greater detail. The basic financial statements of the City of Fort Worth (Table 2–4) will serve as a point of reference.

Governments classify funds into three broad categories: governmental funds, proprietary funds, and fiduciary funds.

Governmental Funds

These are maintained to account for governments' operating and financing activities. There are four primary types of **governmental funds.**

- *General fund.* This fund accounts for all resources that are not required to be accounted for in other funds; in essence it accounts for all unrestricted resources.

TABLE 2–3
University Social Club Balance Sheet (Alternative Presentation)

Assets:

Cash—Unrestricted			$ 7,169
Cash—Restricted			
For Dining		$3,000	
For Debt Service		7,831	10,831
House			800,000
Total Assets			$818,000

Liabilities and Fund Balances:

Mortgage Note Payable			$800,000
Fund Balances			
Unrestricted—General Fund		$7,169	
Restricted—for Dining		3,000	
Restricted—for Debt Service		7,831	18,000
Total Liabilities and Fund Balances			$818,000

TABLE 2–4
City of Fort Worth, Texas

Combined Balance Sheet
September 30, 1996
With Comparative Totals for September 30, 1995
(000's omitted)

	Governmental Fund Types				Proprietary Fund Types	
	General	Special Revenue	Debt Service	Capital Projects	Enterprise	Internal Service
Assets and Other Debits:						
Cash and Cash Equivalents	$45,732	$16,787	$15,544	$104,744	$40,629	$4,352
Cash and Investments held by Trustees	0	0	0	0	0	0
Receivables:						
Taxes	18,419	4,100	0	0	0	0
Grants and Other Governments	11,232	7,019	0	0	0	0
Assessments	0	0	0	3,405	0	0
Levied, Unbilled Assessments	0	0	0	253	0	0
Sale of Land	0	0	0	0	2,209	0
Loans	0	6,765	0	0	0	0
Interest	0	21	0	0	0	0
Accounts and Other	9,319	228	1,144	3,130	28,472	63
Allowance for Doubtful Accounts	(23,430)	0	0	0	(3,403)	0
Due From Other Funds	10,824	0	297	1,858	0	0
Deferred Bond Issue Costs	0	0	0	0	2,312	0
Inventories (at cost)	2,003	0	0	0	2,853	1,973
Other	0	0	0	0	26	83
Deposits and Other	611	0	0	0	0	0
Long-term Loans Receivable, Net	0	0	0	0	0	0
Restricted Assets:						
Cash and Cash Equivalents	803	0	0	0	115,745	0
Cash and Cash Equivalents held by Trustees	0	0	0	0	13,948	0
Grants Receivables	0	0	0	0	4,376	0
Accounts and Other Receivables	0	0	0	0	1,073	0
Property, Plant and Equipment:						
Land	0	0	0	0	49,630	1,888
Buildings	0	0	0	0	38,314	6,065
Improvements Other than Buildings	0	0	0	0	801,679	1,336
Machinery and Equipment	0	0	0	0	135,264	10,183
Construction in Progress	0	0	0	0	144,063	0
Investment in D/FW International Airport	0	0	0	0	0	0
Investment in Railtran	0	0	0	0	0	0
Accumulated Depreciation	0	0	0	0	(268,015)	(7,799)
Amount Available in Debt Service	0	0	0	0	0	0
Amount to be Provided for Retirement of General Long-Term Liabilities	0	0	0	0	0	0
Total Assets and Other Debits	$75,513	$34,920	$16,985	$113,390	$1,109,175	$18,144

- *Special revenue funds.* These funds are established to account for revenues that are restricted to expenditures for specific purposes.

- *Capital projects funds.* These funds are used to account for resources held for the acquisition or construction of major capital facilities.

- *Debt service funds.* These funds are used to account for resources set aside for the payment of interest and principal on long-term debt.

Fiduciary Fund Types	Account Groups		Totals Primary Government		Discretely Presented	Totals Reporting Entity	
Trust and Agency	General Fixed Assets	General Long-Term Liabilities	(Memorandum Only) 1996	1995	Component Units	(Memorandum Only) 1996	1995
$16,595	$0	$0	$244,383	$223,076	$465	$244,848	$223,350
915,422	0	0	915,422	819,725	0	915,422	819,725
0	0	0	22,519	18,405	0	22,519	18,405
0	0	0	18,251	16,998	0	18,251	16,998
0	0	0	3,405	3,690	0	3,405	3,690
0	0	0	253	696	0	253	696
0	0	0	2,209	3,282	0	2,209	3,282
306	0	0	7,071	6,315	0	7,071	6,315
0	0	0	21	15	0	21	15
5,964	0	0	48,320	57,373	6	48,326	57,379
0	0	0	(26,833)	(25,715)	0	(26,833)	(25,715)
0	0	0	12,979	14,580	0	12,979	14,580
0	0	0	2,312	2,222	0	2,312	2,222
0	0	0	6,829	7,063	0	6,829	7,063
0	0	0	109	114	0	109	114
0	0	0	611	579	0	611	579
7,487	0	0	7,487	6,534	0	7,487	6,534
25	0	0	116,573	124,401	0	116,573	124,401
0	0	0	13,948	1,436	0	13,948	1,436
0	0	0	4,376	2,223	0	4,376	2,223
0	0	0	1,073	894	0	1,073	894
0	20,008	0	71,526	71,872	0	71,526	71,872
0	144,429	0	188,808	177,339	0	188,808	177,339
0	521,395	0	1,324,410	1,293,934	0	1,324,410	1,293,934
0	86,286	0	231,733	208,808	0	231,733	208,808
0	129,542	0	273,605	191,670	0	273,605	191,670
0	8,450	0	8,450	8,450	0	8,450	8,450
0	16,584	0	16,584	16,584	0	16,584	16,584
0	0	0	(275,814)	(273,381)	0	(275,814)	(273,381)
0	0	16,700	16,700	15,394	0	16,700	15,394
0	0	377,181	377,181	372,299	0	377,181	372,299
$945,799	$926,694	$393,881	$3,634,501	$3,366,875	$471	$3,634,972	$3,367,155

Proprietary Funds

Proprietary funds are used to account for the business-type activities of a government—those that are carried out as they would be in the private sector.

There are two types of proprietary funds:

- *Enterprise funds.* These funds are used to account for business-type activities in which the government sells goods or services to the general public.

TABLE 2–4 (Continued)
City of Fort Worth, Texas

Combined Balance Sheet
September 30, 1996
With Comparative Totals for September 30, 1995
(000's omitted)

	Governmental Fund Types				Proprietary Fund Types	
	General	Special Revenue	Debt Service	Capital Projects	Enterprise	Internal Service
Liabilities:						
Accounts and Contracts Payable	$6,120	$893	$0	$1,887	$8,039	$1,256
Estimated Claims Payable	1,105	0	0	0	0	0
Participants Compensation Payable	0	0	0	0	0	0
Accrued Compensation	7,046	690	0	39	4,592	2,538
Payable to Railtran	0	0	0	0	0	0
Current Portion of Obligations under Capital Lease	0	0	0	0	0	521
Payable to Federal Government	0	0	285	0	0	0
Due To Other Funds	0	5,956	0	534	2,089	2,305
Other	999	911	0	0	307	15
Payable From Restricted Assets:						
Construction Accounts Payable	0	0	0	0	3,486	0
Current Portion of Enterprise Debt	0	0	0	0	16,857	0
Accrued Interest Payable	0	0	0	0	2,106	0
Customer Deposits	0	0	0	0	4,969	0
Certificates of Obligation Payable	0	0	0	0	2,975	0
Other Revenue Bonds Payable	0	0	0	0	208,112	0
Bond Discounts	0	0	0	0	(2,769)	0
General Obligation Bonds Payable	0	0	0	0	10,797	0
Texas Water Development Board Bonds Payable	0	0	0	0	84,565	0
Commercial Paper Debt	0	0	0	0	0	0
Due to Other Funds	0	0	0	0	2,095	0
Deferred Revenue	2,485	10,844	0	5,621	3,787	0
Obligations Under Capital Lease	0	0	0	0	0	411
Landfill Closure and Postclosure Liability	0	0	0	0	2,951	0
Total Liabilities	17,755	19,294	285	8,081	354,958	7,046
Fund Equity and Other Credits:						
Contributions	0	0	0	0	357,233	12,204
Investment in General Fixed Assets	0	0	0	0	0	0
Retained Earnings:						
Reserved - Debt Service	0	0	0	0	16,441	0
Unreserved	0	0	0	0	380,543	(1,106)
Fund Balances:						
Reserved for Encumbrances	186	0	0	0	0	0
Reserved for Inventories	2,003	0	0	0	0	0
Reserved for Endowments and Loans	0	0	0	0	0	0
Reserved for Employee Retirement Benefits	0	0	0	0	0	0
Reserved for Debt Service	0	0	6,885	0	0	0
Unreserved:						
Designated for Authorized Expenditures	1,458	15,626	0	105,863	0	0
Designated for Debt Service	0	0	9,815	0	0	0
Designated for Insurance Expenditures	24,190	0	0	0	0	0
Undesignated	29,921	0	0	(554)	0	0
Total Fund Equity and Other Credits	57,758	15,626	16,700	105,309	754,217	11,098
Total Liabilities, Fund Equity and Other Credits	$75,513	$34,920	$16,985	$113,390	$1,109,175	$18,144

Fiduciary Fund Types	Account Groups		Totals Primary Government			Totals Reporting Entity	
Trust and Agency	General Fixed Assets	General Long-Term Liabilities	(Memorandum Only) 1996	1995	Discretely Presented Component Units	(Memorandum Only) 1996	1995
$442	$0	$0	$18,637	$17,311	$88	$18,725	$17,311
0	0	14,669	15,774	11,832	0	15,774	11,832
39,179	0	0	39,179	33,992	0	39,179	33,992
0	0	34,682	49,587	43,146	0	49,587	43,146
6,005	0	0	6,005	9,454	0	6,005	9,454
0	0	0	521	492	0	521	492
7,860	0	0	8,145	6,711	0	8,145	6,711
0	0	0	10,884	13,286	0	10,884	13,286
42	0	0	2,274	8,458	0	2,274	8,458
0	0	0	3,486	2,194	0	3,486	2,194
0	0	0	16,857	16,178	0	16,857	16,178
0	0	0	2,106	2,325	0	2,106	2,325
0	0	0	4,969	4,754	0	4,969	4,754
0	0	24,720	27,695	20,140	0	27,695	20,140
0	0	0	208,112	154,152	0	208,112	154,152
0	0	0	(2,769)	(2,506)	0	(2,769)	(2,506)
0	0	319,556	330,353	342,588	0	330,353	342,588
0	0	0	84,565	70,880	0	84,565	70,880
0	0	0	0	39,730	0	0	39,730
0	0	0	2,095	1,294	0	2,095	1,294
0	0	0	22,737	28,021	0	22,737	28,021
0	0	254	665	1,307	0	665	1,307
0	0	0	2,951	2,756	0	2,951	2,756
53,528	0	393,881	854,828	828,495	88	854,916	828,495
0	0	0	369,437	364,211	0	369,437	364,211
0	926,694	0	926,694	869,811	0	926,694	869,811
0	0	0	16,441	23,989	0	16,441	23,989
0	0	0	379,437	318,066	0	379,437	318,066
0	0	0	186	2,024	0	186	2,024
0	0	0	2,003	1,518	0	2,003	1,518
257	0	0	257	215	0	257	215
882,025	0	0	882,025	789,241	0	882,025	789,241
0	0	0	6,885	6,945	0	6,885	6,945
9,989	0	0	132,936	93,834	383	133,319	94,112
0	0	0	9,815	8,449	0	9,815	8,449
0	0	0	24,190	18,767	0	24,190	18,767
0	0	0	29,367	41,312	0	29,367	41,312
892,271	926,694	0	2,779,673	2,538,382	383	2,780,056	2,538,660
$945,799	$926,694	$393,881	$3,634,501	$3,366,877	$471	$3,634,972	$3,367,155

TABLE 2-4 (Continued)
City of Fort Worth, Texas

Combined Statement of Revenues, Expenditures and Changes in Fund Balances
Year Ended September 30, 1996
With Comparative Totals for Year Ended September 30, 1995
(000's omitted)

| | Governmental Fund Types | | | |
	General	Special Revenue	Debt Service	Capital Projects
Revenues:				
General Property Taxes	$132,965	$0	$0	$0
Other Local Taxes	66,003	23,658	0	0
Assessments	0	0	0	1,088
Charges for Services	12,950	0	0	0
Licenses and Permits	31,317	0	0	0
Fines and Forfeitures	9,470	0	0	0
Revenue from Use of Money and Property	9,198	1,472	6,480	1,110
Intergovernmental	1,190	50,765	0	0
Other	907	0	0	0
Contributions	0	147	0	11,089
Total Revenues	264,000	76,042	6,480	13,287
Expenditures:				
Current:				
General Administration	11,640	14,294	0	80
Public Safety	119,696	9,610	0	0
Transportation and Public Works	23,329	3,153	0	0
Parks and Community Services	16,974	2,033	0	0
Public Library	7,750	209	0	0
Public Health	5,603	2,820	0	0
Public Events and Facilities	9,416	0	0	0
Nondepartmental	14,122	0	0	0
Employment and Training	0	10,935	0	0
Planning and Development	3,702	959	0	0
Fiscal Services	4,044	0	0	0
Housing	302	11,502	0	0
Claims and Premiums	0	0	0	0
Capital Outlay	0	6,694	0	32,223
Debt Service:				
Principal Retirement	0	0	39,268	0
Interest and Service Charges	0	0	18,924	0
Total Expenditures	216,578	62,209	58,192	32,303
Excess of Revenues Over (Under) Expenditures	47,422	13,833	(51,712)	(19,016)
Other Financing Sources (Uses):				
Proceeds from Long-Term Debt	0	0	0	36,185
Operating Transfers In - Other Funds	12,765	2,407	53,018	13,765
Operating Transfers From Primary Government	0	0	0	0
Operating Transfers Out - Other Funds	(66,909)	(4,071)	0	(5,875)
Operating Transfers To Component Units	(210)	0	0	0
Total Other Financing Sources (Uses)	(54,354)	(1,664)	53,018	44,075
Excess of Revenues and Other Sources Over (Under) Expenditures and Other Uses	(6,932)	12,169	1,306	25,059
Fund Balances, Beginning of Year, as Previously Reported	64,690	3,457	15,394	80,250
Restatements:				
Eliminate Railtran Activity	0	0	0	0
Implementation of GASB No. 22	0	0	0	0
Prior Years' Operating Transfer	0	0	0	0
Fund Balances, Beginning of Year, as Restated	64,690	3,457	15,394	80,250
Residual Equity Transfer In (Out)	0	0	0	0
Fund Balances, End of Year	$57,758	$15,626	$16,700	$105,309

| Fiduciary Fund Types | Totals Primary Government | | Discretely Presented Component Units | Totals Reporting Entity | |
| Expendable Trust | (Memorandum Only) | | | (Memorandum Only) | |
	1996	1995		1996	1995
$0	$132,965	$127,287	$0	$132,965	$127,287
0	89,661	62,492	0	89,661	62,492
0	1,088	1,295	0	1,088	1,295
0	12,950	12,232	0	12,950	12,232
0	31,317	30,554	0	31,317	30,554
0	9,470	7,818	0	9,470	7,818
975	19,235	17,761	37	19,272	17,788
0	51,955	33,829	991	52,946	34,773
90	997	3,868	0	997	3,868
2,739	13,975	11,793	0	13,975	11,793
3,804	363,613	308,929	1,028	364,641	309,900
1,893	27,907	16,585	1,132	29,039	17,576
0	129,306	115,627	0	129,306	115,627
0	26,482	23,004	0	26,482	23,004
0	19,007	16,876	0	19,007	16,876
0	7,959	7,183	0	7,959	7,183
0	8,423	7,932	0	8,423	7,932
0	9,416	7,320	0	9,416	7,320
0	14,122	12,776	0	14,122	12,776
0	10,935	12,620	0	10,935	12,620
0	4,661	4,196	0	4,661	4,196
0	4,044	3,514	0	4,044	3,514
0	11,804	5,485	0	11,804	5,485
0	0	1,110	0	0	1,110
2,419	41,336	36,001	0	41,336	36,001
0	39,268	37,823	0	39,268	37,823
0	18,924	20,759	0	18,924	20,759
4,312	373,594	328,811	1,132	374,726	329,802
(508)	(9,981)	(19,882)	(104)	(10,085)	(19,902)
0	36,185	0	0	36,185	0
1,787	83,742	75,498	0	83,742	75,706
0	0	0	210	210	0
(349)	(77,204)	(74,449)	0	(77,204)	(74,449)
0	(210)	0	0	(210)	0
1,438	42,513	1,049	210	42,723	1,257
930	32,532	(18,833)	106	32,638	(18,645)
9,059	172,850	185,330	277	173,127	185,419
0	0	(1,231)	0	0	(1,231)
0	0	7,049	0	0	7,049
0	0	2,326	0	0	2,326
9,059	172,850	193,474	277	173,127	193,563
0	0	(1,793)	0	0	(1,793)
$9,989	$205,382	$172,848	$383	$205,765	$173,125

TABLE 2-4 (Continued)
City of Fort Worth, Texas

Combined Statement of Revenues, Expenses and Changes in Retained Earnings (Deficit)/Fund Balances
Year Ended September 30, 1996
With Comparative Totals for Year Ended September 30, 1995
(000's omitted)

	Proprietary Fund Types		Fiduciary Fund Types		Total	
	Enterprise	Internal Service	Pension Trust	Nonexpendable Trust	(Memorandum Only) 1996	1995
Operating Revenues:						
Charges for Services	$173,737	$27,786	$0	$0	$201,523	$180,495
Interest Income	0	0	29,568	26	29,594	23,653
Contributions	0	0	24,118	0	24,118	21,365
Net Appreciation in Fair Value of Investments	0	0	81,321	0	81,321	110,190
Other	6,191	0	0	0	6,191	5,488
Total Operating Revenues	179,928	27,786	135,007	26	342,747	341,191
Operating Expenses:						
Personal Services	25,804	15,157	0	0	40,961	40,881
Supplies and Materials	9,146	7,015	0	0	16,161	14,446
Contractual Services	77,476	5,778	0	0	83,254	80,672
Depreciation	25,574	1,232	0	0	26,806	27,447
Benefit Payments	0	0	39,279	0	39,279	37,637
Refunds	0	0	2,149	0	2,149	2,605
Provision for Loan Losses	0	0	0	0	0	96
Other	0	0	795	0	795	658
Total Operating Expenses	138,000	29,182	42,223	0	209,405	204,442
Operating Income (Loss)	41,928	(1,396)	92,784	26	133,342	136,749
Nonoperating Revenues (Expenses):						
Interest Income	10,170	101	0	16	10,287	8,716
Gain (Loss) on Sale of Property and Equipment	542	(302)	0	0	240	559
Interest and Service Charges	(17,178)	0	0	0	(17,178)	(15,777)
Other Revenue	816	318	0	0	1,134	1,255
Landfill Closure and Postclosure Costs	(194)	0	0	0	(194)	(166)
Total Nonoperating Revenues (Expenses)	(5,844)	117	0	16	(5,711)	(5,413)
Income (Loss) before Operating Transfers	36,084	(1,279)	92,784	42	127,631	131,336
Operating Transfers In	$546	$784	$0	$0	$1,330	$1,634
Operating Transfers Out	(6,136)	(1,732)	0	0	(7,868)	(2,892)
Total Operating Transfers In (Out)	(5,590)	(948)	0	0	(6,538)	(1,258)
Net Income (Loss)	30,494	(2,227)	92,784	42	121,093	130,078
Depreciation Related to Property, Plant and Equipment Acquired through Contributions from Federal Government	5,303	0	0	0	5,303	5,638
Increase (Decrease) in Retained Earnings/Fund Balances	35,797	(2,227)	92,784	42	126,396	135,716
Retained Earnings/Fund Balances, Beginning of Year, as Previously Reported	340,934	1,121	789,241	215	1,131,511	996,588
Restatements (Note A.17):						
Prior Years' Operating Transfer	0	0	0	0	0	(2,326)
Prior Years' Recalculation of Depreciation	20,253	0	0	0	20,253	0
Loans Receivable	0	0	0	0	0	(260)
Retained Earnings/Fund Balances, Beginning of Year, as Restated	361,187	1,121	789,241	215	1,151,764	994,002
Residual Equity Transfer In	0	0	0	0	0	1,793
Retained Earnings (Deficit)/Fund Balances, End of Year	$396,984	($1,106)	$882,025	$257	$1,278,160	$1,131,511

- *Internal service funds.* These funds are used to account for business-type activities in which the customers are other government departments or agencies.

Governmental funds may be characterized as **expendable funds,** in that their resources are received from taxes, fees, or other sources and then spent. There is no expectation that the funds will be reimbursed for services rendered to customers or other departments. By contrast, proprietary funds are said to be **nonexpendable** (or **revolving**) **funds.** The government may make an initial contribution to establish a proprietary fund, but thereafter the fund is expected to "pay its own way" (at least in part) through customer charges.

Fiduciary Funds

Fiduciary funds are used to account for resources held by the government as either a trustee (a party that administers property for a beneficiary) or an agent (one who acts on behalf of another). There are two types of fiduciary funds:

- *Trust funds.* These are used most commonly to account for assets over which the government acts as a trustee (e.g., a pension fund) or which must be invested and the income only (not the principal) may be expended.

- *Agency funds.* These are generally used to account for assets that the government holds temporarily for other parties (e.g., taxes collected by one government on behalf of another).

Whereas a government should have only one general fund, it may have any number of the other types of funds. Note the special revenue columns in Table 2–4; they indicate the combined totals of all the special revenue funds maintained by the city. For example, the city may maintain a separate special revenue fund for each revenue source that is restricted. Similarly, it may maintain a separate capital projects fund for each of its major capital projects and a separate debt service fund for each issue of outstanding bonds.

Having provided an overview of the funds structure, we now take a more comprehensive look at each of the main types of funds.

WHAT'S NOTABLE ABOUT EACH TYPE OF GOVERNMENTAL FUND?

THE GENERAL FUND

The general fund is used to account for all resources that are not legally or contractually restricted or arbitrarily set aside for specific activities. All funds are not created equal; the general fund is the master. In a city or other general purpose government, it embraces most major governmental functions—police, fire, street maintenance, sanitation, and administration.

Why does one single fund cover so many functions? Recall the rationale for fund accounting. Funds are established mainly to assure that governments adhere to resource restrictions. A government's fund structure rarely mirrors its organizational structure. Funds divide a government into categories of *resource restriction*, not functional departments or operations. To keep their accounting systems as simple as possible, governments should establish the minimum number of funds to assure legal compliance or efficient administration. Governments finance their general operations mainly with unrestricted resources, such as property taxes. Therefore, they can legally intermingle these resources and can properly account for all activities financed with unrestricted resources in a single fund.

By noting the assets and liabilities reported in a fund, a statement user can draw meaningful inferences as to the fund's measurement focus and basis of accounting. The balance sheet of the general fund presented in Table 2–4 includes assets other than cash. Were the general fund accounted for on a cash basis, its only asset would be cash. Therefore, the general fund is accounted for on a basis broader than simply cash.

At the same time, however, the balance sheet in Table 2–4 shows neither long-lived assets nor long-term debt. Obviously the city owns police cars, fire equipment, computers, and buildings. Moreover, it probably financed some of its long-lived assets with long-term debt. Were the general fund accounted for on a full accrual basis (full economic resources measurement focus), these assets and liabilities would be reported on the balance sheet. Instead, they have apparently been written off as acquired (and listed in the fixed assets and long-term debt account groups). Therefore, the general fund is accounted for on a basis between cash and full accrual (i.e., a *modified* accrual basis) and has a measurement focus between cash and all economic resources (i.e., current financial resources). This basis and measurement focus will be discussed in depth beginning in Chapter 4.

SPECIAL REVENUE FUNDS

Special revenue funds are established to account for resources legally restricted for specified purposes. Examples of typical restrictions include

- gasoline tax revenues that must be used for highway maintenance

- lottery fund proceeds that must be used for education

- a state law-enforcement grant that must be used to supplement the police department budget

- private donations that must be used to repair and maintain parks and other recreational facilities

As suggested by the mix of assets and liabilities reported on the balance sheet, all governmental funds use a common basis of accounting. Accordingly, almost all of the guidelines pertaining to the general fund set forth in this text can be extended to special revenue funds and other governmental funds.

DEBT SERVICE FUNDS

Debt service funds are a special type of special revenue fund. They are maintained to account for resources restricted to the payment of principal and interest on long-term debt. Debt service funds have much in common with sinking funds (resources set aside to retire debt) maintained by businesses.

Conspicuously missing from the balance sheet of a debt service fund is the obligation for the debt being serviced. This should come as no surprise. First, the purpose of the debt service fund is to account for the *resources* being accumulated to service the debt, not the debt itself. Second, because it is a governmental fund, the debt service fund does not recognize long-term obligations. The long-term debt, for which resources are being accumulated in a debt service fund, is reported only in the general long-term debt account group.

The one exception to this general rule, that the debt being serviced is excluded from the debt service funds, applies to interest and principal that have matured and are therefore *current* obligations. They would be reported as *matured interest payable* or *matured bonds payable*. But this exception is of only slight practical import. On the day the interest or principal matures, it should be paid and the obligation satisfied. Therefore, on year-end financial statements the liability for interest or principal should be reported only when payment is due but for some reason has been delayed.

Debt service funds derive their resources from other funds (e.g., transfers from the general fund) or from taxes or fees dedicated to debt service. Fund resources are expended to pay principal and interest.

When governments accumulate resources to service their long-term obligations, they commonly invest them in commercial paper, Treasury bills, and other financial instruments that, while secure, still provide a reasonable return. Typically, therefore, many debt service fund transactions relate to the purchase and sale of marketable securities and the recognition of investment earnings and related costs.

CAPITAL PROJECTS FUNDS

Capital projects funds, like debt service funds, are categorized as governmental funds and are a special type of special revenue fund. They are maintained to account for the financial resources to be used for the acquisition or construction of major capital facilities. Governments often issue bonds to finance a specific project. The resources received are restricted to that project and must be placed in a restricted fund. Capital projects funds typically derive their resources from the proceeds of bonds. However, they may also receive resources that were initially received by other funds and subsequently earmarked for the acquisition of capital assets.

Just as debt service funds are used to account for the resources accumulated to service a debt—but not the debt itself—so, too, are capital projects funds used to account for the resources set aside to purchase or construct long-lived assets, but not the assets themselves. The assets, whether in the form of construction in progress or of completed projects, are reported in the fixed assets account group.

Moreover, as with the resources accumulated to service debts, governments must invest any excess cash awaiting expenditure for capital projects. Therefore, many transactions of typical capital projects funds, like those of debt service funds, relate to investment activities.

WHAT'S NOTABLE ABOUT EACH TYPE OF PROPRIETARY FUND?

The financial statements of the two types of proprietary funds—the enterprise funds and the internal service funds—are strikingly different from those of the governmental funds. As shown in Table 2–4, their balance sheets report both fixed assets and long-term debt. Moreover, the fund equity section is divided into two classifications—contributions and retained earnings. Thus, the balance sheet looks decidedly like that of a business.

Proprietary funds are used to account for activities that are operated in a businesslike manner where the intent is to recover costs primarily through user charges. Because one of a government's typical objectives in providing the service is to at least break even, the government officials responsible for the activity require the same types of financial information as their counterparts in industry. For example, they need data on the full cost (including depreciation) of the services provided so that they are able to establish prices. Outsiders, such as the tax or rate payers, concerned with the activity's performance or fiscal condition need the same general information as would corporate shareholders. For this reason, proprietary funds are accounted for in essentially the same manner as private businesses. As suggested by their balance sheets, they employ the full accrual basis of accounting, and their measurement focus is on all economic resources. We will address the issue of which activities should properly be accounted for in proprietary funds, but will devote little attention to specific principles and procedures. Most students, though unaware of it, have been learning about proprietary funds since they began studying accounting.

ENTERPRISE FUNDS

Governmental units accounted for in enterprise funds provide services to the public at large. Examples include:

- utilities, such as electric, gas, and water

- golf courses

- hospitals

- mass transportation

- parking garages

- airport and harbor facilities

- housing authorities

Many government enterprises are financed similarly to businesses. Although a government enterprise does not sell stock to the general public, it may issue bonds (called revenue bonds). The principal and interest of the bonds are payable exclusively out of the revenues of the fund itself—not out of the general revenues of the government at-large. Therefore, the resources of the fund must be kept intact and cannot be commingled with those of the government's other funds.

INTERNAL SERVICE FUNDS

Departments accounted for in internal service funds provide goods or services to other departments within the same government (or occasionally to other governments). They bill the receiving departments at rates intended to cover the cost of the goods or services. Although there are no specific guidelines as to which intragovernment activities should be accounted for in an internal service fund, the following are examples:

- a vehicle repair service that maintains and services the cars and trucks of the police department, fire department, and sanitation department

- a motor pool that acts as an intragovernment rental car agency

- an electronic data processing department that maintains records and performs computer services for all other departments

- a store that sells office supplies to the other government departments

- a print shop that provides government-wide printing services

Internal service funds are typically established with a contribution of resources from the general fund, or some other fund. Thereafter, they are expected to be self-sustaining.

Because internal service funds sell their goods and services to other departments, most of their transactions are with other funds. However, internal service fund accounting is relatively straightforward, as long as each fund is seen as a separate accounting entity. When an internal service fund bills another department, it would recognize both a revenue and a receivable. Simultaneously, the fund that accounts for the other department would record both an expenditure and a payable. Most of the departments to which an internal service fund sells its goods or services are likely to be accounted for in the government's general fund or one of its other enterprise funds, since most governmental operations (as opposed to accumulations of resources for specific purposes) are accounted for in those funds.

WHAT'S NOTABLE ABOUT EACH TYPE OF FIDUCIARY FUND?

TRUST FUNDS

Kohler's Dictionary for Accountants defines a trust fund as a "fund held by one person (trustee) for the benefit of another, pursuant to the provisions of a formal trust agreement."[2]

Governments usually maintain trust funds to account for two types of resources:

- gifts, the terms of which specify that the amounts are to be invested, and income only is to be used for a specified purpose. For example, a donor may establish an *endowment* (the income of which is expendable but the principal of which must be maintained) to support a city's botanical gardens, museum, or recreational facilities. This type of trust fund is referred to as a *nonexpendable* trust fund since the resources (the principal) cannot be expended.

- pension contributions of both employer and employees. The activities of public employee retirement systems are accounted for in **pension trust funds.**

Governments can also establish *expendable* trust funds, mainly to account for the revenues generated by nonexpendable trust funds. In these situations the expendable trust funds are, in essence, special revenue funds and are accounted for as such.

For reasons that will be identified in Chapter 11 pertaining to fiduciary funds, nonexpendable trust funds are accounted for like proprietary funds. They use a full accrual basis of accounting and focus on all economic resources. Government pension funds, on the other hand, are accounted for by special rules that are as intricate as

---

[2] W. W. Cooper and Yuji Ijiri, eds., *Kohler's Dictionary for Accountants*, 6th ed. (Englewood Cliffs, N.J.: Prentice-Hall, Inc., 1983), p. 516.

those that have been established by the FASB for their private-sector counterparts. These, too, will be elaborated upon later in the text.

AGENCY FUNDS   Agency funds are used to account for assets held on behalf of other governments, funds, or individuals. Mostly they are established to maintain control over

- taxes collected by one government for the benefit of another
- special assessments collected to repay debt that the government services but for which it is not responsible
- refundable deposits
- pass-through grants—those requiring a government (such as a state) to distribute funds to other parties (such as school districts or individuals) but for which the government has no financial involvement and for which it performs no significant administrative functions, such as selecting recipients or monitoring performance

Custodial in nature, agency funds are not used to account for significant governmental operations. Consequently, agency funds are a student's delight—entities of the utmost simplicity. Their balance sheets show only assets (commonly cash and investments) and liabilities (the amounts owing to the beneficiaries)—no fund balances. The funds report no revenues and no expenditures.

In summary, governments maintain three main types of funds: governmental, proprietary, and fiduciary. The governmental funds, all of which are accounted for on a modified accrual basis, include the general fund, special revenues funds, capital project funds, and debt service funds. The proprietary funds, which are used to account for business-type activities and accordingly are on a full accrual basis, include enterprise funds and internal service funds. The fiduciary funds include trust funds, which are also accounted for on full accrual basis, and agency funds, which report only assets and liabilities, no revenues or expenditures.

WHAT IS INCLUDED IN A GOVERNMENT'S COMPREHENSIVE ANNUAL FINANCIAL REPORT (CAFR)?

So far we have discussed the basic funds maintained by a government. A clear distinction must be drawn, however, between the questions of what funds an organization maintains and how it reports on the funds. The next two sections explain how governments currently report on their funds and how they are likely to do so in the future.

The complete annual report, known as a **comprehensive annual financial report (CAFR),** consists of more than just the basic statements (of which the balance sheet and the statement of revenues, expenditures, and changes in fund balances are illustrated in Table 2–4). Indeed, the annual reports of states, cities, counties, and other general purpose governments are notable for their bulk. The reports of medium to large cities may exceed 200 pages, few of which contain pictures or other touches of frivolity. Government accountants are not typically compensated by the page. Why, then, are the reports so lengthy?

As previously noted, government reports are directed to a wide range of users.

Whereas most users are content with statements that aggregate data from the various funds, others require specific information on fund types or key individual funds. Accordingly, generally accepted accounting principles direct that a government's CAFR present information on at least two levels of detail, the **general purpose financial statements (GPFS)** and the **combining statements.** They may also be required to present information at a third level, the *individual funds,* if a government has but one fund of a particular type or when fair presentation necessitates greater detail on the individual funds than can be captured in the combining statements.

At the top level, the general purpose financial statements provide an overview of all funds and account groups. Also known as *combined* (not to be confused with the *combining* statements of the next level), they include one column for each *type* of fund and account group. The GPFS encompass five separate reports:

GENERAL PURPOSE FINANCIAL STATEMENTS (GPFS)

- a combined balance sheet for all funds and account groups
- a combined statement of revenues, expenditures, and changes in fund balance for all *governmental* (as opposed to propriety) funds
- a statement comparing budgeted and actual revenues and expenditures for the general and special revenue funds (and any other governmental funds for which budgets are prepared) (This statement will be discussed in the next chapter, which pertains to budgets.)
- a statement of revenues and expenses and changes in fund balances for all *proprietary funds.*
- a statement of cash flows for all *proprietary* funds.

As illustrated in Table 2–4, the combined balance sheet encompasses all types of funds—governmental, proprietary and fiduciary. However, separate statements of revenues, expenditures (or expenses), and changes in fund balances (or retained earnings) are prepared for governmental funds and for proprietary and fiduciary funds. This division is advantageous in that it emphasizes that governmental funds are on a modified accrual basis whereas proprietary and fiduciary funds are on a full accrual basis.

GPFS are intended to be "liftable." That is, they should be able to stand apart from the statements at lower levels of reporting without being misleading. Accordingly, they must also include GASB-mandated note disclosures and supplementary data.

As shown in Table 2–4, the "totals" columns of statements that combine funds of different types are marked "memorandum only." This designation is intended to warn statement users that the data have only been combined, *not consolidated.* The totals column represents a simple summation of the amounts in the other columns. No interfund items have been eliminated. Therefore, the assets and liabilities may be overstated by interfund receivables and payables, and revenues and expenditures may be inflated by interfund purchases and sales.

There are sound reasons why the statements are not consolidated. Recall the primary rationale for fund accounting. Governments, as well as other not-for-profits, segregate their resources into funds to assure adherence to legal or contractual restrictions. The resources in the various funds are *not interchangeable.* Surpluses in capital projects or debt service funds, for example, may not be used to offset deficits in the general fund or in special revenue funds. Combined, or even consolidated, totals may camouflage serious economic stress by aggregating the data of fiscally weak funds with those of the fiscally strong.

Further, as indicated previously, whereas governmental funds are accounted for on a modified accrual basis, proprietary funds are on a full accrual basis, so they cannot readily be consolidated.

COMBINING STATEMENTS AND INDIVIDUAL FUND STATEMENTS

Combining statements (which the GASB distinguishes from *combined* statements) present information on the funds that constitute a fund type. Each fund is reported in a separate column. Each statement's totals column ties the statement to an appropriate fund-type column on the entity's GPFS. Thus, there might be one combined statement for special revenue funds, another for capital projects funds, and a third for debt service funds.

Together, the combining statements and the individual fund statements must include (either as one column of a combining statement or as a stand-alone statement) all of the same basic reports as required for the general purpose financial statements—balance sheets; statements of revenues, expenditures and changes in fund balances (or changes in retained earnings for proprietary funds); statements of budget to actual comparisons (for governmental funds that have legally adopted budgets); and statements of cash flow (for proprietary funds).

HOW IS THE STRUCTURE OF FINANCIAL REPORTS LIKELY TO CHANGE?

As this text is being written the GASB is considering ways to both modify and supplement the current presentation of fund data. If adopted, the changes will give a dramatic new look to government's financial statements.

As emphasized previously, each fund is a separate accounting and fiscal entity. For internal purposes both governments and not-for-profits can—and should—prepare separate sets of financial statements for each fund. The proposed changes will not affect the reports of individual funds.

Although external users may require information on individual funds, they likely also make decisions based on the fiscal condition of the government as a whole. Therefore, they need aggregated financial data. But how should governments and not-for-profits present such data? The possibilities are limitless, ranging from a multicolumn spreadsheet (one column for each fund) to business-type consolidated statements.

To satisfy user needs for information on both individual funds and the entity as a whole, the board has proposed that governments present two sets of financial statements. One will be similar to the current GPFS, as illustrated in Table 2–4. This proposed set of statements would differ primarily in the way individual funds are displayed, not in the underlying accounting principles. The other would be radically different in that it changes both the underlying accounting principles and the way in which the funds are combined.

Fund Perspective

In the set of GPFS most like those of the current reporting model, governments will be required to display data for each governmental fund type. They would also be required to prepare separate statements for each of the other two types of funds—proprietary and fiduciary. Moreover, they will no longer present the two account groups—general fixed assets and general long-term debt—on the same combined balance sheet as other funds. Instead, they will prepare, and include in notes to the statements, two new schedules, a schedule of changes in capital assets and a schedule of changes in long-term liabilities. These two schedules would account for all increases and decreases during the year in the major categories of long-lived assets and long-term obligations. Table 2–5 illustrates the proposed balance sheet for governmental funds.

The structure of the proposed statement of revenues, expenditures, and changes in fund balance from the fund perspective will correspond to that of the balance sheet. Thus, the statement for governmental funds will present the same fund types and major funds as the related balance sheet, and the government will display the proprietary and fiduciary funds on separate statements.

Entity-Wide Perspective

The radically different set of statements will present the financial information from the perspective of the entity at-large rather than the individual funds or fund types. Governments will be required to aggregate the data from all of its funds into two columns—one for governmental activities; the other for business-type activities. A third column will be required to show **component units**—government entities that are legally independent of the reporting gov-

TABLE 2–5
Proposed Fund Perspective Balance Sheet

Sample City Balance Sheet Governmental Funds
December 31, 2002

	General Fund	Special Revenue Funds	Debt Service Funds	Capital Projects Funds
Assets:				
Cash and Cash Equivalents	$3,418,485	$ 3,797,635	$ 842,004	$ 1,141,648
Investments	—	—	3,141,980	23,729,732
Receivables, Net	3,644,561	2,963,659	—	364,340
Receivable From Other Funds	1,370,757	—	—	—
Receivable From Other Governments	—	253,778	—	1,461,319
Liens Receivable	791,926	3,195,745	—	—
Inventories	182,821	—	—	—
Total Assets	$9,408,550	$10,210,817	$3,983,984	$26,697,039
Liabilities:				
Accounts Payable	$3,408,680	$ 366,591	$ 151,922	$ 1,981,473
Payable to Other Funds	—	25,369	—	—
Payable to Other Governments	94,074	—	—	—
Deferred Revenue	4,250,430	6,273,045	—	261,000
Total Liabilities	7,753,184	6,665,005	151,922	2,242,473
Fund Balances:				
Reserved	1,015,039	1,179,752	3,832,062	6,587,305
Unreserved	640,327	2,366,060	—	17,867,261
Total Fund Balances	1,655,366	3,545,812	3,832,062	24,454,566
Total Liabilities and Fund Balances	$9,408,550	$10,210,817	$3,983,984	$26,697,039

Source: Exposure Draft, *Basic Financial Statements—and Management's Discussion and Analysis—for State and Local Governments* (Governmental Accounting Standards Board: Norwalk, Conn.: 1997).

ernment, but within the reporting government's control. These will be discussed in Chapter 12. More significantly, however, the statements will focus on *all economic resources* and accordingly, will be prepared on a *full accrual* basis. Hence, the balance sheet (called a statement of net assets) will report on both long-lived assets and long-term debt. Table 2–6 illustrates the proposed entity-wide balance sheet (called a *statement of net assets*) and Table 2–7 illustrates the proposed statement of activities.

The statement of activities (comparable to an income statement) will be strikingly different from that to which both users and preparers are accustomed. Most noticeably, it will highlight the net cost of a government's programs. As illustrated in Table 2–7, the upper portion of the statement will indicate program expenses. From these will be deducted the revenues that can be directly associated with these expenses. Most programs of a government are financed with general revenues, such as taxes, and hence, the revenues cover only a small por-

TABLE 2–6
Proposed Entity-Wide Perspective Balance Sheet (Statement of Net Assets)

Sample City Statement of Net Assets
December 31, 2002

| | Primary Government | | | |
	Governmental Activities	Business-Type Activities	Total	Component Units
Assets:				
Cash and Cash Equivalents	$ 13,597,899	$ 10,279,143	$ 23,877,042	$ 303,935
Investments	27,365,221	—	27,365,221	7,428,952
Receivables, (Net)	12,833,132	3,609,615	16,442,747	4,042,290
Internal Receivables	175,000	—	—	—
Inventories	322,149	126,674	448,823	83,697
Capital Assets, Net (See Note 1)	170,022,760	151,388,751	321,411,511	37,744,786
Total Assets	224,316,161	165,404,183	389,545,344	49,603,660
Liabilities:				
Accounts Payable	6,783,310	751,430	7,534,740	1,803,332
Internal Payables	—	175,000	—	—
Deferred Revenue	1,435,599	—	1,435,599	38,911
Long-Term Liabilities (See Note 2)	92,538,378	78,908,559	171,446,937	28,532,790
Total Liabilities	100,757,287	79,834,989	180,417,276	30,375,033
Net Assets:				
Invested in Capital Assets, Net of Related Debt	90,701,684	73,088,574	163,790,258	15,906,392
Restricted for:				
Capital Projects	24,715,566	—	24,715,566	492,445
Debt Service	3,020,708	1,451,996	4,472,704	—
Community Development Projects	4,811,043	—	4,811,043	—
Other Purposes	3,214,302	—	3,214,302	—
Unrestricted (Deficit)	(2,904,429)	11,028,624	8,124,195	2,829,790
Total Net Assets	$123,558,874	$ 85,569,194	$209,128,068	$19,228,627

Source: Exposure Draft, *Basic Financial Statements—and Management's Discussion and Analysis—for State and Local Governments* (Governmental Accounting Standards Board: Norwalk, Conn.: 1997).

TABLE 2-7
Proposed Entity-Wide Statement of Activities

Sample City Statement of Activities
For the Year Ended December 31, 2002

	Primary Government						Component Units
		Program Revenues		Net (Expense) Revenue			Net (Expense) Revenue
Functions/Programs	Expenses	Charges for Services	Grants and Contributions	Governmental Activities	Business-Type Activities	Total	
Primary Government:							
General Government	$ 9,571,410	$ 3,146,915	$ 843,617	$ (5,580,878)	$ —	$ (5,580,878)	
Public Safety	34,844,749	1,198,855	1,369,993	(32,275,901)		(32,275,901)	
Public Works	10,128,538	850,000	2,252,615	(7,025,923)		(7,025,923)	
Engineering Services	1,299,645	704,793		(594,852)		(594,852)	
Health and Sanitation	6,738,672	5,612,267	575,000	(551,405)		(551,405)	
Cemetery	735,866	212,496		(523,370)		(523,370)	
Culture and Recreation	11,532,350	3,995,199	2,450,000	(5,087,151)		(5,087,151)	
Community Development	2,919,389		2,580,000	(339,839)		(339,839)	
Interest on Long-Term Debt	6,068,121			(6,068,121)		(6,068,121)	
Water	3,594,733	4,159,350	1,159,909		1,723,526	1,723,526	
Sewer	4,912,853	7,170,533	486,010		2,743,690	2,743,690	
Parking Facilities	2,796,283	1,344,087			(1,452,196)	(1,452,196)	
Total Primary Government	$95,143,609	$28,394,495	$11,717,144	(58,046,990)	3,015,020	(55,031,970)	
Component Units:							
Landfill	$ 3,382,157	$ 3,857,858	$ 11,397				$ 487,098
Public School System	31,186,498	705,765	3,937,083				(26,543,650)
Total Component Units	$34,568,655	$ 4,563,623	$ 3,948,480				(26,056,552)
General Revenues:							
Taxes:							
Real Estate				34,168,449	—	34,168,449	21,893,273
Other				13,308,487	—	13,308,487	—
Grants and Contributions Not Restricted to Specific Programs				1,457,820	—	1,457,820	6,461,708
Interest and Investment Earnings				1,958,144	601,349	2,559,493	881,763
Miscellaneous				884,907	104,925	989,832	22,464
Total General Revenues				51,777,807	706,274	52,484,081	29,259,208
Excess (Deficiency) of Revenues Over Expenses Before Special Item				(6,269,183)	3,721,294	(2,547,889)	3,202,656
Special Item:							
Gain on Sale of Park Land				2,653,488	—	2,653,488	—
Excess (Deficiency) of Revenues Over Expenses				(3,615,695)	3,721,294	105,599	3,202,656
Transfers				501,409	(501,409)	—	—
Change in Net Assets				(3,114,286)	3,219,885	105,599	3,202,656
Net Assets—Beginning				126,673,160	82,349,309	209,022,469	16,025,971
Net Assets—Ending				$123,558,874	$85,569,194	$209,128,068	$19,228,627

Source: Exposure Draft, *Basic Financial Statements—and Management's Discussion and Analysis—for State and Local Governments* (Governmental Accounting Standards Board: Norwalk, Conn.: 1997).

tion of total expenses. However, programs providing goods or services on a business-type basis are typically financed with user charges intended to cover all, or a significant portion, of the expenses. Other programs may be supported in whole or part by outside grants or contributions.

The lower portion of the statement will present the revenues of the government at-large—those that cannot be tied to specific programs. These revenues include most taxes, general purpose grants, and investment income. The lower portion of the statement will also link the beginning and end of period net assets (per the balance sheet) with the excess of revenues over expenses.

In accord with the full accrual basis, the statement of activities will include charges for depreciation, as well as for other accruals, among the expenses for each program. Therefore, unlike the corresponding fund perspective statement of revenues and expenditures, it will indicate the full cost of a government's programs. In this way it will promote the objective of providing information on interperiod equity, making clear whether the revenues of the period have covered the full cost of providing services.

As this text goes to press the new reporting model is still in the proposal stage and extremely controversial. Nevertheless, as appropriate, we shall address the accounting and reporting ramifications of the proposed changes—especially the requirement that the entity-wide statements be prepared on a full accrual basis—throughout the text. If adopted, the GASB's final pronouncement will undoubtedly differ from what has so far been put forth. But even if never adopted, or adopted only with significant changes, it provides a useful counterpoint to the current model, highlighting its shortcomings.

HOW DO THE FUND STRUCTURES OF COLLEGES AND UNIVERSITIES AND OTHER NOT-FOR-PROFITS' FUNDS DIFFER FROM THOSE OF GOVERNMENTS?

The fund structures of not-for-profits may appear to have little in common with those of governments. They may bear other titles and differ in measurement focus and basis of accounting. Nevertheless, both not-for-profits and governments establish funds for the same general purposes and account for similar types of transactions.

The FASB, which establishes the accounting standards for not-for-profits, is concerned exclusively with external reporting. Therefore, it has established standards as to how not-for-profits must aggregate and display their financial information in general-purpose, external financial reports. These standards are substantially different from those of the GASB. The FASB, however, has provided no guidance on the types of funds they must maintain for purposes of internal accounting and control.

The fund structure of not-for-profits, like that of governments, should reflect restrictions imposed upon resources. In a not-for-profit entity, the restrictions are most commonly established by donor stipulation rather than law.

To illustrate the fund structure of not-for-profits, the following section describes the fund structure of colleges and universities. Many of the funds maintained by colleges and universities are common to other types of not-for-profits. However, the actual funds maintained by any individual not-for-profit depend on its unique circumstances and the information requirements of its managers and constituents. After all, the fund structure of a large metropolitan hospital would not be appropriate for a small rural cemetery association.

As pointed out in Chapter 1, government colleges and universities are within the purview of the GASB, whereas private colleges and universities are within that of the FASB. As a consequence, for purposes of external reporting, the financial statements of the private colleges and universities must adhere to the same standards as those applicable to other not-for-profits. By contrast, those of government colleges and universities may follow the "AICPA model"—that described in an AICPA industry guide, *Audits of Colleges and Universities*. Nevertheless, both private and government colleges may maintain the same fund structure, even though for purposes of external reporting, the form of their statements may be quite different. In subsequent chapters we will discuss the FASB requirements as to how not-for-profits should aggregate the data from the various funds and present them on their external financial statements.

Table 2–8, which will be referred to in the discussion that follows, presents the balance sheets of Pennsylvania State University. Although Pennsylvania State University is a government university, it better illustrates the fund structure of colleges and universities than does that of a private institution. That's because the FASB reporting standards require not-for-profits to classify their assets in three categories—unrestricted, temporarily restricted, and permanently restricted.[3] These categories typically cut across fund boundaries. By contrast, the AICPA model requires colleges and universities to report by fund type. Irrespective of how they report to outsiders, both private and government universities maintain similar fund structures.

Colleges and universities, like both governments and almost all other not-for-profits, maintain a current operating fund to account for their day-to-day activities. In addition, they maintain other funds to account for specially designated resources. Thus, they would establish funds to account for restricted gifts or grants, resources set aside to service debt, assets reserved for the acquisition of plant and equipment, and money held on behalf of others.

CURRENT FUNDS

The **current funds** of the university are equivalent to a government's general fund and its special revenue funds. Like a government, a university maintains a single *current operating fund* plus as many *current restricted funds* as needed. For purposes of reporting, Penn State combines all of its current funds, both unrestricted and restricted, into a single balance sheet. However, the fund balance section of the current funds' combined balance sheet distinguishes between the restricted and unrestricted fund balances. It further divides the unrestricted balances into designated and undesignated categories. Restricted balances represent resources limited by outside parties, such as grantors and donors, for particular purposes. They would include resources reserved for scholarships, specific research projects, and particular academic programs. Designated balances, by contrast, signify resources set aside by the university's own governing board. They should be classified as unrestricted because the governing board has the authority to redirect them to other activities.

LOAN FUNDS

As implied by their title, **loan funds** account for resources dedicated to student loans. A type of restricted fund, their assets are principally loans receivable and investments. They do not typically have liabilities of consequence, except if the university itself has borrowed the funds that it lends. Fund balances are ordinarily increased by gifts and grants and by investment earnings. They are decreased by administrative costs and by provisions for bad debts.

---

[3] Financial Accounting Standards Board, *Statement of Financial Accounting Standards No. 117*, "Financial Statements of Not-for-Profit Organizations" (Norwalk, Conn.: 1993).

TABLE 2–8

The Pennsylvania State University Balance Sheets, June 30, 1995 and 1994

Assets

	June 30, 1995	June 30, 1994
Current Funds:		
Cash and Temporary Investments	$ 24,417,946	$ 18,029,177
Investments—at Cost (Approximate Market Value, $179,091,000 and $158,854,000)	175,214,982	161,491,737
Accrued Interest Receivable	5,806,944	6,045,826
Inventories	17,991,905	16,542,295
Prepaid Expenses and Deferred Charges	9,314,647	10,268,162
Accounts Receivable—		
U.S. Government	39,876,744	40,551,372
Other, Net of Allowances of $37,338,541 and $38,097,082	106,845,156	98,262,358
Total Current Funds	$379,468,324	$351,190,927
Loan Funds:		
Cash and Temporary Investments	$ 1,049,494	$ 127,539
Investments—At Cost (Approximate Market Value, $8,127,000 and $8,256,000)	7,942,767	8,393,840
Accrued Interest Receivable	1,096,988	959,678
Loans to Students, Net of Allowances of $9,403,529 and $9,754,566—		
Perkins Loans	28,756,474	27,480,695
Health and Human Services Student Loans	1,350,829	1,273,573
Other	6,872,549	6,212,430
Total Loan Funds	$ 47,069,101	$ 44,447,755
Endowment and Similar Funds:		
Cash and Temporary Investments	$ 3,082,093	$ 2,138,223
Accounts Receivable	890,584	540
Accrued Interest Receivable	251,734	218,644
Investments—At Cost		
Land-Grant Fund—On Deposit With State Treasurer (At Cost, Which Approximates Market Value)	517,000	517,000
Other (Approximate Market Value, $359,599,000 and $309,407,000)	331,599,354	302,352,251
Total Endowment and Similar Funds	$336,340,765	$305,226,658

Liabilities and Fund Balances

	June 30, 1995	June 30, 1994
Current Funds:		
Notes Payable—Due Within One Year	$ 29,000,000	$ 30,000,000
Accounts Payable	90,829,901	84,132,977
Accrued Salaries and Wages	36,424,948	36,631,491
Accrued Payroll Taxes	3,365,761	3,096,217
Students' Deposits	2,891,590	2,711,999
Deferred Revenues	52,820,617	45,374,457
Accrued Postretirement Benefits	292,488,682	271,665,531
Fund Balances—		
Restricted	101,864,550	91,245,301
Unrestricted		
Designated	(232,505,602)	(216,791,176)
Undesignated	2,224,877	3,124,130
Total Current Funds	$379,468,324	$351,190,927
Loan Funds:		
Fund Balances		
U.S. Government Grants	$ 28,442,722	$ 26,958,375
University Funds—Restricted	18,626,379	17,489,380
Total Loan Funds	$ 47,069,101	$ 44,447,755
Endowment and Similar Funds:		
Annuities payable	$ 9,981,274	$ 8,896,200
Fund Balances		
Endowment	216,472,396	194,942,902
Quasi Endowment—Unrestricted	39,882,561	33,902,625
Quasi Endowment—Restricted	56,069,707	54,845,549
Annuity Funds	13,934,827	
Total Endowment and Similar Funds	$336,340,765	$305,226,658

Plant Funds

Assets

Plant Funds:		
Unexpended		
Cash and Temporary Investments	$ 11,721	$ 3,430
Accounts Receivable	6,628,807	7,410,628
Accrued Interest Receivable	2,803,743	2,852,413
Investments—At Cost (Approximate Market Value, $169,445,000 and $162,563,000)	165,594,797	165,281,211
Deposits With Trustee Under General Obligation Bonds (At Cost, Which Approximates Market Value)	—	4,532,873
Total Unexpended	175,039,068	180,080,555
Renewals and Replacements		
Accrued Interest Receivable	3,973,341	3,943,566
Investments—At Cost (Approximate Market Value, $240,143,000 and $224,757,000)	234,690,192	228,512,081
Total Renewals and Replacements	238,663,533	232,455,647
Retirement of Indebtedness		
Accrued Interest Receivable	$ 2,493,554	$ 2,521,015
Investments—At Cost (Approximate Market Value, $150,714,000 and $143,688,000)	147,284,804	146,094,684
Deferred Bond Costs	12,133,799	12,740,459
Total Retirement of Indebtedness	161,912,157	161,356,158
Investment in Plant		
Land	29,280,980	28,079,747
Buildings	1,197,642,275	1,143,144,646
Improvements Other Than Buildings	184,721,020	160,380,563
Equipment	582,636,135	544,171,682
Total Plant	1,994,280,410	1,875,776,638
Less Accumulated Depreciation	(892,987,842)	(817,605,670)
Total Investment in Plant	1,101,292,568	1,058,170,968
Total Plant Funds	$1,676,907,326	$1,632,063,328
Agency Funds:		
Cash and Temporary Investments	$ 12,019,507	$ 10,849,474
Accounts Receivable	1,817,306	416,537
Accrued Interest Receivable	717,967	760,414
Investments—At Cost (Approximate Market Value, $30,897,000 and $32,527,000)	29,932,329	32,778,359
Total Agency Funds	$ 44,487,109	$ 44,804,784

Liabilities and Fund Balances

Plant Funds:		
Unexpended		
Bonds Payable	$ 40,739	$ 2,755,828
Fund Balances		
Restricted	28,536,898	24,088,542
Designated	146,461,431	153,236,185
Total Unexpended	175,039,068	180,080,555
Renewals and Replacements		
Fund Balances—Designated	238,663,533	232,455,647
Total Renewals and Replacements	238,663,533	232,455,647
Retirement of Indebtedness		
Accrued Bond Interest	$ 7,819,282	$ 7,992,488
Fund Balances—Designated	154,092,875	153,363,670
Total Retirement of Indebtedness	161,912,157	161,356,158
Investment in Plant		
Notes Payable—Due Within One Year	26,100,000	29,000,000
Bonds Payable	409,862,261	421,639,172
Capital Lease Obligations	20,537,076	22,751,739
Contractual Payments Withheld	1,661,769	2,080,472
New Investment in Plant	643,131,462	582,691,585
Total Investment in Plant	1,101,292,568	1,058,170,968
Total Plant Funds	$1,676,907,326	$1,632,063,328
Agency Funds:		
Federal Taxes Withheld	$ 10,303,189	$ 8,580,367
Accrued Postretirement Benefits	19,363,227	19,990,062
Deposits Held in Custody for Others	14,820,693	16,234,355
Total Agency Funds	$ 44,487,109	$ 44,804,784

ENDOWMENT FUNDS

Endowment funds are analogous to nonexpendable trust funds. They are used most commonly to account for gifts specifying that the donated amount be invested and that only the investment income be expended. The donors may either stipulate the purpose for which the income must be expended or leave it to the discretion of the university.

Suppose, for example, a wealthy alumnus establishes a "chair" in accounting. The donation is to be invested; the investment yield is to be used to supplement the chair holder's salary and to finance his or her research and other professional activities. The university accounts for the principal in an endowment fund. As income is earned, the receipts are transferred to a restricted current fund—restricted because the earnings can be used only to support the chair holder.

Quasi-endowment funds, like current designated funds, account for sums set aside for specific activities by the university's governing board, rather than outside parties. As with other endowments, only the income, not the principal, is expendable.

Annuity funds and **life income funds** are special types of endowment funds. They are used to account for gifts that provide a return to the donor (or a person designated by the donor) for a specified term or for the remainder of his or her life. Thereafter, what remains of the gift will revert to the university. For example, a donor may want to contribute his fortune to a university while he is alive, but still reap all or a portion of the earnings from it. He can accomplish this (and perhaps also be rewarded with advantageous tax treatment) by attaching to his gift the stipulation that he receive either a stated annual sum (an **annuity**) or a percentage of the investment earnings from his gift (**life income**) until his death.

PLANT FUNDS

University **plant funds,** which embrace the government equivalent of capital projects and debt service funds and the debt and asset account groups, seemingly differ the most from corresponding government funds. However, variations in terminology and display must be distinguished from dissimilarities of substance.

Universities divide their plant funds into four categories, one of which, called investment in plant, is more in the nature of an account group than a fund:

- Unexpended (a capital projects fund for acquisition and construction of new plant and equipment)
- Renewals and replacements (a capital projects fund for renewal and replacement of existing plant and equipment)
- Retirement of indebtedness (a debt service fund)
- Investment in plant (a combined fixed assets and long-term debt account group)

These funds are grouped under the rubric *plant* because they account for plant itself, for resources set aside to construct or purchase plant, or for resources set aside to service the debt that financed the plant. But why comparable funds of governments are not so classified and titled is an open question.

Universities, like governments, maintain separate plant funds for each project or issue of bonds if the resources assigned to that project or issue of bonds cannot be intermingled with those of others. Therefore, the balance sheets presented in the financial statements for the various subdivisions of plant funds may be an aggregate of the balance sheets of more than one fund of the same type.

Plant Funds—Unexpended

The unexpended plant funds, the university version of capital projects funds, account for resources reserved for the construction or purchase of plant and equipment. Universities finance the construction of capital projects by issuing bonds, accepting gifts or grants, or by setting aside general operating revenues. To assure that the resources are used only for their intended purposes, they are accounted for in specially dedicated funds.

The assets of an unexpended plant fund consist mainly of cash and investments. In contrast to the capital projects funds of a government, the liabilities include the long-term debt incurred to acquire the fund's assets. The debt attaches to the related assets.

Plant Fund—Renewals and Replacements

The plant funds for renewals and replacement are nothing more than additional capital projects funds. The resources in these funds, however, are committed to the renewal and replacement of existing plant and equipment rather than the acquisition of new facilities.

Plant Funds—Retirement of Indebtedness

The retirement of indebtedness plant funds correspond to a government's debt service funds. Their assets, mostly cash and investments, are held for the retirement of debt and the payment of interest. Like government debt service funds, university retirement of indebtedness funds exclude the liabilities for the actual debt to be retired; they are reported in the investment in plant subgroup of plant funds.

Plant Funds—Investment in Plant

The investment in plant fund combines government's two account groups, the general fixed assets account group and the general long-term debt account group. It "lists" the university's long-term assets, such as land, buildings, construction in progress, improvements other than buildings, equipment, and library books. These assets are offset on the credit side of the balance sheet by:

- the long-term obligations, if any, incurred to finance the assets
- "investment in plant," the excess of the recorded value of the plant over the remaining debt outstanding

AGENCY FUNDS

The agency funds of a university are virtually identical to those of a government. They are maintained to account for resources that the institution holds as a custodian or fiscal agent for "outsiders," such as student organizations and employees. The accounting for these funds is as straightforward as for governmental agency funds; the funds have only assets and liabilities, no fund balances.

ACCOUNTING FOR BUSINESS-TYPE ACTIVITIES

Universities, no less than governments, engage in business-type activities. They operate restaurants, computer and book stores, dormitories, and intercollegiate sports programs. In addition, they have departments, such as print shops, conference and catering facilities, and supplies stores that sell their goods and services to other university departments. Universities, like governments, maintain separate sets of accounts for each proprietary activity. In that way they can measure its performance and control its resources.

The financial statements of Penn State do not explicitly set forth resources directed to business-type activities. Instead, like the statements of other colleges and universities, they incorporate them in their *current unrestricted funds*, sometimes netting both assets and liabilities and revenues and expenses under the caption *auxiliary enterprises*. What is the rationale for this difference in accounting practice? The best answer is an explanation, not a justification. University and government accounting practices have developed out of different traditions; different boards and rule-making authorities have set the standards.

FUND ACCOUNTING AS A CONVENIENCE, NOT A MANDATE

Although the GASB mandates fund accounting for governments, the FASB imposes no similar requirement upon other not-for-profits. As stressed earlier, fund accounting is an expedient means of control that helps assure that governments or other organizations use resources only for the purposes for they have been dedicated. But it is not the only means. After all, private businesses also must account for resources that are restricted (e.g., income taxes withheld from employees, sales taxes collected from customers, advance payments on government contracts, proceeds from bond issues that must be spent on specific projects). Yet they do not employ fund accounting.

Unless fund accounting is mandated by law, not-for-profit organizations need not employ fund accounting for purposes of internal accounting and administration. They must, however, comply with FASB requirements that they classify their net assets by degree of donor-imposed restrictiveness—unrestricted, temporarily restricted, or permanently restricted.

GASB's Proposed New Model for Government Colleges and Universities

As this text goes to press, the GASB is proposing a new reporting model for government colleges and universities. Similar to the model that it has recommended for state and local governments, it would require that colleges and universities prepare two set of financial statements—one from an entity-wide perspective; the other from a funds perspective. The entity-wide statements would be on a full accrual basis; the fund perspective statements would be on a modified accrual basis (e.g., capital assets would be reported as expenditures when acquired rather than as used over time.) If adopted, the proposed model would affect mainly the manner in which colleges and universities report on their funds. It would not affect the basic fund structure as described in this section. In their statements from a fund perspective, colleges and universities would continue to report the resources of, and activities in, each of the major fund types.

WHAT IS INCLUDED IN THE FINANCIAL REPORT OF A NOT-FOR-PROFIT ENTITY?

The financial reports of not-for-profit entities are comparable in size, form, and content to those of businesses. They must include only three primary statements—a statement of position (balance sheet), a statement of activities, and a statement of cash flow. Unlike governments, not-for-profits need not present separate data on each of their major funds or even fund types. Although the FASB imposes some unique accounting and reporting requirements on not-for-profits, for the most part they are subject to business standards.

The FASB permits not-for-profits considerable flexibility as to the form of the primary statements. Table 2–9 illustrates the statements of position and activities of a private university. This university presents the required information on donor restrictiveness on the statement of position simply by disaggregating the equity section into the three classes of net assets. It indicates the changes during the year in each of the classes of net assets by dividing the statement of activities into three columns. In Chapter 6 we will further examine the form and content of these statements.

TABLE 2–9
Case Western Reserve University
Consolidated Balance Sheet
June 30, 1996
(in Thousands)

Assets:

Cash and Temporary Investments	$ 23,685
Accounts and Loans Receivable, Net	95,837
Pledges Receivable, Net	35,979
Prepaid Expenses and Other Assets	12,680
Investments	848,599
Property, Plant, Equipment and Books, Net	384,133
Funds Held in Trust by Others	231,694
Total Assets	$1,632,607

Liabilities:

Accounts Payable and Accrued Expenses	$ 36,546
Deferred Income and Deposits	11,712
Annuities Payable	27,805
Refundable Advances	3,314
Bonds and Notes Payable	129,256
Refundable Federal Student Loans	20,487
Total Liabilities	$ 229,120

Net Assets:

Unrestricted	$ 808,017
Temporarily Restricted	29,268
Permanently Restricted	566,202
Total Net Assets	$1,403,487
Total Liabilities and Net Assets	$1,632,607

SUMMARY

Governments and not-for-profits organize their accounting systems on the basis of *funds*. Funds are independent fiscal and accounting entities, each with a self-balancing set of accounts. Fund accounting is an effective means of establishing control and accountability over restricted resources.

Account groups are lists of assets and liabilities that have not been recognized within a fund because they are outside its measurement focus.

The fund structure of a government or not-for-profit is typically based on the nature of restrictions, not on the entity's organization chart. Four types of governmental funds account for the operating and financing activities of a government:

- The general fund accounts for resources that are *not* restricted and thereby not reported in any other fund.

- Special revenue funds account for resources that must be used for specific purposes as stipulated by legislation or by outside parties, such as grantors or donors.

- Capital projects funds account for resources reserved for the construction, acquisition, or improvement of fixed assets.

- Debt service funds account for resources set aside for the payment of interest and the retirement of debt.

Two types of proprietary funds account for business-type activities of a government:

TABLE 2–9 **(Continued)**
Case Western Reserve University
Consolidated Statement of Activities
For the Year Ended June 30, 1996
(in Thousands)

	Unrestricted	Temporarily Restricted	Permanently Restricted	Total
Operating Revenues:				
Student Tuition and Fees	$126,006			$ 126,006
Less: Student aid	(39,401)			(30,401)
	86,605			86,605
Endowment Income	33,760	$ 784	$ 868	35,412
Grants and Contracts	138,494	94		138,588
Gifts and Pledges	11,856	8,234	19,550	39,640
State of Ohio Appropriations	5,049			5,049
Recovery of Indirect Costs	37,128			37,128
Organized Activities	2,309			2,309
Other Sources	11,973	21		11,994
Auxiliary Services	27,364			27,364
Net Assets Released From Restrictions	19,061	(18,187)	(874)	—
Total Operating Revenues	373,599	(9,054)	19,544	384,089
Operating Expenses:				
Instructional	108,079			108,079
Sponsored Research and Training	108,894			108,894
Other Sponsored Projects	35,305			35,305
Libraries	9,382			9,382
Student Services	8,125			8,125
Operation and Maintenance of Physical Plant	11,290			11,290
University Services	36,317			36,317
Auxiliary Enterprises	26,634			26,634
Total Operating Expenses	344,026	—	—	344,026
Net Operating Revenues	29,573	(9,054)	19,544	40,063
Nonoperating Revenues and Expenses:				
Investment and Other Income	71,710	(272)	32,119	103,557
Net Unrealized Appreciation in the Fair Market Value of Investments	10,765	76	2,018	12,859
Actuarial Adjustment to Annuities Payable	(176)		(5,774)	(5,950)
Loss on Disposal of Equipment	(1,783)			(1,783)
Nonoperating Revenues, Net	80,516	(196)	28,363	108,683
Increase (Decrease) in Net Assets	110,089	(9,250)	47,907	148,746
Beginning Net Assets	697,928	38,518	518,295	1,254,741
Ending Net Assets	$808,017	$29,268	$566,202	$1,403,487

- Enterprise funds account for activities in which the government sells goods or services to the general public.
- Internal service funds account for activities in which the customers are other government departments or agencies.

Two types of fiduciary funds account for resources held by a government as a trustee or agent.

- Trust funds account for endowments that are themselves unexpendable but the earnings thereon can be spent. They also account for pensions and other amounts in which the government controls assets in a trust or fiduciary capacity.
- Agency funds account for resources that the government holds temporarily on behalf of others.

In the government balance sheet, the totals column represents a simple summation of the amounts in each column. It does not present consolidated data.

For internal purposes, each fund must have its own set of accounts from which independent financial statements can be prepared. For external purposes, however, these statements may be aggregated in a variety of combinations. In fact, generally accepted accounting principles require that governments' comprehensive annual financial reports present information at a minimum of two levels of detail: general purpose (combined) statements in which each column represents a different fund type and combining statements, one for each fund type, in which each column represents an individual fund.

The fund structures of other not-for-profits are dictated by the unique characteristics of the entity and the information needs of its managers, governing board, and constituents. The fund structure of colleges and universities, for example, is similar to that of governments, although some of the titles are different. Most notably, colleges and universities include in their plant funds an unexpended fund and a fund for the renewal and replacement of assets, both of which are comparable to governments' capital projects funds. Similarly, the plant funds include a fund for the retirement of indebtedness, which is, in essence, a debt service fund.

For purposes of external reporting, not-for-profits aggregate and present their fund data quite differently than governments. The FASB requires that not-for-profits classify their net assets into three categories: unrestricted, temporarily restricted, and permanently restricted.

Although the GASB dictates that entities within its purview employ fund accounting, the FASB does not. Not-for-profits, therefore, employ fund accounting because it enhances internal control, not because it is required.

EXERCISE FOR REVIEW AND SELF-STUDY

Note to Students: Solutions to the Exercises for Review and Self-Study may be found at the end of each chapter, following the problems.

The newly created County Recreation District established the following funds and account groups, each of which is a separate fiscal and accounting entity:

- a *general fund* to account for resources that are unrestricted
- a *capital projects fund* to account for the proceeds of bonds, which will be issued to finance the construction of recreational facilities
- a *debt service fund* to account for resources set aside to pay principal and interest on the bonds
- an *internal service fund* to account for the operations of an equipment repair department that will provide services to several departments that are accounted for within the general fund
- a *general fixed asset account group* to report fixed assets (other than those of the equipment repair department)
- a *general long-term debt account group* to report the bonds payable.

The district's first-year transactions are summarized as follows (all dollar amounts in millions).

Prepare appropriate journal entries to record the transactions. Based on the entries, prepare a combined balance sheet, a combined statement of revenues, expenditures, and changes in fund balances for the governmental funds and a statement of revenues, expenses, and changes in fund balance for the internal service fund.

1. It levies taxes of $300, of which it collects $250. It expects to collect the remaining $50 shortly after year-end. The taxes are unrestricted as to how they may be used.

2. It incurs $240 in general operating expenditures, of which it pays $170.

3. It issues long-term bonds of $500. The bonds must be used to finance the acquisition of recreational facilities, and therefore they are recorded in a restricted fund, the *capital projects fund.* The capital projects fund is a governmental fund. As such, it is not accounted for on a full accrual basis. It does not recognize long-term debt as an obligation. Accordingly, the inflow of resources is accounted for as "bond proceeds," an account that, like a revenue, increases fund balance. The account is typically classified as "other financing sources" in a statement of revenues, expenditures, and changes in fund balances to distinguish it from operating revenues.

4. The district acquires $400 of recreational facilities using the resources available in the capital projects fund. Just as the capital projects fund recognizes the bond proceeds as a revenue, so too it records the acquisition of the equipment as an expenditure.

5. The bond indenture (agreement) requires that the district periodically set aside funds to repay the principal of the debt. Therefore, the district transfers $40 from the general fund to the fund specially created to account for resources restricted for debt service. This transaction must be recorded in the two affected independent accounting entities, the general fund and the debt service fund.

6. The repair service, which is accounted for in an internal service fund, acquires $10 of equipment, giving a long-term note in exchange. Internal service funds are *proprietary* funds and as such are accounted for as if they were businesses. They are accounted for on a full accrual basis; they focus on all economic resources. Hence, they recognize both long-term assets and long-term obligations.

7. The repair service bills the district's other departments $15 and collects the full amount in cash. The other departments are all accounted for in the general fund. The service incurs cash operating expenses of $12 and recognizes $2 of depreciation.

QUESTIONS FOR REVIEW AND DISCUSSION

1. Distinguish between *funds* as the term is used in governmental as contrasted with business accounting.

2. Upon examining the balance sheet of a large city you notice that the total assets of the general fund far exceed those of the combined total of the city's ten separate special revenue funds. Moreover, you observe that there are no funds for public safety, sanitation, health and welfare, and general administration—all important functions of the government. Why do you suppose the city hasn't attempted to "even-out" the assets in the funds? Why does it not maintain funds for each of its major functional areas?

3. In what significant way does an account group differ from a fund? Why do governments maintain account groups?

4. Why are there generally no capital projects (work in progress or other long-lived assets) in governments' *capital projects* funds? Why are there generally no long-term debts in their *debt* service funds?

5. The balance sheets of both enterprise funds and internal service funds report long-lived assets and long-term debt. What does that tell you about the funds' measurement focus and basis of accounting? Are the fixed assets of these funds likely to be recorded in a fixed asset account group? Are the long-term debts likely to be recorded in a long-term debt account group? Explain.

6. As will be emphasized later in this text, depreciation is recorded in *proprietary* funds but not in *governmental* funds. What is the rationale for recording depreciation in proprietary funds?

7. Why must the totals column on a combined balance sheet bear the warning label "memorandum only"?

8. The combined balance sheets of some not-for-profit organizations are in the form of only a single column. Does this indicate that the entity has opted not to employ fund accounting? Explain.

9. What are a university's counterparts to a government's capital projects and debt service funds? What are the counterparts to a government's fixed assets and long-term debt account groups? What are the similarities; what are the differences?

10. What types of resources are accounted for in *agency* funds? What is notably different about agency funds relative to governments' other funds?

EXERCISES

2-1

Measurement focus is closely tied to basis of accounting.

A newly established not-for-profit organization engaged in the following transactions.

1. A donor pledged $1,000,000, giving the organization a legally enforceable 90-day note for the full amount.

2. The donor paid $300,000 of the amount pledged.

3. The organization purchased a building for $600,000, paying $120,000 and giving a 30-year mortgage note for the balance. The building has a 30-year useful life. When appropriate, the organization charges a full year's depreciation in the period of acquisition.

4. It hired employees. By the end of the period they had earned $4,000 in wages, but had not yet been paid.

The organization accounts for its activities in a single fund.

a. Prepare journal entries to record the transactions, making the following alternative assumptions as to the organization's measurement focus:
- cash only
- cash plus current financial resources (i.e., cash plus short-term receivables less short-term payables)
- all economic resources

You need not be concerned with entries that might be made in account groups rather than the fund itself.

b. Based on your entries, prepare appropriate statements of revenues and expenses and balance sheets.

2-2

Account groups report assets and liabilities that, owing to a narrow measurement focus, are not reported on the balance sheet.

A city accounts for its general fund (its only fund) on a modified accrual basis, giving recognition to all assets and liabilities except fixed assets and long-term obligations. In a particular period it engaged in the following transactions.

1. It issued $20 million in long-term bonds.

2. It acquired several tracts of land at a total cost of $4 million, paying the entire amount in cash.

3. It sold a portion of the land for $1 million, receiving cash for the entire amount. The tract sold had cost $0.8 million.

4. It repaid $2 million of the bonds.

5. It lost a lawsuit and was ordered to pay $9 million over three years. It made its first cash payment of $3 million.

a. Prepare journal entries to record the transactions in the general fund.

b. Prepare appropriate journal entries in the general fixed assets and the general long-term debt account groups.

2-3

Funds are separate fiscal and accounting entities, each with its own self-balancing set of accounts.

The newly established Society for Ethical Teachings maintains two funds—a general fund for operations and a building fund to accumulate resources for a new building.

In its first year it engaged in the following transactions.

1. It received cash contributions of $200,000, of which $40,000 were restricted for the acquisition of the new building.

2. It incurred operating costs of $130,000, of which it paid $120,000 in cash.

3. It earned $3,000 of interest (the entire amount received in cash) on resources restricted for the acquisition of the new building.

4. It transferred $17,000 from the operating fund to the new building fund.

5. It paid $12,000 in fees (accounted for as expenses) to an architect to draw up plans for the new building.

a. Prepare journal entries to record the transactions. Be certain to indicate the fund in which they would be made.

b. Prepare a statement of revenues, expenses, and changes in fund balance and a balance sheet. Use a two-column format, one column for each of the funds.

2-4

Typical transactions can often be identified with specific types of funds.

A city maintains the following funds:

1. general
2. special revenue
3. capital projects
4. debt service
5. enterprise
6. internal service
7. trust
8. agency

For each of the following transactions, indicate the fund in which it would most likely be recorded:

a. The city collects $3 million of taxes on behalf of the county in which it is located.

b. It spends $4 million to pave city streets, using the proceeds of a city gasoline tax dedicated for road and highway improvements.

c. It receives a contribution of $5 million. Per the stipulation of the donor, the money is to be invested in marketable securities and the interest from the securities is to be used to maintain a city park.

d. It collects $800,000 in landing fees at the city-owned airport.

e. It earns $200,000 on investments set aside to make principal payments on the city's outstanding bonds. The bonds were issued to finance improvements to the city's tunnels and bridges.

f. It pays $4 million to a contractor for work on one of these bridges.

g. It pays $80,000 in wages and salaries to police officers.

h. It purchases from an outside supplier $40,000 of stationery that it will "sell" to its various operating departments.

2-5

The primary funds maintained by a not-for-profit organization have counterparts in a government.

The column on the left sets forth funds that are typically maintained by a not-for-profit organization; that on the right presents funds and account groups characteristic of a government. Match each fund in the left-hand column with its closest counterpart on the right. Some of the funds or account groups of a government may be associated with two or more of the not-for-profits' funds, inasmuch as those of the not-for-profits are more specialized or restricted than those of the government.

Not-For-Profits	*Government*
1. Agency	a. Capital projects
2. Endowment	b. General
3. Plant—unexpended	c. Special revenue
4. Plant—renewals and replacements	d. Agency
	e. General fixed asset account group
5. Plant —retirement of indebtedness	f. General long-term debt account group
6. Current operating	g. Trust
7. Current restricted	h. Debt service

2-6

Multiple Choice Questions from CPA Examinations

Items 1–3 are based on the following data relating to Lely Township:

Printing and binding equipment used for servicing all of Lely's departments and agencies, on a cost-reimbursement basis	$100,000
Equipment used for supplying water to Lely's residents	$900,000
Receivables for completed sidewalks to be paid for in installments by affected property owners	$950,000
Cash received from federal government, dedicated to highway maintenance, which must be accounted for in a separate fund	$995,000

1. How much should be accounted for in a special revenue fund or funds?
   a. $995,000
   b. $1,050,000
   c. $1,095,000
   d. $2,045,000

2. How much should be accounted for in an internal service fund?
   a. $100,000
   b. $900,000
   c. $950,000
   d. $995,000

3. How much should be accounted for in an enterprise fund?
   a. $100,000
   b. $900,000
   c. $950,000
   d. $995,000

4. The following revenues were among those reported by Ariba Township in 1995:

Net rental revenue (after depreciation) from a public parking garage owned by Ariba	$40,000
Interest earned on investments held in a trust fund for employees' retirement benefits	$100,000
Property taxes	$6,000,000

What amount of the foregoing revenues should be accounted for in Ariba's governmental-type funds?
   a. $6,140,000
   b. $6,100,000
   c. $6,040,000
   d. $6,000,000

5. Kew City received a $15 million federal grant to finance the construction of a center for rehabilitation of drug addicts. The proceeds of this grant should be accounted for in the
   a. special revenue funds.
   b. general fund.
   c. capital projects funds.
   d. trust funds.

6. The following proceeds received by Grove City in 1995 are legally restricted to expenditure for specific purposes:

Donation by a benefactor mandated to an expendable trust fund to provide meals to the needy	$300,000
Sales taxes to finance the maintenance of tourist facilities in the shopping district	$900,000

What amount should be accounted for in Grove's special revenue funds?
   a. $0
   b. $300,000
   c. $900,000
   d. $1,200,000

7. The following funds were among those on Kery University's books at April 30, 1995:

Funds to be used for acquisition of additional properties for University purposes (unexpended at 4/30/95)	$3,000,000
Funds set aside for debt service charges and for retirement of indebtedness on University properties	$5,000,000

How much of these funds should be included in plant funds?
   a. $0
   b. $3,000,000
   c. $5,000,000
   d. $8,000,000

8. In 1995, the Board of Trustees of Burr Foundation designated $100,000 from its current funds for college scholarships. Also in 1995, the foundation received a bequest of $200,000 from an estate of a benefactor who specified that the bequest was to be used only for hiring teachers to tutor handicapped students. What amount should be accounted for as current restricted funds?
   a. $0
   b. $100,000
   c. $200,000
   d. $300,000

2-7

Multiple Choice Questions from CPA Examinations

1. Maple Township issued the following bonds during the year ended June 30, 1995:

Bonds issued for the garbage collection enterprise fund that will service the debt	$500,000
Revenue bonds to be repaid from admission fees collected by Maple's zoo enterprise fund	$350,000

   What amount of these bonds should be accounted for in Maple's general long-term debt account group?
   a. $0
   b. $350,000
   c. $500,000
   d. $850,000

2. During 1995, Spruce City reported the following receipts from self-sustaining activities paid for by users of the services rendered:

Operation of water supply plant	$5,000,000
Operation of bus system	$900,000

   What amount should be accounted for in Spruce's enterprise funds?
   a. $0
   b. $900,000
   c. $5,000,000
   d. $5,900,000

3. The following financial resources were among those received by Seco City during 1995:

For acquisition of major capital facilities	$6,000,000
To create an expendable trust	$2,000,000

   With respect to the foregoing resources, what amount should be recorded in special revenue funds?
   a. $0
   b. $2,000,000
   c. $6,000,000
   d. $8,000,000

4. The following information for the year ended June 30, 1995, pertains to a proprietary fund established by Burwood Village in connection with Burwood's public parking facilities:

Receipts from users of parking facilities	$400,000
Expenses:	
Parking meters	210,000
Salaries and other cash expenses	90,000
Depreciation of parking meters	70,000

   For the year ended June 30, 1995, this proprietary fund should report net income of
   a. $0
   b. $ 30,000
   c. $100,000
   d. $240,000

5. The following items were among Wood Township's expenditures from the general fund during the year ended June 30, 1995:

Furniture for Township Hall	$10,000
Minicomputer for tax collector's office	$15,000

   The amount that should be classified as fixed assets in Wood's general fund balance sheet at June 30, 1995, is
   a. $25,000
   b. $15,000
   c. $10,000
   d. $0

6. The following information pertains to Timber City's long-term debt:

Cash accumulations to cover payment of principal and interest on general long-term obligations	$350,000
Proprietary fund obligations	$100,000

   How much of these cash accumulations should be accounted for in Timber's debt service funds?
   a. $0
   b. $100,000
   c. $350,000
   d. $450,000

7. On July 31, 1995, Sabio College showed the following amounts to be used for

Renewal and replacement of college properties	$200,000
Retirement of indebtedness on college properties	$300,000
Purchase of physical properties for college purposes, but unexpended at 7/31/95	$400,000

   What total amount should be included in Sabio's plant funds at July 31, 1995?
   a. $900,000
   b. $600,000
   c. $400,000
   d. $200,000

PROBLEMS

....

Continuing Problem

Review the annual report that you obtained.

a. Identify the main types of funds used to account for the entity being report upon. Provide examples of the specific funds within each fund type.

   1. Why are the resources of these funds not being accounted for in the entity's general fund?

   2. Does the report contain an organization chart? If so, how does the entity's organizational structure compare with its fund structure?

b. In which of the fund types are fixed assets and long-term debts reported? On what basis of accounting do you suppose these fund types are maintained? Do the notes to the financial statements indicate the basis of accounting (e.g., cash, modified accrual) of the entity's fund types?

c. Does the general long-term debt account group report an account "amount available for debt retirement" (or one comparable)? Can you reconcile the balance in this account with the balance in the entity's debt service fund?

d. Compare the total balance in the general fund in the current year with that in the previous year? Which statement in the report accounts for the change?

e. What is the population of the entity being reported upon? What are its major industries? Where did you find this information?

f. Are the financial statements audited? By whom?

g. Was the entity's annual report of the previous year awarded a "certificate of achievement for excellence in financial reporting" by the Government Finance Officers Association? If so, what is the significance of this award?

2-1

Account groups report assets that are denied recognition within funds.

    Entrepreneur Consultants, a state agency, was established to provide consulting services to small businesses. It maintains only a single general fund. Owing to the limited scope of its activities, the agency's financial adviser recommended that it account for its operations on a cash basis and maintain only a single fund. Nevertheless, the adviser urged that the agency keep accounting control over both its fixed assets and its long-term obligations. Therefore, it also maintains two account groups, one for fixed assets and the other for long-term obligations.

GAAP would prohibit a government agency from using the cash, rather than the modified accrual, basis. Assume, however, that for this agency the results would be the same.

    During its first month of operations the agency engaged in, or was affected by, the following transactions and events.

- It received an unrestricted grant of $100,000.
- It purchased five computers at $2,000 each.
- It paid wages and salaries of $6,000.
- It borrowed $24,000 from a bank to enable it to purchase an automobile.
- It purchased the automobile for $24,000.
- It made its first payment on the note—interest of $200.
- It destroyed one of its computers in an accident. The computer was not insured.

   a. Prepare journal entries in the general fund to record each of the transactions. Prepare appropriate journal entries in each of the account groups to record assets and liabilities that would not be recognized in the general fund.

   b. Prepare a balance sheet for both the general fund and the two account groups.

   c. Prepare a statement of revenues and expenditures for the general fund.

2-2

Even at this early stage of the course it is possible to reconstruct journal entries from a balance sheet.

    The Sherill Utility District was recently established. Its balance sheet, after one year, is presented below. You are to prepare journal entries to summarize all transactions in which the district engaged. You might note the following additional information:

- The general fund received all of its revenue, $150 million, from taxes. It had operating expenditures, excluding transfers to other funds, of $100 million.
- The general fund transferred $20 million to the debt service fund. Of this, $15 million was to repay the principal on bonds outstanding; $5 million was for interest.
- The bonds were used to finance construction of plant and equipment.

    You need not make closing entries. Do not be concerned with the specific titles of accounts to be debited or credited (e.g., whether a transfer from one fund to another should be called a "transfer," an "expense" or an "expenditure," or whether proceeds from bonds should be called "bond proceeds" or "revenues").

Sherill Utility District
Balance Sheet as of End of Year 1
(in Millions)

	General Fund	Capital Projects Fund	Debt Service Fund	Fixed Asset Account Group	Long-term Debt Account Group	Total (Memorandum Only)
Assets:						
Cash	$30					$ 30
Investments		$90	$20			110
Construction in Process				$ 40		40
Amount Available in Debt Service Fund					$ 15	15
Amount to Be Provided in Debt Service Fund					115	115
Total Assets	$30	$90	$20	$ 40	$130	$310
Liabilities and Fund Balances:						
Accounts Payable				$ 40		$40
Investment in Fixed Assets					$130	130
Bonds Payable						
Fund Balances	$30	$90	$20			140
Total Liabilities and Fund Balances	$30	$90	$20	$ 40	$130	$310

2-3

Funds can be "consolidated" but only at the risk of lost or misleading information.

The note and balance sheet on the following page were adapted from the financial statements of the Williamsburg Regional Sewage Treatment Authority (dates have been changed):

Fund Types

The transactions of the authority are accounted for in the following governmental fund types:

General fund—To account for all revenues and expenditures not required to be accounted for in other funds.

Capital projects fund—To account for financial resources designated to construct or acquire capital facilities and improvements. Such resources are derived principally from other municipal utility districts to which the Williamsburg Regional Sewage Treatment Authority provides certain services.

a. Recast the balance sheets of the two funds into a single *consolidated* balance sheet. Show separately, however, the restricted and the unrestricted portions of the consolidated fund balance account (not each individual asset and liability). Be sure to eliminate interfund payables and receivables.

b. Which presentation, the unconsolidated or the consolidated, provides more complete information? Explain. Which presentation might be seen as misleading? Why? What, if any, advantages do you see to the presentation that is less complete and more misleading?

c. Would it be possible to present the data in the same general format as the consolidated balance sheet yet still provide as much information as in the original balance sheets? Explain.

2-4

The more complete presentation is not always the easiest to understand.

Bertram County maintains a fund accounting system. Nevertheless, its comptroller (who recently retired from a position in private industry) prepared the following balance sheet (in millions):

Williamsburg Regional Sewage Treatment Authority Balance Sheet October 31, 1996		
	General	Capital Projects
Assets:		
Cash	$ 751	$ 5,021
Time Deposits		16,398
Due on Insurance Claim	9,499	
Due From General Fund		9,000
Due From Participants	66,475	4,414
Total Assets	$76,725	$34,833
Liabilities and Fund Equity:		
Accounts Payable	$17,725	
Due to Capital Projects Fund	9,000	
	26,725	
Fund Balance	50,000	34,833
Total Liabilities and Fund Equity	$76,725	$34,833

Assets:		
Cash		$ 600
Investments		1,800
Construction in Progress		500
Fixed Assets		1,200
Total Assets		$4,100
Liabilities and Fund Balance:		
Bonds Payable		$1,700
Fund Balance		
Reserved for Capital Projects	$ 600	
Reserved for Debt Service	200	
Unreserved	1,600	2,400
Total Liabilities and Fund Balance		$4,100

The fund balance reserved for debt service represents entirely *principal* (not interest) on the bonds payable.

a. Recast the balance sheet, as best you can, into separate balance sheets for each of the funds and account groups that are apparently maintained by the county. Assume that the county uses a modified accrual basis of accounting that excludes recognition in its funds of both fixed assets and long-term debt. Assume also that cash and investments are divided among the funds in proportion to fund balances.

b. In your opinion, which of the two presentations gives the reader a more complete picture of the county's financial status. Why? Which presentation is easier to understand?

2-5

Consolidated balances are not substitutes for individual fund balance sheets.

The balance sheets of the town of Paris are presented on page 77.

a. Recast the balance sheets in the form of a single "consolidated" balance sheet. Be sure to eliminate any interfund (intragovernment) payables and receivables. Add together the amounts in each column (but show on a separate line the fund balance for each type of fund).

b. Put yourself in the place of an analyst. The town mayor presents you with the consolidated balance sheet. He asserts that the town is in excellent fiscal condition as measured by the exceedingly "healthy" fund balance. Based on your having seen the combined balance sheet that shows the individual fund-types, why might you be skeptical of his claim?

c. Comment on why a consolidated balance sheet is no substitute for a combined balance sheet that reports on fund types.

2-6

Is fund accounting less appropriate for businesses than for not-for-profits?

A newly formed not-for-profit advocacy organization, the Center for Participatory Democracy, requests your advice on setting-up its financial accounting and reporting system. Meeting with the director, you learn the following:

Town of Paris
Combined Balance Sheet

	General Fund	Special Revenue Fund	Capital Projects Fund	Debt Service Fund	Endowment Fund	Fixed Assets Account Group	Long-term Debt Account Group	Total (Memorandum Only)
Assets:								
Cash	$ 38	$ 20	$ 35	$340	$ 10			$ 443
Investments	105	60	480	136	960			1,741
Due From Other Funds		120	46	39				205
Fixed Assets						$1,450		1,450
Amount Available in Debt Service Fund							$ 515	515
Amount to Be Provided in Debt Service Fund							800	800
Total Assets	$143	$200	$561	$515	$970	$1,450	$1,315	$5,154
Liabilities and Fund Balances:								
Accounts Payable	$ 8							$ 8
Due to Other Funds	205							205
Investment in Fixed Assets						$1,450		1,450
Bonds Payable							$1,315	1,315
Fund Balances	(70)	$200	$561	$515	$970			2,176
Total Liabilities and Fund Balances	$143	$200	$561	$515	$970	$1,450	$1,315	$5,154

- Member dues can be expected to account for approximately 80 percent of the organization's revenues.
- The organization plans to seek grants from private foundations to carry-out research projects pertaining to various political causes.
- The center has already received a gift of $100,000. The donor specified that the funds are to be placed in investment-grade securities and only the income is to be used to support center activities.
- The center leases office space but owns its furniture, fixtures, and office equipment.
- The center has taken out a five-year term loan of $100,000. Although the loan is not due until its term expires, the organization intends to set aside $17,740 each year with the prospect that, properly invested, these payments will provide the necessary $100,000.

   a. Do you believe that the center should establish its accounting system on a fund basis? If so, why?

   b. Assume you answered "yes" to question a. What specific fund-types or account groups do you think the center should set up? If you need additional information, specify what it is. Explain.

   c. Suppose, alternatively, the center was a privately owned, profit-oriented consulting firm that would provide political advice to its clients. The firm would charge its clients a fixed fee each month, in return for which they would receive periodic newsletters and the opportunity to meet with the firm's partners. In addition, the firm expects to enter into contracts to carry out specific research projects for its clients. Would you now recommend that the firm establish its accounting system on a fund basis (assuming, of course, that it would prepare its external financial reports in accordance with generally accepted accounting principles applicable to businesses)? Explain.

2-7

Business-type financial statements may be appropriate for some, but not all, not-for-profits.

The balance sheet of the Hillcrest Home Care Service, a not-for-profit organization providing assistance to the elderly, is presented below:

Hillcrest Home Care Service
Balance Sheet as of December 31
(in Thousands)

Assets

Current Assets:

Cash and Cash Equivalents	$ 115
Investments	232
Accounts Receivable (Net of Estimated Uncollectibles of $60,000)	652
Total Current Assets	999

Equipment:

Medical and Office Equipment	75
Vehicles	60
	135
Less Accumulated Depreciation	(52)
Net Equipment	83

Other Assets:

Deferred Finance Charges	15
Total Assets	$1,097

Liabilities and Fund Balances

Current Liabilities:

Current Maturities of Long-term Note	$ 18
Accounts Payable	50
Accrued Vacation Costs	346
Estimated Third-party Payer Settlements	35
Total Current Liabilities	449
Long-term Debt Less Current Maturities	110

Fund Balances:

Unrestricted	160
Temporarily Restricted	273
Permanently Restricted	105
Total Fund Balances	538
Total Liabilities and Fund Balances	$1,097

   a. As best you can tell from the balance sheet, what are Hillcrest's measurement focus and basis of accounting? Explain.

   b. What is the most likely reason that some assets are classified as temporarily restricted and others as permanently restricted?

   c. Suppose you are the independent CPA who audited the financial statements of Hillcrest. The controller of a town, also one of your clients, reviews the financial statements of Hillcrest and observes that they look remarkably like those of private businesses. He wonders why:
   - the statements of his town are so seemingly complex, consisting of not one, but several, separate balance sheets and statements of operations
   - his town must report fixed assets in an "account group" rather than the main operating fund
   - the statements of his town can't be more like those of Hillcrest

   What would be your most likely response?

2-8

A hospital's balance sheet tells much about its basis of accounting.

The balance sheet of a not-for-profit hospital is shown on page 79. The balance sheet is intended to display the hospital's fund structure. Inasmuch as it does not conform to FASB standards, it is inappropriate for external reporting.

a. On what basis of accounting is the general fund maintained? How can you tell?

b. Why doesn't the hospital maintain an *investment in plant* fund or account group?

c. Are the plant replacement and expansion funds on a cash basis of accounting? How can you tell?

d. Why do you suppose that the unrestricted fund assets "whose use is limited (designated) by board for capital improvements" are not reported in a *restricted* fund?

e. Suppose the hospital were to present its balance sheet in three columns, one each for unrestricted, temporarily and permanently restricted resources. Which of the funds would most likely be reported in each of the columns?

f. What funds in a government are likely to be most comparable to the specific purpose funds?

Central States Rehabilitation Hospital
Balance Sheet as of December 31
(in Thousands)

Assets		Liabilities and Fund Balances	
General Fund			
Current Assets:		*Current Liabilities:*	
Cash and Equivalents	$ 3,103	Accounts Payable	$ 3,200
Patients Accounts Receivable	15,700	Accrued Expenses	3,400
Supplies	1,817	Estimated Third-party	
Other Current Assets	404	Settlements	2,408
		Other Current Liabilities	2,700
Total Current Assets	$21,024	Total Current Liabilities	$11,708
Noncurrent Assets:		*Noncurrent Liabilities:*	
Assets Whose Use Is Limited		Estimated Cost of	
(Designated) by Board for Capital		Malpractice	$ 4,760
Improvements	$21,000	Long-term Debt	34,000
Property, Plant, and Equipment			
(Net of Allowance for Depreciation)	42,500		
Other Assets	7,300	Fund Balance	41,356
Total Noncurrent Assets	70,800	Total Liabilities and	
Total Assets	$91,824	Fund Balance	$91,824
Donor Restricted Funds			
Specific Purpose Funds			
Cash	$ 389	Accounts Payable	$205
Investments	250	Deferred Grant Revenue	80
Grants Receivable	613	Fund Balance	967
		Total Liabilities and	
Total Assets	$ 1,252	Fund Balance	$ 1,252
Plant Replacement and Expansion Funds			
Cash	$ 25		
Investments	250		
Pledges Receivable	110		
Total Assets	$ 385	Fund Balance	$ 385
Endowment Funds			
Cash	$ 1,600		
Investments	4,200		
Total Assets	$ 5,800	Fund Balance	$ 5,800

2-9

The balance sheet of a college provides considerable information as to its accounting practices.

Review the June 30, 1993 balance sheet of Dartmouth College, which appears on pages 81–82. As discussed in the chapter, private colleges may no longer present a balance sheet in this format, even though they may continue to maintain the four types of funds reported in the various columns. This "old-style" balance sheet is illustrated in this example because it focuses on the individual fund types rather than on the college as a whole.

a. Suppose that Dartmouth received a gift restricted for research in biology. In which of the columns would the gift be accounted for? Explain

b. On what basis of accounting (e.g., cash, modified accrual, full accrual) are the current funds accounted for? How can you tell?

c. True or false: As of June 30, 1993, the total assets of the college as a whole were $1.328 billion. Explain.

d. The college reports $283 million in land, buildings, construction in progress, and equipment. Yet its "investment in plant" is only $121 million. How do you account for the difference?

e. What is the distinction between resources that are "restricted" and those "designated by the college"?

f. The college receives a gift of $50 million. Terms of the gift specify that the proceeds are to be invested, but permit the college to expend both principal and interest in support of operations. However, it is the policy of the college to expend only income. How would this gift most likely be reflected on the balance sheet? Explain.

g. Each year the college sets aside a portion of its general revenue to repay its debt. How would the funds "saved" for this purpose be reported on the balance sheet?

h. The college provides loans to students. As best you can tell, what is the source of the funds advanced to the students?

i. An alumnus of the college recently complained to you. "The college has almost a billion dollars in fund balances, yet it still asks for contributions so that it can pay its faculty and mow the grass." How would you respond to the alumnus?

Dartmouth College
Balance Sheet
at June 30, 1993
(With Comparative Totals for 1992)
(in Thousands)

	Current Funds	Loan Funds	Endowment and Other Funds	Plant Funds	Total 1993	Total 1992
Assets:						
Cash and Temporary Investments	$18,567	$6,946	$29,611	$10,853	$65,977	$80,194
Deposits with Trustees		2,736		45,974	48,710	15,405
Accounts Receivable:						
Student Accounts	3,046				3,046	2,831
Grants and Contracts	9,377				9,377	4,885
Receivable for Investments Sold			781		781	15,121
Other Accounts Receivable	11,726	57			11,783	11,230
Inventories	1,990				1,990	1,804
Deferred Charges	5,628	550		6,317	12,495	8,093
Notes Receivable (Less Allowances of $1,569 and $1,526, Respectively)	93	43,779			43,872	40,001
Loans to Other Funds	8,557		6,879		15,436	15,172
Investments	24,940	1,180	796,116	9,345	831,581	732,603
Land, Buildings, Construction in Progress and Equipment, Net of Depreciation				283,181	283,181	266,498
Other Interfund Advances	6,825			(6,825)		
Total Assets	90,749	55,248	833,387	348,845	1,328,229	1,193,837
Liabilities:						
Accounts Payable and Other Liabilities	23,024	56	1,627	1,704	26,411	18,455
Payable for Investments Purchased			2,955		2,955	21,758
Annuities Payable			4,609		4,609	3,110
Deferred Revenue	12,654			18	12,672	12,807
Advances for Grants and Contracts	6,776				6,776	6,000
Loans From Other Funds		32		15,404	15,436	15,172
Notes and Bonds Payable		24,505		188,466	212,971	158,356
Total Liabilities	42,454	24,593	9,191	205,592	281,830	235,658
Net Assets	$48,295	$30,655	$824,196	$143,253	$1,046,399	$958,179

Dartmouth College
Balance Sheet (continued)
at June 30, 1993
(With Comparative Totals for 1992)
(in Thousands)

	Current Funds	Loan Funds	Endowment and Other Funds	Plant Funds	Total 1993	Total 1992
Fund Balances:						
Current Funds:						
Unrestricted	$702				$702	$610
Designated by the College	24,775				24,775	28,883
Restricted:						
Unexpended Gifts	13,570				13,570	17,981
Unexpended Endowment Income	9,248				9,248	9,697
Loan Funds:						
U.S. Government Advances		$13,012			13,012	12,179
Other Advances		1,540			1,540	1,375
College Loan Funds		7,050			7,050	6,192
Dartmouth Educational Loan Corporation		9,053			9,053	8,039
Endowment and Other Funds						
True Endowment			$503,883		503,883	449,037
Quasi-Endowment			239,789		239,789	212,492
Life Income Funds			80,524		80,524	75,498
Plant Funds:						
Unexpended				$19,478	19,478	14,477
Renewals and Replacements				2,146	2,146	1,258
Retirement of Debt				1,084	1,084	416
Investment in Plant				120,545	120,545	120,045
Total Fund Balances	$48,295	$30,655	$824,196	$143,253	$1,046,399	$958,179

SOLUTION TO EXERCISE FOR REVIEW AND SELF-STUDY

1. General fund

Cash	$250	
Taxes receivable	50	
Tax revenues		$300

To record the levy and collection of taxes

2. General fund

Operating expenditures	$240	
Cash		$170
Accounts payable		70

To record operating expenditures

3. Capital projects fund

Cash	$500	
Bond proceeds		$500

To record proceeds of the bond issue

Although the district does not report the obligation in a fund, it still wants to maintain accounting control over it. Therefore, it records the obligation in an extra-balance sheet "list" of long-term obligations, the general long-term debt account group.

General long-term debt account group

Amount to be provided	$500	
Bonds payable		$500

To record the bonds payable

4. Capital projects fund

Expenditure—acquisition of facilities	$400	
Cash		$400

To record the acquisition of facilities

From an accounting perspective the facilities have been written off when acquired. Yet the district wants to make statement users aware of their existence. Hence, it records the facilities in its list of fixed assets, the general fixed asset account group.

General fixed asset account group

Fixed assets—facilities	$400	
Investment in fixed assets		$400

To record the fixed assets

5. General fund

Transfer to debt service fund	$40	
Cash		$40

To record the transfer of cash to the debt service fund (the transfer account is similar to an expenditure account)

Debt service fund

Cash	$40	
Transfer from general fund		$40

To record the transfer of cash from the general fund

A minor adjustment is called for. The entry in the general long-term debt account group (the list of obligations) to record the initial issue of bonds indicated that $500 was the "amount to be provided." With this transfer only $460 remains to be provided.

General long-term debt account group

Amount available in debt service fund for debt repayment	$40	
Amount to be provided		$40

To adjust the general long-term debt account group to reflect the resources now available to repay the debt.

6. Internal service fund

Equipment	$10	
Long-term note		$10

To record acquisition of plant and equipment

Neither the equipment nor the long-term debt need be "listed" in the account groups. They are properly recognized within the internal service fund itself.

7. Internal service fund

Cash	$15	
Operating revenues		$15

To record operating revenues

Operating expenses	$12	
Cash		$12

To record cash operating expenses

Depreciation expense	$2	
Equipment		$2

To record depreciation (Alternatively the credit could have been made to a contra-account, "accumulated depreciation.")

The revenues of the internal service fund are expenditures to the general fund.

General fund

Expenditures	$15	
Cash		$15

To record repair services received

Table 2–10 shows the resultant balance sheets of each of the funds and account groups and explains the reason for the changes in the governmental and proprietary fund balances during the year. Since account groups are not funds, and therefore do not have fund balances, they are excluded from the exhibit showing the changes in governmental fund balances.

TABLE 2–10

County Recreation District
Combined Balance Sheet
End of First Year

	Governmental Funds			Proprietary Funds	Account Groups		
	General Fund	Capital Projects Fund	Debt Service Fund	Internal Service Fund	General Fixed Asset Account Group	General Long-term Debt Account Group	Total (Memorandum Only)
Assets:							
Cash	$25	$100	$40	$ 3			$ 168
Taxes Receivable	50						50
Fixed Assets (Less Depreciation)				8	$400		408
Amount Available in Debt Service Fund						$ 40	40
Amount to Be Provided in Debt Service Fund						460	460
Total Assets	$75	$100	$40	$11	$400	$500	$1,126
Liabilities and Fund Balances:							
Accounts Payable	$70						$ 70
Investment in Fixed Assets					$400		400
Long-Term Notes				$10			10
Bonds Payable						$500	500
Fund Balances	5	100	$40	1			146
Total Liabilities and Fund Balances	$75	$100	$40	$11	$400	$500	$1,126

TABLE 2–10 (Continued)
County Recreation District
Combined Statement of Revenues, Expenditures, and Changes in Fund Balances—Governmental Funds
End of First Year

| | Governmental Funds | | | |
	General Fund	Capital Projects Fund	Debt Service Fund	Total (Memorandum Only)
Revenues:				
Tax Revenues	$300			$300
Expenditures:				
Operating Expenditures	255			255
Acquisition of Facilities		$400		400
Total Expenditures	255	400		655
Excess of Revenues Over Expenditures	45	(400)		(355)
Other Financing Sources (Uses):				
Bond Proceeds		500		500
Transfer to Debt Service Fund	(40)			(40)
Transfer From General Fund			$40	40
Total Other Financing Sources and Uses	(40)	500	40	500
Net Increase in Fund Balance	$ 5	$100	$40	$145

TABLE 2–10 (Continued)
County Recreation District
Statement of Revenues, Expenses, and Changes in Fund Balance—Internal Service Fund
End of First Year

Operating Revenues		$15
Less: Operating Expenses	$12	
Depreciation Expense	2	14
Net Income (Increase in Fund Balance)		$ 1

CHAPTER 3

Issues of Budgeting and Control

LEARNING OBJECTIVES

After studying this chapter you should understand:

- the key purposes of budgets
- the need for more than one type of budget
- the various ways of classifying expenditures
- the benefits of performance budgets
- the key phases of the budget cycle
- why budgets are generally prepared on a cash basis

- the limitations of actual-to-budget comparisons
- how budgets enhance control
- the means by which governments incorporate budgets into their accounting systems
- how an encumbrance system prevents overspending
- the circumstances under which budgetary and encumbrance entries are most beneficial

Budgets are to governments and not-for-profits what the sun is to the solar system. Trying to understand government and not-for-profit accounting without recognizing the centricity of the budget would be like trying to comprehend the earth's seasons while ignoring the sun. As emphasized in Chapter 1, **budgets** are the key financial instruments in both governments and other not-for-profit entities:

> Budgeting is an essential element of the financial planning, control, and evaluation processes of governments. Every governmental unit should prepare a comprehensive budget covering all governmental, proprietary, and fiduciary funds for each annual (or, in some states, biennial) fiscal period.[1]

Governments and not-for-profits are disciplined by their budgets, not the competitive marketplace. With few exceptions, significant decisions—whether political or managerial—are reflected in their budgets. As also pointed out in Chapter 1, a key objective of financial accounting and reporting is assuring that an entity obtains and uses its resources in accordance with its budget. Budgeting exerts a major influence on accounting and reporting principles and practices.

The main purpose of this chapter is to provide an overview of budgets and the budgeting process, and thereby establish a basis for appreciating the relationship between budgeting and accounting. The first part of this chapter discusses functions of budgets, the different types of budgets, schemes of account classification, budgeting cycles, budgetary bases, and the significance of budget to actual comparisons. The second part shows how governments (and, to a lesser extent, other not-for-profits) promote budgetary compliance by integrating the budget into their accounting systems. They do this primarily by preparing journal entries to record both the budget and the goods and services that have been ordered but not yet received.

Although this chapter will describe budgetary procedures and related accounting practices mainly in the context of governments, most of the points can properly be extended to all not-for-profits. For example, whereas the legislatures of governments *appropriate* funds for expenditure (a term reserved for governments), the boards of directors or trustees of private-sector not-for-profits authorize or approve outlays—performing essentially the same function. However, the budget of a government has the force of law and officials may be subject to severe penalties for violating it. To prevent overspending, governments are required to institute certain accounting controls, such as integrating both the budget and purchase orders into their accounting systems, that are optional for not-for-profits.

WHAT ARE THE KEY PURPOSES OF BUDGETS?

Budgets are intended to carry out at least three broad functions:

- *Planning*. In a broad sense planning comprises *programming* (determining the activities that the entity will undertake), resource *acquisition*, and resource *allocation*. It is concerned with specifying the type, quantity, and quality of services that will be provided to constituents, estimating service costs, and determining how to pay for the services.

---

[1] *Codification of Governmental Accounting and Reporting Standards* (Norwalk, Conn.: Governmental Accounting Standard Board), 1996, Section 1700.101.

- *Controlling and administering.* Budgets help assure that resources are obtained and expended as planned. Managers use budgets to monitor resource flows and point to the need for operational adjustments. Legislative bodies, such as city councils or boards of trustees, use budgets to impose spending authority over executives (such as city managers or executive directors), who in turn use them to impose authority over their subordinates (such as department heads).

- *Reporting and evaluating.* Budgets lay the foundation for end-of-period reports and evaluations. Actual-to-budget comparisons reveal whether revenue and spending mandates were carried out. More importantly, when tied to an organization's objectives, budgets can facilitate assessments of efficiency and effectiveness.

WHY IS MORE THAN ONE TYPE OF BUDGET NECESSARY?

The benefits of the budgetary process cannot be fully achieved by a single budget or type of budget. A well-managed government or not-for-profit—just like a well-managed business—should prepare budgets for varying periods of time from multiple perspectives. These include:

- *appropriation budgets,* which are concerned mainly with current operating revenues and expenditures

- *capital budgets,* which focus on the acquisition and construction of long-term assets

- *flexible budgets,* which relate costs to outputs and are thereby intended to help control costs, especially those of business-types activities

APPROPRIATION BUDGETS

A government's *current* or *operating* budget covers its general fund. The operating budget is almost always an **appropriation** budget—one incorporating the legislatively granted expenditure authority, along with the related estimates of revenue. In most jurisdictions the operating budget must, by law, be balanced. Public attention focuses on the budget because it determines the amount of taxes and other revenues that must be generated to cover expenditures. Owing to the appropriation budget's influence upon accounting principles and practices, this chapter will direct attention mainly to this type of budget.

Governments may require that appropriation budgets be developed and approved for special revenue, debt service, or capital projects funds. However, they may be unnecessary if a government has established adequate control over spending by other means. For example, by accepting a federal grant and creating a special revenue fund to account for it, the government may implicitly approve expenditure of the grant resources. Similarly, by issuing bonds, it may authorize spending for specified capital projects. Still, principles of sound management dictate that a nonappropriation budget—a financial plan not subject to appropriation—be prepared each year for such funds and organizational units. Budgets of some type are almost always necessary if activities are to be effectively planned, controlled, and evaluated.

CAPITAL BUDGETS

Although the accounting cycle is traditionally one year, the budgeting process commonly extends for a considerably longer period. The needs of an organization's constituents must be forecast and planned for years in advance.

A **capital budget,** in contrast to an appropriation budget, typically covers multiple years, often as many as five. It concentrates on the construction and acquisition of long-lived assets such as land, buildings, roads, bridges, and major items of equipment. These assets can be expected to last for many years. Therefore, in the interests of interperiod equity, they will generally be financed with long-term debt rather than taxes of a single year. The capital budget is, in essence, a plan setting forth when specific capital assets will be acquired and how they will be financed.

Capital budgets are closely tied to operating budgets. Each year a government must include current-year capital spending in its operating budget. If the capital projects are financed with debt, however, the capital expenditures will be offset with bond proceeds and will not affect the operating budget's surplus or deficit.

Legislators are sometimes more extravagant with capital than operating resources. Capital projects, they reason, can be financed with debt rather than taxes, and thus will not impact the surplus or deficit of the general fund, the budget of which must be balanced. Their error is in failing to take into account the additional operating costs associated with new long-term assets. Roads must be repaired, buildings maintained, and equipment tuned up. Further, in future years the debt must be serviced with interest and principal payments made from operating resources.

FLEXIBLE BUDGETS

Proprietary funds, which account for business-type activities, are generally not subject to the same statutory budget requirements as governmental funds. Nevertheless, budgets are as important to proprietary funds as they are to businesses and governmental funds. As a rule, governments should prepare the same types of budgets for proprietary funds as would a private enterprise carrying out similar activities. For certain, they should prepare a series of **flexible budgets,** each of which contains alternative budget estimates based on varying levels of output. Unlike **fixed budgets,** flexible budgets capture the behavior of costs, distinguishing between fixed and variable amounts. Fixed budgets may be appropriate for governmental funds where the expenditures and level of activity are pre-established by legislative authorization. Flexible budgets are especially suited to proprietary funds in which the level of activity depends on customer demand.

HOW ARE EXPENDITURES AND REVENUES CLASSIFIED?

How financial data are presented affects how they are used. Therefore, accountants, public administrators, political scientists, and economists have directed considerable attention to the form and content of budgets. They are aware that the way the budget is prepared and presented can significantly impact the allocation of resources among organizations, programs, and activities.

EXPENDITURES

The GASB advises that "multiple classification of governmental expenditure data is important from both internal and external management control and accountability standpoints" as it "facilitates the aggregation and analysis of data in different ways for different purposes and in manners that cross fund and organizational lines." Suggested classifications include:

- by *fund,* such as the general fund, special revenue funds, and debt service funds
- by *organizational unit,* such as the police department, the fire department, the city council, and the finance office

- by *function or program* (a group of activities carried out with the same objective), such as general government, public safety, sanitation, and recreation
- by *activity* (line of work contributing to a function or program), such as highway patrol, burglary investigations, vice-patrol
- by *character* (the fiscal period they are presumed to benefit), such as "current expenditures," which benefit the current period, "capital outlays," which benefit the current and future periods, and "debt service," which benefits prior, current, and future periods
- by *object classification* (the types of items purchased or the services obtained), such as salaries, fringe benefits, travel, and repairs[2]

REVENUES

In contrast to expenditures, revenues present less significant issues of classification. Most revenues are not designated for specific purposes; therefore, their classification is relatively straightforward. The GASB recommends that revenues be classified first by fund (i.e., the columns on a statement of revenues and expenditures) and then by source (i.e., the rows). Suggested major source classifications include:

- taxes
- licenses and permits
- intergovernmental revenues
- charges for services
- fines[3]

Most governments divide these classifications into numerous subclassifications, such as property taxes, sales taxes, and hotel taxes.

WHY ARE PERFORMANCE BUDGETS NECESSARY?

The traditional, and most commonly prepared, budget is referred to as an **object classification budget** because it is characterized by the expenditure classification that categorizes objects, such as the types of goods or services to be acquired. Table 3–1 illustrates an excerpt of this type of budget for one department.

The primary virtue of an object classification budget is that it facilitates control. The managers who prepare the budget, and the legislators who pass it, establish rigid spending mandates and thereby direct, in detail, how every dollar should be spent. But this strength may also be a shortcoming:

- By expediting control, an object classification budget discourages planning. It encourages top-level decision makers to focus on specific line-items rather than on overall entity objectives, strategies, and measurable performance targets. Thus, for example, the officials of a school district may focus on the need for increased appropriations for salaries, fuel, supplies, and food while failing to consider how the additional outlays will affect the school's primary educational mission.

---

[2] GASB *Codification*, Section. 1800.116.

[3] GASB *Codification*, Section. 1800.115.

TABLE 3-1
Excerpt from an Object Classification Budget

Expenditure Detail Public Safety

Departmental Summary	FY 1998 Budget	FY 1997 Estimate	FY 1996 Actual
Full-Time Wages	$1,307,000	$1,348,300	$1,283,147
Part-Time Wages	26,200	44,000	52,014
Casual Wages	27,000	15,000	138
Temporary Wages	0	3,800	2,748
Longevity	24,000	21,800	21,257
Overtime	140,500	24,700	27,127
Auto Allowance	46,000	44,400	44,700
Retirement	158,000	142,300	135,077
Social Security (FICA)	120,000	106,000	100,385
Group Insurance	290,000	290,000	265,515
Worker's Compensation	61,300	61,000	54,583
Total Personnel	**$2,200,000**	**$2,101,300**	**$1,986,691**
Office Supplies & Equipment	15,900	14,700	14,302
Postage	23,000	23,500	28,910
Operating Supplies & Equipment	28,500	29,900	18,915
Fuel & Lube	21,200	25,900	17,307
Uniforms & Wearing Apparel	6,000	4,400	1,461
Health-Related Supplies	26,800	32,300	19,257
Telephone Charges	9,200	8,700	6,420
Electricity Charges	9,400	7,300	4,633
Gas Charges	3,100	2,700	2,097
Water & Sewer Charges	3,600	2,500	2,270
Printing Costs	9,100	9,600	7,463
Professional Services	500	500	150
Advertising Costs	3,000	1,300	4,924
Building Maintenance	2,000	2,200	0
Vehicular Maintenance	27,500	26,500	24,855
Equipment Maintenance	2,500	1,980	2,899
Lease & Rent	5,100	5,100	1,629
Travel & Training	12,900	11,600	8,491
Special Services	100,100	83,400	87,482
Hospitality	600	500	753
Fixed Assets	0	2,200	2,931
Total Operating Expenses	**$ 310,000**	**$ 296,760**	**$ 257,149**
Capital Outlay	**$ 25,000**	**$ 71,700**	**$ 61,110**
Total Expenditures	**$2,535,000**	**$2,469,790**	**$2,304,950**

- It promotes bottom-up, rather than top-down budgeting, with each unit presenting its fiscal requirements for approval in the absence of coordinated sets of goals and strategies.
- It overwhelms top-level decision makers with details. As a consequence, the decision makers are induced to take budgetary short-cuts, such as increasing all expenditures by a fixed percentage;

- By failing to relate specific *inputs* (factors used to provide goods and services) to *outputs* (units of service) or *outcomes* (accomplishments in terms of organizational objectives), it limits post-budget evaluation to whether spending mandates were observed.

Owing to these deficiencies, many governments and not-for-profits have adopted **performance budgets** in place of, or as a supplement to, objective classification budgets. Performance budgets focus on measurable units of efforts, services, and accomplishments. They are formulated so that dollar expenditures are directly associated with anticipated units of outputs or outcomes. Comprehensive performance budgeting systems require managers to specify objectives, consider alternative means of achieving them, establish workload indicators, and perform cost–benefit analyses.

To be sure, other sound managerial approaches can overcome the limitations of object classification budgeting. Performance budgets, however, institutionalize effective decision processes and help assure that they are carried out.

The most common type of performance budgets are **program budgets,** whereby resources and results are identified with programs rather than traditional organizational units, and expenditures are typically categorized by activity rather than by object.

Table 3–2 illustrates an excerpt from a program budget. Program budgeting will be discussed in detail in Chapter 14.

WHAT ARE THE KEY PHASES OF THE BUDGET CYCLE?

Budgeting practices in neither governments nor not-for-profits are standardized; they differ from entity to entity. However, irrespective of whether the budget is of object classification or performance type, in most organizations budgeting is a continuous, four-phase process:

- preparation
- legislative adoption and executive approval
- execution
- reporting and auditing

PREPARATION

Budgets are most commonly prepared by an organization's executive branch (e.g., the office of the mayor or executive director) and submitted to the legislative branch (e.g., a city council or board of trustees) for approval. In some jurisdictions, particularly states, the legislature may either prepare its own budget (a legislative budget as opposed to an executive budget) or join with the executive branch in developing a common budget.

Budgeting generally necessitates flows of policies and information to and from all parties involved in the budgetary process. Legislators, for example, will apprise the executive branch as to what they think is politically feasible for revenue measures. Department heads will inform the legislative or executive budget committees as to what they see as their requirements. The committees, in turn, will develop guidelines for funding priorities and establish ranges of funding increases and cuts.

The preparation of a budget requires both forecasts and estimates. Relatively few types of revenues can be determined accurately in advance of the budget period. These types are limited mainly to those that are contractually established (e.g., from

TABLE 3−2
Excerpt from a Program Budget
Summary of Request

Agency Code: 111	Agency Name: Department of Environmental Quality	Prepared By: John Daily	Date: 08/01/96		

Goal/Objective/Strategy	Expended 1995	Estimated 1996	Budgeted 1997	Requested 1998	Requested 1999
Goal 1: Improve Air Quality in Texas					
Reduce Air Pollutants to Reach Federal Standards by 2000					
Implement EPA's Ozone Policy	$10,500,000	$11,100,000	$11,000,000	$11,125,000	$11,125,000
Promote and Enforce Local Air Quality Programs	250,000	250,000	250,000	250,000	250,000
Reduce Air Toxics Emissions by 40 Percent b/w 1995 and 2001					
Implement Comprehensive Air Toxics Program	4,800,000	5,000,000	5,000,000	5,000,000	5,000,000
By 2001, Analyze 90 Percent of Potential Cases of Toxic Chemical Exposure Through Air Pollution					
Conduct Ongoing Studies of Toxic Chemical Exposure	500,000	500,000	500,000	1,250,000	1,250,000
Total, Goal 1	$16,050,000	$16,850,000	$16,750,000	$17,625,000	$17,625,000
Goal 2: Improve Water Availability and Water Quality					
Increase Compliance to 90 Percent of Regulated Sites by 2001					
Enforce Water Quality Standards	$ 4,200,000	$ 4,200,000	$ 4,000,000	$ 4,000,000	$4,000,000
Monitor Maintenance Standards in Water Districts	800,000	800,000	800,000	800,000	800,000
By 2001, Increase by 12 Percent the Amount of Water Available for Beneficial Use					
Negotiate Water Rights With Local and Other Entities	1,400,000	1,400,000	1,500,000	1,190,000	1,125,000
Total, Goal 2	$ 6,400,000	$ 6,400,000	$ 6,300,000	$ 5,990,000	$ 5,925,000

lease agreements), have been previously promised (e.g., grants from other governments), or are set by law and affect a known number of parties (e.g., special assessments). Most, however, depend on factors that are largely outside the government's control. Tax revenues, for example are influenced by economic conditions; revenues from fines and fees are affected by the predilections of the citizenry.

Some expenditures are fixed by legislative fiat or can be determined accurately. Examples of these types of expenditures include salaries of key officials (assuming no turnover), grants to other organizations, acquisitions of equipment, payments of interest, and repayments of debt. Others, however, are affected by acts of God or man. Snow removal, parades for championship sports teams, repair of equipment, and purchases of fuel are some examples of unpredictable expenditures.

The literature of public budgeting is replete with descriptions of forecasting models and techniques. Yet, as is made clear in the accompanying description of budgeting at the federal level (see In Practice), the models or techniques are no better than the underlying assumptions. Moreover, as indicated by an actual study (see the second In Practice), the differences between actual results and budgetary estimates can be substantial.

Significant errors in budget estimates, irrespective of direction or cause, thwart the political process and may lead to a distribution of resources that misrepresent what was expressed by voters through their elected representatives. Moreover, insofar as budgets are used by investors or creditors, they may contribute to misguided fiscal decisions and misallocation of resources.

LEGISLATIVE ADOPTION AND EXECUTIVE APPROVAL

When the budget is presented to a legislature for consideration, it is typically turned over to one or more committees for review. In some legislatures, such as the U.S. Congress, the committees that act on revenues are separate from those that recommend expenditures. Moreover, the committees authorizing new programs may be different from those determining the amount to be spent on them. The committees typically make recommendations to the legislature as a whole; the legislature may revise their proposals as it deems appropriate.

Upon agreeing to the budget, a legislature officially adopts it by enacting an *appropriation* measure authorizing expenditures. Legislatures differ in the degree of control that they exert over the details of appropriations. Some appropriate lump sums to departments or programs, giving the executive branch the flexibility to allocate the resources among the various object classifications. Others go further, specifying not only the departments or programs, but also the object classifications on which authorized funds can be expended. Then, any subsequent shifts from one classification to another require legislative approval.

Property taxes are commonly *levied* (authorized by the legislature) annually. Most other revenues, such as income and sales taxes, are not authorized each year unless there is to be a change in rates or other provisions.

EXECUTION

The budget is executed (carried out) by an organization's executive branch. In some jurisdictions, expenditures are apportioned to particular months or quarters by allotments. **Allotments** are periodic allocations of funds to departments or agencies, usually made by the chief executive's office, to assure that an entire year's appropriation is not dissipated early in the period covered by the budget. They also prevent a department or agency from spending resources that may not be available in the event that actual revenues fall short of budgeted revenues.

FEDERAL BUDGETARY LEGERDEMAIN

When you project a federal budget, someone must make crucial economic assumptions. Many federal payments, such as Social Security, are tied to the inflation rate, so first you must decide what that rate is likely to be. Since income taxes depend on corporate profits and thus on Gross National Product (GNP), you need to know how much you can reasonably expect GNP to go up (or possibly even down). Interest payments on federal debt depend on the market interest rate, so you must have some idea of what that rate is likely to be. These numbers, and others, are interrelated: move one, and they all move.

Every forecaster, including the Office of Management and Budget (OMB), the Treasury, and the Congressional Budget Office (CBO), has a complex computer model of government finances and the economy. If you enter one set of numbers, the model will give you a complete, consistent set of output numbers on which the budget is based. But what are the "best" numbers and assumptions to use? That depends in large part on who your boss is. The OMB, in the executive office of the president, tends to generate numbers that will make the president look good—usually low inflation, high real growth, low interest rates, and a shrinking budget deficit.

David Stockman, head of the OMB during a portion of the Reagan administration, in his remarkable book *The Triumph of Politics*, tells how the Reagan administration arrived at its economic input numbers in the spring of 1981. Competing groups of experts were haggling over the numbers. As the deadline approached for locking up the Reagan budget, Stockman called in Murray Weidenbaum, chairman of the Council of Economic Advisers, and made a political deal. If Weidenbaum would agree to a "reasonably high" real growth rate, Stockman would accept whatever inflation rate was consistent with it.

When the "deal" was announced at the final economic meeting, there were grumbles from all of the contending factions. Finally someone turned to Weidenbaum and asked, "What model did this come from, Murray?"

"Weidenbaum," wrote Stockman, "glared at his inquisitor a moment and said, 'It came right out of here.' With that he slapped his belly with both hands. 'My visceral computer.'" And thus were determined the economic assumptions that would shape a $745 billion national budget.

Source: Joseph J. DioGuardi, *Unaccountable Congress, It Doesn't Add Up* (Washington, D.C.: Regnery Gateway, 1992), p. 16. Reprinted with permission. DioGuardi claims to be the first *practicing* Certified Public Accountant to be elected to Congress. He served in the House of Representatives (Republican, New York) from 1985 to 1988. In this book he reveals the deceptions used by the federal government to mask spending of billions of dollars.

As shall be discussed in a following section, governments integrate their budgets into their accounting systems. In that way they are able to monitor continually how revenues and expenditures to date compare with the amounts that have been estimated or authorized. Moreover, to enhance control and facilitate end-of-period budget-to-actual comparisons, they use the same account structure for their budgets as for their actual revenues and expenditures.

Governments, like businesses, should issue interim financial statements to report on their progress in executing their budgets. Per the GASB *Codification*:

IN PRACTICE

A study of 125 U.S. cities having populations more than 100,000 revealed substantial variances between estimated and actual revenues and expenditures.

For all *revenues* combined, sixty-eight cities (54 percent) overestimated revenues. Twenty-nine (23 percent) overestimated revenues by more than 5 percent and twenty (16 percent) underestimated them by more than 5 percent. Thus, 39 percent of the sample had variations greater than 5 percent.

For all *expenditures* combined, the average budget variance was considerably larger than for revenues. Eighty-nine cities (71 percent) overestimated expenditures. Of these, sixty-four (51 percent) overestimated expenditures by more than 5 percent. Eleven cities (9 percent) underestimated expenditures by more than 5 percent. Hence, 60 percent of the sample had variances greater than 5 percent.

This study revealed that budget estimates were significantly biased in the direction of conservatism. However, the data were drawn from a single year (1983), one of relative prosperity for local governments. Were the study repeated using data from the late 1980s and early 1990s, a period of economic lethargy, the bias might have been in the opposite direction.

Source: Michael H. Granof and Alan Mayer, "A Focus on Government Budgets" (with Alan Mayper), *The CPA Journal*, vol. LXI (July 1991), 28–33.

MISESTIMATING REVENUES AND EXPENDITURES

Appropriate interim budgetary reports should be prepared during the fiscal period to facilitate management control and legislative oversight of governmental fund financial operations. Such reports are important both to revenue and expenditure control processes and to facilitate timely planning and budgetary revisions.[4]

REPORTING AND AUDITING

To complete the budget cycle, information on how the budget was executed must be provided to the analysts and governing officials who must prepare and adopt the subsequent budget. At a minimum, both governments and not-for-profits should include in their annual financial statements or supplementary reports budget-to-actual comparisons for each of the funds for which they have adopted budgets. These comparisons will be discussed later in this chapter.

Performance budgets, unlike traditional object classification budgets, create the basis for evaluating and auditing organizational efficiency and effectiveness. These budgets specify anticipated outputs or outcomes in a quantifiable, measurable form. They thereby provide auditors (both internal and independent) with objective benchmarks by which to gauge organizational accomplishments and to compare them with budgetary expectations. By assessing performance, instead of mere compliance with budgetary spending mandates, auditors can transform the audit from what administrators may perceive as an annoyance into an essential element of the management process. Performance audits will be addressed in Chapter 15.

---

[4] GASB, *Codification*, Section. 2900.102.

ON WHAT BASIS OF ACCOUNTING ARE BUDGETS PREPARED?

Despite the importance of budgets and the influence of budgeting on financial reporting, both the GASB and the FASB establish generally accepted principles only for financial reporting, not for budgeting. Budgetary principles are established either by individual governments or organizations or by the governments or organizations that supervise them (e.g., states may establish the principles for their cities, towns and districts; national association may establish principles for their local chapters).

Although it lacks the authority to establish standards for budgeting, the GASB nevertheless recommends that governments prepare their annual budgets for governmental funds on the modified accrual basis—the same basis they are required to use for external reporting.[5] Although the modified accrual basis does not allow for balance sheet recognition of long-term assets and debts, it does permit a wide array of transactions and events to be recognized when they have their substantive economic impact, not merely when they result in cash inflows and outflows.

Many governments, however, reject the GASB's advice. They opt to prepare budgets on a *cash* basis or a slightly modified cash basis.

Governments that budget on a cash basis assign revenues and expenditures to the period in which the government is expected to receive or disburse cash. Some governments modify the cash basis by requiring that **encumbrances** (commitments to purchase goods or services) be accounted for as if they were the equivalent of actual purchases. Others may permit certain taxes or other revenues to be recognized in the year for which they were budgeted, rather than received, as long as they will be received within a specified period of time.

RATIONALE FOR BUDGETING ON THE CASH BASIS

Governments have valid reasons for budgeting on a cash basis. After all, bills must be paid with cash, not receivables or other assets; therefore, the required cash must be on hand in the year the payments have to be made. And goods or services must be paid for in the year of acquisition (or in the periods set forth in a borrowing agreement), not necessarily in the year or years in which the benefits will be received.

Correspondingly, when a government is able to defer payments, it need not have the cash on hand until disbursements are required. Taxpayers are understandably reluctant to part with their dollars so that the government can retain the cash as "savings" until the year needed. Suppose, for example, that government employees are permitted to defer until future years vacations that are earned in a current year. Although the services of the employees unquestionably benefit the period in which the vacations are earned, the government does not need—and the taxpayers might object to providing—the cash for the vacation payments until the employees actually take the vacations. Thus, in the face of a balanced budget requirement, the cash basis of accounting assures that the government receives in taxes and other revenues only what it is required to disburse.

---

[5] GASB, *Codification*, Section 1700.116.

ADVERSE CONSEQUENCES OF THE CASH BASIS

The adverse consequences of the cash basis should not be overlooked. The cash basis may distort the economic impact of a government's planned fiscal activities. A budget that is balanced on a cash basis may be decidedly unbalanced as to economic costs and revenues. It may give the appearance of a budget that has achieved interperiod equity when it really has not.

The cash basis permits a government to balance its budget by taking any number of steps that artificially delay cash disbursements and advance cash receipts. Consider, for example, the quintessential budget-balancing tactic employed by the federal government and a number of states and local governments: changing the date on which employees are paid from the last day of the month to the first of the next month. In the year of the change the government is able to pay its employees for one fewer payroll periods than it would otherwise.

On the revenue side, a comparable scheme works equally well: advancing the due date of taxes or fees from early in the following budget year to late in the current year, thereby picking up an extra tax or fee payment in the year of the change. This tactic, like that of delaying the payday, can only be employed once for each revenue or expenditure. New devices (such as the uncommon ones described in In Practice) must continually be developed.

The deleterious consequences of cash basis budgeting are exacerbated by the use of fund accounting. Because each fund is a separate accounting entity, governments can readily transfer resources from a fund that has a budget surplus or that does not require a balanced budget to one that needs extra resources. Some governments budget interfund "loans" for the last day of one fiscal year and repayment for the first day of the next. Others delay for one day required payments from the general fund to other funds.

These "one shot" budget balancing techniques would generally not affect revenues and expenditures as reported in the annual financial statements. Governments *must* prepare the external financial reports of their governmental funds on a modified accrual basis. As defined by the GASB, the modified accrual basis requires that short-term loan proceeds, whether from another fund or from an outside source, be accounted for as liabilities rather than revenues. Similarly, most required outlays are reported as expenditures in the period to which they apply, irrespective of when they are actually paid.

Cash basis budgeting complicates financial accounting and reporting. Governments must maintain their accounts to facilitate preparation of two sets of reports—one that demonstrates compliance with the budgetary provisions and one in accordance with GAAP.

WHAT CAUTIONS MUST BE TAKEN IN BUDGET-TO-ACTUAL COMPARISONS?

As emphasized in Chapter 1, a primary objective of government financial reporting is to "demonstrate whether resources were used in accordance with the entities' legally adopted budget."[6] Accordingly, generally accepted accounting principles dictate that governments include in their annual reports a comparison of actual results with the budget for each governmental fund for which an annual budget has been adopted.

---

[6]GASB *Codification*, 1996, Appendix A, para. 77.

IN PRACTICE

On April 1, 1991—April Fools Day—New York's Governor Cuomo announced the sale of Attica prison *to the state itself* for over $200 million—all of which was counted as general revenues. The buyer was a state agency that financed the purchase by floating bonds. The bonds were backed by the state and were, therefore, economic obligations of the state. The purchaser immediately leased the prison back to the state under terms specifying that the "rent" payments would be exactly equal to the debt service on the bonds. In essence, the state balanced its operating budget with a loan in the amount of the prison's sales price. The benefits of the loan were reaped by the taxpayers of the year of the transaction; principal and interest will be paid by the taxpayers of the future.

In the previous year, the state sold its Cross Westchester Expressway to the New York Thruway Authority—also to itself—but that transaction was only for $20 million. Following the lead of its neighbor, New Jersey sold a portion of its highway system to a state-owned agency, the New Jersey Turnpike Authority.

One can only marvel at such ingenuity and wonder what these governments will do for an encore. Perhaps, they will repurchase the assets and sell them, at a profit, to the same or another state agency.

BALANCING THE BUDGET BY SELLING ASSETS TO YOURSELF

Actual results in the budget-to-actual comparisons, per the GASB, should generally be those reported in the statement of revenues and expenditures. If the budgeted amounts are determined differently from the actual results, however, then the comparisons would have little meaning.

Legally adopted budgets may not be readily comparable to amounts reported in the GAAP-based financial statements, owing to several factors. These include:

DIFFERENCES IN HOW BUDGET AND ACTUAL RESULTS ARE DETERMINED

- *Differences in Basis.* As previously noted, governments often prepare their budgets on a cash or near-cash basis, whereas their financial statements must be prepared on a modified accrual basis.

- *Differences in Timing.* As shown in its budget, a government may appropriate resources for a particular project rather than for a particular period. For example, in approving resources for a construction project, the government will typically establish the total amount that can be spent. It will not allocate resources to specific years. By contrast, the annual report of the fund in which the project is accounted would have to present the expenditures year by year. Moreover, governments may permit departments to carry over to subsequent years resources not spent in the year for which they were budgeted. Thus, expenditures in a particular year may not have been budgeted in that year.

- *Differences in Perspective.* Governments may structure their budgets differently than their financial reports. For example, a government may budget on the basis of programs. The programs, however, may be financed by resources accounted for in more than one fund. Thus, the amounts expended in each of the funds cannot be compared to any particular line-item in the budget.

- *Difference in the Reporting Entity.* As you will learn in Chapter 12, GAAP requires that a government's reporting entity include organizations that are legally independent of the government yet, in political or economic reality, an integral part of it. For example, a city may create a financing authority—a separate legal entity—to issue bonds on behalf of the city. If the city has political control over the authority (e.g., the mayor appoints the majority of the governing board) or is responsible for its financial affairs (e.g., approves its budget), then GAAP dictates that the authority be reported upon in the city's financial statements. Yet because the authority is a separate legal entity, the city may exclude it from its legally adopted budget.

The GASB requires that governments present the comparison of budget to actual data on the budgetary rather than GAAP basis. Moreover it mandates that all differences, including those of basis, timing, perspective, and entity, be disclosed and reconciled either on the face of the comparison report or in accompanying notes.[7]

Table 3–3 presents the budget-to-actual comparison of the city of Fort Worth's general fund.

MAY REFLECT AMENDED, NOT INITIAL, BUDGET

A budget-to-actual comparison is intended to demonstrate legal compliance. According to GAAP, the budget-to-actual comparison should reflect *amended*, rather than original, budget data.[8] Consequently, the comparison may provide no information as to the reliability of *initial* budget estimates, thereby limiting its usefulness to most statement users.

Governments are not only permitted to amend their budgets during the year, they are required to do so should they elect or need to spend more than was originally appropriated. Governments may modify their budgets as a result of unanticipated events, changed economic conditions, or operating inefficiencies.

Budgets may be amended up to the last day of the year. Thus, governments do not generally report unfavorable expenditure variances, since they do not typically violate spending mandates. Correspondingly, they often are unable to report greater than anticipated revenues as favorable variances. If they elect to spend the unexpected receipts, they would have to amend the budget to reflect the added revenues.

HOW DO BUDGETS ENHANCE CONTROL?

Owing to the adverse consequences of violating budgetary mandates, both governments and not-for-profits can build safeguards into their accounting systems that help assure budgetary compliance. These include preparing journal entries both to record the budget and to give recognition to goods and services that have been ordered but not yet received. We begin the discussion by describing the basic books of account maintained by governments and not-for-profits and showing how they accommodate these safeguards.

THE BASIC BOOKS OF ACCOUNT

The basic books of account of both governments and not-for-profits correspond to those of businesses. They consist, either in manual or electronic form, of:

- *journals,* in which journal entries are recorded. Most transactions are entered initially in a special journal, such as a property tax cash receipts journal, a parking fines cash receipts journal, a purchases journal, or a cash disbursements journal. Both nonroutine transactions and account totals from special journals are recorded in a general journal.

---

[7] GASB, *Codification*, Sections 2400.104, 2400.123 and 2400.902.

[8] GASB, *Codification*, Section 2400.103.

TABLE 3–3
Excerpt of Budget-to-Actual Schedule of Revenue and Expenditures, City of Fort Worth, Texas

Statement of Revenues, Expenditures, and Changes in General Fund Balance
Budget (GAAP Basis) and Actual
Year Ended September 30, 1996
(000's omitted)

	Actual	Budget	Variance Favorable (Unfavorable)
Revenues:			
General Property Taxes	$132,965	$132,847	$118
Other Local Taxes	66,003	63,410	2,593
Charges for Services	12,950	11,357	1,593
Licenses and Permits	31,317	31,574	(257)
Fines and Forfeitures	9,470	7,673	1,797
Revenue from Use of Money and Property	9,198	7,284	1,914
Intergovernmental	1,190	1,252	(62)
Other	907	1,062	(155)
Total Revenues	264,000	256,459	7,541
Expenditures:			
General Administration	11,640	12,049	409
Public Safety	119,696	120,335	639
Transportation and Public Works	23,329	23,329	0
Parks and Community Services	16,974	16,974	0
Public Library	7,750	7,935	185
Public Health	5,603	5,625	22
Public Events and Facilities	9,416	9,480	64
Nondepartmental	14,122	14,948	826
Planning and Development	3,702	3,703	1
Fiscal Services	4,044	4,044	0
Housing	302	343	41
Total Expenditures	216,578	218,765	2,187
Excess of Revenues Over Expenditures	47,422	37,694	(9,728)
Other Financing Sources (Uses):			
Operating Transfers In - Other Funds	12,765	7,167	5,598
Operating Transfers Out - Other Funds	(66,909)	(67,137)	228
Operating Transfers Out - Component Units	(210)	0	(210)
Total Other Financing Uses	(54,354)	(59,970)	5,616
Excess of Revenues and Other Financing Sources Over (Under) Expenditures and Other Financing Uses	(6,932)	(22,276)	15,344
Fund Balance, Beginning of Year	64,690	64,690	0
Fund Balance, End of Year	$57,758	$42,414	$15,344

- *ledgers,* in which all balance sheet and operating accounts are maintained. The general ledger consists of control accounts that summarize the balances of the detailed subsidiary accounts that are maintained in subsidiary ledgers.

A city or other general purpose government is likely to maintain hundreds of accounts. For example, the control, account general property taxes, may be subdivided as follows:

General property taxes

Real property (e.g., land and buildings)

Personal property

Tangible personal (e.g., business inventories, machinery, household furnishings, and vehicles)

Intangible personal (e.g., stocks, bonds, and bank deposits)

In addition, these accounts would be further divided into accounts for each individual taxpayer.

Similarly, one branch of the expenditure tree for police might be structured as follows (with only a small number of the object classification accounts displayed):

Police

Crime control and investigation

Crime laboratory

Salaries

Regular

Overtime

Social Security contributions

Rentals

Land and buildings

Equipment and vehicles

Supplies

Custodial

Fuel

Office

BUDGETARY CONTROL FEATURES

As in a ledger for a business, each account consists of columns for debits, for credits, and for the balance (the difference between the two.) However, the ledger accounts of governments (and some not-for-profits) incorporate budgetary control features not conventionally found in those of businesses.

The ledger accounts for revenues incorporate an additional debit column, estimated revenues. In this column the government posts the revenue side of an entry (to be described and illustrated in the next section) to record the budget. The difference between the estimated revenues (a debit), actual revenues collected to date (credits), and any unusual adjustments (debits or credits) equals the amount of budgeted revenues still to be collected. Thus, for example, the subledger account "Real Property Taxes" might appear as follows (dates and references omitted):

Revenues—Real Property Taxes

Estimated Revenues (Dr.)	Actual (Cr.)	Adjustments (Dr. or Cr.)	Balance (Dr. or Cr.)
15,000,000	2,300,000		12,700,000
	1,100,000		11,600,000
	500,000		11,100,000

Based on the data shown, the government budgeted real property tax revenue of $15 million and has collected $3.9 million to date. Therefore, $11.1 million remains to be collected.

Similarly, the ledger accounts for expenditures incorporate *two* extra columns. One column, appropriations, corresponds to estimated revenues. In this column the government posts a credit for the amount appropriated per the budget. In the second extra column the government posts, as debits, encumbrances—*commitments* to purchase goods or services. The difference between the appropriation (a credit), resources encumbered (debits), actual expenditures to date (also debits), and any unusual adjustments equals the amount of the appropriation that is still uncommitted and is therefore available to be spent (the unencumbered balance). Thus, crime laboratory expenditures might appear as follows:

Expenditures—Crime Laboratory

Appropriations (Cr.)	Encumbrances (Dr.)	Expenditures (Dr.)	Adjustments (Dr. or Cr.)	Unencumbered Balance
300,000		50,000		250,000
		30,000		220,000
	15,000	40,000		165,000

This account indicates that the government appropriated $300,000 for the crime laboratory. To date it has spent $120,000 and has outstanding commitments for goods and services of $15,000. Therefore, it has $165,000 available for future spending.

WHAT ARE THE DISTINCTIVE WAYS GOVERNMENTS RECORD THEIR BUDGETS?

By recording its budget, a government builds into its accounting system a gauge that warns of excesses in spending and deficiencies in collections. This gauge serves only an *internal* control function. The budgetary entries are reversed-out at year-end and have no impact on year-end financial statements. To external report users, budgetary entries are irrelevant. Nevertheless, because of their significance in controlling costs, students need to be aware of how they affect the accounts.

CREDITING OR DEBITING THE BUDGETED DEFICIT OR SURPLUS DIRECTLY TO FUND BALANCE

Most students initially find budgetary entries counterintuitive and confusing. Mainly, that's because when a government records its budget it *debits* estimated revenues and *credits* appropriations (in effect, estimated expenditures). Most students, of course, are used to crediting revenues and debiting expenditures. The practice of debiting estimated revenues and crediting appropriations makes sense, however, when you understand that each estimated revenue and appropriation account will be tied directly to its related *actual* revenue and *actual* expenditure account. The resulting differences equal the revenues yet to be earned and the appropriations still available to be spent. Thus (ignoring encumbrances):

Estimated revenues (Dr.) − Actual revenues (Cr.) = Revenues still to be earned

and

Appropriations (Cr.) − Actual expenditures (Dr.) = Balance available for expenditure

Moreover, the entries appear to put the cart before the horse. The difference between the debit to estimated revenues and the credit to appropriations is offset by fund balance. Thus, the entity's fund balance may be increased or decreased upon merely *adopting* the budget—that is, wishes and whims—rather than actual transactions. Fortunately, as with other widely used bookkeeping procedures that allow accounts to be temporarily in error (e.g., periodic inventory methods), the entries cause no harm as long as appropriate adjustments are made prior to the preparation of financial statements.

EXAMPLE *Recording the Budget*

A school district adopts a budget calling for total revenues of $400 million and total expenditures of $390 million. The following entries would record the budget:

(b1)

Estimated revenues	$400	
Fund balance		$400
To record estimated revenues		

(b2)

Fund balance	$390	
Appropriations		$390
To record appropriations (estimated expenditures)		

The entries illustrated in this chapter will be made only to control accounts. In reality, corresponding entries would be made to the estimated revenue and appropriation *subaccounts* that support the control accounts. The sum of the debits and credits to the subaccounts should, of course, equal the entries to the respective control accounts.

Suppose that during the year both revenues and expenditures were as estimated and that all transactions were for cash. The transactions would be recorded with standard revenue and expenditure entries (with appropriate entries to the subaccounts as well):

(1)

Cash	$400	
Revenues		$400
To record revenues		

(2)

Expenditures	$390	
Cash		$390
To record expenditures		

At year-end, each of the budgeted and actual revenues and expenditures accounts would be *closed* (i.e., reversed) to fund balance. Thus:

(cl 1)

Appropriations	$390	
Fund balance	10	
Estimated revenues		$400
To close budgetary accounts		

(cl 2)

Revenues	$400	
Expenditures		$390
Fund balance		10
To close revenues and expenditures		

The net effect of the entries is to increase fund balance by the difference between the actual revenues and expenditures—the same increase as would have been recorded had the budgetary entries not been made.

Suppose alternatively that actual revenues and expenditures differed from what were budgeted—for example, that actual revenues were $420 and actual expenditures were $415. Actual revenues and expenditures would have been recorded as follows:

(1a)

Cash	$420	
Revenues		$420
To record revenues		

(2a)

Expenditures	$415	
Cash		$415
To record expenditures		

Closing entries would take the same form as illustrated previously:

(cl 1a)

Appropriations	$390	
Fund balance	10	
Estimated revenues		$400
To close budgetary accounts		

(cl 2a)

Revenues	$420	
Expenditures		$415
Fund balance		5
To close revenues and expenditures		

In this situation, as shown in the T-accounts presented in Figure 3-1, year-end fund balance would again be the difference between *actual* revenues and *actual* expenditures. Actual revenues were $420 and actual expenditures were $415. Ending fund balance, after the closing entries have been posted, is thus $5—the same as if the budgetary entries had not been made.

The components of both the budgetary and the closing entries could, of course, have been combined differently. For example, appropriations and expenditures (rather than appropriations and estimated revenues) and revenues and estimated revenues (rather than revenues and expenditures) could have been closed in the same entry. The net impact on fund balance would have been the same.

AN ALTERNATIVE METHOD: CREDITING OR DEBITING THE DIFFERENCE BETWEEN REVENUES AND EXPENDITURES TO "BUDGETARY FUND BALANCE"

Some governments maintain an account called *budgetary fund balance*. In recording the budget they debit or credit this account instead of fund balance. Budgetary fund balance is a temporary account. At year-end, the appropriations and estimated revenues are closed to this account, so that after the closing entries are made its balance is always zero.

Governments prefer (in some cases, must take) this approach so as to avoid contaminating the actual fund balance with appropriations and estimated revenues. The actual fund balance is affected only by authentic revenues and expenditures, which, as in the example, are closed at year-end, to fund balance. It reflects only genuine transactions, not forecasts (and in some cases mere hopes) of what will occur during the year.

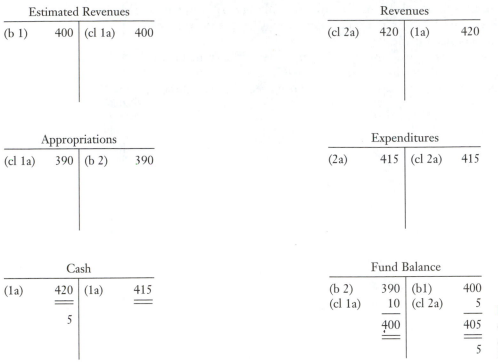

FIGURE 3-1 Illustration of Budgetary Entries.

(Assuming Differences Between Budgeted and Actual Amounts)

HOW DOES ENCUMBRANCE ACCOUNTING PREVENT OVERSPENDING?

Governments and some not-for-profits record encumbrances to help prevent overspending the budget. The entry to record an encumbrance is usually prepared when a purchase order is issued, a contract is signed, or a commitment is made (e.g., when a university makes faculty and staff appointments for a semester or year). Most organizations do not encumber all anticipated expenditures. Many, for example, do not encumber salaries and wages, expenditures below a specified amount, and expenditures that are adequately controlled by other means.

THE BASIC ENTRIES

The entry to record an encumbrance reduces the budgeted amount available for expenditure (as if the amount had already been spent) and concurrently designates a portion of what would otherwise be *unreserved* fund balance as *reserved for encumbrances* (i.e., for expenditures to which the organization is committed). The entry is reversed as the goods or services are received and expenditures are recorded.

Whereas both budgetary entries and encumbrances are mainly internal control devices, encumbrances are of slightly greater concern to external parties since they have a minor impact on general purpose financial statements. Outstanding commitments at year-end are reported on the entity's *balance sheet* as a reservation of fund balance and accordingly reduce the unreserved portion of fund balance.

EXAMPLE   *The Encumbrance Cycle—Year 1*

A university contracts for repair services that it estimates will cost $5,000. The following entry will reserve the funds to meet the anticipated expenditure:

Encumbrances	$5,000	
Reserve for encumbrances		$5,000
To encumber $5,000 for repair services		

In addition to these control account entries, corresponding entries would be made in the repair-related subaccounts (e.g., encumbrances—electrical contractors).

The reserve for encumbrances account is a balance sheet account—a reservation of fund equity. The encumbrance account, although most definitely *not* an expenditure, is similar to an expenditure in that at year-end any remaining balance will be closed to unreserved fund balance. The encumbrance account indicates the net amount that was transferred during the period from unreserved fund balance to fund balance reserved for encumbrances.

The repairs are completed and, as anticipated, the university is billed for $5,000. The repair expenditure must be recorded with the usual entry:

Expenditures	$5,000	
Accounts payable		$5,000
To record repair expenditures		

In addition, the reserve for encumbrance is no longer required. The services have been received and the expenditure has been charged. The reserve must be eliminated by reversing the entry establishing it:

Reserve for encumbrances	$5,000	
Encumbrances		$5,000
To reverse the encumbrance entry upon receipt of services		

At year-end the expenditures would be closed out in standard fashion, thereby reducing fund balance.

Consider two alternative possibilities. Assume first that the contractor *completes* the repairs but bills the university for only $4,800, not the encumbered $5,000. The university must now record an expenditure for the actual amount to be paid:

Expenditure	$4,800	
Accounts payable		$4,800
To record repair expenditures		

As before, it must eliminate the *entire* reserve. With regard to the repairs, the university has no further commitment; it therefore needs no reserve:

Reserve for encumbrances	$5,000	
Encumbrances		$5,000
To reverse the encumbrance entry upon receipt of services		

If the contractor's bill were for more than the encumbered amount, the same approach would be taken. The expenditure would be charged for the amount to be paid; the full amount of the reserve would be eliminated. The university's error in encumbering less than its actual commitment would have no consequences for financial reporting. At worst, it temporarily increased the university's risk of overspending its budget.

As the second possibility, assume that in the current period the contractor completes only 40 percent of the repairs and accordingly bills the university for only $2,000. It expects to fulfill the remainder of its contract in the following period. In this situation, only a part of the encumbrance entry can be reversed; the university still has an outstanding commitment for $3,000. Thus:

Expenditures	$2,000	
Accounts payable		$2,000
To record repair expenditures		
Reserve for encumbrances	$2,000	
Encumbrances		$2,000
To reverse the encumbrance entry upon the contractor's completion		
of $2,000 of the $5,000 in anticipated services		

At year-end, the expenditures and the encumbrances would be closed to fund balance. (The reserve for encumbrances need not be closed because it is a balance sheet account). Continuing with the last set of assumptions (expenditures of $2,000; balance in the encumbrances account of $3,000), the following closing entry would be in order:

Fund Balance	$5,000	
Expenditures		$2,000
Encumbrances		$3,000
To close expenditures and encumbrances		

As a consequence of these entries, $3,000 of the university's fund balance—the amount committed for completion of the repairs—remains reserved for encumbrances.

ACCOUNTING FOR COMMITMENTS OUTSTANDING AT THE START OF A YEAR

Governments differ in how they budget—and therefore how they account—for commitments outstanding (left over from the prior year). Many governments require that the cost of goods or services be charged against budgeted appropriations of the year in which they are received. In other words, all appropriations lapse at year-end. To satisfy its outstanding commitments, a government must reappropriate the funds for the following year or meet them out of whatever resources were budgeted for the following year within an applicable expenditure classification.

Other governments, either for all or only selected types of commitments (particularly long-term projects) allow appropriations to continue into future years. When the goods or services are received, they are charged against the budget of the year of appropriation.

In the circumstances in which appropriations lapse and the government charges the cost of goods or services against appropriations of the year in which they are received, the accounting for commitments made in a previous year is relatively simple. At the start of the new year the government need only restore the encumbrances that were closed at the end of the previous year. This can be accomplished by reversing the closing entry (i.e., debiting encumbrances and crediting fund balance). By restoring the encumbrances, both the reserve for encumbrances (which, as a balance sheet account, was never closed) and the encumbrances would have the same balances as if the closing entries had not been made. Thereafter, the entries to record the fulfillment of the commitments would be the same as if the goods or services were received in the year the encumbrances and the reserve were initially established.[9]

EXAMPLE   *The Encumbrance Cycle—Year 2*

At the end of the first year—the start of the second—the university had $3,000 of outstanding commitments for repairs. The following entry would restore the $3,000 of encumbrances for repairs:

Encumbrances	$3,000	
Fund balance		$3,000

To restore encumbrances at the start of the new year

When the contractor completes the repairs, the university will charge expenditures for the amount billed and reverse the encumbrances and the reserve for encumbrances:

Expenditures	$3,000	
Accounts payable		$3,000

To record repair expenditures

Reserve for encumbrances	$3,000	
Encumbrances		$3,000

To reverse the encumbrances entry upon the contractor's completion of the remaining $3,000 of repairs

The following additional example, by focusing on a single commitment, highlights the impact of the encumbrance procedures on fund balance. Note that over the two-year period the total reduction in fund balance equals the total expenditures.

---

[9] If the appropriation does not lapse and the government charges the cost of goods or services against appropriations of the year in which the commitment was made, then the encumbrance should *not* be restored. Instead, when the commitment is fulfilled, the expenditure should be "dated" to indicate that it is applicable to the previous year. Thus, for example:

Expenditures—19×0	$3,000	
Accounts payable		$3,000

To record repair expenditures

These expenditures would then be closed to the previously established reserve for encumbrances:

Reserve for encumbrances	$3,000	
Expenditures—19×0		$3,000

To close expenditures for the previous year and eliminate the applicable reserve for encumbrances

EXAMPLE   *Impact of Encumbrances on Fund Balance*

Year 1

As of January 1, a government's general fund balance sheet shows the following:

Cash	$1,000
Fund balance—unreserved	$1,000

During the year, the government orders $1,000 of supplies (which are to be charged as expenditures when received):

(a)

Encumbrances	$1,000	
Reserve for encumbrances		$1,000

To encumber $1,000 for supplies on order

Part of the supplies order costing $800 is received and paid for in cash:

(b)

Supplies expenditures	$800	
Cash		$800

To record the receipt of, and payment for, supplies

(c)

Reserve for encumbrances	$800	
Encumbrances		$800

To reverse the encumbrance entry for the portion of the supplies order received

The government prepares the following year-end closing entries:

(cl 1)

Fund balance—unreserved	$1,000	
Encumbrances		$200
Supplies expenditures		800

To close encumbrances and expenditures

Year 2

The government expects to honor its commitment for the supplies on order. However, its budgeting policies dictate that the cost of the supplies on order be charged as expenditures of the year in which they are received. Therefore, at the start of the new year it restores the encumbrances that had been closed at the end of the prior year:

(d)

Encumbrances	$200	
Fund balance—unreserved		$200

To restore encumbrances

It receives, and pays for, the remainder of the supplies. However, the additional charges are only $150, not $200 as encumbered:

(e)

Supplies expenditures	$150	
Cash		$150

To record the receipt of, and payment for, supplies

(f)

Reserve for encumbrances	$200	
Encumbrances		$200

To reverse the encumbrance entry for the remainder of the supplies

It prepares appropriate year-end closing entries:

(cl 2)

Fund balance—unreserved	$150	
Supplies expenditures		$150

To close expenditures (Note: the balance in the encumbrances account is zero; it need not be closed.)

Figure 3-2 summarizes the entries to the accounts. The government began the two-year period with an unreserved fund balance of $1,000. During the two years it incurred expenditures of $950. As shown in the T-account, its unreserved fund balance at the end of the second year is $50—the same as if an encumbrance system were not being employed.

Encumbrances

(a)	1,000	(c)	800
		(cl 1)	200
(d)	200	(f)	200

Supplies Expenditures

(b)	800	(cl 1)	800
(e)	150	(cl 2)	150

Cash

Beg Bal	1,000	(b)	800
Yr 1 Bal	200		
		(e)	150
Yr 2 Bal	50		

Reserve for Encumbrances

(c)	800	(a)	1,000
		Yr 1 Bal	200
(f)	200		
Yr 2 Bal	0		

Fund Balance

(cl 1)	1,000	Beg Bal	1,000
		Yr 1 Bal	0
(cl 2)	150	(d)	200
		Yr 2 Bal	50

FIGURE 3-2 Summary of Budget Entries

The fund's balance sheet at the end of each of the two years and a schedule explaining the change in unreserved fund balance follow:

Balance Sheet

	End of Year 1	End of Year 2
Cash	$200	$ 50
Fund Balance		
Reserved for Encumbrances	$200	$ 0
Unreserved	0	50
Total Fund Balance	$200	$ 50

Schedule of Changes in Unreserved Fund Balance

	Year 1	Year 2	Total
Revenues	$ 0	$ 0	$ 0
Expenditures	800	150	950
Excess of Revenues Over Expenditures	(800)	(150)	(950)
Less: Increase/(Decrease) in Reserve for Encumbrances	200	(200)	0
Net Change in Unreserved Fund Balance During the Year [Increase/(Decrease)]	(1,000)	50	(950)
Add: Beginning of Year Balance	1,000	0	
End of Year Balance	0	50	

Note: If the appropriations did not lapse, then the entry to restore the encumbrances would *not* have been made. Instead, when the goods were received, the following entries would be necessary:

Supplies expenditures—year 1	$150	
Cash		$150

To record the receipt of, and payment for, supplies

(f)

Reserve for encumbrances	$200	
Supplies expenditures—year 1		$150
Fund balance		50

To close the supplies expenditures—year 1 and eliminate the reserve for encumbrances

ARE BUDGETARY AND ENCUMBRANCE ENTRIES REALLY NEEDED?

Not all governments or not-for-profits integrate their budgets into their accounting systems or encumber the cost of goods or services for which they are committed. Under what circumstances should they do so? The general answer is that they should do so when the benefits of added control are worth the costs (in both dollars and inconvenience).

Consistent with this answer, governments are more likely to establish these controls than are other not-for-profits because the penalties for overspending their budgets are likely to be more severe. Similarly, governments are more likely to implement these mechanisms in their general fund than in some other governmental funds, such as their capital projects funds or their debt service funds, since adequate controls may already be in place in those funds. For example, sufficient controls over the cost of a capital project may be established simply by assuring that the agreed upon price with the contractor is within the amount of bond proceeds. The expenditures of a debt service fund may be set by the payments of principal and interest spelled out in the bond indentures.

Modern computer systems make it possible for the controls provided by both budgetary entries and encumbrances to be achieved by means other than formal journal entries. For example, a government can simply "load" the budget into its computer. The computer can be programmed to issue a warning whenever actual expenditures and commitments exceed a specified percentage of budgeted expenditures.

SUMMARY

Almost all aspects of management in government and not-for-profit organizations revolve around the entities' budgets. The budget is at the center of planning, controlling, administering, evaluating, and reporting functions.

Budgets can take many forms. Appropriation budgets indicate governments' estimated revenues and authorized expenditures. Capital budgets concentrate on long-lived assets. Flexible budgets, which governments use for proprietary funds, contain alternative budget estimates based on different levels of output. Performance budgets focus on measured units of effort and accomplishment and relate costs to objectives.

Most governments follow a four-phase cycle for budgeting: preparation, legislative adoption and executive approval, execution, and reporting and auditing.

For legislative purposes, most governments prepare cash or near-cash budgets. But these may fail to capture the economic cost of carrying out government activities and are not an adequate basis for planning and assessing results.

To demonstrate that they complied with their budgets, governments are required to include in their annual reports a budget to actual comparison on a budget basis. However, the revenues and expenditures from the budget may not be readily comparable to those in GAAP-based statements. Differences may be attributable to basis of accounting (e.g., cash vs. modified accrual), timing (e.g., period over which a project will be completed vs. a single year), perspective (e.g., program vs. object classification) and reporting entity (legal vs. economic). Therefore, governments must both explain and reconcile the differences between budgeted and actual amounts.

The accounting systems of governments are similar to businesses in that they use comparable journals and ledgers. However, they differ in that they include corporate budgetary control features to ensure adherence to spending mandates. In addition, they encumber goods and services on order to prevent themselves from overcommitting available resources.

EXERCISE FOR REVIEW AND SELF-STUDY

To enhance control over both revenues and expenditures, a not-for-profit health care agency incorporates its budget in its accounting system and encumbers all commitments. You have been asked to assist the agency in making the entries to record the following transactions.

a. Prior to the start of the year, the agency's trustees adopted a budget in which revenues were estimated at $5,600 (all dollar amounts in this exercise will be expressed in thousands) and expenditures of $5,550 were appropriated (authorized). Record the budget using only the control (summary) accounts.

b. During the year, the agency engaged in the following transactions. Prepare appropriate journal entries.

  1. It collected $5,800 in contributions, grants, and other revenues.

  2. It ordered goods and services for $3,000.

  3. During the year it received and paid for $2,800 of goods and services that had been previously encum-

bered. It expects to receive the remaining $200 in the following year.

  4. It incurred $2,500 in other expenditures for goods and services that had not been encumbered.

c. Prepare appropriate year-end closing entries.

d. Prepare a balance sheet showing the status of year-end asset and fund balance accounts.

e. Per the policy of the agency's trustees, the cost of all goods and services are to be charged against the budget of the year in which they are received, even if they had been ordered (and encumbered) in a previous year. The next year, to simplify the accounting for the commitments made in the prior year, the agency reinstated the encumbrances outstanding at year-end. Prepare the appropriate entry.

f. During the year, the agency received the remaining encumbered goods and services. However, the total cost was only $150, rather than $200 as estimated. Prepare the appropriate entries.

QUESTIONS FOR REVIEW AND DISCUSSION

1. Why is it important that governments and other not-for-profits coordinate their processes for developing *appropriations* budgets with those for developing *capital* budgets?

2. Why may *flexible* budgets be more important to a government's proprietary (business-type) activities than to its governmental activities?

3. What is the main advantage of an *object classification* budget? What are its limitations? How do *performance* budgets overcome these limitations?

4. Why do most governments and not-for-profits budget on a cash or near-cash basis even though the cash basis does not capture the full economic costs of the activities in which they engage?

5. A political official boasts that the year-end excess of revenues over expenditures was significantly greater than was budgeted. Are "favorable" budget variances necessarily a sign of efficient and effective governmental management? Explain.

6. What are *allotments?* What purpose do they serve?

7. Why may a government's year-end results, reported in accordance with generally accepted accounting principles, not be readily comparable with its legally adopted budget?

8. The budget to actual comparisons incorporated in the financial statements of many governments may be of no value in revealing the reliability of budget estimates made at the start of the year. Why? How can you rationalize this limitation of the budget to actual comparisons?

9. In what way will budgetary entries and encumbrances affect amounts reported on year-end balance sheets or operating statements?

10. Why do many governments consider it unnecessary to prepare appropriation budgets for, and incorporate budgetary entries into the accounts of, their capital projects funds?

EXERCISES

3-1

A county engages in basic transactions.

Kilbourne County engaged in the following transactions in summary form during its fiscal year. All amounts are in millions.

1. Its commissioners approved a budget for the current fiscal year. It included total revenues of $860 and total appropriations of $850 million.

2. It ordered office supplies for $20.

3. It incurred the following costs, paying in cash.

Salaries	$610
Repairs	$ 40
Rent	$ 25
Utilities	$ 41
Other operating costs	$119

4. It ordered equipment costing $9.

5. It received the equipment and was billed for $10, rather than $9 as anticipated.

6. It received the previously ordered supplies and was billed for the amount originally estimated. The county reports the receipt of supplies as expenditures; it does not maintain an inventory account for supplies.

7. It earned and collected revenues of $865.

a. Prepare journal entries as appropriate.
b. Prepare closing entries as appropriate.
c. What would have been the difference in the year-end financial statements, if any, had the county not made the budgetary entries?

3-2

Encumbrances are recorded in a capital projects fund similar to a general fund.

Wickliffe County authorized the issuance of bonds and contracted with the USA Construction Company (UCC) to build a new sports complex. During 1998, 1999, and 2000 it engaged in the transactions that follow. All were recorded in a capital projects fund.

1. In 1998 the county issued $310 million of bonds (and recorded them as "bond proceeds," an account comparable to a revenue).

2. It approved the contract for $310 million and encumbered the entire amount.

3. It received from UCC an invoice for construction to date for $114 million, an amount that the county recognized as an expenditure.

4. It paid UCC the amount owed.

5. In 1999 it received from UCC an invoice for an additional $190 million.

6. It paid the amount in full.
7. In 2000 UCC completed the sports facility and billed the county an additional $7 million. The county approved the additional costs, even though the total cost was now $311, $1 million more than initially estimated.
8. The county transferred $1 million from the general fund to the capital projects fund.
9. The county paid the $7 million.
   a. Prepare the journal entries, including closing entries, to record the transactions in the capital projects fund. Assume that expenditures do not have to be appropriated each year. Hence, the county need not reestablish encumbrances at each year subsequent to the first. Instead, it can close the expenditures of the second and third years to reserve for encumbrances rather than fund balance.
   b. What other funds or account groups, other than the capital projects fund, would be affected by the transactions?

3-3

Both budgeted and actual revenues and expenditures are closed to the fund balance.

   The budgeted and actual revenues and expenditures of Seaside Township for a recent year (in millions) were as presented in the schedule that follows.

a. Prepare journal entries to record the budget.
b. Prepare journal entries to record the actual revenues and expenditures. Assume all transactions resulted in increases or decreases in cash.
c. Prepare journal entries to close the accounts.
d. Determine the net change in fund balance. Does it equal the net change in actual revenues and expenditures?

	Budget	**Actual**
Revenues:		
Property Taxes	$ 7.5	$ 7.6
Sales Taxes	2.1	2.4
Other Revenues	1.6	1.5
Total Revenues	$11.2	$11.5
Expenditures:		
Wages and Salaries	$ 6.2	$ 6.1
Supplies	3.1	3.0
Other Expenditures	1.3	1.2
Total Expenditures	$10.6	$10.3
Increase in Fund Balance	$ 0.6	$ 1.2

3-4

Encumbrance accounting has no lasting impact on fund balance.

   London Township began year 1 with an unreserved balance of $10 million in its bridge repair fund, a capital projects fund.

At the start of the year, the governing council appropriated $6 million for the repair of two bridges. Shortly thereafter, the town signed contracts with a construction company to perform the repairs at a cost of $3 million per bridge.

   During the year the town received and paid bills from the construction company as follows:

• $3.2 million for the repairs on Bridge 1. The company completed the repairs, but owing to design changes approved by the town, the cost was $0.2 million greater than anticipated. The town did not encumber the additional $0.2 million.
• $2.0 million for the repairs, which were not completed, on Bridge 2.

   At the start of the following year, the governing council reappropriated the $1 million to complete the repairs on Bridge 2. During that year the town received and paid bills totaling $0.7 million. The construction company completed the repairs, but the final cost was less than anticipated—a total of only $2.7 million.

a. Prepare journal entries to record the events and transactions over the two-year period. Include entries to appropriate, reappropriate, encumber, and reencumber, the required funds, to record the payment of the bills, and to close the accounts at the end of each year.
b. Determine the unreserved fund balance at the end of the second year. Is it equal to the initial fund balance less the total cost of the repairs?

3-5

Encumbrances have an impact on unreserved fund balance, but do not affect total fund balance.

   At the start of its fiscal year on October 1, 1998, Fox County reported the following (all dollar amounts in thousands):

Fund balance:	
Reserved for encumbrances	$200
Unreserved	400
Total fund balance	$600

During fiscal 1998, the county (all dollar amounts in thousands):

• estimated that revenues for the year would be $6,300.
• appropriated $6,500 for operations.
• ordered goods and services estimated to cost $6,000. Of these, the county received (and used) goods and services that it had estimated would cost $5,000. Actual cost, however, was $5,200.
• received (and used) all goods that it ordered in the previous year. Actual cost was only $180.
• recognized actual revenues of $6,400.
   a. Prepare a schedule, similar to that illustrated in the text, of changes in unreserved fund balance.

b. Show how the total fund balance (including the reserved and unreserved portions) would be displayed at year-end.

c. Does the total fund balance at the beginning of the year, plus the actual revenues, minus the actual expenditures, equal the total fund balance at the end of the year.

3-6

Multiple Choice Questions from CPA Examinations

1. For state and local governmental units, generally accepted accounting principles require that encumbrances outstanding at year-end be reported as
   a. expenditures.
   b. reservations of fund balance.
   c. deferred liabilities.
   d. current liabilities.

2. The estimated revenues control account balance of a governmental fund type is eliminated when
   a. the budgetary accounts are closed.
   b. the budget is recorded.
   c. property taxes are recorded.
   d. appropriations are closed.

3. The expenditures control account of a governmental unit is increased when

	A purchase order is approved	The budget is recorded
a.	No	No
b.	No	Yes
c.	Yes	Yes
d.	Yes	No

4. The budget of a governmental unit, for which the appropriations exceed the estimated revenues, was adopted and recorded in the general ledger at the beginning of the year. During the year, expenditures and encumbrances were less than appropriations, whereas revenues equaled estimated revenues. The budgetary fund balance account is
   a. credited at the beginning of the year and not changed at the end of the year.
   b. credited at the beginning of the year and debited at the end of the year.
   c. debited at the beginning of the year and not changed at the end of the year.
   d. debited at the beginning of the year and credited at the end of the year.

5. Which of the following accounts of a governmental unit is debited when a purchase order is approved?
   a. Appropriations control
   b. Vouchers payable
   c. Fund balance reserved for encumbrances
   d. Encumbrances control

Items 6 through 8 are based on the following data:

The Board of Commissioners of Vane City adopted its budget for the year ending July 31, 1995, comprising estimated revenues of $30 million and appropriations of $29 million. Vane formally integrates its budget into the accounting records.

6. What entry should be made for budgeted revenues?
   a. Memorandum entry only
   b. Debit estimated revenues receivable control, $30,000,000
   c. Debit estimated revenues control, $30,000,000
   d. Credit estimated revenues control, $30,000,000

7. What entry should be made for budgeted appropriations?
   a. Memorandum entry only
   b. Credit estimated expenditures payable control, $29,000,000
   c. Credit appropriations control, $29,000,000
   d. Debit estimated expenditures control, $29,000,000

8. What entry should be made for the budgeted excess of revenues over appropriations?
   a. Memorandum entry only
   b. Credit budgetary fund balance, $1,000,000
   c. Debit estimated excess revenues control, $1,000,000
   d. Debit excess revenues receivable control, $1,000,000

Items 9 and 10 are based on the following data:

Albee Township's fiscal year ends on June 30. Albee uses encumbrance accounting. On April 5, 1996, an approved $1,000 purchase order was issued for supplies. Albee received these supplies on May 2, 1996, and the $1,000 invoice was approved for payment.

9. What journal entry should Albee make on April 5, 1996 to record the approved purchase order?

	Debit	Credit
a. Memorandum entry only		
b. Encumbrances control	$1,000	
Fund balance reserved for Encumbrances		$1,000
c. Supplies	1,000	
Vouchers payable		1,000
d. Encumbrances control	1,000	
Appropriations control		1,000

10. What journal entry or entries should Albee make on May 2 upon receipt of the supplies and approval of the invoice?

	Debit	Credit
a. Appropriations control	$1,000	
Encumbrances control		$1,000
Supplies	1,000	
Vouchers payable		1,000
b. Supplies	1,000	
Vouchers payable		1,000

c. Fund balance reserved		
for encumbrances	1,000	
Encumbrances control		1,000
Expenditures control	1,000	
Vouchers payable		1,000
d. Encumbrances control	1,000	
Aropriations control		1,000
Fund balance	1,000	
Vouchers payable		1,000

3-7

Multiple Choice Questions from CPA Examinations

1. The budgetary fund balance reserved for encumbrances account of a governmental fund type is increased when
   a. a purchase order is approved.
   b. supplies previously ordered are received.
   c. appropriations are recorded.
   d. the budget is recorded.

2. The appropriations control account of a governmental unit is debited when

	The budgetary accounts are closed	Expenditures are recorded
a.	No	Yes
b.	No	No
c.	Yes	No
d.	Yes	Yes

3. Lake City incurred $300,000 of salaries and wages in its general fund for the month ended May 31, 1995. For this $300,000, Lake should debit
   a. fund balance-unreserved, undesignated.
   b. encumbrances control.
   c. appropriations control.
   d. expenditures control.

4. When Rolan County adopted its budget for the year ending June 30, 1996, $20 million was recorded for estimated revenues control. Actual revenues for the year ended June 30, 1996, amounted to $17 million. In closing the budgetary accounts at year-end,
   a. revenues control should be debited for $3,000,000.
   b. estimated revenues control should be debited for $3,000,000.
   c. revenues control should be credited for $20,000,000.
   d. estimated revenues control should be credited for $20,000,000.

Items 5 through 10 are based on the following information:

Maple Township uses encumbrance accounting, and formally integrates its budget into the accounting records for its general fund. For the year ending June 30, 1996, the Township Council adopted a budget comprising estimated revenues of $10 million, appropriations of $9 million, and an estimated transfer of $300,000 to the debt service fund. The following additional information is provided:

For the month of April 1996, salaries and wages expenditures of $200,000 were incurred.

On April 10, 1996, an approved $1,500 purchase order was issued for supplies. These supplies were received on May 1, 1996, and the $1,500 invoice was approved for payment.

5. On adoption of the budget, the journal entry to record the budgetary fund balance should include a
   a. debit of $700,000.
   b. credit of $700,000.
   c. debit of $1,000,000.
   d. credit of $1,000,000.

6. Budgeted revenues would be recorded by a
   a. debit to estimated revenues control, $10,000,000.
   b. debit to estimated revenues receivable, $10,000,000.
   c. credit to estimated revenues, $10,000,000.
   d. credit to other financing sources control, $10,000,000.

7. Budgeted appropriations would be recorded by a
   a. debit to estimated expenditures, $9,300,000.
   b. credit to appropriations control, $9,300,000.
   c. debit to estimated expenditures, $9,000,000.
   d. credit to appropriations control, $9,000,000.

8. What journal entry should be made on April 10, 1996, to record the approved purchase order?

	Debit	Credit
a. Expenditures control	$1,500	
Encumbrances control		$1,500
b. Encumbrances control	1,500	
Expenditures control		1,500
c. Encumbrances control	1,500	
Fund balance reserved for encumbrances		1,500
d. Encumbrances control	1,500	
Appropriations control		1,500

9. What journal entries should be made on May 1, 1996, upon receipt of the supplies and approval of the invoice?

	Debit	Credit
a. Encumbrances control	$1,500	
Appropriations control		$1,500
Supplies expense	1,500	
Vouchers payable		1,500
b. Fund balance reserved for encumbrances	1,500	
Encumbrances control		1,500
Expenditures control	1,500	
Vouchers payable		1,500
c. Appropriations control	1,500	
Encumbrances control		1,500

Expenditures control	1,500	
Vouchers payable		1,500
d. Expenditures control	1,500	
Encumbrances control		1,500
Supplies expense	1,500	
Vouchers payable		1,500

10. What journal entry should be made to record the salaries and wages expenditure incurred for April?

	Debit	Credit
a. Salaries and wages expense	$200,000	
Vouchers payable		$200,000
b. Appropriations control	200,000	
Vouchers payable		200,000
c. Encumbrances control	200,000	
Vouchers payable		200,000
d. Expenditures control	200,000	
Vouchers payable		200,000

3-8

Multiple Choice Questions from CPA Examinations

1. The encumbrances control account of a governmental unit is increased when

	A voucher payable is recorded	The budgetary accounts are closed
a.	No	No
b.	No	Yes
c.	Yes	Yes
d.	Yes	No

2. Oro County's expenditures control account at December, 31, 1995, had a balance of $9 million. When Oro's books were closed, this account should have
   a. been debited.
   b. been credited.
   c. remained open.
   d. appeared as a contra account.

3. The estimated revenues control account of a governmental unit is debited when
   a. the budget is closed at the end of the year.
   b. the budget is recorded.
   c. actual revenues are recorded.
   d. actual revenues are collected.

4. Harbor City's appropriations control account at December 31, 1995, had a balance of $7 million. When the budgetary accounts were closed at year-end, this balance should have
   a. been debited.
   b. been credited.
   c. remained open.
   d. appeared as a contra account.

5. At December 31, 1995, Alto Township's committed appropriations that had not been expended in 1995 to-

taled $10,000. These appropriations do not lapse at year-end. Alto reports on a calendar-year basis. On its December 31, 1995, balance sheet, the $10,000 should be reported as
   a. vouchers payable— prior year.
   b. deferred expenditures.
   c. fund balance reserved for encumbrances.
   d. budgetary fund balance—reserved for encumbrances.

Items 6 through 10 are based on the following:
Cliff Township's fiscal year ends on July 31. Cliff uses encumbrance accounting. On October 2, 1995, an approved $5,000 purchase order was issued for supplies. Cliff received these supplies on November 2, 1995, and the $5,000 invoice was approved for payment by the general fund.

Cliff's governing body adopted its general fund budget for the year ending July 31, 1996, comprising estimated revenues of $50 million and appropriations of $40 million. Cliff formally integrates its budget into the accounting records.

6. What accounts should Cliff debit and credit on October 2, 1995, to record the approved $5,000 purchase order?

	Debit	Credit
a.	Encumbrances control	Appropriations control
b.	Appropriations control	Encumbrances control
c.	Encumbrances control	Budgetary fund balance—reserved for encumbrances
d.	Budgetary fund balance—reserved for encumbrances	Encumbrances control

7. What accounts should Cliff debit and credit on November 2, 1995, upon receipt of the supplies and approval of the $5,000 invoice?

	Debit	Credit
a.	Budgetary fund balance—reserved for encumbrances	Encumbrances control
	Expenditures control	Vouchers payable
b.	Encumbrances control	Budgetary fund balance—reserved for encumbrances
	Appropriations control	Vouchers payable
c.	Appropriations control	Encumbrances control
	Supplies inventory	Vouchers payable

d. Encumbrances   Appropriations control
    control

    Expendiutures   Vouchers payable
    control

8. When Cliff records budgeted revenues, estimated revenues control should be
   a. debited for $10,000,000.
   b. credited for $10,000,000.
   c. debited for $50,000,000.
   d. credited for $50,000,000.

9. To record the $40 million of budgeted appropriations, Cliff should

   a. debit estimated expenditures control.
   b. credit estimated expenditures control.
   c. debit appropriations control.
   d. credit appropriations control.

10. The $10 million budgeted excess of revenues over appropriations should be
    a. debited to budgetary fund balance—unreserved.
    b. credited to budgetary fund balance—unreserved.
    c. debited to estimated excess revenues control.
    d. credited to estimated excess revenues control.

PROBLEMS

Continuing Problem

Review the annual report that you obtained.

a. Examine the schedules that compare budgets to actual results and any notes pertaining to budgets.

   1. Are budgets prepared for all governmental funds? If not, for which funds are budgets not prepared? Do the notes indicate why budgets are not prepared?

   2. Do the notes tell whether the budgetary comparisons are based on original or amended budgets?

   3. Are the overall revenue and expenditure variances favorable or unfavorable? Would you expect them to be unfavorable in total (even if some individual variances are unfavorable)? Why?

   4. Is the budget adopted on a basis consistent with generally accepted accounting principles? If not, what are the differences?

   5. Are there any other differences between the budgets and actual results that invalidate comparisons? If so, what are they? Do the statements contain schedules that reconcile differences between the budget as reported and what would be a GAAP-based budget?

b. Examine the combined balance sheet and any notes pertaining to appropriations and encumbrances.

   1. Are any portions of the general fund, or other governmental fund, balances reserved for encumbrances?

   2. Do the notes indicate the government's policy as to whether annual appropriations lapse at year-end? If so, what is the policy?

   3. Do the notes describe the government's practices as to encumbrances? If so, what are its practices?

3-1

Is accrual-based budgeting preferable to cash-based budgeting?

The Disability Research Institute receives its funding mainly from government grants and private contributions. In turn, it supports research and related projects carried out by universities and other nonprofit organizations. Most of its government grants are "matching" awards. That is, the government will reimburse the institute for the funds that it disburses to others.

The institute estimates the following as to the forthcoming year:

- It will be awarded $5,000,000 in government grants, all of which will be paid out to subrecipients during the year. Of this amount, only $4,500,000 will be reimbursed by the government during the year. The balance will be reimbursed in the first six months of the next year. It will also receive $200,000 in grant funds that were owing from the previous year.

- It will receive $600,000 in pledges from private donors. It expects to collect $450,000 during the year and the balance in the following year. It also expects to collect $80,000 in pledges made the prior year.

- It will purchase new furniture and office equipment at a cost of $80,000. It currently owns its building that it had purchased for $800,000 and additional furniture and equipment that it acquired for $250,000. The building has a useful life of 25 years; the furniture and equipment have a useful life of five years.

- Employees will earn wages and salaries of $340,000, of which they will be paid $320,000 during the forthcoming year and the balance in the next year.

- It will incur other operating costs of $90,000, of which it will pay $70,000 in the forthcoming year and $20,000 in the next year. It will also pay another $10,000 in costs incurred in the previous year.

   a. Prepare two budgets, one on a cash basis, the other on a *full* accrual basis. For convenience show both on the same schedule, the cash budget in one column and the accrual in the other.

b. Comment on which budget best shows whether the institute is covering the economic cost of the services that it provides.

c. Which is likely to be more useful to

1. institute managers?
2. members of the institute's board of trustees?
3. bankers from whom the institute seeks a loan?

3-2

Missing data can be derived, and journal entries constructed, from information in the accounts.

The following schedule shows the amounts related to expenditures that a nonprofit welfare organization debited and credited to the indicated accounts during a year (not necessarily the year-end balances), *excluding* closing entries. The organization records its budget, encumbers all of its expenditures, and initially vouchers all payments.

Some information is missing. You are to determine the missing data and construct all entries (in summary form), excluding closing entries, that the organization made during the year.

	Debits	**Credits**
Cash	$ 0	$28
Vouchers payable	?	?
Estimated expenditures (Appropriations)	0	55
Encumbrances	?	?
Expenditures	30	0
Reserve for encumbrances	32	50
Fund balance	?	0

3-3

A city imposes an overhead charge on one of its departments to alleviate its fiscal problems.

A city's visitors' bureau, which promotes tourism and conventions, is funded by an 8 percent local hotel occupancy tax (a tax on the cost of a stay in a hotel). Inasmuch as the visitors' bureau is supported entirely by the occupancy tax, it is accounted for in a restricted fund.

You recently received a call from the director of the visitors' bureau. She complained that the city manager is about to impose an overhead charge of a specified dollar amount on her department. Yet the statute creating the hotel occupancy tax specifies that the revenues can be used only to satisfy "direct expenditures" incurred to promote tourism and bookings at the city's convention center. The manager says that she understands the city is having difficulty balancing its budget, but fails to see how the charge to her department will do much to alleviate the city's fiscal problems.

a. In light of the city's fiscal problems, what is the most likely motivation for the new charge? Will the new overhead charge achieve its objective?

b. What would be the impact of the new charge on the city's annual financial statements, prepared in accordance with GAAP (which requires that the city account for its governmental funds on a modified accrual basis)? Would the impact be the same if the city accounted for its governmental funds on a cash basis?

c. Suppose that the city were to both budget and prepare its financial statements on a consolidated basis in which all funds were combined? Would the charge have an impact on either the budgeted or reported net surplus?

d. In what way might the charge have a substantive impact on the city's economic condition?

e. Assuming that the city provided accounting, legal, and purchasing services to the visitors' bureau, do you think the charge would be consistent with the statutory requirement that the hotel occupancy tax be used to meet only "direct expenditures" related to tourism and use of the convention center (an issue not addressed in this text)?

3-4

Government activities may be less "profitable" than they appear.

A city prepares its budget in traditional format, classifying expenditures as to fund and object. In 1993, amid considerable controversy, the city authorized the sale of $20 million in bonds to finance construction of a new sports and special events arena. Critics charged that, contrary to the predictions of arena proponents, the arena could not be fiscally self-sustaining.

Five years later, the arena was completed and began to be used. After its first year of operations, its general managers submitted the following condensed statement of revenues and expenses (in millions):

Revenues from Ticket Sales	$5.7	
Revenues from Concessions	2.4	$8.1
Operating Expenses	6.6	
Interest on Debt	1.2	7.8
Excess of Revenues Over Expenses		$0.3

At the city council meeting at which the report was submitted the council member who championed the center glowingly boasted that his prophecy was proving correct; the arena was "profitable."

Assume that the following information came to your attention:

• The arena is accounted for in a separate enterprise fund.

• The arena increased the number of overnight visitors to the city. City administrators and economists calculated that the additional visitors generated approximately $0.1 million in hotel occupancy tax revenues. These taxes are dedicated to promoting tourism in the city. In addition, they estimated that the ticket and concession sales, plus the economic activity generated by the arena, increased general sales tax revenues by $0.4 million.

- The city had to improve roads, highways, and utilities in the area surrounding the arena. These improvements, which cost $6 million, were financed with general obligation debt (reported in the city's general long-term debt account group). Principal and interest on the debt, paid out of general funds, were $0.5 million. The cost of maintaining the facilities was approximately $0.1.

- On evenings in which events were held in the arena, the city had to increase police protection in the arena's neighborhood. Whereas the arena compensated the police department for police officers who served within the arena itself, those that patrolled outside were paid out of police department funds. The police department estimated its additional costs at $0.1 million.

- The city provided various administrative services (including legal, accounting, and personnel) to the arena at no charge at an estimated cost of $0.1 million.

- The city estimates the cost of additional sanitation, fire, and medical services due to events at the center to be approximately $0.2 million.

  a. Would you agree with the council member that the arena was fiscally self-sustaining?

  b. In which funds would the additional revenues and expenditures be budgeted and accounted for?

  c. Comment on the limitations of both the traditional object classification budget and fund accounting system in assessing the economic costs and benefits of a project such as the sports and special events arena.

  d. What changes in the city's budgeting and accounting structure would overcome these limitations? What additional problems might these changes cause?

3-5

To what extent do the unique features of government accounting make a difference on the financial statements?

The transactions that follow relate to the Danville County Comptroller's Department over a two-year period.

Year 1

- The county appropriated $12,000 for employee education and training.
- The department signed contracts with outside consultants to conduct accounting and auditing workshops. Total cost was $10,000.
- The consultants conducted the workshops and were paid $10,000.
- The department ordered books and training materials, which it estimated would cost $1,800. As of year-end, the materials had not yet been received.

Year 2

- The county appropriated $13,500 for employee education and training.

- The department received and paid for the books and training materials that it ordered the previous year. Actual cost was only $1,700. The county's accounting policies require that the books and training materials be charged as an expenditure when they are received (as opposed to being recorded as inventory and charged as an expenditure when used).

- It authorized employees to attend various conferences and training sessions. Estimated cost was $10,500.

- Employees submitted $10,800 in reimbursement requests for the conferences and training sessions they attended. The department paid them the requested amounts, and at year-end did not expect to receive any additional reimbursement requests.

  a. Prepare all required journal entries that would affect the expenditure subaccount "education and training," including budgetary and closing entries. Assume that all appropriations lapse at year-end (thus, all expenditures in Year 2 would be charged against that year's appropriation of $13,500).

  b. Indicate (specifying accounts and dollar amounts) how the transactions would be reported on the county's general fund:
     - balance sheet
     - statement of revenues and expenditures

  c. Suppose, alternatively, that the county did not record its budget and did not encumber its commitments. What would be the difference in the year-end financial statements?

  d. Assume instead that appropriations for goods on order at year-end do not lapse. When the goods are received they are charged as expenditures against the budget of the year in which they were encumbered. How would this change affect your entries and the year-end financial statements? How would it affect the amount that the department had available to spend in year 2 on goods or services not previously ordered?

3-6

Different budget to actual comparisons serve different purposes.

The following information was drawn from a county's general fund budgets and accounts for a particular year (in millions):

	Amended Budget	Original Budget	Actual Results (Budget Basis)
Revenues:			
Property Taxes	$46.6	$42.5	$53.0
Sales Taxes	16.3	13.6	15.1
Licenses and Permits	1.1	1.0	1.0
Other	3.2	2.9	3.4
Total Revenues	67.2	60.0	72.5

Expenditures:

General Government	$18.2	16.2	18.1
Public Safety	29.2	25.1	28.5
Sanitation	9.7	9.4	9.6
Culture and			
Recreation	8.1	7.8	8.1
Interest	1.4	1.4	1.4
Total Expenditures	66.6	59.9	65.7
Excess of			
Revenues over			
Expenditures	$ 0.6	$ 0.1	$ 6.8

You also learn the following:

	Beginning of Year	End of Year
Encumbrances (Commitments)		
Outstanding	$2.7	$1.1
Supplies Inventories on Hand	1.8	1.0
Wages and Salaries Payable	0.5	0.7
Property Taxes Expected to be		
Collected Within 60 Days	1.7	2.5

- For purposes of budgeting, the county recognizes encumbrances as the equivalent of expenditures in the year established; for financial reporting, it recognizes expenditures when the goods or services are received, as required by GAAP.

- For purposes of budgeting, it recognizes supplies expenditures when the supplies are acquired; for financial reporting, it recognizes the expenditure when the supplies are consumed.

- For purposes of budgeting, it recognizes wages and salaries when paid; for financial reporting, it recognizes the expenditures when the employees perform their services.

- For purposes of budgeting, it recognizes as revenues only taxes actually collected during the year; for financial reporting, it recognizes taxes expected to be collected within the first 60 days of the following year.

a. Prepare the following four separate schedules in which you compare the budget to actual results and compute the budget variance. You need present only the *total* revenues, *total* expenditures, and excess of revenues over expenditures.

1. actual results on a budget basis to the amended budget (the comparison typically included in financial statements)
2. actual results on a budget basis to the original budget
3. actual results as would be reflected in the financial statements to the amended budget restated so that it is on a financial reporting basis

4. actual results as would be reflected in the financial statements to the orginal budget restated so that it is on a financial reporting basis

b. The county executive has boasted that the "better than anticipated results" (based on the comparison of the schedule that appears in the financial statements) are evidence of "sound fiscal management and effective cost controls" on the part of the county administration. Do you agree?

c. Which of the three schedules best demonstrates legal compliance? Explain.

d. Which schedule best demonstrates effective management? Explain.

3-7

A city's note to its financial statements provides considerable insight into its budget practices.

Shown below is an excerpt from a note, headed *Budgets*, from the City of Raleigh, North Carolina's annual report for the fiscal year ended June 30.

a. The note distinguishes between the "budget ordinance" and the "more detailed line item budgets."
1. Provide examples of expenditures that you would expect to see in the budget ordinance.
2. Provide examples of expenditures that you would expect to see in the line-item budgets.

b. Why do you suspect that budgetary control is not exercised in trust and agency funds?

c. Generally accepted accounting principles require that governments reconcile differences between the entity's budget practices and GAAP in either the financial statements themselves or in accompanying notes. Raleigh's actual-to-budget comparison contained no such reconciliation. Why do you think a reconciliation was also omitted from the notes?

d. Explain how Raleigh's appropriation process would differ between that for its general fund and that for its capital projects fund. How would this difference most likely affect the city's budgetary entries?

e. The city is not required by GAAP to report on the amendments to its budget. Of what use to a statement reader is the note's schedule comparing, by fund, the original and amended budgets?

Note D. Budgets

Budgetary control is exercised in all funds except the trust and agency funds. The budget shown in the financial statements is the budget ordinance as amended at the close of the day of June 30. The City is required by the General Statutes of the State of North Carolina to adopt an annual balanced budget by July 1 of each year. The General Statutes also provide for balanced project ordinances for the life of projects, including both capital and grant activities, which are expected to extend beyond the end of the fiscal year. The City Council officially adopts the annual budget ordinance and all project ordinances and has the authority to amend such ordinances as necessary to recognize new resources or reallocations of budget. At June 30, the effect of such amendments, less eliminating transfers, was as follows:

	Original Budget	Total Amendments	Budget June 30
General fund	$145,259,996	$2,965,856	$148,225,852
Special revenue funds	49,087,784	5,034,632	54,122,416
General capital projects funds	135,304,688	4,038,509	139,343,197
Proprietary funds	145,984,461	2,557,523	148,541,984
Internal service funds	845,657	16,640	862,297

All budgets are prepared on the modified accrual basis of accounting as is required by North Carolina law. Appropriations for funds that adopt annual budgets lapse at the end of the budget year. Project budgeted appropriations do not lapse until the completion of the project.

Budget control on expenditures is limited to departmental totals and project totals as specified in the budget ordinances. Administrative control is maintained through the establishment of more detailed line-item budgets, which correspond to the specific object of the expenditure. All budget transfers, both at the ordinance and the line-item levels, are approved by the City Council. The City Manager is authorized to transfer line-item budgeted amounts up to $1,000 within a fund prior to their formal approval by the City Council.

Encumbrances represent commitments related to unperformed contracts for goods or services. Encumbrance accounting—under which purchase orders, contracts, and other commitments for the expenditure of resources are recorded to reserve that portion of the applicable appropriation—is utilized in all funds. Outstanding encumbrances at year-end for which goods or services are received are reclassified to expenditures and accounts payable. All other encumbrances in the annual budgeted funds are reversed at year-end and are either cancelled or are included as reappropriations of fund balance for the subsequent year. Outstanding encumbrances at year-end in funds that are budgeted on a project basis automatically carry forward along with their related appropriations and are not subject to an annual cancellation and reappropriation.

3-8

Different types of funds justify different practices as to budgets and commitments.

Review the budget note to the City of Raleigh's financial statements presented in the previous problem.

Assume that the city engaged in the following transactions in 1997 and 1998.

- In 1997 it signed a service contract with a private security company. The company agreed to provide security services to the city for one year at a cost of $72,000 ($6,000 per month). By year-end the company provided, and the city paid for, services for three months.
- In 1998, the company performed, and the city paid for, the remaining nine months of the contract. However, owing to agreed-upon changes in the services provided by the company, the total charges for 1998 were reduced from $54,000 to $50,000.

  a. The city properly budgeted for the services and appropriated the funds consistent with policies set forth in the note. Prepare all budgetary, encumbrance, and expenditure entries relating to the service contract that would be required in 1997 and 1998. In 1997, when the city signed the contract, it appropriated the entire $72,000. Then, at the start of 1998, inasmuch as the city expended only $18,000 in 1997, it reappropriated $54,000.

  1. Assume first that the contract was accounted for in Raleigh's *general fund*.
  2. Assume next that it was accounted for in a *capital projects fund* established for the construction of its Walnut Creek Amphitheatre. The city prepares annual financial statements for capital projects funds, but does not close out its accounts. Moreover, it prepares budgets for the entire project, not for particular periods. The project was started in 1997 and completed in 1998.

  b. Justify the city's practice of accounting differently for commitments in the two types of funds.

3-9

Journal entries can be derived from a city's ledger.

On the following page is an excerpt from a city's subsidiary ledger for the first two months of its fiscal year. Missing is the column that explains or references each of the entries.

a. Prepare the journal entries that were most likely made in the account, adding to each a brief note of explanation. Each line of the account records a single transaction (e.g., the receipt of an invoice); however, the entries on January 1 were made before the city engaged in any actual transactions (i.e., with outside parties).

b. The appropriation for consulting fees was intended to last for the entire year. Apparently, the city is spending or committing funds at a faster pace than planned. Can you propose an additional control mechanism to help assure that the funds are spent evenly throughout the year?

Fund: General government
Account: Consulting fees

Date	Encumbrances Dr. (Cr.)	Expenditures Dr. (Cr.)	Appropriations Cr. (Dr.)	Available Balance
1/1			$78,000	$78,000
1/1	$ 7,900			70,100
1/5	(4,000)	$ 3,000		71,100
1/14		4,500		66,600
2/5	6,000			60,600
2/15	(3,200)	3,400		60,400

3-10

Speeding up tax collections helps balance a state's appropriations budget.

The following is an excerpt from *Against the Grain*, a series of recommendations by Texas's State Comptroller as to how to "save" $4.5 billion and thereby balance the state's budget:

Require an Annual August Remittance of One-Half of August's Sales Tax Collections by Monthly Taxpayers. The Legislature should require sales taxpayers to remit half of August's collections during that month.

Background

Currently, sales tax payments are remitted either monthly, quarterly, or annually. They also may be prepaid either on a quarterly or a monthly basis.

Monthly taxpayers, including those who collect taxes on their own purchase or use of taxable items, are required by law to remit to the state all tax collections—less any applicable discounts—by the twentieth day of the month following the end of each calendar month. The state's fiscal year ends on August 31.

Recommendation

The Legislature should require all monthly taxpayers to remit one-half of each August's sales tax collections during that month. Specifically, sales taxes collected between August 1 and August 15 would be due with their regular August 20th payment. Monthly taxpayers would remit tax in the usual manner during all other months.

This is not a prepayment plan, but a speeding up of the remittance of actual taxes collected and owed to the state. This would impose an additional burden and would reduce taxpayer cash flow, but should be considered as preferable to a tax increase.

Implications

An annual payment by monthly filers of taxes actually collected during the first fifteen days of August would increase August's collections and decrease September's collections. Although the initial imposition of this proposal might temporarily inconvenience some taxpayers, the prompt payment to the state of some of its sales tax revenues—collected, but not yet remitted—will enhance the revenue stream at a critical time each fiscal year. During the first year of implementation, all months would have normal collection patterns except August, which would be larger than usual, thereby producing a fiscal gain.

Each following year would see smaller than normal (current) collections in September and larger collections in August. These differences would essentially offset each other. It is important to stress that failure to speed up collections each year after implementation would cause a fiscal loss. The gain to the general fund in the year of implementation would be $215 million.

Fiscal Year	Gain to the General Revenue Fund
1994	$215,113,000
1995	0
1996	0
1997	0
1998	0

a. On what basis is it likely that the State prepares its appropriation budget? Explain.

b. Do you believe the State will be better off, in economic substance, as the result of the proposed change?

c. According to the comptroller (last paragraph), the change would have no impact on revenues of future fiscal years as long as collections are also speeded up in those years. Do you agree? If so, is there any reason not to adopt the proposal?

3-11

Multiple funds provide multiple sources of revenue.

The following is a recommendation from *Against the Grain*, a series of proposals by the State Comptroller of Texas on how the state could enhance revenues and decrease expenditures:

> Amend the Lottery Act to Abolish the Lottery Stabilization Fund. The state should amend the Lottery Act to abolish the Lottery Stabilization Fund requirement and use the income to fund critical services.

Background

The State Lottery Act requires the establishment of a Lottery Stabilization Fund. The fund will contain lottery revenue in excess of the Comptroller's Biennial Revenue Estimate. The Lottery Stabilization Fund is then to provide revenue to the General Revenue Fund if the lottery fails to generate monthly revenue as estimated.

In months that lottery revenue exceeds one-twelfth of the annual estimate, the Comptroller is required to deposit $10 million plus the amount of net lottery revenue in excess of the estimate to the Lottery Stabilization Fund. The Act provides only two circumstances under which revenue could be transferred from the Lottery Stabilization Fund to the General Revenue Fund. In months that lottery revenue is less than 90 percent of one-twelfth of the annual estimate, the difference is to be transferred from the Lottery Stabilization Fund to general revenue. The Act also provides for the transfer of one-half of the balance of the Lottery Stabilization Fund to the General Revenue Fund on the first day of every biennium.

In view of the seriousness of the state's fiscal situation, the Legislature should set aside the stabilization fund requirement. The state already maintains a significant "rainy day" fund, and effective revenue forecasting should be adequate to avoid problems with potential future revenue stream instability.

Recommendation

The state should repeal the provision in the State Lottery Act that establishes the Lottery Stabilization Fund. This action would provide additional revenue to the General Revenue Fund to be used for state programs at the Legislature's discretion.

Implications

Releasing Lottery Stabilization Funds would increase the available revenue for state programs without increasing taxes. General revenue is reduced by at least $10 million in months when lottery revenue exceeds one-twelfth of the annual lottery estimate. In effect, the state is penalized for correctly estimating lottery revenue and operating the lottery efficiently. Repealing the provision that establishes this fund would remove this penalty.

This action would increase general revenue about $65 million per year in fiscal 1994 and 1995.

a. Explain briefly how the Comptroller's recommendation would increase general revenue by $65 million per year. In what way would the proposal affect the fiscal well-being of the state?

b. What impact would the Comptroller's recommendation have on the state's budget if the state were to prepare a "consolidated" budget—one in which all funds were combined?

c. With reference to this recommendation, what are the advantages and disadvantages of budgeting on the basis of individual funds as opposed to all funds combined?

SOLUTION TO EXERCISE FOR REVIEW AND SELF-STUDY

a. Estimated revenues $5,600
    Appropriations $5,550
    Fund balance 50
To record the budget

The budget would specify in detail the revenues anticipated and expenditures appropriated. Hence, the corresponding subledger accounts should be debited and credited for amounts estimated or authorized.

b.
1. Cash $5,800
    Revenues $5,800
To record revenues

2. Encumbrances $3,000
    Reserve for encumbrances $3,000
To encumber resources reserved to fulfill commitments for goods and services on order

3. Expenditures $2,800
    Cash $2,800
To record expenditures

    Reserve for encumbrances $2,800
        Encumbrances $2,800
To unencumber funds for goods and services already received that have been charged as expenditures

| 4. Expenditures | $2,500 | |
| Cash | | $2,500 |

To record other expenditures

c. Revenues	$5,800	
Estimated revenues		$5,600
Fund balance		200

To close revenue and estimated revenue accounts

Appropriations	$5,550	
Expenditures		$5,300
Encumbrances		200
Fund balance		50

To close expenditures, encumbrances, and appropriations

The agency's closing entries deviate slightly from those illustrated earlier in the text in which the budget accounts were closed in one entry and the actual accounts in another. The end result is the same regardless of the grouping used for the closing entries.

d. The following schedule summarizes the impact of the transactions on fund balance:

Revenues	$5,800
Expenditures	5,300
Increase in Total Fund Balance	500
Less: Encumbrances (Transfer from Unreserved to Reserved Fund Balance)	200
Net Increase in Unrestricted Fund Balance	$300

The following balance sheet shows the status of year-end asset and fund balance accounts:

| Cash | $500 |

Fund balance	
Reserved for encumbrances	$ 200
Unreserved	300
Total fund balance	$ 500

| e. Encumbrances | $200 | |
| Fund balance | | $200 |

To restore encumbrances of the previous year

| f. Expenditures | $150 | |
| Cash | | $150 |

To record expenditures

| Reserve for encumbrances | $200 | |
| Encumbrances | | $200 |

To unencumber funds for goods and services already received and charged as expenditures (the entire $200 is reversed, inasmuch as the entire order has been fulfilled; no additional amount need be reserved).

CHAPTER 4

Recognizing Revenue in Governmental Funds

LEARNING OBJECTIVES

After studying this chapter you should understand:

- why governments focus on current financial resources and use the modified accrual basis to account for their governmental funds
- the key features of the modified accrual basis of accounting
- the fundamental differences between the modified and the full accrual bases of accounting
- how each of the following types of revenues are accounted for under the modified accrual basis

- property taxes
- sales taxes
- income taxes
- licenses and permits
- fines
- grants
- investment gains and losses
- interest and dividends
- donations

We now turn to what are among the most intractable questions of government and not-for-profit accounting: When should revenues and expenditures be recognized, and how should the related assets and liabilities be measured?

In Chapters 4 and 5 we consider revenue and expenditure recognition in governments, while in Chapter 6 we address revenue and expenditure recognition in other not-for-profit entities. Most of the examples in this and the next chapter will implicitly be directed toward governments' general funds. However, the discussion is equally applicable to all *governmental* funds, including special revenues funds, capital projects funds, and debt service funds. In Chapter 10 we examine the same issues as they apply to *proprietary* funds (those that account for business-type activities).

WHY AND HOW DO GOVERNMENTS USE THE MODIFIED ACCRUAL BASIS?

RATIONALE FOR THE MODIFIED ACCRUAL BASIS

The foundation for our discussion of revenue and expenditure recognition was laid in Chapter 1. In that chapter we pointed to two key objectives of financial reporting:

- providing information as to the extent the entity achieved interperiod equity (i.e., whether current-year revenues were sufficient to pay for current-year services)
- demonstrating whether the entity obtained and used its resources in accordance with its legally adopted budget

As suggested in Chapter 1, no set of financial statements prepared on a single basis of revenue and expenditure recognition can adequately fulfill both objectives. Therefore, standard setters must choose among three courses of action:

- adopt principles that fulfill one of the objectives, but not the other
- adopt principles that compromise the two objectives, fulfilling both to some extent, but neither one adequately
- develop a reporting model that incorporates more than one basis of revenue and expenditure recognition—either statements that embrace more than one basis of accounting or else two or more sets of statements within the same report

Generally accepted accounting principles (GAAP) require that governmental funds focus on financial resources and be accounted for on a modified accrual basis. They reflect the second approach, that of fulfilling both objectives, but neither satisfactorily. However, as shall be discussed in a section to follow, the GASB's proposed dual perspective model (described in Chapter 2) will require the preparation of two separate sets of financial statements, and thereby is consistent with the third approach.

RELATIONSHIP BETWEEN MEASUREMENT FOCUS AND BASIS OF ACCOUNTING

The criteria by which an entity determines when to recognize revenues and expenditures necessarily stem from its measurement focus and its basis of accounting. As pointed out in Chapter 2, *measurement focus* refers to *what* is being reported upon—that is, *which* assets and liabilities are being measured. *Basis of accounting* refers to *when* transactions and events are recognized. The two concepts obviously are closely linked. If an entity opts to focus on cash, then it will necessarily adopt a *cash basis of accounting.* Correspondingly, if it elects to focus on *all economic resources* (both current and long-term assets and liabilities), then it will adopt a *full accrual basis of accounting.*

Measurement focus and basis of accounting can be viewed as a continuum. As depicted in Figure 4-1, on one end is a cash focus and correspondingly the cash basis of accounting. On the other end is a focus on all economic resources and thus the full accrual basis. Between the two are any number of "modified accrual" (or "modified cash") bases of accounting in which the focus is on resources in addition to cash but not on the full array of economic resources.

If, as is common, a government's budget is on a cash or near-cash basis, then a basis of accounting near the cash end of the continuum best satisfies the reporting objective of demonstrating that resources were obtained in accordance with the legally adopted budget. A basis on the full accrual end of the continuum best fulfills the interperiod equity objective. Any basis between the extremes would compromise the two objectives, satisfying both objectives to some extent, but neither one completely.

OVERVIEW OF THE MODIFIED ACCRUAL BASIS

Per generally accepted practices of today, governmental funds are accounted for on a modified accrual basis. The measurement focus is on "determination of *financial position and changes in financial position* (sources, uses, and balance of financial resources)."[1]

Financial resources, though not explicitly defined in the official literature, has been operationalized to encompass "expendable financial resources"—cash, and other items that can be expected to be transformed into cash in the normal course of operations (less current liabilities). The "other items" include investments and receivables but *not* fixed assets.

As shall be discussed in Chapter 5, inventories and prepaid items are also reported on the balance sheet, even though they do not fall within the conventional view of a financial resource. A frequently cited justification for this apparent inconsistency is that these assets will not ordinarily be transformed into cash (e.g., inventories will be consumed, not sold for cash), but they generally will result in short-term cash savings in that the entity will not have to expend additional cash to acquire them.

The current claims against financial resources include wages and salaries payable, accounts payable, and deferred credits. They exclude long-term obligations such as the noncurrent portions of bonds payable, and the liabilities for vacation pay, sick leave pay, and legal judgments. Consistent with conventional relationships between balance sheet and operating statement accounts, revenues and expenditures are accompanied by an increase or decrease in net financial resources (as opposed to increases or decreases in net economic resources, as would be true under the full accrual basis).

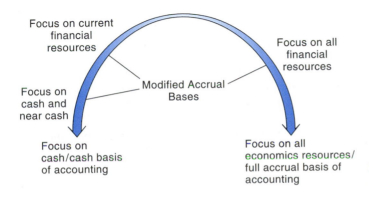

FIGURE 4-1   Measurement Focus and Basis of Accounting

---

[1] *Codification*, Section 1300.102.

As noted by the National Council on Governmental Accounting (NCGA, the GASB's predecessor), the accrual basis of accounting "is the superior method of accounting for the economic resources of any organization" because "it results in accounting measurements based on the substance of transactions and events, rather than merely when cash is received or disbursed, and thus enhances their relevance, neutrality, timeliness, completeness and comparability."[2]

RECOGNITION OF REVENUE

Accepting the accrual basis of accounting still leaves unresolved the thorny issue of when revenues should be recognized. What key economic event in the revenue generation process should trigger the recognition of revenue and the corresponding increase in net assets? In business accounting, revenues are ordinarily recognized when a firm has exerted a substantial portion of its production and sales effort and the amount of cash to be eventually collected can reasonably be assured and estimated. But standard setters, as well as individual firms, still have to grapple with the problem of when the various types of revenue transactions satisfy these criteria. To enhance consistency of practice, standard setters have established specific guidelines for the recognition of such diverse revenues as those from ordinary sales, sales of real estate, installment sales, interest, loan origination fees, license and royalty fees, and construction contracts.

The revenue-recognition issues facing governments are less tractable than those of businesses. Unlike the revenues of businesses, those of governments are not typically generated through processes of production and sales. They are not "earned" in the same sense as those of businesses. Some, such as property taxes, are realized through government fiat. Others, such as grants, are brought about by the acts of other governments. For many of these revenues, the generation process comprehends several key events, any one of which can be rationalized as an appropriate point of recognition.

In governments, revenues are intrinsically associated with expenditures; they are generated solely to meet expenditures. Budgets are formulated so that each period's estimated revenues are expected to cover its appropriated expenditures. Therefore, whereas business accounting principles dictate that the collection of cash must be reasonably assured before revenue can be recognized, existing government accounting principles (as promulgated by the NCGA and endorsed by the GASB) tie the recognition of revenues to the expenditures that they are intended to cover. The principles direct that revenues become susceptible to accrual only when they are both *measurable* and *available to finance expenditures of the fiscal period.*

MEANING OF "AVAILABLE TO FINANCE EXPENDITURES OF THE FISCAL PERIOD"

Expenditures of a current period may either require cash outlays during the period or create liabilities that have to be satisfied shortly after the end of the period. For example, goods or services that a government receives toward the end of one year would ordinarily not have to be paid for until early in the next year. *Available* means "collectible within the current period or soon enough thereafter to be used to pay liabilities of the current period."[3]

Liabilities as used herein refers only to **current liabilities.** Recall that long-term liabilities are outside of the measurement focus of governmental funds and hence are

---

[2] GASB *Codification*, Section 1600.103.

[3] GASB *Codification*, Section 1600.106.

not recorded by them. As shall be discussed in the following chapter, transactions that result in long-term liabilities are not recorded as expenditures.

How many days after the close of the year must revenues be received to satisfy the criteria of having been received soon enough to pay the liabilities of the current period? With respect to *property taxes*—and property taxes only—existing standards provide that, in the absence of unusual circumstances, revenues should be recognized only if cash is expected to be collected within *sixty (60) days* of year-end.[4]

However, because existing standards provide no specific guidance as to time periods for recognition of other revenues, this "sixty-day rule" has become a widely used benchmark for all types of revenues, not just property taxes.

As pointed out in Chapter 2, the GASB has proposed requiring two separate sets of financial statements, one from a funds perspective and the other from an entity-wide perspective. The statements from the funds perspective, which are similar to those prepared today, will focus on financial resources and will therefore be on a modified accrual basis. Those on an entity-wide basis will focus on all economic resources and will therefore be on a full accrual basis. The two sets taken together are intended to satisfy adequately both the interperiod equity and the budgetary compliance objectives.

IMPLICATIONS OF PROPOSED CHANGES ON REVENUE AND EXPENDITURE RECOGNITION

The requirement for the entity-wide statements opens up a new set of accounting issues: What should be the criteria for recognizing specific revenues and expenditures under a full, rather than a modified, accrual basis? The GASB has proposed that at the entity-wide perspective, governments should apply FASB pronouncements whenever they are applicable and do not conflict with GASB pronouncements. The FASB, however, has not addressed the predominant revenue and expenditure recognition questions unique to governments (e.g., recognition of taxes, fines, licenses, and sabbatical leaves).

As this text goes to press, the GASB is in the process of addressing some of these issues. In 1997, it issued an exposure draft of a pronouncement pertaining to "nonexchange" transactions—those in which a government obtains resources by mandate of law rather than through purchase or sales of goods or services. Nonexchange transactions are distinguished from exchange transactions, those involving voluntary transfers of assets or other benefits of approximately equal value.

Previously, in 1990, the GASB issued Statement No. 11, *Measurement Focus and Basis of Accounting—Governmental Fund Operating Statements*. Statement No. 11 shifted the measurement focus to what it defined as "financial resources"—cash, claims to cash (for example, debt securities of another entity and accounts and taxes receivable), claims to goods and services (for example, prepaid items), consumable goods (for example, supplies inventories), and equity securities. This measurement focus fell short of "full economic resources" in that it excluded fixed assets and related long-term debt. With the notable exception that long-lived assets would not be depreciated, Statement No. 11 moved government fund accounting in the direction of full accrual accounting. Accordingly, it provided guidance as to how the main types of revenues and expenses should be recognized under a full accrual basis.

In Statement No. 17, the GASB delayed indefinitely the implementation of Statement No. 11, having decided that it first needed to reexamine the entire reporting model. It is now almost certain that the Board will never implement Statement No. 11 in the form in which it was issued. The statement was intended to overhaul the current funds-perspective statements, but the Board has since abandoned that project in favor of the dual-perspective statements.

---

[4] GASB *Codification*, Section P70.103.

We will use the reporting model exposure draft to highlight the issues that a shift to the full accrual basis presents and to provide insight into the direction to full accrual accounting that the Board appears to be taking. Bear in mind, however, that the specific guidelines of the exposure draft are likely to be modified if and when a final pronouncement is issued. When an issue has not been addressed in the exposure draft but has been in Statement No. 11, we may point out the Statement No. 11 approach. Even though it may never be implemented, Statement No. 11 presents viable full-accrual alternatives to current modified-accrual practices.

In the following sections we discuss the key revenues of state and local governments: property, sales and income taxes; fines, licenses and permits; grants, investment earnings, donations, and sales of fixed assets. We present both the current recognition principles as well as the alternative "full accrual" principles that will be needed to prepare the proposed entity-wide statements.

HOW SHOULD PROPERTY TAXES BE ACCOUNTED FOR?

FUNDAMENTALS OF PROPERTY TAXES

Property taxes are the bread and butter of local governments. Although gradually being supplemented by other taxes and fees, they still account for more than 26 percent of local government revenues (See Figure 1-1 in Chapter 1).

Classified as *ad valorem taxes* (based on value), property taxes are most typically levied against real property (land and buildings). However, many jurisdictions also include personal property, such as automobiles, boats, and business inventories, and intangible assets, such as securities and bank deposits, within the tax base.

Property taxes are levied against the *assessed* value of taxable assets. Most jurisdictions are required to assess property at 100 percent of its *appraised* fair market value. Many, however, assess property as a fraction of appraised value (perhaps in the hope of discouraging taxpayer protests) and then adjust the tax rate upward to offset the reduction in tax base.

Governments establish the property tax rate by dividing the amount of revenue required of the tax by the assessed value of the property subject to tax. For example, if a government needs $400 million in tax revenue and its jurisdiction has $22 billion in taxable property, then the tax rate would be the $400 million in needed revenue divided by the $22 billion in taxable property—1.818 percent, or 18.18 *mils* (dollars per thousand).

In reality the computation is somewhat more complex, as allowances have to be made for discounts, exemptions, and taxes that will be delinquent or uncollectible. Most jurisdictions experience a relatively low rate of bad debts on property taxes, since they are able to impose a *lien* (right to seize and sell) on the taxed property. However, it may take several years before the government is actually able either to collect from a property owner or to seize and sell the property.

Many jurisdictions grant discounts for early payment. For example, taxpayers may be allowed discounts of 3 percent, 2 percent, and 1 percent for paying, respectively, three months, two months, or one month prior to the due date. If they pay after the due date, they are generally subject to both interest and penalties.

Not all property within a jurisdiction is subject to tax. Property held by other governments and religious institutions is ordinarily exempt. In addition, many jurisdictions grant *homestead* exemptions to homeowners on their primary residences. These exemptions include both basic allowances, often of a fixed dollar amount (e.g., $5,000), which are available to all taxpayers, and supplementary amounts to senior citizens or members of other designated classes. Thus, if a residence were assessed at $200,000 but the homeowner were granted a $5,000 exemption, the property's net assessed value would be $195,000. If the tax rate were 18.18 mils, the tax would be $195,000 multiplied by .01818, or $3,545.

Several events in the property tax timeline have potential accounting significance:

SIGNIFICANT EVENTS IN THE REVENUE GENERATION PROCESS

- the legislative body levies the tax, establishing the tax rate and estimating the total amount to be collected
- administrative departments determine the amount due from the individual property owners, enter the amounts on the *tax roll* (a subsidiary ledger that supports the taxes receivable control account), and send out tax notices (bills) to property owners
- The taxes are collected, most prior to the due date, some afterward
- The taxes are due and any taxes not collected are classified as delinquent

The *stated* due date must be distinguished from the *substantive* due date. Some jurisdictions establish a due date but do not impose interest and penalties until a later date. The substantive due date is that date on which interest and penalties begin to accrue.

The question facing governments is which of the events is sufficiently significant to warrant revenue recognition, subject to the measurable and available constraint.

IN PRACTICE

The following is a note from the financial statements of Stamford Connecticut. It illustrates how one city applies the "available to meet current-year expenditures" criterion. Note how the amount of property taxes recognized as revenue depends on the amount of liabilities outstanding.

HOW STAMFORD, CONNECTICUT, ACCOUNTS FOR PROPERTY TAXES

(k) Revenue Recognition—Property Taxes

GASB Codification Section P 70 states that:

"Property tax revenues are recognized when they are available. Available means . . . receivable within the current period . . . and expected to be collected soon enough thereafter to be used to pay liabilities of the current period. Such time thereafter shall not exceed 60 days. If, because of unusual circumstances, the facts justify a period greater than 60 days, the governmental unit should disclose the period being used and the facts that justify it."

Further, GASB Codification Section 1600 provides that the current liabilities are matched with expendable available resources. Accordingly, at year-end the City determines the amount of (i) current liabilities that will be paid subsequent to August 31 (the Liabilities) and (ii) property taxes that will be collected subsequent to that date (the Property Taxes). If the Liabilities exceed the Property Taxes, the City applies the matching concept of expendable available financial resources without regard to the 60-day limitation. If the Property Taxes exceed the Liabilities, the 60-day limitation is applied and any excess property taxes are deferred.

Source: City of Stamford, Connecticut, Notes to General Purpose Financial Statements, June 30, 1993.

In this and subsequent chapters, we shall spotlight accounting issues by placing them within the context of short examples. We shall prepare journal entries so as to emphasize the impact of the possible options on both the statement of operations and the balance sheet. In many of the examples, a single entry may be used to summarize what in practice would be many individual entries. The illustrated entry is intended to show the impact of the described events on the year-end financial statements. In most of the examples we shall assume, for convenience, that the entity's fiscal year ends on December 31, even though the fiscal year of most governments ends on the last day of June, July, August, September, or October.

EXAMPLE　*Property Taxes*

A city levies property taxes of $515 million for 1997. In 1997 it collects $410 million. It collects $30 million of the remaining 1997 taxes during each of the first three months of 1998 and estimates that the $15 million balance will be uncollectible.

In addition, in 1997 it collects $20 million in taxes applicable to 1998. Taxes are due on May 31 of each year and the government has the right to impose a lien on the taxed property if it has not received payment by that date.

Current Standards

Currently accepted accounting principles instruct that, inasmuch as property taxes are assessed to finance the budget of a particular period, the revenue should be recognized in that period, provided that the "measurable and available" criteria are met. "Available" with regard to property taxes means "then due, or past due and receivable within the current period, and collected within the current period or expected to be collected soon enough thereafter to be used to pay liabilities of the current period. Such time thereafter shall not exceed 60 days."[5]

In the example, therefore, the total amount of revenue to be recognized in 1997 would be $470 million—the $410 million due and collected during the year and applicable to it, plus the $60 collected in the first sixty days of the next year. The following entries for 1997 would operationalize the current guidance:

Property taxes receivable	$515	
Deferred property tax revenue		$500
Allowance for uncollectible property taxes		15
To record the property tax levy		
Cash	$410	
Property taxes receivable		$410
To record the collection of cash in 1997		

---

[5] *Codification*, Section P70.103. An August 1997 GASB exposure draft would eliminate the phrase "then due, or past and receivable within the current period." As the standards are currently worded, if a government imposes a January 1, 1999 due date on its 1998 property taxes, it could not recognize as revenue the 1998 taxes until 1999. The proposed change would permit the government to recognize the taxes in 1998 as long as they were collected no later than 60 days after December 31, 1998.

```
Deferred property tax revenue                        $410
     Property tax revenue                                      $410
```
To recognize revenue on the taxes collected

```
Deferred property tax revenue                        $ 60
     Property tax revenue                                      $ 60
```
To recognize revenue on the taxes to be received in the first 60 days of 1998 (Since this entry would be made as of the year-end, it may appear to recognize only an *estimate* of the tax receipts of the first sixty days of 1998. In reality the government would record its actual collections. Few governments are able to close their books and prepare financial statements within sixty days of year-end. Therefore, by the time they close their books and prepare financial statements, they are able to determine exactly how much revenue from collections subsequent to year-end must be recognized.)

```
Cash                                                 $ 20
     Deferred property tax revenue                             $ 20
```
To record collection of property taxes received in advance of the year to which they are applicable (The taxes collected in advance are intended to cover 1998 expenditures. Hence, they should be recorded in 1998 and thereby matched with the expenditures.)

An equally acceptable means of recording the initial tax levy would be to recognize (credit) revenue rather than *deferred* revenue. Thus, the first entry would be:

```
Property taxes receivable                            $515
     Property tax revenue                                      $500
     Allowance for uncollectible property taxes                  15
```
To record the property tax levy

As taxes are collected during the year, accounts receivable would be reduced:

```
Cash                                                 $410
     Property taxes receivable                                 $410
```
To record the collection of cash in 1997

Then, at year-end, the government would "back-out" any previously recognized revenue that would not be collected in time to satisfy the sixty-day test. The uncollected amounts would be transferred to *deferred revenue:*

```
Property tax revenue                                 $ 30
     Deferred property tax revenue                             $ 30
```
To correct accounts for taxes previously recognized as revenue but that will not be collected within 60 days of year-end

This approach requires fewer entries and results in the same year-end balances. However, it causes revenue to be recognized on the basis of the tax levy rather than the collection of cash. Thus, it undermines the budgetary entries, discussed in Chapter 2, that facilitate an ongoing comparison between the budgeted revenues and the results to date.

Irrespective of approach, outstanding taxes receivable should be reclassified as delinquent so they are not intermingled with the current receivables of the following year:

```
Property taxes receivable—delinquent                 $ 90
     Property taxes receivable                                 $ 90
```
To reclassify uncollected taxes as delinquent

This entry has no impact on revenues, expenditures, or net assets (and hence on fund balance). It provides statement readers with additional information as to the status of property taxes receivable. An increase in delinquent property taxes relative to property tax revenues should serve as warning of a possible economic downturn in the government's jurisdiction or ineffective tax collection practices on the part of the government.

As the delinquent property taxes are collected, they would be recorded as follows:

Cash	$ 60	
Property taxes receivable—delinquent		$ 60

To record the tax collections of the first two months of 1998, which had been recognized as revenue of 1997

Cash	$ 30	
Deferred property tax revenue	30	
Property taxes receivable—delinquent		$ 30
Property tax revenue (1998)		30

To record the tax collections of the third month of 1998, which had not *been recognized as revenue of 1997*

Despite their powers to enforce their claims against recalcitrant taxpayers, governments are not always able to collect the full amount of tax levies. In some instances, seized property cannot be sold at prices sufficient to cover outstanding balances. In others, the costs of recovery would be inadequate to cover the expected yield, so the governments elect not to exercise all available legal options.

As a government writes off uncollectible taxes, it should offset the reduction in taxes receivable with a corresponding reduction in the allowance for uncollectibles. Thus, if the $15 million of taxes (now classified as delinquent) were written off:

Allowance for uncollectible property taxes	$ 15	
Property taxes receivable—delinquent		$ 15

To write off delinquent taxes

This entry has no impact on revenues, expenditures, net assets, or fund balance. The government gave substantive accounting recognition to the potential uncollectible taxes in the period in which it established the allowance for uncollectible taxes.

Governments may accrue interest charges and penalties on delinquent taxes as they impose them. However, they should recognize revenue only when it is measurable and available. Until those criteria are satisfied, they should offset interest and penalties receivable with deferred revenue rather than actual revenue.

POSSIBLE DIFFERENCES UNDER ENTITY-WIDE (FULL ACCRUAL) STATEMENTS

The exposure draft on nonexchange transactions directs that a government should generally recognize revenue from property taxes and similar types of nonexchange transactions when it has an enforceable legal claim on the resources. For property taxes this would usually be when the government has the right to impose a lien on the taxed property (which is often the date the taxes are due). However, governments should delay recognizing revenue until applicable *time requirements* are satisfied. Time requirements are stipulations as to when the resources may be used. They are generally imposed by legislation or by the entity, such as the donor or grantor, that provides the resources. For example, property taxes are generally assessed and budgeted for a particular year and are intended to be spent no earlier than that period.

The consequence of the guidelines is that a government should generally recognize property tax revenues when the taxes are due. If, however, they are due prior to the year for which they are assessed, the government should delay recognition until the year for which they are assessed. Property taxes collected prior to the year for which they are assessed should be reported as deferred revenues (a liability).

In contrast to current practices, the exposure draft abandons the measurable and available test for the entity-wide statements. It allows governments to accrue by year-end all property taxes they expect to receive, irrespective of how long in the future the cash will be collected. In the example, therefore, the city could recognize $500 million in revenue—the $410 million actually collected during the year plus the entire $90 million that it expects to collect. The following entry summarizes the 1997 activity pertaining to the 1997 taxes:

Cash	$410	
Property taxes receivable—delinquent	105	
Property tax revenue		$500
Allowance for uncollectible property taxes		15

To summarize 1997 property tax activity pertaining to 1997 taxes

For most governments the change will have little impact on their statements of operations. In the absence of major fluctuations in taxes levied and collected, the amount of revenue recognized in any particular year will remain relatively constant; revenue gains owing to the new end-of-year accruals will be offset by revenue losses attributable to the taxes that will now be recognized in the previous year. However, the effect on the balance sheet will be more pronounced, because the full amount of the accruals will be reported as additions to both assets and fund balance.

HOW SHOULD SALES TAXES BE ACCOUNTED FOR?

SIGNIFICANT EVENTS IN THE "EARNING" PROCESS

Sales taxes are imposed on customers that purchase goods or services. The merchant providing the goods or services is responsible for collecting, reporting, and transmitting the taxes.

Sales taxes, along with income taxes, are categorized as *taxpayer-assessed*. Unlike property taxes, which are government-assessed, the sales tax base is determined by parties other than the beneficiary government. Thus, the government has to wait for, and rely upon, tax returns to become aware of the proceeds to which it is legally entitled.

Three significant dates underlie sales tax transactions:

- the date of the sales transaction and the collection of the tax by the merchant
- the date the merchant is required to file the tax return and transmit the taxes (generally the same)
- the date the merchant actually files the return and transmits the taxes

The date of the sale is arguably the most significant of the three dates, since the transaction producing the tax takes place then, the amount of the tax is established, and the liability of the merchant to transmit the tax is created. However, the government is not entitled to the tax until the date the return is to be filed and the tax paid. Moreover, except for unusual circumstances, such as when a merchant files a return but fails to make timely payment, the government does not know what the amount will be until it actually receives the tax.

EXAMPLE   *Sales Taxes*

In December 1997 merchants collect $20 million in sales taxes. Of these, $12 million are collected prior to December 15 and must be remitted by February 15, 1998; the remaining $8 million must be remitted by March 15, 1998.

Current Standards

Current standards were adopted in 1994 shortly after the GASB deferred implementation of Statement No. 11.[6] They were intended as a temporary measure pending the Board's adoption of the dual perspective model or some alternative. Prior standards held that it was "neither necessary nor practical" to accrue taxpayer-assessed taxes, such as sales and income taxes, and therefore indicated that they should be accounted for on a cash basis. Nevertheless, many states accrued sales tax revenue as of the date of sale, even if the merchants were not required to remit the tax until the following fiscal year.

The new standards are intended both to:

- enhance the consistency of revenue recognition standards by extending to both sales and income taxes the measurable and available criteria that apply to property taxes and other revenues
- legitimize the practices of the states that were already accruing sales taxes as of the date of sale

Accordingly, current standards require that "revenues from taxpayer-assessed taxes, net of estimated refunds, should be recognized in the accounting period in which they become susceptible to accrual—that is, when they become both *measurable* and *available* to finance expenditures of the fiscal period."

The standards provide no guidance, however, as to how to interpret the terms *measurable and available.* They simply note that applying the "susceptible to accrual" criterion "requires judgment, consideration of the materiality of the item in question, and due regard for the practicality of the accrual, as well as consistency in application." They are silent as to whether the sixty-day rule is applicable to sales taxes as it is to property taxes and as to whether taxes should be considered measurable on the date they are collected by the merchants (measurable by the merchants) rather than on the date merchants file returns and remit the taxes (measurable by the government).

---

[6] *Codification*, Section 1600.111 (Based on GASB Statement No. 22, *Accounting for Taxpayer-Assessed Tax Revenues in Governmental Funds*, 1994).

Assume that the state opts to accrue taxes as of the sale date, subject to their being received soon enough after year-end to be available to finance 1997s expenditures. It further determines that it will consider taxes received before February 15 as satisfying the available criteria. Therefore, it recognizes only the $12 million that it received before February 15, deferring recognition of the $8 million to be received by March 15 to 1998:

Sales taxes receivable	$20	
Sales tax revenue		$12
Deferred sales tax revenue		8

To summarize December sales tax activity

POSSIBLE DIFFERENCES UNDER ENTITY-WIDE (FULL ACCRUAL) STATEMENTS

The exposure draft on nonexchange transactions includes sales taxes within the rubric of **derived tax revenues.** These result from a government's power to tax transactions between two or more parties other than the government. They also include income taxes and similar taxes based on earnings or consumption. In general, according to the draft, sales taxes and other derived taxes, should be recognized as revenue *at the time of the underlying transaction.* For sales taxes, this would be at the time of the sale.

Even if the assets received from a sales or other derived tax are restricted for a specific purpose (i.e., subject to *use stipulations*) the government can still recognize revenue at the time of the underlying transaction. However, on its balance sheet it should report the resultant net assets (fund equity) as "restricted" until the restrictions are met.

If, in unusual circumstances, a government were to collect a tax before the underlying transaction took place, it should delay recognizing revenue until the period of the transaction. It should offset the cash received with deferred revenue. Similarly, if taxes were subject to time restrictions and could be used only in a specified year, then the government should not recognize revenue until that period.

In the example, therefore, the government would be able to recognize the entire $20 million of taxes collected by merchants in December, the month in which the underlying transaction took place.

Sales taxes receivable	$20	
Sales tax revenue		$20

To summarize December sales tax activity

Although the government would probably be unaware by year-end of the amount of December taxes collected by the merchants, it would ordinarily have that information by the time it prepared its financial statements for the year. Therefore, it could make the necessary accrual entry as of year-end.

SALES TAXES COLLECTED BY ANOTHER GOVERNMENT

Sales taxes are levied by both state and local governments. However, to avoid duplication of effort, most states collect and administer the sales taxes imposed by their local governments. For example, a state may impose a 5 percent sales tax, allowing local governments to add an additional 2 percent on sales within their jurisdictions. The state will collect the entire 7 percent tax, acting as an agent for the local governments with respect to their 2 percent.

The issue facing local governments is whether they can properly recognize revenue as soon as the state satisfies the recognition criteria or whether they must delay recognition until a later date—either when the state notifies them of the amount collected on their behalf or actually transmits the tax to them.

EXAMPLE   *Sales Taxes Collected by State*

Assume a slight variation of the previous example. In November and December 1997 merchants collect $20 million in sales taxes. Of these, $5 million are remitted to the state, as due, by December 15, 1997; the remaining $15 million are due on January 15, 1998. The state remits the taxes to the city 30 days after it receives them.

Current Standards

Current standards permit the city to accrue the taxes collected by the state at year-end, provided that they would be received by the city in time to satisfy its budgetary obligations of the preceding year. In other words, the city should recognize revenues as if the taxes had been received directly, as long as they will actually be received in time to meet the "available" criteria.

In this example, the city could recognize, as revenue of 1997, the entire $20 million in taxes collected by the state in both December 1997 and January 1998:

Sales taxes receivable	$20	
Sales tax revenue		$20
To summarize December sales tax activity		

However, if it were the practice of the state to remit the taxes to the city ninety days after receipt—subsequent to when the city could use them to meet 1997 expenditures—then the city could recognize none of the taxes as 1997 revenues.

POSSIBLE DIFFERENCES UNDER ENTITY-WIDE (FULL ACCRUAL) STATEMENTS

The exposure draft does not distinguish between taxes collected by the government itself or those collected on its behalf by another government. Therefore, the city could recognize the entire amount of December taxes, just as if it had collected them itself.

HOW SHOULD INCOME TAXES BE ACCOUNTED FOR?

Forty-six states and a few major cities, such as New York, Philadelphia, and Detroit, impose personal or corporate income taxes.[7] Some of these states impose what they call a "franchise" tax on businesses, but they base the tax on income.

---

[7] U.S. Bureau of the Census, *State Government Finances: 1992* and *City Government Finances: 1990–91.*

Income taxes present especially vexatious issues of revenue recognition, owing to their multistage administrative processes. Consider, for example, the following:

- The tax is based on income of either a calendar year or a fiscal year elected by the taxpayer, but such year might not coincide with the government's fiscal year.

- Taxpayers are required to remit tax payments throughout the tax year, either through payroll withholdings or periodic payments of estimated amounts. Within three or four months after the close of the year, they are required to file a tax return in which they inform the government of the actual amount of tax owed. At that time, they are expected to make a final settlement with the government, by either paying additional taxes due or requesting a refund of overpayments. Thus, the taxes received by the government during the year may be more or less than the amount to which they are entitled.

- Governments review all tax returns for reasonableness and select a sample for audit. Moreover, some taxpayers are delinquent on their payments. Thus, taxes continue to trickle in for several years after the due date. Although governments can reliably estimate the amount of late collections based on historical experience, they may not have a legal claim to the taxes until taxpayers either file their returns or agree to the adjustments resulting from an audit.

EXAMPLE   *Income Taxes*

In 1997 a state collects $95 million in income taxes based on taxpayer income of that year. In the first sixty days of 1998 it collects $5 million more in 1997 taxes. These payments are required under the state's system of tax withholdings and estimated payments. Between March 1, 1998, and April 15, 1998, the state collects an additional $15 million (net of refunds) as taxpayers file their 1997 tax returns. The state estimates that over the next three years, as it audits returns, it will collect another $6 million in taxes.

Also in 1997, as the result of audits of prior-year returns, the state bills taxpayers for an additional $4 million in taxes. Of these, it collects $2 million during 1997 and $1 million of the balance by February 1998.

The state issues its 1997 statements on April 30, 1998.

Current Standards

Current standards beg the key issues. As indicated in the discussion of sales taxes, taxpayer-assessed taxes "should be recognized in the accounting period in which they become susceptible to accrual—that is, when they become both *measurable* and *available* to finance expenditures of the fiscal period."

In the example, based on this meager guidance, the state could recognize $100 million in income tax revenue based on 1997 earnings—the $95 million of 1997 taxes collected in 1997 and the $5 million collected in the first sixty days of 1998 (assuming it chooses sixty days as the criterion for "availability"). It could also recognize the $3 million collected in 1997 and the first sixty days of 1998 attributable to audits of prior year returns. It could not recognize revenue on any taxes collected after the first sixty days of 1998.

Cash	$97	
Income taxes of 1997 receivable	20	
Income taxes of prior years receivable	2	
Income tax revenue—1997		$100
Income tax revenue—prior years		3
Deferred income tax revenue—1997		15
Deferred income tax revenue—prior years		1

To summarize 1997 income tax activity (The income taxes of 1997 that are receivable include both the $5 million to be collected in the first sixty days and the $15 million to be collected between the end of the sixty-day period and April 15, 1998).

POSSIBLE DIFFERENCES UNDER ENTITY-WIDE (FULL ACCRUAL) STATEMENTS

The exposure draft, provides no guidance on income taxes other than what was indicated previously with regard to sales and other derived taxes. That is, derived taxes should generally be recognized as revenue in the period in which underlying transactions take place. For income taxes, the underlying transactions would be those that produce the income on which the tax is based. Thus, inasmuch as income taxes are seldom collected before the underlying income is earned, governments can recognize as revenue the income taxes that it collects and expects to collect. Assuming the taxes applicable to prior year had not yet been recognized as revenue, the following entry would be appropriate.

Cash	$97	
Income taxes of 1997 receivable	20	
Income taxes of 1997 expected to be assessed as a result of future audits	6	
Income taxes of prior years receivable	2	
Income tax revenue—1997		$121
Income tax revenue—prior years		4

To summarize 1997 income tax activity

The proposed pronouncement is intended to be a set of broad guidelines rather than a rulebook. Accordingly, it gives entities considerable flexibility in establishing revenue recognition policies. Most governments are likely to recognize as revenue of a current year only amounts that they have actually collected or have a firmly established legal claim upon by the time they issue their financial statements. Unlike the government in our illustration, few can be expected to recognize as revenue amounts they expect to collect as a consequence of audits not yet conducted.

HOW SHOULD LICENSES AND PERMITS BE ACCOUNTED FOR?

UNIQUE CHARAC-TERISTICS

Governments issue licenses (or permits) that allow citizens and businesses to carry out regulated activities over a specified period of time. However, the license period may not coincide with the government's fiscal year.

The primary concern relating to licenses is whether the revenue should be recognized when a license is issued and cash is received (usually concurrently) or whether it should be spread out over the period covered by the license. In other words, is the significant economic event the collection of cash or is it the passage of time?

The issue is by no means clear-cut in light of the following characteristics of licenses:

- Some license fees are intended to cover the cost of services provided to the licensee or related to the activity in which the licensee engages. For example, the funds generated from restaurant licenses may be used to inspect restaurants and thereby protect restaurant customers. Similarly, bicycle registration fees may support bicycle safety programs. Other fees, however, may bear little relation to the cost of services provided and may be imposed mainly as a source of general revenues.

- Generally, license fees are not refundable. Therefore, unless a license fee is tied to specific services, once the government receives the fee, it has no further obligation, either actual or contingent, to the licensee.

EXAMPLE   *License Fees*

In June 1997 a city imposed license fees on barber and beauty shops for the first time. It collected $360,000. The fees are intended to cover the cost of health inspections. The licenses cover the one-year period from July 1 to June 30.

Current Standards

Current standards state simply: "Fines and forfeits, golf and swimming fees, inspection charges, parking fees and parking meter receipts, and the vast multitude of miscellaneous revenues are also best recognized when cash is received." [8]

The following entry, therefore, would summarize the 1997 activity:

Cash	$360,000	
Revenue from license fees		$360,000
To summarize 1997 license fee activity		

POSSIBLE DIFFERENCES UNDER ENTITY-WIDE (FULL ACCRUAL) STATEMENTS

The exposure draft on nonexchange transaction makes no mention of licenses and permits. Statement No. 11, however, illustrates one approach to recognizing revenue on a full accrual basis.

Statement No. 11 distinguishes between license fees that are tied to services

---

[8] *Codification*, Section 1600.113.

and those that are not. In situations in which the fees were tied to services, it encouraged governments to allocate the revenue over the periods covered by the licenses. This treatment would be especially appropriate, it noted, when fees were due in the period preceding the license period or the fees covered more than one fiscal period. When the fees were not tied to services it permitted governments to recognize as revenue the entire amount of fees when they were received.

In this example, the fees are tied to inspection activities, so they may be allocated over the twelve-month period covered. Six months of revenue would be recognized in the year ending December 31, 1997; the balance would be deferred to the year ending December 31, 1998:

Cash	$360,000	
Revenue from license fees		$180,000
Deferred revenue from license fees		180,000
To summarize 1997 license fee activity		

Thus, under the modified accrual basis (as implemented by current standards), license fees are recognized as revenue when cash is received. Under the full accrual basis (if the guidelines of Statement No. 11 were to be adopted) license fees could be recognized as revenue over the period of the license.

HOW SHOULD FINES BE ACCOUNTED FOR?

KEY DATES AND EVENTS

Although the question of when a government "earns" its revenues from fines is seldom important in terms of dollar amount, it is nevertheless provocative. Consider, for example, the several dates and events relating to parking tickets and other traffic violations:

- Tickets are issued; based on historical experience the government can estimate the percentage of tickets that will actually be paid.
- Violators must either pay or protest the fines by specified dates; if they do not protest, the government has a legal claim to the basic fines plus penalties for late payment.
- If ticketed parties opt to protest, hearings are scheduled and held; if they are found guilty, the government now has its legal claim to the basic fine plus penalties for late payment.

EXAMPLE   *Fines*

In November 1997 police issue $200,000 in parking tickets. Of the fines assessed, $130,000 are paid without protest by the due date of December 31, 1997. Of the balance, $22,000 will either "trickle in" or be collected after hearings are held and violators are found guilty. It is estimated that $48,000 will be uncollectible.

Current Standards

As noted in the section dealing with licenses and permits, current standards indicate that parking tickets and "the vast majority of miscellaneous revenues are . . . best recognized when cash is received."

Hence, the following entry would be required:

Cash	$130,000	
Revenues from parking fines		$130,000

To summarize 1997 parking fine activity related to November tickets

POSSIBLE DIFFERENCES UNDER ENTITY-WIDE (FULL ACCRUAL) STATEMENTS

The exposure draft on nonexchange transactions does not address fines. However, as pointed out in the discussion pertaining to property taxes, it says that in the absence of requirements as to when or for what purposes resources from imposed nonexchange transactions must be used, revenue should be recognized when the government has an enforceable legal claim. A government would normally have a legal claim from a fine when the protest period expires, a court imposes a penalty, or the offender pays the penalty. The government should, of course, make appropriate allowances for uncollectibles.

In this example, the following entry would summarize the city's parking fine activity on a full accural basis:

Cash	$130,000	
Parking tickets outstanding (receivable)	70,000	
Revenues from parking fines		$152,000
Allowance for uncollectible parking fines		48,000

To summarize 1997 parking fine activity related to November tickets

HOW SHOULD GRANTS AND SIMILAR INTERGOVERNMENTAL REVENUES BE ACCOUNTED FOR?

Grants and similar intergovernmental revenues take many forms and, hence, the principles of revenue recognition must be based on the particular characteristics of the award. Among the typical types of intergovernmental revenues are the following:

- *Restricted grants* are payments intended for specified purposes, projects, or activities. They are the most common form of grants, usually made to reimburse specific types of expenditures.

- *Unrestricted grants* are payments that are unrestricted as to purpose, project, or activity.
- *Entitlements* are payments, usually from a higher level government, to which a state or local government is automatically entitled in an amount determined by a specified formula. Entitlements are often designated for broad functional activities, such as education.
- *Shared revenues* are revenues raised by one government, such as a state, but shared on a predetermined basis with other governments, such as cities.
- *Payments in lieu of taxes* are amounts paid by one government in place of property taxes they are not required to pay. Such payments constitute an important source of revenue for governments whose jurisdictions include many facilities of other governments. For example, the federal government, the property of which is tax exempt, may make payments to school districts in which military bases are located to compensate them for educating military dependents.

As with other governmental revenues, the key event in the "earnings" process is subject to debate. Suppose, for example, a grant must be used to support a specific activity. Should the recipient recognize revenue when it is awarded the grant, as it carries out the required activity, or when it receives the cash (which may be before, while, or after, it performs the activity)? The following two examples help to explain why different types of grants may necessitate different guidelines.

EXAMPLE No. 1: *Unrestricted Grant*

In June 1998 a school district is notified that, per legislature-approved formulas, it has been awarded $15 million in assistance. The funds must be used to supplement teachers salaries, acquire equipment, and support educational enrichment programs.

EXAMPLE No. 2: *Restricted Grant*

In December 1998 a city is awarded a grant of $400,000 to train its social workers. During 1999 it expends $300,000 on training, for which it is reimbursed $250,000. It expects to be reimbursed for the $50,000 balance early in 2000 and to expend and be reimbursed for the remaining $100,000 of its grant in 2000.

Current Standards

Consistent with the recognition criteria for other revenues, current standards provide that grants, entitlements, and other intergovernmental revenues should be recognized when they become "susceptible to accrual—that is both measurable and available."[9] However, the standards do not specify the conditions that must be satisfied for the awards to be considered measurable and available. Instead, they advise that "legal and contractual requirements should be carefully

[9] *Codification*, Section G60.

reviewed for guidance." The standards point out that some awards, usually entitlements or shared revenues, "are restricted more in form than in substance. Only a failure on the part of the recipient to comply with prescribed regulations will cause a forfeiture of the resources." These revenues should be recorded as revenue at the time of receipt, or even earlier "if the susceptible to accrual criteria are met." For other revenues, mainly grants that must be used for a specific purpose, "expenditure is the prime factor for determining eligibility, and revenue should be recognized when the expenditure is made."

Implicit in the current standards is the concept that a government "earns" entitlements and other awards for which no specific performance is required at the time the award is made. Hence, once the award is announced, revenue can be recognized as soon as the resources are available. By contrast, when the award is restricted and the government must carry out specified activities either to receive the funds or to be legally entitled to keep funds received in advance, the government "earns" the awards only as it carries out the activities.

In both of the examples, the government is required to carry out specific activities: in the first instance it must pay its teachers, purchase equipment, or carry-out enrichment programs, whereas in the second instance it must provide training courses for social workers. In the first example, however, the performance requirement is more of form than substance; the state demands nothing of the district that it would not otherwise do. Once the award is announced, the recipient has no further conditions that must be satisfied before the funds are available for expenditure. Accordingly, the revenue may be recognized when the award is announced, as long as the funds will be received in time to be available to meet 1998 expenditures. Thus, the following entry would be appropriate in 1998:

Awards receivable from state (or cash, to the extent received)	$15	
Revenue from state awards		$15
To recognize 1998 revenue from state assistance		

In the second example, the city will be reimbursed only for qualifying costs. It earns the award, and should recognize revenue, only as it incurs the expenditures. Therefore, in 1999 it may recognize revenue in an amount no greater than its expenditures of $300,000:

Cash	$250,000	
Grants receivable	50,000	
Revenue from grants		$300,000
To record 1999 grant activity		

If the government considered it important to give accounting recognition to the $100,000 balance of the grant not yet reported as revenue, the following supplementary entry would provide the appropriate information yet have no impact on either the operating surplus or deficit or fund balance:

Grant receivable	$100,000	
Deferred revenue from grants		$100,000
To record the balance of the grant awarded but not yet earned		

POSSIBLE DIFFERENCES UNDER ENTITY-WIDE (FULL ACCRUAL) STATEMENTS

The exposure draft on nonexchange transactions classifies grants as voluntary nonexchange transactions—those in which resources are voluntarily given or received without a commensurate return of benefits. Consistent with the other provisions of the draft, governments should recognize revenue from grants as soon as they have satisfied all substantive eligibility requirements, including those as to when and for what purposes the grant must be used.

In the first example, that in which it did not have to satisfy substantive performance requirements, the government could recognize revenue as soon as the grant was announced. Thus, the entry would be the same as under current standards:

Awards receivable from state (or cash, to the extent received)	$15	
Revenue from state awards		$15

To recognize 1998 revenue from state assistance

In the second example, the government must incur allowable costs to be eligible for the grant. Therefore, it may recognize revenue only as it incurs the costs and the appropriate entry would also be the same as under current standards:

Cash	$250,000	
Grants receivable	50,000	
Revenue from grants		$300,000

To record 1999 grant activity

In both examples, in contrast to what is permitted by current standards, the governments could recognize the revenue irrespective of when the cash was expected to be received; the resources would not have to satisfy the measurable and available criteria.

ACCOUNTING FOR PASS-THROUGH GRANTS

Some types of grants—those for which the recipient is required to distribute the resources to other parties or for which payment is made directly to a third party for the benefit of the recipient—raise the additional question of whether the grant should even be recognized by the recipient government. Suppose, for example, a state receives federal funds earmarked for each of its local school districts. Should the state record the receipt of the funds as a revenue and the disbursement as an expenditure? Or alternatively, should it omit the grant from both its budget and its accounts on the grounds that, with regard to these funds, it is nothing more than an agent of the federal government?

Grants that a government must transfer to, or spend on behalf of, a secondary recipient are referred to as **pass-through grants.** Pass-through grants vary in the extent of responsibility they impose on the primary recipient. For example, a state may receive federal funds over which it has no discretion in determining how, or in what amounts, they can be disbursed. Once it distributes the funds, it has no responsibility for monitoring how they are spent. At the other extreme, a state may be permitted to distribute federal funds within broad guidelines and it will be held accountable for assuring that the funds are used in accordance with federal specifications.

In the past, some governments opted to exclude pass-through funds from both their revenues and expenditures. Perhaps wanting to show that they held the line on spending, they accounted for the funds "off the budget"—often in agency funds in which only assets and liabilities are reported.

To reduce diversity of practice, in 1994 the GASB stated that "as a general rule, cash pass-through grants should be recognized as revenue and expenditures or expenses in governmental, proprietary, or trust funds."[10] Only in those "infrequent cases" in which the government serves as only a "cash conduit" may pass-through grants be reported in an agency fund. A government serves as a "cash conduit" the GASB explains, if it "merely transmits grantor-supplied moneys without having `administrative involvement.'" *Administrative involvement* would be indicated if the government selected the secondary recipients of the funds (even based on grantor-established criteria) or monitored compliance with grant requirements.

ACCOUNTING FOR FOOD STAMPS

Food stamps are a form of pass-through assistance. The federal government gives the stamps to the states, which distribute them in accord with specified guidelines. Until 1994, many governments gave no balance sheet or operating statement recognition to food stamps. Then, in its pronouncement on pass-through grants, the GASB asserted that food stamps received and distributed should be recognized as both a revenue and an expenditure.

EXAMPLE   *Food Stamps*

In 1999 a state receives $100 million in food stamps, of which it distributes $95 million.

Current Standards

According to the GASB, *state* governments should report both the revenue and the expenditure concurrently, when the stamps are distributed. They should be measured by the stamps' face value.

Moreover, the GASB directed that state governments report food stamps on hand at year-end as an asset (stated at face value). Inasmuch as governments should recognize revenue from food stamps only as the stamps are distributed, not when they are received, the credit offsetting the stamp inventory should be to "deferred revenue."

The following entries summarize the transactions:

Expenditures—food stamps	$95	
Revenues—food stamps		$95
To record the receipt and distribution of food stamps		
Inventory of food stamps	$5	
Deferred revenues—food stamps		$5
To recognize food stamps on-hand at year-end		

[10] Originally issued as Statement No. 24, "Accounting and Financial Reporting for Certain Grants and Other Financial Assistance," *Codification*, Section G60.

States sometimes involve local governments in the food stamp distribution process. Nevertheless, overall administrative responsibility for the program rests with the states. The local governments serve mainly as agents of the state. Although the GASB does not deal with the issue of how local governments should account for their role in the food stamp programs, most governments have not been reporting stamps received and distributed as either revenues or expenditures. They have, however, been recognizing administrative costs as expenditures and administrative fees charged to the state as revenues.

ACCOUNTING FOR ON-BEHALF PAYMENTS

In the multigovernment system of the United States, one government may make payments for employee fringe benefits "on behalf" (for the direct benefit) of another. For example, a state may contribute to a pension plan for school teachers on behalf of the independent school districts that employ the teachers.

The key issue as to **on-behalf payments** is whether, and in what circumstances, the beneficiary government should recognize the payments as if it had received, and then spent, a cash grant—that is, should it recognize a revenue and an offsetting expenditure, or should it give no recognition at all to the transactions?

As with so many other accounting issues, the challenges of standard setting are compounded by the variety of forms that a transaction can take. Some state on-behalf payments, for example, are made in lieu of pensions or other compensation that the beneficiary local government would otherwise have been required by state law to provide on its own. Other payments are made by the state to cover programs or activities in which the local government would otherwise not engage. Some accountants believe that beneficiary governments should recognize only the on-behalf payments that cover costs for which they are legally responsible.

EXAMPLE   *On-Behalf Payments*

A state government is responsible for funding the state's teacher retirement system. In 1999 it contributes $3 million to the system on behalf of an independent school district.

Current Standards

The GASB ruled, as another part of its grants project, that the recipient government should recognize both a revenue and a corresponding expenditure for *all* on-behalf payments. Despite the objections of two of its five members, it required recognition irrespective of whether or not the beneficiary government was legally responsible for the payments.

The school district would make the following entry:

Pension expenditures	$3	
State aid—pensions		$3
To record the on-behalf pension payments made by the state		

Correspondingly, the state would also record an expenditure:

State aid to school districts (expenditure) $3
  Cash $3
To record the contribution to the pension fund on behalf of an independent school district

A paying government should classify its on-behalf payments in the same manner as similar cash grants to other entities. For example, if it classifies other educational grants as educational expenditures, then it should classify the payments to the pension fund as educational expenditures, not pension expenditures.

HOW SHOULD INVESTMENT GAINS AND LOSSES BE ACCOUNTED FOR?

Investments, whether they be in debt or equity securities, fluctuate in value. Government portfolios generally contain mainly short-term debt securities. Because they are short-term, their values are not greatly influenced by swings in interest rates. Some portfolios, however, also hold longer-term instruments that are considerably more sensitive to changes in interest rates. In recent years, some governments—often in violation of both accepted standards of sound fiscal management and common sense—have speculated in "derivatives" and other instruments that are extremely sensitive to interest rate changes.

Until 1993, both the GASB and the FASB directed that the governments, not-for-profit organizations, and most businesses within their purview report short-term investments at either historical cost or the lower of historical cost or market value. In that year, the FASB broke with tradition, and required businesses to divide their investment portfolios into three categories: trading securities (those that enterprises intend to hold for only a short period of time); held-to-maturity securities (mainly long-term bonds); and available-for-sale securities (other securities, such as stock held for the long-term). They must carry their portfolios of both trading securities and available-for-sale securities at "fair" (i.e., market) values.[11] However, the Board explicitly exempted not-for-profits from the purview of the statement, opting to deal with them in a separate project.

In 1995, as the result of the promised project, the FASB extended its "mark-to-market" directives to not-for-profits.[12] However, inasmuch as the requirement that investments be classified into the three categories was intended mainly to accommodate specialized industries, such as banks and insurance companies, it was omitted from the not-for-profit pronouncement. Instead, the statement requires that all debt and equity securities (except those accounted for by the equity method or those of consolidated subsidiaries) be stated at fair value. Moreover, gains and losses on investments, both realized and unrealized, must be recognized as such and reported in the statement of activities.

The reasons for reporting investments at fair value are as compelling for government organizations as for business and other not-for-profits. Those frequently advanced include the following:

---

[11] Statement of Financial Accounting Standards No. 115, *Accounting for Certain Investments in Debt and Equity Securities.*

[12] Statement of Financial Accounting Standards No. 124, *Accounting for Certain Investments Held by Not-for-Profit Organizations.*

- For virtually all decisions involving investments, fair value is more relevant than historical cost.

- Investments are often held as cash substitutes. They can be liquidated with a phone call to the entity's broker.

- Fair values are objective; up-to-the-minute prices are available from computer and telephone information services.

- The performance of investment managers, and their employer governments, is measured by total return—dividends, interest, and changes in fair values.

- To be sure, prices that go up can also come down. But financial statements report on performance within specified periods. An increase in the value of a security in a particular year is indicative of sound investment performance in the year it occurs. A subsequent decline in the following year reflects poor performance in that year. Insofar as government officials are expected to achieve specified investment goals, statement users are entitled to the information needed to assess how well they have done.

EXAMPLE   *Investment Income*

The following table summarizes the 1999 investment activity in a county's general fund (all amounts in thousands):

	Cost	Fair Value on Jan. 1	Purchases	Sales (proceeds)	Fair Value on Dec. 31
Security A	$120	$120			$140
Security B	520	$540			540
Security C	200	200		$250	0
Security D	90		$ 90		75
	$930	$860	$ 90	$250	$755

Current Standards

Following the FASB's lead, in 1997 the GASB determined that governments, like businesses and not-for-profits, should state their investments as fair value. GASB Statement No. 31, *Accounting and Financial Reporting for Certain Investments and for External Investment Pools*, requires that investment income, including changes in fair value, be reported in the operating statement or other statement of activities of all entities and funds.

The Board made a notable exception for short-term securities that are not subject to the same volatility as long-term instruments. Governments are permitted to report money market investments having a remaining maturity at time of purchase of one year or less at amortized cost rather than market value. These investments would include certificates of deposits, commercial paper, and U.S. Treasury obligations.

Per the new pronouncement, the investments should be reported on the county's December 31, 1999, statements at their fair value—$755. The gain or loss to be reported on the county's 1999 operating statement can be determined by subtracting investment inputs from outputs. The inputs are the securities on hand at the start of the year (stated at fair value as of the beginning of the year) plus the purchases during the year. The outputs are the securities on hand at year-end (stated at fair value as of year-end) plus the proceeds from the sale of securities during the year. Thus:

Outputs

Fair value, December 31	$755	
Sales	250	$1,005

Inputs

Fair value, January 1	$860	
Purchases	90	950
Increase (decrease) in fair value of investments		$ 55

The following entry would therefore be appropriate:

Investments	$55	
Increase in fair value of investments		$55

To record the increase in the fair value of the investments

Many local governments invest what would otherwise be idle cash in investment pools, maintained by their states or other governmental units. These investment pools are similar to mutual funds. Each participant purchases shares in the underlying portfolio. Statement No. 31 specifies that governments should state their investments in a pool at the fair value per share of the pool's underlying portfolio. Each period they should recognize the change in fair value as a gain or loss.

How should interest and dividends be accounted for?

The GASB has not yet provided specific directives as to when governments should recognize interest and dividends on their investments. However, by recording the changes in fair value governments will automatically accrue interest and dividends as they are earned.

EXAMPLE *Interest Income*

On December 1, a town purchased a $1,000, two-year discount note for $891, a price that reflects an annual yield of approximately 7 percent. As a discount note, the security provides no periodic payments of interest. However, assuming no change in prevailing interest rates or other factors that would also affect fair value, the note's fair value can be expected to increase by approximately $5 the first month. On December 31, if the fair value of the note were $876, the following entry would recognize the $5 of investment income, attributable in economic substance to the interest earned:

Investments	$5	
Increase in fair value of investments		$5

To record the increase in the fair value of the investments

If the security were a short-term Treasury note (one-year or less) the government would not look to fair value to adjust the security. Instead, it would amortize the initial discount over the life of the note. If, for example, the initial discount on a six-month, 6 percent, $1,000 note were $15, the following entry would recognize one month's interest income:

Discount on note (or Investments)	$5	
Interest income		$5

To record one-month's interest

The impact of the two approaches on both net assets and change in fund balance is the same. Both would give recognition to the interest earned and the resultant change in the value of the underlying security.

HOW SHOULD DONATIONS BE ACCOUNTED FOR?

Governments sometimes receive donations of either financial or fixed assets. Gifts are commonly associated with special purpose governments or units of governments, such as school districts, hospitals, colleges, and museums. However, they may also be received by general purpose governments, often to support parks and cultural programs.

Current Standards

Authoritative pronouncements currently in effect do not address donations. In concept, however, donations are comparable to grants, so that consistency would suggest that they be accounted for in a similar way. Thus, they would be recognized when they are both measurable and available. For unrestricted gifts, this would ordinarily be when cash is received. For restricted gifts it would be when the resources are expended for the designated purpose.

POSSIBLE DIFFERENCES UNDER ENTITY-WIDE (FULL ACCRUAL) STATEMENTS

The exposure draft on nonexchange transactions makes it clear that donations are to be accounted for like grants. Therefore, revenue may be recognized as soon as the government satisfies the conditions for the contribution. If a government receives an unconditional pledge of a donation (one for which no further action is required by the government), then it can recognize both the pledge receivable and the corresponding revenue at the time of the pledge. If it receives a gift that is contingent upon it fulfilling certain requirements, then it must delay revenue recognition until it has met those requirements. Suppose, for example, an alumnus of a government university promises to match all other contributions to a scholarship fund up to a maximum of $1 million. That is, the matching funds are contingent upon the university receiving the other funds. In a particular year the university receives $350,000. The university could recognize as revenue $350,000 of the alumnus's pledge, plus the $350,000 from the other sources.

ACCOUNTING FOR GIFTS OF FIXED ASSETS

Gifts of fixed assets present an especially intriguing issue, mainly because fixed assets are not reported in governmental funds. Both current standards and the proposed exposure draft on nonexchange transactions are silent on the issue. However, the guidance of Statement No. 11 could readily be applied within the framework of both the existing fund perspective statements and the proposed entity-wide statements.

EXAMPLE   *Gifts of Fixed Assets*

A school district receives a donation of two automobiles, each having a fair market value of $20,000. Needing only one, it intends to keep one and sell the other.

Statement No. 11 distinguishes between donated fixed assets that a government intends to use and those that it intends to sell. Fixed assets intended for use should not be recorded in a governmental fund as assets; correspondingly, the receipt of the fixed assets should not be recognized as revenue. The assets can be recognized only by recording them in the general fixed assets account group—the "list" of fixed assets. Thus, the vehicle intended for use would not be recorded in either the general fund or any other governmental fund. It would be recorded in the general fixed assets account group:

Vehicles	$20,000	
Investment in fixed assets (from		
donations)		$20,000

To record a donated vehicle (general fixed assets account group)

By contrast, fixed assets held for sale are unlike fixed assets held for use. From the perspective of the recipient government, they are the equivalent of marketable securities or other short-term investments. They are expected to be transformed soon into cash. Therefore, fixed assets intended to be sold should be recorded in governmental funds, and donations of these assets should be recognized as revenues. They should not be recorded in the general fixed assets account group. Thus, the entry in a governmental fund would be:

Vehicles held for sale	$20,000	
Revenue from donations		$20,000

To record the gift of a vehicle that the school district intends to sell

A related question arises. What must a government do to support its contention that it intends to sell the donated fixed asset? The only acceptable evidence, per Statement No. 11, is that prior to the issuance of financial statements, it has already sold the assets or entered into a contract to sell them.

> ## POSSIBLE DIFFERENCES UNDER ENTITY-WIDE (FULL ACCRUAL) STATEMENTS
>
> Under an entity-wide full accrual basis of accounting, a donation of fixed assets would be accounted for just as a donation of any other type of asset. The government would recognize both the revenue and the property received in an appropriate fund (e.g., the general fund). There would be no need to record the assets in a general fixed assets account group (since account groups are not reported in entity-wide full accrual statements) or to distinguish between property held for use and that held for sale.

HOW SHOULD SALES OF FIXED ASSETS BE ACCOUNTED FOR?

Governments sell fixed assets for the same reasons as businesses—the services the assets impart can more economically be provided by another means or by replacement assets. The unique accounting problem faced by governments when they sell general fixed assets is that the financial resources received are accounted for in a governmental fund, but the assets that are sold are listed in the general fixed assets account group.

EXAMPLE   *Sales of Fixed Assets*

On December 31, 1998, a city purchases a new police car for $30,000. On January 2, 1999, the vehicle is damaged in an accident. The vehicle is uninsured; the city is able to sell the nearly demolished vehicle for $5,000.

Current practice requires the following, seemingly odd, entry:

Cash	$5,000	
Other financing sources—sale of vehicle		$5,000

To record the sale of general fixed assets

"Seemingly odd" because "other financing sources" is reported on a statement of revenues, expenditures, and changes in fund balance (below the revenues and expenditures). Although not exactly a revenue, it is similar to a revenue in that it may be budgeted as a revenue and results in an increase in fund balance.

From an accounting perspective, therefore, the accident that destroyed a $30,000 vehicle left the government $5,000 better off; that is, the governmental fund's assets and fund balance increased by $5,000. This outcome, while bizarre—and not suggestive of appropriate means by which governments should reduce their deficits—is inevitable when the measurement focus of governmental funds excludes fixed assets. As indicated in Chapter 2, when governmental fund resources are used to acquire an asset, its cost is written off (charged as an expenditure) as it is paid for. Consequently, the police vehicle, which is clearly evident to most citizens, is invisible to the governmental fund's accountant.

Of course, when the vehicle is destroyed, it would have to be removed from the general fixed assets account group. Thus, the following entry would be required in the general fixed assets account group:

Investment in fixed assets	$30,000	
Vehicles		$30,000

To record the destruction of a police car

Before you get overly exercised over this anomalous accounting outcome, consider that business accounting may produce a similar result. The fixed assets of businesses are carried at historical cost less depreciation—amounts that may be considerably less than fair market values. Suppose that a vehicle owned by a business was destroyed in an accident and that the vehicle was insured for any amount that exceeded its book value. That accident, too, would cause the business to report a gain owing to the mishap.

Both businesses and governmental funds state their fixed assets at amounts bearing little relationship to their economic worth. Whereas businesses carry them at historical cost, less depreciation, governmental funds report them at zero. In the GASB-proposed, entity-wide, full accrual statements, governments would report their fixed assets and would recognize gains and losses from sales, on the same basis as businesses.

SUMMARY

Governmental funds focus on current financial resources and correspondingly are on a modified accrual basis of accounting. Revenues are recognized when a key underlying event takes place and the cash to be received is both measurable and available to finance expenditures of the current budgetary period. By contrast, in the entity-wide, full accrual statements that the GASB has proposed, revenues would be recognized when earned irrespective of when cash will be received.

Because there are several events in the time line for most types of government revenues, governments and standard-setting authorities must determine which event is the most significant and should thereby warrant revenue recognition. Current practices include the following:

- Property taxes are recognized in the year for which they are levied, provided they are either collected in that year or expected to be collected soon enough thereafter (generally no more than sixty days) to pay liabilities of the current period.
- Taxpayer assessed taxes, such as sales taxes and income taxes, are recognized in the period in which they become both measurable and available to finance the expenditures of the fiscal period. Sales taxes are generally recognized in the period of sale as long as they will be remitted by the merchant soon enough to pay the liabilities of the current period. Income taxes are generally recognized in the year to which the related income has

been earned provided they are collected during that year or shortly thereafter.

- Fines, license fees, permits, and most miscellaneous revenues are recognized as cash is received.
- Restricted grants are generally recognized as the related expenditures are made; unrestricted grants, such as entitlements, are recognized when the award is made, subject to the availability criterion.
- Per a GASB standard that was only recently adopted, investments must be marked-to-market. Changes in the fair value of securities, including those attributable to anticipated payments of dividends and interest, are recognized as revenue as they take place.
- In the absence of specific GASB standards, donations are commonly recognized as cash is received.
- Increases in fund balance from the sale of fixed assets are recognized as the sales take place. Inasmuch as fixed assets are not reported in government funds, their book value is zero. Therefore, the increase in fund balance from the sale of a fixed asset is equal to the sales proceeds.

The GASB is in the process of developing the guidelines for recognizing revenue for the proposed entity-wide, full accrual statements. The exposure draft on nonexchange transactions points to the approach that the GASB is taking. Under a full accrual basis, governments would recognize revenues when the underlying transaction or event takes place, irrespective of whether cash has yet to be received.

However, if the government must meet specified restrictions as to when or how they can use the resources received or to be received in the future, then they would have to delay recognizing revenues until these constraints are satisfied.

The issues addressed in this chapter can never be resolved definitively by a rulemaking authority. There are no "correct" answers that are beyond challenge—no more so than in business accounting.

EXERCISE FOR REVIEW AND SELF-STUDY

The Town of Malvern engages in the following transactions during its fiscal year ending September 30, 1998. All dollar amounts are in thousands.

1. During fiscal 1998 the town levied property taxes of $154,000, of which it collected $120,000 prior to September 30, 1998, and $5,000 over each of the next six months. It estimated that $4,000 will be uncollectible.

2. On November 20, 1998, it received $12,000 from the state for sales taxes collected on its behalf. The payment was for sales made in September that merchants were required to remit to the state by October 15.

3. In April the town was awarded a state employment-training grant of $400 covering the period June 1, 1998, through May 31, 1999. The grant required the town to distribute the funds to local community job training centers according to prescribed criteria and to monitor how the funds were spent by the centers. In fiscal 1998 the town received the entire $400 but spent only $320.

4. The town requires each vendor who sells in its "farmers' market" to obtain an annual permit. The funds generated by the sale of these permits are used to maintain the market. The permits, which cover the period from June 1 through May 31, are not refundable. In May 1998 the town issued $36 of permits.

5. On September 1, 1998, with $500 in funds available for temporary investment, the town acquired two-year, 6 percent U.S. Treasury notes. The notes pay interest upon maturity. On September 30, the market value of the notes was $540.

6. Several years earlier the town received a donation of a parcel of land, upon which it expected to build. During fiscal 1998 it opted to sell the land for $135. When acquired by the town, the land had a market value of $119.

Prepare summary journal entries to reflect their impact on year-end financial statements. Base your entries on generally accepted accounting principles now in effect. In addition, indicate whether, and how, they would likely change if the statements were to be prepared on a full accrual basis.

QUESTIONS FOR REVIEW AND DISCUSSION

1. Why is a choice of *basis of accounting* inexorably linked to *measurement focus?*

2. What are the current measurement focus and basis of accounting of governmental funds? Why do governmental funds *not* focus on all economic resources and use a full accrual basis of accounting?

3. As a general rule, when are revenues recognized in governmental funds? What is the rationale for this rule?

4. In what significant way would the criteria for recognizing property tax revenues be different if they were accounted for on a full accrual basis?

5. What is the earliest point in the sales tax collection process that revenues may be recognized? How can you justify recognizing revenue on the basis of this event?

6. A government recognizes revenues from some licenses and permits at the time cash is received. It recognizes revenues from others pro-rata over the period covered by the license. How can you justify such seemingly inconsistent practices?

7. What special problems do governments face in measuring the income taxes associated with a particular year?

8. Explain the distinction between expenditure-driven grants and entitlements. How does this distinction affect the way both types of grants are accounted for?

9. What are pass-through grants? Under what circumstances must a recipient government report them as both a revenue and an expenditure?

10. A student comments: "A government destroys a recently acquired car, sells the remains for scrap, and its general fund surplus for the year increases. That's ridiculous. Government accounting makes so much less sense than private sector accounting." Explain why the situation described by the student arises. Does government accounting, in fact, differ so much from business accounting?

11. Until recently governments were not permitted to recognize revenue on increases in the value of investments. What arguments might you present in support of the current position that investments be stated at fair value and that changes in fair value be recognized as either revenues or expenditures?

EXERCISES

4-1

Property taxes are not necessarily recognized as revenue in the year collected.

The fiscal year of Duchess County ends on December 31. Property taxes are due March 31 of the year they are levied.

a. Prepare journal entries (excluding budgetary and closing entries) to record the following property-tax related transactions in which the county engaged in 1998 and 1999.

1. On January 15, 1998, the county council levied property taxes of $170 million for the year ending December 31, 1998. Officials estimated that 1 percent would be uncollectible.
2. During 1998 it collected $120 million.
3. In January and February 1999, prior to preparing its 1998 financial statements, it collected an additional $45 million in 1998 taxes. It reclassified the $5 million of 1999 taxes not yet collected as delinquent.
4. In January 1999, the county levied property taxes of $190 million, of which officials estimated 1.1 percent would be uncollectible.
5. During the remainder of 1999 the county collected $2.5 million in taxes relating to 1998, $160 million relating to 1999, and $1.9 million (in advance) applicable to 2000.
6. In December 1999 it wrote off $1 million of 1998 taxes that it determined would be uncollectible.

b. Suppose the county were to account for property taxes on a full accrual basis of accounting rather than the currently accepted modified accrual basis. How would your entries differ? Explain.

4-2

Grants are not necessarily recognized as revenue when awarded.

Columbus City was awarded a state grant of $150,000 to assist its adult literacy program. The following were significant events relating to the grant:

- The city, which is on a calendar year, was notified of the award in November 1998.
- During 1999 it expended $30,000 on the literacy program and was reimbursed for $20,000. It expected to receive the balance in January 2000.
- In 2000 it expended the remaining $120,000 and was reimbursed by the state for the $10,000 owing from 1999 and the amount spent in 2000.

a. Prepare journal entries to record the events.
b. Suppose instead that the city received the entire $150,000 in cash at the time the award was announced in 1998. How much revenue should the city recognize in each of the three years? Explain.
c. Suppose alternatively that the state awarded the city an unrestricted grant of $150,000, which the city elected to use to support the adult literacy program. The city received the entire $150,000 in cash at the time the award was announced in 1998. How much revenue should the city recognize in each of the three years? Explain.

4-3

The accounting for contributions may depend on how they will be used.

Green Hills County received the following two contributions during a year:

- A developer (in exchange for exemptions to zoning restrictions) donated several acres of land that the county intended to convert to a park. The land had cost the developer $1.7 million. At the time of the contribution its fair market value was $3.2 million.
- A local resident donated several acres of land to the county with the understanding that the county would sell the land and use the proceeds to fund construction of a county health center. The land had cost the resident $2.5 million. At the time of the contribution its fair market value was $2.9 million.

a. Prepare journal entries to record the contributions. Be sure to specify the appropriate fund or account group in which they would likely be made.
b. Suppose the county sold the land intended for the health center for $3 million. Prepare an appropriate journal entry.
c. Comment on and justify any differences in the way you accounted for the two contributions.

4-4

Sales taxes should be recognized when "measurable and available."

A state requires "large" merchants (those with sales over a specified dollar amount) to report and remit their sales taxes within fifteen days of the end of each month. It requires "small" merchants to report and remit their taxes within fifteen days of the end of each quarter.

In January 1999, large merchants remitted sales taxes of $400 million owing to sales of December 1998. In February 1999, they remitted $280 million of sales taxes owing to sales of January 1999. In January small merchants remitted sales taxes of $150 million owing to sales of the fourth quarter of 1998.

a. Prepare an appropriate journal entry to indicate the impact of the transactions on the state's financial statements for the year ending December 31, 1998.

b. Suppose, instead, that 10 percent of the taxes received by the state were collected on behalf of a city within the state. It is the policy of the state to remit the taxes to the city thirty days after it receives them. Prepare an appropriate journal entry to indicate the impact of the transactions on the city's financial statements for the year ending December 31, 1998.

c. Suppose, instead, that it were the policy of the state to remit the taxes to the city ninety days after it receives them. How would your response to part b differ? Explain.

4-5

Income taxes should be recognized as revenue when measurable and available.

The fiscal year of a major state ends on September 30. Its income tax, however, is based on income as reported on federal tax returns. The federal tax, for most taxpayers, is based on a calendar year. As with the federal income tax, taxpayers must remit their taxes throughout the year, either through wage and salary withholdings or by making quarterly estimated payments. Then, when they file their return (due April 15 of each year), they must either pay any additional amounts or they may claim a refund for overpayments.

During its fiscal year ending September 30, 1999, the state collected income taxes as follows:

- Between January 1, 1999, and April 15, 1999 it collected $1.9 billion in income taxes (net of refunds) as taxpayers filed their returns for calendar year 1998.

- Between October 1, 1998, and September 30, 1999, it collected $4.2 billion in income taxes that were either withheld by employers or reported and paid by taxpayers on estimated tax returns. None of these taxes had been recognized as revenue in the prior fiscal year. They were applicable to both the 1998 and the 1999 calendar years.

- In the sixty days subsequent to September 30, 1999, it collected $0.7 billion in taxes withheld and reported by taxpayers on their estimated returns. They were applicable to the 1999 calendar year.

- As the result of audits conducted prior to September 30, 1999, the state assessed taxpayers $0.3 billion in taxes in addition to any taxes included in the amounts already indicated. As of December 1, 1999, the state had not yet collected any of these taxes. It estimates that it will collect only $0.2 billion of this amount and have to write-off the other $0.1 billion.

Indicate the amount of taxes that satisfies the "measurable and available" criterion and should thereby be recognized as revenue in the fiscal year ending September 30, 1999.

4-6

The recognition of revenue from fines does not necessarily reflect the amount "earned."

In August 1999, the last month of its fiscal year, Spiedrap Township issued $88,000 of tickets for parking and traffic violations. Of these, the township collected $45,000. It expects to collect an additional $20,000 within sixty days of the close of the fiscal year and $3,000 subsequent to that. It will have to write off the balance.

a. Based on current standards, how much revenue should the township recognize from the tickets issued in August 1999? Explain.

b. How might your answer change if the township accounted for fines on a full accrual basis?

4-7

Questions adopted from the Uniform CPA Examination.

1. Under the modified accrual basis of accounting for a governmental unit, revenues should be recognized in the accounting period in which they
   a. are earned and become measurable.
   b. are collected.
   c. become available and measurable.
   d. become available and earned.

2. Fixed assets donated to a governmental unit should be recorded
   a. at estimated fair value when received.
   b. at the lower of donor's carrying amount or estimated fair value when received.
   c. at the donor's carrying amount.
   d. as a memorandum entry only.

3. A public school district should recognize revenue from property taxes levied for its debt service fund when
   a. bonds to be retired by the levy are due and payable.
   b. assessed valuations of property subject to the levy are known.
   c. funds from the levy are measurable and available to the district.
   d. proceeds from collection of the levy are deposited in the district's bank account.

4. Property taxes levied in fiscal year 1997 to finance the general fund budget of fiscal year 1998 should be reported as general fund revenues in fiscal year 1998
   a. regardless of the fiscal year in which collected.
   b. for the amount collected in fiscal year 1998 only.
   c. for the amount collected before the end of fiscal year 1998 only.
   d. for the amount collected before the end of fiscal year 1998 or shortly thereafter.

5. Which of the following accounts of a governmental unit is credited when taxpayers are billed for property taxes?
   a. Appropriations
   b. Taxes receivable—current
   c. Estimated revenues
   d. Revenues

6. Which of the following funds of a governmental unit recognize revenues in the accounting period in which they become available and measurable?

	General Fund	Enterprise Fund
a.	Yes	No
b.	No	Yes
c.	Yes	Yes
d.	No	No

7. The following information pertains to property taxes levied by Oak City for the calendar year 1998:

Collections during 1998	$500,000
Expected collections during the first 60 days of 1999	100,000
Expected collections during the balance of 1999	60,000
Expected collections during January 2000	30,000
Estimated to be uncollectible	10,000
Total levy	$700,000

   What amount should Oak report for 1998 net property tax revenues?
   a. $700,000
   b. $690,000
   c. $600,000
   d. $500,000

8. The following information pertains to Cobb City:

1997 governmental fund revenues that became measurable and available in time to be used for payment of 1997 liabilities	$16,000,000
Revenues earned in 1995 and 1996 and included in the $16,000,000 indicated above	2,000,000
Sales taxes collected by merchants in 1997 but not required to be remitted to Cobb until January 1998	3,000,000

For the year ended December 31, 1997, Cobb should recognize revenues of
   a. $14,000,000.
   b. $16,000,000.
   c. $17,000,000.
   d. $19,000,000.

9. Pine City's year end is June 30. Pine levies property taxes in January of each year for the calendar year. One-half of the levy is due in May and one-half is due in October. Property tax revenue is budgeted for the period in which payment is due. The following information pertains to Pine's property taxes for the period July 1, 1998, to June 30, 1999:

	Calendar Year	
	1998	1999
Levy	$2,000,000	$2,400,000
Collected in:		
May	950,000	1,100,000
July	50,000	60,000
October	920,000	
December	80,000	

   The $40,000 balance due for the May 1999 installments was expected to be collected in August 1999. What amount should Pine recognize for property tax revenue for the year ended June 30, 1999?
   a. $2,160,000
   b. $2,200,000
   c. $2,300,000
   d. $2,400,000

10. In November 1997, Maple Township received an unexpected state grant of $100,000 to finance the purchase of school buses, and an additional grant of $5,000 was received for bus maintenance and operations. Only $60,000 of the capital grant was used in the current year for the purchase of buses, but the entire operating grant of $5,000 was disbursed in the current year. The remaining $40,000 of the capital grant is expected to be expended during the year ending June 30, 1999. What amount should be reported as grant revenues for the year ending June 30, 1998?
   a. $5,000
   b. $60,000
   c. $65,000
   d. $100,000

PROBLEMS

Continuing Problem

Review the annual report that you obtained.

a. What are the main sources of the government's revenues, including those reported in special revenue funds?

b. Does the report indicate the accounting basis for any of these revenues?

c. Does the government use a different basis for recognizing revenues in its budget than in its financial statements?

d. Does the government's balance sheet report "deferred revenue?" Can you tell why this revenue has been deferred?

e. What is the government's property tax rate?

f. At what percentage of fair market value is property assessed?

g. When are property taxes due? When do interest and penalties begin to accrue?

h. What is the assessed value of property within the government's jurisdiction? Does the report indicate the value of property that is exempt from taxation?

4-1

Disproportionate assessments lead to inequities.

The town of Blair determines that it requires $22.5 million in property tax revenues to balance its budget.

According to the town's property tax assessor, the town contains taxable property that it assessed at $900 million. However, the town permits discounts for early payment that generally average about 2 percent of the *amount levied.* Further, the town grants homestead and similar exemptions equal to 3 percent of the property's *assessed value.*

a. Calculate the required tax rate, expressed in mils.

b. A resident's home is assessed at $300,000. He is permitted a homestead exemption of $10,000 and a senior-citizens' exemption of $5,000. What is the resident's required tax payment prior to allowable discounts for early payment?

c. Blair assesses property at 100 percent of its fair market value. Sussex, a nearby town in the same county, assesses property at only 80 percent of fair market value. The county bases its own tax assessments on the assessments of the individual towns. However, it grants no exemptions or discounts. Its tax rate is 8 mils.

   1. A taxpayer in Sussex owns a home with a market value of $300,000—the same as that of the Blair resident. Compute and compare the amount of county tax that would be paid by each resident.

   2. Comment on why governments find it necessary to "equalize" tax assessments based on assessments of other governments?

4-2

A change to the full accrual basis may have little impact upon reported revenues.

A city levies property taxes of $4 billion in June 1998 for its fiscal year beginning July 1, 1998. The taxes are due by January 31, 1999. The following (in millions) indicates actual and anticipated cash collections relating to the levy:

June 1998	$ 100
July 1998—June 1999	3,600
July 1999—August 1999	80
September 1999—June 2000	150

The city estimates that $30 will eventually have to be re-

funded, owing to taxpayer appeals as to the assessed valuation of their property and $70 will be uncollectible.

a. Prepare a journal entry that summarizes the city's property tax activity for the fiscal year ending June 30, 1999, based on:

   1. the modified accrual basis (i.e., currently accepted accounting principles)

   2. the full accrual basis (e.g., those under consideration)

b. Indicate the differences in amounts that would be reported on both the balance sheet and the statement of revenue, expenditures, and changes in fund balances on a full accrual basis?

c. Suppose that in the following year the tax levy and pattern of collections were identical to those of the previous year. What would now be the difference in amounts reported on the balance sheet and the statement of revenue, expenditures, and changes in fund balances on a full accrual basis?

4-3

This case is adapted from an actual dispute between a Community College system and the Government Finance Officers Association. The association denied the college its Certificate of Achievement For Excellence in Financial Reporting owing to what it said were violations of generally accepted accounting principles. It claimed that the college gave premature recognition to property tax revenues; the college insisted that its accounting was in accord with principles that are generally accepted.

Background

NCGA Interpretation No. 3, "Revenue Recognition—Property Taxes" (incorporated into the GASB's *Codification of Governmental Accounting and Financial Reporting Standards* in section P70) is silent as to what constitutes a due date. It provides that revenues from property taxes should be recognized in the fiscal period for which it was levied, provided the "available" criteria are met. As indicated in the text, *available* means "then due, or past due and receivable within the current period, and collected within the current period or expected to be collected soon enough thereafter to be used to pay liabilities of the current period. Such time thereafter should not exceed 60 days." But it provides no guidance as to what is meant by *due.*

The GFOA's *Governmental Accounting, Auditing and Financial Reporting* (GAAFR, 1994 edition) gives more specific guidance as to *due date,* but it does not have the authoritative standing of NCGA Interpretation No. 3, a GASB-endorsed pronouncement. GAAFR explains that "although the term 'due' is not defined in the authoritative literature, it is recommended that property taxes be considered due only as of the last day before interest or penalties begin to accrue. For example, if taxpayers are accorded an automatic 15-day 'grace period' before penalties or interest accrue, the 'due date' would be the last day of the grace period, rather than the date on which payment was originally requested." The GAAFR indicates in a footnote that its recommendation is based on Statement No. 11.

Issues

Waukesha County Technical College (WCTC) levies taxes in October of each year. The tax rate is based on its budget, which is implemented in July. The taxes are used to finance the budget of the then-current fiscal year, which extends from July 1 to June 30.

WCTC sends out its tax bills in December. It gives taxpayers a choice of two payment schedules. They can opt either to pay their entire obligation by the last day of February or to pay half by January 31 and half by July 31. They will be charged neither interest nor penalties as long as they make their payments on schedule. If they miss a scheduled payment, then interest and penalties will accrue from the previous January 31—not from the date of the missed payment. The tax bills clearly state (in bold type) that the total tax is due on January 31, even though taxpayers are permitted the installment option.

The recognition issue arises over the taxes that must be paid by July 31. The college recognizes taxes as revenues of the budget year ending the previous June 30, arguing that the taxes are due on January 31. If, however, July 31 is considered the due date, as the GFOA contends, then taxes collected in July must be accounted for as revenues of the year ending the following June 30, not that for which they were budgeted.

The issue is not trivial. For WCTC, July collections are a hefty 30 percent of its total levy. Moreover, the outcome of the dispute will affect not only WCTC but other Wisconsin Technical Colleges and school districts in Wisconsin, Ohio, and Illinois. These districts have tax calendars similar to those of WCTC, and many have comparable policies of revenue recognition.

a. Defend the position of the WCTC that taxes paid by July 31 should be considered revenues as of the fiscal year ending the previous June 30.

b. Defend the position of the GFOA that the taxes should be considered revenues of the following year.

4-4

Do current principles capture the economic essence of sales tax transactions?

A state imposes a sales tax of 6 percent. The state's counties are permitted to levy a tax of an additional 2 percent. The state administers the tax for the counties, forwarding the proceeds to the counties 15 days after they receive the proceeds from the merchants.

The state requires merchants to file a return and transmit collections either monthly, quarterly, or annually, depending on the amount of taxable sales made by the merchant. This problem pertains only to taxes that must be paid quarterly.

Merchants must file their returns and transmit their taxes within one month after the end of a quarter. The quarters are based on the calendar year. Thus, taxes for the quarter ending March 31 are due by April 30; those for the quarter ending June 30 are due by July 31.

The fiscal year of both the state and its counties ends on September 30.

For the quarter ending September 30, 1998, merchants collected and paid (in October) $300 million in taxes. Of these, 80 percent ($240 million) are applicable to the state; 2 percent ($6 million) are applicable to Cayoga County.

a. Prepare journal entries to summarize the state's sales tax activity for its share of taxes for the quarter ending September 30, 1998:
   1. based on currently accepted accounting principles
   2. on a full accrual basis

b. Prepare journal entries to summarize the county's sales tax activity for the quarter ending September 30, 1998:
   1. based on currently accepted accounting principles
   2. on a full accrual basis

Be concerned only with any entries that would affect the fiscal year ending September 30, 1998.

c. Some critics have charged that both current standards and the proposed full accrual standards allow for premature recognition of sales tax revenue. What do you think is the basis for their position? What arguments can be made in defense of both current and proposed practices?

4-5

Accounting for income taxes is especially difficult because the tax year may not coincide with the fiscal year.

A state's tax calendar with respect to individual income taxes is as follows:

• Employers must submit monthly withholdings from employees by the fifteenth day of the month following that for which the taxes were withheld.

• Individuals must file estimated returns and pay any tax due on April 15th, June 15, September 15, and December 31. The tax due on each date is one-quarter of the difference between what taxpayers estimate will be withheld from their salaries throughout the *calendar* year and the total estimated tax for the year.

• Individuals must file a return by April 15 of each year and must pay any remaining tax owed (or request a refund of any overpayments) from the previous *calendar* year.

The state is on an August 31 fiscal year. It issues its annual financial statements in November and uses October 31 as the cut-off date for all accruals.

The following data may be relevant to the amount of income tax revenue to be recognized during the state's fiscal year ending August 31, 1998 (all amounts in millions).

• From January 1, 1998, through August 31, 1998, the state receives withholding taxes applicable to calendar-year 1998 of $300.

• From September 1, 1998, through October 31, 1998, it receives withholdings (both late and on-time) of $25 applicable to August 1998.

- From September 1, 1997, through August 31, 1998, it receives $150 for the quarterly payments due September 15, 1997, through June 15, 1998.
- From September 1, 1998, through October 31, 1998, it receives $40 for the quarterly payments due on September 15, 1998. These taxes are not necessarily applicable to income earned by the end of the state's August 31, 1998, fiscal year.
- Between January 1, 1998, and August 31, 1998, it receives $1,200 in taxes for the 1997 calendar year that were due on April 15, 1998 (along with the 1997 tax returns). It estimates that an additional $20, reported on the April 15, 1998, tax returns will continue to trickle in by October 31, 1998.
- Owing to actual audits between April 15, 1998, and August 31, 1998, it collects an additional $12 in 1997 taxes. Moreover, it estimates that as the result of audits to be conducted in the future, it will collect an additional $6 in 1997 taxes.

Determine the amount of revenue that the state should recognize in its fiscal year ending August 31, 1998. The state accounts for income taxes on the modified accrual basis that incorporates the criteria that for revenues to be recognized they must be "measurable and available to finance expenditures of the current period." Assume that resources are considered available if collected within sixty days of the end of the fiscal year.

4-6

Recognition of revenues from license fees should take into account the purposes to which the fees will be put.

Kyle Township charges residents $100 per year to license household pets. As specified in a statute enacted in 1997, residents are required to purchase a license by October 1st of each year; the license covers the period October 1 through September 30.

The license fees are not refundable. The statute authorizing the fees specifically states that the revenues are to be used to support the township's animal control program. The program, which will be carried out throughout the year, is not expected to receive financial support from any other sources.

During the calendar year 1997 (which corresponds to the township's fiscal year), the township collected $36,000 in license fees for the 1997–98 licensing period.

a. Irrespective of official pronouncements, prepare what you consider to be appropriate entries to record the collection of cash and recognition of revenue in 1997. Justify your entries.

b. Suppose, alternatively, that the township does not carry out an animal control program and the fees are imposed strictly to generate revenues. Would you still make the same entries? Explain and justify.

c. Suppose, instead, that the township does carry out an animal control program. Although the license fee is

levied to help support the program, the revenues are not legally restricted for that purpose. Appropriations for the program may be influenced by the amount of fee revenues collected but not specifically tied to them. How would this circumstance affect the timing of revenue recognition in each of the above situations?

d. Comment briefly on the extent to which your entries are consistent with the GASB goal of reporting on budgetary compliance. The township budgets on a cash basis.

e. Comment briefly on whether your entries are consistent with:
   1. current generally accepted accounting principles
   2. the full accrual basis of accounting

4-7

Recognition of grant revenue may be affected by timing of both expenditures and reimbursements.

Manor County was awarded a state grant to establish evening athletic programs for at-risk youth. The $3.6 million award, to cover the *calendar* year 1998, was announced on November 15, 1997.

According to the terms of the grant, the county will be reimbursed for all qualifying costs within thirty days of when it files an appropriate request-for-reimbursement form.

During 1998 the county incurred $300,000 of costs each month. It filed a reimbursement claim shortly after the end of each month and received a reimbursement check approximately forty-five days after the end of the month in which it incurred the costs. Hence, it received twelve checks, the first on March 15, 1998, and the last on February 15, 1999.

The county operates on a fiscal year beginning October 1.

a. Prepare journal entries to summarize the county's grant-related activity for its fiscal year ending September 30, 1998.

b. Suppose, alternatively, that the state would reimburse the county for its costs in four installments, the first on June 30, 1998, and the last on March 31, 1999. What journal entry would you now make to recognize revenue? Explain.

4-8

The distinction between an entitlement and an expenditure-driven grant is not always obvious.

A city received two state grants in fiscal 1998. The first was an award for a maximum of $800,000, over a two-year period, to reimburse the city for 40 percent of specified costs incurred to operate a job opportunity program. During 1998, the city incurred allowable costs of $1.4 million (paid in cash) on the program. It was reimbursed for $500,000 and anticipates that it will receive the balance of what it is owed for 1998 early in fiscal 1999.

The second was an award of $600,000, also to cover a two-year period, to assist the city in administering a day-care program. Given only to selected cities, the award was based on several criteria, including quality of program and need for assistance. The amount was calculated as a percentage of the funds incurred by the city on the program in the prior year. Although the award must be spent on the day-care program, there are no specific matching requirements. During the year the city received the entire $600,000. It spent $550,000 (in cash) on the program.

a. Prepare entries to summarize the grant activity during 1998.

b. In a few sentences justify any differences in your approach to the two grants.

4-9

It's not always obvious whether governments should recognize grants and awards as revenues and expenditures.

For each of the following grants and awards, indicate whether the recipient government should recognize both revenues and expenditures. In a sentence or two, justify your response.

a. As the result of damaging floods, New York State receives disaster assistance relief that it must distribute in predetermined amounts to specified cities and towns. The governor had appealed to the president to declare the affected areas as being in a "state of emergency," but the state has no responsibility for monitoring how the funds are spent by the localities.

b. Cleveland receives money from the state to distribute to private health and welfare organizations within the city. The organizations applied for the funds directly to the state, but Cleveland is responsible for assuring that the approved programs are audited by independent CPAs.

c. Santa Fe serves as a representative of the state in administering the federal food stamp program. State governments, which participate in the program, receive stamps from the federal government. The federal government establishes eligibility requirements and the scale of benefits. The states, however, are responsible for selecting the recipients and distributing the stamps.

Some states involve both local governments and private institutions, such as banks and check-cashing outlets, in the administrative process. Under a contract with the state, Santa Fe, for example, checks the eligibility of stamp applicants and distributes the stamps to them. It serves all stamp applicants and recipients who come to its offices, irrespective of whether they are residents of the city. It receives an annual fee for its administrative services.

d. Arlington township is responsible for all costs of operating its volunteer fire department, with one exception. Its volunteer firefighters receive medical insurance

through a state program. The state pays 80 percent of their insurance premiums; they pay the rest. The township has no legal responsibility for providing insurance benefits to its firefighters. The insurance program was adopted by the state mainly to encourage citizens to join the volunteer departments.

4-10

Recording investments at fair-value may provide a measure of income similar to that if investments were stated at amortized historical cost, but is it consistent with the "measurable and available" criteria?

On August 2, thirty days prior to the end of its August 31 fiscal year, a government issues $3 million of general obligation bonds. The proceeds are being accounted for in a capital projects fund (a governmental fund). To earn a return on the bond proceeds before they have to be spent, the government invests $1 million in each of three financial instruments:

- a 60-day discount note with a face value of $1,010,000. The note pays no interest. The purchase price of the note is $1 million (a price that provides an annual yield of 6 percent—0.5 percent per month).

- a two-year note that pays interest at an annual rate of 6 percent. Both interest and principal are payable upon the maturity of the note.

- shares in an investment pool of government debt securities that provides a fixed return of 6 percent per year. The pool pays no dividends; the returns are reflected as an increase in the value of the shares.

a. Assuming no changes in prevailing interest rates between the date of purchase and year-end, what would you expect to be the market value of each of the three investments? Explain.

b. Prepare journal entries, as appropriate, to record investment income and changes in market values as of the year ending August 31.

c. Why might it be said that your entry for the two-year note is inconsistent with the general rule that revenues should be recognized only when they are "measurable" and "available?" Why might it also be argued that it is perfectly consistent with it?

4-11

Policy changes and other measures will have varying effects on reported revenues.

The board of trustees of an independent school district is contemplating several policy changes and other measures, all of which it intends to implement within the fiscal year that ends August 31, 1998. It requests your advice on how the changes would affect the reported general fund revenues. For each of the proposals, indicate the impact on revenues (or accounts comparable to revenues, such as proceeds from sale of fixed assets) and provide a brief explanation. Base your response on generally accepted accounting principles and practices of today.

a. Allow a two-month "grace period" for the payment of property taxes. District property taxes for the fiscal year ending August 31 are currently payable in ten installments. The final installment is due on July 31. The proposed change would give taxpayers a two-month grace period before interest and penalties are assessed. Thus, if the change were implemented, interest and penalties on the final installment, which is due on July 31, 1998, would begin to accrue on September 30, 1998, rather than on July 31. The district estimates that the change would affect $2 million in receipts.

b. Sell a parcel of land that the district purchased three years earlier for $450,000. Current market value is $500,000.

c. Request that a donation be advanced from September 1998 to August 1998. An alumnus of a district high school has promised to donate to the district laboratory equipment having a fair market value of $400,000 along with real estate having a fair market value of $300,000. The district intends to use the equipment in student labs. It plans to sell the real estate as soon as possible and, in fact, has an acceptable offer from a buyer.

d. Redeem the district's shares in the State School District Temporary Investment Fund, a state-managed investment pool in which school districts can temporarily invest cash. The shares were initially purchased for $98,000. Current redemption value is $101,000.

e. Sell parking permits to students in the semester prior to that for which they are applicable. The district sells parking permits to students at the beginning of the fall semester. The permits cover the period from September 1 through June 30. To reduce the start-of-year administrative burden upon staff, the district proposes to begin sale of the permits the previous spring. It estimates that in spring 1998 it will sell $6,000 of permits that would otherwise be sold the following September.

SOLUTION TO EXERCISE FOR REVIEW AND SELF-STUDY

1. Current practice:

Cash	$120,000	
Property taxes receivable	34,000	
Property tax revenue		$130,000
Deferred property tax revenue		20,000
Allowance for uncollectibles		4,000

To record property tax revenue

Revenue would be recognized on actual collections plus those of the sixty days following the end of the period; hence, $120,000 plus $10,000. The $20,000 of taxes expected to be collected in the following four months would be reported as deferred revenue.

Full accrual basis

Cash	$120,000	
Property taxes receivable	34,000	
Allowance for uncollectibles		$ 4,000
Property tax revenue		150,000

To record property tax revenue

Revenue would be recognized on all actual and anticipated collections.

2. Current practice:

Sales taxes receivable	$12,000	
Sales tax revenue		$12,000

To record sales taxes

Current standards direct that sales taxes should be accrued when measurable and available. Most states have interpreted this to allow for accrual of taxes that are collected by merchants prior to year-end but are payable to the state subsequent to year-end. If the state (in effect the town's agent) can recognize the taxes as revenue, then so can the town, as long as the taxes will be received in time (widely considered sixty days) to meet the expenditures of the year to which they are applicable.

Full accrual basis

Sales taxes are derived from the sales transaction. The sales transactions took place in September. Therefore the entire amount of revenue could be recognized irrespective of when the state collected the taxes or distributed them to the city.

3. Current practice:

Cash	$80	
Expenditures	320	
Grant revenues		$320
Deferred revenue		80

To record grant expenditures and revenues

The revenue from this *expenditure-driven* grant would be recognized as the related costs are incurred. Hence, only the funds that were expended can be recognized as revenue; the difference between the cash receipts ($400) and the expenditures ($320) must be reported as deferred revenue.

Full accrual basis

The government is eligible for the grant only as it makes the required expenditures. Therefore, as under current practices, it would recognize revenue only to the extent of the $320 actually expended.

4. Current practice:

Cash	$36	
Revenue from permits		$36

To recognize revenue from permits

Current standards indicate that miscellaneous revenues, such as those from permits, are best recognized as cash is received.

Full accrual basis

Cash	$36	
Deferred revenue		$24
Revenue from permits		12

To recognize revenue from permits

Although the GASB has not issued specific standards pertaining to licenses and permits, the full accrual accounting would suggest that when revenues from licenses and permits are tied to expenditures, a government should allocate them over the period covered by the license or permit. Therefore, the portion of the fees applicable to the four months (June through September) of the 1998 fiscal year should be recognized as revenue; the balance should be deferred.

5. **Current practice:**

Investment in notes	$500	
Cash		$500

To record investments

Investment in notes	$40	
Investment revenue		$40

To record the increase in the fair value of notes

The notes would be stated at fair value and the increase in value would be recognized as revenue.

Full accrual basis

No change would be required.

6. **Current practice:**

Cash	$135	
Proceeds from sale of land		$135

To record the sale of land

When it was acquired, the land would have been recorded in the *general fixed assets account group* at its fair market value. It would not be reported as an asset in the general fund. Therefore, in the general fund (or other governmental fund) the entire proceeds would be reflected as an increase in fund balance.

The following entry would remove the land from the general fixed assets account group:

Investment in fixed assets—donations	$119	
Land		$119

To remove the land from the general fixed assets account group

Full accrual basis

Cash	$135	
Donated land		$119
Gain on sale of land (revenue)		16

To record the sale of land

Under the full accrual basis, the donation land would have been recognized as revenue when the land was received. The increase in market value would be recognized at time of sale.

CHAPTER 5

Recognizing Expenditures in Governmental Funds

LEARNING OBJECTIVES

After studying this chapter you should understand:

- the modified accrual basis of accounting for expenditures and the rationale for differences between that basis and the full accrual basis
- how each of the following expenditures are accounted for:
  - wages and salaries
  - compensated absences
  - pensions
  - claims and judgments
  - acquisition and use of materials and supplies
- prepayments
- acquisition and use of fixed assets
- interest and principal on long-term debt
- the different types of interfund transfers and how they are reported
- what constitutes other financing sources and uses
- the overall rationale for, and limitations of, the current fund perspective statements

In the previous chapter we addressed the question of when revenue should be recognized in governmental funds. We turn now to the other side of the ledger and consider when expenditures should be recognized. We shall follow the same general pattern in that for each major expenditure we will first present the current standards of recognition—those consistent with a funds perspective and a modified accrual basis of accounting. Then we shall discuss the changes required by the entity-wide perspective's full accrual basis of accounting.

HOW IS THE ACCRUAL CONCEPT MODIFIED FOR EXPENDITURES?

THE DISTINCTION BETWEEN *EXPENDITURES* AND *EXPENSES*

Under the modified accrual basis of accounting governmental funds are concerned with **expenditures** rather than **expenses.** Expenditures are decreases in net financial resources, whereas expenses are reductions in overall net assets. Expenditures are generally recognized when resources are acquired; expenses when resources are consumed. Simply stated, owing to convention, expenditures are the expenses of governmental funds—those outflows that are recognized in accordance with the modified, as opposed to the full, accrual basis. Under the full accrual basis the expenditures would be termed *expenses*.

THE VIRTUES OF ACCRUAL ACCOUNTING AND THE RATIONALE FOR MODIFICATIONS

As pointed out in the previous chapter, the National Council on Governmental Accounting (NCGA, the GASB's predecessor) asserted that the *accrual* basis "is the superior method of accounting for the economic resources of any organization" because it "results in accounting measurements based on the substance of transactions and events, rather than merely when cash is received or disbursed, and thus enhances their relevance, neutrality, timeliness, completeness, and comparability." Accordingly, "use of the accrual basis to the fullest extent practicable is recommended in the government environment."[1]

We have seen that the accrual concept is applied differently in governmental funds than in businesses or in proprietary funds, which are accounted for as if they were businesses. Governmental accounting is heavily influenced by governmental budgeting. Owing to the importance of the budget, expenditures are closely tied to cash flows and near-cash flows rather than to flows of economic resources. In addition, governmental funds report only current, not long-term, liabilities. They focus on obligations that must be funded by current, not future, taxpayers.

Although the general principles of accrual accounting apply to governmental funds, there are key differences between how they are applied in governmental funds and in businesses. As suggested by the accompanying In Practice, the differences are consistent with the concept that under the modified accrual basis of accounting expenditures are decreases in net current financial resources—current assets less current liabilities. But unlike those in business, liabilities are considered current only when they must be liquidated with available financial resources—not as in businesses when they must be paid within a year.

In the context of governmental funds, **financial resources** refers to current financial resources—cash and other assets that are expected to be transformed into cash

---

[1] GASB *Codification*, Section 1600.103.

in the normal course of operations. *Net* financial resources refers, then, to financial resources less the *current* claims against them.

Just as governments have considerable flexibility in determining what constitutes a receivable (and hence, in recognizing revenue), they have similar leeway in establishing what constitutes a *current* liability (and correspondingly, in recognizing expenditures). To give symmetry to the accounting model, many governments use a cut-off period of sixty days—the same as is often used for receivables. Obligations expected to be paid within that period are considered current and hence recorded in governmental funds; those expected to be paid after that period are seen as noncurrent and thereby reported in the general long-term debt account group (the "list" of long-term obligations). Analogously, costs that have to be paid within sixty days are reported as expenditures (decreases in net financial resources) of the current period; those that do not are reported as expenditures of future periods. Other governments adopt a one-year cut-off (corresponding to the rule-of-thumb in business organizations).

Governments recognize expenditures when their expendable available financial resources are reduced. That is, they either make cash payments or obligate themselves to make cash payments shortly after the end of the period (and such payments are not offset by increases in other current assets or reductions in other short-term liabilities). Transactions that create only long-term obligations are not recognized as expenditures of a current period. There are exceptions, however. As discussed later in the section pertaining to fixed assets, expenditures are also recognized when acquisitions of long-lived assets are financed with installment debt and capital leases.

POSSIBLE DIFFERENCES UNDER ENTITY-WIDE (FULL ACCRUAL) STATEMENTS

The GASB's proposed entity-wide statements provide for a measurement focus upon, and balance-sheet recognition of, all economic resources, including fixed assets and long-term obligations. Correspondingly, they should be on a full accrual basis.

As indicated in the previous chapter, the GASB has proposed that in their entity-wide statements governments should apply FASB pronouncements unless they specifically conflict with those of GASB. In that chapter, we encountered numerous issues as to how to adapt the full accrual basis of accounting to revenues that are unique to governments. In this chapter, we shall face far fewer implementation problems, as most government expenditures are similar to those of businesses.

HOW SHOULD WAGES AND SALARIES BE ACCOUNTED FOR?

Wages and salaries may be earned in one fiscal year but paid in the next. Most governments pay their employees periodically—on a specified day of a week or month. Whenever the end of a pay period or the pay date does not coincide with the end of the fiscal year, then the government must carry over wages earned in one year until the next. Therefore, the question arises as to whether the wages and salaries should be reported as expenditures in the period earned or paid.

EXAMPLE   *Wages and Salaries*

A city pays its employees for the two-week period ending December 27, 1997, on January 2, 1998. The portion of the payroll applicable to December 1997 is $40 million, an amount included in the city's 1997 budget.

Current Standards

The GASB *Codification* does not specially address wages and salaries. Hence, the general principles of modified accrual accounting apply. Wages and salaries should be recognized in the period in which the employees earn their wages and salaries, as long as the government's obligation will be liquidated with expendable available financial resources.

In the example, the employees will be paid within days of year-end and with resources budgeted for 1997 expenditures—resources that would generally be assumed to be available and expendable. Thus (ignoring the usual payroll-related taxes, withholdings, and benefits):

Payroll expenditures	$40	
Accrued wages and salaries		$40
To record the December payroll (in 1997)		

The entries in this chapter will designate an **object** classfication (such as payroll, insurance, supplies, etc.). Alternatively, they could have designated an *organizational unit* (such as police department, fire department, sanitation department) or a *function or program* (such as public safety, general government, culture and recreation). Although the financial statements of most governments report expenditures by organizational unit, function or program, the expenditures are typically charged initially to an object account.

POSSIBLE DIFFERENCES UNDER ENTITY-WIDE (FULL ACCRUAL) STATEMENTS

Wages and salaries are already recognized on an accrual basis; no change would be required by a shift to a full accrual basis. The GASB has not provided any special guidance on how to account for wages and salaries.

HOW SHOULD COMPENSATED ABSENCES BE ACCOUNTED FOR?

Governments compensate employees for time not worked for a variety of reasons: vacations, holidays, sick leave, sabbatical leave, jury duty, and military reserve. In concept, the accounting issues are similar to those of wages and salaries earned in one period but paid in another. But there are differences as well. Most significantly, compensated absences are earned in one period, but they may not be paid until several periods later. Hence, the liability cannot be considered current. In addition, the amount of compensation to be paid is not always certain. First, some employees may leave the organization before they take all the time-off to which they are entitled. Second, the amount of compensation is almost always based on the employee's wage or salary rate in effect when the time off is taken, not when it is earned.

IN PRACTICE

WHY DO GOVERNMENT ACCOUNTANTS GO 'ROUND IN CIRCLES?

Standard-setting bodies have not yet explicitly defined *current liability*, thereby leaving open the meaning of *net financial resources* and, in turn, of *decreases in net financial resources* (i.e., expenditures).

In its discussion of long-term liabilities, the **Codification of Governmental Accounting and Financial Reporting Standards** implies that current liabilities consist only of obligations requiring "current appropriation and expenditure of governmental fund resources." It states:

> Further, just as general fixed assets do not represent financial resources available for appropriation and expenditure, the unmatured principal of general long-term debt does not require current appropriation and expenditure of governmental fund financial resources. To include it as a fund liability would be misleading and dysfunctional to the current period management control (for example, budgeting) and accountability functions. (*Codification*, Section 1500.104)

In a discussion of compensated absences, it further reinforces this concept of a governmental fund liability as an obligation to be paid out of resources that are available for expenditure:

> In governmental funds, liabilities usually are not considered current until they are normally expected to be liquidated with *expendable available financial resources*. (emphasis added, *Codification*, Section C.60.104).

The guidance may seem straightforward, but in fact is circular. A governmental fund liability is a liability that will be liquidated with "expendable available financial resources." What then are *expendable available financial resources*? As discussed in the previous chapter, *available* means "collectible within the current period or soon enough thereafter to be used to pay liabilities of the current period." Thus, *current* (i.e., governmental fund) liabilities are defined in terms of "available financial resources" and "available financial resources" in terms of current liabilities.

ACCOUNTING FOR VACATIONS

As in the private sector, government employees are almost always granted paid vacation after completing a specified period of service. The number of vacation days generally varies with years of employment. While on vacation, employees are paid at their current wage rate, irrespective of when they earned their vacation. From their perspective, the paycheck they receive for vacation days is usually indistinguishable from that received for working days. Employers, however, usually charge the expenditure to a vacation pay account instead of their standard wages or salary account.

EXAMPLE   *Vacation Leave*

City employees earn $8 million in vacation leave. Of this amount, they are paid $6 million in 1997 and defer the balance until future years. The leave *vests* (i.e., employees are legally entitled to it, even if they resign or are discharged) and can be taken any time up to retirement or as additional compensation at the time of retirement.

Current Standards

Current standards state that vacation leave and comparable compensated absences should be accrued as a *liability* as the benefits are earned by the employees if *both* of the following conditions are met:

- The employees' rights to receive compensation are attributable to services already rendered.
- It is probable that the employer will compensate the employees for the benefits through paid time off or some other means, such as cash payments at termination or retirement.

The compensation should be based on the wage or salary rates in effect at the balance sheet date, and employers should adjust for benefits that are expected to lapse.[2]

Although this guidance may appear to sanction accrual of vacation pay, there is a catch. The pronouncement goes on to explain that, in governmental funds, the accounting should be consistent with the modified accrual basis of accounting. That is, "the amount of the compensated absences recognized as expenditures in these funds should be the net amount accrued during the year that normally would be liquidated with *expendable available financial resources* (emphasis added)." The balance of the compensation should be reported in the general long-term debt account group (GLTDAG).

The following entry, in the general fund or other appropriate governmental fund, would give effect to the GASB standard:

Vacation pay expenditure	$6	
Cash (or wages payable)		$6
To record vacation pay		

The $2 million deferred until future periods should not be recognized as either an expenditure or a liability in the governmental fund. Instead, it should be reported in the GLTDAG:

Amount to be provided for vacation pay	$2	
Liability for vacation pay		$2
To record long-term liability for vacation pay (GLTDAG)		

The deferred amount should, of course, be recognized in the general fund as an expenditure in the years the vacations are taken and paid for.

---

[2] *Codification*, Section C.60.104.

> ## POSSIBLE DIFFERENCES UNDER ENTITY-WIDE (FULL ACCRUAL) STATEMENTS
>
> Consistent with the accrual concept as applied in the FASB model, the proposed entity-wide statements provide for balance sheet recognition of long-term liabilities. Accordingly, the "standard" accrual entry would be appropriate:
>
> | | | |
> |---|---|---|
> | Vacation pay expense | $8 | |
> | Cash (or wages payable) | | $6 |
> | Accrued vacation pay | | $2 |
> | *To record vacation pay* | | |

ACCOUNTING FOR SICK LEAVE

It might appear as if sick leave is a compensated absence with characteristics similar to those of vacation leave and should, therefore, be accounted for in the same way. However, there is at least one critical distinction between the two types of leave. Vacation leave, along with most other types of paid time off, is within the control of the employee or the employer. Separately or together, for example, they decide when the employee will take a vacation or a paid holiday. Sick leave, by contrast, is beyond the control of both the employer and the employee.

In the public sector, sick leave most commonly accumulates, but either a portion or none of it vests. That is, employees can store sick days that they don't take in a particular year until they need it. However, if they resign or are terminated, they are not entitled to compensation for all of their unused leave.

EXAMPLE   *Sick Leave*

A city allows employees one day of sick leave a month and permits them to accumulate any sick leave that they do not take. If they terminate after at least ten years of service, they will be paid for unused sick leave up to thirty days. In 1999, employees earned $12 million of sick leave that they did not take during the year. The city estimates that of this amount $8 million will be paid to employees in future years as sick leave, $1 million will be paid to ten-year employees upon their termination, and $3 million will not be paid.

Current Standards

Current standards state that sick leave should be recognized as a liability only insofar as "it is probable that the employer will compensate the employees for the benefits through cash payments *conditioned on the employees' termination or retirement ('termination benefits')*" (emphasis added). In other words, sick leave should be recorded only to the extent that it will *not be paid to employees who are sick*. Instead, it should be recorded only when expected to be paid to employees upon their discharge, resignation, or retirement.[3]

---

[3] *Codification*, Section C.60.105. This section incorporates the guidance of GASB Statement No. 16, *Accounting for Compensated Absences*, issued in 1992.

The standards are grounded in the rationale that sick leave, other than the portion that vests, is contingent upon an employee getting sick. The key economic event, therefore, is not the employee's service, but rather his or her illness.[4]

In the example, therefore, the city would recognize a liability only for the $1 million to be paid in termination benefits.[5] However, as with vacation pay, only the portion of the liability expected to be liquidated with expendable available financial resources may be recorded in a governmental fund. Assuming, therefore, that none of the termination benefits will be paid with funds budgeted for the current year, no entry is required in the general or other governmental fund. The obligation would be recognized only in the GLTDAG:

Amount to be provided for sick pay termination benefits	$1	
Liability for sick pay termination benefits		$1

To record sick pay termination benefits (GLTDAG)

POSSIBLE DIFFERENCES UNDER ENTITY-WIDE (FULL ACCRUAL) STATEMENTS

Recognition of sick leave on a full accrual basis would not affect the measurement of the obligation, only where and when it is reported. As with vacation pay, both the expense and the obligation would be reported on the entity-wide financial statements in the period the sick leave is earned. Thus,

Sick leave termination benefit expense	$1	
Accrued sick leave		$1

To record sick leave termination benefits

ACCOUNTING FOR SABBATICAL LEAVE

Government entities, mainly colleges, universities, and public schools, may offer employees sabbatical leaves. After a specified term of service, commonly seven years, employees (usually teachers) may be granted a paid leave of either a semester or an academic year.

As with sick leave, sabbatical leaves may appear to be similar to vacations and should be accounted for as such. Few teachers, however, perceive them as a time for rest and relaxation. Vacations are provided as a fringe benefit in lieu of salaries and wages. They are compensation for service already rendered. Sabbaticals, by comparison, are typically offered to benefit both the employee and the employer in the fu-

---

[4] FASB Statement No. 43, *Accounting for Compensated Absences*, draws a similar distinction between sick leave and other types of compensated absences. Whereas employers are required to accrue the costs of other types of compensated absences, they are not required to accrue a liability for nonvesting sick leave.

[5] The *Codification* provides detailed guidance as to how governmental entities should estimate the amounts to be paid upon termination.

ture, not the past. Employees are commonly required to perform research or public service, to take courses, or to engage in other activities that will enhance their job-related abilities.

The accounting issue relating to sabbaticals is when should the employer should first recognize the sabbatical costs. There are three possibilities:

- as they are earned by the employee in the period leading up to the leave
- over the course of the leave
- over the years to be benefited from the leave (e.g., from the end of one leave until the start of the next)

EXAMPLE *Sabbatical Leave*

A public university grants faculty members a one-year leave after each seven years of service to engage in research, further study, or other authorized activities. In a particular year it paid $2 million to faculty on leave. In addition, it estimated that faculty "earned" $2.4 million toward leaves they are likely to take in the future.

Current Standards

Current standards prescribe that the accounting for sabbatical leave depends on the purpose of the leave. If the leave is to provide employees with relief from their normal duties so they can perform research, obtain additional training, or engage in other activities that would "enhance the reputation or otherwise benefit the employer," then the sabbatical should be accounted for in the period the leave is taken. No liability should be accrued in advance of the leave. If, however, the leave is for "compensated unrestricted time off," then the government should accrue a liability during the period that the leave is earned.[6]

In the example, the sabbatical leaves are restricted to approved activities. Therefore, they should be accounted for during the period of the leave; the university need not accrue amounts expected to be paid in the future. Only the amounts actually paid to employees on leave should be recorded as an expenditure:

Sabbatical leave expenditure	$2	
Cash (or salaries payable)		$2
To record the salaries of faculty on sabbatical		

If, by contrast, the leave were unrestricted as to purpose and a liability must be accrued in advance, then, as with other compensated absences, only the portion expected to be liquidated with expendable available resources would be reported in a governmental fund. The balance of the liability would be recorded in the GLTDAG.

---

[6] *Codification*, Section C.60.106.

The accounting for compensated absences, including vacation pay, sick leave, and miscellaneous leave, represents the *first* major difference between how the accrual basis is applied in governmental funds and businesses.

POSSIBLE DIFFERENCES UNDER ENTITY-WIDE (FULL ACCRUAL) STATEMENTS

As with other compensated absences, the main difference under a full accrual basis would be that the proportionate share of the leave to be accrued in advance would be recognized as an expense when earned, not paid. Thus:

Sabbatical leave expense	$2.4	
Accrued sabbatical leave		$2.4

To record the sabbatical leave earned by faculty

In addition, the standard entry would be required to record the amount paid in the current year:

Accrued sabbatical leave	$2.0	
Cash (or salaries payable)		$2.0

To record amount paid to teachers currently on leave (assuming leave-pay was previously accrued as it was earned)

The switch to the full accrual basis would not affect the criteria as to whether the sabbatical costs should first be recognized prior to, or during, the leave.

HOW SHOULD PENSIONS BE ACCOUNTED FOR?

Pensions are sums of money paid to retired or disabled employees owing to their years of employment. Under a typical plan, an employer makes a series of contributions to a special fund over the working lives of its employees. Under some plans the employees also contribute.

Calculating the employer contribution to the plan is necessarily complex and based on a number of estimates such as employee life expectancy, employee turnover, and anticipated earnings of fund investments. The issue of how to compute the required annual contribution and the related question of how to measure and report a pension plan's actuarial liability will be addressed in Chapter 11, which deals with fiduciary funds.

In this chapter, we address the relatively straightforward concern of how a *governmental* fund should report the expenditure for its required annual contribution, assuming that the contribution has been properly calculated. In its simplest form, the required annual contribution is the share of the pension costs attributable to a particular period (i.e., the pension benefits earned by the employees in that period). If the government makes its required contribution in full, the amount to be reported as an expenditure is obvious; it would be the amount of the contribution. But what if it pays into the pension fund only a portion, or none, of the required contribution? Should the expenditure be the required contribution, which is indicative of the economic value of the pension benefits provided to the employees? Or should it be merely the actual payment, which is likely to be indicative of the amount budgeted for pension costs?

EXAMPLE *Pension Contributions*

A city is informed by its actuary that it should contribute $55 million to its pension fund, an amount calculated in accordance with generally accepted accounting and actuarial principles. It elects, however, to contribute only $45 million.

Current Standards

Current standards for pensions, as set forth in GASB Statement No. 27, *Accounting for Pensions by State and Local Governmental Employers*, are consistent with those for other compensated absences. The expenditure should be the amount that will be liquidated with expendable available financial resources.

Although, in the example, the economic cost of providing employees with pension benefits would be $55 million, the city would report an expenditure of only $45 million. The balance would be reported as a liability, but only in the GLTDAG, not in a governmental fund. Thus, the following entry would be required in the general or other appropriate governmental fund:

Pension expenditure	$45	
Cash (or current pension liability)		$45
To record the pension expenditure		

And, in the GLTDAG:

Amount to be provided for pensions	$10	
Pension liability		$10
To record the pension liability (GLTDAG)		

Pension accounting represents the *second* difference between how the accrual concept is applied in governmental funds and in businesses.

POSSIBLE DIFFERENCES UNDER ENTITY-WIDE (FULL ACCRUAL) STATEMENTS

Consistent with the FASB approach to pension accounting, in their entity-wide statements governments should report as their pension expense their required annual contribution—the amount representative of the economic cost—not an amount based on the government's predilection to contribute. This approach also conforms to that directed by Statement No. 27 as it applies to proprietary funds, which are currently accounted for on a full accrual basis. Thus:

Pension expense	$55	
Cash (or current pension liability)		$45
Pension liability		10
To record the pension expense and liability		

How should claims and judgments be accounted for?

Governments face many types of claims and judgments. Common examples include those arising from:

- injuries to employees (e.g., workers' compensation)
- negligence of government employees (e.g., medical malpractice in city hospitals, failure to properly repair streets, auto accidents, wrongful arrests)
- contractual disputes with suppliers
- employment practices (e.g., civil rights violations, sexual harassment, wrongful discharge)

As in the private sector, the key accounting questions relating to claims and judgments are when and in what amounts expenditures and liabilities should be reported. These questions arise, first because of the considerable length of time between when an alleged wrong takes place and when the claim is ultimately resolved and, second, because of the uncertainties as to the likelihood and dollar amount of a required payment.

In governmental funds, the major constraint in accounting for claims and judgments is identical to that faced in accounting for compensated absences. The event causing the claim or judgment usually precedes by one or more years the actual disbursement of financial resources. Yet, the current accounting model has no place on the balance sheet for long-term obligations.

EXAMPLE   *Claims and Judgments*

A county is sued for personal injuries resulting from negligence on the part of a road maintenance crew. The county attorney estimates that the case will ultimately be settled for $400,000, but that the slow pace of the judicial process indicates it will be at least five years until any required payment must be made. Inasmuch as the county uses a discount rate of 10 percent to evaluate all long-term projects, officials determine the "present value" of the eventual payment will likely be only $248,369.

Current Standards

Current standards for recognizing the liability for claims and judgments are drawn from FASB Statement No. 5, *Accounting for Contingencies.* A liability for claims and judgments should be recognized when information available before the issuance of financial statements indicates:

- it is probable that an asset has been impaired or a liability has been incurred at the date of the financial statements, *and*
- the amount of the loss can be reasonably estimated[7]

---

[7] *Codification*, Section C.50.110.

> However, as with compensated absences, only the portion of the total liability that would be paid with available financial resources would be reported in the governmental fund. The balance would be reported in the GLTDAG. Thus, the expenditure would be reported in the period that the liability is liquidated, not when the offending incident took place or a settlement was agreed upon or imposed. The standards make no mention of discounting. Therefore, the liability should be recorded at "face" rather than economic value.

In the example, the county estimates its liability to be $400,000, no portion of which is expected to be liquidated with available financial resources. Thus, no entry would be required in the general or other governmental fund. The liability would be entered in the GLTDAG:

Amount to be provided for claims and judgments	$400,000	
Liability for claims and judgments		$400,000
To record estimated cost of settling lawsuit (GLTDAG)		

The standards require that in the year the liability is first recognized, the following information be reported either on the face of the governmental fund statements or in explanatory notes:[8]

Expenditures:

Claims and judgments ($400,000 less $400,000 recorded as long-term obligations)	$0

The accounting for claims and judgments is the *third* difference in the application of the accrual concept.

POSSIBLE DIFFERENCES UNDER ENTITY-WIDE (FULL ACCRUAL) STATEMENTS

As with compensated absences and pensions, the full accrual basis would require that the expense be recognized at the time the loss liability first satisfies the criteria of FASB Statement No. 5. Thus:

Claims and judgments (expense)	$400,000	
Liability for claims and judgments		$400,000
To record estimated cost of settling lawsuit		

How should the acquisition and use of materials and supplies be accounted for?

The acquisition and use of materials and supplies (and the related issue of prepaid expenditures, to be discussed in the next section) present unique accounting problems

---

[8] *Codification*, Section C.50.101–C.50.118

in governmental funds. Materials and supplies (and prepaid items) are not strictly *expendable available financial resources*, in that they will neither be transformed into cash nor can they be used to satisfy governmental fund obligations. Nevertheless, having supplies on hand obviates the government from needing to purchase the items in the future. But if materials and supplies are not strictly expendable available financial resources, they are neither long-term nor fixed assets. Therefore, they do not qualify for recognition in the general fixed assets account group.

Unlike businesses, governments do not generally acquire inventories with the intention of either reselling them or using them in manufacturing processes. They do, however, maintain inventories of office supplies, road maintenance and construction materials, spare parts, and other materials needed to carry out day-to-day operations.

Among the primary issues pertaining to governmental fund materials and supplies are:

- the timing of the expenditure; specifically, should governmental funds recognize an expenditure when they *acquire*, *pay for*, or *use* the materials and supplies?

- the reporting of the asset; specifically, should inventory be reported as an asset, even though it is not strictly an expendable available financial resource?

EXAMPLE   *Supplies*

During the year a city purchases supplies that cost $3.5 million, pays for $3 million of the supplies, and uses $3.3 million of them. At the start of the year it had no inventory on hand. Hence, at year-end it has $0.2 million of supplies available for future use.

Current Standards

Current standards permit a choice. Government may recognize inventory items either when purchased (the *purchases* method) or when consumed (the *consumption* method). However, irrespective of which method is used, significant amounts of inventory should be reported on the balance sheet.[9] Governments may *not* account for inventories on a payment (cash) basis.

In the example, irrespective of whether it uses the purchases or the consumption method, the government would record the payment for the goods purchased with the conventional entry:

Accounts payable	$3.0	
Cash		$3.0
To record payment of amounts owed to suppliers		

The Purchases Method

Using the **purchases method**, a government would record the *purchase* of the inventory as an expenditure. Thus, in the example:

---

[9] *Codification*, Section 1600.123.

Supplies expenditure	$3.5	
Accounts payable		$3.5

To record the acquisition of supplies

Although the accounting is seemingly unambiguous, there's a complexity. Current standards state that significant amounts of inventory must be reported on the balance sheet. Metaphorically, they prescribe that governments must eat their cake yet have it too. By writing off the inventory upon acquisition, governments implicitly deny its existence. How, then, can governments account for the full amount of the inventory acquired as an expenditure, yet still report the unused inventory as an asset? Simple, according to current standards! Show the inventory as an asset, offset by a fund balance reserve. The following entry would do the trick:

Supplies inventory	$0.2	
Fund balance—reserve for supplies inventory		$0.2

To record the inventory on hand at year-end

The year-end entry increases reported assets and increases reserved fund balance. It has no impact on either expenditures or unreserved fund balance.

In subsequent years, the supplies inventory and the fund balance reserve would be adjusted to reflect the change in inventory during the year. If, at the conclusion of the following year, inventory on hand were only $150,000, then both supplies inventory and the reserve would be reduced by $50,000 (the difference between the $200,000 on hand at the end of the previous year and the $150,000 on hand at the end of the current year):

Fund balance—reserve for supplies inventory	$0.05	
Supplies inventory		$0.05

To adjust supplies inventory and related reserve to reflect inventory on hand (following year)

The Consumption Method

Using the consumption method, a government would account for inventory the same as would a business, with one additional, albeit optional, feature—the establishment of an inventory reserve. As it acquires inventory, the government would record it as an asset:

Supplies inventory	$3.5	
Accounts payable		$3.5

To record the acquisition of supplies

Then, as it uses the inventory, it would record an expenditure and reduce the balance in the inventory account:

Supplies expenditure	$3.3	
Supplies inventory		$3.3

To record the consumption of inventory

At year-end, the inventory balance would be $0.2 million—the amount of supplies on hand. The reported expenditure would be $3.3 million—the amount of supplies consumed.

Some accountants, however, see the inventory balance as tainted, for it is not an expendable available financial asset in the same way as are cash, investments, and receivables. They contend it should be offset, not by "fund balance—unreserved," but rather by "fund balance—reserve for inventories." Therefore, they would propose the following additional entry:

Fund balance—unreserved	$0.2	
Fund balance—reserve for inventories		$0.2

To reclassify fund balance to reflect year-end inventory

The reserve would indicate the portion of fund balance—that relating to the inventories—not available for future appropriation. The balance in the reserve would always equal the balance in inventory. Therefore, each year-end the government would adjust it to reflect any changes in inventory during the year.

Other accountants oppose establishing the reserve, arguing that the reserve adds confusion to an already complicated balance sheet. Current standards represent something of a compromise. They require governments that use the consumption method to establish the reserve only if they must maintain minimum amounts of inventory that are not available for use and therefore cannot be expended.[10] For most governments, therefore, the reserve is discretionary.

Inventory accounting, specifically the option to use the purchases method, is the *fourth* difference in how expenditures are accrued in governments and businesses.

POSSIBLE DIFFERENCES UNDER ENTITY-WIDE (FULL ACCRUAL) STATEMENTS

The GASB has not proposed or issued any pronouncements on inventory accounting in entity-wide statements. The purchases method, however, has no place GAAP as established by the FASB and would appear to be inconsistent with full accrual accounting. Hence, inventory should be accounted for on a consumption basis.

HOW SHOULD PREPAYMENTS BE ACCOUNTED FOR?
....

Prepaid expenditures are comparable economically to inventories. For example, a government purchases an insurance policy. As with materials and supplies, it will consume a portion in one period and the balance in the following periods. Or, by paying rent in one period, it acquires the right to use property in a subsequent period.

EXAMPLE   *Prepayments*
....

On September 1, 1999, a town purchases a two-year insurance policy for $60,000 (a cost of $2,500 per month).

---

[10] *Codification*, Section 2200.903.

Current Standards

Current standards offer governments the same choice in accounting for prepaid expenditures as they do for inventories: they may use either the purchases or the consumption method. "Expenditures for insurance and similar services extending over more than one accounting period need not be allocated between or among accounting periods" the *Codification* states. Instead, they "may be accounted for as expenditures of the period of acquisition."[11]

In contrast to the current standards for inventories, however, the *Codification* does *not* prescribe that governments using the *purchases* method report material amounts of prepayments on the balance sheet.

If the town were to use the *purchases* method, it would make the following entry in 1999:

Insurance expenditure	$60,000	
Cash (or accounts payable)		$60,000
To record purchase of a two-year insurance policy		

No additional entries would be required either in 1999 or the subsequent two years.

If the town were to use the *consumption* method, then it would make the following entry upon purchasing the insurance policy:

Prepaid insurance	$60,000	
Cash (or accounts payable)		$60,000
To record purchase of a two-year insurance policy		

Then, each month for the next two years (or at year-end by way of a summary entry) it would record both an expenditure and a reduction in the balance of prepaid insurance:

Insurance expenditure	$ 2,500	
Prepaid insurance		$ 2,500
To recognize insurance expenditure for one month		

Whereas under the purchases method, the town would recognize the full $60,000 as an expenditure in 1999, under the consumption method it would recognize only $10,000, the economic cost of four months of insurance.

Current Standards

Current standards do not distinguish between "current" and "long-term pre-payments." Thus, the unused portion of a three-year insurance policy would be reported as an asset the same as a one-year policy.

The accounting for prepayments, specifically the option to use the purchases method, is the *fifth* difference in the way in which expenditures are accounted for on the full accrual basis by businesses and by governments.

---

[11] *Codification*, Section 1600.123.

> ### POSSIBLE DIFFERENCES UNDER ENTITY-WIDE (FULL ACCRUAL) STATEMENTS
>
> The use of the purchases method in full accrual entity-wide statement is as inappropriate for prepayments as for inventories. Only the consumption method may be used.

HOW SHOULD FIXED ASSETS BE ACCOUNTED FOR?

Fixed assets provide services in periods beyond those in which they are acquired. In that regard, the accounting issues pertaining to fixed assets are comparable to those of each of the costs addressed so far in this chapter. A three-year insurance policy benefits a government over the period covered by the policy, irrespective of whether it is paid for before, during, or subsequent to the policy period. Similarly, a computer with a three-year useful life benefits the government over the same number of years regardless of the timing of payments.

In businesses, the cost of a fixed asset is recorded on the balance sheet when the asset is acquired. Over the asset's productive life, the cost is allocated, through the process of depreciation, to the periods in which it provides its benefits. In that way, the cost of the asset is matched to the revenues that it helps to generate.

Governmental funds could, of course, account for fixed assets in the same way as businesses. Many statement users and accountants have suggested that they should. As emphasized earlier, however, governmental accounting aims to provide information as to both the extent to which interperiod equity was achieved and whether resources were used in accordance with the entity's legally adopted budget. Governments must budget and appropriate the resources for fixed assets in the periods when they are to be paid for, not those in which they will be used. Therefore, accounting practices in which fixed asset expenditures are tied to services rather than to payments may not provide the sought-after budget-related information.

EXAMPLE *Fixed Assets*

A village purchases road maintenance equipment for $90,000 and pays for it at the time of acquisition. The equipment is expected to have a useful life of three years.

Current Standards

As pointed out in previous chapters, current standards preclude governments from reporting "general fixed assets" on governmental fund balance sheets.[12] Instead, the acquisition of fixed assets is reported as an expenditure in the period requiring the outflow of expendable available financial resources. According to the GASB *Codification:*

---

[12] General fixed assets are all fixed assets other than those reported in proprietary or fiduciary funds.

The primary purposes for governmental fund accounting are to reflect its revenues and expenditures—the sources and uses of its financial resources—and its assets, the related liabilities, and the net financial resources available for subsequent appropriation and expenditure. These objectives can most readily be achieved by excluding general fixed assets from the governmental fund accounts and recording them in a separate GFAAG (General Fixed Assets Account Group).[13]

Further, per the *Codification:*

Expenditures, not expenses, are measured in governmental fund accounting. To record depreciation expense in governmental funds would inappropriately mix two fundamentally different measurements—expenses and expenditures. General fixed asset acquisitions *require* the use of governmental fund resources and are recorded as expenditures. General fixed asset sales proceeds *provide* governmental fund financial resources. Depreciation expense is neither a source nor a use of governmental fund financial resources, and thus is not properly recorded in the accounts of such funds.[14]

Thus, in the example, the following entry would be appropriate when the assets are acquired:

Fixed assets—expenditure	$90,000	
Cash		$90,000
To record the acquisition of equipment		

As noted previously, the equipment would be recorded in the GFAAG:

Equipment	$90,000	
Investment in fixed assets		$90,000
To record the acquisition of equipment (GFAAG)		

Regardless of the argument as to whether fixed assets should, in fact, be depreciated (which will be taken up in Chapter 8), note an obvious inconsistency. Assume that the government *rented* equipment for a three-year period, paying the entire rental costs in advance. Then, if the rental equipment agreement qualified as an operating rather than a capital lease, the government would be permitted to account for the prepaid rent using the *consumption* method, thereby spreading the rent expenditure over the life of the rental agreement.

ACQUISITION OF FIXED ASSETS FINANCED WITH DEBT

The main accounting issue presented by the acquisition of fixed assets with debt is that the purchase of the asset is not coincident with the repayment of the debt—and hence, in effect, with the cash outflows required to obtain the asset.

When governments issue bonds to acquire assets, they often account for the debt proceeds in a capital projects fund. However, governments may also account for asset-related obligations in other governmental funds, such as the general fund or special revenues funds. The debt may take the form of conventional notes, installment notes, or capital leases. The accounting for capital projects funds will be discussed in Chapter 7. At this time it should be noted, however, that because capital projects funds are governmental funds, the same general principles of accounting apply.

---

[13] *Codification,* Section 1400.107.

[14] *Codification,* Section 1400.116.

EXAMPLE   *Installment Notes*

As in the previous example, a village purchases road maintenance equipment for $90,000. This time, however, the equipment is acquired on an installment basis with three annual installments of $36,190—the amount required to liquidate a loan of $90,000 over three periods at an interest rate of 10 percent.

Inasmuch as long-term obligations are not reported in governmental funds, current standards require that the proceeds of long-term debt be reflected as "other financing sources" in the recipient fund's operating statement.[15]

Thus, were the village to *borrow* $90,000 cash, the following entry would be appropriate in the governmental fund receiving the proceeds:

Cash	$90,000	
Other financing sources—installment		
note proceeds		$90,000
To record a loan of $90,000		

Were the government to use the proceeds to acquire a fixed asset, the governmental fund entry illustrated in the previous example would be appropriate:

Fixed assets—expenditure	$90,000	
Cash		$90,000
To record the acquisition of equipment		

In the example at hand, the government borrowed the purchase price, acquired the asset, but at the time of acquisition did not actually receive or pay cash. Hence, it could properly make the following combining entry that eliminates the debit and credit to cash:

Fixed assets—expenditure	$90,000	
Other financing sources—installment		
note proceeds		$90,000
To record the acquisition of equipment		

The related accounting question is how the loan repayment should be recorded. Specifically, to what type of account should the payment be charged, since no long-term liability is reported on the governmental fund balance sheet?

Current practice requires that the repayment be charged as an expenditure. Thus, the following entry would recognize the first payment of principal and interest:

Debt service expenditure (note principal)	$27,190	
Debt service expenditure (interest)	9,000	
Cash		$36,190
To record the first payment of installment note interest (10 percent of $90,000) and		
principal		

Subsequent payments would be recorded in the same way, with only the division of the payment between principal and interest changing from period to period. The equipment would be recorded in the GFAAG and the long-term debt in the GLTDAG.

The series of entries may be disconcerting in that it results in the asset being recorded as an expenditure twice—once when acquired and again as the loan is repaid. Nonetheless, the double-counting does not cause fund balance to be misstated, because the expenditure recorded upon acquisition of the asset is offset by "other financing sources"—a credit to fund balance that adds back the amount of the charge.

---

[15] *Codification*, Section 1800.110.

CAPITAL LEASES

A capital lease is the equivalent of a purchase-borrow transaction. In economic substance, the lessee (the party that will use the property) becomes the owner of the leased asset. The lessee treats the lease as a purchase of the asset. It makes periodic payments, each of which represents a partial repayment of the amount "borrowed" (the value of the property at the inception of the lease), plus interest. By contrast, an operating lease is a conventional rental arrangement under which the lessor remains the owner of the property both in legal form and in economic substance. FASB Statement No. 13, *Accounting for Leases* established criteria to distinguish between operating and capital leases. These criteria have been adopted by the GASB.

EXAMPLE *Capital Leases*

Instead of purchasing the $90,000 of equipment, the village leases it under an arrangement that satisfies the criteria of a capital lease. The term of the lease is three years. The village agrees to make three annual payments of $36,190, an amount that reflects interest at an annual rate of 10 percent.

Current standards specify that capital leases should be accounted for in the same manner as other forms of long-term debt.[16] Thus, in the example, the village would record the lease in the same way as it did the installment purchase, varying only the account descriptions:

Fixed assets—expenditure	$90,000	
Other financing sources—capital lease		$90,000

To record the acquisition of equipment under a capital lease

Debt service expenditure (lease principal)	$27,190	
Debt service expenditure (lease interest)	9,000	
Cash		$36,190

To record the first lease payment consisting of interest (10 percent of $90,000) and principal

As with the installment note, subsequent payments would necessitate a different division of the payment between principal and interest. The equipment would be recorded in the GFAAG and the debt principal ($90,000) in the GLTDAG.

The accounting for fixed assets, whether they are acquired for cash or paid for over time, is the *sixth* difference between expenditure accruals in businesses and governments. The GASB *Codification* notes that "depreciation and amortization are allocations, not accruals, and that 'accrual' in a governmental fund accounting context does not mean that depreciation, amortization, and similar allocations should be recognized." Irrespective of whether depreciation is an allocation or an accrual, however, the practice of not recognizing depreciation is counter to the way the accrual method is applied in business accounting.[17]

---

[16] *Codification*, Section L20.

[17] *Codification*, Section 1600.101.

> ## Possible Differences Under Entity-Wide (Full Accrual) Statements
>
> The proposed entity-wide model requires that fixed assets be reported on the statement of net assets (a balance sheet) at historical cost, net of accumulated depreciation. Correspondingly, the statement of activities (a statement of revenues and expenses) would include a charge for the depreciation of the assets. The accounting for fixed assets will be discussed in greater detail in Chapter 8.

How should interest and principal on long-term debt be accounted for?

Interest on long-term debt is a major expenditure for many governments. Most typically, government debt takes the form of bonds, which pay interest twice per year. Many governments accumulate the resources to pay both the interest and principal on their debts in a debt service fund (a governmental fund). However, the original source of payments is likely to be either general revenues or revenues specially dedicated for debt service. As the scheduled payments from the debt service fund must be made, the government transfers the necessary cash from the general fund or a special revenue fund.

Long-term debts, as previously emphasized, are not recorded as liabilities in governmental funds; they are "listed" in the GLTDAG. When bonds or other forms of debt are issued, the increase in (debit to) cash is offset by a credit to "bond proceeds," an operating statement account, rather than to "bonds payable," a balance sheet account. Therefore, when the bonds are repaid the offset to cash cannot be to a liability account. Instead, it must be to an expenditure or comparable operating statement account.

The key accounting issues with regard to long-term debt interest and principal arise because debt service payments may extend beyond a fiscal year. A six-month interest payment may cover some months in one year and some in another. A principal repayment covers the entire time the debt has been outstanding. Should the expenditures be allocated proportionately among the years (i.e., accrued) or should they be recognized entirely in the year of payment?

In light of the position articulated in the *Codification* that the accrual basis "is the superior method of accounting for the economic resources of any organization," the answer may appear obvious—allocate proportionately among the years. But bear in mind that debt service involves large dollar amounts. Taxpayers obviously prefer to provide resources only as they are required to satisfy current obligations. Most governments budget (appropriate) resources for principal and interest only for the period in which they must make actual payments. They do not set aside resources for payments to be made in the future. Therefore, the goal of reporting on budgetary compliance, in contrast to that of reporting on interperiod equity, would suggest that the expenditures be recognized entirely in the year the payments are due.

EXAMPLE   *Long-Term Debt*

A state issues $100 million of twenty-year bonds on August 1, 1998, at an annual rate of 6 percent. Interest of $3 million per semiannual period is payable on January 31 and July 31. The bonds are sold for $89.3 million, a price that reflects an annual yield of 7 percent (semiannual yield of 3.5 percent). The first payment of the interest is due on January 31, 1999.

Current Standards

Current standards specify that neither interest nor principal on long-term debt should be accrued in advance of the year in which it is due. Both should be accrued only in the period in which they are due. Until then, they are not current liabilities; they will not require the liquidation of expendable available financial resources.

In the example, the government would make *no entry* in 1998 to accrue either interest or principal on the debt. It would not record an interest expenditure until January 31, 1999, when the first interest payment is due. The following entry would then be required in the fund out of which the payment was to be made:

Debt service, interest—expenditure	$ 3	
Matured interest payable		$ 3
To record obligation for interest due		

When the bonds mature in July 2018 the government would make a comparable entry to record the obligation for principal:

Debt service, principal—expenditure	$100	
Matured bonds payable		$100
To record obligation for matured bonds payable		

At that time, the debt would be removed from the GLTDAG.

ADVERSE CONSEQUENCES OF FOCUS ON CASH PAYMENTS

Consistent with the standards that neither interest nor principal should be accrued until due, current standards make no provision for recognizing and amortizing bond discounts or premiums. As a result, the reported interest expenditure fails to capture the true economic cost of using borrowed funds. Instead it indicates merely the required interest coupon payments. In the example, the state borrowed only $89.3 million (the amount of the proceeds), not $100 million (the face value). Its true economic cost of using the borrowed funds in the six months ending January 31, 1999, was $3.1 million ($89.3 million times the effective interest, or yield, rate of 3.5 percent per period), not $3.0 million (the required payment). Nevertheless, as illustrated, the state would record an interest expenditure equal to the $3.0 million required payment.

The failure of current standards to recognize premiums and discounts may not be particularly serious when the difference is small between a bond's coupon rate and yield rate. But when the difference is large, it results in financial statements that seriously distort borrowing costs. Consider an extreme case. A government issues $100 million in twenty-year **zero coupon bonds.** The bonds are sold for $25.26 million, a price that would provide an annual yield of 7 percent. As implied by their name, these bonds pay zero interest each period. Instead, they are sold at a deep discount, in this case a discount of $74.74 million. Upon maturity, the investor, who loaned the government $25.26 million, would receive $100 million. Inasmuch as $25.26 million is the present value of $100 million discounted at a rate of 3.5 percent for forty periods, the bonds would provide a return of 3.5 percent (compounded) per semiannual period.

Under current standards the government would record *no* interest or principal costs until the bonds mature. In the period of maturity it would recognize the entire $100 million as a debt service expenditure.

Current standards make one exception to the general rule that neither interest nor principal be accrued. If resources to service the debt are transferred from one fund to another in a current year for payment of principal and interest due early the next year, then both the expenditure and related liability *may* be (not *required* to be) recognized in the recipient fund. Suppose that in the example, in 1998 the general fund transferred to the debt service fund $2.5 million of the $3 million interest payment due on January 31, 1999. The debt service fund would, of course, recognize the cash received as an asset and would record an increase in fund balance. Per the standard, to avoid reporting a misleadingly high fund balance, the debt service fund would be permitted also to accrue the related interest expenditure. Thus:

ACCRUAL OF INTEREST AND PRINCIPAL WHEN RESOURCES ARE TRANSFERRED

Debt service, interest—expenditure	$2.5	
Accrued interest payable		$2.5

To accrue interest in the amount of resources received from the general fund

The accounting for interest and principal is the *seventh* difference in the application of the accrual concept.

POSSIBLE DIFFERENCES UNDER ENTITY-WIDE (FULL ACCRUAL) STATEMENTS

Just as the proposed entity-wide statement standards would require that long-lived assets be recorded at cost less an accumulated depreciation, they would require that long-term debt be reported at face value less any unamortized premiums or discounts. Thus, the state would record the issuance of the bonds as follows:

Cash	$ 89.3	
Discount on bonds payable	10.7	
Bonds payable		$100.0

To record the issuance of operating debt

Then as it pays interest, it would record the payment ($3.0 million), the interest expense (the yield rate times the net carrying value of the bonds), and the amortization of the premium or discount (the difference between the two). As of December 31, 1998, the end of the first period, in which no interest was yet paid, the following entry would be appropriate to accrue five months' interest:

Interest expenditure	$2.6	
Accrued interest payable		$2.5
Discount on bond payable		0.1

To accrue five months' interest (interest expenditure = ⅚ of the effective interest rate of 3.5 percent times the effective liability of $89.3 million; accrued interest payable = ⅚ of the required payment of $3.0 million; discount on bond payable = the difference between the two, i.e., ⅚ of the total amount of bond discount to be amortized at time of the first interest payment)

Long-term debt will be addressed in detail in Chapter 9.

HOW SHOULD INTERFUND TRANSACTIONS BE ACCOUNTED FOR?

As stressed in Chapter 2, each of a government's funds is an independent fiscal and accounting entity. When the focus is on individual funds, many types of transactions between funds create revenues and expenditures. Yet when the government is viewed as a whole, these transactions are nothing more than intragovernmental transfers. If certain types of transactions were classified as revenues of one fund and expenditures of another, then the revenues and the expenditures of the government as a whole would be overstated.

EXAMPLE #1   *Interfund Transactions*

A government transfers $3 million from its general fund to a debt service fund for payment of interest. When the debt service fund pays the interest, it will record the payment as an expenditure.

Should the general fund record the payment to the debt service fund as an expenditure and the debt service fund record the receipt as a revenue? As independent entities, both funds incur expenditures; the debt service fund also earns revenue. Yet if each fund recognizes an expenditure, the government as a whole would recognize the interest cost as an expenditure twice (once in the general fund when the resources are transferred to the debt service fund and again when the interest is paid out of the debt service fund).

EXAMPLE #2   *Interfund Transactions*

A government department, which is accounted for in the entity's general fund, acquires $30,000 of supplies from a supply center that is accounted for in an internal service fund.

The internal service fund will report the cost of the supplies "sold" as an expenditure. Should the general fund also report an expenditure? If it does not, then its reported expenditures—the measure of the cost of general government operations—would be less than if it had purchased the same supplies from outside vendors.

Current Standards

The *Codification* differentiates between two types of interfund transfers:

- *Residual equity transfers.* These are nonrecurring or nonroutine transfers of equity between funds. For example, the general fund may contribute resources to an internal service fund or an enterprise fund to provide an initial base of capital. Or, the funds may return all or a portion of the contributions. Also, upon being discontinued, a special revenue fund may transfer its remaining assets to the general fund.

- *Operating transfers.* These encompass all other interfund transfers between governmental funds and are usually classified as operating transfers because governments routinely make such transfers.

Both types of transfers should be reported apart from revenues and expenditures. Operating transfers should be reported on the governmental fund's operating statement in the section "other financing sources (uses)." Residual equity transfers should be shown as a direct addition to, or deduction from, beginning fund balance—that is, either on a separate schedule of changes in fund balance or on that portion of an operating statement that reconciles beginning and ending fund balances.

Current standards require that all interfund transactions be reported as *interfund transfers*, not revenues or expenditures, with two exceptions:

- *Quasi-external transactions.* These are transactions that would be treated as revenues or expenditures if they involved organizations *external* to the government unit. They include payments in lieu of taxes from an enterprise fund to the general fund, internal service fund charges to other funds, and routine contributions from the general fund to a pension fund.

- *Reimbursements.* These are transactions in which a fund that an expenditure should properly be charged to reimburses some other fund to which the expenditure was initially charged. For example, a special revenue fund might reimburse the general fund for an expenditure made on its behalf. The reimbursement should be recorded as an expenditure by the reimbursing fund and as a reduction in expenditures by the recipient fund.[18]

In the first example, the payment of interest by the general fund to the debt service fund does not satisfy the criteria for either of the two exceptions and would therefore be recorded by the general fund as an operating transfer, not an expenditure:

Operating transfer-out to debt service fund	$3	
Cash		$3
To record transfer from general fund to debt service fund		

---

[18] *Codification*, Section 1800.102–1800.107.

The debt service fund would make a corresponding entry to recognize the operating transfer-in.

Cash	$ 3	
Operating transfer-in from general fund		$ 3

To record transfer to debt service fund from the general fund

In the second example, by contrast, the payment by the general fund to the internal service fund for supplies would qualify as a quasi-external transaction and therefore would be reported in the general fund as an expenditure:

Supplies expenditure	$30,000	
Cash		$30,000

To record the "purchase" of supplies

The internal service fund would make a corresponding entry recognizing $30,000 in sales revenue.

Cash	$30,000	
Sales revenue		$30,000

To record the "sale" of supplies

POSSIBLE DIFFERENCES UNDER ENTITY-WIDE (FULL ACCRUAL) STATEMENTS

As implied by their title, entity-wide statements present revenues and expenditures from the perspective of the entity, not individual funds. Reported expenses would be those of the entity as a whole, not of individual funds. Interfund revenues and expenditures would be eliminated and double-counting thereby avoided.

WHAT CONSTITUTES OTHER FINANCING SOURCES AND USES?

Governmental funds receive or use resources from transactions that, under a full accrual basis, would affect long-term assets or liability accounts. For example, if a business issues long-term debt, it would establish a long-term liability. However, the measurement focus of governmental funds excludes both fixed assets and long-term liabilities. Therefore, resources received from the issuance of bonds cannot be recorded as liabilities. Although similar to revenues in that they increase fund balance, they lack the characteristics of conventional revenues in that they will need to be repaid. Similarly, the proceeds from the sale of equipment can neither reduce a reported asset nor be interpreted as a revenue.

Generally accepted accounting and reporting standards direct that certain resources flows that would otherwise affect long-term assets or liabilities be classified on statements of revenues, expenditures, and changes in fund balances as other financing sources and uses. The main types of other financing sources and uses are:

- proceeds of long-term debt
- proceeds from the sale of fixed assets
- present value of assets and liabilities created by capital leases
- payments to bond "escrow" agents who maintain accounts for the eventual re-payment of long-term obligations

Operating transfers to other funds are also reported under the heading "other financing sources and uses." Residual transfers, by contrast, because they do not involve ordinary operations, are typically shown below the line "excess of revenues and other financing sources over expenditures and other financing uses."

How should revenues, expenditures, and other financing sources and uses be reported?

Current Standards

Revenues, expenditures, and other financing sources and uses should be reported on a statement of operations. Depending on the level of reporting, the statement could combine either all funds (a *combined* statement) or selected funds (a *combining* statement) or present the data for an individual fund. The statement may take a variety of formats. It should, however, indicate the following:

- revenues
- expenditures
- excess of revenues over or under expenditures
- other financing sources and uses, including operating transfers
- excess of revenues and other sources over or under expenditures and other uses
- beginning fund balance
- residual transfers
- ending fund balance

Fort Worth's general fund operating statement is presented in Table 5–1.

POSSIBLE DIFFERENCES UNDER ENTITY-WIDE (FULL ACCRUAL) STATEMENTS

The proposed entity-wide statement of operations, renamed the **Statement of Activities,** differs dramatically from the conventional operating statements of both governments and businesses. Most prominently, the statement presents the *net cost* of each of the government's programs. The net cost of a program is its total expenses, less any revenues that can be directly associated with it. These

TABLE 5–1
City of Fort Worth

**Comparative Statements of Revenues, Expenditures
and Changes in Fund Balance
Years Ended September 30, 1996 and 1995
(000's omitted)**

	1996	1995
Revenues:		
General Property Taxes	$132,965	$127,287
Other Local Taxes	66,003	62,492
Charges for Services	12,950	12,232
Licenses and Permits	31,317	30,554
Fines and Forfeitures	9,470	7,818
Revenue from Use of Money and Property	9,198	8,868
Intergovernmental	1,190	1,853
Other	907	3,842
Total Revenues	264,000	254,946
Expenditures:		
General Administration	11,640	10,432
Public Safety	119,696	112,439
Transportation and Public Works	23,329	20,640
Parks and Community Services	16,974	14,930
Public Library	7,750	6,880
Public Health	5,603	5,233
Public Events and Facilities	9,416	7,320
Nondepartmental	14,122	12,776
Planning and Development	3,702	3,374
Fiscal Services	4,044	3,514
Housing	302	213
Claims and Premiums	0	1,110
Total Expenditures	216,578	198,861
Excess of Revenues Over Expenditures	47,422	56,085
Other Financing Sources (Uses):		
Operating Transfers In – Other Funds	12,765	3,048
Operating Transfers Out – Other Funds	(66,909)	(59,461)
Operating Transfers Out – Component Units	(210)	0
Total Other Financing Uses	(54,354)	(56,413)
Excess of Revenues and Other Financing Sources Under Expenditures and Other Financing Uses	(6,932)	(328)
Fund Balance, Beginning of Year, as Previously Reported	64,690	37,800
Restatement for Implementation of GASB No. 22	0	7,049
Fund Balance, Beginning of Year, as Restated	64,690	44,849
Residual Equity Transfer In	0	20,169
Fund Balance, End of Year	$57,758	$64,690

revenues would include fees and charges, grants and subsidies from other governments, and dedicated taxes. For example, a state law-enforcement grant would be deducted from public safety costs; an electric utility's customer charges would be deducted from its operating costs. Revenues that cannot be associated with specific programs are deducted from the net cost of the programs of the entity as a whole. These would include most of the revenues that would be accounted for in the general fund, since by definition general fund revenues are unrestricted.

The main virtue of this reporting format is that it is directly compatible with the financial reporting objective of providing enough information to determine whether current year revenues were sufficient to pay for current year services. In addition, because it aggregates costs by program it will help to facilitate both budgeting and evaluation. This new look was illustrated in Chapter 2, Table 2–7.

WHAT IS THE SIGNIFICANCE OF THE CURRENT FINANCIAL STATEMENTS?—AN OVERVIEW

The ultimate question faced by governmental fund financial statement readers is, "What does it all mean?" A governmental fund balance sheet presents the entity's resources at a particular point in time; its operating statement accounts for the net change in those resources during a particular period of time. All measurements, however, are in accord with GAAP.

As made apparent in this and the previous chapter, governmental fund revenues and expenditures would frequently not be determined on the same basis for purposes of budgeting as for financial reporting. Examples of significant differences include:

- for purposes of budgeting, governments may recognize taxes as revenues only as collected; in accord with GAAP, they must recognize them as revenues only when they are both measurable and available to finance expenditures of the fiscal period

- for purposes of budgeting, governments may recognize license fees as revenues as the licenses are issued; consistent with GAAP, they may allocate the revenues over the years covered by the license

- for purposes of budgeting, governments may account for wages and salaries on a cash basis; as required by GAAP, they must accrue compensation expenditures as long as the payments will be made with expendable available financial resources

- for purposes of budgeting, governments may account for supplies and prepayments on a cash basis; as permitted by GAAP, they may use the consumption method

Consequently, the reported revenues and expenditures, and the resultant surplus or deficit, may not be comparable with corresponding budgeted amounts.

Moreover, the balance sheet may not present a clear picture of either resources available for appropriation or the claims against those resources. It may not reflect taxes and other receivables that the government may be able to use to cover expenditures of the following and future years. Correspondingly, it may not show all of the claims against the fund's resources, such as those for deferred compensation, interest, and legal judgments. At the same time, however, some reported assets, such as prepaid amounts, might not be available for future appropriation. Therefore, the reported fund balance may not be representative of the net resources legally available for future appropriation.

The operating statement also cannot be counted on to reveal the true economic costs of government operations or the economic value of resources that it actually received or to which it became entitled during the year. Because they are based on modified rather than full accrual accounting, governmental fund operating statements fail to recognize both increases and decreases in such assets and liabilities as taxes and grants receivable, inventories and prepayments (if the purchases method is used), buildings and equipment, deferred compensation payable, and bonds payable. Correspondingly, the balance sheet cannot be relied upon to show the true economic value of all the assets available to the government and the claims against them.

The current standards of revenue and expense recognition satisfy both the interperiod equity and the budgetary compliance objectives of financial reporting, but only to a limited extent. The proposed entity-wide statements are intended to provide greater information on the economic costs of operations and on the economic value of resources. However, in the absence of other changes in principles, the fund perspective statements will continue to fall short of indicating budget-based revenues and expenditures and the resources that are legally available for appropriation.

The limitations of fund perspective statements, both current and proposed, do not, by themselves, imply criticisms of either the statements themselves or the rulemaking authorities responsible for them. As suggested in Chapter 1, it is questionable whether a single set of financial statements can satisfy each of the key accounting and reporting objectives. Both the strength and the weakness of current standards is that they represent a compromise among objectives.

IN PRACTICE

THE USEFULNESS OF REPORTED FUND BALANCE

A new member of the National Council on Governmental Accounting (the predecessor of the GASB) attended his first meeting of the standard-setting organization. In a morning session devoted to a proposed pronouncement, the discussion centered around the impact of the recommended standard, both on operating statement surplus or deficit and on fund balance.

At lunch, the new member asked others at his table, all of whom regularly utilized financial statements, what use they made of reported fund balance. All agreed they paid no attention to it. First, they said, the information is several months out of date by the time the financial statements are issued. Second, the reported fund balance fails to indicate the resources that are actually available to them for future appropriation.

SUMMARY

Rulemaking authorities assert that "use of the accrual basis to the fullest extent practicable is recommended in the government environment." But they have substantially modified the accrual basis from the way it is applied in businesses (and government proprietary funds).

As pointed out in the previous chapter, for revenues to be recognized, not only must a key underlying event take place, but also the resources to be received must be *measurable and available to finance expenditures of the fiscal period.*

In this chapter, we stressed that governmental fund expenditures are defined as "decreases in *net financial resources*" in contrast to *expenses*, which represent outflows or consumption of *overall net assets*. As a consequence, we identified seven differences in how the accrual concept is applied in governments as opposed to businesses:

- Vacations, sick leave, and other compensated absences are not accrued unless they will be liquidated with current financial resources.
- The reported pension expenditure includes only the governmental fund's actual contribution for the year, not, as in businesses, the actuarially required contribution.
- Claims and judgments are reported as expenditures only insofar as they will be paid out of current financial resources.
- Inventory may be accounted for using either a purchases or a consumption method, but significant amounts of inventory must be reported in the financial statements regardless of the accounting method used.
- Prepaid items may also be accounted for on either a purchases or a consumption basis, but significant amounts of prepayments need not necessarily be reported on the balance sheet.

- The costs of fixed assets are reported as expenditures when the assets are acquired; fixed assets are not depreciated.
- Repayment of long-term capital debt is reported as an expenditure as payments are made; interest on the debt is ordinarily not accrued.

The proposed entity-wide statements, in sharp contrast to the funds perspective statements, would be on a full accrual basis. All of the differences would be eliminated. Further, the proposed operating statement, called a *statement of activities*, would directly relate program revenues to program expenses. Funds perspective statement would continue to be part of the proposed model, albeit with modifications (to be discussed in Chapter 12).

In the following chapter we consider issues of revenue and expenditure recognition similar to those discussed in this and the preceding chapter. In that chapter, however, we address them in the context of not-for-profit entities rather than governments.

EXERCISE FOR REVIEW AND SELF-STUDY

For years beginning January 1, 1999, the City of Arbor Hills will finance its parks and recreation activities with a special property tax levy. Accordingly, it will account for resources related to parks and recreation in a special revenue fund.

a. Prepare journal entries to summarize the transactions that affected the special revenue fund in 1999.

1. The fund received $6 million from the city's general fund. The city had initially deposited the special parks and recreation fund tax levy in the general fund.

2. During the year the parks and recreation employees earned $4.5 million in wages and salaries. Of this amount, the city paid $4.1 million in 1999 and is to pay the balance early in 2000.

3. Parks and recreation employees earned $.26 million in vacation leave and were paid for $.20 million. The city estimates that it will pay the entire balance in the future.

4. The employees earned $0.17 million in sick leave but were paid for only $0.14 million. The leave accumulates but does not vest.

5. According to city actuaries, employees earned $.37 million in pensions. However, the city had budgeted only

$.30 million. During the year it contributed to its pension fund $.25 million and plans to contribute an additional $.05 million in early January 2000.

6. During 1999 the city ordered $.80 million in parks and recreation supplies. Of this amount, it received $.70 million, used $.55 million, and paid for $.50 million. The city uses the *purchases* method to account for supplies inventory.

7. In January 1999 the city purchased $1 million in parks and recreation equipment. It paid $.20 million in cash and gave an installment note for the balance. The first payment on the note ($.30 million plus interest of $0.05 million) is due on January 12, 2000.

b. Prepare a statement of revenues, expenditures, and changes in fund balance and a balance sheet for the Parks and Recreation Fund as of December 31, 1999.

c. Indicate any assets or liabilities that would be reported in other funds or account groups as a consequence of the transactions engaged in by the Parks and Recreation Fund.

QUESTIONS FOR REVIEW AND DISCUSSION

1. What is the distinction between *expenditures* and *expenses* as the terms are used in governmental accounting?

2. A government expects to pay a bill relating to its current

fiscal year sometime in the following year. An official of the government requests your advice as to whether the anticipated payment should be charged as an expenditure of the current or the following year. Specifically, he wants guidance on the number of days that distinguish a current from a noncurrent obligation. How would you respond?

3. Under pressure to balance their budgets, governments at all levels have resorted to fiscal gimmicks, such as delaying the wages and salaries of government employees from the last day of the month to the first day of the following month. In the year of the change they thereby had one fewer pay periods. How would the change affect the reported expenditures of a governmental fund under GAAP?

4. Currently accepted accounting standards require that, if specified conditions are satisfied, the costs of compensated absences be accrued as a liability as the benefits are earned by employees. Yet even if a government adheres to these standards it may not necessarily have to record a governmental-fund expenditure indicative of the amount accrued and the liability recognized. How can that be? Explain and justify.

5. A government permits its employees to accumulate all unused vacation days and sick leave. Whereas (in accord with current standards) it may have to "book" a liability for the unused vacation days, it may not have to record an obligation for the unused sick leave. Explain and justify the applicable standards.

6. A government accounts for inventory on the consumption basis. Why do some accountants believe that it should offset the year-end inventory balance with a fund balance reserve when no comparable reserve is required for cash, taxes receivable, or most other assets?

7. A government accounts for inventory on the purchases basis. Why *must* it offset its year-end inventory balance with a fund balance reserve?

8. Many accountants note that most governments' "bottom line" (i.e., its excess of revenues over expenditures) would not be greatly affected by a change in the accounting model requiring them to record and depreciate capital assets in governmental funds. That's because they typically finance capital acquisitions with long-term debt. Repayment occurs evenly over the term of the debt, which approximates the economic life of the asset. Assuming their assumption as to means of financing to be correct, does what they say make sense? Explain.

9. Governments are not required to accrue interest on long-term debt even if the interest is applicable to a current period and will be due the first day of the following year. Explain and justify the standards that permit this practice.

10. A school district accounts for its pension costs in a governmental fund. In a particular year the district's actuary calculates the district's required contribution for the year to be $18 million. The district, however, had only budgeted $15 million and chooses to contribute only what was budgeted. What should the district report as its pension expenditure for the year? Explain.

11. A city's electric utility transfers $40 million to its general fund. Of this amount, $30 million is a return of the general fund's initial contribution of "start-up capital." The balance is a payment in lieu of property taxes that a private utility operating in the city would have had to pay. Explain how each element of the transfer would be reported in the general fund's operating statement.

12. True or false? A government's unreserved general fund balance at year-end is ordinarily indicative of the amount that the government has available for appropriation in future years. Explain and provide an example to support your answer.

EXERCISES

....

5-1

The purchases method differs from the consumption method.

The Boyd School District began a recent fiscal year with $3,000 of supplies in stock. During its fiscal year, it engaged in the following transactions relating to supplies:

- It purchased supplies at a cost of $22,000.
- It paid for $19,000 of the supplies.
- It used $20,000 of the supplies and therefore had $5,000 in supplies inventory at year end.

The district establishes inventory reserves as appropriate.

a. Record the transactions, assuming that the district uses the purchases method.

b. Record the transactions, assuming that the district uses the consumption method.

c. Comment on any differences between the two as they would affect:
   1. the district's balance sheet
   2. its statement of revenues and expenditures

5-2

Irrespective of how fixed assets are acquired, they are recorded differently in governmental funds than in businesses.

In a recent year Ives Township acquired eight police cars at a total cost of $200,000. The vehicles are expected to have a useful life of four years.

a. Prepare the journal entries that the township would

make in its general fund in the year of acquisition, assuming that:

1. It paid for the cars in cash at the time of acquisition.
2. It leased the cars agreeing to make four equal payments of $63,095, starting in year of acquisition, an amount that represents the annuity required to liquidate a loan of $200,000 at 10 percent interest. The lease would satisfy the criteria necessary to be accounted for as a capital lease.
3. It issued $200,000 in installment notes to the car dealer, agreeing to repay them in four annual payments of $63,095, starting in year of acquisition.

b. Comment on any other entries in other funds or account groups that would be required.

5-3

Expenditures for vacations do not necessarily reflect the amounts the employees have earned.

In 1999, employees of Pecos River County earned $5 million in vacation pay. They were paid for $4.2 million but deferred taking the balance of their earned vacations until subsequent years. Also, employees were paid $.7 million for vacation earned in previous years.

a. Prepare journal entries in the general fund and any other appropriate funds or account groups to reflect the vacation pay earned in 1999.
b. Prepare journal entries in these same funds and account groups to reflect the payments for vacation days that had been earned in prior years.

5-4

Obligations for sick leave may not be recognized as liabilities if they are to be paid to employees who become ill.

Lemon County permits employees to accumulate any sick leave that they do not take. If employees do not use accumulated sick leave, then they will be paid for those days upon retirement or termination (up to a maximum of 45 days). In 1999 employees earned $4 million in sick leave. Of this amount they were paid $3.1 million. The county expects that they will be paid for $0.6 million as they take sick days in future years and for $0.2 million upon retirement or termination. The balance of $0.1 will not have to be paid.

a. Based on current standards, prepare journal entries in the general fund and any other appropriate funds to reflect the sick leave earned and paid for in 1999.
b. What is the rationale for the standards that underlie your entries?

5-5

The manner in which a transfer is accounted for depends on its nature.

Prepare general fund journal entries to record the following cash transfers that a city made from its general fund

to other funds. Be sure your entry reflects the nature of the transfer.

a. $4,000,000 to provide start-up capital to a newly established internal service fund that will account for the city's data processing activities
b. $50,000 to pay for data processing services provided by the data processing internal service fund
c. $38,000 to reimburse the capital projects fund for equipment rental costs that it incurred on behalf of activities accounted for in the general fund
d. $300,000 to pay the electric utility fund for four months of electric service
e. $600,000 to enable the debt service fund to make timely payments of principal and interest on outstanding general obligation debt

5-6

Prepayments may be accounted for on a purchases or consumption basis.

During its fiscal year ending June 30, 1998, the Parkville Independent School District enters into a two-year lease for office space covering the period May 1, 1998, through April 30, 2000. Annual rent is $60,000. The lease specifies that the entire rent for each year is to be paid, in advance, on May 1.

a. Prepare journal entries to record the lease payments and the lease expenditures for fiscal years ending June 30, 1998, 1999, and 2000, assuming that the district uses the consumption method.
b. Prepare journal entries to record the lease payments and the lease expenditures for the same years assuming that the district uses the purchases method.

5-7

Multiple Choice Questions from CPA Examinations

1. When a snowplow purchased by a governmental unit is received, it should be recorded in the general fund as a(an)
   a. encumbrance.
   b. expenditure.
   c. fixed asset.
   d. appropriation.
2. When a capital lease of a governmental unit represents the acquisition of a general fixed asset, the acquisition should be reflected as
   a. an expenditure but not as another financing source.
   b. another financing source but not as an expenditure.
   c. both an expenditure and another financing source.
   d. neither an expenditure nor another financing source.
3. Expenditures of a governmental unit for insurance extending over more than one accounting period
   a. must be accounted for as expenditures of the period of acquisition.
   b. must be accounted for as expenditures of the periods subsequent to acquisition.

c. must be allocated between or among accounting periods.

d. may be allocated between or among accounting periods or may be accounted for as expenditures of the period of acquisition.

4. Which of the following transactions is an expenditure of a governmental unit's general fund?
   a. contribution of enterprise fund capital by the general fund
   b. transfer from the general fund to a capital project fund
   c. operating subsidy transfer from the general fund to an enterprise fund
   d. routine employer contributions from the general fund to a pension trust fund

5. Operating transfers received by a governmental-type fund should be reported in the Statement of Revenues, Expenditures, and Changes in Fund Balance as
   a. an addition to contributed capital.
   b. an addition to retained earnings.
   c. an other financing source.
   d. a reimbursement.

Questions 6–10 are based on the following information. Rock County has acquired equipment through a noncancellable lease-purchase agreement dated December 31, 1996. This agreement requires no down payment and the following minimum lease payments:

December 31	Principal	Interest	Total
1997	$50,000	$15,000	$65,000
1998	50,000	10,000	60,000
1999	50,000	5,000	55,000

6. What account should be debited for $150,000 in the general fund at inception of the lease if the equipment is a general fixed asset and Rock does not use a capital projects fund?
   a. Other financing uses control
   b. Equipment
   c. Expenditures control
   d. Memorandum entry only

7. What account should be credited for $150,000 in the general fixed assets account group at inception of the lease if the equipment is a general fixed asset?
   a. Fund balance from capital lease transaction
   b. Other financing sources control—capital leases
   c. Expenditures control—capital leases
   d. Investment in general fixed assets—capital leases

8. What journal entry is required for $150,000 in the general long-term debt account group at inception of the lease if the lease payments are to be financed with general government resources?

Debit	*Credit*
a. Expenditures control	Other financing sources control
b. Other financing uses control	Expenditures control
c. Amount to be provided	Capital lease payable
d. Capital lease payable	Amount to be provided

9. If the lease payments are required to be made from a debt service fund, what account or accounts should be debited in the debt service fund for the December 31, 1997, lease payment of $65,000?

a. Expenditures control	$65,000
b. Other financing sources control	$50,000
Expenditures control	15,000
c. Amount to be provided	$50,000
Expenditures control	15,000
d. Expenditures control	$50,000
Amount to be provided	15,000

10. If the equipment is used in enterprise fund operations and the lease payments are to be financed with enterprise fund revenues, what account should be debited for $150,000 in the enterprise fund at inception of the lease?
    a. Expenses control
    b. Expenditures control
    c. Other financing sources control
    d. Equipment

PROBLEMS

Continuing Problem

Review the annual report that you obtained.

a. How does the government classify its expenditures, by function or by "object"?

b. For what purposes or activities are its major expenditures?

c. On what basis does the government account for its in-ventories (purchases or consumption)? Does it maintain a reserve for inventories?

d. On what basis does it account for insurance or other prepaid items? How can you tell?

e.. What is the nature of any transfers to or from the general fund?

f. Did any general fund expenditures exceed budgeted

amounts? If not, what is the most likely reason there were no unfavorable variances?

g. Explain the nature of any general fund balance sheet reserves related to expenditures.

h. Identify any notes that pertain to expenditures.

5-1

All paid time off may not be the same.

A city has adopted the following plan as to compensated time off:

- City employees are entitled to a specified number of days each year for holidays and vacation. The number depends on length of service (e.g., 20 days for employees with fewer than 5 years of service, 25 days for employees with between 5 and 10 years, 30 days for employees with over 10 years). Employees may accumulate up to forty days, which they can either carry over to future years or be compensated for upon termination.

- Employees are also entitled to seven sick days per year. They may carry over to future years up to sixty sick days. However, upon termination they can be paid for no more than twenty unused days.

During 1999 the city paid employees $4.2 million for holidays and vacations during the year. Of this amount, $0.4 million was for days carried over from previous years. In addition, employees earned $0.5 million in time off that they expect to use, and be paid for, in the future.

The city also paid $1.5 million in sick leave. Of this amount, $0.3 million was carried forward from previous years. The city estimates that employees earned an additional $0.8 million in unused sick leave. Of this, $0.5 million will eventually be paid for as time off, $0.2 million will be paid upon termination, and $0.1 million will lapse.

a. Prepare journal entries (in the general fund and any other appropriate funds or account groups) to record the holiday and vacation compensation.

b. Prepare journal entries (in the general fund and any other appropriate funds or account groups) to record the sick leave.

c. Justify any differences between the two sets of entries.

d. Suppose additionally that for the first time in 1999 the city offered up to eight weeks of paid maternity leave to eligible employees. In 1999 the city paid $0.2 million to employees on leave. In addition, employees earned an estimated $0.3 million in leave to be taken in the future. Consistent with your previous entries and justifications, explain how (and why) you would account for this leave (which is not specifically addressed by current GASB pronouncements).

5-2

The guidance on sabbatical programs leaves much to the judgment of school officials and their accountants.

The Allendale School District recently signed a contract with its teachers' union. The contract provides that all teachers will receive a one-semester sabbatical leave after seven continuous years of employment. The preamble to the contract provision stresses that the leave is intended for "renewal, additional education and academic enrichment." It provides examples of the types of activities it is intended to promote: formal post-baccalaureate courses, service with public or nonprofit organizations, and independent study and research.

The contract indicates that the leave is guaranteed to all teachers who satisfy the time in service and other specified criteria. Although teachers must apply for the leave, the district is required to approve it if the criteria are met. If a teacher opts not to take the leave after seven years, then he or she may accumulate it and either take it in the future or receive payment for it upon retirement. Teachers do not have to report to the school officials either on what they plan to accomplish while on leave or what they actually accomplished.

School officials estimate that the new sabbatical provision will add to its annual compensation costs approximately $3,000 per currently employed teacher per year (after taking account of teachers who will never satisfy the leave criteria). The district currently employs 2,500 teachers. The program will be phased in gradually; the first teachers will be eligible to take their leaves in four years.

Another school district, the Balcones West School District, which is not unionized, adopted a similar sabbatical program the same year. However, the Balcones West program does not guarantee teachers a leave. Instead they must be granted the leave on the basis of an interview and lengthy application, which includes a schedule of planned activities. Teachers who win approval for the leave must agree to work for the district for at least one year subsequent to the leave. If they fail to return to the district, they will be required to reimburse the district for salary and benefits received while on leave. Moreover, they must submit a written report to the district on their accomplishments during the leave.

Balcones West officials estimate that the cost of its leave will be approximately $2,000 per currently employed teacher per year. The district currently employs 1,000 teachers. As with the Allendale district, the program will be phased in gradually and the first teachers will be eligible for leaves in four years.

Prepare any entries that you would recommend that (1) the Allendale District and (2) the Balcones West District prepare in the first year after adopting their sabbatical programs. Specify the fund or account groups in which your entries would be made. Explain and justify your answers, citing relevant accounting standards.

5-3

Inventory transactions can be derived from year-end balances.

The following schedule indicates selected accounts from a city's *preclosing* 2000 and *postclosing* 1999 trial balances:

All of the amounts shown relate only to supplies. All purchases during the year were paid in cash.

a. Assume that the city uses the *consumption* method to account for supplies.
1. Reconstruct all journal entries relating to supplies that were made in 2000.
2. Make any additional entries that would be required at year-end 2000 to close the accounts.

b. Assume instead that the city uses the *purchases* method to account for supplies. However, assume also that the supplies inventory balance as reported on the preclos-

ing December 31, 2000, balance sheet is $54,000 (not $81,000 as shown in the schedule), even though actual supplies on hand are still $81,000. (This adjustment is necessary because under the purchases method inventory is maintained throughout the year at the beginning of year balance; it is adjusted only at year-end when the closing entries are made.)
1. Reconstruct all journal entries relating to supplies that were made in 2000.
2. Make any additional entries that would be required at year-end 2000 to close the accounts.

	December 31, 2000 (Preclosing)	December 31, 1999 (Postclosing)
Expenditures	$315,000	-------
Supplies Inventory	81,000	$54,000
Encumbrances	36,000	-------
Reserve for Encumbrances	45,000	9,000
Reserve for Supplies	54,000	54,000

5-4

Generally accepted accounting practices pertaining to inventories may not fulfill the objectives of financial reporting.

The following is an excerpt from a note to the financial statements of the city of Dallas:

> The city prepares its annual appropriated General Fund, Debt Service Fund and Proprietary operating funds budgets on a basis (budget basis) which differs from generally accepted accounting principles (GAAP basis). . . . The major differences between the budget and GAAP bases are that encumbrances are recorded as the equivalent of expenditures (budget) rather than a reservation of fund balance (GAAP) in the Governmental Funds.

The city accounts for inventories on the *purchases* basis. One of the city's departments, which is accounted for in the general fund, budgeted $195,000 in supplies expenditures for fiscal 1999. It began the 1999 fiscal year with $30,000 of supplies on hand. It also had $12,000 of supplies on order. During the year it ordered an additional $180,000 of supplies, received (and paid for in cash) $185,000 of supplies, and consumed $178,000 of supplies.

a. Prepare all journal entries, consistent with GAAP, including budgetary and encumbrance entries that the department should make in 1999.

b. Indicate the accounts and amounts related to supplies that the city would report on its year-end statement of operations and balance sheet.

c. By how much did the department over or underspend its supplies budget (on a budget basis)?

d. Comment on the extent to which the city's operating statement provides a basis to:
1. assess the "true" economic costs associated with supplies
2. determine whether the city adhered to budgetary spending mandates

e. Suppose that in the last quarter of the year, department officials realized that the department was about to overspend its supplies budget. They therefore ceased placing new orders for supplies. However, they imposed no restrictions on the use of supplies and thereby allowed the supplies inventory to decline to near zero.
1. What impact would these cost-cutting measures have on supplies expenditures as reported in an actual-to-budget comparison (on a budget basis)?
2. What impact would the year-end measures have on reported supplies expenditures (per GAAP)? Would your response be different if the city accounted for supplies on the consumption basis?

5-5

Can a government sell assets to itself to generate revenue?

A city is having fiscal problems in 1999. It expects to report a deficit in its general fund, the only fund that is statutorily required to be balanced.

To eliminate the anticipated deficit the city opts to "sell" its city hall—to itself—for $5 million. The city establishes a "fixed asset financing agency," which will be accounted for in a fund other than the general fund. It structures the transaction as follows:

- The financing agency pays the city $5 million in 1999 in exchange for "ownership" of city hall. The city hall has been carried as an asset in the city's general fixed asset account group.

- The agency acquires the necessary cash by issuing twenty-year, 6 percent, notes. The notes will be repaid in twenty annual installments of $435,920. The notes are guaranteed by the city at large. Hence, they are ultimately a liability of the general fund.

- The agency leases the city hall back to the city at large. Lease payments are to be paid out of general fund resources.

a. Prepare journal entries in the general fund to record the sale and concurrent lease-back of the city hall. The lease-back satisfies the criteria of a capital lease transaction.
b. Prepare journal entries in the general fund to record the first lease payment, which was made in 1999.
c. Will the transaction, in fact, reduce the 1999 anticipated fund deficit? Briefly justify the accounting principles that underlie this type of accounting.

5-6

How an acquisition is financed may dictate the annual reported expenditure.

The Mainor School District is about to establish a thirty-machine computer lab. It is considering six alternative means of acquiring and financing the machines:

1. Buy the machines outright; cost will be $60,000.
2. Buy the machines and finance them with a $60,000, three-year, 10 percent-interest term note. The district will repay the note and pay the entire interest with a single payment of $79,860 when the note matures.
3. Buy the machines and finance them with a $60,000, three-year, 10 percent-interest, *installment* note. The district will repay the note (plus interest) in three end-of-year installments of $24,127 each.
4. Lease the equipment under a standard operating lease. The district will make three end-of-year lease payments of $24,127 each.
5. Lease the equipment under an operating lease, but pre-pay the entire rent ($60,000) in advance.
6. Lease the equipment, but structure the lease so that it satisfies the criteria of a capital lease. The district will make three $24,127 end-of-year lease payments.

The district estimates that the equipment has a useful life of three years.

a. Prepare a table in which for each alternative you indicate the net expenditure that the district would record in its general fund in the year of purchase and the following two years. Ignore any expenditures that are offset by "other financing sources." For the fifth option (the operating lease with the rent paid in advance), assume first that the district accounts for prepayments on the purchases basis and then that it accounts for them on the consumption basis.
b. Determine the present value (using a discount rate of 10 percent) of the cash payments under each option.
c. Comment on any incentives that district officials might have either to spread out the payments over the three-year period (either by a lease or borrowing arrangement) or to postpone the full payment until the third year, rather than to pay for the computers entirely in the year of acquisition.
d. Suppose instead that the district accounts for the equipment in a proprietary fund and follows generally accepted accounting principles for businesses. Comment on any significant differences in how the six options would be accounted for in a proprietary fund instead of

a governmental fund. How would each year's reported expense be determined?

5-7

Accounting practices for interest expenditures may neither reflect actual economic costs nor mirror those for interest revenues.

A town plans to borrow about $10 million and is considering three alternatives. A town official requests your guidance on the economic cost of each of the arrangements and advice as to how they would affect the town's reported expenditures.

a. For each of the town's three alternatives, determine (1) What would be the town's economic cost of using the funds in the year ending December 31, 1999? and (2) What would be the amount of interest expenditure that the town would be required to report for the year ending December 31, 1999?
   1. The town would issue $10 million of twenty-year, 6 percent coupon bonds on September 1, 1999. The bonds would be issued at par. The town would be required to make its first interest payment of $300,000 on February 28, 2000.
   2. The town would issue $10 million of twenty-year, 6 percent bonds on July 1, 1999. The bonds would be sold for $9,552,293, a price that reflects an annual yield (effective interest rate) of 6.4 percent. The town would be required to make its first interest payment of $300,000 on December 31, 1999.
   3. The town would issue $32,071,355 in twenty-year zero coupon bonds on July 1, 1999. The bonds would be sold for $10 million, an amount that reflects an annual yield of 6 percent. The bonds require no payment of principal or interest until June 30, 2019.
b. Suppose that the town elects the first option and issues $10 million twenty-year, 6 percent coupon bonds at par on September 1, 1999. The town establishes a debt service fund to account for resources that it sets aside to pay principal and interest on the bonds. On December 31, 1999, the town transfers $200,000 from the general fund to the debt service fund to partially cover the first interest payment of $300,000 that is due on February 28, 2000.
   1. How would the transfer be reported in the general fund?
   2. How would the transfer be reported in the debt service fund? What options are available to the town to record 1999 interest in the debt service fund?
c. Suppose that the town borrowed $10 million on September 1, 1999 and temporarily invested the proceeds in two-year, 6 percent Treasury notes. The first payment of interest, $300,000, is payable on February 28, 2000.
   1. What would be the town's economic gain from investing the funds in the year ending December 31, 1999? Ignore borrowing costs.
   2. How much investment revenue should the town report for the year ending December 31, 1999? Assume there was no change in prevailing interest rates.

5-8

Not all interfund transactions are classified as "transfers."

The following information was abstracted from a note, headed "Interfund Transactions," to the financial statements of Independence, Missouri.

Interfund Charges for Support Services

Interfund charges for support services (which would otherwise be acquired from outsiders) and rent paid to the General Fund during fiscal 1993 were as follows:

	Interfund Charges	Rent
Tourism Fund	$ _____	$ 4,372
Power and Light Fund	1,285,011	230,933
Water Fund	522,244	36,883
Sanitary Sewer Fund	629,442	34,243
Central Garage Fund	152,330	3,411
	$2,589,027	$309,842

Rent charges, which consist of leased office space and computer charges, are included in other revenue of the general fund.

Payments in Lieu of Taxes

The payments of $5,161,609, $628,371, and $880,637 in fiscal year 1993 by the power and light, sanitary sewer, and water (enterprise) funds, respectively, to the general fund in lieu of taxes represent franchise taxes and real estate taxes on plant in service. The franchise tax rate, established by City ordinance at 9.08 percent for 1993, is applied to gross billed operating revenues less amounts written off to arrive at the franchise tax due the General Fund. Real estate taxes are charged at a set amount.

Interfund Operating Transfers

Interfund operating transfers for fiscal year 1993 were as follows:

	Transfer To	Transfer From
General	$ 173,617	$ 944,327
Special Revenue		307,772
Debt Service	930,000	
Capital Projects	440,551	157,918
Enterprise		3,000
Internal Service		140,604
Expendable Trust	9,453	
Total Operating Transfers	$1,553,621	$1,553,621

a. Based on the information provided, prepare four journal entries (for support services, rent, payments in lieu of taxes, and interfund operating transfers) to record the transfers into the general fund. Be sure the account titles you use make clear the nature of the transaction (e.g., revenue, operating transfer, equity transfer).

b. Justify any differences in how you classified the interfund transactions.

5-9

Analysts may (depending on account classification) be able to derive information on cash flows from a statement of operations and balance sheets.

Highbridge County imposes a motor fuel tax to finance road maintenance. It therefore accounts for all road maintenance in a special revenue fund. The fund's operating statement and balance sheet are presented as follows.

Road Maintenance Special Revenue Fund
Statement of Revenues, Expenditures, and Changes in Fund Balance
Year Ending December 31, 1998
(in Thousands)

Motor Fuel Tax Revenues		$710
Expenditures:		
Wages and Salaries	$410	
Contribution to Pension Fund	35	
Supplies	190	
Acquisition of Equipment	90	
Legal Settlement	3	
Other Expenditures	70	798
Excess of Revenues Over Expenditures		(88)
Other Financing Sources:		
Proceeds of Long-Term Debt		90
Increase in Supplies Inventory		8
Total Other Financing Sources		98
Excess of Revenue and Other Financing Sources Over Expenditures		10
Fund Balance, Beginning of Year		69
Fund Balance, End of Year		$ 79

Balance Sheet
As of December 31
(in Thousands)

	1998	1997
Assets:		
Cash	$26	$17
Motor Fuel Taxes Receivable	15	11
Prepaid Expenditures	18	22
Supplies Inventory	40	32
Total Assets	$99	$82
Liabilities and Fund Balances:		
Accounts Payable (for Supplies)	$ 6	4
Accrued Wages and Salaries	7	9
Claims and Judgments Payable	3	0
Current Obligation to Pension Fund	4	0
Total Liabilities	20	13

Fund Balance		
Reserve for Encumbrances		
(Supplies)	12	16
Reserve for Inventories	40	32
Unreserved	27	21
Total Fund Balance	79	69
Total Liabilities and Fund Balance	$99	$82

a. The county prepares its budget for the road maintenance special revenue fund on a strict cash basis—no accruals whatsoever. Based on the information in the financial statements, prepare a schedule in which you account for all inflows and outflows of cash. The county reports inventories on a *purchases* basis. Be sure that your schedule accounts for the entire $9,000 increase in cash during the year.

b. Are you able to determine from the statements any of the following?
1. the actual amount of any claims and judgments incurred during the year
2. the fund's *required* contribution to its pension fund
3. the interest cost applicable to the long-term debt issued

If not, would this information be reported in any other fund or account group? Explain.

c. Most governments do not classify their expenditures by object classification as in this example. Instead they report them by function, such as general government, public safety, recreation, and so on. However, they present their assets and liabilities in a fashion similar to that in the example. Is it possible, therefore, to derive information on cash flows from the statement of operations and balance sheets? Explain. Why do you think governments report expenditures by function rather than by object classification?

5-10

Fund balance deficits may not be all bad.

The balance sheet and schedule of revenues, expenditures, and changes in fund balance for Boulder, Colorado's Permanent Parks and Recreation Fund, a special revenue fund, for the year ending December 31, 1993 follow:

Boulder Colorado
Schedule Of Revenues, Expenditures, And Changes In Fund Balance
Year Ended December 31, 1993
(Amounts in 000's)

Revenues:

General Property Taxes	$ 855
Other Taxes—Development Excise	663
Development Fees	13
Golf Expansion Fees	138
Interest Earnings	42
Lease/Rent From Land	24
Other	209
Total Revenues	1,944

Expenditures:

Culture and Recreation	1,881
Interest	119
Total Expenditures	2,000
Excess (Deficiency) of Revenues Over Expenditures	(56)
Other Financing Uses Operating Transfers Out	(123)
Excess (Deficiency) of Revenues and Other Sources Over Expenditures and Other Uses	(179)
Fund Balance, Beginning of Year	(367)
Fund Balance, End of Year	$ (546)

Balance Sheet
as of December 31, 1993

Assets:

Cash and Equivalents	$ 3
Investments at Cost or Amortized Cost	902
General Property Taxes Receivable	938
Accrued Interest	8
Other	9
Due From Other Funds	14
Restricted Asset, Cash for Special Purposes	4
Total Assets	$1,878

Liabilities and Fund Equity

Liabilities:

Vouchers and Accounts Payable	$ 120
Salaries and Wages Payable	9
Advances From Other Funds	1,357
Deferred Revenue—General Property Taxes	938
Total Liabilities	2,424

Fund Equity:

Reserved For:	
Encumbrances	112
Special Purposes	24
Unreserved	(682)
Total Fund Equity	(546)
Total Liabilities and Fund Equity	$1,878

A note to the financial statement states the following:

Fund Deficits

The Permanent Parks and Recreation Fund has a fund balance deficit of $546,539. This deficit is the result of the Permanent Parks and Recreation Fund expenditures: one-half of the cost of a central irrigation system for city parks and the acquisition of Roper fields for soccer fields. The cost of the central irrigation system was shared with the Water Utility Fund to improve water conservation. The Permanent Parks and Recreation Fund has funded these projects through interfund loans with December 31, 1993 balances of: Water Utility Fund ($52,870), and Flood Control Utility Fund ($1,274,524).

a. Suppose that you are the chief accountant of the Parks and Recreation Department. A member of the city council accuses you and your department of mismanagement as evidenced by the substantial fund deficit. How would you defend yourself? What is the significance of the fund deficit?

b. Prepare journal entries (as best you can with the information provided) in the Permanent Parks and Recreation Fund to record:
   1. the acquisition of the central irrigation system and the Roper fields (assuming that the cost of the assets is equal to the December 31, 1993, interfund loan balances even though the acquisition was, in fact, made prior to 1993 and a portion of the balances had already been repaid by December 31, 1993)
   2. the interfund loans

c. A schedule of changes in general fixed assets by function and activity indicates the following with respect to parks and recreation:

General Fixed Assets as of January 1, 1993	$24,100
Additions, 1993	1,291
Deductions, 1993	(373)
General Fixed Assets as of December 31, 1993	$25,018

How are the additions (which are other than the irrigation system and the soccer fields) and deductions most likely reflected in financial statements of the Permanent Parks and Recreation Fund?

d. Another note to the financial statement indicates that the Boulder city council levies property taxes by December 15 of each year. The taxes are payable in full by April 15, or in two installments by June 15, of the following year. Prepare the 1993 property tax entries (in summary form) most likely made in the Permanent Parks and Recreation Fund.

5-11

The amount available for appropriation may not always be obvious from the balance sheet.

A recent balance sheet of Dallas, Texas showed the following (in thousands):

Assets:

Cash and Equivalents	$49,182
Property Taxes Receivable	5,265
Sales Taxes Receivable	25,911
Accounts Receivable	11,388
Accrued Interest	781
Due From Other Funds	674
Inventories at Cost	3,517
Total Assets	$96,718

Liabilities:

Accrued Payroll	$12,468
Accounts Payable	5,712
Accrued Vacation and Sick Leave	5,081
Due to Other Funds	527
Deferred Revenue	9,067
Housing Discrimination Case Settlement	1,894
Other	5,238
Total Liabilities	39,987

Fund Equity:

Reserved for Encumbrances	14,469
Unreserved:	
Designated for Contingencies	19,670
Undesignated	22,592
Total Fund Equity	56,731
Total Liabilities and Fund Equity	$96,718

a. Which method, consumption or purchases, does the city use to account for inventories? How can you tell?

b. In the examples in the text, liabilities for accrued vacation and sick pay and for claims and judgments were not recognized in governmental funds. Yet the Dallas balance sheet shows liabilities for both. What is the most probable explanation? (Dallas's general long-term debt account group also reports obligations, in substantially greater amounts than is shown in the general fund, both for vacation and sick pay and for the housing discrimination case settlement).

c. A note to the financial statements indicates the following:

Deferred revenues arise when a potential revenue does not meet both the "measurable" and "available" criteria for recognition in the current period. Deferred revenues also arise when resources are received by the government before it has a legal claim to them, as when grant monies are received prior to the incurrence of qualifying expenditures. In subsequent periods, when both revenue recognition criteria are met, or when the city has a legal claim to the resources, the liability for deferred revenue is removed from the combined balance sheet and revenue is recognized.

Assume that Dallas prepares its general fund budget on a cash basis (even though, in fact, it budgets on a basis similar to the modified accrual basis). A city official comments: "For next year we expect to budget $600 million in expenditures. Therefore, as long as we collect at least $543 million ($600 million less approximate fund equity of $57 million) in taxes and other revenues we shall end the year with a positive fund balance."

1. Do you agree with the official? Review each of the assets and liabilities presented on the balance sheet. Indicate which are likely to generate cash (or, with respect to liabilities, require the use of cash) that will be available to meet the city's budgeted expenditures. (For example, taxes receivable, but not inventories, will generate cash that can be used to meet expenditures.) Note also any assets or obligations *not* reported on the balance sheet that might either provide additional cash or require the use of cash.

2. With the data on the balance sheet, are you able to determine the amount of cash (and claims against it) that will be generated by the reported net assets (i.e., fund balance)? Do you agree with the member of the National Council on Governmental Accounting that a governmental fund balance fails to provide information on the resources available for future appropriation?

SOLUTION TO EXERCISE FOR REVIEW AND SELF-STUDY

a. *Journal entries* (in millions)

1. The transfer from the general fund would qualify as a *quasi-external transaction* since the property taxes would have been recorded as revenue if deposited directly in the parks and recreation fund.

Cash	$6.00	
Property tax revenue		$6.00

To record property tax revenues

2. The general rule is that revenues and expenditures are recognized in governmental funds, such as special revenue funds, on an accrual basis. There are exceptions, but wages and salaries are *not* among them.

Wages and salaries— expenditure	$4.50	
Cash		$4.10
Accrued wages and salaries		.40

To record wages and salaries

3. Vacation leave should be accrued as a liability as long as employees have earned the time off and the employer is expected to compensate employees for it in the future. However, only the portion of the liability expected to be liquidated with expendable available financial resources should be reported as a governmental fund obligation. The balance should be reported as a liability in the GLTDAG.

Vacation pay expenditure	$0.20	
Cash		$0.20

To record vacation pay

4. Unused sick leave should be accrued only insofar as employers expect to compensate employees for the leave as a termination benefit. In this case, the leave only accumulates, it does not vest. Thus, the city will not have to compensate employees for leave not taken as a termination benefit. It should charge as an expenditure only the amount that was liquidated with expendable financial resources. It need *not* report a liability in the GLTDAG.

Sick leave expenditure	$0.14	
Cash		$0.14

To record sick-leave pay

5. Pension costs should be reported as an expenditure only insofar as they were, or will be, liquidated with expendable financial resources (in this case, actual amounts paid plus amounts to be paid early in the following year). The difference between what the city *should* contribute and what it *actually* contributes should be reported as a liability in the GLTDAG.

Pension expenditure	$.30	
Cash		$.25
Current obligation to pension fund		.05

To record pension contributions

6. Since the city accounts for inventories on the purchases method, it should report as an expenditure only the supplies actually acquired. However, it should give balance sheet recognition to material amounts of inventory on hand at year-end and should establish reserves for both encumbrances and inventories on hand.

Supplies expenditure	$.70	
Cash		$.50
Accounts payable		.20

To record supplies purchased

Encumbrances	$.10	
Reserve for encumbrances		$.10

To give recognition to supplies ordered but not yet received

Supplies inventory	$0.15	
Fund balance—reserve for supplies		$0.15

To record the inventory on hand at year-end

7. Fixed assets should be recognized as expenditures as acquired. Noncurrent debt issued to finance them should be reported as "other financing sources." Interest and principal on long-term debt need not be recognized as expenditures until they are due.

Fixed assets—expenditures	$1.00	
Other financing sources—		
installment note proceeds		$0.8
Cash		0.2

To record the acquisition of equipment

b. Statements

Statement of Revenues, Expenditures, and Changes in Fund Balance
Year Ending December 31, 1999

Property Tax Revenue		$6.00
Expenditures:		
Wages and Salaries	$4.50	
Vacation Pay	.20	
Sick Leave	.14	
Pensions	.30	
Supplies	.70	
Acquisition of Fixed Assets	1.00	6.84
Excess of Revenues Over Expenditures		(0.84)
Other Financing Sources:		
Proceeds of Installment Notes		0.80
Increase in Supplies Inventory		0.15
Total Other Financing Sources		0.95
Excess of Revenues and Other Financing Sources Over Expenditures		0.11
Fund Balance, Beginning of Year		0
Fund Balance, End of Year		$0.11

Balance Sheet
As of December 31, 1999

Assets:

Cash	$0.61
Supplies Inventory	0.15
Total Assets	$0.76

Liabilities and Fund Balances:

Accounts Payable	$0.20
Accrued Wages and Salaries	0.40
Current Obligation to Pension Fund	0.05
Total Liabilities	0.65

Fund Balance:

Reserve for Encumbrances	0.10
Reserve for Inventories	0.15
Unreserved	(0.14)
Total Fund Balance	0.11
Total Liabilities and Fund Balance	$0.76

Note: The increase in supplies inventory must be reported as an "other financing source" since the addition of the inventory to assets was offset directly by a credit to fund balance (albeit "fund balance—reserve for supplies"). It was not credited to a revenue account and thereby not included among the items that affect the "excess of revenues over expenditures."

c. The following assets or liabilities would be reported in other funds or account groups:

General Fixed Asset Account Group

Parks and Recreation Equipment	$1.00

General Long-Term Debt Account Group

Obligation for Vacation Pay	$0.06
Obligation for Pensions	0.07
Installment Note	0.80

CHAPTER 6

Revenues and Expenditures in Other Not-For-Profit Organizations

Governments and not-for-profit organizations confront similar accounting and reporting issues. However, they do not necessarily resolve them alike. Differences in standards can be partly explained—and indeed, justified—by differences in the entities characteristics and resultant differences in constituents' information needs. For example, not-for-profits lack the authority of law to generate revenues and they have greater flexibility in administering their budgets. Differences in standards may also be attributed to dissimilarities in the composition and perspectives of the standard-setting authorities. This chapter will first address accounting and reporting issues that the FASB has already considered and that affect all not-for-profits. Then it shall consider the issues facing two types of specialized entities—hospitals and other health care institutions, and universities.

WHO'S IN CHARGE?

Whereas the Governmental Accounting Standards Board has standard-setting jurisdiction over all governments, the Financial Accounting Standards Board has jurisdiction over all other not-for-profits. As a consequence, even similar types of organizations may fall within the province of different boards. A state university or city hospital would be under the authority of the GASB whereas comparable nongovernment institutions would be under the control of the FASB.

Although the FASB began operations in 1973, it did not establish standards targeted specifically at not-for-profit organizations until 1987, when it issued Statement No. 93, *Recognition of Depreciation by Not-for-Profit Organizations*. Until then, the AICPA articulated the accounting and reporting practices of not-for-profit organizations through a series of industry audit guides. Individual guides dealt with colleges and universities, hospitals and other health care providers, voluntary health and welfare organizations, and other not-for-profit entities. Separate AICPA committees were responsible for each of these publications, causing inconsistencies in the accounting and reporting guidelines. However, because the FASB pronouncements were now common to all not-for-profits, in 1996 the AICPA eliminated the inconsistencies and consolidated its audit guides into two:

1. *Health Care Organizations* covers hospitals, clinics, health maintenance organizations, nursing homes, and home health organizations.

2. *Not-for-Profit Organizations* covers all other not-for-profits, including colleges and universities.

Both guides incorporate the latest FASB pronouncements. However, they also provide guidance as to issues not addressed by FASB.

As will be evident in this chapter, the accounting practices of not-for-profits are more compatible with those of businesses than of governments. Like their GASB counterparts, the FASB and AICPA pronouncements emphasize the superiority of the accrual basis over the cash basis of accounting. But they are far less indulgent of modifications of, and exceptions to, the accrual basis. As a consequence, not-for-profits generally do not distinguish between *expenses* and *expenditures*. The term *expenses* is the one commonly used. Moreover, the FASB has been moving to minimize the differences between business and not-for-profit accounting and reporting.

WHAT SHOULD BE THE FORM AND CONTENT OF FINANCIAL STATEMENTS?

As emphasized in Chapter 2, not-for-profits, like governments, account for their resources in funds, each of which is a separate accounting entity. As in governments, most entities maintain an unrestricted operating (or general) fund, as well as one or more restricted funds. Accordingly, the journal entries to be proposed in this chapter will be made in the individual funds. However, the FASB is not concerned with the specific funds maintained by not-for-profits. Instead, it is interested in how entities report their overall financial position and results of operations. A key issue, therefore, is whether not-for-profits should display separately each of the funds, consolidate them into single column presentation, or aggregate the funds in a way that would combine groups of funds. Although this chapter is concerned primarily with revenue and expense recognition, it will soon become apparent that how funds are combined directly impacts how and when certain types of revenues and expenses are reported.

In 1993 the FASB issued Statement No. 117, *Financial Statements of Not-for-Profit Organizations*, which established standards for the form and content of financial statements. The Statement provides that not-for-profits must issue three primary financial statements:

REPORTING ASSETS AND LIABILITIES

- a statement of financial position (balance sheet)
- a statement of activities
- a statement of cash flows

The balance sheet and statement of activities will be discussed in this chapter; the statement of cash flows will be discussed in Chapter 12.

Statement No. 117 provides for considerably more aggregation of financial data than do corresponding GASB pronouncements. Per Statement No. 117, not-for-profits must classify their **net assets** into three categories based on the existence or absence of donor-imposed restrictions:

- **unrestricted net assets**
- **temporarily restricted net assets**—mainly resources that must be used either for specific purposes, in specific periods, or when specified events have occurred
- **permanently restricted net assets**—ordinarily endowments, the principal of which must permanently remain intact, with only the income available for expenditure

Temporarily restricted net assets can take several forms. Resources that must be used for research, for specific programs, or for acquisition of plant and equipment would be temporarily restricted as to *purpose*. The resources would be released from the restriction when the organization incurred expenses that satisfied the donor's stipulations. A **term endowment** would be temporarily restricted as to *time*. A term endowment is a gift from which only the income is available for expenditure for a specified period of time. Once the period of time has expired, then the principal of the gift is also available for expenditure. Pledges that will not be received until future periods may also be seen as subject to time restrictions. They are unavailable for expenditure until then. An **annuity** would be temporarily restricted pending the occurrence of a *specified event*. An annuity is a gift that provides the donor with income until his or her death. Upon death, the balance of the gift reverts to the donee for either restricted or unrestricted purposes.

Even assets classified as unrestricted are not necessarily free of all restrictions—only those imposed by donors. Restrictions imposed by the organization's members, its own governing board, or by outside parties other than donors, such as bondholders and regulatory authorities, do not affect how net assets should be classified.

Statement No. 117 does not detail how net assets must be presented. It merely requires that the balance sheet present six totals: total assets, total liabilities, total net assets, total unrestricted assets, total temporarily restricted assets, and total permanently restricted assets. However, in an illustrative balance sheet, it combines the organization's assets, liabilities, and net assets (i.e., fund balances) from all of its funds and presents them in a single column. Net assets are then broken down into the three required categories of restrictiveness. Information as to the nature and amount of restrictions may be shown on the face of the balance sheet or in notes to the financial statements. If shown on the face of the balance sheet, separate line items may be added to the two categories of restricted net assets (e.g., "restricted for acquisition of plant" or "restricted for scholarships"). As another (but not the only other) possibility, the three categories of assets may be presented in three separate columns, with specific resources, as well as net assets, assigned to each of the three categories.

The FASB statement also directs that data as to the liquidity of the organization's assets and liabilities be reported either on the face of the financial statements or in the accompanying notes. Most organizations satisfy this requirement by categorizing their assets and liabilities as either current or noncurrent. For not-for-profits (unlike governments), there is little ambiguity as what constitutes a current asset or liability. The definitions of business accounting control. Per *Accounting Research Bulletin 43*, Chapter 3a, current assets are resources reasonably expected to be realized in cash or sold or consumed during the normal operating cycle of the business. Current liabilities are obligations whose liquidation is expected to require the use of existing resources classified as current assets, or the creation of other current liabilities. Table 6–1 presents the balance sheet of the American Health Association, a voluntary health and welfare organization.

REPORTING REVENUES AND EXPENSES

Statement No. 117 directs that revenues and expenses be reported in a **statement of activities**. Like the balance sheet, the statement of activities should focus on the organization as a whole, rather than on individual funds. Further, it should report the changes in each of the three categories of net assets. The FASB specifies that the statement of activities must break out gains and losses recognized on investments and other assets from revenues and expenses, but otherwise leaves the form and content of the statement to the individual organization. Therefore, as in the balance sheet, organizations can present the information in respect to the three categories of net assets in separate sections of the statement (several rows each for the different categories) or in three separate columns.

As would be expected, the statement instructs that revenues be reported as increases in one of the three categories of net assets, depending on donor-imposed restrictions. However, in a controversial decision, the Board concluded that *all expenses should be reported as decreases in unrestricted net assets*. The Board reasoned that donors restrict only how the contributed resources may be used. They do not control expenses. "Expenses result from the decisions of an organization's managers about the activities to be carried out and how and when particular resources are to be used," it explained. In other words, donors do not determine the activities in which an organization engages. Their control is limited to dictating the activities for which their contributions will be used to pay.

TABLE 6–1
Voluntary Health and Welfare Organization

American Health Association, Local Affiliate
Statement of Financial Position as of June 30, 1996

Assets	Unrestricted	Temporarily Restricted	Permanently Restricted	Total
Current Assets:				
Cash and Cash Equivalents	$ 806,383	$ —	$ —	$ 806,383
Short-Term Investments	8,884,309	288,073	—	9,172,382
Accrued Investment Income	192,427	—	—	192,427
Accounts Receivable—				
Federated and Nonfederated	—	694,382	—	694,382
National Center	20,382	—	—	20,382
Bequest Receivable	—	286,000	—	286,000
Pledges	84,601	19,000	—	103,601
Other	70,719	—	—	70,719
Educational and Campaign Material Inventory	250,670	—	—	250,670
Prepaid Expenses	79,410	—	—	79,410
Total Current Assets	10,388,901	1,287,455	—	11,676,356
Noncurrent Assets:				
Accounts Receivable—				
Pledges, Net of Discount of $1,000	—	19,000	—	19,000
Charitable Gift Annuity—National Center	40,500	—	—	40,500
Long-Term Investments	6,622,538	331,695	2,383,620	9,337,853
Beneficial Interest in Perpetual Trust	—	—	2,767,900	2,767,900
Contributions Receivable from Charitable Remainder Trust	—	4,963,216	—	4,963,216
Land, Buildings and Equipment, at Cost				
Less Accumulated Depreication of $2,344,393	3,921,690	—	—	3,921,690
Total Noncurrent Assets	10,584,728	5,313,911	5,151,520	21,050,159
TOTAL ASSETS	$20,973,629	$6,601,366	$5,151,520	$32,726,515
Liabilities and Net Assets				
Current Liabilities:				
Payable to the National Center				
Campaign Share	$ 3,181,641	$ 414,241	$ —	$ 3,595,882
Purchased Material	137,781	—	—	137,781
Accounts Payable and Accrued Expenses	585,896	—	—	585,896
Research Awards Payable Within One Year	3,315,845	—	—	3,315,845
Total Current Liabilities	7,221,163	414,241	—	7,635,404
Noncurrent Liabilities:				
Payable to the National Center				
Campaign Share	—	1,240,804	—	1,240,804
Annuity Obligation	19,640	—	—	19,640
Research Awards Payable After One Year,				
Net of Discount of $50,000	1,983,172	—	—	1,983,172
Post Retirement Benefit Obligation	932,246	—	—	932,246
Total Noncurrent Liabilities	2,935,058	1,240,804	—	4,175,862
Total Liabilities	10,156,221	1,655,045	—	11,811,266

TABLE 6-1 (Continued)				
Assets	**Unrestricted**	**Temporarily Restricted**	**Permanently Restricted**	**Total**
Net Assets:				
Unrestricted				
Net Investment in Land, Building and Equipment	3,921,690	—	—	3,921,690
Designated by the Governing Board for				
Programs and Operations for the Ensuing Fiscal Year	6,697,513	—	—	6,697,513
Research Designated to Future Years	177,345	—	—	177,345
Charitable Gift Annuity—National Center	20,860	—	—	20,860
Temporarily Restricted				
Land, Buildings, and Equipment	—	168,953	—	168,953
Research	—	232,759	—	232,759
Public Health Education	—	354,341	—	354,341
Community Services	—	467,856	—	467,856
Charitable Remainder Trust	—	3,722,412	—	3,722,412
Permanently Restricted				
Endowment Funds	—	—	2,383,620	2,383,620
Beneficial Interest in Perpetual Trust	—	—	2,767,900	2,767,900
Total Net Assets	10,817,408	4,946,321	5,151,520	20,915,249
TOTAL LIABILITIES AND NET ASSETS	$20,973,629	$6,601,366	$5,151,520	$32,726,515

As a consequence of this requirement, a not-for-profit must make two sets of journal entries whenever it spends restricted resources. The first, in a restricted fund, records the decrease in cash or other assets and the release of the restrictions (a decrease in restricted net assets); the second, in an unrestricted fund, records the expense and the release of the restriction. This entry has no effect on unrestricted net assets, inasmuch as it consists of an expense (a debit) offset by the bookkeeping equivalent of a transfer in (a credit).

EXAMPLE   *Reporting Revenues and Expenses*

The Professional Accountant's Association receives a $50,000 contribution to promote "truth in budgeting" among state and local governments. In the same year it spends the funds for the stipulated purpose.

Inasmuch as the contribution is restricted as to purpose, it would be recorded in a temporarily restricted fund:

Cash	$50,000	
Revenue from contributions		$50,000

To record the receipt of a temporarily restricted contribution (restricted fund)

When the association expends the resources for the stipulated purpose, it would account for the reduction in cash as "resources released from restriction." Thus:

Resources released from restriction	$50,000	
Cash		$50,000

To record the disbursement of cash in satisfaction of contributor restrictions (restricted fund)

"Resources released from restriction" is comparable to "other financing sources (or uses)," such as operating transfers. It would be reported in the statement of activities as negative revenue (a negative revenue rather than an expense because, as indicated, restricted funds do not report expenses).

At the same time, an unrestricted fund would recognize the expense and a corresponding increase in net assets:

Program expense	$50,000	
Resources released from restriction		$50,000
To record an expense and the release of contributor restrictions (unrestricted fund)		

To be sure, the Board's approach adds complexity to the financial reporting process. However, it permits not-for-profits, in contrast to governments, to report all expenses in a single column and thereby show more clearly the full cost of organizational operations.

The Board permits an important exception to the requirement that all restricted contributions be classified upon receipt as restricted. It gives not-for-profits the option of reporting restricted contributions as unrestricted if the restriction has been met in the same period as the contribution is made.

Table 6–2 presents the statement of activities of the American Health Association.

To fulfill its stated goal, financial reporting should provide information as to an organization's service efforts (See excerpts from statement of objectives in Table 1–4 of Chapter 1). The FASB mandates that either the statement of activities or the accompanying notes report expenses by *function*—that is, by program services or supporting activities. As a result of this requirement, the statement indicates to users not only the activities on which the organization is spending its resources, but more importantly the proportion of resources that are being directed toward substantive, as opposed to administrative, undertakings.

Voluntary health and welfare organizations must also report expenses by "natural" (i.e., object) classification, such as salaries, rent, electricity, and interest. The dual classification should be presented in matrix form in a separate financial statement. Other not-for-profits are encouraged, but not required, to provide information about expenses by their natural classification. Although the distinction between voluntary health and welfare organizations and other types of not-for-profits is not always clear, voluntary health and welfare organizations are formed to provide services to a community rather than to its own members. Examples include the United Way, Boy and Girl Scouts, the American Heart Association, and most social service agencies.

Table 6–3 illustrates the American Health Association's schedule of expenses.

WHAT ARE THE MAIN TYPES OF CONTRIBUTIONS, AND HOW SHOULD PLEDGES BE ACCOUNTED FOR?

Contributions, a mainstay means of support for many not-for-profits, encompass all *nonreciprocal* receipts of assets or services. A nonreciprocal receipt is one for which the recipient gives nothing in exchange. As defined by the FASB in its 1993 pronouncement, *Accounting for Contributions Received and Contributions Made* (Statement No. 116), contributions may be made in cash, marketable securities, property and equip-

TABLE 6–2
Voluntary Health and Welfare Organization

American Health Association, Local Affiliate,
Statement of Activities for the Year Ended June 30, 1996

	Unrestricted	Temporarily Restricted	Permanently Restricted	Total
Revenue:				
Public Support				
Received Directly				
Contributions	$ 2,603,328	$ 263,759	$ —	$ 2,867,087
Contributed Services	85,160	—	—	85,160
Capital Campaign	—	9,486	—	9,486
Special Events	10,528,221	12,500	—	10,540,721
Special Event Incentives	(1,802,014)	—	—	(1,802,014)
Net Special Events	8,726,207	12,500	—	8,738,707
Legacies and Bequests	1,327,126	788,844	270,000	2,385,970
Total Received Directly	12,741,821	1,074,589	270,000	14,086,410
Received Indirectly				
Allocated by Federated Fund-Raising Organizations	—	694,382	—	694,382
Allocated by Unassociated and Nonfederated Fund-Raising Organizations	142,472	—	—	142,472
Total Received Indirectly	142,472	694,382	—	836,854
Total Public Support	12,884,293	1,768,971	270,000	14,923,264
Other Revenue				
Grants from National Center	87,180	—	—	87,180
Program Fees	302,530	—	—	302,530
Sales of Educational Materials	1,106,074	—	—	1,106,074
Membership Dues	68,103	—	—	68,103
Investment Income	806,041	107,433	—	913,474
Perpetual Trust Revenue	—	64,732	—	64,732
Gains on Sale of Fixed Assets	6,468	—	—	6,468
Unrealized Gain on Perpetual Trust Contribution	—	—	308,100	308,100
Gains on Investment Transactions	—	103,544	—	103,544
Miscellaneous Revenue	96,296	—	—	96,296
Total Other Revenue	2,472,692	275,709	308,100	3,056,501
Net Assets Released from Restrictions:				
Satisfaction of Research Restrictions	704,264	(704,264)	—	—
Satisfaction of Program Restrictions	118,256	(118,256)	—	—
Satisfaction of Equipment Acquisition Restrictions	20,298	(20,298)	—	—
Satisfaction of Geographic Restrictions	266,000	(266,000)	—	—
Expiration of Time Restrictions	513,898	(513,898)	—	—
Total Net Assets Released From Restrictions	1,622,716	(1,622,716)	—	—
Total Public Support and Other Revenue	$16,979,701	$ 421,964	$578,100	$17,979,765

TABLE 6-2	(Continued)		
	Unrestricted	**Temporarily Restricted**	**Permanently Restricted**	**Total**

	Unrestricted	Temporarily Restricted	Permanently Restricted	Total
Expenses:				
Program Services				
Research—to Acquire New Knowledge Through Biomedical Investigation	$ 3,659,784	$ —	$ —	$ 3,659,784
Public Health Education—to Inform the Public About the Prevention and Treatment of Cardiovascular Diseases and Stroke	3,565,704	—	—	3,565,704
Professional Education and Training—to Improve the Knowledge, Skills, and Techniques of Health Professionals	971,708	—	—	971,708
Community Services—to Provide Organized Training in Emergency Aid, Blood Pressure Screening, and Other Community-Wide Activities	2,050,768	—	—	2,050,768
Total Program Services	10,247,964	—	—	10,247,964
Supporting Services				
Management and General—Providing Executive Direction, Financial Management, Overall Planning, and Coordination of the Association's Activities	1,069,084	—	—	1,069,084
Fund-Raising—Activities to Secure Vital Financial Support from the Public	2,487,090	—	—	2,487,090
Total Supporting Services	3,556,174	—	—	3,556,174
Total Program and Supporting Services Expenses	13,804,138	—	—	13,804,138
Allocation to the American Health Association, Inc. (National Center) for National Research and Other Activities	3,467,527	—	—	3,467,527
Total Expenses and Allocation to National Center	17,271,665	—	—	17,271,665
Change in Net Assets before Cumulative Effect of Change in Accounting Principles	(291,964)	421,964	578,100	708,100
Cumulative Effects of Changes in Accounting Principles	(520,508)	3,844,838	2,459,800	5,784,130
Change in Net Assets	(812,472)	4,266,802	3,037,900	6,492,230
Net Assets, Beginning of Year	11,629,880	679,519	2,113,620	14,423,019
Net Assets, End of Year	$10,817,408	$4,946,321	$5,151,520	$20,915,249

TABLE 6-3

Voluntary Health and Welfare Organization

American Health Association, Local Affiliate,
Statement of Functional Expenses for the Year Ended June 30, 1996

Account Title	Special Event Incentives	Program Services Research	Program Services Public Health Education	Program Services Professional Education and Training	Program Services Community Services	Program Services Sub Total	Supporting Services Management and General	Supporting Services Fund-Raising	Supporting Services Sub Total	Total
Salaries	$ —	$ 86,541	$1,600,091	$ 158,077	$ 951,992	$ 2,796,701	$ 366,639	$1,109,774	$1,476,413	$4,273,114
Payroll Taxes	—	6,915	131,026	13,005	78,838	229,784	30,150	90,125	120,275	350,059
Employee Benefits	—	9,169	283,924	26,003	171,947	491,043	65,398	194,719	260,117	751,160
Occupancy	—	4,501	146,862	12,827	84,405	248,595	36,220	103,152	139,372	387,967
Telephone	—	2,641	82,012	7,404	55,080	147,137	19,459	58,594	78,053	225,190
Supplies	—	1,015	76,404	5,343	30,400	113,162	20,832	24,382	45,214	158,376
Rental and Maintenance of Equipment	—	1,952	70,242	3,617	40,394	116,205	18,506	47,729	66,235	182,440
Printing and Publication	—	3,900	587,178	549,617	338,437	1,479,132	26,616	338,334	364,950	1,844,082
Postage and Shipping	—	4,092	188,810	27,479	64,285	284,666	26,826	194,228	221,054	505,720
Visual Aids, Films and Media	—	47	6,197	2,123	1,581	9,948	10,602	4,755	15,357	25,305
Conferences and Meetings	—	24,681	77,137	106,291	55,776	263,885	137,827	44,357	182,184	446,069
Other Travel	—	3,559	76,541	14,162	44,183	138,445	62,452	87,244	149,696	288,141
Professional Fees	—	85,787	72,449	29,184	32,479	219,899	134,282	62,031	196,313	416,212
Awards and Grants	—	3,419,771	—	—	—	3,419,771	—	—	—	3,419,771
Other Expenses	—	503	20,979	3,218	12,642	37,342	79,495	27,639	107,134	144,476
Depreciation and Amortization	—	4,710	145,852	13,358	88,329	252,249	33,780	100,027	133,807	386,056
Total Expenses Before Allocation to National Center	—	3,659,784	3,565,704	971,708	2,050,768	10,247,964	1,069,084	2,487,090	3,556,174	13,804,138
Allocation to the National Center	—	2,285,083	257,928	190,933	187,582	2,921,526	375,167	170,834	546,001	3,467,527
Total Functional Expenses and Allocation to the National Center	—	5,944,867	3,823,632	1,162,641	2,238,350	13,169,490	1,444,251	2,657,924	4,102,175	17,271,665
Special Event Incentives	1,802,014	—	—	—	—	—	—	—	—	1,802,014
Total Functional Expenses, Allocation to National Center, and Incentives	$1,802,014	$5,944,867	$3,823,632	$1,162,641	$2,238,350	$13,169,490	$1,444,251	$2,657,924	$4,102,175	$19,073,679

ment, utilities, supplies, intangible assets (such as patents and copyrights) and the services of professionals and craftsmen.[1]

Contributions also include **unconditional promises**, that is, **pledges**, to give those items in the future. Thus, pledges are regarded as contributions. They exclude, however **conditional promises** to give these items in the future. A conditional promise depends on a specified future and uncertain event to bind the donor. For example, a university alumnus may pledge funds to construct a new physics laboratory if the university is successful in winning a government research grant.

Contributions must be distinguished from exchange transactions. A contribution is a transfer of assets in which the donor does not expect to receive equal value in return. An exchange transaction is a reciprocal transfer in which each party receives and gives up resources of commensurate value. For example, if a private corporation were to give a not-for-profit research foundation funds to study the cause of a disease with the expectation that the results would be published in a scientific journal, the transaction would be considered a contribution. If, on the other hand, it would give the funds with the contractual agreement that it would have the rights to resultant patents, then the transaction would be an exchange transaction.

DISTINGUISHING A CONTRIBUTION FROM AN EXCHANGE TRANSACTION

The difference between the two are not always obvious. When people join the Friends of the Library Association, do they do so to support the library's scholarly activities or to benefit from the right to attend member-only lectures? Do they send money to their local public radio station to promote classical music or to receive the coffee mugs offered as a premium? Do they join the Association of Senior Citizens to advance the interests of the elderly or to take advantage of low-cost life and auto insurance offers?

Distinguishing between asset transfers and exchange transactions and contributions requires the exercise of judgment. Factors to be taken into account should include the recipient's intent in soliciting the resources, the party that establishes the amount of resources transferred (e.g., the transferor or the transferee), and the penalties assessed if either party fails to deliver what has been promised.

As previously discussed, the classification of resources into the three categories of restrictiveness is based on *donor* stipulation. Hence, only contributions need be categorized. Exchange transactions are always classified as unrestricted; by definition, the resources received are not subject to donor restrictions. They should be accounted for as ordinary commercial transactions.

The recognition of unrestricted gifts of cash and other assets (that have not been preceded by a pledge) has never been a major issue. Not-for-profits, irrespective of type, have recognized gifts of cash and other assets as revenue upon receipt. Gifts of assets other than cash have been measured at their fair (i.e., market) value.

ACCOUNTING FOR PLEDGES

But when should not-for-profits recognize pledges—promises to make donations of cash or other assets in the future? Organizations generally lack legally enforceable claims against fickle donors. Even if they do have legally enforceable claims, they may be reluctant to act on them because the likely benefit is exceeded by the costs in both goodwill and legal fees. Pledges may be legally enforceable when the organization has acted on a pledge and thereby incurred costs. Suppose, for example, relying on a donor's promise to finance a new building, an organization engages an architect to draw up plans. The donor reneges. The organization may have a valid claim upon the donor for its losses.

More importantly, pledges receivable, albeit assets, are not available for expenditure. They cannot be used to pay employees or suppliers. Recognition of pledges

---

[1] Paragraph 5.

might give the unwarranted impression that the organization has excess spendable funds and thereby has less of a need for further fiscal assistance.

On the other hand, many organizations have sufficient experience to be able to estimate with reliability the percentage of pledges that will be uncollectible and, like merchants, can establish appropriate allowances for uncollectibles. Further, they can borrow against the pledges and spend the proceeds. Arguably, therefore, there is no more justification for a not-for-profit than for a merchant to delay revenue recognition until cash is in hand.

Until the FASB standardized practice, some types of not-for-profits recognized revenue upon receipt of a pledge. Most, however, consistent with their conservative accounting traditions, chose to wait until cash had been collected.

Businesses measure receivables at the present value of anticipated cash flows (except for short-term receivables, those for which the impact of discounting would be immaterial). They adjust the stated amount of a receivable to take into account both anticipated defaults and the time value of money. Prior to the FASB pronouncement on contributions, not-for-profits that recorded pledges reduced their carrying value to take into account anticipated defaults. They did not, however, discount the face value to take into account the time value of money.

EXAMPLE *Pledges*

In November 1999, a public broadcasting station conducts its annual pledge drive and receives telephone pledges of $700,000. By year-end December 31, it collects $400,000 of the pledges.

Based on previous experience it estimates that $60,000 of the balance will be uncollectible. In addition, it receives a pledge from a local foundation to contribute $100,000 at the end of each of the next three years.

Current Standards

The FASB, over the vociferous objections of many of its constituent not-for-profit organizations, decided that unrestricted pledges should be reported as revenue in the period received; organizations need not wait until pledges are fulfilled. They should measure the pledges at "the present value of estimated future cash flows using a discount rate commensurate with the risk involved." That is, they should take into account both anticipated bad debts and the time value of money. However, they need not discount pledges to be collected within one year.

To avoid recognizing contributions as revenue before they are available for expenditure, not-for-profits should consider pledges of cash to be received in future periods as subject to *time restrictions*. The FASB concluded that by promising to make payments in the future, donors implicitly restricted the donated resources to support of future, not current, activities. Hence, the recipient organizations should classify them as *temporarily restricted*. When the cash is received and available for expenditure, they should release resources from the temporarily restricted category and transfer them to the unrestricted category.

The standard allows an option to recognize pledges that are restricted, either as to time or use, as unrestricted if the restriction has been met in the same period as the donation is made.

Thus, the following entries, in both unrestricted and temporarily restricted funds, summarize the results of the year's pledge drive:

Pledges receivable	$400,000	
Revenues from contributions		$400,000

To record the pledges of cash to be paid in the current year (in an unrestricted fund)

Cash	$400,000	
Pledges receivable		$400,000

To record the collection of cash (in an unrestricted fund)

These pledges need not be reported as being subject to time restrictions and thereby recorded in a temporarily restricted fund. They fall under the exception that when time restrictions are satisfied within the same year, the revenue can be reported as unrestricted.

Pledges receivable	$300,000	
Pledges receivable—allowance for uncollectibles		$ 60,000
Revenues from contributions		240,000

To record the pledges expected to be collected in future periods (in a temporarily restricted fund)

As the pledges are collected in subsequent years, the resources would be released from the temporarily restricted category and added to the unrestricted category. Thus, if $75,000 were collected:

Resources released from restriction	$75,000	
Pledges receivable		$75,000

To release the resources from restriction upon collection of cash (temporarily restricted fund)

Cash	$75,000	
Resources released from restriction		$75,000

To record the collection of cash (unrestricted fund)

Were the station to determine that 10 percent is an appropriate discount rate, then the present value of the annuity of $100,000 per year for three years would be $248,690. The present value of an annuity of $1 for three periods, discounted at a rate of 10 percent, is $2.4869. Hence, the present value of the annuity of $100,000 is $100,000 × 2.4869. The appropriate discount rate is the prevailing *risk-free* interest rate. The risk-free rate should be used because by establishing an allowance for uncollectibles the government will have already factored in the risk of loss from bad debts.

Pledges receivable	$248,690	
Revenues from contributions		$248,690

To record a pledge of three annual payments of $100,000, the present value of which, discounted at 10 percent, is $248,690 (temporarily restricted fund)

Each year, as the $100,000 is received, the station would recognize interest at a rate of 10 percent on the net balance of the pledge (the pledge receivable less the remaining discount) and record the excess as a reduction of the pledges receivable. Interest for the first year would be 10 percent of $248,690, or $24,869. Thus, when the first installment is received:

Resources released from restriction	$75,131	
Pledges receivable		$75,131

To release the resources upon collection of cash in the first year (temporarily restricted fund)

Cash	$100,000	
Contributions—interest revenue		$24,869
Resources released from restriction		75,131

To record the first year's payment of $100,000 (unrestricted fund)

In the two subsequent years, as the balance in pledges receivable is reduced, greater proportions of the $100,000 would be assigned to principal and lesser proportions to interest. By the end of the third year the balance in the pledges receivable account would be reduced to zero. The interest should be reported as additional contributions.

The FASB position on the time value of money contrasts with that of the GASB. The GASB requires both receivables and payables (including long-term obligations) to be recorded at their stated values.

WHEN SHOULD USE-RESTRICTED CONTRIBUTIONS BE RECOGNIZED?

In concept, a not-for-profit's *use-restricted contributions* are equivalent to a government's restricted grants. Use-restricted contributions can be used only for specified purposes. Before the FASB issued its pronouncement on contributions, most not-for-profits accounted for restricted contributions like governments account for restricted grants. That is, they recognized revenue from restricted grants as they expended the funds for the specified purpose. In that way, they matched the revenues to the expenses to which they were related.

As a consequence of this practice, organizations failed to give timely recognition to transactions that clearly enhanced their welfare. A restricted gift, no less than an unrestricted gift, provides an economic benefit; it helps the organization to carry out its mission.

EXAMPLE   *Use-Restricted Contributions*

In 1999 The Lyric Opera Society receives a $150,000 contribution to fund a production of Gilbert and Sullivan's *H.M.S. Pinafore*, to be performed in 2000.

Current Standards

Per FASB Statement No. 116, restricted contributions are accounted for no differently than unrestricted contributions. Restricted contributions, including pledges, are recognized as revenues in the period received, irrespective of when the resources will be expended. As discussed previously, for reporting purposes, distinctions must be drawn among resources that are unrestricted, temporarily restricted and permanently restricted.

Thus, the Lyric Opera Society would report its gift in a temporarily restricted fund:

Cash	$150,000	
Revenues from contributions		$150,000

To record a temporarily restricted gift (in a temporarily restricted fund)

When, in 2000, the Society expends the resources, it would record the release of the funds in the restricted fund and the expenditure in its current operating fund:

Resources released from restriction	$150,000	
Cash		$150,000

To record the release of restrictions (in the temporarily restricted fund)

Production expenses	$150,000	
Resources released from restriction		$150,000

To record the expenditure of funds previously restricted (in an unrestricted fund)

The expenditure of the funds raises a related issue. Suppose the society budgeted an additional $150,000 or more of its own resources to finance the production. When it spent the first $150,000 was it spending its own resources or the donated resources?

Per the FASB, as long as the organization incurs an expense for a purpose for which the restricted resources are available, it can consider the restriction as having been released. The only exception is that if the organization receives resources from two external donors, both of which restrict resources for the same purpose, then it cannot release the two restrictions with the expenditure of the same resources.

IN PRACTICE

A GIFT WITH STRINGS ATTACHED

Is it really possible to restrict a gift? Yes, but not as easily as it may appear. Resources are fungible and can readily be transferred from one account to another.

Suppose, for example, you contribute $100,000 to your favorite university, stipulating that the gift must be used to support teaching and research in accounting. The chairman of the accounting department would no doubt be delighted by your generosity and sense of priorities. His joy might be short-lived, however, if the university president reduced the department's standard budget allocation by $100,000, claiming that the accounting department is now less needy than other departments.

To be sure, donors can add covenants to gift agreements that minimize the likelihood that their wishes will be circumvented. But these are difficult to enforce and many organizations would be unwilling to accept unusual controls upon their administrative prerogatives.

Only by limiting a gift to activities that the organization would not otherwise undertake can a donor be certain that the gift will support the intended activity.

SHOULD CONTRIBUTIONS OF SERVICES BE RECOGNIZED?

Not-for-profits benefit from the services of volunteers. The services range from professional assistance that would otherwise have to be paid for at commercial rates to those that are part of the normal activities carried out by an organization's members. Consider some examples:

- An advertising agency develops a fund-raising campaign for a not-for-profit welfare agency
- An attorney provides free legal counsel to a hospital
- An attorney is a member of the board of directors of a performing arts association, and is frequently called upon for legal guidance

- Nurses are paid considerably less than the prevailing wage by a hospital maintained by a religious order of which they are members
- Community members perform odd jobs at a local hospital, such as carrying meals to patients, staffing the reception desk, and maintaining the hospital's library and recreation area
- Church members paint the church facilities and construct a children's play center

In each of these examples, the organization receives an economic benefit from the contributed services. Correspondingly, it incurs a cost in that it "consumes" the services provided. Yet it is not obvious whether the values of these contributed services can be reliably measured and, if they can, whether they should be accorded financial statement recognition.

EXAMPLE   *Service Contributions*

The Northern New Mexico Clinic, a not-for-profit health care provider, recruits a local contractor to repave its parking lot. Had the contractor billed the clinic at standard rates, the cost would have been $12,000.

Current Standards

Recognizing the diverse nature of contributed services, the FASB in Statement No. 116 prescribes that they should be recognized only if they are of a *professional nature* and of the type that the *entity would ordinarily have had to pay for* had they not been donated. It establishes two conditions, either of which must be met, for recognition:

- The services create or enhance nonfinancial assets.
- The services require specialized skills, are provided by individuals possessing those skills, and would typically need to be purchased if not provided by donation. Services requiring specialized skills, according to the FASB, are those provided by accountants, architects, carpenters, doctors, electricians, lawyers, nurses, plumbers, teachers and other professionals, and craftsmen.[2]

The services received by the Northern New Mexico Clinic satisfy both of these conditions. Hence, the clinic should recognize both a revenue and a corresponding expense:

Repair and maintenance expense	$12,000	
Revenue from contributed services		$12,000

To recognize revenue and the related expense from contributed services

---

[2] Paragraph 9.

A veterans association conducts an annual fund-raising campaign to solicit contributions from members of the community. In prior years the association's own members made the phone calls. This year, a local telemarketing company agreed to contact the potential donors.

The association should not recognize the contributed services of the firm because neither of the two conditions is met. The services do not create nonfinancial assets. Moreover, they do not require specialized skills and, based on experience, the association would otherwise not have purchased the services.

A local welfare organization benefits from the services of two CPAs. One is its treasurer, a position that must be filled by a member of its board of directors, all of whom are unpaid. The second, who is not a member of the board, provides ongoing accounting services (e.g., making monthly journal entries, closing the books, and preparing annual financial statements). Were it not for the services of this CPA, the organization would have to engage a part-time bookkeeper or accountant.

The welfare organization should not recognize the services of the treasurer. Although the organization benefits from his professional advice, his services are offered as an unpaid board member, not as a professional accountant. Therefore, neither condition is satisfied.

The other CPA provides services that require special skills and would otherwise have to be purchased. Therefore, the second condition is satisfied and the welfare organization should recognize his contributed services.

EXAMPLES OF CONTRIBUTED SERVICES

SHOULD RECEIPTS OF COLLECTION ITEMS BE RECOGNIZED AS REVENUES?

Not-for-profits, especially museums, universities, and libraries, receive contributions of works of art, rare books, and historical artifacts. These works often have considerable monetary value and may be the organization's most significant assets.

Museums and other not-for-profits have generally resisted suggestions that they give accounting recognition to contributions of collectibles. Similarly, some institutions have avoided capitalizing collectibles that they have purchased, especially if the acquisitions were from resources that were either donated or restricted for collectible purchases.

Not-for-profits believe they have sound reasons for not wanting to give accounting recognition to works of art and other collectibles. These resources are extremely difficult to value and, indeed, from the perspective of art curators, only the most Philistine of accountants would even consider placing a dollar sign beside a "priceless" work of art. At the same time, works of art are *not* assets, in that they cannot be associated with future cash receipts or savings. When retained, they are a drain upon resources because they require ongoing protection. They generate cash only upon sale. To report them as assets, the not-for-profits contend, would result in financial statements that are as surrealistic as some of the art itself.

Current Standards

Statement No. 116 encourages not-for-profits to recognize contributions of collectibles as revenues and to capitalize their entire collections. However, it states that entities *need not* (note: not *cannot*) recognize contributions of collectibles as long as the items satisfy *all* of the following conditions:

- They are held for public exhibition, education, or research in furtherance of public service rather than financial gain
- They are protected, kept unencumbered, cared for, and preserved
- They are subject to an organizational policy that requires proceeds from sales of collection items be used to acquire other items for collections

If not-for-profits elect not to capitalize their collections, then they must disclose, in notes to the statements, the details of items both purchased and "deaccessed."[3]

WHEN SHOULD CONDITIONAL PROMISES BE RECOGNIZED?

Donors may promise to contribute to a not-for-profit on condition that a specified event take place or that the entity take specified actions. Conditional promises to give must be distinguished from *restricted* contributions. A restricted gift is one that must be used for a particular purpose. A conditional promise, by contrast, is one in which the donor will provide the resources only if the specified condition is satisfied. The resources to be provided may be either restricted or unrestricted.

In practice, the distinction between a restricted gift and a conditional gift may be ambiguous. A donor may pledge resources that can be used only to support a particular activity, such as a conference. Although the promise is not explicitly conditioned upon the entity holding the conference, the donor is not likely to provide the resources if the conference is not held. Such a restricted gift is not much different from a conditional gift—one in which the donor promises to provide resources to the organization if and when it holds the conference.

A conditional promise unquestionably is an economic benefit to a not-for-profit entity, as long as there is a positive probability that the conditions can be met. Yet, if there is reasonable uncertainty that the conditions will be met, the entity may be premature in recognizing revenue until it has "earned" the right to the contribution by satisfying the conditions.

EXAMPLE   *Conditional Promises*

The City Symphony is conducting a campaign to provide financing for a new auditorium. In 1999 a private foundation agrees to match 50 percent of all other contributions up to $1 million (that is, each $1 of its gift is conditioned upon the symphony raising $2 from other sources). During the year, the symphony receives $500,000 in other donations.

---

[3] Paragraphs 11-13.

Current Standards

Statement No. 116 stipulates that conditional promises to give shall be recognized when the conditions on which they depend are substantially met.

In 1999 the symphony satisfied the conditions to receive $250,000 of the foundation's donation:

Pledges receivable	$250,000	
Revenues from contributions		$250,000

To record the fulfillment of conditions necessary to receive the foundation's matching funds.

WHEN SHOULD GAINS AND LOSSES ON INVESTMENTS BE RECOGNIZED?

Current Standards

As discussed in Chapter 4, the FASB, in Statement No. 124, *Accounting for Certain Investments Held by Not-for-Profit Organizations*, prescribed that not-for-profits, like businesses, must report their investments at fair value and recognize the changes in fair value as they occur. They need not, however, classify the investments into the three categories (trading, available-for-sale, and held-to maturity) as required of businesses. Therefore, even debt securities that are expected to be held to maturity must be stated at fair value. The only exempt securities are investments accounted for under the equity method, investments in consolidated subsidiaries, and those for which the fair value is not readily determinable. The fair value of an equity security is generally considered to be "readily determinable" if the security is traded on a major exchange or over the counter.

Per Statement No. 124, interest, dividends, and gains and losses from changes in the fair value of securities should be reported on the statement of activities as increases or decreases in *unrestricted* net assets—unless their use is temporarily or permanently restricted by explicit donor stipulation or law. However, even investment income and gains from restricted assets may be recognized as increases in unrestricted assets if the restrictions are met in the same reporting period and the organization follows the same policy with respect to contributions received.

EXAMPLE *Investment Gains*

In June 1999, the Children's Welfare Association receives a grant of $100,000, which it classifies as temporarily restricted. To earn a return until it needs the funds, the Association invests the proceeds in Treasury notes. As of December 31, 1999, the fair market value of the notes is $103,000. The following entry in an *unrestricted* fund would be appropriate:

Investments	$3,000	
Investment earnings—appreciation in fair value		$3,000

To record the increase in fair value

The investments would now be divided into the two fund categories:

Unrestricted	$ 3,000
Temporarily Restricted	100,000
Total	$103,000

If the securities were subsequently sold for $103,000, entries in both an unrestricted and restricted fund would be needed:

Cash	$100,000	
Investments		$100,000
To record the sale of securities in a temporarily restricted fund		
Cash	$3,000	
Investments		$3,000
To record the sale of securities in an unrestricted fund		

SHOULD DEPRECIATION BE REPORTED?

As emphasized in previous chapters, owing to their focus upon budgets, governments do not currently charge **depreciation** in their governmental funds. Not-for-profits, like governments, generally budget on a cash or near-cash basis and governing boards, managers, and external constituents are vitally concerned with actual-to-budget comparisons. The major challenge faced by managers and governing boards of most not-for-profits is meeting day-to-day cash demands. Inasmuch as depreciation is not a cost that requires cash, they have little or no interest in it; it does not enter into their financial deliberations or decisions.

On the other hand, as important as the budget is to not-for-profits, it does not have the same force of law as it does for governments. Therefore, not-for-profit statement users (particularly outsiders to whom general purpose financial statements are directed) may place greater weight on reporting objectives calling for information on the cost of services than on budgetary compliance. Depreciation represents the cost of consuming assets; in any comparison of service efforts with accomplishments, it may be too significant to ignore.

EXAMPLE   *Depreciation*

A not-for-profit job placement service acquires a personal computer for $3,000. It pays for the computer out of a fund restricted for the acquisition of equipment. Estimated useful life is three years.

Current Standards

The FASB, in its Statement No. 93, *Recognition of Depreciation by Not-for Profit Organizations*, mandates that not-for-profits "shall recognize the cost of using up the future economic benefits or service potentials of their long-lived tangible assets—depreciation." It requires that they disclose depreciation expense and accumulated depreciation for the period.

The Board did not indicate the specific funds in which not-for-profits should account for fixed assets and report depreciation. Some not-for-profits account for fixed assets, and charge depreciation, in their current operating funds; others maintain special plant funds. However, owing to Statement No. 117, *Financial Statements of Not-for-Profit Organizations*, the fund in which the entity records depreciation has no reporting significance. As discussed previously, Statement No. 117 requires that all expenses be reported as decreases in *unrestricted* net assets. Thus, whether the depreciation is initially recorded in a current operating fund or a plant fund, it would still be reported in the unrestricted column or section of the statement of activities.

The following entries would record the acquisition of the computer and first-year depreciation:

Resources released from restriction	$3,000	
Cash		$3,000

To record the release of restricted assets to acquire the computer (in a restricted fund)

Equipment	$3,000	
Resources released from restriction		$3,000

To record the purchase of the computer (in an unrestricted fund)

Depreciation expense	$1,000	
Accumulated depreciation		$1,000

To record first year depreciation (in an unrestricted fund)

COMPREHENSIVE EXAMPLE *Museum of American Culture*

This example, which focuses on the Museum of American Culture, synthesizes several of the principles presented so far. We start with the museum's balance sheet as of December 31, 1998 (presented in Table 6–4), account for the transactions in which the museum engaged during 1999 (journalized in the body of the text), and prepare selected financial statements as of December 31, 1999 (presented in Table 6–5).

The museum engages in two main programs: curatorial and exhibits, and education. These are backed by two support functions: fund raising and administration.

The AICPA's audit and accounting guide, *Not-For-Profit Organizations*, provides the most comprehensive and authoritative accounting guidance for museums. It covers not-for-profit organizations as diverse as colleges and universities, cemetery associations, civic organizations, fraternal associations, labor unions, professional associations, religious organizations, and performing arts organizations. It does not, however, cover health care organizations, which are addressed in a separate guide.

The key transactions in which the museum engaged during the year (in summary form) are described as follows (000s omitted):

TABLE 6–4
Museum of American Culture

Statement of Financial Position
December 31, 1998
(in Thousands)

Assets
Current Assets:

Cash	$ 120
Investments	4,210
Pledges Receivable	165
Less: Allowance for Uncollectibles	(15)
	150
Supplies Inventory	20
Prepaid Expenses	50
Total Current Assets	4,550
Property, Plant and Equipment	2,100
Less: Accumulated Depreciation	(540)
	1,560
Total Assets	$6,110

Liabilities
Current Liabilities:

Wages and Salaries Payable	$ 8
Accounts Payable	250
Total Liabilities	258

Net Assets

Unrestricted	2,002
Temporarily Restricted	850
Permanently Restricted (Endowments)	3,000
Total Net Assets	5,852

Accrual of Wages and Salaries

The museum paid wages and salaries expenses of $1,045, including amounts owing from the prior year. At year-end, employees had earned an additional $6, which was slated to be paid early in 2000. Museums, like other not-for-profits, are on an accrual basis. Hence, a provision must be made for the wages and salaries earned, but not yet paid.

    FASB Statement No. 117, *Financial Statements of Not-for-Profit Organizations*, provides that the statement of activities set forth expenses by *function*. The museum allocated the wages and salaries to its functions as indicated in the following entry:

Wages and salaries—curatorial and exhibits	$780	
Wages and salaries—education	85	
Wages and salaries—fund raising	50	
Wages and salaries—administration	130	
Cash		$1,039
Accrued wages and salaries		6

To record wages and salaries (in an unrestricted fund)

Other Operating Expenses; Inventory

The museum incurred other operating expenses of $280 ($200 in curatorial and exhibit costs, $30 for education, $10 for fund raising, and $40 for administration). The expenses are, of course, accounted for on an accrual basis and must be allocated to the organization's functions.

The museum accounts for both supplies inventory and prepaid items on the *consumption basis.* Unlike governments, not-for-profits are not permitted the option of the purchases basis. The FASB grants no exception to the accrual basis for either inventories or prepayments.

During the period, the museum purchased $5 more of supplies than it used and, as a consequence, inventory increased by the same amount. Moreover, it reduced its balances in accounts payable by $3 and in prepaid expenses by $7. It disbursed a total of $281 in cash relating to the operating expenses:

Other operating expenses—curatorial and exhibits	$200	
Other operating expenses—education	30	
Other operating expenses—fund raising	10	
Other operating expenses—administration	40	
Accounts payable	3	
Inventory	5	
Cash		$281
Prepaid expenses		7

To record other operating expenses (in an unrestricted fund)

Acquisition Of Fixed Assets; Long-Term Debt

The museum acquired $20 of new furniture and fixtures in exchange for a long-term note of the same amount. Although many not-for-profits account for both their fixed assets and related long-term debt in a plant fund (discussed in Chapter 8), this museum accounts for them in its operating fund. For reporting purposes, the results would be the same. The assets are reported in the unrestricted funds along with other unrestricted resources:

Property, plant and equipment	$20	
Notes payable		$20

To record the acquisition of fixed assets (in an unrestricted fund)

Unlike governments, not-for-profits must account for interest on the long-term note on the accrual basis.

Depreciation

The museum recognized depreciation of $210. Inasmuch as it reports its fixed assets in its operating fund, it also records depreciation in that fund:

Depreciation expense—curatorial and exhibits	$160	
Depreciation expense—education	15	
Depreciation expense—fund raising	5	
Depreciation expense—administration	30	
Allowance for depreciation		$210

To record depreciation (in an unrestricted fund)

Admissions and Memberships

The museum's main operating revenues are derived from admissions and membership fees. In 1999 they totaled $505:

Cash	$505	
Revenues—admissions and memberships		$505

To record revenues from admissions and members (in an unrestricted fund)

Interest and Dividends

The museum earned $280 in interest and dividends on its investments, most of which are held in an endowment fund. For this particular museum, the endowment income is unrestricted and thereby should be recorded in the operating fund and reported as unrestricted income. Were it restricted for a specific purpose, it would be recorded in a temporarily restricted fund and reported as temporarily restricted income. The endowment principal itself is accounted for in a permanently restricted fund. For internal bookkeeping purposes, many not-for-profits initially account for endowment interest and dividends in the endowment fund and then transfer them to the beneficiary funds. For external reporting purposes, however, the investment income should be reported as revenue of the beneficiary fund:

Cash	$280	
Investment earnings—interest and dividends		$280

To record dividends and interest (in an unrestricted fund)

Changes in Fair Values

During the year, the fair value of the museum's investments increased by $100. Assuming that there are no explicit legal or donor-imposed restrictions requiring that gains from the appreciation of the endowment portfolios be added to the principal of the endowment, the increase in fair value would be recognized as unrestricted investment earnings—the same as dividends and interest.

Investments	$100	
Investment earnings—appreciation in fair value		$100

To record appreciation in fair value (in an unrestricted fund)

Revenues and Expenses of Auxiliary Enterprises

The museum operates a gift shop. In 1999 revenues and expenses totaled $470 and $350, respectively.

Governments account for their business-type activities in enterprise funds. These funds are accounted for on the full accrual basis and, for purposes of external reporting, are not combined with governmental funds.

Inasmuch as not-for-profits account for their general operations on an accrual basis, there is less need to separate their business from their non-business activities. Although it is usually convenient to account for "auxiliary" activities (i.e., business-type activities) in separate funds, for external purposes they are usually reported along with other operations and the resources classified as unrestricted. Many not-for-profits aggregate their auxiliary revenues on one line and their auxiliary expenses on another. Others break out the revenues and expenses by individual, or types of, enterprises. The following summary entry would capture the museum's 1999 auxiliary activities:

Expenses applicable to auxiliary activities	$350	
Cash	120	
Revenues from auxiliary activities		$470

To record the activities of auxiliary activities (in an unrestricted fund)

Insofar as the revenues and expenses affected accounts other than cash, such as inventory, prepaid expenses, and allowance for depreciation, then those balance sheet accounts, rather than cash, would be debited or credited.

Unrestricted and Time-Restricted Pledges

During the year, the museum conducted a fund-raising campaign. As of year-end it received cash of $338 and pledges for an additional $180. Of the pledges, it estimates that $20 will be uncollectible.

Contributions, including unconditional promises to pay, should be recognized as revenue upon receipt. However, the pledges outstanding, inasmuch as they are unavailable for expenditure (and thereby subject to time restrictions), should be reflected as an increase in restricted resources.

Cash	$338	
Revenue from unrestricted contributions		$338

To record unrestricted contributions (in an unrestricted fund)

Pledges receivable	$180	
Allowance for uncollectible pledges		$ 20
Revenue from unrestricted contributions		$160

To record pledges subject to time restrictions (in a temporarily restricted fund)

For convenience, "revenue from unrestricted contributions" has been reduced by the "allowance for uncollectible pledges." Many not-for-profits would record this estimate as bad debt expense rather than as a reduction of revenues.

During the year, it collected $145 of time-restricted pledges receivable outstanding from prior years and wrote off $10 as uncollectible:

Cash	$145	
Resources released from restriction		$145

To record cash collected on outstanding pledges (in an unrestricted fund)

Allowance for uncollectible pledges	$ 10	
Resources released from restriction	145	
Pledges receivable		$155

To release resources from time restrictions and to write off uncollectible pledges (in a temporarily restricted fund)

Purpose Restricted Contributions

The museum received a $90 contribution from a patron who required that the gift be used to acquire additional works of art. During the year, the museum used the gift, along with $620 of resources that had previously been restricted, to add to its collection.

Because the gift is restricted (and in this instance the museum did not expect to expend it in the current year), it accounted for in a temporarily restricted fund:

Cash	$90	
Revenue from restricted contributions		$90

To record contributions restricted for acquisition of art (in a temporarily restricted fund)

This museum, like most others, elects *not* to capitalize its art collection. Therefore, the costs to acquire the new art would be reported as an expense. However, because not-for-profits must report all expenses in an unrestricted fund, the resources must be released from the restricted fund to the current fund:

Resources released from restriction	$710	
Cash		$710

To record the release of restricted resources upon acquiring new art (in temporarily restricted fund)

Acquisition of art—expense	$710	
Resources released from restrictions		$710

To record the acquisition of art (unrestricted fund)

To pay for the art, the museum sold $500 of unrestricted investments. There was no gain or loss on sale inasmuch as the museum carried the investments at fair value:

Cash	$500	
Investments		$500

To record the sale of investments

Volunteer Services

The museum benefits from the services of volunteer guides. Guides are essential to the operations of the museum and were it not able to attract volunteers, the museum would have to hire them. Nevertheless, the guides do not have to possess specialized skills (those characteristic of craftsmen or professionals), and therefore the museum may not recognize the value of their services as either revenues or expenses.

Table 6–5 summarizes the 1999 transactions in a statement of activity, a year-end balance sheet, and a schedule of program and support expenses.

TABLE 6–5
Museum of American Culture

Statement of Activity
For the Year Ending December 31, 1997 (in Thousands)

	Unrestricted	Temporarily Restricted	Endowment Fund	Total
Support and Revenues:				
Admissions and Memberships	$ 505			$ 505
Investments— Dividends and Interest	280			280
Investments— Appreciation	100			100
Revenue from Auxiliary Enterprises	470			470
Unrestricted Contributions, Including Pledges	338	$160		498
Restricted Contributions		90		90
Total Support and Revenues	1,693	250		1,943
Expenses:				
Program				
Curatorial and Exhibits	$1,140			$1,140
Education	130			130
Support Services				
Fund Raising	65			65
Administration	200			200
Acquisition of Art	710			710
Expenses of Auxiliary Enterprises	350			350
Total Expenses	$2,595			$2,595
Excess (Deficiency) of Support and Revenue Over Expenses	(902)	250		(652)
Resources Released from Restrictions	855	(855)		
Net (Decrease) in Fund Balances	(47)	(605)		(652)
Net Assets, Beginning of Period	$2,002	$850	$3,000	$5,852
Net Assets, End of Period	$1,955	$245	$3,000	$5,200

TABLE 6–5 (Continued)
Museum of American Culture

Statement of Financial Position
December 31, 1999
(in Thousands)

Assets
Current Assets:

Cash	$ 68
Investments	3,810
Pledges Receivable	190
Less: Allowance for Uncollectibles	(25)
	165
Supplies Inventory	25
Prepaid Expenses	43
Total Current Assets	4,111
Property, Plant and Equipment	2,120
Less: Accumulated Depreciation	(750)
	1,370
Total Assets	$5,481

Liabilities
Current Liabilities:

Wages and Salaries Payable	$ 14
Accounts Payable	247
Total Current Liabilities	261
Note Payable	20
Total Liabilities	281

Net Assets:

Unrestricted	1,955
Temporarily Restricted	245
Permanently Restricted (Endowments)	3,000
Total Fund Balances	5,200

TABLE 6–5 (Continued)
Museum of American Culture

Schedule of Program and Support Expenses
For the Year Ending December 31, 1999
(in Thousands)

	Curatorial & Exhibit	Education	Fund Raising	Administration and Other	Total
Wages and Salaries	$ 780	$ 85	$50	$130	$1,045
Other Operating Expenses	200	30	10	40	280
Depreciation	160	15	5	30	210
Acquisition of Art				710	710
Auxiliary Enterprise				350	350
Total	$1,140	$130	$65	$1,260	$2,595

WHAT UNIQUE ISSUES DO HEALTH CARE PROVIDERS FACE?

Health care in the United States is in the midst of a massive economic reorganization in which the divisions between business, not-for-profit, and government providers are becoming increasingly blurred. Consequently, the accounting distinctions among health care providers in the three sectors are also becoming less significant. Moreover, with the FASB's issuance of Statement No. 117, *Financial Statements of Not-for-Profit Organizations*, the differences in financial reporting between not-for-profit health care providers and other types of not-for-profit organizations are now only minimal. Therefore, in this section of the text, we limit our discussion to transactions that are either unique, or of special importance, to health care providers.

The accounting and reporting practices of health care organizations have been strongly influenced by the Healthcare Financial Management Association and the *American Hospital Association*, both of which are industry associations, and the AICPA. Until recently, external financial reporting was governed mainly by AICPA industry audit guides pertaining to hospitals and other types of health care organizations. Now that the FASB is taking an active interest in not-for-profit accounting, many of the guides' directives have been superseded by FASB pronouncements such as Statements No. 116 (contributions) and No. 117 (financial statements). Nevertheless, the AICPA's current industry guide, *Health Care Organizations* (which unlike earlier versions deals with both hospitals and other types of health care providers) is the primary authoritative source for issues not addressed by the FASB.

Health care may be provided by individual practitioners (including physicians, therapists, and counselors), hospitals, out-patient clinics, medical service and retirement institutions, and a wide range of not-for-profit specialty organizations (such as screening clinics, support organizations, and research institutes). Until recently, most health care organizations billed their patients (or third-party payers such as insurance companies) for services actually rendered. Today, an increasing percentage of medical care is provided through health maintenance organizations (HMOs) or related types of health plans that provide services to members in return for fixed, periodic payments. These HMOs or health plans may subcontract with hospitals, physicians associations or other medical groups to provide specialized services in exchange for *capitation* (per person) fees. The capitation fees are generally based on number of persons covered and expected costs to be incurred rather than actual services provided.

To a greater extent than most other not-for-profits, health care organizations must be concerned with their costs. Many other not-for-profits focus mainly on fund raising; they then adjust the level of services to available revenues. Health care organizations charge for their services. Often the amount of fees charged are limited by competition or pre-established reimbursement rates. Therefore, they must be vitally interested both in determining and controlling the cost of their services.

FUND STRUCTURE

The basic financial statements of not-for-profit health care organizations are similar in all major respects to those of the museum illustrated in the previous section. The balance sheet and statement of activities should distinguish among unrestricted, temporarily restricted, and permanently restricted resources. The statement of activities should classify the revenues as unrestricted, temporarily restricted, and permanently restricted but should report expenses only as decreases in unrestricted resources.

Hospitals and health organizations typically maintain one or more unrestricted operating funds, as well as several temporarily and permanently restricted funds. The general operating funds report both financial resources and property plant and equipment. Temporarily restricted funds are typically established to account for donated resources received for particular purposes. These purposes include specified programs or services (e.g., geriatric care, research, community education) as well as replacement of, or additions to, plant and equipment. In addition, temporarily restricted funds include term endowment funds, annuity funds, and life income funds.

Two points regarding temporarily restricted funds warrant emphasis:

- Temporarily restricted funds related to plant and equipment generally account only for *resources* restricted to the purchase or construction of plant and equipment. They do not usually account for the plant and equipment itself. Plant and equipment is typically reported in the general operating fund. (A notable exception involves fixed assets acquired by gift. These assets may be subject to restrictions that expire as the asset is depreciated, and hence, they may be accounted for in temporarily restricted funds.)

- An organization may opt to establish temporarily restricted funds to account for resources designated by its governing board for specific purposes (e.g,. to replace plant and equipment). For purposes of external reporting, however, board-designated resources are *not* considered restricted and should therefore be reported along with other unrestricted operating resources. They may, however, be classified within the unrestricted fund as "assets whose use is limited" (or some similar category).

As with the other not-for-profits, permanently restricted funds encompass mainly ordinary endowments (funds the principal of which must remain intact and only the earnings are expendable).

Like other not-for-profits (as well as governments), health care organizations may maintain numerous funds of each of the three categories. For reporting purposes, however, the funds should be combined by category.

CLASSIFICATION OF REVENUES AND EXPENSES

The statement of activities of a health care organization is relatively straightforward. Revenues are displayed by category (often in columns): unrestricted, temporarily restricted, and permanently restricted. They are divided into at least two classifications (usually rows): patient care revenues and other revenues. Patient care revenues include:

- routine services (such as room, board, and general nursing)
- other nursing services (such as operating room services)
- professional services (such as physicians' services, laboratories, and pharmacy)

Other revenues include:

- contributions
- educational services
- miscellaneous sources (such as rental of space, auxiliary enterprises, and fees charged for medical records)

In addition, revenues from capitation fees should generally be shown apart from other types of revenues.

Expenses are reported exclusively within the unrestricted category. They may be classified either by function or by object. However, per Statement No. 117, if the expenses are classified by object, then the functional classification must be presented in the notes.

The statement of activities must also indicate resources released from restriction and any transfers between funds. Likely functional and natural (object) classifications of expenditures include the following:

Functional	*Natural*
• Nursing services	• Salaries and wages
• Other professional services	• Employee benefits
• General services	• Fees to individuals and organizations
• Fiscal services	• Supplies and other expense
• Administrative services	• Purchased services
• Bad debts	• Bad debts
• Depreciation	• Depreciation
• Interest	• Interest

RECOGNIZING FEE-FOR-SERVICE PATIENT-CARE REVENUES

Health care organizations may provide patient services over an extended period of time. Yet patients are often billed only at the conclusion of their stay at the facility.

In reality, most patients pay either none, or only a small portion, of their bills themselves. Health care organizations derive most of their revenues from third parties, such as Medicare, Medicaid, Blue Cross, and other insurance companies and health plans. These third parties pay the hospital or other health care provider based on contractual or other predetermined rates. For example, in most circumstances, Medicare reimburses hospitals based on the nature of patients' illnesses. Under its Prospective Payment System (PPS), it classifies patient care into diagnosis-related groups (DRGs) and allows a specified rate for each group. In some circumstances, however, it reimburses specified allowable costs. The amounts paid by the third-party payers are almost always less than the provider's "standard" billing rate.

At the time they provide patient care, hospitals and other health care providers cannot always be certain as to the portion of their standard charges that they ultimately will be paid. Usually the amount is known for certain only when they receive payment. In fact, under some "retrospective" payment arrangements, payments are based on total costs incurred during a particular period. Although the third-party payer makes interim payments during the period, a final determination may not be reached until after the end of the period.

Inasmuch as many patients who are uninsured cannot afford the costs of an extended hospital stay or expensive medical procedures, health care providers may face high rates of bad debts. Moreover, unlike businesses, providers often serve patients who they know will be unable to pay the amounts billed.

Owing to the uncertainty of the amounts that they will actually collect for their services, hospitals face salient issues of when and how to report their patient-care revenues and value their related receivables.

EXAMPLE *Patient-Care Revenues*

During a particular week a hospital records $400,000 in patient charges. The charges applicable to patients that were actually discharged from the hospital (including charges incurred in prior weeks) were $395,000.

The hospital estimates that 80 percent of the charges will be billed to third party payers, who will, on average, pay only 75 percent of the invoiced amounts.

The remaining 20 percent will be billed to patients who are uninsured. Of this 20 percent, 60 percent will be uncollectible.

Current Standards

According to the AICPA audit guide, revenue from health care services is usually recorded "when coverage is provided to an enrollee or the service is provided to a patient or resident."[5] Thus, the patient discharge method (at one time a popular basis for revenue recognition) is *inappropriate*.

Further the guide advises:

> Revenue and the related receivables for health care services are usually recorded in the accounting records on an accrual basis at the provider's *full established rates*. The provision for contractual adjustments (that is, the difference between established rates and third-party payer payments) and discounts (that is, the difference between established rates and the amount collectible) are recognized on an *accrual basis* and deducted from gross revenue to determine net service revenue. Contractual adjustments, discounts, and an allowance for uncollectibles are recorded to report the receivables for health care services at net realizable value. [emphasis added][6]

Bad debts, as implied in the recommended classification of expenses, should be reported as an expense, not a deduction from revenues.

The following entries would be consistent with these guidelines:

Patient accounts receivable	$400,000	
Patient revenues		$400,000

To record one week's patient revenues

Revenue from patient services—estimated contractual adjustments	$80,000	
Patient accounts receivable—allowance for contractual adjustments		$80,000

To establish an allowance for contractual adjustments (25 percent of the 80 percent of the $400,000 that will be paid by third parties)

Bad debt expense	$48,000	
Patient accounts receivable—allowance for bad debt		$48,000

To establish an allowance for bad debts (60 percent of the 20 percent of the $400,000 that will be paid directly by patients)

RECOGNIZING CAPITATION FEE REVENUES

Health care organizations receive capitation fees when they contract either with an individual or with an insurance company or other third-party payer to provide covered services during a specified period of time. Typically an organization receives the payments at the beginning of each month and is obligated to provide the services during the month. Sometimes the organization also assumes the risk of having to refer a patient to other organizations for diagnosis or treatment and to pay for those services.

---

[5] Paragraph 10.04.

[6] Paragraph 5.03.

EXAMPLE   *Capitation Fee Revenues*

A physicians group receives $300,000 in capitation fees from the Hartford Insurance Company to provide comprehensive health care to members of the company's health plan. During the month it provides services for which it would bill, at standard rates, $240,000. In addition, it refers patients to hospitals and other health care providers for which it expects to be billed $18,000.

Current Standards

Per the AICPA audit guide, revenue from capitation fees "is earned as a result of agreeing to provide services to qualified beneficiaries and not as a result of actually providing the care."[7]

Therefore, the physicians group should recognize revenue in the period covered by the capitation fees. Correspondingly, it should establish a liability for any related costs for which it has not yet paid.

Thus:

Cash	$300,000	
Revenue from capitation fees		$300,000
To record capitation fees received		
Patient referrals (expense)	$18,000	
Obligations for patient referrals		$18,000
To record liability for patient referrals		

The amount for which it would have billed at standard rates is therefore irrelevant.

ACCOUNTING FOR AND REPORTING CHARITY CARE

Health care organizations provide uncompensated patient care as a matter of both policy and law. The *Hospital Survey and Construction Act of 1946* (Public Law 79-725, usually referred to as the *Hill-Burton Act*), stipulates that hospitals receiving federal construction funds must provide a certain amount of charitable care. This care does not result in cash inflows and consequently, it can be argued, should not qualify for recognition either as revenue or as receivables. On the other hand, charity care is conceptually similar to patient care for which third parties will reimburse the hospital or other provider for less than full rates (in the case of charity care, at zero) or patient care in which substantial bad debts are anticipated.

EXAMPLE   *Charity Care*

A hospital values care provided to indigent patients at $300,000, based on standard billing rates. However, it anticipates collecting for none of its services.

---

[7] Paragraph 1.19.

Current Standards

The AICPA audit guide specifies that gross revenue should *exclude* charity care. However, it also makes clear that health care organizations are obligated to disclose their policies for providing charity care and should indicate the amounts provided based on the provider's "rates, costs, units of service, or other statistics."[8]

The guide recognizes that distinguishing bad debt expense from charity care requires judgment. However, it notes that "charity care represents health care services that are provided but are never expected to result in cash flows," whereas it defines bad debt expense as "the provision for actual or expected uncollectibles resulting from the extension of credit."[9] The key distinction is that an entity provides charity care in the expectation that it will not receive compensation but incurs bad debts by providing service in the hope of at least partial payment.

Thus, in the example, the hospital need not make an entry to record the value of the charitable care. It should, however, explain its policies and report the total value of the care provided in notes to the financial statements.

IN PRACTICE

The following are excerpts from an article published shortly after Austin's municipal hospital, which had previously reported that it was profitable, disclosed that it was in fact facing a major deficit.

COLLECTION OF ERRORS ADD UP TO $21 MILLION DEBACLE

Behind the now infamous $21 million shortfall at Brackenridge Hospital is a collection of several problems, not one. They came to light as Richard Lewis, who took over Sept. 1 as the hospital's chief financial officer, began reviewing the closing of the books for the 1993 fiscal year, which ended Sept. 30. . . .

Mostly, the $21 million shortfall centered on accounting for projected income from big institutional payers—the federal government, health maintenance organizations and preferred provider organizations—that pay only part of the full charge for a patient's medical services. "They booked some $70 million worth of deductions," Dunkerley said. But $70 million wasn't enough: "They made some errors in math; they made some errors in the accounting."

City official Betty Dunkerley and Brackenridge official Richard Lewis outline some of what they say are accounting errors at the hospital:

• About $4.1 million involved Medicare "contractual allowances." A contractual allowance, or discount, is the amount of money Medicare and Medicaid, fed-

---

[8] Paragraphs 10.03; 10.20.

[9] Paragraph 7.2 and glossary.

eral health insurance programs, will not pay of a hospital's full bill. Like other hospitals, Brackenridge needs to know how much money it can expect to come in, not just how much it has billed, to project income and plan accurately. Of the $4.1 million, $1.53 million was money the hospital received from Medicare but was booked twice in the process of accounting for the contractual allowances when the books were closed for the fiscal year, Lewis said.

- About $8.6 million involved patients who were billed at full service rates and only later were identified as Medicaid patients. When patients are admitted with no insurance, Lewis said, the hospital assumes none of the bill will ever be paid. But thanks to an aggressive program to recover as much money as possible from Medicaid, Brackenridge often does collect part of the bill charged to such patients.

- $4.5 million resulted when accountants did not book enough discounts given to HMOs and PPOs until the hospital was paid for its service. While awaiting payment, therefore, the accountants were reporting that the full payment—not the discounted payment—would be paid.

- $3.4 million came from reconciling the hospital's general ledger with its more detailed subsidiary ledger, which lists individual patients and their accounts. "I'll just be up front with you," Lewis said. "That was bad accounting."

Source: Austin American Statesman, January 23, 1994. Reprinted with permission.

Under Medicare and other arrangements with third-party payers, health care organizations may be entitled to reimbursement for allowable costs. For example, a county government might agree to share the cost of a not-for-profit hospital's emergency room. The government would reimburse the hospital for an established percentage of all direct costs (including depreciation) as well as allocated overhead costs. The third-party payers, however, may not necessarily reimburse the allowable costs in the same period in which the organization expenses the costs in its financial statements. The differences would arise when an organization:

ACCOUNTING FOR TIMING DIFFERENCES BETWEEN COSTS INCURRED AND COSTS REIMBURSED

- uses straight-line depreciation for reporting purposes but claims reimbursement on an accelerated basis

- reports gains and losses from the early extinguishment of debt in the year of extinguishment for purposes of financial reporting (per FASB Statement No. 76, *Extinguishment of Debt*) but must delay recognition for purposes of reimbursement

- capitalizes certain interest costs for purposes of financial reporting (per FASB Statement No. 34, *Capitalization of Interest*) but recognizes them as expenses for purposes of reimbursement

If the organization were to recognize an expense in one period and the reimbursement in another, then there would be a clear mismatch of revenue and expenses. However, if it were to recognize reimbursement revenue in a period before (or after) it were actually reimbursed, it would be recognizing revenue in a period before (or after) it actually had use of the resources.

Reimbursement timing differences are conceptually similar to a business's income tax timing differences. Such differences occur when a revenue or expense is recognized for reporting purposes in one period, but in another for tax purposes. Current FASB standards require that these differences be accounted for so that the reported tax expense is tied to reported income, irrespective of when the taxes actually have to be paid.

EXAMPLE   *Timing Differences*

In 1997 a hospital acquires $600,000 of medical equipment with an estimated useful life of three years. For purposes of financial reporting, it charges depreciation on a straight-line basis—$200,000 per year. A third-party payer, however, allows reimbursement on a double-declining balance basis—$400,000 in 1997, $133,333 in 1998, and $66,667 in 1999.

Current Standards

Reimbursement revenues should be matched to related expenses and the differences between revenue recognized and amounts actually reimbursed should be debited or credited to a balance sheet account comparable to deferred income taxes.

In this example, the hospital should record straight-line depreciation in the usual way in each of the three years:

Depreciation expense	$200,000	
Allowance for depreciation		$200,000

To record depreciation in 1997 (identical entries would also be made in 1998 and 1999)

The hospital should recognize reimbursement revenue in the amount of the expense to be reported on its current-year financial statements, even if this expense differs from the actual amount to be reimbursed. Thus, in this example, even though the reimbursement will differ each year, the amount recognized as revenue should be the same. The difference between the amount of the reimbursement and the amount recognized as revenue should be either debited or credited to a balance sheet account, deferred (or advanced) reimbursement. The amount recognized as the deferred (or advanced) reimbursement in the first year would automatically be reversed by the last. Thus:

1997

Cash	$400,000	
Reimbursement revenue		$200,000
Reimbursements received in advance of the related depreciation charge (a liability)		200,000

To record the reimbursement for equipment acquired in 1997

1998

Cash	$133,333	
Reimbursements received in advance of the related depreciation charge	66,667	
Reimbursement revenue		$200,000

To record the reimbursement for equipment acquired in 1997

1999

Cash	$ 66,667	
Reimbursements received in advance of the related depreciation charge	133,333	
Reimbursement revenue		$200,000

To record the reimbursement for equipment acquired in 1997

Timing differences must be distinguished from *permanent* differences. Suppose the hospital bought the same $600,000 of equipment as in the example, but the third-party would reimburse only 80 percent of the costs. Assume further (to avoid complicating the issue) that the third party would reimburse depreciation charges on the same basis used by the hospital (the straight-line basis). Thus, the hospital would be reimbursed for $160,000 each year (80 percent of $200,000). In these circumstances the difference between what the hospital charges as an expense and the amount for which it will be reimbursed is not a temporary (or timing) difference but a permanent difference. The hospital would recognize revenue of $160,000 per year—the amount actually received. No special adjustments would be necessary.

Malpractice claims have become an accepted, if unwanted, concern of health care organizations and a routine element of their financial reports. Potential losses arising from malpractice claims are obviously consequential, so most entities transfer a portion of their risk to independent insurers. However, even if all or a portion, of the risk is insured, litigation costs can still be daunting. The key accounting and reporting issues relate to when and how much of a loss should be recognized owing to both unsettled claims and claims that have not yet been filed.

ACCOUNTING FOR AND REPORTING MALPRACTICE CONTINGENCIES

EXAMPLE *Malpractice Claims*

A hospital has been charged with negligence in the death of a patient. Although no claim has yet been filed, past experience indicates that the hospital is almost certain to be sued.

Current Standards

Current standards for malpractice and other claims are drawn from FASB Statement No. 5, *Accounting for Contingencies*, and are therefore the same as for businesses. They provide that a health care organization should accrue an estimated loss by a charge to operations as soon as both of the following conditions are met:

- it is probable that an asset has been impaired or a liability has been incurred
- the amount of the loss can be reasonably estimated

If either of these conditions are not met, but there is at least a *reasonable possibility* that a loss will be incurred, then the organization should disclose the nature of the contingency and estimate the possible loss or the range of the loss (or state that an estimate cannot be made).

Thus, the cost of a malpractice claim should be accrued when the incident giving rise to the claim occurs, as long as the eventual loss can be reasonably estimated. Obviously, health care organizations face considerable practical difficulties in estimating the amounts for which claims will eventually be settled, particularly those that have not yet been asserted. Nevertheless, the organization can draw upon both its own past experience and industry data. Moreover, it does not have to assess each incident individually. It can group together similar incidents and thereby take advantage of statistical relationships. The total accrued cost should take into account litigation fees, but should be reduced by anticipated insurance recoveries.

In the example, the hospital would be required to charge an expense (a loss) in the period of the incident if it were able to make a reasonable estimate of the amount. If it were unable to estimate the amount, then it would be required to disclose the details of the incident. Assuming the best estimate of the loss was $300,000, the following entry would be appropriate:

Anticipated legal claims (expense)	$300,000	
Commitments and contingencies (liability)		$300,000

To record the estimated cost of settling a potential malpractice claim

REPORTING "RETROSPECTIVE" INSURANCE PREMIUMS

Another aspect of the question as to when and how malpractice claims should be reported is that of reporting malpractice insurance expense. Some insurance policies make provisions for "retrospectively rated premiums." These policies require that, at the expiration of the policy, the premium costs be adjusted to take into account actual loss experience. Thus, if claims during the period are greater than anticipated, the insured will have to pay more; if claims are less, then it will receive a refund. As a consequence, the insured does not always know by year-end what that year's actual insurance costs will be. These types of policies do not provide true insurance coverage (except, perhaps for claims above a specified amount), since the insured is being charged for all, or a portion, of actual losses.

EXAMPLE   *Retrospective Premiums*

In June 1999 a health maintenance organization (HMO) entered into an insurance contract for the period July 1, 1999 through June 30, 2000. The basic premium was $120,000 for the year, which the HMO paid in advance. However, the policy also contained a complex formula for premium adjustments upon the termination of the policy. Prior to preparing its financial statements for the year ended December 31, 1999, the HMO estimated, based on both asserted and unasserted claims, that it would have to pay an additional $50,000 in premiums resulting from incidents in 1999.

Current Standards

The AICPA audit guide indicates that the insured entity should charge the basic premium as an expense pro rata over the term of the policy. In addition, it should accrue additional premiums or refunds based on the FASB Statement No. 5 criteria for recognition of losses. If it is unable to estimate losses from claims, then it should disclose the contingencies in the notes.

The following entry would be required for 1999:

Malpractice insurance expense	$110,000	
Prepaid insurance (basic premium)	60,000	
Cash		$120,000
Commitments and contingencies (liability)		50,000

To record 1999 malpractice insurance expense (basic premium of $60,000 for six months plus anticipated claims adjustment of $50,000) and prepaid insurance for 2000 (basic premium of $60,000)

DIFFERENCES BETWEEN GOVERNMENT AND NOT-FOR-PROFIT HOSPITALS

Although government hospitals are within the purview of the GASB and not-for-profit hospitals are under the jurisdiction of the FASB, there are relatively few differences in their accounting practices. GAAP for governments direct that government hospitals should be accounted for in enterprise funds and should follow the requirements of the AICPA's health care audit guide (including all amendments and interpretations).[11]

WHAT UNIQUE ISSUES DO COLLEGES AND UNIVERSITIES FACE?

APPLICABLE STANDARDS

U.S. higher education is characterized by a diversity unparalleled in other countries. Not only is our system dichotomized between public and private institutions, but colleges and universities range in size from small liberal arts colleges of a few hundred students to multicampus systems of a hundred thousand or more students.

The standard-setting environment for colleges and universities is not only confusing, but is in a state of transition. Prior to the formation of the GASB, almost all colleges and universities based their accounting and reporting on guidelines established by the AICPA, in cooperation with the National Association of College and

---

[11] GASB *Codification*, Section H50. Notable exceptions relate to the statement of cash flows and the measurement of pension expense. Both GASB and the FASB have issued separate statements on these issues, which conflict in significant respects. The differences will be taken up in subsequent chapters.

University Business Officers (NACUBO). The guidelines were set forth in the AICPA industry audit guide, *Audits of Colleges and Universities* (1973), which was modified and supplemented by an AICPA Statement of Position (SOP) No. 74-8, *Financial Accounting and Reporting By Colleges and Universities*. As the GASB was being created, the allocation of standard-setting responsibility became a source of controversy. Constituents of the FASB argued that it should have jurisdiction over all colleges and universities and those of the GASB asserted that GASB should have responsibility for at least government-operated institutions. When the GASB was created in 1984 it was agreed (and later reaffirmed in 1989) that the FASB would have jurisdiction over all not-for-profit (private) colleges and universities and the GASB would have jurisdiction over all government (public) colleges and universities.

Today, not-for-profit colleges and universities follow the FASB pronouncements and the applicable AICPA accounting and auditing guide, *Not-for-Profit-Organizations*. However, on specific issues not addressed by these, they still look to the 1973 AICPA college and university guide.

The GASB is in the process of completely overhauling current college and university accounting practices, comparable to its revising the government model. As a stop-gap measure, until it completes its work, it issued Statement No. 15, *Governmental College and University Accounting and Financial Reporting Models* giving government colleges and universities two accounting and reporting options:

- the "standard" government model applicable to cities, states, and all other government entities
- the AICPA model as set forth in the 1973 AICPA college and university audit guide as amended by Statement of Position No. 78-4, *Financial Accounting and Reporting By Colleges and Universities*, and GASB pronouncements up to 1989 (the date of the college and university jurisdiction agreement), and all applicable provisions cited in GASB's Codification, Section Co5, *Colleges and Universities*

Most government colleges and universities follow the AICPA model. The standard model was not specifically designed for colleges and universities, but it is nevertheless adhered to by many community colleges, especially those that have independent taxing authority and are thereby similar to other local governments.

The following discussion addresses issues common to both government and private colleges and universities. It points out the differences between the 1973 AICPA college and university audit guide followed by government institutions and the latest FASB pronouncements and AICPA not-for-profit audit guide followed by their private counterparts. It does not address the "standard" government model; that is being dealt with throughout the text in all sections dealing with state and local governments.

IN PRACTICE

WHICH SET OF STANDARDS DO WE FOLLOW?

Most colleges and universities are clearly either public or private. Some, however, face an accounting and reporting identity crisis.

Cornell University, for example, consists of both public and private colleges. The public ("statutory") colleges include its School of Industrial and Labor Relations, College of Veterinary Medicine and College of Agriculture and Life Sciences. The private ("endowed") colleges include its College of Arts and Sciences, School of Management, Law School, and Graduate School.

The college has chosen to adhere to the FASB standards.

Fund Structure

As emphasized earlier, FASB Statement No. 117 requires that, for purposes of reporting, all not-for-profits, including colleges and universities, group their funds into only three categories: unrestricted; temporarily restricted, and permanently restricted. Private colleges and universities may continue to maintain the same funds as their public counterparts; for reporting purposes, however, they must aggregate them into the three categories.

Colleges and universities are sustained mainly by revenues from tuition, fees, contributions, grants, and investment income. Many of their revenues are restricted for specific purposes. The 1973 AICPA audit guide recommends that they establish the following types of funds (as discussed in Chapter 2):

- Current funds
- Loan funds
- Endowment funds
- Annuity and life income funds
- Plant funds
- Agency funds

Many private colleges and universities continue to maintain these funds for purposes of internal accounting and control. Government colleges and universities that adhere to the AICPA model not only maintain them for purposes of internal accounting and control, but must also structure their external reports around them.

CLASSIFICATION OF REVENUES AND EXPENSES

FASB Statement No. 117 does not specify how revenues and expenses should be classified. But most colleges and universities, both governmental and private, classify revenues by source and expenses by function. Common categories of revenues include:

- Tuition and fees
- Government appropriations
- Government grants and contracts
- Gifts and private grants
- Endowment income
- Revenues from auxiliary enterprises
- Gains (or losses) on sales of investments

Common categories of expenditures include:

- Education and general
  - instruction and departmental research
  - extension and public service
  - libraries
  - student services
- Sponsored research
- Operation and maintenance of plant
- General administration
- Expenses of auxiliary enterprises

- Depreciation
- Interest
- Provision for uncollectible student loans

DEPRECIATION

FASB Statement No. 93, *Recognition of Depreciation by Not- for-Profit Organizations*, requires all not-for-profits, including colleges and universities, to report depreciation.

By contrast, the 1973 AICPA audit guide prohibits colleges and universities from charging depreciation as an operating expense (although they are permitted to report an allowance for depreciation in the investment in plant section of their plant fund). Moreover, The GASB, in its Statement No. 8, *Recognition of Depreciation by Not-for-Profit Organizations* (Codified in Section Co5), specifically directs government colleges and universities *not* to change their accounting and reporting practices in response to FASB Statement No. 93. Therefore, whereas private colleges and universities are required to charge depreciation, public colleges and universities are prohibited from doing so.

RECOGNIZING TUITION AND FEE REVENUES AND RELATED EXPENSES

The issue of when tuition and fee revenue should be recognized arises mainly because most colleges and universities end their fiscal year in the summer months, their "slow" season. Therefore, summer semesters or quarters may overlap fiscal years. Fall or spring terms, however, generally take place entirely within a single fiscal year.

Several events or transactions could be justified as a point of revenue recognition for tuition and fees:

- as students pay their tuition or fees (i.e., a cash collection basis)
- the start of a semester
- the last date at which refunds can be claimed
- the passage of time (i.e., if a semester overlaps two fiscal years, then the revenue could be allocated between the years based on the number of semester days in each year)

EXAMPLE   *Tuition and Fee Revenues*

The fiscal year of a college ends July 31. In June 1999 a college collects $6 million in tuition and fees for its summer semester that begins on June 1 and ends on August 15. It also collects $9 million for the following fall semester, which begins on September 5. Faculty salaries applicable to summer session courses are $500,000. Of this amount, $400,000 is paid in June and July and $100,000 in August.

> ## Current Standards
>
> The 1973 AICPA audit guide states that "revenues and expenditures of an academic term, such as a summer session, which is conducted over a fiscal year-end, should be reported totally within the fiscal year in which the program is predominantly conducted."

Thus, in the example, the entire summer semester tuition and fees, as well as the related faculty salaries, should be recognized in the year ending July 31, 1999:

Cash	$6,000,000	
Revenue from tuition and fees		$6,000,000

To record revenue for the summer semester beginning June 1, 1999

Faculty salaries relating to the summer		
semester—expense	$500,000	
Cash		$400,000
Deferred faculty salaries relating to the		
summer semester (liability)		100,000

To record the faculty salaries applicable to the summer semester beginning June 1, 1999

In this example it is assumed that faculty salaries, but not other operating costs, can be tied directly to summer courses. Therefore, the faculty salaries have been matched to the tuition revenues and fees. The other operating costs would be accounted for as "period" costs and expensed as incurred.

The $9 million in tuition and fees applicable to the fall semester should be recognized as revenue in the year ending July 31, 2000, and should therefore be reported as deferred revenue when received in June 1999:

Cash	$9,000,000	
Deferred revenue—fall semester tuition		
and fees (liability)		$9,000,000

To record tuition and fees applicable to the fall semester beginning September 5, 1999

Neither FASB pronouncements nor the AICPA not-for-profits audit guide addresses the issue of tuition revenue, so the 1973 AICPA college and university guide remains the most authoritative source of guidance for both government and not-for-profit institutions.

CONTRIBUTIONS

FASB Statement No. 116 changes the way not-for-profit colleges and universities should recognize contributions. As discussed earlier, unless contributions, including pledges, are conditional, they must be recognized as revenue when received.

The 1973 audit guide, however, gives colleges and universities the option of recognizing revenue when pledges are either made or fulfilled. Therefore, government colleges and universities retain this option. Most choose to recognize revenue only when pledges are fulfilled (and cash is received).

ACCOUNTING FOR AND REPORTING GRANTS

For many colleges and universities, reimbursement grants for research and related activities are a mainstay of financial support. Grantors, especially the federal government, do not expect recipients to earn a "profit" from their grants; they expect the grants merely to cover the costs of the specified research or other activities. Nonetheless, almost all grants provide reimbursement for "indirect costs" or overhead, and Office of Management and Budget rules detail how overhead allowances on federal grants should be computed.[12]

The most controversial accounting issue as to research grants is the same as that discussed in Chapter 4 pertaining to government grants: When should revenue and expenses be recognized, inasmuch as the various stages in the grant process

---

[12] Office of Management and Budget Circular A-21, *Cost Principles for Educational Institutions.*

(award, fulfillment of terms, and payment) may occur in different accounting periods?

EXAMPLE   *Grants*

In 1999 a private university's accounting department receives a $300,000 federal grant to carry out research in government budgeting. Of this amount, $180,000 is to cover faculty salaries and $120,000 is to cover overhead. During 1999 the department began the research and paid faculty members $45,000. It was reimbursed by the federal government for $75,000 (the direct costs incurred plus a proportionate share of the overhead).

Current Standards

Per FASB Statement No. 116, grants (excluding those that are exchange transactions in which the grantors expect to receive reciprocal value) are a form of contributions and should be accounted for as such. Reimbursement grants are conditioned upon the grantee's incurring qualifying costs. Therefore, they should be accounted for as conditional grants. They should be recognized as revenue only as the grantee incurs qualifying costs.

The AICPA 1973 college and university audit similarly requires that revenue from reimbursement grants be recognized as costs are incurred. However, unlike FASB pronouncements and the not-for-profit audit guide, it stipulates that the portion of grants applicable to direct costs should be accounted for in a restricted fund. Since overhead costs cannot be tied to any specific activities or projects and can thereby be used for general purposes, they should be reported in an unrestricted fund.

The following entries would be appropriate in 1999:

Sponsored research—expense	$45,000	
Cash		$45,000

To record faculty salaries (in an unrestricted fund)

The overhead costs incurred are not broken out separately because by their very nature they cannot be. They are subsumed in categories such as maintenance, administration, and library costs.

Due from federal government	$75,000	
Government grants and contracts—		
direct reimbursement (revenue)		$45,000
Government grants and contracts—		
reimbursement for overhead (revenue)		$30,000

To record the amount due from the federal government for reimbursement of direct costs (in an unrestricted fund)

Cash	$75,000	
Due from federal government		$75,000

To record the collection of cash from the federal government (in an unrestricted fund)

In this illustration, the resources received from the federal government are restricted for specified research. Nevertheless, the transactions are recorded entirely in the unrestricted category because it is assumed that the university will exercise its option to report restricted promises to give as unrestricted if the restriction has been met in the same period as the donation is made.

The exercise for review and self-testing further illustrates these practices of non-government colleges and universities.

POSSIBLE DIFFERENCES UNDER A REVISED GASB MODEL

In 1997 the GASB proposed that the two models currently available to government colleges and universities (the AICPA model and the "standard" government model) be replaced with a new, dual perspective, model similar to the proposed government reporting model.[13] Like the government model, the college and university model would require that institutions prepare two sets of statements—one from an entity-wide perspective, the other from a funds group perspective.

The entity-wide statements would consolidate and display an institution's funds in a single column and would be on the full-accrual basis of accounting. Long-lived assets would depreciated.

The funds group perspective statements would be similar to those that are part of the AICPA model. They would show separately data on the fund types (i.e., current unrestricted, current restricted, loan, endowment, annuity, life income, and agency) and would focus on total financial resources. Long-lived assets would be reported in a plant fund and would be reported as expenditures when acquired. They would not be depreciated.

SUMMARY

The Financial Accounting Standards Board sets accounting standards for not-for-profits other than governments. The FASB, like the GASB, acknowledges the superiority of the accrual basis of accounting, but it is far less indulgent of modifications and exceptions. For example, unlike governments, not-for-profits are permitted no exceptions for inventories, prepayments, or interest.

The financial statements of not-for-profits classify resources into three categories: unrestricted, temporarily restricted, and permanently restricted. All expenses should be reported as changes in *unrestricted* resources. In contrast, governments, can report expenses in both restricted and unrestricted funds.

Not-for-profits should recognize as revenue all unconditional contributions, including both pledges and restricted donation, when they are received. However, they should recognize conditional contributions only as the conditions are satisfied. By contrast, governments recognize revenue from grants, which are similar to contributions, only when the resources received are both measurable and available for expenditure.

Not-for-profits, according to the FASB, should recognize contributed services only if they are of a professional nature and are of the type that would have to be paid for if not donated. They are also encouraged, but not required, to recognize and capitalize donations of art objects as long as they are held for public exhibition, are properly cared for, and will not be sold for purposes other than the acquisition of other collectibles.

Not-for-profits generally report both plant and

---

[13] Proposed Statement of the Governmental Accounting Standards Board, *Basic Financial Statements—and Management's Discussion and Analysis—for Public Colleges and Universities,"* 1997.

equipment and related debt as unrestricted resources. They state the assets net of depreciation, and report depreciation as an expense. Governments, in their governmental funds (both unrestricted and restricted) focus only on financial resources, thereby excluding fixed assets and related debt from the balance sheet; they do not report depreciation as an expenditure.

Most of the accounting practices followed by hospitals are similar to those of other not-for-profits. Hospitals, more than most other not-for-profits, however, must be concerned with costs. In addition, owing to reimbursement arrangements with third parties, bad debts, malpractice claims, and insurance premiums, they face uncertainty as to revenues to be realized and costs to be incurred. Accordingly, the AICPA has established criteria as to when appropriate revenues or expenses should be recognized.

Colleges and universities are unique in that the accounting and reporting models of private and government institutions differ considerably. Whereas private colleges and universities use the same general model as other not-for-profits, government institutions may adopt either the AICPA model or the "standard" governmental model. The resultant differences include practices as to fund structure, depreciation, and recognition of revenue from contributions. Both, however, follow similar policies as to when to recognize tuition revenue for semesters that overlap fiscal years (in the fiscal year in which the program is predominantly conducted), and for reimbursement grants (as the costs are incurred).

In the next chapter we turn our attention to how both governments and not-for-profits face common issues of accounting for and reporting fixed assets and long-term debt.

EXERCISE FOR REVIEW AND SELF-TESTING

The balance sheet and statement of activities of New Hampshire College (adapted from the financial statements of a well-known New England college) are presented in Table 6–7. The statements are as of June 30, 1999, and all amounts, both in the statements and in the text that follows, are in thousands.

a. In addition to the tuition and fees reported on the statement of activities (all of which were received in cash), the college received $4,000 in tuition applicable to the 1999 summer semester, which runs from June 15 to August 15. Prepare a summary journal entry to record the tuition and fees collected for the year ended June 30, 1999.

b. Prepare appropriate summary entries to record grant and contract revenues and expenses.

c. Among the college's restricted funds is a plant fund that accounts for resources reserved for the acquisition of facilities. During the year, the college used $24,000 of fund resources to acquire plant and equipment. Prepare appropriate journal entries to record the acquisition of the plant and equipment.

d. What was the college's "profit" on the inn that it operates? On its student housing and dining?

e. The college accounts for student loans in a restricted "student loans" fund. What is the amount owed to the college by students? How much interest on student loans did the college earn during the year? Is the interest on the loans available for general purposes, or is it restricted? Explain.

f. Why is endowment income not reported in the permanently restricted funds? How much of the 1999 endowment income must be used for specific purposes? Why are gains on investments reported in the permanently restricted funds?

g. During the year the college received the following pledges:

- $2,500 from an alumnus to construct a new wing to its science building
- $4,500 to be used for general educational purposes
- $5,000 to be used to acquire investment-grade securities; only the earnings from these securities may be used to support teaching, research, and other routine activities of the college
- up to $1,000 to be used to match other expected contributions to a scholarship fund in honor of a recently retired faculty member

Indicate how each of the pledges would be accounted for.

TABLE 6–7
New Hampshire College

Statement of Financial Position
For Year Ending June 30, 1999

	Unrestricted	Temporarily Restricted	Permanently Restricted	Total
Assets:				
Current				
Cash and Temporary Investments	$ 18,567	$ 36,309	$ 29,611	$ 87,487
Grants and Contracts Receivable		30,200		30,200
Pledges Receivable	4,000			4,000
Other Receivables	14,772	57	781	15,610
Total Current	$ 37,339	$ 66,566	$ 30,392	$ 134,297
Noncurrent				
Student Loans Receivable		36,954		36,954
Inventories	1,990			1,990
Deferred Charges	5,628	6,867		12,495
Investments	24,940	10,525	796,116	831,581
Land, Buildings and Equipment (Net of $89,241 Accumulated Depreciation)	283,181			283,181
Other Assets	15,475		6,879	22,354
Total Noncurrent	$ 331,214	$ 54,346	$ 802,995	$ 1,188,555
Total Assets	$ 368,553	$ 120,912	$ 833,387	$ 1,322,852
Liabilities:				
Current				
Accounts Payable	$ 23,024	$ 1,760	$ 1,627	$ 26,411
Deferred Revenue	12,672			12,672
Other Current Liabilities		1,399		1,399
Total Current	$ 35,696	$ 3,159	$ 1,627	$ 40,482
Notes and Bonds Payable	188,466	24,505		212,971
Other Liabilities		15,436	7,564	23,000
Total Noncurrent	188,466	39,941	7,564	235,971
Total Liabilities	$ 224,162	$ 43,100	$ 9,191	$ 276,453
Net Assets	$ 144,391	$ 77,812	$ 824,196	$ 1,046,399

New Hampshire College

Statement of Activities
For the Year Ending June 30, 1999

	Unrestricted	Temporarily Restricted	Permanently Restricted	Total
Revenues:				
Tuition and Fees	$ 96,662			$ 96,662
Grants and Contracts		$52,820		52,820
Private Gifts	16,503	33,868	$20,396	70,767
Endowment Income	12,382	18,548		30,930
Other Investment Income	1,593	3,619		5,212
Departmental Sales and Service	13,544			13,544
Athletic Income	1,308			1,308
Income from Museums and				
Other Programs	15,713			15,713
Auxiliary Enterprises				
Student Housing and Dining	20,117			20,117
College Inn	5,806			5,806
Rentals, Recreational and Other Facilities	11,871			11,871
Interest on Student Loans		1,856		1,856
Gains on Investments		1,649	73,552	75,201
Total Revenues	$209,405	$98,454	$93,948	$401,807
Expenses:				
Instruction and Department Research	64,697			64,697
Grants and Contracts	47,661			47,661
Libraries, Computers and Other				
Academic Support	37,406			37,406
Student Services	15,677			15,677
General Administration	13,326			13,326
Plant Operation and Maintenance	20,667			20,667
Financial Aid	26,616			26,616
Athletics and Physical Education	6,207			6,207
Auxiliary Enterprises				
Student Housing and Dining	18,999			18,999
College Inn	6,564			6,564
Rentals, Recreational and Other Facilities	11,079			11,079
Interest on Debt	6,602			6,602
Depreciation Expense	9,381			9,381
Other Expenses	8,707			8,707
Total Expenses	$293,589	$ 0	$ 0	$293,589
Excess (Deficiency) of Revenues				
Over Expenses	(84,184)	98,454	93,948	108,218
Resources Released from Restrictions	124,518	(124,518)		0
Change in Net Assets	$ 40,334	$(26,064)	$93,948	$108,218

QUESTIONS FOR REVIEW AND DISCUSSION

1. Provide an example of resources that are temporarily restricted as to (a) purpose (b) time (c) occurrence of a specific event. Provide an example of permanently restricted resources.

2. A not-for-profit organization receives a restricted gift. When, and in which type of fund, should it recognize the revenue? When, and in which type of fund, should it recognize the related expense? What is the reason for the apparent inconsistency between the fund-type in which the revenues and expenses are reported?

3. Parents of a college junior pledge to donate $1 million to her college upon her expected graduation, one year in the future. When, and in what amount, should the university recognize revenue? The university applies a discount rate of 10 percent to all pledges. Would your response be the same if the parents pledged to donate the funds only if and when the daughter was graduated? Why do many not-for-profits object to the standards pertaining to revenue recognition of pledges?

4. Members of the National Accounting Association, a not-for-profit organization, are charged annual dues of $150. Of this amount, $50 is restricted, per association policy, to covering the cost of the association's journal, which every member receives. In what category of restrictiveness should the association report the portion of revenues associated with the journal? Explain.

5. In what significant way do not-for-profits account for investments differently than businesses?

6. In a recent month a CPA provided ten hours of volunteer time to the Society for the Visually Impaired. He devoted seven hours to maintaining the organization's financial records and three to recording tapes of newspapers and magazine articles. If volunteers had not provided these services, the organization would have had to hire professionals. Should the organization give accounting recognition to the CPA's services?

7. A museum received gifts of two valuable paintings. It recorded the value of one of the two as an asset and recognized the corresponding revenue. It gave no accounting recognition to the other. What might be a legitimate explanation for such an apparent inconsistency?

8. Hospitals and other health care organizations provide services knowing that they will collect from third-party payers, such as insurance companies, considerably less than their established billing rates. In addition, they provide services to uninsured patients, aware that they will collect either none or only a small portion of the amounts to be billed. Comment on how these organizations distinguish between charity care, bad debts, and contractual adjustments, and indicate how each affects the amount of revenue from patient care that they should report.

9. What is meant by "retrospective" insurance premiums, and how should they be reported?

10. How can a hospital or other not-for-profit avoid a mismatch of revenues and expenses when they recognize expenses in one period for purposes of financial reporting but in another for purposes of obtaining reimbursement from an outside party? Give an example of how this situation can arise.

11. How do not-for-profits differ from governments in the way they account for business-type activities, such as dining halls, gift shops, and admission fees?

EXERCISES

6-1

Minor differences in the terms of a contribution may justify major differences in revenue recognition.

Upon meeting with the executive director of the Crime Victims Advocacy Group, the president of a private foundation agreed to contribute $100,000 in support of the group's proposed program to provide legal assistance to victims of violent crimes. Suppose that the foundation's formal letter acknowledging its pledge was worded in three different ways:

1. "We are pleased to pledge $100,000 in support of your group's efforts to assist victims of violent crimes."

2. "We are pleased to pledge $100,000 in support of your group's efforts to develop a new program to provide legal assistance to victims of violent crimes."

3. "We are pleased to pledge $100,000 upon your developing a new program to provide legal assistance to victims of violent crimes."

For each of the three options:

a. Prepare the journal entries that should be made upon

receipt of the letter from the foundation. Assume that it was unlikely that the pledge would be fulfilled in the same period as it was made.

b. Prepare the journal entries that should be made to record the expenditure of $100,000 on activities related to the legal assistance program.

c. Prepare the journal entries that should be made upon receipt of the $100,000 check, assuming that it was received shortly after the legal assistance program was established and the group spent the $100,000 on program-related activities.

d. Comment on why minor differences in wording might justify major differences in accounting.

Be sure to indicate the type of fund in which your entries would be made.

6-2

Some, but not all, contributions of goods and services are given accounting recognition.

In each of the following scenarios, an organization receives a contribution in kind. Prepare journal entries, as necessary, to give them accounting recognition. For each, tell why you made an entry or why you did not.

a. A local not-for-profit art museum receives advertising for its yearly benefit from radio station WLOU. The air time would have cost the museum $1,000.

b. Volunteers for "Breakfast on Bikes," a voluntary health and welfare organization, deliver hot meals to the elderly three times a week. Each of the ten volunteers works about six hours per week. All of the volunteers have permanent jobs with pay averaging $8.10 an hour.

c. Lynn Simms, a local CPA, maintains the books and records of her church. Although her normal billing rate is $60 per hour, she accepts no payment from the church. She works on church matters approximately four hours a week.

d. A construction company allows a not-for-profit community association to use its bulldozer at no cost to clear land for a new baseball park. If the association had to rent the bulldozer it would have incurred costs of $1,400.

6-3

Investment gains and losses have to be recognized as they occur— and have to be assigned to the appropriate category of net assets.

During 1998 University Hospital received a contribution of marketable securities that were to be placed in a permanent endowment fund. Neither donor stipulations nor applicable state law requires that capital gains or increases in value be added to the endowment principal. The income from the securities was to be restricted for research in pulmonary diseases. The following schedule indicates the value of the securities as of the date of receipt (labeled "cost"), the fair value at December 31, 1998, and the unrealized gains and losses of the year.

Endowment Portfolio as of December 31, 1998
(in thousands)

	Cost	Fair Value	Unrealized Gain (Loss)
Northwest Industries	$260	$275	$15
Campbell Corp.	317	304	(13)
St. Regis, Inc.	141	171	30
	$718	$750	$32

a. Prepare a journal entry to record the unrealized net gain during the year. Be sure to indicate the type of fund (e.g., unrestricted, temporarily restricted, permanently restricted) in which the entry would be made. Assuming no other transactions and no other assets in the relevant funds, show how the investments would be reported on the hospital's year-end 1998 balance sheet.

b. During 1999, the hospital sold Northwest Industries for $280. Prepare appropriate journal entries to record the sale. Credit the gain to the same account in which you credited the unrealized appreciation of 1998.

c. As of December 31, 1999, the market value of Campbell Corp. had increased to $320; that of St. Regis, Inc. to $180. Prepare a journal entry to record the unrealized gain during the year. Show how the hospital would report the investment portfolio on its December 31, 1999, balance sheet. You may combine the cash and securities of each type of fund into a single account.

6-4

The basis for recognizing patient care revenue is not always obvious.

In a particular month Northwest Medical Clinic reported the following:

1. It provided direct care services to patients, billing them $400,000. Of this amount it received $120,000 in cash, but as a consequence of bad debts it expects to collect a total of only $330,000.

2. It provided direct care to patients covered by insurance and who are members of various group health plans for which, at standard rates, it would have billed $650,000. However, owing to contractual arrangements with the payers it actually billed them for, and expects to collect, only $480,000.

3. It provided charity care, for which it would have billed, at standard rates, $82,000.

4. It received capitation fees of $1,400,000 from health care plans and provided services to members of those plans, for which it would have billed, at standard rates, $1,600,000.

Prepare appropriate journal entries to recognize revenue.

6-5

Fixed assets are accounted for differently in not-for-profits than governments.

Discovery Barn, a not-for-profit science center for children, received a contribution of $30,000 explicitly designated for the acquisition of computers. During the year it acquired $21,000 of computers, which it estimated have a useful life of three years. It is the policy of the organization to charge an entire year's depreciation in the year of acquisition.

Prepare all required journal entries, being certain to indicate the type of fund in which each entry would be made.

6-6

Multiple Choice Questions from CPA examinations.

1. FASB Statement No. 117, *Financial Statements of Not-for-Profit Organizations*, focuses on
   a. basic information on financial statements of the organization as a whole.
   b. standardization of funds nomenclature.
   c. inherent differences between not-for-profit organizations and governments that impact reporting presentations.
   d. distinctions between current fund and non-current fund presentations.

2. Lea Meditators, a not-for-profit religious organization, elected early adoption of FASB Statement No. 116, *Accounting for Contributions Received and Contributions Made*. A storm broke glass windows in Lea's building. A member of Lea's congregation, a professional glazier, replaced the windows at no charge. In Lea's Statement Of Activities, the breakage and replacement of the windows should
   a. not be reported.
   b. be reported by note disclosure only.
   c. be reported as an increase in both expenses and contributions.
   d. be reported as an increase in both net assets and contributions.

3. Valley's community hospital normally includes proceeds from sale of cafeteria meals in
   a. deductions from dietary service expenses.
   b. routine service revenues.
   c. patient service revenues.
   d. miscellaneous (auxilliary service) revenues.

4. Which of the following normally would be classified as "other" operating revenues of a hospital?

Revenues from Educational Programs	Unrestricted Gifts
a. No	No
b. No	Yes
c. Yes	No
d. Yes	Yes

5. Lema Fund, a voluntary welfare organization funded by contributions from the general public, received unrestricted pledges of $200,000 during 1999. It was estimated that 10 percent of these pledges would be uncollectible. By the end of 1999, $130,000 of the pledges had been collected. It was expected that $50,000 more would be collected in 2000 and that the balance of $20,000 would be written off as uncollectible. What amount should Lema include under public support in 1999 for net contributions?
   a. $200,000
   b. $180,000
   c. $150,000
   d. $130,000

6. An organization of high school seniors assists patients at Leer Hospital. These students are volunteers and perform services that the hospital would not otherwise provide, such as wheeling patients in the park and reading to patients. Leer has no employer–employee relationship with these volunteers, who donated 5,000 hours of service to Leer in 1997. At the minimum wage rate, these services would amount to $18,750; it is estimated that the fair value of these services was $25,000. In Leer's 1997 statement of revenues and expenses, what amount should be reported as nonoperating revenue?
   a. $25,000
   b. $18,750
   c. $6,250
   d. $0

7. In 1996, Pyle Hospital received a $250,000 pure endowment fund grant. Also in 1996, Pyle's governing board designated, for special uses, $300,000, which had originated from unrestricted gifts. What amount of these resources should be accounted for as part of general (unrestricted) funds?
   a. $0
   b. $250,000
   c. $300,000
   d. $550,000

8. Funds established at a college by donors who have stipulated that the principal is nonexpendable but that the income generated may be expended by current operating funds would be accounted for in the
   a. quasi-endowment fund
   b. endowment fund
   c. term endowment fund
   d. agency fund

9. Hospital financial resources are required by a bond indenture to be used to finance construction of a new pediatrics facility. In which of the following hospital fund types should these resources be reported?
   a. permanently restricted
   b. temporarily restricted
   c. unrestricted
   d. bond indenture

6-7

Multiple Choice Questions from CPA Examinations

1. In 1996, a private university's board of trustees established a $100,000 fund to be retained and invested for scholarship grants. In 1997, the fund earned $6,000, which had not been disbursed at December 31, 1997. What amount should be added to its permanently restricted fund balances for 1997?
   a. $0
   b. $6,000
   c. $100,000
   d. $106,000

2. In hospital accounting, restricted funds are
   a. not available unless the board of directors removes the restrictions.
   b. restricted as to use only for board-designated purposes.
   c. not available for current operating use; however, the income generated by the funds is available for current operating use.
   d. restricted as to use by the donor.

Questions 3–5

The following information pertains to Lori Hospital for the year ended May 31. In March, a $300,000 unrestricted bequest and a $500,000 pure endowment grant were received. In April, a bank notified Lori that the bank received $10,000 to be held in permanent trust by the bank. Lori is to receive income from this donation.

3. Lori should report the $300,000 unrestricted bequest as
   a. other revenue.
   b. operating revenue.
   c. a direct credit to the fund balance.
   d. a credit to operating expenses.

4. The $500,000 pure endowment grant
   a. may be expended by the governing board only to the extent of the principal, since the income from this fund must be accumulated.
   b. should be reported as nonoperating revenue when the full amount of principal is expended.
   c. should be recorded as a memorandum entry only.
   d. should be accounted for as restricted funds upon receipt.

5. The $10,000 donation being held by the bank in permanent trust should be
   a. recorded in Lori's restricted endowment fund.
   b. recorded by Lori as nonoperating revenue.
   c. recorded by Lori as other operating revenue.
   d. disclosed in notes to Lori's financial statements.

6. Community College, a private institution, had the following encumbrances at December 31:

Outstanding purchase orders	$12,000
Commitments for services not received	50,000

What amount of these encumbrances should be reported as liabilities in Community's balance sheet at December 31?
   a. $62,000
   b. $50,000
   c. $12,000
   d. $0

7. Financial resources of a college or university that are currently expendable at the discretion of the governing board and that have not been restricted externally nor designated by the board for specific purposes should be reported internally in the balance sheet of which fund?
   a. board-designated current fund
   b. restricted current fund
   c. unrestricted current fund
   d. general fund

8. At the end of the year, Cramer University's unrestricted net assets comprised $15 million of assets and $9 million of liabilities (including deferred revenues of $300,000). What is the fund balance of Cramer's unrestricted net assets?
   a. $5,700,000
   b. $6,000,000
   c. $6,300,000
   d. $15,000,000

9. The following funds were among those held by a private college at December 31:

Principal specified by the donor as nonexpendable	$500,000
Principal expendable after five years	300,000
Principal designated from current funds	$100,000

What amount should State College classify as permanently restricted endowment funds?
   a. $100,000
   b. $300,000
   c. $500,000
   d. $900,000

10. Which of the following financial statements should not-for-profit hospitals prepare?
    a. balance sheet and income statement
    b. balance sheet, income statement, and statement of changes in financial position
    c. statement of financial position, statement of activity, and statement of cash flows
    d. balance sheet, statement of revenues and expenses, statement of changes in fund balance, and statement of funds flows

PROBLEMS

6-1

A multifund balance sheet can readily be recast so that it conforms with FASB standards.

A balance sheet of Brown University, issued prior to the effective date of FASB Statement No. 117, is shown on page 264.

Recast the fund balance section of the balance sheet so that it presents the fund balances in the three categories required by Statement No. 117. Assume the assets and liabilities are to be shown in a single column (i.e., the totals column of the balance sheet presented). However, divide the fund balance section into three separate sections, each of which conforms to one of the three categories required by Statement No. 117. Report each fund balance on the new balance sheet within one of the three categories.

Make appropriate assumptions as to the type of restriction that applies to each of the funds.

6-2

Pledges must be distinguished by the extent to which they are restricted.

A private college receives the following pledges of support.

a. As part of its annual fund drive, alumni and friends of the college pledge $8 million. The college estimates that about 15 percent of the pledges will prove uncollectible.

b. A CPA firm promises to establish an endowed chair in the accounting department by donating $500,000. The professorship agreement will provide that the funds be used to purchase investment-grade securities and that the income from the securities be used to supplement the salary of the chairholder and support his or her academic activities.

c. A private foundation promises to donate $100,000 to be used to support a major revision of the college's accounting curriculum.

d. An alumnus pledges $25,000 to the college's loan fund, which is used to make loans to students requiring financial assistance.

e. The college is seeking support for construction of a new athletic field house. A local real estate investor promises to donate ten acres of land on which a fieldhouse could be built if the college is able to raise the funds required to construct the building. The land has a market value of $1 million.

Indicate the fund type (unrestricted, temporarily restricted, or permanently restricted) in which each of the contributions should be recorded and the amount of revenue, if any, that should be recognized when the pledge was made. Briefly explain your response.

6-3

A single contribution may affect all three types of funds.

The following events and transactions relate to a single contribution.

a. A high-tech firm pledged to contribute $1 million in the company's common stock to a university's business school if the school would establish a new program in the management of information technology. The securities were to be placed in an endowment fund and the annual dividend earnings were to be used to purchase computer hardware and software.

b. The business school established the program and thereby satisfied the conditions to receive the contribution.

c. The business school received the stock and placed it in an endowment fund.

d. In the first year after receiving the stock, the business school earned $30,000 in cash dividends. They were credited to an appropriate fund.

e. The business school purchased $20,000 of computer equipment.

f. The computer equipment was estimated to have a useful life of four years (no salvage). The school charged one-year's depreciation.

Prepare journal entries to record these events and transactions. Be sure you indicate the type of fund in which the entries would be made.

6-4

The distinction between contributed services that warrant financial statement recognition and those that do not is not always clear.

For each of the following situations, indicate whether the organization should recognize the described contributed services as revenue (offset by a corresponding expense). Briefly justify your response or identify key issues.

a. Nellie Wilson, the noted country-western singer, performs a benefit concert for the Save-Our-Farms Association, a political advocacy group. Wilson, who would normally charge $60,000 per concert, did not accept a fee.

Brown University

Balance Sheet as of June 30, 1992
(in Thousands)

	Total	Current Funds	Loan Funds	Endowment Funds	Plant Funds
Assets:					
Cash	$110,922	$45,268	$ 590	$ 61,555	$ 3,509
Investments	507,503	9,042		456,126	42,335
Accounts Receivable	15,070	14,499	426		145
Notes Receivable	26,000		26,000		
Inventories and Pre-Paid Expenses	5,047	5,047			
Land, Buildings and Equipment (Less Accumulated Depreciation)	196,897				196,897
Due From (to) Other Funds		11,338	(3,376)	3,323	(11,285)
Total Assets	$861,439	$85,194	$23,640	$521,004	$231,601
Liabilities and Fund Balances:					
Accounts Payable—Accrued Liabilities	$ 29,788	$20,836		$ 6,597	$ 2,355
Deferred Revenues	5,424	5,424			
Agency Accounts	10,375	10,375			
Bonds Payable	88,399				88,399
Total Liabilities	$133,986	$36,635	$ —	$ 6,597	$ 90,754
Fund Balances					
Current Funds					
Designated	20,445	20,445			
Restricted	28,114	28,114			
Student Loans Funds Established by Gift and Grants	23,640		23,640		
Endowment and Similar Funds					
Unrestricted Quasi-Endowment Funds	59,644			59,644	
Restricted Quasi-Endowment Funds	68,352			68,352	
True Endowment Funds	369,399			369,399	
Life Income Funds	17,012			17,012	
Plant Funds					
Unexpended	19,452				19,452
Retirement of Indebtedness	6,306				6,306
Net Investment in Plant	115,089				115,089
Total Fund Balances	$727,453	$48,559	$23,640	$514,407	$140,847
Total Liabilities and Fund Balances	$861,439	$85,194	$23,640	$521,004	$231,601

b. Camp Chi-Wan-Da, a summer camp for disadvantaged youth, benefits from the services of four physicians, each of whom spends two weeks at the camp providing medical services to the campers. The doctors receive free room and board but no salary. Camp association standards require that a camp of Chi-Wan-Da's size either have a physician on the premises or one on call.

c. The Taconic Music Festival, a performing arts association, needed new practice facilities. The architecture firm of Lloyd-Wright designed the facilities for the association without charge and local merchants provided the building materials. All construction work was carried out by community volunteers, only a few of whom had professional experience in the building trades.

d. A neurologist serves on the board of trustees of the Neurological Disease Foundation, an organization that funds clinical research. He was asked to serve because of his expertise in the area of neurological research and chairs the board's committee that selects grant recipients.

e. Daughters of Charity Hospital draws its nursing staff from members of its religious order. The nurses do not get paid a salary. Instead, they receive free room and board and a living allowance. The total cost to the hospital is approximately 60 percent of what it would have to pay in salary and benefits in the open market. In addition, the hospital benefits from the services of "candy stripers" and other volunteers, who staff the hospital's gift shop, carry meals to patients, and perform a variety of other important functions. Were it not for these volunteers, the hospital would have to hire additional personnel to carry out many of their duties.

6-5

Should exchange transactions be accounted for differently than contributions?

In December 1997, the Consumer Association of America (CAA), a not-for-profit research organization, received a $6 million grant from the Sporting Goods Manufacturers Association (SGMA) to develop a football helmet that will provide better protection against head injuries. The grant was intended to cover $4 million of direct costs and $2 million of overhead costs. The grant contract stipulated that the SGMA would make its payment to the CAA upon receiving invoices from CAA for the actual direct costs incurred. It further required that the research results be reported only to the SGMA and not be made publicly available. Each reimbursement payment for direct costs incurred would also include an appropriate proportion of indirect costs (i.e., an additional $.50 for each $1 of direct costs).

In 1998 the CAA carried out and completed the research for which it contracted. Direct costs were, as estimated, $4 million. It submitted the necessary invoices and received payment in full.

a. Prepare required journal entries for 1997 and 1998. Be sure to indicate whether each entry should be made to an unrestricted or temporarily restricted fund. You need not, however, record the indirect costs themselves (inasmuch as, by their very nature, they are not tied directly to the grant).

b. Assume instead that in December 1997 the CAA received from the National Sports Association (NSA) a pledge of $6 million. The donation is for research relating to football helmets. The NSA is a not-for-profit agency and the results of any research will be in the public domain. In January 1998 the CAA received the contribution. Throughout the remainder of 1998 it carried out its football-related research (incurring $4 million of direct costs). Prepare the required journal entries for 1997 and 1998 and indicate whether each entry should be made to an unrestricted or temporarily restricted fund.

c. Comment on any differences between the two awards that might justify differences in revenue recognition.

d. Suppose instead that the NSA promised to make its contribution only upon receiving a report that the research had actually been completed. Would your approach have been different? Explain.

6-6

Not-for-profits must account for timing differences in reimbursements, just as businesses must account for timing differences in taxes.

The Round Hill Health Clinic, a not-for-profit medical center that services a rural population, is reimbursed by Williams County for 60 percent of certain allowable costs.

In each of the three years, 1997 through 1999, the clinic incurs $600,000 of allowable, reimbursable costs. In addition, the following two items affected the clinic:

- the 1997 purchase of $60,000 of equipment. For purposes of external reporting, the clinic depreciates this equipment over a period of three years. The county, however, reimburses the clinic (at the 60 percent rate) entirely in the year of acquisition.
- the 1997 loss of $10,000 on early extinguishment of debt. For purposes of external reporting, the clinic recognizes the entire loss in the year the debt is extinguished. The county, however, reimburses the clinic (at the 60 percent rate) over what would have been the remaining life of the debt—in this instance, two years.

a. Prepare a schedule in which you compare, for each of the three years, the expenses that the clinic would report on its financial statements with those for which it would be reimbursed (use two columns—reportable and reimbursable).

b. Prepare journal entries for each of the three years to record the reimbursement.

6-7

This example, drawn from the actual financial statements of a major urban hospital, illustrates the main types of transactions (in summary form) in which hospitals engage.

The December 31, 1997, balance sheet of Mosholu Medical Center, a major urban hospital and research center, is shown on page 267. All amounts are in thousands.

The following transactions and events occurred in 1998 (all dollar amounts in thousands):

1. The hospital provided $705,943 in patient care at standard rates. On average, it expects to collect approximately 75 percent ($529,457) of this amount, owing mainly to discounts allowed third-party providers. Further, it expects that 5 percent of the 75 percent ($26,473) will have to be written off as bad debts.

2. It collected $480,125 in patient accounts and it wrote off $50,000 of bad debts.

3. It also provided $52,000 in charity care which it never expected to collect.

4. It earned $15,040 in investment income, of which $10,080 is unrestricted and $4,960 is temporarily restricted.

5. It purchased plant and equipment of $242, all of which was paid for with restricted resources.

6. It charged depreciation of $29,262.

7. It received unrestricted pledges of $2,070 and temporarily restricted pledges of $120. It collected all of the unrestricted pledges and $100 of the temporarily restricted pledges.

8. It earned other operating revenues (including those from auxiliary enterprises) of $135,000.

9. It incurred $430,650 in wages and salaries, of which it paid $425,000. The balance was accrued. It also incurred $200,000 in other operating expenses (including those of auxiliary enterprises), of which it paid $198,500. The balance was vouchered (and thereby credited to accounts payable).

10. It incurred and paid $210,200 in costs related to restricted contracts and grants (amounts that were not included in any other expense category). It was reimbursed for $206,800 and expects to be reimbursed for the balance in the future. In addition, it received $3,000 in advances on other grants.

11. The other operating expenses include insurance costs. However, under "retrospective" insurance policies, the hospital anticipates having to pay an additional $3,500 in premiums.

   a. Prepare journal entries to record the transactions. Be sure to indicate whether each entry would affect unrestricted, temporarily restricted, or permanently restricted fund-types.

   b. Prepare a statement of activities for 1998 and a balance sheet as of December 31, 1998.

6-8

Is there a sound reason for accounting for contributions to a not-for-profit university differently than a government university?

In January, 1997, Kirkland University receives a pledge of $200,000, to be used exclusively to support research in a specialized area of communication disorders. The university's fiscal year ends on July 31.

In December, 1997 (the following fiscal year), Kirkland receives the pledged contribution of $200,000 and spends $150,000 on qualifying research.

a. Prepare all required journal entries to reflect the transactions described. Indicate the type of fund in which the entries would be made.

   1. Assume first that Kirkland is a private, not-for-profit, university.

   2. Assume instead that Kirkland is a public university that opts to adhere to the "standard" government model that is applicable to cities, states, and all other government entities.

b. On what grounds, if any, can you justify different methods of accounting for the same transaction merely because one institution is a private university and the other a government university?

6-9

Based on actual statements (although the name of the organization has been changed), this problem illustrates the impact of FASB Statement No. 117 on financial statements and raises some provocative reporting issues.

The balance sheet and statement of activities from the 1993 financial report of The Portland War on Drugs (PWOD), a voluntary health and welfare organization, follows on pages 268 and 269. The statements reflect the provisions of FASB Statement No. 116, *Accounting for Contributions Received and Contributions Made*, but not Statement No. 117, *Financial Statements of Not-for-Profit Organizations*.

a. Recast the statement of activities (as shown in program format) so that it conforms with Statement No. 117, *Financial Statements of Not-for-Profit Organizations*.

b. Assuming that the PWOD does not maintain endowment funds, would its balance sheet also have to be recast to conform to Statement No. 117?

c. A note to the financial statements indicates that "certain grant revenue is recorded as deferred revenue to properly match the revenue with the related expenses in subsequent periods." Suppose that in August 1993, the PWOD was awarded a $20,000 reimbursement grant from the Oregon Commission on Drug Abuse to cover the costs of a youth services program. The program was to be carried out in the period September 1, 1993, through January 31, 1994. The Commission paid the PWOD $5,000 at the time it announced the award.

Prepare an appropriate journal entry for the year

Mosholu Medical Center
Balance Sheet as of December 31, 1997

	Unrestricted	Temporarily Restricted	Permanently Restricted
Assets:			
Current Assets			
Cash	$ 2,449	$ 252	$ 3
Receivables for Patient Care ($110,465 Less Allowance for Contractual Adjustments and Doubtful Accounts of $45,755)	64,710		
Other Receivables	13,059	11,343	
Marketable Securities	109,085	61,691	17,133
Other Current Assets	27,853		
Total Current Assets	$217,156	$73,286	$17,136
Noncurrent Assets			
Property Plant and Equipment ($512,184 Less Accumulated Depreciation of $223,259)	288,925		
Other Assets	11,522		
Total Noncurrent Assets	$300,447	$ 0	$ 0
Total Assets	$517,603	$73,286	$17,136
Liabilities and Fund Balances:			
Current Liabilities			
Accounts Payable	$ 55,960		
Accrued Wages and Salaries	56,942		
Total Current Liabilities	112,902		
Noncurrent Liabilities			
Long-Term Debt	292,370		
Deferred Revenue and Other Noncurrent Liabilities	96,609	10,323	
Total Noncurrent Liabilities	388,979	10,323	
Total Liabilities	501,881	10,323	$ 0
Fund Balance	15,722	$62,963	17,136
Total Liabilities and Fund Balance	$517,603	$73,286	$17,136

ending August 31, 1993, in which you recognize the $5,000 as deferred revenue. Indicate whether it would be made in an unrestricted or restricted fund. Comment on why you agree or disagree with the decision to recognize the $5,000 as "deferred revenue," as opposed to simply "revenue."

d. The notes to the statements also include a schedule (required of voluntary health and welfare organizations) in which the organization's revenues and expenses are shown by both fund and "natural" (i.e., object) classification. The organization maintains funds for each of the programs indicated in the statement of activities. In summary form, in which the funds are combined by whether they are restricted or unrestricted, the schedule is presented on page 269.

Another note to the statements states:

Property and Equipment. Property and equipment purchased with grant proceeds are expensed as acquired. Title to assets purchased with grantor funds remains with the grantor agency. At August 31, 1993, PWOD held assets with a historical cost of approximately $321,000 in this capacity. Assets purchased with unrestricted funds are capitalized and depreciated on a straight-line basis with an estimated useful life of five years.

The Portland War on Drugs

Balance Sheet as of August 31, 1993

Assets:

Current Assets

Cash	$227,112
Accounts Receivable	50,661
Prepaid Expenses and Other	47,787
Total Current Assets	$325,560
Office Equipment (Net of Accumulated Depreciation of $648)	5,815
Total Assets	$331,375

Liabilities and Fund Balance:

Current Liabilities

Accounts Payable	$229,500
Deferred Revenue	1,922
Total Current Liabilities	231,422

Fund Balance

Unrestricted	51,013
Restricted	48,940
Total Fund Balance	99,953
Total Liabilities and Fund Balance	$331,375

---

1. What was the amount of assets purchased in 1993?
2. Present arguments in defense of the practice described in this note.
3. Present arguments in favor of an alternative practice, such as capitalizing the assets, depreciating them over their useful lives, and deferring the reimbursement revenue so that it is matched to the depreciation (the approach illustrated in the section of the chapter dealing with hospitals).

6-10

The statements of an actual performing arts company (name changed) must be recast to conform to recent FASB pronouncements.

The May 31, 1994, balance sheet and statement of activities of The Little Theater (TLT), a community performing arts company, are presented on pages 270 and 271. The statements were issued prior to the effective dates of both Statements No. 116, *Accounting for Contributions Received and Contributions Made* and 117, *Financial Statements of Not-for-Profit Organizations*. Hence, they are *not* in accord with generally accepted accounting principles of today.

Among the notes to the statements are the following:

Revenue Recognition

Revenue from advance season ticket sales is deferred when sold and recognized at the beginning of the applicable ticket season. Revenue from ticket sales for specific performances is recognized when the performance is held. Also, revenue from contributions and tuition received in the current period for the next performance season is deferred and recognized at the beginning of the performance year. Such amounts are reflected on the balance sheet as deferred revenue.

Contributions restricted by the donor for particular operating purposes or for plant acquisitions are deemed to be earned and reported as revenue when the TLT has incurred expenditures in compliance with the specific restrictions.

Deferred Revenue

Deferred revenues consist of the following at May 31, 1994, and 1993:

	1994	1993
Ticket Sales	$ 94,416	$108,829
Contributions	26,570	48,514
Tuition	221,288	10,090
Total	$142,274	$167,433

The Portland War on Drugs

Statement of Activities for the Year Ending August 31, 1993

	Unrestricted	Temporarily Restricted	Total
Revenue:			
Community Mobilization	$1,066,383		$1,066,383
Youth Services	340,028	$ 7,485	347,513
Adult Services	174,172		174,172
Gold Star		162,455	162,455
Conferences	87,481	545,981	633,462
Other	26,718	14,822	41,540
Total Revenue	$1,694,782	$730,743	$2,425,525
Expenses:			
Community Mobilization	1,096,731		$1,096,731
Youth Services	340,028	2,533	342,561
Adult Services	174,172		174,172
Gold Star		143,104	143,104
Conferences	83,587	460,565	544,152
Other	20,020	50,128	70,148
Total Expenses	$1,714,538	$656,330	$2,370,868
Excess (Deficiency) of Revenues Over Expenses	(19,756)	74,413	54,657
Fund Balance (Deficit) Beginning of Year	68,696	(23,400)	45,296
Fund Balance, End of Year	$ 48,940	$ 51,013	$ 99,953

The Portland War on Drugs

Statement of Activities for the Year Ending on August 31, 1993, Natural Classifications
(Per Notes to Financial Statements)

	Unrestricted	Temporarily Restricted	Total
Revenue:			
Grant receipts	$1,623,139	$ 65,000	$1,688,139
Sales	2,083	166,745	168,828
Conferences	15,567	453,045	468,612
Other	53,993	45,953	99,946
Total Revenue	$1,694,782	$730,743	$2,425,525
Expenses:			
Personnel	976,862	86,093	1,062,955
Contractual Services	87,902	64,516	152,418
Travel and Transportation	116,907	297,230	414,137
Equipment Purchases	25,783		25,783
Supplies and Operating	507,084	208,491	715,575
Total Expenses	$1,714,538	$656,330	$2,370,868
Excess (Deficiency) of Revenues Over Expenses	$ (19,756)	$ 74,413	$ 54,657

Contributed Services

A substantial number of volunteers have donated significant amounts of their time in the TLT program services and its fund-raising campaigns. However, since no objective basis exists for recording and assigning values to their services, such activities are not reflected in the accompanying financial statements.

a. In what way is the TLT's policy of revenue recognition with respect to restricted contributions inconsistent with FASB Statement No. 116?

b. Suppose that the only restricted contributions were those that were reported as deferred revenue. The restrictions on the $48,514 of contributions that were deferred as of May 31, 1993, were satisfied in fiscal 1994, and therefore the contributions were recognized as revenue in that year.

1. Recast the statement of activities for 1994 so that it is in conformity with GAAP as currently applicable. For convenience you may combine all revenues (other than "contributions and special events") and all expenses into single amounts.

2. Also recast the balance sheets for May 31, 1993 and 1994 so that they are in conformity with GAAP. For convenience you may show only total assets, total liabilities and fund balances (both unrestricted and restricted components). Be sure that the fund balances as of year-end 1993, plus the change in fund balances (per your revised statement of activities) equals the fund balances as of year-end 1994.

c. Do you believe that the note pertaining to contributed services is consistent with the provisions of FASB Statement No. 116? If not, how would you rewrite it to explain why the contributed services were not reflected in the financial statements?

d. Suppose that you were TLT's independent auditor. The controller of the organization suggested that, in the future, TLT recognize revenue from ticket sales at the time a sale is made rather than when the performance takes place. Neither the FASB nor the AICPA has provided official guidance as to when performing arts organizations should recognize revenue from ticket sales. Consistent with other policies established by FASB, would you sanction the change?

The Little Theater

Balance Sheet as of May 31

	1994	1993
Assets:		
Cash	$ 75,253	$ 6,915
Certificates of Deposit	3,971	3,852
Accounts Receivable	16,922	8,495
Prepaid Expenses and Other Assets	16,120	19,714
Total Current Assets	$112,266	$ 38,976
Leasehold Improvements, Furniture and Equipment, Net of Accumulated Depreciation	183,880	187,309
Total Assets	$296,146	$226,285
Liabilities and Fund Balance:		
Accounts Payable and Accrued Expenses	$ 26,591	$ 50,225
Workers' Compensation Payable—Current	10,910	10,910
Deferred Revenue	142,274	167,433
Notes Payable	42,203	79,107
Total Current Liabilities	$221,978	$307,675
Workers' Compensation Payable	4,359	15,265
Total Liabilities	$226,337	$322,940
Fund Balance	69,809	(96,655)
Total Liabilities and Fund Balance	$296,146	$226,285

The Little Theater

Statement of Activities
for the Year Ending May 31, 1994

Revenues:

Ticket Sales	$ 800,067
Contributions and Special Events	420,984
Tuition	223,865
Touring Income	47,000
Other	8,454
Total Revenues	$1,500,370

Expenses:

Salaries, Wages and Payroll Taxes	864,734
Marketing	164,903
Facilities	128,120
Other	68,770
Special Events	47,439
Production	39,024
Touring	20,916
Total Expenses	1,333,906
Excess of Revenues Over Expenses	166,464
Fund Balance (Deficit), Beginning of Year	(96,655)
Fund Balance, End of Year	$ 69,809

SOLUTION TO EXERCISE FOR REVIEW AND SELF-TESTING

a. *Tuition and fees*

Cash	$100,662	
Tuition and fees		$96,662
Deferred revenue		4,000

To record tuition and fees (in an unrestricted fund)

The summer session tuition collected in the fiscal year ended June 30, 1999, would be recognized as revenue in the following fiscal year, inasmuch as the major portion of the summer semester would be carried out in that year.

b. *Grants and contracts*

Grants and contracts receivable	$52,820	
Grants and contracts (revenue)		$52,820

To record revenue from grants and contracts (in a temporarily restricted fund)

Grants and contracts	$47,661	
Resources released from restrictions		$47,661

To record expenses incurred to fulfill grants and contracts, both government and private (in an unrestricted fund)

Resources released from restrictions	$47,661	
Cash		$47,661

To record the payment of cash in connection with the grant and contract expenses (in a temporarily restricted fund)

Note that only some of the grants and contracts must have been reimbursement-type. If all were reimbursement-type, then the grant and contract expenses would be at least as great as the revenues.

c. *Acquisition of plant and equipment*

Land, buildings, and equipment	$24,000	
Resources released from restrictions		$24,000

To record the acquisition of plant and equipment (in an unrestricted fund)

Resources released from restrictions	$24,000	
Cash		$24,000

To record the payment of cash for the plant and equipment (in a temporarily restricted plant fund)

The resources were recorded initially in a temporarily restricted plant fund, but as plant and equipment is acquired it must be recorded in an unrestricted fund.

d. *Auxiliary enterprises*

	College Inn	Housing and Dining
Revenues	$5,806	$20,117
Expenses	6,564	18,999
Excess of revenues over expenses	$ (758)	$ 1,118

e. *Student loans*

Per amounts reported in the temporarily restricted funds, the college is owed $36,954 in principal and it earned $1,856 in interest. The interest is restricted, most probably for purposes related to student loans, as evidenced by its being reported in a restricted rather than an unrestricted fund.

f. *Endowment income*

The endowment income (unlike the endowment principal) is available for expenditure by the college and therefore must be reported as revenue of either unrestricted or temporarily restricted funds. The distribution depends on whether the income must be used for specific purposes or is available for general purposes. In 1999, $18,548 of the earnings were restricted, the balance unrestricted. The $73,552 of gains on investments is most likely reported in the permanently restricted funds because, by law or donor stipulation, they must be added to principal, not made available for expenditure.

g. *Pledges*

- the pledge of $2,500 to construct the wing to the science building would be reported as revenue and a receivable in a plant fund (a temporarily restricted fund)

- the pledge of $4,500 for general purposes could be reported as revenue and a receivable in an unrestricted fund if it were to be fulfilled in the same year as it were made; otherwise it would be reported in a temporarily restricted fund

- the $5,000 to purchase investment grade securities would be reported in an endowment fund (a permanently restricted fund)

- the pledge of $1,000 in matching funds is a *conditional contribution* and as such would *not* be reported as revenue and a receivable until the conditions upon which the pledge is contingent (i.e., obtaining the other contributions) are satisfied

CHAPTER 7

Accounting for Capital Projects and Debts Service

As indicated in previous chapters, both governments and other not-for-profits maintain separate funds (accounting and reporting entities) for resources to be used to acquire long-lived assets and to service debt. Governments classify these funds as *governmental*, as opposed to proprietary. In other not-for-profits, the resources in these funds are categorized as either *unrestricted* or *temporarily restricted*, depending on their source. For the most part, the principles of revenue and expenditure recognition presented in earlier chapters are applicable to these funds. Nevertheless, since these funds are used to account for transactions having unique features and involving sizable amounts of resources, they warrant special consideration.

Our concern in this chapter is with the *resources* to acquire assets and to service debts, not with the assets or debts themselves. In governments, the resources to acquire fixed assets, especially those that are financed with debt, are generally accounted for in **capital projects funds.** However, they may also be accounted for in the general fund or even special revenue funds, particularly if their costs are relatively low. Since the general and special revenue funds, like the capital projects funds, are governmental funds, the accounting entries and issues are similar. The resources to service debts are typically accounted for in **debt service funds.** Accounting for the assets and liabilities themselves will be addressed in Chapters 8 and 9.

In other not-for-profits, resources for both purposes may be accounted for in specially designated **plant funds.** However, as emphasized in the previous chapter, for external reporting purposes these funds are combined with the resources from other funds and presented in one of the three resource classifications as to restrictiveness. An exception relates to the plant funds of government colleges and universities that elect to use the AICPA reporting model. This model will be discussed later in this chapter.

In this chapter we shall first discuss capital projects and debt service funds in governments, along with the related issues of special assessments, arbitrage, and debt refunding. Then we will deal with how not-for-profits account for capital acquisitions and debt service.

HOW DO GOVERNMENTS ACCOUNT FOR CAPITAL PROJECTS FUNDS?

Governments establish capital projects funds to account for resources dedicated to the purchase and construction of capital facilities (other than those to be financed by proprietary and trust funds). They may maintain a separate fund for each major project or combine two or more projects in a single fund. Capital facilities include buildings, infrastructure projects (such as roads, bridges, airports, and sewer systems), and plant and equipment.

REASONS FOR MAINTAINING CAPITAL PROJECTS FUNDS

Governments *must* maintain capital projects funds for resources that are *legally restricted* for the acquisition of capital assets. Some governments also maintain capital projects funds for resources they have set aside for capital purposes at their own discretion. Although this practice may be permitted, it may mislead statement users into assuming that the resources are legally restricted when they are not.

Major capital projects are most commonly financed with bonds or other forms of long-term debt, but they may also be funded by grants, special tax levies, or assessments. Restrictions on capital project resources usually stem from debt covenants or from legislation authorizing the taxes or assessments. Generally the restrictions are exceedingly specific as to how the resources may be used. For example, the funds may be used only for the construction of a particular bridge or the purchase of a narrowly defined type of equipment.

Capital projects funds are, in essence, special revenue funds. Accordingly, the principles of revenue and expenditure spelled out in Chapters 4 and 5, which are applicable to all governmental funds, are also appropriate for capital projects funds. Capital projects funds are accounted for on the **modified accrual basis.** If the proposed entity-wide statements were to be prepared, then the funds would be accounted for on a full accrual basis (as discussed in previous chapters with respect to governmental funds in general) and consolidated with the government's other funds.

BASIS OF ACCOUNTING

As pointed out previously, budgetary entries give formal accounting recognition to the budget and enhance control. They help assure that expenditures do not exceed authorizations.

BUDGETARY ENTRIES

Governments generally budget capital expenditures on the basis of projects rather than periods. Therefore, they may not find it necessary to prepare an annual budget, to make annual budgetary entries, or to include comparisons of actual-to-budget expenditures for the year in their financial statements.

Nevertheless, budgetary accounts are as useful in maximizing control over project expenditures as period expenditures. Therefore, the GASB requires budgetary account integration in circumstances in which control cannot readily be established by means other than a budget. Integration is essential, for example, "where numerous construction projects are being financed through a capital projects fund or where such projects are being constructed by the government's labor force."[1]

On the other hand, when a government can establish control by entering into a fixed-price contract with a single vendor or construction company, then budgetary entries are not necessary.

The budgetary entries for capital projects would follow the pattern illustrated in Chapter 3 for other governmental funds. Budgetary entries are strictly an internal control mechanism; they do not affect year-end financial statements.

Government long-term obligations can take many forms, the most common of which are bonds. Bonds are formal certificates of indebtedness, most frequently issued by governments for the long-term. The discussion in this section can be generalized to other forms of debt, such as leases and certificates of obligation, which often differ from bonds more in legal form than in economic substance.

REPORTING BOND PROCEEDS AND ISSUE COSTS

Governmental funds, including capital projects funds, do not report long-term obligations. Therefore, when the proceeds of bonds or other long-term obligations are received by a capital projects fund, they must be accounted for as "other financing sources."

When governments issue bonds, they seldom receive in cash an amount exactly equal to the bonds' face value. There are at least two sources of the difference between face value and cash received:

- *Issue costs.* The bond underwriters (the brokers and dealers who will distribute the securities to other brokers and dealers or sell them directly to investors)

---

[1] *Codification*, Section 1700.119.

charge for their services and will withhold a portion of the gross proceeds as their fees.

- *Premiums and discounts.* The bond **coupon rate** (the stated interest rate) is rarely exactly equal to the market rate at the time of sale. Bonds may be printed with a coupon rate days or weeks prior to the issue date. Market rates fluctuate constantly, and the market rate that will prevail at the time of issue cannot be determined accurately in advance. The exact rate that the bonds will yield is established by issuing the bonds at a price greater or less than face value. A bond sold to yield an interest rate *greater* than the coupon rate will be sold at a *discount.* Because the prevailing rate is greater than the coupon rate, the bond is of less value to an investor than a bond with a comparable face value paying the prevailing rate; hence, the investor will pay less than the face value for it. Conversely, a bond sold to yield an interest rate *less* than the coupon rate will be sold at a *premium.* Because the prevailing rate is less than the coupon rate, the bond is of greater value than a bond with a comparable face value paying the prevailing rate.

Whenever they can separate the underwriting and other issue costs from the discounts or premiums, governments should report the issue costs as an expenditure.

EXAMPLE   *Bond Issue Costs*

A city issues $10 million of bonds at a premium of $.2 million. It incurs $.6 million in issue costs, and thereby nets $9.6 million.

The following entry would be appropriate:

Cash	$9.6	
Expenditure—bond issue costs	.6	
Other financing source—bond proceeds (face value)		$10.0
Other financing source—bond proceeds (bond premium)		.2

To record the issuance of bonds and related issue costs

Of course, the face value of the obligation will concurrently be recorded in the general long-term debt account group.

ACCOUNTING FOR BOND PREMIUMS AND DISCOUNTS

Bond premiums and discounts become an accounting issue only insofar as there is uncertainty as to how the "excess" cash will be disposed of and the manner of compensating for any cash deficiency.

EXAMPLE   *Bond Premiums and Discounts*

A government authorizes two highway construction projects, Project #1 and Project #2, each to cost no more than $50 million. To finance the projects, it issues two series of bonds, Series #1 and Series #2, each with a face value of $50 million. Both mature in thirty years (60 semiannual periods) and pay interest at an annual rate of 6 percent (semiannual rate of 3 percent). Owing to prevailing interest rates of 5.9 percent on the issue date, Series #1 is issued for $50.699 million (a *premium* of $.699 million). However, as a consequence of subsequent increases in prevailing interest rates to 6.1 percent, Series #2 is issued for $49.315 million (a *discount* of $.685 million).

The initial entries to record both bond issues are straightforward:

Cash	$50.699	
Other financing sources—bond proceeds		
(face value)		$50.000
Other financing sources—bond proceeds		
(bond premium)		.699

To record the issue of Series #1

Cash	$49.315	
Other financing sources—bond proceeds		
(bond discount)	.685	
Other financing sources—bond proceeds		
(face value)		$50.000

To record the issue of Series #2

Both projects were authorized to cost no more than $50 million. Therefore, the $.699 million premium should not be used to add unauthorized frills to the planned highway. Instead, it should be applied to future interest payments. The bonds were printed with a coupon rate of 6 percent. Owing to favorable market conditions, the government was able to borrow funds at only 5.9 percent. Still, its annual cash interest payments will be $3.0 million (6 percent of $50 million)—not $2.95 million (5.9 percent of $50 million). The premium of $.699 million can be seen as interest that investors paid the government "up front" to receive "extra" interest of $0.1 million each year over the life of the bonds. Accordingly, the government should transfer the $.699 premium to the *debt service fund*—the fund that will be used to accumulate the resources required to pay the interest and principal on the bonds. The following entry would give effect to this policy:

Other financing use—operating transfer		
of bond premium to debt service fund	$0.699	
Due to debt service fund		$0.699

To record the premium payable to the debt service fund

Accounting for the discount is generally not the mirror image of that for the premium. A bond discount, like a bond premium, adjusts the bond issue price so as to align the coupon rate with the prevailing rate. Because of the unfavorable market conditions, the government had to pay interest at a rate greater than the bond coupon rate. Therefore, it received less than the face value of the bonds; less than it apparently planned to spend on the capital project. When the bonds are issued at a premium, the capital projects fund can transfer resources to the debt service fund. However, when the bonds are issued at a discount the debt service fund would not have resources available for transfer to the capital projects fund. Therefore, the government has a choice. It can either reduce the scale of the project or make up the deficiency by some other means. If it elects to reduce the scale of the project, then no further journal entries are required. If it opts to fund the shortfall by other means, then the source of the funds will dictate the additional accounting entries. For example, if the government were to appropriate $.685 million of general fund resources, then the following capital projects fund entry would be necessary:

Due from general fund	$0.685	
Other financing sources—operating		
transfer from general fund		$0.685

To record anticipated transfer from the general fund to compensate for the bond discount

COMPREHENSIVE EXAMPLE   *Main Types of Transactions Accounted for in Capital Projects Funds*

The voters of New City authorize the issuance of $20 million in general obligation bonds to finance the construction of a new highway. The project is expected to cost $30 million (including bond issue costs), with the additional $10 million to be financed with a state grant.

Authorizing the Project and Recording the Budget

The city is required to account for the resources in a fund dedicated exclusively to this project. It elects to adopt a budget and integrate it into its accounts.

Estimated bond proceeds	$20.00	
Estimated grant revenues	10.00	
Fund balance		$30.00
To record estimated revenues and other financing sources		

Fund balance	$30.00	
Appropriations		$30.00
To record appropriations (estimated expenditures)		

Issuing the Bonds

The city issues $20 million of bonds. Owing to favorable market conditions, the bonds are sold for $20.2 million. After deducting issue costs of $.15 million, the sale nets $20.05 million.

Cash	$20.05	
Issues costs (expenditures)	$0.15	
Other financing sources—bond proceeds (face value)		$20.00
Other financing sources—bond proceeds (bond premium)		$0.20
To record the issuance of bonds		

Upon issuing the bonds, the city would record the face value of the liability in its general long-term debt account group:

Amount to be provided from general government resources	$20.00	
General obligation bonds payable		$20.00
To record general obligation bonds payable (general long-term debt account group)		

Transferring the Premium to the Debt Service Fund

The city transfers the premium to the debt service fund.

Other financing use—operating transfer of bond premium to debt service fund	$0.05	
Cash		$0.05
To transfer the bond premium, net of issue costs, to the debt service fund		

Encumbering Available Resources

The city signs several construction-related contracts for goods and services to cost $16 million. Capital projects funds, no less than the general fund, can avoid overspending by encumbering fund balance in the amount of purchase orders and similar commitments.

Encumbrances	$16.00	
Reserve for encumbrances		$16.00
To encumber $16 million for contracts signed		

Recording Grants

The city receives $8 million of its grant from the state. To be consistent with the approach taken in other governmental funds, the recognition of grant revenue should be expenditure driven. Hence, the city should record the advance payment from the state as deferred revenue.

Cash	$8.00	
Deferred revenue (grants)		$8.00
To record the advance from the state		

Recording Expenditures

The city receives and pays contractor invoices of $15 million for construction and related services.

Expenditures—construction related	$15.00	
Cash		$15.00
To record construction and related expenditures		

Capital projects funds are maintained to account for resources that will be expended on capital projects, not for the capital projects themselves. Therefore, construction outlays are charged as expenditures, not construction in process. If it is the practice of the government to give accounting recognition to infrastructure assets (some governments do; some don't), then it would record the construction in process in its general fixed assets account group. Infrastructure assets include roads, bridges, curbs and gutters, streets and sidewalks, drainage systems, and lighting systems. They are immovable and of value only to the governmental unit. The appropriate entry in the general fixed assets account group would be:

Construction in process	$15.00	
Investment in fixed assets		$15.00
To record construction in process (general fixed assets account group)		

Upon recording the expenditures in the capital projects fund, the city must reverse the related encumbrance accounts and recognize the revenue that was previously deferred.

Reserve for encumbrances	$15.00	
Encumbrances		$15.00

To reverse the encumbrance entry upon receipt of services

Deferred revenue (grants)	$ 8.00	
Revenue from grants		$ 8.00

To recognize grant revenue upon incurring allowable costs

This entry is based on the assumption that the government recognizes grant revenue as soon as it has incurred any costs that the grant is permitted to cover. Hence, it does not divide its costs between those applicable to the bonds and those applicable to the grant.

Recognizing Investment Earnings

The city invests $5 million in U.S. Treasury notes so as to earn a return on temporarily available cash.

Marketable securities	$5.00	
Cash		$5.00

To record the purchase of Treasury bills

As of year-end it has earned $0.15 million in interest, but it does not expect to actually receive the interest until the notes mature. However, the accrued interest is reflected in the market price of the notes. As observed in Chapter 4, GASB pronouncements now require that appreciation in the fair value of investments be recognized as revenue.

Marketable securities	$0.15	
Investment revenue		$0.15

To recognize appreciation in investments

Closing the Accounts

If a government needs to prepare an operating statement that shows revenues, expenditures, and similar accounts for the particular year, then it can readily close these accounts, along with the related budgetary accounts, in the manner illustrated in Chapter 3. Closing the accounts would reduce the balances in these accounts to zero and enable the government to record the revenues and expenditures of the following year. If the budget is for the entire project, not for a particular year, then the government would have to restore the budgetary accounts at the start of the next year in the amount of the balances not yet expended.

However, if the government intends to prepare reports that indicate only cumulative amounts of revenues and expenditures over the life of the project, then there is no need to close the accounts. They can remain open until the project is completed. Then, the accounts can be closed and remaining resources disposed of in accordance with the government's policy or applicable legal or contractual specifications. Generally the transfer of unspent resources to another fund would be classified as a residual equity transfer.

Table 7–1 presents an operating statement and balance sheet for the capital projects fund.

TABLE 7–1
Capital Projects Fund—Construction of Highway

Statement of Revenues, Expenditures and Changes in Fund Balance (in Millions)
For the City's Fiscal Year

Revenues:	
Grant from State	$ 8.00
Investment Revenue	0.15
Total Revenues	$ 8.15
Expenditures:	
Bond Issue Costs	0.15
Construction Related	15.00
Total Expenditures	$15.15
Excess of Revenues Over Expenditures	(7.00)
Other Financing Sources (Uses):	
Proceeds of Bonds (Including Premium)	20.20
Transfer of Premium to Debt Service Fund	(0.05)
Total Other Financing Sources (Uses)	$20.15
Excess of Revenues and Net Financing Sources Over Expenditures	13.15
Fund Balance, Beginning of Year	0
Fund Balance, End of Year	$13.15

Balance Sheet
As of the End of the City's Fiscal Year

Assets:	
Cash	$ 8.00
Marketable Securities	5.15
Total Assets	$13.15
Fund Balance:	
Reserved for Encumbrances	$ 1.00
Unreserved	12.15
Total Fund Balance	$13.15

How Do Governments Account for Resources Dedicated to Debt Service?

Debt service funds are maintained to account for resources accumulated to pay interest and principal on long-term debt. Debt service funds do *not* account for the long-term debt itself. Indeed, the only circumstances in which the principal of debt is reported as an obligation is when it has matured but actual payment has been delayed.

REASONS FOR MAINTAINING DEBT SERVICE FUNDS

The GASB *Codification* directs that debt service funds be established when:

- legally required
- financial resources are being accumulated for principal and interest payments maturing in future years[2]

Legal mandates to maintain debt service funds are commonly incorporated into agreements associated with the issuance of the debt. Lenders want assurance that the funds will be available to make timely payments of interest and principal. Therefore, they may require that the borrower maintain a specified amount, perhaps one year's interest, in a "reserve" fund—similar to the way a landlord requires a tenant to provide a deposit of one month's rent.

Debt service funds may receive their resources from several sources:

- transfers from the general fund
- special taxes restricted to the payment of debt (e.g., to construct a new high school, a school district may dedicate a portion of its property tax to the repayment of high school bonds)
- special assessments (charges to an identifiable group of residents who will receive a disproportionate share of the benefits of a project for which long-term debt was issued)

As with capital project funds, governments may be required to maintain several independent debt service funds or may be permitted to combine some or all into common funds.

BASIS OF ACCOUNTING

Like capital projects funds, debt service funds are *governmental* funds, which are accounted for on the modified accrual basis.

As discussed in Chapter 5, the GASB *Codification* stipulates that "the major exception to the general rule of expenditure accrual relates to unmatured principal and interest on general long-term debt." Until the period in which they must be paid, interest and principal are *not* considered current liabilities of the debt service fund, as they do not require the expenditure of existing fund assets. Moreover, the resources required for payment are unlikely to be appropriated—and transferred to the debt service fund—until the period in which the interest and principal actually must be paid, not before. "To accrue the debt service fund expenditure and liability in one period but record the transfer of financial resources for debt service purposes in a later period would be confusing and would result in overstatement of debt service fund expenditures and liabilities and understatement of the fund balance," according to the *Codification*.[3] The Codification makes clear, however, that when the general fund appropriates resources for debt service in one year for payment in the next, then the government *may* (but is not required to) accrue the expenditure and related liability in the debt service fund.

In contrast to the manner in which the expenditures for debt service are accounted for, the interest *revenue* on bonds held as investments is, in effect, accrued as earned, since investments must be stated at fair value and interest earned but not yet paid affects fair value.

---

[2] *Codification*, Section 1300.107.

[3] *Codification*, Section 1600.122.

Both budgets and budgetary entries are less needed, and accordingly, less common in debt service funds than in other governmental funds. Insofar as debt service funds receive their resources from other funds, then, overall internal control is established by the budgets in other funds. Moreover, the expenditures of debt service funds are typically limited to payments of principal and interest, the amount and timing of which are established by the terms of the outstanding debt.

However, if the resources of a debt service fund are derived mainly from special taxes or assessments, then an appropriations budget, and suitable accounting entries, may help enhance internal control and demonstrate legal compliance. In many circumstances the decision of whether to adopt an appropriations budget is beyond the control of accountants; it is specified in legislation authorizing the debt or establishing the fund.

BUDGETARY ENTRIES

COMPREHENSIVE EXAMPLE *Main Types of Transactions Accounted for in Debt Service Funds*

In January 1999, Carver City establishes a debt service fund to account for a serial issue of $100 million, 6 percent bonds sold at a premium of $0.2 million. Principal is to be repaid evenly over a period of twenty years beginning on December 31, 1999. Interest is payable semiannually, beginning June 30, 1999. Of the bond proceeds, $2 million is to be retained in the debt service fund as a reserve for payment of interest and principal.

The debt is to be repaid from a voter-approved addition to the property tax, plus earnings from debt service fund investments. However, any revenue shortage is to be made up by a general fund appropriation. Although the revenues generated by the property tax are expected to increase over time, the city estimates that in 1999 it will collect only $8 million, far less than the required interest and principal payments.

Serial bonds, as distinguished from term bonds, which mature on a single specified date, are repaid in installments over the life of the issue. The first installment may be delayed for several years after they have been issued, and uniform payments may not be required. The amount of principal repaid with each installment, although established in advance, may vary from year to year. Serial bonds are, in essence, nothing more than a collection of term bonds, each of which matures at a different time.

Recording the Budget

The city estimates its revenues and expenditures as reflected in the entry that follows:

Estimated revenues—investments	$ 60,000	
Estimated revenues—property taxes	8,000,000	
Estimated transfer-in— capital projects fund	2,200,000	
Estimated transfer-in—general fund	2,940,000	
Appropriations—interest		$6,000,000
Appropriations—principal		5,000,000
Fund balance		2,200,000

To record the budget

Transferring in the Bond Premium and the Amount to be Held as a Reserve

The bonds are issued and the proceeds are placed in a capital projects fund. The premium of $200,000 and the $2 million to be held in reserve are transferred from the capital projects fund to the debt service fund.

Cash	$2,200,000	
Other financing source—		
operating transfer from the		
capital projects fund		$2,200,000

To record the transfer in of the bond premium and the amount to be placed in reserve

The debt itself would be recorded in the general long-term debt account group:

Amount to be provided from general government		
resources	$100,000,000	
General obligation bonds payable		$100,000,000

To record bonds payable (general long-term debt account group)

Recognizing Investment Earnings

The city purchases as an investment $1 million (face value) long-term U.S. Treasury bonds. Acquired in the secondary market, the bonds pay interest at a rate of 6 percent annually (3 percent each semiannual period) and mature in seven years. They are purchased for $894,369—a price that provides an effective yield of 8 percent annually (4 percent semiannually).

Investment in bonds	$894,369	
Cash		$894,369

To record purchase of bonds as an investment

As discussed previously, investments will be carried at fair value. Therefore the bond discount need not be reported separately from the bonds.

During the year the city receives two semiannual interest payments of $30,000 (3 percent of $1 million). At the same time the fair value of the bonds increases by $5,775 in the first period and by $6,006 the second period. In the absence of changes in prevailing interest rates, the fair value of the bonds can be expected to increase each period by the amount by which the discount would otherwise be amortized. In that way, their fair value at maturity would be equal to their face value. In this instance, the increases in value can be attributed entirely to the amortization of the discount.

Cash	$30,000	
Investment in bonds	5,775	
Investment revenue		35,775

To record the first period's interest.

Cash	$30,000	
Investment in bonds	6,006	
Investment revenue		36,006

To record the second period's interest.

Recognizing Tax Revenue

During the year the city collects $7.5 million of the $8.0 million in dedicated property taxes due during the period. It expects to collect the balance within 60 days of year-end.

Cash	$7,500,000	
Property taxes receivable	500,000	
Property tax revenue		$8,000,000
To record property taxes		

Property taxes are recognized as revenue on the same basis as if recorded in the general fund or any other special revenue fund. Taxes restricted for a specific purpose may be recorded initially in the general fund, especially if, as in this situation, they are part of a larger tax levy. However, it is preferable that they be reported directly in the fund to which they are dedicated.

Recording the Transfer from the General Fund

During the year the city, as budgeted, transfers $2,940,000 from the general fund to the debt service fund:

Cash	$2,940,000	
Other financing source— operating transfer from the general fund		$2,940,000
To record the transfer from the general fund		

Recording the Payment of Interest and Principal

The city makes its first payment of interest on the $100 million of bonds, as due, on June 30:

Expenditure—debt service, interest	$3,000,000	
Matured interest payable		$3,000,000
To record the obligation for the first payment of interest		

Matured interest payable	$3,000,000	
Cash		$3,000,000
To record the first payment of interest		

Many governments use a bank or other fiscal agent to distribute payments of interest and principal to bondholders. If they do, then any cash transferred to the fiscal agent should be reported as an asset "cash with fiscal agent." "Cash with fiscal agent," along with the liability "matured interest (or principal)," should be reduced as the fiscal agent reports that it made the required payments to the bondholders.

Although the second payment of interest and the first payment of principal are due on December 31, 1999, the city does not actually mail the checks until January 2, 2000. Nevertheless, the expenditure and related obligation must be recognized when the payments are due:

Expenditure—debt service, interest	$3,000,000	
Expenditure—debt service, principal	5,000,000	
Matured interest payable		$3,000,000
Matured bonds payable		5,000,000
To record the obligation for the second payment of interest and the first payment of principal		

As the bonds mature, the bonds payable account in the general long-term debt account group would simultaneously be reduced:

General obligation bonds payable	$5,000,000	
Amount to be provide from general government resources		$5,000,000

To record maturity of bonds payable (general long-term debt account group)

Closing the Accounts

At year-end, the city would have to close the non–balance sheet accounts:

Appropriations—interest	$6,000,000	
Appropriations—principal	5,000,000	
Other financing source—operating transfer from the general fund	2,940,000	
Other financing source—operating transfer from the capital projects fund	2,200,000	
Property tax revenue	8,000,000	
Investment revenue	71,781	
Estimated revenues—investments		$ 60,000
Estimated revenues—property taxes		8,000,000
Expenditure—debt service, interest		6,000,000
Expenditure—debt service, principal		5,000,000
Estimated transfer-in—capital projects fund		2,200,000
Estimated transfers-in—general fund		2,940,000
Fund balance		11,781

To close the accounts

Table 7–2 presents a 1999 operating statement and balance sheet for the debt service fund.

HOW DO GOVERNMENTS HANDLE SPECIAL ASSESSMENTS?

Governments sometimes construct capital projects or provide services that primarily benefit a particular group of property owners rather than the general citizenry. To assign the costs to the beneficiaries, they assess (i.e., charge) those taxpayers the entire, or a substantial share, of the cost of the project or services. Generally, the majority of property owners within the area must vote their approval of the particular project or services and of the assessments. They can ordinarily pay the assessments in installments over several years, but must pay interest on unpaid balances.

TABLE 7–2
Debt Service Fund

Statement of Revenues, Expenditures, and Changes in Fund Balance
For Year Ending December 31, 1999

Revenues:	
Property Taxes	$8,000,000
Investments	71,781
Total Revenues	$8,071,781
Expenditures:	
Debt Service, Interest	6,000,000
Debt Service, Principal	5,000,00
Total Expenditures	$11,000,000
Excess (Deficiency) of Revenues Over Expenditures	$(2,928,219)
Other Financing Sources:	
Operating Transfer from the General Fund	2,940,000
Operating Transfer from the Capital Projects Fund	2,200,000
Total Other Financing Sources	$5,140,000
Excess of Revenues and Other Financing Sources Over Expenditures	2,211,781
Fund Balance, Beginning of Year	0
Fund Balance, End of Year	$2,211,781

Balance Sheet as of December 31, 1999

Assets:	
Cash	$ 8,805,631
Property Taxes Receivable	500,000
Investment in Bonds	906,150
Total Assets	$10,211,781
Liabilities and Fund Balance:	
Matured Interest Payable	$ 3,000,000
Matured Bonds Payable	5,000,000
Total Liabilities	$ 8,000,000
Fund Balance	2,211,781
Total Liabilities and Fund Balance	$10,211,781

REASONS FOR SPECIAL ASSESSMENTS

Cities and towns often levy special assessments when taxpayers in areas beyond their jurisdiction either want to be annexed to the city or town or want to benefit from certain of its facilities and services. In some circumstances, the area to be assessed may be designated a special purpose government district (such as a local improvement district) and may be authorized to levy and collect the assessments. In others, the assessments are levied and administered by the city or town itself.

Most often, special assessments are levied for infrastructure improvements, such as water and sewer lines, sidewalks, roads, and street lights. They could also be for discrete projects such as parks, tennis courts, swimming pools, and recreation centers.

Special assessments for services are normally levied when a community wants greater services than the government would normally provide. For example, a community that would otherwise be protected by a volunteer fire department may request that it be serviced by a professional fire department. Or, a neighborhood may petition the city to maintain and provide electricity for its street lights (in addition, perhaps, to installing the lights themselves), to provide trash collection service, or to snow-plow its roads. Assessments for services present few, if any, unique accounting and reporting problems. They should be accounted for in the fund that best reflects the nature of the assessment and the services to be provided—usually either the general fund, a special revenue fund, or an enterprise fund.

Inasmuch as the enhancements in either infrastructure or services may provide at least some benefits to the citizenry at large (for example, improved roads are not for the exclusive use of the taxpayers who live along them), governments may share in the cost of the improvements. Therefore, the projects may be financed in part by direct government contributions, by general obligation debt, or by special revenue debt (debt to be repaid from user fees, such as water and sewer charges).

Governments assure collectibility of the assessments by attaching liens against the affected properties. Thus, they can foreclose upon delinquent property owners and can prevent the properties from being sold or transferred until the assessments are current.

Like other financing mechanisms, special assessments may be subject to misuse. The accompanying In Practice insert illustrates an alleged impropriety in the use of service-type assessments.

ALLEGED ABUSE OF SPECIAL ASSESSMENTS

A Michigan lawmaker has introduced a bill intended to put an end to alleged abuses of special assessments. As reported in *The Bond Buyer* (April 10, 1996), owing to resistance to property tax hikes, several Michigan towns have established special districts to provide basic services, such as fire and police protection and ambulance transportation. The services are to be financed by assessments against property owners.

The assessments have come under attack because they are based on the state equalized value of property. This value, established by the state for purposes unrelated to the service district assessments, is generally higher than the taxable value of the property. Under Michigan law, however, property taxes must be based on the taxable value of the property.

Opponents of the practice contend that the assessments are really property taxes and are being used to circumvent the state limitations on property taxes. To curb their use they have proposed legislation that would eliminate special service districts that are used for any purposes other than infrastructure improvements.

Bond analysts took a dim view of the efforts to end the alleged abuses. They warned that by closing off an important source of revenues, the legislation could negatively affect the credit standing of Michigan municipalities. It would add to their fiscal pressures, making it more difficult for them to repay their obligations and to maintain essential services.

Capital improvement special assessments involve two distinct, albeit overlapping, phases—the construction and financing phase and the debt service phase.

In the first phase, a project is authorized and the property owners are assessed. To finance the project, the government issues long-term debt. It then undertakes construction.

In the second phase, the property owners pay their assessments and the debt is serviced. Whereas the first phase is usually fairly short—the time required to complete the project—the second may extend over many years.

Until the late 1980s special assessments were accounted for in a special type of fund called a *special assessment fund.* Today, however, special assessments are accounted for just as are any other capital projects. The construction phase is accounted for in a capital projects fund. The debt service phase is accounted for in a debt service fund.

When a government issues debt to finance a special assessment capital project, it should place the proceeds in a capital projects fund. It should account for issue costs, bond premiums and discounts, and construction costs no differently than those relating to other projects. If the government is responsible for the debt (see discussion to follow), it should report it in the general long-term debt account group. It *may* report both construction in process and the completed project in the general fixed assets account group. It *may*, rather than *should*, because most governments exclude infrastructure assets from the general fixed assets account group.

When the government levies the special assessments, it should recognize them in a debt service fund. Consistent with the principle that revenue should be recognized only when both measurable and available, it should report the assessments receivable initially as *deferred* revenue, rather than revenue. Only as it collects the assessments (or the assessments become available to meet current-year expenditures) should it recognize them as revenue. It should report contributions from the general fund or other sources just as if they were for other types of projects.

The government should account for interest and principal payable on special assessment debt in a debt service fund, no differently than that on debt relating to other projects. Thus, it should recognize expenditures (and a corresponding liability) only when the payment is actually due. It need not accrue either interest or principal. However, if the government charges interest on the unpaid balance of assessments, then "as a practical matter" the interest revenue may be accrued when due, rather than when earned, "because it approximately offsets the related interest expenditure that is also recognized when due."[4]

Accounting for special assessments is illustrated in the exercise for review and self-study at the end of this chapter.

The key accounting issue pertaining to special assessments is if, and under what circumstances, a government should report the special assessment debt as its own debt. Special assessment debt is the primary responsibility of the property owners on whom the assessments are levied. In economic substance, though not necessarily legal form, it is usually an obligation of the property owners, not the government. Arguably, therefore, the government need not report the debt on its own financial statements.

In most circumstances, however, the government is linked to the debt in some manner. These ties can be in a variety of arrangements:

ACCOUNTING FOR SPECIAL ASSESSMENT PROJECTS AND THE RELATED DEBT

GOVERNMENT OBLIGATIONS AS TO PROPERTY OWNERS' DEBT

[4] GASB *Codification*, Section S40.115.

- The government itself may issue the debt (as general obligation debt) with the expectation that the special assessments will be sufficient to cover the debt service.

- To help make the debt more marketable, and lower the interest rate, the government may either back the debt with its full faith and credit or guarantee it with some other type of commitment.

- The government may have no legal commitment for the debt, but nevertheless may assume responsibility for it so as to protect its own credit standing.

- The government may agree to share in the cost of the project and thereby to be responsible for a specified proportion of the debt.

Current Standards

Current standards require that a government account for the debt as its own as long as it *is obligated in some manner* to assume responsibility for the debt in the event of property owner default. Conditions that would indicate that a government is obligated in some manner for the debt include the following:

- The government is obligated to honor any special assessment deficiencies.

- The government establishes a fund to pay off the debt as it matures, to purchase or redeem it prior to maturity, or to satisfy any commitments or guarantees in the event of default.

- The government explicitly indicates by contract, such as the bond agreement or offering statement, that in the event of default it *may* cover delinquencies, even if it has no legal obligation to do so.

- Legal decisions within the state or previous actions by the government make it probable that the government will assume responsibility for the debt in the event of default.

Put more strongly, the government is *obligated in some manner* unless:

- it is *prohibited* (by constitution, charter, contract, or statute) from assuming the debt in the event of property owner default, *or*

- it is not legally liable for assuming the debt and makes no statement, or gives no indication that it will, or may, honor the debt in the event of default[5]

If the government is obligated in some manner for the special assessment debt, then it should account for the project as just described. That is, the construction phase should be reported in a capital projects fund, the debt service phase in a debt service fund, the fixed assets (as appropriate) in the general fixed assets account group, and the special assessment debt in the general long-term debt account group.

If the government is not obligated for the debt but simply collects the assessments from the property owners and forwards them to the bondholders, then it should:

---

[5] *Codification*, Section S40.116.

- report the debt service transactions in an *agency* fund (reflecting the government's role as a mere agent)

- report construction activities, like other capital improvements, in a capital projects fund

- report fixed assets (including infrastructure assets if it is the government's practice to capitalize them) in the general fixed assets account group

- disclose in notes to the financial statements the amount of debt and its role as an agent of the property owners, though it *need not* report the long-term debt in the general long-term debt account group[6]

Governments sometimes assess property owners for projects that they would ordinarily account for in enterprise funds. These projects typically involve infrastructure associated with utilities, such as water, sewer and electric power lines, and related facilities. Current accounting principles give governments an option in accounting for special assessments that finance these types of enterprise fund assets:

ACCOUNTING FOR SPECIAL ASSESSMENTS IN ENTERPRISE FUNDS

- They can account for the projects as they would other projects (i.e., in capital projects and debt service funds), except that the cost of the improvements should be capitalized on the enterprise fund's balance sheet and should be offset by contributed capital. The contributed capital should be reported net of any resources provided by the enterprise fund itself for construction. Moreover, the enterprise fund should report as a liability only the portion of special assessment debt that is either a direct obligation of the enterprise fund or is expected to be paid from enterprise fund revenues.

- They can report all of the transactions and balances relating to the special assessments within the enterprise fund.[7]

The GASB permits the choice because it sees merit in accounting for all enterprise-related special assessment transactions and balances within a single fund. On the other hand, in many instances enterprise funds cannot access the assessments receivable and are not responsible for the debt if the property owners default. Therefore, the board believes that a flexible standard, adaptable to many different types of legal arrangements, is appropriate.

POSSIBLE DIFFERENCES UNDER ENTITY-WIDE (FULL ACCRUAL) STATEMENTS

Were governments to prepare the proposed entity-wide, full accrual statements, they would display neither the debt service nor capital projects funds in separate columns. These funds would be combined with all other funds and account groups. However, inasmuch as the resources of both the capital projects and the debt service funds may be restricted by the bond indentures for asset acquisition or debt service, this information should be clearly conveyed. This can be accom-

---

[6] *Codification*, Section S40. 119.

[7] *Codification*, Section S40. 123.

plished by displaying the government's net assets (i.e., its fund balances—assets minus liabilities) into three sections: capital, resticted, and unrestricted. The capital component would include the government's capital assets, less its capital-related debt. The restricted would show the net assets set aside in capital projects, debt service, and other restricted funds. Thus:

Net Assets:

Invested in Capital, Net of Related Debt		$xxxx
Restricted for:		
Capital Projects	$xxxx	
Debt Service	xxxx	
Other Purposes	xxxx	xxxx
Unrestricted		xxxx
Total Net Assets		$xxxx

WHY IS ARBITRAGE A CONCERN OF GOVERNMENTS?

Arbitrage, as it applies to municipalities (i.e., state and local governments), refers to the issuance of debt at relatively low, tax-exempt rates of interest and the investment of the proceeds in taxable securities yielding a higher return. Arbitrage is of major concern to governments and can have important financial and accounting consequences for both capital projects and debt service funds.

The interest paid on debt issued for *public* purposes by state and local governments is not subject to federal taxation. The federal government draws the distinction between public and private purposes so as to restrict governments from providing assistance to private corporations by substituting their own low-interest, tax-exempt debt for that of the companies.

State and local governments can issue bonds for public purposes at lower interest rates than either the federal government or private corporations. Taking into account the required taxes on the taxable bonds, the tax-exempt bonds can provide a return equivalent to that on the taxable bonds. For example, a 6 percent tax-exempt bond provides a return to an investor in a 30 percent tax bracket equal to that of an 8.571 percent taxable bond $[6.0\% \div (1 - .30) = 8.571\%]$.

Arbitrage subverts the federal government's rationale for exempting state and local debt from federal taxation—that of indirectly subsidizing state and local governments by enabling them to save on interest costs. At one time it was argued that the federal government did not have the constitutional right either to regulate the issuance of state and local debt or to tax the interest on it. Today the federal government does regulate the issuance of state and local debt and it is widely believed that a tax on municipal bond interest could withstand constitutional challenges.

Were governments permitted to engage in arbitrage, they could generate virtually unlimited amounts of earnings simply by issuing their own bonds and investing the proceeds in higher yielding risk-free federal government securities. Using the federal securities as collateral for their own bonds, they could assure that their own debt was also risk free.

To prevent municipalities from reaping the benefits of arbitrage, the federal government has added restrictions to the Internal Revenue Code and accompanying regulations.

As previously discussed, governments typically spend the proceeds of bonds over the period of project construction. Major projects may take several years to complete. Moreover, governments may transfer a portion of the proceeds from a capital projects fund to a debt service fund, either because the proceeds include a premium or the debt covenants stipulate that they must maintain a reserve fund to guard against default. Sound fiscal management dictates that proceeds held for anticipated construction costs, for future debt service, or as bondholder required reserves be invested in interest-earning securities, such as those issued by the U.S. government.

COMPLEXITY OF FEDERAL REGULATIONS

The tax provisions are complex because they must allow for legitimate temporary investment of funds, yet at the same time prevent arbitrage abuse. To achieve this objective the federal government has produced a set of regulations so complex that few governments can administer them without assistance from outside experts. In essence, they are of two types:

- *arbitrage restrictions.* Primarily developed in 1969, these provisions establish a general rule prohibiting arbitrage. But they set forth several exceptions. Issuers are permitted to invest both construction funds and reserve funds for limited periods of time (e.g., 85 percent of the proceeds must be spent within three years).

- *arbitrage rebates*. Instituted as part of the Tax Reform Act of 1986, these regulations require that all arbitrage earnings, with some exceptions (e.g., the proceeds are spent within six months, or 75 percent of the proceeds are spent on construction within two years), be remitted to the federal government.

By failing to comply with these mandates a government can compromise the tax-exempt status of its bonds, thereby subjecting itself to bondholder litigation and political embarrassment.

ACCOUNTING PROBLEMS

The main accounting problems arise because the regulations permit issuers to calculate and remit their required rebates as infrequently as every five years. Moreover, the arbitrage earnings may be measured over multiyear, rather than annual, periods. At the conclusion of any one year, then, the government may be unable to determine its expenditure and related liability for that year. Thus, although the GASB has not yet issued a pronouncement pertaining to arbitrage, it is clear that governments must estimate their rebate obligations and recognize an appropriate expenditure and liability.

In practice, governments take two approaches to accounting for the estimated rebates. Some report the rebates as a deduction from interest revenue (a debit) offset by a payable to the U.S. government. Others, however, treat the obligation as if it were a claim or judgment. In the debt service fund or capital projects fund in which the arbitrage is earned, they recognize (as both an expenditure and a liability) only the portion of the obligation to be liquidated with currently available resources. They report the balance of the obligation in the general long-term debt account group.

HOW CAN GOVERNMENTS BENEFIT FROM DEBT REFUNDINGS?

Governments, as well as other not-for-profits, retire debt prior to maturity for a variety of reasons. For example, owing to greater revenues than anticipated they may be able to pay off bonds earlier than planned. Or, they may elect to sell facilities financed by the debt and to use the proceeds to liquidate the obligations.

In this section, however, we will be concerned with **bond refundings**—the early retirement of existing debt so that it can be replaced with new debt. Governments refund—that is, **refinance**—their debt to take advantage of more favorable (lower) interest rates, to shorten or lengthen the debt payout period, or to rid themselves of restrictive bond covenants (such as those that prevent them from incurring new debt).

GENERAL RULE AS TO POTENTIAL FOR ECONOMIC GAINS

As a general rule, if a government must retire outstanding debt by repurchasing it in the open market and paying a price reflective of current interest rates, then there would be no benefit to refunding—even in the face of prevailing interest rates that are substantially lower than those on the existing debt. There would be no economic gain because the premium to retire existing bonds would exactly offset the present value of the future interest savings. A simple example will demonstrate the point.

EXAMPLE   *Debt Refundings*

A government has bonds outstanding that pay interest at an annual rate of 8 percent (4 percent per semiannual period). The bonds mature in ten years (20 periods). In the years since the bonds were issued, annual interest rates on bonds with similar risk characteristics have decreased to 6 percent. Owing to the decline in interest rates, each of the government's bonds ($1,000 face value) is selling in the secondary market for $1,148.77.

The **economic cost** to the government of the debt, assuming that it will remain outstanding until maturity in ten years is $1,148.78—the same as its market value. "Economic cost" means the *present value of all future payments*, based on the *prevailing* interest rate of 6 percent (3 percent per period). Hence, the economic cost is the twenty semiannual interest payments of $40 each and a single principal payment of $1,000:

Present value, at 3 percent, of $1,000 principal (a single sum) be paid at the end of 20 periods (present value of $1 = $.55368)	$ 553.68
Present value, at 3 percent, of $40 interest (an annuity) to be paid at the end of each of 20 periods (present value of an annuity of $1 = $14.87748)	595.10
Total economic cost of existing bonds	$1,148.78

Were the government to retire the debt, it would have to pay the market value of $1,148.78. Assuming that it still needs the funds initially borrowed, it would have to issue new bonds to obtain the required $1,148.78. Inasmuch as current market rates have now fallen to 6 percent, it could reduce its semiannual interest payments from $40 to $34.46 (3 percent of $1,148.78). The present value of all future payments on the new debt (based on the prevailing annual interest rates of 6 percent (3 percent per period) would also be $1,148.78:

Present value, at 3 percent, of $1,148.78 principal (a single sum) to be paid at the end of 20 periods (present value of $1 = $.55368)	$ 636.07
Present value, at 3 percent, of $34.46 interest (an annuity) to be paid at the end of each of 20 periods (present value of an annuity of $1 = $14.87748)	512.68
Total economic cost of new bonds	$1,148.75

The slight discrepancy of three cents is attributable to rounding. It is, of course, no coincidence that the economic cost of the new bonds is the same as their face value. The present value of bonds issued at par is always the same as their face value.

The economic cost of the new bonds is the same as that of the existing bonds. Hence, there is no economic gain to refunding.

REALIZING ECONOMIC GAINS— EXCEPTIONS TO THE GENERAL RULE

There are exceptions, however, to the general rule that there is no benefit to refunding. First, *yield curves* (the relationship between interest rates and time to maturity) may be such that by refunding the existing bonds with new bonds having a different maturity (and thus different prevailing interest rates and prices) the government can obtain true economic savings. Second, bonds are often issued with specified **call prices.** These give the issuer the opportunity to redeem (call) the bonds at a preestablished price, irrespective of the current market price. The call price places a ceiling on the bond's market price. After all, why would an investor pay more for a bond than its call price, knowing that the government could, at its discretion, buy back the bond at the call price? If a government can redeem a bond at a call price less than the economic value of the existing bonds (i.e., what the market price of the bonds would be in the absence of a call provision) then, of course, it could realize an economic saving.

Suppose, in the example, the bonds contained a call provision giving the government the opportunity to redeem the bonds at a price of $1,050. The government refunds the existing debt, issuing $1,050 of new bonds at the prevailing annual interest rate of 6 percent for ten years—an obligation having a present economic value of $1,050. The government would thereby realize a economic gain of $98.78—the existing bonds' economic cost of $1,148.78 less the new bonds' economic cost of $1,050.00.

Most call provisions do not become effective until a specified number of years after the bonds have been outstanding. By delaying the effective date, an issuer is able to assure investors that they will receive their agreed-upon return for the indicated period and thereby enhance the marketability of its bonds.

Even if a call provision is not yet effective, the government can still lock in the savings that would result from a decline in prevailing interest rates. They can do this through a process known as **in-substance defeasance**—an advance refunding in which the borrower *economically*, although not legally, satisfies its existing obligations. Issuing new debt, the government places in trust sufficient funds to make all required interest payments through the earliest call date and to redeem the debt on that date.

EXAMPLE   *In-Substance Defeasance*

A government has outstanding the same 8 percent, ten years to maturity bonds described in the previous example. The call provision permits the government to redeem the bonds at a price of $1,050 per bond, but the earliest call date is five years (ten semiannual periods) in the future. Prevailing interest rates are 6 percent (3 percent per period).

To defease the bonds in substance the government would have to place $1,122.50 with a trustee. This amount, determined as follows, is based on an assumption that the bond proceeds will be invested in securities earning the prevailing annual interest rate of 6 percent (3 percent per period):

Present value, at 3 percent, of the $1,050 (a single sum) required to redeem the bonds after 10 periods (present value of $1 = $.74409)	$ 781.30
Present value, at 3 percent, of the $40 interest to be paid at the end of each of 10 periods (present value of an annuity of $1 = $8.53020)	341.21
Total economic cost of redeeming the bonds in 5 years (10 periods)	$1,122.51

The government would borrow the required $1,122.51 at an annual rate of 6 percent, an obligation that would have an economic cost of $1,122.51. This amount, if invested in securities earning 6 percent, would be just sufficient to make the required ten interest payments of $40 and the single principal payment of $1,050.

Most commonly (though not necessarily) the maturity date of the new bonds would be the same as those on the existing bonds. If so, the government would have the same amount of time to repay the debt as it had originally planned.

The total economic cost of taking no action is that of the existing bonds, determined previously to be $1,148.78. Therefore, the economic saving from defeasing the bond, in substance, is $26.27 per each $1,000 of existing bonds outstanding— $1,148.78 less $1,122.51.

Reporting the in-Substance Defeasance in Governmental Funds

The in-substance defeasance would generally be reported in the debt service fund. The accounting is straightforward:

Cash	$1,122.51	
Other financing source—proceeds of refunding bonds		$1,122.51

To record the issuance of the refunding (the "new") bonds

Other financing use—payment to trustee	$1,122.51	
Cash		$1,122.51

To record the transfer of cash to the trust responsible for servicing and redeeming the existing bonds.

Current Standards

Assuming that an in-substance transaction satisfies certain conditions intended to assure that the government has, in economic substance, no further responsibility for the existing debt, then it may remove the existing bonds from its general long-term debt account group and replace them with the new bonds. Among the conditions are:

- the debtor irrevocably places cash or other assets with an escrow agent in a trust to be used solely for servicing and retiring the debt
- the possibility of the debtor having to make future payments on the debt is remote
- the assets in the escrow fund must be essentially risk-free, such as U.S. government securities[8]

In addition, the government must detail the transaction in notes to the financial statements, indicating the resultant economic gain or loss.

RECOGNIZING THE GAIN OR LOSS IN PROPRIETARY FUNDS

The more controversial accounting question arises with regard to refundings undertaken by proprietary funds. As stressed previously, proprietary funds, unlike, governmental funds, report long-term liabilities within the funds themselves. Suppose, therefore, the bonds described in the previous example were issued initially at par and are thereby reported in a proprietary fund at face value of $1,000. Were the bonds to be defeased by placing $1,122.51 in trust, then the following entry would be in order to remove the existing debt from the books:

"Loss" (past, present, or future?)	$ 122.51	
Bonds payable	1,000.00	
Cash		$1,122.51

To record the in-substance defeasance of the existing bonds

As demonstrated previously, the government realizes an economic *gain* by defeasing the debt prior to maturity. Yet because the book value of debt is less than the reacquisition price, it is forced to recognize an "accounting" loss. As implied by the parenthetical question in the entry, the salient accounting issue relates to the disposition of the loss. There are at least three possibilities:

- *Recognize the loss over the prior years in which the debt has been outstanding.* The loss is attributable to declines in interest rates (and corresponding increases in bond prices) over those years. Given perfect foresight as to when, and at what amount, it would have defeased the debt, the issuer would have amortized the anticipated difference between issue price and reacquisition price over those years. However, in reality it is impractical to do that upon defeasance, because several years of previous financial statements would need to be restated.

- *Recognize the loss at the time of defeasance.* Accepting that it is impractical to assign the loss to the periods the debt was actually outstanding, this policy would recognize it as soon as feasible. Immediate recognition may be objectionable, however, in that the operating results of that period would be distorted. Not only would the government be required to report a loss when in economic substance it realized a gain, but, as if to compound the fiscal injury, it would be forced to recognize the entire amount in single period.

- *Defer the loss, and amortize it over future years.* This approach is grounded on the assumption that the defeasance is merely a substitution of new debt for existing debt with a corresponding adjustment in interest rates.

---

[8] *Codification*, Section D20.103

Current Standards

The GASB opted for the third method. It requires that the difference between the book value of the existing debt and the reacquisition price be deferred and amortized over the *remaining life of the existing debt or the new debt, whichever is shorter.*[9] This period of amortization is consistent with an interpretation that the new debt is merely a restructured version of the old. The GASB does not permit the amortization to extend past the maturity date of the existing debt because it sees any debt outstanding beyond that date as essentially a new borrowing for an additional period of time.

The GASB standards as to amortization of the difference between book value and reacquisition cost are squarely at odds with those established by the Accounting Principles Board (APB), the predecessor of the FASB. The APB, in its Opinion 26, *Early Extinguishment of Debt*, stipulated that the gains and losses must be fully recognized in the year of the refunding. The APB opinion is applicable to both businesses and not-for-profits, and accordingly results in another significant difference in accounting and reporting practices between governments and their not-for-profit counterparts—a difference of special poignancy because it is difficult to make relevant economic distinctions between the two types of entities.

What needs to be emphasized is that the reported gain or loss from defeasance, whether amortized over several periods or recognized as once, may be counter to the economic gain or loss. Entities may be tempted, therefore, to defease debt at an economic loss just so they can report an economic gain.

HOW DO OTHER NOT-FOR-PROFITS ACCOUNT FOR CAPITAL PROJECTS AND DEBT SERVICE?

Not-for-profit organizations, like governments, borrow to acquire long-lived assets. Therefore, they face comparable issues of accounting and reporting for resources restricted to the acquisition of capital projects and the servicing of debt. However, owing to differences in both basis of accounting and overall structure of the reporting model, they do not always resolve them in the same manner as governments.

Prior to the effective date of FASB Statement No. 117, *Financial Statements of Not-for-Profit Organizations*, not-for-profits reported resources designated for both capital projects and debt service in a variety of ways. Statement No. 117, however, substantially reduced the diversity of practice.

As described in Chapter 6, Statement No. 117 requires that not-for-profits classify their resources into three categories: unrestricted, temporarily restricted, and permanently restricted. The classification is based on restrictions imposed exclusively by *donors*. The statement makes clear that assets restricted by contractual agreements with suppliers, creditors, and other outside parties should be classified as *unrestricted*, and information about significant restrictions should be provided in notes to the financial statements. Thus, even the proceeds of bonds, restricted for specific projects,

---

[9] *Codification*, Section D.20.109.

should be reported as unrestricted. Similarly, resources designated for specific purposes by the organization's governing board should also be considered unrestricted. Therefore, unless restricted by donors, resources set aside for both capital projects and debt service are reported as unrestricted resources.

Resources restricted by either creditors or a governing board may be shown on lines separate from other unrestricted resources on the statement of financial position. Thus, the net asset (i.e., equity) section of a balance sheet might appear as follows:

Donor Restricted		
Permanently Restricted		$XXX
Temporarily Restricted		$XXX
Other		
Designated by Board for [Purpose]	$XXX	
Undesignated	XXX	XXX
Net Assets		$XXX [10]

As emphasized in Chapter 6, not-for-profits are accounted for on the full accrual basis, not the modified accrual basis. They account for both bonds (including the payment of principal and interest) and fixed assets the same as do businesses. The issuance of bonds is recorded with a debit to cash and a credit to *bonds payable*; the repayment with the reverse. Disbursements for the construction or purchase of plant and equipment are recognized with a debit to **fixed assets** and a credit to cash. The consumption of the assets is recognized with a debit to **depreciation** expense and a credit to *accumulated depreciation*.

As a consequence of these principles, resources accumulated for capital assets may be accounted for and reported in either a restricted or an unrestricted fund depending on their source. For example, a hospital would account for the proceeds of bonds issued to finance capital improvements in its current (unrestricted) operating fund. Its entries would be the same as those of any business. At the same time, it would account for the proceeds of contributions restricted to capital improvements in a donor restricted fund. As the improvements are made, it would transfer the resources to the current operating fund and record the new capital assets therein.

Table 7–3 (on page 300) shows how resources reserved for the acquisition of plant and the repayment of debt might be reported on the balance sheet of a hospital.

For purposes of internal control, not-for-profits may continue to maintain funds that are the equivalent of capital projects and debt service funds. For purposes of **external reporting**, however, Statement No. 117 rendered these types of funds irrelevant.

Nevertheless, the not-for-profit equivalent of capital projects and debt service funds cannot yet be relegated to the archives of accounting history. *Government universities* that elect to follow the AICPA model as set forth in the AICPA industry audit guide, *Audits of Colleges and Universities* (see the discussion of this option in Chapter 6) must still maintain these types of funds.

Under the AICPA model, colleges and universities maintain four separate funds, all of which are classified as **plant funds**:

THE AICPA MODEL

- an *unexpended plant fund,* comparable to a capital projects fund, for resources for the acquisition of plant and equipment
- a *renewal and replacement fund,* similar to the unexpended plant fund and also comparable to a capital projects fund, for resources for the renewal and replacement of physical plant

---

[10] *Statement No. 117,* para. 100.

	Unrestricted	Temporarily Restricted	Permanently Restricted
TABLE 7–3			
Illustration of How Net Assets Reserved for the			
Acquisition of Plant and Equipment Might Be Reported			
Excerpts from the Statement of Financial Position of Sylvan Valley Hospital (in Thousands)			
Net Assets:			
Unrestricted			
Net Investment in Land, Buildings and Equipment	$8,500		
Designated for Debt Service on Bonds Outstanding	600		
Other	475		
Temporarily Restricted			
For Construction of New Wing and Acquisition of Equipment		$1,300	
For Pediatric Program		158	
Permanently Restricted Endowment Funds			$1,590
Total Net Assets	$9,575	$1,458	$1,590

Note: In this illustration, $1,300 of the hospital's net assets are donor restricted for the acquisition of capital assets.

- a ***retirement of indebtedness fund,*** comparable to a debt service fund, for resources for the retirement of indebtedness
- an ***investment in plant fund,*** comparable to the general fixed assets account group, for the plant and equipment itself

These funds differ from their governmental counterparts in a significant respect: each records not only assets, but also *related bonds payable* and other long-term obligations.

The functions of these funds and the relationships among them can readily be illustrated with an example involving a public university.

COMPREHENSIVE EXAMPLE   *A Public University*

Recording the Issuance of Bonds and Donations

State University issues $8 million of bonds to purchase an office building and receives a $12 million donation to construct a library.

The proceeds of the bonds and the donations would be recorded in the *unexpended plant fund:*

Cash	$20.0	
Bonds payable		$ 8.0
Fund balance (donations)		12.0
To record issuance of bonds (in the unexpended plant fund)		

Under the AICPA model, increases and decreases in plant fund balances are reported in a statement of changes in fund balances. They are excluded from the statement of revenues and expenditures. The additions and deductions are not considered to be revenues and expenditures, although they are similar. In the example, therefore, they are charged or credited directly to fund balance (with a parenthetical notation, to facilitate the preparation of a statement of changes in fund balances, indicating the reason for the change).

Recording the Purchase and Construction of the Plant Assets

State University purchases the office building for $8 million and incurs $3 million in construction costs on the library.

The purchase of the building and the construction of the library would be recorded initially in the unexpended plant fund. The costs would be recorded as *assets*.

Buildings	$8.0	
Construction in process	3.0	
Cash		$11.0

To record the purchase and construction of plant facilities (in the unexpended plant fund)

Periodically (typically at year-end) the new assets would be transferred to the *investment in plant fund*. Moreover, the liabilities "stick" to the related assets. Therefore, they too must be transferred.

Bonds payable	$ 8.0	
Fund balance (expended for plant)	3.0	
Buildings		$8.0
Construction in process		3.0

To remove the buildings, construction in process, and related debt from the unexpended plant fund

Construction in process	$ 3.0	
Buildings	8.0	
Bonds payable		$8.0
Investment in plant (expended for plant)		3.0

To record the newly acquired assets (in the investment in plant fund)

As an alternative, the construction in process could be accounted for in the unexpended plant fund until the project is completed. At that time, the construction in process would be removed from the unexpended plant fund and the completed asset recorded in the investment in plant fund.

Inasmuch as the investment in plant fund records only fixed assets and related debt, the difference between the two is referred to as "investment in plant" (i.e., the university's equity in the plant) rather than "fund balance."

Accounting for the Debt Service

The university transfers $1.8 million from its current unrestricted fund to the *retirement of indebtedness fund* for the payment of principal and interest on the bonds. Deposited in an interest-bearing account, the resources earn $0.1 million in interest revenue. During the period, the university repays $.6 million of the bonds and incurs (and pays) $.2 million in interest.

Cash	$1.9	
Fund balance (transfer from current funds)		$1.8
Fund balance (interest earned)		0.1

To record transfer and interest revenue (in the retirement of indebtedness fund)

Although the entry is not shown in this example, the university would also, of course, record the transfer-out in its current unrestricted fund.

Fund balance (interest cost)	$0.2	
Fund balance (repayment of debt)	0.6	
Cash		$0.8

To record the debt service expenditures (in the retirement of indebtedness fund)

The retirement of indebtedness fund accounts for the resources set aside for the payment of interest and the repayment of debt. Neither the debt itself, nor the related fixed assets, are recorded in this fund. Accordingly, the contributions to the fund are recorded as increases in fund balance and the payments of both interest and principal as decreases in fund balance.

As the debt is repaid, the university must reduce the balance of the bonds payable in the investment in plant fund:

| Bonds payable | $0.6 | |
| Investment in plant (repayment of debt) | | $0.6 |

To reflect the partial repayment of the bonds (in the investment in plant fund)

The balances in each of the plant funds could be reported as unrestricted or restricted, depending on whether the resources are merely designated for a specific purpose by the governing board or whether they are legally or contractually limited to the purpose implied by the fund. Table 7–4 presents a statement of changes in plant fund balances and a balance sheet based on the entries illustrated.

Were the university to accumulate resources for the renewal and replacement of existing plant, it would report them in a *renewal and replacement fund.* This fund would be accounted for identically to the unexpended plant fund (and, hence, is not included in the example).

TABLE 7–4
State University Statement of Changes in Fund Balances (in Millions)

	Unexpended	Retirement of Indebtedness	Investment in Plant
Revenues and Other Additions			
Donations	$12.0		
Interest		$0.1	
Expended for Plant			$3.0
Repayment of Debt			0.6
Total Revenues	$12.0	$0.1	$3.6
Expenditures and Other Deductions			
Plant Facilities	3.0		
Interest		0.2	
Repayment of Debt		0.6	
Total Expenditures	$3.0	$0.8	—
Excess of Revenues Over Expenditures	9.0	(0.7)	3.6
Transfer from Current Funds		1.8	
Increase in Fund Balance	$9.0	$1.1	$3.6

TABLE 7–4 (Continued)
State University Balance Sheet (in millions)

	Unexpended	Retirement of Indebtedness	Investment in Plant
Assets			
Cash	$9.0	$1.1	
Construction in Process			$ 3.0
Buildings			8.0
Total Assets	$9.0	$1.1	$11.0
Liabilities and Fund Balances			
Bonds Payable			$ 7.4
Fund Balances	$9.0	$1.1	3.6
Total Liabilities and Fund Balances	$9.0	$1.1	$11.0

Note: Most colleges and universities present this plant fund information as part of more comprehensive statements that include current and other funds. Thus, the statement of changes in fund balance would include current fund revenues and expenditures. Moreover, the balance sheets may be presented in "pancake" (layered), rather than columnar, form.

POSSIBLE DIFFERENCES UNDER A REVISED GASB MODEL

As indicated in Chapter 6, GASB has proposed a new dual perspective model for colleges and universities similar to that for other governmental entities. The model would require that colleges and universities prepare two sets of statements—one from an entity-wide perspective; the other from a fund group perspective.

Per a GASB exposure draft, in their entity-wide financial statements, colleges and universities would report capital assets as either a single line item or detailed by major class of assets. The assets would be reported net of accumulated depreciation. Related bonds and other long-term obligations would be included among the liabilities. The excess of the capital assets over the liabilities would be reported as part of fund balance and would be classified as to the nature of the balance (e.g., invested in capital assets, restricted for capital projects, restricted for debt service.) Depreciation would be included among reported expenses.

In the funds group perspective statements, colleges and universities would display the various plant funds (those currently maintained under the AICPA model) is a single column. On the balance sheet, long-lived assets would be reported at historical cost. Accumulated depreciation would not be deducted. As in the entity-wide statements, related obligations would be reported as liabilities and the difference between the capital assets and the related obligations would be reported as part of fund balance (also classified as to nature). On the statement of revenues, expenditures, and changes in fund balances, expenditures for the acquisition of capital assets would be reported in the plant fund group. If capital assets were acquired with resources from another fund group, the resources would be shown as a transfer to the plant fund group. Depreciation would not be recognized as an expenditure.

The proposed model would require that colleges and universities include in the notes to the financial statements schedules of changes both in capital assets and in long-term liabilities. The two schedules would show, by type of asset and liability, the beginning balance, the additions and reductions during the year and the ending balance. The schedule of changes in capital assets would also show the same type of information for accumulated depreciation.

SUMMARY

Both government and other not-for-profit organizations maintain special funds to account for resources set aside for the purchase and construction of long-lived assets and for the service of long-term debt. Governments both account for, and report, these resources in capital projects and debt service funds.

Governments account for capital projects and debt service funds on a modified accrual basis. The principles of revenue and expenditure recognition are the same for these funds as for the general fund and special revenue funds. Accordingly, these funds do not report either long-term assets or long-term liabilities, and interest on long-term debt outstanding need not be accrued. The long-term assets and liabilities are reported in the general fixed assets and the general long-term debt account groups.

Special assessments are accounted for just as any other capital projects: The construction phase is accounted for in a capital projects fund, and the debt service phase is accounted for in a debt service fund. Even though the debt issued to finance special assessment projects is often the responsibility of the property owners rather than the government, the government should nevertheless report it as its own as long as it is obligated for it in some manner (e.g., it is prohibited from making payments on the debt or it gives no indication that it will, or may, honor the debt in the event of default). Governments may account for enterprise-related special assessments either in an enterprise fund or in the funds in which they account for other types of assessments.

Arbitrage, which refers to the issuance of debt at relatively low, tax-exempt interest rates and the investment of the proceeds in taxable securities yielding a higher return, subverts the federal government's rationale for exempting state and local debt from federal taxation. Consequently, the federal government has established complex regulations to deter municipalities from engaging in this practice. These regulations cause accounting problems, mainly because they require governments to rebate their arbitrage earnings and expose them to substantial penalties if they are violated.

As a general rule, bond refundings do not bring economic gains to a government, unless the government is able to call the bonds at less than their market value. However, even if the call date is in the future, a government can lock in the economic gains from the future call through an in-substance defeasance—a transaction in which the government sets aside the resources necessary to make all required interest and principal payments on the bonds to be refunded.

Like governments, other not-for-profits may account for resources set aside for capital acquisition and debt service activities in separate funds. Unlike governments, however, for purposes of reporting they combine these resources with those of other funds, classifying them as to whether they are donor restricted or unrestricted. Also, unlike governments, they account for both capital acquisition and debt service activities on a full accrual basis.

Government colleges and universities can elect to use the AICPA accounting and reporting model. Using this model, the colleges and universities account for and report their capital project and debt service activities in four types of plant funds: unexpended (for resources for the acquisition of new capital assets), renewal and replacement (for resources for the renewal and replacement of existing capital assets), retirement of indebtedness (for resources for the repayment of debt) and investment in plant (for capital assets and related debt).

In the next two chapters we consider issues associated with the long-lived assets and the long-term obligations of both governments and not-for-profits.

EXERCISE FOR REVIEW AND SELF-STUDY

With the approval of neighborhood property owners, the White City council voted to construct sidewalks in a newly annexed neighborhood, assess the property owners for the cost, and issue debt to finance the project.

a. For the 1999 transactions that follow, prepare journal entries in White City's capital projects and debt service funds:

1. The city council assessed the property owners the estimated cost of $8,000,000. The assessments are payable over a five-year period ($1,600,000 per year) with interest at 6 percent annually on the unpaid balance. The first installment is due on December 31, 1999.
2. The city issued $8,000,000 of five-year, 6 percent, serial bonds. The bonds were issued at a premium of $200,000, but the city incurred issuance costs of $150,000. It transferred the premium (net of the issuance costs) to the debt service fund.
3. It constructed the sidewalks.
4. It collected the first $1,600,000 installment of the assessments, along with $480,000 in interest.

5. It made one payment of $240,000 interest on the bonds. The next payment of interest, along with $1,600,000 of principal, is due in January 2000.

b. The bond agreement permits the city to redeem the $1,600,000 of bonds that are due in January 2004 one year early in (January 2003), at par, without penalty. In January 2001 (with six semiannual periods until the January 2004 maturity date) interest rates decrease to an annual rate of 4 percent and the city has the opportunity to defease the bonds "in substance."

1. What is the "economic cost" of the $1,600,000 of bonds outstanding as of January 2001, assuming that the city would have to make six additional interest payments of $48,000 (the semiannual coupon rate of 3 percent times $1,600,000) plus a principal payment of $1.6 million? Base your valuation on the prevailing interest rate of 4 percent (2 percent per period).

2. How much would the city have to place with a trustee in January 2001 so that it would have sufficient resources on hand to retire the bonds in January 2003—i.e., the *four* required interest payments of $48,000 through January 2003 and the one payment of principal of $1,600,000. Assume the funds placed with the trustee would earn interest at the annual rate of 4 percent (2 percent per period).

3. Assume the city would borrow the funds to be placed with the trustee by issuing bonds yielding the prevailing rate of 4 percent. What would be the "economic cost" of this new debt? How does it compare with that of the old debt?

QUESTIONS FOR REVIEW AND DISCUSSION

1. Although many governments prepare budgets for both capital projects and debt service funds and integrate them into their accounts, budgetary control over these funds is not as essential as for other governmental funds. Do you agree? Explain. If budgets are prepared for capital projects funds, in what significant way may they differ from those prepared for other funds.

2. When bonds are issued for capital projects, premiums are generally not accounted for as the mirror image of discounts. Why not?

3. It is sometimes said that in debt service funds the accounting for interest revenue is inconsistent with that for interest expenditure? Explain. What is the rationale for this seeming inconsistency?

4. Until recently governments maintained a unique type of fund to account for special assessments. This fund recorded the construction in process, the long-term debt and the assessments receivable. Explain briefly how governments account for special assessments today.

5. Special assessment debt may be, in economic substance and/or legal form, an obligation of the assessed property owners rather than a government. Should the government, therefore, report it in its statements as if it were its own debt? What are the current standards as to when a government should recognize special assessment debt as its own obligation?

6. What is *arbitrage?* Why does the Internal Revenue Service place strict limits on the amount of arbitrage that a municipality can earn?

7. Under what circumstances can a government refund outstanding debt and thereby take advantage of a decline in interest rates?

8. What is meant by an *in-substance defeasance*, and how can a government use it to lower its interest costs? How must it recognize a gain or loss on defeasance if it accounts for the debt in a proprietary fund? How do the GASB standards pertaining to in-substance defeasances differ from those of the FASB?

9. A private college issues bonds that must be used for the construction of a science center. Where on the college's balance sheet should the bond proceeds be reported? Why?

10. A municipal government and a not-for-profit social service agency each repay $1 million of principal on outstanding bonds. Both had previously "saved" and set aside sufficient resources to make the required payments. Compare the impact of the transactions on the financial statements of the two entities.

EXERCISES

7-1

Capital projects funds account for construction expenditures, not for the assets that are being constructed.

The Wickliffe City Council authorizes the restoration of the city library. The project is to be funded by the issuance of bonds, a grant from the state, and property taxes.

a. Prepare journal entries in the capital projects fund to reflect the following events and transactions.

1. The city approves (and gives accounting recognition to) the project's budget of $9,027,000, of which $6,000,000 is to be funded by general obligation bonds, $2,500,000 from the state, and the remaining $527,000 from the general fund. The city estimates that construction costs will be $8,907,000 and bond issue costs $120,000.
2. The city issues 9 percent, 15-year bonds that have a face value of $6,000,000. The bonds are sold for $6,120,000, an amount reflecting a price of $102. The city incurs $115,000 in issue costs; hence, the net proceeds are $6,005,000.
3. The city transfers the net premium of $5,000 to its debt service fund.
4. It receives the anticipated $2,500,000 from the state and transfers $527,000 from the general fund.
5. It signs an agreement with a contractor for $8,890,000.
6. It pays the contractor $8,890,000 upon completion of the project.
7. It transfers the remaining cash to the debt service fund.

b. Prepare appropriate closing entries.

7-2

The accounting for bond premiums is not the mirror image of that for bond discounts.

Pacific Independent School District issued $100 million of general obligation bonds to finance the construction of new schools. The bonds were issued at a premium of $.6 million.

a. Prepare the capital projects fund journal entries to record the issue of the bonds and the transfer of the premium to an appropriate fund.

b. Suppose, instead, that the bonds were issued at a discount of $.6 million but that the project will still cost $100 million. Prepare the appropriate entries.
  1. Contrast the entries in this part and in part a.
  2. Indicate the options available to the school district and tell how they would affect the entries required of the district.
  3. Suppose the government chose to finance the balance of the project with general revenues. Prepare the appropriate capital projects fund entry.

7-3

Governments can seldom realize an economic gain by refunding bonds in the absence of call provisions.

A government has outstanding $100 million of twenty-year, 10 percent bonds. They were issued at par and have sixteen years (32 semiannual periods) until they mature. They pay interest semiannually.

a. Suppose current prevailing interest rates had decreased to 8 percent (4 percent per period). What amount would you estimate the bonds were trading at in the open market?

b. Suppose the government elected to purchase the bonds in the market and retire them. To finance the purchase it issued sixteen-year (32-period) bonds at the prevailing rate of 8 percent (4 percent per period). What would be the "economic cost" (i.e., the present value of anticipated cash flows) of issuing these bonds? Would the government realize an economic gain by retiring the old bonds and issuing the new?

c. Suppose a call provision permitted the government to redeem the bonds for a total of $101 million. Could the government realize an economic gain by recalling the bonds and financing the purchase by issuing $101 million in new, 8 percent, sixteen-year bonds?

7-4

Debt service funds account for resources accumulated to service debt, not the debt itself.

On July 1, a city issued, at par, $100 million in 6 percent, twenty-year general obligation bonds. It established a debt service fund to account for resources set aside to pay interest and principal on the obligations.

In the year it issued the debt, the city engaged in the following transactions involving the debt service fund.

1. It estimated that it would make interest payments of $3 million and have interest earnings of $30,000 from investments. It would transfer from the general fund to the debt service fund $2.97 million to pay interest and $.5 million to provide for the payment of principal when the bonds mature. Further, as required by the bond indentures, it would transfer $1 million of the bond proceeds from the capital project fund to the debt service fund to be held in reserve until the debt matures.
2. Upon issuing the bonds, the city transferred $1 million of the bond proceeds from the capital projects fund. It invested $977,254 of the funds in twenty-year, 6 percent Treasury bonds that had a face value of $1 million. The bond discount of $22,746 reflected an effective yield rate of 6.2 percent.
3. On December 31, the city received $30,000 interest on the Treasury bonds. This payment represented interest for six months. Correspondingly, the market value of the bonds increased by $294 reflecting the amortization of the discount.
4. On the same day the city transferred $2.97 million from the general fund to pay interest on the bonds that it had issued. It also transferred $.5 million for the eventual repayment of principal.
5. Also on December 31, it made its first interest payment of $3 million to bondholders.
  a. Prepare appropriate journal entries in the debt service fund, including budgetary and closing entries.
  b. The bonds issued by the city pay interest at the rate of 6 percent. The bonds in which the city invested its reserve have an effective yield of 6.2 percent. Why might the difference in rates create a potential liability for the city?

7-5

Using the AICPA model, public universities record long-lived assets, the related debt, and resources accumulated to service the debt in plant funds.

A public university engaged in the following transactions:

1. It issued $50 million in bonds to finance the construction of classroom facilities.
2. It incurred $40 million of construction costs, completing one building at a cost of $25 million.
3. It transferred $4 million from an unrestricted current fund to a retirement of indebtedness plant fund.
4. It paid bondholders $3 million in interest and $1 million as a return of principal.
   a. Prepare journal entries to record the transactions in appropriate plant funds. Be sure to indicate the type of plant fund in which each entry would be made.
   b. Describe briefly how the balance sheet of a public university that follows the AICPA model would differ from that of a not-for-profit university that follows the FASB not-for-profit model.

7-6

Multiple Choice Questions from CPA Examinations

1. Kew City received a $15 million federal grant to finance the construction of a center for rehabilitation of drug addicts. The proceeds of the grant should be accounted for in the
   a. special revenue funds.
   b. general fund.
   c. capital projects funds.
   d. trust funds.

2. The basis of accounting for a capital projects fund is the
   a. cash basis.
   b. accrual basis.
   c. modified cash basis.
   d. modified accrual basis.

3. Dale City is accumulating financial resources that are legally restricted to payments of general long-term debt principal and interest maturing in future years. At December 31, 1997, $5 million has been accumulated for principal payments and $.3 million has been accumulated for interest payments. These restricted funds should be accounted for in this way:

	Debt Service Fund	General Fund
a.	$0	$5,300,000
b.	$300,000	$5,000,000
c.	$5,000,000	$300,000
d.	$5,300,000	$0

4. A public school district should recognize revenue from property taxes levied for its debt service fund when
   a. bonds to be retired by the levy are due and payable.
   b. assessed valuations of property subject to the levy are known.
   c. funds from the levy are measurable and available to the district.
   d. proceeds from collection of the levy are deposited in the district's bank account.

5. Wood City, which is legally obligated to maintain a debt service fund, issued the following general obligation bonds on July 1, 1997:

Term of bonds	10 years
Face amount	$1,000,000
Issue price	101
Stated interest rate	6%

Interest is payable January 1 and July 1. What amount of bond premium should be amortized in Wood's debt service fund for the year ended December 31, 1997?
   a. $1,000
   b. $500
   c. $250
   d. $0

6. In connection with Albury Township's long-term debt, the following cash accumulations are available to cover payment of principal and interest on

Bonds for financing a water treatment plant (a utility)	$1,000,000
General long-term obligations	400,000

The amount of these cash accumulations that should be accounted for in Albury's debt service fund is
   a. $0
   b. $400,000
   c. $1,000,000
   d. $1,400,000

7. Tott City's serial bonds are serviced through a debt service fund with cash provided by the general fund. In a debt service funds statement, how are cash receipts and cash payments reported?

	Cash Receipts	Cash Payments
a.	Revenues	Expenditures
b.	Revenues	Operating transfers
c.	Operating transfers	Expenditures
d.	Operating transfers	Operating transfers

8. The following information pertains to certain monies held by Blair County at December 31, 1998, that are legally restricted to expenditures for specified purposes:

Proceeds of short-term notes to be used by the county's electric utility	$ 8,000
Proceeds of long-term debt to be used for a major capital project	$90,000

What amount of these restricted monies should Blair account for in special revenue funds?
   a. $0
   b. $8,000
   c. $90,000
   d. $98,000

9. Central County received proceeds from various towns and cities for capital projects financed by Central's long-term debt. A special tax was assessed by each local government, and a portion of the tax was restricted to repay the long-term debt of Central's capital projects. Central should account for the restricted portion of the special tax in which of the following funds?
   a. internal service fund
   b. enterprise fund
   c. capital projects fund
   d. debt service fund

10. The debt service fund of a governmental unit is used to account for the accumulation of resources for, and the payment of, principal and interest in connection with a

Trust Fund	Proprietary Fund
a. No	No
b. No	Yes
c. Yes	Yes
d. Yes	No

11. Lisa County issued $5 million of general obligation bonds at 101 to finance a capital project. The $50,000 premium was to be used for payment of principal and interest. This transaction should be accounted for in the
   a. capital projects funds, debt service funds, and the general long-term debt account group.

   b. capital projects funds and debt service funds only.
   c. debt service funds and the general long-term debt account group only.
   d. debt service funds only.

12. Financing for the renovation of Fir City's municipal park, begun and completed during 1995, came from the following sources:

Grant from state government	$400,000
Proceeds from general obligation bond issue	500,000
Transfer from Fir City's general fund	100,000

   In its 1995 capital projects fund operating statement, Fir City should report these amounts as

	Revenues	Other Financing Sources
a.	$1,000,000	$0
b.	$900,000	$100,000
c.	$400,000	$600,000
d.	$0	$1,000,000

13. In what fund type should the proceeds from special assessment bonds issued to finance construction of sidewalks in a new subdivision be reported?
   a. agency fund
   b. special revenue fund
   c. enterprise fund
   d. capital projects fund

PROBLEMS

Continuing Problem

Review the annual report that you obtained.

a. How many capital projects funds does the government maintain? For what purposes?

b. How many debt service funds does it maintain? For what types of debts?

c. Are there any unusual features in these funds (accounts or reporting practices either not addressed in the chapter or at variance with those presented)?

d. Select one of the capital projects funds.
   1. What were the main sources of resources for the fund?
   2. Does the government maintain a debt service fund for the debt, the proceeds of which were recorded in the capital projects fund?
   3. Are the assets purchased or constructed with fund assets reported elsewhere in the report? If so, where?

e. Did any of the capital projects funds receive resources from special assessments? If so, are assessments receivable recorded in one of the debt service funds?

f. Did the government refund or defease any debts during the year? How can you tell? Was there an economic gain on the transaction? How did the government account for any accounting gain or loss?

7-1

The financial statements of an actual capital projects fund leave it to the report reader to draw inferences as to key transactions.

The accompanying statements of the parks, recreation, and municipal capital improvement bond fund (a capital projects fund) were drawn from a recent annual report (dates changed) of Boulder, Colorado. According to a note in the report (the only one pertaining to the fund), the fund is maintained "to account for bond proceeds to be utilized for the construction and refurbishment of parks and recreation facilities and the refurbishment of other municipal facilities."

a. The variances in expenditures between budget and actual are substantial. What is the most likely explanation?

b. A schedule of long-term debt payable (in the statistical section of the report) indicates that only $7,000 of parks, recreation, and municipal capital improvement

Parks, Recreation, and Municipal Capital Improvement Bond Fund
Balance Sheet December 31, 1997
(in thousands)

Assets:

Receivables	$ 2
Investments	5,874
Total Assets	$5,876

Liabilities and Fund Equity:

Liabilities

Accrued Wages and Salaries	$ 4
Construction Contracts Payable	202
Due to Other Funds	220
Total Liabilities	$ 426

Fund Equity

Reserved for Encumbrances	431
Reserved for Bond Projects	5,019
Total Fund Equity	5,450
Total Liabilities and Fund Equity	$5,876

bonds were authorized and issued. How do you reconcile that amount with the proceeds from bonds payable reported in the schedule of revenues and expenditures?

c. Another schedule of operating transfers between funds (in the same section) indicates that the $131 was transferred to the general fund. What conclusions can you draw as to whether interest on fund investments must be used either to repay the capital improvement bonds or to construct and refurbish city facilities?

d. How much of fund resources did the government spend during the year on capital improvements?

e. How do you explain the absence in the balance sheet of "construction in process"?

f. Why is the entire fund balance "reserved"?

7-2

The financial statements of a debt service fund may reveal less information than is apparent.

The balance sheet and a comparative schedule (actual to budget) of revenues, expenditures, and changes in fund balance of the City of Boulder, Colorado's general obligation debt service fund (date changed) is presented as follows.

Parks, Recreation, and Municipal Capital Improvement Bond Fund
Schedule of Revenues, Expenditures, and Changes in Fund Balance—Budget and Actual
Year Ended December 31, 1997 (in thousands)

	Budget	Actual
Revenues:		
Interest Earnings	$ 75	$ 131
Expenditures:		
Capital Outlay		
General Government—		
Facility	1,552	425
Culture and Recreation—		
Facility	5,500	1,177
Total Expenditures	7,052	1,602
Deficiency of Revenues Over		
Expenditures	(6,977)	(1,471)
Other Financing Sources (Uses)		
Proceeds From Bonds Payable	7,052	7,052
Operating Transfers Out	(75)	(131)
Total Other Financing		
Sources (Uses)	6,977	6,921
Excess of Revenues and Other		
Sources Over Expenditures and		
Other Uses	$ 0	$5,450
Fund Balance, Beginning of Year		0
Fund Balance, End of Year		$5,450

General Obligation Debt Service Fund
Balance Sheet
December 31, 1997 (in thousands)

Assets:

Equity in Pooled Cash and Cash Equivalents	$	18
Cash With Fiscal Agent		21
Investments, at Market Value		1,527
Receivables—Accrued Interest		2
Due From Other Funds		44
Total Assets		$1,612

Liabilities and Fund Equity:

Liabilities

Vouchers and Accounts Payable	$	1

Fund Equity

Reserved for Special Purposes		1
Unreserved, Undesignated		1,610
Total Fund Equity		1,611
Total Liabilities and Fund Equity		$1,612

General Obligation Debt Service Fund
Schedule of Revenues, Expenditures, and Changes in Fund Balance—Budget and Actual
Year Ended December 31, 1997 (in thousands)

	Budget	Actual
Revenues:		
Investment Earnings	$ -	$ 151

Expenditures:

Administrative Services	25	22
Debt Service Payments		
Principal	2,592	2,592
Interest	4,088	4,088
Total Expenditures	$6,705	$6,702
Excess (Deficiency) of Revenues		
Over Expenditures	(6,705)	(6,551)
Other Financing Sources (Uses)		
Operating Transfers-in	6,292	6,292
Operating Transfer-out	(10)	(10)
	$6,282	$6,282
Excess (Deficiency) of Revenues		
and Other Sources Over		
Expenditures and Other Uses	$ (423)	(269)
Fund Balance, Beginning of Year		382
Residual Equity Transfer		1,498
Fund Balance, End of Year		$1,611

a. Of what significance is the *deficiency* of revenues over expenditures? Is it an indication of poor management?

b. The fund reported a smaller deficit than was budgeted. Is this variance a sign of good management? Explain.

c. Can you assess whether the fund will have the fiscal wherewithal to satisfy its obligations of principal and interest as they come due? Explain.

d. The fund reported a residual equity transfer-in of $1,498. The statement of changes in fund balance of a related capital projects fund indicates a residual transfer-out of the same amount. What is a likely explanation for the transfer?

e. A schedule of operating transfers indicates that the transfers-in were as follows:

From the General Fund	$2,080
From the Permanent Parks and Recreation Fund	25
From the Transportation Fund	15
From the Open Space Fund (to Account for the Acquisition of Greenbelt Land)	3,944
From the Major Maintenance and Equipment Replacement Fund	228
Total	$6,292

The major maintenance and equipment replacement fund is a capital project funds; each of the other funds,

other than the general fund, is a special revenue fund. What are the most likely reasons for the transfers?

7-3

The construction and financing phase of a special assessment project is accounted for in a capital projects fund; the debt service phase in a debt service fund (see the next problem).

Upon annexing a recently developed subdivision, a government undertakes to extend sewer lines to the area. Estimated cost is $10 million. The project is to be funded with $8.5 million in special assessment bonds and a $1.0 million grant from the state. The balance is to be paid by the government out of its general fund. Property owners are to be assessed an amount sufficient to pay both principal and interest on the debt.

During the year, the government engaged in the following transactions, all of which would be recorded in a capital projects fund.

1. It recorded the capital project fund budget. It estimated that it would earn $.20 million in interest on the temporary investment of bond proceeds, an amount that will reduce the required transfer from the general fund. It estimated that bond issue costs would be $.18 million.

2. It issued $8.5 million in bonds at a premium of $.30 million and incurred $.18 million in issue costs. The premium, net of issue costs, is to be transferred to a newly established debt service fund.

3. It received the $1 million grant from the state, recognizing it as deferred revenue until it incurred at least $1 million in construction costs.

4. It invested $7.62 million in short-term (less than one year) securities.

5. It issued purchase orders and signed construction contracts for $9.2 million.

6. It sold $5 million of its investments for $5.14 million, the excess of selling price over cost representing interest earned. By year-end the investments still on hand had increased in value by $.06 million, an amount that also could be attributed to interest earned.

7. It received invoices totaling $5.7 million. As permitted by its agreement with its prime contractor, it retained (and recorded as a payable) $.4 million pending satisfactory completion of the project. It paid the balance of $5.3 million.

8. It transferred $.12 million to the debt service fund.

9. It updated its accounts, but did not close them inasmuch as the project is not completed and its budget is for the entire project, not for a single period.
   a. Prepare appropriate journal entries for the capital projects fund.
   b. Prepare a statement of revenues, expenditures, and changes in fund balance, in which you compare actual and budgeted amounts.

c. Prepare a year-end balance sheet.

d. Does your balance sheet report the construction in process? If not, where might the construction in process be reported?

7-4

The debt service phase special assessment bonds are accounted for in a debt service fund (see the previous problem).

As indicated in the previous problem, a government issued $8.5 million of special assessment bonds to finance a sewer-extension project. To service the debt, it assessed property owners $8.5 million. Their obligations are payable over a period of five years, with annual installments due on March 31 of each year. Interest at an annual rate of 8 percent is to be paid on the total balance outstanding as of that date.

The bonds require an annual principal payment of $1.5 million each year for five years, due on December 31. In addition, interest on the unpaid balance is payable twice each year, on June 30 and December 31 at an annual rate of 8 percent.

The government agreed to make up from its general fund the difference between required debt service payments and revenues.

At the start of the year, the government established a debt service fund. During the year it engaged in the following transactions, all of which would affect that fund.

1. It prepared, and recorded in its accounts, its annual budget. It estimated that it would collect from property owners $1.3 million in special assessments and $.5 million of interest on the unpaid balance of the assessments. In addition, it expected to earn interest of $.08 million on temporary investments. It would be required to pay interest of $.68 million and make principal payments of $1.7 million on the outstanding debt. It anticipated transferring $.5 million from the general fund to cover the revenue shortage.

2. It recorded the $8.5 million of assessments receivable, estimating that $.2 million would be uncollectible.

3. The special assessments bonds were issued at a premium (net of issue costs) of $.12. The government recognized the anticipated transfer of the premium to the debt service fund.

4. During the year the government collected $2.0 million in assessments and $.4 million in interest (with a few property owners paying their entire assessment in the first year). During the first sixty days of the following year it collected an additional $.1 million in assessments and $.01 in interest, which were due the previous year.

5. It transferred $.12 million (the premium) from the capital projects fund.

6. It purchased $.8 million of six-month treasury bills as a temporary investment.

7. It made its first interest payment of $.34 million.

8. It sold the investments for $.85 million, the difference between selling price and cost representing interest earned.

9. It recognized its year-end obligation for interest of $.34 million and principal of $1.7 million, but did not actually make the required payments.

10. It prepared year-end closing entries.

a. Prepare appropriate journal entries for the debt service fund.

b. Prepare a statement of revenues, expenditures, and changes in fund balance in which you compare actual and budgeted amounts.

c. Prepare a year-end balance sheet.

d. Does your balance sheet report the balance of the bonds payable? If not, where might it be reported?

7-5

Special assessment debt may take different forms.

A city agrees to extend water and sewer lines to an outlying community. To cover the cost, the affected property owners agree to special assessments of $12 million. The assessments are to be paid over five years, with interest at the rate of 6 percent per year.

For each of the following situations describe how the city should account for the special assessment debt.

a. The city finances the project by issuing special assessment bonds. The bonds are to be repaid with the special assessment revenues, which the city will account for, as received from property owners, in a debt service fund. The newly constructed lines will be accounted for as general fixed assets.

b. The project is financed by bonds issued by a specially created municipal utility district, which is not part of the city's financial reporting entity. Although the city is to construct and own the lines, the utility district is responsible for collecting the assessments and making all required principal and interest payments. The city has no legal responsibility for the debt but has indicated to the bond underwriters in a letter that it accepts a "moral obligation" to assume the debt in the event the municipal utility district defaults.

c. The project is financed by bonds issued by a specially created municipal utility district, which is not part of the city's financial reporting entity. The city has agreed to collect the assessments and make all required principal and interest payments on behalf of the municipal utility district. The city is constitutionally prohibited from assuming responsibility for this type of debt.

d. The project is carried out, and the bonds are issued, by the city's water and sewer utility, which is accounted for in an enterprise fund.

7-6

Bond refundings may result in an economic gain but a book loss. When should the loss be recognized?

Colgate County issued $1 million of thirty-year, 8 percent term bonds to finance improvements to its electric utility plant. The bonds, accounted for in an enterprise fund, were issued at par.

After the bonds were outstanding for ten years, interest rates fell and the county exercised a call provision to redeem the bonds for $1.1 million. The county obtained the necessary cash by issuing $1.1 million in new, twenty-year, 6 percent bonds.

a. Prepare the entry that the county should have made in its enterprise fund to record the issuance of the original debt (the same entry as in business accounting).

b. Prepare the entry that the county should have made to record the interest expense and payment each semiannual period.

c. Prepare the entry that the county would make to record the redemption of the original debt. Be sure your entry is in accord with GASB standards.

d. Did the county incur an *economic* gain or loss by refunding the debt? Of how much?

e. Suppose, instead, that the county could have predicted that it would redeem the debt after it had been outstanding for ten years (20 periods) for $1.1 million.
   1. What entry should it have made to record the issuance of the bonds?
   2. Over how many periods should the county have amortized the bond discount?
   3. During the ten years that the bonds were outstanding, what would have been the average reported interest expense each semiannual period taking into account the amortization of the bond discount. (Assume that the county amortizes bond discounts on a straight-line basis. Although straight-line amortization is not conceptually sound, it provides a measure of the average amortization that would result if the more correct, compound interest method were used.)
   4. Prepare the journal entry the county would have made to record interest expense each semiannual period.

f. What is the economic nature of the refunding loss that the county would have to report? In what sense is it really a loss? When did it occur?

g. Compare your response to part f with both GASB and FASB standards pertaining to recognizing refunding gains and losses. Why would it not be practical to recognize the loss in the periods in which it actually occurs?

7-7

Debtors may be able to realize an economic gain by defeasing their debt "in substance."

A hospital has outstanding $100 million of bonds that mature in twenty years (40 periods). The debt was issued at par and pays interest at a rate of 6 percent (3 percent per period). Prevailing rates on comparable bonds are now 4 percent (2 percent per period).

a. What would you expect to be the market price of the bonds, assuming that they are freely traded? Would there be an economic benefit for the hospital to refund the existing debt by acquiring it at the market price and replacing it with new, "low-cost" debt?

b. Assume the bonds contain a provision permitting the hospital to call the bonds in another five years (10 periods) at a price of $105 and that any invested funds could earn a return equal to the prevailing interest rate of 4 percent (2 percent per period). What would be the economic saving that the hospital could achieve by defeasing the bonds "in substance"?

7-8

A debt service fund reports both routine principal and interest payments as well as an in-substance defeasance.

The statement on page 313 is from a recent annual report of the City of Fort Worth, Texas. It was accompanied by the following notes:

Defeasance of Prior Debt

During the year, the City issued $194,520 of general obligation bonds. The proceeds were used to refund debt obligations with a face value of $181,985. A portion of the proceeds from the issuance of the bonds was placed in an irrevocable escrow account and invested in U.S. obligations that, together with interest earned thereon, would provide an amount to call the bonds on the appropriate call dates. The advance refunding resulted in an economic gain of $4,816.

Arbitrage

The City of Fort Worth frequently issues bonds for capital construction projects. These bonds are subject to the arbitrage regulations. At September 30, the liability for rebate of arbitrage was $560 for general obligation bonds and $51 for enterprise bonds, respectively. These amounts are included in the "Payable to Federal Government" category of the debt service and enterprise funds.

a. Based on your knowledge of debt service funds, what is the most likely source of "revenue from use of money and property?"

b. Explain in your own words the significance of "proceeds from refunding bonds" and "payment to refunded bond escrow account." (Do not attempt to reconcile the amounts in the statement with those in the footnotes; a portion of the bonds refunded was accounted for in a proprietary fund.)

c. The note pertaining to the bond defeasance also indicates that the refunding resulted in an accounting loss of $536, which was reported in the water and sewer fund, an enterprise fund. How is it possible that the city had an economic gain but an accounting loss? Why is a loss reported in an enterprise fund but not this type of debt service fund?

City of Forth Worth	
Statement of Revenues, Expenditures, and Changes in Fund Balance **Year Ended September 30 Debt Service Fund (000s omitted)**	
Revenues:	
Revenues From Use of Money and Property	$ 6,170
Expenditures:	
Defeasance of Certificates of Obligation	1,837
Principal Retirement	39,842
Interest and Service Charges	26,659
Total Expenditures	68,338
Excess of Revenues Over (Under) Expenditures	$(62,168)
Other Financing Sources (Uses):	
Proceeds From Refunding Bonds	190,009
Proceeds From General Obligation Bonds	9,617
Operating Transfers-in	55,565
Payment to Refunded Bond Escrow Account	(186,860)
Operating Transfer-out	(1,995)
Total Other Financing Sources	$ 66,336
Excess of Revenues and Other Financing Sources Over Expenditures and Other Financing Uses	4,168
Fund Balance, Beginning of Year	10,401
Fund Balance, End of Year	$ 14,569

d. What is the most likely source of the operating transfer-in? What was its purpose?

e. What is the most likely reason that the city had an obligation to the federal government for arbitrage? Is the liability necessarily an indication of poor management?

7-9

For purposes of external reporting, not-for-profits, unlike governments, do not distinguish between plant and other types of resources.

In 1998, the Northwest Ballet Association (NBA), a not-for-profit performing arts organization, undertook a major capital campaign to fund a new theater, expected to cost $10 million. It was quickly able to raise $6 million, all of which was donor-restricted. It borrowed the balance, issuing a five-year, 8 percent term note for $4 million.

During the year, the NBA broke ground on the project and incurred construction costs of $3.4 million. It earned $.52 million in interest on temporary investments. It incurred and paid $.32 million in interest on the note. In addition, as required by the note, it placed $.7 million in a reserve fund (a specially dedicated bank account) for the repayment of the debt.

a. To show how these transactions would be reflected on the NBA's financial statements, prepare a December 31, 1998, statement of financial position and statement of activities. Assume that these were the only transactions

in which the organization engaged and that all available cash, except that in the reserve fund, had been invested in short-term marketable securities. Be sure to properly classify all resources as to whether they are temporarily restricted or unrestricted.

b. Comment briefly on whether the contributions from donors and the proceeds from the bonds should be reported as restricted or unrestricted.

c. Comment briefly on whether the $.7 million in the reserve fund should be reported as restricted or unrestricted.

7-10

The FASB model has a decidedly different look than the AICPA model.

The plant fund balance sheets that follow were adapted from those of Ohio State University (several account balances have been combined). They are consistent with the AICPA model.

a. Recast the balance sheets, as best you can, to reflect how the balances would be reported under FASB Statement No. 117, *Financial Statements of Not-for-Profit Organizations*.

1. Assume all restrictions on the resources were imposed by either bondholders or the university's trustees. Why is this assumption significant?

2. Assume also that all the amounts "due from" and

"due to" are from or to restricted funds. Why is this assumption important?

b. What, in your opinion, are the key advantages of the AICPA approach relative to that of the FASB? What are the disadvantages?

The Ohio State University Balance Sheet—Plant Funds Only June 30, 1993 (in millions)

Unexpended

Assets:

Cash and Cash Equivalents	$ (4)
Investments	48,726
State Appropriations Receivable	26,809
Due from Other Funds	422
Other Receivables	264
Total Assets	$ 76,217

Liabilities and Fund Equity:

Due to Other Funds	$ 7,976
Bonds Payable	49,162
Fund Equity	
Restricted	26,809
Unrestricted—Designated	(7,730)
Total Liabilities and Fund Equity	$ 76,217

Renewals and Replacements

Assets:

Cash and Cash Equivalents	$ 75
State Appropriations Receivable	18,511
Due from Other Funds	49,365
Total Assets	$67,951

Liabilities and Fund Equity:

Accounts and Interest Payable	$ 800
Due to Other Funds	5,410
Fund Equity	
Restricted	18,511
Unrestricted—Designated	43,230
Total Liabilities and Fund Equity	$67,951

Retirement of Indebtedness

Assets:

Deposits with Trustees	$15,545
Due from Other Funds	29,474
Other Receivables	3,097
Total Assets	$48,116

Liabilities and Fund Equity:

Accounts and Interest Payable	$ 1,012
Fund Equity	
Restricted	17,903
Unrestricted—Designated	29,201
Total Liabilities and Fund Equity	$48,116

Investment in Plant

Assets:

Due from Other Funds	$ 1,535
Land, Improvements, and Buildings	1,063,913
Equipment, Furniture, and Library Books	533,475
Construction in Process	129,003
Total Investment in Plant	$1,727,926

Liabilities and Fund Equity:

Accounts and Interest Payable	$ 1,535
Bonds Payable	219,043
Net Investment in Plant	1,507,348
Total Investment in Plant	$1,727,926

7-11

A hospital's footnote distinguishes between the book value and the economic value of long-term debt.

The financial report of Montefiore Medical Center, which operates a major New York City hospital, included the following item in a summary of long-term debt outstanding:

	December 31	
	1993	**1992**
	(In thousands)	
Revenue bonds payable	$4,178	$4,303

An explanatory note indicated the following:

The proceeds from the 8.625 percent revenue bonds, dated November 1, 1979, issued by the Dormitory Authority of the State of New York, were used by the Medical Center to construct a parking garage. The fair value of these bonds was estimated to be approproximately $5.1 million and $5.4 million at December 31, 1993, and 1992, respectively, using a discounted cash flow analysis based on the Medical Center's incremental borrowing rates for similar types of borrowing arrangements. The bonds are payable serially through June 30, 2010, at increasing annual amounts ranging from $130,000 in 1994 to $500,000 in 2010. Bonds may be redeemed before maturity, for which call premiums are 0.5 percent through June 30, 1994, after which call premiums cease. Under the terms of the revenue bonds agreement, certain escrow funds are required to be maintained. At December 31, 1993, escrow assets aggregated approximately $1.2 million, which exceeded minimum escrow requirements.

a. Why would the *fair* value of the bonds, as calculated by the center, be so much greater than their *face* value?

b. The note indicates that the "bonds are payable *serially.*" What does that mean?

c. Assuming that prevailing interest rates remain constant, why would the market price of the bonds be greater prior to, than after, June 30, 1994?

d. Is it likely that the market value of the bonds is as great as the fair value calculated by the center? Explain.

e. Where, in your opinion, should the resources held in escrow (i.e., with an independent trustee) be reported on the center's balance sheet? Should they be classified as *restricted assets?*

SOLUTION TO EXERCISE FOR REVIEW AND SELF-TESTING

a. *Journal entries*

1.

Assessments receivable— current	$1,600,000	
Assessments receivable— deferred	6,400,000	
Revenues		$1,600,000
Deferred revenues		6,400,000

To record the assessments (debt service fund, the fund that will account for resources used to service the debt)

The first-year assessments may be recognized as revenues as they will be available for current-year expenditure. The balance must be deferred.

2.

Cash	$8,050,000	
Expenditures—bond issue costs	150,000	
Other financing sources— bond proceeds (face value)		$8,000,000
Other financing sources— bond proceeds (bond premium)		200,000

To record the issuance of the bonds (capital projects fund, the fund that will account for resources used to construct the project)

Other financing use— operating transfer of bond premium to debt service fund	$50,000	
Cash		$ 50,000

To record transfer-out of the bond premium to the debt service fund (capital projects fund)

Cash	$50,000	
Other financing sources— operating transfer from capital projects fund		$50,000

To record transfer-in of the bond premium to the debt service fund (debt service fund)

Inasmuch as the city issued the debt in its name (and is thereby obligated in some manner for repayment), the bonds themselves should be recorded as a liability in the general long-term debt account group.

Amount to be provided from special assessments	$8,000,000	
Bonds payable		$8,000,000

To record bonds payable (general long-term debt account group)

3.

Expenditures—construction	$8,000,000	
Cash		$8,000,000

To record construction of the sidewalks (capital projects fund)

If it is the government's practice to capitalize infrastructure assets, then the sidewalks should be recorded in the general fixed assets account group:

Sidewalks	$8,000,000	
Investment in infrastructure		$8,000,000

To record the construction of the sidewalks (general fixed asset account group)

4.

Cash	$2,080,000	
Assessments receivable—current		$1,600,000
Interest revenue		480,000

To record collection of interest (6 percent of $8,000,000) plus the first assessment installment (debt service fund)

The availability of the resources to repay the debt can be reflected in the general long-term debt account group.

Amount available to repay debt	$1,600,000	
Amount to be provided from special assessments		$1,600,000

To record availability of resources to repay debt (general long-term account group)

5.

Expenditures—interest	$240,000	
Cash		$240,000

To record interest (debt service fund)

As the debt service fund is a governmental fund and thereby accounted for on the modified accrual basis, neither the interest nor the principal due in 2000 need be accrued.

b. *Debt defeasance*

1.

Present value, at 2 percent, of $1,600,000 principal (a single sum) to be paid at the end of 6 periods (present value of $1 = $.88797)	$1,420,754
Present value, at 2 percent of $48,000 interest (an annuity) to be paid at the end of each of 6 periods (present value of an annuity of $1 = $5.60143)	268,869
Total economic cost of "old" bonds	$1,689,623

2.

Present value, at 2 percent, of $1,600,000 principal (a single sum) to be paid at the end of 4 periods (present value of $1 = $.92384)	$1,478,153
Present value, at 2 percent of $48,000 interest (an annuity) to be paid at the end of each of 4 periods (present value of an annuity of $1 = $3.80773)	182,771
Amount that would have to be placed with trustee	$1,660,924

3. The economic cost of the new bonds would be the same as the amount required to be borrowed. Hence, the economic savings is the difference between the old bonds and the new—$1,689,623 minus $1,660,924—$28,699.

CHAPTER 8

Long-Lived Assets and Investments in Marketable Securities

LEARNING OBJECTIVES

After studying this chapter you should understand:

- why and how governments account for fixed assets in a general fixed assets account group
- why and how governments account for transactions involving donated assets, trade ins, and infrastructure

- the virtues and limitations of current practices as to depreciation and asset valuation
- how not-for-profits other than governments account for and report fixed assets
- why investments in marketable securities may be of high risk and thereby present special problems of accounting and reporting

The accounting for both long-lived assets and investments, albeit for different reasons, should be of vital concern to statement users and preparers. Long-lived assets are a key component of many of the services provided by government and not-for-profits. They include its police cars, administrative buildings, and its utility lines and roads. If they are inadequate to meet the demands for services to be delivered in the future, then the organization will either have to reduce its services or come up with the financial resources to enhance the assets. At the same time, existing stocks of fixed assets have to be either maintained or replaced, thereby necessitating an ongoing commitment of financial resources. In addition, the constituents of governments and not-for-profits generally want, and are entitled to, assurance that the organization is using its assets efficiently and effectively.

Whereas the previous chapter was concerned with the *resources* that are used to acquire long-lived, "general" assets, this chapter is directed to the assets themselves. Although the accounting issues relating to long-lived assets facing both governments and other not-for-profits (as well as businesses, in fact) are similar, the accounting practices that have evolved are currently quite different. Therefore, the first part of the chapter will be directed to governments; the second to other not-for-profits.

A third part of the chapter will address marketable securities held for *investment*. Investments are at the opposite end of the liquidity spectrum from fixed assets and present contrasting issues of both disclosure and control. They are of critical concern to both governments and other not-for-profits. Unlike long-lived assets, they are subject to significant risks of declines in market values as well as of fraud and mismanagement on the part of both the financial institutions with whom they deal and of their own employees. The entity needs to inform statement users of these risks and to establish policies and procedures to manage and control them.

WHAT ACCOUNTING PRACTICES DO GOVERNMENTS FOLLOW FOR CAPITAL ASSETS?

The objectives of reporting **fixed assets** are set forth in GASB's *Objectives of Financial Reporting*:

> Financial reporting should provide information about a governmental entity's physical and other nonfinancial resources having useful lives that extend beyond the current year, including information that can be used to assess the service potential of these resources. This information should be presented to help users assess long- and short-term capital needs.[1]

Although current practices predate the establishment of the GASB and, hence, of the GASB objectives, the objectives are relevant in assessing the practices.

REPORTING FIXED ASSETS IN AN ACCOUNT GROUP

General fixed assets—capital assets that, by definition are associated with the government as a whole, rather than with any specific fund—are accounted for in the **general fixed assets account group (GFAAG)**. General fixed assets are distinguished from the assets of proprietary funds, (enterprise funds and internal service funds) and of fiduciary funds (pension and other trust funds in which land, buildings, and other fixed assets are held as investments).

---

[1] Concepts Statement Number 1, paragraph 78 (*Codification*, Appendix B, paragraph 78).

Nonfinancial in character, general fixed assets are excluded from governmental funds because the measurement focus of governmental funds is on financial resources. Therefore, in governmental funds, the costs of fixed assets are reported as expenditures when the assets are acquired rather than capitalized as assets and subsequently written off as the assets are consumed.

As emphasized previously, the general fixed asset account group is little more than a list of government-owned assets. The list, however, is in double-entry form, with the assets (the debits) offset with an equity-type account called investment in general fixed assets (the credits). The list takes the double-entry form mainly so that the assets can be displayed as part of the multicolumn combined balance sheet, along with a government's other assets and liabilities. If the list reported only assets, but not the offsetting account "investment in general fixed assets," then the totals of the combined balance sheet would be out of balance. The City of Fort Worth's schedule of fixed assets is shown in Table 8–1.

The fundamental entries in the general fixed assets account group are simple. When an asset is acquired (and the expenditure properly recognized in a governmental fund) the following entry is made:

Fixed assets (specify type)	$XXXX	
Investment in fixed assets (specify source of resources)		$XXXX

To add fixed assets to the general fixed assets account group

When an asset is sold or retired the entry is reversed:

Investment in fixed assets (specify source of resources)	$XXXX	
Fixed assets (specify type)		$XXXX

To remove fixed assets from the general fixed assets account group

TABLE 8–1
City of Fort Worth
Schedule of General Fixed Assets

	1996	1995
General Fixed Assets:		
Land	$ 20,008	$ 20,008
Buildings	144,429	132,995
Improvements Other than Buildings	521,395	512,254
Machinery and Equipment	86,286	76,871
Construction in Progress	129,542	102,649
Investment in D/FW International Airport	8,450	8,450
Investment in Railtran	16,584	16,584
Total General Fixed Assets	$926,694	$869,811
Investment in General Fixed Assets:		
Gifts and Other	$ 47,571	$21,610
Capital Projects Funds	725,102	698,594
Federal Grants	54,909	50,804
State Grants	3,133	2,956
General Fund	95,979	95,847
Total Investment in General Fixed Assets	$926,694	$869,811

The following entry would be made in the general fund or whichever other fund received the sale proceeds:

Cash	$XXXX	
Other financing sources (sale of fixed assets)		$XXXX

To record the sale of a fixed asset

The most common classifications for general fixed assets include:

- land
- buildings
- equipment
- improvements other than buildings
- construction in progress.

However, "softer" assets, such as library books and recordings, computer software (whether purchased or developed in-house), and intangibles, such as water rights, may also be capitalized and included in the GFAAG. As will be discussed later in this chapter, governments have the option of including infrastructure assets in the GFAAG.

Many governments divide the investment in general fixed assets into categories, based on the source of the resources used to acquire the fixed assets (e.g., "investment in fixed assets—general fund"). Typical sources include:

- the general fund
- special revenue funds
- capital projects funds
- donations

PLACING VALUE ON CAPITAL ASSETS

When a government acquires an asset, it should follow the same general guidelines used by businesses to determine the costs to be capitalized. Thus, capitalized value should include all costs necessary to bring an asset to a serviceable condition. For purchased assets the capitalized cost should include purchase price (less any discounts, such as those for prompt payment or for favored customers), plus transportation and installation costs. For an asset such as land, it would include legal fees, title fees, appraisal costs, closing costs, and costs of demolishing existing structures that cannot be used (less recoveries from salvage).

For constructed assets it would include direct labor and materials, overhead costs, architect fees, and insurance premiums during the construction phase. Although businesses must capitalize interest on assets that they construct for their own use, governments are *permitted*, but are not required, to do so. For businesses, capitalization of interest facilitates a better match of costs with revenues. Interest costs are added to the cost of the asset and depreciated (recognized as an expense) over the asset's productive life. For governments, however, the interest is reported as a fund expenditure, irrespective of whether capitalized in the GFAAG. Therefore, the advantages of capitalization are less compelling and few governments exercise the capitalization option. However, per GASB guidelines, all governments are required to state their capitalization policy in a note to their financial statements.

PLACING VALUE ON DONATED ASSETS

The general fixed assets account group is used to keep track of fixed assets for general government use, regardless of whether purchased or donated. Donations can come from outside parties or divisions within the government that are accounted for in proprietary funds.

EXAMPLE   *Donated Assets*

A local resident donates a parcel of land to a city for use as a site for a new art museum. The land cost the resident $30,000 but it has a fair market value of $150,000.

At the same time, the city transfers construction equipment from its electric utility (accounted for in a proprietary fund) to its plant maintenance department (accounted for in the general fund). The equipment initially cost $50,000. It is recorded on the books of the proprietary fund at $20,000 (cost less accumulated depreciation) and has a fair market value of $25,000.

Current Standards

Governments should state assets donated from parties outside the reporting entity at their fair market value at the time of the gift. However, when the government transfers a fixed asset from a proprietary fund to the GFAAG, it should normally record the asset at one of the two following values:

- the value on the books of the proprietary fund. Because proprietary funds recognize depreciation on fixed assets, this value would typically be original cost less accumulated depreciation
- the original cost of the asset[2]

Both these options assure that the GFAAG value is derived from the original cost to the government as a whole. The virtue of the first option is that it retains an existing value; unlike the second, it does not result in a change in asset value (from cost less accumulated depreciation to original cost) based solely on an internal transfer. The advantage of the second is that it assures consistency in the GFAAG; all assets are stated at the original cost to the government; none are reported at cost less accumulated depreciation (assuming that it is the government's policy not to depreciate assets in the GFAAG, an issue to be dealt with shortly).

If the city elects the first option, the appropriate entry in the GFAAG would be:

Equipment	$ 20,000	
Land	150,000	
Investment in general fixed assets—proprietary fund		$ 20,000
Investment in general fixed assets—donations		150,000

To record donation of land from a resident and the transfer of equipment from the utility fund

The utility fund would record an operating transfer to the plant maintenance department. As discussed in Chapter 4, the government need recognize the donations as revenue in a *governmental* fund only it if intends to sell the asset, not if it expects to use it.

Governments, like businesses, trade in old assets for new. As in businesses, the accounting issues arise because the form of a transaction may differ from its economic substance.

ACCOUNTING FOR TRADE-INS

---

[2] *Governmental Accounting, Auditing and Financial Reporting* (Chicago: Governmental Finance Officers Association, 1994), p. 107.

EXAMPLE   *Trade-ins*

A government trades in an old automobile for a new one. The old automobile had cost $15,000; its fair market value at the time of trade is $6,000. The new automobile has a "sticker" (suggested retail) price of $25,000. The dealer allows the government a trade-in allowance of $8,000 ($2,000 more than fair market value) and a preferred-customer discount of $3,000. Thus, the government is required to pay only $14,000 cash for the new vehicle.

Current Standards

Governments should record trade-ins so that the new asset is stated at its fair market value without taking into account the trade. In contrast to business accounting, no distinction need be made between trades for similar or dissimilar assets. The fair market value, however, should reflect the economic substance of the transaction, not arbitrary (or artificial) trade-in allowances and discounts.

In the example, the facts suggest that irrespective of discounts and allowances, the fair market value of the new automobile is only $20,000—the actual consideration of the $14,000 cash plus the used vehicle that has a fair market value of $6,000. Thus, the entry to record the new vehicle would be:

Equipment	$20,000	
Investment in general fixed assets		$20,000
To record new equipment obtained in a trade-in transaction		

The entry to remove the old asset would be:

Investment in general fixed assets	$15,000	
Equipment		$15,000
To remove equipment surrendered in a trade-in transaction		

REPORTING ACCUMULATED DEPRECIATION

GASB standards with respect to accumulated depreciation are brief and to the point:

> Recording accumulated depreciation in the general fixed assets account group is optional. Where it is recorded, the entry should increase the *Accumulated Depreciation* account(s) and decrease the *Investment in General Fixed Assets* account(s).[3]

Most governments do not record accumulated depreciation. However, as will be evident in the next part of this chapter, GASB standards regarding depreciation differ significantly from those of the FASB for not-for-profit organizations but will most likely change dramatically if the GASB adopts its proposed reporting model.

Remember, *governmental* funds record neither fixed assets nor depreciation. As a consequence, nowhere in their financial statements do governments report the consumption of *general* (as opposed to proprietary fund) fixed assets. General fixed assets are reported at acquisition cost in the GFAAG until they are sold or retired.

---

[3] *Codification*, Section 1400.118.

Limitations of Current Practice

Current practice regarding depreciation has several limitations:

- The GFAAG reports assets at their initial value, irrespective of how much of the asset has already been consumed. An automobile that is days away from the scrap heap is reported at the same value as when it was fresh out of the showroom.

- The reported value provides no indication of the worth of the asset's future services to the government.

- The entire cost of an asset is reported as an expenditure in a governmental fund at the time of acquisition. Subsequently, the cost of consuming the asset goes unreported.

- It is a prime objective of governmental financial reporting to provide information as to whether current revenues are sufficient to cover the cost of current services. Without data on the portion of an asset consumed within a period, this objective cannot be fulfilled.

- Depreciation is currently reported by proprietary and trust funds. The statement of revenues and expenditures of governmental funds, however, indicates only the outflow of the financial resources, not the reduction in the long-lived assets. Thus, different funds within the same set of financial statements employ different bases of accounting.

These deficiencies are made all the more apparent in light of demands by federal, state, and private funding agencies that depreciation be included as an allowable (reimbursable) cost. When these agencies give reimbursement-type grants to state and local governments, they typically cover the cost of fixed assets—but only the portion consumed in the period covered by the grant. Thus, governments are often required to maintain depreciation records, even if they do not incorporate the data into their financial reports. As a consequence, only parties with the authority to demand information supplementary to the annual reports are able to obtain the information on depreciation; the citizenry may be left in the dark.

Justification for Current Practice

Still, the debate over depreciation is by no means one-sided. There are persuasive arguments for not reporting either depreciation or accumulated depreciation:

- Owing to the importance of the budget in governments, financial statement users are concerned primarily with flows of financial resources. Depreciation-related information would do little to facilitate the decisions or assessments made by most statement users.

- When given the opportunity to rank types of information in terms of importance, statement users of all categories have placed low priority on depreciation and accumulated depreciation. In a survey sponsored by the GASB, only 40 percent of respondents indicated that they favor reporting depreciation in the general fund.[4]

- Depreciation is a construct that facilitates income determination. Inasmuch as governments do not measure income, depreciation is unnecessary.

[4] See David B. Jones, *The Needs of Users of Governmental Financial Reports* (Norwalk, Conn.: Governmental Accounting Standards Board, 1985), p. 69.

- Depreciation is necessarily subjective, reflecting arbitrary estimates (such as useful life and residual value) and determinations (such as whether to calculate the charge on a straight-line or accelerated basis). This characteristic detracts from the credibility of financial statements in the private sector and arguably would do the same for those in government.

REPAYMENT OF DEBT AS A SURROGATE FOR DEPRECIATION

In governmental funds, the measurement focus is upon flows of *financial* resources, not long-lived assets. Nevertheless, governmental funds may better capture the cost of consuming long-lived assets than is at first apparent.

Governments generally finance their major fixed assets, particularly their infrastructure assets, by issuing long-term bonds. Since long-term bonds, like corresponding assets, are not given balance sheet recognition in governmental funds, the repayment of debt is reflected as an expenditure. To the extent that the bonds are in serial form and are repaid over the life of the associated asset, then the general fund, or other governmental fund, reports an annual expenditure—repayment of bond principal—that is a surrogate for an annual depreciation charge. For example, if a government finances a $100,000, twenty-year asset with debt to be repaid evenly over twenty years, then the annual expenditure (in the form of debt repayment) would be $5,000— the same as if the asset had been depreciated over its twenty-year economic life.

REPORTING INFRASTRUCTURE

A government's infrastructure is its fixed assets that are immovable and of value only to the government. They include roads, sidewalks, drainage systems, bridges, tunnels, and lighting systems. Although many citizens take the nation's infrastructure for granted, public officials, investors, and economists are expressing serious concern over it. In the last quarter-century, spectacular failures have called attention to the deteriorating condition of much of the country's public physical plant. For example, in the 1970s New York City was forced to close a portion of its West Side Highway, a scenic drive along the Hudson River, because the road had become unsafe and the city was unable to come up with the cash to repair it. In 1982 the residents of Jersey City, New Jersey, had to go without water for three days owing to a breakdown in the city's aqueduct system. Then in 1983, Connecticut's Mianus River Bridge on Interstate 95, the main east coast highway, collapsed, killing three people. Numerous research studies have confirmed that there is an increasing gap between the nation's infrastructure requirements and its ability to pay for them.

Infrastructure may be a national problem, but it must be solved mainly at the state and local level. After all, most roads and highways (apart from those that are part of the Interstate System), bridges, and drainage, water and public power systems, are the responsibility of state and local governments.

Governments are accountable for infrastructure assets and it is difficult to see how the objectives of financial reporting can be fulfilled without comprehensive information, not only as to the expenditures for infrastructure (which is currently provided) but also on their status. For example, data on infrastructure are essential if government financial reports are to achieve the following general goals set forth in the GASB's *Objectives of Financial Reporting*:

- to help users assess the economy, efficiency, and effectiveness with which government used the resources within its command

- to determine whether the entity's financial condition position improved or deteriorated during the reporting period

DEPRECIATION ACCOUNTING CAN INFLUENCE CAPITAL EXPENDITURE DECISIONS

Depreciation may also serve as a cognitive reminder to government decision makers as to the need to replace long-lived assets as they physically deteriorate. Given a choice between allocating available resources between current services and long-lived assets that will provide benefits over an extended period of time, government officials are more likely to opt for the current services. Depreciation, however, may be one means of mitigating the bias against the capital outlays.

Virtually all capital budgeting models focus on cash flows. They exclude depreciation (except, of course, as it affects income taxes) because depreciation is merely an allocation of asset cost over years of asset use. Still, depreciation expense may cue the decision makers to increase spending on long-term assets.

To examine the impact of depreciation accounting on capital budgeting decisions, researchers carried out a laboratory experiment in which 216 subjects were randomly assigned to twelve groups.[5] Each group was given a different combination of information as to fixed assets (e.g., no information, depreciation expense, a complete history of past capital expenditures), and various levels of an initial stock of capital resources. They were asked to make a series of budget allocations between current services and capital outlays.

The study found that when participants were provided with either the complete history of capital expenditures or depreciation expense, they allocated a greater proportion of their budget to the capital outlays. The researchers concluded that their results were consistent with the premise that depreciation accounting can influence capital expenditure decisions. Depreciation accounting, they suggested, provides decision makers with other information that they could not obtain elsewhere and in a more explicit form (such as asset age and remaining service life). Further, depreciation may act as a surrogate for a more detailed recap of past expenditures (which would likely be impractical to include in financial reports) and thereby offsets a natural bias in favor of current expenditures.

- to provide information about a government's physical and other nonfinancial resources having useful lives that extend beyond the current year, including information that can be used to assess the service potential of those resources

- to help users assess long and short-term capital needs

Current Standards

GASB standards as to infrastructure, like those as to depreciation, are succinct and clear:

> Reporting public domain or "infrastructure" fixed assets—roads, bridges, curbs and gutters, streets and sidewalks, drainage systems, lighting systems and similar assets that are immovable and of value only to the governmental unit—is optional. The accounting policy in this respect should be disclosed in the Summary of Significant Accounting Policies. Appropriate legal and descriptive records (for example, deeds, maps, and listings) should be maintained for *all* fixed assets, however, for both management and accountability purposes.[6]

[5] "Depreciation and Capital Investment Decisions," by S.J. Kachelmeier and M.H. Granof, *Journal of Accounting and Public Policy*, vol. II, (Winter 1993).

[6] *Codification*, Section 1400.109.

Few governments elect to include infrastructure in their GFAAG, but as might be expected, the option to exclude has been a source of controversy. For many governments, infrastructure assets constitute their primary resources in terms both of initial cost and importance. Indeed for some, such as counties, their main raison d'etre is the construction and maintenance of roads, bridges, drainage systems, and the like.

Several reasons have been advanced to justify current practices of excluding infrastructure assets from the GFAAG:

- A key reason for maintaining accounting control over assets is to prevent fraud or abuse. But infrastructure assets cannot be stolen or misused.

- Another important reason for reporting assets is to enable statement users to assess whether the assets have been used efficiently. Governments are not expected to earn a monetary return on infrastructure. Therefore, a comparison between a measure of output (performance) and any monetary value that might be assigned to the assets in the GFAAG is not likely to be meaningful.

- A third reason for reporting assets is so that statement users can consider alternative uses for them. Infrastructure assets, however, cannot be either sold or moved. They seldom have alternative uses.

- It would be extremely difficult to obtain data on the cost of infrastructure assets constructed in the past, as would be necessary if the balance sheet were to present a comprehensive picture of assets in use. Many of a government's infrastructure assets may not have been constructed as part of a single project. Instead they evolved over time. For example, a government does not typically construct a four-lane highway through virgin fields or forests. More likely, a highway begins as a footpath and metamorphoses over generations to an unpaved road, a paved road, and a two-lane highway. Correspondingly, although infrastructure assets must be continually maintained, many, like roads and utility lines, have indeterminate useful lives.

In brief, it is argued, the information that would be reported on the face of a balance sheet facilitates no decisions and therefore, the cost of record keeping and reporting is not worth the benefits.

PROPOSAL TO PROVIDE MORE INFORMATION

In 1986 the GASB issued a resolution urging governments to experiment in providing information about their infrastructure. Concurrently, it sponsored a research study to explore the types of information that financial statement users might find helpful. A report on the study identified the following six types of information that governments could provide and asked a sample of statement users to assess the utility of each:[7]

- *Historical cost.* The purchase price or construction cost plus any additional costs incurred in placing an asset in its intended location and condition

- *Replacement cost.* The cost of acquiring or constructing an asset today that is identical to or has the same service potential as an asset already owned (a good indicator of an asset's current value)

- *Constant dollar cost.* The historical cost of an asset adjusted for changes in the purchasing power of the dollar (i.e., inflation)

[7] Relmond P. Van Daniker and Vernon Kwiatkowski, *Infrastructure Assets: An Assessment of User Needs and Recommendations for Financial Reporting* (Norwalk, Conn.: Governmental Accounting Standards Board, 1986).

- **Budget-to-actual data.** The amounts budgeted for the acquisition of assets compared to the amounts actually spent
- **Financial plans.** Estimates of resources that are expected to be available for the acquisition of assets and the projects that are expected to be undertaken
- **Engineering information.** Estimates of the useful lives of assets and assessments of their condition, as might be reported in aging schedules showing the construction date of major assets categorized by type (bridges, roads, etc.)

The users who participated in the study included citizens, investors, managers, legislators, and academics. Although the groups differed significantly in how they evaluated each type of information, they all agreed that **historical cost** information is the *least* useful. Similarly, most concurred that **constant dollar cost** information (historical cost data adjusted for inflation) was the second least useful. This finding is ironic, since the fixed asset account group now provides only historical cost data. At the other end of the scale, they ranked engineering and financial plan information first and second as to their usefulness. These types of information are the least financial in nature, suggesting perhaps that if accountants are to be relevant, they must reach beyond their traditional boundaries.

As pointed out earlier in the text, government assets, especially infrastructure, can be seen as liabilities as much as assets. Infrastructure assets must be maintained and, like an individual's car, home, and college-age children, are a continuing drain upon fiscal resources.

    Governments can postpone asset upkeep costs, but they cannot avoid them. For some assets, engineers have developed sophisticated maintenance schedules that minimize long-term costs. For example, streets and highways should be resurfaced after a specified number of years. If governments delay beyond that period, then the costs to repair the further deterioration will outweigh the financial benefits of having put off the expenditures.

    Deferred maintenance costs are defined as "delayed repair, or upkeep, measured by the outlay required to restore a plant or individual asset to full operating characteristics."[8]

    They could be measured as the amount necessary to bring the assets up to their expected operating condition. Deferred maintenance costs may be interpreted as a potential call upon government resources—an obligation that is being passed on to taxpayers of the future. They are an indication that taxpayers of the past or present have not paid for the maintenance costs applicable to the services received.

    In the GASB infrastructure study, at least 84 percent of the academic, investor, legislator, and citizen groups were in favor of including information on deferred maintenance in annual financial reports. Only managers (who would be responsible for providing the data) were less enthusiastic, with only 52 percent advocating inclusion.[9]

    Despite the apparent demand for information on deferred maintenance costs, the GASB is unlikely in the foreseeable future to require governments to provide it. The main obstacle is the obvious measurement problems. Governments currently lack reliable standards for determining either the full or the current operating capacity of infrastructure assets or for calculating the cost of eliminating the gap between the two.

THE QUESTION OF DEFERRED MAINTENANCE

---

[8] W.W. Cooper and Y. Ijiri, eds., *Kohler's Dictionary for Accountants*, 6th ed. (Englewood Cliffs, N.J.: Prentice-Hall, 1993), p. 155.

[9] Van Daniker and Kwiatkowski, p. 112

More likely, the GASB will require the disclosure of actual infrastructure maintenance and repair costs over an extended period of time, perhaps ten years. With such data, statement users will be able to establish expenditure trends and thereby spot major variances. This type of information is no substitute for a dollar estimate of future repair and maintenance obligations facing a government. Nevertheless, it may serve as a warning flag, highlighting both expenditure increases (signaling that perhaps maintenance costs will continue to increase) and decreases (indicating possibly that the maintenance expenditures have been postponed to the future). The conclusions to be drawn from the data will be left to the statement users.

REPORTING CHANGES IN FIXED ASSETS

GASB standards require that governments either present a "statement of changes in general fixed assets," or include comparable information in notes.[10] Although the standards do not specify the content of the report, most governments show the beginning balance, the additions, the retirements, and the ending balance. Some divide the additions column into additions by acquisition and additions by construction; some also include a column for assets transferred to and from the various government functions or activities. The City of Fort Worth's schedule is presented in Table 8–2. Note how, as is common, the schedule of fixed assets (Table 8–1) shows the assets by asset type, whereas the schedule of changes in fixed assets (Table 8–2) categorizes them by function and activity. Of course, the total beginning- and end-of-year assets per the two schedules are the same.

LIMITATIONS OF INFORMATION REPORTED ABOUT LONG-TERM ASSETS

In reality readers can learn very little from the information provided on long-term assets. The schedule of changes in general fixed assets, along with the GFAAG balance sheet, are inadequate to facilitate any significant decisions or judgments involving long-term assets that statement users are likely to make.

Consider, for example, typical questions relating to fixed assets that either city officials or external parties might ask:

- *Should the city they sell an asset and replace it with another?* For this decision the recorded amount, indicative of the initial cost of the asset, is irrelevant. It is a "sunk cost" and has no bearing on cash flows of the future. By contrast, the current market price of the asset—that for which it could be sold—is of direct concern.

- *Are assets being used efficiently?* As with the previous question, the historical cost of the assets is irrelevant. Suppose that the city owns two parcels of land, which it uses as sports fields. Both have the same market value. It would make no sense to assert that one is being used more efficiently than the other merely because it was acquired earlier and at a lower price.

- *Is the city replacing assets that it sells or retires?* The comparison between additions and book value of retirements would shed little light on whether the city is maintaining its asset base, since it would relate assets at current prices with those of the past.

- *Are the city's assets adequately insured?* The adequacy of insurance must be assessed by comparing the amount of coverage with the cost of replacing the assets.

---

[10] *Codification*, Section 2200.109(b).

TABLE 8-2
City of Fort Worth
Schedule of Changes in General Fixed Assets

	General Fixed Assets October 1, 1995	Additions	Retirements	General Fixed Assets September 30, 1996
General Administration:				
Mayor and Council	$ 43	$ 8	$ 11	$ 40
City Manager	1,978	0	479	1,499
Internal Audit	32	4	0	36
City Secretary	121	0	10	111
Legal	34	80	0	114
Human Resources and Risk Management	337	30	0	367
City Services	1,760	0	483	1,277
Environmental Management	982	432	5	1,409
Total General Administration	5,287	554	988	4,853
Public Safety:				
Police	45,019	3,007	2,407	45,619
Fire	38,267	1,401	1,236	38,432
Emergency Preparedness (Fire)	537	0	0	537
Municipal Court	1,319	94	101	1,312
Total Public Safety	85,142	4,502	3,744	85,900
Transportation and Public Works	609,097	32,270	647	640,720
Parks and Community Services	63,001	2,296	434	64,863
Public Library	16,327	758	69	17,016
Public Health	1,831	218	97	1,952
Public Events and Facilities:				
Culture and Tourism	6,645	0	0	6,645
Public Events and Facilities	43,326	465	23	43,768
Total Public Events and Facilities	49,971	465	23	50,413
Nondepartmental	239	722	0	961
Zoo	60	20,575	0	20,635
Planning and Development:				
Development	861	157	66	952
Planning	111	54	0	165
Total Planning and Development	972	211	66	1,117
Fiscal Services	3,143	76	180	3,039
Housing:				
Housing	9,639	578	107	10,110
Human Relations Commission	68	13	0	81
Total Housing	9,707	591	107	10,191
Investment in International Airport	8,450	0	0	8,450
Investment in Railtran	16,584	0	0	16,584
Total General Fixed Assets	$869,811	$63,238	$6,355	$926,694

The best that can be said about the information provided by governments on fixed assets is that it is characterized by all the limitations of business statements, plus one key additional (albeit debatable) deficiency: it provides no indication of the proportion of the assets already consumed. To be sure, fixed asset reporting is not a strong point of governmental accounting, and the GASB recognizes that substantial improvements are needed before its own objectives of reporting are satisfied.

IN PRACTICE

WHY DO GOVERNMENT ASSETS LAST SO LONG?

Extant governmental accounting standards provide only for a general fixed assets account group (GFAAG), which in practice is simply a running total of all prior capital expenditures with no accounting indication of physical deterioration over time. Worse, although governments are technically obliged to remove assets from the GFAAG once useful lives have expired, many governmental entities systematically ignore this requirement.

To support this claim, we selected a random sample of fifty annual reports from the mid- to late-1980s from U.S. cities with populations over 100,000. We then examined the *equipment* category in the schedule of changes in general fixed assets to isolate an asset group with a finite and (reasonably short) useful life. The median deletion rate for equipment was 4.16 percent, implying an average useful life of twenty-four years (1/.0416) for equipment assuming that all deletions reflect retirements upon the expiration of useful life (see note below). This assumption is clearly unrealistic, since some deletions may reflect sales, trade-ins, or transfers of assets in advance of useful life expiration. Therefore, twenty-four years is a conservative estimate of the implied useful life of equipment, supporting our contention that many fixed assets remain on the books long after they have become useless or obsolete. None of the fifty cities in our sample disclosed any allowance for depreciation within the general fixed assets account group.

Note: We used the median as opposed to the mean deletion rate because rates for certain cities were extreme. For example, the fiscal 1988 annual report for Sunnyvale, California, showed equipment deletions of $6.1 million from a beginning balance of only $4.2 million. There was no explanation of how more assets could be deleted than actually existed at the beginning of the year.

Source: Excerpt from a Research Study, "Depreciation and Capital Investment Decisions," by S.J. Kachelmeier and M.H. Granof, *Journal of Accounting and Public Policy*, vol. XII (Winter 1993). Reprinted with permission of the publisher, Elsevier Science Inc.

Addendum. These findings were discussed with government specialists representing most of the independent CPA firms that audited the cities in the sample. Their reaction was that their firms direct relatively little time to auditing fixed assets because compared to other government resources, there is both scant risk of fraud, theft, or other abuse and statement users are seldom concerned with the reported data.

POSSIBLE DIFFERENCES UNDER ENTITY-WIDE (FULL ACCRUAL) STATEMENTS

The revamped reporting model as proposed by the GASB would dramatically alter the way in which governments account for their capital assets. As emphasized previously, the new entity-wide statements would be on a full accrual basis and would focus on all economic resources. Therefore, long-lived assets would be reported on the statement of net assets (the balance sheet) at historical cost net of accumulated depreciation. Correspondingly, the statement of activities would include a charge for depreciation.

As proposed by the GASB, infrastructure assets would be reported in the same manner as other capital assets. Thus, they too would be reported at cost less accumulated depreciation.

As indicated in Chapter 7, the equity side of the balance sheet would report net assets (total assets less total liabilities) in three sections:

- Invested in capital assets, net of related debt
- Restricted net assets (e.g., for capital project, for debt service and for other purposes)
- Unrestricted net assets

The GASB blueprint for the new reporting structure also calls for supplementary schedules of changes in both capital assets and long-term liabilities. The schedule of changes in capital assets would present, by asset classification (such as land, buildings, equipment, works of art), the beginning balance, the additions, the sales and retirements, the depreciation charges, and the ending balance. It would be similar to that currently prepared (see the statement of Fort Worth in Table 8–2), except that it would include all capital assets—those currently reported in the GFAAG as well as in proprietary funds—and, of course include data as to depreciation.

This new schedule has important ramifications not only for the entity-wide statements but also for the fund-perspective statements. Because it includes the same information currently displayed in the balance sheet column of the general fixed assets account group, it obviates the need for that column. Therefore, in their fund-perspective balance sheets, governments would no longer have to report on the GFAAG.

HOW DO OTHER NOT-FOR-PROFITS ACCOUNT FOR CAPITAL ASSETS?

Other not-for-profit organizations, which are under the jurisdiction of the FASB, generally account for long-lived assets as do businesses, rather than governments. Long-lived assets are accorded balance sheet recognition and depreciated over their useful lives.

Not-for-profits usually classify their fixed assets (excluding those held in endowment funds as investments, such as real estate) as *unrestricted*. They report fixed assets on the balance sheet as would businesses. Thus, for example:

Land	$4,000,000
Buildings and Equipment	7,000,000
Less: Accumulated Depreciation	(2,000,000)
	5,000,000
Total Property and Equipment	$9,000,000

They also, however, have the option of classifying donated fixed assets and fixed assets acquired with donations restricted for the acquisition of those assets as temporarily restricted. These assets are then released from their restrictions as they are consumed (i.e., depreciated). The depreciation expense, like all other expenses of not-for-profits, is charged to the unrestricted assets. The rationale for this treatment is that the assets are subject to time restrictions.

FASB STANDARDS REGARDING DEPRECIATION

Not-for-profits are governed by FASB Statement No. 93, *Recognition of Depreciation by Not-for-Profit Organizations* (1987). This statement stipulates that "not-for-profit organizations shall recognize the cost of using up the future economic benefits or service potentials of their long-lived tangible assets—depreciation" and mandates disclosure of depreciation expense for the period, balances of major classes of depreciable assets, and a description of the depreciation method used.

FASB Statement No. 117, *Financial Statements of Not-for-Profit Organizations*, directs that not-for-profits classify their expenditures by function (i.e., activity), rather than by natural classification. Therefore, most organizations allocate depreciation to the functions and report the total depreciation charge only in notes to the financial statements, not in the statement of activities itself. Of course, they also deduct accumulated depreciation from the depreciable assets as shown on their balance sheets.

The Board grounded its depreciation requirement in its conclusion that "accrual accounting is presently considered superior to the cash basis and the so-called 'modified cash' and 'modified accrual' bases because, among other things, other bases do not faithfully represent costs incurred during a period." Reliable information about the cost of assets used by a not-for-profit organization to provide services "is useful to resource providers and others in assessing how the organization carried out its services."[11]

Consistent with the accepted practice of not charging depreciation on land, the economic value of which is not diminished by either time or usage, the Board makes an exception for "individual works of art or historical treasures whose economic benefit or service potential is used up so slowly that their estimated useful lives are extraordinarily long." Entities need not depreciate these types of assets.

STANDARDS OF THE FASB VERSUS THOSE OF THE GASB

Earlier we considered what statement-readers can learn from the information that governments provide about their fixed assets. We concluded that the information is inadequate to facilitate key decisions or assessments made by parties either external or internal to the organization.

Not-for-profits, unlike governments are required to report both depreciation expense and accumulated depreciation. Both depreciation and accumulated depreciation are based on *historical costs*. As a consequence, they add either little or nothing to the

---

[11]Paras. 21 and 22.

In its "Basis for Conclusions," the FASB asserted that many benefits would result from recording depreciation. [In the opinion of the Harvard Business School Faculty], depreciation on assets acquired with an entity's own resources is necessary in order to report on the maintenance of financial capital, but the other alleged benefits do not exist.

Depreciation expense amortizes the cost of assets acquired at various times in the past, at various price levels, and often by different managers from those responsible for operations in the current period. It does not report the current cost of using depreciable assets. Depreciation expense is therefore not a useful number for measuring the accountability, efficiency, effectiveness, or other aspects of the performance of current management, or of the "service effort" or "service potential" of the entity. Moreover, depreciation is not a valid number in a comparison of various organizations, unless their assets were acquired at similar price levels.

As an extreme, but indicative example, consider two buildings at Harvard University. Massachusetts Hall is a brick building housing the President and other senior officials, with 20,300 square feet of floor space. It was built in 1720 at a cost of 3,500 British pounds, and it was renovated in 1925 at a cost of $175,000. (Its replacement cost is more than $2 million but statement No. 93 relates only to historical cost.) About 100 feet away is a wooden gate house with 60 square feet of space. It was built in 1983, at a cost of $51,272. The sum of the depreciation expense on these two assets is a meaningless number.

The Board also asserted that recording depreciation expense helps in facilitating the custody and safekeeping of the organization's resources, and in showing whether an organization can continue to provide services. Recording the cost or fair value of assets acquired may be useful for these purposes, but depreciation as such has not a slight relevance to them.

Although the Board asserted that depreciation expense is useful for many purposes, it gave not one shred of evidence from the literature or from its own research that these benefits exist. It did not conduct research on this crucial matter, other than that provided in the responses to the Exposure Draft, and these responses clearly do not support the assertion. The weight of evidence, some of which became available after the issuance of that statement, does not support this assertion.

Source: Excerpts of the February 12, 1989, letter from several Harvard Business School Faculty to the FASB protesting statement No. 93 *Recognition of Depreciation in Not-for-Profit Organizations.*

ARGUMENTS AGAINST RECOGNIZING DEPRECIATION (PER THE HARVARD BUSINESS SCHOOL FACULTY)

decision-making value of the historical cost information without depreciation. The depreciation-adjusted statements will no more enable a statement-reader to answer the questions raised in the previous section than the modified accrual statements without depreciation.

To help place the deficiencies of fixed asset reporting in perspective, it is essential to raise the same questions about business accounting. The answers, of course, will be the same. The deficiencies are inherent in any accounting system that is based on historical, rather than current, costs. The point to be made is *not* that a current cost system is necessarily preferable to an historical cost system—obviously it has its own attendant problems. Instead, it is that fixed asset accounting—in governments and not-for-profits as well as businesses—provides little information that facilitates the decisions or assessments of statement readers.

Neither the FASB nor the GASB has seriously entertained an accounting model in which long-lived assets are reported at **replacement cost**. Harvard University has experimented with such an approach (see Table 8–3). The resultant statements, although not conventional, were in accord with generally accepted accounting principles because they presented the assets at historical cost (and disclose information as to historical cost depreciation in notes) as well as replacement values.

ACCOUNTING FOR PLANT ASSETS UNDER THE AICPA COLLEGE AND UNVERSITY MODEL

As discussed and illustrated in Chapter 7, the AICPA college and university model, which is currently used only by governmental colleges and universities, displays long-lived assets in an **investment in plant fund.** The assets of the fund are generally classified as:

- land
- buildings
- improvements other than buildings
- equipment
- library books

Government colleges and universities that adhere to the AICPA model are *not* required to report accumulated depreciation; however, many elect to do so.

The liabilities of the fund (which has more of the characteristics of an account group than a fund) are the obligations relating to the recorded assets. The difference between the two is reported as "net investment in plant."

The liabilities reported in the investment in plant fund are reduced when paid with resources from other funds, such as the current unrestricted fund or the plant fund for retirement of indebtedness. Correspondingly, net investment in plant is increased. Similarly when assets of the fund are reduced either through sale, retirement, or recognition of depreciation, "net investment in plant" is also reduced.

EXAMPLE *Plant Assets*

The investment in plant fund of a university (based on actual balances of Pennsylvania State University) reflects the following (in millions):

Investment in Plant—Assets

Land	$ 27
Buildings	1,043
Improvements Other Than Buildings	145
Equipment	517
Total Plant	1,732
Less: Accumulated Depreciation	(757)
Total Investment in Plant	$ 975

Investment in Plant—Equities

Notes Payable	$ 29
Bonds Payable	406
Capital Lease Obligations	6
Contractual Payments Withheld	5
Net Investment in Plant	529
Total Investment in Plant	$ 975

During the following year the university engaged in the transactions that follow (in millions). The entries indicated are only those that will affect the investment in plant fund, not the plant funds in which financial resources may be received or disbursed. These were illustrated in the previous chapter.

It acquired equipment of $90.

Equipment	$90	
Net investment in plant		$90
To record acquisition of equipment		

It sold or retired equipment that had cost $60 on which depreciation of $55 had previously been recognized.

Accumulated depreciation	$55	
Net investment in plant	5	
Equipment		$60
To record the retirement of equipment		

It repaid $30 million of principal on its bonds and $2 on its capital leases.

Bonds payable	$30	
Capital lease obligations	2	
Net investment in plant		$32
To record the repayment of debt		

It recognized $57 of depreciation.

Net investment in plant	$57	
Accumulated depreciation		$57
To recognize depreciation		

The depreciation would *not* be recognized as an expenditure in any of the university's other funds. It is recorded only as a reduction of the assets and a corresponding reduction in net investment in plant.

WHAT ISSUES ARE CRITICAL AS TO INVESTMENTS IN MARKETABLE SECURITIES AND OTHER FINANCIAL INSTRUMENTS?

The standards for valuing investments in marketable securities, such as stocks, bonds, and notes, and for recognizing interest, dividends, and gains and losses (both realized and unrealized) have been discussed in previous chapters. However, the concerns of governments, not-for-profits, and their constituents with regard to investments extend beyond issues of accounting. Investments in marketable securities and related financial instruments such as commodity options allow organizations to enhance their

TABLE 8–3
Excerpts from the Balance Sheet and Accompanying Note of Harvard University
June 30, 1996 and 1995 (in Thousands of Dollars)

	1996	1995
Facilities (See Note)		
Replacement Cost	$4,018,220	$3,980,217
Accumulated Replacement Cost Depreciation	(1,181,682)	(1,185,581)
Net Replacement Cost	2,836,538	2,794,636
Adjustment to Historical Cost	1,204,592	1,260,877
Net Historical Cost	$1,631,946	$1,533,759

The University capitalizes and depreciates the major costs associated with acquiring, constructing, and renovating facilities. Land is presented at its original historical cost when known. Equipment and furniture are generally expensed when purchased.

In order to highlight and better quantify the scope and condition of the University's facilities, supplementary replacement cost data are presented on the face of the Balance Sheet, in the Statement of Changes in Net Assets of the General Operating Account, and in the notes.

The major categories of capitalized facility costs as of June 30, 1996 are summarized as follows (in thousands of dollars):

	Net Historical Value	Current Year Additions	Replacement Cost Depreciation	Estimated Replacement Value	Gross Square Feet (in Millions)	Average Estimated Useful Life
Housing	$ 337,950	$ 43,886	$24,590	$1,014,556	5.8	35 years
Laboratories	293,842	20,750	20,561	760,387	2.9	31
Classrooms and Offices	306,420	34,091	17,273	792,261	3.3	39
Libraries	45,944	4,724	8,674	397,838	1.4	39
Museums/Assembly	71,879	4,555	7,876	361,278	1.2	39
Athletics	45,866	655	2,699	118,225	0.7	37
Service Facilities	145,178	11,043	7,661	275,602	1.2	37
Other	215,831	4,495	1,869	235,574	0.3	35
Construction in Progress	169,036	19,657	—	62,499	—	
Totals	**$1,631,946**	**$143,856**	**$91,203**	**$4,018,220**	**16.8**	

Note:
Accumulated historical cost depreciation was $486.9 and $441.2 million at June 30, 1996 and 1995, respectively.

Harvard maintains a program of regularly planning for and estimating the cost of major maintenance and renovation of buildings. Replacement cost values and depreciation information have been developed in support of these efforts. This information is integral to planning, managing, and reporting the costs of maintaining the University's facilities. The replacement cost values shown in the preceding table represent reasonable estimates of the current cost to replace existing structures with facilities of comparable utility, or, in the case of historic structures, to reproduce them through modern methods. They do not purport to present the market value of facilities. These estimates are based on building use, on detailed records of the size, type, and quality of construction, and on relevant construction cost indices related to each of the University's buildings. Each building's effective age was developed using available information regarding building condition and acquisition or construction date, together with life expectancy guidelines. These estimates are periodically compared to detailed building surveys and appraisals and are updated annually to reflect inflation or deflation in construction costs.

revenues and, in some cases, to better manage their risks. But they also present special hazards. This section of the chapter discusses the reasons why governments and not-for-profits purchase marketable securities and related financial instruments and identifies some of the perils associated with them.

Both governments and other not-for-profits may have large pools of cash available for investments. The following are among the major sources:

- Governments and not-for-profits periodically receive large amounts of cash—from donations, tax collections, tolls, fees for services, etc. A fundamental rule of cash management is the less cash on hand, the better. As long as the cash is not required to meet required expenditures of the same day, it should be placed in short-term—even overnight—securities.

- They maintain reserve funds to repay debts or to "save," either for a particular purpose or for a "rainy day."

- They accumulate resources in pension funds.

- They maintain permanent endowments, which are established to generate investment revenues.

Their reasons for investing this cash in marketable securities are, for the most part, similar to those of businesses—to earn a return on resources that would otherwise be unproductive.

Many governments invest their funds directly in stocks, bonds, notes, and other financial instruments. Others, especially smaller units, participate in **investment pools,** maintained by other governments. For example, most states operate investment pools for their cities, counties, and school districts. These pools enable these units to gain the benefits of increased portfolio size—lower trading costs, greater opportunity to diversify, and ability to pay for sophisticated investment advice.

Until recently the investment activities of governments and not-for-profits received relatively little attention from accounting standard-setting authorities. Generally, governments and not-for-profits were satisfied with "conservative securities" that provided steady, if relatively modest, returns. Accordingly, their risks of loss were low.

Within the last decade, however, treasurers and other officials responsible for their organizations' investments have come under considerable pressure to increase their portfolio yields. In part, the demands can be attributed to the need for their organizations to maintain or enhance services in the face of increasing costs. Also, though, the treasury function has become more professional. No longer can treasurers simply divide their available resources among local banks or friendly brokerage houses. Today, their performance—and consequently, their salary increases and opportunities for advancement—are more likely to be tied to the yields on the portfolios they control. In the face of these incentives it is easy for portfolio managers to ignore a fundamental concept of finance: the greater the returns, the greater the risk.

At the same time, the range of investment "products" offered by Wall Street has increased dramatically. Succumbing to aggressive sales tactics from brokers and dealers, many treasurers purchase securities that they don't understand and that are clearly unsuited to their institutions' investment objectives.

When governments and not-for-profits restricted their portfolios to conventional financial instruments, the accounting issues of asset classification (e.g., current or noncurrent) and valuation (cost or market) and of revenue recognition (upon change in value or only upon sale) were far more tractable than they are today. The new financial instruments are often multifaceted, and extremely difficult to value. In addition, identical types of financial instruments can be held for diametrically opposed purposes (e.g., to increase risk or to decrease risk).

SPECIAL RISKS OF REPURCHASE AGREEMENTS

In the mid-1980s it became clear that existing requirements were inadequate to assure that investors of all types (governments, not-for-profits and businesses) fully disclosed their investment risks. One main problem centered around repurchase agreements. A **repurchase agreement** (referred to as a "repo") is a short-term investment in which an investor (a lender) transfers cash to a broker-dealer or other financial institution (the "counterparty") in exchange for securities. The broker-dealer or other financial institution promises to repay the cash, plus interest, in exchange for the same (or in some cases different) securities.

Repurchase agreements usually have either short-term (some times overnight) maturities or open-ended maturities in which the interest rates may be changed daily and the agreement may be terminated at any time by either party. To facilitate the transactions, the investor may not actually take custody of the securities (in effect, the collateral) that back its investment. Instead the securities may be retained by the counterparty (perhaps in its trust department) or by its agent. Moreover, the securities may be held in the name of the counterparty rather than the investor.

The major risk to the government (or other investor) from a repurchase transaction is that the counterparty will be unable to repay cash and that either the government will be unable to obtain the securities or that the securities will have decreased in value. As might be expected, for some governments that invested in repurchase agreements the risk became the reality.

Governments and other not-for-profits may also enter into **reverse repurchase agreements.** A reverse repurchase agreement—*reverse repo*—is one in which the government or other party is a borrower rather than an investor. The broker-dealer or other financial institution transfers cash to the government in exchange for securities and the government agrees to repay the cash plus interest and return the securities.

SPECIAL RISKS OF DERIVATIVES

The 1980s and 1990s saw many governments and not-for-profits invest in derivatives. A derivative is defined as a security whose value depends on (is *derived* from) that of some underlying asset (such as a share of stock), a reference rate (such as a prevailing interest rate) or an index (such as the Standard & Poor's index of stock prices). Derivatives embrace many types of securities, ranging from the ordinary to the esoteric. For example, they include ordinary stock options (such as puts and calls), debt instruments that are backed by pools of mortgages, and interest-only or principal-only "strips" (bond-like securities in which the obligations to pay principal and interest are traded separately). Most derivatives are highly volatile instruments and can enable an investor to achieve gains, or cause it to incur losses, greatly out of proportion to the change in the value of the securities or assets to which they are linked.

Ironically, many types of derivatives were developed to *reduce* overall investment risks. Hence, they may have a legitimate place in the portfolios of even the most conservative organizations. However, they were widely misused by some governments and not-for-profits as means of speculation.

IN PRACTICE

FROM OPULENCE ON WALL STREET TO WRECKAGE ON MAIN STREET

E.S.M. Government Securities Inc. was a small firm that had somehow transferred the opulence of Wall Street to Ft. Lauderdale, Florida. Its headquarters surrounded a courtyard and was furnished like a penthouse. Its officers paid themselves lavish salaries and bonuses and lived every bit of it: one kept show horses on his estate, another had a seventy-foot yacht. But as it turned out, a large share of the tab for their high living may have been picked up by some plain folks on Main Street.

E.S.M. lay in wreckage last week. The Securities and Exchange Commission had charged it with a massive fraud, and a court-appointed receiver was trying to figure out how a firm that had lost a total of $196.5 million since it started in 1976 had managed to stay afloat as long as it had. When it finally did collapse, E.S.M. left unpaid claims of about $300 million, mostly owed to municipalities such as Toledo, Ohio, Harrisburg, Pennsylvania, and Beaumont, Texas, and some thrift institutions.

The City of Toledo, which stood to lose $19 million, suspended two top financial officers. One of the thrifts, the Home State Savings Bank in Cincinnati, was forced to close and offer itself up for sale—an event that led to a run on several other thrifts in the area whose deposits were insured not by a federal agency but by a state fund that appeared inadequate to cover the anticipated losses. In at least one case, panicky depositors camped outside their thrift overnight to be first in line to withdraw in the morning. Then-governor Richard Celeste finally closed seventy other state-chartered and state-insured thrifts for three days (they were scheduled to open again Monday) until the state could work out an emergency plan to keep them viable.

For the most part, the losers may have been stung simply because they were too trusting. Many of the municipalities and thrifts became E.S.M. customers because they had spare cash to invest. They, in effect, lent money to the firm through repurchase agreements, or "repos," which are common in the government-securities business. Technically, the municipalities and thrifts bought government securities from E.S.M., which promised to repurchase them at a higher price at a later date—that higher price representing the "interest" on the customers' investments. The deals seemed riskproof, since the purchased securities themselves were the collateral. But unlike bigger investors who insist on holding the actual securities they are buying, E.S.M.'s customers were content with the firm's promise that the securities were on deposit in New York banks. They weren't.

E.S.M. apparently increased its inflow of funds by pledging the same securities more than once. And to get more securities to pledge, it made "reverse repos" with the same kind of small customers, buying government paper and selling it back later at a higher figure. Customers were fooled further by audited reports showing that E.S.M. had a healthy balance sheet. What happened, says Thomas Tew, E.S.M.'s receiver, is that the firm charged its losses to affiliated firms whose books seemingly were not reviewed by outside accountants. Tew sued E.S.M.'s auditor, Alexander Grant & Co., charging it with "professional negligence" of "outrageous character."

E.S.M.'s downfall began when American Savings and Loan Association of Florida decided to phase out its dealings with the firm. The institution demanded the return of the securities it had put up with E.S.M., apparently in reverse repo deals, but the firm could not make good on all of the obligations. Ronald Ewton, E.S.M.'s chairman and one of its cofounders, resigned in February. But the funds apparently kept flowing out of the firm right up to the end.

Source: "Fallout From a Failure," *Newsweek* (March 25, 1985), p. 72. Reprinted by permission of publisher, © 1995 *Newsweek, Inc.* All rights reserved.

Texas, Other Governments, Trade in Commodities Futures

Texas, along with other governments, is becoming a big-time player in the commodities market. But it's not because they've become bored with their own lottery operations. Quite the contrary; their goal is not to take risks, but to reduce them. If the word *hedging* does not yet appear in the codification of government accounting standards, you can be certain that it will soon.

Texas uses commodity options to protect its tax revenues from sudden drops in the price of oil. Texas expects to generate $500 million from its oil severance tax. For every barrel of the black gold produced in the state, the Treasury receives 4.6 percent of the sales price. A sharp drop in price, such as in 1986 when it nose-dived from almost $25.82 to 11.36, can play havoc with the state's budget.

To lock in a set price, the state is experimenting with oil options. Here's how they work.

The State purchases *put options* on crude oil. Each option permits it to sell (or "put") a thousand barrels of oil at an established price to the party that sold the option on a specified date. If the market price on the exercise date is below the established price, then the option has value—the difference between the established price and the market price. The state either exercises the option or sells it in the open market, thus making a "profit" and covering the cost of the oil itself. The greater the decline in market price, the greater the gain to the state. If, however, the market price on the specified date is above the established option price, then the option has no value and the state will allow it to expire. Its loss is limited to the amount that it paid to acquire the option (the "premium" cost).

The Texas Treasury can be viewed as the de facto owner of 4.6 percent (the severance tax rate) of all the oil produced in the state. Therefore, for each 1,000 barrels of oil that it wants to protect against a decline in revenue, it must buy puts on 46 barrels.

Suppose that on June 1, the State buys puts on 100,000 barrels of oil, thereby protecting 2,173,913 barrels (100,000 divided by 4.6 percent). Since put contracts are typically written in units of 1,000 barrels, it would be required to buy 100 contracts. Assume that on the date the puts are purchased the prevailing market price is $21 per barrel and that this is the price that the state wants to lock in for purposes of severance tax collection three months hence. Therefore it buys puts with $21 as the strike price and October 1 as the expiration date. The cost of each contract might be approximately $1,100 including commissions—$110,000 for the 100 contracts.

If, on the expiration date, the market value of oil has fallen to $18 per barrel, then the market value of each contract can be expected to approximate $3,000—[($21 − $18) × 1,000 barrels]—or $300,000 for the 100 contracts. This amount will be just sufficient to offset the loss on the severance tax revenue from the $3 per barrel price drop (2,173,913 barrels times $3 per barrel times the tax rate of 4.6 percent). The state will sell the options for the $300,000 and its net loss on the entire transaction will be $110,000, the cost of the options.

If on the expiration date, the price of oil is $21 or more, then the options will have no value and the state will be out the $110,000 that it paid for them. However, the state will still reap the benefits from the increased tax revenue owing to the rise in oil prices, and this additional revenue may be sufficient to offset all or at least a part of the option cost.

Futures Options May Have Broad Use

Trading in options is not just for states like Texas, whose tax base is tied to commodities. They may be a way to limit risk on the expenditure portion of a government's operating statement. The Metropolitan Atlanta Rapid Transportation Authority (MARTA) has entered into "energy swaps" (a special type of hedging arrangement) to protect itself from increases in the price of the diesel fuel needed to power its 700 buses. The hedging concept may make good sense for other large energy users, such as public utilities—especially those that are unable to adjust revenues rapidly in response to cost increases.

Futures and options may also have an appeal beyond commodities. Governments can also hedge both interest revenues and interest expenses. By reducing their risks, governments may be able not only to improve budgeting, but also to increase net investment returns and to reduce net financing costs. However, such strategies should only be used when government personnel are skilled and experienced in such strategies.

Source: *Government Accounting and Auditing Update* (October 1992). Reprinted by permission of publisher, RIA Group-Warren/Gorham Lamont.

The most spectacular of losses were incurred by Orange County, California, in 1994. They were so severe they caused the County to file for bankruptcy. The county not only invested its own funds in highly speculative instruments (only a small proportion of which were derivatives), but those of an investment pool maintained for school districts and other governments within the county. The In Practice that follows highlights the nature of the transactions in which it engaged.

IN PRACTICE

"Orange County's disastrous foray into Wall Street's high-rolling world of leverage and derivatives came to a brutal end yesterday when the county and its investment funds filed for bankruptcy under Chapter 9 of the federal Bankruptcy Code."

So began the lead article of the *Wall Street Journal* (December 7, 1994). "It is the largest such filing by a municipality ever," it continued. The decision, it said, "affects not only the county's $7 billion in outstanding public debt, but all 180 municipalities and local government agencies that had invested in the county's fund."

The following excerpts from an article in *Barron's* (December 5, 1994), which was published well before the full extent of the Orange County debacle became known and prior to the declaration of bankruptcy provides insight into where the county went wrong.

INCREASING RISK AND COURTING DISASTER

Peter Pan Portfolio

Orange County bet that interest rates would stay low forever

Perhaps the biggest mistake being made in assessing the $1.5 billion or more in financial losses announced last week in Orange County, California, is to lump them with the derivatives losses suffered earlier this year by the likes of Procter & Gamble and Gibson Greetings. It's true that Orange County Treasurer Robert Citron did have a heavy dose of derivatives in his $20 million portfolio. But his problem was more fundamental and old-fashioned: He ran a highly leveraged bond operation, yet he chose to ignore the fact that his strategy's success depended on interest rates staying low. Obviously, it didn't work out that way.

When rates shot up this year, the 69-year-old Citron did what many bond managers around the country consider inexcusable: He put his head in the sand and pretended that nothing significant was wrong.

A critical flaw in Citron's approach was that he never believed in adjusting the value of his securities based on changes in rates. Some West Coast wags have taken to calling it the Peter Pan Portfolio, noting that its reporting technique is based on the idea, however mistaken, that "ya gotta believe" things will work out.

Citron's operation was something like a mutual fund that never cut its share price to account for a stock-market plunge. For his part, Citron argued that he was holding the bonds until maturity, so current market value didn't matter. Which might have been a defensible position if he hadn't borrowed so much money to leverage his investments. In the end, the rising costs of those borrowings are what put the squeeze on Orange County.

"The county leadership should never have allowed this to happen," says John Mooriach, a Costa Mesa accountant who made Citron's handling of the investment the centerpiece of an unsuccessful bid to win Citron's job this spring. Adds Mooriach: "If you want to make a killing, that's fine, but do it with your own money. Don't play with the taxpayers' money."

Citron's disastrous exploits spell trouble for Southern California. The fund's losses, which could easily exceed the $1.5 billion estimated last week, will damage the already strained finances of Orange County because the county and dozens of government units within the county held more than 90% of the investments in the fund.

The largest holder is Orange County, with 37% of the portfolio, followed by the Orange County Transportation Authority, with a 15% holding, and 87 school districts, with a collective 18% stake. Othes include the Orange County Sanitation District, Transportation Corridor Agencies, Irvine Ranch Water District, the Moulton Niguel Water District and the Orange County Water District.

In all, Citron took in $7.5 billion from nearly 200 local governments and agencies statewide and pyramided those funds through aggressive use of borrowing into a $20 billion investment pool. In Orange County many government units were forced to put money into the fund, but for other municipalities, which didn't have to invest with Citron, the lure was yield. At a time when a conservative state-run fund open to municipalities was paying 4% annually, Citron offered 7%–8%.

This proved irresistible to cash-strapped local government officials, who have seen their budgets cut by the state's recession.

Not only did municipalities place their operating and reserve funds into the Orange County pool, but some actually sold short-term debt in the bond market and invested through a separate Citron-run program, basically trying to profit through arbitrage.

What Citron and his fans chose to ignore were some obvious risks. It was dangerous enough that Citron primarily bought five-year bonds, generally those issued by such quasi-government agencies as the Federal National Mortgage Association and Federal Home Loan Banks. But he compounded the risk by purchasing from these agencies volatile, five-year derivatives known as "structured" notes, and then leveraging the entire pool by a factor of three. The idea was to earn about 5% on the base investment and then a bonus on the leveraged portion of the fund based on a rate spread between the 5% yield on the bonds and the cost of financing them, which at times was as low as 8%.

This worked wonderfully in 1992 and 1993, allowing the fund to earn 8% returns. But this year, as rates have risen, trouble hit. In fact, the structure of Citron's investment pool probably gave it a risk greater than that of the 30-year Treasury bond, the most volatile and interest-sensitive government security.

Current Disclosure Requirements for Governments

Recognizing that the then-current standards of providing information on investments were inadequate, the GASB in 1986 issued Statement No. 3, *Deposits with Financial Institutions, Investments (including Repurchase Agreements), and Reverse Repurchase Agreements*. Statement No. 3 mandates extensive note disclosures, not only as to repurchase agreements but also as to all investments and deposits with banks and other financial institutions. Most prominently it requires governments to classify its bank balances and other investments into three categories of credit risk (the risk that the other party to an investment transaction will not fulfill its obligations). For bank balances the required classifications are:

- insured or collateralized with securities held by the entity or by its agent in the entity's name
- collateralized with securities held by the pledging financial institution's trust department
- uncollateralized

For other investments, including repurchase agreements they are:

- insured, registered in the name of the government or held by the government or its agent in the government's name
- uninsured and unregistered, with securities held by the other party's trust department or agent in the government's name
- uninsured and unregistered in the government's name and held by the other party or the other party's agent

In addition, it requires governments to indicate both the carrying value and the market value of their investments.[12]

In 1994, the GASB issued a technical bulletin reaffirming previous standards that governments must disclose their relevant accounting policies as to investments and provide any other information to assure that the financial statements are not misleading. It also, however, interprets existing provisions as implying that a government must reveal any violations of legal, regulatory, or contractual provisions by investing in derivatives. Further, it says, the government must explain the nature of derivative transactions, indicate the reasons why they were entered into, and include a discussion of its exposure to credit risk (that of the other party defaulting), market risk (that of changes in interest rates or market prices), and legal risk (that of the transaction being determined to be prohibited by law, regulation, or contract).[13]

Table 8–4 presents the required investment disclosures of Raleigh, North Carolina.

---

[12] *Codification*, Sections I.50.164.

[13] Technical Bulletin No. 94-1, *Disclosures about Derivatives and Similar Debt and Investment Transactions*.

TABLE 8-4
City of Raleigh, North Carolina
Investment Note

Investments. State statutes authorize the City to invest in obligations of the U.S. Treasury, obligations of any agency of the United States of America (provided the payment of interest and principal of such obligations is fully guaranteed by the United States), certain non-guaranteed federal agencies, certain high quality issues of commercial paper and bankers' acceptances, and the North Carolina Capital Management Trust, a Securities and Exchange Commission registered mutual fund.

The City is permitted to enter into repurchase agreements that consist of the purchase of securities with a simultaneous agreement to sell them in the future at the original price plus a contracted rate of interest. All repurchase agreements entered into by the City require delivery of the purchased security to the City's third party safekeeping agent, providing the City a margin against a decline in market value. On June 13, 1996, the City entered into a master repurchase agreement with a financial institution for the investment of the proceeds from the May 21, 1996 sale of $50,215,000 general obligation bonds.

The City's investments are categorized at year-end to give an indication of the level of custodial risk assumed. Column 1 represents investments that are insured or registered or for which the securities are held by the City or its agent in the City's name. Column 2 represents uninsured and unregistered investments for which the securities are held by the counterparty's trust department or agent in the City's name. Column 3 represents uninsured and unregistered investments for which the securities are held by the counterparty or its trust department or agent but not in the City's name. Investments in mutual funds are exempt from risk categorization. At June 30, 1996, the City's investments are categorized as follows:

	Category			Carrying Amount	Market Value
	1	2	3		
U.S. Government Securities	$ 14,853,906	$ –	$ –	$ 14,853,906	$ 14,853,906
U.S. Government Agencies	81,618,633	–	–	81,618,633	80,145,693
Bankers' Acceptances	26,682,375	–	–	26,682,375	26,682,375
Commercial Paper	53,965,639	–	–	53,965,639	53,965,639
Master Repurchase Agreement	49,509,718	–	–	49,509,718	50,844,766
	$226,630,271	$ –	$ –	$226,630,271	$226,492,379
Investment in Mutual Funds				54,347,238	54,347,238
				$280,977,509	$280,839,617

Investment income is allocated to the various funds based on their equity in a pooled acount. Each fund's equity of pooled cash and investments is presented in the accompanying financial statements. A summary of cash and investments at June 30, 1996 is as follows:

Petty Cash and Change Funds	$ 21,095
Deposits	10,129,476
Investments	280,977,509
	$291,128,080

CURRENT DISCLOSURE REQUIREMENTS FOR NOT-FOR-PROFITS

Although the FASB pronouncements pertaining to financial instruments apply to not-for-profits as well as to businesses, they were clearly formulated with businesses rather than not-for-profits in mind. Therefore, they address a wider range of financial instruments, including those such as foreign currency contracts that would not normally be held by not-for-profits. The disclosure requirements are set forth mainly in three statements:

- No. 105, (1990) *Disclosure of Information about Financial Instruments with Off-Balance-Sheet Risk and Financial Instruments with Concentrations of Credit Risk.* Directed mainly at instruments such as interest rate swaps (a transaction in which a party trades a promise of fixed interest payments for variable payments), foreign currency contracts, and futures contracts, the statement mandates that the nature, terms and risks of these instruments be described.

- No. 107, (1991) *Disclosures about the Fair Value of Financial Instruments.* This statement requires the disclosure of fair market value for short-term and long-term investments, including derivatives and other nonconventional securities.

- No. 119, (1994) *Disclosures about Derivative Financial Instruments and Fair Value of Financial Instruments.* Issued after several corporations incurred major losses in derivatives, this statement expands upon Statement No. 107 to require considerably more detail as to an organization's derivative transactions, including dollar amounts, nature, terms, trading gains and losses and reasons as to why they were undertaken.

Problem 9 in the problem section of this chapter illustrates the disclosures of the Carnegie Foundation, a not-for-profit with over $1 billion in investments.

SUMMARY

Governments commonly report their general fixed assets, as opposed to those in proprietary and fiduciary funds, in the general fixed assets account group. This account group is essentially a double-entry list showing government-owned assets (debits) offset by an equity-type entry, investments in general fixed assets (credits).

Although governments are permitted to adjust their GFAAG assets for accumulated depreciation, most opt to state them at acquisition cost. However, the GASB's proposed reporting model would require that in their entity-wide statements, governments account for their long-lived assets on a full accrual basis. They would thereby be required to record an annual depreciation charge and offset asset cost with accumulated depreciation.

Governments are not currently required to report infrastructure assets in the GFAAG. However, spectacular failures of infrastructure in the United States have raised questions about this practice and the GASB has proposed that these assets be included in the entity-wide statements.

In contrast to governments, other not-for-profits report their fixed assets similarly to businesses. They value the assets at cost, less accumulated depreciation and recognize depreciation on their statements of activities. Even so,

the accounting is based on historical cost and thereby fails to facilitate adequately the decisions of most statement users.

Investments are of concern because of the substantial risk that investors can incur losses through default, declines in value, and even fraud. In recent years, interest in investments has been heightened by major losses caused by purchases of overly speculative securities. These securities included repurchase agreements (a short-term investment in which the investor transfers cash to a broker-dealer or other financial institution in exchange for securities) and derivatives (a security whose value depends on that of some underlying asset such as a share of stock, a reference rate, or an index). The major risk to a government or other investor from a repurchase agreement is that the counterparty will be unable to repay cash and that either the government will unable to obtain the securities or that securities will decline in value. The major risk from a derivative is that the value of the underlying securities will decline causing the value of the derivative to decline by a disproportionately greater amount. Through their standards, both the GASB and the FASB require disclosure of a wide range of investment information.

EXERCISE FOR REVIEW AND SELF-STUDY

In January 1999, Oneida County and Oneida College (a private, not-for-profit institution) each purchased for $5 million a building to be used as a library. Both buildings were funded from private contributions. Each entity anticipated that its building's useful life would be forty years (with no residual value).

a. Prepare appropriate journal entries to record the acquisitions.

b. Prepare entries that would be made at the end of the first fiscal year to adjust, as necessary, the fixed asset values. Assume that the Oneida County accounts for assets as do most other governments.

c. Suppose that after forty years both buildings were still in service. The replacement cost of each was $12 million.

    1. At what value (net of accumulated depreciation) would each of the organizations report its library building?

    2. Provide an example, if possible, of one decision or assessment to be made (e.g., for which the buildings should be insured, whether they should be sold, whether they should be renovated) for which the book value (historical cost), as reported, would be a relevant consideration for either entity. Explain and justify your response, telling specifically how the information would be taken into account.

d. Both the county and the college established a maintenance plan specifying that the buildings should be repainted on a five-year cycle. In 2009 both institutions were short of resources and decided to defer the scheduled painting for an additional two years. Under current standards, how would each of the organizations be required to account for and report the deferral?

QUESTIONS FOR REVIEW AND DISCUSSION

1. Why are *general* fixed assets reported in an account group rather than a fund?

2. At what value are general fixed assets recorded in the general fixed assets account group (GFAAG) when they are acquired? At what value are they recorded initially if received by donation from outside parties? At what value are they recorded if they were previously recorded in an enterprise fund, such as a utility fund? What is the rationale for each of the options if they were previously recorded in an enterprise fund?

3. What are some key limitations of stating general fixed assets at cost rather than cost less accumulated depreciation and of not reporting depreciation in governmental funds?

4. What are the key arguments in defense of the current practice of not reporting depreciation in governmental funds?

5. It is widely acknowledged that information on infrastructure, in contrast to that on depreciation, is considered important by many users. Why, then, are governments *not* required to report infrastructure assets in the GFAAG?

6. How, in general, do not-for-profits other than governments account for their fixed assets? In which category of resources do they ordinarily classify fixed assets? Suppose a not-for-profit is considering the sale of a fixed asset. For purposes of this decision, would the book value of the asset as determined by GAAP for not-for-profits be more useful than the book value as determined by GAAP for governments? Explain.

7. Why do many users consider information on deferred maintenance to be of particular significance?

8. What is a repurchase agreement, and what are its special risks to a government that invests in it?

9. What are the differences between market risk, credit risk, and legal risk? Suppose a local government invests in twenty-year U.S. government bonds. Assess each of the three risks.

10. What are derivatives? Why may they be especially high-risk securities?

EXERCISES

8-1

The general fixed assets account group accounts for assets that are not accounted for in governmental funds.

   A city engaged in the following transactions during a year.

1. It acquired computer equipment at a cost of $40,000.
2. It completed construction of a new jail, incurring $245,000 in new costs. In the previous year the city had incurred $2.5 million in construction costs. The project was accounted for in a capital projects fund.
3. It sold for $16,000 a fire department vehicle that it had acquired three years earlier for $28,000. The city does not record depreciation on general fixed assets.
4. It traded in a four-year-old sanitation department vehicle for a new model. The old vehicle had initially cost $27,000 and its fair market value at the time of trade was $17,000. The city paid an additional $30,000 cash for the new model. The "sticker price" of the new model was $52,000.
   a. Prepare appropriate journal entries in the general fixed assets account group.
   b. Prepare an appropriate journal entry in the general fund to record the sale of the fire department vehicle.

8-2

The accounting for trade-ins must reflect economic substance rather than form.

   Twin City recently replaced its existing computer system. The existing system was recorded in the general fixed assets account group at $350,000, its acquisition cost of seven years earlier.

   The city contracted to purchase the new equipment from Computer Services, Inc. at a price of $800,000. However, Computer Services granted the city a trade-in allowance on the existing equipment of $150,000. Hence, the city paid only $650,000 cash, an amount that was appropriated from general funds.

   The city had previously sought to sell its existing system; the highest bid it obtained was $70,000. Although the list price of the new system is $800,000 Computer Services frequently grants customers a discount of 10 percent off list price.

a. What is the most likely fair market value of the new equipment?
b. Prepare required journal entries to record the transaction.

8-3

Under the AICPA model, government universities account for both assets, accumulated depreciation, and related debt in the investment in plant fund.

   The following summarizes the history of Sharp Hall, the main foreign language classroom building at a state university that adheres to the AICPA reporting model.

1. In 1975, the university constructed the building at a cost of $1.5 million. Of this amount $1 million was financed with bonds and the balance from unrestricted university funds.
2. In the ten years from 1975 through 1984, the university recorded depreciation, based on a useful estimated life of thirty years.
3. In the same period, the university repaid $750,000 of the bonds.
4. In 1985, the university renovated the building at a cost of $3 million. The entire amount was financed with unrestricted university funds. The renovation was expected to extend the useful life of the building for twenty-five more years—i.e., until 2010.
5. In the fifteen years from 1985 through 1999, the university recorded depreciation. Depreciation was calculated by dividing the undepreciated balance of the original cost, plus the costs of renovation, over the anticipated remaining life of twenty-five years.
6. In the same period, the university repaid the $250,000 balance of the debt.
7. In 2000, the university demolished the building so that the land on which it is situated could be converted into a practice field for the women's soccer team.
   a. Prepare the journal entries to summarize the history of the building. Include only those that would be made in the investment in plant fund.
   b. Comment on how, if at all, the "loss" from demolishing the building would be recognized in either the investment in plant fund or any other fund.

8-4

Private colleges account for fixed asset transactions differently than do government colleges.

   Prepare entries to record the transactions described in the previous exercise. Assume now, however, that the university is private.

8-5

The initial value to be assigned to an asset is not always obvious.
   A city acquired general fixed assets as follows:

1. It purchased new construction equipment. "List" price was $400,000, but the city was granted a 10 percent "government discount." The city also incurred $12,000 in transportation costs and paid $4,000 to its own employees to customize the equipment.

2. It received a donation of land to be set aside for a nature preserve. The land had cost the donor $300,000. At the time of the contribution it was valued on the city's tax rolls at $1.7 million. However, independent appraisers estimated its fair market value at $1.9 million

3. It transferred a vehicle from its utility, which is accounted for in an enterprise fund, to the police department. The vehicle had cost the utility $40,000. At the time of the transfer, it had a book value (cost less accumulated depreciation) of only $15,000. The city estimated its replacement value at $18,000.

4. It constructed a new maintenance facility at a cost of $2 million. During the period of construction the city incurred an additional $110,000 in interest on funds borrowed to finance the construction.

Indicate the value that the government should assign to these assets in the general fixed assets account group. Justify briefly the value you assigned and, as appropriate, indicate any other acceptable alternatives.

8-6

Multiple Choice Questions from CPA examinations.

1. The following information pertains to a computer that Pine Township leased from Karl Supply Co. on July 1, 1995, for general township use:

Karl's cost	$5,000
Fair value at July 1, 1995	$5,000
Estimated economic life	5 years
Fixed noncancellable term	30 months
Rental at beginning of each month	$135
Guaranteed residual value	$2,000
Present value of minimum lease payments at July 1, 1995 using:	
Pine's incremental borrowing rate of 10.5%	$5,120
Karl's implicit interest rate of 12.04%	$5,000

On July 1, 1995, what amount should Pine capitalize in its general fixed assets account group for this leased computer?
   a. $0
   b. $3,000
   c. $5,000
   d. $5,120

2. The following are Boa City's fixed assets:

Fixed assets used in proprietary fund activities	$1,000,000
Fixed assets used in governmental type trust funds	$1,800,000
All other fixed assets	$9,000,000

What aggregate amount should Boa account for in the general fixed assets account group?
   a. $9,000,000
   b. $10,000,000

   c. $10,800,000
   d. $11,800,000

3. One feature of state and local government accounting and financial reporting is that fixed assets used for general governmental activities
   a. often are not expected to contribute to the generation of revenues.
   b. do not depreciate as a result of such use.
   c. are acquired only when direct contribution to revenues is expected.
   d. should not be maintained at the same level as those of businesses so that current financial resources can be used for their government services.

4. Dodd Village received a gift of a new fire engine from a local civic group. The fair value of this fire engine was $400,000. The entry to be made in the general fixed assets account group for this gift is

	Debit	Credit
a. Memorandum entry only	–	–
b. General fund assets	$400,000	
Private gifts		$400,000
c. Investment in general fixed assets	$400,000	
Gift revenue		$400,000
d. Machinery and equipment	$400,000	
Investment in general fixed assets from private gifts		$400,000

5. Fixed assets donated to a governmental unit should be recorded
   a. at estimated fair value when received.
   b. at the lower of donor's carrying amount or estimated fair value when received.
   c. at the donor's carrying amount.
   d. as a memorandum entry only.

6. Old equipment, which is recorded in the general fixed assets account group, is sold for less than its carrying amount. The sale reduces the investments in general fixed assets balance by the
   a. difference between the cost of the equipment and the sales price.
   b. difference between the carrying amount of the equipment and the sales price.
   c. selling price of the equipment.
   d. carrying amount of the equipment.

7. The recording of accumulated depreciation in the general fixed assets account group is
   a. never allowed.
   b. dependent on materiality.

c. optional.

d. mandatory.

8. Fixed assets should be accounted for in the general fixed assets account group for the

	Enterprise Fund	Special Revenue Fund
a.	Yes	No
b.	Yes	Yes
c.	No	Yes
d.	No	No

9. Which of the following accounts would be included in the fund equity section of the combined balance sheet of a governmental unit for the general fixed assets account group?

	Investment in General Fixed Assets	Fund Balance Reserved for Encumbrances
a.	Yes	Yes
b.	Yes	No
c.	No	No
d.	No	Yes

10. When fixed assets purchased from general fund revenues were received, the appropriate journal entry was made in the general fixed assets account group. What account, if any, should have been debited in the general fund?

a. no journal entry

b. fixed assets

c. expenditures

d. due from general fixed assets account group

11. On March 2, 1995, Finch City issued ten-year general obligation bonds at face amount, with interest payable March 1 and September 1. The proceeds were to be used to finance the construction of a civic center over the period April 1, 1995, to March 31, 1996. During the fiscal year ended June 30, 1995, no resources had been provided to the debt service fund for the payment of principal and interest.

On June 30, 1995, Finch's combined balance sheet should report the construction in progress for the civic center in the

	Capital Projects Fund	General Fixed Assets Account Group
a.	Yes	Yes
b.	Yes	No
c.	No	No
d.	No	Yes

12. If a primary government's general fund has an equity interest in a joint venture, all or a portion of this equity interest should be reported in the

a. general fixed assets account group.

b. trust fund

c. agency fund

d. internal service fund.

13. Fixed assets of a governmental unit, other than those accounted for in propriety funds or trust funds, should be accounted for in the

a. general fund.

b. capital projects fund.

c. general long-term debt account group.

d. general fixed assets account group.

PROBLEMS

Continuing Problem

Review the annual report that you obtained.

a. Does the government's schedule of its fixed assets contain any unusual features not discussed in the text?

b. What was the total amount of fixed assets added during the year? What was the amount retired? Where is this information provided (e.g., in notes to the financial statements or in a schedule included adjacent to that which classifies the general fixed assets by type)?

c. Does the government provide any information as to infrastructure in either notes or supplementary schedules?

d. What is the government's policy as to depreciation? Where is it described?

e. Does the government provide a schedule in which its assets are classified by function?

f. Does the government categorize its investments into the required three categories of risk? What percentage of its investments are in Category 1? Are these investments necessarily more secure (i.e., bearing less overall risk) than those in the other categories? Explain.

g. Does the government own any "unusual" securities such as derivatives; has it entered into repurchase agreements? If so, does the report contain an explanation of these transactions?

h. Does the market value of its investments exceed their cost?

8-1

The entries to record fixed assets can easily be derived from the schedules of general fixed assets and changes in general fixed assets.

The City of Tucson included the following schedule of general fixed assets in its annual report of June 30, 1993:

General Fixed Assets

Land	$106,555,867
Buildings	180,875,999
Improvements and Equipment	137,120,255
Construction Work-in-Process	38,889,841
Total General Fixed Assets	$463,441,962

Investment in General Fixed Assets

From General Obligation Bonds	$136,167,591
From Current Revenues	204,090,771
From Federal Grants	50,061,697
From Other Sources	4,608,015
From HUD Grants and Housing Fund Operating Revenue (Public Housing Assets) (Note 1)	68,513,888
Total Investment in General Fixed Assets	$463,441,962

Note 1. The federal government has an interest in some fixed assets purchased with federal grant monies. This interest may include the right to approve sale of assets or require return of the assets or sale proceeds.

The report notes that infrastructure assets of approximately $378,654,172 are not included in these schedules.

Another schedule included in the report summarizes the changes in the general fixed asset as shown below.

a. Prepare the 1993 journal entries made by the city in its general fixed assets account group affecting *buildings* and *construction work in process*, assuming that all additions and deletions involved assets funded from current revenues.

b. Suppose the city were to repay, with resources provided from current revenues, the entire $136,167,591 in general obligation bonds that funded the acquisition of fixed assets. What journal entry would the city make in the general fixed asset account group?

c. Suppose the city were to sell a public housing project that was funded, in part, by a federal grant. The buildings had cost $6 million when acquired ten years earlier. The sales price was $4 million of which $1 million had to be returned to the federal government (per note 1). What entry would the city make in the general fixed assets account group? Describe any entries it would make in other funds.

d. What percentage of its total general fixed assets (including infrastructure assets) does the city include in its general fixed assets account group?

8-2

The journal entries affecting the general fixed assets account group are straightforward.

In the year it was established, a road maintenance district engaged in the following transactions involving fixed assets (all dollar amounts in thousands):

1. It acquired machinery and equipment for $700, with general fund resources.
2. It incurred costs of $2,500 to construct a building, and financed construction with general obligation bonds.
3. It incurred additional costs of $500, financed from resources of a special revenue fund, to complete the building.
4. It acquired equipment having a fair market value of $60 in exchange for $20 cash (from general fund resources) plus used equipment for which the district had paid $50 but which had a fair market value at the time of the trade of only $40.
5. It sold equipment for $70 that had been acquired for $90.
6. It received a donation of land from one of the towns within the district. The land had cost the town $120, but at the time of the contribution had a fair market value of $500.

City of Tucson
Schedule of Changes in Fixed Assets

	Balance June 30, 1992	Additions	Transfers and Deletions	Balance June 30, 1993
Land	$100,298,761	$ 8,575,641	$ 2,318,535	$106,555,867
Buildings	173,307,375	11,241,166	3,672,542	180,875,999
Improvements and Equipment	122,911,080	24,777,538	10,568,363	137,120,255
Construction Work in Process	44,449,433	6,209,591	11,769,183	38,889,841
	$440,966,649	$50,803,936	$28,328,623	$463,441,962

7. It repaid out of general revenues $200 of the general obligation bonds used to finance the constructed building.

8. It retired equipment, for which it had paid $7, after it was destroyed in an accident. The district recovered $3 in an insurance claim.
   a. Prepare general fixed assets account group entries.
   b. Prepare a year-end general fixed assets account group balance sheet.

8-3

Which is the preferred value to be assigned to donated assets?

A city's road maintenance department received "donations" of two types of assets:

- From the county in which the city is located it received earth-moving equipment. The equipment had cost the county $800,000 when it was acquired five years earlier. Accounted for in county proprietary funds, its book value, net of accumulated depreciation, at the time of donation, was $500,000. Its fair market value was $530,000.

- From the city's own utility fund (a proprietary fund) it received motor vehicles that had cost the city $400,000 when acquired three years earlier. At the time of transfer, the vehicles were recorded on the utility's books at $180,000, net of accumulated depreciation. Their fair market value was $225,000.
   a. Prepare the entry to record the earth-moving equipment in the city's general fixed asset account group.
   b. Prepare two alternative entries in the city's general fixed assets account group, each reflective of available options, to record the receipt of the motor vehicles.
   c. Briefly justify each of the three entries. Comment on the significance of each of the resultant book values for decisions or assessments to be made by statement users.

8-4

The significant entries involving fixed assets affect a government's funds, in addition to (or instead of) its general fixed assets account group.

The City of Tiberius engaged in the following transactions affecting fixed assets:

1. It issued bonds for $30 million to construct new highway interchanges. During the year, it began construction on the interchanges, incurring $12 million in costs. It is the city's policy to capitalize infrastructure improvements.

2. It purchased new vehicles and equipment for its fire department at a cost of $2 million (paid out of general tax revenues).

3. It sold, for $5 million, an office building that had been used for general administration. The building had cost $6 million when acquired eight years earlier (with a long-term note that had since been repaid out of general revenues). The proceeds from sale are unrestricted.

4. It incurred $1 million in costs to construct a swimming pool. The resources had previously been collected from neighborhood residents who had approved a special assessment for the pool and other recreational facilities. They had been placed in a capital projects fund.

5. It incurred costs of $3 million to improve the city jail. The resources had been provided from a federal grant restricted for law enforcement and related activities.

6. It acquired $12 million in electrical generating equipment in exchange for a long-term note. The equipment is to be used by the city's electrical utility, which is accounted for in an *enterprise fund.*
   a. Prepare required journal entries in the city's general fixed assets account group as well as any funds that would be affected by the transactions.
   b. Why are long-lived assets recorded in a general fixed assets account group rather than an actual fund?

8-5

Governments sometimes add to, but do not delete, their fixed assets.

The following totals were drawn from the City of Independence, Missouri "Schedule of Changes in Fixed Assets by Function and Activity," included in the City's financial statements for the year-ending June 30, 1993:

General Fixed Assets, July 1, 1992	$33,276,151
Additions/Transfers In	459,430
Deletions/Transfers Out	(265,795)
General Fixed Assets, June 30, 1993	$33,469,786

The complete schedule disaggregates the data by function (e.g., general government, public safety, public works, health and welfare, culture and recreation) and subfunction (e.g. park maintenance, recreation, tourism). Another schedule, "Schedule of General Fixed Assets by Source," shows the beginning and ending balances of the specific types of assets:

	1993	1992
Land	$ 8,209,380	$ 8,209,380
Buildings	9,293,847	9,292,611
Improvements Other Than Buildings	1,088,307	1,088,307
Office Furniture and Equipment	4,863,535	4,536,506
Mobile Equipment	7,834,277	8,073,945
Other Equipment	2,180,440	2,075,402
	$33,469,786	$33,276,151

a. Assume that the assets, excluding land, had an average useful life of twenty years. What percentage of the total assets, excluding land, would you expect to be retired each year?

b. What percentage of the assets (beginning of year values), excluding land, were actually retired during 1993 (assuming that all deletions/transfers out represent retirements)?

c. What is the average useful life of the assets as implied by this percentage?

d. Assume that the entire $265,795 of the deletions and transfers out apply to the mobile equipment. What would be the useful life of the equipment as suggested by the percentage of the equipment retired?

e. Do you think it is likely that the city is conscientious about removing assets from the general fixed assets account as they are taken out of service?

8-6

Expenditures for amortizing debt principal may be a rough surrogate for depreciation.

A school district constructs a new high school at a cost of $24 million. It finances the project by issuing thirty-year general obligation serial bonds, payable evenly over the outstanding term ($800,000 per year). District officials estimate that the school will have a useful life of thirty years (with no residual value).

a. Prepare summary entries in a capital projects fund to record the issuance of the bonds and construction of the school.

b. Prepare the entry in the general fixed assets account group.

c. Assume that the district repays the bonds out of current revenues.
   1. Prepare the entry that it would make each year in its general fund to record the bond principal payments.
   2. Prepare the entry that it would make each year in its general fixed assets account group.

d. Assume that the school district must balance its budget; all general fund expenditures must be covered by general fund tax and other revenues. A member of the district's board of trustees pointed out that, owing to an unanticipated increase in property values, the district enjoyed a budget surplus in the previous two years and consequently had accumulated $4 million in "savings." She argued that the district should have borrowed only $20 million and financed the balance out of savings. Further, she contended, since prosperous times were expected to continue for the next several years the district should have issued bonds repayable over ten years rather than thirty. Focusing exclusively on issues of "interperiod equity," how would you defend the financing arrangement actually entered into by the district?

e. Suppose, instead, that the district was a private, not-for-profit organization rather than a government. It reported all fixed assets, as well as related obligations, as unrestricted resources and recorded annual depreciation charges. How would the reported expenditures of this organization differ from those of the governmental school district? If this organization were required to balance its budget, would it have to raise any more or less revenue each year than the governmental school district? Would your response be the same if the repayment schedule on the bonds differed from the pattern of depreciation (e.g., the bonds were repaid over only ten years or depreciation were charged on an accelerated basis)?

8-7

Public and private colleges account for their fixed assets quite differently.

Colton University, a public institution that adheres to the AICPA college and university model, reported the following in its investment in plant fund (in millions):

Investment in Plant—Assets

Land	$ 20
Buildings	810
Improvements Other Than Buildings	95
Equipment	288
Books and Related Assets	30
Total Plant	$1,243
Less: Accumulated Depreciation	(511)
Total Investment in Plant	$ 732

Investment in Plant—Equities

Notes Payable	$ 80
Bonds Payable	100
Net Investment in Plant	552
Total Investment in Plant	$ 732

During the year the university engaged in the following transactions affecting plant (in millions):

1. It acquired land at a cost of $30, giving a long-term note for the entire amount.

2. It sold for $7 equipment that had initially cost $11 and on which accumulated depreciation of $8 had been recorded.

3. It repaid $10 of outstanding bonds.

4. It constructed tennis courts, a soccer field and various other athletic facilities at a cost of $2, paid in cash.

5. It purchased equipment for $17 and books for $1, paid in cash.

6. It recognized depreciation of $120 on its assets.

a. Prepare the entries the university would make during the year that affect its investment in plant fund and prepare an end-of-year balance sheet. Also indicate which other university funds would be affected by the transactions.

b. Suppose, instead, that Colton University is a *private institution* and adheres to FASB standards. Prepare all journal entries that the university would make, assuming that both the assets and all resources used to acquire them are *unrestricted*.

c. Indicate what you see as the advantages of the FASB as opposed to the AICPA approach.

8-8

Inspired by Orange County, this problem tries to show the risks of investing in seemingly safe securities.

Bear County maintains an investment pool for school districts and other governments within its jurisdiction. Participating governments contribute cash to the pool, which is operated like a mutual fund, and receive in return a proportionate share of all dividends, interest, and gains. They also, of course, must share in any losses.

The governments may withdraw part or all of their funds at any time, receiving their share of the pool's resources. As of year-end 1999, the value of the Bear County investment pool was approximately $1.2 billion.

Governments have been eager to place their funds in the Bear County pool because it has provided historically higher returns than they could earn independently. The individual governments must restrict their investments to short-term, highly liquid securities, inasmuch as they will likely have need for cash within days, weeks, or months. By contrast, the investment pool can invest a substantial portion of its resources in longer-term, higher-yielding securities, since it is unlikely that all of the participating governments will withdraw their funds at the same time.

The county pool places its funds only in U.S. government notes and bonds or securities guaranteed by the U.S. government. Hence, there is virtually no default risk; the county can be certain that it will receive timely payment of principal and interest.

a. Assume that the county invests $1-billion of the $1.2 billion of its portfolio in 10-year, 6 percent, government bonds (retaining the balance in cash and short-term securities). Shortly after it purchases the bonds, prevailing interest rates on comparable securities increase to 8 percent. What would you expect would be the *market value* of the bonds after the increase in rates? [*Hint:* The bonds pay interest semiannually. Therefore, using a discount rate of 4 percent per period (one-half the prevailing rate of 8 percent) calculate the present value of $1-billion principal to be received

in 20 periods. Then, using the same discount rate of 4 percent, determine the present value of the 20 interest payments of $30 million each (based on one-half the coupon rate of 6 percent).]

b. Suppose that the county invests $1 billion in the ten-year, 6 percent bonds just described. However, it also finances the purchase of an additional $1 billion of similar bonds by entering into reverse repurchase agreements. In effect, therefore, it borrows $1 billion, putting up the ten-year bonds as collateral. Inasmuch as the loan is short-term, the interest rates are only 4 percent—substantially lower than on the long-term bonds.

1. Determine the net percentage return on the $1 billion in the portfolio, taking into account the total interest received on the entire $2 billion and the total interest paid (exclude consideration of the $.2 billion held in cash and short-term securities).

2. Suppose that short-term interest rates were to increase to 7 percent and long-term interest rates were to increase to 8 percent. What will be the total market value of the portfolio, net of the amount borrowed (and excluding consideration of the $.2 billion in cash and short-term securities)?

In the face of the sharp decline in the market value of the investment portfolio, county officials assured participating governments that they have nothing to be concerned about, since:

- The county intends to hold all bonds to maturity and therefore the fluctuations in market values are not relevant.

- Based on historical experience, the county will have sufficient funds on hand to meet all routine withdrawals.

3. If you were the treasurer of a participating government would you be comforted by the statements of the county officials? Explain. Would it make sense for you to withdraw your funds from the pool?

4. Suppose you—and treasurers of other governments—were not comforted and did, in fact, withdraw funds from the pool. What would be the probable consequences to both the pool and the pool participants?

8-9

Note disclosures pertaining to investments are not always easy to interpret (and this text could not possibly cover all types of investments held by governments and not-for-profits).

As of September 30, 1993, the Carnegie Corporation of New York, a major philanthropic foundation, reported investments on its balance sheet, at market value, of $1,168,613,050. A note indicated that they were composed of the following:

	Cost	Market Value
Equities		
Common Stock	$ 281,873,447	$ 336,933,800
Convertibles	4,091,209	5,176,829
Fixed Income		
Short Term	143,649,433	143,190,813
Long Term	341,803,775	367,836,412
Limited Partnership		
Interests		
Real Estate	14,214,747	11,370,831
Venture Capital	7,082,124	17,361,069
Hedge Funds	196,782,795	274,997,705
Other Investments	22,496,641	11,745,591
Total	$1,011,944,171	$1,168,613,050

The following are additional excerpts from the note:

As a result of its investing strategies, the corporation is a party to off-balance-sheet S&P 500 index futures contracts. Changes in the market values of these futures contracts are recognized currently in the statement of changes in fund balance, using the marked-to-market method.

Off-balance-sheet futures contracts involve, to varying degrees, elements of market risk and credit risk in excess of the amounts recorded on the balance sheet. Market risk represents the potential loss the corporation faces due to the decrease in the value of off-balance-sheet financial instruments. Credit risk represents the maximum potential loss the corporation faces due to possible nonperformance by obligors and counter-parties of the terms of their contracts.

The corporation held 384 S&P 500 index futures contracts long at September 30, 1993, representing contract values of $88.1 million. The corporation also held 52 thirty-year bond futures contracts-short and 46 ten-year note futures contracts-short at September 30, 1993, with contract values totaling $11.5 million.

Securities sold, not yet purchased, recorded net in the corporation's investment accounts of $73.7 million in 1993 have market risk to the extent that the corporation, in satisfying its obligations, may have to purchase securities at a higher value than recorded.

a. What is meant by *fixed income* securities, as the term is used in the schedule of investments?

b. The note indicates that the corporation "is a party to off-balance-sheet S&P 500 index futures contracts." It also explains that the corporation faces an element of market risk "due to the decrease in the value of off-balance-sheet financial instruments." What is a "futures contract?" Why are they "off the balance sheet"? How could changes in their market value be recognized in the statement of changes in fund balance if the securities themselves are not reported on the balance sheet? [*Hint:* Futures contracts are, in essence, options to pur-

chase securities in the future. The amounts paid for the options are, in fact, reported on the balance sheet; the values of the underlying securities are not.]

c. How could securities be sold before they are purchased (as discussed in the note's last paragraph)?

d. Explain in your own words how the market risk relating to a futures contract differs from the credit risk.

e. A futures contract-long represents the obligation to purchase securities; a futures contract-short represents the obligation to sell securities. What would most likely be the impact on the market value of the thirty-year bond futures contracts-long of an increase in long-term interest rates? Explain.

8-10

This problem is based on an annual report issued prior to the FASB requirement that investments be carried at market values and provides insight into the disclosure deficiencies that the requirement was intended to ameliorate.

The following was taken from the 1993 financial statements of Pepperdine University, a private institution.

Investments

Where permitted by gift agreements and/or applicable regulations, certain investments have been grouped in one of three investment pools designated as Pool A, Pool B, and Pool C. Pooled investments and allocation of pooled investment income are accounted for on a unit market method. The following schedule summarizes data pertaining to each pool for the year ended July 31, 1993:

	Pool A	Pool B	Pool C
Unit Market Value at End of Year	$215.55	$117.13	$102.23
Units Owned at End of Year:			
Current Funds			
Restricted		2,644	544
Endowment Funds	456,152		1,879
Annuity and Life			
Income Funds		43,774	23,641
Plant Funds		198,713	23,891
Total Units	456,152	245,131	49,955
Net Ordinary Investment Income Per Weighted Average Unit	$ 6.10	$ 7.45	$ 2.05

It is the university's policy to invest and maintain a diversified investment portfolio. The following schedule summarizes the assets in pooled investments and the assets held by certain funds as separate investments at July 31, 1993. The market values of the investments are estimates based on quoted market prices, and analytical pricing methods, such as discounted cash flow, for investments for which there is no market. The market values are considered fair values. The university investment portfolio is composed of the following:

	Carrying Value	Market Value
Cash and Cash Equivalents	$ 4,370,000	$ 4,370,000
Short-term Investments	82,000	82,000
Publicly Traded Stocks	59,591,000	65,810,000
Bonds	50,085,000	53,920,000
Notes Receivable	18,446,000	21,149,000
Privately Held Stocks	10,154,000	10,154,000*
Equity in Wholly Owned Entities	13,352,000	13,352,000*
Real Estate	29,182,000	29,182,000*
Assets Held by Trustees	3,880,000	3,986,000
Other	7,249,000	7,159,000
Total	$196,391,000	$209,164,000

*Listed at carrying value

Investments at carrying value and market value by fund are as follows:

	Carrying Value	Market Value
Current Unrestricted Funds	$ 3,675,000	$ 4,153,000
Current Restricted Funds	8,182,000	8,193,000
Loan Funds	1,351,000	1,351,000
Endowment Funds	106,135,000	113,904,000
Annuity and Life Income Funds	36,947,000	38,566,000
Plant Funds	40,101,000	42,997,000
Total	$196,391,000	$209,164,000

The summary totals below segregate pooled assets from those separately invested:

	Carrying Value	Market Value
Pooled Investments	$122,664,000	$132,139,000
Separately Invested	73,727,000	77,025,000
Total	$196,391,000	$209,164,000

a. From the information in the note, determine the return on investment (based on year-end market values) of each of the three pools, taking into account only *ordinary investment income* (excluding gains or losses in market values). Why do these returns on investment provide, at best, a very limited indication of investment performance?

b. What is the most likely explanation for the substantial difference in percentage return among the pools? (Note, in particular, that the resources of the funds are not allocated uniformly among the pools. Consider the possibility that the funds have different investment objectives.)

c. Based on the schedule summarizing the investments by pools, what is the total market value of the pooled investments? Can you verify this value with other information in the note?

d. Indicate whether, and explain why, the note does or does not, provide information that enables one to determine:

1. the gains in market value of the investments during the year

2. if the yield on bonds was greater or less than that in the previous year or better or worse than that of a widely cited index

3. the type of assets held by each fund

4. whether the overall investment performance of the university was better than in the previous year

SOLUTION TO EXERCISE FOR REVIEW AND SELF-STUDY

a. *Oneida County*

Library building	$5,000,000	
Investment in fixed assets —contributions		$5,000,000

To record the acquisition of the library (general fixed assets account group)

Additional entries would have to be made in a governmental fund, such as a capital projects funds, to record the receipt and disbursement of the contributed resources.

Oneida College

Library building	$5,000,000	
Donated revenues		$5,000,000

To record the acquisition of the library (unrestricted resources)

This entry summarizes the donation of the funds and the acquisition of the building. If the donated resources were reported initially as restricted, then additional entries would be required to record the "transfer" from the restricted to the unrestricted category. The focus in this example is on the asset itself, not the contribution of the resources.

b. *Oneida County*

Most governments do *not* report their long-lived assets net of depreciation; hence, there is no need for a year-end adjustment.

Oneida College

Depreciation expense	$125,000	
Accumulated depreciation		$125,000

To record depreciation expense

The college would account for depreciation just as if it were a business.

c. **1.** The county would report the building at the initial cost of $5 million; the college at the initial cost of $5 million less accumulated depreciation of $5 million—hence, zero.

   2. There are few, in any, decisions or assessments for which the historical cost of an asset is relevant (excluding, of course, decisions or assessments in which historical costs are specified, as when a bank demands that an organization maintain particular financial ratios, which are defined in terms of historical cost book values).

d. Under current standards, neither organization would have to account for or report the deferral of maintenance.

CHAPTER 9

Long-Term Obligations

LEARNING OBJECTIVES

After studying this chapter you should understand:

- why information on long-term debt is important to statement users
- the significance of bankruptcy in a governmental and not-for-profit context
- why and how governments account for long-term obligations in a general long-term debt account group
- the nature of demand bonds, bond anticipation notes, tax anticipation notes, and revenue anticipation notes, and how they should be accounted for and reported
- the reasons why governments lease assets, and how they are accounted for and reported

- why governments issue revenue bonds
- what is meant by overlapping debt, and how it is computed
- what is meant by conduit debt, and how it is accounted for and reported
- the significance of other types of information that users want about debt, including credit enhancements, debt margin, payout schedules, reserve funds, and key ratios
- how not-for-profits other than governments account for long-term debt
- the role of rating agencies

This chapter is directed to long-term obligations, including liabilities—such as bonds that are accorded balance sheet recognition—and other commitments such as loan guarantees that may be disclosed only in notes. Liabilities may be interpreted as negative long-lived assets. They present comparable issues of valuation and reporting and, for the most part, are accounted for as mirror images of their asset counterparts, which were discussed in Chapter 8. Governments exclude long-term liabilities from governmental funds and report them instead in the general long-term debt account group. Not-for-profits report them as they would other assets or short-term liabilities. Long-term liabilities are important to governments and not-for-profits for the same reasons they are to businesses. They represent claims upon the entity's resources; failure to satisfy them can seriously jeopardize the entity's ability to provide the services expected of it.

The first major section of the chapter sets forth the goals of long-term debt reporting. The next section raises the intriguing question of whether governments and not-for-profits, like businesses, can go bankrupt if they fail to meet their obligations. The following section is directed to the "debits and credits" of accounting for long-term debt by governments. The fourth section addresses the issue of what types of obligations should be included within the rubric "**long-term debt**" for reporting, legal, and analytical purposes. The fifth discusses credit enhancements and other features of debt that are of concern to statement users. The sixth deals with long-term debt in not-for-profits, a topic that requires relatively little attention in that, for the most part, long-term debts (like long-term assets) are accounted for in not-for-profits as they are in businesses. The concluding section pertains to bond ratings, a subject common to both governments and not-for-profits.

WHY IS INFORMATION ON LONG-TERM DEBT IMPORTANT TO STATEMENT USERS?

The issues addressed in this chapter are closely tied to a key objective of financial reporting. As stated by the GASB:

> *Financial reporting should provide information about the financial position and condition of a government entity.* Financial reporting should provide information about resources and obligations, both actual and contingent, current and noncurrent. The major financial resources of most governmental entities are derived from the ability to tax and issue debt. As a result, financial reporting should provide information about tax sources, tax limitations, tax burdens and debt limitations.[1]

The FASB has set forth similar objectives for not-for-profits, emphasizing the importance of information on liquidity and cash flows.

Information on long-term debt is especially important to statement users because an entity's failure to make timely payments of interest and principal can have profound repercussions, both for its creditors and itself. Creditors will obviously incur losses.

---

[1] Concept Statement Number 1, paragraph 79.

But insofar as governments and not-for-profits rely on debt to fund acquisitions of infrastructure, building, and equipment, a loss of credit standing can seriously harm their ability to provide the services expected of them.

A key message of this chapter is that statement users must look beyond the basic financial statements to establish the amount and nature of the debt burden of both governments and not-for-profits. The balance sheets of these entities cannot be relied upon to disclose all of their obligations, and they do not provide sufficient data to assess their economic value. Hence, users must pay particular attention to note disclosures, supplementary data in the annual reports' statistical sections, and, if necessary, public data available outside the annual reports.

CAN GOVERNMENTS AND NOT-FOR-PROFITS GO BANKRUPT?

An entity's failure to satisfy claims against it can produce dire results, including bankruptcy. In such a situation both governments and not-for-profits can seek protection under the Federal Bankruptcy Code—just as can individuals and businesses. Not-for-profits are covered under the same chapter of the code as businesses; a special section of the code (Chapter 9) is directed to governments.

Whereas bankruptcy filings by major governments may be rare (Orange County being a notable exception), those of smaller units, especially utility districts, are much more common. In 1994 at least fifteen governments petitioned for bankruptcy; in years of economic downturn the number has been substantially greater. Other cities, such as New York, Yonkers (New York), Bridgeport (Connecticut), Philadelphia, and Washington, D.C., avoided bankruptcy only by being brought under the authority of "financial control boards" by higher-level governments.

As suggested by the accompanying In Practice, the concept of municipal bankruptcy is elusive. Governments have the power to tax and in return are expected to provide certain essential services. In a sense, their access to resources is limited only by the wealth of their population. Correspondingly, their expenditures can be reduced to zero by cutting back on services. In reality, however, there are practical limits to both their taxing authority and the extent to which they can eliminate services. Raise taxes above a certain level and both residents and businesses flee the jurisdiction, thereby reducing overall revenues. Reduce services beyond a certain point and the safety and overall well-being of the community are impaired.

When a court declares a government bankrupt, it temporarily transfers control over its affairs to an independent trustee. The eventual outcome, with the court's approval, is generally a settlement with creditors and a reorganization, sometimes with the jurisdiction being permanently incorporated into another government.

Bankruptcy represents the ultimate fiscal failure, resulting in almost certain losses to creditors. But creditors can also experience losses, even in the absence of bankruptcy. New York City, for example, responded to its mid-1970s crisis by obtaining creditor agreement to a voluntary debt "restructuring." Even though creditors may have eventually been repaid the full face value of their loans, payments were delayed and interest was reduced. Thus, the economic loss was as real (if not necessarily as great) as if the city had filed for bankruptcy.

How destitute must a city be before it can qualify for legal protection under the federal Bankruptcy Code? Very, according to a U.S. bankruptcy court ruling rejecting the City of Bridgeport's petition to be considered a debtor under Chapter 9. It must be able to prove not only that it is in deep financial trouble, but that it will be unable to pay its debts in its current fiscal year or, based on an adopted budget, in its next fiscal year.

The Bridgeport decision was in response to the city's attempt to become the first major government in decades to take refuge in the federal Bankruptcy Code. The city's petition was opposed by both the State of Connecticut and the city's own Financial Review Board that was established in 1988 to fund the government's deficits and restore it to fiscal stability.

DECISION HELPS CLARIFY CONCEPT OF MUNICIPAL BANKRUPTCY

Must Be Insolvent

To be considered for bankruptcy under Chapter 9 of the Bankruptcy Code an entity must satisfy several criteria, the most significant of which is that it must be **insolvent**. According to the statute this means:

- it is generally not paying its debts as they become due *or*
- it is unable to pay its debts as they become due.

Up to the time it filed its petition, the city had not defaulted on its obligations and therefore did not satisfy the first criterion. Hence, the key question in the case revolved around the second criterion, whether it would be "unable to pay its debts as they become due."

The testimony of Bridgeport officials left no doubt that the city's fiscal condition would eliminate it as a contender for the All-American City award:

- The chief of police estimated that the city had 21 percent fewer police officers than is required to provide basic, adequate service. He indicated that some neighborhoods were controlled by drug dealers and pointed out that the detective staff was so overworked that there was almost no investigation of property crime, even though the auto-theft rate was the nation's second highest.
- The director of public works testified that reduced garbage collections created a rodent and arson hazard. Moreover, the city could afford only one street sweeper for its 275 miles of streets.
- Other officials disclosed that the city had to close two of its four senior citizen programs. Branch libraries were open only one day per week, while the main library was open only 20 hours per week.

Interpretation Should Be Prospective

In opposing the city's bankruptcy petition, the state argued that since the city *had been* paying all of its debts, it was also *able* to pay those same debts. Therefore, it asserted, the city was not insolvent. The city, by contrast, maintained that the statute required a prospective interpretation—it might not in the future be able to pay its debts. The Court held with the city that the insolvency standard is not limited to current debts.

Nevertheless, the Court rejected Bridgeport's claim that it would be unable to pay its debts in the future. Pointing to a $16 million proposed budget deficit for fiscal 1991–92, the city argued that the excess of expenditures over revenues was sufficient proof of insolvency. The Court, however, declared that solvency should be assessed in terms of *cash flow*, not the operating budget. Bridgeport, it noted, had substantial cash reserves in a "contingency" fund resulting from a bond sale.

This fund could be drawn upon to satisfy current obligations and could be replenished in the future. Therefore, it said, it is apparent that Bridgeport would be able to pay its 1991–92 obligations. "I conclude," the judge said, "that to be found insolvent a city must prove that it will be unable to pay its debts as they become due in its current fiscal year or based on an adopted budget, in its next fiscal year." Bridgeport, it decided, did not meet that burden of proof.

Source: *Government Accounting and Auditing Update*, October 1991. Reprinted by permission of publisher, RIA Group/Warren, Gorham, Lamont.

HOW DO GOVERNMENTS ACCOUNT FOR LONG-TERM OBLIGATIONS?

General long-term debt has been defined as:

the *unmatured principal* of bonds, warrants notes, special assessment debt for which the government is obligated in some manner, or other forms of noncurrent or long-term *general obligation* debt that is not a specific liability of any proprietary fund or trust fund.[2]

General long-term debt is the obligation of the government at large and is thereby backed by the government's general credit and revenue raising powers. It is distinguished from *revenue* debt, which is secured only by designated revenue streams, such as from utility fees, highway tolls, rents, receipts from student loans, or patient billings.

The long-term debts of governments by no means include *all* their financial obligations—no more than do those of businesses. As a general rule, only debts resulting from past transactions for which the government *has already received a benefit* are recognized. Reported obligations thereby exclude commitments for payments of interest when the government has not yet enjoyed the use of the borrowed funds, the salary of a city manager that, although contractually guaranteed, has not been earned, future rent payments that are established by a noncancellable operating lease, and amounts owing under long-term service contracts when the promised services have not yet been provided.

REPORTING IN AN ACCOUNT GROUP RATHER THAN A FUND

As previously emphasized, governmental funds focus on financial resources. A long-term obligation does not require current-year appropriation or expenditure of governmental fund financial resources. Therefore, as noted by the National Council of Governmental Accountants (NCGA), "to include it as a governmental fund liability would be misleading and dysfunctional to the current period management control (for example, budgeting) and accountability functions."[3]

When the proceeds of long-term debt are received by **governmental funds**, the debit to cash (or other assets) is offset by "other financing sources—bond proceeds," or some comparable account signifying an inflow of resources, not by a liability. Just as the existence of buildings, vehicles, and other long-term assets are ignored in governmental funds, so also are long-term debts, including the portion of bonds, notes, claims and judgments, and obligations for sick-leave and vacations for which payment is not required out of resources appropriated for the current year. As a consequence,

[2]*Codification*, Section 1500.103.

[3]*Codification*, Section 1500.104.

long-term debt includes amounts arising out of operating as well as capital transactions. As emphasized in previous chapters, the expenditures relating to these operating transactions will be charged in the periods in which the resources are appropriated for payment—in effect, when the long-term debts are liquidated—not necessarily in those in which the government reaped the benefits.

ACCOUNTING FOR TRANSACTIONS IN THE GENERAL LONG-TERM DEBT ACCOUNT GROUP

Long-term debt and other noncurrent obligations are relegated to the **general long-term debt account group (GLTDAG)**. Like the general fixed asset account group, the GLTDAG is essentially a list. It is presented in double-entry form so that when included with other funds and account groups in a combined balance sheet the debts of the "totals" column will equal the credits.

GLTDAG liabilities are offset by two types of accounts:

- amounts to be provided from general government resources to satisfy the obligations
- amounts available in debt service funds to satisfy the obligations

Although they have debit balances, these offsetting accounts are by no means assets of the GLTDAG, which is not a fiscal entity. Instead, they are simply artificial constructs to give the account group symmetry.

"Amounts available in the debt service funds" are government resources set aside in debt service funds for debt retirement. If the resources in the debt service funds were dedicated exclusively to the retirement of the *principal* of outstanding long-term debt, then the GLTDAG "amounts available" in debt service funds should equal the fund balances of those debt service funds. Often, however, governments use their debt service funds to accumulate resources for the payment of both principal and interest. Because the GLTDAG should properly report only the amounts available for the repayment of *principal*, the balance in the debt service funds may exceed the "amounts available" of the GLTDAG. Nevertheless, some governments report in their GLTDAG the entire balance in the debt service funds, thereby giving the misleading impression that all of it is available for the repayment of principal.

The GLTDAG also reports special assessment debt for which the government may be obligated in some manner, even though the debt is expected to be repaid from the assessments rather than the governments' general revenues.[4] These obligations, as well as the offsetting "amounts available" or "amounts to be provided," should be reported separately from the government's direct debts.

Table 9–1 presents the balance sheet of Fort Worth's GLTDAG.

As illustrated in the following example, the entries in the GLTDAG are no more complicated than those in the general fixed assets account group. Indeed, the balance sheet for Fort Worth's GLTDAG was based exclusively on comparable entries.

EXAMPLE   *Entries to the GLTDAG*

- A government issues $50 million of general obligation bonds.

Amount to be provided from general government resources	$50.0	
General obligation bonds payable		$50.0

To record general obligation bonds payable

---

[4] Refer to the discussion of special assessments in Chapter 7, *Accounting for Capital Projects and Debt Service*.

TABLE 9-1		
City of Fort Worth General Long-Term Debt Account Group		

Comparative Balance Sheets
September 30, 1996 and 1995
(000s omitted)

	1996	1995
Assets		
Amount Available in Debt Service	$16,700	$15,394
Amount to be Provided for Retirement		
of General Long-Term Liabilities	377,181	372,299
Total Assets	$393,881	$387,693
Liabilities		
Estimated Claims Payable	$14,669	$9,512
Accrued Compensation	34,682	30,567
Certificates of Obligation Payable	24,720	16,840
General Obligation Bonds Payable	319,556	330,399
Obligations Under Capital Lease	254	375
Total Liabilities	$393,881	$387,693

Correspondingly, the cash proceeds of the debt would be recorded in a governmental fund (Dr. cash; Cr. bond proceeds), such as the general fund or a capital projects fund.

- The government transfers $3.4 million from its general fund to a debt service fund. Of this, $1.4 million is for interest and $2.0 million for principal.

Amount available in debt service funds	$ 2.0	
Amount to be provided from general		
government resources		$ 2.0

To recognize accumulation in the debt service fund of resources for the repayment of principal

The transfer of the entire $3.4 million would be recognized in both the general fund and the debt service fund. Only the resources accumulated for the repayment of principal would be recorded in the GLTDAG.

- The government invests the resources of the debt service fund and earns interest of $0.1 million, all of which is intended for the repayment of principal.

Amount available in debt service funds	$ 0.1	
Amount to be provided from general		
government resources		$ 0.1

To recognize accumulation in the debt service fund of resources for the repayment of principal

This entry assures that the "amount available" and "amount to be provided" accounts show the current status of the resources both available, and still to be provided, for debt repayment.

- The government repays $2.0 million of bond principal.

General obligation bonds payable	$ 2.0	
Amount available in debt service funds		$ 2.0
To record repayment of debt		

As the debt is repaid, both the liability and the amount available are reduced. As with the other entries, the substantive transaction (that involving the actual flow of resources) would be recorded in a debt service fund or other appropriate governmental fund.

The government incurs $4.6 million in compensation costs for vacations and holidays to be taken in future years.

Amount to be provided from general		
government resources	$ 4.6	
Compensated absences payable		$ 4.6
To record noncurrent compensated absences		

Compensated absences and claims and judgments are *not* recognized in governmental funds as either expenditures or liabilities until the period in which they must be liquidated with current financial resources. Therefore, they must be reported in the GLTDAG. The liability for compensated absences should be based on wage and salary rates in effect at the *balance sheet date*. Therefore, to take into account changes in wages and salaries the liability may have to be recalculated and adjusted each year.

- The government acquired an office building by entering into a thirty-year lease that satisfies the criteria of a *capital* lease. The present value of the lease payments (which equals the fair market value of the building) is $12 million.

Amount to be provided from general		
government resources	$12.0	
Capital lease payable		$12.0
To record capital lease payable, long-term obligation		

As shall be discussed later in this chapter, capital lease obligations are the equivalent of bonds and other types of long-term debt.

In practice, governments are unlikely to make all of the illustrated entries as the related events occur. Instead, they may make them only at year-end, to bring the accounts up to date so that the general-purpose financial statements can be prepared.

RECORDING LIABILITIES AT FACE VALUE

Long-term obligations are ordinarily recorded in the GLTDAG at face value. Bond issue costs, such as underwriter commissions, rating agency charges, attorney fees, and bond insurance costs, are not taken into account. They are charged as expenditures in the capital projects, or other funds, receiving the bond proceeds.

Bond premiums and discounts are also not accounted for in the GLDTAG, unless they are substantial. As a consequence, what is reported in the GLTDAG is usually indicative only of the amount that the government will be required to pay when the obligation matures. It does not provide users with information as to the amount actually borrowed (i.e., the debt proceeds) or the amount for which the liability could currently be liquidated.

The difference between the face value of a bond and the amount for which it is issued is reflected in the bond premium or discount. A bond is sold at a premium whenever its specified interest rate (its **coupon rate**) is greater than interest rates prevailing at the time of issuance (the **yield rate**). It is sold at a discount whenever the specified rate is less than the prevailing rates. The greater the difference between coupon rate and yield rate and the greater the number of years to maturity, the greater the premium or discount.

In recent years many governments have issued both "deep discount" and "superpremium" bonds. For these types of bonds the discrepancy between face value and issue price can be substantial. **Zero coupon bonds** are the ultimate in deep discount bonds. As their name implies, they pay no interest; the entire return to lenders is provided as the difference between the issue price and the face value.

Suppose, for example, that a government were to issue $1 million of thirty-year zero coupon bonds at a price that reflects a yield of 8 percent (4 percent per 60 semi-annual periods.) The bonds would be sold for only $95,060 (the present value $1 million discounted at 4 percent for 60 periods). Thus, the government's initial liability would be only $95,060. The difference between that amount and the $1 million to be paid represents compounded interest.

To avoid the blatant distortions that would result from recording the bonds at face value rather than unamortized issue price, the **Government Finance Officers Association (GFOA)** advises governments to record deep discount and super-premium debt initially at issue price and subsequently amortize the premium or discount. It defines deep discount bonds as those in which the stated interest rate is less than 75 percent of the yield rate.[5] The GASB has delayed dealing with deep discount and superpremium bonds until it addresses the broader issues of defining, reporting, and valuing all liabilities.

Were a government to report the zero coupon bonds at issue price rather than face value, then upon issuing the bonds, it would record them in the GLTDAG as follows:

Amount to be provided for retirement		
of long-term debt	$95,060	
General obligation bonds payable		$95,060

To record the issuance of $1 million of zero coupon bonds

Then, in each semiannual period it would increment the value by 4 percent of the previous balance to take into account the liability for interest:

Amount to be provided for retirement		
of long-term debt	$ 3,802	
General obligation bonds payable		$ 3,802

To recognize interest for the first period that the bonds are outstanding

These entries do not affect the *expenditure* as reported in the governmental fund responsible for the payment of interest. In that fund, as indicated in Chapter 5, only the interest actually due in a particular period (zero, for all periods except the last) is reported as an expenditure.

---

[5] *Governmental Accounting, Auditing and Financial Reporting.* (Chicago: Government Finance Officers Association, 1994), p. 117. The association fails to define superpremium bonds, so presumably the same percentage difference between the two values would be appropriate.

Zero coupon bonds are merely exaggerated versions of all bonds issued at premiums or discounts. By failing to account for premiums and discounts, current practice distorts both periodic interest costs and the GLTDAG liability.

ALTERNATIVES TO "FACE VALUE"

Both present value and market value have been proposed as alternative bases of reporting all long-term debts—not only bonds and notes, but also those arising from claims and judgments and from deferred compensation.

Present Value of Future Cash Flows

The present value of a liability indicates the economic sacrifice required if an entity is to fulfill its obligation. Were liabilities to be stated at present value, they would be recorded initially at the present value of all cash flows associated with the obligation—that is, both principal and interest payments. Thereafter, the present value would be adjusted each period to reflect only the remaining payments, not those already made. The discount rate would be established when the obligation was first recorded and would *not* be adjusted subsequently to take into account changing interest rates. Thus, the present value would be determined by actual transactions engaged in by the entity, and thereby would be firmly rooted in the historical cost tradition.

Suppose a city is negotiating the settlement of a lawsuit. The plaintiff demands $5 million payable at the start of the next fiscal year; the city counters with an offer of $5 million payable in five annual installments of $1 million. If the city's *cost of capital* (either the rate it would have to pay to borrow the required funds or the rate it would otherwise earn if it had the funds available for investment) were 8 percent, then the city's offer of the five payments of $1 million would have a present value of only $3,992,710 ($1 million times $3.99271, the present value of an annuity of $1 discounted at 8 percent). Under current accounting principles, the city would report a GLTDAG obligation of $5 million, irrespective of which proposal were agreed upon. Unquestionably, however, the present (discounted) values of the two settlements ($5 million versus $3,992,710) better indicate the required economic sacrifices.

For long-term bonds and notes issued at par (i.e., with no premium or discount), present value would be the same as face value. For bonds and notes issued at more or less than par, present value would be the same as issue price. For both these types of liabilities, therefore, present value can be determined objectively. For other liabilities, present value would have to be calculated using an appropriate discount rate such as the entity's cost of capital or a rate that was used in negotiating the agreement establishing the liability.

Proposals to state long-term liabilities at present, rather than face, values cannot be seen as calling for radical change. Obligations under capital leases have long been stated at the present value of future payments. Moreover, the FASB is reviewing liability reporting for both businesses and not-for-profits and is almost certain to require that most, if not all, long-term obligations be reported at their present values. In addition, the GASB mandates that government-operated insurance pools discount agreed-upon settlements of claims that require specified payments on fixed dates in the future.[6]

---

[6] *Codification*, Section C50.120.

An accountant lucky enough to win the state lottery may have the opportunity to strike a blow for truth in government accounting as well as advertising. Lottery prizes are almost always paid out over an extended period of time, commonly twenty years. When presented with the first $3 million installment of a much publicized prize of $60 million, for example, the winner should graciously thank the government official presenting the check. But he or she should also point out that, contrary to the government's advertisements and publicity campaigns, the economic value of the prize (assuming a discount rate of 6 percent) is only $34,409,764—sufficient to provide a comfortable living, but nevertheless only 57 percent of the prize's stated value.

For many governments the issue of valuing the prize liability on their balance sheets never arises. Rather than appropriating funds over the payout period, they satisfy the obligation immediately by setting aside sufficient resources (e.g., $34,409,764) in a trust fund, or purchasing an "annuity" from a private financial institution, to assure that the required payments are made.

VALUING A LOTTERY PRIZE

Market Value of the Obligation

Corresponding to market values of assets, market values of obligations point to the amount for which liabilities can be liquidated. Market values of outstanding debt securities are driven mainly by prevailing interest rates but are influenced by other factors, such as the issuer's financial condition. At the same time, however, the issuer's financial condition may be affected by the market value of its debts.

Virtually all decision models relating to bond retirement and refunding decisions incorporate market, not historical, values as their parameters. Suppose, for example, that a hospital issues thirty-year, 4 percent, bonds for $10 million (at par). Five years later interest rates increase to 8 percent and as a consequence the market value of the bonds decreases to $5.7 million.

In assessing the fiscal health of the hospital, the market value of $5.7 million may be more relevant than the historical value of $10 million. As of the date that the value is determined, the hospital can liquidate the entire $10 million liability for $5.7 million by purchasing the bonds in the secondary markets. Indeed, in deciding whether it should purchase the bonds, it should compare the cash flows to be received and paid in the future with the $5.7 million to be paid out immediately. It need not take into account the original issue price. That value, the equivalent of a sunk cost, will not affect any future cash flows. Over time, the effectiveness of hospital officials in managing its debt should be assessed, at least in part, by measuring the changes in the market value of outstanding debt. Declining market values would imply that the hospital correctly forecast interest rate trends and was able to lock in low-cost financing prior to interest rate increases.

The case in favor of reporting liabilities at market values has become increasingly compelling now that both the FASB and GASB require entities in their purview to report investments at market values. If a government has long-term debt outstanding and, at the same time, holds long-term bonds as an investment, then the market value of both are affected by prevailing interest rates—albeit in opposite directions. It would be both inconsistent and misleading to show changes on one side of the balance sheet while ignoring those on the other.

The primary argument in favor of historical, rather than market price-based, reporting is that the market value information will not be used. This contention is most convincing when the entity has no intention of retiring the debt until it matures, and therefore is not concerned with period-to-period fluctuations. In its Statement No. 115, *Accounting for Certain Investments in Debt and Equity Securities*, the FASB recognized the legitimacy of this point by allowing businesses to report "held-to-maturity" debt securities at cost (or amortized cost), whereas all other investments must be reported at market. However, as noted in Chapter 4, the FASB did not permit other not-for-profits to report their held-to-maturity debt securities at cost.

WHAT CONSTITUTES A GOVERNMENT'S LONG-TERM DEBT?

The basic entries required to account for liabilities are, for the most part, unambiguous. However much less clear is when an obligation should be characterized as a liability and whether it should be classified as long-term or short-term.

The issue of whether an obligation should be reported as a long-term rather than a current liability is especially consequential in governments, because it determines not only in which *section* of a balance sheet, but also on *which* balance sheet, it should be reported. Governments account for short-term liabilities—those expected to be liquidated with currently available assets—within governmental funds. They exclude long-term liabilities (except for those relating to proprietary and trust funds) from governmental funds, reporting them instead in the GLTDAG. Thus, if assets are held constant, short-term debt reduces a government's general fund (or other governmental fund) balance, whereas long-term debt does not.

DEMAND BONDS: CURRENT OR LONG-TERM LIABILITIES?

Demand bonds are obligations that permit the holder (the lender) to demand redemption within a specified period of time, usually one to thirty days after giving notice. They are referred to as *put bonds* because the right of redemption is the equivalent of a put (or sell) option. Although demand bonds may have maturity periods of up to thirty years, their redemption date is not only uncertain but is beyond the issuers' control. Issuers cannot classify them with confidence as long-term (i.e., GLTDAG) obligations because they may have to redeem them at any time. Yet they may be overly conservative in classifying them as short-term obligations, since they may not have to redeem them until maturity.

One apparent resolution to the classification dilemma is for the issuer to estimate the proportion of bonds likely to be called within the short-term (similar to estimating the proportion of receivables that will be uncollectible). It would classify these as governmental fund obligations and the balance as GLTDAG liabilities. But this solution is specious in that it fails to consider the inherent characteristics of the bonds and the reasons for redemption.

Inherent Characteristics and Reasons for Redemption

Demand bonds are issued to permit the borrower to take advantage of the lower interest rates paid on short-term obligations. If prevailing short-term rates increase, then the bondholders will no longer find them attractive. They will demand redemption so that they can use the funds to purchase higher-yielding bonds. Since the economic conditions motivating redemption are common to all bondholders, the issuer should expect that if some bonds are presented for redemption, they all will. In substance, therefore, demand bonds, taken by themselves, are short-term, not long-term, instruments, because the lender has made no long-term commitments and assumed no long-term risks.

Most issuers provide for the possibility of redemption by arranging with a financial institution to convert the bonds to long-term notes. In a contract called a *take-out agreement*, the financial institution promises to lend the issuer sufficient funds to repay the bonds. The payback period on the notes is usually long-term, sometimes ten years or more. Thus, the demand bonds, together with the take-out agreement, can rightfully be viewed as a long-term instrument.

Current Standards

In a 1984 interpretation, GASB tied the classification of demand bonds to the take-out agreement. Demand bonds that are exercisable within one year of the balance sheet date, it said, should be reported as *long-term* liabilities in the GLTDAG as long as the entity has entered into a take-out agreement that satisfies the following criteria:

- it does not expire within one year
- it is not cancelable by the lender or prospective lender during that year
- the lender or prospective lender is financially capable of honoring the take-out agreement[7]

If the demand bonds do not satisfy these criteria, then they should be reported as liabilities of the governmental fund receiving the proceeds. Usually this would be a capital projects fund.

EXAMPLE   *Demand Bonds*

A government issues $20 million of demand bonds and obtains an acceptable take-out agreement from a bank. It would record the bonds like any other long-term obligation:

Amount to be provided from general
   government resources $20
     Bonds payable $20
To record the issuance of demand bonds (in the GLTDAG)

Correspondingly, it would record the proceeds in a governmental fund:

Cash $20
   Proceeds from sale of demand bonds $20
To record the proceeds of the demand bonds (in a capital projects fund or other fund receiving the bond proceeds)

---

[7] *Codification*, Section D30.108. The statement does not specify the interest rate to be paid by the borrower on loans resulting from the take-out agreement. Thus, in the event the bonds had to be redeemed, the issuer might have to pay a considerably higher interest rate on the new loan than on the old.

If the demand bonds do not qualify as long-term debt because the government did not obtain an acceptable take-out agreement, then it would record the bonds as a governmental *fund* liability, in the fund receiving the proceeds, as if they were current obligations:

Cash	$20	
Bonds payable		$20

To record the issuance of demand bonds (in a capital projects fund or other fund receiving the bond proceeds)

No entry would be required in the GLTDAG.

BOND ANTICIPATION NOTES

Bond anticipation notes (BANs) present an issue similar to that of demand bonds—should the debt be classified as current (and thereby reported as a governmental fund liability) or as long-term (and reported in the GLTDAG)? BANs are short-term notes issued by the lender with the expectation that they will soon be replaced by long-term bonds. Governments issue BANs after obtaining necessary voter and legislative authorization to issue long-term bonds. The BANs enable them to postpone issuing the bonds in the hope of obtaining more favorable long-term interest rates or to begin work on construction projects without having to wait until it has cleared the lengthy administrative and legal hurdles to issue the bonds.

If a government can, as planned, refund the BANs with long-term bonds, then the notes are, in essence, long-term obligations; the government will not have to repay them with current financial resources. However, if it is unable to refund them, then it must repay them when due—and must have on hand the requisite cash.

The issue of whether to classify the BANs as short-term or long-term is not as intractable as that of demand bonds. Governments do not typically issue financial statements until at least three months after the close of the fiscal year. By then, they have usually either issued the long-term bonds or consummated an agreement to do so.

Current Standards

GAAP provide that a government may recognize BANs as long-term obligations if, by the *date the financial statements are issued*, "all legal steps have been taken to refinance the bond anticipation notes and the intent is supported by an ability to consummate refinancing of the short-term note on a long-term basis."[8] Evidence of this comes through meeting the conditions set forth by the FASB in Statement No. 6, *Classification of Short-term Obligations Expected to be Refinanced*:

- The entity has already refinanced the BANs; or
- It has entered into a financing agreement
  - that does not expire within one year of the balance sheet date and is noncancellable by the lender
  - that has not been violated as of the balance sheet date and
  - is capable of being honored by the lender

---

[8] *Codification*, Section B50.101.

EXAMPLE   *Bond Anticipation Notes*

A government issues $3 million of ninety-day BANs. Because the government expects to roll them over into long-term bonds, it would record them initially in the GLTDAG:

Amount to be provided from general government resources	$3	
Bond anticipation notes payable		$3

To record the issuance of a BAN (in the GLTDAG)

Simultaneously, it would record the proceeds of the BANs in a governmental fund, such as a capital projects fund:

Cash	$3	
Proceeds from sale of bond anticipation notes		$3

To record the proceeds of the BANs (in a capital projects fund or other funds receiving the bond proceeds)

When the government replaces the BANs with the actual bonds, it would reclassify its GLTDAG liability:

Bond anticipation notes payable	$3	
Bonds payable		$3

To record the conversion of the BANs to bonds (in the GLTDAG)

If, however, by the time the financial statements were issued, it were unable to demonstrate the ability to refinance the BANs, then it would remove the liability from the GLTDAG: Thus:

Bond anticipation notes payable	$3	
Amount to be provided from general government resources		$3

To remove the BANs from the GLTDAG

Simultaneously it would "correct" the initial entry to the governmental fund in which the proceeds were recorded, so that the BANs are recorded as a liability rather than source of financial resources:

Proceeds from sale of bond anticipation notes	$3	
Bond anticipation notes payable		$3

To record the BANs as a short-term fund obligation (in a capital projects fund or other fund receiving the bond proceeds)

TAX ANTICIPATION AND REVENUE ANTICIPATION NOTES

Governments usually do not receive their taxes or other revenues evenly throughout the year. Property taxes, for example, may not be due until three or more months after the start of a fiscal year. To meet cash needs earlier in the year, governments can issue **tax anticipation notes (TANs)** and **revenue anticipation notes (RANs)**—short-term notes payable out of specified streams of revenues.

Like bond anticipation notes, TANs and RANs are a means of borrowing against expected cash proceeds. But unlike bond anticipation notes, they will *not* be converted into long-term instruments. Therefore, they must be accounted for in the funds in which the related revenues will be reported; they cannot be relegated to the GLTDAG.

EXAMPLE   *Tax Anticipation Notes*

A government issues $5 million of TANs, backed by property taxes that will be recorded in the general fund. The appropriate general fund entries to record both the issuance and subsequent repayment of the notes are as follows:

Cash	$5	
Tax anticipation notes payable		$5
To record the issuance of a TAN		
Tax anticipation notes payable	$5	
Cash		$5
To record the repayment of a TAN		

CAPITAL VERSUS OPERATING LEASES

Governments, like businesses, may enter into both **capital leases** and **operating leases**. Capital leases are, in essence financing arrangements. The **lessee** (the party that will use the asset) "purchases" an asset in exchange for a long-term note. Operating leases are conventional rental agreements, giving the lessee the right to use property for a portion of its useful life. Operating leases are typified by the daily automobile rental and the long-term rental of office space.

Current Standards

The GASB has adopted the criteria of FASB Statement No. 13, *Accounting for Leases*, to distinguish between a capital lease and an operating lease. A capital lease meets *any one* of the following four conditions:

- The lease transfers ownership of the property from the lessor to the lessee by the end of the lease term.

- The lease contains an option permitting the lessee to purchase the property at a bargain price (i.e., an amount substantially less than market value).

- The lease term is equal to or greater than 75 percent of the estimated economic life of the leased property.

- The present value of rental and other minimum lease payments equals or exceeds 90 percent of the fair value of the leased property.

An operating lease does not meet all of these four conditions.

CAPITAL LEASES

Similarities and Differences from Other Long-term Financing Arrangements

A capital lease may be structured like an ordinary mortgage note or a coupon bond. The **lessor** (the lender) may be a manufacturer, retailer, or financing institution. If it were a financing institution it would first purchase the property from the retailer or manufacturer on behalf of, and for lease to, the ultimate user (the purchaser/ borrower). The financing institution may even sell shares in the lease (called *certificates of participation*) to investors for whom the shares would be an alternative to bonds or notes. If the lessee were a government, then the shares might be exempt from federal taxation, just as if they were the government's bonds. Assets commonly acquired under capital leases include heavy equipment, communications systems, motor vehicles, and buildings.

Collateral

Capital leases are almost always secured only by the leased assets, not by the issuer's full faith and credit. The leased assets, however, are often inadequate as collateral. First, if seized by the lessor (the lender) they may have only limited value. If a government were to abrogate its lease, it may do so for the very reason that the property is of less value than anticipated (e.g., it has become technologically obsolete). Second, seizing government property may be extremely costly in terms of bad publicity and public ill-will. After all, which local bank or finance company would like to be shown on the six o'clock news repossessing a city's ambulance or emergency communications equipment?

Nonappropriation and Nonsubstitution Clauses

Government leases characteristically contain a **nonappropriation clause or fiscal funding clause.** This provision, by stipulating that the payments for each year must be separately appropriated by the legislative body, permits the government to cancel the lease at the end of each year. However, to mitigate this clause, a lessor might add provisions to the lease agreement that would make it economically impractical for the lessees to cancel. For example, the contract may contain a **nonsubstitution clause** prohibiting the lessee from replacing the leased property with similar property. Thus, the government would be unable to evoke the nonappropriation clause without impairing its ability to maintain essential services.

Rationale for Leasing

Governments enter into *operating leases* for the same reasons as individuals and businesses:

- They need an asset for only a small part of its useful life.
- They wish to avoid risks of ownership, such as declines in market value and technological obsolescence.
- They have neither available cash nor credit to purchase the asset.

But why would governments opt for *capital leases* rather than conventional buy and borrow arrangements? Owing to the nature of the collateral and the inclusion of nonappropriation clauses, capital leases are decidedly less attractive to lenders than comparable full faith and credit instruments. Therefore, they invariably bear higher effective interest rates.

Capital leases may be an effective means of circumventing debt limitations. Restrictions on the amount of debt that state and local governments are permitted to borrow were first imposed in the 1840s. During a period of rapid growth between 1820 and 1837, many states financed public works, such as railroads and canals, with general obligation debt. The bond proceeds were invested in the stock of private rail and canal companies, with the expectation that dividends from these companies would be sufficient to service the debt. When the economy collapsed in 1837, many companies failed and governments were forced to default on their bonds.

To ensure fiscal discipline in the future, state governments limited the amount of debt they or their subdivisions could incur. The original limitations were expressed as fixed dollar amounts. Today, however, they are generally set as a percentage of the assessed value of the jurisdiction's property. Alternatively, the limits can be established indirectly through restrictions on tax increases, balanced budget mandates, or requirements that voters approve either all debt or debt above a specified amount.

The extent to which lease obligations are considered as debt, and thereby subject to debt limitations, has been the object of extensive litigation. The outcomes vary by state, but in at least twenty-six states the courts have upheld capital leases as being beyond the purview of debt restrictions. As might be expected, the court decisions have often run counter to prevailing accounting and financial wisdom. For example, in some states the courts have keyed their opinions to the nonappropriation clauses, asserting that because the lease payments are subject to annual authorization the leases lack the characteristics of long-term debts.

Leasing is especially popular in municipalities in which the debt limitations take the form of voter approvals. It is a convenient means of acquiring assets that public officials might consider more essential to the public welfare than does the electorate.

Current Standards

Per both FASB and GASB standards, capital leases are accounted for as if the reporting entity purchased an asset and issued long-term debt. The classification of the arrangement as a capital or an operating lease and the resultant accounting is independent of its legal status as to debt limitations.

If the lease meets the criteria of a capital lease, then the entity would record both the acquired asset and the incurred debt at the *present value* of the required lease payments—an amount that would ordinarily be equal to the fair market value of the property. The discount rate would be that agreed upon by the lessor and lessee in establishing the lease payments (which could also be derived mathematically from the market price of the property and the schedule of lease payments).

A government would account for the leased asset and the related lease liability just as it would an installment purchase. It would report the asset in the GFAAG and the obligation in the GLTDAG. Concurrently, in a governmental fund, such as the general fund or a capital projects fund, it would charge the acquisition of the asset as an expenditure, and credit "other financing sources—capital leases."

As the government makes each lease payment it would report the outlay as a governmental fund expenditure, dividing it between "debt service expenditure—interest" (the discount rate times the remaining principal balance) and "debt service expenditure—principal."

EXAMPLE *Capital Leases*

A municipality agrees to lease an office building for its remaining twenty-year economic life. The building has a fair market value of $3 million. Based on an interest rate of 6 percent, annual lease payments are set at $261,554 (the amount required to liquidate a $3 million, twenty-year, 6 percent loan in equal annual installments).

The municipality would record the lease as follows in the GFAAG, the GLTDAG, and the appropriate governmental fund:

General fixed assets account group

Buildings	$3,000,000	
Investment in fixed assets		$3,000,000

To record the acquisition of a building by capital lease

General long-term debt account group

Amount to be provided for repayment		
of capital leases	$3,000,000	
Capital lease obligations		$3,000,000

To record the obligation incurred by capital lease

Governmental fund

Fixed assets—expenditure	$3,000,000	
Other financing sources—capital lease		$3,000,000

To record the acquisition of equipment under a capital lease

Of the first payment of $261,554, $180,000 would be for interest (6 percent of $3 million); the balance of $81,554 would be for principal. Thus:

General long-term debt account group

Capital lease obligations	$ 81,554	
Amount to be provided for repayment		
of capital leases		$81,554

To recognize reduction of lease obligation owing to first lease payment

Governmental fund

Debt service expenditure (lease principal)	$81,554	
Debt service expenditure (lease interest)	180,000	
Cash		$261,554

To record the first lease payment

If the government had a policy of recording depreciation on fixed assets, then it would reduce the balance of the GFAAG building account by an appropriate amount (e.g., $150,000 if it uses the straight-line method).

If a government were to use the leased assets for activities accounted for in an enterprise fund, then it would account for capital leases just as would a business. Consistent with FASB Statement No. 13, it would record both the asset and the corresponding liability as if it had purchased the asset and borrowed the required funds. It would depreciate the asset over the term of the lease (or the economic life of the property if it expects to receive ownership upon the expiration of the lease). As it makes each lease payment it would charge a portion of the payment to interest (the discount rate times the remaining principal balance) and the remainder to principal. Similarly, not-for-profits organizations would also be guided by the provisions of FASB Statement No. 13. They too would account for capital leases as purchase/borrow transactions.

Both governments and not-for-profits are required to disclose the specifics of their capital and operating lease obligations. The note disclosures of Fort Worth are presented in Table 9–2. A separate note indicates that the city had no material operating lease commitments.

LINKS BETWEEN REVENUE BONDS AND GENERAL OBLIGATION BONDS

Revenue bonds, unlike general obligation (GO) bonds, are backed only by specific revenues, usually from a government's business-type activities. They are generally reported in proprietary funds, and are thereby accounted for as if they were issued by a business. Nevertheless, revenue bonds are integrally linked to GO bonds and the government's debt burden cannot be assessed without taking both into account.

Even if a government is legally responsible for servicing its revenue debt only out of designated revenues, fiscal reality may dictate that it back the bonds with its full faith and credit. Were a government to default on the revenue debt of one of its component units (for example, a utility, convention center, parking garage, or airport), the

TABLE 9-2
City of Fort Worth—Note Disclosures as to Leases

Leases

Obligations under capital leases represent the remaining principal amounts payable under lease purchase agreements for the acquisition of various equipment. These leases are recorded as capital leases in the Office Services Fund, Information Systems Fund, General Fixed Assets Account Group, and General Long-Term Liabilities Account Group. Amortization of the leased assets is included in depreciation expense in the Proprietary Funds. The leased equipment in the Office Services Fund, the Information Systems Fund, and the General Fixed Assets Account Group has an original cost totaling $3,148.

The following is a summary of capital lease transactions of the City for the year ended September 30, 1996:

Capital Lease Obligations, October 1, 1995	$1,799
Additions	0
Principal Payments	613
Capital Lease Obligations, September 30, 1996	$1,186

Future minimum lease payments, by year and in the aggregate, under capital leases and the present value of the net minimum capital lease payments as of September 30, 1996 are as follows:

Year Ending September 30,	General Long-Term Liability	Office Services	Information Systems	Total
1997	$144	$25	$537	$706
1998	131	2	275	408
1999	0	0	89	89
2000	0	0	66	66
2001	0	0	0	0
Total Minimum Lease Payments	275	27	967	1,269
Less Amount Representing Interest	21	0	62	83
Present Value of Net Minimum Capital Lease Payments	$254	$27	$905	$1,186

fiscal community is likely to view the failure as one of the government at large. Thus, the credit standing of the entire government would be severely diminished and the government would either be denied access to the credit markets or would be admitted only by paying a substantial interest penalty.

Governments generally have a choice whether to finance revenue-generating activities with GO or revenue bonds. Because revenue bonds (like capital leases) are not backed by the government's full faith and credit, they almost always bear higher interest rates than comparable GO bonds. Why then would a government issue the more costly revenue bonds? At least two reasons can be cited, both of which point to the interrelationship between the two types of securities:

- Revenue bonds, because they are not obligations of the government at-large, are usually not subject to voter approvals or other forms of voter oversight. Therefore, revenue bonds are another means of circumventing constitutional or legislative constraints on GO borrowing.

- By issuing revenue bonds the government can readily incorporate costs of debt service into user fees. Thus, the facilities financed by the bonds will be paid for out of user charges, not taxes or other general revenues. The costs will be shared among the constituents of the government in proportion to benefits received rather than the factors on which other taxes or revenues are based. Revenue bond-financing may be especially appropriate when parties residing outside of the government's property tax jurisdiction are to be the major users of the facilities. These parties might otherwise escape paying for the assets.

In addition, it should be noted that whereas any single incremental issue of revenue bonds is likely to be more costly that a comparable issue of GO bonds, the choice between the two types of debt may not affect the issuer's total borrowing costs. A government's total revenues and other resources available to service its debt are not changed by the type of debt issued. Accordingly, it's overall risk of default remains the same irrespective of whether it issues GO or revenue bonds. The mix of bonds affects only the distribution of the risk among the bondholders. By issuing revenue bonds, the government shifts a portion of the risk—and the attendant interest costs—to the revenue bondholders, who are in a less secured position than the GO bondholders. Were it to issue only GO bonds, however, the same risk and interest costs would have to be assumed by the GO bondholders and the interest rates on the GO bonds would then increase.

Overlapping debt refers to the obligations of property owners within a particular government for their proportionate share of debts of other governments with overlapping geographic boundaries. Concern for overlapping debt arises because the property located in one government's jurisdiction may serve as the tax base for one or more other governments.

OVERLAPPING DEBT

Suppose, for example, a town is located within a surrounding county. The taxable property of the town is assessed at $600 million; that of the county (including the town) is assessed at $800 million. The town has outstanding debt of $30 million; the county has outstanding debt of $50 million.

Based on the ratio of the value of the property within the town to that within the entire county, the town supports 75 percent ($600 million/$800 million) of the county's debt. Thus, the town's overlapping debt would be 75 percent of the county's $50 million debt—$37.5 million. The taxable property of the town also supports 100 percent of the town's own direct debt of $30 million. Its combined overlapping and direct debt would be $67.5 million—overlapping debt of $37.5 million plus direct debt of $30 million.

Insofar as property taxes are the mainstay revenue of local governments, financial analysts look to the ratio of assessed value of property to total debt outstanding as a primary measure of ability to sustain both existing and proposed liabilities. They obviously would run the risk of overstating the town's fiscal capacity if they took into account only the town's direct debt and ignored that of the county—which will be repaid from taxes on the same property as that of the town.

The computation of overlapping debt may be more complicated than suggested by the previous illustration since governments may be overlapped by not one, but several, taxing authorities. Moreover, the boundaries of the governments may not be concentric; instead, only a portion of one entity may lie within the geographical boundaries of another. The general principal of computing overlapping debt is the same as in the simple example, however. A government's share of each other entity's debt is determined by the percentage of the other entity's property that is within the government's boundaries.

Because the overlapping debt is not an actual liability of the reporting entity, a government cannot report it on its own balance sheets. Owing to its analytical significance, however, a government should include a schedule of overlapping debt as supplementary information in the statistical section of its annual report.

EXAMPLE   *Overlapping Debt*

The property of a city is located within a total of five governmental units as shown in the following schedule and in Figure 9-1.

	Outstanding Debt	Assessed Valuation of Taxable Property
	(in Millions)	
County	$320	$2,000
School District	160	2,000
Library District	12	2,400
Hospital District	40	4,000
City	400	1,800

The city's *direct* debt is $400 million. The city's share of debt of the overlapping jurisdictions is based on the ratio of the assessed value of the city's own property to that of each of the other jurisdictions. Thus:

		Share of City		
	Debt	Proportion	Percent	Amount
		(Dollar Amounts in Millions)		
Direct Debt				
City	$400	$1,800/$1,800	100%	$400
Overlapping Debt				
County	320	$1,800/$2,000	90%	288
School District	160	$1,800/$2,000	90%	144
Library District	12	$1,800/$2,400	75%	9
Hospital District	40	$1,800/$4,000	45%	18
Total Overlapping Debt				459
Total Direct and Overlapping Debt				$859

The schedule indicates that the city's property (assessed at $1,800 million) supports not only $400 million of the city's own debt but $459 million of other governments with overlapping geographic boundaries.

CONDUIT DEBT

Conduit debt refers to obligations issued in the name of a government on behalf of a nongovernmental entity, such as a business or not-for-profit organization. The debt is expected to be serviced entirely by the nongovernmental entity and usually takes the form of revenue bonds or certificates of participation. Often the government retains title to the property financed by the obligations and leases it back to the beneficiary. Other times, it simply loans the resources to the beneficiary. The lease or loan payments are typically established so as to match the payments on the debt. The bonds are payable exclusively from the debt payments. Generally the debt is secured by the property financed by the bonds and in the event of default the bondholders have claims only on the property and the lease or loan payments. Therefore, conduit debt is also referred to as **noncommitment debt**.

Conduit debt is a form of government assistance to the beneficiary organizations in that it enables them to obtain financing at lower rates than if they issued the debt themselves. The lower rates can be obtained because interest on debt issued by a government is exempt from federal income taxes, whereas that on debt issued by the beneficiary may

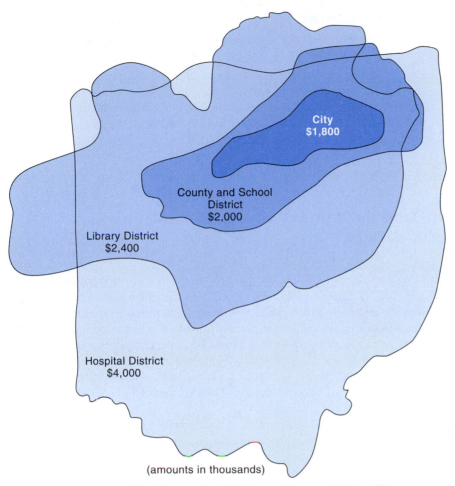

FIGURE 9-1 Diagram of Overlapping Jurisdictions and Assessed Value of Property

be taxable. Bonds that a government issues to attract a private corporation to its jurisdiction are known as **industrial development bonds**. Although the bonds benefit and will be repaid by the corporation, not the government, they nevertheless qualify as tax exempt municipal debt. The federal government imposes strict limitations on the dollar amount of industrial development bonds that can be issued within each state. These limitations constrain municipalities from transferring to corporations the interest-rate subsidies that Congress intended for governments.

The key reporting question relating to conduit debt is the extent to which the issuing government should account for the obligations as if they were its own.

Current Standards

Although many governments elect to report conduit obligations in either their GLTDAG or a proprietary fund, the GASB has ruled that **note disclosure** is sufficient. The following information, it said, must be provided:

- a general description of the conduit debt transactions

- the aggregate amount of all conduit debt obligations outstanding
- a clear indication that the issuer has no obligation for the debt beyond the resources provided by related leases or loans
- for any "major" issuance, the name of the specific nongovernmental third party, the financial maturity date, and the outstanding amount. A "major" issuance is one that has an outstanding balance greater that 10 percent of the aggregate conduit debt outstanding.[9]

WHAT OTHER INFORMATION DO USERS WANT TO KNOW ABOUT OUTSTANDING DEBT?

The magnitude and nature of an entity's obligations, each with its own unique characteristics and risks, is obviously of major concern to the entity's creditors as well as other statement users. As might be expected, both governments and other not-for-profits direct a substantial portion of their annual financial reports to long-term debt. The disclosures pertaining to long-term debt are far more comprehensive than those relating to long-term assets. They typically include not only technical features of the debt, such as interest rates, payout schedules, and collateral, but also selected financial ratios that incorporate debt. Excerpts from the disclosures of Fort Worth pertaining only to GO debt is presented in Table 9–3.

The economic burden of long-term debt is dependent on the issuer's ability to pay. Ability to pay is tied to a wide range of financial, social, economic, political, and administrative factors, only some of which are reported in financial statements. This section, will focus on some of these factors, but will be limited to those tied directly to the debt itself. Broader measures of ability to pay will be considered in Chapter 12, which is directed to financial analysis.

CREDIT ENHANCEMENTS

An issuer can enhance the security of its bonds by replacing its credit standing with that of a more fiscally sound entity. Two such means are by acquiring bond insurance and by obtaining the moral obligation of another issuer to back its debt.

Bond Insurance

Bond and other forms of debt insurance guarantee the timely payment of both interest and principal. Although it is purchased by the bond issuers, it is intended to protect the bondholders.

Written mainly by a small number of specialized companies, the two largest of which are American Municipal Bond Assurance Corp. (AMBAC) and Municipal Bond Insurance Association (MBIA), bond insurance may appear costly. Premiums range from 0.1 percent to 2.0 percent of principal and interest, depending on the risk. However, municipal bond insurance often results in net savings to the issuer in that the leading bond rating services automatically raise the rating of any covered issue to AAA (the highest.) The higher the bond rating the lower the interest cost.

---

[9] *Codification*, Section C65.

TABLE 9-3
City of Forth Worth—Note Disclosure

NOTE H: DEBT OBLIGATIONS

Changes in Long-Term Debt Obligations and Other Liabilities

The following is a summary of changes in long-term debt obligations of the City for the year ended September 30, 1996:

	Range of Interest Rates %	Balance at October 1, 1995	Issued	Other Increase	Retired	Other Decrease	Balance at September 30, 1996
General Long-Term Liabilities:							
General Obligation Bonds	3.75/8.5	$330,399	$26,350	$ 0	$37,193	$ 0	$319,556
Certificates of Obligation	4.75/8.5	16,840	9,835	0	1,955	0	24,720
Accrued Compensation		30,567	0	4,115	0	0	34,682
Estimated Claims Payable		9,512	0	6,398	0	1,241	14,669
Obligation Under Capital Lease	5.95/6.98	375	0	0	120	1	254
Total General Long-Term Liabilities		387,693	36,185	10,513	39,268	1,242	393,881

Summary of changes in long-term debt obligations, continued:

	Range of Interest Rates %	Balance at October 1, 1995	Issued	Other Increase	Retired	Other Decrease	Balance at September 30, 1996
Propriety Fund Types:							
Bonded and Contractual Debt:							
Enterprise Funds:							
Water and Sewer Revenue Bonds	2.85/6.6	238,391	82,785	0	14,001	0	307,175
Water and Sewer General Obligations	3.9/6.7	12,380	0	0	1,284	0	11,096
Water and Sewer Commercial Paper	3.55/3.9	39,730	0	0	39,730	0	0
Total Water and Sewer		290,501	82,785	0	55,015	0	318,271
Municipal Airport Certificates of Obligation	6.8/7.0	3,625	0	0	325	0	3,300
Municipal Parking Revenue Bonds	7.25/8.0	851	0	0	209	0	642
Solid Waste Revenue Bonds	6.6	250	0	0	250	0	0
Municipal Golf General Obligations	3.9/8.5	1,202	0	0	109	0	1,093
Total Enterprise Funds		296,429	82,785	0	55,908	0	323,306
Internal Service Funds:							
Office Services Obligation Under Capital Lease	6.96	52	0	0	25	0	27
Information Systems Obligation under Capital Lease	5.53/6.63	1,372	0	0	467	0	905
Total Internal Service Funds		1,424	0	0	492	0	932
Total Proprietary Fund Types		297,853	82,785	0	56,400	0	324,238
Total Long-Term Liabilities		$685,546	$118,970	$10,513	$95,668	$1,242	$718,119

(continued)

> ### TABLE 9-3 (Continued)
> ### City of Forth Worth—Note Disclosure
>
> *General Long-Term Liabilities Account Group*
>
> The General Long-Term Liabilities Account Group consists of General Obligation Bonds and Certificates of Obligation, as well as other long-term liabilities. Principal and interest payments on debt obligations are secured solely or in part by ad valorem taxes levied on all taxable property within the City.
>
> General Obligation Bonds and Certificates of Obligation indentures require the City to levy the tax required to fund interest and principal at maturity or at least 2% of the principal whichever is greater. At September 30, 1996, $16,700 (with $6,885 being reserved exclusive for bond covenants) is available in the Debt Service Fund to service General Obligation Bonds and Certificates of Obligation.

Moral Obligation Debt

Bonds or notes issued by one entity (usually a state agency) but backed by the promise of another entity (usually the state itself) to make up any debt service deficiencies are referred to as **moral obligation debt**. The obligation is described as "moral" because it is not legally enforceable.

Moral obligation debt is motivated mainly by a state's intent to avoid voter approvals or to circumvent debt limitations. To issue debt that would otherwise be proscribed, a state, with legislative approval, borrows in the name of a state agency, sometimes one formed specifically to issue the debt. To enhance the credit-worthiness of the agency, the state supports the bonds with a promise to cover debt service shortages.

The state does not typically place its full faith and credit behind its pledge. Rather, it promises only to seek future appropriation for any required debt service payments. This promise may be of only dubious value. When New York State issued moral obligation bonds, for example, the promise took the form of a so-called moral makeup clause, wherein the state budget director was required to ask for an appropriation to make up any shortfall in its debt service reserve fund. However, the legislature was not committed to honoring the budget director's request.

Moral obligation bonds obviously are not as secure as the state's general obligation bonds, and rating agencies typically assign them a rating at least one grade below that of the state's general obligation bonds. Still, the rating is likely to be significantly higher than if the bonds were issued by the state agency without the backing of the state.

DEBT MARGIN

As discussed earlier, governments may be limited in the amount of debt that they can incur. The difference between the amount of debt outstanding (computed according to applicable legal provisions, not necessarily as reported on the issuer's balance sheets) and the amount of debt allowed is described as **debt margin**.

EXAMPLE   *Debt Margin*

A government's general obligation bond debt is legally limited to 6 percent of the assessed value of taxable property within its jurisdiction. The assessed value of the property is $1 billion and therefore the government can issue a maximum of $60 million in debt. If the government currently has $45 million of debt outstanding, then its legal debt margin is $15 million (25 percent of its limit).

Payout schedules can take a variety of forms, ranging from those in which a substantial portion of principal is repaid early in the bond's life to those in which it is paid entirely at the end. A typical payout schedule is one in which 50 percent of the debt is retired in ten years. Often, but by no means always, this is accomplished through a twenty- to twenty-five-year serial bond issue with an equal proportion of the issue maturing each year. Usually lenders see a faster retirement schedule as positive, as long as it does not place too great a fiscal strain upon the issuer. Schedules in which the payout is strung-out over thirty to forty years, while not uncommon, are viewed as negative.

Sound fiscal policy dictates that the payout schedule correspond to the useful life of the property being financed. Indeed, the very rationale for borrowing is that the burden of paying for long-lived assets should be borne by the parties who will use them. When the schedule is shorter than the useful life, then only the early-year users will pay for the assets. When it exceeds the useful life, then parties beyond the period of use will be required to pay for them and, in effect, a portion of the debt will be financing operations rather than capital assets.

PAYOUT SCHEDULES

As discussed in Chapter 7 on debt service funds, to assure that an issuer keeps current on its principal and interest payments, lenders commonly stipulate that it maintain a reserve fund. Usually the amount to be set aside is based on principal and interest payments—for example, the highest year's debt service. A reserve fund can generally be dipped into only for the final year's debt service or in the event that the issuer is otherwise unable to make its required payments. From the perspective of a lender, the reserve fund provides a cushion against difficult fiscal times and thereby makes the bond a more attractive investment.

RESERVE FUNDS

Investors and other statement users look to a variety of bond-related ratios and other data to assess ability to pay and risk of default. The most notable of these include:

COMMON RATIOS AND PAST HISTORY

- ***Debt service costs as a percentage of total general fund and debt service fund expenditures.*** Similar to the times–interest earned ratio that is widely used in business, this ratio is usually considered high if it exceeds 20 percent of total general and debt service fund expenditures.

- ***Debt per capita and debt as a percentage of taxable property.*** Both of these ratios are measures of *fiscal capacity*. They relate the bonded debt, not to resources or resource flows within the government, but to the ultimate sources of a government's revenues. As with most ratios involving long-term obligations, debt can be expressed with varying degrees of inclusiveness. For example, debt could be limited to GO debt or could also include revenue debt. Moreover, it could incorporate only the issuer's direct debt or both the direct and overlapping debt.

- ***Past history.*** As any banker will testify, character dominates all quantifiable measures in capturing a borrower's credit standing. Users want information as to whether past payments were made on time. Whereas the bond community may forgive borrowers for unintentionally missing or being late on payments, they may be less tolerant of an issuer who evades payments through bankruptcy or comparable legal maneuvers.

Ratios pertaining to revenue bonds will be discussed in the following chapter dealing with business-type activities. The long-term debt of hospitals, universities, and other not-for-profits are often of this type.

POSSIBLE DIFFERENCES UNDER ENTITY-WIDE (FULL ACCRUAL) STATEMENTS

The proposed reporting model would affect the accounting and reporting for long-term liabilities, much as it would long-lived assets. The entity-wide statements would be on the full accrual basis, so that both long-lived assets and long-term liabilities would be within their measurement focus. Thus, the entity-wide balance sheet would include bonds payable, accrued compensated absences, claims and judgments, and capital lease obligations—all of which are now excluded from governmental funds and instead relegated to the GLTDAG. For purposes of entity-wide reporting, the issuance and repayment of long-term debt would be accounted for and reported as it is by businesses, by not-for-profits and by government enterprises.

As discussed in Chapter 8, the equity section of the entity-wide balance sheet would report net assets (total assets less total liabilities) in three sections: invested in capital assets, net of related debt; restricted net assets and unrestricted net assets. The capital portion of equity would be determined by subtracting the long-term debt from the capital assets that they financed.

The proposed reporting model calls for a schedule of changes in long-term liabilities comparable to that described in Chapter 8 for capital assets. It would show, for each category of liability, the beginning balance, the year's additions and repayments and the ending balance. It would be similar to the schedule of changes in long-term debt obligations and other liabilities that the City of Fort Worth includes in its notes (as presented in Table 9–3). The GLTDAG, like the GFAAG, would no longer be required.

HOW DO NOT-FOR-PROFITS ACCOUNT FOR LONG-TERM OBLIGATIONS?

The accounting and reporting practices of not-for-profits have not been controversial and, in fact, have been given only limited attention by the standard-setting organizations. In large measure this is because most not-for-profit organizations are not capital intense and their liabilities are generally small in relation to their assets. Hospitals, nursing homes, and universities are notable exceptions. These types of institutions have historically looked to the bond markets or to large institutional lenders to finance the construction of buildings and the acquisition of equipment. Moreover, in recent years, not-for-profits, such as museums, professional and trade associations, research institutions, and endowed foundations have also had public offerings of debt. The borrowing arrangements into which not-for-profits enter can be as large and as complex as those of many businesses and governments. In the bond markets the obligations of not-for-profits are generally tied to the municipal rather than corporate market.

Unlike governments, not-for-profits do not typically maintain separate account groups for fixed assets and long-term capital debt. Instead, they account for their debts in the same funds (usually either an operating fund or a plant fund) as the assets that they finance. For purposes of external reporting, however, they must classify their *net assets*, irrespective of which fund they are accounted for, into the three categories of *donor* restrictiveness. Inasmuch as debt proceeds are not *donor* restricted (although they may be restricted by bondholders) they are accounted for as unrestricted. Therefore, not-for-profits are not likely to face serious questions of liability classification.

Not-for-profits generally account for and report their obligations as do businesses. They record their debt at either face value or, if the debt is issued at a premium or discount, at the unamortized issued price. Each period they amortize the premium or discount, offsetting the unamortized premium or discount with a decrease or increase, respectively in interest expense.

EXAMPLE *How Not-For-Profits Account for Long-Term Obligations*

A hospital issues $10 million of 6 percent, twenty-year term bonds at a price of $10,234,930 (i.e., a premium of $234,930). The issue price provides an effective yield of 5.8 percent.

The hospital would record the issuance of the bonds as follows:

Cash	$10,234,930	
Bonds payable		$10,000,000
Bond premium		234,930
To record the issuance of bonds		

Upon making its first semiannual interest payment of $300,000, it would report interest expense of $296,813, which represents the per period yield rate of 2.9 percent (one-half of 5.8 percent) times $10,234,930, the book value of the liability (bonds payable plus bond premium). Thus:

Interest expense	$296,813	
Bond premium	3,187	
Cash		$300,000
To record the first semiannual payment of interest		

This entry would reduce the unamortized premium to $231,743, so the interest expense to be reported when the second payment is made would be only $296,721 (2.9 percent of $10,231,743):

Interest expense	$296,721	
Bond premium	3,279	
Cash		$300,000
To record the second semiannual payment of interest		

Government colleges and universities that adhere to the AICPA model continue to report by individual fund. The long-term debts "attach" to the assets with which they are associated and are thereby reported in the same plant fund as the assets that they finance. As illustrated in Chapter 7, when the institution initially issues debt, it records both the proceeds and the debt in the **unexpended plant fund**. Then as the plant or equipment is purchased or constructed, both the assets and the debt are transferred to the **investment in plant fund**.

WHAT ARE BOND RATINGS AND WHY ARE THEY IMPORTANT?

The leading bond rating agencies, *Standard & Poor's* (S&P), *Moody's Investors Service*, and *Fitch's Investor Service* will assign quality rating to the debt instruments of any issuer (government, not-for-profit, and business) that requests it. Their fees, paid by the issuers generally, range from $2,500 to $65,000.

The agencies base their ratings on a comprehensive review of all factors affecting the issuer's ability to pay. A review would include analyses of the debt instrument itself, the issuer's financial reports and budgets, key demographic data, and a range of economic statistics. It would also incorporate interviews with city officials and assessments of their competence.

The rating services continue to monitor an issuer even after they have assigned an initial rating and expect the issuer to update them continually with current information. A rating generally remains in effect until the issuer's next offering of comparable securities. Sometimes, however, as a result of new developments the agencies will change their initial classification.

The classification scheme of Standard & Poor's for municipal debt (which includes that of not-for-profits as well as governments) is presented in Table 9–4.

Debt ratings are of critical concern to both issuers and investors because they affect the debt's marketability and hence its interest rate. In fact, many institutions are legally prohibited from investing in securities classified by a specified rating service as less than "investment grade."

As suggested by the experience of Washington, D.C. (see accompanying In Practice) a rating service downgrade, even though it generally does nothing more than

---

TABLE 9–4
Debt Rating Definitions of Standard and Poor's

Investment Grade

AAA – Debt rated 'AAA' has the highest rating assigned by S&P. Capacity to pay interest and repay principal is extremely strong.

AA – Debt rated 'AA' has a very strong capacity to pay interest and repay principal and differs from the hightest rated issues only in a small degree.

A – Debt rated 'A' has a strong capacity to pay interest and repay principal although it is somewhat more susceptible to adverse effects of changes in circumstances and economic conditions than debt in higher rated categories.

BBB – Debt rated 'BBB' is regarded as having an adequate capacity to pay interest and repay principal. Whereas it normally exhibits adequate protection parameters, adverse economic conditions or changing circumstances are more likely to lead to a weakened capacity to pay interest and repay principal for debt in this category than in higher rated categories.

Speculative Grade

Debt rated 'BB,' 'B,' 'CCC,' 'CC,' 'C' is regarded as having predominantly speculative characteristics with respect to capacity to pay interest and repay principal. 'BB' indicates the least degree of speculation and 'C' the highest. While such debt will likely have some quality and protective characteristics, these are outweighed by large uncertainties or major risk exposures to adverse conditions.

Source: Municipal Finance Criteria (New York: Standard & Poors, 1996) p. 4.

FALLING BOND RATINGS ADD TO A CITY'S WOES

Expressing serious doubt that city leaders can balance the municipal budget in the current fiscal year, Moody's Investors Service, a Wall Street credit rating firm, today lowered Washington's rating to junk bond status.

The decision by Moody's to drop the city's rating on about $1 billion in general obligation bonds to below investment-grade levels followed similar action on Tuesday by Standard & Poor's Corporation, which lowered the District of Columbia's rating to one level above junk-bond status.

With Washington facing a projected budget deficit of $722 million and Congress poised to wrest more control of the city's finances, the rating changes have a double-barreled impact. The city will have to pay higher interest on future loans, and Mayor Marion S. Barry Jr. will have more trouble restructuring the city's current debt to save $70 million, as outlined in his deficit-reduction plan earlier this month.

Mr. Barry today declared himself helpless to fight the rating changes and, in his strongest language yet, blamed his predecessor, Sharon Pratt Kelly, for the crisis.

"I have been in office for one month and 14 days," he said at an afternoon news conference. "As you look at all these problems, please refer to the one who was in office when they occurred."

He chided Mrs. Kelly for failing to make deeper budget cuts or to conduct yearly audits. Mrs. Kelly, now a fellow at Harvard University, did not return a telephone message seeking comment. She said that she managed the best she could, given the $300 million deficit she said she inherited from Mr. Barry, who had served as mayor the previous twelve years before his imprisonment on a drug charge.

The rating changes increased the likelihood that city leaders would be forced to ask the federal government for help. Mr. Barry said he wanted to avoid that step, knowing that financial relief from Congress would reduce his autonomy.

With the lower ratings, Mr. Barry acknowledged that the city would have difficulty going back into the bond market, especially after city officials had to wage a strong campaign in December to secure $250 million in loans. That transaction is under investigation by the Securities and Exchange Commission because the deficit, described in the prospectus as $40 million for 1994, was said to be $631 million in 1995.

Source: "Washington Bond Rating Falls, Adding to City's Fiscal Woes," © *The New York Times*, February 16, 1995. Reprinted by permission.

spotlight information that was already widely known, can be a traumatic fiscal event for an issuer. Almost always it increases the issuer's interest costs, thereby adding to its fiscal anguish.

Despite the significance attached to bond ratings, investors should no more rely solely on them, than they should a report of a stock brokerage firm. The rating agencies are fallible and they are neither prophets nor seers. Their ratings are merely opinions, not guarantees. The information on which they base their ratings—all of which is in the public domain—is subject to varying interpretation and an independent analysis may provide insights in addition to, or at variance with, those of the agencies.

SUMMARY

The basic financial statements of governments and not-for-profits do not disclose all of the entities' obligations and fail to provide sufficient data to assess their economic burden. Hence, users must seek other sources to establish the amount and nature of debt burden, because an entity's failure to make timely payments of interest and principal can have profound repercussions.

Whereas bankruptcy filings by major governments are rare, those of small units are more common. Because governments have taxing authority, their access to resources seems almost unlimited. Nevertheless there are practical limits to the extent of taxing and service cutbacks.

Liabilities associated with governmental funds are consigned to the general long-term debt account group. Like the general fixed assets account group, the long-term debt account group is essentially a list in double-entry form. Except when the liabilities are issued at deep discounts or superpremiums, they are reported at face value—the amount the government will be required to pay when the obligation matures.

Demand bonds may be reported as long-term debt only if the issuer has entered into a take-out agreement assuring that if the bonds are presented for redemption the debt can be refinanced. Similarly, bond anticipation notes may be reported as long-term debt only if the issuer has already refinanced the notes or has a binding refinancing agreement. In contrast, tax anticipation notes and revenue anticipation notes are not converted into long-term investments, so they cannot be accounted for as long-term obligations.

Leases that meet the criteria of capital leases and are thereby, in essence, financing arrangements are also reported as long-term debt. Capital leasing arrangements are often motivated by an effort to avoid the debt limitations and voter approvals to which conventional general obligation bonds are subject. But whether, in fact, they can be used for that purpose is a matter of state law and judicial decisions.

Revenue bonds and overlapping debts, though not strictly full faith and credit liabilities of the reporting governments, impose financial obligations on their citizens and should be taken into account in assessing the capacity of the government to sustain new and existing debt. In contrast, conduit debt is a legal obligation of the issuer, but it may not be an economic obligation because it is expected to be repaid by the beneficiary, not the issuer.

Although the ultimate ability of a government to repay its debt depends on fundamental financial, social, economic, political, and administrative factors, creditors must also be concerned with features of the debt itself: credit enhancements such as moral obligations and bond insurance, debt margin (the difference between allowable debt and outstanding debt), debt payout schedule, reserve fund requirements, and debt rating.

Not-for-profits, in contrast to governments, account for long-term debts as do businesses and generally report them as claims against unrestricted assets.

Bond ratings are of critical concern to issuers and investors because they affect the debt instrument's marketability and hence its interest rate. Nevertheless, the ratings are opinions, not guarantees.

EXERCISE FOR REVIEW AND SELF-STUDY

A city agrees to lease an emergency communications system. The term of the lease, which is noncancellable, is ten years. The lease gives the city options to purchase the system at several points during the lease, always at less than expected fair market value. It provides for annual payments of $1,086,944, an amount reflective of an $8 million loan (the fair value of the asset) and interest at a rate of 6 percent.

a. Prepare an entry, if required, to record the lease in the general long-term debt account group. What additional entries would be required in the city's other account groups and in its capital projects (or other governmental) fund?

b. Prepare entries, as required, in the same account groups and funds to record the first payment of rent. Assume that the government does not depreciate fixed assets.

c. Suppose, instead, that the city financed the acquisition of the equipment with bonds that could be redeemed at any time at the option of the holder. The bonds paid interest at the rate of 6 percent. At year-end prevailing rates of interest had decreased to 5 percent. The city does *not* have a take-out agreement providing for refinancing if the bonds are presented for payment. How should the city record the debt?

d. The city is permitted to issue a maximum of $30 million of general obligation bonds. It already has $19 million of qualifying debt outstanding. What would be the city's debt margin after issuing $8 million of new debt subject to the limits?

e. The city is served by an independent school district that includes the city as well as nearby towns. The assessed value of taxable property within the city is $600 million; that of the school district is $800 million. The school district has $48 million of debt outstanding. What is the city's overlapping debt with respect to the school district?

QUESTIONS FOR REVIEW AND DISCUSSION

1. What unique issues arise when a government, as opposed to a business, is declared bankrupt?

2. What is the distinction between *general obligation* debt and *revenue* debt? Which one is likely to bear higher interest rates?

3. Will the general long-term debt account group (GLTDAG) debit balance, "Amounts available in the debt service funds," always be equal to the total fund balances in the debt service funds? Explain.

4. At what value would a government report bonds payable in its GLTDAG? Why might this amount differ from the amount actually borrowed? Why might it differ from the amount for which the government can liquidate its bond obligations?

5. What are *demand* bonds? When can they be reported as long-term, rather than current, obligations?

6. If, under GAAP, capital leases are considered long-term obligations, why, in many jurisdictions, are they not subject to debt limitations?

7. What is *overlapping debt* and why is it of significance to financial analysts and other users of a government's financial statements?

8. What is *conduit debt*? Why are governments required to report it only in notes to their financial statements, not on their balance sheets?

9. What distinguishes *moral obligation* bonds from other types of debt? Why would one government assume a moral obligation for another government's bonds?

10. Why are bond ratings of vital concern to bond issuers?

11. Not-for-profits account for their long-term obligations more as businesses than governments. Do you agree? Explain.

EXERCISES

9-1

The general long-term debt account group records only obligations; not the debt proceeds.

The City of Fairfield engaged in the following transactions:

1. It issued $10 million of general obligation bonds to finance the construction of an office building.

2. It transferred $1.6 million from the general fund to the debt service fund. Of this amount, $1.0 million was for principal repayment and $0.6 million for interest.

3. It repaid the $1.0 million of bond principal.

   a. Prepare the journal entries that the city should make in the general long-term debt account group (GLTDAG).

   b. Describe any other entries that the city should make in its governmental funds.

9-2

The accounting for BANs may depend on events subsequent to year-end.

In anticipation of issuing long-term bonds, a state issues $200 million of sixty-day BANs to finance highway construction. The government expects to roll-over the BANs into long-term bonds within sixty days.

a. Prepare appropriate journal entries to record the following, assuming that the state's fiscal year ends on May 31:

   1. Issuance of the $200 million, 60 day BANs on May 1, 1998

   2. Conversion of the BANs to long-term bonds on June 18, 1998.

   State the funds or account groups in which your entries would be made.

b. How would your entries for the year ending May 31, 1998, differ if the state had neither converted the bonds as of the date the financial statements were issued nor entered into an agreement to convert the bonds? Indicate the entries that would now be appropriate.

9-3

The general long-term debt account group is affected by entries in governmental funds.

The following transactions directly affected a city's general fund and other governmental funds. Prepare journal entries to reflect their impact upon the general long-term debt account group.

1. City employees earned $7.7 million in vacation pay during the year, of which they took only $6.6 million. They may take the balance in the following three years.

2. The employees took $0.5 million of vacation days that they had earned in previous years.

3. The city settled a claim brought against it during the year by a building contractor. The city agreed to pay $10 million immediately and $10 million at the end of the following year.

4. The city issued $100 million in general obligation bonds at a price of $99.7 million—i.e., a discount of $0.3 million.

5. It transferred $4 million from the general fund to the debt service fund. Of this, $3 million was for the first payment of interest; the balance for repayment of principal.

6. The government earned $0.2 million in interest on investments held in the debt service fund. The funds are available for the repayment of debt principal.

9-4

Capital leases create both assets and liabilities.

Pearl City leases an emergency communications system. The term of the lease is ten years, approximately the useful life of the equipment. Based on a sales price of $800,000 and an interest rate of 6 percent, the city agrees to make annual payments of $108,694. Upon the expiration of the lease the equipment will revert to the city.

a. Prepare appropriate journal entries in the general (or capital projects) fund, the general fixed assets account group, and the general long-term debt account group to record the signing of the lease.

b. Prepare appropriate journal entries in the same funds and account groups to record the first payment on the lease. The city records depreciation on equipment using the straight-line method.

c. Will your entries to record the final payment on the lease be the same as the first? Explain.

9-5

Not-for-profits account for bonds similarly to businesses.

The Cleveland Historical Society issues $40 million of 6 percent, fifteen-year bonds at a price of $36.321 million to finance the construction of a new museum. The price reflects an annual yield of 7.0 percent.

a. Prepare the journal entry to record the issuance of the bonds. Indicate the category of funds (e.g., unrestricted, temporarily restricted, permanently restricted) in which the entry would be made.

b. Prepare the journal entry to record the first *semiannual* payment of interest.

c. Prepare the journal entry to record the second *semiannual* payment of interest.

9-6

Multiple Choice Questions from CPA examinations.

1. Grove Township issued $50,000 of bond anticipation notes at face amount and placed the proceeds into its capital projects fund. Although it intended to refinance the notes, Grove was unable to consummate refinancing. In the capital projects fund, what account should be credited to record the $50,000 proceeds?
   a. Other financing sources control
   b. Revenues control
   c. Deferred revenues
   d. Bond anticipation notes payable

2. Which of the following accounts would be included in the asset section of the combined balance sheet of a governmental unit for the general long-term debt account group?

Amount Available in Debt Service Funds	Amount to be Provided for Retirement of General Long-Term Debt
a. Yes	Yes
b. Yes	No
c. No	Yes
d. No	No

3. Unmatured general obligation bonds payable of a governmental unit should be reported in the liability section of the
   a. general fund.
   b. capital projects fund.
   c. general long-term debt account group.
   d. debt services fund.

4. The portion of special assessment debt maturing in five years, to be repaid from general resources of the government, should be reported in the
   a. general fund.
   b. general long-term debt account group.
   c. agency fund.
   d. capital projects fund.

5. A major exception to the general rule of expenditure accrual for governmental units relates to unmatured:

Principal of General Long-Term Debt	Interest on General Long-Term Debt
a. Yes	Yes
b. Yes	No
c. No	Yes
d. No	No

6. Flac City recorded a twenty-year building rental agreement as a capital lease. The building lease asset was reported in the general fixed assets account group. Where should the lease liability be reported in Flac City's combined balance sheet?
   a. general long-term debt account group
   b. debt service fund
   c. general fund
   d. A lease liability should not be reported.

7. Bell City entered into a capital lease agreement on December 31 to acquire a general fixed asset. Under this agreement, Bell is to make three annual payments of $75,000 each on principal, plus interest of $22,000, $15,000, and $8,000 at the end of each of the next three years. At the beginning of the lease, what amount should be debited to expenditures control in Bell's general fund?
   a. $270,000
   b. $225,000
   c. $ 75,000
   d. $ 0

8. Maple Township issued the following bonds during the year ended June 30:

Bonds issued for the garbage collection enterprise fund that will service the debt	$500,000
Revenue bonds to be repaid from admission fees collected by the Township zoo enterprise fund	350,000

   What amount of these bonds should be accounted for in Maple's general long-term debt account group?
   a. $0
   b. $350,000
   c. $500,000
   d. $850,000

9. The following obligations were among those reported by Fern Village at December 31:

Vendor financing with a term of two months when incurred on December 15, in connection with equipment maintenance	$ 150,000
Long-term bonds for financing of capital asset acquisition	3,000,000
Bond anticipation notes due in six months, issued as part of a long-term financing plan for capital purposes	400,000

   What aggregate amount should Fern Village report as general long-term capital debt at December 31?
   a. $3,000,000
   b. $3,150,000
   c. $3,400,000
   d. $3,550,000

10. On April 1, Oak County incurred the following expenditures in issuing long-term general obligation bonds:

Issue costs	$400,000
Debt insurance	90,000

   When Oak County establishes the accounting for operating debt service, what amount should be deferred and amortized over the life of the bonds?
   a. $0
   b. $90,000
   c. $400,000
   d. $490,000

11. On June 28, Silver City's debt service fund received funds for the future repayment of bond principal. As a consequence, the long-term debt account group reported
   a. an increase in the amount available in debt service funds and an increase in the fund balance.
   b. an increase in the amount available in debt service funds and an increase in the amount to be provided for bonds.
   c. an increase in the amount available in debt service funds and a decrease in the amount to be provided for bonds.
   d. no changes in any amount until the bond principal is actually paid.

PROBLEMS

Continuing Problem

Review the annual report that you obtained. With respect to long-term liabilities, pay particular attention to information included in both the notes and the supplementary statistical information.

a. Does the government's general long-term debt account group balance sheet contain unusual features not discussed in the text?

b. What is the total of the city's bonded debt, including both general obligation and revenue bonds?

c. What is the ratio of the city's annual debt service expenditures for general obligation debt to total governmental fund expenditures? Is this ratio provided, or did you have to compute it?

d. What is the percent of total general obligation debt to assessed value of property? What is the amount of general obligation debt per capita?

e. What is the city's legal debt margin?

f. What ratings have been assigned by Moody's Investors Service and Standard & Poor's?

g. Based on currently outstanding debt, what will be the city's required debt service payment in 2000? How can you tell?

h. Does the city have obligations under capital leases? If so, how much? Does the statement reveal if the city has obligations under operating leases? If so, does it indicate the present value of those obligations?

i. What is the total amount of the city's overlapping debt?

j. How much new debt did the city issue in the last year? How much did it retire or refund?

9-1

The entries in the GLTDAG are straightforward.

The East Eanes School District engaged in, or was affected by, the following events and transactions during its fiscal year ending June 30, 1999. For each, prepare an appropriate journal entry (if necessary) in the district's general long-term debt account group and indicate how it would be reported in other funds or account groups.

1. Teachers and other personnel earned $350,000 in vacations and other compensated absences which they did not take but for which they expect to be paid in the future.

2. The district settled a suit brought by a student, agreeing to pay $3 million by December 31, 2000.

3. The district issued $8 million in GO bonds to finance an addition to its high school. By year-end, it had expended $1 million in construction costs.

4. The district signed a three-year lease for office space. Annual rent is $40,000 per year.

5. It acquired school buses and other vehicles, financing them with an eight-year capital lease. Annual lease payments are $140,000. Had the district purchased the equipment outright, the price would have been $800,000.

6. The district transferred $500,000, representing the final year's principal payment, to a reserve fund required by the bond indenture.

7. To smooth out cash flows, the district issued ninety-day tax anticipation notes of $950,000.

8. The district paid teachers and other personnel $150,000 for compensated absences earned in previous years.

9-2

Not-for-profits, but not governments, report their effective liabilities and interest costs; neither reports changes in market values.

On January 1, both a public school district and a private school issued $6 million of 6 percent coupon, fifteen-year bonds to finance a new building. The bonds, which require semiannual payments of interest, were issued for $6,627,909, a price that provides an annual yield of 5 percent (a semiannual yield of 2.5 percent). The school district adheres to GAAP for governments; the private school adheres to GAAP for not-for-profits.

a. Prepare the journal entries that each entity would make to record the issuance of its bonds. Be sure to indicate the funds, account groups or category of restrictiveness in which they would be recorded. Comment on whether the liability recorded by each entity represents the amount actually borrowed.

b. Prepare the entries that each entity would make to record the first payment of interest. Indicate the value at which the bonds would be reported immediately following the payment. Comment on whether the expenditure as a percentage of the recorded liability reflects the yield rate at which the bonds were issued.

c. Suppose that immediately following the first payment of interest, prevailing interest rates fell to 4 percent. For how much could the entities liquidate their obligations by acquiring all outstanding bonds in the open market? [*Hint:* Determine the present value (based on the prevailing interest rate of 2 percent per period) of the remaining 29 coupon payments of $180,000 and the repayment of the $6 million of principal.] Comment on whether this amount would be reported in the entities' financial statements. Comment also on why and how this amount might be of interest to statement users.

9-3

Demand bonds may provide the issuer with the disadvantages, but not the advantages, of long-term debt.

On January 1, 1999, a city issues $2 million in 7 percent demand bonds. Although the bonds have a term of ten years, they contain a "put" option permitting the holder to present the bonds for redemption, at par, any time after December 31, 2000. The bonds pay interest semiannually.

a. Prepare journal entries to record the bonds assuming:

1. the city has entered into a qualifying take-out agreement

2. the city has not entered into a qualifying take-out agreement

Be sure to indicate the specific funds or account groups in which you would make your entries.

b. Suppose that on January 1, 2001, prevailing interest rates for bonds of similar credit risk had fallen to 4 percent. A bondholder needed immediate cash for personal reasons. Assuming that the bonds were publicly traded, do you think the bondholder would redeem his bonds? Do you think that any other bondholders would redeem their bonds? Explain.

c. Suppose, instead, that prevailing interest rates had increased to 9 percent. Do you think that the bondholder needing cash would redeem his bonds? Do you think that the other bondholders would redeem their bonds?

d. Suppose that, since it is not mandated by the applicable GASB pronouncement, the take-out agreement does not specify the interest rate at which the financing institution would provide the funds necessary for the city to redeem its bonds. If prevailing rates had increased to 9 percent, at approximately what rate is it likely the financing institution would loan the city the required funds?

e. Comment on the extent to which the demand bonds provide the city with one of the primary benefits of issuing long-term debt—the guarantee of a fixed interest rate over the life of the bond. To what extent does it burden the city with the corresponding disadvantage—being required to pay no less than the stated rate over the life of the bond (or otherwise retire the bonds at market prices)?

9-4

BANs, TANs, and RANs may sound alike, but they are not necessarily accounted for alike.

In August 1999 voters of Balcones, a medium-sized city, approved a $15 million general obligation bond issue to finance the construction of recreational facilities. So as to begin construction immediately, without waiting to complete the lengthy process of issuing long-term bonds, the city issued $4 million in bond anticipation notes (BANs). The notes matured in March 2000, but the city had the right to prepay them any time prior to maturity.

On February 15, 2000, the city issued $15 million of 6 percent twenty-year GO bonds. Upon receiving the proceeds it repaid the BANs, along with $80,000 in interest.

a. Prepare a journal entry to indicate how the city should report the BANs its December 31, 1999, financial statements, assuming that it issued the statements after February 15, 2000. Be sure to indicate the fund or account group in which it would make the entry.

b. Suppose that the city did not refinance the BANs prior to the date the financial statements were issued. What other evidence must the city present to justify reporting the BANs as long-term obligations? Prepare a journal entry to indicate how the city should report the BANs if it is unable to provide this evidence.

c. Assume, also, that the city experienced a cash flow shortage in November 1999. Anticipating tax collections in January 2000, it issued $2 million in tax anticipation notes (TANs) due February 2000. In February 2000, instead of repaying the notes, it "rolled them over" for an additional six months. In which fund or account group should the city report the TANs? Explain.

d. Assume further that in July 1999 the city was awarded a $1 million reimbursement grant. It expected to receive the grant funds in January 2000. Inasmuch as it expected to incur many of the expenditures covered by the grant in 1999, it issued $1 million in six-month revenue anticipation notes (RANs). As of December 31, the city did not repay the notes but had secured the written agreement of the lender that they could be extended for an additional six months. How should the city report the RANs on its December 31, 1999, financial statements? Explain.

9-5

Accountants and lawyers may have differing concepts of debt.

Officials of Danville, determining that the city needed additional administrative space, decided to acquire an available office building. Aware that it was unlikely that city voters would approve a bond issue to finance the purchase of the building, they decided instead to lease the property.

If the city had purchased the building outright, the acquisition price would have been $5 million. If it issued general obligation bonds at the prevailing interest rate of 6 percent and elected to service the debt with equal payments over twenty years, then annual interest and principal payments (assuming annual compounding) would have been $435,923.

The city arranged for a financial institution to purchase the building and lease it to the city for twenty years. The lease specified annual payments of $435,923 and gave the city the option to purchase the building for $1 at the expiration of the agreement. The financial institution would sell shares in the lease to the public, just as if the city had issued bonds to acquire the building.

The lease also contained a nonappropriation clause stipulating that the city would make "good faith" efforts to adhere to its payment schedule but that its obligation was limited to amounts that the city council appropriated annually.

a. Prepare journal entries to record the lease transaction, assuming that the city records debt proceeds and fixed asset expenditures in a capital projects fund and that it does not depreciate fixed assets.

b. Prepare journal entries to record the first payment of interest. Indicate how the entries to record the second payment would differ from the first.

c. Suppose you were asked to represent the Danville

Taypayers Association, a group of citzens opposed to the acquisition of the building. The association contended that under the city's charter, the city was required to obtain voter approval for all general obligation debt over $1 million. The lease, it said, was the equivalent of general obligation debt. Therefore, it charged, the lease violated the city's charter and should be be voided. What arguments would you make in support of the association's position?

d. Suppose, instead, that you were asked to represent the city. What arguments would you make to support the contention of city officials that the lease is not the equivalent of general obligation debt?

9-6

Overlapping debt can significantly alter key measures of debt capacity.

The following information was taken from the City of Wyoming, Michigan's schedule of direct and overlapping debt:

Name of Government Unit	Net Debt Outstanding	Percentage Applicable to City
City of Wyoming	$ 22,863,510	100.00%
Kent County	125,653,951	13.40
Kent County Intermediate School District	1,766,795	13.55
Wyoming Public Schools	3,956,922	99.24
Godwin Heights Public Schools	1,338,501	85.96
Kelloggsville Public Schools	2,363,037	61.97
Grandville Public Schools	10,734,809	13.58
Kentwood Public Schools	25,502,958	.55
Godfrey Lee Public Schools	3,204,362	100.00

a. The schedule does not indicate the origin of the percentages of the debt applicable to the city. What is the most likely way these percentages were derived?

b. Compute the total amount of the City of Wyoming's direct and overlapping debt.

c. Another schedule in the city's annual report indicates that the city's ratio of net direct debt to assessed value of property is 1.861 percent and that net debt per capita is $354.47. The schedule reports that assessed value of property is $1,228,774,900 and that the population is 64,500. What would be the ratio of *total net direct debt*

and overlapping debt to assessed value of property? What would be the total net direct and overlapping debt per capita?

d. Why might a statement user be at least as concerned with the ratios that include overlapping debt as with those limited to direct general obligation debt?

9-7

Operating leases, as well as capital leases, represent long-term fiscal commitments.

The following schedule was taken from the notes to the financial statements of Beth Israel Medical Center, a nonprofit hospital. Dates have been changed.

Future minimum payments under capitalized leases and non-cancellable operating leases with initial or remaining terms of one year or more.

	Capitalized leases	Operating leases
	(in thousands)	
1998	$ 756	$11,696
1999	560	7,949
2000	415	6,388
2001	242	5,475
2002 and Thereafter	116	25,079
Total Minimum Lease Payments	$2,089	$56,587
Less Amount Representing Interest	271	
Present Value of Minimum Payments	$1,818	

a. Where on the medical center's balance sheet, if at all, would each of the amounts reported on the schedule, be reflected (or combined with other amounts)?

b. What is the significance of *amount representing interest*?

c. Prepare a journal entry to record the 1998 capital lease payments. Assume that the leases incorporate an interest rate of 6.56 percent (a rate that when used to discount each of the lease payments yields $1,818, the total present value of minimum payments).

d. Prepare a journal entry to record the 1998 operating lease payments.

e. Suppose that the medical center's cost of capital is 6.56 percent and that the $25,079 in operating lease payments for 2002 and thereafter are for a period of five years from 2002 through 2006 (in equal amounts of $5,016). What is the present value of the center's operating lease obligations from 1998 through 2006? [*Hint*: Discount each of the payments at a rate of 6.56 percent. If possible, use the present value functions of a calculator or a computer spreadsheet program; otherwise, use an interest rate of 7 percent]. Of what significance is this amount to a statement user (i.e., why might it be as important as the actual debt reported on the balance sheet)?

9-8

Entries in governmental funds can be reconstructed from transactions affecting the GLTDAG.

The following is an excerpt from a note included in the financial statements of The Metropolitan Government of Nashville and Davidson County, regarding bonds and other obligations.

Transaction summary for the year ended June 30, 1994

	General Long-term Debt Account Group	
	General Obligation Bonds and Notes Payable	Other Obligations Payable
Bonds, Notes, and Other Obligations Payable, July 1, 1993	$503,341,423	$85,423,817
New Bonds and Notes Issued	121,398	
Other Additions		
Unfunded Pension Obligation		67,968,390
Compensated Absences		38,588,966
Claims and Judgments		2,342,000
Landfill Closure		5,425,804
Bonds, Notes, and Other Obligations Retired	(30,179,281)	
Other Retirements		
Unfunded Pension Obligation		(69,153,390)
Compensated Absences		(28,061,416)
Claims and Judgments		(4,294,790)
Arbitrage Rebate		(57,009)
Landfill Closure		(2,348,564)
Bonds, Notes and Other Obligations Payable, June 30, 1994	$473,283,540	$95,833,808

a. Prepare the entries, in the GLTDAG and the general fund (or other appropriate governmental funds) to re-

cord the transactions affecting compensated absences. Be sure to indicate the significance of each of your entries (i.e., what the amounts debited and credited represent).

b. Prepare the entries in the GLTDAG, the capital projects fund, and the debt service fund (or other appropriate governmental funds) to record the issuance and retirement of bonds and notes.

c. Pension accounting will be discussed in Chapter 11 dealing with fiduciary funds. However, based on what you know about other expenditures and obligations, what is the significance of the $67,968,390 addition to the GLTDAG labeled "unfunded pension obligation"? What is the significance of the $69,153,390 reduction?

d. What is the most likely reason for the reduction of the liability "arbitrage rebate"? In which fund or account group was the initial expenditure (or reduction in revenue) most likely recorded? [Hint: See Chapter 7.]

9-9

Legal debt margins do not typically include all of a government's obligations.

The following was taken from the statistical section of the City of Wyoming, Michigan's annual report (see also Problem 6).

Computation of Legal Debt Margin for General Obligation Bonds as of June 30, 1994		
Value of Assessed Property (Excluding Certain Industrial and Commercial Properties)		$1,139,255,400
Debt Limit—Ten Percent of Assessed Value		113,925,540
Amount of Debt Applicable to Debt Limit:		
Total Bonded Debt	$27,442,000	
Less:		
Assets Available for Debt Service	1,770,453	
Revenue Bonds Not Subject to Debt Limitations	2,025,000	
	3,795,453	
Total Amount of Debt Applicable to Debt Limitations		$ 23,646,547
Legal Debt Margin		$ 90,278,993

Assume that in its fiscal year ending June 30, 1994, the city issued an additional (net of repayments) $30,000,000 of general obligation bonds and $6 million in revenue bonds. It increased its bond reserves (assets available for debt service) by $200,000. Moreover, owing to both a recession and a change in valuing property, the assessed value of its property decreased by 5 percent.

a. What is the maximum the city could issue in general obligation bonds as of June 30, 1994?

b. Suppose the city:

1. signed a five-year agreement with a waste disposal firm. The firm agreed to provide services to the city for $50,000 per year. The city could not cancel the contract unless the firm failed to deliver the specified services.

2. signed a five-year lease to acquire equipment. The useful life of the equipment was also five years. Annual payments were $50,000 per year and the city had the option to purchase the equipment at the end of its useful life for $1. The lease agreement was based on an interest rate of 8 percent and contained a "nonappropriation clause," which local courts recognized as being decisive with respect to whether the debt was subject to the legal debt margin.

How would each be reflected in the city's GLTDAG? If you were writing the legislation establishing debt limits, would you make either leases or service contracts subject to the limits?

c. As indicated in the schedule, and as is typical of most debt limitations, the debt margin does not apply to revenue bonds. What do you think is the reason for this exemption? What argument could you make that revenue bonds should not be exempt?

9-10

University plant funds can readily be recast from an AICPA to an FASB presentation.

A university maintains several plant funds as shown in the condensed balance sheets that follow. The fund structure and presentation is consistent with the AICPA college and university reporting model. Although this model has been superseded by FASB Statement No. 117, *Financial Statements of Not-for-Profit Organizations*, it may still be used for *internal* purposes by not-for-profit colleges and universities. Moreover, it may be used for *both* internal and external purposes by government colleges and universities.

Plant Funds (in Thousands)		
Unexpended Plant Funds		
Assets:		
Cash		$ 9,000
Investments		27,000
Total Assets		$ 36,000
Liabilities and Fund Balances:		
Bonds Payable		$24,000
Fund Balance		
Restricted by Donors		
for Specified Projects	$4,000	
Unrestricted	8,000	12,000
Total Liabilities and Fund Balances		$ 36,000
Funds for Renewals and Replacements		
Assets:		
Cash		$ 4,500
Investments		85,100
Total Assets		$ 89,600
Liabilities and Fund Balances:		
Fund Balance		$ 89,600
Funds for Retirement of Indebtedness		
Assets:		
Cash		$ 21 600
Investments		25,600
Total Assets		$ 47,200
Liabilities and Fund Balances:		
Fund Balance		$ 47,200
Investment in Plant		
Assets:		
Construction in Process		$ 3,500
Equipment		39,300
Land		12,000
Buildings		127,800
Total Plant		182,600
Less Accumulated Depreciation		(78,200)
Total Investment in Plant		$104,400
Liabilities and Fund Balances:		
Notes Payable		$ 20,000
Bonds Payable		39,000
Capital Lease Obligations		8,500
Net Investment in Plant		36,900
Total Investment in Plant		$104,400

a. Prepare the journal entries that would be required to record the following transactions:

1. Using the cash in its retirement of indebtedness fund, the university repays $20 million of the bonds recorded in the investment in plant fund.

2. Using unexpended plant fund resources, which had previously been borrowed, it incurs $3 million in construction costs.

3. It recognizes depreciation of $7 million.

4. It issues long-term notes of $5.5 million to restore (i.e., renew) an old classroom building.

b. Recast the plant funds (*prior* to the entries required in part a) as they would appear in external reports in accord with Statement No. 117. Allocate the cash and investments (in the unexpended funds) to the donor-restricted category based on donor restricted fund balance as a proportion of total liabilities and net assets.

c. Comment briefly on the advantages and disadvantages of each presentation.

SOLUTION TO EXERCISE FOR REVIEW AND SELF-STUDY

a. The lease would satisfy the criteria of a capital lease and therefore the city would record the long-term debt in the GLTDAG:

Amount to be provided from
general government
resources $8,000,000
   Capital lease
     payable $8,000,000
To record the obligation incurred by the capital lease

At the same time it would record the asset in the general fixed assets account group:

Equipment $8,000,000
   Investment in fixed assets $8,000,000
To record the fixed assets acquired by capital lease

It would record the expenditure in its capital projects (or other governmental) fund:

Fixed assets—expenditures $8,000,000
   Other financing sources—
     debt proceeds $8,000,000
To record the expenditure and offsetting receipt of resources

b. Of the first payment of rent, $480,000 (6 percent of $8 million represents interest and $606,944 represents principal. The city must reduce the balance in the GLTDAG by the portion applicable to the principal:

Capital lease payable $ 606,944
   Amount to be provided from
     general government resources $ 606,944
To record the reduction of debt upon the first lease payment

The lease payment would be recorded in the capital project (or other governmental) fund:

Capital lease
  expenditure—interest $ 480,000
Capital lease
  expenditure—principal   606,944
  Cash $1,086,944
To record the first lease payment

c. Since the city does not have a take-out agreement, it cannot record the bonds as long-term obligations—irrespective of whether prevailing interest rates are higher or lower than those of the bonds. It must record the debt as a short-term obligation of the capital projects (or some other governmental) fund. Thus:

Fixed assets—expenditures $8,000,000
   Demand bonds payable $8,000,000
To record the acquisition of the fixed asset as financed with demand bonds that do not satisfy the criteria of long-term debt

The acquired assets would be recorded, as before, in the GFAAG.

d. After issuing the $8 million of new debt, the city would have total debt outstanding of $27 million. Its debt margin would be only $3 million—10 percent of its $30 million limit.

e. Of the school district's taxable property, 75 percent ($600 million of $800 million) is located within the city. Therefore, the city is responsible for 75 percent of its debt—$36 million.

CHAPTER 10

Business-Type Activities

Governments and not-for-profits engage in a variety of functions that are similar to those carried out by businesses. They range in size from the small gift shops of churches to multibillion-dollar regional power authorities.

Thus, in this chapter we will look at accounting principles applicable to business accounting. As shall soon be evident, the business-type activities of governments and not-for-profits are accounted for similarly to corresponding enterprises in the private sector. Their financial statements are on a full rather than a modified accrual basis, and their measurement focus is on all economic resources, not merely financial resources.

We shall direct relatively little attention, therefore, to the general principles (such as those of revenue and expense recognition) of full accrual accounting. Since these are the same as those of businesses, they are covered in other courses dealing with financial accounting.

Instead, our objectives are more specific:

- to consider criteria for distinguishing between business and governmental activities and to raise pertinent questions as to whether and why these activities should be accounted for differently

- to address several selected accounting issues that are unique to government enterprises

- to set forth the purposes, and assess the consequences, of using internal service funds to account for goods and services provided by one government department to another

- to present examples of the information needed to assess revenue bonds—the type of debt associated both with a government's business-type activities and with not-for-profit organizations

WHAT TYPES OF FUNDS INVOLVE BUSINESS-TYPE ACTIVITIES?

Governments segregate their business-type activities into *proprietary* funds, of which there are two types:

- *Enterprise funds* account for operations in which goods or services are provided to the general public.

- *Internal service funds* account for operations in which goods or services are provided by one government department to other departments within the same government or to other governments.

Some of the accounting and reporting issues pertaining to business-type activities are common to enterprise funds and internal service funds. However, each fund has unique features, so at the risk of repetition, we shall devote separate sections to each of the fund types.

Governments account for proprietary funds, both enterprise and internal service, on a full accrual basis. They recognize revenues as earned and *expenses* (rather than expenditures) as incurred, irrespective of when cash is received or paid. They accord balance sheet recognition to both long-lived assets and long-term debt, depreciating the long-lived assets and amortizing any premiums or discounts on long-term debt.

Not-for-profits, in contrast to governments, account for their business-type activities, both internal and external, within their current operating funds. However, the current operating funds of not-for-profits, unlike those of governments, are on a full rather than a modified accrual basis. Therefore, not-for-profits, like governments, account for their business-type operations on a full accrual basis, giving balance sheet recognition to long-lived assets and long-term debt. The resources associated with these activities are generally donor-unrestricted and hence, are so classified per the guidelines of Statement No. 117, *Financial Statements of Not-for-Profit Organizations.*

WHY DO GOVERNMENTS AND NOT-FOR-PROFITS ENGAGE IN BUSINESS-TYPE ACTIVITIES?

Governments and not-for-profits engage in a wide variety of activities that are also carried out by for-profit businesses. For example:

- Governments provide waste removal, electric and other utility services, maintain hospitals (often in competition with stockholder-owned hospitals), and operate swimming pools, tennis courts, and golf courses.
- Universities sell computers, books and clothing, sponsor professional-like sports teams, operate cafeterias and restaurants, and maintain dormitories.
- Churches, synagogues, hospitals, museums, and zoos sell religious artifacts, gifts, posters and books.
- Girl Scouts sell cookies; Boy Scouts sell candy.

In the United States, prevailing political and economic doctrine dictates that goods and services should be provided mainly by the private business sector. Why, then, do governments and not-for-profits engage in activities similar to those carried out by private enterprise? Several reasons can be cited:

- The activities provide resources that would otherwise have to be raised by taxes, contributions, tuition, or other means. Gifts shops, for example, may be major sources of revenue for museums; government-owned utilities may generate cash as well as electricity.

IN PRACTICE

IN PRACTICE: UNIVERSITIES IN BUSINESS GENERATE REVENUES

Housing, computer centers, conference rooms, bookstores, and such become more important sources of income as colleges' costs rise faster than tuition, says the National Association of College and University Business Officers. Some 70 percent of schools now run such services "aggressively," and that is likely to top 90 percent in a few years, says the group's Robin Jenkins. Approaches vary. Student's use spurs growth in service revenue, but so does business use of facilities.

In California, UCLA has two on-campus hotels, while the University of Southern California makes money selling merchandise and licensing the USC logo. Michigan State University got almost $3 million in gross revenue last year by letting out facilities for summer conferences. Franklin & Marshall College, a private school in Lancaster, Pennsylvania, built a retail-office complex on campus that generates $350,000 a year.

Source: "Universities Push Auxiliary Services To Generate More Revenue," *The Wall Street Journal*, April 27, 1995. © Dow Jones and Company, Inc. All rights reserved worldwide.

- The activities complement and support the main mission of the entity. Thus, for example, college cafeterias, book stores, and sports programs are an integral part of a university environment.

- The entity wants control over the activity. Thus, universities operate dormitories not necessarily because they can do so at less cost than a private contractor, but so they can maintain authority over them. Similarly, some cities and counties have rejected proposals to sell their hospitals to private firms so as to keep them entirely within their command.

- The entity can provide the services more cheaply or efficiently than can a private firm. This may be especially true if the government or not-for-profit is not subject to the income, property or sales taxes that would be charged to private businesses. Public housing authorities, for example, have an inherent cost advantage over private landlords in providing apartments to low income families in that their properties are not subject to property taxes.

- The entity either wants to subsidize the activity or assure that the goods or services are available at less than market rates. Thus, a city might maintain a bus service or a public golf course, even though it is unprofitable.

In recent years, both governments and not-for-profits have come under attack for operating activities that critics believe should be carried out in the private sector. Opponents of large government have urged the **privatization** of services, claiming that, lacking the profit motive, governments are inherently inefficient. Merchants have charged tax-exempt universities and museums with unfair competition in selling books, computers, and other items at less than prevailing prices.

The issue of whether business-type activities should be carried out by governments and not-for-profits is beyond the scope of this text. But the reasons why they carry them out are directly pertinent to the questions of both how to distinguish business-type from governmental activities and how to account for them.

HOW ARE PROPRIETARY ACTIVITIES DISTINGUISHED FROM OTHER GOVERNMENT ACTIVITIES?

LACK OF UNIFORMITY IN DEFINITIONS AND STANDARDS

Both the criteria for distinguishing business-type from governmental activities and the need for separate funds and accounting principles for the two types of activities are sources of controversy. Current standards allow governments considerable discretion in determining which of their activities may be accounted for in proprietary funds.

Because proprietary (business-type) activities are carried out for a wide range of purposes, there is no obvious way to differentiate them from other governmental operations.

Current Standards

Current standards, established by the National Council on Governmental Accounting (NCGA), dictate that activities to be accounted for in proprietary funds are those:

- financed and operated in a manner similar to private business enterprises—where the entity's intent is to finance or recover the costs (expenses,

> including depreciation) of providing goods or services to the general public on a continuing basis primarily through user charges
>
> *or*
>
> - where the governing body has decided that periodic determination of revenues earned, expenses incurred, and/or net income is appropriate for capital maintenance, public policy, management control, accountability, or other purposes[1]

The current standards fail to establish clear boundaries between business and other types of activities. Consequently, they allow governments broad discretion in determining which of their activities to account for in proprietary funds. Consistent with the current standards, any activity can qualify for proprietary fund accounting as long as it is financed at least partially by fees and the government either declares its intent that the activity be self-sustaining or "decides" that income determination (i.e., full accrual) accounting is "appropriate." The result, quite understandably, is that there is little uniformity among governments as to whether similar activities are accounted for in governmental or proprietary funds.

CONTROVERSY AS TO THE NEED FOR SEPARATE FUNDS AND ACCOUNTING PRINCIPLES

Irrespective of how business-type activities are defined, an equally fundamental question is whether and why they should be accounted for differently than governmental activities; in particular, why they should be accounted for on a full rather than a modified basis of accounting.

Key reasons cited for using business-type accounting to account for proprietary-fund activities include:

- The full accrual basis of accounting (i.e., a measurement focus upon all economic resources) captures all the resources and obligations, including fixed assets and long-term obligations, associated with an activity. It thereby provides a more complete picture of the entity's fiscal status and operating results.
- The measurement focus on all economic resources is more consistent with the GASB's objectives that financial reporting should provide information to determine whether current-year revenues were sufficient to pay for current-year services and to assist users in assessing service efforts, costs, and accomplishments.
- Full accrual accounting provides information on depreciation, which is an essential cost of operations.
- Business-type accounting facilitates comparisons with similar private enterprises.

At the same time, there are cogent arguments against separate accounting principles for proprietary activities:

- Two separate measurement focuses and bases for accounting within the same set of financial statements are confusing and confound attempts to combine the statements of individual funds into a single consolidated report that presents an overview of the entity as an economic whole.
- As suggested earlier, there are no clear-cut distinctions between business and nonbusiness activities. Despite many similarities, governmental activities cannot—and should not—be compared to activities carried out in the private sector. A government should have sound political and economic reasons—other than merely earning a profit—for conducting a particular activity in the public sector. If it does not, then it should be privatized. These reasons, by themselves, should suggest that the activities be assessed by criteria other than profits—the *bottom line* of business-type financial reports.

---

[1] GASB *Codification*, Section 1300.104.

- Surveys of statement users indicate that information on depreciation is not of high priority to governmental decision makers. They are concerned mainly with the ability of revenues to cover debt service rather than depreciation. This applies especially to users interested in toll roads, tunnels, and bridges.

Closely tied to the issue of whether proprietary activities should be accounted for using separate accounting principles is whether they should be accounted for and reported in separate funds. A key rationale for fund accounting and reporting in general is that legally restricted resources should be reported apart from those that are unrestricted. The resources directed to proprietary activities, especially those accounted for in internal service funds, are often not legally restricted. They can be used for all purposes of government and are subject to the claims of general creditors. As will be discussed later in this chapter, governments generally present restricted proprietary fund assets (usually owing to revenue bond covenants) separately from those that are unrestricted. Both, however, are presented within the same fund.

Obviously, there are compelling reasons to account *internally* for each of a government's business-type activities in separate funds. Separate funds facilitate budgeting, planning, and control. However, when resources that are not legally restricted are reported upon apart from unrestricted resources, statement users may have difficulty determining the total resources available for future appropriation or payment to creditors. They may be misled into thinking that unrestricted resources are, in fact, restricted.

In contrast to governments, the financial reports of not-for-profits are guided by the underlying principal that unrestricted resources, even if used to carry out business-type activities, should be reported upon in a common fund. Not-for-profits have traditionally reported upon their business-type activities within their current unrestricted funds, even though they may have maintained separate sets of books for each separate enterprise. This practice has been officially sanctioned by FASB Statement No. 117, *Financial Statements of Not-for-Profit Organizations*, which requires not-for-profits to intermingle all resources, irrespective of whether they are associated with business or non-business activities, unless they are *donor* restricted.

Nevertheless, the arguments in favor of reporting upon proprietary activities apart from governmental activities are also persuasive. Up to the point of "information overload," more information is better than less. If managers need separate reports to assess the performance and fiscal status of business-type activities, so too do citizens, investors, and other statement users. Insofar as statement users are concerned with the total amount of unrestricted resources, they can readily add together the resources in unrestricted proprietary funds with those in the general and other unrestricted funds.

POSSIBLE DIFFERENCES UNDER ENTITY-WIDE (FULL ACCRUAL) STATEMENTS

The proposed dual-perspective model would retain the distinctions between governmental and proprietary funds. The two types of funds would continue to be shown in separate columns on the combined entity-wide statements, and proprietary funds would still be reported on a full accrual basis.

Under the proposed model, governments would have less discretion in choosing whether to account for an activity in a proprietary or a governmental fund. As recommended by the GASB, any activity that charges users a fee for its services

> *may* be accounted for in a proprietary fund. In addition, an activity *must* be accounted for in a proprietary fund if it satisfies any one of the following criteria:
>
> - The activity issues debt that is secured *solely* by a pledge of the net revenue from fees and charges of the activity.
> - State or local laws or regulations require that the activity recover the costs of providing services, including capital use charges or debt service, with fees and charges.
> - The pricing policies of the activity establish fees and charges designed to recover the costs of providing services, including capital use charges or debt service.

ACCOUNTING PRINCIPLES FOR PROPRIETARY FUNDS

In general, proprietary funds are accounted for like businesses; they adhere to the pronouncements of the FASB. However, pronouncements issued by the GASB that conflict with a FASB pronouncement override the FASB pronouncements. For example, in 1989 the GASB issued its Statement No. 9, *Reporting Cash Flows of Proprietary and Nonexpendable Trust Funds and Governmental Entities that Use Proprietary Fund Accounting* requiring proprietary funds to prepare a cash flows statement that differs in significant respects from that mandated by the FASB's Statement No. 95, *Statement of Cash Flows*. Moreover, other FASB statements require disclosures that go beyond those mandated by GASB for governments' nonbusiness activities.

To avoid having both to consider the applicability to governments of all future FASB pronouncements and to issue "negative" standards (those telling governments that they don't have to adhere to a FASB pronouncement) the GASB issued Statement No. 20, *Accounting and Financial Reporting for Proprietary Funds and Other Governmental Entities that Use Proprietary Fund Accounting*. This statement gives governments an option between two approaches to applying FASB pronouncements:

- *Option #1.* A government must apply to its proprietary activities all FASB pronouncements *issued on or before November 30, 1989*, unless they conflict with, contradict, or are replaced by GASB pronouncements. In addition, they must comply with any post–November 30, 1989, pronouncements that have been specifically adopted by GASB.
- *Option #2.* A government must apply to its proprietary activities all FASB pronouncements, *irrespective of when they were issued*, unless they conflict with, contradict, or are replaced by GASB pronouncements.

Thus, the standard requires all governments, irrespective of which approach they choose to follow, to adhere to all FASB pronouncements issued *on or before the 1989 cut-off date* (unless those pronouncements have been overridden by specific GASB statements). Then, if they elect the first approach, they must adhere to *none* of the subsequent FASB pronouncements (unless they were specifically adopted by the GASB). By contrast, if they elect the second approach, they must adhere to *all* of the subsequent FASB pronouncements (unless they specifically conflict with GASB pronouncements). They cannot cherry-pick the most appealing statements and reject the others.

November 30, 1989, while not yet as notable as June 15, 1215, (the signing of the Magna Carta) or July 4, 1776, (the signing of the Declaration of Independence) owes its significance to what future accounting historians will likely see as an equally significant proclamation—the "Jurisdiction Determination of the Board of Trustees of the Financial Accounting Foundation." The key feature of this agreement is a new hierarchy of generally accepted accounting principles, establishing that the GASB has the final standard-setting authority over *all* government entities, including hospitals, universities, and other proprietary activities. Thus, if the GASB issues a statement that conflicts with one issued by the FASB, the GASB statement must be followed by the entities within its jurisdiction.

Table 10–1 presents the balance sheet and the statement of revenues, expenses, and changes in retained earnings of one of Fort Worth's enterprise funds, its water and sewer fund. Key features to note include the following:

- The two statements are similar in form and content to those of comparable businesses; they are on a full accrual basis and accordingly, long-lived assets are not only reported upon on the balance sheet but are stated net of accumulated depreciation.

- As shall be addressed in a following section, restricted assets are shown apart from unrestricted assets. The restricted assets may include resources received from grants (e.g., a federal grant for facilities upgrades) and bonds as well as those set aside per terms of bond indentures for debt service. Similarly, the liabilities to be paid from restricted assets are broken out from other obligations.

- The fund equity is divided into two parts: capital contributions from the city itself, the federal government and developers; and retained earnings.

TABLE 10–1
City of Fort Worth Water and Sewer Fund

Comparative Balance Sheets
September 30, 1996 and 1995
(000's omitted)

	1996	1995
Assets:		
Current Assets:		
Cash and Cash Equivalents	$33,636	$31,070
Accounts and Other Receivables	24,796	26,479
Allowance for Doubtful Accounts	(3,403)	(2,891)
Inventories (at cost)	2,780	2,518
Deferred Bond Issue Costs	2,312	2,222
Total Current Assets	60,121	59,398
Restricted Assets:		
Cash and Cash Equivalents	111,986	120,002
Cash and Cash Equivalents held by Trustees	13,948	1,436
Grants Receivables	995	562
Accounts and Other Receivables	1,073	894
Total Restricted Assets	128,002	122,894
Property, Plant and Equipment (at cost):		
Land	14,844	14,844
Buildings	23,218	23,218
Improvements Other than Buildings	700,075	678,885
Machinery and Equipment	128,138	114,836
Construction in Progress	132,107	82,070
Accumulated Depreciation	(221,415)	(223,570)
Net Property, Plant and Equipment	776,967	690,283
Total Assets	$965,090	$872,575

TABLE 10–1 (Continued)
City of Fort Worth Water and Sewer Fund

Comparative Balance Sheets
September 30, 1996 and 1995
(000's omitted)

	1996	1995
Liabilities and Fund Equity:		
Current Liabilities:		
Accounts and Contracts Payable	$6,644	$3,108
Accrued Compensation	3,428	3,060
Payable to Federal Government	0	49
Due To Other Funds	0	190
Other	196	716
Payable From Restricted Assets:		
Construction Accounts Payable	2,845	2,007
Current Portion of Enterprise Debt	16,420	15,285
Accrued Interest Payable	1,994	2,094
Total Current Liabilities	31,527	26,509
Payable From Restricted Assets:		
Customer Deposits	4,562	4,376
Other Revenue Bonds Payable	207,470	153,510
Bond Discount	(2,769)	(2,506)
General Obligation Bonds Payable	9,816	11,096
Texas Water Development Board Bonds Payable	84,565	70,880
Commercial Paper Debt	0	39,730
Deferred Revenue	1,453	1,494
Total Liabilities	336,624	305,089
Fund Equity:		
Contributions:		
Municipal	3,215	3,215
Federal Government	93,079	92,962
Developers and Others	129,468	124,946
Total Contributions	225,762	221,123
Retained Earnings:		
Reserved:		
Debt Service	16,183	23,494
Unreserved	386,521	322,869
Total Retained Earnings	402,704	346,363
Total Fund Equity	628,466	567,486
Liabilities and Fund Equity	$965,090	$872,575

- The statement of revenue, expenses, and changes in retained earnings includes an unusual item relating to depreciation: "Depreciation Related to Property, Plant and Equipment Acquired through Contributions from Federal Government." This change, which is unique to governments, shall be discussed in a later section dealing with depreciation.

Proprietary funds are also required to present a statement of cash flows. This statement shall be discussed in Chapter 12 pertaining to financial reporting.

TABLE 10–1 (Continued)
City of Fort Worth Water and Sewer Fund

Comparative Statements of Revenues,
Expenses and Changes in Retained Earnings
Years Ended September 30, 1996 and 1995
(000's omitted)

	1996	1995
Operating Revenues:		
Charges for Services	$149,957	$131,365
Other	5,564	4,851
Total Operating Revenues	155,521	136,216
Operating Expenses:		
Personal Services	20,761	21,301
Supplies and Materials	8,231	8,151
Contractual Services	61,717	60,085
Depreciation	19,771	20,564
Total Operating Expenses	110,480	110,101
Operating Income	45,041	26,115
Nonoperating Revenues (Expenses):		
Interest Income	9,192	7,562
Interest and Service Charges	(16,797)	(15,330)
Other Revenue	745	717
Total Nonoperating Expenses	(6,860)	(7,051)
Income before Operating Transfers	38,181	19,064
Operating Transfers-In	134	134
Operating Transfers-Out	(3,705)	0
Total Operating Transfers-In (Out)	(3,571)	134
Net Income	34,610	19,198
Depreciation Related to Property, Plant and Equipment Acquired through Contributions from Federal Government	1,478	1,765
Increase in Retained Earnings	36,088	20,963
Retained Earnings, Beginning of Year, as Previously Reported	346,363	325,400
Restatements:		
Prior Years' Recalculation of Depreciation	20,253	0
Retained Earnings, Beginning of Year, as Restated	366,616	325,400
Retained Earnings, End of Year	$402,704	$346,363

Government enterprises are disciplined by the marketplace rather than by their budgets. Both their revenues and expenses, unlike those of governmental funds, are determined by "customer" demand, not by legislative fiat. Principles of sound management dictate that governments, like businesses, prepare annual budgets. However, the budgets of proprietary funds play a decidedly different role than those of

THE NEED FOR PROPRIETARY FUNDS BUDGETS

governmental funds. Like those of businesses, they facilitate planning, control, and evaluation. They are not, however, the equivalent of either spending authorizations or tax levies. Accordingly, governments neither have to get formal legislative approval for their proprietary fund budgets nor incorporate them into their accounting systems. Moreover, in their annual reports they need not compare the budgeted amount with actual results.

Governments, like businesses, should ordinarily prepare several different types of budgets. For example, they should formulate:

- a cash budget to facilitate cash management and help assure that they will have adequate, but not excessive, cash on hand
- a capital budget to plan the acquisition of fixed assets
- a flexible budget, indicating anticipated fixed and variable costs at different levels of output, to help control costs

WHAT ACCOUNTING ISSUES ARE UNIQUE TO ENTERPRISE FUNDS OF GOVERNMENTS?

Although governments have adopted the business accounting model to account for their proprietary funds, they nevertheless face several unique issues. Three such issues pertain to capital contributions, restricted assets, and landfills.

CAPITAL CONTRIBUTIONS

The equity section of an enterprise fund's balance sheet looks very much like that of a corporation in that it distinguishes contributed capital from retained earnings. It does not, however, report stockholders' equity, because government enterprises do not generally have stockholders. The entry to record a capital contribution is straightforward.

Suppose, for example, a government transferred $10 million from its general fund to its utility fund, either to make an initial or supplementary capital contribution. In its general fund the government would report the transfer-out as a residual equity transfer:

Residual equity transfer-out (contribution to utility fund)	$10	
Cash		$10

To record a capital transfer to the utility fund

In its utility fund it would recognize the transfer as an addition to contributed capital:

Cash	$10	
Contributed capital—general fund		$10

To record a capital contribution from the general fund (The credit could also have been made to "residual equity transfer-in," in which case the "residual equity transfer-in" would then be closed to "contributed capital.")

Distinguishing Capital Contributions from Other Types of Receipts

Enterprise funds often obtain their capital from both internal (i.e., other funds) and external (e.g., new customers, developers, and other governments) sources. The key accounting issue is how to determine whether a receipt is a capital contribution, an operating transfer, a revenue, or a loan. Consider several examples of different types of nonroutine receipts:

- *Tap (system development) fees.* A city charges new customers of an electric or water utility a tap fee to hook up to an existing system. The amount of the fee may exceed the cost of connecting the customer to the system; part may cover the customer's share of the capital cost of the system already in place.

- *Impact fees.* A municipal utility district charges developers a fee for anticipated improvements, such as new water and sewer lines, that will be required because of new development. Unlike tap fees, these fees cannot necessarily be associated with specific projects or improvements.

- *External subsidies.* A municipal transit authority receives a federal grant both to purchase new buses and to defray operating costs.

- *Internal subsidies.* A county hospital receives an annual transfer from the county's general fund based on the number of indigent patients that it serves. The transfer enables the hospital both to cover operating expenses and to acquire new equipment.

- *Debt forgiveness.* A state provides a loan to its state-operated liquor stores. The stores have historically been unprofitable and there is little possibility of the loan ever being repaid.

Although the GASB has considered the issue of how enterprise funds should distinguish between capital contributions and other inflows of resources, it has not yet resolved it. In the absence of authoritative standards, practice is diverse. Some governments, for example, report tap fees and impact fees as revenues; others as contributions to capital. Similarly, some governments report grants to acquire fixed assets as capital grants; others as revenues or operating transfers. Current GASB standards dictate only that grants "received for proprietary fund operating purposes, or ones which may be utilized for either operations or capital expenditures at the discretion of the recipient government should be recognized as 'nonoperating' revenues," and that "such resources restricted for the acquisition or construction of capital assets should be recorded as contributed equity."[2]

The Government Finance Officers Association (GFOA) provides additional guidance as to tap fees. It advises that the portion of tap fees equal to connection costs actually incurred be reported as contributed capital and the balance be recognized as nonoperating revenue. By contrast, it states, it is acceptable to account for impact fees as either capital contributions or nonoperating revenue.[3]

EXAMPLE *Capital Contributions*

A utility charges a developer $3,000 to hook into a water line. The actual cost to the utility of the connection is only $1,200. The following entries would be appropriate:

Fixed assets (e.g., pipelines) and/or operating expenses	$1,200	
Accounts payable		$1,200
To record the cost of connecting a customer to a water line		

---

[2] GASB *Codification*, Section G60.110

[3] *Governmental Accounting, Auditing and Financial Reporting* (Chicago: Government Finance Officers Association, 1994), p.131.

Accounts receivable	$3,000	
Contributed capital—developers		$1,200
Nonoperating revenues—tap fees		1,800
To record the billings for a tap fee		

Contributed Capital and Depreciation

Governments depreciate their fixed assets in the same manner as do businesses—a debit to depreciation expense and a credit to accumulated depreciation. The GASB, however, allows governments an unusual option. If a government has acquired fixed assets from capital grants restricted to the acquisition of fixed assets (usually received from higher-level governments), then instead of closing the depreciation expense to retained earnings, it may close it to contributed capital. The rationale is that if the assets acquired with the capital are being dissipated, then so also should the offsetting capital. By reducing reported capital rather than retained earnings, the government would more clearly indicate whether it is maintaining the capital contributed by grantors.

Even if the government elects to close depreciation expense to contributed capital, according to the GASB, it must nevertheless include the depreciation among its expenses. Then, however, in reconciling beginning- and end-of-year retained earnings, it would "add back" the depreciation that had been incorporated in earnings.[4]

EXAMPLE *Depreciation of Assets Acquired with Contributed Capital*

A utility reported:

- $14 million of revenues
- $2 million in operating transfers-in
- $8 million in expenses other than depreciation
- $4 million in depreciation, of which $1 million was on assets acquired with capital grants that had been recorded as an increase in capital
- $8 million in beginning-of-year retained earnings
- $7 million in beginning-of-year contributed capital from grants (the initial balance of which was $10 million, prior to reduction of $3 million relating to depreciation)
- $9 million in contributed capital from other sources

The utility would make the usual entries to record all revenues and expenses including depreciation. Thus, to record depreciation:

Depreciation expense	$4	
Accumulated depreciation		$4
To record depreciation expense		

---

[4] GASB *Codification*, Section G60.116.

At year-end it would make the following entry to close the depreciation account:

Retained earnings	$3	
Contributed capital	1	
Depreciation expense		$4

To close depreciation expense, $1 million of which is on assets acquired with capital contributions

On its year-end statement of revenues, expenses, and changes in retained earnings (in abbreviated form) it would report the depreciation and the depreciation add-back as follows:

Revenues	$14
Expenses Other Than Depreciation	8
Depreciation Expense	4
Total Expenses	$12
Income Before Operating Transfers	2
Operating Transfers-in	2
Net Income	$ 4
Add: Depreciation on Fixed Assets Acquired With Capital Grants	1
Increase in Retained Earnings	5
Retained Earnings, Beginning of Year	$ 8
Retained Earnings, End of Year	$13

At year-end it would report fund equity on its balance sheet as follows:

Contributed Capital		
Capital Grants	$10	
Less: Amortization	(4)	$ 6
Other Sources		9
Total Contributed Capital		$15
Retained Earnings		13
Total Fund Equity		$28.

The depreciation add-back option is favored by some government officials in that it may enable them to avoid having to report a retained earnings deficit. It is looked upon with decided disfavor by accounting theoreticians, as it promotes the misguided notion that specific assets can be associated with specific liability and equity accounts.

POSSIBLE DIFFERENCES UNDER ENTITY-WIDE (FULL ACCRUAL) STATEMENTS

As indicated in Chapter 8, the GASB has proposed replacing the current equity section of the balance sheet, now divided between contributed capital and retained earnings, with one that categorizes net assets into three categories: capital, restricted, and unrestricted. As part of the change, *all* resource inflows would be reported initially on the operating statement and subsequently closed to one of the three net asset accounts. No inflows, whether they be direct contributions from other funds or tap or impact fees from developers, would be reported as direct additions to a contributed capital account. Similarly, depreciation expense could no longer be closed to contributed capital.

RESTRICTED ASSETS

Government enterprises are, in key respects, reporting entities within reporting entities. Although accounted for in a single fund, they issue debt and are responsible for servicing it. Accordingly, some of their resources, like those of their parent governments, may be restricted. For example:

- Bond proceeds may have to be used for the construction or acquisition of specific assets.
- Resources may have to be set aside for the repayment of bond principal or the payment of interest.
- Customer deposits may have to be segregated from other resources to assure that they are available for return.

To indicate that assets are restricted, governments may (but are not required to) report their restricted enterprise-fund assets in a separate section of the balance sheet. Since these assets are mainly financial assets, such as cash and investments—the same type as would be accounted for in a capital projects fund or debt service fund—they are usually shown between the unrestricted current assets and the long-lived assets.

To further highlight the restrictions on the assets, governments may also reserve a portion of retained earnings (as they reserve a portion of fund balance in governmental funds for inventories or encumbrances). They should not, however, reserve retained earnings for assets that are already offset by a liability, such as bonds payable. Suppose, for example, a government issues bonds, the cash proceeds of which are restricted for the construction of a specific project. The bonds would be recorded as a payable, representing a claim against the cash received. There is no need for an additional claim (a reserve) against the same assets.

EXAMPLE   *Revenue Bonds as Restricted Assets*

A government issues $10 million in revenue bonds that are restricted for the construction of plant and equipment. The following entry would be appropriate:

Restricted assets—revenue bond construction account	$10	
Revenue bonds payable		$10

To record the issuance of revenue bonds

Subsequently, the government sets aside $2 million cash to repay the revenue bonds:

Restricted assets—revenue bond debt service account	$2	
Cash		$2

To record the designation of cash as restricted

At the same time, it reserves an appropriate portion of retained earnings to indicate that the assets restricted for repayment of debt are not available for expenditure or other purposes.

Retained earnings	$2	
Retained earnings—restricted for repayment of revenue bonds		$2

To reserve a portion of retained earnings to reflect resources restricted for repayment of debt.

LANDFILL COSTS

One of the most pressing economic and political issues of the foreseeable future will be how to maintain—and pay for—a clean environment. Both governments and private industry will face billions of dollars of costs to dispose of wastes, to prevent additional pollution, and to clean up messes that have been made in the past. Because the magnitude of the costs is so large, and the timing, specific amounts and distribution of cash outlays are so uncertain, the associated accounting issues are necessarily complex. So far, the GASB has addressed only one aspect of the issues—accounting for landfill costs.[5]

Governments account for landfills in either governmental or enterprise funds, depending mainly on whether they charge usage fees. Since most governments do charge usage fees, they are generally accounted for in enterprise funds. The GASB standards to be discussed are equally applicable to both enterprise and governmental funds with regard to the calculation of the *amount* of the landfill liability to be reported. But, inasmuch as the two types of funds differ in their measurement focus and basis of accounting, they differ as to *where* the liability should be reported and *when* the related expenditure must be charged.

Landfills provide benefits over the period that they accept waste, often thirty or forty years. However, both state and federal regulations make landfill operators responsible for properly closing their landfills and subsequently caring for and monitoring them. Therefore, an operator must incur sizable costs when it closes the landfill and for an extended period, as long as twenty years, thereafter.

The accounting problems pertaining to closure and postclosure costs are comparable to those of pensions. The benefits are received over the years when the landfill accepts the waste (or, in the case of pensions, when employees provide their services). Although some costs may be incurred prior to the point of closure, most are incurred in the years of closure (retirement) and beyond. Moreover, the actual costs to be incurred are subject to unpredictable factors.

Current Standards

Consistent with the pension accounting principles in both industry and government, the GASB has directed that proprietary funds allocate closure and postclosure costs to the years in which the landfill accepts its waste rather than when they are paid. Therefore, in each year of a landfill's useful life, the government should recognize as both an expense and an increase in a liability an appropriate portion of the estimated total costs for closure and postclosure care.

Total costs would include:

- cost of equipment expected to be installed and facilities expected to be constructed near or after the date that the landfill stops accepting waste (e.g., gas monitoring and collection systems, storm water management systems, ground water monitoring wells, etc.)
- cost of final cover
- cost of monitoring and maintaining the landfill during the postclosure period

The amount to be added to a liability account at the end of each year would be based on the percentage of the landfill actually used up to that point. It would equal the percentage of the landfill used during the year times the total estimated costs. At any point during the life of the landfill, the balance in the liability account would equal the sum of the yearly amounts added to the account less any costs incurred.

---

[5] GASB *Codification*, Section L10.

From a slightly different perspective, the amount to be added to a liability each year—and to be charged as the expense for that year—would be the total amount that should have been recognized as an expense (added to the liability) up to the date of computation, less the amount that has actually been recognized so far. Thus, the amount to be added each year (the current year expense) equals:

$$\frac{\text{Estimated total cost} \times \text{landfill capacity used to date}}{\text{Total landfill capacity}} - \text{Amounts recognized in the past}$$

Both costs and capacity would be based on *current* conditions at the time of the computation. Each year, however, the government would reestimate both the total landfill capacity and the total closure and postclosure costs, thus taking into account inflation, new regulatory requirements, and technological improvements since the previous computation.

The GASB does *not* deal with the issue of when governments should *finance* closure and postclosure costs. Therefore, a government does not necessarily have to "fund" the costs during the landfill's useful life; it merely has to report both an expense and a liability for them. Moreover, in contrast to the manner in which it would compute its pension liability, it need not explicitly take into account the time value of money in making any of its calculations.

The example that follows illustrates how a government would account for a landfill in an enterprise fund. If it accounted for the landfill in a governmental fund, only the journal entries, not the total liability or the amount to be added each year would differ. Inasmuch as governmental funds do not report long-term obligations, the liability for the closure and postclosure costs would be reported only in the general long-term debt account group, not the fund itself. Correspondingly, the governmental fund would not report an annual expenditure for the amount added to the liability account. As with other long-term obligations, a fund expenditure would be charged only in the period that the liability is to be liquidated with currently available financial resources. The result, therefore, is that with respect to the expenditure, the government is on a "pay-as-you-go" basis.

EXAMPLE   *Landfill Costs in an Enterprise Fund*

At the start of year 1, a government opens a landfill, which it elects to account for in an enterprise fund. It estimates that total capacity will be 4.5 million cubic feet, that the site will be used for thirty years, and that total closure costs will be $18 million.

Year 1

During year 1 the government uses 90,000 cubic feet of the landfill. At year-end, it estimates that total capacity will still be 4.5 million cubic feet but that closure related costs will now be $18,036,000. The required expense addition to the liability would be computed as follows:

Total estimated costs	$18,036,000
Proportion of landfill used (90,000/4,500,000)	.02
Required expense (addition to liability)	$ 360,720

Journal Entry

Landfill expense	$360,720	
Liability for landfill costs		$360,720

To record the landfill liability and expense for year 1

The end-of-year balance in the liability account would be $360,720.

Year 2

In year 2, the government uses 120,000 cubic feet of the landfill. At year-end, it estimates that total closure-related costs have increased to $18,526,600 and that landfill capacity has decreased to 4,275,000 cubic feet. Thus:

Total Estimated Costs	$18,526,600
Proportion of Landfill Used to Date	
(90,000 + 120,000)/4,275,000	.049122
Amount That Should Have Been Added to the	
Liability to Date (Cumulative Expense)	910,079
Less: Amount Recognized Previously	360,720
Required Expense (Addition to Liability)	$ 549,359

Journal Entry

Landfill expense	$549,359	
Liability for landfill costs		$549,359

To record the landfill liability and expense for year 2

The end-of-year balance in the liability account would be
$360,720 + $549,359 = $910,079.

Year 3

In year 3, the government uses 135,000 cubic feet of the landfill. At year-end, it estimates that total closure-related costs have increased to $18,840,254 and that landfill capacity has remained at 4,275,000 cubic feet. During the year the government also spends $277,221 on closure-related costs.

Total Estimated Costs	$18,840,254
Proportion of Landfill Used to Date	
(90,000 + 120,000 + 135,000)/4,275,000	.080700
Amount That Should Have Been Added to the	
Liability to Date (Cumulative Expense)	1,520,442
Less: Amount Recognized Previously	910,079
Required Expense (Addition to Liability)	$ 610,363

Journal Entry

Landfill Expense	$610,363	
Liability for landfill costs		$610,363

To record the landfill liability and expense for year 3

As the government actually incurs the closure-related costs of $277,221, it would record the payment as follows:

Liability for landfill costs	$277,221	
Cash		$277,221

To record the payment of closure or postclosure costs

It would not matter if these costs were incurred for the acquisition of fixed assets (e.g., earth-moving equipment) or for operating purposes (e.g., salaries). When the government incurs the costs, it reduces the previously established liability. It does *not* record as capital assets the equipment and facilities included in the estimate of closure-related costs. The end-of-year balance in the liability account would be $360,720 + $549,359 + $610,363 − $277,221 = $1,243,221.

WHAT ARE INTERNAL SERVICE FUNDS AND HOW ARE THEY ACCOUNTED FOR?

Recall that internal service funds are used to account for governmental units or departments that provide goods or services to other departments or agencies on a cost reimbursement basis. Like other funds, they are *accounting* rather than organizational entities. Most commonly the accounting entities correspond to related organizational units, such as data processing or vehicle repair centers. Sometimes, however, an internal service fund may be established to account for an activity for which there is no parallel organizational unit. For example, an internal service fund may be used to account for "self-insurance," which may be administered by a finance or accounting department.

REASONS FOR ESTABLISHING

Internal service funds are intended to promote efficiency in the acquisition, distribution, and use of goods and services. The department providing the goods or services is, in effect, a profit center. Therefore, it is expected to keep its costs in line with its revenues and to satisfy the requirements of its "customers." At the same time, the customers are charged for the goods or services that they receive and thereby have incentives to demand only what they can optimally use. In addition, internal service funds are a means of allocating the costs of functions and activities to the departments that are the ultimate beneficiaries.

Internal service funds, like enterprise funds, may be established at the discretion of each individual government. Current guidance permits governments to establish funds, not only when legally required, but also "to achieve sound and expeditious financial administration and reporting."[6] Only rarely are all the resources assigned to internal service funds legally restricted. Therefore, it would usually be as proper for a government to account for them in its general fund or some other governmental fund as in an internal service fund.

Current practice reflects the absence of specific standards for establishing internal service funds, and the range of activities that some governments account for in internal service funds is far-reaching. Examples include:

- supplies stores
- legal, accounting, auditing, and personnel services
- maintenance and janitorial services
- insurance
- fixed asset lasing

WAYS OF ACCOUNTING FOR INTERNAL SERVICE FUNDS

Internal service funds, like enterprise funds, use business-type accounting. Therefore, they follow the FASB model and are subject to the same guidelines and options (i.e., whether or not to adopt either none or all of the post-FASB 1989 pronouncements) as discussed in connection with enterprise funds.

---

[6] GASB *Codification*, Section 1200.107.

Internal service funds derive their revenues from other governmental funds (or, in some circumstances from other governments). Although they may provide services to a large number of different departments, most of their revenues are generally earned from a small number of funds—typically, the general fund and the enterprise funds. Nevertheless, some internal service funds, particularly those established to account for accounting or data processing activities, may provide services to capital projects, debt service, and other restricted governmental funds.

Per the principles of accrual accounting, the revenues of an internal service fund are recognized when earned, not necessarily when cash is received. Thus, internal funds ordinarily recognize revenue as they deliver the goods or services. However, they might also recognize revenue uniformly over time—as would be appropriate for a fund that leases assets or underwrites insurance.

The expenses of internal service funds are the costs incurred to produce the goods and services. These, too, are recognized on a full accrual basis. They thereby include both depreciation on fixed assets and amortization of bond premiums and discounts. Correspondingly, internal service funds account for, and report on their balance sheets, both fixed assets and long-term debt.

Table 10–2 presents the balance sheet and statement of revenues, expenses, and changes in retained earnings of Fort Worth's office services internal service fund, a fund "used to account for the city's mailroom, motor pool, copy machines, print shop

TABLE 10–2
City of Fort Worth Office Services Fund

Comparative Balance Sheets
September 30, 1996 and 1995
(000's omitted)

	1996	1995
Assets:		
Current Assets:		
Cash and Cash Equivalents	$649	$599
Accounts and Other Receivables	6	6
Inventories (at cost)	188	283
Total Current Assets	843	888
Machinery and Equipment (at cost)	606	632
Accumulated Depreciation	(264)	(287)
Net Machinery and Equipment	342	345
Total Assets	$1,185	$1,233
Liabilities and Fund Equity:		
Current Liabilities:		
Accounts Payable	$108	$27
Accrued Compensation	56	54
Current Portion of Obligations under Capital Lease	25	25
Total Current Liabilities	189	106
Obligations under Capital Lease	2	27
Total Liabilities	191	133
Fund Equity:		
Contributions	352	352
Retained Earnings	642	748
Total Fund Equity	994	1,100
Total Liabilities and Fund Equity	$1,185	$1,233

**Comparative Statements of Revenues,
Expenses, and Changes in Retained Earnings
Years Ended September 30, 1996 and 1995
(000's omitted)**

	1996	1995
Operating Revenues:		
Charges for Services	$1,437	$1,551
Operating Expenses:		
Personal Services	515	434
Supplies and Materials	276	211
Contractual Services	531	546
Depreciation	58	60
Total Operating Expenses	1,380	1,251
Operating Income	57	300
Nonoperating Revenues (Expenses):		
Interest Income	35	35
Loss on Sale of Machinery and Equipment	(23)	(3)
Total Nonoperating Revenues	12	32
Income before Operating Transfers	69	332
Operating Transfers Out	(175)	(175)
Net Income (Loss)	(106)	157
Retained Earnings, Beginning of Year	748	591
Retained Earnings, End of Year	$642	$748

and graphics activities." Note that except for some governmental-specific accounts, such as fund equity contributions on the balance sheet and operating transfers-out on the statement of revenues, expenses, and changes in retained earnings, the statements could readily be those of a private service business. Internal service funds, like enterprise funds, are required also to prepare a statement of cash flows, which will be discussed in Chapter 12.

The budgets of internal service funds, like those of enterprise funds, seldom require legislative approval, and are almost never incorporated into the funds' accounting system. Like those of enterprise funds, the revenues and expenditures are driven by customer demand rather than specific legislative action. Moreover, control over the demand may be established by the budgets of the funds receiving the internal service fund's goods or services. Governments should, of course, prepare the same types of budgets (cash, flexible, capital, etc.) as would be expected of any business that provides similar goods or services.

The example that follows highlights the key features of internal service fund accounting.

EXAMPLE *Internal Service Fund Accounting*

Establishment of Fund

A government establishes an internal service fund to account for a new data processing department. It transfers $0.6 million from its general fund to the internal service fund as an initial contribution of capital.

Cash	$0.6	
Capital contribution—general fund		$0.6

To record the capital contribution from the general fund

The general fund would record the contribution as a **residual equity transfer.** (The internal service fund could also have recorded the contribution initially as a residual equity transfer and then closed the transfer account to the capital account.)

Issuing Long-term Debt

The government issues $1.0 million in general obligation bonds to support the new department. It intends to service the debt entirely from the revenues of the data processing fund.

Cash	$1.0	
Bonds payable		$1.0

To record the long-term debt

Even though the bonds are general obligation bonds, they can be recorded in the internal service fund rather than the general long-term debt account group (GLTDAG) as long as the government intends to repay them from the internal service fund. As a consequence, the GLTDAG cannot be relied upon to provide a complete listing of all general obligation debt. Since the government at-large is liable for the debt in the event that resources are unavailable from the internal service fund, the government should disclose its "contingent" liability in notes to the financial statements.

Acquisition of Fixed Assets

The department acquires long-lived assets (buildings, computers, furniture, etc.) for $1.4 million.

Fixed assets (specified in detail)	$1.4	
Cash		$1.4

To record the acquisition of fixed assets

Billings to Other Departments

For services rendered during the year, the department bills the utility fund for $0.3 million, and the police department, the fire department and all other departments accounted for in the general fund for $0.8 million.

Due from general fund	$0.8	
Due from utility fund	0.3	
Operating revenues		$1.1

To record billing to other departments

Correspondingly, the general fund would report an expenditure, and the utility fund an expense, for the amounts billed. The two funds would recognize expenditures or expenses, rather than intra-governmental transfers, since these transactions qualify as *quasi-external* transactions—costs that would be characterized as expenditures or expenses if the services were provided by outside vendors.

Depreciation and Other Expenses

The data processing department incurred $0.2 in depreciation and $0.7 in other operating expenses. In addition, it acquired $0.1 in supplies inventory that remained on hand at year-end.

Depreciation expense	$0.2	
Other operating expenses (specified in detail)	0.7	
Supplies inventory	0.1	
Accounts payable		$.08
Accumulated depreciation		.02

To record depreciation and other expenses

Other transactions, such as those involving purchases of investments, the use of materials and supplies, and accrual of interest, would be accounted for in the same manner as they would in a comparable business.

BASIS FOR ESTABLISHING BILLING RATES

Internal service funds are used to account for goods and services provided to other governmental units on a cost reimbursement basis. This dictum implies that billing rates should be established so as to cover costs. As any student of management accounting can appreciate, however, cost can have several different meanings: full cost; incremental cost; opportunity cost; and direct cost.

In practice, cost has been interpreted to mean full cost. Internal service funds are expected, over time, neither to earn profits nor to incur losses. As a consequence, billing rates should reflect all operating costs, including depreciation, interest, and other indirect costs.

The accumulation of retained earnings surpluses or deficits may suggest that billing rates either exceed or are less than actual costs. However, governments may intentionally establish rates that exceed cost. This enables them to accumulate the resources required either to replace existing assets or to expand the asset base to meet anticipated increases in demand.

Ironically, the practice of establishing billing rates at full cost may subvert a key objective of internal service funds—that the supplying and receiving departments each provides or takes an optimal quantity of goods and services. As illustrated in the accompanying In Practice, full cost prices do not reflect the cost of providing incremental amounts of goods or services. Therefore, they may encourage departments to purchase either more or fewer goods or services than is optimal from the perspective of the government as a whole.

RAMIFICATIONS FOR OTHER FUNDS

The accounting and operating practices of departments accounted for in internal service funds have critical implications not only for the internal service funds themselves but also for the other funds with which they have transactions.

Duplicate Reported Expenses

Costs reported by internal service funds are reported twice within the same set of financial statements. They are reported once by the internal service fund providing the goods and services and a second time by the fund that is billed for them. Correspondingly, revenues are also reported twice: once by the fund receiving them from outside parties (as taxes or fees) and again when earned by the internal service fund. If statement users understand that each of a government's funds is an independent fiscal and accounting entity, these results are not necessarily harmful. But they give special significance to the "memorandum only" warning that appears over the "totals" column of a government's combining statements—a column that overstates both expenses and revenues of the government as a whole.

IN PRACTICE

A city accounts for a vehicle repair unit in an internal service fund and bills departments at full cost. The unit's fixed costs are $80,000 per month; its variable costs are $40 per hour. On average it provides 4,000 hours of service per month. Accordingly, its billing rate is $60 per hour:

FULL COST PRICING MAY ENCOURAGE DYSFUNCTIONAL DECISIONS

Fixed costs per month	$ 80,000
Variable costs (4,000 hours @ $40)	160,000
Total costs per month	$240,000
Number of hours	÷ 4,000
Cost per hour	$ 60

The police department receives a bid of $3,000 from an outside garage to repair one of its vehicles.

The repair service calculates that the job will take sixty hours and therefore submits an estimate to the police department of $3,600 (60 hours @ $60 hours). Since the price is greater than $3,000, the police department accepts the outside bid.

Assuming that the repair service had the necessary capacity to carry out the repairs, its fixed costs would have been unaffected by the job for the police department. It would have incurred only the additional variable costs of $2,400 (60 hours @ $40).

From the perspective of the city as a whole, the police department's decision to use the outside garage was dysfunctional. The city passed up the opportunity to receive $3,000 of incremental benefits in exchange for incremental costs of $2,400.

Transfer of Depreciation to Governmental Funds

Governmental funds do not report fixed assets; they do not charge depreciation. However, insofar as an internal service fund incorporates depreciation expense into its billing rates, the depreciation charge is transferred, along with all other costs, to the funds that it bills.

The impact on reported expenditures of a governmental fund can be telling. Suppose one government accounts for a motor pool in an internal service fund; another in its general fund. The motor pool of each government serves only other departments that are accounted for in the government's general fund. The general fund of the government maintaining the internal service fund will record the cost of the motor pool vehicles over their useful lives (through the depreciation expense incorporated into the billing rates). That of the other government will record the cost as the vehicles are acquired or paid for.

Detract from Objectivity of Financial Statements

An internal service fund should establish its billing rates so it covers its costs. Yet cost is an elusive concept. It depends on estimates (such as useful life of assets), choices among accounting methods (as to expense recognition, depreciation, inventory), and bases of overhead allocation. Although generally accepted accounting principles may establish broad guidelines for cost determination, they leave considerable latitude for individual companies or governments.

Owing to the leeway permitted governments in establishing costs, neither the billing rates nor the total revenues of an internal service fund can be seen as being objective. And if its revenues are not objective, then neither are its excess of revenues over expenses, its retained earnings, nor its net assets.

The inevitable subjectivity of individual internal service fund financial statements might be of only minor concern to statement users if the impact were limited to the internal service fund statements. But it is not. The revenues of an internal service fund are the expenditures and expenses of other funds. Thus, if the revenues of an internal service fund are subjective, then so also are the expenditures of the general fund and all other funds to which the internal service provides goods or services. And if their expenditures are subjective then so too are their annual excess of revenues over expenditures, their fund balances and their net assets.

By controlling billing rates, government officials can fine-tune the reported excess of revenues over expenditures of the general fund—the fund most subject to balanced budget requirements and public scrutiny. For example, faced with pressure to hold down general fund expenditures, a government can delay imposing rate increases that would otherwise be warranted. Or, with an eye to maximizing cost recovery under a state or federal grant, it can increase the internal service fund charges to the programs whose costs are eligible for reimbursement.

Obscure Fund Balance Surpluses or Deficits

By adjusting the billing rates, government officials can transfer surpluses or deficits (i.e., positive or negative fund balances) from the general fund to the internal service fund. These surpluses or deficits might be prohibited if they remained in the general fund. Suppose, for example, government officials see a need to set aside resources for the replacement of long-lived assets or for a rainy day. They recognize, however, that if the general fund were to report a surplus, legislators would seek either to increase spending or to reduce taxes.

The officials could achieve their objective by increasing the billing rates of an internal service fund, thereby transferring resources from the general fund to the internal service fund. The reserve would be maintained in the internal service fund rather than the general fund. To be sure, the reserve would be reflected in the retained earnings of the internal service fund. But the internal service fund may not be as carefully examined as the general fund. Since retained earnings is a conglomeration of undistributed earnings for many years and many purposes, the reserve could readily be obscured.

WHAT SPECIAL PROBLEMS ARE CREATED WHEN AN INTERNAL SERVICE FUND OR THE GENERAL FUND ACCOUNTS FOR "SELF-INSURANCE"?

Many governments, seeking ways to reduce costs, elect to "self-insure" all or a portion of their risks, especially those for less than catastrophic losses. Independent insurance companies set premiums at rates that allow them to cover anticipated claims, administrative costs, and capital costs. For the portion of its policy applicable to routine losses, such as from automobile accidents or worker injuries, an insured entity's premiums are almost always based on the entity's own claims history. Self-insurance may provide an opportunity for the government to reduce the portion of the premium that covers the administrative and capital costs.

GASB permits governments to account for their self-insurance activities in either a general fund or an internal service fund.[7] Irrespective of which is used, the insurance "department" (which may be only an accounting entity rather than an organizational unit) operates as if it were an independent insurance company. It periodically bills other departments for premiums and it pays their claims as losses are incurred.

Self-insurance presents intriguing and controversial issues of accounting. The term **self-insurance** is an oxymoron. The essence of insurance is the transfer of risk to an outsider. When a government self-insures, it retains the risk itself, irrespective of whether it accounts for the activity in an internal service fund or a general fund. Therefore, self-insurance is no insurance.

ACCOUNTING FOR INSURANCE PREMIUMS

The key accounting issues pertain to when, and in what amount, the insured departments should recognize expenditures for premiums paid and the insurance departments recognize revenues for the insurance premiums received.

Suppose a government accounts for its insurance activities in an internal service fund and all the departments that it insures are accounted for in the general fund. The general fund, therefore, pays annual premiums to the internal service fund.

If the general fund paid these premiums to an outside insurance company, the premiums would be recorded as an expenditure. Consistent with the principles that quasi-external transactions be accounted for as expenditures, it might appear that premiums paid to the internal service fund should also be accounted for as an expenditure.

Some accountants point out, however, that payments for self-insurance premiums are different than other types of charges from internal service funds. The general fund does not actually transfer risk to the internal service fund. Except for the portion of the premiums that cover losses actually incurred, it simply sets aside funds to provide for possible losses in the future. In that regard the transaction is comparable to a transfer of resources to a debt service fund for the future repayment of bonds. Therefore, the accountants contend, only the portion of the premium that covers actual losses should be reported as an expenditure in the general fund. The excess should be accounted for as an operating transfer. Correspondingly, only the portion of the premium that represents a reimbursement for actual losses should be recognized as a revenue in the internal service fund.

Current Standards

The GASB has held that as long as specified criteria are satisfied, an internal service insurance fund can recognize revenues, and the insured funds (departments) can recognize expenditures, for the full amount of the premiums billed.

An internal service insurance fund, it has ruled, can use any basis to establish its premiums that the government considers appropriate as long as the premiums satisfy either of the following conditions:

- The total charge covers the actual losses incurred by the fund.
- The total charge is based on an actuarial method or historical cost method and adjusted over time so that internal service fund revenues and expenses are approximately equal.

[7]GASB *Codification*, Section C50.

The premiums can also include a provision for expected catastrophe losses.

If the premiums satisfy either of these criteria, then the internal service insurance fund may recognize revenue upon billing the insured funds. Correspondingly, the insured funds may recognize an expenditure. If, however, the premiums exceed the amount that satisfies these criteria, the excess should be reported as an operating transfer from the insured funds to the internal service fund. If they are less, the resultant deficit in the internal service fund should be charged back to the insured funds and reported as an expenditure in those funds.

Consistent with FASB Statement No. 5, *Accounting for Contingencies*, the internal service insurance fund should recognize its expenses for claims expenses and liabilities when:

- It is probable that an asset has been impaired or a liability incurred.
- The amount of loss can be reasonably estimated.

EXAMPLE   *Insurance Premiums*

A government maintains an internal service fund to insure all government vehicles for loss and damage and for liability to third parties. It establishes premiums using actuarial techniques intended to assure that over time the premiums will cover claims, administrative expenses, and catastrophic losses. In a particular year, the internal service fund bills the general fund $260,000 and the utility fund $130,000—a total of $390,000. Of this amount $25,000 is for potential catastrophes. During the year it incurs $360,000 in claims losses, none of which resulted from catastrophes.

The internal service fund would recognize as revenues the entire $390,000 in premiums:

Cash	$390,000	
Revenues—insurance premiums		$390,000
To record premium revenue		

At the same time, the general fund would recognize an expenditure of $260,000 and the utility fund an expense of $130,000.

The internal service fund would also recognize claims expenses for the actual $360,000 of losses:

Expenses—claims	$360,000	
Claims liability (or cash)		$360,000
To record losses incurred		

As a consequence of closing the revenue and expense accounts at year-end, retained earnings will increase by $30,000. Of this sum, $25,000 is attributable to the premiums for the potential catastrophes. GASB standards direct that this amount should be designated in the notes to the statements as intended for catastrophes.

ACCOUNTING FOR SELF-INSURANCE IN A GENERAL FUND

Although this chapter is directed toward proprietary funds, this section digresses to contrast how self-insurance activities would be accounted for in a general fund rather than an internal service fund.

Current Standards

The GASB stipulates that when self-insurance activities are accounted for in a general fund, the amount of premium revenue recognized by the general fund should be limited to actual claims expenditures (i.e., those losses that satisfy the criteria of FASB Statement No. 5.) Correspondingly, total expenditures and expenses recognized by the general fund and any other insured funds should be limited to the same amounts. Any amounts charged to the other funds (including the general fund itself) in excess of the actual claims should be accounted for as operating transfers. The differences in accounting principles are justified according to the GASB, because the general fund neither transfers risk nor actual resources to either an outside party or to a separate fund.

EXAMPLE *Self-Insurance in a General Fund*

Assume the same facts as in the previous example except that the insurance activities are accounted for in the general fund. The insurance "department" bills other general fund departments for $260,000 in premiums and the utility fund for $130,000, a total of $390,000. As before, the government incurs only $360,000 in actual claims.

The general fund would recognize the claims, as would an internal service fund (except that the general fund would report the claims as an expenditure rather than an expense):

Expenditure—claims	$360,000	
Claims liability (or cash)		$360,000
To record losses incurred		

However, the maximum that the insurance department could recognize as premium revenues from the other departments would now be $360,000—the amount of the actual claims. Of this, one-third ($130,000/$390,000), or $120,000, would be attributable to the utility fund and two-thirds ($260,000/$390,000), or $240,000, to the other general fund departments. The $10,000 that the utility fund paid above its share of the allowable premium revenue would be reported as an interfund transfer. Thus, the general fund would record the billings to the utility fund as follows:

Cash	$130,000	
Revenues—insurance premiums		$120,000
Operating transfer-in (from utility fund)		10,000
To record premiums collected from utility fund		

The utility fund would recognize a premium expense of $120,000 and an operating transfer-out of $10,000.

Although the insurance department would also record the billings to the other departments accounted for in the general fund, the entries are not shown here. Because the insurance department is also accounted for in the general fund, there would be no impact on the financial statements. Intrafund revenues and expenditures would net out.

WHAT DO USERS WANT TO KNOW ABOUT REVENUE DEBT?

In the previous chapter we highlighted the main types of ratios and other data that investors and other statement users look to in assessing a government's ability to repay its general obligation debt. In this section we do the same as to revenue debt.

Revenue bonds encompass the debt that will be paid from a dedicated revenue stream produced by the assets that the debt financed. These assets typically include utilities, convention centers, stadiums, parking facilities, and similar fee-generating projects. Revenue bonds also incorporate the debt of most not-for-profits, including health care organizations, universities, and museums.

In light of the vast array of entities that issue revenue bonds, it is difficult to generalize as to the data needed by users. The salient fiscal characteristics of a private nursing home, for example, may differ considerably from those of a private university. Nevertheless, some types of information are central to the evaluation of any revenue-backed security. Among the types identified by Standard & Poor's, a leading bond rating service, are the following:[8]

- *Security Provisions.* Revenue bonds are secured by specific fees or taxes. These may include user charges (such as highway tolls, college tuition, and hospital billings) or dedicated taxes (such as a sales tax restricted for debt service or a gasoline tax restricted for highway improvements).

- *Competition.* Revenue bonds, unlike general obligation bonds, are often used to support activities that are competitive. For example, hospitals, universities, airports, parking garages, and museums compete with other public and private institutions that provide similar services. Whereas, the general obligation (GO) bonds are backed by the full faith and credit of the government—and thus by its power to tax—revenues bonds are backed only by specified revenues. Competition introduces a credit risk not normally associated with GO bonds.

- *Service area.* Projects financed by revenue bonds do not necessarily serve areas that are within predetermined geographic boundaries. For example, a university may attract students from throughout the world. A hospital may compete statewide for patients. The broader the geographic base of a revenue stream, the less likely it is to be affected by local economic downturns.

- *Revenue-raising flexibility.* Some user charges can be raised more easily than others. For example, a city may be constitutionally prohibited from increasing a restricted sales tax, whereas a hospital may have considerable flexibility in increasing patient charges. The greater the revenue-raising flexibility, the less the credit risk.

The specific information depends, of course, on the nature of the institution. Table 10–3 outlines the factors that Standard & Poor's deems important in evaluating private colleges and universities. The list is especially notable for the prominence of nonfinancial factors. It shows that even to assess the ability of the bond issuer to service its debt—the primary concern of a rating service—users must look beyond conventional financial statements. Table 10–4 summarizes the key factors that Standard and Poor's focuses on in evaluating the revenue bonds of not-for-profit health care organizations.

---

[8] The information requirements presented in this section were drawn from *Municipal Finance Criteria* (New York: Standard & Poor's Rating Group, 1994).

TABLE 10–3
Factors Focused on by Standard & Poor's in Evaluating the Revenue Bonds of Private Colleges and Universities

I. Student demand

    A. Enrollment trends, including the reasons for upward or downward cycles

    B. Flexibility in admissions and programs

        1. The acceptance rate (a college that accepts almost all applicants is more vulnerable to a decline in demand than one that is highly selective and admits only a small percentage)

        2. Geographic diversity (the wider the geographic diversity, the less likely that an economic downturn will affect enrollment)

        3. Student quality (strong student quality, as measured by class rank, standardized test scores and other factors, enhances a school's ability to withstand a decline in enrollment)

        4. Faculty (the higher the percentage of tenured faculty, the less likely that the university's program offerings can change to reflect current demand)

        5. Program offerings (the more specialized the programs, the greater the risk of an enrollment decline owing to changes in the work force)

        6. Competition (schools that are the first choice of its students are less threatened by widespread enrollment declines than those that are their second or third selections)

        7. Attrition (high attrition may be a sign of student dissatisfaction and a precursor to declining demand)

II. Finances

    A. Revenues

        1. Diversification (a diverse revenue base, in which a substantial portion of revenue is from grants, endowment income, dormitories and sources in addition to tuition, tends to mitigate shortfalls in any single revenue stream)

        2. Ability to raise revenues through tuition adjustments (low rates in comparison with competitors indicates room for increases)

    B. Expenditures

        1. Ability to reduce expenditures (a high ratio of fixed to variable costs limits flexibility)

        2. Amounts being retained to build up plant and endowment (large amounts of resources being transferred to plant and endowment funds signify the availability resources that could be redirected to debt service)

    C. Operating results (modest surpluses convey that revenues are sufficient to meet expenditures, but one- or two-year deficits are not necessarily a problem)

    D. Endowment

        1. Comparison with debt level

        2. Amount per student

        3. Proportion that is unrestricted (the greater the proportion, the greater the flexibility)

    E. Debt (a ratio of maximum annual debt service to unrestricted current fund expenditures greater than 10 percent generally indicates an excessive debt burden)

III. Management

    A. Ability to foresee and plan for potential challenges

    B. Strategies and policies that appear realistic and attainable

    C. A track record indicative of an ability to deal with new situations and problems

    D. A history of management continuity

IV. Legal provisions

    A. Security pledges (debt secured by enterprise revenues, such as dormitory rentals, is seen as weaker than that backed by general revenues or tuition revenues)

(continued)

B.   Covenants (provisions requiring the institution to set certain rates and fees at specified levels may enhance the security of the bonds)

C.   Debt service reserve policies (the existence of reserve funds enhances the security of the bonds, especially those that are backed strictly by enterprise revenues)

D.   Credit enhancements such as loan guarantees or bond insurance

Source: Drawn from *Municipal Finance Criteria (New York: Standard & Poor's* 1996), pp. 94–97.

TABLE 10-4
Factors Focused on by Standard & Poor's in Evaluating the Revenue Bonds of Health Care Organizations

I.   Demand and service area characteristics
A.   Trends in volume, such as number of outpatient procedures, number of inpatient and outpatient surgeries, and observation days
B.   Utilization rates
C.   Demographic factors, including age distribution
D.   Economic factors, such as unemployment rates and local wealth levels

II.   Institutional characteristics and competitive profile
A.   Size, age, and level of board certification of medical staff
B.   Ability to attract and retain new doctors
C.   Relationships with physicians groups that may provide financial incentives for doctors to remain loyal to the organization

III.   Management and administrative factors
A.   Depth and experience of management team and ability to deal effectively with hospital staff, to promote sound budgeting, to control financial and personnel resources, and to provide strong leadership.
B.   The strength of management information systems

IV.   Financial factors
A.   Trends in revenue growth and profitability
B.   Financial flexibility as indicated by the ratio of fixed to variable costs
C.   Market position
D.   Costs in comparison with competitors
E.   Strength of income statement as indicated by operating margins, debt service coverage, and debt burden
F.   Strength of balance sheet as indicated by days' cash on hand, cash flow to total debt ratio, and debt to capitalization ratio

Source: Drawn from *Municipal Financial Criteria (New York: Standard & Poor's,* 1996), pp. 76–79

SUMMARY

Governments account for and report business-type activities in proprietary funds. Activities carried out with outside parties are accounted for in enterprise funds; those with other departments within the government or with other governments are accounted for in internal service funds.

Not-for-profits, like governments, often maintain separate funds for their business-type activities. Unlike governments, however, for purposes of external reporting they combine them with their other activities, since generally the assets associated with their business-type activities are not donor restricted.

Both governments and not-for-profits account for their business-type activities using business-type accounting. They apply a full accrual, all economic resources model.

Governments and not-for-profits engage in business-type activities for many reasons. For example, the activities provide resources that otherwise would have to be raised through taxes or contributions and they complement and support their main mission.

Current standards do not establish clear boundaries between government and business-type activities. Therefore, governments have considerable discretion in determining which of their activities may be accounted for in enterprise funds, and considerable diversity exists among governments.

Moreover, current standards do not yet address issues unique to governments' business-type activities. For example, they are silent as to how capital contributions should be distinguished from other inflows of resources or how restricted enterprise-fund assets should be reported on the balance sheet. As a consequence, current practice is not uniform.

Current standards do, however, specify how governments should account for landfills. Landfills may be accounted for in either governmental funds or enterprise funds, depending on whether the government charges usage fees. Irrespective of fund, however, governments must report a liability for the estimated costs of closing and monitoring a landfill when it will be taken out of service. The amount of the liability should be based on the proportionate share of the landfill used to date.

Internal service funds are established to promote efficiency in the acquisition, distribution, and use of goods and services. Like enterprise funds, they use the full accrual method of accounting. Internal service funds bill the funds to which they provide services at rates intended to cover their costs. However, in the absence of standards as to how the costs should be calculated, governments have considerable flexibility in establishing those rates.

By their very nature, internal service funds affect the other funds with which they have transactions. The consequences of accounting for activities in internal service funds rather than governmental funds are that revenues and expenditures are counted twice within the same set of financial statements, depreciation charges are incorporated in the expenditures of the funds billed, and surpluses and deficits can be transferred from the funds billed to the internal service funds.

Many government accounts maintain internal service funds to account for self-insurance. Self-insurance, however, does not result in a transfer of risk to outsiders. Therefore, the GASB has established standards as to the policies by which governments can determine the premium revenue to be recognized by self-insurance funds and the expenditures to be charged by the funds that they insure.

Government business-type activities are often supported by revenue bonds, which are backed by specific revenue streams such as dedicated taxes or user charges. The ability of the issuer to maintain these streams can seldom be evaluated by focusing exclusively on factors reported in the financial statements. Users must look to the entire range of elements that affect the entity's operating environment.

EXERCISE FOR REVIEW AND SELF-STUDY

The balance sheet and statement of operations of the Lower Colorado River Authority (LCRA), one of the nation's largest government owned utilities is presented on pages 430 to 431. The authority uses proprietary fund accounting.

a. On what basis of accounting (i.e., cash, accrual, modified accrual) are the statements prepared? How can you tell?

b. Is it necessary for the LCRA to adopt a budget comparable to that of a governmental fund and to incorporate it into its accounting system by making annual budgetary entries?

c. As do many private utilities, the LCRA reports both its assets and equities in reverse order from a typical government or private corporation. What might be a possible explanation?

d. A note to the statements states that "the LCRA's Bond Resolutions require separate funds to be established for designated purposes." How are these funds reported?

e. What is the significance of the accounts "unamortized net losses on refunded debt," and "unamortized gains on refunded debt?" Would you expect to see a comparable accounts on the balance sheet of a private utility? (Refer to the discussion on debt refunding in Chapter 7.)

f. In reconciling beginning- and end-of-year "capital derived from earnings," (in the capitalization section of the balance sheet), the LCRA adds to the beginning balance "Current depreciation on utility plant acquired or constructed with contributions." What is the significance of this amount? What entry did the LCRA make to record its total depreciation expense? What entry did it make to close the depreciation account?

g. According to a note to the financial statements:

Due to regulation of its rates by its Board and to a lesser extent by the State Utility Commission, the LCRA is subject to the requirements of FASB Statement No. 71, Accounting for the Effects of Certain Types of Regulation. Accordingly, certain costs may be capitalized as a regulatory asset that would otherwise be charged to expense. A regulatory asset is recorded when it is probable that future revenue in an amount at least equal to the capitalized costs will result from inclusion of those costs in future rates. . . . Any regulatory asset is amortized over the life of LCRA's outstanding long-term debt.

How are the regulatory asset and subsequent amortization reflected on the balance sheet; on the statement of operations?

h. What percent of the LCRA's "Total Capitalization and Liabilities" has been (a) contributed from governments or other parties; (b) derived from earnings; (c) borrowed in the form of long-term debt?

i. Suppose that the LCRA were to charge a major industrial customer $200,000 to hook into its power distribution system. The actual costs to the LCRA of the connection were only $150,000. How should the receipt of the $200,000 be accounted for?

Lower Colorado River Authority

Balance Sheet

	June 30,	
	1996	**1995**
Assets:		
Property, Plant & Equipment		
Utility Plant in Service		
Electric	$ 1,523,021	$ 1,461,017
Water and Wastewater	31,163	25,585
	1,554,184	1,486,602
Accumulated Depreciation	(505,470)	(460,715)
	1,048,714	1,025,887
Construction Work in Progress	29,333	43,807
Oil and Gas Property, Net	30,365	39,619
Utility Plant, Net	1,108,412	1,109,313
Other Physical Property, Net	15,132	8,647
Total Property, Plant & Equipment	$ 1,123,544	$ 1,117,960
Cash & Investments in Restricted Funds (Includes Cash and Cash Equivalents of $38,114 and $54,645)		
General Improvement and Construction Funds	16,890	11,931
Debt Service Funds	160,469	159,246
Contingency and Other Restricted Funds	9,066	8,929
Net Amount Due to Revenue Fund	(13,417)	(4,216)
Total Cash & Investments in Restricted Funds	$ 173,008	$ 175,890
Current Assets		
Cash & Investments in Revenue Fund (Includes Cash and Cash Equivalents of $42,684 and $21,141)	55,805	32,067
Accrued Interest Receivable	2,558	1,711
Net Amount Due from Restricted Funds	13,417	4,216
Total Cash & Investments in Revenue Fund	$ 71,780	$ 37,994
Account Receivable (Net of Allowance for Doubtful Accounts of $576 and $561)	53,899	41,590
Inventories		
Fuel	36,768	40,256
Material and Supplies	23,295	22,531
Other	13,873	14,220
Total Current Assets	$ 199,615	$ 156,591
Deferred Charges		
Costs to be Recovered from Future Revenues	155,665	174,683
Contract Extension Settlement with Major Customers	15,877	16,652
Unamortized Debt Expense	16,413	16,474
Other Deferred Charges	34,935	33,468
Total Deferred Charges	$ 222,890	$ 241,277
Total Assets	$ 1,719,057	$ 1,691,718
Capitalization and Liabilities:		
Capitalization		
Capital derived from earnings		
Balance, beginning of year	$ 425,798	$ 393,871
Net income for the year	28,574	31,524
Current depreciation on utility plant acquired or constructed with contributions	403	403
Balance, end of year	$ 454,775	$ 425,798
Contributed capital	10,944	11,347
Unrealized losses on investments	(2,501)	(710)
Total capitalization	$ 463,218	$ 436,435

	June 30,	
	1996	**1995**
Capitalization and		
Liabilities (continued):		
Long-term Debt		
Capital reimbursable		
to U.S. Government	3,621	3,779
Senior, junior and		
subordinate lien		
revenue bonds		
(includes amounts due		
within one year		
of $40,931 and $38,145,		
respectively)	1,208,448	1,142,288
Unamortized net losses		
on refunded debt	(183,218)	(177,804)
Subordinate debt:		
commercial paper	98,000	193,000
Total long-term debt	$ 1,126,851	$ 1,161,263
Liabilities Payable		
from Restricted Funds		
(includes amounts		
due within one year		
of $31,143 and		
$33,904, respectively)	32,304	35,162
Current Liabilities Payable		
from Revenue Fund	54,437	33,260
Deferred Credits and		
Other Long-term		
Liabilities	42,247	25,598
Total Capitalization		
and Liabilities	$ 1,719,057	$ 1,691,718

Lower Colorado River Authority

Statements of Operations

	Year Ended June 30,	
	1996	**1995**
Operating Revenues		
Sales of electricity	$ 407,352	$ 369,617
Water and irrigation	12,709	11,427
Natural gas	8,350	8,574
Other	10,192	7,565
Total operating		
revenues	$ 438,603	$ 397,183
Operating Expenses		
Fuel	143,147	134,723
Purchased power	14,286	3,352
Operation	84,673	79,061
Maintenance	25,299	24,922
Depreciation		
and amortization	60,192	58,440
Total operating		
expenses	$ 327,597	$ 300,498
Operating income	$ 111,006	$ 96,685
Interest and Other		
Income	7,628	15,837
Income before interest		
expense and prior costs		
recovered from revenues	118,634	112,522
Interest Expense	74,534	72,388
Income before prior		
costs recovered		
from revenues	44,100	40,134
Prior Costs Recovered		
from Revenues	(15,526)	(8,610)
Net Income	$ 28,574	$ 31,524

QUESTIONS FOR REVIEW AND DISCUSSION

1. You are the independent CPA for a medium-sized city. The city manager asks your guidance as to whether, according to generally accepted accounting principles, the municipal golf course should be accounted for in an enterprise fund. What would be your response?

2. How would you compare the accounting for enterprise funds with that of (a) businesses and (b) governmental funds? Summarize the reasons both for and against accounting for enterprise funds differently than governmental funds.

3. Business accounting is governed by the pronouncements of the Financial Accounting Standards Board. Enterprise funds are generally accounted for using the accounting principles applicable to businesses. Must, therefore, a government adhere to all pronouncements of the FASB in accounting for its enterprise funds? Explain.

4. When governments charge depreciation in their enterprise funds, they sometimes account for it as a reduction in contributed capital rather than retained

earnings. What is the rationale for this practice? What is an argument against it?

5. A government accounts for a municipal landfill in an enterprise fund. How will it determine how much to charge as an expense (and add to a liability) each year that the landfill is in use? Suppose, instead, that it accounts for the landfill in a governmental fund. What will be the amount charged as an expenditure?

6. For what types of activities are internal service funds used to account? Provide several examples. Is a government *required* to account for the activities you cite in an internal service fund, or may it account for them instead in its general fund?

7. It is sometimes asserted that the absence of specific principles as to what constitutes "cost" detracts from the objectivity of the financial statements not only of internal service funds but also the general fund. In what sense might this be true?

8. "Self-insurance," it is often said, is an oxymoron. Why? If it is, what are the implications as to whether a government should be permitted to recognize self-insurance premiums as a general fund expenditure when paid to an internal service fund?

9. In what way must a government account for premium revenue differently if it accounts for self-insurance in an internal service fund rather than its general fund?

10. You have been given the responsibility of assigning a bond rating to a hospital. Indicate five factors that are unlikely to be reported upon in the hospital's financial statements that you would consider essential to your assessment.

EXERCISES

10-1

Internal service funds are accounted for similarly to businesses.

William County opted to account for its duplication service center in an internal service fund. Previously the center had been accounted for in the county's general fund.

During the first month in which it was accounted for as an internal service fund the center engaged in the following transactions.

1. Five copiers were transferred to the internal service fund from the general fixed assets account group. At the time of transfer they had a fair market value of $70,000.

2. The general fund made an initial cash contribution of $35,000 to the internal service fund.

3. The center borrowed $270,000 from a local bank to finance the purchase of additional equipment and renovation of its facilities. It issued a three-year note.

4. It purchased equipment for $160,000 and paid contractors $100,000 for improvements to its facilities.

5. It billed the county clerk's office $5,000 for printing services, of which the office remitted $2,500.

6. It incurred, and paid in cash, various operating expenses of $9,000.

7. The fund recognized depreciation of $1,500 on its equipment and $900 on the improvements to its facilities.
   a. Prepare journal entries in the internal service fund to record the transactions.
   b. Comment on the main differences resulting from the shift from the general fund to an internal service fund in how the center's assets and liabilities would be accounted for and reported.

10-2

Enterprise funds face unique problems in accounting for restricted assets.

The Louisville City bus system engaged in the following transactions.

1. It issued $10,000,000 in 8 percent revenue bonds to finance the acquisition of new buses. The bonds were issued at par.

2. Consistent with a bond covenant, the system set aside 1 percent of the bonds' gross proceeds for repair contingencies. Correspondingly, it designated an equal dollar amount of retained earnings as reserved for repairs.

3. The bus system accrued nine month's interest ($600,000) at year-end.

4. The bus system incurred $50,000 of repairs costs, paying for them with the cash set aside for repair contingencies.
   a. Prepare appropriate journal entries.
   b. Comment on how assets set aside for repairs, as required by bond covenants, would be accounted for if the bus system were reported in the government's general fund.

10-3

Governments can elect to close depreciation to contributed capital.

Drebinsville accounts for its airport in an enterprise fund. The city recently was awarded a $4 million federal grant to upgrade its airport facilities. It used the funds to acquire navigation and communication equipment, which it estimates has a useful life of five years (with no salvage.)

The city accounts for the grant as a direct contribution to capital and elects to close depreciation to contributed capital. It charges depreciation on a straight-line basis.

a. Prepare journal entries to record the capital contribution, to acquire the equipment, to recognize first-year depreciation, and to close the depreciation expense at year-end.
b. Assume that the enterprise fund began the year with retained earnings of $8 million and had net income, taking into account depreciation on the equipment, of $5 million. Show how the fund would report its change in retained earnings (starting with net income) on its year-end statement of revenues, expenses, and changes in retained earnings.
c. Assume further that the enterprise fund began the year with contributed capital of $20 million, all from sources other than capital grants. Show how it would report its fund equity on its year-end balance sheet.

10-4

The insurance expense recognized by an enterprise fund depends on the type of carrier.

The water and waste-water utility (enterprise) funds of three cities each paid $1 million in casualty insurance premiums.

City A is insured by a small independent insurance company. City B is self-insured and accounts for its insurance activities in an internal service fund. City C is self-insured and accounts for its insurance activities in its general fund.

Each of the insurers collected a total of $10 million in premiums from all of the parties that it insures, including the city utility funds. Of this amount each paid out $8 million in actual claims. The balance was held in reserve for major catastrophes.

Prepare the journal entry that each of the three utility funds should make to record its insurance payment and expense for the year. Comment on any differences.

10-5

Landfill expenses depend on estimates that may change from year to year.

In 1998 Marquette County opened a landfill that was expected to accept waste for four years. The following table indicates estimates that county officials made at the end of each of the four years.

Year	Total Capacity (millions of cubic feet)	Capacity Used This Year (millions of cubic feet)	Expected Closure Costs (millions of dollars)
1998	10	4	$ 8
1999	10	2	9
2000	12	2	10
2001	12	4	10

Determine the amount of the total expected closure costs ($10 million) that should be assigned to each of the years that the landfill accepts waste.

10-6

Multiple Choice Questions from Previous CPA Examinations

1. Which of the following funds of a governmental unit recognizes revenues in the accounting period in which they become available and measurable?

	General Fund	Enterprise Fund
a.	Yes	No
b.	No	Yes
c.	Yes	Yes
d.	No	No

2. The comprehensive annual financial report (CAFR) of a governmental unit should contain a combined statement of revenues, expenditures, and changes in fund balances for:

	Governmental Funds	Propriety Funds
a.	Yes	No
b.	Yes	Yes
c.	No	Yes
d.	No	No

3. The comprehensive annual financial report (CAFR) of a governmental unit should contain a combined statement of revenues, expenses, and changes in retained earnings for:

	Account Groups	Proprietary funds
a.	Yes	Yes
b.	Yes	No
c.	No	No
d.	No	Yes

4. Which of the following does not affect an internal service fund's net income?
   a. depreciation expense on its fixed assets
   b. operating transfers in
   c. operating transfers out
   d. residual equity transfers

5. Bay Creek's municipal motor pool maintains all city-owned vehicles and charges the various departments for the cost of rendering those services. In which of the following funds should Bay Creek account for the cost of such maintenance?
   a. general fund
   b. internal service fund
   c. special revenue fund
   d. special assessment fund

6. The following information for the year ended June 30, 1995, pertains to a proprietary fund established by Burwood Village in connection with Burwood's public parking facilities:

Receipts from users of parking facilities $400,000

Expenditures

Purchase of parking meters	210,000
Salaries and other cash expenses	90,000
Depreciation on parking meters	70,000

For the year ended June 30, 1995, this proprietary fund should report net income of

a. $0
b. $30,000
c. $100,000
d. $240,000

7. Hull City has established a separate internal service (self-insurance) fund to pay claims and judgments of all of Hull City's funds. In 1995, payments to the insurer fund amounted to $500,000, while the actuarially determined amount was $400,000. The payments to the insurer fund should be accounted for as

	Expenditure	*Operating Transfer*
a.	$0	$0
b.	$100,000	$400,000
c.	$400,000	$100,000
d.	$500,000	$0

8. During 1995, Spruce City reported the following receipts from self-sustaining activities paid for by users of the services rendered:

Operation of water supply plant	$5,000,000
Operation of bus system	900,000

What amount should be accounted for in Spruce City's enterprise funds?

a. $0
b. $900,000
c. $5,000,000
d. $5,900,000

9. The following equity balances are among those maintained by Cole City:

Enterprise funds	$1,000,000
Internal service funds	400,000

Cole City's proprietary equity balances amount to

a. $1,400,000
b. $1,000,000
c. $400,000
d. $0

10. The following transactions were among those reported by Cliff County's water and sewer enterprise fund for 1991:

Proceeds from sale of revenue bonds	$5,000,000
Billings to customer households	3,000,000
Capital contributed by subdividers	1,000,000

In the water and sewer enterprise fund's statement of revenues, expenses, and changes in fund balance for the year ended December 31, 1991, what amount should be reported as revenues?

a. $9,000,000
b. $8,000,000
c. $3,000,000
d. $4,000,000

10-7

Multiple Choice Questions from Previous CPA Examinations.

1. During the year ended December 31, 1995, Leyland City received a state grant of $500,000 to finance the purchase of buses, and an additional grant of $100,000 to aid in the financing of bus operations in 1995. Only $300,000 of the capital grant was used in 1995 for the purchase of buses, but the entire operating grant of $100,000 was spent in 1995.

   If Leyland City's bus transportation system is accounted for as an enterprise fund, how much should it report as grant revenues for the year ended December 31, 1995?
   a. $100,000
   b. $300,000
   c. $400,000
   d. $500,000

2. Which of the following fund types would include retained earnings in its balance sheet?
   a. special revenue
   b. capital projects
   c. expendable pension trust
   d. internal service

3. Customers' security deposits that cannot be spent for normal operating purposes were collected by a governmental unit and accounted for in the enterprise fund. A portion of the amount collected was invested in marketable debt securities and a portion in marketable equity securities. How would each portion be classified in the balance sheet?

	Portion in Marketable Debt Securities	*Portion in Marketable Equity Securities*
a.	Unrestricted asset	Restricted asset
b.	Unrestricted asset	Unrestricted asset
c.	Restricted asset	Unrestricted asset
d.	Restricted asset	Restricted asset

4. Which of the following funds of a governmental unit uses the same basis of accounting as the enterprise fund?
   a. internal service fund
   b. expendable trust funds
   c. special revenue funds
   d. capital projects funds

5. Which of the following bases of accounting should a government use for its proprietary funds in measuring financial position and operating results?

Modified Accrual Basis	Accrual Basis
a. No	Yes
b. No	No
c. Yes	Yes
d. Yes	No

6. An enterprise fund would be used when the governing body requires that

   I. accounting for the financing of an agency's services to other government departments be on a cost-reimbursement basis.

   II. user charges cover the costs of general public services.

   III. net income information be provided for an activity.

   a. I only
   b. I and II
   c. I and III
   d. II and III

7. Gem City's internal service fund received a residual equity transfer of $50,000 cash from the general fund. This $50,000 transfer should be reported in Gem City's internal service fund as a credit to
   a. revenues.
   b. other financing sources.
   c. accounts payable.
   d. contributed capital.

8. Eureka City should issue a statement of cash flows for which of the following funds?

Eureka City Hall Capital Projects Fund	Eureka Water Enterprise Fund
a. No	Yes
b. No	No
c. Yes	No
d. Yes	Yes

9. Through an internal service fund, New County operates a centralized data processing center to provide services to New County's other governmental units. In 1992, this internal service fund billed New County's parks and recreation fund $150,000 for data processing services. What account should its internal service fund credit to record this $150,000 billing to the parks and recreation fund?
   a. data processing department expenses
   b. intergovernmental transfers
   c. interfund exchanges
   d. operating revenues control

10. The town of Hill operates municipal electric and water utilities. In which of the following funds should the operations of the utilities be accounted for?

   a. enterprise fund
   b. internal service fund
   c. agency fund
   d. special revenue fund

10-8

Multiple Choice Questions from Previous CPA Examinations

1. For governmental units, depreciation expense on assets acquired with capital grants externally restricted for capital acquisitions should be reported in which type of fund?

Governmental Fund	Proprietary Fund
a. Yes	No
b. Yes	Yes
c. No	No
d. No	Yes

2. For which of the following funds do operating transfers affect the results of operations?

Governmental Funds	Proprietary Funds
a. No	No
b. No	Yes
c. Yes	Yes
d. Yes	No

3. During the year, a city's electric utility, which is operated as an enterprise fund, rendered billings for electricity supplied to the general fund. Which of the following accounts should be debited by the general fund?
   a. appropriations
   b. expenditures
   c. due to electric utility enterprise fund
   d. other financing uses operating transfers out

4. The billings for transportation services provided to other governmental units are recorded by the internal service fund as
   a. interfund exchanges.
   b. intergovernmental transfers.
   c. transportation appropriations.
   d. operating revenues.

5. A state government had the following activities:

State-operated lottery	$10,000,000
State-operated hospital	3,000,000

Which of the above activities should be accounted for in an enterprise fund?
   a. neither one
   b. only the first
   c. only the second
   d. both of them

6. The orientation of accounting and reporting for all proprietary funds of governmental units is
   a. income determination.
   b. project.
   c. flow of funds.
   d. program.

PROBLEMS

Continuing Problem

Review the annual report that you obtained.

a. Note the activities accounted for in both internal service funds and enterprise funds. Comment on whether any of these activities would ordinarily be accounted for in a general or other governmental fund.

b. What percent of the government's assets and its long-term obligations are accounted for in enterprise funds? In internal service funds?

c. Did any of the internal service funds report significant operating surpluses or deficits (as a percentage of revenues) for the year? Have any accumulated significant retained earnings balances or deficits over the years?

d. Have the government's enterprise funds been "profitable"? If so, what has the government done with the "earnings"? Has it transferred them to the general fund?

e. Does the government maintain a municipal landfill? If so, in which fund is it accounted for? Does the government report an obligation for closure or post-closure costs?

f. Is it the government's policy to charge a portion of enterprise fund depreciation against contributed capital rather than retained earnings? How can you tell?

g. Has the government issued revenue bonds? For what purposes? From what sources of revenue will the debt be serviced?

h. Does the report indicate how the government manages its risks? Does it carry outside insurance or does it "self-insure"? If the latter, then in what fund does it account for its insurance activities?

10-1

Enterprise funds are accounted for like comparable businesses; nevertheless, they have their quirks.

The Green Hills Water District was established on January 1, to provide water service to a suburban development. It accounts for its operations in a single enterprise fund. During the year it engaged in the following transactions:

1. It issued $6,000,000 of revenue bonds.

2. It purchased, for $4,500,000, the plant and equipment of the private water company that previously served the area.

3. It incurred $500,000 in costs to improve and expand its plant and equipment.

4. It billed customers for $1.8 million, of which it collected $1.5 million.

5. It collected $200,000 in tap connection fees from developers. The actual cost of the hook-ups (paid in cash and not included in transaction #4) was $140,000.

6. It incurred the following operating costs (all paid in cash):

- Purchases of water, $850,000
- Labor and contract services, $320,000
- Interest, $80,000
- Supplies and miscellaneous, $60,000

7. It recognized depreciation of $350,000 on its fixed assets.

8. As required by its bond indentures, it placed $100,000 of the bond proceeds in a restricted account. The resources are dedicated to the repayment of the bond principal.

a. Prepare journal entries to record the transactions.

b. Prepare a year-end statement of revenues, expenses, and changes in retained earnings.

c. Prepare a year-end balance sheet.

d. In some jurisdictions, water districts may account for their operations entirely in an enterprise fund or in several funds, as if they were full-service governments. If a water district chose the latter, then it would report all revenues and operating expenditures in its general fund and would maintain other funds and account groups as appropriate. Describe briefly how the financial statements of the Green Hills Water District would differ if it chose to prepare its financial statements as if it were a full service government. Be specific (note changes in fixed assets, long-term debt, etc.).

10-2

The premiums charged by self-insurance funds depend on whether they are accounted for in internal service or governmental funds.

Believing that it is more economical to manage its risks internally, a county elects not to purchase commercial insurance. Instead, it sets aside resources for potential claims in an internal service "self-insurance" fund.

In a recent year, the fund recognized $1.5 million for claims filed during the year. Of these it paid $1.3 million.

Based on the calculations of an independent actuary, the insurance fund billed, and collected, $2.0 million in premiums from the other county departments insured by the fund. Of this amount $1.2 million was billed to funds accounted for in the general fund and $0.8 million to the county utility fund. The total charge for premiums was based on historical experience and included a reasonable provision for future catastrophe losses.

a. Prepare the journal entries in the internal service fund to record:

1. the claims recognized and paid
2. the premiums billed and collected

b. Suppose instead that the county accounted for self-insurance within its general fund. As in part a, of the $2.0 million in premiums charged, $1.2 million were billed to the other departments accounted for in the general fund and $.8 million to the utility department.

1. Prepare the general fund journal entry to record the claims recognized and paid.
2. Prepare the general fund entry to record the premiums billed and collected from the *utility* fund. (Those billed and collected from the other general fund departments would "net out" against their premium expenditures for purposes of external reporting.)

c. What would be the net expenses (i.e., expenditures less premium revenues) reported by the general fund if the self-insurance were accounted for (1) in the internal service fund and (2) in the general fund? What would be the total expenses charged by the utility fund if the self-insurance were accounted for (1) in the internal service fund and (2) in the general fund? Comment on the rationale for standards that permit such differences.

10-3

The differences in accounting for an activity in an internal service fund rather than the general fund may be striking.

A school district establishes a vehicle-repair shop that provides service to other departments, all of which are accounted for in its general fund. During its first year of operations the shop engages in the following transactions:

- It purchases equipment at a cost of $24 million and issues long-term notes for the purchase price. The useful life of the equipment is eight years, with no residual value.
- It purchases supplies at a cost of $4 million. Of these it uses $3 million. In its *governmental* funds, the district accounts for supplies on a *purchases* basis.
- It incurs $13 million in other operating costs.
- It bills other departments for $19 million.

For purposes of *external* reporting, school district officials are considering two options:

- Account for the vehicle-repair shop in an internal service fund.
- Account for the vehicle-repair shop in the general fund

a. For each of the following items indicate the amounts that would be reported in the year-end financial statements of (1) the internal service fund assuming that the school dis-

trict selected the first option and (2) the general fund assuming that it selected the second option.

1. Billings to other departments (revenues)
2. Cost of supplies (expense or expenditure)
3. Expenses or expenditures relating to acquisition or use of equipment
4. Other operating costs
5. Equipment (asset)
6. Accumulated depreciation
7. Inventory (asset)
8. Notes payable
9. Reserve for inventory

b. What would be the total expenses reported in the internal service fund, assuming that the school district selected the first option?

c. What would be the total amount of expenditures reported in the *general fund*, assuming that the school district: (1) selected the first option; (2) selected the second option.

10-4

Internal service funds can be used to reduce general fund expenditures.

A city maintains an internal audit department and accounts for it in its general fund. In the coming year, the department will purchase $300,000 of computer and other office equipment, all of which will be paid for out of current resources (i.e., not with debt).

City officials have given top priority to reducing general fund expenditures. To that end, the city comptroller has proposed accounting for the internal audit department in an internal service fund rather than the general fund.

As envisioned by the comptroller, the audit department would bill each of the units (all of which are accounted for in the general fund) for each audit performed. Fees would be established so that they would cover all audit department costs. The fund would be established by a transfer of $300,000 from the general fund to cover the cost of the new equipment.

The city estimates that for the coming year the audit department's operating costs, excluding any costs relating to the new equipment, will be $1,600,000. The equipment is expected to have a useful life of five years.

a. Assume that the city accepts the comptroller's suggestion. Prepare journal entries in the internal service fund to record:

1. the transfer-in of the $300,000
2. the acquisition of the equipment
3. the operating and other costs
4. the billings to, and collection of cash from, the general fund

b. Prepare journal entries in the general fund to record:
  1. the transfer-out of the $300,000
  2. the billings from, and payment of cash to, the internal service fund

c. Would the establishment of the internal service fund result in a decrease in overall government costs (e.g., cash outflows)? Would it result in a reduction in reported general fund expenditures? Explain.

d. Suppose that in the following year, the city does not plan to acquire additional fixed assets. Comment on whether reported general fund expenditures would be greater if the internal service fund were to be established than if it were not.

10-5

A city's financial statements and related disclosures as to one of its internal service funds raises intriguing questions.

The balance sheet and statement of revenues, expenses, and changes in retained earnings of a medium-sized city's Support Services internal service fund are as follows:

Support Services Fund	

Balance Sheet

Assets:

Pooled Investments and Cash	$ 546,463
Prepaid Expenses	239,582
Total Current Assets	$ 786,045
Property Plant and Equipment	3,587,524
Less Accumulated Depreciation	(2,007,684)
Net Property, Plant and Equipment	1,579,840
Total Assets	$2,365,885

Liabilities and Equities:

Accounts Payable	$ 39,034
Accrued Payroll	854,956
Accrued Compensated Absences	291,470
Due to Other Funds	89,876
Total Current Liabilities	$1,275,336
Accrued Compensated Absences	2,049,902
Total Liabilities	$3,325,238

Fund Equity:

Contributions from Municipality	1,531,325
Retained Earnings—Unreserved	(2,490,678)
Total Fund Equity	$ (959,353)
Total Liabilities and Fund Equity	$2,365,885

Statement of Revenues, Expenses, and Changes in Retained Earnings

Revenues:

Billings to Other Departments	$20,340,426

Expenses

Operating Expenses Before Depreciation	32,228,281
Depreciation	122,544
Total Expenses	$32,350,825
Operating Income (Loss) Before Transfers	(12,010,399)
Operating Transfers-In	9,083,006
Net Income (Loss)	$(2,927,393)
Retained Earnings, Beginning of Year	436,715
Retained Earnings, End of Year	$(2,490,678)

The financial statements provide a limited amount of additional information as to the Support Services Fund:

- The Support Services Fund "includes the activities of the various support service departments";
- It is one of four internal service funds. The other three account for fleet maintenance, information system and utility customer services;
- The transfer-in was from the general fund.

The city's general fund reported the following (in millions):

Revenues	$188
Expenditures	227
Excess (Deficiency) of Revenues Over Expenditures	(39)
Net Operating Transfers-In	43
Excess of Revenues Over Expenditures and Operating Transfers-In	4
Fund Balance, Beginning of Year	25
Net Equity Transfers-Out	(1)
Fund Balance, End of Year	$ 28

a. The financial statements do not provide additional information as to what constitutes "support services." What likely activities might support services include?

b. What is the significance of the balance sheet deficit in "retained earnings—unreserved"? What concern might it raise as to the proper application of accounting principles?

c. What is the significance of the internal service fund's operating deficit as it relates to the general fund's excess (deficiency) of revenues over expenditures?

d. Suppose that the city accounted for the support services in its general fund. Approximately how much more or less would its "excess of revenues over expenditures and operating transfers-in" have been?

e. If you were the city's independent auditor, what changes in billing practices might you propose the city consider?

10-6

The rates to be charged by internal service funds may not be obvious—and can have a significant impact on who pays the costs of government.

A city maintains an internal service fund to account for a maintenance department. The department provides services to all city departments, which, with one exception, are accounted for in the city's general fund. That exception is the department responsible for the city's golf course. It is accounted for in an enterprise fund.

The maintenance department estimates that it provides approximately 20,000 hours of service per year. However, the volume is seasonal. During the "slack season"—four summer months—it provides approximately 1,400 hours of service per month; during the eight other months it provides approximately 1,800 hours of service per month.

The department has determined its fixed costs to be $33,333 per month ($400,000 per year) and its variable costs to be $10 per hour ($200,000 per year, if it provides 20,000 hours of service).

The departments accounted for in the general fund request 17,600 hours of service per year. The department in charge of the golf course requests the remaining 2,400 hours of service per year. However, all of its service is requested during the summer months—600 hours per month. Were it not for the demands of the golf course department, the maintenance unit would otherwise have substantial excess capacity during the slack months, as no other department would require those 600 hours of service per month.

a. Suppose that the maintenance department determines its billing rates on an annual basis, based on total estimated costs for the year.

1. What would be the cost per hour of service?

2. How much of the total costs for the year would be billed to the golf course enterprise fund? How much would be billed to the general fund?

b. Suppose, instead, that the maintenance department determines its billing rates on a monthly basis, based on total costs for each month.

1. What would be the cost per hour of service in the busy months (when it provides 1,800 hours of service)?

2. What would be the cost per hour of service in the slack months (when it provides only 1,400 hours of service)?

3. How much of the total annual costs would be billed to the golf course enterprise fund? How much of the total annual costs would be billed to the general fund?

c. If you were in charge of the golf course, why would you argue that both billing policies are unfair?

d. What difference might the choice of policies have on the distribution of costs among the city's tax and fee payers?

10-7

Some government enterprises "add back" depreciation on contributed assets.

The City Transit Authority (CTA), which uses proprietary fund accounting, presented the following beginning-of-year condensed balance sheet (in millions):

Working Capital		$12
Buses and Equipment	$90	
Less: Accumulated Depreciation	30	60
Total Assets		$72
Contributed Capital—City		$65
Retained Earnings		7
Total Equity		$72

During the year the CTA was awarded a $20 million federal grant restricted for the acquisition of capital assets. It used the funds to acquire buses and equipment.

At year-end it reported the following revenues and expenses (in millions):

Operating Revenues		$52
Depreciation Expense	$10	
Other Expenses	45	55
Net Income (Loss)		$(3)

Of the depreciation expense, $6 million applied to the buses and equipment on hand at the beginning of the year and $4 million to those acquired with the federal grant. It is the practice of the CTA to report contributed capital restricted to the acquisition of plant and equipment net of accumulated depreciation on the related assets.

a. Prepare summary journal entries to record the year's depreciation expense and to close the account at year-end.

b. Prepare a combined statement of revenues, expenses, and changes in retained earnings.

c. Prepare a year-end balance sheet. Be sure that it shows separately, net of amortization, the portion of capital contributed attributable to the federal grant.

d. At year-end, how much of the contributed capital can be identified with the buses and equipment acquired with the federal funds? Is it possible to determine how much of the retained earnings and the remaining contributed capital is associated with buses and equipment and how much is associated with the working capital?

e. In one or two sentences, justify the practice of reducing contributed capital by the amount of depreciation charged on related assets. Based on your response to part d, comment on any apparent reporting inconsistencies attributable to the practice.

10-8

A government's reported landfill closing expense may exceed its required cash payments.

A municipality expects to use a landfill evenly throughout the twenty-five years from January 1, 1997, to December 31, 2021. Upon closing the landfill it estimates that it will incur closing costs of $300,000. Thereafter, it anticipates, it will have to monitor the site yearly for the following thirty years at an annual cost of $10,000.

The government intends to pay for the closure and monitoring costs evenly over the twenty-five years that the landfill is in use (1997 through 2021) by making annual cash contributions to a trust fund. The resources of the trust fund will be invested in government securities that can be expected to earn interest at a rate of 5 percent.

a. How much would the municipality need in the trust fund as of December 31, 2021, to satisfy its monitoring obligations for the next 30 years? [*Hint:* What is the present value of an annuity of $10,000 for 30 years?] How much would it need in the fund to pay the closing costs?

b. How much would it have to contribute to the fund during each of the twenty-five years that it adds to the landfill to have a sufficient amount in the fund at the end of 2021 to satisfy its obligations for *both* the closure and the monitoring costs? [*Hint:* The required sum (based on the calculations in part a) is the equivalent of the future value of a 25-year annuity of unknown amount (x) compounded at a rate of 5 percent.]

c. Per the GASB reporting standards, what amount would the government have to report as its landfill closure and monitoring expenses during each of the twenty-five years (1997 through 2021) irrespective of how much it actually contributes to the trust fund? Assume that the costs were as estimated.

d. If the government were to make the contributions as you calculated in part b, but charged the expenses that you calculated in part c, would it be overstating its closure and monitoring expenses? Explain. What might be a factor that mitigates the overstatement of the expenses?

10-9

Landfill costs must be reported as expenses during the periods of use—but only in enterprise funds.

In 1998 a city opens a municipal landfill, which it will account for in an enterprise fund. It estimates capacity to be 6 million cubic feet and usable life to be twenty years. To close the landfill, the municipality expects to incur labor, material, and equipment costs of $3 million. Thereafter, it expects to incur an additional $7 million of costs to monitor and maintain the site.

a. In 1998, the city uses 300,000 feet of the landfill. Prepare the journal entry to record the expense for closure and postclosure costs.

b. In 1999 it again uses 300,000 feet of the landfill. It revises its estimate of available volume to 5.8 million cubic feet and closure and postclosure costs to $10.2 million. Prepare the journal entry to record the expense for closure and postclosure costs.

c. In 2017, the final year of operation, it uses 350,000 feet of the landfill. The actual capacity has proven to be only 5 million cubic feet and closing costs are now estimated to be $15 million. Through the year 2016, the municipality had used 4,650,000 cubic feet and had recorded $14.2 million in closure and postclosure costs. In 2017, it actually incurs $5 million in closure costs, the entire amount of which is paid in cash.

　1. Prepare the journal entry to record the expense for closure and postclosure cost.

　2. Prepare the journal entry to record the actual closure costs paid.

d. Suppose, instead, that the landfill was accounted for in the government's general fund. Indicate how the entries would differ from those in the enterprise fund.

10-10

Based on actual circumstances, this minicase illustrates an issue faced by government-operated utilities (one that has not been addressed by standard setters and is not discussed in the text).

The City Electric Utility (CEU), which a city accounts for in its enterprise fund, provides cash rebates to customers who install insulation, storm windows, or energy-saving appliances. The payments are intended to reduce the demand for electricity and thereby enable the CEU to avoid having to add generating capacity.

Like many government-operated utilities, the CEU establishes rates based on a number of factors, of which cost is only one. It is the policy of the city, for example, to make substantial transfers each year from the CEU to its general fund. Utility fees are thereby a form of taxation and the revenue requirements of the general fund are taken into account in setting the rates.

The CEU controller has raised the question of whether the rebates should be charged as an expense as paid or should be capitalized and charged as an expense over time (i.e., amortized). Moreover, he asks, if the costs should be capitalized and charged as an expense over time, then what should be the basis for determining the length of the amortization period?

Required: Write a brief memo in which you recommend to the controller how the rebates should be accounted for. Be sure to support your position.

SOLUTION TO EXERCISE FOR REVIEW AND SELF-STUDY

a. The statements are based on the full accrual basis of accounting as evidenced by the presence on the balance sheet of property plant and equipment, accumulated depreciation, deferred charges and credits, and long-term liabilities.

b. Both the revenues and the expenses of the LCRA are determined by the demand for its goods and services. It is not possible for the entity to budget its revenues and expenses as if they could be determined by legislative fiat. The entity should, of course, prepare budgets—just as would any private utility. There would be little point, however, to incorporating them into its accounting system.

c. For utilities, the long-lived assets and capital structure (including long-term debt) are of far greater significance than the current assets and liabilities; hence, they are presented first.

d. The authority reports its restricted fund assets and liabilities in separate sections of the balance sheet, "Cash & Investments in Restricted Funds," and "Liabilities Payable from Restricted Funds."

e. As discussed in Chapter 7, when a government refunds its debt, it does not have to recognize the gains or losses on refunding at the time of the transaction. Instead, it can amortize them over the shorter of the refunded debt or the associated new debt. By contrast, organizations under the purview of the FASB must recognize the gains or losses immediately.

f. Governments are permitted to close depreciation expense to contributed capital rather than retained earnings on assets acquired with capital grants. In that way, when they depreciate the assets they correspondingly reduce the related capital accounts. The entry to record depreciation expense would be the standard depreciation entry:

Depreciation and amortization expense (total)	$60,192	
Accumulated depreciation		$60,192

To record depreciation expense

That to close the depreciation expense at year-end would be:

Capital derived from earnings	$59,789	
Contributed capital	403	
Depreciation expense		60,192

To close depreciation to capital derived from earnings (the equivalent of retained earnings) and to contributed capital

Note that in the capitalization section of its balance sheet the LCRA added the reported income for the year to beginning of year capital derived from earnings. It then added the current-year's depreciation on assets acquired with contributions. Presumably, this portion of depreciation (as shown in the above entry) was charged directly to contributed capital.

g. The regulatory asset is reported on the balance sheet as an asset (under deferred charges) as "Costs to be recovered from future revenues." The costs that were previously deferred are subtracted from income on the statement of operations as "Prior Costs Recovered from Revenues."

h. Of the LCRA's $1,719,057,000 in total capital and liabilities, $10,944,000 (0.64 percent) has been contributed from governments or other parties; $454,775,000 (26.5 percent) has been derived from earnings; and $1,126,851 (65.6 percent) has been borrowed in the form of long-term debt.

i. The $150,000 portion of the tap fee representing the hook-up costs should be charged as a contribution to capital. The $50,000 balance should be recognized as revenue.

Fiduciary Funds

When one thinks of the assets of either governments or not-for-profits, it is natural to conjure up images of highways, buildings, police cars, research laboratories, and so on. In fact, however, both governments and not-for-profits are among the nation's largest holders of stocks, bonds, and similar securities. Indeed, government pension funds, university endowment funds, and private charitable foundations are among the most powerful and influential of corporate investors.

This chapter will be directed to **fiduciary funds,** which are described in the GASB *Codification*, as being established:

> to account for assets held by a governmental unit in a trustee capacity or as an agent for individuals, private organizations, other governmental units, and/or other funds. These include (a) expendable trust funds, (b) nonexpendable trust funds, (c) pension trust funds, and (d) agency funds.[1]

Fiduciary funds are of special interest to both statement preparers and statement users, not only because they may contain vast amounts of resources, but also because the assets are highly liquid and are therefore subject to risk of loss both through fraud and reduction in value. Moreover, organizations and their constituents rely on these resources as a main source of current and future income.

Although the GASB explains fiduciary funds in the context of governments, its description is equally applicable to not-for-profits. Indeed, for the most part, the general principles and issues to be discussed in this chapter are common to both governments and not-for-profits. This chapter will deal first with trust funds and then with pension and agency funds.

WHAT ARE NONEXPENDABLE TRUST FUNDS AND HOW DO THEY DIFFER FROM EXPENDABLE TRUST FUNDS?

Nonexpendable trust funds are used to account for resources donated to an organization with the stipulation that only the income earned from the assets can be expended. Depending on donor preferences, the income may be restricted for specific programs or activities or may be unrestricted.

The typical nonexpendable trust fund, herein used synonymously with **endowment,** requires that its principal be preserved in perpetuity. However, some endowments, referred to as **term endowments,** permit the principal to be expended after a specified number of years.

Governments report upon their endowments in a separate column in their combined balance sheets or statements of revenues and expenses. Not-for-profits categorize them as **permanently restricted net assets,** unless they are term endowments, in which case they would be classified as temporarily restricted.

The following are but a few examples of endowments that are maintained by governments and not-for-profits:

- Universities maintain endowments—the income from which maybe either restricted or unrestricted—and rely upon them as major sources of general operating revenues. Some take the form of "chairs" or "professorships." Assigned to spe-

---

[1] *Codification*, Section 1100.103.

cific faculty members, they provide salary supplements and support teaching and research. Other endowments help to finance scholarships, teaching awards, research, or general operations.

- Private foundations, such as the Ford and Carnegie foundations are, in essence, endowment funds. With billions of dollars in assets, they promote a wide array of educational, social welfare, and scientific activities.

- Public schools sometimes maintain endowments, albeit generally small, to provide ongoing support for specific activities, such as band or science enrichment programs.

- Municipalities establish endowments to account for gifts in support of nature centers, performing arts centers, and parks.

- Churches and synagogues maintain endowments to sponsor lectures, music programs, or youth activities.

Expendable trust funds are distinguished from nonexpendable trust funds in that in expendable trust funds *both* the principal and interest may be expended. The resources of expendable trust funds are typically derived from the income of nonexpendable trust funds. Some governments and not-for-profits (but not all, as will be discussed in the following section) transfer to an expendable trust fund the cash earned from the investments held in their nonexpendable trust funds. If the cash is not immediately needed, then it is used to acquire new income-producing investments. At any time, however, both the earnings on those investments as well as the investments themselves are subject to expenditure.

In essence, expendable trust funds are nothing more than ordinary operating funds. If the resources are unrestricted, then they are similar to a general fund; if restricted for special purposes, then they are the equivalent of special revenue funds. Because of their similarity to ordinary operating funds, they are accounted for as such. This chapter, therefore, will direct only minimal attention to expendable trust funds; the accounting principles for expendable trust funds have been set forth in earlier chapters dealing with operating funds.

SHOULD INVESTMENT INCOME BE REPORTED IN AN EXPENDABLE OR A NONEXPENDABLE FUND?

The income from nonexpendable trust funds is intended to benefit other funds and must eventually be transferred to them. At issue, however, is whether, investment earnings should first be recognized as revenue within the nonexpendable funds and then be transferred to the beneficiary funds or whether it should be recorded directly in the beneficiary funds.

The significance of the issue is mainly in whether the income should be reported in the recipient fund as revenue or as an operating transfer. If reported as revenue, then it would be incorporated into "excess of revenues over expenditures." If reported as an operating transfer, however, it would be shown "below the line" and included among "other financing sources." The impact on fund balance is the same; the difference is one of statement user perception. When investment income is reported as revenue an organization's ongoing operations may appear to be generating a larger surplus (or incurring a smaller deficit) than if shown as a transfer-in.

Current Standards in Governments

In governments, although the issue is not explicitly addressed in the GASB *Codification*, it is common practice to account for all nonexpendable trust fund income within the nonexpendable fund itself. Periodically (either at the discretion of government officials or as required by law, contract, or donor stipulation) the income (net of investment expenses, if applicable) is transferred to the beneficiary funds.

Current Standards in Other Not-for-Profits

Per Statement No. 117, *Financial Statement of Not-for-Profit Organizations*, income from endowment investments should generally be reported directly as either unrestricted or temporarily restricted revenues. Income from endowment revenues should be reported as permanently restricted—and thus in the endowment fund itself—only if, in fact, it is unavailable for expenditure.[2] This would be the case if a donor were to specify that all income for a stated period of time must be added to, and permanently retained in, the endowment principal. Of course, for purposes of internal reporting, an institution may report the endowment income initially in the endowment fund and then transfer it to the beneficiary fund.

WHY IS IT IMPORTANT FOR NONEXPENDABLE TRUST FUNDS TO BE ACCOUNTED FOR ON A FULL ACCRUAL BASIS?

Both governments and not-for-profits account for nonexpendable trust funds on a full accrual basis. The full accrual basis helps to assure that they do not dissipate their assets by inappropriately basing their distributions on cash flows rather than economic earnings. For governments, this means that they apply the same principles as they do in their proprietary funds. Most of the transactions in endowment funds involve investments in stocks, bonds, and similar types of securities. Consistent with the accrual basis of accounting, interest, and dividends are recognized as earned, not necessarily when cash is received.

Organizations may also invest their resources in nonliquid assets, such as commercial real estate or equity securities of nonpublic corporations. These investments, too, are accounted for on a business-type basis. Therefore, the governments or not-for-profits should generally charge depreciation or amortization on all long-lived assets that decline in value over time.

The importance of charging depreciation can be illustrated by the example that follows.

RECOGNIZING DEPRECIATION

---

[2] Paragraph 20.

EXAMPLE　*Charging Depreciation*

A trust fund receives a contribution of a commercial office building having a fair market value of $20 million. The donor stipulates that only the income, not the principal, can be used to carry out the purposes of the gift. The estimated useful life of the building is twenty years (with no residual value). The trust expects to earn $1 million per year in rent revenue, net of *cash* operating expenses. Consistent with the wishes of the donor, the trust will each year distribute all of its reported income, but none of its principal.

If the trust were not to charge depreciation, then its reported earnings would be $1 million per year—the rent revenue net of cash operating expenses. It would therefore distribute $1 million per year. By contrast, if it were to charge depreciation its reported earnings would be zero per year—net rent revenue of $1 million less depreciation of $1 million ($20 million divided by 20 years).

Irrespective of whether or not the trust charges depreciation, the economic value of the building at the end of its twenty-year life can be expected to be zero (i.e., it would generate no additional cash receipts), assuming that the initial estimate of useful life was correct.

The following table compares the consequences of charging, and not charging, depreciation over the period of twenty years (in millions):

	Do Not Depreciate	Depreciate
Total Assets (Building), Beginning of Period 1	$20	$20
Net Cash Receipts ($1 Million Per Year)	20	20
Depreciation Expense ($1 Million Per Year)	0	20
Net Income and Hence Total Cash Distributions	(20)	(0)
Cash Balance, End of Period 20	0	20
Market Value of Building, End of Period 20	0	0
Total Assets (Cash and Building), End of Period 20	0	20

By charging depreciation, the trust reduces its reported income—and thus its cash distributions—to reflect the ongoing decline in the value of the building. It thereby preserves the principal at $20 million, consistent with the expectations of the donor. At the end of the twenty-year period, it no longer has a building of value, but has $20 million in other assets; in this example, cash.

By not charging depreciation, the trust is, in effect, distributing not only its cash earnings, but also a portion of the building. At the end of the twenty-year economic life of the building, it is left with neither a building nor any compensating assets.

Donors may explicitly stipulate that depreciation need not be charged against revenues in determining expendable income. Moreover, in some jurisdictions, in the absence of donor stipulations, the trust is not required to charge depreciation. Even so, inasmuch as the fixed asset is losing economic value over time, sound accounting dictates that depreciation be charged and that any distributions in excess of net income (after depreciation) be explicitly reported as distributions of principal.

SHOULD INVESTMENT GAINS BE CONSIDERED NET ADDITIONS TO PRINCIPAL OR EXPENDABLE INCOME?

The primary accounting issue pertaining to endowments relates to whether, in the absence of specific donor or legal stipulations, investment gains and losses, including unrealized appreciation, should be recognized as a component of expendable income or nonexpendable principal. The issue has economic consequences that reach far beyond the content of financial reports; it affects the amount of resources available for operations and is likely to influence the organization's investment policies.

Whether gains on the sale of investments (capital gains) or gains from appreciation should be accounted for as income or as an adjustment to principal is undoubtedly one of the most provocative questions related to fiduciary funds. But it is as much of a legal as an accounting question. If a particular policy is required either by donor stipulation or law, then that policy will dictate accounting practice.

DIFFERING POLICIES OF GOVERNMENTS AND NOT-FOR-PROFITS REGARDING INVESTMENT GAINS

Parties establishing endowments often stipulate that gains from the sale of investments be added to the principal (the "corpus") of the endowment and not incorporated into income. Thus, the gains will not be expendable; they will be available only for reinvestment. However, in the absence of donor stipulations or other applicable legal provisions, the governing board of the recipient institution is generally free to appropriate investment gains for current use.

The widespread practice of accounting for gains as adjustments to fund balances rather than income is grounded in the need to protect endowment principal from inflation. In the long-term, owing to inflation, the market value of a corporation's common stock can be expected to increase, even in the absence of substantive changes in supply and demand relationships. Thus, when an endowment sells that stock, the gain may represent nothing more than a decrease in the purchasing power of a dollar.

Although it may protect an endowment from inflation, a policy of automatically assigning investment gains to principal rather than income may have the perverse consequence of encouraging institutions to adopt less than optimum investment strategies.

EXAMPLE *Investment Gains*

A university's policies require that all investment gains, both realized and unrealized, be added to endowment principal. The university has to choose between one of two stock portfolios as an investment for a $1 million endowment. The first portfolio contains the common stock of "high-tech" companies that pay either no, or very small, dividends. The returns will be almost entirely from appreciation. The second contains an extremely conservative mix of bonds, preferred stocks, and the common stocks of well-established industrial firms, all of which pay high dividends or interest. The endowment fund managers estimate that the first portfolio will provide a total return (appreciation plus dividends) of 14 percent per year; the second only 6 percent per year (almost all interest and dividends).

Assuming that the university needs the income to be generated by the endowment, it has little choice but to select the second portfolio; the first provides no accessible resources. Yet the first provides the greater returns and—were the university to periodically liquidate a portion of the portfolio—the greater cash flows.

Current Standards for Governments

Current GASB pronouncements do not explicitly address the question of how trust fund investment gains should be accounted for. However, inasmuch as investments must now be stated at fair value and gains and losses in value recognized as revenues and expenses, then, in the absence of specific legal or donor-imposed restrictions, governments should account for them just as they do dividends and interest. That is, they should report them initially in the nonexpendable trust fund. Then, if they are permitted to spend the income from appreciation and opt to do so, they should periodically transfer resources to the recipient fund, accounting for the transaction as an operating transfer.

Current Standards for Other Not-For-Profits

The FASB, in Statement No. 117, not only takes a decidedly different position than the GASB, but also refashions traditional practice. It says:

> "A statement of activities shall report gains and losses recognized on investments and other assets (or liabilities) as increases or decreases in *unrestricted* net assets unless their use is temporarily or permanently restricted by explicit donor stipulations or by law."

Thus, whereas traditional practice requires an entity to add gains to, or subtract losses from, the balance of the nonexpendable fund unless it is legally required to debit or credit them to an expendable fund, Statement No. 117 mandates the opposite. Not-for-profits must report endowment gains or losses as an addition to either unrestricted or temporarily restricted funds unless they are explicitly required by law or donor stipulation to account for them in the endowment fund.[3]

In explaining the new requirement, the FASB notes that restricted net assets result only from donor or legal stipulations that limit their use. In the absence of such stipulations, government boards are at liberty to authorize the expenditure of appreciation gains, and therefore it is improper to classify them as permanently restricted. Since not-for-profits, like governments, must state their investments at market value, appreciation gains include those that are both realized and unrealized.

DIFFERING POLICIES OF GOVERNMENTS AND NOT-FOR-PROFITS AS TO INVESTMENT LOSSES

The issue of accounting for net investment losses—those that reduce the value of an endowment below the amount contributed to it—is especially intriguing, because investment losses are not the mirror image of investment gains. Whereas investment gains can be distributed to other funds, investment losses cannot always be recovered from them.

---

[3] Paragraph 22.

EXAMPLE   *Investment Losses*

At the start of a year, an organization has an endowment fund to which donors had contributed $1 million in securities. In addition, as a result of previous investment gains, it has $10,000 of securities that are temporarily restricted for programs specified by the endowment donor. Thus, the total value of its investment portfolio, both permanently restricted and temporarily restricted, is $1,010,000. During the year, owing to losses on the sale of securities, the value of the portfolio declines by $25,000 to $985,000.

The key question is whether, in the absence of specific legal requirements or donor stipulations, the organization should reduce the stated value of its permanently restricted endowment fund to an amount below the $1 million original contribution or whether it should compensate for the loss from other sources, such as the temporarily restricted net assets or unrestricted net assets.

Current Standards for Governments

Neither the GASB nor its predecessor organizations has yet addressed explicitly the issue of investment losses. However, as noted previously, in the absence of specific provisions to the contrary, most governments report all types of investment income initially in a nonexpendable trust fund. If they are permitted to appropriate the gains for expenditure, they then transfer resources to an appropriate recipient fund. Therefore, if all of the losses were applicable to securities held in the nonexpendable fund, they would reduce the fund by the amount of the losses. If some of the losses were applicable to securities held in a restricted fund, then they would reduce the balance in that fund. Thus, in the event of losses, the balance in an unexpendable fund could be reduced below the amount contributed by the donors and expected to be preserved in perpetuity.

In the example, if the $25,000 in losses were uniform across the portfolio then $24,752 [$25,000 × ($1,000,000/$1,010,000)] would be assigned to the nonexpendable fund and $248 [$25,000 × ($10,000/$1,010,000)] to the expendable fund.

Current Standards for Other Not-For-Profits

Per FASB Statement No. 124, *Accounting for Certain Investments Held By Not-for-Profit Organizations*, unless a not-for-profit is required by donor or legal stipulation to do otherwise, it should first charge investment losses (both realized and unrealized) to **temporarily restricted net assets** to the extent that donor-imposed restrictions on previously recognized net appreciation have not yet been met.

It should charge any remaining losses to unrestricted net assets. If, in a subsequent year, investment gains restore the value of the investments to their original value, then organizations should credit them to unrestricted assets.

In the example, therefore, the organization should continue to report the endowment principal at $1 million. It should charge the first $10,000 of the $25,000 loss to temporarily restricted net assets (thereby reducing the balance of those net assets to zero) and the remaining $15,000 to unrestricted net assets. Thus (assuming a beginning-of-year balance in unrestricted assets of zero):

	Permanently Restricted	Temporarily Restricted	Unrestricted	Total
Beginning of Year	$1,000,000	$10,000	$ 0	$1,010,000
Investment Losses		(10,000)	(15,000)	(25,000)
End of Year	$1,000,000	$ 0	$(15,000)	$ 985,000

Suppose, in the example, that in the following year, the organization realizes $27,000 in investment gains, thereby increasing the total value of the portfolio from $985,000 to $1,007,000. The organization would credit to unrestricted net assets the first $15,000—the amount previously deducted from unrestricted assets. It would credit the $12,000 balance to temporarily restricted net assets. Thus:

	Permanently Restricted	Temporarily Restricted	Unrestricted	Total
Beginning of Year	$1,000,000	$ 0	$ (15,000)	$ 985,000
Investment Gains		12,000	15,000	27,000
End of Year	$1,000,000	$12,000	$ 0	$1,012,000

The end result is intuitively appealing. Since receiving its initial donation of $1 million the organization experienced net investment gains of $12,000 ($10,000 – $25,000 + $27,000). The entire amount of the net gain is available for expenditure for the donor-specified programs and is thereby classified as temporarily restricted—just as if there had been only a total gain of $12,000 without any losses and subsequent recoveries of the losses.

AGREEMENT ON HOW TO ACCOUNT FOR GAINS OR LOSSES ON EXPENDABLE RESOURCES

Expendable income from an endowment fund that is not immediately needed may be invested in temporarily revenue-producing securities, such as equity or debt securities. Therefore, an organization may reap gains or incur losses on its expendable endowment resources just as it does on its nonexpendable resources.

A question is sometime raised, therefore, of whether gains or losses on securities purchased with expendable resources are expendable or nonexpendable. This issue, however, can be resolved without debate. Although there may be confusion on the point by accounting students, there are no substantive legal or accounting issues. Expendable resources, whether held in an expendable fund or in an endowment fund awaiting transfer to an expendable fund, are, by definition, expendable. Therefore, the gains on expendable resources are also expendable.

HOW CAN INSTITUTIONS PROTECT AGAINST INFLATION, YET REAP THE BENEFITS OF CURRENT INCOME?

Institutions can readily protect against inflation, yet simultaneously reap the benefits of current income, by taking a *fixed rate of return* (often referred to as a *total return*) approach to the distribution of income. The fixed rate of return approach requires the institution to make available for current expenditure a fixed percentage of its endowment portfolio, irrespective of actual interest and dividends. The fixed (or "spending") rate would be based on long-term estimates of anticipated appreciation, inflation, dividends, and interest.

EXAMPLE   *Fixed Rate of Return Approach*

A private university expects to earn an annual return of 10 percent on its $1 million portfolio, divided as follows:

Interest and Dividends	$ 40,000
Appreciation	60,000
Total Return	$100,000

It anticipates an annual inflation rate of 3 percent per year. Thus, it expects its real (inflation-adjusted) return to be only 7 percent (10 percent less 3 percent).

Consistent with the fixed rate of return concept, the university permits annual spending of only 7 percent of its endowment principal—$70,000 the first year. The first-year excess of $30,000 is to be added to the principal and reinvested.

The apparent—and one-time controversial—accounting issue faced by organizations that take a total return approach is whether the fund in which the endowment *income* is reported should recognize as investment revenue the amount *transferred to* it or the amount *actually earned by* the endowment fund. However, under current practice for governments and Statement No. 117 for not-for-profits, the answer is now clear.

A fixed rate of return approach has no special accounting standing. Both governments and not-for-profits must account for investment income, including appreciation, as described in the previous sections.

In the example, therefore, if endowment income does not legally have to be added to principal, then the entire $100,000 would be reported as donor unrestricted (or donor temporarily restricted) income. Insofar as the university authorizes the expenditure of only $70,000, opting to retain $30,000 as if it were permanently restricted, then the unspent $30,000 would be classified as donor unrestricted (or donor temporarily restricted) assets. However, to show that the university intends to treat the sum as if it were an endowment, it could classify the $30,000 as "Designated by Board as a Nonexpendable Endowment"—a subcategory of unrestricted (or donor temporarily restricted) fund balance.

Thus, if the $30,000 were unrestricted, the university might present the equity section of its balance sheet as follows:

Net Assets:		
Permanently Restricted		$1,000,000
Unrestricted		
Designated by Board as a		
Nonexpendable Endowment	$30,000	
Undesignated	70,000	100,000
Total Fund Balances		$1,100,000

HOW ARE THE MAIN TYPES OF TRANSACTIONS RECORDED IN NONEXPENDABLE TRUST FUNDS?

As indicated, nonexpendable trust funds are accounted for on a full accrual basis. Therefore, the accounting is comparable to that of a business or a proprietary fund. This example presents the main types of transactions affecting an endowment fund. The entries are only illustrative of the general approach to fiduciary fund accounting. There can be as many variations as there are individual funds.

EXAMPLE   *Recording Transactions in Nonexpendable Trust Funds*

Establishing the Endowment Fund

A town receives a bequest of $12 million in cash and a commercial office building to support its zoo. The building, to be held as an investment, has a market value of $5 million and an anticipated useful life of twenty years. The donor stipulates that income only may be used to support the activities of the zoo. However, any investment gains beyond an amount required to protect the endowment from declines in the value of the dollar may be appropriated for zoo use as if they were ordinary income. The bequest is to be accounted for in a nonexpendable trust fund.

Cash	$12,000,000	
Office building	5,000,000	
Fund balance		$17,000,000

To record the bequest of cash and an office building

Alternatively the gift could have been credited to "endowment contributions," an account that would be closed at year-end to fund balance.

Recording the Budget

The town estimates its first-year income and prepares a budget.

Budgets are almost never recorded in a nonexpendable trust fund. The distribution of the income to expendable funds is generally governed by donor or legal stipulation and the actual appropriation of the income for substantive purposes can be more directly and effectively controlled by the budget of the expendable fund to which the income is distributed. Hence, no journal entries are required.

Purchases of Securities

The town purchases common stock for $2 million and bonds having a face value of $10 million. The bonds are twenty-year 9 percent bonds that yield 10 percent and pay interest annually. They are acquired for $9,149,000. Both securities are recorded at cost.

Common stock	$ 2,000,000	
Bonds	9,149,000	
Cash		11,149,000

To record the purchase of stocks and bonds

Interest Revenue

The town collects its first payment of bond interest, $900,000.

Cash	$ 900,000	
Interest revenue		$ 900,000

To record first payment of interest

The interest to be recognized as revenue is based on the cash received. Inasmuch as the bonds will be stated at fair value, the amortization of the bond discount will be incorporated implicitly into the revenue from appreciation.

Building Revenue and Expenses, Including Depreciation

The town collects rent on the office building of $1,000,000 and incurs cash operating expenses of $200,000. It also recognizes depreciation of $250,000

Cash	$800,000	
Building operating expenses	200,000	
Rent revenue		$1,000,000

To record building rent and operating expenses

Depreciation expense	$250,000	
Office building—accumulated depreciation		$250,000

To record depreciation (building cost of $5 million depreciated over 20 years)

Unrealized Appreciation

Owing mainly to decreases in prevailing interest rates, the market value of the bonds increases by $751,000 to $9,900,000. The market value of the stock increases by $200,000 to $2,200,000. The town recognizes the changes in value.

Bonds	$751,000	
Common stock	200,000	
Investment income—appreciation		$ 951,000

To record appreciation in the value of the securities

The town sells the bonds for $9,900,000, the amount to which the carrying value of the bonds had been adjusted immediately prior to sale.

Cash	$ 9,900,000	
Bonds (face value)		$ 9,900,000
To record the sale of bonds		

Administrative Costs

The town incurs $20,000 of costs in administering the fund.

Administrative expenses	$ 20,000	
Cash		$ 20,000
To record administrative costs		

Closing Revenue and Expense Accounts

The town closed its revenue and expense accounts, other than gains on investments.

Interest revenue	$ 900,000	
Rent revenue	1,000,000	
Building operating expenses		$ 200,000
Depreciation expense		250,000
Administrative expenses		20,000
Income available for transfer to an expendable fund		1,430,000
To close revenue and expense accounts		

"Income available for transfer to an expendable fund" is a temporary account, similar to "income summary" in a business. It is established mainly to show the distributable income in a single account.

Distribution of Investment Gains Between Principal and Income

The town determines that the prevailing inflation rate is 4%. Per the donor's stipulations, any annual investment gains greater than the inflation rate are expendable. Thus:

Investment Income—Appreciation (Per Unrealized Appreciation Entry)		$ 951,000
Beginning of Year Balance in the Endowment Fund	$17,000,000	
Inflation Rate	× .04	
Amount to be Retained in a Nonexpendable Fund		(680,000)
Amount of Investment Income—Appreciation Available for Distribution to an Expendable Fund		$ 271,000

The following entry would affect the distribution of the investment gains between principal and income:

Investment income—appreciation	$951,000	
Fund balance		$ 680,000
Income available for transfer to an expendable fund		271,000
To close the investment income—appreciation account and distribute the balance between fund balance and income available for transfer		

Transfer to Expendable Fund

The town transfers the total distributable income ($11,430,000 + $271,000) to an expendable fund (assume a fund restricted for zoo operations).

Operating transfer to expendable zoo operations fund	$ 1,701,000	
Cash		$ 1,701,000
To transfer available income to expendable zoo fund		

Correspondingly, of course, the expendable zoo fund records an operating transfer-in of the same amount.

Closing Remaining Accounts

To complete the bookkeeping process the government closes both the operating transfer and the income available for transfer accounts:

Income available for transfer to an expendable fund	$ 1,701,000	
Fund balance		$ 1,701,000
To close the income available account		

Fund balance	$ 1,701,000	
Operating transfer to expendable zoo operations fund		$ 1,701,000
To close operating transfer account		

Table 11–1 presents a summary statement of revenues, expenses, and changes in fund balance and a balance sheet.

Differences If the Trust Were Maintained by a Not-For-Profit Organization

Were the trust fund established for a not-for-profit organization rather than a government, the accounting and reporting would differ in the following respects:

- For purposes of external reporting, the interest income and the appropriate share of the investment gains would be reported in the statement of activities directly as increases in donor-restricted resources; they would be shown as investment income, not operating transfers.

- The investment income would most probably be aggregated and reported on a single line. However, an organization is free to present the details within the statement itself or in a separate schedule.

Table 11–2 illustrates how a not-for-profit organization would likely report upon the zoo expendable and nonexpendable funds. To keep Table 11–2 comparable to Table 11–1, it is assumed that, per donor stipulation, expendable income is determined as previously calculated for the government.

TABLE 11–1
Governmental Zoo Funds

Statement of Revenues, Expenditures/Expenses, and Changes in Fund Balances

	Expendable Zoo Fund (Special Revenue)	Nonexpendable Zoo Fund (Endowment)
Revenues:		
Interest		$ 900,000
Rent		1,000,000
Investment Income—Appreciation		951,000
Total Revenues		2,851,000
Expenses:		
Building Operating Expenses		200,000
Depreciation Expense		250,000
Administrative Expenses		20,000
Total Expenses		470,000
Excess of Revenues Over Expenses		2,381,000
Operating Transfer to Expendable Fund	$1,701,000	(1,701,000)
Excess of Revenues Over Expenses and Transfers	1,701,000	680,000
Contributions to Establish Nonexpendable Fund		17,000,000
Ending Fund Balance	$ 1,701,000	$ 17,680,000

Balance Sheet

	Expendable Zoo Fund (Special Revenue)	Nonexpendable Zoo Fund (Endowment)
Assets:		
Cash	$ 1,701,000	$ 10,730,000
Common Stock		2,200,000
Office Building (Net of Accumulated Depreciation of $250,000)		4,750,000
Total Assets	$ 1,701,000	$ 17,680,000
Liabilities and Fund Balance:		
Fund Balance	$ 1,701,000	$ 17,680,000

WHY ARE PENSIONS SO IMPORTANT?

Pension funds are a type of fiduciary fund, yet they are far more complex than the usual endowment fund. Owing to their dollar magnitude, they must be at the heart of an assessment of a government's or not-for-profit's fiscal well-being.

A **pension** is a sum of money paid to retired or disabled employees owing to their years of employment. Although the employees earn their pensions—and the employer benefits from their services—during their years of employment, the actual cash payments do not have to be made to the employees until their years of retirement. Thus, there may be a mismatch of many years between the benefits received and the cash payments.

TABLE 11-2		
Not-For-Profit Zoo Funds		
Statement of Activities		
	Temporarily Restricted	Permanently Restricted
Income from Investments Including Both Realized and Unrealized Gains	$1,701,000	$ 680,000
Contributions to Establish Nonexpendable Fund		17,000,000
Net Assets (End of Year)	$1,701,000	$17,680,000

Statement of Financial Position

Assets:

Cash	$12,431,000
Common Stock	2,200,000
Office Building (Net of Accumulated Depreciation of $250,000)	4,750,000
Total Assets	$19,381,000

Net assets:

Temporarily Restricted	$ 1,701,000
Permanently Restricted	17,680,000
Total Net Assets	$19,381,000

Both employer liabilities for unpaid pensions and the resources set aside for eventual payment can be gargantuan. The assets of CALPERS, the California Public Employees Retirement System, total more than $80 billion; those of the New York State Teachers Retirement System are more than $35 billion. These funds face pressures similar to large mutual funds to maximize earnings while protecting against investment losses.

The road to governmental fiscal failure is paved with inadequately funded pensions. In the years following World War II, New York City substantially expanded its work force. In exchange for smaller increases in direct wages and salaries, the city offered some groups of employees exceedingly generous retirement benefits. In the subsequent years the city failed to contribute adequately to its pension funds, sometimes basing its contributions on outmoded actuarial tables. By the mid-1970s, when many of the employees hired after the war reached retirement age, the required pension outlays consumed so large a portion of the city's current budget that they were a major cause of its fiscal crisis and its resultant forced reorganization.

How Does a Defined Contribution Plan Differ From a Defined Benefit Plan?

There are two types of pension plans. The first, and by far the simpler to account for, is a **defined contribution plan**. Under a defined contribution plan, an employer agrees to make a series of **pension contributions**. Typically, the amount is expressed as a percentage of each employee's salary and very often the pension fund is totally independent of the employer. For example, a college may contribute 8 percent of faculty member's salary to TIAA-CREF (Teachers Insurance and Annuity Association-College Retirement Equities Fund—an independent, nonprofit retirement plan), provided that the faculty member also contributes a corresponding percentage. TIAA-CREF invests the contributions and upon retirement the employee can begin to withdraw the funds, plus accumulated earnings. The actual benefits to be received by the employee depend on the fund's investment performance. As implied by the plan's name, the employer defines (specifies) the inputs, its contributions; it makes no guarantees as to the outputs, the payments to be made to its employees when they retire.

Defined contribution plans present few financial or accounting complexities. The employer reports an annual expense for the amount that it is obligated to contribute to the pension fund. Hence, this chapter will be concerned mainly with the second type of plan, the **defined benefit pension plan**.

Under a defined benefit plan, the employer specifies the benefits—the actual pension payments—that the employee will receive. Usually the benefits will vary according to length of service and salary. For example, a college might promise to pay faculty members 2.5 percent of their average annual salaries during their last three years of service for each year of employment. If a faculty member with thirty years of service earned an average of $100,000 during the three years prior to his retirement, he would be guaranteed an annual pension of $75,000 (2.5 percent × 30 years × $100,000). In contrast to the defined contribution plan, the employer guarantees the outputs (the payments to the retirees), not the contributions to the pension fund. It is therefore up to the employer to assure that it sets aside sufficient resources each year to make the required payments.

Both funding and accounting decisions relating to defined benefit plans are complex, mainly because of the uncertainties as to the amounts that will have to be paid to the retirees and that will be earned on fund investments. Sound financial policy and the need to report upon interperiod equity dictate that the costs of pensions be allocated to the periods in which employees perform their services and earn their pension benefits—not those in which they receive the cash benefits. However, the actual cost cannot be known for sure until the employees receive all the benefits that they have been promised. These will not be known until the employees (and sometimes their spouses if they are also entitled to benefits) have died. The key uncertainties affecting the actual cost of a defined benefit pension plan include:

- Employee life expectancy
- Employee turnover rates (Employees usually must accumulate a minimum number of work years before qualifying for even minimum benefits and must satisfy other conditions relating to length of employment and age to qualify for full benefits.)
- Future wage and salary rates
- The investment returns on pension fund assets

The amount that an employer must provide each year to meet its future **pension obligations** can be calculated actuarially. Actuaries are statisticians who compute insurance risks and premiums. They have also been described as "accountants without personality."

An **actuarial cost method** is the means of allocating the total cost of expected benefits over the total years of employee service. Actuarial cost methods have much in common with depreciation methods. Whereas a depreciation method allocates the cost of long-lived assets over the periods in which the assets provide service, an actuarial method allocates pension costs over the periods in which employees provide service. Just as depreciation can be allocated in many different patterns (e.g., straight-line or double declining) so, too, can pension costs.

What is the Relation Between an Employer and Its Pension Trust Fund?

Assets that have been set aside for pensions are generally legally restricted and are held for the benefit of employees. Therefore, they are accounted for in a trust fund. Government pension trusts that are organizationally separate from their sponsoring governments are often referred to as **Public Employee Retirement Systems (PERS)**.

Some pension plans are established by a single employer and cover only the employer's own employees. Others are established by a sponsoring organization, such as a state or a county for employees of governments within its jurisdiction. Under one type of multiple employer plan (an *agent* multiple employer plan), separate accounts are maintained and actuarial computations are made for each employer. In substance, therefore, each employer has its own plan; the sponsoring agent merely provides administrative and investment services. Under another type of multiple employer plan (a *cost-sharing multiple employer plan*) all employees are placed in a common pool. Their employers share all risks and costs and make contributions at the same rate.

A pension trust fund, whether maintained by the employer itself or an outside party, is an independent financial and accounting entity. If maintained by the employer, then the employer must include it in its financial statements just as it does its other funds. If maintained by an outside party, then the employer must disclose information as to its financial condition in notes to its financial statements.

The assets of a pension trust fund consist mainly of cash, securities, and other income-producing assets. Its economic obligations (irrespective of whether and when they are given accounting recognition) are the pension benefits that have been earned by its employees—both those already retired and those currently in the work force.

Even if pension trust funds are independent fiscal and accounting entities, they are inexorably linked to their sponsoring employers and the individual funds from which the pension contributions will be received. Under a defined benefit plan an employer is ultimately liable for the benefits to be paid to retirees. Therefore, the liabilities of the pension trust fund are, in economic substance, those of the employer. Similarly, if the trust fund assets increase or decrease in value, the ultimate benefits or costs revert to the employer in that its future contributions can be greater or less.

In this chapter, we shall first discuss how *employers* should account for and report their pension costs, obligations, and assets. Our attention will be on the funds used to account for the pension contributions, not the pension trust fund. We shall then turn to issues relating to the pension trust funds.

Our focus in the chapter will mainly be on governments, and more specifically on GASB Statements No. 25, *Financial Reporting for Defined Benefit Pension Plans and Note Disclosure for Defined Contribution Plans* and No. 27, *Accounting for Pensions by State and Local Governmental Employers* (both issued in 1994). We emphasize governments rather than other not-for-profits in this text primarily because pensions tend to be of greater significance to governments than to not-for-profits. Not-for-profits often participate in defined contribution rather than defined benefit plans and the plans are usually maintained by independent financial institutions. The accounting for pensions of not-for-profits that do maintain defined benefit plans is governed by FASB Statements No. 35 *Accounting and Reporting by Defined Benefit Pension Plans*, and No. 87, *Employers' Accounting for Pensions*. Consequently, there are few accounting issues or issues that are either troublesome or different than those faced by businesses.

WHAT ISSUES DOES A GOVERNMENT EMPLOYER FACE IN ACCOUNTING FOR ITS PENSIONS?

DIFFERENCES FROM PRIVATE-SECTOR STANDARDS

As the GASB carried out its project on pension accounting and reporting, it faced a fundamental question. In light of the similarity between pensions in the private and public sectors, should the GASB simply adopt the FASB's pension pronouncements and apply them to governments? In other words, is there an economic rationale for different principles and practices?

To a minority of the Board, the answer was yes, the GASB should indeed adopt the relevant FASB pronouncements (albeit with some modifications). To a majority, however, pensions of governments are sufficiently different from those of businesses to justify their own set of accounting standards. Relevant distinctions between businesses and governments include the following:

- In governments, short-term measures of financial condition are less important than in businesses. Businesses, unlike governments, can be bought and sold. In some circumstances the pension plans of businesses can be liquidated and any excess of plan assets over obligations to current employees and retirees can either be used for other corporate purposes or be distributed to stockholders. Thus, point-in-time values of plan assets and obligations are of critical concern to current and potential investors. Governments, by contrast, can be assumed to have a "perpetual" existence and it is unlikely that their pension plans will be dissolved.

- In governments, a primary objective of financial accounting is reporting on budgetary compliance. Therefore (as emphasized throughout this text), the need for expenditure measures that capture the full economic cost of services must be tempered with the need for those that are comparable to amounts that have been budgeted and appropriated.

- Many federal statutes that influenced the development of pension standards for businesses are inapplicable to governments.

THE BASIS FOR DETERMINING THE ANNUAL PENSION COST

In considering possible bases for determining a government's annual pension cost, one must be careful to distinguish between pension *cost* and pension *expenditure*. In governmental funds an expenditure represents a decrease in net financial resources. Costs that result in liabilities that will not be liquidated with available financial resources are not recognized as expenditures. Hence, whereas *expenditure* refers to the amount that will be liquidated with financial resources, *cost* measures the full value of economic resources to be sacrificed. As shall be evident later in this chapter, governments are required to disclose their full pension costs, even if they do not recognize the costs as expenditures.

Governments have a choice among several widely accepted actuarial methods to determine the amount that they should contribute to their pension plans each year. The method that they choose, as well as what they actually contribute, are beyond the purview of the GASB. The GASB is empowered only to establish accounting and reporting standards. It has no authority to mandate the funding (contribution) practices of individual governments.

In developing standards on pension cost, the GASB had to choose between two competing approaches. The first dictates that *for purposes of external reporting*, all governments determine their pension cost according to a specified actuarial method and other assumptions. They would have to use these methods and assumptions, even if they use others to establish their actual funding schedule. This approach would permit the board to develop principles that capture the full economic costs of pensions and assure that they are allocated among periods in what the board considers the most appropriate pattern. Equally important, it would assure that reported pension costs among all governments are comparable.

The second approach allows each government to use the same actuarial methods and assumptions to determine its reported pension cost as it does its actual funding schedule. This approach would assure that a government's budgeted and reported expenditures are comparable to its required contribution per its own actuarial procedures. Moreover, it would reduce the complexity of financial statements, as it would eliminate the need to explain and reconcile differences between what should have been contributed per the government's own actuarial procedures and what should have been contributed per a board-specified formula.

The board adopted the second approach—but with constraints. It said that a government's annual pension cost should equal its *annual required contribution* (as determined by its own actuaries), as long as the contribution satisfies specified guidelines. The guidelines are intended to give governments reasonable flexibility in their choice of actuarial methods and assumptions but at the same time prohibit those methods and assumptions that are clearly unacceptable (such as the pay-as-you-go method, whereby expenditures are recognized only as payments are made to retirees).

Minimum Criteria for Acceptable Annual Required Contribution

The criteria that an employer's annual required contribution must satisfy to be considered acceptable include the following:

- The contribution must consist of the employer's *normal cost* plus a provision for amortizing the employer's unfunded actuarial accrued liability. This requirement is discussed in more detail in the section that follows.

- Actuarial assumptions, including those pertaining to mortality, changes in compensation rates, and investment earnings, must be in accordance with standards of the Actuarial Standards Board, the actuarial equivalent of the FASB and the GASB.

- The actuarial value of pension plan assets must be *market-related*. That is, in calculating the employer's annual required contribution, the actuary does not necessarily have to value plan assets at their market price as of a specific date, but rather, can look to average values over a period of three to five years. The advantage of using an extended period rather than a point in time is that changes in value can be recognized over several years rather than a single year, thereby dampening year-to-year swings in the annual required contribution.

- Assumptions as to investment earnings rates and future inflation should be based on long-term projections, rather than on those for a single year.

Determination of Normal Cost

The employer's normal cost is the portion of the present value of pension plan benefits that is allocated to a particular year by an actuarial cost method. The GASB requires that normal cost be based on one of six specified actuarial methods. These bear such esoteric names as "projected unit credit," "entry age normal," and "frozen entry age normal." The normal cost is computed by actuaries and the specifics of the various methods are beyond the scope of this text.

Unfunded Actuarial Accrued Liability and Amortization

The employer's unfunded actuarial accrued liability is the excess of the actuarially computed pension liability over the pension plan's assets. For example, if an actuary has determined that a government's current employees and retirees have earned a total of $50 million of pension benefits (computed in accordance with an appropriate actuarial method) and the value of the plan's investments total $45 million, then the unfunded actuarial accrued liability would be $5 million.

An unfunded actuarial accrued liability can result from several circumstances. These include:

- *Transition losses.* When an employer applies GASB Statement No. 27 for the first time, it may have to recognize a pension liability that previously it did not.
- *Actuarial losses.* As a result of changes in actuarial methods or actuarial assumptions, the pension liability may increase.
- *Improvements in pension benefits.* If an employer increases pension benefits, then it may have a significant increase in its pension liability. For example, if an employer increases pension benefits from 60 to 65 percent of a final year's salary (and the change is applicable to all employees, including those who are about to retire), then the employer's liability would increase.
- *Special termination benefits.* By sweetening pension benefits as an incentive for employees to retire early, employers will increase their pension obligations. For example, to trim its work force without having to discharge employees, an employer may reduce the number of years of service employees must accumulate to get full pension benefits.

For convenience we have set forth the circumstances in terms of changes that increase the pension liability. Decreases are accounted for in a corresponding fashion. Plans can also be overfunded, in which case the liability is negative.

To mitigate possible spikes in pension expenditures, the GASB requires an employer to amortize these components of its unfunded actuarial accrued liability, rather than recognize them in a single period. Each of the circumstances that contributes to the liability causes increases in the employer's pension costs. Were the employer required either to fund the increased costs entirely in the year of the change, or to report an expenditure equal to the full amount of the additional costs, then its pension contribution or expenditure for that year would be unduly large.

GASB permits employers to amortize the unfunded liability over ten to forty years (although the 40-year maximum decreases to 30 years after GASB Statement No. 25, pertaining to pension *plans* (rather than the employer) has been in effect for 10 years).

EXAMPLE *Unfunded Actuarial Accrued Liability*

An employer's normal pension cost is $40 million. Owing to an improvement in pension benefits, its actuarial pension obligation increases by $20 million. If the employer elects to amortize the additional cost over the maximum of forty years, then the employer would add $0.5 million to its normal costs each year. Its total annual required contribution would therefore be $40.5 million—the normal cost plus the amortization of the unfunded liability. (In reality, owing to a required interest charge on unfunded obligations and other technical adjustments, the calculation is considerably more complex than implied by this presentation.)

The GASB permits such a long amortization period, so as to minimize the volatility of employer pension costs. However, critics of the statement, including two members of the GASB who dissented to its issuance, have charged that this range is far too broad and the maximum number of years is too great. The maximum period, they note, is far longer than the working lives of most employees. In fact, because the GASB permits governments to amortize the unfunded actuarial accrued liability over an "open" period—one that begins again at each actuarial valuation date—the effective maximum number of years can be even greater than 40. The benefits to the employer could not possibly be that long and the costs, therefore, should be amortized over a shorter period, perhaps an average of employee service lives.

In particular, critics object to allowing the termination benefit component of the liability to be spread over the same number of years as the other components. Employees who are eligible for early retirement would almost always have retired in a few years anyway, they contend. Therefore the benefits to the employer could not possibly last for forty years, the permissible maximum amortization period. They further point out that the FASB, in Statement No. 74, *Accounting for Special Termination Benefits Paid to Employees*, requires comparable benefits in businesses to be charged off entirely in the year they are granted.

An employer would almost always report its pension costs in the same fund as it charges the related wages and salaries. Owing to a different basis of accounting, the pension expense or expenditure would be determined differently in proprietary as opposed to governmental funds. The pension expense for employees of a utility fund would be accounted for in a propriety fund, while the pension expenditure for policemen would be accounted for in the general (governmental) fund.

REPORTING PENSION COSTS

EXAMPLE *Reporting Pension Costs*

A city maintains a defined benefit plan for its employees. During the year the city contributed $25 million to its pension fund, even though its actuary calculated the required contribution, consistent with GASB guidelines, to be $32 million.

In a Propriety Fund

If the pension costs are to be accounted for in a proprietary fund, and thus on the full accrual basis, then the reported pension expense would be the same as the pension cost—the required contribution as determined by the employer's actuary. As discussed previously, the individual employer has considerable flexibility in calculating its pension cost, but it must satisfy the GASB-imposed criteria.

Insofar as the employer makes its required contribution, it need not report a pension liability. However, if it contributes less than what is required, it must account for the difference as a liability, "net pension obligation."

In the example, inasmuch as the annual required contribution ($32 million) as calculated in accord with GASB guidelines exceeds the employer's contribution ($25 million), the following entry would be appropriate:

Pension expense	$32	
Cash		$25
Net pension obligation		7

To record the annual pension contribution and expense

In each subsequent year, the net pension obligation would be adjusted by the difference between the required contributions (the pension expense) and the actual contributions. Were cumulative pension contributions to exceed the cumulative reported expenses, then the excess would be reported as a net pension asset.

In a Government Fund

In a governmental fund, which is accounted for on a modified accrual basis, the reported pension expenditure would be the contribution to be liquidated with expendable available financial resources—that is, the amount actually contributed plus contributions expected to be made with current-year resources shortly after the end of the current year. The difference between the annual required contribution and the amount reported as the expenditure would be recognized as an increase to the net pension obligation—a *long-term* liability that would be reported in the general long-term debt account group (GLTDAG). Thus, the pension expenditure would be only the $25 million contributed to the pension fund; the $7 million difference between the annual required contribution and the actual contribution would be reported as a long-term liability:

General (or other governmental) fund

Pension expenditure	$25	
Cash		$25

To record the annual pension contribution and expenditure

General long-term debt account group

Amount to be provided for pension payments	$7	
Net pension obligation		$7

To record the difference between the annual required contribution and the actual pension contribution

As in the proprietary fund, the net pension obligation would be adjusted each year for differences between pension expenditures and pension contributions. However, unlike in the proprietary fund, if at any time the contributions exceeded the assets, the government would not report either a negative liability in the GLTDAG or an asset in the fixed asset account group. It would simply report no asset or liability.

When an employer first adopts Statement No. 27, it must determine whether it has an actuarial liability—that is, whether it undercontributed in past years. If so, the liability (the pension liability at transition) should be reported as the initial net pension obligation.

In truth, the pension information disclosed in the body of an employer's financial statements provides relatively little insight into an employer's pension costs and obligations. The following are but a few of its limitations:

- Insofar as employment costs and obligations are divided among several funds, so, too, are pension expenditures and liabilities.

- The reported liability does not capture the full economic obligation to current and future pensioners; it is merely the difference between required annual contributions to the pension fund and actual contributions.

- Since employers have considerable flexibility in actuarial methods and assumptions, neither the pension expenditures nor obligations are readily comparable among employers.

To compensate for these limitations the GASB directs that employers provide extensive information about both their pension costs and obligations and the financial condition of the underlying pension plan. The required disclosures include the following:

- a detailed description of the pension plan, including the types of benefits provided
- the employer's funding policy, including employer and employee contribution rates for the current and past two years
- the components of the pension cost and the changes in the net pension obligation
- key assumptions used in determining the pension costs and liability, including actuarial method, inflation rate, projected salary increases, and investment rate
- the actuarial value of plan assets and liabilities for the current and past two years
- significant ratios, such as funding ratio (actuarial value of plan assets to actuarial value of plan liabilities) and ratio of unfunded actuarial accrued liabilities to annual covered payroll for the current and past two years.

Table 11–3 indicates the pension disclosures as illustrated by the GASB in Statement No. 27. The statement is effective for fiscal years beginning after June 15, 1997.

LIMITATIONS OF THE INFORMATION REPORTED IN THE BASIC FINANCIAL STATEMENTS

HOW SHOULD THE PENSION PLAN BE ACCOUNTED FOR?

In this section we shift our attention from the funds that provide the pension contributions to the pension trust fund that receives them.

The GASB issued Statement No. 25, *Financial Reporting for Defined Benefit Pension Plans and Note Disclosure for Defined Contribution Plans*, concurrently with Statement No. 27, *Accounting for Pensions by State and Local Governmental Employers*. Its objective was to assure that the information provided by both pension plan and employer were consistent.

As seen by the GASB, the main objective in pension plan accounting and reporting should be to provide useful information for assessing:

- the stewardship of plan resources and the ongoing ability of the plan to pay benefits
- the effect of plan operations and benefit commitments on the contributions required of both employers and employees

Therefore, according to the GASB, the plans should provide information on:

- plan assets, liabilities, and net assets available for benefits
- year-to-year changes in plan net assets available for benefits
- the funded status of the plan from a long-term perspective
- the contribution requirements of employers and employees

TABLE 11–3
Employer Pension Disclosures as Illustrated by the GASB

Note disclosure

Note X. Pension Plan

Plan Description. The City's defined benefit pension plan, Dill Employees Pension Plan (DEPP), provides retirement and disability benefits, annual cost-of-living adjustments, and death benefits to plan members and beneficiaries. DEPP is affiliated with the Municipal Employees Pension Plan (MEPP), an agent multiple-employer pension plan administered by the Columbine Retirement System. Article 39 of the Regulations of the State of Columbine assigns the authority to establish and amend the benefit provisions of the plans that participate in MEPP to the respective employer entities; for DEPP, that authority rests with the City of Dill. The Columbine Retirement System issues a publicly available financial report that includes financial statements and required supplementary information for MEPP. That report may be obtained by writing to Columbine Retirement System, State Government Lane, Anytown, USA 01000 or by calling 1-800-555-PLAN.

Funding Policy. DEPP members are required to contribute 8% of their annual covered salary. The City is required to contribute at an actuarially determined rate; the current rate is 11% of annual covered payroll. The contribution requirements of plan members and the City are established and may be amended by the MEPP Board of Trustees.

Annual Pension Cost. For 19X2, the City's annual pension cost of $2,590,000 for DEPP was equal to the City's required and actual contributions. The required contribution was determined as part of the December 31, 19X1 actuarial valuation using the entry age actuarial cost method. The actuarial assumptions included (a) 7.5% investment rate of return (net of administrative expenses), (b) projected salary increases ranging from 5.5% to 11.5% per year, and (c) 2% per year cost-of-living adjustments. Both (a) and (b) included an inflation component of 5.5%. The actuarial value of DEPP assets was determined using techniques that smooth the effects of short-term volatility in the market value of investments over a four-year period. DEPP's unfunded actuarial accrued liability is being amortized as a level percentage of projected payroll on a closed basis. The remaining amortization period at December 31, 19X1 was 14 years.

Three-Year Trend Information for DEPP
(Dollar Amounts in Thousands)

Fiscal Year Ending	Annual Pension Cost (APC)	Percentage of APC Contributed	Net Pension Obligation
6/30/X0	$2,409	100%	$0
6/30/X1	2,511	100	0
6/30/X2	2,590	100	0

Required supplementary information

Schedule of Funding Progress for DEPP
(Dollar amounts in thousands)

Actuarial Valuation Date	Actuarial Value of Assets (a)	Actuarial Accrued Liability (AAL) —Entry Age (b)	Unfunded AAL (UAAL) (b–a)	Funded Ratio (a/b)	Covered Payroll (c)	UAAL as a Percentage of Covered Payroll ((b–a)/c)
12/31/W9*	$49,629	$52,838	$3,209	93.9%	$21,367	15.0%
12/31/X0	55,088	57,615	2,527	95.6	22,276	11.3
12/31/X1	59,262	62,817	3,555	94.3	23,551	15.1

* Revised economic and noneconomic assumptions due to experience review.

The most fundamental issue faced by the GASB relates to the form and content of the basic financial statements. Specifically, the main question the Board had to address was whether information as to current plan assets and activities could be combined with actuarial data into the same set of financial statements.

The Board determined that the two types of information are fundamentally different in character and need to be reported in different ways. Therefore, it decided that the primary financial statements, a balance sheet (statement of net assets available for benefits) and statement of activities (statement of changes in net assets available for benefits), should report only on net plan assets, excluding actuarially determined benefits to current and future retirees. The actuarial obligations and related information should be reported in supplementary schedules and notes.

Because they exclude actuarial liabilities, the statement of net assets available for benefits and the statement of changes in net assets available for benefits do not depend on the estimates and assumptions discussed earlier. Net assets consist mainly of three categories of resources:

- *Receivables.* These are generally short-term, primarily contributions actually due on the reporting date from employees and employers, and investment interest and dividends.

- *Investments.* These include the stocks, bonds, and real estate acquired with employer and employee contributions. Pension plan investments, including real estate, should be reported at *fair* (ie., market) value.

- *Assets used in plan operations.* These include the buildings, equipment, furniture, and fixtures used in administering the plan. Generally minor in relation to investments, they should be stated at *cost less accumulated depreciation.*

The statements of net assets available for benefits and changes in such asset are illustrated in Table 11–4.

REPORTING NET PLAN ASSETS

REPORTING AND CALCULATING ACTUARIAL INFORMATION

Per Statement No. 25, pension plans should report their actuarial information in notes to the basic financial statements and in two supplementary schedules.

In establishing standards for reporting the actuarial information, the GASB confronted an issue similar to that relating to pension costs being reported by employers: Should all plans have to use the same actuarial procedures, or should they be permitted to base their data on the procedures that they actually use?

The Board decided that measures based on the actual procedures used by a plan would be more useful to statement users. It elected not to impose a standardized measure. Instead, it established guidelines to assure that the reported measures are reasonable—indeed, the *same* guidelines as those that apply to employer pension costs. Thus, for example, the pension costs and liabilities must be calculated by one of the six Board-approved actuarial methods, the annual cost must include the normal cost plus a provision for amortizing the unfunded actuarial accrued liability and the amortization period can be no longer than forty years (reduced to 30 years for years beginning after June 15, 2007).

The two required supplementary schedules are a *schedule of funding progress* and a *schedule of employer contributions.* Each should include information for a period of *six* years. The schedule of funding progress should include the following information:

TABLE 11-4
Statements of Plan Net Assets
and Changes in Net Plan Assets as Illustrated by the GASB

Statement of Plan Net Assets as of June 30, 19X2 (in thousands)

Assets:

Cash and Short-Term Investments	$ 66,129
Receivables	
Employer	16,451
Employer—Long-Term	
Interest and Dividends	33,495
Total Receivables	49,946
Investments, at Fair Value	
U.S. Government Obligations	541,289
Municipal Bonds	33,585
Domestic Corporate Bonds	892,295
Domestic Stocks	1,276,533
International Stocks	461,350
Mortgages	149,100
Real Estate	184,984
Venture Capital	26,795
Total Investments	3,565,931
Properties, at Cost, Net of Accumulated	
Depreciation of $5,164 and $4,430, Respectively	6,351
Total Assets	3,688,357

Liabilities:

Refunds Payable and Other	4,212
Net Assets Held in Trust for Pension Benefits	**$3,684,145**

Statement of Changes in Net Plan Assets for Year Ending June 30, 19X2 (in Thousands)

Additions:

Contributions	
Employer	$137,916
Employer—Long-Term	
Plan Member	90,971
Total Contributions	228,887
Investment Income	
Net Appreciation (Depreciation) in Fair Value of Investments	(241,408)
Interest	157,371
Dividends	123,953
Real Estate Operating Income, Net	10,733
	50,649
Less Investment Expense	54,081
Net Investment Income	(3,432)
Total Additions	225,455

Deductions:

Benefits	170,434
Refunds of Contributions	15,750
Administrative Expense	4,984
Total Deductions	191,168
Net increase	34,287
Net Assets Held in Trust for Pension Benefits	
Beginning of Year	3,649,858
End of Year	$3,684,145

- actuarial value of plan assets
- actuarial accrued liability
- the total unfunded actuarial accrued liability (the difference between the actuarial value of plan assets and the actuarial accrued liability)
- the actuarial value of assets as a percentage of the actuarial accrued liability (the funded ratio)
- the annual covered payroll
- the ratio of the unfunded actuarial accrued liability to annual covered payroll

The schedule of employer contributions should indicate:

- the dollar amount of the annual required contributions applicable to that year
- the percentage of the annual required contributions that the employer actually contributed
- contributions from other sources, such as a state government

The notes to the basic statements and the schedules should detail keys terms of the plan, actuarial methods used, important actuarial assumptions, and factors that significantly affect trends in the amounts reported (such as changes in benefits, population and actuarial assumptions).

Table 11–5 presents the schedule of funding progress and a schedule of employer contributions as recommended by the GASB in Statement No. 25.

TABLE 11–5
Schedules of Funding Progress and Employer Contributions as Illustrated by the GASB

Schedule of Funding Progress (Dollar Amounts in Thousands)

Actuarial Valuation Date	Actuarial Value of Assets (a)	Actuarial Accrued Liability (AAL) —Entry Age (b)	Unfunded AAL (UAAL) (b − a)	Funded Ratio (a/b)	Covered Payroll (c)	UAAL as a Percentage of Covered Payroll ((b − a)/c)
12/31/W6	$2,005,238	$2,626,296	$621,058	76.4%	$ 901,566	68.9%
12/31/W7	2,441,610	2,902,399	490,789	83.1	956,525	51.3
12/31/W8	2,709,432	3,331,872	622,440	81.3	1,004,949	61.9
12/31/W9*	3,001,314	3,604,297	602,983	83.3	1,049,138	57.5
12/31/X0	3,366,946	3,930,112	563,166	85.7	1,093,780	51.5
12/31/X1	3,658,323	4,284,961	626,638	85.4	1,156,346	54.2

Schedule of Employer Contributions (Dollar Amounts in Thousands)

Year Ended June 30	Annual Required Contribution	Percentage Contributed
19W7	$100,729	100%
19W8	106,030	100
19W9	112,798	100
19X0	118,735	100
19X1	124,276	100
19X2	137,916	100

The issue of whether pension plans should base their actuarial values for purposes of *external reporting* on standardized procedures or on the actuarial procedures has important economic consequences, because the values impact employer contributions.

Prior to the implementation of Statement No. 25, pension plans were required by GASB Statement No. 5, *Disclosure of Pension Information by Public Employee Retirement Systems and State and Local Government Employers* to present a standardized measure of their pension obligations. As a consequence, the New York State retirement system reported that its pension plan was *overfunded*—that plan assets exceeded the actuarial value of its liabilities—when, in fact, based on the methods used by the plan's own actuaries, it was not.

As might be expected, when the governor and members of the state legislature became aware of the plan's overfunded status, they sought to reduce the state's contributions to the plan. Plan trustees objected, claiming that the reported values misleadingly characterized the plan's financial status.

When plan trustees complained to the GASB that the standardized measure was having what they considered adverse economic consequences, the Board defended the standardized measure, claiming that it was serving its intended purpose. That purpose, it said, was to enable comparisons with other pension plans and to raise a warning flag as to under- or overfunded conditions. Funding decisions, it argued, do not have to be consistent with GAAP-based financial statements. The statements merely provide information, which the governments are free to accept, supplement, or reject as they deem appropriate.

Obviously, Statement No. 25 represents a sharp turnabout in Board opinion from that expressed in Statement No. 5.

A STATE LEGISLATURE IS INFLUENCED BY THE REPORTED PENSION OBLIGATION

HOW SHOULD POSTEMPLOYMENT HEALTH CARE BENEFITS BE ACCOUNTED FOR?

We now focus our attention, albeit only briefly, on postemployment health care benefits—employee benefits that are substantively similar to pensions. Some employers, in fact, provide health care benefits to retirees through their defined benefit pension plans. Postemployment health care benefits present all of the issues associated with ordinary pension benefits—and then some. The ultimate net cost of providing health care benefits to retirees is subject to the same uncertainties of ordinary pension benefits—mortality rates, investment rates, turnover rates, and so on. In addition, however, the cost will depend on medical technology and the institutional and economic structure of health care—factors difficult to predict five years in the future, to say nothing of the potential 60 to 80 years between the start of an employee's career and the end of his or her life.

The GASB considered how defined benefit pension plans should account for and report on postemployment plans as part of its project on pensions. It chose, however, to provide only "interim" guidance, pending completion of a more comprehensive project that also included other types of postemployment benefits.

Per the interim standards, a defined benefit pension plan that administers a postemployment health care plan should include in its annual report two statements in addition to those that apply to the ordinary pension benefits:

- a statement of postemployment health care plan assets
- a statement of changes in postemployment health care plan net assets

These statements are not illustrated in this chapter. They would be virtually identical to the comparable statements of pensions.

The plan need *not* include supplementary schedules of funding progress and employer contributions comparable to those required for ordinary pension benefits. Moreover, it need *not* provide any actuarial information, such as the annual required contribution or the actuarial accrued liability. Thus, until the GASB issues a final pronouncement on postemployment benefits, the financial statements will provide only minimal information on the fiscal status of the health care portion of the plan itself or the employer's costs and obligations.

Even though the GASB has provided only minimal guidance as to postemployment health care benefits, the potential significance of these benefits should not be underestimated. Most governments that offer these benefits fund them on a pay-as-you go basis. Therefore, they have neither set aside the resources, nor reported the expenditure, for the benefits being earned today. But the bills will eventually be presented and have to be paid.

WHAT ACCOUNTING ISSUES DO AGENCY FUNDS PRESENT?

Agency funds are the other main category of fiduciary funds. Associated mainly with governments, they are used to account for resources held by one entity in a capacity as a trustee or an **agent** (a representative) of another. Agency funds are the simplest of all funds to account for. They are custodial in nature. Assets always equal liabilities. There are no fund balances—and therefore no changes in fund balances—upon which to report. Budgets are unnecessary.

Because agency funds are custodial in nature, they do not carry out operations that affect the governments that administer them. Nevertheless, governments should prepare agency fund balance sheets and statements that show the changes in assets and liabilities. The assets and liabilities should be measured on the modified accrual basis.

The journal entries of an agency fund present few problems. An increase in assets is generally offset with a liability—amounts due to the party on whose behalf the assets are being held.

EXAMPLE   *Agency Funds*

To reduce billing and collection costs, a county collects property taxes for the independent school district with which it shares common boundaries. The county bills taxpayers for both itself and the school district on a single invoice. The county maintains an agency fund to account for the school district's taxes. At the start of a year it held $0.3 million in cash not yet remitted to the school district.

During the year, the county collects $4.5 million of taxes on behalf of the school district. The following entry would be appropriate in the county's agency fund:

Cash	$4.5	
Due to school district		$4.5
To record the collection of taxes		

To enhance administrative control over the collection and distribution of taxes, some governments might record a receivable (e.g., school district taxes receivable) and a corresponding liability (e.g., due to school district) upon being notified of the tax levy by the other government. However, the agent government does not have a legal liability to the other government until it actually collects the taxes, and it is not responsible for losses resulting from uncollectible taxes. To emphasize this point in this example, we avoid recording both the receivable and the liability. Further, since taxpayers will make a single payment for the taxes of both governments, many governments initially account for both their own taxes and those of the other government in a common agency fund. Periodically they apportion the receipts between the other government and itself. To avoid complicating the example, we assume that the government accounts for only the school district taxes in an agency fund.

To earn interest on the funds received, the county invests $4.0 million in short-term securities.

Investments	$4.0	
Cash		$4.0
To record purchase of short-term securities		

It earns, but does not yet collect, $0.1 million in interest. The interest would be accounted for on an accrual basis. Assuming that by agreement with the school district all investment risks and rewards are those of the district, not the county, the interest would be recognized as due to the school district

Interest receivable	$0.1	
Due to school district		$0.1
To record interest earned		

It sells $2.9 million of the investments.

Cash	$2.9	
Investments		$2.9
To record the sale of investments		

It distributes $3.0 million to the county.

Due to school district	$3.0	
Cash		$3.0
To record distribution of assets to school district		

At year-end, its balance sheet and statement of changes in assets and liabilities (combined into a single statement) would appear as follows:

Property Tax Collection Agency Fund Statement of Changes in Assets and Liabilities (in millions)				
	Beginning Balance	Additions	Deductions	Ending Balance
Assets:				
Cash	$0.3	$ 7.4	$7.0	$0.7
Interest Receivable		0.1		0.1
Investments	0.0	4.0	2.9	1.1
Total Assets	$0.3	$11.5	$9.9	$1.9
Liabilities:				
Due to School District	$0.3	$ 4.6	$3.0	$1.9

The challenging—and sometimes controversial—questions relate to when an agency fund should be established. Consider, for example, two issues.

ESTABLISHING AGENCY FUNDS

Special Assessments

A government issues debt that is to be serviced entirely from special assessments. The government collects the assessments from the assessed property owners, temporarily invests any funds on hand, and makes the required payments to the bondholders or the bond trustee. Although it anticipates that it will service the debt entirely from the assessments, the government may, to a variety of degrees, be liable for any shortages. For example, it may formally guarantee the debt, it may be required to cover delinquencies until foreclosure proceeds are received from defaulting property owners, or it may explicitly indicate that in the event of default it *may* cover delinquencies even if not legally obligated to do so.

As pointed out in the previous discussion of special assessments (Chapter 7), a government should account for special assessment resources in an agency fund only when it is not obligated for the related debt *in any manner*, it held. "Any manner" would include any indication that it is either legally obligated for the debt or may assume responsibility for it, even if not legally obligated.[4]

Pass-Through Grants

Governments routinely receive grants that they are required to "pass-through" to secondary recipients. Although the assets can be used only to benefit the secondary recipients, depending on the terms of the award, the governments may have varying responsibilities for administering the grants. For example, some grants require the government to disburse funds to parties named by the grantor. Others require the government to select the recipients and subsequently monitor their performance. Thus, in some circumstances the government may be a mere agent for the grantor; in others the government may have substantive control over the funds.

Per GASB Statement No. 24, *Accounting and Financial Reporting for Certain Grants and Other Financial Assistance*, a government may account for the proceeds of a pass-through grant only when it serves as a *cash conduit*. It serves as a cash conduit when it

---

[4] *Codification*, Section S40.119.

merely transmits funds to the recipient without having any administrative involvement in the grant program. Administrative involvement includes monitoring compliance with grant requirements, selecting recipients, or allocating discretion in how the funds are allocated.[5]

ACCOUNTING FOR AGENCY RELATIONSHIPS BY NOT-FOR-PROFITS

Not-for-profit organizations other than governments also act as agents for other parties. To enhance internal control, not-for-profits may account for the resources held for others in agency funds. For purposes of external reporting, however, they must classify all net assets into one of the three categories of donor restrictiveness. Agency relationships imply an obligation to the party for whom assets are held. Therefore, not-for-profits, like governments, must offset changes in agency assets with corresponding changes in liabilities—not revenues or expenses. Irrespective of whether agency assets are classified as restricted or unrestricted, they would have no impact on the organization's net assets.

The difficult issue faced by not-for-profits is similar to that faced by governments—distinguishing between an agency and an operating transaction. Although the FASB has not yet provided guidance on drawing the distinction, the AICPA's audit guide, *Not-for-Profit Organizations*, indicates that an agency transaction is one in which an organization has little or no discretion in receiving the resources received.[6]

Consider, for example, three transactions in which the recipient organization has virtually no discretion over an apparent contribution:

- A college receives funds that must be used to provide financial aid for a specified student (as opposed to a class of students, such as those with grade-point averages of 3.5 or better from which the university can select the recipients)

- A welfare organization receives contributions of furniture and clothing to assist a specific local family whose home was destroyed by a storm (as opposed to all victims of the storm)

- A church sponsors a food drive for a local food bank (as opposed to collecting the food and distributing it directly to the ultimate recipients)

In each of these situations, the recipient would debit an asset for the fair value of the resources received. But it would credit a liability, "Resources held for others," rather than a revenue.

SUMMARY

Fiduciary funds are used to account for resources held by one organization as a trustee or agent for others. The two main categories of fiduciary funds are trust funds, including pension funds, and agency funds.

Nonexpendable trust funds, also called endowments, are used to account for resources donated to an organization with the stipulation that only income earned from the assets can be expended, not the principal. In expendable trusts, both the principal and the interest may be expended. Governments typically record investment income in a nonexpendable trust fund and then transfer it to the beneficiary funds. Not-for-profits, however, report it directly in the beneficiary funds.

Nonexpendable trust funds should be accounted for on a full accrual basis. The full accrual basis encompasses changes in all resources, not just cash, and thereby helps to

---

[5] *Codification*, Section G60.104.
[6] Paras. 5.03–5.18.

assure that a trust does not dissipate its principal through excessive spending.

Governments typically recognize endowment fund investment gains and losses in the endowment fund itself. Then, if they are permitted to spend the gains, they transfer them to a beneficiary fund.

By contrast, in the absence of specific legal or donor-imposed stipulations, not-for-profits are required to recognize expendable gains, including unrealized appreciation, as additions to either unrestricted or temporarily restricted net assets. However, they must charge investment losses first to temporarily restricted net assets to the extent that donor-imposed restrictions on previously recognized gains have not yet been met and then to unrestricted net assets. Thus, they must preserve the balance in the endowment fund.

The resources of expendable trust funds, by definition, are expendable. Therefore, investment gains are available for expenditure and investment losses decrease the resources available for expenditure.

The fixed rate of return approach requires an institution to make available for current expenditure a fixed percentage of its endowment portfolio. For accounting purposes, however, the actual earnings should be recognized as investment revenue, irrespective of whether they are greater or less than the stated fixed percentage.

Because of their dollar magnitude, pensions are of vital concern to statement preparers and users. Defined contribution plans—which are becoming increasingly popular—are simple to account for because the employer defines the inputs and makes no guarantees as to outputs. Therefore, the reported expenditures are generally the agreed-upon contributions. Defined benefit plans are far more complex because the employer defines the outputs and is required to contribute a sufficient amount to pay the required benefits when its employees retires. But inasmuch as the benefits are subject to uncertainties, the funding and accounting determinations have to be based on estimates and allocations.

Although a government employer and its pension trust fund may each be independent legal and reporting entities, the two are inexorably linked. The government must assure that the trust fund has sufficient resources to pay retirees. Ultimately, albeit indirectly, it benefits from investment and actuarial gains and incurs the cost of corresponding losses.

According to GASB standards, each employer should report as its pension costs its annual required contribution to its pension plan as long as that contribution satisfies certain criteria of reasonableness as to actuarial methods and assumptions. If the government accounts for its pension costs in a governmental fund, then the recognized expenditure should be the portion of the pension cost to be liquidated with expendable available financial resources. The difference between the cumulative annual pension costs and the cumulative contributions should be reported as a liability in the general long-term debt account group. If it accounts for its pension costs in a proprietary fund, then the recognized expenditure should be the annual required pension contribution and the difference between the cumulative pension cost and the cumulative contributions should be reported as a fund liability.

As a consequence of the GASB standards, the basic financial statements of government employers do not provide information on the entity's unfunded actuarial liability to current and future retirees. The actuarial data must be reported in supplementary notes and schedules.

Pension plans include in their basic financial statements information only on net plan assets, *excluding* actuarial obligations. Like the employers, they should report actuarial information in supplementary schedules and notes. Moreover, like employers, they have broad discretion in how they determine their actuarial values. However, the actuarial values of the plans must be consistent with those reported by the employers.

Agency funds are the simplest of funds for which to account. They are custodial in nature, so assets must equal liabilities. They have no fund balances, and hence no changes in fund balances to account for and report.

EXERCISE FOR REVIEW AND SELF-STUDY

The following note was taken from the June 30, 1999, financial statements of a state government:

Pension Plan

- *Plan Description.* The state contributes to the State Employees Pension Plan (SEPP), a single-employer defined benefit pension plan administered by the State Retirement System. SEPP provides retirement, disability, and death benefits to plan members and beneficiaries. Cost-of-living adjustments are provided to members and beneficiaries at the discretion of the state legislature.

- *Funding Policy.* The contribution requirements of plan members and the state are established and may be amended by the state legislature. Plan members are required to contribute 8.1 percent of their annual covered salary. The state is required to contribute at an actuarially determined rate; the current rate is 12.9 percent of annual covered payroll.

- **Annual Pension Cost and Net Pension Obligation.** The state's annual pension cost and net pension obligation to SEPP for the current year were as follows (dollar amounts in thousands):

Annual required contribution	$ 206,874
Contributions made	(196,374)
Increase (decrease) in net pension obligation	10,500
Net pension obligation beginning of year	57,332
Net pension obligation end of year	$ 67,832

The annual required contribution for the current year was determined as part of the June 30, 1999, actuarial valuation using the entry age actuarial cost method. The actuarial assumptions included (a) 7.7 percent investment rate of return (net of administrative expenses) and (b) projected salary increases ranging from 6.5 percent to 9.5 percent per year. Both (a) and (b) included an inflation component of 5.4 percent. The unfunded actuarial accrued liability is being amortized over twenty-three years.

Three-Year Trend Information

(Dollar Amounts in Thousands)

Fiscal Year Ending	Annual Pension Cost (APC)	Percentage of APC Contributed	Net Pension Obligation
6/30/97	$179,664	99.1	$56,187
6/30/98	187,559	99.4	57,332
6/30/99	206,874	94.9	67,832

a. This plan is a single employer plan. What is the difference between a single employer plan and a multiple employer plan?

b. Suppose the plan were a defined contribution plan rather than a defined benefit plan. What would be the major difference in how the state's contributions were determined?

c. Suppose the state were to change its actuarial projections of salaries, increasing them by an average of 1 percent? Suppose it would change its assumed investment rate, decreasing it by 1 percent. How would these changes affect the present value of the state's pension obligation to current employees? How would they affect the annual required contribution for the current year— (that is, would they increase it by the full amount of the increase in the obligation)? Explain.

d. What does the "net pension obligation" represent? Suppose the wages and salaries of the employees covered by the pension plan are accounted for entirely in the state's general fund. In which fund or account group would the "net pension obligation" be reported?

e. Suppose, instead, the wages and salaries of the employees covered by the pension plan are accounted for entirely in an enterprise fund. In which fund or account group would the "net pension obligation" be reported?

f. Assume the wages and salaries of the employees covered by the pension plan are accounted for entirely in the state's general fund. Prepare the general fund journal entry to record the 1999 pension expenditure. What additional journal entry would have to be made in another fund or account group?

g. Assume, instead, that the wages and salaries of the employees covered by the pension plan are accounted for entirely in an enterprise fund? Prepare the enterprise fund journal entry to record the 1999 pension expense.

h. What is the significance of the "percent of APC contributed"? How was it derived?

i. What is meant by the "unfunded actuarial accrued liability"? How does it differ from the net pension obligation? Why is it being amortized rather than added to the pension expenditures of the years in which its components were first recognized?

j. As indicated in the note, the pension plan's unfunded actuarial accrued liability increased by $206,874 and the state contributed only $196,374. How would the receipt of the $196,374 affect the balance sheet of the pension *plan*? How would the increase of $206,874 in the actuarial accrued liability affect the balance sheet of the plan?

k. Suppose that during the year retirees were entitled to $150,000 of current-year benefits. How would the liability be reflected on the balance sheet of the plan?

QUESTIONS FOR REVIEW AND DISCUSSION

1. What is the rationale for accounting for nonexpendable fiduciary funds on a full, rather than a modified, accrual basis? Why is it important that depreciation be charged on long-term assets held as fiduciary fund investments?

2. Suppose that you are the independent auditor for a local performing arts association that recently received a sizable endowment. The association has asked whether gains, both realized and unrealized, from the appreciation of endowment investments

should be accounted for as expendable or nonexpendable resources. What primary factors should determine your response? How should FASB pronouncements influence your recommendation?

3. You are the sole contributor to a philanthropic foundation. You must specify whether investment gains should be expendable or nonexpendable. Present the key arguments in favor and against permitting the gains to be expendable.

4. A not-for-profit college has adopted a "fixed rate of return" approach to the distribution of investment income. Each year it transfers 6 percent of its endowment value to expendable funds, irrespective of actual earnings. Suppose that in year one the fund actually earns 8 percent; in year two it earns 4 percent. Assuming the endowment earnings are not restricted for any particular purpose, how much should the college report as unrestricted earnings in each of the two years? How should the difference, if any, between what is transferred and what is reported be classified and accounted for?

5. A not-for-profit organization has an endowment fund which, at the start of the year, has a value of $1 million—the amount initially contributed to establish the fund. Owing to investment losses, the year-end balance decreased to $950,000. In a previous year, the organization had added $30,000 of endowment fund investment gains to temporarily restricted assets. Of this amount, $20,000 has already been spent. How should the $50,000 of investment losses be accounted for?

More specifically, what should be the reported value of the endowment fund? In which category of assets should the losses be recognized?

6. Distinguish between a defined benefit plan and a defined contribution plan. Why does a defined benefit plan present far more complex accounting issues than a defined contribution plan?

7. How should an employer determine its annual pension cost? What minimum GASB criteria must it satisfy?

8. Why may a government's reported pension expenditure differ from its annual required contribution?

9. Why do the fundamental financial statements (statement of net assets available for benefits and statement of changes in net assets available for benefits) of a pension plan provide inadequate information to assess the plan's funding status? Where would a statement user look for more comprehensive information?

10. Why are the problems of accounting for postemployment health care benefits even more intractable than those of accounting for pensions? Do you believe that current reporting standards assure that statement users have sufficient information to assess whether government employers have adequately funded their postemployment health care benefits?

11. Why do the balance sheets of agency funds contain only assets and liabilities, but no fund balances? Why is it often unclear whether the resources relating to a particular activity should be accounted for in an agency fund or a governmental fund?

EXERCISES

11-1

Nonexpendable trust funds are accounted for on a business-like basis.

Christopher City received a contribution of $520,000 to provide care and maintenance of a city park. The donor stipulated that all income, including both realized and unrealized investment gains, be used to support the park.

a. Record journal entries for the following, assuming that the gift is to be accounted for in a nonexpendable trust fund.
  1. The gift was composed of the following assets:
     • Cash, $20,000
     • Marketable securities, $100,000 (fair market value)
     • A building, $400,000 (fair market value); estimated useful life, 40 years
  2. The city leased the building as office space to Brooks Law Firm. It collected $46,000 in rent and incurred

expenses, other than depreciation, of $15,000. The city records depreciation based on the straight-line method.
  3. The city sold $20,000 of the marketable securities for $26,000. At year-end the remaining securities had a market value of $97,000.
  4. It earned and received dividends of $5,000.

b. The city closed the trust's revenue and expense accounts and transferred the total amount available for expenditure to a special revenue fund. It then closed the transfer account. Prepare the entries to make the transfer and close the accounts.

c. Prepare the trust fund's year-end balance sheet.

d. Suppose the trust fund, contrary to generally accepted accounting principles, accounted for its activities on a modified accrual basis and therefore did not record depreciation. How much would be available for transfer to an expendable fund? What is the rationale for accounting for nonexpendable trust funds on a full accrual basis?

11-2

Expendable trust funds apply accounting principles that differ significantly from those of nonexpendable trust funds.

The McCracken County Humane Society (MCHS), which is part of the county's reporting entity, established an expendable trust fund to account for contributions related to its pet neutering program. The program is funded from contributions, volunteer time, donated services from local veterinarians and interest earned from a nonexpendable trust fund.

The following transactions and events occurred in a recent year:

1. The MCHS conducted a "walk your pet day" fundraising drive. The event raised $12,000, of which $2,000 were in pledges expected to be collected shortly after year-end.
2. The society acquired food and medicine at a cost of $6,000 (on account). During the year, it used $3,000 of these supplies. The society accounts for supplies on a consumption basis.
3. The society earned, and transferred to the expendable trust fund, interest of $450 on investments accounted for in the nonexpendable trust fund, the income of which is dedicated to the support of the pet neutering program.
4. The society paid $5,000 on its accounts payable.
5. During the year marketable securities held by the expendable trust increased in value from $13,000 to $13,100.

a. Prepare journal entries to record the events and transactions.
b. Comment on the distinctions between the accounting principles applicable to expendable as opposed to nonexpendable trust funds. Comment also on the distinction between the principles applicable to nonexpendable trust funds and special revenue funds.

11-3

Recorded pension expense is not always influenced by actuarial computations.

Hayward City maintains a defined benefit pension plan for its employees. In a recent year the city contributed $5 million to its pension fund. However, its annual required contribution as calculated by its actuary was $7 million. The city accounts for the pension contributions in a governmental fund.

a. Record the pension expenditure and related liability in the proper fund and account group.

b. Suppose in the following year the city contributed $6 million to its pension fund, but its annual required contribution per its actuary was only $5 million. Prepare the appropriate journal entries.

11-4

Investment losses need not impair the principal of not-for-profits' endowment funds.

In 1998, the Rubin Center for the Arts received a $2 million endowment, the income of which was to be used to support local artists. The center invested the proceeds in securities. In 1998, owing to interest, dividends and changes in market prices, the value of the endowment increased by $120,000. Of this amount, the center spent $80,000 on programs that were consistent with the endowment's restrictions. In 1999, owing to a market downturn, the portfolio incurred net losses of $60,000. In 2000, it had net earnings of $70,000. In neither 1999 nor 2000 did the center use any endowment resources to support its programs.

In the absence of donor specifications and applicable statutes, what would be the balances, at the end of 1998, 1999, and 2000, in the center's (a) permanently restricted endowment fund and (b) related temporarily restricted fund? Indicate also any impact on unrestricted funds.

11-5

Endowment funds should be accounted for on a full accrual basis.

The Nebraska Institute of Science (NIS) pools all of its endowment funds so that it can obtain the benefits of a large and diverse investment portfolio. The institute recently acquired a commercial office building as an investment property. The cost was $12 million and its economic life was expected to be fifteen years. Upon acquiring the building, NIS signed a fifteen-year lease with a tenant. The annual rent was $1.3 million, with the tenant responsible for all maintenance and other operating costs.

a. Suppose that the NIS did not charge depreciation and distributed to expendable funds the entire "income" earned on the office building.
   1. What would be the total amount distributed over the fifteen-year life of the building?
   2. Assuming that NIS's estimate of economic life was correct, what would likely be the market value of the building when the lease expired? Would NIS have had available any cash for the acquisition of other assets that would compensate for the decline in value of the building?
b. Suppose NIS charged depreciation and distributed to expendable funds the entire "income" earned on the office building.
   1. What would be the total amount distributed over the fifteen-year life of the building?

2. Assuming that NIS's estimate of economic life was correct, what would likely be the market value of the building when the lease expired? Would NIS have had available any cash for the acquisition of other assets to compensate for the decline in value of the building?

11-6

Multiple Choice Questions from Previous CPA Examinations.

1. At December 31, 1995, the following balances were due from the state government to Clare City's various funds:

Capital projects	$300,000
Trust and agency	100,000
Enterprise	80,000

   In Clare City's December 31, 1995, combined balance sheet for all fund types and account groups, what amount should be classified under governmental funds?
   a. $100,000
   b. $180,000
   c. $300,000
   d. $480,000

2. Stone Corp. donated investments to Pine City and stipulated that the income from the investments be used to acquire art for the city's museum. Which of the following funds should be used to account for the investments?
   a. endowment fund
   b. special revenue fund
   c. expendable trust fund
   d. nonexpendable trust fund

3. In 1995, a state government collected income taxes of $8 million for the benefit of one of its cities that imposes an income tax on its residents. The state remitted these collections periodically to the city. The state should account for the $8 million in the:
   a. general fund
   b. agency funds
   c. internal service funds
   d. special assessment funds

4. Which of the following funds frequently does not have a fund balance?
   a. general fund
   b. agency fund
   c. special revenue fund
   d. capital projects fund

Questions 5–7 are based on the following:

   Elm City contributes to and administers a single-employer defined benefit pension plan on behalf of its covered employees. The plan is accounted for in a pension trust fund. Actuarially determined employer contribution requirements and contributions actually made for the past three years, along with the percentage of annual covered payroll, were as follows:

	Contribution Made		Actuarial Requirement	
	Amount	*Percent*	*Amount*	*Percent*
1999	$11,000	26	$11,000	26
1998	5,000	12	10,000	24
1997	None	None	8,000	20

5. What account should be credited in the pension trust fund to record the 1999 employer contribution of $11,000?
   a. revenues control
   b. other financing sources control
   c. due from special revenue fund
   d. pension benefit obligation

6. To record the 1999 pension contribution of $11,000, what debit is required in the governmental-type fund used in connection with employer pension contributions?
   a. other financing uses control
   b. expenditures control
   c. expenses control
   d. due to pension trust fund

7. In the notes to Elm City's 1999 financial statements, employer contributions expressed as percentages of annual covered payroll should be shown to the extent available for a minimum of how long?
   a. 1 year
   b. 2 years
   c. 3 years
   d. 12 years

8. In which of the following funds should the debt service transactions of a special assessment issue for which the government is not obligated in any manner be reported?
   a. agency fund
   b. trust fund
   c. internal service fund
   d. general fund

9. Which type of fund can be either nonexpendable or expendable?
   a. trust fund
   b. special revenue fund
   c. enterprise fund
   d. debt service fund

PROBLEMS

Continuing Problem

Review the annual report that you obtained.

a. For what purposes does the government maintain trust funds? Does the government maintain expendable as well as nonexpendable trust funds?

b. Does the government contribute to one or more pension plans? Are they defined benefit or defined contribution plans? If they are defined benefit plans, are they single employer (maintained by the government itself) or multiple employer?

c. Does the government report a pension expense or expenditure? If so, in which funds?

d. Does the government report a pension liability? If so, in which funds or account groups?

e. Do notes to the financial statements indicate the components of the government's pension cost? Do they indicate the value of plan assets and the actuarially determined obligations?

f. Does the financial report contain the financial statements of the pension plan? Does it indicate that the pension plan issues its own reports and that these are publicly available?

g. Does the report indicate that the government provides postemployment health care benefits? If so, what is the nature of these benefits?

h. For what purposes does the government maintain agency funds?

11-1

The accounting for trusts is dependent upon donor stipulations.

To promote computer education, a leading computer manufacturer donates $4 million to the Kerrville Independent School District. The donor stipulates that the district is to establish an endowment, from which income only is expendable. Income is defined to include interest, dividends, and investment gains. All income is to be recorded initially in a nonexpendable endowment fund. Each year the district is to transfer to an expendable endowment fund (i.e., a special revenue fund) all income of the year that exceeds the rate of inflation as measured by the consumer price index times the beginning fund balance. The expendable funds are to be used exclusively to acquire computer-related materials and to provide computer training for teachers.

In the year the contribution was received, the district:

- purchased bonds having a face value of $3,000,000 for $2,970,000 and common stock of $1,000,000
- received $180,000 in interest and recognized an increase of $3,000 in the fair value of the bonds

- sold $500,000 of the common stock at a gain of $50,000 and used the proceeds to purchase additional common stock
- transferred expendable income to a newly established special revenue fund (During the year the consumer price index increased by 5 percent.)

a. Prepare journal entries, including closing entries, in the nonexpendable endowment fund to record the year's transactions.

b. Prepare a statement of revenues, expenses, and changes in fund balance for the nonexpendable endowment fund.

c. Some donors stipulate that no investment gains are expendable. What is the most probable purpose of that restriction? What is its limitation? In what way is the approach taken by the donor in this example preferable?

11-2

Investment losses cannot be accounted for as the mirror image of investment gains.

On December 31, 1996, The Child Crisis Center establishes an endowment fund with a $5 million gift of securities. Income from the endowment is to be used exclusively to support a nutrition program. Expendable income is defined in the indenture agreement so as to include all investment gains, both realized and unrealized. Investment gains and losses are to be accounted for as recommended by the FASB.

During 1997, the endowment earns $100,000 in interest and dividends and spends the entire amount on the nutrition program. The value of its securities portfolio increases by $500,000 from $5,000,000 to $5,500,000.

During 1998 the endowment again earns $100,000 in interest and dividends and spends the entire amount on the nutrition program. This year, however, the value of its securities portfolio decreases by $800,000 from $5,500,000 to $4,700,000.

During 1999 the endowment continues to earn and spend $100,000 in interest and dividends. This year the portfolio recovers $400,000 of its investment losses and at year-end is worth $5,100,000.

At the start of 1997, the center had a cash balance of $600,000 in an unrestricted fund. Over the three-year period, this balance was unaffected by transactions other than those just described.

a. Prepare a schedule for each of the three years (1997 through 1999) in which you summarize the transactions as they affect permanently restricted, temporarily restricted, and unrestricted net assets.

b. At the beginning of 1998, the year of the loss, the total value of the security portfolio was $5.5 million. Of this amount, the initial $5 million was classified as permanently restricted; the balance as temporarily restricted. Assuming that you adhered to the FASB pronouncement, how much of the loss did you assign to the permanently restricted assets and how much to the temporarily restricted assets? How can you justify this division of the loss?

11-3

Choice of accounting basis may determine whether endowment principal will be preserved.

On January 1, 1998, the JKG Foundation received a $10 million bequest consisting of a commercial warehouse building and $5 million of cash.

The foundation immediately invested the $5 million cash in twenty-year, 7 percent, corporate bonds having a face value of $4,485,512. The bonds, which pay interest annually, were purchased to yield 6 percent. The total premium was $514,488, and hence total purchase price was $5 million. The annual interest payments (7 percent of the face value) are $313,986. In 1998, the fair value of the bonds decreased by $13,986, an amount equivalent to the first year's amortization of the bond premium.

The JKG Foundation leased-out the warehouse for $600,000 per year. The useful life of the building is twenty years.

Per the terms of the bequest, income only is available for spending. However, neither the terms nor the applicable law specifies how income is to be determined.

a. Determine the amount available in 1998 for expenditure, assuming that the foundation calculates income:

1. on a cash basis
2. on a full accrual basis, recognizing changes in the market value of the securities and depreciating (on a straight-line basis) the warehouse

b. Assume that the foundation spent all of its income. Prepare both a cash-basis and an accrual-basis balance sheet.

c. Is there a difference in fund balance between the two balance sheets? If not, can it be said that one basis of accounting better preserves endowment principal? Explain.

11-4

Differences in accounting may make a significant difference in resources available for expenditure.

The following statement of activities and statement of assets and fund balances are those of the Pew Memorial Trust, a foundation that supports nonprofit activities in the areas of culture, education, the environment, health and human services, public policy, and religion. All amounts are in millions. The statements are for years prior to the issuances of FASB Statements No. 116 and 117.

Statement of Activities
For the Year Ended December 31, 1993

Revenues Collected:		
Interest	$	53
Dividends		71
Income from Investments	$	124
Expenditures Allocable to the Production of Income		4
Revenues Collected Available for Distribution		120
Expenditures Paid:		
Grant Payments		105
General and Administrative Expenditures		8
Total Expenditures Paid	$	113
Excess of Revenues Collected Over Expenditures Paid		7
Net Gain on the Sale of Securities		86
Fund Balance at the Beginning of Year		1,522
Fund Balance at End of Year	$	1,615

Statement of Assets And Fund Balances

	December 31, 1993		December 31, 1992	
	Market Value	Book Value	Market Value	Book Value
Assets:				
Cash and Cash Equivalents	$ 71	$ 71	$ 46	$ 46
Bonds and Notes	615	590	698	667
Stocks	1,589	903	1,428	765
Other Investments	26	25	23	22
Assets Held for Charitable Use	26	26	22	22
Total Assets	$2,327	$1,615	$2,217	$1,522
Fund Balance:				
Appropriated	$ 200	$ 199	$ 188	$ 188
Unappropriated	2,127	1,416	2,029	1,334
Total Fund Balance	$2,327	$1,615	2,217	1,522

Note No. 1 to the financial statements states:

The accounts of The Pew Charitable Trust are maintained on the basis of cash receipts and disbursements and do not include interest and dividends receivable, amortization of bond premiums, accretion of bond discounts, or other liabilities. At the time that grants are approved, the committed amounts are recorded as funds appropriated in the statement of assets and fund balances.

a. In what critical way are these statements in violation of generally accepted accounting principles?

b. Based on the information provided, are *realized* gains on the sale of investments available for expenditure, or are they added to the principal of the endowment? Are *unrealized* gains available for expenditure? Explain.

c. Suppose that effective January 1, 1993, the trust was permitted to expend all future gains on investments, both realized and unrealized. How much more would have been available for expenditure in 1993 than is indicated on the statement of activities?

11-5

Expendable trust funds may be different in character than non-expendable funds.

On January 1, 1998, the balance sheet of a city's trust funds for the acquisition of library books showed the following (in thousands):

	Nonexpendable	Expendable
Cash	$ 1,400	$ 120
Marketable Securities		
(at Cost)	10,000	160
	11,400	280
Building	20,000	
Less: Accumulated		
Depreciation	(4,000)	
	16,000	
Total Assets	$ 27,400	$ 280
Fund Balance	$ 27,400	$ 280

The endowment was established in 1990 with a contribution of cash, securities, and real estate having a market value of $24 million. The endowment agreement stated that *income only* (excluding both realized and unrealized investment gains) could be used to acquire library books.

The building has a useful life of forty years with no expected salvage value.

The following table provides information about cash transactions and other events (excluding depreciation) during 1998 (in thousands):

	Nonexpendable	Expendable
Interest and Dividends		
Received (in Cash)	$ 760	$ 60
Rent Received (in Cash)	1,800	
Cash Expenditures for		
Building Maintenance	400	
Sales Price of		
Securities Sold	800	20
Book Value of		
Securities Sold	200	15
Increase During the Year in		
Market Value of Securities		
on Hand at Year-End	150	12

As of January 1, 1998, all prior-year earnings of the nonexpendable fund had been transferred to the expendable fund and are therefore available for expenditure.

a. Prepare in good form a schedule in which you calculate the total amount available at December 31, 1998, for the acquisition of books.

b. Did you account for the investment gains in the expendable fund in the same way as in the nonexpendable fund? If not, justify any differences.

11-6

Pension expenditures are reported differently in government than proprietary funds.

Pebble City maintains a defined benefit pension plan for its employees. In a recent year, the city's consulting actuary calculated that the city's annual required contribution for the year was $6 million. Its determination was consistent with the GASB-specified parameters. The city records 50 percent of its payroll in its general fund and 50 percent in an enterprise fund.

a. During the year the city contributed the entire $6 million to the pension fund. Prepare the pension journal entries that the city should make to record its pension contribution, expenditure, and obligation (if any) in all applicable funds and account groups (excluding the pension plan itself).

b. Assume the city contributed only $5.6 million. Prepare the appropriate journal entries.

c. How can you justify the differences in the reported expenditures/expense between the two funds?

11-7

The basic financial statements of a pension plan provide only limited amounts of information as to its economic condition.

The following information relates to the Lincoln County Firefighters Pension Plan (dollar amounts in millions):

Beginning-of-Year Balances

Cash and cash equivalents, January 1	$ 67
Marketable securities and other investments at fair value, January 1	3,180
Current liabilities to retirees, January 1	4
Actuarial accrued liability, January 1	3,430

Transactions During the Year

Contributions received during the year from employers and employees	138
Benefits to which retirees were entitled during the year	120
Benefits actually paid to retirees, including amounts owed from prior year	122
Interest and dividends earned during the year	145
Net appreciation in fair value of marketable securities and other investments (i.e., realized and unrealized gains) during the year	36
Investment and administrative expenses	45

End-of-Year Balances

Cash on hand, December 31	92
Marketable securities and other investments at fair value, December 31	3,307
Current liabilities to retirees, December 31	2
Actuarial accrued liability, December 31	3,690

a. Prepare a statement of net assets available for benefits (balance sheet) as of January 1. You may not have to include all of the data provided.

b. Prepare a statement of changes in net assets available for benefits (statement of activities) for the year.

c. Prepare a statement of net assets available for benefits (balance sheet) as of December 31.

d. Comment on the significance of the data provided that you did not include in your statements. Where in the plan's financial statements would this information be reported?

e. Determine the amount of the unfunded actuarial accrued liability as of December 31, assuming that the actuarial value of the plan assets is the same as their fair value. (Sometimes actuaries use average values over several years rather than point in time values as of the balance sheet date.)

11-8

A pension plan's financial statements provide useful, but limited, information as to the plan's fiscal condition.

The following are Rockville School District Teachers Retirement Plan's statement of plan net assets (balance sheets) for 1999 and 1998, and statement of changes in plan net assets for 1998.

All dollar amounts are in millions.

Statement of Net Plan Assets As of December 31

	1999	1998
Assets:		
Cash	$ 210	$ 440
Due from Employer	39	46
Interest and Dividends Receivable	87	81
Investments in Stocks and Bonds (at Fair Value)	9,176	8,831
Total Assets	$ 9,512	$ 9,398
Less: Benefits Payable	6	37
Net Assets Available for Benefits	$ 9,506	$ 9,361

Statement of Changes in Net Plan Assets For the Year Ended December 31, 1999

Additions:	
Employer Contributions	$ 541
Interest and Dividends	630
Total Additions	$ 1,171

Deductions:

Net Depreciation in Value of Investments	621
Benefits to Which Retirees are Entitled for Year	394
Administrative Expenses	11
Total Deductions	$ 1,026
Net Increase	145
Plan Assets, December 31, 1998	9,361
Plan Assets, December 31, 1999	$ 9,506

a. Prepare a summary journal entry to record the employer contributions recognized during the year, the cash actually received from the employer during the year, and the change in the contributions receivable from previous years.

b. Prepare a journal entry to record the benefits paid to retirees.

c. Should the net depreciation in value of investments include unrealized as well as realized losses? Why?

d. Based on the data provided, are you able to determine the obligation of the plan attributable to benefits earned by current and retired employees? Are you able to determine whether the financial health of the plan has improved or deteriorated in 1999? If not, where could you find this information?

11-9

Supplementary schedules provide the actuarial information necessary to assess a plan's fiscal status.

The following information was reported in a state's Police Officers Pension Plan's schedule of funding progress. Dollar amounts are in millions.

	Valuation Date December 31	
	1998	1997
Value of Assets (a)	$ 2,411	$ 2,005
Actuarial Accrued Liability (b)	$ 2,902	$ 2,626
Unfunded Actuarial Accrued Liability (b – a)	$ 491	$ 621
Funded Ratio (a/b)	83%	76%
Covered Payroll (c)	$ 957	$ 902
Unfunded Actuarial Accrued Liability as a Percent of Covered Payroll ((b – a)/c)	51%	69%

The plan's schedule of employer contributions indicated that the employers' annual required contribution was $106 million in 1998 and $100 million in 1997. In both years the employers contributed 100 percent of those amounts.

a. Based on the limited data available, do you think that the fiscal health of the plan improved in 1998? Explain, citing the specific factors you took into account and telling why they are significant.

b. Suppose you were asked to prepare a schedule explaining the change in the value of assets. What factors might account for increases and decreases in this amount?

c. Suppose that you were asked to prepare a schedule explaining the change in the actuarial accrued liability? What factors might account for increases and decreases in this amount?

d. What is the total amount that employers should report as pension expenditures in 1998? How much must they add to, or subtract from, their pension liability accounts?

11-10

The major issue relating to agency funds is when they should be established.

Consider each of the following situations. Indicate whether (and why or why not) you think that the government should account for the transactions and resources in an agency fund or a governmental fund. Not all the situations have been explicitly addressed in the text. Therefore, you may have to generalize from those that have been discussed.

a. A county establishes a deferred compensation plan for its employees. Under the plan, the county withholds up to 5 percent of employees' wages and salaries. It contributes none of its own funds. The county invests the funds on behalf of the employees. All investment risks and rewards are those of the employees, not the county. Upon reaching a specified age, employees can begin to withdraw their share of the funds.

b. A city extended sewer and water lines to a recently annexed community. Per agreement with the community, the improvements are to be paid for entirely by local residents. To finance the improvements, the city issued ten-year notes on behalf of the residents. It assessed the residents for the amount of the debt, plus interest. The city guaranteed the notes and agreed to collect the assessments from the residents and make appropriate payments to the noteholders. However, the city's role is primarily one of an intermediary. The residents, not the city, are expected to service the debt.

c. A state receives a federal law-enforcement grant intended to assist local communities in hiring additional police officers. The federal granting agency selects the cities and counties that are to receive the awards and determines the amounts they are to receive. The federal government, not the state, is responsible for monitoring grant compliance. The state's only responsibility is to write the checks to the cities and counties.

d. A state receives a federal educational grant intended to assist local school districts in hiring additional teachers. The federal granting agency establishes the criteria that the state is to use in determining the school districts to receive the awards and the amounts they are to receive. The district has no discretion in selecting recipients other than to apply the specified criteria.

e. A county collects sales taxes that it distributes among itself and the towns within its jurisdiction. The taxes are levied by the county and are divided among the recipient governments in accordance with a formula set forth in the legislation that authorized the tax.

11-11

The types of transactions affecting an agency fund (although not necessarily the exact amounts) can be derived from its statement of changes in assets and liabilities.

The following statement is that of the Sewer User Fee Fund of Tucson, Arizona, a fund that "accounts for sewer user fees collected by the city and remitted to Pima County":

a. Prepare summary journal entries to record:

  1. the recognition of interest
  2. the receipt of interest
  3. collection of $30,000 in sewer fees not previously recognized as receivables
  4. payments to other governments of $45,000

b. Suppose $10,000 of the accounts receivable must be written off as uncollectable. Prepare an appropriate journal entry.

Statement of Changes in Assets and Liabilities (in Thousands)				
	Balance July 1, 1993	Additions	Deductions	Balance June 30, 1994
Assets:				
Cash/Deposits/Pooled Iinvestments	$ 578	$55,227	$55,079	$ 726
Due from Other Funds	7	439	438	8
Accounts Receivable	1,786	28,082	27,971	1,897
Interest Receivable	1	31	29	3
Total Assets	$2,372	$83,779	$83,517	$2,634
Liabilities:				
Accounts Payable	$ 2	$27,511	$27,512	$ 1
Due to Other Governmental Agencies	2,370	55,914	55,651	2,633
Total Liabilities	$2,372	$83,425	$83,163	$2,634

SOLUTION TO EXERCISE FOR REVIEW AND SELF-STUDY

a. A single employer plan covers the employees of only one employer (e.g., in this example, the employees of the state). A multiple employer plan covers the employees of more than one employer (e.g., when a state maintains a plan for the employees of all counties within the state).

b. If the plan were a defined contribution plan, the state would contribute a fixed percentage of employees' wages and salaries. No actuarial computations would be required.

c. If the state increased its projection of salary increases, then the current employees would be entitled to greater pensions upon their retirement. Similarly, if it decreased the assumed investment rate, then the contributions to date would have been inadequate. Hence, the actuarial liability for pension benefits already earned would increase. This change would increase the state's annual required contribution of the current year, but not by the full amount. As indicated in the note, the liability is being amortized over twenty-three years. Hence, the annual required contribution for the current year would increase by only one twenty-third of the total increase in the actuarial liability. In addition, the changes in salary and investment rates would affect the computation of the normal cost. It would thereby have an impact on the annual required contributions of both current and future years.

d. The net pension obligation represents the cumulative difference between what the state should have contributed to the pension plan (the annual required contribution) and what it actually contributed. If wages and salaries, and hence pensions, are accounted for in the general fund, then the net pension obligation (a long-term liability) would be reported in the state's general long-term debt account group.

e. If pensions are accounted for in an enterprise fund, then the net pension obligation would be reported in that fund.

f. The reported pension expenditure would be the actual contribution to the pension fund. The difference between the annual required contribution ($206,874) and the actual contribution ($196,374) would be added to the net pension obligation in the GLTDAG. Thus:

General Fund

Pension expenditure	$196,374	
Cash		$196,374

To record the annual pension contribution and expenditure

General Long-Term Debt Account Group

Amount to be provided		
for pension payments	$10,500	
Net pension obligation		$10,500

To record the difference between the annual required contribution and the actual pension contribution

g. The reported pension expense would be the required annual contribution to the pension fund. Thus:

Enterprise Fund

Pension expense	$206,874	
Cash		$196,374
Net pension obligation		10,500

To record the annual pension contribution and expense

h. The percent of APC (annual pension cost) contributed represents the percentage of the annual required contribution as computed by the government's actuaries (consistent with the GASB guidelines) that was actually contributed. Thus, for 1999:

Actual Contribution	$196,374
Annual Required Contribution	÷ 206,874
Percent of Annual Pension Cost Contributed	94.9%

i. The unfunded actuarial accrued liability is the excess of the actuarially computed pension liability over the pension plan's assets. By contrast, the net pension obligation is the cumulative difference between what the employer should have contributed to the pension plan and what it actually contributed. The unfunded actuarial accrued liability relates to the pension plan (and thereby indirectly to the employer), whereas the net pension obligation relates directly to, and is reported on the balance sheet of, the employer. It is being amortized mainly so that changes in the liability, attributable for example to plan improvements, do not affect reported expenditures or expenses entirely in the year in which they take place and thus make the expenditures or expenses appear excessively volatile.

j. The state's contribution would increase the plan's cash and, correspondingly, its net assets. The increase in the actuarial liability, however, would have no impact on the plan's balance sheet. The plan's balance sheet reports only actual liabilities (those currently due to retirees), not actuarial obligations.

k. The payment would increase liabilities, thereby reducing net assets. Thus:

Retiree benefits	$150,000	
Due to retirees (liability)		$150,000

To record current obligations to retirees

"Retiree benefits" would be closed to net assets.

CHAPTER 12

Issues of Reporting, Disclosure, and Financial Analysis

LEARNING OBJECTIVES

After studying this chapter you should understand:

- why the make-up of a government's or not-for-profit's reporting entity is an issue
- the criteria that the GASB has established to determine the units that constitute a government's reporting entity
- the various ways of reporting component units
- the criteria that the FASB has established to determine the units that constitute a not-for-profit's reporting entity

- how governments and not-for-profits each report cash flows, and the rationale for the differences
- the main elements of a government's comprehensive annual financial report (CAFR)
- the critical factors to be taken into account in assessing a government's financial condition

This chapter, the final chapter that deals mainly with external reporting, presents an overview of the annual financial report. It begins by considering the issue of the reporting entity—what related organizations a primary entity must incorporate into its financial reports. The chapter then addresses how organizations should report upon cash flows. Thereafter it highlights the structure of the annual report and the need for statistical information to supplement the financial statements. It concludes by focusing on key indicators of a government's financial condition and thereby draws on information in the funds and account groups discussed in the previous chapters.

WHY IS THE REPORTING ENTITY AN ISSUE FOR GOVERNMENTS?

The composition of the reporting entity has proven one of the least tractable issues facing business, government, and not-for-profit standard setters. As has long been recognized in the business sector, an organization's legal entity may differ from its economic entity. If a company controls another company, then its economic entity comprises the company itself plus its subsidiaries. Yet satisfactory definitions of control have proven illusive, and the FASB is thoroughly reviewing existing standards for consolidated reporting.

The reporting entity issue in the government sector can be delineated by the example and subsequent variations to it that follow.

EXAMPLE   *The Reporting Entity*

A city operates an electric generating facility that supplies power exclusively to its municipal subway system. The facility needs costly capital improvements, but owing to debt limitations the city is unable to borrow the required funds. To circumvent the limitations, the city forms a new unit of government, a public power authority, to which it transfers the generating facility. The facility is to be governed by a board of directors, the members of which will be the same officials that compose the city council. The authority will issue city-backed bonds, which it will repay from revenues earned from the sale of electricity to the city.

In this example, the power authority, though an independent legal entity, is within the economic and political control of the city, no less than if it were another city department. City council members govern the authority, and the city is obligated for its debt. The city is the sole beneficiary of its resources. Therefore, if the city's financial statements were to report on all of its economic assets and liabilities, they would have to encompass the assets and liabilities of the authority.

Consider, however, a continuum of modifications to the example:

- The authority's governing board, rather than being composed of city council members, is appointed by the city's mayor.
- The authority's governing board is independently elected, but the city retains the right to approve the authority's budget.
- The governing board is independently elected, and the city has no right to approve the authority's budget.

In this sequence of variations the city's ability to control the authority is gradually reduced and the economic borders between the city and the authority are made more pronounced. Consequently, with each variation the rationale for including the authority within the city's reporting entity is diminished. But where should standard setters draw the line?

This sequence of variations oversimplifies the problem, however, in that it focuses exclusively on whether the city *controls* the authority. In fact, the extent to which entities are economically intertwined cannot be assessed on the single vector of control. Economic interdependence may be influenced by whether one organization shares geographic boundaries with the other, is responsible for its debts, must fund its deficits, can benefit from its surpluses, and is a major source of its revenues. Rule-making authorities have had to develop a multidimensional framework of standards that is appropriate for the over 80,000 U.S. governments, all of which are tied to at least one other government.

The following are but a very small sample of common intergovernmental relationships in the United States:

- housing authorities established by cities to provide low-cost financing for residents of the cities
- turnpike commissions established by states to finance and operate toll roads
- volunteer fire departments partially funded by counties or towns
- universities that receive state funds but are controlled by independently elected boards of regents

WHAT CRITERIA HAVE BEEN ESTABLISHED FOR GOVERNMENT REPORTING ENTITIES?

The current standards for governments are set forth in GASB Statement No. 14, *The Financial Reporting Entity*. This statement establishes the criteria for determining both the units that should be included in a reporting entity and how they should be reported.

TYPES OF UNITS COMPOSING THE REPORTING ENTITY

Per Statement No. 14, a financial reporting entity should consist of a **primary government** and its **component units**.

A *primary government* can be a state government, a general purpose local government such as a municipality or a county, or a special purpose state or local government. Statement No. 14 explicitly states that "a primary government is any state government or general purpose local government (municipality or county)." Under the U.S. system of federalism, local governments are subunits of the states in which they are located and are subject to state control. Were the definition of a primary government not to explicitly include general purpose local governments, then virtually all cities, towns, and counties would be component units of their states rather than primary governments.

Special purpose governments include a vast array of authorities and districts, such as school districts, municipal utility districts and transportation authorities. To qualify as a primary government a special purpose government must have a separately elected governing body, be legally separate from other primary governments, and be *fiscally independent* of other governments. Fiscally independent implies that the government has the authority, without approval from other governments, to:

- determine its budget
- levy taxes and set rates
- issue bonds

A *component unit* is a legally separate government for which the elected officials of the primary government are financially accountable. A component unit may also be an organization whose exclusion would cause a primary government's statements to be misleading or incomplete because of the nature and relationship between the two. Such a relationship would exist if the potential component unit were created solely to benefit the primary government. For example, to help New York City out of its financial difficulties in the mid-1970s, the State of New York established the Municipal Assistance Corporation (known as "Big MAC"). The function of the corporation was to supervise the city's fiscal affairs and to issue bonds on its behalf. Since the city was financially accountable to the corporation, not the other way around, the corporation would not qualify as a component unit, were it not for this "misleading or incomplete" provision.

The key criterion as to whether a primary government is financially accountable for another government—thus qualifying the other government as a component unit— is that the primary government either *appoints a voting majority of the unit's governing body* or a majority of the unit's governing body is composed of primary government officials.

MEANING OF FINANCIALLY ACCOUNTABLE COMPONENT UNITS

In addition, the relationship between the two governments must satisfy either of two additional criteria:

- ability of the primary government to *impose its will* upon the potential component unit
- the potential for the organization to *provide specific financial benefits to, or impose specific financial burdens on*, the primary government

The factors indicative of the primary government *being able to impose its will* upon a potential component unit (of which only one need be met) include the following:

- It can remove appointed members of the potential component unit's governing board.
- It has the authority to modify or approve the unit's budget.
- It can approve or modify the unit's fee charges.
- It can veto, overrule, or modify decisions of the unit's governing board.
- It can appoint, hire, reassign, or dismiss the unit's managers responsible for day-to-day operations.

The potential for a unit to *provide specific financial benefits to, or impose specific financial burdens* on, a primary government would exist if the primary government is:

- entitled to the potential component unit's financial resources
- legally obligated for, or has assumed the obligation to finance, the unit's deficits or is otherwise obligated to support the unit's operations
- obligated "in some manner" for the unit's debt, whether that obligation is expressed or implied

EXAMPLE   *Financially Accountable Component Units*

The Jefferson Hospital District was established to furnish medical aid and hospital care to indigent persons residing in Jefferson County. The district is governed by a board of trustees that sets policy for the district and oversees its day-to-day operations. The district is located entirely within Jefferson County and the county's commissioners' court appoints the members of the district's board of trustees. The commissioners' court has the authority to approve the hospital district's budget.

The hospital district is a component unit of the county. It satisfies the two criteria of financial accountability in that:

- the county appoints the voting majority of the district's elected board
- the authority to approve the district's budget gives it the ability to impose its will on the district

As a general rule, a potential component unit is fiscally accountable to a primary government *only* if the primary government controls the appointment of its governing board. However, Statement No. 14 provides for an exception. A potential component unit may be considered financially accountable to a primary government, even if its board is independently elected and thereby outside the influence of the primary government. Financially accountability may also be indicated by *fiscal dependency*. A unit is fiscally dependent on the primary government if it is unable to determine its own budget, levy taxes or set rates, or issue bonds without approval of the primary government.

EXAMPLE   *Fiscal Dependency*

A school district has its own independently elected governing board. Nevertheless, the board of supervisors of the surrounding county must approve the district's budget and tax rates.

The school district would be financially accountable to the county in that it is financially dependent upon it. Thus, even though the county has no control over the district's governing board, the district would nevertheless satisfy the criteria of a component unit.

WAYS OF REPORTING COMPONENT UNITS

Per Statement No. 14, a primary government should include a component unit in its financial statements in either of two ways:

- *discrete presentation:* reporting the unit in a single column, apart from the data of the primary government, as if the unit were another fund or account group
- *blending:* combining the unit's transactions and balances as if they were part of the primary government—that is, aggregating the unit's special revenue funds, capital projects funds, debt service funds, general fixed assets account group, and so on with the corresponding funds and account groups of the primary government and reporting them in the same columns

Discrete presentation is the default means of reporting. **Blending** is appropriate only when the relationship between the primary government and the component unit is so close that the two governments, albeit legally separate, are substantively the same. Either of the following two circumstances would indicate that the two units are substantively the same and should be blended:

- The two units are controlled by governing boards having the same members.
- The component unit provides services solely to the primary government. A common example of this type of relationship is when a financing authority issues debt and acquires property exclusively for lease to the primary government. This criterion is satisfied only when the component unit provides the services to the primary government itself, not to the same citizens that are served by the primary government.

Discrete Presentation

Discrete presentation can take a variety of forms. Common to all, however, is that the discrete columns should be presented to the right of the "totals" columns of the primary government. For example:

Totals— Memorandum Only Primary Government	Component Unit No. 1	Component Unit No. 2	Totals— Memorandum Only Reporting Entity

Within that general framework, the primary government can select from an array of options:

- It can report each of its component units in a separate column (as just shown).
- It can combine selected component units having similar characteristics (e.g., all power authorities) into one column.
- It can combine all component units accounted for on a governmental (modified accrual) basis into one column and all accounted for on a proprietary (full accrual) basis into another.
- It can combine all component units, both governmental and proprietary—even though they use different bases of accounting—into a single column.

Irrespective of which form of discrete presentation it chooses, the primary government must disclose, in either the statements themselves or in accompanying schedules and notes, detailed information as to each *major* component unit. This information should include the component unit's key balance sheet and statement of revenues and expenditures accounts.

Blending

When a primary government blends one or more component units into its own financial statements, it combines the funds of the component units with its own. However, because most statement users require information on the primary government's general fund, Statement No. 14 makes an exception. A primary government must keep its own general fund intact, not aggregate it with the general funds of its component units. It should blend the general funds of the component units with its own *special revenue funds*—that is, add them to the special revenue funds column. Table 12–1 contains excerpts of Fort Worth's note on its component units, some of which it blends and some of which it reports discretely.

TABLE 12–1
City of Fort Worth *Note re: Reporting Entity*

In evaluating the City's financial reporting entity, management has considered all potential component units. The decision to include a potential component unit in the financial reporting entity was made by applying the criteria set forth in GASB Statement No. 14. Complete financial statements for the individual component units may be obtained at the City's offices. The following blended component units although legally separate from the City are reported as part of the primary government:

Fort Worth Housing Finance Corporation—The Fort Worth Housing Finance Corporation (FWHFC) was created pursuant to the Texas Finance Corporation Act. The FWHFC was organized for the purpose of financing the cost of residential ownership and development of single family dwellings for persons of low and moderate income. Although it is legally separate from the City, the members of the Board of the FWHFC and the members of the City Council are essentially the same. Due to the financial management responsibility of the City and the general oversight given by the City, the FWHFC has been included in the City's general purpose financial statements as a Special Revenue Fund.

Taxing Increment Reinvestment Zone Number Two—The Taxing Increment Reinvestment Zone Number Two was created pursuant to the Texas Tax Increment Financing Act, Tax Code, Sections 311.001 through 311.017, as amended. The purpose of the Zone is to promote the development of the Texas Motor Speedway. In fiscal year 1996, this Zone had no financial activity. In the future it will be included in the City's general purpose financial statements as a Special Revenue Fund.

Taxing Increment Reinvestment Zone Number Three—The Taxing Increment Reinvestment Zone Number Three was created pursuant to the Texas Tax Increment Financing Act, Tax Code, Sections 311.001 through 311.017, as amended. This Zone was previously Taxing Increment Reinvestment Zone Number One from January 1995 until December 1995 when it was dissolved due to a lack of fiscal activity. The purpose of the Zone is to finance public improvements to the area such as; construction of an underground parking garage and central park, the upgrade of the Tandy subway system and streetscape improvements along heavily traveled pedestrian corridors. In fiscal year 1996, this Zone had no financial activity. In the future it will be included in the City's general purpose financial statements as a Special Revenue Fund.

The following legally separate entities are noted as discretely presented component units of the City in a separate column in the combined financial statements to emphasize that they are legally separate from the primary government. Discretely presented component units are entities that are legally separate from the City, but for which the City is financially accountable or whose relationship with the City are such that exclusion would be misleading or incomplete.

Fort Worth Public Improvement District No. 1—The Fort Worth Improvement District No. 1 was created by resolution of the City Council pursuant to Texas Statute Article 1269 paragraph 4.1. The purpose of the District to furnish improvements and services which provide enhancements for the City within the District. Special assessments are levied on property within the District to pay for these improvements and services. Due to this component unit directly benefiting the City itself rather than the citizens of the City, the Fort Worth Improvement District No. 1 has been included in the City's general purpose financial statements as a Discretely Presented Component Unit.

Fort Worth Public Improvement District No. 2—The Fort Worth Improvement District No. 2 was created by resolution of the City Council pursuant to Sections 372.002 and 372.005 of the Public Improvement District Assessment Act. The purpose of the District is to provide an enhanced level of services and improvements in a specific geographic area. Special assessments are levied on property within the District to pay for these improvements and services. Due to this component unit directly benefiting the City itself rather than the citizens of the City, the Fort Worth Improvement District No. 2 has been included in the City's general purpose financial statements as a Discretely Presented Component Unit.

TABLE 12-1 (Continued)
City of Fort Worth *Note re: Reporting Entity*

Fort Worth Public Improvement District No. 3—The Fort Worth Improvement District No. 3 was created by resolution of the City Council pursuant to Chapter 372, Local Government Code. The purpose of the District is to provide an area revitalization by installing accent paving, pedestrian benches, lighting and trees and other enhancements. Special assessments are levied on property within the District to pay for these improvements and enhancements. Due to this component unit directly benefiting the City itself rather than the citizens of the City, the Fort Worth Improvement District No. 3 has been included in the City's general purpose financial statements as a Discretely Presented Component Unit.

Fort Worth Public Improvement District No. 4—The Fort Worth Improvement District No. 4 was created by resolution of the City Council pursuant to Chapter 372, Local Government Code. The purpose of the District is to provide an area enhancement by landscaping, construction and maintenance of an irrigation system and fencing and providing supplemental security patrol services. Special assessments are levied on property within the District to pay for these improvements and services. Due to this component unit directly benefiting the City itself rather than the citizens of the City, the Fort Worth Improvement District No. 4 has been included in the City's general purpose financial statements as a Discretely Presented Component Unit.

No audited financial statements are available.

The City's officials are also responsible for appointing the members of the boards of other organizations, but the City's accountability for these organizations does not extend beyond making the appointments. The City appoints the board members of the following:

Trinity Housing Finance Corporation
Lone Star Airport Improvement Authority
Alliance Airport Authority
Fort Worth Development Corporation
Sunbelt Industrial Development Corporation

Joint ventures in which the City has an equity interest are (1) Dallas/Fort Worth International Airport and (2) Railtran. The City's investment in these joint ventures are recorded in the General Fixed Assets Account Group.

WAYS OF REPORTING OTHER TYPES OF UNITS

Joint Ventures

Governments sometimes enter into joint ventures with other governments. A **joint venture** is a contractual arrangement, whereby two or more participants agree to carry out a common activity, with each sharing in both its risks and rewards. For example, two cities (e.g., Dallas and Fort Worth) may join together to construct and operate an airport.

If a government has invested in a joint venture and thereby has an equity interest in it (i.e., owns a share of it) then it should account for the investment as an asset. If it made the investment with proprietary fund resources, it would record the asset in a proprietary fund. It would account for gains and losses on the *equity* basis (the same as a corporation accounts for unconsolidated subsidiaries in which it has a 20 percent or more interest). If it made the investment from a governmental fund, then it would record it in the general fixed assets account group, since long-term assets are not recorded in the general fund. The government would recognize revenue in the governmental fund based on the usual recognition criteria for that fund. Generally, for example, it would recognize revenues from the joint venture as the venture declares dividends and they become measurable and available.

Related Organizations

Statement No. 14 defines a **related organization**, as an entity that satisfies the criterion of financial accountability (that is, the primary government appoints a voting majority of its governing board) but neither of the other two criteria (that is, the primary government cannot impose its will upon the organization and there is no potential for the organization to provide specific financial benefits to, or impose specific financial burdens upon, the primary government). Hence, a related organization does not qualify as a component unit and cannot therefore be incorporated into the primary government's basic financial statements. Nevertheless, per Statement No. 14, the primary government should describe each organization to which it is related and indicate the nature of the relationship.

Affiliated Organizations

As defined by the GASB, an "affiliated organization" is a legally independent entity directly tied to a primary government.[1] In addition, the organization must qualify as a tax-exempt organization under the Internal Revenue Code, Section 501(c)(3), and its affiliation with the primary government must be set forth both in its articles of incorporation and in its application to the Internal Revenue Service for tax-exempt status.

Affiliated organizations may be distinguished from both component units and related organizations in that the primary government does not appoint a majority of their governing boards, and they are not fiscally dependent on the primary government.

In a typical arrangement, a government university's development foundation would be established as a 501(c)(3) organization. Its main mission would be to raise funds for the university. Although it would work closely with the university, it would be governed by an independent board of trustees.

Other examples of entities that should be considered as potential affiliated organizations include:

- a university's football booster club
- a hospital's fund-raising foundation
- a "friend's of the library" association

Per the GASB, a primary government should report an affiliated organization as a component unit, using discrete presentation, if either condition holds

- it has the ability to impose its will (as discussed earlier) on the organization
- there is the potential for the organization to provide specific financial benefits to, or impose specific financial burdens on, the primary government

If the affiliated organization does not satisfy these tests, then the primary government should report it as a related entity—that is, by describing it in footnotes.

---

[1] The discussion in this section is based on an exposure draft, *The Financial Reporting Entity—Affiliated Organizations* (December 1994). The final pronouncement, when issued, is intended as a supplement to GASB Statement No. 14.

EXAMPLE   *Summary of Statement No. 14*

A legally separate financing authority was created to enhance the availability of low and moderate income housing in a state by providing mortgage loans to purchasers of residential homes. The governing board of the authority is appointed by the governor. The authority determines its own budget, holds title to property in its own name, and controls its own day-to-day operations. Mortgage loans are made according to guidelines included in the authority's enabling legislation. The authority is permitted to issue debt, subject to a statutory limitation. All bonds issued to provide mortgage loans are secured by first mortgages on the related properties and are payable from the proceeds of mortgage repayments. In the event that the authority determines that funds will not be sufficient for the payment of the principal and interest on its bonds during the next succeeding state fiscal year, the chairman of the authority certifies to the governor the amount required to pay such principal and interest. The governor is obligated to include these amounts in the state budget. However, the legislature has no obligation to appropriate funds for the authority.[2]

The flowchart in Figure 12-1 can be used to assess whether, and if so, how the financing authority should be incorporated into the financial statements of the state:

- Is the financing authority legally separate? Yes.
- Does the state appoint a voting majority of its board? Yes.
- Is the state able to impose its will on the financing authority? There is no evidence that any one of the factors indicative of an ability to impose will are present.
- Is there a financial benefit/burden relationship? Yes, the state is obligated, in "some manner," for the authority's debt. It must include the debt in its budget. Therefore, the agency would qualify as a component unit
- Are the governing boards of the state and the authority the same? No.
- Does the authority provide services entirely or almost entirely to the state? No. Therefore, the state should report the authority as a component unit, using discrete presentation.

Controversy Surrounding Statement No. 14

The objective of the GASB in promulgating Statement No. 14 was to assure that a government's financial statements include information on all organizations for which it is accountable. Yet in the eyes of critics, the statement requires governments to cast out nets that are both too wide and too fine, thereby drawing into their reporting entities organizations for which they are only remotely accountable. In the summary illustration the state would have to include the financing authority in its reporting entity even if, in reality, it had only a minimum degree of accountability for its activities and obligations. For example, if the governor's appointees to the board served for nonrenewable terms and could not be removed from office except for cause, then the governor may have little ability to influence them. Similarly, if it were highly improbable that the authority would default on its obligations, and, even if it did, that the legislature would appropriate the funds to make up the deficiencies, then the state would bear little financial risk. Nevertheless, the board believed that the majority-rule criteria, coupled with the other requirements (i.e., imposition of will or financial benefit/burden) provided reasonable assurance that governments would have to include in their reporting entity only other governmental units for which they were legitimately accountable.

---

[2] Drawn from a GASB "implementation guide," *Guide to Implementing Statement No. 14 on the Reporting Entity*.

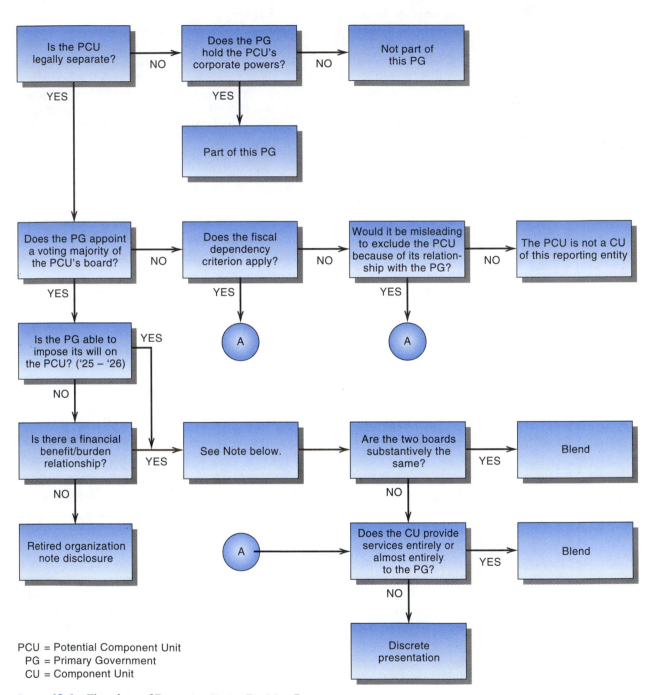

PCU = Potential Component Unit
PG = Primary Government
CU = Component Unit

Figure 12-1   Flowchart of Reporting Entity Decision Process
Source: Codification. Section 2100.901

In addition, critics have charged that when a government aggregates two or more component units into a single column for discrete presentation, the information loses significance. This is especially true, they note, when the aggregated units use different bases of accounting (i.e., modified accrual and full accrual). Some critics have dubbed the aggregated discrete column the *big blob*. However, in defense of GASB Statement No. 14, proponents note that the information loss caused by aggregating component units into a single column is no greater than that when two or more special revenue funds, capital projects funds, or enterprise funds are similarly combined.

WHAT ISSUES DOES A NOT-FOR-PROFIT FACE IN ESTABLISHING ITS REPORTING ENTITY?

Relationships among not-for-profits can be as varied as those among governments. For the most part, however, the relationships manifest three basic (although overlapping) characteristics:

- *Ownership.* An organization may own all or part of another entity. For example, one hospital may own another hospital; a college may own a research laboratory.
- *Control.* An organization may control another entity by having the power to appoint the majority of its governing board. For example, a health care organization may establish a fund-raising foundation, specifying that the foundation's governing board be composed of the organization's own officers.
- *Economic interest.* An organization may have an economic interest in another entity because the entity holds or utilizes resources on its behalf, the entity produces income or provides services to it, or the organization guarantees the debt of the entity. In the absence of ownership or control of the board, the economic interest may be expressed in a contract or affiliation agreement. For example, per affiliation agreements, a national fraternal organization may have the authority to establish operating policies and standards for its local chapters; a professional association may provide funding for a political action committee that lobbies on its behalf.

Accordingly, a not-for-profit organization faces the same fundamental issues as a government: What types of related entities should it include in its reporting entity? How should it include them?

WHAT ARE THE CURRENT STANDARDS FOR OTHER NOT-FOR-PROFITS?

According to a 1994 AICPA Statement of Position, *Reporting of Related Entities by Not-for-Profit Organizations*, (No. 94-3), a not-for-profit entity should include (and should *consolidate*) the financial statements of a related not-for-profit organization in the following two circumstances:

- It has a controlling financial interest in the organization through direct or indirect ownership of a majority voting interest.
- It has both control of the organization and an economic interest in it. Control can be evidenced by either a majority ownership or a majority voting interest in the organization's *governing board* (as opposed to the organization itself).

If the not-for-profit organization can exercise control of an entity in which it has an economic interest by means other than majority ownership or majority voting interest in the governing board, it is permitted, but not required, to consolidate that entity.

The FASB is currently addressing the issue of how all organizations, both not-for-profits and businesses, should account for entities to which they are related. When issued, its pronouncement will supersede that of the AICPA.

In a 1995 exposure draft, *Consolidated Financial Statements: Policy and Procedures*, the FASB proposed that organizations would have to consolidate all entities that they control, unless the control is merely temporary. In the draft it defines *control* as the power over assets—the ability to use or direct the use of another entity's assets as if they were one's own. More specifically, it says, control enables one entity to use or direct the use of assets of another by:

- establishing the controlled entity's policies and its capital and operating budgets
- hiring, firing, and determining the compensation of managers responsible for implementing the controlled entity's policies and decisions

Control, the statement explains, permits the parent to use the subsidiary's assets for its own benefit. Thus, for example, within the limits imposed by donors, a not-for-profit organization can use the assets of the entity that it controls to further its own mission, as if the assets were its own.

The proposed standard cites several circumstances that would lead to a presumption that an entity can exercise effective control. The two most directly applicable circumstances to not-for-profits are that the entity has:

- the powers to direct the other organization to provide all future net cash inflows or other future economic benefits to itself
- the unilateral ability to dissolve the other organization and assume control of its assets

Effective control, according to the draft, can also be indicated by circumstances in addition to those that would lead to an automatic presumption of control, including:

- an ability to cast a majority of the votes usually cast in an election of directors
- an entity's position as the sole creator of another entity
- a relationship between two or more entities that requires them to work together to fulfill a common charitable purpose. Such a relationship would exist, for example, when one entity formed a separate organization for the primary purpose of:
  - holding and investing assets to generate income for itself
  - holding assets to pay its debts
  - raising contributions for itself

EXAMPLE   *Not-For-Profit Reporting Entity*

A private university establishes a foundation specifically to solicit gifts for athletics and to manage a newly established athletic fund to which the university would transfer contributed funds. The university's board of trustees appoints the foundation's board of directors. Its articles of incorporation stipulate that its sole purpose is to raise and manage money for the benefit of the university's athletic program. They also state that the foundation's name or purpose cannot be changed without the consent of the university. Further, its bylaws provide that if the foundation is dissolved, its assets shall be distributed to the university.

Under these circumstances, the foundation would satisfy the consolidation criteria of both the AICPA statement of position and the FASB exposure draft. By appointing a majority of its members the university controls the governing board and, in that benefits from its revenues, has an economic interest in the foundation.

The proposed FASB standard emphasizes that the mere association of two or more entities in a common federation or association does not imply that the federation or association has the authority to control some of the members' activities. For example, local not-for-profits, like franchisees, may operate under the name of a national organization and agree to be bound by its standards and policies. As long as the national organization lacks the power to control the assets of the local units, however, it does not satisfy the exposure draft's criteria for effective control.

Similarly, local churches may either join or be established by an archdiocese, presbytery, or other central organization. Although the central organization may have considerable influence over the churches' practices and policies, it usually has only limited control over their finances. Therefore, it should not consolidate the statements of the local churches with its own.

HOW SHOULD CASH FLOWS BE REPORTED?

To this point in the text we have focused mainly on the balance sheet and the statement of activities. We now consider other components of a complete annual report.

As pointed out in Chapter 4, accounting rule-making authorities have recognized the accrual basis as being "superior" to the cash basis of accounting. The accrual basis "results in accounting measurements based on the substance of transactions and events, rather than merely when cash is received or disbursed, and thus enhances their relevance, neutrality, timeliness, completeness and comparability."[3]

Nonetheless, cash has a significance that transcends that of other assets. Cash is the medium of exchange in our society; organizations default on obligations owing to shortages of cash. In 1987, the FASB in Statement No. 95, *Statement of Cash Flows*, required businesses to include a statement of cash flows in their financial statements. It thereby gave the statement equal standing with the balance sheet and income statement. In 1989, the GASB, in Statement No. 9, *Reporting Cash Flows of Proprietary and Nonexpendable Trust Funds and Governmental Entities That Use Proprietary Fund Accounting* did the same for governments, albeit only for their business-type activities.

FASB Statement No. 95 applied initially only to businesses, not to not-for-profits. In 1993, however, FASB Statement No. 117, *Financial Statements of Not-for-Profit Organizations*, made Statement No. 95 applicable to not-for-profits as well.

The GASB does not yet require governments to prepare a statement of cash flows for *governmental* activities. There is less need for a statement of cash flows for governmental funds in that governmental funds are accounted for on a modified

---

[3] *Codification*, Section 1600.103.

accrual basis. Therefore, the statement of revenues and expenditures focuses—if not on cash itself—then on resources that are near-cash and are currently available for disbursement.

The preparation of a statement of cash flows can be complex and tedious, but it presents few, if any conceptual problems. In essence, the statement is a summary of an entity's cash account. The main issues, which both the FASB and the GASB have had to address, pertain to transaction classification.

DIFFERENT STANDARDS FOR GOVERNMENTS THAN FOR BUSINESSES

The GASB and FASB standards for statements of cash flows establish differing classification schemes. FASB Statement No. 95 requires that cash transactions be classified into three categories:

- *Cash flows from operating activities,* such as receipts from sales of goods and services, interest, and dividends and disbursements for goods and materials, interest and taxes

- *Cash flows from financing activities,* such as proceeds from issuing stocks and bonds and payments for dividends and repayments of loans

- *Cash flows from investing activities,* such as receipts and disbursements from the sale and purchase of marketable securities and long-lived assets

These categories have obvious limitations if applied to governments. Governments typically characterize their activities as either operating or capital. Capital activities—those involving the acquisition and financing of long-lived assets—are often both budgeted and accounted for apart from operating activities. Yet the FASB classification scheme draws no distinction between the two.

To remedy this deficiency the GASB developed a classification scheme with four categories:

- *Cash flows from operating activities*
- *Cash flows from noncapital financing activities*
- *Cash flows from capital and related financing activities*
- *Cash flows from investing activities*

Table 12–2 sets forth the main transactions included in each category.

The GASB and FASB standards also differ in how interest should be reported. In a significant departure from the precedent of FASB Statement No. 95, the GASB pronouncement requires that government enterprises classify interest paid as a *financing* activity and interest received as an *investing* activity rather than an operating activity. Whether interest paid is classified as a capital rather than a noncapital financing activity would depend on how the underlying debt is classified. The GASB maintains that by classifying interest received and disbursed in the same categories as purchases and sales of the underlying securities, governments provide a more complete picture of the cash flows associated with financing and investing activities.

Like FASB Statement No. 95, GASB Statement No. 9 permits governments to report their cash flows using the indirect method but encourages them to use the *direct* method. The direct method explicitly reports the operating cash flows in a way that makes clear their source or use (e.g., cash receipts from customers, cash payments to employees). The indirect method, by contrast, reconciles operating cash flows to operating income. Thus, the reporting entity would add to, or subtract from, operating income any differences between cash flows (e.g., cash receipts from customers, cash payments to employees) and the related revenues or expenses (e.g., sales revenues,

> ### TABLE 12–2
> ## Classification of Cash Receipts and Disbursements Per GASB Statement No. 9, *Reporting Cash Flows of Proprietary and Nonexpendable Trust Funds and Governmental Entities that Use Proprietary Fund Accounting*

Cash Flows from Operating Activities

Inflows
- Sales of goods or services, including collections of receivables
- Grants for operating activities
- Quasi-external operating transactions with other funds
- All other cash receipts not defined as capital, financing, or investing transactions

Outflows
- Payments to acquire materials for providing services, including payments on accounts payable
- Payments to employees
- Grants to other governments for operating activities
- Quasi-external operating transactions with other funds
- All other cash payments not defined as capital, financing, or investing transactions

Cash Flows from Noncapital Financing Activities

Inflows
- Proceeds from bonds, notes, or other debt instruments not clearly attributable to the acquisition, construction, or improvement of capital assets
- Grants from other governments that are not specifically restricted for capital purposes or are for specific activities considered to be operating activities of the grantor government (e.g., a grant to finance an operating deficit)
- Receipts from property and other taxes collected for the governmental enterprise that are not specifically restricted for capital purposes

Outflows
- Repayments of amounts borrowed for noncapital purposes
- Interest payment on amounts borrowed for noncapital purposes
- Grants to other governments except for those specific activities that are considered to be operating activities of the grantor government
- Cash paid to other funds, except for quasi-external operating transactions

Cash Flows from Capital and Related Financing Activities

Inflows
- Proceeds from issuing bonds, notes, or other debt instruments for the acquisition, construction, or improvement of capital assets
- Capital grants
- Receipts from the sale of capital assets
- Special assessments and property taxes to finance capital assets

Outflows
- Payments to acquire, construct, or improve capital assets
- Repayments of capital debt
- Interest on capital debt

Cash Flows from Investing Activities

Inflows
- Receipts from sales of marketable securities
- Interest and dividends received from investments
- Withdrawals from investment pools
- Collections of loans made by the government (except for program loans)

Outflows
- Purchases of marketable securities
- Disbursement for loans (except for program loans)

wage and salary expense). The GASB's willingness to allow governments a choice between the two methods is noteworthy in light of the FASB's experience with the same reporting option. Despite the FASB's expressed preference for the direct method, the overwhelming majority of businesses elect to use the indirect method.

Fort Worth's statement of cash flows for its municipal parking fund is presented in Table 12–3.

DIFFERENT STANDARDS FOR NOT-FOR-PROFITS THAN FOR GOVERNMENTS

In requiring a statement of cash flows for not-for-profits the FASB faced a dilemma. On the one hand, many experts, including a task force of the AICPA, asserted that with respect to cash flows the operations of not-for-profits more closely parallel those of governments than of businesses. Not-for-profits, like governments, draw the distinction between cash flows attributable to operations and those that are restricted for capital and comparable long-term purposes, such as permanent endowment funds. Accordingly, the experts contended, the FASB should adopt a four-way classification scheme similar to that established by the GASB.

On the other hand, however, by requiring a four-way scheme the FASB would be widening the gulf between business and not-for-profit reporting, thereby countering

---

TABLE 12–3
City of Fort Worth Municipal Parking Fund

Comparative Statements of Cash Flows
Years Ended September 30, 1996 and 1995
(000's omitted)

	1996	1995
Cash Flows from Operating Activities:		
Operating Income	$ 229	$ 264
Adjustments to Reconcile Operating Income to Net Cash Provided by Operating Activities:		
Depreciation	55	54
Change in Assets and Liabilities:		
Increase in Accounts and Other Receivables	(1)	(2)
Increase (Decrease) in Accounts Payable	4	(8)
Increase in Accrued Compensation	5	1
Net Cash Provided by Operating Activities	292	309
Cash Flows from Capital and Related Financing Activities:		
Acquisition and Construction of Property, Plant and Equipment	(3)	(1)
Principal Paid on Long-Term Debt	(209)	0
Interest Paid on Long-Term Obligations	(179)	0
Net Cash Used for Capital and Related Financing Activities	(391)	(1)
Cash Flows from Investing Activities:		
Interest Income Received	48	47
Net Cash Provided by Investing Activities	48	47
Net Increase (Decrease) in Cash and Cash Equivalents	(51)	355
Cash and Cash Equivalents, Beginning of Year	1,038	683
Cash and Cash Equivalents, End of Year	$ 987	$1,038

Note: This particular fund apparently had no cash flows from noncapital financing activities.

a trend toward, and apparent objective of, narrowing it. Emphasizing the importance of comparability between businesses and not-for-profits, the FASB elected to apply the three-way scheme to not-for-profits.

Owing to the types of contributions engaged in by not-for-profits, the FASB was required to modify Statement No. 95 so that it would be more germane to not-for-profits. For example, it stipulated that cash flows from *financing* activities should include both contributions restricted for long-term purposes and interest and dividends from investments restricted for long-term purposes. By contrast, other contributions and interest and dividends on investments not restricted for long-term purposes could be classified as *operating* cash flows.

The statement of cash flows of the American Health Association is presented in Table 12–4.

WHAT OTHER ELEMENTS MAKE UP THE COMPREHENSIVE ANNUAL FINANCIAL REPORT?

Generally accepted accounting principles mandate that governments prepare a **comprehensive annual financial report (CAFR).** The CAFRs of multipurpose governments, no matter what the entity's size, are imposing—even overwhelming—documents. The purpose of this section is to provide an overview of the CAFR and, in particular, to put into perspective the vast amount of information it incorporates.

The GASB *Codification* describes financial reporting as a pyramid. As illustrated in Figure 12-2, it consists of five levels. However, generally only two (although sometimes as many as four) levels need be part of the CAFR.

The pyramid rests on the individual transactions in which the government engages (the bottom level). Although aggregated and summarized in the financial statements, they are not reported upon directly in the CAFR.

Governments may present condensed summary data (the top level) in any fashion that they choose. Some issue "popular" reports in the form of newspaper advertisements, brochures, and even wall calendars. But the summary data, like the transactions, need not be part of the CAFR.

Of the remaining four levels, only the general purpose financial statements and the combining statements by fund type must be included in the CAFR. Individual fund and account group statements and schedules are required only if the information required by GAAP cannot be satisfied at the other levels of reporting.

The CAFR is divided into three major sections:

- introductory section
- financial section
- statistical section

SIGNIFICANT COMPONENTS OF THE INTRODUCTORY SECTION

The most significant component of the introductory section is the letter of transmittal, usually from the government's chief financial officer (often co-signed by the city manager or other chief executive officer) and addressed to the governing board and the citizenry. Similar to the management discussion and analysis that is now a required part of private sector reports, the letter of transmittal may serve as a written "state of the city" address. The Government Finance Officers Association (GFOA) recommends that the transmittal letter discuss local economic conditions, provide an

TABLE 12-4
Statement of Cash Flows of a Not-for-Profit Organization

American Health Association, Local Affiliate, Inc.
Statement of Cash Flows
for the Year Ended June 30, 1996

Cash Flows	
Change in Net Assets	$ 6,492,230
Adjustments to Reconcile Change in Net Assets to Net Cash	
Provided By Operating Activities	
Depreciation and Amortization	386,056
Unrealized Gain on Perpetual Trust Contributions	(308,100)
Gains on Investment Transactions	(103,544)
Gain on Sale of Fixed Assets	(6,468)
Contributions Restricted to Investment in Property	(9,486)
Contributions to Endowment Funds	(270,000)
Increase in Accrued Investment Income	(57,260)
Increase in Federated and Nonfederated Receivable	(13,516)
Increase in National Center Receivable	(20,382)
Decrease in Other Receivable	116,532
Decrease in Bequest Receivable	314,000
Decrease in Pledges Receivable	2,812
Decrease in Educational and Campaign Material Inventory	78,454
Increase in Other Assets	(21,255)
Increase in Perpetual Trust	(2,459,800)
Increase in Charitable Gift Annuity	(40,500)
Increase in Charitable Remainder Trust	(4,963,216)
Increase in Payable to National Center	1,332,258
Increase in Accounts Payable and Accrued Expenses	808,360
Increase in Research Awards Payable	225,508
Increase in Annuity Obligation	19,640
Decrease in Deferred Revenue and Support	(413,959)
Net Cash Provided by Operating Activities	**$ 1,088,364**
Cash Flows from Investing Activities	
Purchase of Equipment	(724,492)
Proceeds from Sale of Equipment	200,217
Proceeds from Maturities of Investments	7,730,368
Purchase of Investments	(8,216,079)
Net Cash Used in Investing Activities	**$(1,009,986)**
Cash Flows from Financing Activities	
Contributions to Endowment Funds	270,000
Proceeds from Contributions Restricted to Investment in Property	9,486
Net Cash Provided by Financing Activities	**$ 279,486**
Net Increase in Cash and Cash Equivalents	**357,864**
Cash and Cash Equivalents (at Beginning of Year)	**448,519**
Cash and Cash Equivalents (at End of Year)	**$ 806,383**
Supplemental Data	
Noncash Investing and Financing Activities-Gifts of Equipment	$ 30,000

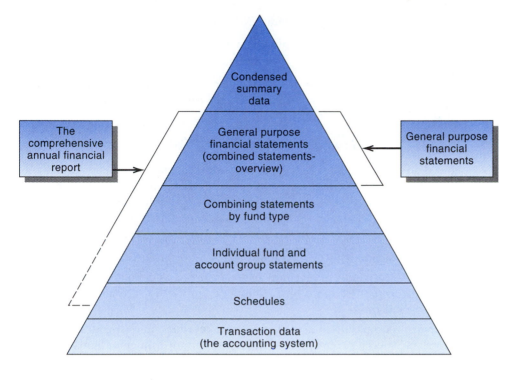

— Required
—— May be necessary

Figure 12-2 The Financial Reporting Pyramid

Source: Governmental Accounting Standards Board Codification, Section 1900.114.

overview of the government's financial status, describe major initiatives, and summarize key budgetary and accounting practices.[4]

The letter of transmittal is not a part of the financial statements and is thereby not within the scope of the independent auditors' report. Government officials, especially those subject to election, are not beyond occasionally "puffing," so the letter of transmittal should not be afforded the same credibility as the information subject to audit.

The introductory section would also contain a *certificate of achievement for excellence in financial reporting* if one has been awarded by the GFOA. The certificate of achievement is awarded to governments whose annual reports conform to GFOA standards. The GFOA does not, however, audit the government's books and records and does not therefore vouch for the accuracy of the underlying information. Subsequent to Orange County's 1994 multibillion dollar investment losses, reporters questioned GFOA officials as to how, in light of obvious fiscal mismanagement, the county was awarded a certificate of achievement. The officials had to painstakingly explain that investment losses are by no means necessarily indicative of improper financial reporting and that even if they were, the certificate of achievement is not an endorsement of the underlying data.

---

[4] *Governmental Accounting, Auditing and Financial Reporting* (Chicago: Government Finance Officers Association, 1994), p. 216–218.

IMPORTANT PARTS OF THE FINANCIAL SECTION

The financial section consists of the auditor's report plus:

- the general purpose financial statements (GPFS)
- combining statements
- individual fund and account group statements (which are generally not necessary if adequate information on the individual funds and account groups is provided in the combining statements)

The General Purpose Financial Statements (GPFS)

As discussed in Chapter 2, the general purpose financial statements present an overview of all funds and account groups. These are the statements in which each column represents a **fund type** or account group (e.g., general fund, special revenue funds, capital projects funds, fixed asset account group). The general purpose financial statements are composed of the five basic statements:

- a combined balance sheet for all funds and account groups
- a combined statement of revenues, expenditures, and changes in fund balance for all governmental funds and component units that are accounted for as governmental funds
- a statement comparing budgeted and actual revenues and expenditures for the general and special revenue funds (and any other governmental funds for which budgets are prepared)
- a statement of revenues and expenses and changes in fund balances for all proprietary and nonexpendable trust funds and component units that are accounted for as proprietary funds
- a statement of cash flows for all proprietary and nonexpendable trust funds and component units that are accounted for as proprietary funds

The general purpose financial statements contain the complete set of notes and other disclosures required by generally accepted accounting principles. Thus, they are *liftable*; they can stand alone. If included (along with the auditor's report) in a bond offering statement or similar document, they constitute full and fair presentation in accordance with GAAP.

The Combining Statements

The combining statements, like the general purpose financial statements, are a required component of the CAFR's financial section. The combining statements support the general purpose financial statements. They provide the detail as to each of the individual funds included in the columns of the general purpose financial statements. Thus, whereas each column of the **combined statements** would provide information as to a fund type or account group, each column of the **combining statements** would report on an individual fund or account group. The "totals" column of a combining statement would tie into the respective column on the combined statement. Moreover, because each combining statement deals only with a specific fund type, it is possible to present the data in greater detail (e.g., to disaggregate broad categories of revenues and expenses into narrower categories) than is practical on the combined statements.

Most governments limit their combining statements to a balance sheet, statement of revenues, expenditures, and fund balances, and (for proprietary funds only) a statement of cash flows.

Individual fund statements are not generally required, inasmuch as they would usually be superfluous; the information would be the same as a corresponding column in the combining statements. They are necessary, though, if it is impractical to present information required for complete and fair presentation in the combining statements. Moreover, governments may elect to present individual fund statements so as to show actual-to-budget information for particular funds (especially in the face of legal requirements that budgets be prepared for those funds) or to provide comparative data for the prior fiscal year.

PROPOSED CHANGES TO THE FISCAL SECTION

As discussed in previous chapters, the GASB has proposed a major modification to the financial section of the CAFR. Governments would now be required to prepare financial statements from both an entity-wide and a funds perspective.

The proposed entity-wide statement of activities differs dramatically from the traditional statement. The revenues and expenses would be categorized by program, rather than by object. Thus, it would highlight programs such as public safety, sanitation, and administration as opposed to specific costs such as salaries, travel, and rent. As discussed previously, all revenues and expenses would be recognized on a full accrual basis.

The proposed entity-wide statement is illustrated in Chapter 2, (Table 2–4) As is obvious, the statement is likely to be initially confusing. Unlike a statement with which you are likely to be familiar, it is designed to highlight the net cost of each program that must be paid for with general (unrestricted) revenues. However, upon more careful examination, it becomes apparent that the statement not only contains more information than is incorporated into conventional statements, but is quite easy to understand.

Reduced to its simplest form, the top part of the statement shows the net operating cost for each program—that is, the total expenses (in the first column), less any revenues that can be directly associated with the program (in the columns marked program revenue). The bottom part of the statement indicates the government's unrestricted revenues—those it must rely on to cover its net program costs. See Example below.

EXAMPLE   *Proposed Entity-Wide Statement of Activities*

A sanitation district has two programs: collection and recycling. In a recent year, collection expenses were $100 million and recycling expenses were $30 million. The district billed residents $90 million in fees for collection and received a $10 million federal recycling grant. It recognized $35 million in unrestricted property taxes. The following is an abbreviated statement of activities:

| Program | Expenses | Program Revenues | | Net Costs |
		Fees	Grants	
Collection	$100	$90		($10)
Recycling	30		$10	(20)
Total	$130	$90	$10	($30)
Nonprogram Revenue:				
Property Taxes				35
Excess of Revenue Over Expenses				$ 5

As emphasized previously, the *funds* perspective statements would still be prepared on a modified accrual basis. However, the form and content of the financial statements would be modified. Separate sets of statements would be presented for governmental funds, for proprietary funds, and for fiduciary funds.

Most prominently, the balance sheet and the statement of revenues and expenditures for the governmental funds would include one column for the general fund and at least one column for each fund type (thus, at least one column for special revenue funds, capital projects funds, debt service funds) additional columns for each major fund (a major fund being defined as one in which fund assets, liabilities, revenues, or expenses are at least 10 percent of the relevant fund type).

As discussed in Chapters 8 and 9, information on the long-term assets and liabilities now reported in the fixed assets and general long-term debt account groups would be presented only in supplementary schedules of changes in capital assets and long-term debt. Table 12–5 illustrates the proposed funds perspective statement of revenues, expenditures, and changes in fund balances.

In a major change from current practice, the statement of actual to budget revenues and expenditures for the general fund would have to include two columns for the budgeted amounts—one that shows the budget as initially adopted (the original budget) and one that shows the budget as amended throughout the year (the final budget). The statement would thereby enable users to assess not only whether the government operated within legal constraints (per the final budget), but also whether its initial estimates were reliable.

Along with the core financial statements, entities would be required to present an analytical discussion of their fiscal condition and operating results. This section, *Management's Discussion and Analysis of Financial Condition and Results of Operations* (MD&A), would be similar to that required of businesses. It would include an explanation of the objectives of the two financial reporting perspectives, an analysis of significant differences in operating results from the previous year, an assessment of budgetary variances, a description of debt activity during the year, and an interpretation of known trends, events, commitments, and uncertainties.

CRITICAL ASPECTS OF THE STATISTICAL SECTION

The GASB *Codification* lists fifteen statistical tables a government should include in its CAFR unless the information is clearly inapplicable to that type of entity. These are presented in Table 12–6.

These supplementary disclosures (which are not within the scope of the auditor's report) are of value because of a key limitation of government financial reports, which was pointed out in Chapter 1. Governments have the power to tax. They can thereby command the resources of their constituents. The fiscal wherewithal of a government cannot be assessed merely by examining the resources actually within the government's control. The resources *potentially* within its control must also be taken into account.

Both Orange County, California, and Bridgeport, Connecticut sought the protection of bankruptcy courts in the 1990s. Their financial statements were equally dismal. Yet their overall fiscal condition was dramatically different. Orange County was one of the wealthiest communities in the country, while Bridgeport was one of the poorest. If Orange County defaulted on its debts or reduced public services, it did so not because it did not have access to the necessary resources, but rather because the citizenry *elected* not to draw upon them.

The statistical section supplements the financial statements. The required tables fall into two broad categories. The first are those that provide additional information

TABLE 12–5
Proposed Funds Perspective Statement of Revenues, Expenditures, and Changes In Fund Balances

For the Year Ended December 31, 2002

	General Fund	Special Revenue Funds	Debt Service Funds	Capital Projects Funds
Revenues				
Property Taxes	$29,280,163	$ —	$ 4,605,192	$ —
Other Taxes	13,025,392	—	—	—
Fees and Fines	606,946	—	—	—
Licenses and Permits	2,287,794	—	—	—
Intergovernmental	6,119,938	3,951,287	—	1,457,820
Charges for Services	11,374,460	30,708	—	—
Interest	552,325	215,204	146,604	836,589
Miscellaneous	881,874	66,270	—	2,939
Total Revenues	64,128,892	4,263,469	4,751,796	2,297,348
Expenditures				
Current Operating:				
General Government	8,630,835	53,622	11,820	490,124
Public Safety	33,729,623	—	—	—
Public Works	4,975,775	3,721,542	—	—
Engineering Services	1,299,645	—	—	—
Health and Sanitation	6,070,032	—	—	—
Cemetery	706,305	—	—	—
Culture and Recreation	11,411,685	—	—	—
Community Development	—	2,879,389	—	—
Debt Service:				
Principal	—	75,000	3,375,000	—
Interest and Other Charges	—	—	5,215,151	—
Capital Outlay:	—	—	—	16,718,649
Total Expenditures	66,823,900	6,729,553	8,601,971	7,208,773
Excess (Deficiency) of Revenues Over Expenditures	(2,695,008)	(2,466,084)	(3,850,175)	(14,911,425)
Other Financing Sources (Uses)				
Proceeds of Refunding Bonds	—	—	38,045,000	—
Proceeds of Long-Term Capital Febt	—	—	—	18,829,560
Payment to Bond Refunding Escrow Sgent	—	—	(37,284,144)	—
Transfers In	129,323	134,500	3,991,298	1,269,722
Transfers Out	(2,163,759)	(348,046)	—	(2,273,187)
Total Other Financing Sources and Uses	(2,034,436)	(213,546)	4,752,154	17,826,095
Special Item				
Proceeds from Sale of Park Land	3,476,488	—	—	—
Net Change in Fund Balance	(1,252,956)	(2,679,630)	901,979	2,914,670
Fund Balances—Beginning	2,908,322	6,225,442	2,930,083	21,539,896
Fund Balances—Ending	$ 1,655,366	$ 3,545,812	$ 3,832,062	$ 24,454,566

Source: GASB Exposure Draft, *Basic Financial Statements—and Management's Discussion and Analysis—for State and Local Governments* (Appendix E: Illustrations) 1997

TABLE 12–6
Statistical Tables Required for the CAFR

- General Governmental Expenditures by Function—Last Ten Fiscal Years
- General Revenues by Source—Last Ten Fiscal Years
- Property Tax Levies and Collections—Last Ten Fiscal Years
- Assessed and Estimated Actual Value of Taxable Property—Last Ten Fiscal Years
- Property Tax Rates—All Overlapping Governments—Last Ten Fiscal Years
- Special Assessment Billings and Collections—Last Ten Fiscal Years (if the government is obligated in some manner for related special assessment debt)
- Ratio of Net General Bonded Debt to Assessed Value and Net Bonded Debt per Capita—Last Ten Fiscal Years
- Computation of Legal Debt Margin, (if not presented in the GPFS)
- Computation of Overlapping Debt (if not presented in the GPFS)
- Ratio of Annual Debt Service for General Bonded Debt to Total General Expenditures—Last Ten Fiscal Years
- Revenue Bond Coverage—Last Ten Fiscal Years
- Demographic Statistics.
- Property Value, Construction, and Bank Deposits—Last Ten Fiscal Years
- Principal Taxpayers
- Miscellaneous Statistics

Source: *Governmental Accounting Standards Board Codification,* Section 2800.103

or insights into data reported in current or previous financial statements. These include, for example, tables that show ten-year trends in expenditures, revenues, tax collections, and bond coverage.

The second are those that report on economic conditions within the government's jurisdiction. These include tables that indicate the largest taxpayers, overlapping debt, and trends in the value of property, new construction and bank deposits. They provide insight into the government's *fiscal capacity*—the economic base that the government can draw upon for its resources.

HOW CAN A GOVERNMENT'S FISCAL CONDITION BE ASSESSED?

Assessing a government's financial condition (i.e., its ability to finance its services and satisfy its obligations on a continuing basis) is a daunting task. Not only is a government's fiscal condition directly dependent upon economic, political, social, and demographic factors within its jurisdiction, it is also intertwined with those of other governments that provide financial aid or serve the same constituents.

CONSULTING THE COMPREHENSIVE ANNUAL FINANCIAL REPORT

The CAFR is probably the single richest source of data as to a government's fiscal condition. But the data of any one period, by themselves, are little more than a collection of numbers. They provide a scant basis on which to assess the government's past performance or make predictions as to its future. They are useful only when related to other data in the form of ratios, trends, and comparisons. Although the CAFR reports some of these relationships, it is mainly a source of raw data. The burden of analysis and interpretation falls on individual users. As suggested by the accompanying In Practice, sophisticated users are sufficiently knowledgeable to custom tailor, and supplement, the data to their own needs.

IN PRACTICE

Since New York City's 1975 bond default, the accounting profession has borne the blame for permitting the city to issue financial reports that masked its fiscal deterioration. But now, almost two decades later, a research study may relieve government accountants of some of their guilt. The study concludes that whereas the reports did, indeed, overstate revenues and understate expenses, they failed to fool the bondholders. The bondholders "saw through" the misstatements and priced the bonds just as they would had the city's financial statements been prepared on the basis of GAAP.

Published in the *Journal of Accounting and Public Policy* (Fall 1992), the study by Dartmouth accounting professor Virginia Soybel correlates the yields on New York City bonds with two sets of accounting measures. The first was drawn from the financial statements as actually issued by New York. The second was based on the same financial statements, but now adjusted to conform to GAAP. The author finds that the bond yields are far more sensitive to the measures based on the adjusted rather than the unadjusted statements. This indicates, she reasons, that bondholders were aware of New York's slide toward default despite the misleading financial statements, and apparently based their investment decisions on other information.

Measured Risk by Comparing Bond Yields

Soybel carried out her study in three main stages. First she investigated the behavior of New York City bond yields relative to other bond yields for the fifteen-year period from 1961 to 1975. During this period the city's bonds were rated Baa, Baa-1, or A. She found, however, that the bond markets judged the New York bonds more risky than the average municipal bonds with a Baa rating. That is, the yields on the New York bonds were higher than the average yields for Baa bonds. In fact, even in periods during which Moody's rated the City's bonds Baa-1 or A, the yields on the New York bonds were higher than those on the average Baa bonds.

Second, Soybel reconstructed New York's financial statements for the same fifteen years so that they conformed to GAAP. She was able to do this by consulting numerous sources in addition to the financial statements. Most of these would not have been available to investors at the time, and they included documents such as reports on a SEC investigation and a New York State audit, both of which were prompted by the City's bond default. For example, New York had been issuing revenue anticipation notes (RANs) in expectation of federal and state aid and had been recognizing the proceeds as revenue. Soybel backed out these proceeds and instead recognized the federal and state aid as revenue when it was received.

Third, Soybel examined the relationship between the accounting ratios (both adjusted and unadjusted) and the differences between New York's bond yields and the average Baa yields. The aim was to determine whether the differences in bonds yields (measures of the bonds' risk) were more sensitive to the ratios based on the original or the adjusted accounting data. Based on sophisticated statistical tests, she found that the differences in yields were more closely tied to the *adjusted* ratios—those that, presumably, portrayed the financial condition of the city more accurately then the unadjusted versions. Thus, she concluded, "the evidence presented in my paper indicates that over the fifteen years leading to the default, the market measured New York's relative risk in a manner consistent with the city's financial deterioration, as revealed *ex post*, although that deterioration was not clear *ex ante* in the City's reported financial information."

Source: Adapted from *Government Accounting and Auditing Update* (March 1993). Reprinted by permission of publisher, RIA Group/Warren, Gorham, Lamont.

The CAFR is intended to provide information relevant to a wide range of decisions; it is not designed to be the sole source of information for any particular decision. Bond rating agencies, for example, require governments applying for a bond rating to supplement their CAFRs with additional documents, such as budgets, long-range forecasts and plans, biographical summaries of key officials, and economic reports.

Assessing financial condition in government is especially challenging in light of the small number of bond defaults and bankruptcy filings among general-purpose governments. In the business sector, the ability of ratios and similar indicators to predict fiscal stress can be evaluated statistically by constructing regression or similar models in which the ratio and other indicators are associated with actual failures. In the public sector, owing to the small number of bankruptcies and defaults, there is considerably less evidence as to which indicators actually point to impending failure. Hence, the indicators to be presented in this section, while widely accepted, have not been statistically validated.

The discussion that follows is intended merely to suggest some of the indicators and relationships that users, such as rating agencies, take into account in assessing financial condition.

VIEWING OPERATING DEFICITS WITH CAUTION

Operating deficits should be to financial analysts as red flags are to bulls. They should get their attention, yet they should not distract their focus away from other, more consequential, targets.

A widely used rule of thumb holds that two consecutive years of operating deficits connote serious fiscal distress. But operating deficits as a measure of fiscal performance have inherent limitations and must be interpreted with considerable caution.

First, operating deficits (as well as all other accounting measures) result from the application of generally accepted accounting principles. As stressed throughout this text, these principles represent compromises among competing objectives and were not developed to facilitate any particular decisions. The resultant accounting revenues and expenditures may not necessarily have been determined on the most appropriate basis for the purpose at hand.

Second, operating deficits are reported fund by fund; a deficit reported in the "totals" column carries the warning label "memorandum only." The financial health of a government cannot be assessed by focusing exclusively on the general fund or any other specific fund. Funds resources (especially cash and other liquid assets) may be fungible. They may be transferable from fund to fund. Yet on the other hand, fund accounting rests on the rationale that resources in individual funds are restricted for specific purposes and that resources in one fund cannot necessarily be used to satisfy obligations in others.

There are no all-purpose guidelines as to whether and when operating deficits—or for that matter, any financial indicators—should be analyzed at the fund or the government-wide level. By focusing on individual funds, analysts can readily fail to take into account opportunities to transfer resources from one fund to another. By focusing on the government as a whole, however, they may ignore restrictions on how the resources in specific funds may be used.

Third, operating deficits, whether government-wide or of individual funds, even if over a period of two or more years, do not necessarily signify deteriorating financial condition. If a government has accumulated excessive surpluses in the past, it may elect, quite sensibly, to draw them down by running planned deficits over the following several years.

In governments, more revenue is not necessarily preferable to less. Revenues must cover expenditures but they need not exceed them. A key step in assessing the adequacy of revenues, therefore, is to associate trends in revenues with those in expenditures.

Both revenues and expenditures are closely correlated with size of constituency. To compare the revenues and expenditures of the same government over time or of one government with another, it is necessary to take into account differences in population. For many analytical purposes, revenues and expenditures are best expressed *per capita*.

A stable revenue base is generally characterized by several diverse sources of revenues, so that a decline in one source will not necessarily be contemporaneous with declines in others. Moreover, the revenues should be linked to population, so that costs of providing for a larger population are automatically offset by a broader revenue base. For example, a state government that generates its revenue from a mix of property taxes, incomes taxes, sales taxes, user fees, and intergovernmental aid is more likely to have a stable revenue base than one that relies primarily on taxes on oil production.

The following ratios spotlight the stability of a government's revenues:

- *Intergovernmental revenues to total operating revenues.* Governments generally want to maximize the amount of resources received from other governments. Failure to take advantage of appropriate intergovernmental grants can rightfully be interpreted as a sign of poor management. But what a granting government gives, it can also take away. Therefore, a high, or increasing, ratio of intergovernmental revenues to total revenues is a sign of risk and hence a negative fiscal characteristic.

- *Restricted revenues to total operating revenues.* Restricted revenues decrease the flexibility of governments to respond to changing conditions and may lead to a misallocation of resources. State gasoline taxes, for example, may be dedicated to highway construction, and thereby be unavailable to meet pressing needs for new schools. Therefore, low percentages of restricted revenues are preferred to high percentages.

- *One-time revenues to total operating revenues.* By definition, one-time revenues cannot be ongoing. As suggested earlier in the text, these revenues may result from substantive measures, such as sales of assets, or merely "one-shot" technical adjustments, such as changes in the due date of taxes or license fees. Some can be motivated by opportunities to enhance productivity; others by a need to balance the budget. A high proportion of one-time revenues is generally a decidedly negative characteristic.

- *Property tax revenues to total operating revenues.* Property tax revenues are considered a stable source of revenue and a high ratio of property tax revenues to other, less stable, revenues is a positive attribute.

- *Uncollected property taxes to total property taxes levied.* A high rate of uncollected property taxes may signal an underlying weakness in the economy and hence warn of an impending reduction in revenues, not only from property taxes, but from other sources as well.[5]

Expenditures are a measure of the cost of services provided. Changes in per capita expenditures can be the result of several factors, some positive, some negative. For example, increases in expenditures can be attributable to:

- decreases in productivity or increases in prices (that is, the government provides the same services but at greater cost)

---

[5] These and several other ratios presented in this section have been adapted from Sanford M. Groves and Maureen Godsey Valente, *Evaluating Financial Condition, A Handbook for Local Government* (Washington, D.C.: International City Management Association, 1986).

- changes in the number, quality, or mix of services owing to *favorable* economic conditions (e.g., new housing developments or new industries that require a city to enhance its infrastructure)
- changes in the number, quality, or mix of services owing to *unfavorable* economic factors (e.g., added unemployment that requires the city to provide free medical care for a larger number of citizens)

Ratios that may be used to identify changes in spending patterns and thereby signal the need for an investigation into the cause of the change include the following:

- ***Number of employees to population or payroll expenditures to total expenditures.*** Without evidence of corresponding increases in the level or quality of services, increases in payroll costs may be a consequence of decreased productivity or higher wage rates.

- ***Expenditures for specific functions to total expenditures.*** Disproportionate increases in expenditures for specific functions (such as public safety, health and welfare, or recreation) may indicate new policies or circumstances that presage additional increases in the future.

- ***Nondiscretionary expenditures to total expenditures.*** Governments typically control only a limited percentage of their total costs. Others are dictated by contractual agreements (such as leases), debt commitments, and mandates from higher levels of government. The higher the percentage of nondiscretionary expenditures, the less flexibility the government has to reduce (or limited increases) in spending.

Analysts must also be cognizant of one-time reductions in expenditures. Some, such as a decrease in snow removal costs caused by an unusually snow-free winter, may be for legitimate reasons. Others, such as a postponement in the purchase of needed goods or services, may be only artificial, representing the government equivalent of "window dressing."

ASSESSING THE BALANCE SHEET

The balance sheet reports on a government's resources and claims against these resources. Therefore it provides an indication of a government's ability to perform the services expected of it and to fulfill its obligations. In this text, key issues in assessing the burden of a government's long-term obligations and the adequacy of its long-term assets have already been addressed in the chapters dealing with the general long-term debt and the general fixed assets account groups.

Of all a government's balance sheet accounts—particularly those of its governmental funds—fund balance typically draws the greatest attention. In large part, fund balance is so highly visible because it embodies all other balance sheet accounts and in government funds is indicative of net available financial resources.

Most governments try to maintain positive fund balances so as to be better able to cope with unforeseen expenditures or revenue shortfalls, and analysts view with concern declining fund balances. However, the significance of fund balance can easily be overstated. Fund balance is nothing more than the accumulation of annual surpluses and deficits and is therefore subject to the limitations ascribed earlier to operating deficits. If, as is common, the budgetary principles applicable to a particular government differ from the generally accepted accounting principles on which reported fund balance is based, the fund balance may not necessarily denote the resources legally available for expenditure. In addition, since it is established by the application of modified accrual accounting, the fund balance of governmental funds excludes the government's equity in both fixed assets and receivables not expected to be collected in time to satisfy current obligations—resources that obviously affect financial condition. Similarly, it fails to take into account claims against the government's resources, many of which are captured in the general long-term debt account group as "amounts to be provided." The fund balances of proprietary funds, on the other hand, reflect values based on historical costs, which have little or no bearing on financial condition.

The adequacy of fund balance is often measured by the ratio of *unreserved* fund balance to operating revenues:

$$\frac{\text{unreserved fund balance}}{\text{total operating revenues}}$$

Other factors being equal, a trend of decline in the ratio is seen as a sign of deteriorating financial condition.

A government's balance sheets are most useful in assessing **liquidity** (the ability to cover short-term obligations). Liquidity in governments can be measured just as it is in businesses—by comparing some or all current assets to current liabilities. Because a government's inventories are not usually for sale and will not be a source of cash, most analysts exclude inventories. Thus, the current ratio includes only cash, short-term investments (i.e., near cash) and receivables:

$$\frac{\text{cash, short-term investments and receivables}}{\text{current liabilities}}$$

A more rigorous form of the ratio also excludes receivables:

$$\frac{\text{cash and short-term investments}}{\text{current liabilities}}$$

As in business, analysts can key in on a specific balance sheet account by comparing it to the revenue or expenditure (or a similar inflow or outflow measure) with which it is associated. For example, the extent to which property taxes are being collected on a timely basis can be evaluated by dividing property taxes receivable (or uncollected property taxes) by the total property tax levy for the year. Similarly, a build-up in unfunded pension obligations can be detected by dividing the total pension liability (as reported in both funds and account groups) by the annual required pension contribution.

Ironically, no analysis of a government's fiscal condition can be meaningful if it fails to consider the status of the entity's infrastructure—assets that may not even be accorded accounting recognition. Analysts must therefore obtain from sources other than the CAFR information on the age, condition, and capacity of infrastructure and assess the demands that infrastructure maintenance and improvement will place on future years' revenues.

EVALUATING ECONOMIC FACTORS

The ultimate ability of a government to perform the services expected of it and to meet its obligations will be determined not by the resources currently on hand, but by those within the government's command. Thus, the economic base of the community that the government serves is of prime importance in assessing the government's financial condition.

Fiscal Effort

A government's **fiscal effort**—the extent to which it is taking advantage of its fiscal capacity—may be measured by comparing the revenues that it generates from its own sources (i.e., total revenue, excluding grants from other governments) with either the wealth or income of its taxpayers. Income can be captured by measures such as median family income; wealth by total appraised (market) value of property. Thus, fiscal effort equals:

$$\frac{\text{Revenue from own sources}}{\text{Median family income}} \quad \text{or} \quad \frac{\text{Revenue from own sources}}{\text{Total appraised value of property}}$$

As these ratios increase, the government exerts greater fiscal effort and thereby uses a greater portion of its fiscal capacity. It has less remaining capacity to handle increases in fiscal burdens that might result from emergencies or increased demands for services.

Demographic and Social Considerations

Population size and composition greatly impact a community's economic base. Population trends, however, are not usually discernible over short periods and therefore should be analyzed over at least a decade, not merely two or three years.

Increases in population are often associated with expanding economies and the creation of new businesses. Growth, however, may have its fiscal downside, especially in the short-term. As new developments are constructed and families, often with young children, move into the community, the government may have to extend its infrastructure, construct new schools, and enhance its social services.

The composition of a population is as critical as its size. Factors of particular importance include age (the elderly require extensive medical care; the young require education), income distribution, educational level, and labor skills.

Closely tied to demographic considerations are sociological factors such as crime rates, percentage of citizens requiring public assistance, and the percentage of residents owning their own homes. These factors affect the extent and level of services that the government will have to provide, as well as its ability to raise revenues.

Industrial Base

The potential of an economy to generate tax and other revenues depends on the composition of its taxpayers. If the leading taxpayers are in a variety of industries, the government's revenue stream is less likely to be adversely affected by recessions, technological developments, changes in consumer tastes or similar factors that may have an impact on some industries but not others. In addition, some industries may be riding a wave of expansion, whereas others are caught in an undertow of decline. Some companies, perhaps because of high capital investments or historical ties, are likely to remain in a community. Others, maybe because their facilities are aging or they can reduce operating costs by relocating abroad, may be candidates for early departure.

TAKING INTO ACCOUNT OTHER FACTORS

Leadership Characteristics

The ability of a government to exercise decisive leadership both in planning for the future and in responding to crises adds strength to its fiscal condition. This ability can be influenced by several factors. These include:

- *Formal structure of the government and the powers that are granted to key officials.* In some governments, the chief executive officers have the authority to make major spending decisions on their own, without legislative approval. In others, even minor decisions are subject to lengthy administrative or legislative processes.
- *Degree of political competition.* In the absence of political competition, as might be evidenced by closely contested elections, the chief executive officer may be able to act swiftly and forcefully, irrespective of requirements for formal legislative approval.

- *Competence and integrity of government officials.* Bright, experienced, and honest officials are a necessary, if not necessarily sufficient, condition for fiscal well-being.

- *Relations with other governments.* These are affected not only by the power of home rule (the authority to act without the approval of the state or some other government) but also by personal and political relationships among the officials of the various levels of government.

- *Community's political climate.* Politics and economics go hand in hand. Albeit a highly subjective factor, a favorable political climate makes it easier for a community to achieve its social, environmental, or educational goals while assuring that the costs are distributed equitably.

The Budget

The CAFR reports on what has happened in the past, but financial condition is assessed with an eye to the future. Therefore, analysts should pay as much attention to budgets and plans (such as a five-year capital improvement plan) as to financial statements. A sound budget should be attainable, take into account potential uncertainties that can affect both revenues and expenditures, and provide for changes in population size and requirements. The analyst should also, of course, test the integrity of the budget by comparing previous budgets with actual results.

SUMMARY

The extent to which government entities are intertwined and the many types of U.S. governments have made it necessary for rule-making authorities to develop a multidimensional framework for defining reporting entities.

According to the GASB, a primary government should include a potential component unit in its reporting entity if the unit is financially accountable to it. A potential component unit is financially accountable if the primary government can appoint a majority of its governing board and it is either able to impose its will on the entity or the unit is able to provide specific financial benefits to, or impose specific financial burdens on, the primary government.

Per an FASB exposure draft, by contrast, a not-for-profit should consolidate another organization in its financial statements if it is able to control that entity. Control is the ability to use or direct the use of the entity's assets as if they were one's own—for example, by establishing its budget or operating policies or by hiring and firing management.

The GASB requires a four-way classification of cash flows instead of the three-way classification required of businesses. The additional category is motivated by the need to distinguish between capital and noncapital financing transactions. Although the FASB recognizes that a similar four-way classification might also be more suitable for not-for-profits, it sees a need to maintain consistency between business and not-for-profit reporting. Therefore, it adopted the three-way classification statement, with slight modification, for not-for-profits.

The most significant component of the introductory section of the annual financial report is the letter of transmittal. This letter is similar to a state-of-the-government address and reports on the overall fiscal health of the entity.

The financial section of the report consists of the general-purpose financial statements, combining statements, and, if needed, individual fund and account group statements. The general purpose financial statements contain a combined balance sheet, statements of revenues and expenditures (or expenses) for both governmental and proprietary funds, actual-to-budgetary comparisons for governmental funds for which budgets are prepared, and statements of cash flows for proprietary funds.

The statistical section, which can consist of fifteen types of tables, is valuable because of its supplementary disclosures. The tables provide additional information or insights into the data reported in current or previous financial statements and report on economic conditions within the government's jurisdiction.

Several financial ratios are significant indicators of a government's financial condition. Nevertheless, because the financial condition of a government is so intertwined with that of both its constituents and other governments, a broad range of economic, political, demographic, and administrative factors must also be taken into account.

EXERCISE FOR REVIEW AND SELF-STUDY

The suburban town of Evansville experienced considerable growth in the five years between 1993 and 1998. Table 12–7 was drawn from the town's CAFR. Based on the limited information provided, you are to assess whether the town's fiscal condition has improved or deteriorated in that period. You may ignore the impact of inflation and assume that all significant revenues and expenditures are reported in the general fund.

a. Has the town's debt burden increased or decreased between 1993 and 1998?

b. Based on revenues from its own sources, has the government imposed a greater burden upon its constituents? Assess the burden in terms of both population and wealth.

c. Is the town more liquid in 1998 than it was in 1993?

d. Does the town have a proportionately greater general fund balance in 1998 than in 1993?

e. Has there been any change in the mix of revenues from more to less stable revenues?

f. Has the annual burden of debt service increased?

g. Is there any evidence that the growth in population has forced a change in mix of services provided?

h. Propose at least five additional questions (the answers to which would not be obvious from the financial statements) you would raise before you would draw conclusions as to whether the fiscal condition of the town improved between 1993 and 1998?

TABLE 12–7
Selected Information From CAFR
1993 versus 1998
(All Dollar Amounts, Including Per Capita Amounts, in Thousands)

	1993		1998	
	Actual	**Per Capita**	**Actual**	**Per Capita**
Population	73,706		95,818	
Total Assessed Value of Property	$1,885,000	$25.57	$2,827,500	$29.51
Total Property Tax Levy	21,560	0.29	32,340	0.34
General Fund Cash and Investments	2,280	0.03	3,457	0.04
General Fund Total Assets	18,201	0.25	19,307	0.20
General Fund Total Liabilities	12,952	0.18	14,388	0.15
General Fund Reserved Fund Balance	510	0.01	307	0.00
General Fund Unreserved Fund Balance	4,739	0.06	4,612	0.05
General Fund Total Tax Revenues	36,764	0.50	56,617	0.64
General Fund Total Expenditures	39,174	0.53	60,328	0.63
General Fund Debt Service Expenditures (1)	5,793	0.08	9,633	0.10
General Fund Revenue from Own Sources	38,600	0.52	56,550	0.59
General Fund Total Revenues	40,063	0.54	61,697	0.64
General Fund Intergovernmental Revenue	1,463	0.02	5,147	0.05
General Fund Public Safety Expenditures	13,654	0.19	24,301	0.25
General Fund Health and Welfare Expenditures	2,979	0.04	4,915	0.05
Direct Debt	35,849	0.49	72,900	0.76
Overlapping Debt	27,159	0.37	47,875	0.50

(1) Includes Transfers to Debt Service Fund

QUESTIONS FOR REVIEW AND DISCUSSION

1. Per GASB Statement No. 14, what is the key criterion as to whether a government should be included as a *component unit* in the reporting entity of another government?

2. How does *discrete presentation* differ from *blending*? When is each appropriate?

3. What is the primary deficiency of discrete presentation as it must be applied according to Statement No. 14?

4. Per the proposed FASB standard, what is the main criterion as to when a not-for-profit organization must include another organization in its reporting entity? What types of circumstances would provide evidence that this criterion is satisfied?

5. Indicate two significant ways in which the statement of cash flows of the GASB differs from that of the FASB.

6. What are the three main sections of the Comprehensive Annual Financial Report? What are the main components of the financial section? Must all of these components be included in every CAFR?

7. The text notes that two consecutive years of operating deficits are generally seen by analysts as a sign of serious fiscal distress. Suppose that a government has had several years of *general fund* surpluses. Are they necessarily a sign of financial strength?

8. Why might analysts be concerned if a government has an unusually high ratio of intergovernmental revenues relative to a comparable government? Why might they be concerned if the same ratio is unusually low.

9. What is meant by fiscal capacity and fiscal effort? Why are they of significance in assessing a government's financial condition?

10. Why do some analysts see the budget of a government as being of no less importance than its CAFR in assessing financial condition?

11. The GASB requires governments to list their principal taxpayers in their CAFR's statistical section. In what way does this information contribute to an analysis of financial condition?

EXERCISES

12-1

Governments must apply the criteria of GASB Statement No. 14 in determining whether and how to include a related entity in its reporting entity.

A city is considering whether and how it should include the following related organizations in its reporting entity.

1. Its school system, which, although not a legally separate government, is managed by a school board elected by city residents. The system is financed with general tax revenues of the city and its budget is incorporated into that of the city at large (and thereby is subject to the same approval and appropriation process as other city expenditures).

2. Its fixed asset financing authority is a legally separate government that leases equipment to the city. To finance the equipment, the authority issues bonds that are guaranteed by the city and expected to be paid from the rents received from the city. The authority leases equipment exclusively to the city.

3. Its housing authority, which provides loans to low-income families within the city, is governed by a five-person board appointed by the city's mayor.

4. Its hospital is owned by the city but managed under contract by a private hospital management firm.

5. Its water purification plant is owned in equal shares by the city and two neighboring counties. The city's interest in the plant was acquired with resources from its water utility (enterprise) fund.

6. Its community college, a separate legal entity, is governed by a board of governors elected by city residents and has its own taxing and budgetary authority.

Based on the very limited information provided, indicate whether and how the city should report the related entity.

12-2

Cash flows of a government must be presented in four categories, rather than the three used by businesses.

The following list of cash flows was taken from the statement of cash flows of Grand Junction's internal service fund. All amounts are in thousands.

Cash on hand at beginning of year	$ 122
Interest from investments	45
Wages and salaries paid	(3,470)
Purchases of supplies	(1,650)
Collections (for services) from other funds	6,380
Interest on long-term debt	(150)
Repayment of loans to other funds	(880)
Purchase of fixed assets	(900)
Proceeds of revenue bonds	800
Purchases of investments	(440)
Proceeds from sale of fixed assets	23
Proceeds from sale of investments	33
Loans from other funds	600

Recast the list into a statement of cash flows, adding a line for cash on hand at the end of the year.

12-3

Ratios can help users in assessing fiscal condition.

The data that follow were taken from the CAFR of Chaseville, a mid-sized midwestern city with a population of 82,000. All dollar amounts are in thousands.

Total assessed value of property	$2,300,000
Total property tax levy	42,500
General fund cash and investments	3,120

General fund total assets	19,500
General fund total liabilities	16,230
General fund reserved fund balance	780
General fund unreserved fund balance	5,789
General fund total tax revenues	38,756
General fund total expenditures	44,600
General fund debt service expenditures	4,500
General fund revenue from own sources	46,500
General fund total revenues	48,865
General fund intergovernmental revenue	2,003
General fund public safety expenditures	9,321
General fund health and welfare expenditures	4,567
Direct debt	70,000
Overlapping debt	46,486

Indicate and calculate the ratios that would best be used to compare Chaseville with similar cities as to whether:

1. it is more dependent upon revenues from other governments
2. it is directing a greater share of its expenditures toward public safety
3. it has the necessary liquid resources to be better able to meet its short-term obligations as they come due
4. it has a greater available general fund balance relative to revenues to meet future needs
5. its citizens pay a higher tax rate
6. its citizens pay more in taxes per person
7. it is a wealthier city, in that its citizens own relatively more property
8. it exerts greater fiscal effort

12-4

The GASB flowchart can be used to guide decisions as to whether and how to incorporate a potential component unit.

A town's library system is a legally constituted government entity. It is governed by a ten-person board. Six of the members are appointed by the town's council; the other four are selected by the other members of the board. The members serve staggered terms of three years. Once appointed, the members can be removed from office only for illegal activities.

The town provides 95 percent of the library system's resources and thereby can control the total amount spent by the system. However, the governing board adopts the system's budget and the budget need not be approved by the town. The board also controls the day-to-day operations of the system.

Using the flowchart presented in the text, indicate whether and how the town should incorporate the library system into its own financial statements.

12-5

A government's comprehensive annual financial report (CAFR) is divided into four main sections.

The following statements, schedules, tables, or other types of data are found in the annual report of a typical municipality.

1. A combining balance sheet of all special revenue funds
2. A certificate of achievement for excellence in financial reporting
3. Data on general revenues, by source, for the past ten years
4. The letter of transmittal
5. A combined balance sheet for all funds and account groups
6. A note providing data as to the government's pension contributions and its net pension obligation for the past three years
7. Data on property tax collections for the past ten years
8. An income statement for the city's utility fund that presents details not shown in any of the combining statements
9. A statement comparing budgeted and actual revenues and expenditures for special revenue funds
10. A statement of cash flows for all proprietary funds (including nonexpendable trust funds and component units that are accounted for as proprietary funds)

For each of these items indicate whether it would be found in

- the introductory section
- the financial section
- the statistical section

If it would be found in the financial section, specify whether it would be included in:

- the general purpose financial statements (GPFS)
- combining statements
- individual fund and account group statements

PROBLEMS

Continuing Problem

Review the annual report that you obtained.

a. Read the letter of transmittal and note any items of special interest.

b. Did the government's auditors issue an "unqualified" report?

c. Do the notes to the financial statements indicate the related entities that are included within the reporting entity? Do they indicate any units that are not included? Do they explain why these units are either included or excluded?

d. How are the component units presented in the general purpose financial statements? If they are discretely presented, how are they aggregated? What percent of total assets are represented by discretely presented component units?

e. Review the various combining statements. Do they tie-in to the combined statements that are included in the general purpose financial statements?

f. Does the CAFR include statements of any individual funds or account groups?

g. Do the general purpose financial statements include a statement of cash flows for the enterprise and internal service funds? Is it in the format described in the text?

h. What is the municipality's population? How has it changed over the last decade?

i. Have property tax levies increased or decreased relative to the total market value of the property?

j. Does the report provide information as to the median income of residents?

12-1

Public housing authorities are typical of the related entities toward which GASB Statement No. 14 is directed.

A city established a public housing authority (PHA) to fund the construction of low-income residential homes within city limits. The PHA is governed by a nine-person board of trustees. New trustees are nominated by the board itself, but are formally appointed by the city council. However, the city council has never rejected a board nominee. The trustees have complete responsibility for the day-to-day operations of the authority, but are required to obtain city council endorsement of the authority's annual budget and must submit audited annual financial statements to the council. The PHA is permitted to issue its own debt, which is guaranteed by the federal government.

Approximately 90 percent of the PHA's day-to-day operating costs are paid by the Housing and Urban Development Department (HUD, a federal agency) and 10 percent by the city.

The sources of the funds used by the authority to perform its functions are as follows:

- Authority-issued bonds (which will be repaid by tenant rents)—60 percent
- Direct federal subsidies—30 percent
- Direct city subsidies—10 percent

a. Should the city include the PHA in its reporting entity as a component unit per the provisions of GASB 14? If so, how? Explain your response?

b. Suppose the same facts except that the PHA did not directly fund the construction of homes. Instead, it lent money to the city's housing department, which, in turn, lent the funds to home buyers.

c. Suppose, instead, that the city council also served as the PHA's board of trustees. How, if at all, would your response differ? Explain.

12-2

State governments face especially difficult issues as to whether to incorporate their "independent" agencies in their reporting entity.

A state established the Mohansic River Power Authority to construct and operate dams and to provide electric power to rural areas. The authority, a state-owned corporation, is governed by an independent board of directors, the ten members of which are appointed by the governor. They can be removed only for criminal misconduct or comparable misdeeds.

The board of directors has complete control over the authority's operations. The authority does not need approval to issue debt, to sign contracts, or to hire managers. Its debt is not guaranteed by the state. Per the authority's charter, any excess of revenues over expenditures is to be used for capital expansion or improvements or to offset future deficits.

Because the authority is a public utility, the rates that it charges its customers must be approved by the state's public utility commission. However, the public utility commission considers the authority's request for rate adjustments just as if the authority were a private utility.

a. Do you believe that the state should include the authority in its reporting entity? If so, how? Justify your response, with reference to the GASB criteria. (This problem is based on an actual situation; there is not a clear-cut solution).

b. Suppose, instead, that the governor could remove members of the board at will. Would your answer be the same? Explain.

c. Suppose the members can serve indefinitely on the board, subject to annual reappointment by the governor. Would your answer be the same? Explain.

12-3

Discrete presentation allows for two or more entities to be combined into a single column. The results may not always be meaningful.

Hawkins County is related to two component units that it is required to include in its reporting entity. The first, a housing authority, maintains three funds or account groups: a general fund, a special revenue fund, and a general fixed assets account group. The second, a transportation authority, has but one fund, an enterprise fund. The township itself has only a general fund and a general fixed assets account group.

The balance sheets, in highly condensed form, of all three entities are as follows (in millions):

Hawkins County

	General Fund	General Fixed Assets Account Group
Cash and Investments	$200	
Fixed Assets		$ 70
Total Assets	$200	$ 70
Investment in Fixed Assets		$ 70
Fund Balance	$200	
Total Equities	$200	$ 70

Transportation Authority

Cash and Investments	$ 50
Fixed Assets	800
Less: Accumulated Depreciation	200
Net Fixed Assets	600
Total Assets	$650
Fund Balance	$650

Housing Authority

	General Fund	Special Revenue Fund	General Fixed Assets Account Group
Cash and Investments	$10	$ 5	
Fixed assets			$20
Total Assets	$10	$ 5	$20
Investment in Fixed Assets			$20
Fund Balance	$10	$ 5	
	$10	$ 5	$20

a. Assume that both component units qualify for discrete presentation. The county elects to combine the two units in a single column. Prepare a combined balance sheet in which you show the totals column for the county, the column in which the component units are presented, and the totals column for the reporting entity.

b. Comment on the significance of the column in which the two component units are presented. What special problems of interpretation are presented by the balance in fixed assets?

c. Suppose instead that the county is required to blend the housing authority (but not the transportation authority). Prepare a combined balance sheet in which you show the blended funds of the county and the totals for the county. You need not show the column in which the transportation authority would be presented or the totals column for the entire reporting entity.

12-4

The relationships between governments and other organizations can take a variety of forms.

A large city is associated with several organizations. Based on the limited amount of information provided about each, indicate how the municipality should report on the organization in its financial statements. Give a brief rationale. If you require additional information, state specifically what you need and how you would use it.

a. The city, in partnership with the surrounding county, established a public benefit corporation to construct and operate a special events center. Each party contributed $3 million as initial capital and each controls 50 percent of the places on a six-member board of governors. Each shares equally in any profits and is equally responsible for any deficits. The city made its contribution out of its general fund.

b. The city's high schools have booster clubs that are established as legally separate not-for-profit entities under Section 501(c)(3) of the IRS Code. The purpose of the clubs is to provide financial and moral support for the schools' athletic teams. The governing boards of the clubs are elected by club members. The city has no control over the clubs' budgets, but the schools are the main recipients of their revenues.

c. The city's performing arts center is governed by a five-person board appointed by the mayor. The center is self-sufficient; it receives no funds from the city. It is empowered to issue debt, but the debt is in its own name and not guaranteed by the city. The board members serve terms of five years and are not eligible for reappointment. They can be removed only for cause. The city has no control over the center's budgets, operating policies or contracts.

d. The city's elementary schools have parent–teacher associations that are governed by their membership. The purpose of the associations is to support school activities. The associations are not tax-exempt under Section 501(c)(3) of the IRS code. The schools do not approve the associations' budgets.

e. The city's college maintains a fund-raising foundation that was created as a 501(c)(3) entity. The foundation is governed by an independent board of trustees, new members of which are elected by the continuing members. The city does not approve the foundation's budget, but the college's president has the authority to approve all operating expenses. As specified in the city's charter, all funds collected by the foundation are for the benefit of the college.

12-5

The cash flow statement for a government hospital would differ from that of a not-for-profit hospital.

The following represent a hospital's inflows and outflows of cash:

- Patient service fees received
- Government grants for operating purposes
- Government grants for specific research programs
- Contribution restricted for construction of a new building
- Salaries and wages
- Supplies
- Interest paid on long-term debt
- Interest paid on short-term operating debt
- Acquisition of fixed assets
- Purchases of marketable securities
- Proceeds from sale of marketable securities
- Interest received from investments
- Dividends received from investments
- Proceeds of long-term debt to finance a new building
- Proceeds of short-term borrowings for operating purposes

a. Categorize the cash inflows and outflows as they would be reported in a statement of cash flows assuming that the hospital is government-owned.

b. Do the same, this time assuming that the hospital is a not-for-profit.

c. Why did the GASB opt for a four-way classification, whereas the FASB retained the three-way classification?

12-6

This problem reviews the fundamentals of the statement of cash flows (indirect method)—a topic not addressed in this text as it is typically covered in courses in financial accounting.

The following was adopted from the statement of cash flows of the Motor Pool Internal Service Fund of Nashville Tennessee.

Cash Flow From Operating Activities

Operating Income	$ 1,791,679
Adjustments to Reconcile Operating Income to Net Cash Provided by (Used In) Operating Activities:	
Depreciation	793,011
Increases in Accounts and Other Receivables	(6,514)
Decrease in Due from Other Funds	347,353
Increase in Inventory	(2,947)
Decrease in Other Assets	9,337
Decrease in Accounts Payable	(1,900,256)
Increase in Accrued Payroll	12,613
Decrease in Due to Other Funds	(918,816)
Total Adjustments	(1,666,219)
Net Cash Provided by Operating Activities	125,460

Cash Flows from Noncapital Financing Activities

Operating Transfers Out	(257,043)

Cash Flows from Capital and Related Financing Activities

Acquisition of Property Plant and Equipment	(1,093,852)
Proceeds from the Sale of Equipment	82,992
Net Cash Used in Capital and Related Financing Activities	(1,010,860)

Cash Flows from Investing Activities

Purchases of Investments	(3,021,941)
Proceeds from the Sale and Maturities of Investment Securities	2,008,276
Interest on Investments	82,994
Net Cash Used in Investing Activities	(930,671)
Net Decrease in Cash and Cash Equivalents	(2,073,114)
Cash and Cash Equivalents at Beginning of Year	4,009,716
Cash and Cash Equivalents at End of Year	$ 1,936,602

a. Why is depreciation added to operating income?

b. Why are increases in accounts and other receivables subtracted from operating income?

c. Why are decreases in accounts payable subtracted from operating income?

d. Did the motor pool replace the fixed assets that it consumed (assuming that consumption can be measured by depreciation expenditure)?

e. Summarize briefly why, in light of operating income of $1,791,679, cash and cash equivalents decreased by $2,073,114.

f. How would the statement of cash flows differ if prepared on a "direct" basis (that encouraged by the GASB)?

12-7

Citizens of wealthier cities may not only have a lighter tax burden, but they may receive more intergovernmental assistance.

The following data were drawn from the CAFRs of two northern Virginia cities (all dollar amounts are in thousands):

	Fairfax	Manassas
Population	20,200	27,856
Value of taxable property	$1,933,472	$1,948,337
Property tax levy	18,664	24,534
Total general fund revenues	38,397	36,092
General fund tax revenues	31,861	29,706
Intergovernmental revenues	5,050	2,351

a. Based on the limited data provided, which city has the greater resources upon which to draw?

b. Which city imposes the greater tax burden on its population based on

1. per capita total general fund taxes?
2. per capita property taxes?
3. tax rate (i.e., property taxes as a percent of property value)?

c. Which city receives a greater amount of assistance from other governments

1. as a percentage of its total general fund revenues?
2. per capita?

12-8

Environmental regulators see the financial forests, but not the trees.

The U.S. Environmental Protection Agency (EPA) requires owners of municipal solid waste landfills to demonstrate that they have the financial capability of satisfying the costs of closing and subsequently caring for the landfills that they operate. Per EPA regulations, one way for a local government to demonstrate financial capability is by satisfying certain financial standards. In particular, a government must meet the following four ratios:

1. cash plus marketable securities to total expenditures greater than or equal to 0.05
2. annual debt service to total expenditures less than or equal to 0.20
3. long-term debt issued and outstanding to capital expenditures less than or equal to 2.00
4. current cost estimates for closure, postclosure, corrective action to total revenue less than or equal to 0.43

The regulations provide no interpretative guidance except to imply that the ratios are to be based on financial statements prepared in accordance with generally accepted accounting principles.

Suppose you are engaged as a consultant to a state agency that has to administer the regulations. In the course of examining the evidence of financial capability supplied by municipal landfill operators, state officials raised the following questions as to how the ratios should be calculated:

1. Should the ratios be based only on a government's general fund or should they encompass funds in addition to the general fund?
2. Assuming the ratios should not be based exclusively on the general fund, should they include proprietary funds (i.e., does use of the term *expenditures* imply that expenses should be excluded)?
3. Should the ratios incorporate restricted as well as unrestricted funds?
4. Should revenues and expenditures be those of the "totals" column of the combined statement of revenues and expenditures, or should interfund transactions be eliminated?

5. Should capital expenditures include only the acquisition of long-lived assets financed with long-term debt, or should it also include long-lived assets paid for from the general fund? Should capital expenditures include only those for the year in question, or an average of several years?

a. Propose answers to these questions that you believe are most consistent with the EPA's objective of assuring financial capability. For each question not only recommend an appropriate policy, but both justify it and cite any potential limitations.

b. Suggest at least three additional questions that you believe need to be addressed.

12-9

Changes in mix of revenues and expenditures must be interpreted with care.

The data that follow were drawn from the city of Boulder, Colorado's CAFR. They are from two statistical-section schedules showing the mix of revenue and expenditures for a ten-year period. They include amounts only from the general fund, special revenue funds, and debt service funds.

	1993	1984
	(Amounts in Thousands)	
Revenues		
Sales and Use Taxes	41,941	18,750
General Property Taxes	9,501	4,900
Other Taxes	9,673	3,756
Charges for Services	5,004	2,524
Intergovernmental	10,114	6,840
Proceeds from Bonds and Notes		16,330
Other	8,246	5,692
Total Revenues	$ 84,479	$ 58,792
Expenditures		
General Government and Administration	$ 10,222	$ 3,975
Public Safety	17,466	10,786
Public Works	16,472	7,499
Housing and Human Services	6,195	4,093
Culture and Recreation	16,764	9,016
Acquisition of Real Estate and Open Spaces	11,315	11,706
Debt Service	10,816	2,886
Other	2,323	
Total Expenditures	$91,573	$49,961

a. As a consultant for a citizens' association, you have been asked to determine whether there have been significant changes in the way the city acquires and spends its resources. Prepare a schedule in which you the compare the mix of revenues and of expenditures of 1993 with that of 1984. Note and comment on any items that might distort a straightforward comparison of revenues and expenditures.

b. Comment on any changes between the two years that you consider significant.

c. Expenditures for debt service increased significantly. What are the most likely reasons for the increase? Is it necessarily a sign of increased financial stress?

12-10

Strong financial statements are not necessarily indicative of strong financial condition.

The following information was taken from the CAFRs of two cities of approximately the same size in the same state.

	Riverside	Lakeview
	(Dollar Amounts in Thousands)	
Population	92,000	96,000
Number of Employees	1,050	1,420
Total Operating Revenues	$120,000	$ 170,000
Property Tax Levy	83,000	102,000
Total Operating Expenditures	112,000	174,000
Cash, Investments and Receivables	27,000	15,000
Current Liabilities	9,000	12,000
Unreserved General Fund Balance	7,000	1,000
General Obligation Debt	21,000	32,000
Total Appraised Value of Property	965,000	1,620,000

a. Compare the financial condition of the two cities based on the following indicators:

1. Per capita operating expenditures
2. Per capita general obligation debt
3. Operating surplus (deficit)
4. Liquid assets/current liabilities
5. Unreserved general fund balance/total operating revenues
6. Per capita number of employees

b. Compare the financial condition of the two cities based on the following additional measures:

1. Operating revenue/total appraised value of property
2. Property taxes/total appraised value of property
3. Per capita total appraised value of property

c. What conclusions can be drawn from the two sets of measures? Comment on the apparent discrepancy between them.

SOLUTION TO EXERCISE FOR REVIEW AND SELF-STUDY

a. As measured by both per capita direct debt (discussed in Chapter 9) and percentage of total assessed value of property, the debt burden increased substantially. Per capita direct debt increased from $.49 to $.76 (all dollar amounts in thousands). Direct debt as a percentage of total assessed value of property increased from 1.90 percent to 2.58 percent:

	1993	1998
Direct Debt	$ 35,849	$ 72,900
Total Appraised Value of Property	1,885,000	2,827,500
Direct Debt as a Percentage of Appraised Value of Property	1.90%	2.58%

Similarly, overlapping debt also increased both per capita and as a percentage of assessed value of property.

b. Based on population, the government is imposing a somewhat greater revenue burden on its constituents in 1998 than in 1993. Per capita revenue from own sources increased from $.52 to $.59. Relative to wealth (i.e., assessed value of property), however, it is imposing a slightly lighter burden:

	1993	1998
Total Revenue from Own Sources	$ 38,600	$ 56,550
Total Appraised Value of Property	1,885,000	2,827,500
Revenue from Own Sources as a Percentage of Appraised Value of Property	2.05%	2.00%

c. Liquidity can be measured by the ratio of cash and investments to current liabilities. Based on liabilities of the general fund only (all of which can be assumed to be current), the town is more liquid in 1998 than it was in 1993:

	1993	1998
General Fund Cash and Investments	$ 2,280	$ 3,457
General Fund, Total Liabilities	12,952	14,388
Cash and Investments as a Percentage of General Fund Liabilities	17.6%	24.03%

d. Based on a comparison of unreserved general fund balance to total general fund revenues, the town's reserves have been diminished:

	1993	1998
General Fund Unreserved Fund Balance	$ 4,739	$ 4,612
General Fund, Total Revenue	40,063	61,697
General Fund Unreserved Fund Balance as a Percentage of General Fund Revenues	11.83%	7.48%

e. Property taxes are often considered a stable form of revenue. The percentage of revenue received from property taxes has remained approximately the same:

	1993	1998
Total Property Tax Levy	$ 21,560	$ 32,340
General Fund, Total Revenues	40,063	61,697
Property Tax Levy as a Percentage of Total General Fund Revenues	53.82%	52.42%

However, intergovernmental revenues, generally considered more subject to risk, increased:

	1993	1998
General Fund Intergovernmental Revenue	$ 1,463	$ 5,147
General Fund, Total Revenues	40,063	61,697
General Fund Intergovernmental Revenue as a Percentage of Total General Fund Revenues	3.65%	8.34%

f. The per capita burden of debt service has increased from $.08 to $.10, but debt service as a percentage of general fund expenditures has increased only slightly:

	1993	1998
Total Debt Service Expenditures	$ 5,793	$ 9,633
Total General Fund Expenditures	39,174	60,328
Debt Service as a Percentage of Total General Fund Expenditures	14.79%	15.97%

g. Between 1993 and 1998 expenditures for public safety increased substantially relative to other expenditures whereas those for health and welfare increased slightly.

	1993	1998
Public Safety Expenditures	$ 13,654	$ 24,301
Total General Fund Expenditures	39,174	60,328
Public Safety Expenditures as a Percentage of Total General Fund Expenditures	34.85%	40.28%
Health and Welfare Expenditures	$ 2,979	$ 4,915
Total General Fund Expenditures	39,174	60,328
Health and Welfare Expenditures as a Percentage of Total General Fund Expenditures	7.60%	8.15%

h. Additional questions to be raised include the following:

- Did the revenues or expenditures of either year include substantial "one-shot" transactions?
- What changes were there in the mix of industries on which the town relies for its revenues?
- What changes were there in the characteristics of the population (e.g., in age, income, and educational distribution)?
- What changes were there in per capita income?
- What is the condition of the town's infrastructure? Is it adequate for the future?
- What are the town's forecasts of revenue and expenditures for the next five years?
- How do the ratios and forecasts of this city compare with those of similar cities?

CHAPTER 13

Using Cost Information to Manage and Control

With this chapter the text takes a turn. In previous chapters, we focused mainly on general purpose financial reports and how they can be used to assess the financial condition of governments and other not-for-profits. Chapters 13 through 15 deal primarily with how financial data and related information can be used to plan, administer, and evaluate these organizations. So far we have covered topics typically categorized as financial accounting and widely associated with external users; now we will cover those classified as managerial accounting and identified with managers and other internal parties. As noted in Chapter 1, however, the boundaries between internal and external accounting are less well defined in government and not-for-profit entities than in businesses. The "outside" constituencies of governments and not-for-profit organizations (such as citizens or members) may play an active role in establishing policies, allocating resources, and assessing accomplishments.

Recall from Chapter 1 that in key respects managing a government or not-for-profit organization is much the same as managing a business. In this chapter we expand upon this point, demonstrating that the managerial accounting concepts applicable to businesses are, for the most part, relevant for governments and not-for-profits. Indeed, the chapter covers few concepts that are not addressed in managerial and cost accounting courses. Here we consider **cost accounting** in a government and not-for-profit context and emphasize that the material dealt with in those managerial accounting courses is as germane to governments and not-for-profits as to businesses.

As we shall see, conventional, business-type management accounting may be necessary for government and not-for-profit organizations, but it is hardly sufficient. It focuses mainly on maximizing net inflows of cash rather than on achieving the organization's other objectives. In Chapter 14, we consider these other goals.

How are the Decision Criteria of Governments and Not-for-Profits Similar to Those of Businesses Despite Different Objectives?

Although businesses are concerned with maximizing profit, relatively few of their decisions are actually directed toward profits. The typical organizational unit of a business is either a cost center or a revenue center, not a profit center. Hence, its objective is either to maximize revenues or to minimize costs. For example, the foreman in charge of a road maintenance crew for a private contractor may have no influence on revenues; he is held accountable for controlling costs. In that regard, his objective is the same as that of a foreman of a government road maintenance crew.

An overriding theme of this chapter is that managers of governments and not-for-profits, no less than those of businesses, must be aware of the impact of their decisions on **incremental receipts** and disbursements. Incremental receipts and disbursements are those that would be different if one alternative were chosen over another. Only future receipts and disbursements can be affected by a decision. Past benefits and costs are irrelevant unless they affect the future. Similarly, costs that are common to two or more activities are relevant only if they will change as a consequence of a decision.

For some decisions, especially those relating to reimbursement, pricing, and resource allocation, managers may need to focus on the **full cost** of goods or services. Full cost includes a proportionate share of costs that are common to two or more goods or services. This chapter will address issues of allocating overhead and other common costs and also consider the relationship between full cost of goods or services and the fees that should be charged for them. It will pay particular attention to controversies as to when and how charitable organizations should allocate costs between fund-raising and programmatic activities.

A secondary theme of this chapter is that variance analysis is as fundamental to cost control in governments and not-for-profits as in businesses. We shall develop this theme by highlighting the importance of cost standards and flexible budgets.

WHY MUST FIXED COSTS BE DISTINGUISHED FROM VARIABLE COSTS?

Of the many ways in which costs can be classified, the most significant from the perspective of managers is by degree of variability. Information on variability is essential if managers are to determine the effect of their actions on costs to be incurred in the future or are to assess deviations between actual results and amounts that were budgeted.

Fixed costs remain the same over fairly broad ranges of volume. **Variable costs** are those that change in direct proportion to volume. Volume refers to the quantity or output of the activity under consideration. Common measures of output in government and not-for-profit organizations include patients and clients served, students enrolled, miles of road repaired, and number of documents processed.

Fixed costs are *not unchanging*. The costs of heating and air conditioning a medical clinic or an employment service may be highly volatile. Nevertheless, they should be classified as fixed rather than variable, as long as they vary with the outside air temperature, not with the number of patients or clients served.

SIGNIFICANCE OF RELEVANT RANGE

In practice, no costs are completely fixed or variable. They are fixed or variable only within a particular range of output. The salaries of school cafeteria managers, for example, are fixed as long as a school district can serve its population within the same number of schools (assuming one manager per school). Once the district has to add another school, the cost becomes variable. Thus, within a range of zero to 1,000 students (assuming 1,000 to be the capacity of a single school) cafeteria managers' salaries may be fixed; within a range of zero to 5,000 they would be variable, because additional managers would have to be hired as new schools are added.

Similarly, the cost of food in a school cafeteria is variable within small ranges. Each incremental student requires another container of milk, an extra serving of dessert. In practice, however, inasmuch as many items of food cannot be purchased in single units, the addition of one—or even ten—students will not increase total food costs. Thus, within a range of zero to 10 they may be fixed, within a range of zero to 100 they would be variable.

As illustrated in Figure 13-1, both managers' salaries and food costs can be shown graphically as step functions. Within a relevant range (appropriate for a decision at hand) fixed costs can be depicted as a horizontal line, variable costs as an upward sloping line.

Costs behave in a variety of ways and cost "curves" take an assortment of shapes. For example, old-age survivors and disability insurance (Social Security) taxes are a fixed percentage of each employee's wages and salaries up to a specified ceiling; thereafter, they are zero. By contrast, the lease on a copy machine may specify a fixed monthly charge plus a per-copy charge once a minimum number of copies has been made. This per-copy charge may decrease as the number of copies increase. Graphs of

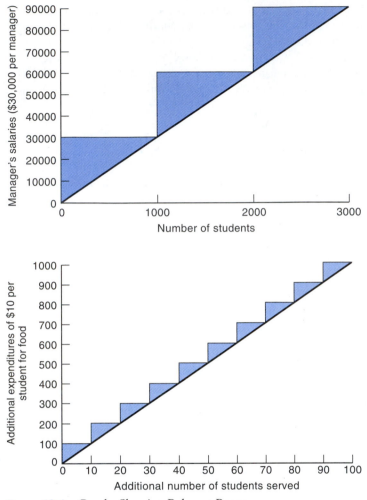

FIGURE 13-1 Graphs Showing Relevant Range

these costs are illustrated in Figure 13-2. For virtually all decisions, including preparation of budgets and evaluation of performance, managers must be explicitly aware of how the costs will behave within the relevant range.

LIMITATIONS OF AVERAGE COST

Average (per unit) cost is arrived at by dividing total costs for a specified number of units of output by the number of units of output.

EXAMPLE *Average Cost*

....

The fixed costs to operate a school cafeteria are $200,000 per year and variable costs are $400 per student. If the cafeteria serves 1,000 students, then the average cost per student is $600:

Fixed Costs		$200,000
Variable Cost Per Student	$ 400	
Number of Students	× 1,000	400,000
Total Cost		$600,000
Number of Students		÷ 1,000
Average Cost Per Student		$ 600

There are few types of decisions for which average cost is appropriate and for which a manager would not be better served by disaggregating the average cost into fixed and variable elements. For example, faced with a decision to increase enrollment by thirty students, the average cost of $600 provides little useful information. The cost of additional students would not be $600 per student; it would be only the variable costs of $400 per student.

Despite its limitations, average cost is a common—and often misused—expression of cost. It is not unusual for managers of both governments and not-for-profits to argue for an increase in their budgets proportionate to an expected increase in services provided. Thus, if they anticipate a 3 percent increase in services, they will assume that average cost will remain constant and will request a 3 percent increase in appropriations—missing the obvious point that depending on the behavior of costs, the increase in output may require a less than, or greater than, proportionate increase in appropriations.

WHY IS IT IMPORTANT TO IDENTIFY INCREMENTAL COSTS AND BENEFITS?

A financial decision involves a choice between two or more possibilities, both of which ordinarily cause the decision maker to incur costs and to reap benefits. The objective of the decision maker is to select the option that provides the greater net benefit—the margin between benefits and costs.

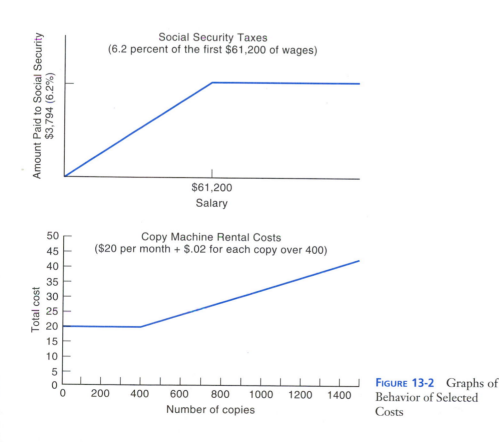

FIGURE 13-2 Graphs of Behavior of Selected Costs

In any type of organization the benefits must ultimately be tied to the entity's objectives. In governments and not-for-profits the objectives are sometimes less well defined than in business. Fortunately, though, for most decisions managers do not have to specify all the costs and benefits associated with each option. They need only be concerned with the costs and benefits that will differ among the choices. They need not take into account those that will be unaffected by the selection. For many decisions, the costs and benefits that are the least tangible and most difficult to define and quantify will be the same irrespective of the option chosen. Often, in fact, the only differential costs or benefits will be the cash inflows or outflows—the same as in many business decisions. When this is so, the objective of the decision is either to maximize net cash inflow or to minimize net cash outflow. For example, a decision by a mental health clinic as to whether to focus on in-patient or out-patient care may indeed involve costs and benefits that are difficult both to identify and to quantify. But the more common types of decisions—whether to acquire a new software package for its computer, for example—can likely be narrowed to questions of cash flow.

The general concept that only incremental costs and benefits—those that will make a difference—are relevant has at least two corollaries: Sunk costs are irrelevant and allocated costs are irrelevant.

IRRELEVANCE OF SUNK COSTS

Sunk costs need not and should not be incorporated into an analysis of costs and benefits. Sunk costs are costs that have already been incurred. They cannot be recovered, and therefore they do not matter. The examples that follow are intended to highlight this point.

EXAMPLE   *The Foolish Overhaul*

A health and welfare organization recently spent $10,000 to repair and overhaul its copy machine. The machine makes copies at a cost of approximately $.06 per copy, an amount that includes paper, supplies, electricity, and maintenance, all of which are variable costs.

The day after the machine was returned to service, a representative of a copy machine company offered to lease the organization a technologically superior machine at a rate based entirely on number of copies—$.02 per copy. Additional variable costs, such as paper and toner, would bring the total cost of each copy to $.05. The period of the lease would be three years—a period that, by coincidence, is the same as the remaining life of the overhauled machine.

The administrator of the agency rejected the offer outright. "We just spent $10,000 to repair the machine," he noted. "Surely, there's no point in abandoning the machine until we can recover our investment in the overhaul."

Is the position of the administrator fiscally sound?

The answer is unequivocally in the negative. The $10,000 overhaul is a sunk cost; it cannot be recovered. The only relevant costs are those to be incurred in the future. With the benefit of hindsight, it is clear that the administrator erred in overhauling the old machine. The question he faces now is whether to compound the mistake by spending $.06 to make copies when, by signing the lease, he could reduce the cost to $.05.

The following example, inspired by an actual nuclear disaster (that fortunately was only fiscal), reinforces the point, albeit from a slightly different perspective, that sunk costs are irrelevant.

EXAMPLE   *The Nuclear Disaster*

A mid-sized city constructed a nuclear power plant at a cost of $3 billion, financing it with thirty-year bonds that required annual debt service, including principal and interest, of $218 million.

The plant took five years longer to construct than was anticipated, and by the time it was completed, it was obvious that the project should never have been undertaken. Owing to new safety and environmental standards and declining prices for conventional fuels, the city would be able to meet its electricity demands more economically by purchasing electricity from independent utilities. In fact, the city estimated that by purchasing electricity from independent utilities it could save $103 million per year in cash outlays (excluding debt service on the nuclear plant bonds).

Unfortunately, the city could not sell the new plant—despite advertisements in national newspapers, there were no interested buyers. Its only options were to abandon the plant or to operate it. If it elected to abandon the plant it would have had to incur approximately $10 million in annual monitoring costs. Moreover, it would have had to continue to service the debt.

City officials estimated that the useful life of the plant would be thirty years, and that all of its cost estimates would be applicable over the life of the plant.

The city council chose to put the plant in service and reject the opportunity to purchase electricity from outside sources. It argued that if it abandoned the plant it would have had to recognize an immediate loss of $3 billion, an amount that would not be compensated for by the annual cash savings of $93 million (the operating savings of $103 million less the $10 million in monitoring costs). Moreover, it could not see paying $218 million per year in principal and interest on an abandoned plant.

Did the city make the fiscally sound decision?

This case has much in common with "The Foolish Overhaul." The $3 billion spent to construct the plant is irrelevant to the decision at hand. Whether the plant is retained on the balance sheet or is written off has no impact on future cash flows. Similarly, the $218 million in annual debt service is equally extraneous; it must be paid irrespective of whether the plant is operated or abandoned.

The only relevant costs are those to be incurred in the future, the net annual cash savings of $93 million. Therefore, as awkward as it might be to abandon a $3 billion plant, it is the proper course of action.

Suppose, instead, that the utility officials estimated that excluding debt service, the annual cost to operate the nuclear facility would be $700 million, determined as follows:

Depreciation on Nuclear Plant ($3 Billion Over 30 Years)	$100
Cash Operating Costs	600
Total Annual Costs	$700

The city could purchase its electricity from outside sources for $620 million (and would incur $10 million annually to monitor the abandoned plant). Should it still take advantage of the apparent cost savings and abandon the plant?

Depreciation is nothing more than an allocation of a cost incurred in the past and, hence, the accounting recognition of a sunk cost. Sunk costs are not relevant, irrespective of how they are reported on the general purpose financial statements. Therefore, in this example, the relevant comparison is between the annual $600 million in cash operating costs to be incurred if the plant is placed in operation and the annual $630 million in electricity purchase and monitoring costs to be incurred if electricity is obtained from outsiders. Therefore, the city should place the plant in service; its annual cash outlays in the future would be $30 million less.

INAPPLICABILITY OF ALLOCATED COSTS

The general rule that only incremental costs should be taken into account applies also to *allocations* of common costs. Allocation in the process of charging costs to the various activities, processes, operations, or products in proportion to benefits received. Common costs are irrelevant to decisions affecting individual activities, processes, operations, or products, except to the extent that they will be either increased or decreased in *total*. Circumstances in which allocated costs should be taken into account will be discussed later in this chapter in the section dealing with the pricing of goods and services.

EXAMPLE   *Allocated Costs*

The Health–North Rehabilitation Hospital operates a speech clinic to provide therapy for its patients. The clinic is staffed by three therapists, each of whom contracts with the hospital to provide services at a rate of $50 per hour. On average, the therapists bill the hospital for 390 hours per month, a total of $19,500.

The clinic is operated as a profit center and each month is allocated a share of hospital overhead as follows:

Building Occupancy Costs ($1 Per Square Foot of Space; 2,000 Feet @ $1)	$2,000
Administrative Costs ($.20 Per Dollar of Independent Contractor Costs; $19,500 × $.20)	3,900
Total Speech Clinic Overhead	$5,900

Accordingly, the Cost Per Therapy Hour is $65.13:

Direct Costs Per Month (390 Hours @ $50)	$19,500
Allocated Overhead	5,900
Total Costs Per Month	$25,400
Number of Therapy Hours Per Month	+ 390
Cost Per Therapy Hour	$ 65.13

Physicians Practice Associates, a local health maintenance organization (HMO), has proposed that the clinic provide outpatient speech therapy to its members. It estimates that it would refer patients for approximately fifty hours of therapy per month. It has offered to pay $58 per hour. Should the hospital accept the offer?

If the hospital accepts the offer, it would receive $2,900 per month in additional revenue (50 hours @ $58). Assuming that it would not be required to add either space or administrative personnel, it would incur only $2,500 in additional costs (the $50 per hour to be paid to the speech therapists). Therefore, by accepting the offer, it would increase its monthly cash flow by $400 per month.

Note, however, that the decision criteria of the clinic is not necessarily congruent with that of the hospital at large. If the clinic is being allocated overhead at the $.20 per dollar paid to the therapists, then for purposes of internal performance evaluation its incremental cost of providing the service would be $60 per hour [$50 + ($.20 × $50)], not merely the direct contract costs of $50. Given a choice, therefore, the clinic would presumably reject the offer, even though it would benefit the hospital as a whole.

Allocated costs are relevant to a decision if they would be changed by it. For example, if by accepting the offer the hospital would incur additional administrative costs of $500 per month—$100 more than the net direct cash inflow—then obviously the HMO's proposal would no longer be to its advantage.

HOW CAN ORGANIZATIONS ASSESS THE FISCAL BENEFITS OF CONTRACTING OUT?

In the next two sections we discuss contracting out and pricing—two types of decisions to which the concepts of incremental costs are central. In addressing both these decisions we emphasize that only costs that will actually change need be taken into account. Both sunk costs and allocated costs are irrelevant.

Contracting out—engaging an outside, private-sector firm to provide services that have previously been performed in-house—has been one of the most compelling movements of the 1990s. When governments contract out they are said to **privatize** the affected activity, and in recent years considerable public attention has been centered upon privatization initiatives at all levels of government. Yet the ideology of contracting out (also referred to as *outsourcing*) has permeated both private corporations and not-for-profit organizations with equal potency.

Decisions to contract out can have consequences that range from the marginal to the momentous—a university's department of accounting may get cheaper and fresher coffee by arranging with an independent service company to supply coffee and service its coffee machine; an eastern European country may transfigure its economy by selling its major industries to private investors.

Examples abound of services that are being contracted out by governments and not-for-profits:

- A hospital engages an outside cleaning service to replace its own maintenance staff.
- A university contracts with a catering concern to take over its cafeterias and snack bars.
- A county turns over the operation of its jails to a prison-management company.
- A school district contracts with a private bus operator to transport its students.
- A theater company transfers its ticket-sales operations to an independent ticket agency.

A full discussion of the advantages and disadvantages of contracting out is well beyond the scope of this text. Nevertheless, among the most frequently offered reasons for the practice are the following:

- It brings the efficiencies and lower costs that are associated with both competition and specialization.
- It encourages innovation, as the firm providing the service can draw upon the ideas gleaned from a variety of organizations, not just the one to which it provides the service.
- It opens new career paths for the employees that perform the activities. For example, a member of a hospital's small maintenance staff may have scant opportunity to advance in the organization. Yet if employed by a service firm that employs many maintenance workers, that person may have the chance for promotion to supervisory and management positions.

The fiscal aspects of a decision to contract out are mainly additional applications of the general principle that one should select the option that provides the greater incremental benefits (least costs). In practice, however, the decision to contract out may become extraordinarily complex, often requiring an inordinate number of estimates and assumptions.

EXAMPLE   *Contracting Out*

A data processing company has offered to assume responsibility for a hospital's accounting and information management functions, currently carried out by the hospital's data-processing department. The company would charge the hospital $1,350,000 each year of a three-year contract.

The hospital has provided the following cost information as to the data-processing department being considered for elimination. It assumes that the costs will remain constant over the three years of the contract:

Salaries, wages, and benefits	$ 730,000
Equipment rental	180,000
Phone and other utilities	56,000
Training, travel, and other miscellaneous costs	80,000
Depreciation of computer software	19,000
Depreciation of computer hardware	320,000
Total direct costs	$1,385,000
Overhead allocated from other departments	176,000
Total departmental costs	$1,561,000

It has also determined the following:

- The hardware could be sold for $400,000.
- Were the data processing department eliminated, hospital overhead could be reduced by $22,000 per year.
- The cost of administering the contract would be $45,000 per year.
- The department was planning to spend approximately $25,000 per year to upgrade its software and $240,000 per year to upgrade its hardware.

Based on this limited amount of information, the analysis, as presented in Table 13–1, should focus on the incremental costs—the changes in the cash flows. Thus the analyst should:

- identify the differential cash flows associated with each of the two options.
- determine the present value of the cash flows.
- select the option in which the net cash outflows are the least (or the net cash inflows the greatest).

For purposes of the decision at hand, the differential cash flows associated with the option to reject the offer (i.e., to continue to perform the services in-house) include the costs of upgrading both the hardware and the software. They exclude, however, depreciation on previously purchased hardware and software. Depreciation, as pointed out earlier, is an allocation of a sunk cost; it does not require a cash outflow.

The overhead costs assigned to the "reject" alternative include only the $22,000 above what would be incurred if the offer were accepted. The remaining $154,000 in overhead costs are irrelevant in that they would stay the same irrespective of whether the offer were accepted or rejected.

The costs of administering the contract are mainly those of interacting with the contractor and of monitoring its performance. They are included in this example so as to emphasize their importance; in practice, they are often overlooked.

TABLE 13–1
Accept or Reject Offer to Contract Out Accounting and Information Functions

Reject Offer	Present Value @ 6%	Year 1	Year 2	Year 3
Salaries, Wages, and Benefits	$1,951,299	$ 730,000	$ 730,000	$ 730,000
Equipment Rental	481,142	180,000	180,000	180,000
Phone and Utilities	149,689	56,000	56,000	56,000
Training, Travel, etc.	213,841	80,000	80,000	80,000
Software Upgrades	66,825	25,000	25,000	25,000
Hardware Upgrades	641,523	240,000	240,000	240,000
Overhead	58,806	22,000	22,000	22,000
Net Outlays	$3,563,125	$1,333,000	$1,333,000	$1,333,000

Accept Offer	Present Value @ 6%	Year 1	Year 2	Year 3
Payment to Contractor	$3,608,566	$1,350,000	$1,350,000	$1,350,000
Cost of Administering Contract	120,286	45,000	45,000	45,000
Total	$3,728,852	$1,395,000	$1,395,000	$1,395,000
Sale of Hardware	(400,000)			
Net Outlays	$3,328,852			

Advantages of Contracting Out

Net Outlays if Contract Is Rejected	$3,563,125
Net Outlays if Contract Is Accepted	3,328,852
Net Saving	$ 234,273

The time value of money must be taken into account in any decision in which all cash flows do not occur simultaneously. Cash to be received or disbursed in the future is worth less than that to be received or disbursed in the present. If the difference in value is likely to be significant then all cash flows must be *discounted* to the present. In the example, cash flows are assumed (for computational convenience) to take place at the end of each period, with the exception that the cash from the sale of the hardware is assumed to be received at the time the contract is signed. Therefore, the cash from the sale of the hardware does not have to be discounted and is included in the present value column rather than in any one of the three contract years. It is assumed that 6 percent is the appropriate discount rate.

As shown in Table 13–1, the present value of the differential net cash outflows if the offer were to be rejected is $3,563,125; if accepted, it is only $3,328,852. Therefore, the offer would result in a net saving of $234,273 and should be accepted.

In practice, the decision to contract out is far more complex than suggested by the example and, unfortunately, the complicating factors are often either ignored or assumed away as if they didn't matter. The following are suggestive of some of these:

FINANCIAL COMPLEXITIES

- *Time horizon.* The contract period may not be an appropriate length of time over which to assess the contracting out opportunity. Once it elects to contract out, an organization cannot simply return to the status quo without financial penalty. Restoration of a department or function that has been abandoned may be extremely costly. Yet the price of renewing the contract for additional periods (either with the same or new contractors) might be greater than that of the

IN PRACTICE

COLLEGES ARE TURNING TO PRIVATE VENDORS FOR MORE AND MORE CAMPUS SERVICES

Many colleges are finding out that if they want something done well, it might be better to hire someone else for the job.

College business officers are signing on with private companies that can provide or manage a variety of campus support services. Its a practice called *outsourcing*, *privatizing*, or *contracting out*, and it is driven by two goals: saving money, by paying a private company to provide a service at a lower cost; or making money, by having someone run a service, then sharing in the profits that the vendor generates.

The most frequently privatized services are bookstores and food-service operations, says Richard D. Wertz, vice-president for business affairs at the University of South Carolina at Columbia and a consultant on outsourcing. But companies are increasingly being sought to provide campus health, computing, custodial, fund-raising, mail-delivery, maintenance, printing, security, and trademark-and-licensing services.

Private colleges have contracted out services for years, but now budget-conscious legislators in many states are pushing all publicly supported institutions to consider the practice.

Even so, outsourcing is moving at a slower pace on the campuses than elsewhere, says William D. Eggers, director of the Privatization Center, a division of the Los Angeles-based Reason Foundation, which assists state governments in privatizing efforts. Colleges, he says, could easily hire private companies to perform as much as 40 percent of their support services.

Some university officials say outsourcing would allow institutions to "buy" expertise and business acumen while improving the level of service.

Clemson University, for example, is seeking a contractor to serve as a chief facilities officer. "The contractor would bring the breadth and depth of a corporate structure to bear on our operations and point out savings well beyond what we would be able to identify ourselves," says Gary A. Ransdell, Clemson's vice-president for administration and advancement.

Privatizing can offer a college the chance to gain new equipment at a company's expense. Under the terms of a contract between Marshall University and Follett College Stores, the company will install more cash registers in the campus bookstore to speed service.

Privatizing also has another benefit, some people believe: It forces university employees to think creatively about ways to save money and improve efficiency.

But privatization also can mean the loss of jobs. Even though difficult economic times have familiarized many colleges with cutbacks, layoffs are still painful on the campuses, which pride themselves on collegiality.

Public employees are "rarely laid off" when services are contracted out, responds Mr. Eggers of the privatization center. A 1989 study of state and county governments by the U.S. Department of Labor—still the definitive work, he says—showed that half of all employees went to work for the company hired by their employers and that most of the others retired or were reassigned.

At George Mason University, most of the employees who have been affected by privatizing have opted for early retirement, were kept on by the contractor, or were retrained and placed elsewhere, says Maurice W. Scherrens, vice president for finance and planning.

One official says the day is coming when there will be almost no limit to what a campus will consider privatizing.

"I think it's only a matter of time before somebody outsources areas of instruction," such as developmental-education programs, says Mr. Davies, the director of Virginia's higher-education council. "There would be people who would say that's horrible. But the essence of creating and maintaining a community is not doing everything yourself."

Source: *The Chronicle of Higher Education, July 7, 1995. Excerpted with permission. Copyright ©*
1995.

initial contract, especially if, as is common, the contractor agrees to a "low-ball" rate for the initial contract.

Varying the time horizon (e.g., carrying out the analysis over two or more contract periods) can markedly affect the cash flow comparisons. Differences in net cash flows would be particularly great, for example, if there are material nonrecurring proceeds, such as from the sale of assets when the contract is first implemented. Moreover, the greater the number of contract periods over which the analysis is carried out, the less the credibility of the cash flow estimates of the more distant years. At the same time, however, owing to discounting, the more distant the receipts or disbursements, the less their impact on the net present value of the cash flows.

- *Value of assets at conclusion of period of analysis.* In the example, the hospital forecast that if it continued to operate the data processing department it would upgrade its hardware and software evenly over the three-year period of analysis. However, no assumption was made as to the disposition of assets at the conclusion of the period. Hence, it was implicitly assumed that the assets had no value at that time.

  To assure that the comparison between the two alternatives is properly balanced, it is necessary either to make an explicit assumption as to an asset's salvage value at the expiration of the contract or to extend the analysis until the end of the asset's useful life. Making an explicit assumption will introduce an additional element of arbitrariness into the comparison, whereas extending the analysis may cause the time horizon to be open-ended. If the organization has assets without concurrent useful lives, then assets will continually have to be retired and replaced, and there will never be a clean cut-off date.

- *Discount rate.* Choice of discount rate can have a dramatic impact on the present value of cash flows and, unless the cash flows are uniform over the period of analysis, may affect the alternatives differently. It is generally agreed that an entity's discount rate should relate to its cost of capital. Yet there is no concurrence as to whether cost of capital should be based on the rate at which an entity can borrow funds (perhaps a tax exempt rate) or invest funds (an opportunity cost). Moreover, it is arguable whether the rate should reflect an average cost of capital, taking into account all of the organization's outstanding debt, or only any new funds to be borrowed.

- *Alternative use of resources.* When an organization discontinues an activity, it may transfer its assets to other departments. Even though the transfer will not involve a flow of cash, it will provide something of value to the recipient departments. Yet the actual worth of assets to those departments might not be clear, especially if the recipient department would not otherwise have purchased the assets. For example, a department might receive more floor space, which adds to its comfort but would not actually be needed until the future. Any cash flow assumptions as to the value of the assets would necessarily be arbitrary.

- *Calculating reductions in overhead.* By its very nature, overhead cannot be easily traced to specific departments. Therefore, the amount to be saved can seldom be established objectively. Suppose, for example, a pool of overhead costs includes the cost of an entity's internal audit department. If an activity is contracted out the audit department may have the luxury of directing greater attention to audits of remaining activities but it may not be able to reduce its staff.

NONFINANCIAL ISSUES

As suggested by the two In Practices, decisions to contract out may have important ramifications that extend far beyond flows of cash. These include:

- *Impact on employees and organizational morale.* Contracting out may permit reductions in the work force. Layoffs are obviously economically and emotionally traumatic for the discharged workers. But they can also diminish the morale of retained employees who may become fearful of losing their own jobs or see a change in the organizational culture and values with which they have become secure. Alternatively, contracting out can improve the outlook of remaining employees by demonstrating that the organization is responding positively to financial exigencies and that it is taking steps to become more efficient and effective.

- *Loss of control and reduction in flexibility.* If an organization outsources an activity it may sacrifice both control and flexibility. When a hospital contracts out for its maintenance service, for example, it may lose its ability to assign personnel to tasks other than those contractually specified, to have employees on the premises except at previously agreed-upon hours, and to provide incentives for above-minimal performance.

- *Political and social values.* Constituents of an organization may believe that certain functions are the responsibility of the organization and cannot be abdicated. Governments, for example, have been slow to privatize prisons, mainly because many citizens see incarceration as an inherent obligation of government. Similarly, university efforts to outsource their food services to popular-name franchises have faced opposition from students who see the businesses as commercial intrusions into their academic environment.

- *Social and economic externalities.* When an organization, especially a government, contracts out it may incur costs or reap benefits only indirectly tied to the activity that is being outsourced. Suppose, for example, that a city sells its electric utility. The new owner hires some of the city's employees but lays off others. The discharged employees may place added demands upon the city's unemployment, medical, and other social welfare services. On the other hand, the property of the new owner, now that it is in private hands, can be added to the tax rolls and thereby generate property tax revenue.

Decisions to contract out are complex and even seemingly minor changes in estimates and assumptions can alter the outcome of an analysis. Moreover, where individuals stand on particular outsourcing decisions may be strongly influenced by their own political persuasions and how the decision will affect them personally. Accordingly, comparative cost analyses should always be viewed with the utmost skepticism.

Privatize City Jails? Here's The Hitch

Throughout his administration, Mayor Rudolph Giuliani has unleased a blizzard of declarations about privatizing government. All have had zeal and purpose, but few have been accompanied by specific plans and verified savings. One of the least plausible is the Mayor's recent proposal to privatize the New York City Department of Correction.

The city's jails and the work force which runs them are critical components of the criminal justice system. The system itself is anchored to the bedrock of the Constitution, jointly protecting the public safety and the rights of the individual. Its efficacy is measured by how it metes out justice, not by cost economies. Otherwise, we could dispense with such luxuries as multiple appeals, retrials and life sentences without parole.

That is not to say there are no savings to be gleaned by privatizing the jails' ancillary services like laundry and food preparation or by revamping management and union work rules.

But to farm out the Correction Department's core custodial and disciplinary functions is a transaction fraught with peril. Witness the scandalous outcome of turning over the Immigration and Naturalization Service's detention center in New Jersey to the Esmor Correctional Services. After a prison uprising there in June, an investigation revealed that Esmor's cost-cutting had produced a staff of poorly paid, undertrained guards who regularly abused inmates.

True, some jurisdictions are now experimenting with privatized prisons, but the savings generally have been small.

One thing is sure. To privatize this sovereign government responsibility, it is essential that contract terms be highly specified and vigilantly monitored. But imposing such requirements would substantially subtract from the advertised savings.

Generally speaking, the privatization of government operations less sensitive than the jail system yields worthwhile savings, but the amounts are usually less than what zealous privateers claim. It works best where quality and output lend themselves to measurement and where there is genuine competition among bidders. How many cans of trash, a garbage collector picks up on a given day is easy to ascertain.

With his privatization ideas—which embrace not only the Correction Department, but the Health and Hospitals Corporation, which runs 11 city hospitals, and the public schools—Mr. Giuliani has loudly jumped on the bandwagon led by other mayors.

To downsize government, they argue, leaders first need to rip up existing programs by the roots and bring in hard-headed private-sector management. Mr. Giuliani's proposals tend to affect programs used disproportionately by the poor, a change that would leave that large and growing group with the fewest choices for quality services.

But even Philadelphia Mayor Edward Rendell, who has been far more aggressive about privatizing than Mr. Giuliani and who didn't blink when municipal workers went on strike in response to the contract he offered them in 1992, has not gotten that much for his efforts. He has saved $25 million from the annual budget, which is nothing to sneeze at, but it is a minute share of the city's $2.5 billion yearly budget.

Privatization is just a small piece of the solution. The rest comes from forcing supervisors and employees, agency workers and private contractors to focus on the bottom line. Only tough management, fueled by competition, can help the city meet its needs. The Mayor must begin by taking a tougher stance against the unions representing city employees.

Virtually the only value of Mr. Giuliani's proposal to privatize the Correction Department is to instill some fear in its largest union, the Correction Officers Benevolent Association. If he manages to get some give on unproductive work rules, he will have accomplished much of what privatization purports to do without forfeiting city responsibilities.

Source: D. Kettl and L. Winnick, "Privatize City Jails? Here's the Hitch," *The New York Times*, August 22, 1995, p. 11. Reprinted by permission, New York Times Co. Copyright © 1995.

HOW SHOULD GOVERNMENTS AND NOT-FOR-PROFITS ESTABLISH PRICES?

Both governments and not-for-profit organizations charge fees for some or all of their services. For businesses the guidelines for establishing prices are relatively unambiguous—charge the price that will maximize net revenues (revenues less the cost of the goods or services). If a business operates in an environment of *perfect competition*, the implementation of that guideline is clear—charge the prevailing market price. At that price it will be able to sell all of its available goods. If it sets the price above the prevailing market price, then it can expect to sell none. If it sets the price below market, then it can expect to sell the same amount of goods as if it had charged the market price (the entire amount available) but would realize less revenue.

For governments and not-for-profit organizations pricing decisions—like most other decisions—are more complex. These entities provide goods or services to achieve objectives other than, or in addition to, profit maximization. Most of the objectives can be grouped into the following five categories:[1]

1. *To provide revenue.* User fees and other charges can either supplement, or substitute for, taxes, contributions, and other revenues.

2. *To ration output.* User charges help to ration output among the various claimants. In a competitive economy, pricing schemes can be used to assure that the output is acquired by the parties that could use it most efficiently. Thus, the federal government auctions off communication licenses and mineral rights in the expectation that the highest bidders will put them to their most profitable use. Universities establish a scale of rates for different parking lots, so that the most desirable spaces will go to those willing to pay for them. New York City charges substantial tolls on roads, bridges, and tunnels leading into Manhattan as a means of rationing the capacity of the borough's streets and parking spaces.

---

[1] See Werner Z. Hirsch, *The Economics of State and Local Government*, (New York: McGraw-Hill, 1970), Chapter 3, "User Charges" and Mary T. Ziebell and Don T. DeCoster, *Management Control Systems in Nonprofit Organizations*, (San Diego: Harcourt Brace Jovanovich, 1991) Chapter 8, "Pricing Decisions," for an extended discussion of reasons for user charges and the bases on which they are established.

3. **To allocate burdens.** User fees are a means of allocating the cost of goods or services to the parties that will benefit from them. For example, a local YMCA may fund the construction of a new gym in whole or part by assessing fees to members who elect to use the facility. Governments finance parking garages by operating them as business enterprises.

4. **To provide demand signals.** User fees can provide information as to the extent that a service is demanded. They indicate the number of potential service recipients that value the service at least as much as the fee being charged. They thereby help the organization to determine the quantity of the service to provide and the amount of resources to be directed to it. By experimenting with different fares a municipal bus system can gauge the value of its service to potential riders.

5. **To regulate demand.** Governments may establish a monopoly over a product, such as alcoholic beverages, and then set prices at a level that discourages consumption. Correspondingly, governments or not-for-profits may establish a below-cost price, such as for inoculations against childhood diseases, to encourage consumption.

The basis on which a user fee is established should, of course, reflect the reason for the fee. Thus, consistent with one or more of the objectives, user fees can range from nominal amounts to amounts greatly in excess of full cost.

Pricing policies can be categorized as being either market- or cost-based. Market-based policies are those in which the prices are influenced mainly by market forces—the relationship between demand and price. Cost-based policies are those in which cost factors dominate. In practice, of course, almost all pricing decisions must take into account both market forces and cost.

Organizations may adopt market-based policies in the interests of "profit" maximization. Taking into account the relationship between price and demand, for example, a not-for-profit may set ticket prices for a fund-raising concert at rates that will generate the greatest revenues. Similarly, a graduate school of business may establish tuition charges for executive development programs at a level reflective of the prevailing rates charged by both professional associations and private business–education companies.

Organizations using cost-based pricing strategies typically use some measure of cost, such as incremental cost or full cost, as a starting point and then decide how much above (or below) that cost they should charge. In Chapter 10, for example, it was noted that internal service funds operate on a cost reimbursement basis and in practice *cost* is usually interpreted to mean *full cost*.

The problem set forth in the following In Practice, pertaining to the prices to be charged by a municipal electric utility, suggests the multiplicity of variables, in addition to cost that may have to be taken into account in establishing user charges. The text provides no specific solution to the utility pricing problem, mainly because it would require the development of a highly complex econometric model.

ESTABLISHING AND TAKING INTO ACCOUNT FULL COST

Even though most pricing decisions should focus on incremental costs and benefits, the significance of the full cost of goods or services should not be minimized. Indeed, over an extended period of time, full cost is often an approximation of incremental cost. Information on the full cost of a product is an important element of pricing decisions. Even if managers elect not to set a price that covers full cost, they should be aware of the magnitude of any subsidy. Federal agencies are required to establish user fees at either market price or full cost.[2]

---

[2] Per Office of Management and Budget Circular No. A-25 (revised).

IN PRACTICE

FACTORS THAT SHOULD ENTER INTO THE PRICING DECISIONS OF A CITY-OPERATED ELECTRIC UTILITY

A city operates an electric utility. The utility provides service not only to all electricity users within its boundaries, but also to neighboring communities. In the jurisdictions in which it operates, the city is a regulated monopoly. Although its rates are subject to approval by a state public utility commission, they are unlikely to be rejected unless they are far out of line with those charged by other power providers within the state.

The rates charged by the utility are considerably in excess of cost. In fact, each year the utility provides approximately 33 percent of the city's general fund revenues. Were it not for the transfer of cash from the utility fund to the general fund, the city would have to increase property tax rates.

The following are but a sample of the factors that the city should properly take into account in setting its utility rates:

- **Elasticity of demand.** Even though the city faces no direct competition for electricity within its boundaries, like any monopolist it faces a downward-sloping demand curve; that is, the higher the price, the less quantity it sells. Therefore, the city must consider the elasticity of the demand for its product—the percentage decline in electricity sold associated with percentage increases in price. Indeed, at some point increases in price will cause decreases in total revenues.

   Moreover, the city faces competition in sales beyond its jurisdiction. If the city sets its price sufficiently high, then the customers outside the city can elect to obtain their power from other sources.

- **Regressivity of user charges relative to alternative revenue sources.** Although the burdens of both electric rates and alternative sources of revenue will fall mainly on city residents, they will not be shared in the same proportions. Some revenue sources will be more regressive than others; that is, the amount that residents pay will decrease more sharply as a percentage of their income or wealth. The regressivity of any particular source of revenue will depend largely on the residents' consumption patterns (e.g., how much electricity they use and how much real property they own).

- **Amount of revenue that could be raised from parties that are exempt from property taxes.** A sizable portion of property within city limits is exempt from property taxes. This includes federal military bases, state office buildings, and real estate owned by religious organizations. The owners of this property are subject to utility charges, but not property taxes.

- **Amount of revenue that could be raised from parties outside of the city.** Electricity users outside of city limits pay utility charges, but not property taxes. Therefore, by increasing utility rates and lowering property taxes, the city is able to transfer a portion of its overall fiscal burden to nonresidents.

- **Federal income tax savings that will accrue to citizens by shifting from utility charges to property taxes.** The Internal Revenue Code permits individuals who itemize deductions to deduct local property taxes, but not utility charges. The federal government thereby pays a share of property taxes. The value of this subsidy is especially difficult to measure because it depends on the amount of property taxes paid by the taxpayers, whether or not they itemize their deductions, and the taxpayers' marginal income tax rates.

The optimum property tax rates and user charges would be those that not only minimize the total amount to be paid by city residents, but that also distribute the revenue burden equitably.

Similarly, full cost is an essential ingredient of decisions as to whether activities or programs should be carried out. To be sure, organizations do not have to cover the full cost of *each* product or service that they provide. But they cannot incur losses on *all* products and services. Information as to full cost, therefore, helps managers compare goods and services and establish priorities among them. As implied in a Chapter 1 In Practice, the enthusiasm with which university officials view their institution's football program will likely be influenced by whether revenues cover full cost or only incremental cost. Further, full cost data is helpful in comparing the efficiency with which two or more units provide similar services. For example, if a state highway department needs to establish which of its districts maintains roads at the least cost per mile, it would require data that encompasses all costs associated with the maintenance, not merely those that vary with output.

Full costs are especially important to government and not-for-profit organizations that are reimbursed for some of their activities, but not others. The means by which overhead is allocated among activities is a frequent source of controversy. Universities, for example, routinely spar with the federal agencies for which they perform contract research over what constitutes a fair allocation of overhead. In fact, to reduce what it considers excessive overhead charges, the federal government has established an elaborate set of cost accounting standards and disclosure rules for colleges and universities.[3]

To determine the full cost of an **object**, it is necessary to assign to it all relevant costs, both direct and indirect. An object is the unit being measured. It could be an activity, program, or product. For example, the object of a hospital might be a patient served. Alternatively, so as to recognize explicitly that the cost of caring for patients depends on their ailments, it could be the cost of treating a patient with a particular diagnosis. In fact, Medicare uses diagnosis-related groups (DRGs) as its object of reimbursement. For a highway department, the cost object might be a single pothole. For an accounting department it might be an activity, such as processing payroll, or a product, such as a single processed voucher.

The development of cost accounting systems of both governments and not-for-profits has generally lagged far beyond that in industry. Only within the last decade have both the federal government and several state governments mandated that their component units provide information on the full cost of programs and activities.

Both the conventional and the more recently developed **activity-based costing (ABC)** means of establishing the full cost of an object are as applicable to governments and not-for-profits as to businesses. Both means of costing will be discussed in this section.

The full cost of an object consists of **direct costs**—direct labor and direct materials—and **overhead**. Direct labor and materials, by definition, can readily be associated with specific units of product. Overhead (indirect) costs are common to more than one object. The conventional and the activity-based costs systems differ only in how they assign the overhead costs to the individual products.

Conventional Approach

Taking the conventional approach, an organization initially assigns all costs to cost centers, some of which are directly associated with the cost object and others of which are only indirectly associated with it. In a governmental or not-for-profit

---

[3] Office of Management and Budget, Circular No. A-21, *Cost Principles for Educational Institutions*. This circular also extends the applicability of certain Cost Accounting Standards Board (CASB) rules to institutions of higher education that receive federal funds and requires them to file a CASB disclosure statement.

environment, the cost centers directly associated with the cost object are referred to as "mission" or "operating" centers. These correspond to *production centers* in a manufacturing concern. The cost centers that are only indirectly associated with the cost object are called *service* or *support* centers (as they are in manufacturing companies).

The costs of the service centers (overhead costs) are **allocated** among the various mission centers. They are then combined with the mission centers' own overhead costs and, based on an *overhead charging rate*, *absorbed* into (or *applied* to) the cost object. An overhead charging rate is predetermined and is used to apply overhead from the mission departments to the cost object (the units of product or service). It is generally computed by dividing the total overhead by a factor of production, such as direct labor or direct materials. Thus, if a mission department estimates that it will incur $100,000 in overhead cost and utilize 5,000 direct labor hours, its overhead charging rate would be $20 per direct labor hour. If a particular service required 30 direct labor hours, then $600 of overhead costs (i.e., 30 hours at $20 per hour) would be charged to that service.

EXAMPLE   *Allocating Cost—Conventional Means*

The Urban Legal Clinic provides assistance to low-income residents of a major city. The clinic's legal staff is divided into two departments (mission centers). One is devoted to criminal matters; the other to civil. Ten attorneys are assigned to the criminal department; six to the civil department. The clinic maintains three support centers: an administrative section; a library; and a secretarial pool.

The clinic is funded in part by a government grant that provides reimbursement on a case by case basis. Accordingly, it must determine the cost of each case that it handles.

The clinic initially charges all building occupancy, insurance, and a wide array of miscellaneous costs to the administrative section. It allocates the cost of this section to the two mission centers and the two other support centers. The costs are allocated on two different bases. Costs associated with building occupancy are allocated on the basis of percentage of floor space occupied (excluding the space occupied by the administrative section itself). All other administrative costs are allocated on the basis of proportionate share of total employees (excluding the employees of the administrative section).

After allocating the administrative costs to the other cost centers, the clinic allocates the costs of the library and the secretarial pool (including the allocated administrative costs) to the two mission centers. The costs of both service centers are allocated on the same basis—proportionate number of employees (although, of course, different bases could also have been used).

As shown in Table 13–2, the criminal department was allocated $338,281 of the $550,000 of total overhead costs. The civil department was assigned $211,719.

Inasmuch as direct labor (attorney's time) is the key component of a case (the cost object), the department applies overhead to each case based on direct labor hours. The department estimates that throughout the year the ten criminal attorneys will charge a total of 15,000 hours to specific cases; the six civil attorneys will charge only 8,000 hours. Therefore, for each hour that a criminal attorney works on a case the clinic will apply $22.55 in overhead ($338,281 divided by 15,000 hours); for each hour that a civil attorney works on a case it will apply $26.46 ($211,719 divided by 8,000 hours).

Suppose, for example, that a criminal attorney spends 90 hours on Case No. 103. The clinic determines that salary and benefits of the attorney are $43 per hour. Moreover, the attorney has incurred $520 in other costs (such as travel, filing fees, long-distance calls, and supplies) that can be directly traced to the case. The total cost to be charged to the case would be $6,420 computed as follows:

Direct Labor (Attorney Salaries and Benefits, 90 Hours @ $43.00)	$3,870
Other Direct Costs	520
Allocated Overhead (90 Hours @ $22.55)	2,030
Total Cost of Case	$6,420

TABLE 13–2
Urban Legal Clinic Allocation of Overhead Costs—Conventional Costing

	Mission Centers		Support Centers			
	Criminal	Civil	Administration	Library	Secretarial	Total
Number of Employees	10	6	4	1	3	24
% Floor Space	30.0%	25.0%	20.0%	15.0%	10.0%	100%
% Floor Space Excluding Administration	37.5%	31.3%		18.7%	12.5%	100%
% Employees Excluding Administration	50.0%	30.0%		5.0%	15.0%	100%
% of Employees in Mission Centers	62.5%	37.5%				100%
Number of Case Hours	15,000	8,000	–	–	–	23,000
Costs Incurred			400,000	60,000	90,000	550,000
Allocation of Administrative Costs:						
Building Occupancy Cost (% Floor Space Excluding Administration)	37,500	31,250	(100,000)	18,750	12,500	0
Other Administrative Costs (% Employees Excluding Administration)	150,000	90,000	(300,000)	15,000	45,000	0
Total Overhead Costs After Allocation of Administrative Costs	187,500	121,250	0	93,750	147,500	550,000
Allocation of Library Costs (% Employees in Mission Centers)	58,594	35,156		(93,750)		0
Allocation of Secretarial Costs (% Employees in Mission Centers)	92,188	55,313			(147,500)	0
Total Allocated Overhead	338,281	211,719	0	0	0	550,000
Number of Case Hours	÷15,000	÷8,000				
Overhead Per Hour	22.55	26.46				

Activity-Based Costing

Under activity-based costing, overhead costs are collected in cost pools. Then, rather than being allocated both to other service departments and to production departments they are assigned directly to the cost objects.

Each of the overhead cost pools should be homogeneous in that the costs should be driven (influenced) by, a common factor. The activity pools can cut across departmental lines, and they can include overhead costs of both mission and service centers.

Once overhead costs are collected in cost pools, they are distributed to the cost objects by a *cost driver*, one for each pool. A cost driver is conceptually similar to an overhead charging rate. However, whereas in practice an overhead charging rate is based on direct labor hours or direct materials, cost drivers are more representative of the factors that influence the amount of overhead costs incurred. The following are examples of cost drivers that might be used to assign various types of overhead costs:`

Type of Cost (Cost Pool)	*Cost Driver*
Materials handling	Materials requisitions
Maintenance	Maintenance hours
Depreciation on equipment	Machine hours
Payroll processing	Labor hours
Accounts payable processing	Vouchers purchases

Figure 13-3 contrasts conventional and activity-based costing.

EXAMPLE   *Cost Allocation—Activity-Based Costing*

Assume the same facts as in Table 13–2, plus the additional information as to the two mission centers (criminal and civil law) presented in Table 13–3, Part I. The legal clinic collects its overhead costs in three pools (administrative, library, and secretarial), which happen to coincide with the entity's organizational structure. The clinic selects the following cost drivers to assign these costs to each of its cases:

Cost Pool	*Cost Driver*
Administrative	Direct labor hours
Library	Research hours
Secretarial	Documents processed

Table 13–3, Part II, indicates the costs assigned to each pool, the estimated number of units of activity for a year, and the resultant overhead cost per unit of activity to be applied to each case. It also indicates the units of activity attributable to a particular case, No. 103, and the amount of overhead that would thereby be applied to it.

Therefore, the total to be charged to the case would be $6,730:

Direct Labor (Attorney Salaries and Benefits, 90 Hours @ $43.00)		$3,870
Other Direct Costs		520
Applied Overhead:		
Administrative	$1,565	
Library	480	
Secretarial	295	2,340
Total Cost of Case		$6,730

Assuming that the estimates incorporated in the overhead charging rate and cost drivers are accurate, both the conventional and the ABC procedures will assure that all overhead costs are assigned to specific cost objects. As is apparent from the examples, however, they will not necessarily distribute the overhead costs among the jobs in the same amounts. Presumably, if the overhead is more strongly influenced by the ABC cost drivers than by the conventional overhead charging rate (the underlying rationale for ABC costing) then the ABC procedures provide the more reliable measure of the resources consumed in providing the goods or services.

I. Conventional Costing

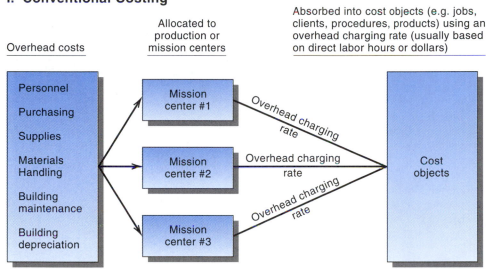

II. Activity-Based Costing

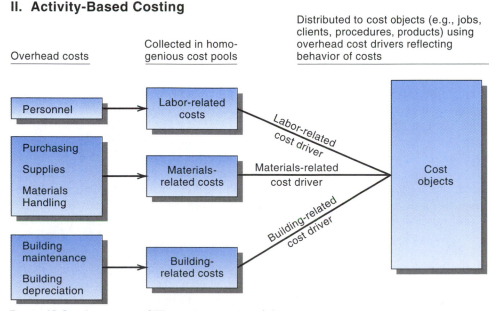

FIGURE 13-3   Conventional Versus Activity-Based Costing

TABLE 13-3
Urban Legal Clinic Allocation of Overhead Costs—Activity-Based Costing

I. Additional Information Required for Activity-Based Costing

	Mission Centers		
	Criminal	Civil	Total
Number of Lawyers	10	6	16
Number of Direct Labor Hours	15,000	8,000	23,000
Documents Processed for Center	4,400	1,400	5,800
Research Hours Conducted	1,200	300	1,500
Units of Activity Attributable to Case No. 103			
Direct Labor Hours	90		
Research Hours	12		
Documents Processed	19		

II. Overhead to be Assigned to Case No. 103 Using Activity-Based Costing

	Administrative	Library	Secretarial
Costs Incurred	$400,000	$60,000	$90,000
Estimated Annual Units of Activity			
Direct Labor Hours	÷ 23,000		
Research Hours		÷ 1,500	
Documents Processed			5,800
Cost Per Unit of Activity	$ 17.39	$ 40.00	$ 15.52
Number of Units Attributable to Case No. 103			
Direct Labor Hours	× 90		
Research Hours		× 12	
Documents Processed			× 19
Overhead to be Applied to Case No. 103	$ 1,565	$ 480	$ 295

How should the costs of fund-raising activities be determined?

Contributors, as well as other users of financial statements, want assurance that their donations are being used mainly to support substantive programs and activities rather than merely additional fund-raising or administrative efforts. To be sure, few individuals drop their coins into a charity's canister contingent upon receiving financial statements. However, private foundations, umbrella agencies such the United Way, and major donors almost always demand detailed financial data prior to making a commitment of resources. Moreover, state and local government regulatory authorities established to deter fraud may require that organizations permitted to solicit funds in their jurisdictions furnish information as to how they spend their resources.

As suggested by the In Practice, some charitable organizations are established mainly to provide salaries and benefits to their officers and staff. Others simply devote an inordinate proportion of their resources to both fund-raising and administration.

Fund-raising activities are often carried out in conjunction with programmatic or administrative activities. Therefore, the costs of the fund-raising activities may not be easily distinguishable from those of the other activities.

IN PRACTICE

For most people, picking the right charity from all the emotional letters, dinner-hour phone calls, and numerous appeals outside the home can be confusing, even risky at times. To be sure, about half of the 1,000 adults questioned in the Gallup poll over the summer expressed concern about how charities spent their money. Around two-thirds said they weren't getting enough information from the groups and three-quarters called for more regulation to ensure charities fulfilled their promises to donors.

EXPERTS CAUTION AGAINST CARELESS GIVING

Experts suggest individuals pick a charitable group in much the same way they would decide on a company in which to invest. After aligning with a particular cause or philosophical belief, it's crucial to regularly check a group's financial statements to determine how much of its total income is spent on programs, versus fund-raising expenses and overhead, including salaries of top officers. The Better Business Bureau and the National Charities Information Bureau also keep an eye on how charities are run, setting strict guidelines for solicitations and regularly publishing a list of groups that meet their standards. Among their requirements: The BBB says 50 percent of a charity's total income should be spent on its programs. The NCIB says 60 percent of every charity dollar spent should go to programs. The vast majority of national charities do meet such standards, both groups report. But there also have been those newsworthy exceptions. United Way of America, for instance, came under fire in 1992 amid charges of mismanagement and lavish spending. The chief executive officer was forced to resign after it was revealed that his annual salary and benefits totaled $435,000, far above the $50,000 to $150,000 average annual income for CEOs of charities.

Part of the problem, experts say, is that there's little government regulation. "People assume there's one government agency out there to regulate charities. There isn't," said Weiner. "Most individuals are not going to know about the finances of a charity unless they ask . . . and most people don't."

Source: Associated Press, December 5, 1993. Used with permission.

Consider, for example the following activities that are intended not only to advance an organization's main mission but also to solicit donations:

- The American Cancer Society takes out newspaper advertisements alerting readers to the seven danger signals of cancer. The ads include a plea for funds, accompanied by a coupon asking for the donor's name, address, and amount of contribution.

- Friends of the Environment conducts a door-to-door campaign seeking signatures on a petition urging a city council not to permit development in a wildlife habitat area. Each person spoken to is asked also to make a financial contribution to aid additional advocacy efforts.

- A hospital mails its annual report, which contains its financial statements and a report on its accomplishments, to trustees, employees, and previous donors. An accompanying letter suggests programs for which additional financial support is needed.

- An organization that seeks to prevent teenage drug abuse conducts a broad-based mail campaign to solicit funds. It includes in each mailing a pamphlet informing teens of ways in which they can "just say no" to their peers.

Each of these situations raises two related questions:

- Should the costs of the activity be apportioned between fund-raising and mission-related programs?
- If so, on what basis should they be apportioned?

In a proposed Statement of Position (SOP), *Accounting for Costs of Materials and Activities of Not-For-Profit Organizations and State and Local Governmental Entities that Include a Fund-Raising Appeal*, the AICPA addressed both of these issues.[4]

CRITERIA FOR ALLOCATING A PORTION OF COSTS TO PROGRAM OR MANAGEMENT FUNCTIONS

The AICPA directs that all costs of a joint activity should be considered fund-raising costs unless three criteria are satisfied: purpose, audience, and content.

Purpose

The purpose of the combined activity is to accomplish a programmatic or management purpose other than public education. Factors that would indicate such a purpose include (in order of importance):

- Whether compensation or fees for performing the activity are based entirely on considerations other than amount of contributions raised. Thus, if personnel are compensated, even in part, on the amount of funds they raise, then the purpose criterion would not be met.
- Whether the organization conducts a similar program or management activity separately from, and on the same scale as, that which is part of the joint activity. Suppose, for example, an environmental organization takes out a full-page newspaper ad appealing for donations and urging readers to recycle trash. The ad would be consistent with the purpose criterion if the organization ran similar full-page ads that promoted recycling but did not ask for donations.
- Other evidence, such as the measures used to assess the results and accomplishments of the joint activity, the qualifications of the parties carrying it out and organizational mission statements, minutes, or plans

Audience

The audience for the materials or activities is selected principally on its need for the program or for its ability to advance program goals in ways other than by financial support. Thus, in the examples presented earlier, the American Cancer Society would satisfy the criterion since its advertisement was directed to a broad segment of society, all the members of which are potential cancer victims. By contrast, the drug abuse organization would not (unless the mailing was specifically targeted at households with teenagers) since most of the recipients of the mailing would unlikely be of the age group toward which the informational pamphlet was aimed.

Content

The materials or activities call for specific actions that will help accomplish the entity's mission beyond providing financial support. For example, they might ask the recipients to take actions that would either improve the recipients' own physical, emotional or

---

[4]This discussion is based on a 1997 draft that the AICPA expected would be issued as a final pronouncement without significant changes.

spiritual well-being or address a societal need. If the materials or activities are in support of management or general functions, then they should fulfill one or more of the entity's management responsibilities, such as reporting on the organization's accomplishments or financial status.

EXAMPLE *Allocating Charitable Costs*

Facts. The Citizens for Educational Reform conducts a telephone campaign, both to solicit funds and to urge the persons called to write their legislators in favor of increased spending for education. The telephone list was purchased from a fund-raising concern and includes only households with incomes in the top 10 percent of the population.

Conclusion. In the absence of compelling evidence that persons in upper-income households are especially likely to contact their legislators in favor of increased spending for education, the campaign would not satisfy the audience criterion, and hence, all costs of the campaign should be reported as fund-raising costs.

Facts. The Protect our Children Society sends a brochure, along with a request for donations, to all citizens within selected areas of a city that have high crime rates. The brochures recommend ways in which parents can shield their children from criminal activity. The brochures were prepared by an outside consultant whose only compensation will be a percentage of the contributions received.

Conclusion. The mailing does not satisfy the purpose criterion, as compensation is based entirely on amount of funds raised.

Facts. The Senior Citizens Coalition sends representatives to speak to senior citizens groups about the virtues of physical exercise. After a presentation, the coalition mails to each person that attended a request for a contribution, along with literature advising how to maintain a healthy lifestyle.

Conclusion. The mailing satisfies all three criteria and its costs should be allocated between fund-raising and educational programs.

MEANS OF ALLOCATION

The proposed SOP allows organizations broad discretion in allocating joint costs between fund raising and other activities. It specifies only that the method should be "rational and systematic," that it should result in an allocation that is reasonable, and that it should be applied consistently. It further emphasizes that costs need not be allocated when a fund-raising activity is only incidental to a substantive program or management activity (e.g., when a single line in an advertisement otherwise devoted entirely to a programmatic purpose provides an address to which contributions may be sent.)

The following three methods are among those that would be considered rational and systematic:

Physical Units Method

The joint costs are allocated on the basis of physical units, such as number of lines, or square inches. Suppose an American Cancer Society newspaper ad costs $10,000. Based on square inches, 80 percent of the ad is directed to information about the disease and 20 percent to an appeal for funds. The organization would allocate $8,000 to its information program and $2,000 to fund-raising.

Relative Direct Costs Method

The joint costs are allocated to each of the component activities based on the identifiable direct costs. Suppose an organization mails to supporters an informational brochure, a flyer asking for a contribution, and a return envelope in which to mail the contribution. The mission-related brochures cost $90,000, whereas the fund-raising flyers and return envelopes cost $10,000. Direct costs thereby total $100,000, 90 percent of which are directed to informational activities and 10 percent to fund-raising. Common mailing costs, including postage and the outside envelope, cost $15,000. Based on the direct costs, the organization would allocate 90 percent ($13,500) of the common mailing costs to informational activities and 10 percent ($1,500) to fund-raising.

Stand-alone Costs Method

The joint costs are allocated to each of the components based on what it would have cost to conduct each of the component activities independently. Suppose in the previous example, it would have cost a total of $100,000 to produce the brochures and mail them separately ($90,000 for the brochures and $10,000 for envelopes and postage). It would have cost $18,000 to send and mail the solicitation flyers and return envelopes ($10,000 for the flyers and $8,000 for the outside envelopes and postage). Hence, total costs would have been $118,000. Based on this amount the organization would allocate the $15,000 in common costs as follows:

Informational Program	$100,000/118,000 × $15,000 =	$12,712
Fund-Raising	$ 18,000/118,000 × $15,000 =	2,288
Total Common Cost Allocated		$15,000

HOW CAN ANALYSES OF VARIANCE BE USED TO CONTROL COSTS AND EVALUATE PERFORMANCE?

Although managers of government and not-for-profit organizations may be aware of the costs incurred in providing goods or services, many are exceedingly lax in compiling cost information in a form that can be used to compare actual costs with budgets and explain the reasons for deviations.

Standard costs and *variable budgets* are at the core of many systems of budgeting, managerial control, and performance evaluation. In private industry they are most commonly associated with manufacturing operations, but they have been adapted, with equal success, to clerical, materials handling, and other support activities. However, they are no less relevant to government and not-for-profit organizations.

As illustrated in the example to follow, the analysis of variances—differences between actual costs incurred and standard costs—is the key not only to identifying less (or greater) than par performance, but to understanding the reasons for it and the particular units that are responsible for it. In this particular example, for instance, the above par performance of one department reporting a favorable variance was attributable not to its own efficiencies but to factors within the control of another department to which it provides services.

A standard cost is a planned or allowable cost per unit of either input or output. Standard costs not only facilitate budgeting, but provide a basis for assessing performance and taking corrective actions, if warranted. Standards can represent ideal levels of performance (goals the organization would like to attain) or merely reasonable expectations based on past performance.

EXAMPLE   *Standard Costs*

The College Assistance Association is dedicated to helping low-income high school students get information about college scholarships and loans and apply for them. It also assists their parents to manage better their finances so as to be able to contribute to their children's college education.

The association fulfills it mission mainly through its counseling service. Students and their parents who avail themselves of the organization's services meet with a counselor for approximately an hour and a half. On the basis of this meeting, the counselor, with the aid of the association's support staff, prepares a written report outlining key recommendations.

In a typical month the association serves 250 clients. Based on both past experience and cost constraints, the association has established a standard time of two hours per client for a counselor's interview and written report. The standard compensation cost per counselor, including benefits, is $20 per hour. However, the actual compensation cost may vary, since all counselors are not paid at the same rate. On average, the counselors collectively provide 500 hours of service per month at a total standard direct cost of $10,000.

The counselors are supported by an administrative staff that establishes appointments and assists in preparing the written reports. The association has determined that its standard fixed administrative costs (including building occupancy costs) should be $4,000 per month. In addition, it has found that some overhead costs vary with the number of direct labor (counselor) hours. It has calculated these costs to be $4 per direct labor hour. Hence, it assigns overhead to each client served at a total rate of $12 per direct labor hour:

Fixed Administrative Overhead Cost	$4,000
Variable Administrative Overhead	
(500 Hours Per Month @ $4)	2,000
Total Administrative Overhead Costs	6,000
Number of Direct Labor (Counselor)	
Hours Per Month	÷ 500
Overhead Per Direct Labor Hour	$ 12

Thus, standard overhead is $24 per client (2 direct labor hours @ $12) and the total standard cost per client is $64:

Direct Labor (Counselor) Costs (2 Hours @ $20)	$40
Administrative (Overhead) Costs (2 Hours @ $12)	24
Total Standard Cost Per Client	$64

In a month that the association serves the usual 250 clients, its expected costs would be $16,000 (250 clients @ $64).

In the month of June the association served only 220 clients, 30 fewer than normal. The counselors charged 470 hours and actual costs were $14,950:

Direct Labor (Counselors)		
400 Hours @ $20	$8,000	
70 Hours @ $15	1,050	$ 9,050
Overhead		
Fixed	$4,100	
Variable	1,800	5,900
Total Actual Costs for June		$14,950

Cost per client served was therefore $67.95 ($14,950 divided by 220 clients), $3.95 per client greater than standard. By itself, the magnitude of the variance, however, provides no insight into its significance or the reasons for it.

Direct Labor Usage and Rate Variance

Actual direct labor for the month was, as shown above, $9,050. Standard for 220 clients is $8,800 (220 clients @ 2 hours per client @ $20 per hour). Hence, direct labor costs were $250 greater than standard.

The direct labor usage (efficiency) and rate variances help explain whether and why direct labor varied from standard. The direct labor *usage* variance focuses on the amount of labor used, assuming that the labor was compensated for at standard rates. Thus:

Direct labor usage (efficiency) variance = (actual labor hours used – standard labor used) × standard wage rate.

For June (U = Unfavorable; F = Favorable):

Actual Labor Hours Used	470
Standard Labor Hours for Actual Output	
(220 Clients @ 2 Hours)	440
Excess Hours Used	30
Standard Wage Rate Per Hour	×$ 20
Labor Efficiency Variance	$600U

The direct labor *rate* variance keys in on the extra costs incurred (or the costs saved) because the actual hours used were compensated at more or less than standard. Thus:

Direct labor rate variance = (actual rate – standard rate) × actual number of hours.

Thus:

Actual Rate ($9,050 Divided by 470 Hours)	$19.2553
Standard Rate	20.0000
Excess of Standard Rate Over Actual Rate	$ 0.7447
Actual Number of Hours	× 470
Labor Rate Variance	$ 350F

The two variances combined explain the $250 excess of actual over standard cost. The variances clarify that the association was "inefficient" in that it used an excessive number of hours to serve its clients and suggest that a possible cause for the excessive hours was that it employed less experienced (or at least less compensated) personnel.

In governments and not-for-profit organizations, the direct labor variances must be interpreted more guardedly than in a manufacturing concern. In a manufacturing concern the output—the product—is likely to be precisely defined. It either meets specifications or it does not. Products that do not meet the specifications are excluded from the count of number of units produced. In governments and not-for-profits, however, each unit of output, especially if it is a unit of service, may differ qualitatively from others. Thus, the June labor usage variance may be high, either because the counselors dealt with an unusually high number of especially difficult cases or because they elected to spend more time with their clients, thereby enhancing the quality of service to them.

Overhead Variances

Actual administrative overhead for the month was only $5,900 ($4,100 fixed and $1,800 variable), whereas standard is $6,000. Three overhead variances—the flexible budget variance, the overhead efficiency variance, and the overhead volume variance—shed light on the reasons for the $100 of apparent savings.

The key to understanding—and thereby controlling—overhead is a **flexible budget.** A flexible budget indicates the expected overhead costs that should be incurred at various levels of activity. It explicitly distinguishes between the fixed and the variable portions of overhead. The variable overhead (administrative costs) of the College Assistance Association varies with the number of counselor hours (direct labor). Its flexible budget for overhead would reflect total overhead costs for several levels of input, four of which are as follows:

| | **Direct Labor Hours** | | | |
	440	**470**	**480**	**Normal 500**
Fixed Overhead	$4,000	$4,000	$4,000	$4,000
Variable Overhead ($4 Per				
Direct Labor Hour)	1,760	1,880	1,920	2,000
Total Overhead	$5,760	$5,880	$5,920	$6,000

In June the counselors charged 470 hours. As indicated in the schedule, budgeted overhead for that level is $5,880. Inasmuch as the association incurred $5,900 in administrative costs, it exceeded its flexible budget by $20 (an unfavorable *flexible budget variance*):

	Fixed Overhead	**Variable Overhead**	**Total**
Actual Costs	$4,100	$1,800	$5,900
Budgeted Per Flexible Budget			
(470 Counselor Hours)	4,000	1,880	5,880
Flexible Budget Variance	$ 100U	$ 80F	$ 20U

The flexible budget variance compares actual overhead with overhead per the flexible budget. The flexible budget takes into account the factors that drive variable overhead. The association's unfavorable variance indicates that costs were greater than budgeted for the actual level of activity. But it does not, by itself, pinpoint responsibility for the variance or even suggest that the variance was within the control of anyone within the association. Additional investigation would be required to determine whether it could be ascribed to inefficiencies (e.g., low productivity) or factors beyond the association's command (e.g., hot weather that boosted air conditioning costs).

The counselors charged 470 hours, but they served only 220 clients. Based on the standard of two hours per client, they should have charged only 440 hours. Inasmuch as variable overhead is a function of direct labor, their extra hours contributed to additional overhead charges. The *overhead efficiency variance* measures the additional overhead costs attributable to the inefficiency in the use of the factor that influences variable overhead. It compares the budgeted overhead costs (per the flexible budget) for the actual input (i.e., direct labor hours) with the budgeted overhead costs for the standard input. Thus:

	Fixed Overhead	Variable Overhead	Total
Budgeted Per Flexible Budget for Actual Input (470 Counselor Hours)	$4,000	$1,880	$5,880
Budgeted Per Flexible Budget for Standard Input (440 Counselor Hours)	4,000	1,760	5,760
Overhead Efficiency Variance	$ 0	$ 120U	$ 120U

In June, the counselors served only 220 clients compared with the expected 250 clients. Had they operated at standard efficiency, 220 clients should have required 440 direct labor hours, as opposed to 500 hours had they served 250 clients. Thus, per the flexible budget they should have incurred $240 less costs—that is, the organization had a favorable *volume variance* of $240:

	Fixed Overhead	Variable Overhead	Total
Budgeted Per Flexible Budget for Standard Input (440 Counselor Hours)	$ 4,000	$ 1,760	$ 5,760
Budgeted Per Flexible Budget for Normal Volume of 250 Clients (500 Counselor Hours)	4,000	2,000	6,000
Overhead Volume Variance	$ 0	$ 240F	$ 240F

The three overhead variances combined account for the total difference between actual and standard overhead at normal volume. They make clear that overall administrative costs were $100 less than standard mainly because the counselors served 30 fewer clients. In fact, had both the counselors and the administrative departments been operating "efficiently," then administrative costs should have been $240 less instead of merely $100 less. However, the counselors spent 30 hours more than standard in serving clients, thereby requiring additional administrative services and causing administrative costs to increase by $120. Further, the administrative department itself incurred $20 more in costs than were budgeted for the services it actually provided. Thus:

Overhead Volume Variance Attributable to Fewer than Normal Clients Served by Counselors	$240F
Overhead Efficiency Variance Attributable to Counselors' Use of More Direct Labor Hours than Standard for the Actual Number of Clients Served	120U
Flexible Budget Variance Attributable to Greater than Standard Amount of Costs Incurred by Administrative Staff in Providing Actual Amount of Service	20U
Net Overhead Variance	$ 100F

SUMMARY

Governments, other not-for-profits, and businesses are typically organized into revenue and cost centers. Their managerial decisions should focus on incremental costs (i.e., those that differ if one alternative is chosen instead of another) because only future receipts and disbursements can be affected by a decision.

Variable costs increase proportionately to changes in volume, whereas fixed costs remain the same. Costs are not intrinsically fixed or variable; they are fixed or variable only within the range that is relevant to the decision at hand. Despite widespread use, the average cost of goods or services is an inadequate measure for most cost-based decisions.

Sunk costs are irrelevant to management decisions. They have already been incurred and have no bearing on the future. Similarly, allocated costs are of concern to managers mainly to the extent that they will differ in total among the decision options. They are irrelevant if only the distribution of the costs among organizational subunits will change.

Contracting out, or outsourcing, can have advantages: efficiencies and lower costs that are associated with competition and specialization, innovation, and enhanced opportunities for employee advancement. Nevertheless, the decision to contract out involves fiscal complexities requiring estimates and assumptions and nonfiscal issues, such as impact on employee and organizational morale and loss of control.

Businesses establish prices to maximize net revenues. Governments and other not-for-profits may have additional objectives, such as rationing output, allocating burdens, providing demand signals, and regulating demand.

Information about full costs helps managers compare goods and services and establish priorities among them. Full costs include direct and overhead costs. There are two approaches to allocating overhead. Under the conventional approach, costs of service centers (overhead costs) are allocated among the various mission (operating) centers, combined with the mission centers' own overhead costs and absorbed in the cost object (based on an overhead charging rate). Under activity-based costing, overhead costs are collected in cost pools (in which costs are influenced by a common factor) that can include the overhead costs of both service and mission centers. The overhead costs are then assigned directly to the cost objects by a cost driver, one for each pool.

Not-for-profit organizations face the problem of how to allocate common costs of fund-raising and program and administrative activities. The AICPA's three general criteria for concluding that a bona fide program or management function has been conducted involve purpose, audience, and content.

Analysis of variance, the differences between actual costs incurred and standard costs, help organizations to understand better the reason for cost overruns and to target responsibility for them.

EXERCISE FOR REVIEW AND SELF-STUDY

The Permits Division of a state's Land Commission processes, on average, 500 permits per month. Each permit takes approximately two hours to complete. The employees who work on the permits are paid on average $22 per hour, including benefits.

The Permits Division is supported by an Administrative Center, which also serves other divisions of the Land Commission. The center has determined that it incurs fixed costs of $20,000 per month and additional costs that vary with the direct labor hours of the divisions to which it provides service. It estimates these variable costs to be $3

per hour. In a typical month it provides service to divisions that accumulate a total of 4,000 direct labor hours. Accordingly, it charges the divisions that it serves $8 for each of their direct labor hours:

Fixed Costs	$20,000
Variable Costs (4,000 d.l.hrs. @ $3)	12,000
Total Administrative Center Costs	$32,000
Estimated Number of d.l.hrs.	
Per Month	÷ 4,000
Overhead Charging Rate	$ 8 per d.l.hr.

The standard costs per permit processed by the Permits Division is therefore $60:

Direct Labor (2 d.l.hrs. @ $22)	$44
Overhead Charged by Administrative Center (2 d.l.hrs @ $8)	16
Total Standard Cost Per Permit	$60

In the month of April, the Permits Division processed 600 documents. Its staff worked 1,150 direct labor hours and were paid compensation of $27,600, an average of $24 per hour. In addition, the division was charged $9,200 by the Administrative Center (1,150 direct labor hours @ $8). Its total costs for the month were therefore $36,800.

The Administrative Center incurred $33,300 in costs. The divisions that it served worked a total of 4,150 direct labor hours. The 150 hours above normal were attributable entirely to the Permits Division.

a. How much in direct labor costs should the Permits Division have incurred to process the 600 permits? Explain the reason for the deviation.

b. How much should the Administrative Center have budgeted for 4,150 hours per a flexible budget? By how much did the Administrative Center exceed this amount?

c. How much should the Administrative Center have budgeted for 4,200 direct labor hours—the total direct labor hours that all the divisions that it serves would have used assuming the Permits Division used the stan-

dard 1,200 direct labor hours rather than the 1,150 hours, to process 600 permits? How much did the Administrative Center save because of the efficiency of the Permits Division in processing the permits with only 1,150 direct labor hours?

d. How many additional direct labor hours should the Permits division have been required to work to process 600 permits rather than the normal 500 permits? How much in additional variable costs should these additional hours have caused the Administrative Center to incur?

e. As just indicated, the Administrative Center budgets $32,000 for a normal month in which 500 permits are processed. In the month of April it incurred $33,300. Do the three overhead variances—volume, efficiency, and flexible budget—account for the entire difference of $1,300?

f. Suppose that a private firm offers to process permits at a cost of $50 per permit. The manager of the Administrative Center estimates that if the offer were accepted, the Center could reduce its fixed costs by $1,000 per month (net of additional costs to administer the contract) and its variable costs by $3 per direct labor hour. Assuming that the Permits Division expects to process 500 permits per month, should the state accept the offer?

g. Suppose the State wants to charge permit applicants just enough "to cover its costs." What is the minimum that it should charge? What is the maximum?

QUESTIONS FOR REVIEW AND DISCUSSION

1. A division head automatically budgets the same amount for fixed costs each month, noting, with seemingly sound logic, that fixed costs are by definition fixed and therefore remain constant. Is this approach reasonable?

2. Why is average cost not relevant for most management decisions?

3. In reality both fixed cost curves and variable cost curves have a similar shape—that of a flight of stairs. Do you agree? If so, what is the difference between the two types of costs?

4. "Obviously, sunk costs need not be taken into account in deciding whether to replace an old machine with a new. But depreciation is not a sunk cost; it is an ongoing cost, just like wages and materials, and therefore too important to be omitted from the decision analysis." Do you agree?

5. A not-for-profit has decided to contract-out its food service to an independent catering company. Based on

a detailed cost analysis, it calculates that it will save several thousands of dollars over the three-year period of the initial contract with the caterer. What pitfalls do you see in restricting the analysis to only the period covered by the initial contract?

6. The decision of a government to contract out an activity cannot be based exclusively on the cash flows directly associated with that activity or the amount to be paid to the contractor. Indicate three "nonfinancial" (or factors not involving direct cash flows) that should be given consideration.

7. Specify three purposes that user charges serve when imposed by either governments or other not-for-profits.

8. Why is it especially important that not-for-profits dependent on contracts or grants from outside parties develop defensible bases for allocating overhead to the various programs and activities that they conduct?

9. In what significant ways do conventional and ABC cost allocation schemes differ?

10. What special abuse does the AICPA address in its proposed statement of position on the allocation of fund-raising costs? What general criteria does it establish as to when common costs of materials and activities that include a fund-raising appeal can be allocated to programmatic, rather than fund-raising, activities?

11. Why are unfavorable overhead efficiency variances and volume variances unlikely to be the fault of the departments that actually provide the services categorized as overhead?

EXERCISES

13-1

The advantages of outsourcing cannot be assessed on the basis of "full" cost.

A state manufactures its own road signs. In a recent year it produced 27,000 signs. Based on the following data, average cost per sign was $3,000:

Direct Materials	$27,200,000
Direct Labor	20,600,000
Manufacturing Overhead:	
Indirect Labor	13,500,000
Depreciation	12,800,000
Plant Manager & Staff	900,000
Pension Expense	2,000,000
Costs Allocated from Other Departments	4,000,000
Total Costs	$81,000,000
Number of Signs	÷ 27,000
Cost Per Sign	$ 3,000

An independent sign manufacturer has offered to produce the signs for an average of $2,400 per sign.

Were the state to accept the offer:

- It would have to continue to employ selected direct labor employees at a cost of $2,000,000. Although these workers would fill other state jobs, their wages would be approximately $800,000 more than the state would otherwise have to pay.
- Owing to early retirement provisions, it would be able to reduce its pension costs by only $1,500,000 per year.
- None of the costs allocated from other departments could be reduced.

a. Which of the costs included in the above computation of average cost are relevant to the state's decision to accept the contract in that they would no longer be incurred? Assume that even if the state were not to accept the offer, it has no plans to replace plant and equipment in the foreseeable future.

b. Based on the limited amount of data, should the state accept the contract? Explain.

c. Why did you include or exclude depreciation expense in your list of relevant costs? Explain. How does that decision bias your analysis?

13-2

Deviations from average cost may not indicate either efficiencies or inefficiencies.

The Children's Health Center serves all residents of Harris County. The center primarily provides immunizations to infant children. During a normal month it serves approximately 450 patients.

Based on prior experience, the center has established a standard time of 30 minutes of medical staff time for each patient visit. The medical staff of the center generally spend a cumulative total of 225 hours per month serving patients. Their average wage or salary rate is $45 per hour. Hence, the standard direct medical staff cost is $10,125 per month (225 hours @ $45).

The center has determined that standard fixed administrative costs are $9,000 per month. In addition, some of the administrative costs vary with the number of hours worked by the medical staff. These have been calculated at $10 per direct medical staff hour.

For a typical month, in which the center serves 450 patients using 225 hours of direct medical staff time, total administrative costs are therefore $50 per direct medical staff hour:

Fixed Administrative Overhead	$ 9,000
Variable Administrative Overhead	
(225 hours @ $10)	2,250
Total Administrative Costs	$11,250
Number of Direct Medical	
Staff Hours	÷ 225 hrs
Overhead Per Direct Labor Hour	$ 50.00

a. Based on the data presented what should be the average cost of serving each patient?

b. Suppose that in a particular month, the center served 500 patients using 260 staff hours. All personnel were paid at the standard rate per hour of $45, so total direct medical costs were $11,700. Total administrative costs were $10,900. Hence, total costs were $22,600 and average cost was $45.20.

1. How much in additional direct medical staff costs can be attributed to the inefficiency of the medical staff (that is, to the above standard number of hours

required to serve the 500 patients) as opposed to the additional number of hours required to serve more than the normal number of patients?

2. How much less administrative overhead did the center actually incur than what it would expect to incur in a normal month (in which it serves 450 patients)?

3. How much administrative overhead should the center have incurred for the 260 direct medical staff hours actually used? What is the difference between the actual overhead and what it should have incurred (a flexible budget variance)?

4. How much administrative overhead should the center have incurred for 250 direct medical staff hours—the standard number of hours to serve 500 patients? What is the difference between what it should have incurred for 260 direct medical staff hours and what it should have incurred for 250 hours (an overhead efficiency variance)?

5. How much administrative overhead should the center have incurred for a normal volume of 450 patients (225 medical staff hours)? What is the difference between what it should have incurred for 250 hours and what it should have incurred for a normal volume of 450 patients (an overhead volume variance)?

6. Do the three elements of the administrative overhead variance as just computed sum to the total administrative overhead variance computed in question 2?

c. Comment on why average cost is of little use for purposes of pinpointing operational efficiencies or inefficiencies.

13-3

Average costs seldom facilitate appropriate decisions.

Westview College maintains a repair and maintenance division that provides services to other divisions of the college on a cost-reimbursement basis.

The division's annual expenditure budget is $1 million. Approximately 30 percent of its costs ($300,000) are fixed; the balance of $700,000 are variable—$35 per service hour provided, based on approximately 20,000 hours of service that it provides in a typical year.

The college permits divisions a choice of obtaining needed services from the repair and maintenance division or from private vendors.

a. Assuming that the policy of the division is to recover all costs, what would be the division's hourly rate for providing service?

b. The food service division needs to have equipment installed. An outside repair firm has agreed to do the job for $4,700 (plus parts and other out-of-pocket costs). The repair and maintenance division has estimated that the work will require 100 hours, and has therefore bid $5,000 (plus parts and other out-of-pocket costs).

1. What would be the savings to the food service division if it accepted the bid from the outside repair firm?

2. What would be the cost or savings to the college as a whole if the food service division accepted the bid of the outside firm?

c. Suppose that in a typical year the repair and maintenance division provides 4,000 of its 20,000 hours of service to the food service division. The food service division decides that in the future it will "outsource" all of its repair and maintenance needs. As a consequence the repair and maintenance division will have to reduce to 16,000 the number of hours its provides.

1. What will be the impact on the rate that it charges to other divisions of the college, assuming that the repair and maintenance division is unable to reduce its fixed costs?

2. What will be the most likely impact on the decisions of the other divisions of the college as to whether to continue to deal with the repair and maintenance division or to obtain service from outside providers?

13-4

Financial reporting losses are not necessarily economic losses.

The Independent Accountants Association, a not-for-profit organization, has occupied its office building for many years. The building, which was purchased for $4 million, currently has a book value (cost less accumulated depreciation) of $1.8 million.

The association needs more space for the next five years. After that, it plans to sell whatever property it owns in its current city and relocate to another part of the country.

It is considering two options. First, it could keep its current building and rent space in an adjoining building for $200,000 per year for the next five years. It estimates that in five years it would be able to sell its current building for $1 million.

Second, it could sell its current building immediately. It has been offered $1.1 million. It would then purchase a new, more spacious building for $2.5 million. It estimates that the new building would retain its value for the next five years and could be sold then for same $2.5 million.

The association uses an annual discount rate of 8 percent to evaluate all capital investment proposals involving the time value of money.

For some members of the association the decision is clear. They would reject the second option in favor of the first inasmuch as the second would require that the association recognize an immediate loss of $700,000 that would not be compensated for with future gains or savings.

a. Are the members correct in asserting that the association would have to recognize an immediate loss of $700,000? Prepare the required journal entry to record the sale of the building if the association selected the second option.

b. Do you agree that the association should select the first option? Prepare an analysis in which you show which of the two options is the more financially favorable.

13-5

Activity-based costing may result in different overhead allocations than conventional costing.

The University of the Hills computer repair and service division is divided into two mission departments—hardware and software—plus an administrative department. In the past, using conventional costing, the department first allocated the costs of the administrative department to each of the mission departments based on billable labor hours. Then it assigned the allocated administrative costs to the individual jobs—also on the basis of billable labor hours. Recently, however, it switched to activity-based costing. It now collects all administrative (i.e., overhead) costs in three pools and applies them to the cost objects (individual jobs) using appropriate cost drivers. The three pools and the cost drivers are as follows:

Pool	*Cost Driver*
Payroll and general overhead (e.g., space, utilities, maintenance)	Billable labor hours
Purchasing and materials handling	Materials requisitions
Accounting and billing	Number of jobs

The following data relate to the month of November:

	Hardware	*Software*	*Total*
Billable labor hours	1,360	1,040	2,400
Number of jobs	340	300	640
Number of requisitions	360	80	440

Total administrative overhead for the month was collected in cost pools as follows:

Payroll and general	$14,000
Purchasing and materials handling	4,000
Accounting and billing	2,000
Total administrative overhead	$20,000

Job #22, undertaken in November, involved the installation of a new hard drive and miscellaneous other repairs to a computer. A single job, it required four billable hours of labor and three materials requisitions. Direct labor, billed at $30 per hour, was therefore $120; direct materials were, $620.

a. Suppose that under conventional costing, the computer and repair service allocated the entire $20,000 in administrative costs to the two mission departments based on billable labor hours. The departments then assigned both the allocated overhead and their own overhead to individual jobs based on billable labor hours. What would be the cost assigned to Job #22?

b. What would be the cost of Job #22 under the new ABC costing procedures?

PROBLEMS

13-1

Variable costs may not always be as variable as they appear.

The Commuter Division of the Metropolitan Transit System (MTS) operates a commuter bus service between a suburban community and the downtown area of a major city.

The division currently operates 10 buses, each of which has a practical capacity of 300 passengers (rides per day). As the number of riders increases, the division can schedule more frequent service. However, each time the number of passengers exceeds the maximum capacity of 300, another bus must be added. The additional bus must be scheduled for the same number of daily trips as the others.

The division currently provides service for approximately 2,900 passengers per day. Inasmuch as the division does not operate on weekends or holidays, it bases all monthly calculations on 22 operating days per month. Thus the division currently provides 63,800 (2,900 × 22) rides per month.

The division leases, rather than purchases, its buses. Operating costs for a recent month were as follows:

Monthly Costs Per Bus

Lease Charges	$ 2,000
Wages of Drivers	4,000
Fuel Costs	2,400
Variable Maintenance and Miscellaneous Costs	800
Total Costs Per Bus	$ 9,200
Number of Buses	× 10
Total Direct Costs of Operating Buses	$ 92,000
Administration, General, and Fixed Maintenance Costs	32,000
Total Monthly Costs	$124,000

The fare for each ride is $2.75; monthly revenues are $175,450 (63,800 rides @ $2.75).

a. The division manager anticipates that ridership will increase by 3 percent. He estimated that earnings (revenues less expenses) will also increase by 3 percent. Do you agree? If not, indicate the amount by which you believe earnings will increase.

b. The division's financial manager, only slightly more knowledgeable about accounting, believes that ridership will increase by five percent. He has determined that earnings will increase by the difference between the additional revenue and the additional variable costs. He has computed variable costs to be $92,000 divided by average monthly ridership of 63,800—that is $1.44 per rider. Do you agree with his computations? If not, determine the amount by which you believe earnings will change?

c. In light of your computations, do you believe that the division should make an effort to increase ridership by 5 percent, or would it be better off by attempting to restrict ridership to its current level?

13-2

Seemingly unprofitable operations may be worth continuing.

The dean of a leading college of business (a former professor of marketing) has asked a joint student–faculty committee to advise him as to whether to discontinue the school's food service. The food service, which provides sandwiches, salads, snacks, and beverages, is located in a corner of a large student lounge and study area. If the service were discontinued, its space would be used to expand the lounge.

The dean's request to the committee was motivated by the following monthly sales and cost data indicating that the service is a drain on business school finances:

Sales	$ 56,000
Cost of Food and Supplies	42,000
Gross Margin	$ 14,000
Other Costs	
Wages and Salaries	8,200
Depreciation of Equipment	1,200
Repairs and Maintenance	3,000
Occupancy Costs	2,700
Other Overhead	1,500
Total Other Costs	$ 16,600
Net Profit (Loss)	($ 2,600)

Upon investigation, the committee learned that the occupancy costs were allocated on the basis of square feet. As best they were able to determine, the only saving in occupancy costs were the service to be discontinued would be $400 per month in electricity. "Other overhead" represents an arbitrary assignment of accounting and administrative costs, none of which would clearly be saved if the service were discontinued.

The committee also learned that the food service estimates it will spend, on average, $2,000 per month to replace existing equipment. Were the existing equipment to be sold today, it would yield only a negligible amount.

a. Based on the available data, and taking into account only financial considerations, do you think the food service should be discontinued? Justify your response.

b. Suppose, instead, that the equipment could be sold today for $60,000. The dean has indicated that the funds would be invested in an account that would earn 6 percent interest per year. How would the sale of equipment affect your analysis? Explain.

13-3

Universities sometimes adopt overhead policies that are especially arbitrary and may be dysfunctional.

Wertimer University, like almost all major research universities, permits its component academic departments, bureaus, and research institutes to enter into research contracts with government agencies, corporations, and other outside organizations. Out of the negotiated price, the university unit must pay all direct costs pertaining to the project for which it contracts. In addition, however, the university charges as overhead 60 percent of the direct wage and salary costs that will be incurred in fulfilling the contract.

The university maintains an office of "contract research," the mission of which is to assist the academic departments, bureaus, and research institutes in obtaining and administering contracts. The cost of maintaining the office is approximately $200,000 per year. For the most part, however, the overhead charged to the units undertaking contract research represents costs that are incurred to support the traditional academic functions of the university—buildings and grounds, maintenance, libraries, laboratories, computer facilities, administration, and so on. These costs are fixed; they cannot be identified with any single contract research project.

Most contracts, particularly those with government agencies, are reimbursement-type agreements. A unit gets reimbursed for all costs, including overhead, that it incurs, but earns no "profit." Some contracts, however, are for a negotiated amount that provides for payment in excess of costs incurred. When such contracts are entered into the unit performing the research is permitted to retain the excess of revenues over costs and use it to supplement university budget allocations. The primary motivation for conducting contract research is that it provides funding for projects that faculty and research associates want to conduct but that otherwise would have no financial support.

In recent years the contract value of sponsored research was $40 million annually.

Critically evaluate the university's policy of imposing a charge for overhead.

a. What do you think are the primary purposes of the charge?

b. What effect do you think it has on the motivation of the various units to obtain research contracts?

c. How do you think the 60 percent charge was arrived at?

d. What objections might be raised to the policy?

e. What alternatives to the policy merit consideration?

13-4

Decisions to contract out are often far more complex than they appear.

The National Association of Professional Accountants (NAPA) operates a printing department that prints the professional pronouncements, brochures, catalogs, and most other printed matter that it distributes to members. The NAPA is deliberating whether to discontinue the operation and contract with independent printers for its requirements. The change would be effective January 1, 1998.

The association has compiled the following data with respect to its printing department:

Direct Labor	$ 180,000
Paper and Supplies	620,000
Repair and Maintenance	30,000
Depreciation of Equipment	50,000
Other Costs (All Cash)	40,000
Allocation of Overhead	70,000
Total Operating Costs	$ 990,000

- The equipment could be sold today for $200,000. Although the printing department was not planning on acquiring new equipment or replacing existing equipment for several years, the equipment would have to be overhauled in December 1999 at a cost of $50,000.

- The space occupied by the printing department could be converted into office space, thereby saving NAPA $15,000 in rental costs. No other overhead costs would be reduced if the printing operations were discontinued.

- NAPA estimates that the cost of satisfying its printing requirements with independent printers would be approximately $850,000 per year. In addition, the association would have to hire an additional media specialist to make arrangements with and work with the independent printers. The cost would be $50,000 per year.

- The association uses a discount rate of 6 percent to make all capital budgeting and comparable decisions.

a. Should NAPA contract out its printing operations as of January 1, 1998? Assume that the association has a three-year time horizon—i.e., through December 31, 2000. For convenience, assume that all cash flows (except those relating to the initial sale of equipment) occur at year-end.

b. Suppose alternatively that the printing department plans to purchase new equipment at the end of 1999 and that the equipment would have a useful life of seven years. How would that affect your analysis?

c. Suppose you were asked to make the decision as to whether to discontinue the printing operation. What other factors would you want to take into account, or what other questions would you raise?

13-5

A mission center must share blame for budget variances in a service center.

The Tri-County Blood Center, a not-for-profit organization that collects and processes donated blood, has several operating units and overhead cost pools.

Per standards established by the collection department, a technician should be able to draw blood from three donors per hour. During a typical month, the five technicians of the department work a total of 880 direct labor hours and draw 2,640 pints of blood. Technicians are paid at the rate of $12 per hour. Hence, the typical payroll for a month is $10,560.

The overhead costs accumulated in a pool of payroll-related costs, such as benefits and insurance, vary with the direct labor *dollars* of the mission centers that it serves. The accountant in charge of the pool has determined that in an average month it incurs fixed costs of $5,000 and variable costs of $.15 per direct labor dollar. Over time, the payroll of the several mission departments, including the collection department, averages $30,000 per month. Hence, the budgeted monthly costs of the payroll-related pool are $9,500 [$5,000 + (.15 × $30,000)].

During September, the collection department drew 2,688 pints of blood. Technicians worked a total of 960 hours, and since some of these hours were compensated at premium rates the wages averaged $12.50 per hour. Total wages were $12,000.

In the same month, the payroll-related cost pool incurred $10,300 of costs. The departments that it serves paid $34,000 in direct labor dollars.

a. Determine the direct cost to the center of the excessive use of labor on the part of the collection department (i.e., the labor efficiency variance). Determine also the cost of having to pay greater than standard wages (the labor rate variance).

b. Determine the total variance of the payroll-related cost pool (i.e., actual costs less those budgeted for a normal month).

1. Of this variance, how much can be attributed to the additional direct labor dollars (i.e., $34,000 less $30,000) of all the departments that it serves?

2. Of the variance attributable to the departments served, how much can be attributed to the collection department (i.e., the difference between the total wages paid by the collection department and the standard wages for the normal volume of 2,640 pints)?

3. Of the variance attributable to the collection department (in number 2), how much is the result of:
   - the 48 greater than normal number of pints processed?
   - the "inefficiency" of the collection department (i.e., the combined direct labor usage and direct labor rate variances as just calculated)?

4. Mission departments other than the collection department incurred $2,560 of direct labor costs more than anticipated. What was the impact of these additional costs on the payroll-related cost pool?

5. Assuming that $600 of the total variance of the payroll-related cost pool (as you might have calculated in part b1) can be attributed to additional direct labor costs incurred by mission departments, how much of the total variance can be assigned to other factors (such as increases in insurance and other benefit rates)?

13-6

When it comes to classifying costs, it's not only what you say, it's when you say it.

Parents Against Underage Drinking (PAUD) recently paid $50,000 to sponsor a series of commercials on a local television station. Each commercial is one minute in length. In the first 45 seconds sports stars plead with teenagers to avoid peer pressure to consume alcoholic beverages. In the remaining 15 seconds a celebrity solicits funds for the organization and gives a telephone number to call, and an address to which to send a contribution. The commercials are scheduled to run during the reruns of *Baywatch*, a program that features magnificent scenery, most of which is scantily clad.

a. How much of the cost of the commercials should PAUD allocate to mission-related programs and how much to fundraising?

1. Assume first that the allocation is to be based on physical units.

2. Assume, alternatively, that the allocation is to be based on "stand-alone costs." The cost of a single 45-second commercial would be approximately $40,000; that of a 15-second commercial would be $20,000.

b. Suppose that the organization elected to run the same series of commercials on reruns of the *Lawrence Welk Show*, a musical variety program that features tunes of the 1950s and appeals primarily to the grandparents of those to whom *Baywatch* is targeted. The cost is the same $50,000. Would your response be the same? Explain.

13-7

Costs of adding capacity do not necessarily mirror those of reducing it.

A northwestern state operates a program of "halfway houses" for teenagers who have run away from home or have been delinquent (arrested for minor drug violations, for example). The halfway houses are located throughout the state and teenagers are assigned to a house that is located within or near their county of residence. The houses provide food and lodging. While they are residing at the houses the teenagers are encouraged to meet, both individually and in groups, with trained counselors who help them work out their problems and pave the way for a return to their homes and schools. In addition, the program provides that each teenager receive a thorough physical exam and medical counseling to help control any physical problems that might contribute to their emotional difficulties.

To date the program has been generally successful. More than 75 percent of the teenagers who spend time at the halfway houses return to their homes, improve their grades at school, and abandon their use of drugs.

Each halfway house can serve 40 teenagers at a time. The average stay is two months; hence, each house serves approximately 240 teenagers per year (i.e., 40 slots each occupied by an average of 6 different teenagers).

There are currently twenty halfway houses in operation throughout the state. Since the program began each of the houses has always been filled to its prescribed capacity. Indeed, there is a waiting list for admission to each of the houses. As a consequence, the administrators of the program see a need to increase the number of teenagers served. They prefer to increase the number of halfway houses, but as an alternative they would increase the prescribed enrollment at each from 40 to a maximum practical capacity of 50. An increase in the number of teenagers served at existing houses may, of course, decrease the quality of service, but the administrators believe that an increase in the stated capacity of each house would better serve the state than no increase at all.

The cost of operating the entire program is $5,240,000; that of operating each of the twenty houses is $262,000. The cost of maintaining a teenager at the center is, on average, $6,550 a year ($1,092 for a two-month stay). The breakdown of costs is as follows:

Annual Cost of Operating a Halfway House (Based on a capacity of 40)	
Rent	$ 12,000
Director	28,000
Counselors (4 @ $20,000)	80,000
Kitchen and Maintenance Employee	16,000
Furniture and Fixtures (See Note A)	6,000
Food ($2,000 Per Teenager Per Year)	80,000
Supplies and Miscellaneous Costs ($300 Per Teenager Per Year)	12,000
Utilities	3,000
Medical and Drugs ($400 Per Teenager Per Year)	16,000
Central Office Costs (See Note B)	9,000
Total Costs Per Center	$262,000

Note A: Total cost of furniture and fixtures is $24,000; useful life is four years. The current stock of furniture will not have to be replaced for at least another two years.

Note B: Central office costs are $180,000. They are divided equally among the twenty centers. Of these costs, $120,000 are fixed; the remainder vary with number of centers ($3,000 per center).

a. Specify the annual costs of increasing the capacity—the incremental cost per place—of each of the existing centers by ten places per center (and thereby serving 60 additional teenagers per center, a total of 1,200 for the 20 centers).

b. Specify the costs of adding 200 places at an additional five centers (a total 1,200 teenagers served). Consider only the costs of the first year.

c. Why might you not recommend the option with the lower cost?

d. Suppose that the state were forced to reduce the scope of the program. The administrator of the program was informed that the budget would be reduced by 15 percent ($786,000). How would you recommend the cuts be effected (i.e., by reducing the number of centers or reducing the number of places at each center)? Consider only savings for the first year. Explain and indicate any factors for which information is not provided that you would want to take into consideration.

13-8

Past errors can easily be compounded by the failure to take advantage of new cost-saving opportunities.

Two years ago, the Democratic Ideals Foundation completed the acquisition and installation of a new computer software system. The director of the foundation has determined that the total cost was approximately $200,000 including purchase price, consulting fees, and training costs.

The system is operating as expected and has resulted in the anticipated efficiencies and cost savings. However, a newer system has been developed which would effect even greater efficiencies and cost savings.

The director estimates that the new system would cost $250,000 to acquire and install, including all costs necessary to bring it to proper operating condition.

The director predicts that the new system would have an economic life of four years, approximately the same as the remaining life of the system just installed. He forecasts that it would result in annual cash operating savings of $80,000 per year.

Despite these savings, the director has elected not to acquire the system, basing his decision on the following analysis:

Cost of the New System		
Direct Outlay	$250,000	
Loss on Abandonment		
of Old System (See Below)	100,000	
Total Cost		$350,000
Less: Annual Savings Attributable		
to New System ($80,000 Per Year		
for 4 Years)		320,000
Net Disadvantage of New System		$ 30,000

The $100,000 loss on the abandonment of the old system was determined as follows:

Cost of Purchasing the Software (Consulting and Training Costs Were Charged as Expenses as Incurred)	$150,000
Less: Amortization to Date, Based on Initial Expected Life of 6 Years (Two Years @ $25,000)	50,000
Net Loss on Abandonment of Old System	$100,000

The analysis, he points out, is conservative in that it actually understates the disadvantages of replacing the old system. First, he notes, the cash savings will occur over several years and have not been discounted back to the present. If discounted at a rate of 8 percent, for example, their present value would be only $264,970. Second, he says, owing to arbitrary accounting conventions only the purchase price of the software has been capitalized and is reflected as a loss. The actual loss, were the consulting and training costs to be factored in, would be much greater.

a. Do you agree with the analysis and decision of the director? If not prepare your own analysis.

b. Suppose that when confronted with your analysis the director asserts that the foundation's auditor has warned him that if a system is acquired, the $100,000 loss would have to be recognized in the foundation's financial statements. Why, he wonders, should a management action that is supposedly in the fiscal interests of the organization result in a reported loss? Is he correct that the foundation would have to recognize a loss? If so, how would you respond to his question?

13-9

Choice of allocation basis may be more than academic.

The Port City Municipal League, a voluntary health and welfare organization, carries out four primary programs:

- Job training
- Emergency home repair
- Alcohol and drug abuse
- Activities for youth

Each of the programs is supported by federal, county, and city reimbursement grants. In addition, the league receives private contributions and dues from the United Way, corporations, and league members.

The following schedule provides information relating to the job training program, the three other mission programs, and the league's administrative activities.

	Job Training	Other Mission Programs	Administrative Activities
Direct Salaries and Benefits	$140,000	$312,000	$148,000
Equipment Maintenance and Rental	14,000	7,000	6,000
Telephone	2,500	4,000	7,200
Supplies	2,900	15,600	1,100
Contractual Services	7,300	220,000	5,000
Other Costs	4,600	9,700	14,500
Occupancy Costs			27,000
Independent Auditor			12,000
Total Costs	$171,300	$568,300	$220,800
Square Feet Occupied	2,000	2,200	3,000
Number of Employees (Full Time Equivalent)	5.6	13.0	6.1

Port City, which finances the job training program, reimburses the league for all direct costs, plus a proportionate share of administrative costs. The sponsors of the other programs, by contrast, either refuse to reimburse for overhead or reimburse only for a set percentage of direct costs.

a. The league currently allocates all administrative costs to the mission programs on the basis of total direct costs—i.e., those that can be identified with a specific program. What would be the total amount that the league should request for reimbursement from Port City for the job training program?

b. Suppose that the league divides its administrative costs into pools and allocates them on the following bases.

Cost Pool	Basis for Allocation (Cost Driver)
Salaries and benefits, contractual services, equipment maintenance and rental, and other costs	Direct salary and benefits
Occupancy costs	Square feet
Independent auditor	Total direct costs
Supplies, telephone	Number of employees

The amount of costs in each pool allocated to each of the mission programs is the program's proportionate share of the cost driver (excluding the share associated with administrative activities). Thus, for example, the job training program would be allocated 5.6/(5.6 + 13.0) of the $8,300 of administrative supplies and telephone costs.

What would be the total amount that the league should request for reimbursement from Port City for the job training program under this alternative basis of allocation? Which of the two allocation schemes is more justifiable? Why?

13-10

Activity-based costing systems provide a basis for establishing charges.

The repair and installation division of a municipal utility has two mission departments—one for repairs, the other for installation. The repair division not only maintains equipment of the utility, but also services equipment of its customers. However, if the equipment is owned by the customer, then the utility bills the customer for actual costs incurred.

The division has established three pools of overhead costs and assigns them to particular jobs as follows:

Cost Pool	Cost Driver
Accounting, supervision, and administration	Direct labor dollars
Vehicle and equipment related costs (including depreciation and maintenance)	Direct labor hours
Materials and supplies related costs (including warehousing and ordering)	Materials usage

The division has accumulated the following data for what it considers to be an "average" month:

	Repairs and Maintenance	Installation	Overhead
Direct Labor Hours	1,600	3,000	
Direct Labor Dollars	$ 32,000	$ 54,000	
Materials Used	340,000	900,000	
Accounting, Supervision, and Administration (Total)			$ 20,000
Vehicle Related Costs (Total)			5,000
Materials Related Costs			7,000

a. For each of the cost drivers determine the cost per unit that the division should assign to a job.

b. Repair Job No. 103 required 8 hours for which employees were paid a total of $190. It required $2,000 of parts and materials. How much should the utility bill the customer assuming that it intends to recover the full cost of providing the service?

SOLUTION TO EXERCISE FOR REVIEW AND SELF-STUDY

a. To process 600 permits, the division should have incurred only $26,400 in direct labor costs (600 permits @ $44) rather than $27,600. The $1,200 excess can be explained by both a labor efficiency variance and a labor rate variance:

Actual Labor Hours Used	1,150
Standard Labor Hours for Actual	
Output (600 Documents @ 2 Hours)	1,200
Excess (Fewer) Hours Used	(50)
Standard Wage Rate Per Hour	×$ 22
Labor Efficiency Variance	$ 1,100F
Actual Rate	$ 24
Standard Rate	22
Excess of Standard Rate Over	
Actual Rate	$ 2
Actual Number of Hours	× 1,150
Labor Rate Variance	$ 2,300U
Total Direct Labor Variance	$ 1,200U

b. The Administrative Center should have budgeted (per a flexible budget) $32,450 for 4,150 hours:

Fixed Costs	$ 20,000
Variable Costs (4,150 d.l.hrs. @ $3)	12,450
Total Budgeted Costs Per Flexible Budget	$ 32,450

Therefore, the flexible budget variance was $850 (unfavorable):

Actual Costs	$ 33,300
Budgeted Per Flexible Budget	
for Actual (4,150) Direct Labor Hours	32,450
Flexible Budget Variance	$ 850U

c. The Administrative Center should have budgeted (per a flexible budget) $32,600 for 4,200 hours:

Fixed Costs	$ 20,000
Variable Costs (4,200 d.l.hrs. @ $3)	12,600
Total Budgeted Costs Per Flexible Budget	$ 32,600

The Administrative Center thereby saved $150, a favorable overhead efficiency variance, owing to the better-than-standard use of labor by the Permits Division:

Total Budgeted Costs Per Flexible Budget	
for Actual (4,150) Direct Labor Hours	$32,450
Total Budgeted Costs Per Flexible Budget	
for Standard (4,200) Direct Labor Hours	32,600
Overhead Efficiency Variance	$ 150F

d. The Permits division should have been required to work an additional 200 hours (2 hours per permit) to process an additional 100 permits. At $3 variable costs per hour, the additional hours should have caused the Administrative Center to incur $600 in additional costs—an unfavorable volume variance.

e. Yes:

Volume Variance	$ 600U
Efficiency Variance	150F
Flexible Budget	850U
Total Overhead Variance	$1,300U

f. If the state accepts the offer, then its costs per month would be $25,000 (500 permits @ $50). If it rejects it, then it would have to incur the following incremental costs relating to the permits:

Direct Labor Costs (500 Permits @ $44)	$22,000
Administrative Overhead	
Fixed (additional amount only)	1,000
Variable (500 Permits @ 2 d.l.hrs @ $3)	3,000
Total Relevant Costs to Be Incurred If	
Offer is Rejected	$26,000

The state could save $1,000 per month in differential costs by accepting the contract and, other factors held constant, should do so.

g. At a minimum the state should seek to recover its *incremental costs*. Thus, it should charge $50 per permit:

Direct Labor Costs	$44
Variable Overhead	6
Total Incremental Costs	$50

More realistically, it should charge at least $52, an amount that takes into account $1,000 of the fixed costs ($2 per permit if 500 permits are processed) that the Administrative Center could save if it did not have to serve the Permits Division.

As a maximum, it should charge the full cost—$60 per permit.

CHAPTER 14

Managing for Results

LEARNING OBJECTIVES

After studying this chapter you should understand:

- the various roles that accountants can play in the management of governmental and other not-for-profit organizations

- how program budgets overcome the limitations of traditional, object classification budgets

- the need for, and characteristics of, sound operational objectives

- the risks of establishing explicit organizational objectives

- the ways in which program budgets link expenditures to objectives

- the advantages and disadvantages of program budgets

- why it is important for organizations to develop and report measures of service efforts and accomplishments that indicate the extent to which they achieved their objectives

- the special problems that governments and not-for-profits face in planning and budgeting their capital expenditures and how they can address them

In Chapter 13 we saw that conventional, business-type management accounting focuses mainly on maximizing net inflow of cash rather than on achieving the organization's other objectives. In this chapter, our emphasis shifts to these other goals of governments and not-for-profits. The central messages of this chapter are that organizations must be managed so as to achieve intended results, and that all phases of the management cycle must be linked to this end.

We first review the management cycle and explain how an organization's operational objectives tie together each of its phases. The role of accountants in each of these phases is described briefly. We then consider several ideal characteristics of operational objectives and show how operational objectives can be incorporated into what are referred to as program budgets. Next we discuss how organizations can report on "service efforts and accomplishments"—in essence, on the extent to which they achieved their objectives. We conclude by showing why and how capital, and capital-related expenditures, no differently than operating expenditures, must be budgeted and planned within the framework of the organization's operational objectives. We address two key steps in the process: benefit-cost analysis and project ranking.

This chapter pertains to topics to which entire courses are directed and as to which there is an extensive body of literature. Nevertheless, as readily will be apparent, the issues raised are not nearly as well-defined as those dealt with in earlier chapters and the options for resolving them are not nearly as clear. Indeed, if only a small portion of the subject matter of this chapter is covered on the CPA or other professional exams, part of the reason could well be that there would be no agreed-upon answers to relevant objective-type questions.

WHAT ROLE DO ACCOUNTANTS PLAY IN THE MANAGEMENT CYCLE OF GOVERNMENTS AND OTHER NOT-FOR-PROFITS?

The development, implementation, and assessment of programs in governments and other not-for-profits (herein referred to as "social" programs) has been diagrammed and described in almost as many different ways as there are textbooks and articles on public and not-for-profit administration. The diagram presented in Figure 14-1 divides the process into four phases—none of which are as well defined or as discrete as might be suggested by the four separate boxes. It is intended to emphasize that accountants can play multiple roles in an entity's fiscal management; they need not be confined to their widely accepted roles of statement preparers and auditors.

As social problems within the purview of an entity arise, teams of area specialists develop and analyze potential solutions (Box 1). They collect and analyze budgetary and related financial information, and compare the potential costs and benefits associated with various options. These teams may be composed primarily of organizational managers but, depending on the size and the magnitude of the entity, may also include policy, program and budget analysts, social scientists, statisticians, and economists. Since much of this data collection and analysis centers upon financial information, accountants can make valuable contributions to this phase of the program cycle.

The proposed options are presented to policy makers—the legislature, board of directors, or other governing body (Box 2). The policy makers select among the options, modify them as they see fit, and appropriate the required resources. They also establish the expected goals. Ideally the goals will be set forth explicitly in a budget,

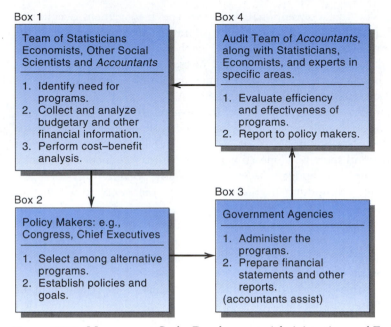

FIGURE 14-1 Management Cycle: Development, Administration, and Evaluation of the Social Programs of Governments and Other Not-For-Profits

appropriations legislation, or other documents, and will take the form of operational objectives that are measurable and quantifiable. Often, however, they are revealed only obliquely through written minutes of legislative debates or changes in the appropriations measures as they work their way through the legislative process. Moreover, they are seldom specific. Accountants, as accountants, have no special role to play in this phase of the program cycle (although accountants are undoubtedly as competent as members of other professions to serve as members of legislatures and other governing boards).

Once adopted, the programs are administered by appropriate agencies and departments (Box 3). These units are responsible for assuring that the program objectives are achieved. Accountants, of course, are key participants in this phase, actively involved in establishing plans and operating budgets, controlling costs, and preparing financial and other operating reports to officials of both the agency itself and to outside entities charged with monitoring the agency.

Finally, the programs are audited (Box 4). Not only are programs' financial statements attested to (a conventional financial audit), but more importantly, the programs are assessed as to the extent to which they achieved their objectives. Accountants are almost always members of audit teams, but they may be joined by statisticians, economists, and specialists in the particular programs. The results of the audit are made available not only to the agencies and departments administering the programs, but also to the policy makers and the analysts involved in budgeting and program analysis.

The cycle then repeats. The team involved in budgeting and program analysis must assess the success of the programs, recommend whether they should be continued, and if so, propose an appropriate level of funding. The audit reports, while by no means the only source of information, can be expected to play a prominent role in their analyses.

From one perspective programming/budgeting and auditing are far apart in the cycle and have little in common. Program/budgeting appears to lead the cycle; auditing concludes it. Programming/budgeting looks to the future; auditing at the past. From another perspective, however, the two phases are next to each other and are functionally similar. The cycle is continuous; it has neither a beginning nor an end. Programming/budgeting decisions must be based on the success of programs in the past; auditing is carried out with an eye to making improvements in the future. Both are linked by the entity's operational objectives and are intended to assure that the entity fulfills the objectives efficiently and effectively.

HOW CAN THE LIMITS OF TRADITIONAL BUDGETS BE OVERCOME?

The proposed budget of the Highland Hills Assistance League, an urban health and welfare agency, is presented in Table 14–1. Typical of budgets prepared by state and local governments and not-for-profit organizations, and referred to as an **object classification budget**, it is backed by schedules that show details of each of the major expenditures—for example, salaries, transportation, and travel costs by department. This agency provides job training, counseling, and training, repairs the homes of low-income families, and carries out youth-oriented programs.

Suppose you were the League's chief executive officer and were required to defend the proposed budget before the board of directors. You were asked:

- Will the requested funds—an increase over the prior year—be sufficient to increase the number of homes repaired? If so, by how many?

- Will they enable the organization to improve its drug prevention program? If so, how will the improvements be measured?

- Will they increase the number of job trainees that obtain well-paying jobs? If so, by how many?

- Will they reduce the community's school drop-out rate? If so, by how much?

Based on the budget alone, it is obvious that you would be unable to respond adequately to the questions. It is equally self-evident that the queries reflect legitimate concerns of the board members and the constituents they represent. By contrast, you would be able to provide data on the amount to be spent on travel, supplies, and rent. These costs should be of concern to the organization's managers. But the organization's members and policy makers are likely to—and should—be more concerned with the relationship between costs and results.

As emphasized throughout this text, the budget is the most significant of financial documents for both governments and not-for-profit organizations. It determines the amount of resources to be received from the various groups of constituents and the programs and activities that the resources will support. Directly or indirectly it affects, or is effected by, virtually all decisions of consequence that a governing body must make. The budget details in financial terms the strategy of the organization to accomplish its mission.

Yet the traditional budget, as illustrated in the exhibit, provides no insight into what the organization's constituents can expect for their contributions. It offers no information as to the extent that the expenditures will advance the entity's mission or better enable it to achieve its objectives.

This chapter is directed mainly to budgeting, performance reporting, and evaluation. These topics are linked with a common thread—the importance of defining the organization's mission, developing broad goals, and establishing operational ob-

TABLE 14-1
Highland Hills Assistance League Proposed Budget

Summary of Support/Revenue and Expenses

	Budgeted	
	FY 98–99	FY 97–98
Support/Revenue:		
Interest on Investments/Endowments	$ 7,200	$ 7,800
Fundraising	75,096	75,000
Individual Contributions	4,860	19,800
Government Grants	1,063,830	800,545
Corporate/Foundations	28,848	37,000
United Way	67,009	60,504
Other	13,009	6,504
Total Support/Revenue	$1,259,852	$1,007,153
Expenses:		
Salaries	$ 638,626	$ 464,785
Employee Benefits	53,737	42,672
Payroll Taxes	55,962	58,012
Professional Fees	46,145	38,004
Rent	106,666	105,360
Equipment Rental and Maintenance	23,166	19,112
Travel and Transportation	25,378	22,030
Subcontracting	211,742	317,614
Promotion and Printing	13,056	9,840
Specific Assistance to Individuals	23,100	13,800
Insurance	5,397	6,000
General and Administrative	29,100	19,727
Total Expenses	$1,232,075	$1,116,956
Surplus/(Deficit)	$ 27,777	$ (109,803)

Note how each of the expenses relates to means of carrying out the agency's activities; none is tied to specific objectives. The budget provides no basis for assessing subsequent performance.

jectives. **Operational objectives** is used herein to signify *specific* sought-after results. Whenever possible, operational objectives should be both quantifiable and measurable. They should be distinguishable from goals, which are more generalized statements of aspirations.

Establishing appropriate objectives is at the heart of budgeting, because if an organization doesn't have a clear idea as to *where* it wants to go, it cannot determine how to get there and when it has arrived. Nevertheless, as shall be stressed in this chapter, the importance of operational objectives is matched by the challenge of establishing them. Virtually no managers of government or not-for-profit organizations deny, or even minimize, the need for operational objectives—but for organizations other than their own. Their own objectives, they may contend, are too intangible to quantify.

WHAT ARE THE CHARACTERISTICS OF SOUND OPERATIONAL OBJECTIVES?

Operational objectives should be central to the functions that compose the management cycle. They should not simply be technical contrivances within the province of budget analysts, accountants, and auditors. Derived from the organization's mission and its goals, they should be the basis for allocating resources, managing day-to-day activities, and distributing rewards and reprimands. Per an often-repeated aphorism, "What we measure is what we manage." This section sets forth ideal characteristics of operational objectives, but at the same time emphasizes that the ideal is not readily attainable.

Operational objectives should be distinguishable from the means of achieving the organization's broad goals. They should not preclude alternative means of accomplishing the desired results. The "true" goal of a state highway department, for example, might be to enable drivers to reduce travel time from home to work rather than the obvious one of building more miles of highway. Building more miles of highway may be one primary means of reducing travel time, but it may not be the only one. Other means may include synchronizing the timing of traffic signals on existing roads and of designating special lanes for buses and other multipassenger vehicles.

SHOULD REPRESENT TRUE ENDS (OUTCOMES), NOT MEANS (OUTPUTS)

Operational objectives should be doable and measurable. In addition, they should be accomplishable within a specific time or by a specified date.

What might be a means at one level within an organization might be an objective at another. For example, the objective of the highway construction division, a unit within the highway department, might well be to build highways. The measure of its performance might be the number of miles constructed.

The distinction between true ends and means is more of a continuum than a dichotomy. Whereas higher order objectives—those that refer to more abstract statements of intent and are generally referred to as "goals"—are associated with true ends, the more specific, readily measurable actions that entities take to achieve the goals are identified with the means.

In ideal circumstances, operational objectives would capture the true ends rather than the means. But owing to difficulties of measurement, this is often not possible. In a city that is expanding in both population and geographic area, it may not be feasible for a highway department to assess its success in reducing travel time. It may be constrained, therefore, to rely on miles of new highway construction as one of its main operational objectives.

The virtues of focusing on true ends rather than means is a central theme of recent management literature. Organizations, the literature has stressed, should be "mission" rather than "rules" driven. Top management should tell lower-level managers and employees what to accomplish rather than how to accomplish it.[1]

Closely tied to the concepts of ends and means, but connoting more precisely specified consequences, are those of **outcomes** and **outputs**. *Outcomes*, like ends, represent the *results* of an activity. *Outputs*, like means, indicate the quantity or units of service provided by the activity. Outcomes reflect accomplishments and typically

---

[1] See, for example, D. Osborne and T. Gaebler, *Reinventing Government: How the Entrepreneurial Spirit is Transforming the Public Sector* (Reading, Mass.: Addison Wesley, 1992), especially Chapter 4, "Mission Driven Government: Transforming Rules-Driven Organizations," pp. 108–37.

include an element of quality—e.g., number of units that satisfy specified criteria. Accordingly, in the ideal organization operational objectives should be expressed as outcomes rather than outputs.

The following are examples of outputs and the outcomes that they may help to effect:

Output	*Outcome*
Number of accounting majors	Number of students passing the CPA exam; number of students in accounting positions after a specified number of years following graduation
Number of criminal investigations carried out	Number of crimes cleared; crime rate
Number of air-quality samples tested	Percentage of population living in areas in which the quality of air meets specified standards; percentage of samples meeting air-quality standards
Number of applicants served by an employment agency	Number of applicants placed in suitable (as specifically defined) jobs
Number of patients served	Percentage of patients cured

SHOULD BE READILY MEASURABLE, YET CAPTURE THE DESIRED OUTCOME

Operational objectives should be readily measurable. Yet often the true outcome of a program cannot easily be quantified, and certainly not described, by any single metric. The aims of an undergraduate accounting program (like those of most other undergraduate programs) include enhancing students' abilities to read, to write, to reason, and to develop sound moral, ethical, and cultural values. In the eyes of many faculty, these goals are at least as important as the more obvious objectives—enabling students to pass the CPA exam or obtain employment in a professional or managerial capacity. They are far more difficult to measure, however, and therefore less likely to be focused or reported upon.

In the absence of measures indicative of true outcomes, organizations must resort to surrogates. However, the less the similarity of the surrogate to the true outcome, the less its utility, and the greater the danger that it will result in dysfunctional behavior (as discussed in the section that follows on the perils of operational objectives.)

SHOULD BE MEASURABLE WITHIN A PERIOD SUFFICIENTLY SHORT TO TAKE CORRECTIVE ACTION

If operational objectives are to be the basis of performance evaluation, then they should not only capture true outcomes, but do so in a timely manner. An objective of an accounting program may be to produce leaders of the accounting profession. However, it generally takes graduates at least fifteen years to fulfill their leadership potential. Most departments are unable to wait that long to learn whether they need to change their curriculum, replace faculty, or adjust admission standards so as to better achieve their objective. Hence, they are required to rely upon expedients, such as percentage of students placed with prestigious employers or who passed the CPA exam.

SHOULD BE PRECISE

Operational objectives should be precise. They should leave little room for individual interpretation. But the precision should not be at the risk of misspecification.

The objective of a park police unit might be "to reduce the number of assaults in city parks and to arrest the perpetrators"—an apparently well-defined goal. Nevertheless, it leaves open issues that if not properly resolved could undermine that objective:

- Should the number of assaults be based on the number of actual or reported incidents? (If actual incidents, then there is no objective way to determine the number, since some incidents may go unreported. If reported incidents, then the department could best achieve the objective by taking its phone off the hook—or, perhaps more realistically, by not encouraging victims to report the incidents.)

- Should "arrest of perpetrators" be based on arrests of suspects, indictments, or on actual convictions? (If based on arrests, then the police could achieve the objective by taking into custody any potential suspects, no matter how low the probability that they are the actual criminals. If based on convictions, however, then the performance of the police unit depends on other city departments, such as the district attorney's office, over which it has no control. If based on indictments, then the problems of the other two indicators are mitigated, but by no means eliminated.)

- Should all assaults be grouped together, or is it preferable to divide them into categories as to degree of severity? (If all assaults are grouped together, then police may have the incentive to concentrate on assaults that are easy to prevent, but not especially severe.)

SHOULD BE MULTIPLE IN MOST CASES

The mission of an organization must generally be expressed through more than one objective. Rarely is a single objective sufficient.

Multiple objectives create special problems of both resource allocation and performance evaluation, since outcomes cannot be assessed on a single scale. A unit or activity that ranks high on one scale may rank low on another. Therefore, the organization may have no obvious way of determining which of its activities or units is the more efficient overall. This limitation may be alleviated to some extent by sophisticated mathematical techniques, such as data envelopment analysis (DEA) and other types of goal programming, that combine the relative strengths of each unit or activity and create a single "frontier" of efficiency.

WHAT ARE THE PERILS OF ESTABLISHING OPERATIONAL OBJECTIVES?

Despite the importance of operational objectives, many organizations are reluctant to establish them. Operational objectives can have adverse consequences. It is critical that they be understood and dealt with forthrightly.

MAY FOMENT CONFLICT

By establishing objectives, an organization invariably signals which of its activities are primary and which are secondary. Arguably, in fact, that is one of the main purposes of the process. Implicitly, therefore, organizations distinguish among the individuals or units that are central to achieving their objectives and those that are merely supportive.

Suppose, for example, an academic department of accounting establishes as one of its objectives "increasing the pass rate on the CPA exam." This objective may be perceived as enhancing the stature of the faculty members who teach the courses from which the CPA examination questions are drawn (e.g., intermediate accounting) at the expense of those responsible for those from which they are not (e.g., accounting history). The elevation in status of some employees at the expense of others will almost certainly create organizational tensions.

Similarly, by being too precise as to their objectives, organizations risk alienating their constituents. Recognizing this reality, political parties, for example, often confine their platforms to vague generalities. University presidents, for fear of offending undergraduate students and their parents, may be reluctant to publicize their objective of creating top-flight research programs.

MAY RESULT IN DYSFUNCTIONAL BEHAVIOR

Objectives are intended to lay the foundation for specific evaluative criteria for the organization as a whole, for the various component units, and ultimately for individual employees. Operating under mandates from governing authorities or top managers to establish objectives, an organization may substitute objectives that are convenient to measure for those that express its true mission. As a consequence, employees may target their efforts toward improving what will be measured rather than what may be ultimately beneficial to the organization and its constituents.

If a stated, but not true, objective of an accounting department is to increase the CPA pass rate, then presumably the department will compile data on exam results. Individual instructors will be under pressure (actual or implied) to assure that their students perform well on the exams and will therefore emphasize exam-related material to the detriment of topics that may be of greater long-term importance to the students.

A main goal of the U.S. involvement in the Vietnam conflict was to assure that South Vietnam was governed by a pro-Western, non-Communist government. Success could not be assured, as in conventional wars, by capturing territory. Instead it had to be achieved by winning the support ("the hearts and minds") of the populace. In what has been widely cited as a quintessential case of placing reliance on misspecified objectives, the U.S. military evaluated both progress and the performance of individual units on "body counts"—a criterion easy to measure but not genuinely indicative of the military's ultimate aim. Contrast the two views of this measure as presented in the following In Practice.

IN PRACTICE

A CLASSIC CASE OF RELIANCE ON MISSPECIFIED OBJECTIVES (TWO PERSPECTIVES OF THE VIETNAM WAR)

I. The Soldier's Perspective

The rugged terrain and frequent night attacks made it very hard to place priority on recovering casualties, which helped prevent accurate counts. Because of such difficulties, field commanders were inclined to estimate the enemy's losses without hard evidence. Although most tried to be accurate, for others, body count became a work of creative fiction. . . . Exaggerated counts never seemed to be questioned higher up. Officers who tried to render accurate body counts had to fight against a current of pressure to produce results—on paper, if not in truth. [This] manipulation of reality affected not only battle news, which was edited and revised until it was acceptable to those higher up, but also friendly casualty reports, pacification reports, food distribution status—anything that lent itself to statistical measurement as a demonstration of progress. [A noted officer] was quoted as saying, "Duplicity was so automatic that lower headquarters began to believe the things they were forwarding to higher headquarters. . . . Paper graphs and charts became the ultimate reality." This situation was reinforced, as [an observer] points out, by the fact that the unquestioned tallies "were readily rewarded by medals, promotions, and time off from field duty."

Incentives offered to the enlisted personnel were usually the result of increasing pressure from above to produce more kills. [A field officer], for example, claimed that his unit was "constantly under pressure to turn in a body count, and the word was out that companies with the greatest number would get to spend more time at Cocoa Beach. It was an accepted thing to cheat on a body count report—all of us had been guilty of this."

Source: James R. Ebert, *A Life in a Year: the American Infantryman in Vietnam, 1965–1972* (Novato, Calif.: Presido Press, 1993) pp. 273–274. © Reprinted with permission.

II. *The Secretary of Defense's Perspective*

But I insisted we try to measure progress. As I have emphasized, since my years at Harvard, I had gone by the rule that it is not enough to conceive of an objective and a plan to carry it out; you must monitor the plan to determine whether you are achieving the objective. If you discover you are not, you either revise the plan or change the objective. I was convinced that, while we might not be able to track something as unambiguous as a front line, we could find variables that would indicate our success or failure. So we measured the targets destroyed in the North, the traffic down the Ho Chi Minh Trail, the number of captives, the weapons seized, the enemy body count, and so on.

The body count was a measurement of the adversary's manpower losses; we undertook it because one of [the commanding general's] objectives was to reach a so-called crossover point, we needed to have some idea what they could sustain and what their losses were.

Critics point to use of the body count as an example of my obsession with numbers. "This guy McNamara," they said, "he tries to quantify everything." Obviously, there are things you cannot quantify: honor and beauty, for example. But things you can count, you ought to count. Loss of life is one when you are fighting a war of attrition. We tried to use body counts as a measurement to help us figure out what we should be doing in Vietnam to win the war while putting our troops at the least risk. Every attempt to monitor progress in Vietnam during my tenure as secretary of defense was directed toward those goals, but often the reports were misleading.

Source: Robert S. McNamara with Brian VanDeMark, *In Retrospect: The Tragedy and Lessons of Vietnam* (New York: Random House, 1995) pp. 237–38. © Reprinted with permission.

HOW DO PROGRAM BUDGETS RELATE EXPENDITURES TO OPERATIONAL OBJECTIVES?

As pointed out in Chapter 3, **performance budgets** explicitly relate expenditures to operational objectives. Accordingly, both governments and not-for-profits use them in place of, or as a supplement to, the traditional **object classification budgets.** **Program budgets**, the most common type of performance budgets, allocate funds by programs rather than by objects. Thus, the governing board of a city would appropriate funds for public safety programs, fire prevention programs, and health programs, rather than for salaries, equipment, or supplies.

Programs are composed of activities that are directed toward a common goal. They are generally carried out within a single organizational unit, but they may also cut across departments. For example, a drug prevention program may involve a city's police department, health department, and education department. When program budgets were first popularized (in the 1960s), considerable emphasis was placed on the advantages of allocating costs to programs, rather than departments, even when the programs involved two or more departments. In practice, however, budgeting across departments is fraught with managerial pitfalls as it blurs the lines of authority and responsibility over the appropriated resources.

Program budgets can take many forms, each reflective of the specific needs and culture of the specific entity. In this chapter we illustrate **zero-base budgeting (ZBB)**, which is one variant of program budgeting. We choose this variant, not because it is the most widely used, but because its requirements are precisely delineated. Those of other forms are more organization-specific. ZBB requires entities to make explicit the decisions and judgments that other forms allow the entities to leave implied. Accordingly, it is more clearly indicative of the strengths and pitfalls of program budgets in general.

The defining feature of ZBB is its mandate that both current and proposed activities be subject to a common review and priority ranking. As implied by its name, all activities must be evaluated from a base of zero. None, irrespective of how long it has been in existence, is exempt from budgetary review. In this respect, ZBB is distinguished from "incremental" budgeting procedures in which the emphasis is primarily on requests for initial funding for new activities or added funding for continuing activities. An implicit assumption of incremental budgeting is that in the absence of affirmative measures to the contrary, activities will continue to be funded at no less than their current level.

In the 1970s ZBB received considerable attention and was adopted by many governments. With great fanfare, President Carter introduced it into the federal government, and states such as Illinois and Texas, as well as many cities and not-for-profits, followed the federal lead. It is currently being promoted by consulting firms (under the name "priority-based budgeting"). Although relatively few organizations use ZBB in its totality, many of its elements are common to the other variants of program budgeting.

FOCUS ON ACTIVITIES

Within programs, expenditures are almost always disaggregated by object and fund. However, so as to tie expenditures more closely to objectives, they should also be broken down by activity and the focus of the budget deliberations should be on the activities rather than the object or the fund. Suppose, for example, the Highland Hills Assistance League, (the organization whose object classification budget was presented in Table 14–1) maintains the following programs:

- employment skills
- housing rehabilitation
- teen substance abuse

The following are examples of activities that might comprise the employment skills programs:

- job-seeking skills (resume-writing, "dress for success," and interviewing skills)
- computer training
- electronics training
- day care (for children of course participants)

At the heart of program budgeting are the materials that must be presented as part of the budget request. Under zero-base budgeting, the budget request takes the form of a **decision package** that must be presented for each activity. Table 14–2 illustrates a decision package for computer training, one of the activities that comprises the employment skills program of the Highland Hills Assistance League. Illustrative of the type of information that many organizations require be presented as part of program budget requests, it includes the following components:

THE DECISION PACKAGE

- the objectives of the activity, expressed in a way that makes clear the desired objectives (e.g., to train unemployed adults for positions requiring word-processing and spreadsheet computer skills)
- alternative means of accomplishing the same objective (e.g., contract with a proprietary business college) and reasons why the alternatives were rejected
- consequences of not performing the activity (e.g., program participants will have no marketable skills)
- inputs (such as dollar amounts and number of employees), quantity or units of service provided (*outputs*) and results (*outcomes*) at various levels of funding (e.g., three sections of the course will be offered, resulting in approximately 200 participants per year being qualified for the job market)

Inasmuch as the objectives of an activity may not change from year to year, much of the ongoing effort of program budgeting can be directed toward the last component, that of estimating the inputs, outputs, and outcomes at various levels of funding.

TABLE 14–2
Example of a Program (Zero-Base) Budget Decision Package
Highland Hills Assistance League

Date: September 17, 1999

Prepared by: Joshua Kalman

Fiscal Year Ending: December 31, 2000

Activity Name: Computer training

Program: Employment skills

Activity Objective: To train unemployed adults in word processing and spreadsheet computer applications and place them in positions requiring those skills.

Activity Description: The organization conducts a six-month course in which participants are first taught the basics of using computers and then are given specific training in word processing and spreadsheet programs. The course, which lasts fifteen weeks, meets four days a week for four hours a day. There is one instructor, plus an assistant, for each section of twenty participants. The classroom in which the course is conducted has one computer for each participant. It is open to students on evenings and Saturdays so that they can practice what they have been taught and do "homework" exercises.

Current (1999) Budget

Total Cost:		
Salaries and Benefits		
Instructor (1)	$38,000	
Assistants (2)	34,000	$ 72,000
Computers		11,000
Software		1,700
Repairs and Maintenance		3,500
Instructional Materials		3,100
Other		$ 94,900
Total		$ 96,200

(continued)

TABLE 14–2 (Continued)
Example of a Program (Zero-Base) Budget Decision Package
Highland Hills Assistance League

The amount budgeted for computers assumes that the organization will replace four computers per year.

Current (1999) Workload (Output) Measures: 3 sections per year, each with 20 participants

Estimated Outcome: Of the 60 participants that enroll in the program, it is estimated that 48 will complete the program, and of these 44 will obtain jobs requiring the skills they acquired.

Estimated direct agency cost per projected successful outcome will be $96,200/44 = $2,186.

Level 1 Request (No More than 80 Percent of Current Level)

Cost: $75,500

Reduce number of sections to two per year, and the number of participants to 40 per year. This will likely reduce the number actually obtaining employment to 29. Staff will work only 34 weeks per year. This cut will not only lessen the extent to which the organization fulfills its mission but will put it at risk of losing key staff members.

The organization will save $10,500 in the instructor's salary and $10,000 in assistants' salaries. In addition, it will save $500 in other costs.

Estimated direct agency cost per projected successful outcome will be $75,500/29 = $2,603.

Level 2 Request (Current level)

Additional Amount, This Level: $20,700
See Current 1999 Budget
Cost: $96,200

Level 3 Request (No More than 5 Percent Above Current Level)

Additional Amount, This Level: $4,200
Cost: $100,400

Increase staff salaries by 5 percent ($3,600) and increase expenditures for software by $600. This will give the staff a deserved salary increase (their first in 2 years), thereby helping to retain them. The acquisition of the software will enable the instructors to expose the participants to word processing programs other than the two with which they currently work, thereby making them more marketable and potentially increasing both their starting and long-term salaries.

Estimated direct agency cost per projected successful outcome will be $100,400/44 = $2,281.

Level 4 Request (No More than 20 Percent Above Current Level)

Additional Amount, This Level: $14,600
Cost: $115,000

Acquire four additional computers @ $3,000 each, plus one printer @ $1,000. This will enable the league to increase the size of each section from 20 to 24, the total number of program participants from 60 to 72, and the estimated number of participants obtaining jobs from 44 to 53.

Open the classrooms to participants for four additional hours per week (on Sunday) so that students, many of whom work on evenings or Saturdays, can get additional practice. This will require additional wages for assistants of $1,600.

Estimated direct agency cost per projected successful outcome will be $115,000/53 = $2,169.

Alternative Means of Accomplishing This Activity:

Contract with Computronics, Inc. a local proprietary school. The school has offered to provide training similar to that of the league for $3,500 per student. This alternative was rejected because the training is far more costly that could be provided in-house and less appropriate to the needs of league clientele.

Consequences of Not Performing This Activity:

A primary mission of the league is to improve economic conditions in the Highland Hills neighborhood by assisting low-income residents to obtain employment. Discontinuing this activity would strike at the heart of the organization's ability to fulfill its mission.

In some organizations, budget requests must include estimates for at least four levels of funding—for example, the current level, two levels above the current level, and one level substantially (perhaps 20 percent) below the current level.

Implicit in the requirement for data at the different levels of funding should be the understanding that the entity will apply appropriate cost accounting procedures (such as those discussed in the previous chapter) to relate inputs to outputs and outcomes. Thus, if the managers of an activity aim to increase outcomes by 20 percent, they should not necessarily request a 20 percent increase in funding. Instead, by taking into account the behavior of each of its costs (i.e., the step functions), they should request the amount actually needed—which could be more or less than 20 percent. By budgeting at discrete levels, organizations thereby minimize *slack* (funds that cannot be used to increase outcomes) and maximize resource productivity.

Once the requests for funding have been prepared, they must be reviewed and ranked. Some organizations leave it up to individual units to establish criteria as to how funding proposals should be ranked; others establish uniform guidelines for all their units. It is not uncommon for organizations to ask units to give top priority to activities that will advance a particular phase of its mission—for example, a social service agency, such as the Highland Hills Assistance League, may determine that in a particular year activities involving children should be given funding preference.

REVIEW AND RANKING

Under the ZBB approach, the decision packages for all activities within a program are combined into a table that ranks the funding proposals. As illustrated in Table 14–3, each discrete level of funding is treated as a separate request. Thus, if the program were to be allocated only $75,500, the entire amount would be directed toward the first level of the computer training course. If the program were granted an additional $80,300, it would be applied to the first level of electronic training (an activity for which a decision package, not illustrated, has been prepared). If it were granted an additional $28,000, it would be used for the first level of day care (another activity for which a decision package, not illustrated, has been prepared). Only if it were granted an additional $20,700 (a total of $222,500) would the second level of the computer training course be funded.

TABLE 14–3
Example of a Program (Zero-Base) Budget Ranking Schedule
Highland Hills Assistance League Employment Skills Program

Rank	Activity Name and Level	2000 Request	2000 Cumulative
1	Computer Training (Level 1 of 4)	$ 75,500	$ 75,500
2	Electronics Training (Level 1 of 4)	80,300	155,800
3	Day Care (Level 1 of 3)	28,000	183,800
4	Job Training Skills (Level 1 of 2)	18,000	201,800
5	Computer Training (Level 2 of 4)	20,700	222,500
6	Day Care (Level 2 of 3)	5,400	227,900
7	Electronics Training (Level 2 of 4)	20,100	248,000
8	Computer Training (Level 3 of 4)	4,200	252,200
9	Electronics Training (Level 3 of 4)	2,400	254,600
10	Computer Training (Level 4 of 4)	14,600	269,200
11	Day Care (Level 3 of 3)	2,800	272,000
12	Electronics Training (Level 4 of 4)	7,900	279,900
13	Job Training Skills (Level 2 of 2)	5,400	285,300

ZBB presupposes that the governing body responsible for appropriating funds will accept the rankings submitted by the program administrators (although they are generally not required to do so). If they do, then they need only specify the total amount to be allocated to a program. That amount will be a cut-off point. Activities above the cut-off will be funded at the level implied by the table; those below will not be funded.

ZBB requires all activities, both new and ongoing, to be reviewed and included in an explicit ranking table. Other forms of program budget focus mainly on the amounts to be added to a program's funding level and do not require budget requests to be explicitly ranked.

The primary virtue of the comprehensive ranking process is that it forces program administrators to weigh the need for new activities against those of existing activities. Administrators can assure funds for a proposed activity by ranking it high, but they risk losing support for activities to which they assign a lower priority.

The ranking table makes a further contribution to efficient resource allocation in that, like the underlying decision packages, it specifies discrete funding levels. It emphasizes that resources above one level, but below another, will not necessarily advance the program's objectives. Thus, it encourages the parties responsible for making appropriations to grant spending authority only at the discrete levels.

The main disadvantage of the comprehensive ranking process—and indeed, the reason why many entities have either abandoned or rejected ZBB—is that it requires budgetary units to provide information that may never be used in the decision process. If an organization has no intention of reducing the funding for certain basic, often essential, activities, then the effort expended in preparing the decision packages for them is likely to be superfluous. Worse yet, the requirement that some activities be compared and ranked with others—none of which are being considered for budget reductions—runs the risk of arousing sentiments of resentment and jealousy among employees associated with the lower-ranked activities.

MAIN ADVANTAGES OF PROGRAM BUDGETING

As implied in the discussion so far, program budgeting has several advantages over conventional object classification budgeting:

- It relates expenditures to objectives. Decision makers are made aware of the specific additional benefits (outcomes) to be derived from additional expenditures.

- It encourages explicit consideration both of alternative means of achieving the same objective and of whether the objective even needs to be achieved.

- It promotes analysis of the behavior of costs and discourages funding at levels other than those that will result in actual increases in results.

- It invites (and in the form of ZBB requires) the periodic review of all programs and activities to assure that they are consistent with the entity's current objectives. Programs and activities that no longer contribute efficiently and effectively to the entity's mission give way to those that do. Program budgeting may incorporate what are, in essence, "sunset" reviews of all activities, thereby encouraging organizations to discontinue activities that have outlived their usefulness.

PITFALLS OF PROGRAM BUDGETS

Despite its several favorable features, program budgeting runs the risk of adding many pitfalls to the budgetary landscape:

- As noted earlier, organizational objectives may provoke conflict. If activities are explicitly ranked, the rankings may send a formal, and unavoidable message, that some endeavors—and the employees engaged in them—are less important than others.

- Program budgeting encourages governing boards, such as a city council, to establish and make known to the public, their funding priorities. This form of candor may run counter to the inclination of both elected and appointed officials to assure each of their different constituencies that their interests—often competing—are of paramount importance.

- It links dollar expenditures with anticipated outcomes. However, even when outcomes can be readily quantifiable, they may not be causally linked to expenditures. The number of students passing the CPA exam may be a desirable (and even readily quantifiable) objective of an accounting department. But increasing the department's budget will not necessarily lead to a measurable increase in the CPA exam pass rate.

  Contemporary forms of program budgeting recognize this limitation and focus mainly on outputs rather than outcomes. Thus, the budget request of an accounting department might key on the link between dollar expenditures and number of students served in total, or perhaps more specifically, number of places in CPA review classes, rather than on the number of students passing the exam.

- It may require extraordinary efforts to implement initially, but thereafter may be applied perfunctorily. When program budgeting is first instituted, budgetary units may have to establish objectives and outcome measures, develop new techniques of cost analysis, and adjust their accounting systems to conform to new budgetary classifications. Managers have to learn to prepare budget requests in new formats. Indeed, many of the benefits of program budgeting may be ascribed to the organizational self-examination that it requires at the outset. Once adopted, however, the organizational units can readily call up prior-year's budget requests on their word processors and merely change the numbers. The advantages of program budgeting can easily be lost if the budgeting process becomes nothing more than a mechanical exercise.

- It may be imposed by the organization's budgetary generals on their troops and thereby be resented by them. Governmental and not-for-profit folklore is replete with anecdotes of senior managers who attend seminars on new budgetary techniques and order that they be implemented immediately. Program budgeting requires the active participation and support of employees at all levels of the organization. Budget requests must be prepared by the parties responsible for individual activities. If program budgeting is to be successfully instituted, then senior-level managers must first convince the lower-level employees of its benefits.

- It may require easily overlooked "technical" adjustments to computer programs and other elements of the accounting and control systems. The required changes may be costly, may result in organizational confusion, and may delay implementation.

- It may present decision makers, especially in large organizations such as state and federal agencies, with so much information that they are overwhelmed by its sheer volume—and hence, likely to ignore much of it.

- It may not live up to the expectations of the participants in the budgetary process and thereby leave them cynical and discouraged. New forms of budgeting are typically promoted as an effort to bring "rationality" to the budget process. But what is rational to one person may be absurd to another. Indeed, to some *rationality* may imply an increase in resources for activities they favor. No widely reported upon empirical evidence suggests that program budgeting alters budgetary allocations. Budgeting is primarily a political process. Irrespective of the elegance or the logic of budgetary proposals, they are unlikely to turn liberals into conservatives or conservatives into liberals. Program budgeting might be useful in challenging the biases of both liberals and conservatives and encouraging them to look beyond the short-term interests of their immediate constituents. But no budgeting system, by itself, can be expected to diminish the influence of the politically powerful nor enhance that of the politically weak.

- The budgeting recommendations and rankings of program officials may be overridden by the ultimate decision makers. As a result, those who expended great effort in preparing their budget requests, only to have their advice ignored or rejected, may become cynical toward the entire budget process.

How should service efforts and accomplishments be reported?

If an organization is to tie its budgets to specific performance objectives, it follows that it should periodically report on the extent to which it has achieved those objectives. It should report upon results (Box 3 of Figure 14-1) and those results should be subject to audit (Box 4).

Leading accounting organizations disagree as to the extent to which information on performance measures should be incorporated into annual general purpose financial statements or other required supplementary reports that would be publicly available. Some say that measures of performance will necessarily be so subjective that they should be outside the scope of financial reporting. There is virtually no disagreement, however, that performance should be assessed and the results reported *within* organizations.

As noted in Chapter 1, the GASB established the following as one of the main objectives of financial reporting:

> "Financial reporting should provide information to assist users in assessing the service efforts costs and accomplishments of the governmental entity." This information helps users assess the government's "economy, efficiency, and effectiveness" and "may help form a basis for voting or funding decisions."[2]

In furtherance of this objective the GASB has conducted extensive research on **service efforts and accomplishment (SEA) indicators**. Most notably, it commissioned a series of studies on how they can be applied in twelve significant areas of state and local government (such as education, fire protection, and mass transit).[3]

These studies led the Board to issue a concepts statement, *Service Efforts and Accomplishment Reporting*, setting forth the criteria that SEA measures should meet.[4]

Although the concepts statement is intended to lay the foundation for the GASB to develop standards for reporting SEA measures to outsiders, for the most part it is

---

[2] Concepts Statement 1, *Objectives of Financial Reporting* (Norwalk, Conn. Governmental Accounting Standards Board, 1987). *Codification*, para. 77.

[3] For a summary of these studies, see *Service Efforts and Accomplishments Reporting: Its Time Has Come (An Overview)*, (Norwalk, Conn.: Governmental Accounting Standards Board, 1990).

[4] Concepts Statement No. 2, 1994.

equally relevant to measures that would be used within an organization. Therefore, this section of the text reflects many of the board's conclusions and recommendations.

Irrespective of whether the GASB should establish standards for SEA reporting, there are compelling reasons why organizations routinely should compile and incorporate performance measures into their management processes:

PERFORMANCE MEASURES

- Measuring and reporting upon performance promotes higher-order accountability among employees at all levels of the organization. Employees are put on notice explicitly that they are expected to achieve certain objectives—objectives that presumably are consistent with the organization's overall mission. Organizations make statements as to what is important by what they measure and report. Whereas traditional statements signal the significance of budgetary compliance and custodianship of resources, SEA reports stress the importance of achieving organizational objectives.

- SEA measures are consistent with both the purposes of financial reporting (both internal and external) and the nature of government and not-for-profit organizations. Financial reporting is intended to indicate the extent to which an organization achieves it objectives. The main objective of businesses is profit (or cash flow) maximization. Hence, their statements emphasize profitability and cash flow. The main objectives of governments and not-for-profits are to provide services, advocate a political or social cause, or carry out research or other activities for the betterment of their constituents. Therefore, reports on their accomplishments should be geared to those objectives.

- SEA reporting fosters sound budgeting and administration. As suggested in Figure 14-1, effective budgeting and administration requires information on the results of previous expenditures. Reports on performance indicate whether previously appropriated resources were used efficiently and effectively.

The GASB concepts statement divides SEA measures into three categories:

MAIN TYPES OF SEA INDICATORS

- **Measures of efforts**—the resources applied to a service (i.e., the *inputs*). Although the primary measure of effort is dollar cost, effort can also be expressed in nonfinancial metrics, such as number of personnel, amount of equipment, and amount of other capital assets (e.g., feet of floor space, or amount of land).

- **Measures of accomplishment**—what was provided and achieved with available inputs. These include both *outputs* and *outcomes* and reflect the organization's operational objectives.

- **Measures that relate efforts to accomplishment**—the GASB subdivides these measures into two categories: efficiency measures and cost–outcome measures.

Efficiency measures relate efforts (inputs) to outputs. Examples include cost per full-time student, cost per passenger-mile, and number of doctors per patient. Cost–outcome measures relate efforts (inputs) to outcomes. Examples include cost per student who passes the bar exam, cost per commuter that arrives at a destination within a specified time, and number of doctors per patient successfully treated.

The GASB concepts statement also emphasizes that these three types of data should be supplemented with explanatory information that can better help users understand the measures presented and put them in proper perspective. The explanatory information can be both quantitative and narrative. The quantitative information can include data on factors beyond the control of the entity, such as on population or the economy. It might include number of students from families below the poverty line or percentage of citizens by age grouping. The narrative information can interpret the data and indicate how the entity is responding to them.

The GASB concepts statement makes no reference to ZBB or other specific systems of program budgeting. It is no coincidence, however, that most variants of program budgeting also requires specification of inputs, outputs, and outcomes. Consistent with the theme of this chapter, both budgeting and assessment must be tied to organizational objectives.

Table 14–4 presents an example of SEA indicators of an Aid to Dependent Children program. Table 14–5 presents examples from a police department crime program.

TABLE 14–4
Service Efforts and Accomplishments
Examples of SEA Indicators—
Aid for Dependent Children Program*

Inputs
- Administrative cost of program
- Total cost
- Total staff-hours used to operate program

Outputs
- Total number of recipients
- Total amount of assistance provided

Outcomes
- Percentage of applications processed within 45 days
- Percentage of cases redetermined within 6 months
- Payment error rates
- Percentage of surveyed who meet predetermined levels of physical health
- Percentage of surveyed who live in adequate housing
- Percentage of grants reduced due to employment of parents
- Percentage of cases not reopened within two years

Efficiency Indicators
- Number of accurate case actions processed per worker
- Administrative cost per case
- Staff-hours per accurate case action

Explanatory Information
- Unemployment rate
- Number of cases per worker
- Percentage of working parent recipients
- Staffing problems

*Source: Adapted from S. Wagner, R. E. Brown, and J. B. Tinnin, "Public Assistance Programs" in *Service Efforts and Accomplishments Reporting: Its Time Has Come* (Norwalk, Conn.: Governmental Accounting Standards Board, 1990), p. 217.

TABLE 14–5
Service Efforts and Accomplishments
Examples of SEA Indicators—
Police Department*

Inputs

- Budget expenditures
- Equipment facilities, vehicles
- Number of personnel; hours expended

Outputs

- Hours of patrol
- Responses to calls for service
- Crimes investigated
- Number of arrests

Outcomes

- Deaths and bodily injury resulting from crime
- Value of property lost due to crime
- Crimes committed per 100,000 of population
- Percentage of crimes cleared
- Response time
- Citizen satisfaction

Efficiency Indicators

- Cost per case assigned
- Cost per crime cleared
- Personnel-hours per crime cleared

Explanatory Information

- Population by age
- Unemployment rate
- Percentage of population below poverty line
- Land area
- Number of calls for service

*****Source:** Adapted from A. Drebin and M. Brannon, "Police Department Programs," in *Service Efforts and Accomplishments Reporting: Its Time Has Come* (Norwalk, Conn.: Governmental Accounting Standards Board, 1990), p. 193.

LIMITATIONS

SEA measures also have obvious limitations. Some of these, along with means of overcoming them, are discussed here.

SEA measures, insofar as they are drawn from an entity's objectives, are unlikely to be any more indicative of the entity's true accomplishments than the stated objectives are of the entity's true goals. Moreover, they are silent as to whether the objectives, even if they are indicative of true goals, are really worth achieving and if they genuinely reflect the values of the organization's constituents. As they do in formulating objectives, organizations must be sure not to sacrifice measurement convenience for substance. Also, as suggested in the discussion of objectives, accomplishments can seldom be described by a single measure. Therefore, several measures may have to be provided.

SEA data may not provide sufficient information to enable meaningful comparisons among organizations, or units within the same organization, since they do not take into account different operating conditions. Consider the following examples of situations in which misleading inferences can easily be drawn:

- A school district uses results on standardized reading and mathematics tests to assess the performance of elementary schools. The scores, by themselves, provide no information on social, economic, and cultural differences in the composition of the schools' student bodies—differences that almost certainly affect test scores.

- A sanitation department measures the efficiency of its several districts as cost per ton of trash collected. The metric fails to take into account district differences in the average distances between homes and in the percentage of the customers that are businesses rather than residences.

Similarly, even comparisons over time within the same organization can be deceptive in the face of changing conditions. The efficiency of a job placement service, as measured by the ratio of clients to placements, may appear to decline as the result of a downturn in the local economy, a factor beyond the control of the service. The failure of SEA measures, by themselves, to take into account differences in circumstances can be mitigated by supplementing the quantitative data with narrative explanations of factors that influence the measures.

SEA data, especially if presented in numerous and lengthy tables, can be mind-numbing. In some circumstances, charts and graphs can more sharply spotlight organizational or temporal differences. At the same time, however, graphs and charts can easily be used to mislead. For example, on a line graph, changes from one year to the next can be made to appear greater by altering the scales of either the horizontal or vertical axis.

SEA data can easily be under- or over-aggregated. A recent study of performance data in four countries revealed that members of parliament did not use the data to the extent anticipated. The members complained that the reports they received failed to provide the "right" amount of information and that they lacked the time or staff assistance to properly interpret them.[5] Level of detail must be tailored to the user. Governing boards, for example would ordinarily benefit most from data that are more aggregated and summarized than those provided to department managers.

AUDITS OF SEA REPORTS

The role of auditors in attesting to reports on service efforts and accomplishments can be similar to that in expressing an opinion on traditional financial statements. If the service efforts and accomplishments can be measured and reported upon, then the measurements can be verified and the reports attested to. In fact, the AICPA now has separate standards for attesting to nonfinancial assertions. They have formed the basis for auditor opinions on matters as diverse as the circulation of newspapers and the distance traveled by golf balls.[6]

As they are in traditional financial engagements, auditors could be required to assess the adequacy of the information systems used to compile the SEA data, to verify that the data are reliable, and to evaluate whether they are fairly presented. This would require that they review the organization's internal control systems and test selected transactions. The auditing profession has not, as yet, developed guidelines and standards as to what constitutes fair presentation of the data and as to how the data should be examined and the underlying information systems tested. It will, of course, have to do so if auditors are to expand the scope of their engagements to cover SEA data. However, by developing standards as to what constitutes fair presentation, it runs the risk of intruding on the judgments and values of elected officials in determining what aspects of performance are important in their jurisdictions.

---

[5] U.S. General Accounting Office, *Managing for Results, Experiences Abroad Suggest Insights for Federal Management Reforms* (GAO/GAD 95–120), 1995. The four countries were Australia, Canada, New Zealand, and the United Kingdom.

[6] See the series of AICPA professional standards, *Statements on Standards for Attestation Engagements*.

Auditors cannot be expected to assess the appropriateness of either the organization's basic objectives or indicators selected to gauge whether they have been achieved. That, as stressed earlier, is the function of legislatures, governing boards, or other policy makers.

Auditing the performance of an entity is far more complex than merely expressing an opinion on organization-prepared SEA reports. "Performance" audits will be discussed in greater detail in Chapter 15.

HOW ARE CAPITAL EXPENDITURES PLANNED AND BUDGETED WITHIN A FRAMEWORK OF OPERATIONAL OBJECTIVES?

Both government and not-for-profit organizations shape their futures through their acquisitions of capital assets. Capital assets may not only be costly, but they may have long lives and have a long-term impact on both operating costs and results. By purchasing or constructing capital assets, organizations make commitments of resources that can generally be revoked only with substantial economic penalty.

In Chapter 1 it was noted that a key difference between businesses and not-for-profits, including governments, is that the latter make significant investments in assets that neither produce revenues nor reduce expenditures. Accordingly, the analysis of proposed outlays may be far more complex and difficult in not-for-profits than in businesses.

In business the general approach to determining whether to acquire an asset (or undertake a project) is to compare the cash outflows associated with the asset (the costs) with the cash inflows or savings that it will provide (the benefits). However, cash has a *time value*, and both the outflows and inflows may occur over a number of years. Therefore, to make the inflows and outflows comparable, they must be *discounted* back to the present. This general approach is consistent with the objective of a business—to maximize net cash flows.

Governments and not-for-profits have objectives other than maximizing net cash flows. Accordingly, they must take an approach to capital budgeting that relates the costs of a proposed acquisition to fulfillment of their own unique goals and operational objectives.

DIFFERENCES BETWEEN CAPITAL AND OPERATING EXPENDITURES

It is widely accepted that interperiod equity dictates that capital assets may be financed and paid for differently than operating expenditures. Capital assets provide benefits over more than one year. Hence, it is asserted, they should be paid for by the taxes—and the taxpayers—of more than one year. It therefore may be not only acceptable, but desirable, to finance capital acquisitions with debt rather than with taxes or other operating revenues. To do otherwise would strongly discourage investment in long-term projects, because in the year of acquisition they may necessitate a significant one-time increase in taxes or decreases in other expenditures.

Insofar as capital projects will be financed with debt rather than operating revenues, it is especially important that they be budgeted and planned for separately. The amount of debt that an organization can issue is almost always limited, either by legal debt limitations or fiscal prudence. Accordingly, a project to be financed with debt must compete for funds, not with all other activities, but only with the others that will be financed out of the same pool of resources.

Separate budgeting and planning also enables an organization's managers and constituents to focus more sharply upon capital outlays; to narrow their attention to a subset of all expenditures. In that way they decrease the likelihood of misguided expenditures—mistakes the entity will have to live with for many years.

CAPITAL IMPROVEMENT PROGRAMS AND BUDGETS

Just as an operating budget, when approved, authorizes operating expenditures, a capital budget sanctions capital outlays. Because of their cost, their longevity and the long lead time required for financing as well as purchase or construction, capital expenditures are usually planned for over a period of at least five or six years. An entity's long-term schedule of capital acquisitions is conventionally termed its **capital improvement program (CIP)**.

Most entities define capital assets as physical properties (almost always above a specified dollar amount). Capital budgets and improvement programs are commonly associated with infrastructure assets, such as buildings, roads, airports, and utilities, and with major items of equipment, such as emergency communication systems, construction equipment, and mainframe computers. However, some organizations also include within the scope of their capital budgets projects other than physical assets—such as toxic clean-ups—that require major outlays and will provide benefits over many years.

Capital budgeting and programming are generally carried out in two stages. In the first, individual projects are screened to determine whether they should be undertaken at all, assuming that the resources will be available to fund them. As part of this stage, the organization compares alternative means of achieving the same objective (e.g., lease or purchase office space) and selects that which will be the most cost-effective. The essence of this stage is **benefit—cost analysis**. The second stage is that of ranking the projects that pass through the initial screen.

BENEFIT–COST ANALYSIS

Benefit–cost analysis is nothing more than a generic term for any form of expenditure analysis that identifies and quantifies the benefits of a proposal and compares them to its costs. In business, the benefits are cash flows; in government and not-for-profits they should be drawn from the entities' own operational objectives. By requiring that the benefits be explicitly identified and quantified, organizations help assure that they are consistent with their own operational objectives and overall mission.

Benefit–cost analysis has often been misused and subjected to ridicule as analysts go overboard in attempting to assign numbers to benefits that are not readily quantifiable. However, to the extent that benefits can be quantified, it provides a reasonable means of deciding whether an asset should be acquired or a project should be undertaken and of ranking competing proposals. Benefit-cost analysis may be used to enhance the objectivity of decision-making. By no means can it eliminate the role of informed judgment, and it should not be used to give the appearance of mathematical precision when such rigor is unjustifiable.

Benefits Are Cash Savings

As stressed in Chapter 13, many types of not-for-profit decisions are comparable to those in businesses and thus are amenable to business-type analysis. Proposed capital acquisitions may affect mainly the cost of achieving desired outcomes, not their quality or quantity. Therefore, the potential benefits of many capital assets or long-term projects can be expressed as cash savings and can be assessed by standard discounting procedures.

The benefits and costs of a project must always be assessed over its entire life cycle. Some assets may be relatively cheap to repair. Over time, however, key parts may have to be replaced, repaired, or overhauled. These costs must be taken into account, especially when selecting among alternatives.

EXAMPLE *Benefits Are Cash Savings*

The Food for the Elderly Center currently relies on a private messenger service to deliver meals to its clients. The cost per year is $20,000. The center is considering acquiring a van and engaging a driver to deliver the meals. The price of the vehicle, to be paid in cash at time of acquisition, is $26,000. Annual estimated operating costs, including insurance, maintenance, repairs, and the wages and benefits of the required part-time driver, are expected to be $12,000. Thus, the center would save $8,000 per year in annual operating costs (the $20,000 cost of the messenger service less the $12,000 in anticipated costs). The estimated useful life of the van is five years. The center uses a discount rate of 10 percent to assess all long-term proposals.

Per the following analysis, the center should accept the proposal:

Annual Anticipated Cash Savings for Five Years:	$ 8,000
Present Value of an Annuity of $1 @10 Percent for Five Years	× 3.7908
Present Value of Annual Benefits (Annual Cash Aavings)	30,326
Less: Cost of Vehicle (Present Value)	26,000
Present Value of Net Cash Savings	$ 4,326

The benefits exceed the costs by $4,326.

It is often useful in comparing the benefits of two or more competing options, especially if projects require initial investments of differing amounts, to express the relationship of cost to benefits (net of all post-acquisition costs) as a ratio:

$$\text{Benefit–cost ratio} = \frac{\text{Present value of net annual benefits}}{\text{Initial investment}}$$

Thus, in this example: $\dfrac{\$30,326}{\$26,000} = 1.16$

Having calculated the quantifiable net benefits of an acquisition, the organization's managers must then weigh them against factors that cannot easily be reduced to numbers. In this example, these might include the potential for improvement (or deterioration) in the quality of delivery service and the risks of unanticipated repair costs.

Of course, as anyone who has studied capital expenditure analysis in other contexts is aware, the computations can be far more complex than is suggested by the example. The example, however, is intended merely to demonstrate that a systematic, discounted cash-flow approach to capital expenditure analysis, is as applicable to governments and not-for-profits as to businesses.

Benefits Are the Same Among Options

Benefit–cost analysis, including present value techniques, is obviously easier to apply when, as in the previous example, the benefits are mainly cash savings rather than gains that are less tangible. But it can also be utilized in circumstances, of which there are many, in which an organization has to select among two or more options, each of will provide the same benefits. For if the benefits are the same, they need not be taken into account.

EXAMPLE   *Choosing Between Options with Similar Benefits*

City Transit, a public authority, is required by its charter to assure that its services are available to mobility-impaired city residents. It is considering three options:

- Install special equipment on selected buses to enable wheel-chair bound passengers to board the vehicles. Installation costs would be $10 million, to be incurred in the current year. Thereafter, maintenance and repair costs would be covered by state and federal grants.

- Purchase and operate a fleet of special transit vans. The initial cost would be $2.5 million. Estimated maintenance, repair, and other operating costs, including the wages of drivers, would be $1.8 million.

- Distribute vouchers to eligible passengers enabling them to use private taxis for a specified number of rides per month. Estimated cost would be $2.4 million per year.

The economic life of both the special equipment and the vans is expected to be five years and is therefore a reasonable period over which to assess the three options. The authority uses a discount rate of 10 percent to evaluate all capital proposals. The following analysis compares the three options:

	Cash Outflow (Thousands)	Present Value of an Annuity of $1 @10%	Present Value of Cash Flow (Thousands)
Option #1, Special Equipment			
Period 0	$10,000	$1.0000	$10,000
Option #2, Acquisition of Vans			
Period 0	$ 2,500	$1.0000	$ 2,500
Periods 1–5	1,800	3.7908	6,823
Total			$9,323
Option #3, Taxis			
Periods 1–5	$ 2,400	$3.7908	$9,098

Based on the present value of the costs and assuming the benefits of all three options to be the same, the authority would select the third option, that of giving taxi vouchers to eligible passengers. It would result in the cash outflows with the least present value.

This example is intended mainly to demonstrate the applicability of present value analysis to circumstances in which the benefits of the options cannot be expressed in monetary units but nevertheless are similar. But it can also be used to highlight two of the inherent limitations of present value analysis.

First, present value analysis may be sensitive to the choice of discount rate. The following analysis replicates the previous one, except that it incorporates a discount rate of 6 percent rather than 10 percent. Note that the order of preference of the three options is reversed. The installation of special equipment is now the least costly.

	Cash Outflow (Thousands)	Present Value of an Annuity of $1 @6%	Present Value of Cash Flow (Thousands)
Option #1, Special Equipment			
Period 0	$10,000	$1.0000	$10,000
Option #2, Acquisition of Vans			
Period 0	$2,500	$1.0000	$ 2,500
Periods 1–5	1,800	4.2124	7,582
Total			$10,082
Option #3, Taxis			
Periods 1–5	$2,400	$4.2124	$10,110

Second, even though the benefits of the options may be similar, they are unlikely to be identical. In the illustration, for example, transportation by taxi as opposed to public buses embodies a very different set of advantages and disadvantages (both physical and psychological) for the affected passengers. Thus, the analysis, which compares only present value of dollar outflows may fail to take into account costs and benefits that are difficult even to describe, let alone measure—factors that, especially in a political environment, are crucial to an ultimate decision.

Benefits Differ among Options

Because of their very purpose, governments and not-for-profit organizations undertake projects that are intended to extend the length, or enhance the quality, of human lives. Moreover, they must make decisions in which the benefits of available options will not be the same.

Benefit–cost analysis requires that costs be compared to benefits. Since they can be compared only when expressed in common terms, organizations must come to grips with the monetary value of human life or various aspects of the quality of human life.

Although it is never easy—nor analytically satisfactory—to place a dollar value on human lives or happiness, both governments and not-for-profit organizations (and their constituents) must constantly do so, either implicitly or explicitly. A decision to purchase an additional ambulance involves a tacit comparison of the cost of the ambulance with the value of the human lives it might save or suffering it might reduce.

One widely used approach to placing an economic value on human life is grounded on future earning capacity. Estimated future earnings of the individuals affected by a proposed program are discounted back to the present. Courts, for example, generally base wrongful death damages on the victim's anticipated earnings. Thus, the life of a 25-year-old medical student is considered far more valuable than that of a 50-year-old homemaker. Similarly, as illustrated in the In Practice, the cost of illnesses is measured as the number of work years lost, both because of temporary disability or death.

An obvious objection to these approaches is that they recognize only the income associated with human life, not the costs. The longer humans live, the more they consume. Moreover, it places no value on dimensions of human existence other than earning power—e.g., that of noncompensatory services, such as housekeeping, and of the emotional support, love, and affection that people provide to others.

Monetization of costs and benefits not only facilities analysis, but serves as a reminder that as long as resources are limited, human life cannot be considered "priceless." Nevertheless, it runs the same risk as quantifying an organization's

IN PRACTICE

Mortality costs are the present value of lifetime earnings lost by all who died in 1985 due to ADM disorders. This cost is the product of the number of ADM deaths and the expected value of future earnings with gender and age taken into account. This method takes into consideration life expectancy at the age of death, changing patterns of earnings at successive ages, varying labor force participation rates, imputed value for housekeeping services, and a 6 percent discount rate to convert aggregate earnings over a lifetime to its present worth.

In 1985, 140,593 people died from ADM disorders—94,765 alcohol abuse deaths, 39,707 mental illness deaths, and 6,118 drug abuse deaths. Included are all deaths for which the underlying cause is coded as alcohol abuse, drug abuse, or mental illness. For alcohol abuse, alcohol-related deaths are included in which alcohol is implicated as a contributing cause of death. For example, about half the deaths due to motor vehicle traffic accidents, two-fifths of deaths from falls, fires, and burns, and three-tenths of drownings are estimated to involve alcohol. Almost all suicides (87 percent) are classified as mental illness suicides; the remaining 13 percent are classified as alcohol-related deaths.

These 140,593 deaths result in almost 4 million person-years lost, or 28 years per death. These deaths represent a loss of $35.8 billion to the economy at a 6 percent discount rate, or $254,716 per death.

For the 94,984 men who died from ADM disorder, an estimated 2.8 million person-years are lost, 29 years per death, valued at $28.6 billion, or $301,566 per death. The 45,608 women who died represent a loss of 1.2 million years, or 26 years per death. Because of the fewer deaths and lower earnings of women, losses are significantly lower than for men, amounting to a total of $7.2 billion, or $157,145 per death. Thus, men account for 68 percent of the ADM deaths, 70 percent of the person-years lost, and 80 percent of the productivity losses for 1985.

Many people who die of ADM disorders are relatively young—38 percent of the victims are aged 15–44. The total of life years lost for this age group, a function of both age and number of deaths, represents 61 percent of the person-years lost to ADM disorders. In terms of lost earnings, this age group accounts for 74 percent of the total. By contrast, 35 percent of ADM deaths are persons 65 years and over, accounting for 12 percent of person-years lost and only 2 percent of productivity losses.

ADM deaths comprise 7 percent of the 2.1 million deaths in the United States in 1985, 12 percent of the total person-years lost, and 20 percent of the total productivity losses.

ADM deaths comprise a disproportionately larger share of deaths at the younger age groups. Almost half, 46 percent, of all ADM deaths are aged 15–24 years, and 30 percent are aged 25–44.

Source: Dorothy P. Rice, Sander Kelman, Leonard S. Miller, and Sarah Dunmeyer, *The Economic Costs of Alcohol and Drug Abuse and Mental Illness: 1985.* Report submitted to the Office of Financing and Coverage Policy of the Alcohol, Drug Abuse, and Mental Health Administration, U.S. Department of Health and Human Services (San Francisco, Calif. Institute for Health and Aging, University of California, 1990). The report also includes an extensive discussion of the methods of estimating economic costs of illnesses, including a review of the relevant literature.

objectives and accomplishments—that of misspecifying the true benefits of a proposal and of thereby promoting decisions that are inconsistent with the true goals of the organization and the values of its constituents. As observed earlier, merely because an outcome can be measured does not make it meaningful.

Ranking assets or projects is never easy. Since all general obligation debt is issued in the name of a government or organization, not its subunits, projects from all divisions must be combined into a common ordering. For obvious reasons, there are no clear-cut criteria that are suitable for comparing projects as diverse as highways and jails. Nevertheless, institutions attempt to discern common denominators. For example, one state government (Massachusetts) assigns general rankings as following:

RANKING PROPOSED CAPITAL ACQUISITIONS

1. needed for legal compliance (e.g., court mandated)
2. needed to preserve an existing facility
3. needed to promote operational efficiency
4. needed to promote additions to capital stock[7]

   Others establish systems that require each program to be scored on a variety of criteria. For a government, these may include:

- benefit–cost ratio
- impact on the economy, including number of jobs and sales to be generated (both directly and indirectly)
- impact on the government's costs and revenues to the extent they are incorporated in the benefit–cost ratio
- proportion of population that will benefit
- effect on environment
- extent of inconvenience and disruptions during construction
- effect on health and safety

If a government or not-for-profit has established the total amount of costs it is willing to incur for capital expenditures, then, as with ZBB, it will undertake all projects the cumulative sum of which is less than the determined maximum. But as with operating expenditures, the process of ranking is seldom as objective as might appear from benefit–cost ratios or other numerical scores assigned to projects. Capital budgeting, no less than operating budgeting, is a political process in which various constituencies and interest groups vie for available resources. In the end, therefore, many organizations make at least some of their capital budgeting decisions the old-fashioned way—by subjective (albeit, hopefully, informed) judgment.

As noted earlier, capital budgets and improvement programs enable an organization's managers and constituents to sharpen their focus upon capital outlays. The downside, however, is that they run the risk of failing to account for the operating and maintenance costs associated with the newly acquired assets.

   As was noted in Chapter 1, many government and not-for-profit assets have more of the characteristics of liabilities than of assets. They provide no cash inflow, yet they

THE DOWNSIDE OF EVALUATING CAPITAL SPENDING SEPARATELY FROM OPERATIONAL SPENDING

---

[7] John L. Mikesell, *Fiscal Administration, Analysis and Applications for the Public Sector*, 4th ed., (Belmont, Calif.: Wadsworth, 1995), p. 225.

must be serviced and maintained. The cost of a capital asset—that which is incorporated in a capital budget—is comparable to the hospital bill for a newborn child. It may be just the tip of a fiscal iceberg. Roads and highways are not only in need of ongoing repair, they must be patroled by police. University buildings must be heated and air-conditioned. Indeed, when proponents of major capital projects, such as sports arenas and convention centers, assure voters that the ventures will "pay for themselves" through leases payments, fees, and added sales tax revenues, they often fail to make mention of the added operating costs, such as for police, fire protection, and administration.

The risk of overlooking operating and maintenance costs can be minimized by explicitly incorporating into the benefit–cost analysis of all proposed projects an itemization of anticipated additional operating costs. Moreover, procedures can be established so when the capital budget is approved, the additional operating costs are automatically added to the operating budget. Table 14–6 presents an excerpt from the capital budget of Columbus, Georgia. Note how the impact on operating expenditures is highlighted.

TABLE 14–6
An Excerpt from a Capital Budget Emphasizing Impact of Additional Operating Costs

New County Jail

Project Description: A new 576-bed prison facility will be constructed in the same vicinity as the current facility. The new prison, housing state prisoners, will replace a 40+-year-old 256-bed prison. The old prison—which houses fewer than 30 county prisoners today—will then be remodeled as an annex for the county jail.

	Prior	FY 95	FY 96	Total
Financing Method				
Direct Revenue				
Grants	$447,000	$7,500,000		$7,947,000
PAA Fund		185,000		185,000
Other CIP Fund Sources				
Balance Forward		389,602	$3,309,700	3,699,302
GF CIP Reallocation	9,700	0		9,700
Total	$456,700	$8,074,602	$3,309,700	$8,141,000
Project Cost				
Land				
Land Improvements		$120,000		$120,000
ROW/Easements				
Legal				
Arch/Eng/CM	$67,098	379,902		447,000
Demolition				
Utility Relocation		100,000		100,000
Road Construction		85,000		85,000
General Construction		4,080,000	2,800,000	6,880,000
Landscaping			9,700	9,700
Public Art Element				
Furnishing/Equipment			500,000	500,000
Administrative				
Total	$67,098	$4,764,902	$3,309,700	$8,141,700
Balance	$389,602	$3,309,700	$ 0	$ 0

(continued)

TABLE 14-6
An Excerpt from a Capital Budget Emphasizing Impact of Additional Operating Costs (Continued)

Benefit to the Community: The Consolidated Government uses inmate labor extensively to offset operating costs in such areas as parks maintenance and waste management. The new prison will add 320 inmates to our "labor pool." Additionally, the old facility will be converted into a county jail annex, providing inexpensive additional beds for county inmates.

Impact on Operating Budget: Using state-of-the-art design methods and theory devised to optimize human resource requirements, the new prison should reduce the operating deficit by increasing revenue potential by increasing the number of prisoners (for which the City receives a per diem). Associated operating costs are expected to increase at a slower rate relative to operating revenues. These actions are expected to decrease the FY 95 projected $430,000 operating deficit by half in future years. The additional inmate labor provided will help to offset anticipate parks' maintenance costs increases due to sales tax supported projects.

SUMMARY

Accountants have a role to play in all phases of the management cycle in governments and not-for-profits: programing and budgeting; appropriating funds; administering; auditing and assessing.

Operational objectives should be the basis for allocating resources, managing day-to-day activities, and distributing rewards and reprimands. Ideally, operational objectives should represent true ends, capture outcomes, be measurable within a sufficiently short period, and be precise. However, in practice, owing to measurement difficulties, many entities express their objectives as outputs rather than outcomes. Moreover, most organizations find that they require multiple objectives to express fully their missions.

Organizations face significant obstacles in establishing operational objectives that facilitate, rather than detract from, their ability to accomplish their missions. In some cases organizations are not clear as to the results they want to achieve or are unable to distinguish results from the means of accomplishing them. In others, the objectives provoke conflict among employees and other constituents or encourage dysfunctional behavior.

Traditional budgets provide no information about the extent to which expenditures advance an entity's mission or enable it to achieve its objectives. By contrast program budgeting helps to ensure that all expenditures are justified in relation to organizational objectives. It encourages consideration of alternative ways of achieving the same objective and of whether the objective is even appropriate for the organization. Further, it helps to assure that the behavior of costs is explicitly taken into account and that programs or activities that have outlived their usefulness are replaced with those that would do more to advance the organization's mission.

Although, ideally, program budgets should link costs to outcomes, in reality increases in costs can not always be causally associated with improvements in outcomes. Therefore, many entities have found it more practical to tie costs to outputs rather than outcomes.

If governments and other not-for-profits are to budget so as to achieve specific performance objectives, it follows that they should report on the extent to which they have achieved those objectives. That is, they must provide information about their service efforts and accomplishments. This information should encompass inputs, outputs, and outcomes. SEA reporting is consistent with the GASB's objectives of reporting, and it promotes higher-order accountability, sound budgeting and forward-looking administration.

Governments and not-for-profits shape their destiny through the acquisition of capital assets, which are not only costly but have long lives. Therefore, the acquisition of capital assets requires commitments that can generally be revoked only with substantial economic penalty. Capital budgeting is usually carried out in two steps: screening (of which benefit–cost analysis is a key aspect) and ranking.

Benefit–cost analysis is a generic term for procedures in which the benefits of a project are compared to its costs. It is a means of assuring that as many benefits and costs as feasible are explicitly identified and quantified. For many decisions the benefits are cost savings. For others, the benefits remain constant irrespective of the means of achieving them. In both these situations the standard discounted cash flow models that are widely used in business can be used to assess whether a project should be undertaken. In other situations, those in which the costs and benefits are intangible, such as number of lives lost or saved, the costs or benefits may be expressed in dollar terms so as to facilitate comparisons.

One of the disadvantages of evaluating capital expenditures apart from operating expenditures is that it is easy to overlook the operating costs associated with newly acquired assets. To assure that these costs are taken into account, organizations should develop procedures that automatically incorporate estimated operating costs in the capital expenditure analysis and correspondingly add them to the expenditures of the operating budget.

EXERCISE FOR REVIEW AND SELF-STUDY

The subway system of a major U.S. city has several overall goals. These include:

- serving a broad segment of society
- providing on-time service
- providing frequent service
- assuring that passengers are safe
- assuring that the environment in which passengers travel, including trains and stations, are clean and pleasant.

a. For each of these goals propose at least *two operational objectives*.

b. Suppose that the system is to report on its service efforts and accomplishments. Propose at least two *input*, *output*, *outcome* and *efficiency* indicators relating to the goal that trains and stations are clean and pleasant.

c. The system is considering enhancing safety at selected stations by installing TV cameras, emergency call boxes, and more modern lights and by making minor structural changes at selected stations. It estimates the cost to be $400,000 per station. In addition, it forecasts that it would be required to spend approximately $30,000 per year to monitor, maintain, and repair the new equipment. It estimates that the useful life of the equipment would be 10 years. The system assesses all proposed capital expenditures using a discount rate of 12 percent. It estimates that the improvements would reduce crime by 10 percent.

1. Based on this limited amount of information is it possible to determine whether the expenditure is economically advantageous?

2. Suppose, instead, the system decided that safety must be enhanced. The alternative to the physical improvements is to provide additional police protection at each station. The cost of the additional police would be approximately $110,000 per year. Taking into account this additional information, is the expenditure on the physical improvements advantageous?

3. If the system were to approve the capital outlays, what changes would have to be made to its *operating* budget?

QUESTIONS FOR REVIEW AND DISCUSSION

1. Indicate four significant criteria that "operational objectives" should satisfy.

2. Why may an organization foment conflict merely by establishing specific objectives?

3. In what key way do program budgets more directly link expenditures to organizational goals than do conventional object classification budgets?

4. What are the key elements of program budgets as exemplified by a zero-base budget decision package for an activity?

5. The ultimate aim of governmental and not-for-profit organizations is to produce *outcomes*. Yet in preparing program budgets, many organizations link expenditures to *outputs* rather than outcomes. Why?

6. Why is it more important for governments and not-for-profit organizations than for businesses to report on service efforts and accomplishments?

7. What are the three main categories of SEA indicators?

8. Describe at least three limitations, both actual and potential, of SEA indicators and tell how they might be overcome.

9. Why is it advantageous to budget for capital outlays apart from operating expenditures?

10. What are the advantages of "monetizing" the value of human lives (often said to be "priceless") in assessing the costs and benefits of a proposed project or activity? What is the most widely used basis for valuing human lives? What are the limitations of this basis?

EXERCISES

14-1

Programs budget more closely tie expenditures to organizational objectives.

The "object classification" budget of a police department includes the following expense categories:

> Salaries
>
> Employee benefits
>
> Supplies
>
> Equipment
>
> Vehicle maintenance, gas, etc.
>
> Dues and subscriptions

Based on your layman's knowledge of the operations of a police department, indicate five or six categories that would likely appear if the budget were recast in program format.

14-2

Organizations should consider desired outputs as well as outcomes.

For each of the following organizations, propose at least one measure of outputs and two of outcomes.

1. The admissions office of a selective private college
2. The sales tax division of a city government
3. A private foundation that provides college scholarships to economically disadvantaged students
4. A municipal housing authority that makes loans to low-income families so as to encourage home ownership
5. The Parkinson Disease Information Service, a not-for-profit organization that provides information to Parkinson patients and their families

14-3

Average costs generally contribute little to the budget process.

The Pleasant Valley School District, which leases its buses from a private transportation company, has determined that the direct costs of operating a bus (including rental fees, driver, and fuel) is $40,000 per year. The district currently operates 30 buses, each of which provides service to 90 children—hence, to a total of 2,700 children. The district also incurs $350,000 per year in fixed costs relating to transportation.

a. Calculate the average cost per child of providing bus transportation.

b. The district expects that next year it will have to provide transportation for an additional 300 children— a total of 3,000.

1. Based on average cost, how much additional cost should the district budget?
2. How much additional costs do *you* think the district should budget?

c. Suppose that the district expects that it will have to provide transportation for another 60 children in addition to the 300—a total of 360. How much more should it budget for the additional 60 children?

14-4

Conventional capital budgeting techniques are a useful starting point for investment decisions.

The Metropolitan Housing Authority is charged with providing housing to low-income residents. The authority is currently assessing two options, each of which would provide homes for 100 families.

Under the first option the authority would construct an apartment building at a cost of $8 million. Tenants would rent their apartments from the authority at subsidized rates. The authority estimates that its net annual cash operating costs (after taking into account the rent paid by the tenants) would be $300,000 per year. The expected useful life of the building would be 20 years.

Under the second option, the authority would make direct cash assistance payments to the tenants and they would arrange for their own housing. The expected annual payment to each family would be $12,000 per year—a total of $1,200,000 per year for 100 families.

The authority evaluates all capital projects using a discount rate of 8 percent.

a. Based on the limited information provided, which option would be the more cost-effective?

b. What other financial or nonfinancial factors should the authority consider in selecting between the two options.

14-5

Benefit–cost ratios may be useful in assessing the benefits of capital investments.

Antonio County is assessing whether it should build a new correctional facility for nonviolent offenders. Currently offenders are housed in the county jail at a cost of approximately $52,000 per year.

The new facility would cost $4 million to construct. However, inasmuch as inmates would be housed in dormitories rather than cells and the need for supervision would be reduced, the cost per inmate could be reduced to $43,000 per year.

The county estimates that if the new facility were constructed, it could accommodate 100 inmates who would otherwise be housed in the jail.

The county assesses all capital projects using a discount rate of 8 percent and uses a time horizon of 10 years to evaluate proposals, such as that for the new facility, for which useful lives are indeterminate.

a. Determine the present value of the net savings that would result from undertaking the proposed project.

b. Calculate a benefit–cost ratio. Based on the limited amount of data provided, should the project be undertaken? Explain.

PROBLEMS

14-1

Object classification budgets can be recast to "program-type" budgets in which expenditures are tied to objectives.

The "object classification" budget of a fire department includes the following expense categories:

- salaries
- employee benefits
- supplies
- equipment
- station maintenance, utilities, etc.
- vehicle maintenance, gas, etc.
- dues and subscriptions

Based on your layman's knowledge of the operations of a fire department, indicate three categories that the department's budget might include if it were recast in "program" format. For each category indicate the following:

a. An appropriate operational objective

b. Possible measures of inputs, outputs, and outcomes

14-2

Inputs, outputs, and outcomes are not always readily distinguishable.

The following are selected measures of service efforts and accomplishments that might be appropriate for a university. For each, indicate whether it is an *input*, *output*, or *outcome* and state the objective with which it would most likely be associated. If it could be more than one, explain why. (For example, number and amount of research grants could be either an input or outcome associated with the objective of increasing the quality and quantity of research. Research grants are given as a reward for past research accomplishments and are therefore an outcome of a successful research program. At the same time, they facilitate research to be conducted in the future and are thereby an input).

1. Tuition revenues
2. Number of students enrolled

3. Number and percentage of students passing the CPA exam
4. Number of articles published by faculty in specified "top tier" journals
5. Scholastic Aptitude Test scores
6. Graduate Record Exam scores
7. Revenues generated by a football program

14-3

Budgets—whether zero-base or any other type—should relate costs to objectives and take into account the actual behavior of costs

Vision for Kids, a clinic funded by the Community Health Plan, a not-for-profit agency, provides eye examinations, eye glasses, and eye-related medical care for children from low-income families. Children are referred to it by school nurses and teachers, physicians, and social workers on the basis of poor performance on a vision screening test.

In its current year, Vision for Kids expects to serve 6,200 children. It will give each child an examination and, if needed, issue a pair of glasses. On average, one pair of glasses is issued for each child, since only children who failed the screening test are referred to the clinic, and some children lose or break their glasses after they have been issued.

The total budget for the current year is $942,000, broken down as follows:

Director	$ 75,000
Ophthalmologist (One Full-Time)	140,000
Optometrists (2 @ 70,000)	140,000
Secretaries (2 @ $30,000)	60,000
Technician	35,000
Nurses (2 @ $40,000)	80,000
Glasses (6,200 @ $60)	372,000
Drugs and Other Supplies	15,000
Other Operating Costs	25,000
	$942,000

Vision for Kids' ability to serve patients is limited by available funds. Were the resources available, it could easily serve twice as many patients. It receives all funds from its parent organization.

The ophthalmologist examines only those children referred to him by one of the optometrists. He is currently examining and treating the maximum number of patients in the available time (approximately 1,300—one out of every four children served by the center). The director estimates, however, that the organization would be able to hire an additional ophthalmologist on a one-quarter-time basis for $30,000 per year.

The director has also determined the following:

- An additional secretary would have to be added when the number of patients reaches 8,000.

- The currently employed ophthalmologist and two optometrists would not accept less than full-time employment. In light of their extensive experience, it would be uneconomical in the long-run to reduce their appointments to less than full time and replace them with part-time personnel (except, of course as a last resort). By contrast, one of the nurses has indicated a willingness to drop down to either three-quarter time or half-time status.

- Additional nurses and ophthalmologists can be added in quarter-time increments. Optometrists can be added only in half-time increments.

- Each optometrist can handle 3,200 patients per year; additional optometrists can be hired on a one-half time basis for $30,000.

- Each nurse can also serve 3,200 patients; nurses can be hired on a quarter-time basis for $10,000.

- The technician can handle at least 10,000 additional patients.

- Variable cost per patient is $64, determined as follows:

Glasses	$60
Drugs and Other Supplies	2
Other Operating Costs	2
Total Variable Costs	$64

The staff has submitted requests for many small items of equipment totaling $50,000 in costs. Although this equipment would not enable the clinic to serve additional patients, it would improve their care.

Prepare a zero-based decision package to be submitted to Vision for Kids parent organization. Consider Vision for Kids to be an activity that is part of a children's health care program. Funding should be requested at the following levels, in addition to the current level:

- 90 percent ($847,800) of the current level
- 105 percent ($989,100) of the current level
- 120 percent ($1,130,400)

These percentage levels, however, should be interpreted only as approximations. If a major increase in efficiency (e.g., cost per unit of outcome) could be effected by operating at a level slightly greater or less than those specified, then the request should be at that level. Similarly, if all funds up to the stated level could not be used productively, then a lesser amount should be requested.

Based on your own judgment provide output and outcome measures, alternative means of carrying out the activity and consequences of not performing the activity.

14-4

Successful outcomes may not necessarily be indicative of effective performance, especially when considered in isolation of factors beyond an organization's control.

The Education Agency of one of the nation's most populous states evaluates public *elementary schools* on the basis of the following inputs and outcomes:

Outcomes

- total campus attendance
- average student scores on standardized tests in math, reading and writing

Inputs

- total number of students enrolled
- average teacher salary
- average teacher experience
- total number of teachers employed in regular education
- total number of teachers employed in special education
- average instructional expenditure per student
- total number of economically disadvantaged students
- total number of limited English proficiency students

The inputs and outputs are factored together to obtain an overall performance rating.

a. Comment on these criteria as a basis for evaluating the performance of elementary schools.

b. Can you propose a means of improving upon these criteria?

14-5

Program-type budgets may not be as management friendly as they may initially appear—especially when the program and organizational structures are incongruent.

A public school district recently converted its budget from an object to a program format. The district is organized into three instructional divisions: elementary school (kindergarten through grade 6); middle school (grades 7 and 8); and high school (grades 9 through 12). In addition, it maintains support divisions for transportation, food services, and administration.

The district's two elementary schools are each organized in a traditional manner. They are headed by a principal and, depending on size, two or three vice-principals. There are up to six classes for each grade; the teachers assigned to a grade form the equivalent of a department.

Each elementary class is within the charge of a single teacher. He or she teaches all the main subjects (reading, science, mathematics, etc.). However, specialist teachers may provide instruction in areas such as computers and physical education.

Under the previous object classification format, all appropriations were broken down by school and, if appropriate, by grade. The main expenditure categories included the following:

- administrator salaries
- teacher salaries
- aides salaries
- support personnel salaries
- supplies
- computer and audio visual equipment
- Library books

Under the new format, the elementary school division has two major programs: basic education and support. These are subdivided into the following activities:

Basic Education

- reading
- mathematics
- social studies
- science
- music
- art
- computer literacy
- physical education

Support

- administration
- library
- computers and visual aids

Teachers' salaries and other costs that cut across programs and activities are allocated to programs and activities on an appropriate basis, such as percentage of classroom hours spent on a subject (for teacher's salaries) or amount of usage (for computers and audio equipment).

The district has set forth specific objectives for each activity. For example, the primary objective for "reading" is "to assure that at least 90 percent of students are reading at or above grade level as measured by [a specified standardized test]." The primary objective for each of the other academic activities is similar.

a. Suppose that you are a member of the district's governing board.

1. Owing to an increase in district population, two first-grade classes will have to be added. Which of the two budget formats (if either) would better permit you to direct additional resources to the first grade?

2. You are concerned that sixth graders are not reading as well as you think they should. You attribute their deficiencies to teachers spending too much time on "frivolous" subjects such as music and art rather than on reading. Which of the two budget formats (if either) would permit you to redistribute resources so that more time is spent on reading?

3. Comment on why the program and activity structure of the district's elementary schools, although closely tied to the schools' educational objectives may not facilitate allocation of resources.

b. Suppose that the district's high school is organized by subject. There is a history department, a mathematics department, a biology department, etc. Would it be more fitting in the high school than in the elementary schools to have a program structure that is tied to academic subject-matter? Why?

14-6

Capital budgeting decisions depend on specification of objectives.

To enhance security in Riverside Park, a city is considering whether it should install a high-tech security system. The system would not only reduce the cost of police patrols but would also deter crime.

The city has received offers from two contractors who have proposed competing systems. System A would cost $4 million; System B would cost $6 million. The city estimates that by reducing the cost of police patrols System A would save $150,000 per year and System B $260,000 per year.

The city uses a discount rate of 10 percent to evaluate all capital outlays. It determines that each of the systems would have an economic life of five years.

a. Considering the cost as the initial investment and the benefits as the present value of the cash savings from reduced police patrols, which of the two systems would cost the least in relation to benefits. Based only on this criterion, should that system be acquired?

b. Suppose that the city estimates that System A is likely to deter 40 violent crimes per year and that System B is likely to deter 50 violent crimes per year. Which of the two would cost the least (considering cost as the initial investment less the present value of savings from reduced police patrols) in relation to benefits?

c. Suppose further that consultants engaged by the city have placed a dollar cost upon violent crime. Taking into account victims' medical bills and lost wages, they estimate the present value of net outflows owing to a violent crime to be $90,000 per victim. Considering the costs as the initial investment and the benefits as the present value of the cash savings (including those from both reduced police patrols and crimes deterred), which of the two systems would cost the least in relation to benefits? Based only on this criterion, should that system be acquired?

14-7

Capital expenditures cannot be assessed in isolation of operating expenditures.

A city is weighing the costs and benefits of a new convention center. The center would be accounted for in an enterprise fund. It would cost $20 million and would be funded from the proceeds of twenty-year revenue bonds. Officials estimate that the center would generate $3.5 million each year in rental and other fees and would cost $1.6 million (excluding interest) to operate.

a. Based on this limited amount of information, should the city construct the convention center? Assume that the term of the bonds is indicative of the center's useful life and that the city's cost of capital is 6 percent.

b. Suppose that city officials estimate that the center would generate an additional $150,000 in general sales taxes and $200,000 in hotel occupancy taxes that are dedicated to promotion of tourism. However, the center would cost the city an additional $250,000 to provide police, fire, and other services in connection with center events. Further, the city utility department (accounted for in an enterprise fund) would have to extend utility lines to the center at an initial cost of $1.7 million and would have to incur annual costs of $50,000 to maintain and repair these lines. None of these operating and utility costs would be charged to the convention center.

Taking into account these costs and revenues, should the city construct the convention center?

c. Assuming that the city were to construct the convention center, what would be the annual impact on revenues and expenses/expenditures (excluding interest and other financing costs) of the following funds?

1. Convention center fund
2. General fund
3. Hotel occupancy tax fund
4. Utility fund

14-8

Conventional capital budgeting techniques can be applied to nonconventional assessments.

The Mount Eden Medical Center is considering establishing a screening program for a virulent form of cancer. If the program were established, the center would have to acquire equipment that would cost $8.2 million. Thereafter, the center would incur operating costs of $400,000 per year. The equipment has a useful life of four years.

The center estimates that it would screen 3,000 high risk patients per year. It calculates that 0.2 percent (6) of these will test positive. With proper treatment, at minimal cost, these patients would be spared the disease. Experts have determined that if they were not screened and, as a consequence developed the disease, they would incur at least $300,000 per year in medical costs, for a period of two years, before succumbing to it. The disease would cut short their working lives by an average of ten years, during which time they would have earned an average of $28,000 per year.

The center uses an interest rate of 10 percent to assess all long-term projects.

a. What would be the *annual* net benefits of the program, taking into account the operating costs (excluding the cost of the equipment), the present value of the medical costs, and the present value of lost earnings?

b. Does the present value of the annual net benefits exceed the cost of the equipment? Based exclusively on this criterion, should the program be established? What reservations would you have as to the significance of your analysis.

c. Assume that the center has decided to establish the screening program. However, the screening could be carried out with equal reliability by physician examinations coupled with laboratory tests rather than with the special equipment. The annual cost, however, would be $3 million. Should the center acquire the equipment or carry out the screening with physician examinations and laboratory tests? Base your analysis on a period of four years, the life of the equipment. Do you have the same reservations about this analysis as you did the previous one?

14-9

Misspecified objectives and performance measures can have dysfunctional consequences.

The Granite Falls Detention Center is a boot camp for criminal offenders aged 18 to 25. "Campers" spend one year at the camp, during which they take vocational courses (mainly in the construction trades), engage in vigorous physical exercise, and are given psychological counseling. Upon completion of the program, they are returned to their hometowns. They fulfill the remainder of any sentence on parole instead of in prison. The overall mission of the center is to prevent recidivism; to assure that, once released, the campers commit no further criminal acts and become productive members of society.

A unit of the state prison system, the center has a limited capacity, which is far less than the number of offenders who would qualify for it. Offenders who are not admitted to the camp are sentenced instead to conventional jails or prisons.

Campers are subject to strict discipline, similar to that in a military training facility. Those who violate camp rules, or fail to make satisfactory progress in courses and other activities, are subject to transfer to prison.

The center is a budgeted program of the state prison system.

In a recent budget, the prison system set forth the objective of the detention center as follows:

> To provide programs of vocational training, physical exercise and psychological counseling for youthful offenders with the aim of preventing them from committing criminal acts after their release and of enabling them to become productive members of society.

At the end of each year the center submitted a report of its performance. Outcome measures included the following:

- percentage of campers released to society (as opposed to being transferred to other prison facilities)
- number of campers completing vocational courses
- number of hours of psychological counselling provided

a. Comment on the program's objective and its outcome measures. Do you believe that they provide a basis on which to assess the program's performance?

b. Indicate ways in which employees of the center could enhance the center's performance as measured by the outcome measures yet which would not be consistent with the center's overall mission.

c. Suppose that the center included as one of its outcome measures "percentage of campers that did not commit a crime within five years." Comment on the virtues and deficiencies of this measure.

14-10

Indiscriminate comparisons of SEA data can be more misleading than enlightening.

The city manager of Midfield summoned the city's sanitation commissioner. He had compared the service efforts and accomplishments data for the sanitation department with those for Lowville, a nearby city of comparable size and population. Midfield fared poorly on virtually all measures. The city manager wanted an explanation.

Both cities used SEA measures that were recommended in a GASB research report (cited in this chapter). These included the following:

Inputs

- expenditures in current and constant dollars
- number of personnel
- number of vehicles

Outputs

- number of customers served
- tons of waste collected

Outcomes

- percentage of scheduled collections missed
- percentage of scheduled collections not completed on schedule
- percentage of streets rated acceptably clean
- average customer satisfaction rating
- number of customer complaints

Efficiency

- cost per ton of solid waste collected
- cost per customer served
- tons of solid waste collected per employee

It is generally acknowledged that comparisons of SEA measures must be supplemented with explanations as to possible differences in operating conditions.

a. Suppose that you were Midfield's sanitation commissioner. List at least seven factors, each of which is likely to be beyond your control, that might explain the apparently poor performance of your department. Specify one or more outcome or efficiency indicators that they would affect.

b. Suppose instead that the city manager had compared the sanitation department's performance of the current year with that of the previous year and noted a deterioration in several of the measures. List at least three factors, each of which is likely to be beyond your control, that might account for the apparent deterioration in performance. Assume that there have been no major changes in the city's population or its policies as to frequency of collection or other factors affecting customer service.

SOLUTION TO EXERCISE FOR REVIEW AND SELF-STUDY

a. Examples of operational objectives

Serving a Broad Segment of Society

- A subway station is located within one-half mile of 90 percent of city residences and places of employment.
- 85 percent of the population can commute between their homes and offices in less than one hour.

Providing On-Time Service

- 90 percent of the trains arrive at stations within 2 minutes of scheduled time.
- No more than 1 percent of trains are subject to major delays (greater than 20 minutes).

Providing Frequent Service

- During rush hours trains are scheduled no more than 6 minutes apart.
- During off-peak hours trains are scheduled no more than 20 minutes apart.

Assuring that Passengers are Safe

- There are no more than 6 reported violent crimes per 1,000,000 passenger trips.
- There are no more than 3 accidents per 1,000,000 miles.

Assuring that the Environment in Which Passengers Travel, Including Trains and Stations, Are Clean and Pleasant.

- At least 80 percent of passengers surveyed are satisfied with the conditions of trains and stations.
- 95 percent of trains departing from the terminal are rated B+ or better by system inspectors.

b. Examples of service effort and accomplishment indicators

Inputs

- dollar cost of cleaning trains and stations
- number of employees engaged in refurbishing trains

Outputs

- number of trains repainted each year
- number of cars cleaned
- number of stations cleaned

Outcomes

- percentage of cars meeting specified standards (e.g., no broken doors, adequate lights, no torn seats, etc.)
- number of passenger complaints about unsatisfactory conditions

Efficiency (Inputs to Outputs or Outcomes)

- cost per car cleaned
- number of maintenance employees per cars meeting specified standards

c. Capital outlays

1. The net economic benefit of expenditures to enhance safety can be determined by comparing the cost of the improvements to the economic savings that will result from fewer crimes. Although it is possible to estimate the dollar costs of crimes (e.g., the lost wages of the victims) the reliability, and hence, the utility, of such estimates are, at best, problematic.

2. If the system must choose between two alternatives, each providing approximately the same benefits, then the merits of each option can be determined using conventional capital budget analysis. Thus, over a ten-year period, using a discount rate of 12 percent:

Present Value of Costs of Hiring Additional Police

Cost Per Year	$110,000
Present Value of An Annuity of $1, 10 Periods, 12 Percent	× 5.6502
Net Present Value	$621,522

Present Value of Capital Improvements

Maintenance and Monitoring Costs Per Year	$ 30,000
Present Value of An Annuity of $1, 10 Periods, 12 Percent	× 5.6502
Present Value of Maintenance and Monitoring Costs Per Year	169,506
Present Value of Initial Outlays	400,000
Net Present Value	$569,506

The cost of the capital improvements is less than that of hiring police; hence, they should be undertaken.

3. The operating budget should account for the operating costs associated with the newly acquired assets. Procedures can be established so when the capital budget is approved, the additional operating costs are automatically added to the operating budget.

CHAPTER 15

Auditing Governments and Not-For-Profit Organizations

LEARNING OBJECTIVES

After studying this chapter you should understand:

- the primary differences between auditing in the government and not-for-profit sectors and in the business sector
- how the Yellow Book has influenced governmental and not-for-profit auditing
- the types of audits that governments conduct
- the standards to which government audits must comply

- how the Single Audit Act and supporting regulations have influenced auditing
- the reports that auditors must prepare as part of a single audit
- the unique characteristics of performance audits
- the key elements of performance audits
- the unique ethical issues facing governmental and not-for-profit accountants and auditors

The theme of the previous chapter was that government and not-for-profit organizations must be managed to achieve their objectives. By extension, therefore, their performance must also be evaluated as to whether they achieved these objectives. In this chapter we consider how governments and not-for-profits organizations are audited—how their accomplishments are attested to and reported upon.

Whereas in the development of financial auditing standards and practices the independent public accounting profession has played the leadership role, in the areas of reporting on compliance and assessing performance, the government and not-for-profit sectors have been at the forefront of progress. The advances in compliance and performance auditing can be attributed mainly to the federal government, especially to the leadership of the **General Accounting Office (GAO)** and the requirements of the **Single Audit Act.** The federal government provides financial assistance, either directly or indirectly through the states, to almost all general-purpose local governments, most colleges and universities, and a substantial portion of not-for-profit entities. As a condition of awarding financial assistance, it requires that the entities submit financial statements that are audited in accord with federally specified standards. It is thereby able to influence the auditing standards applicable to entities as disparate as major state governments and small-town soup kitchens. In addition, inasmuch as the more progressive internal audit departments of corporations began to focus on performance audits as early as the 1960s, the Institute of Internal Auditors, the professional association of internal auditors, has also made substantial contributions to promoting performance auditing and to developing appropriate concepts and practices.

Auditing is a discipline in its own right, and therefore comprehensive coverage is well beyond the scope of this text. The objective of this chapter is to shed light on some of the unique features of government and not-for-profit auditing and to show how federal requirements have affected both state and local governments and not-for-profits. The chapter first discusses the unique features of auditing in the government and not-for-profit sectors. It then addresses the two primary types of audits—financial audits and performance audits. A final section deals with ethical issues facing auditors and accountants—a topic only tangentially related to the main thrust of the chapter, but nevertheless of special concern to government accountants and auditors.

How do Audits of Governments and Not-For-Profits Differ from Those of Businesses?

An **audit** is defined in general-purpose dictionaries as an examination of records or accounts to check their accuracy. Business-sector financial audits are characterized by the attest function. **Attest** means "to affirm to be correct, true, or genuine; corroborate." The attest function adds credibility to the assertions of others—in the case of an independent financial audit, to an entity's financial data as presented by management.

In the government and not-for-profit sectors, auditing extends beyond the attest function. Auditors not only attest to the data reported in financial statements. They also make, and report upon, their own independent evaluations as to whether auditees have complied with appropriate laws, regulations, and terms of grants. Further, they assess whether the auditees have achieved their objectives and carried out their missions efficiently and effectively.

HOW HAS THE YELLOW BOOK INFLUENCED GOVERNMENTAL AND NOT-FOR-PROFIT AUDITING?

In 1972, the U.S. General Accounting Office (GAO) issued the first edition of *Government Auditing Standards (Standards for Audit of Governmental Organizations, Programs, Activities, and Functions)*, commonly referred to (because of the color of its cover) as the **Yellow Book**. The GAO, an agency of Congress, is responsible for auditing all federal agencies and programs. In addition, it is accountable, along with the Department of the Treasury and the **Office of Management and Budget (OMB)**, for prescribing the accounting standards and practices of federal agencies. It is headed by the **Comptroller General of the United States**, who is appointed by the president, with the advice and consent of the Senate, for a term of fifteen years.

Government Auditing Standards was issued to elevate the practice of auditing by both federal agencies and state and local governments. The GAO has no direct authority over state and local governments, but by publishing—and publicizing—the standards, it exerts its influence through the force of persuasion and example.

Federal legislation now requires that the *inspectors general* (the chief auditors) of each federal agency apply the Yellow Book to their own audits. In addition, they must also ensure that all audits for which they are responsible, mainly those of entities to which their agencies provide funds, satisfy the GAO standards. Thus, for example, if a federal department were to make an award to a not-for-profit organization, then that organization's auditors, even if independent CPAs, must adhere to the GAO standards.

When it initially established government accounting standards, the GAO incorporated into them the relevant standards of the American Institute of Certified Public Accountants (AICPA). Since then, the AICPA has also adopted many, but not all, of the GAO standards as they apply to government audits. Hence, while there are no inconsistencies between the GAO and the AICPA standards, the GAO standards may impose requirements in addition to those of AICPA standards.

WHAT TYPES OF AUDITS DO GOVERNMENTS CONDUCT?

Government audits are conventionally characterized as either **financial audits** or **performance audits**. *Government Auditing Standards* further divides each of these two types into two additional categories. Financial audits, it explains, consist of **financial statement audits** and **financial related audits**.

Financial statement audits determine whether an entity's financial statements are presented fairly in accordance with generally accepted accounting principles, and whether the entity has complied with laws and regulations that may have a material effect on the financial statements. *Financial related audits* determine whether financial reports, including those on specific funds or accounts, are either fairly presented or presented in accordance with stated criteria, and whether the entity has complied with specific financial-related requirements, such as those set forth in laws and regulations, grants and contracts.

These descriptions make it clear that financial audits in government differ from those in business in that government audits place greater emphasis upon *compliance*—assuring that the auditee has observed applicable provisions of laws, regulations, grants, and contracts. Nongovernmental audits focus mainly on assuring that the financial statements are in accordance with GAAP—compliance is not an end in itself. They are concerned with violations of laws, regulations, and comparable legal requirements, mainly because they can cause the financial statements to be misleading.

Performance audits, often referred to as **operational audits**, are also of two types: **economy and efficiency audits** and **program audits**.

Economy and efficiency audits assess whether the entity is acquiring, protecting, and using its resources economically and efficiently, and whether it has complied with laws and regulations relating to economy and efficiency. They are intended to assure, for example, that the entity is:

- following sound procurement practices
- avoiding overstaffing
- properly maintaining its resources
- using efficient operating procedures

Program audits determine the extent to which the organization is achieving desired results or benefits, and whether the entity has complied with significant laws, and regulations applicable to its programs. They consider, for example:

- whether the objectives of a new or ongoing program are suitable and relevant
- the factors inhibiting satisfactory performance
- whether management has considered alternatives for conducting the program that might yield desired results more effectively at lower cost

These two types are also conducted simultaneously. In this chapter we focus first upon financial audits, including the requirements of the Single Audit Act. We then consider performance audits.

WHAT LEVELS OF STANDARDS ARE APPLICABLE TO FINANCIAL AUDITS?

Audits of all entities, irrespective of whether governmental or nongovernmental, that are carried out by independent CPAs must first satisfy **generally accepted auditing standards (GAAS)**—the standards of the AICPA. Audits conducted under these standards focus on an entity's financial statements. They result in reports in which the auditors express an opinion as to whether the statements are fairly presented in accordance with generally accepted *accounting* standards—those established or recognized by either the GASB or the FASB.

Agencies that provide funds to governments or not-for-profit entities may stipulate that the audit they require be conducted in accord with a second set of standards, that set forth in *Government Auditing Standards* (the Yellow Book). *Government Auditing Standards* constitute what are known as **generally accepted government auditing standards (GAGAS)**.

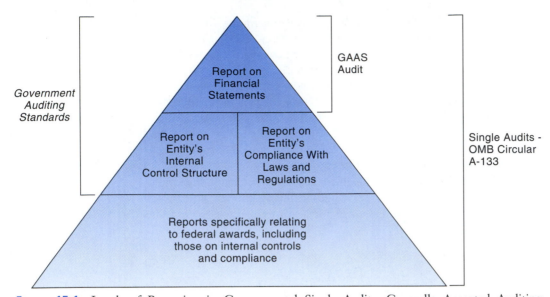

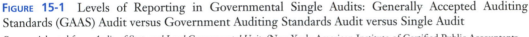

FIGURE 15-1   Levels of Reporting in Governmental Single Audits: Generally Accepted Auditing Standards (GAAS) Audit versus Government Auditing Standards Audit versus Single Audit

Source: Adapted from *Audits of State and Local Governmental Units* (New York: American Institute of Certified Public Accountants, 1996), p. 181.

Audits of governments or not-for-profit entities that are subject to the Single Audit Act must satisfy a third, additional level of standards—those of the Single Audit Act and its supporting circulars.

The diagram in Figure 15-1 shows the types of reports required at each of the three levels of audit, and thereby implies the differences in the scope of the examinations required at each level.

KEY DIFFERENCES BETWEEN GENERAL AND GOVERNMENT AUDITING STANDARDS

Government Auditing Standards for financial audits are modeled after the ten basic "generally accepted auditing standards" of the AICPA. These ten standards were first developed in 1939, but have subsequently been augmented by numerous detailed requirements, most of which are set forth in the AICPA's eighty-plus statements on auditing standards (SASs). Like the AICPA standards, the government auditing standards are divided into three categories:

- General standards
- Field work standards
- Reporting standards

The GAO has supplemented the basic AICPA standards with both additional standards and additional guidance as to how they should be interpreted and implemented. Table 15–1 sets forth the resultant standards, excluding the interpretative and implementation guidance. The discussion that follows highlights some of the key differences between the two sets of standards.

GENERAL STANDARDS

The general standards pertain to the qualifications of the auditors, the independence of both the individual auditors and the audit organization, the auditors' exercise of due professional care and the need for quality control. Although the first three GAO

TABLE 15–1
Government Auditing Standards for Financial Audits

General Standards

1. Qualifications: The staff assigned to conduct the audit should collectively possess adequate professional proficiency for the tasks required.

2. Independence: In all matters relating to the audit work, the audit organization, and the individual auditors, whether government or public, should be free from personal and external impairments to independence, should be organizationally independent, and should maintain an independent attitude and appearance.

3. Due Professional Care: Due professional care should be used in conducting the audit and in preparing related reports.

4. Quality Control: Each audit organization conducting audits in accordance with these standards should have an appropriate internal quality control system in place and undergo an external quality control review.

Field Work Standards for Financial Audits

1. For financial statement audits, generally accepted government auditing standards (GAGAS) incorporate the American Institute of Certified Public Accountants' (AICPA) three generally accepted standards of field work, which are:

   (a) The work is to be adequately planned and assistants, if any, are to be properly supervised.

   (b) A sufficient understanding of the internal control structure is to be obtained to plan the audit and to determine the nature, timing, and extent of tests to be performed.

   (c) Sufficient competent evidential matter is to be obtained through inspection, observation, inquiries, and confirmations to afford a reasonable basis for an opinion regarding the financial statements under audit.

2. The work is to be properly planned, and auditors should consider materiality, among other matters, in determining the nature, timing, and extent of auditing procedures and in evaluating the results of those procedures. Auditors should follow up on known material findings and recommendations from previous audits.

3. Auditors should design the audit to provide reasonable assurance of detecting (1) irregularities that are material to the financial statements and (2) material misstatements resulting from direct and material illegal acts. Auditors should be aware of the possibility that indirect illegal acts may have occurred. If specific information comes to the auditors' attention that provides evidence concerning the existence of possible illegal acts that could have a material indirect effect on the financial statements, the auditors should apply audit procedures specifically directed to ascertaining whether an illegal act has occurred.

4. Auditors should design the audit to provide reasonable assurance of detecting material misstatements resulting from noncompliance with provisions of contracts or grant agreements that have a direct and material effect on the determination of financial statement amounts. If specific information comes to the auditors' attention that provides evidence concerning the existence of possible noncompliance that could have a material, indirect effect on the financial statements, auditors should apply audit procedures specifically directed to ascertaining whether that noncompliance has occurred.

5. Auditors should obtain a sufficient understanding of internal controls to plan the audit and determine the nature, timing, and extent of tests to be performed.

6. A record of the auditors' work should be retained in the form of working papers. Working papers should contain sufficient information to enable an experienced auditor having no previous connections with the audit to ascertain from them the evidence that supports the auditors' significant conclusions and judgments.

Reporting Standards for Financial Audits

1. For financial statement audits, generally accepted government auditing standards (GAGAS) incorporate the American Institute of Certified Public Accountants' (AICPA) four generally accepted standards of reporting, which are:

   (a) The report shall state whether the financial statements are presented in accordance with generally accepted accounting principles.

   (b) The report shall identify those circumstances in which such principles have not been consistently observed in the current period in relation to the preceding period.

   (c) Informative disclosures in the financial statements are to be regarded as reasonably adequate unless otherwise stated in the report.

(continued)

TABLE 15–1 (Continued) **Government Auditing Standards for Financial Audits**

(d) The report shall either contain an expression of opinion regarding the financial statements, taken as a whole, or an assertion to the effect that an opinion cannot be expressed. When an overall opinion cannot be expressed, the reasons therefore should be stated. In all cases where an auditor's name is associated with financial statements, the report should contain a clear-cut indication of the character of the auditor's work, if any, and the degree of responsibility the auditor is taking.

2. Auditors should communicate certain information related to the conduct and reporting of the audit to the audit committee or to the individuals with whom they have contracted for the audit.

3. Audit reports should state that the audit was made in accordance with generally accepted government auditing standards.

4. The report on the financial statements should either (1) describe the scope of the auditors' testing of compliance with laws and regulations and internal controls and present the results of those tests or (2) refer to separate reports containing that information. In presenting the results of those tests, auditors should report irregularities, illegal acts, other material noncompliance, and reportable conditions in internal controls. In some circumstances, auditors should report irregularities and illegal acts directly to parties external to the audited entity.

5. If certain information is prohibited from general disclosure, the audit report should state the nature of the information omitted and the requirement that makes the omission necessary.

6. Written audit reports are to be submitted by the audit organization to the appropriate officials of the auditee and to the appropriate officials of the organizations requiring or arranging for the audits, including external funding organizations, unless legal restrictions prevent it. Copies of the reports should also be sent to other officials who have legal oversight authority or who may be responsible for acting on audit findings and recommendations and to others authorized to receive such reports. Unless restricted by law or regulation, copies should be made available for public inspection.

Source: Government Auditing Standards, 1994 Revision (Washington, D.C.: Comptroller General of the United States), pp. 32–61.

standards (as set forth in Table 15–1) are similar to those of the AICPA, the implementation guidelines differ in that they are tailored specifically to government audits.

Independence

In the private sector auditors cannot be considered independent if employed by the entity they are to audit. However, most government audit agencies are part of the government that they have been established to audit. Therefore, the GAO advises that an audit organization of a government may be considered independent as long as it meets one of the following conditions:

- It is from a different branch (e.g., legislative, executive) of the government than the particular units that it is to examine
- It is headed by an auditor who is elected by the citizens of the government's jurisdiction or who is accountable to the government's legislative body

Continuing Professional Education

The standards' interpretative guidelines require that to meet the test of professional proficiency, auditors must be knowledgeable of government auditing standards and accounting principles. Auditors that perform government audits must complete at least eighty hours of continuing professional education (CPE) every two years, of which twenty-four hours must be related directly to the government environment and to government auditing. The requirement for twenty-four hours of specialized government education goes beyond the CPE standards of both the AICPA and state CPA licensing boards, which make no demands as to specific industry content. It applies to all auditors who participate in government engagements (including those of not-for-profits receiving federal assistance)—even if the engagements constitute only a small part of the auditors' overall practice.

Peer Review

The GAO, but not the AICPA, standards require that each audit organization have "an appropriate internal quality control system in place and undergo an external quality control review." To satisfy this standard the organization must undergo a "peer review" by an independent audit organization at least once every three years. Although peer reviews are not required by the AICPA's general standards, they are mandated by the membership rules of the *Private Companies Practice Section* and the *SEC Practice Section*, two subgroups of the AICPA that firms can volunteer to join.

STANDARDS OF FIELD WORK

The standards of field work are intended to assure that audits are properly planned and supervised, that the auditees' internal control structures are properly reviewed, and that auditors obtain sufficient evidential matter.

Compliance

Both the AICPA and GAO standards require auditors to design their engagements to provide "reasonable assurance" of detecting material misstatements resulting from illegal acts or similar irregularities, such as intentional omissions or fabrications. Because governments and not-for-profits are accountable to the parties from which they receive grants or have contracts, the GAO standards also require auditors to design their audits to provide reasonable assurance of detecting noncompliance with the terms of *contracts or grant agreements*.

Working Papers

Audits of governments and of not-for-profits receiving government funds are often undertaken by independent CPAs or by auditors from one government agency for the benefit of another. Therefore, they may be subject to more frequent and careful quality reviews than those of businesses. Whereas both the AICPA and GAO standards require that auditors document their audit work in "working papers," the GAO standard is more rigorous. Unlike the AICPA standard, it explicitly says that the working papers must contain sufficient information to convince an auditor having no previous connection with the audit that the evidence supports the auditor's conclusions and judgments.

STANDARDS OF REPORTING

The standards of reporting establish the form and content of auditors' opinions on financial statements and on any other required reports.

Compliance and Internal Controls

The AICPA standards of reporting require that auditors explain, in general terms, the nature of their examination. They do not, however, require that the auditors explicitly describe their tests of compliance or their assessments of internal controls.

In light of the importance governments place on both compliance and internal controls, the GAO adds a standard stipulating that auditors must explicitly describe (either in their reports on the financial statements or in separate reports) the scope of their compliance and internal control testing. They must also indicate any irregularities, illegal acts, and other instances of material noncompliance that they found. To put the violations in perspective, the auditors should also indicate the number of infractions and their dollar amount.

The standard makes no distinction between violations that are material and those that are not. It requires auditors to report all violations, except for those that are "clearly inconsequential." In some circumstances, especially if management fails to take appropriate corrective measures, the auditors may also have to notify legal authorities, such as federal inspectors general or state attorneys general.

Public Inspection

Under AICPA standards, auditors are not required to disclose in their audit report either deficiencies in internal control or instances of illegal acts, irregularities, or noncompliance unless they materially affect the financial statements. Usually auditors inform management of their nonmaterial findings in a "management letter," which the entity need not make public.

Under the GAO standards, auditor reports on internal control and compliance are part of the complete audit report. Unless restricted by law or regulation, they must be made available for public inspection.

How have the single audit act and other pronouncements influenced auditing?

In the 1960s the federal government greatly increased the number, dollar magnitude, and complexity of its assistance programs. These programs, which were directed to a wide range of activities including education, health and welfare, job training, and transportation, were typically funded by the federal government but administered by the states. However, the federal agencies in charge of the programs were responsible for auditing them.

As a result of congressional disclosures of severe deficiencies in federal audit practices, the OMB urged that federal agencies rely more on CPA firms and other independent auditors than on their own "in-house" auditors. Nevertheless, federal agencies were interested mainly in whether grant recipients complied with the applicable laws, regulations, and grant provisions. Independent auditors, adhering to then-current standards, focused on financial statements and thereby did not provide the compliance assurances needed by the agencies. Hence, the agencies continued to perform their own audits.

IN PRACTICE

THE AUDITORS' DILEMMA

The requirement that the complete audit report, including details of all deficiencies in internal controls or instances of noncompliance, be made public may place independent CPAs that audit governments in uncomfortable circumstances.

Opponents of the officials responsible for reported irregularities may seize upon the auditors' report to score political points. The officials may respond by questioning the validity of the auditors' findings.

How should the auditors react? Should they defend their findings and thereby jeopardize their relationship with their client? Or should they agree with their client and thereby jeopardize their own reputation?

Further, many grant recipients, especially local governments, received funds from several federal agencies and were subject to audits from each. Although each audit team directed its attention primarily to the grants from its own agency, they all had to review common books and records, accounting systems, and internal controls. The result was both costly duplication of audit effort and inadequate audit coverage of the entity as a whole.

In 1979, the OMB issued a directive calling for organization-wide **single audits** to be performed by CPAs or other independent auditors.[7] The directive did not preclude federal agencies from conducting their own examinations, but instructed them to build on the independent audits.

To give legislative sanction to the directive, Congress enacted the *Single Audit Act of 1984*. Amended in 1996 to make it easier to administer, the act applies to both direct and indirect recipients of federal assistance and requires that organizations receiving more than $300,000 in federal assistance under more than one program be subject to a single audit.

The objectives of a single audit are to assure:

- the financial statements of the entity as a whole can be relied upon
- the entity is adhering to the common set of federal laws and regulations that apply to all recipients of federal aid
- the entity is satisfying the laws, regulations, and provisions that apply to each specific federal award

Whereas prior to the act a recipient of federal funds had to submit audit reports to each agency from which it received funds, now a recipient has to deal with only a single agency. That agency, referred to as the *cognizant* agency, is responsible for ensuring that all audit standards are met and for coordinating the special audit requirements of each of the individual agencies providing funds. The cognizant agency is typically the agency that provides the greatest portion of federal funds to the recipient.

The OMB is primarily responsible for administering the Single Audit Act. It issues circulars that provide detailed guidance as to how the single audit is to be performed. Periodically updated, they address matters such as the nature and scope of internal control reviews, the extent of compliance testing, and the form and content of reports. Until recently, one circular addressed audits of governments and another those of not-for-profits. OMB has now combined these into a single circular, A-133, *Audits of States, Local Governments and Non-Profit Organizations*.

OMB has augmented the guidance of Circular A-133 with a "Compliance Supplement" that details major compliance requirements and key audit procedures. It has also published *Uniform Administrative Requirements for Grants and Cooperative Agreements to State and Local Governments* (referred to as the "Common Rule,") a detailed compendium of additional rules and regulations.

The Single Audit Act specifies that single audits be conducted in accord with the GAO's *Government Accounting Standards*. However, it requires that federal recipients be subject only to financial audits, not to performance audits. Therefore, the sections of *Government Accounting Standards* on performance audits need not be applied.

To provide additional guidance on single and other government-related audits, the AICPA issued SAS No. 74, *Compliance Auditing Considerations in Audits of Governmental*

---

[7] Attachment P, "Audit Requirements" to OMB Circular A-102, *Uniform Administrative Requirements for Grants-in-Aid to State and Local Governments*.

Entities and Other Recipients of Governmental Financial Assistance. By issuing this statement, the AICPA establishes that CPAs who conduct audits of financial assistance but fail to meet the federal audit requirements also fail to adhere to AICPA standards.

WHAT REPORTS RESULT FROM SINGLE AUDITS?

A single audit has two main components:

- an audit of the financial statements conducted under generally accepted government auditing standards
- an audit of federal financial awards

Per Circular A-133, these two types of audits should culminate with the auditors issuing at least four types of reports (which the auditors may combine as they deem appropriate):

- an opinion as to whether the financial statements are fairly presented in accord with generally accepted accounting principles and an opinion as to whether the schedule of expenditures of federal awards is presented fairly
- reports on internal controls related to the financial statements, major programs, and the determination of the overhead costs charged to federal awards
- an opinion as to whether the organization complied with laws, regulations, and the provisions of contracts or grant agreements
- a schedule of findings and questioned costs

REPORT ON SCHEDULE OF EXPENDITURES OF FEDERAL AWARDS

The **schedule of expenditures of federal awards** is a listing of total expenditures made by the organization under each federal program from which it received funding. Its main purpose is to enable the federal grantor agencies to coordinate their audit efforts and assure adequate audit coverage. Per relevant OMB directives, the schedule must identify each program by its number as listed in the *Catalog of Federal Domestic Assistance* (CFDA). It must include expenditures to be reimbursed both directly from the federal government and indirectly through other governments (i.e., "pass-through" awards). The schedule should indicate whether programs are major or nonmajor and may include optional information as to matching contributions, the total amount of the program awards and the time periods that are covered by them.

The Single Audit Act distinguishes between major and nonmajor programs. As might be expected, a higher level of auditing is required of the major programs. The distinction is based on two primary factors:

- the dollar amount of federal funds expended by the program in relation to the dollar amount of total federal funds expended by the organization as a whole
- the inherent risk of the program, taking into account factors such as previous audit findings, the strength of the organization's internal controls, the extent of oversight exercised by federal agencies or other supervisory organizations and whether the program is new or ongoing.

Table 15–2 illustrates a schedule of expenditures of federal awards. The auditors' responsibility for this schedule is to assure that the information presented is materially complete and accurate and that the expenditures are properly categorized.

TABLE 15–2
Urban Assistance Federation
Schedule of Expenditures of Federal Awards for Year Ended December 31, 1998

Grantor/Pass-Through Grantor/Program Title	Federal CFDA Number	Grant Award Number	Expenditures
U.S. Department of Housing and Urban Development			
Passed through City Housing Department			
Community Development Block Grant			
Programs Emergency Home Repair			
11/07/98–10/31/99	15.649*	I C420.1	$487,198
U.S. Department of Labor			
Passed through the State Employment Commission			
Willard-Feyser 7(b) Program			
1/1/98–2/28/99	18.927*	1-027-70	152,188
Passed through the County Private Industry Council			
Project Exceed (III-A)			
5/1/98–9/30/98	18.971*	II A36.98	38,899
U.S. Department of Education			
Passed through the State Commission on Alcohol			
and Drug Abuse			
Drug Free Schools and Communities			
9/1/97–8/31/98	92.604*	12-016-841	87,625
9/1/98–8/31/99	92.604*	12-016-941	73,357
Total Federal Awards			$839,267

* Denotes a major program.

Government Auditing Standards requires auditors to assess, and report upon, the auditee's overall system of internal control. The focus of the Single Audit Act and its supporting circulars is, understandably, on assuring that federal funds are properly spent. Therefore, they stipulate that auditors must assess and report upon whether the organization has internal controls in place to assure that it is managing its federal awards in compliance with applicable laws and regulations.

According to the Single Audit Act and the supporting circulars, auditors should first obtain an understanding of the controls in place to make certain that they are properly designed to assure compliance and then test whether the controls are actually functioning as intended. The extent of testing is spelled out in the circulars and differs for major and nonmajor programs. The auditor's reports should describe the scope of testing and the results of those tests.

REPORT ON INTERNAL CONTROLS

The auditors' tests of, and report on, compliance must be directed both to requirements that are common to all federal awards and to those that are specific to the programs and contracts under which individual awards are made.

OMB compliance supplements set forth nine *general* requirements that "involve significant national policy and for which failure to comply could have a material impact on an organization's financial statements including those prepared for federal programs." They relate to:

- *Political activity.* Per the Hatch Act and the Intergovernmental Personnel Act of 1970, no federal funds can be used for partisan political activities

- *Prevailing wages.* The Davis–Bacon Act requires that the wages of laborers and mechanics employed by contractors of federally funded projects be paid at rates no lower than those prevailing in their region

REPORT ON COMPLIANCE

- *Civil rights.* No person may be excluded from participation in federal assistance programs because of race, color, national origin, age, handicap, and (in some programs) sex or religion
- *Cash management.* Per the Federal Cash Management Improvement Act, recipients of federal funds must maintain systems that minimize the time between the receipt and the disbursement of cash
- *Relocation assistance and real property acquisition.* When public agencies acquire property and thereby displace businesses and households they must follow specified procedures to assure that the parties having to relocate receive fair compensation and adequate relocation assistance
- *Federal financial reports.* Federal funds recipients must periodically report on the status of funds received and disbursed
- *Allowable costs and cost accounting.* Federal grantees and contractors must adhere to cost accounting principles and standards that are set forth in applicable OMB circulars
- *Drug-free workplace.* Federal grantees and contractors that receive funds directly from the federal government must certify that they maintain a drug-free workplace
- *Administrative requirements.* Federal funds recipients must comply with the administrative requirements of the Common Rule and other OMB circulars. These deal with matters such as application procedures, record maintenance and retention, and post-award procedures.

Tests for compliance with these general requirements may seem far afield from audit procedures associated with a traditional financial audit. In practice, however, auditors are not expected to assume the role of detectives or law-enforcement investigators, and their tests may be comparable to those used to assess internal and administrative controls. For example, with regard to political activity, auditors might examine personnel and payroll records to identify employees whose responsibilities or activities include partisan political activity. They would then review the accounts to make certain that neither the salaries of these employees nor related costs were improperly charged to a federally assisted program.

Similarly, auditors do not have to actually test workers for drug use. Instead, they merely have to assure that a drug-free workplace policy has been adopted and is being implemented. Thus, they might make certain that a written policy is in place, verify that the employees have been notified of the policy, and examine records describing the procedures followed when illicit drug use has been suspected.

The specific compliance requirements are set forth in the rules and regulations of each federal program or contract. In general, they relate to matters such as:

- the individuals or groups that are eligible to participate in the program or to receive financial assistance
- the types of goods or services that may be acquired
- the percentage of its own funds that an entity must contribute to a program
- any special reports that the organization must submit to the sponsoring agency

Obviously, the compliance tests for these requirements depend upon the specific provisions of the program or contract.

SCHEDULE OF FINDINGS AND QUESTIONED COSTS

The schedule of findings and questioned costs is, perhaps, the most distinctive—and often the most informative—of the auditors' reports. This report should set forth the particulars of:

- "reportable conditions" (i.e., weaknesses) in internal controls and the procedures used to charge overhead to federal awards
- instances of material noncompliance with provisions of laws, regulations, and contracts or the procedures used to charge overhead to federal awards
- "questioned costs" (i.e., costs that may have been improperly charged to federal awards)
- explanations as to why the auditor's report on compliance may have been other than unqualified
- instances of known fraud

The report should be forward looking in that it should be in sufficient detail so as to allow the audited entity to prepare a plan of corrective action. It should also include the auditor's recommendations as to how the violations could be prevented in the future.

WHAT ARE PERFORMANCE AUDITS?

Financial audits are intended to assure that financial statements are fairly presented and that the organization has complied with applicable laws and regulations. Performance audits, by contrast, focus on organizational accomplishments. Inasmuch as the goals of a government or not-for-profit are seldom limited to profitability or other financial measures, the auditors may have to assess organizational performance on a wide range of nonfinancial dimensions, each of which relates to an entity's individual objectives.

Performance audits are most commonly carried out by "internal" audit departments—organizations that may be independent of the various agencies or departments that they examine, but not separate from the government or other entity at large. They are not typically required by creditors, regulatory agencies, or other outside parties. Therefore, the accounting profession, other than the GAO, has not developed a detailed set of standards for performance audits comparable to those for financial audits.

The GAO standards for performance audits have had a substantial influence on practice mainly because audit departments have elected voluntarily to adhere to them. These standards correspond to the standards for financial audits in that they are divided into the same three sections: general, field work, and reporting. The general standards are common to both financial and performance audits; the field work and reporting standards are similar in many respects to their financial counterparts, but also have features (the most significant of which will be pointed out in this section) that are unique.

Although the two types of performance audits—economy and efficiency audits and program audits—can be carried out independently of each other, they are so closely intertwined that this section of the text will make no distinction between them.

Attest Function versus Independent Assessment

Performance audits differ conceptually from financial audits. In carrying out financial audits the auditors *attest* to the fairness of the assertions of management. These assertions are primarily incorporated in the entity's financial statements and for the most part relate to constructs, such as revenues, expenditures, assets and liabilities, that are well defined and subject to accepted accounting standards of measurement.

KEY DIFFERENCES BETWEEN FINANCIAL AND PERFORMANCE AUDITS

In performance audits, the auditors make independent assessments as to whether an entity is operating economically and efficiently, and is achieving anticipated results. But the constructs to be measured and the standards of measurement, especially those relating to outcomes, are far less clear and precise than those associated with financial audits.

Pointing to this difference in concept, some auditors contend that they should limit their role to testing management's assertions as to performance. Management should be expected to issue a report that sets forth the extent to which the entity achieved its operational objectives. Auditors would then examine management's assertions and express an opinion as to whether they are fairly presented. If management has not established operational objectives and measured whether they have been achieved, then no performance audit would be possible—no more than a financial audit could be conducted if an entity has not accounted for its financial activities and prepared financial statements.

Focus—Organization At Large versus Specific Programs

Financial statement audits focus on the organization as a whole. An entity's statements of activities (or income statement) and balance sheet summarize virtually every transaction in which the entity has engaged. Auditors do not, of course, verify each of these transactions. Nevertheless, each is within the population from which they draw their samples.

Performance audits are almost always carried out on a specific program or activity, not on the organization in its entirety. Unless the entity is extremely limited in its aims, determining whether the organization as a whole is carrying out its mission is generally infeasible. Imagine, for example, attempting to assess the performance of a major university or metropolitan health care center. As long as their various programs have different objectives, are targeted toward different segments of the population, and are conducted by different employees, little is accomplished by performing a single, unified assessment of the complete entity.

Timing—Routine versus Occasional

Financial audits are typically conducted annually. They are routine elements of an organization's operating cycle.

Performance audits, however, are conducted irregularly. Unlike financial audits they need not coincide with the issuance of the entity's annual financial statements.

Audit organizations have limited resources and generally cannot afford to expend them on audits of the same programs year after year. Instead, they target programs that will likely yield the greatest benefits (such as cost savings or improvements in results) per dollar of audit cost. Their prime selection criteria are the dollar magnitude of the program and the probability of significant audit findings. Therefore, they may examine large, high-risk programs with some frequency (perhaps even annually) but small, low-risk programs only occasionally.

Evidence—Well Delineated versus Broad

The evidence examined in financial audits is relatively well delineated and limited to a few major categories: These include:

- books and records that are created by the organization itself, such as journals and ledgers, schedules, canceled checks, purchase orders, and receiving reports
- documents prepared by outside parties, such as invoices, contracts, and notes

- physical assets, such as inventories and fixed assets
- letters of confirmation or assurance from creditors and debtors, banks, and attorneys

Performance audits are characterized by a broader range of evidence, much of which may be engagement-specific. Depending on the objectives of a program, the auditors may have to review—in addition to financial data—economic and demographic statistics, engineering reports, and medical records.

Auditor Knowledge—Financial versus Program

Financial audits are performed mainly by specialists in accounting—CPAs or others with similar educational and experiential backgrounds. For some engagements, nonaccountants with expertise in areas such as computers, statistical sampling, or specific industries (e.g., jewelry appraisers or geologists) may be brought in as consultants to address certain phases of the examination. They generally play only supporting roles.

Owing to the wider range of evidence that must be examined, performance audits may require more program-specific knowledge and fewer traditional accounting skills. Thus, the GAO and many other government audit organizations have on their staff economists, engineers, health care specialists, and statisticians. Often, the contributions of accountants are not so much their knowledge of accounting per se, but rather, their ability to define a problem and resolve it in a logical and orderly manner.

MANNER OF CONDUCTING

In light of the dissimilarities among programs, each performance audit is unique. Consequently, no generic audit program can readily be tailored to specific engagements. Therefore, the following discussion is necessarily general and may not be applicable to all types of performance audits. Table 15–3 lists the GAO's field work and reporting standards for performance audits.

Selecting the Audit Target

As indicated previously, audit organizations target for examination the programs for which the potential for cost savings are the greatest—those in which expenditures and/or risk of inefficiencies or noncompliance is substantial. The extent to which risk is substantial is a matter of auditor judgment. However, the following are examples of factors that add to a program's exposure:

- recently installed and untested computer systems
- past inefficiencies as revealed in previous audits
- ineffective administration or poor results as reflected in reports to supervisory agencies or higher levels of management
- opportunities or incentives for illegal activities
- adverse press reports or "tips" from employees or other knowledgeable parties

Some audit organizations are required either by law or political necessity to perform audits upon the request of members of legislative or other governing bodies to which they are responsible. The GAO, for example, reports to Congress and therefore responds to recommendations, if reasonable, from its members. The audit departments of municipalities may be similarly responsive to suggestions from members of city councils.

TABLE 15–3
Government Auditing Standards for Performance Audits

Field Work Standards for Performance Audits

1. Work is to be adequately planned.
2. Staff are to be properly supervised.
3. When laws, regulations, and other compliance requirements are significant to audit objectives, auditors should design the audit to provide reasonable assurance about compliance with them. In all performance audits, auditors should be alert to situations or transactions that could be indicative of illegal acts or abuse.
4. Auditors should obtain an understanding of management controls that are relevant to the audit. When management controls are significant to audit objectives, auditors should obtain sufficient evidence to support their judgments about those controls.
5. Sufficient, competent, and relevant evidence is to be obtained to afford a reasonable basis for the auditors' findings and conclusions. A record of the auditors' work should be retained in the form of working papers. Working papers should contain sufficient information to enable an experienced auditor with no previous connection to the audit to ascertain the evidence that supports the auditors' significant conclusions and judgments.

Reporting Standards for Performance Audits

1. Auditors should prepare written audit reports communicating the results of each audit.
2. Auditors should appropriately issue the reports to make the information available for timely use by management, legislative officials, and other interested parties.
3. Auditors should report the audit objectives and the audit scope and methodology.
4. Auditors should report significant audit findings, and where applicable, auditors' conclusions.
5. Auditors should report recommendations for actions to correct problem areas and to improve operations.
6. Auditors should report that the audit was made in accordance with generally accepted government auditing standards.
7. Auditors should report all significant instances of noncompliance and all significant instances of abuse that were found during or in connection with the audit. In some circumstances, auditors should report illegal acts directly to parties external to the audited entity.
8. Auditors should report the scope of their work on management controls and any significant weaknesses found during the audit.
9. Auditors should report the views of responsible officials of the audited program concerning auditors' findings, conclusions, and recommendations, as well as corrections planned.
10. Auditors should report noteworthy accomplishments, particularly when management improvements in one area may be applicable elsewhere.
11. Auditors should refer significant issues needing further audit work to the auditors responsible for planning future audit work.
12. If certain information is prohibited from general disclosure, auditors should report the nature of the information omitted and the requirement that makes the omission necessary.
13. The report should be complete, accurate, objective, convincing, and as clear and concise as the subject permits.
14. Written audit reports are to be submitted by the audit organization to the appropriate officials of the auditee and to the appropriate officials of the organizations requiring or arranging for the audits, including external funding organizations, unless legal restrictions prevent it. Copies of the reports should also be sent to other officials who have legal oversight authority or who may be responsible for acting on audit findings and recommendations and to others authorized to receive such reports. Unless restricted by law or regulation, copies should be made available for public inspection.

Source: Government Auditing Standards, 1994 Revision (Washington, D.C.: Comptroller General of the United States), pp. 62–101.

Perhaps most importantly, audit organizations may have to rely on intangible factors to detect programs of high risk. Experienced auditors tend to develop long-term relations with personnel of the departments that they have examined in the past. Often they become as knowledgeable of departments' operations as its most senior managers. Further, like street-wise detectives, they develop an intuitive sense as to where the entity hides its skeletons.

A senior manager of the GAO was asked why so few of his agency's reports are positive toward the programs that they examine; why almost all are critical of at least some aspects of auditees' operations. His response was that owing to limited resources, the GAO lacks the time to bestow compliments. The agency, he said, knows where the problems exist and it goes after them.

WHY PERFORMANCE AUDIT REPORTS ARE SELDOM POSITIVE

Establishing Scope and Purpose

Auditors must begin their engagement by establishing the scope and purpose of the audit. Since an organization's programs and objectives may be ill-defined and overlap, the auditors must delineate specifically the activities and outcomes to be addressed.

Auditors can best establish the scope and purpose of an engagement by taking a preliminary survey, the aim of which is to gain an understanding of the entity's mission, personnel, history, and operating procedures. The survey might include:

- interviews with key executives as to what they see as the mission of the program and its strengths and weaknesses
- a review of the legislation that established the program
- a review of other laws, governing board resolutions, contracts, and administrative regulations to which the organization is subject
- an examination of reports from previous audits (These audits may have been performed by the same or a different audit organization. The importance of these reports as a source of information cannot be overemphasized. Often they spell out deficiencies that existed in the past and provide a map that marks out the entity's problem areas.)
- a review of the entity's financial statements, as well as related schedules that indicate the sources and uses of entity resources
- a search for literature (such as the GASB studies on service efforts and accomplishments) that set forth potentially applicable performance measures and standards of economy and efficiency
- a review of management controls
- a search for newspaper articles, press reports, transcripts of legislative hearings, and other literature that might provide insight into the organization's strengths and weaknesses
- explicit consideration of the organization's vulnerabilities to fraud and mismanagement and the "things that might go wrong"

Discerning the Objectives of the Programs

If the objectives of a program are clearly spelled out, and are both quantifiable and measurable, then the program is readily auditable. The auditors have either to measure the outcomes themselves or to verify the measurements of management or others.

In Chapter 14 we stressed that well-defined operational objectives are central to sound management. Yet auditors cannot always expect managers to have established a clear statement—written, or even oral—as to the intended outcomes of their programs. The absence of clearly articulated objectives should itself be a "reportable" audit finding. Nevertheless, if a program is to be audited, then the auditors may themselves have to discern its objectives. Auditors can take several steps to determine a program's objectives:

- Examine the legislation that created the program or authorized funds for it. Governing bodies can greatly facilitate audits by explicitly incorporating program objectives into their authorization or appropriation measures, but often they do not.
- Study the "legislative history" of the program, including committee reports, various versions of the authorization bills as they passed through the legislative process, statements of the bills' sponsors, and transcripts of committee and floor debates
- Review budgets, especially if they are in a program format
- Read internal performance reports and memos
- Interview program managers and other key personnel

Scheduling Disbursements or Other Populations

As in a financial engagement, auditors will likely have to rely on sampling; they may not be able to review all activities within a program and seldom can test all transactions. To determine which activities and transactions to test, the auditors must be aware of the nature and amount of disbursements. Therefore, they should schedule all outlays, summarizing them as appropriate.

However, depending on the objective of the audit, disbursements might not be the proper population from which to select a test sample. For example, to test whether participants in a job training program satisfied admissions criteria, the auditors would want to obtain a list of either program participants or program applicants.

Assessing Management Controls

The GAO standards require that auditors "obtain an understanding of management controls that are relevant to the audit." These controls encompass the policies and procedures intended to assure that:

- programs meet their objectives
- the data regarding the programs are valid and reliable
- the organization has complied with all laws, regulations, and contractual provisions
- resources are properly safeguarded

The specific controls to be assessed and the means of reviewing them will depend on the objectives of the audit and the nature of the program. Controls that assure that a program meets its objectives may be of a different type than those intended to safeguard assets. In general, however, the procedures that auditors follow to gain an understanding of financial controls are equally applicable to the other types of controls. They include:

- making inquiries of employees
- flow-charting appropriate systems
- reviewing and inspecting policy manuals and other documents records
- preparing and administering questionnaires

Preparing a Written Audit Plan

The GAO standards of field work require that "work is to be adequately planned." To satisfy this standard auditors must prepare a written plan (i.e., an audit program) that sets forth audit goals, procedures, staff assignments, and anticipated reports. Based on the preliminary survey, review of controls and other preliminary steps, the plan should always be seen as tentative, subject to change as additional insights into the entity are obtained during the evidence-gathering process.

Gathering Evidence

The overall objectives of performance audits are typically twofold: to provide information on the extent to which a program achieved its objectives and to explain the reasons for its successes or failures.

In gathering evidence as to program outcomes, auditors must either make their own observations and measurements or rely on those of others—i.e., either the auditee or third parties. If they intend to rely on those of others, then they must either test the data or assure its reliability by other means.

The specific evidence to be gathered stems directly from the program's objectives. For example, if the objective of a computer-training program were to obtain employment for participants, then the auditors would need to obtain appropriate placement data. If it were to improve high school graduation rates, then they would require data on the percentage of students graduating.

The reasons as to why a program failed to achieve its objectives can generally be attributed to one of three fundamental causes. Taken together the three imply the auditors' approach to identifying a program's shortcomings:

- *Shortcoming:* The program's policies and procedures were poorly designed and, therefore, even if properly executed, would not lead to success.

  Auditor approach: The auditors should examine the policies and procedures, including controls, noting any logical or conceptual flaws.

IN PRACTICE

FINDINGS MUST RELATE TO OBJECTIVES

Upon auditing a federal housing program, the GAO reported that the agency in charge failed to fulfill the program's objectives. The purpose of the program, as established by Congress, was to prevent "middle-class" housing from deteriorating into slums. One aspect of the program required the agency to loan funds to homeowners so that they could improve their properties and ensure that they were in compliance with building codes. The GAO charged that the agency directed program funds to areas that were in far worse condition than permitted by the criteria specified in the enabling legislation.

A program official was critical of the GAO report. He claimed that the areas that his department focused on were in far greater need of assistance than those that satisfied the legislative criteria. "The auditors are just a bunch of bean-counters," he said. "They know nothing about the realities of housing".

The GAO auditors rejected the program official's complaints. If the official thinks that the program was misguided and that resources could have been better spent otherwise, they said, he should take his complaint to Congress. "It's our job to inform the members of Congress that the program, as they established it, is not achieving its goals."

- *Shortcoming:* The program's policies and procedures (including those for supervision and review), while properly designed, were not properly executed.

    Auditor approach: The auditors should test the policies and procedures to gauge the extent to which they were being followed.

- *Shortcoming:* The program was inherently flawed owing to incorrect assumptions or failure to take into account significant factors that would affect its success. For example, a computer training program may have been based on the assumption that if participants learned certain skills, they would be able to find employment. In fact, there may be no demand for those skills in the community served. Hence, even if the policies and procedures were properly executed the program was destined to be unsuccessful.

    Auditor approach: The auditors should identify the conditions that would have been necessary for its success and assess whether they were satisfied.

The following example is illustrative of the auditors' approach to evidence gathering.

EXAMPLE   *Evidence Gathering*

A northwest city is becoming a center for the manufacture of silicon chips and other computer-related products. To encourage unemployed young adults (ages 20 to 30) to undertake technical training in skills needed by local businesses (as well as firms that it would like to attract), the city has established a $5 million revolving loan fund. The fund is being used to make low-interest loans to eligible candidates so that they can enroll in suitable programs offered by local community colleges and proprietary schools. The loans of up to $10,000 are repayable over five years, starting when the candidate completes the program. The city makes approximately 150 loans per year. The loan program, which is administered by a specially created educational loan authority, is now in its sixth year of operation.

An audit team assigned to review the loan program has completed its preliminary survey and the other basic steps necessary to prepare an audit plan. It has determined that the program's operating policies and procedures (e.g., qualifications for loan recipients) are consistent with its objectives.

The following are examples of the audit procedures that the audit team should consider:

1. Obtain from the loan authority a schedule indicating all loans made during the period.

2. Select a sample of loans and for each obtain the applicant's loan file.

    a. Verify that the recipient met all specified qualifications and that all appropriate approval guidelines were followed.

    b. Verify that the file contains documents, such as school transcripts, showing that the candidate enrolled in an approved program and made required progress.

    c. Verify the loan recipient's payment history, assuring that the authority properly pursued all delinquencies.

    d. Make certain that the file contains up-to-date records of the loan recipient's employment history subsequent to completing the training program. Confirm its accuracy by corresponding with the employers.

3. Obtain the authority's summary statistics and supporting schedules as to loans made, recipients successfully completing approved training programs and participant employment experience.

    a. Reconcile the supporting schedules to the summary statistics.

    b. Test the accuracy of the supporting schedules by tracing a sample of the information on the schedule to the loan files of individual recipients.

In obtaining and assessing evidence, auditors must document their procedures and findings. By the time the audit is completed, every assertion in the auditors' report should be backed by one or more working papers setting forth the underlying evidence. Auditors should always assume that any unfavorable determinations will be challenged by the managers accountable for them. Therefore, they must be certain their working papers, when subjected to the most hostile of analysis, can withstand assault.

Reporting the Results of the Audit

The GAO standards specify that auditors should prepare timely written reports of each engagement. Auditors' reports on financial statement engagements generally constitute only a few standardized paragraphs in which the auditors explain the scope and nature of their engagement and attest to information included in the statements. Those on performance audits, however, set forth data and findings as generated by the auditors, not merely the auditors' opinion on the assertion of others. Therefore, the auditor's reports are often fifty to one-hundred pages long.

Per the GAO standards, the reports should include:

- an explanation of the audit's objectives and of its scope and methodology
- the significant auditing findings and the auditors' conclusions. The findings should relate to the objectives of the engagement. The report should not only indicate the quantitative measures of performance, but also, if the program did not meet expectations, the reasons as to why. It should back any general assertions with specific examples. As noted by the GAO:

> Conclusions should be specified and not left to be inferred by readers. The strength of the auditors' conclusions depends on the persuasiveness of the evidence supporting the findings and the logic used to formulate the conclusions.[8]

- recommendations as to how to correct problems and improve operations. To be most useful, audits should be as much concerned with the future as with the past. They should be at least as constructive as they are critical.
- an indication of all significant instances of illegal acts or noncompliance with regulations and contractual provisions
- a description of any significant deficiencies in management controls
- a description of any noteworthy accomplishments. This type of information not only adds balance to the report and takes the sharp edge off the report's critical comments, but provides suggestions that can be applied to other areas within the same organization or to outside organizations.

---

[8] *Government Auditing Standards (Standards for Audit of Governmental Organizations, Programs, Activities, and Functions)* (Washington, D.C.: Comptroller General of the United States, 1994), page 91.

The GAO standards also require that the auditors include in the report the views of officials responsible for the program as to the auditors' conclusions and recommendations. To enable them to comment, the auditors should present the officials with a preliminary version of the report and solicit their written observations as to why they agree or disagree with the report and what corrective measures, if any, they plan.

If the auditors agree that the objections of the officials are valid, then they can modify their report before issuing a final version. However, if the auditors do not believe that the officials' protests are legitimate, they can include in their report their reasons why they believe they are invalid—and, in effect, have the last word.

Per the GAO standards, reports on governmental performance audits, like those on governmental financial audits, should be made public, unless their distribution is limited by law or regulation. Some government agencies, such as the GAO, now promote wide distribution of their reports by making them available on the "internet."[9]

Although it is difficult to predict the future of accounting and auditing, it is almost certain that performance auditing will play an increasingly prominent role. As both governments and not-for-profits place greater emphasis on achieving their objectives, it is inevitable that increasing attention will be paid to reports as to the extent that they accomplished what was expected of them.

What Unique Ethical Issues Do Governmental and Not-For-Profit Accounting and Auditing Present?

A unit on professional ethics is commonly incorporated into university-level courses in auditing. The discussion is often divided into two parts. The first addresses philosophical principles of ethical behavior. The second concerns the AICPA's Code of Conduct. The Code of Conduct is mainly a series of practices established by the AICPA to advance the interests of both the accounting profession and the constituents that it serves. The code contains rules relating to independence, integrity, advertising, contingent fees, and form of practice organization.

This section of the text is not intended to duplicate the materials ordinarily addressed in auditing courses—almost all of which are relevant to CPAs carrying out independent audits of governments and not-for-profit organizations. Instead, its purposes are to highlight the characteristics of governments that may justify a special perspective on ethical questions, to set forth an approach to resolving ethical dilemmas (one not unique to the governmental environment), and to illustrate how that approach can be applied to ethical dilemmas.

CHARACTERISTICS OF GOVERNMENTS THAT JUSTIFY A SPECIAL PERSPECTIVE ON ETHICAL QUESTIONS

Governments (and to a lesser extent many not-for-profits) have characteristics that present their employees with ethical decisions different from those faced by employees of businesses. These include the following:

- **Public expectations.** The public holds employees of governments to a higher standard of conduct than those of businesses. Whereas it may accept that private companies—and hence, their employees—act in their own self-interest, it expects government employees to put the welfare of the public above that of themselves.

---

[9] The GAO's home page is at http://www.gao.gov/

- *Guardians of public funds.* Government accountants are guardians of public funds and are accountable to the public as to how they use them. Although corporate managers are accountable to stockholders, the public has far more rigorous standards than investors of what constitutes proper use of resources and is far less tolerant of frivolous expenditures. For example, investors may tolerate lavish entertainment, personal use of company jets, and palatial offices as acceptable management "perks." The public, however, permits few government officials the same luxuries.

- *Activities carried out in open view.* Virtually all government activities are carried out in broad daylight. Public officials are answerable to the public for almost all their actions. Under federal and state "open records" statutes, relatively few types of documents, not even internal memos and correspondence, are immune from public scrutiny. "No comment—that's proprietary information," in response to a reporter's question may be accepted from corporate executives, but it is seldom countenanced from government officials.

- *Special powers.* Governments have powers that businesses do not. For example, they may compel citizens to disclose personal information, such as earnings and holdings of personal property. Moreover, many citizens attach a legitimacy to requests for data from government officials that they would view with suspicion if they came from private businesses. Therefore, government officials have a particular obligation to maintain the confidentially of information that is not in the public domain and not to exceed the limits of their authority in their dealings with the public.

- *Conflicting loyalties.* Government workers are not only government employees, but they are also citizens to whom the government is accountable. Government decisions may be made in a highly charged political atmosphere and may involve the most basic of human values. The government may be led by officials of a political party different from that of an individual employee. Hence, the individual employee may be faced with a conflict between loyalty to his organization and his superiors and that to his own political and moral values.

ANALYZING ETHICAL DILEMMAS

A *dilemma*, by definition, is a situation that requires a choice between two equally balanced alternatives; a predicament that seemingly defies a satisfactory solution. Few ethical dilemmas can be resolved without an individual selecting among, or compromising between, competing ethical values. There is almost never a single "correct" course of action. Nevertheless, by identifying and analyzing the factors relevant to the issue at hand, the individual can better develop available options and understand their consequences.

The following questions are indicative of an approach (merely one of several possibilities) that can be taken to resolve ethical dilemmas:

1. What are the relevant facts? (Although many situations are seemingly complex, there may be only a small number of facts that are genuinely germane).

2. Who are the major parties affected and what are their interests in how the dilemma is resolved?

3. What are the ethical values that are in question? How do they rank in importance? Examples of these values include:

   - honesty and integrity
   - loyalty and obligations to colleagues

- responsibilities to family
- obligation to make full and fair disclosures to appropriate parties
- loyalty and other obligations to one's employer
- responsibilities as a citizen
- pursuit of excellence

4. What are the alternative courses of action?

5. What are the consequences of each course of action? Which values would have to be sacrificed or compromised?

The following example illustrates how these questions may be applied to a specific ethical dilemma.

EXAMPLE   *Ethical Dilemma*

James Klavan is a city's assistant comptroller. Within the last year, the comptroller established an enterprise fund to account for the operation of the city's golf course. Previously the course had been accounted for in the general fund. Generally accepted accounting principles permit a government flexibility as to the types of funds in which it should account for activities financed by user charges. There is no question that under those principles golf-course operations can be accounted for in either a governmental fund or an enterprise fund. The main reason for the change was to shift expenses out of the general fund and thereby help to eliminate a general fund deficit. Were it not for the accounting change, the general fund deficit would have to be offset by increased taxes or reductions in services. However, if the reasons for the change were made public, city officials would unquestionably be charged by political opponents with fiscal gimmickry.

The city comptroller was approached by a reporter covering the publication of the city's annual report. Owing to time constraints, the comptroller referred him to Klavan, his assistant. In the course of an interview, the reporter (who couldn't distinguish a debit from a credit) asked Klavan to explain the change and indicate its significance. Klavan is uncertain as to how to respond.

1. Relevant facts

- The comptroller established an enterprise fund so as to reduce the reported general fund deficit.
- Klavan is aware of the reason for the change and is asked by a reporter for an explanation of its significance.
- Although the change is permissible under generally accepted accounting principles, it was made to eliminate a general fund deficit and thereby avert either increases in taxes or reductions in services.
- Disclosure of the true reason for the change would embarrass both Klavan's immediate superior and the city administration.

2. Major parties affected (other than Klavan)

- The comptroller, who stands to be embarrassed if the reason for the change were made public
- The reporter, who presumably expects a full and fair explanation of the change

- The citizenry, who might be misled by the change (yet might nevertheless support it if it would avert a tax increase or service reduction)

3. Ethical values in conflict

- Loyalty to colleagues and employer (both the comptroller and the city administration)
- Honesty (to reporter)
- Obligation to make full and fair disclosures to appropriate parties
- Responsibilities as a citizen (either to prevent the city from misleading its citizens or, by contrast, to facilitate a means of averting tax increases)

4. Possible courses of action available to Klavan

- Explain the change to the reporter, but obfuscate the reason for it.
- Explain the change and reveal the underlying reason for it.
- Delay responding to the reporter. Tell the comptroller that he will not meet with the reporter unless the comptroller explicitly gives him permission to reveal the reason for the change.

5. Consequences of actions

- If Klavan explains the change to the reporter without revealing the reasons for it, he will not be providing full disclosure and will thereby be dishonest. Moreover, he will be allowing his employer (both the comptroller and the city administration) to mislead the citizenry.
- If he explains the change and reveals the underlying reason for it, he will embarrass both the comptroller and the city (and thereby place his career with the city at risk).
- If he confronts the comptroller and indicates that he will meet with the reporter only if granted permission to reveal the underlying reason for the change, then he will place the comptroller in an uncomfortable position (by suggesting that the comptroller is being deceitful) and thereby jeopardize his relationship with the comptroller and consequently his career with the city.

To be sure, there may be other courses of action available to Klavan. Indeed, the key to resolving most ethical dilemmas is to develop options beyond those that are obvious. There are, unfortunately, no "textbook" solutions.

SUMMARY

In the area of government and not-for-profit auditing the influence of the federal government has been paramount. It has had its impact mainly through the GAO's Yellow Book, *Government Auditing Standards (Standards for Audit of Governmental Organizations, Programs, Activities, and Functions)* and through the Single Audit Act.

The Yellow Book establishes "generally accepted government auditing standards" (GAGAS), which, owing to the Single Audit Act, must now be adhered to in virtually all audits of both governments and not-for-profit organizations that receive federal financial assistance. Although the standards cover both financial statement audits and performance audits, the Single Audit Act requires only financial audits. Like the auditing standards of the AICPA after which they are modeled, they are grouped into three categories: general standards, standards of field work, and standards of reporting.

The primary difference between financial audits as carried out in a government or not-for-profit entity, as opposed to a business, is the greater influence placed upon assuring compliance with laws, regulations, and contractual requirements. The GAO standards, for example, require that audit reports include an explicit description of compliance tests and an indication of compliance violations.

Legislative actions, now codified in the Single Audit Act, direct that recipients of federal aid be subject to a single independent financial audit even though they may receive funds from many agencies. These audits should comprise two elements: (1) an examination in accord with government auditing standards and (2) an audit of federal financial awards. The audit of federal financial awards focuses almost entirely on assuring that a federal funds recipient has satisfied the terms of its grants or contracts. These terms include compliance with both "general" and program-specific requirements. The general requirements, common to all federal awards, relate to matters such as political contributions, civil rights, and drug-free workplaces. The specific program requirements are set forth in the rules and regulations of each program.

Performance audits differ in concept from financial audits in that the auditors do not merely *attest* to assertions of management. Rather, they make their own assessments as to the extent that an entity or program has achieved its objectives. The key to carrying out a performance audit (consistent with the theme of the previous chapter) is in identifying the operational objectives of the target program or activity. If these objectives are quantifiable and measurable, then the auditors have either to make the appropriate measurements or to verify those of others. Hence, performance audits can be as objective as traditional financial engagements.

As emphasized throughout this text, both governments and not-for-profits have objectives other than profit maximization. Accordingly, the conventional operating statements that highlight revenues and expenditures provide little indication of how well an entity is fulfilling its mission. These statements must be supplemented by reports on service efforts and accomplishments that focus on the entity's actual objectives. Correspondingly, audits that merely attest to the fairness of the conventional statements are of only limited value to the constituents of the entity. Performance audits are therefore an important supplement to conventional financial audits. They are unquestionably the wave of the future.

Although government accountants and auditors face ethical dilemmas similar to those in the private sector, they must resolve them in face of the following unique characteristics of government employees: public expectations; status as guardians of public funds; the open environment in which they function; special powers they may have, and conflicting loyalties. Unfortunately, there are no textbook answers to ethical problems; the key to a satisfactory resolution is the development of options beyond the obvious.

EXERCISE FOR REVIEW AND SELF-STUDY

You are the partner of the CPA firm that has been engaged to perform the annual audit of the Euless School District. The district receives approximately $1.5 million per year in federal assistance. This includes $500,000 in annual grants to conduct an experimental high school science enrichment program. The program has now been in existence for three years.

a. You assign one of the firm's managers to be in charge of the audit's field work. The supervisor recently returned from a two-week professional education course in estate and gift taxation. He took the course to satisfy his state's biannual eighty-hour CPE requirement. He took no other CPE courses in the past two years. Why might his appointment be in violation of *Government Auditing Standards*?

b. The auditor manager who was eventually assigned to the engagement inquired as to whether the firm had on hand the most recent version of "Circular A-133" and the "Common Rule." What are these documents, and why are they likely to be relevant to the financial audit of a local independent school district?

c. Soon after the audit staff began the engagement, the school district's chief financial officer called to complain that the auditors were making inquiries of the district's employees as to civil rights policies and the political activities of district administrators. These matters, he asserted, were clearly beyond the scope of a financial engagement. How would you respond to his objection?

d. After your firm completed the financial audit of the district, the school board requested that it conduct a performance audit of the science enrichment program. In what critical way would the performance audit differ conceptually from the financial engagement?

e. Suppose the objectives of the program were not spelled out in the federal legislation that authorized the program. Moreover, the school district had never prepared a written "statement of objectives." What steps would you take to establish the program's objectives?

f. Suppose you are able to establish that a primary objective of the program is to encourage students to enter vocational fields related to science. The grant funds may be used to pay for teachers' training, curriculum devel-

opment projects, equipment and texts, and extracurricular activities related to science.

1. What would be the purpose of preparing a schedule showing how the grant funds were disbursed?

2. How would you recommend the auditors gain an understanding of the internal controls over program expenditures?

3. Inasmuch as the program has been in existence for only three years, how might you assess whether the program has fulfilled its objective?

QUESTIONS FOR REVIEW AND DISCUSSION

1. What is the Yellow Book, and why has it influenced audits both of state and local governments and of not-for-profit organizations?

2. What are the two types of government *financial audits*? In what significant way do financial audits in government and not-for-profit organizations differ from those carried on in businesses?

3. The State Auditor of Missouri is an elected official. In auditing the financial statements of the University of Missouri, what special problems relating to independence would he or she face that a private CPA firm would not? Would he or she be in violation of the GAO standards? Explain, indicating how the GAO standards deal with the apparent conflicts of interest faced by state and local government audit departments.

4. In what way do the GAO standards impose more rigorous continuing professional education requirements than those of the AICPA?

5. In what way do the reporting standards of the GAO differ from those of the AICPA as to (a) public dissemination of the reports; and (b) tests of compliance and internal controls.

6. What is a single audit? What deficiencies in previous practice was the Single Audit Act intended to correct?

7. What are the two main components of a single audit?

8. What are "general" compliance requirements? Provide several examples.

9. What types of matters do "specific" requirements address?

10. It is sometimes said that performance audits are not "true" audits in that they are conceptually different from traditional financial audits. In what way are they conceptually different?

11. In what other significant ways do performance audits differ from financial audits?

12. What are the general criteria that audit organizations use in selecting programs and activities for performance audits?

13. What steps might auditors take to discern the objectives of a program or activity?

14. What are the key features of a performance audit report?

PROBLEMS

15-1

The Yellow Book standards relating to financial audits apply to independent CPA firms as well as government audit departments.

The following descriptions relate to an independent CPA firm that includes among its audit clients municipal-

ities, school districts, and not-for-profit organizations, all of which receive federal financial assistance. Each description presents a possible violation of *Government Auditing Standards* (summarized in Table 15–1). For each description indicate the specific standard at issue and tell why there might be violation.

a. Each year the managing partner appoints a committee of three of its partners to evaluate the quality of the work performed by the firm. The firm is not otherwise reviewed by independent parties.

b. When the firm conducts a financial examination, its primary objective is to determine whether the auditee's financial system is properly designed, the system is operating as intended, and the resultant financial records can be relied upon. Accordingly, the department does not test explicitly for fraud or other illegal activities.

c. The firm has a formal program of continuing professional education. To eliminate the need to pay for the staff to attend outside courses, it brings in outside experts to conduct forty hours per year of training. Each year the training is directed to a specific area. This year's area was changes in the federal tax code; last year's was "how to market the firm."

d. The firm periodically assigns members of its staff on a temporary basis to government and not-for-profit audit clients. The staff members typically serve as financial consultants or as acting financial administrators.

e. The firm may not test compliance with certain federal grant provisions if the grant was examined by the client's internal auditors and no violations were detected.

f. In its single audit of a client's federally assisted program, the firm detected numerous instances of noncompliance with applicable federal regulations. Inasmuch as none of the violations were either serious or material, the firm reported them to the client in its "management letter" but did not mention them in its compliance report to federal officials.

g. As part of all financial audits of federal funds recipients the auditors carefully assess the adequacy of internal controls. They do not, however, prepare a specific report on internal controls or address them in the standard audit report.

15-2

Even programs involving relatively subjective judgments can readily be audited.

A Department of Housing and Urban Development (HUD) program is aimed at conserving and rehabilitating blighted but salvageable urban areas. One element of the program provides that HUD will make rehabilitation grants and low-interest loans to property owners to help them finance the repairs needed to bring their properties into compliance with housing codes.

When Congress authorized the program it did not establish specific criteria as to what constitutes a "blighted but salvageable" area; it left that up to HUD.

A preliminary survey by the GAO has indicated that HUD is directing funds to areas that were far too deteriorated for conservation and rehabilitation to work.

Suppose that you are assigned to the engagement. Outline an approach that you would take to support (or reject) the findings of the preliminary survey.

15-3

Compliance testing may require auditor ingenuity.

The CPA firm of which you are a manager has placed you in charge of the audit of the Thornburg School District. The district receives substantial financial support from the State Education Agency. The state requires aid recipients to have annual single audits conducted by independent CPA firms. The firms are responsible for verifying that recipients have complied with the provisions of all financial awards from the state.

From your preliminary survey you learn that the district received an award of $3 million to provide free hot lunches to elementary schoolchildren of low-income families. The award specifies that only children from families with incomes under $20,000 are eligible to participate in the program. The state requires districts to determine eligibility, but it provides no guidance as to how they are to do so.

Based only on this limited information, it is obviously not possible to develop a specific audit program to assure that the district has complied with the eligibility provisions. However, before you even meet with district officials to discuss the audit, you wish to have a preliminary strategy in mind.

a. As best you can from the limited amount of information provided, design a strategy to test compliance with the eligibility provisions.

b. Suppose that the audit was being conducted under the federal Single Audit Act and the auditors were required to adhere to all of its reporting provisions. As part of your examination you found that 25 students out of 350 in the program failed to meet the eligibility requirements. Assuming that the auditors consider the amounts involved as indicative of a weakness in internal controls, how, if at all, should that finding affect your report on the program?

15-4

A performance audit of investment activities must ascertain whether common-sense controls (not explicitly discussed in this chapter) have been established.

The director of the internal audit department of a mid-sized city, received a memo from a member of the city council that included the following:

> I am certain that you have followed recent press reports of the losses incurred by city and state governments on their investment portfolios. Many of these losses can be attributed to pressures to boost investment returns. These pressures encouraged the investment officers to acquire derivatives and other high-risk securities, which are clearly inappropriate for governments. I am extremely concerned that our city might also be vulnerable to major losses.

The city currently has investments (including those of our retirement funds, bond reserves and endowments) totaling more than $800 million. These are managed by our Office of Investments (a subunit of the Treasury Department). The mission of the office as set forth in the enabling legislation is "to invest prudently the available resources of the city so as to maximize the return to the city."

I note that whereas our independent CPAs have reviewed the city's investment portfolio as part of their annual financial audit, your department has never conducted a performance audit of the office. I urge, therefore, that you do so as soon as feasible. I think it especially important that you report on the extent to which the office has in place the administrative controls, policies, and practices necessary to assure that it is accomplishing its mission.

a. In light of widely accepted criteria for selecting audit targets, do you find it surprising that the internal audit department has never conducted a performance audit of the Office of Investments. Explain, citing relevant criteria.

b. Suppose you are placed in charge of the engagement. Draft a memo to the head of the internal audit department in which you outline the approach you would take in carrying it out. Be as specific as possible, providing examples of the types of administrative controls that you would expect to find in place. Indicate how you would assess whether the Office of Investments is "maximizing the return to the city."

15-5

The key to auditing the effectiveness of a social program is in establishing its objectives.

The Office of Economic Opportunity (OEO) designed "special impact programs" to reduce unemployment, dependency, and community tensions in urban areas with large concentrations of low-income residents or in rural areas having substantial migration to such urban areas. The purpose of these experimental programs, which combine business, community, and manpower development, is to offer poor people an opportunity to become self-supporting through the free enterprise system. The programs are intended to create training and job opportunities, improve the living environment, and encourage development of local entrepreneurial skills.

One area chosen to participate in several special impact programs was Bedford-Stuyvesant. The Bedford-Stuyvesant program was the first and largest such program to be sponsored by the federal government. It has received more than $960 million in federal funds from its inception through the current year. Another $250 million was obtained from private sources, such as the Ford Foundation and the Astor Foundation.

Problems:

Bedford-Stuyvesant is a five-square-mile area with a population of 350,000 to 400,000 in New York City's borough of Brooklyn. The area has serious problems of unemployment, underemployment, and inadequate housing.

Bedford-Stuyvesant's problems are deep-seated and have resisted rapid solution. They stem primarily from the fact that local residents, to a considerable degree, lack the education and training required for the jobs available elsewhere in the city and from the lack of jobs in the area. Unemployment and underemployment, in turn, reduce buying power, which has a depressing effect on the area's economy.

The magnitude of the Bedford-Stuyvesant problems are indicated by the following data disclosed by the U.S. census:

- Of the total civilian labor force, 8.9 percent are unemployed, compared with unemployment rates of 7.1 percent for New York City and 6.8 percent for the New York Standard Metropolitan Statistical Area (SMSA).

- Per capita income is 66 percent that of New York City and 51 percent that of the SMSA.

- Families below the poverty level make up 24.8 percent of the population, compared with 11.4 percent in New York City and 9.2 percent in the SMSA.

- Families receiving public assistance make up 25.4 percent of the population, compared with 9.6 percent in New York City and 7.5 percent in the SMSA.

A number of factors aggravate the area's economic problems and make them more difficult to solve. Some of these are:

- a reluctance of industry to move into New York City
- a net outflow of industry from New York City
- high city taxes and a high crime rate
- a dearth of local residents possessing business managerial experience

The area's housing problems result from the widespread deterioration of existing housing and are, in part, a byproduct of below-average income levels resulting from unemployment and underemployment. They are aggravated by a shortage of mortgage capital for residential housing associated with a lack of confidence in the area on the part of financial institutions.

One of the special impact programs that Bedford-Stuyvesant participates in is intended to stimulate the private economy by providing funds to local businesses, both new and existing. Under this program, begun five years ago, the sponsors propose to create jobs and stimulate business ownership by local residents. At first, investments in local businesses were made only in the form of loans. Later, the sponsors adopted a policy of making equity investments in selected companies to obtain for the sponsors a voice in management. Equity investments totaling about $2.5 million were made in four companies.

Loans are to be repaid in installments over periods of up to 10 years, usually with a moratorium on repayment for six months or longer. Repayment is to be made in cash or by applying subsidies allowed by the sponsors for providing on-the-job training to unskilled workers. Loans made during the first two years of the program were interest free. Later, the sponsors revised the policy to one of charging below-market interest rates. Rates charged are now from 3 to 6.5 percent. This policy change was made to (1) emphasize to borrowers their obligations to repay the loans and (2) help the sponsors monitor borrowers' progress toward profitability.

Prospective borrowers learn of the program through information disseminated at neighborhood centers, advertisements on radio and television and in a local newspaper, and word of mouth. Those who wish to apply for loans are required to complete application forms providing information relating to their education, business and work experience, and their personal financial condition and references. The sponsors set up a management assistance division that employed consultants to supplement its internal marketing assistance efforts and to provide management, accounting, marketing, legal, and other help to borrowers.

The sponsors proposed to create at least 1,700 jobs during the first four years of the loan program by making loans to seventy-three new and existing businesses.

Required

Put yourself in the position of the GAO manager in charge of all audits pertaining to the Office of Economic Opportunity. Your staff has undertaken a preliminary survey of the Bedford-Stuyvesant program and the above information was extracted from its report on the survey.

The New York City field office has been assigned the job of conducting the detailed performance audit of the special impact program just described. Prepare a memo to the New York City field office in which you indicate, in as great detail as is possible from the information provided, the specific steps its staff should perform in conducting an evaluation of the effectiveness of the program.

This problem was based on an actual GAO Audit. Although written by the author, it was previously published in Auditing *(8th ed.), by Jack C. Robertson (Chicago: Irwin, 1996). It is reprinted with permission of McGraw Hill-Irwin ©.*

15-6

Performance audits are often far removed from financial audits, but even seemingly unauditable programs can be evaluated.

The president of a major state university has a problem. A group of alumni are complaining that the university's athletic program is an embarrassment to the university and are demanding that the athletic director be fired. In response, the president has promised an intensive "audit" of the all aspects of the department's performance.

The university has never explicitly established formal goals for the athletic department. Nevertheless, five years prior to this crisis, at the press conference announcing his appointment, the athletic director (with characteristic exuberance and hyperbole) made the following statements:

1. We intend to win national championships in all major sports.
2. Every one of our athletes will be graduated in five years.
3. The student body will once again be proud of its teams, showing its support by attending our games.
4. We will be "number one" as measured by TV appearances and revenues.

Although these comments are obviously visions, rather than operational objectives, they do imply performance indicators that can be objectively assessed.

Suppose that you are placed in charge of the president's promised audit of the athletic department. For each of the four visions, propose objective indicators that could be used to assess the department's performance. Recognizing that you will be unable to make definitive judgments as to whether the department's performance was satisfactory or not, tell what information you would want to provide the president and the university's board of trustees so that they can make an informed judgment as to the quality of the department's performance.

15-7

Assessment of the procurement process may be a central element in an operations audit.

The chairman of a state legislature's finance committee has charged that the Division of Taxation's computer systems are in chaos and, as a consequence, the state is failing to collect hundreds of millions in income taxes to which it is entitled. According to the chairman, the system was improperly designed and many of its component computers, software programs, and peripheral items of equipment have failed to perform as promised.

The overall system had been designed three years earlier by an outside consulting firm. The component computers, software programs, and peripheral items of equipment were purchased by the state from numerous different vendors.

The chairman has charged that the new system, costing $50 million, was a fiscal disaster and demanded that the State Auditor determine the reasons for the failure.

Suppose that you are a senior-level auditor in the State Auditor's Office. You are asked by the State Auditor to head a team to assess whether, in fact, the systems are not working as intended and, if not, why not and who is responsible.

a. Indicate in general terms how you might determine what was intended of the system.
b. Assume that you concluded that the system was not operating as intended. Indicate your general approach to discerning the reason for the failures and to pinpointing responsibility.

15-8

Even when objectives are clearly stated, the reasons why they have not been met may not be easy to discern.

The City on the Lake Convention Center was constructed at a cost of $250 million with the aim of attracting visitors to the area. Taxpayers were assured that the convention center would be self-supporting; that convention-center revenues would be sufficient to cover all expenditures, including debt service. Yet in its first five years of operation the center consistently reported operating deficits.

In a recent report to the city council, the convention center manager indicated that deficits can be attributable to the center's inability to attract sufficient conventions and other events. Whereas convention planners had projected that the center would have events scheduled for at least 250 days during the year, it had so far averaged only 180 days—far fewer than the break-even point.

As the city auditor, you have been requested by the city council to conduct a performance audit to learn why the center has been unable to attract the projected number of conventions and other events and to make recommendations for appropriate changes so that the projections can be met.

Required: Propose, in general terms, an approach to fulfilling the mandate of the city council.

Cases in Ethics

1. Conflicting Responsibilities

Kevin Watkins is a manager of a CPA firm. At the recommendation of the partner-in-charge he applied, and was accepted, for membership on the Accounting Standards Committee of the Government Finance Officers Association. Committee members are selected on their individual qualifications. In appointing members the Association tries to assure that they are drawn from all major constituent groups, but members do not represent their employers.

The Committee has under consideration a resolution urging municipalities to develop measures of service efforts and accomplishment and to report upon them in their annual reports. It is divided on the resolution, but Watkins is convinced of its merits. The partner in charge of Watkin's CPA firm, however, is strongly opposed to it, noting that obtaining the required information would impose a substantial net cost upon the firm.

A voice vote on the resolution is scheduled for the next meeting.

2. Audit Failure

In a management letter following its year-end audit of the City Hospital, the city's independent audit firm questioned the adequacy of the hospital's accounts receivable allowance for contractual adjustments. It noted that owing to contractual changes, the discounts given to insurance companies and HMOs were increasing, and it urged that the hospital carefully review the collectibility of its receivables. It asserted that audit tests revealed numerous required adjustments and as a consequence the hospital

reduced its receivable balance by 7 percent. Nevertheless, the firm warned, additional write-downs would likely be required in the future. The firm had issued an unqualified opinion on the financial statements.

Several months following the audit, the hospital announced that operating losses for the then-current year would far exceed expectations, owing to a 30 percent write-down of accounts receivable. The required write-down was greatly in excess of the allowance for contractual adjustments.

The partner in charge of the engagement was asked by a reporter, who was unaware of the management letter, why the audit of the previous year failed to detect the overstatement of receivables.

3. Charity Begins with the Auditor

In June 1998, Jason King completed his audit of a 1997 grant that a city made to Field of Dreams, a private, not-for-profit organization that sponsors recreational programs for disadvantaged teens. In the course of his testing, King discovered that material disbursements that were clearly applicable to 1998 were charged as 1997 expenditures. The program director acknowledged the overcharges, pointing out that the organization faced a temporary cash shortage in 1997. By charging the costs to 1997, he was able to obtain early reimbursement and thereby avoid a fiscal crisis. He assured King that no dishonesty was intended; he was simply shifting funds from one year to another. Indeed, King was able to verify that the organization did not request reimbursement for the same charges in 1998.

The Field of Dreams grant was a pass-through grant in that the federal government provided the funds. Were this discrepancy set forth as a "reportable condition" in King's single audit report, it is almost certain that the organization would be ineligible for federal awards in the future.

Over the course of several years, King has become familiar with the organization's programs and considers them to be of uncommon value to the community.

4. Undisclosed Losses

The Office of the Treasurer maintains an investment pool for several quasi-independent governments, such as housing authorities and development boards, affiliated with a city. Michelle Ruiz, a senior manager in the Treasurer's Office, recently became aware that the treasurer has been investing pool funds in risky derivatives and has been leveraging the funds by financing the purchase of long-term securities with short-term loans. Because of a sustained rise in interest rates over the past year, the market value of the portfolio is considerably below the contributions of pool participants. If the pool participants were to learn of the losses, it is virtually certain that some would withdraw from the fund immediately, thereby prompting an overall run on the pool.

As long as the losses are kept quiet, it is more than probable that the interest rates will soon decline and that the portfolio will recover its value. Indeed, within the last week the Federal Reserve Bank announced a reduction in its discount rate and the value of the portfolio rebounded slightly. By contrast, a run on the pool would assure that virtually all participants incur substantial losses.

Shortly after Ruiz learns of the losses, she is making a presentation to the media as to the operations of the pool. During a question and answer session she is asked how the pool has performed over the last several years. She explains (truthfully) that over the long-term investment returns have been well above average. She is uncertain, however, as to whether she should add anything as to its short-term results.

5. Politically Uncomfortable Conclusion

In verifying the fixed asset records of the electric utility department, Jean Hanson, staff auditor of a city's internal audit department, noted that several trucks and pieces of equipment were out of service and apparently unrepairable.

Therefore, they should have been written off. She described and documented her conclusions in her working papers.

When she discussed her findings with the manager in charge of the engagement, the manager indicated that she was aware of the problem since it had been raised in previous years. Moreover, she had already discussed it with the internal auditor (the head of the department) and both had agreed that this was not the year to make the required write-off. A large write-off would cause considerable embarrassment to the city manager, the mayor, and members of the city council, all of whom had recently defended the electric utility department against charges that it was mismanaged. Further, the budget of the internal audit department was coming up for consideration before the city council.

Jean Hanson had reason to believe that the working paper in which she described her findings was removed from the audit binder.

SOLUTION TO EXERCISE FOR REVIEW AND SELF-STUDY

a. The appointment of the supervisor would be in violation of *Government Auditing Standards* because the supervisor has not completed the requisite 24 hours of continuing professional education in areas directly related to the governmental environment.

b. The school district receives federal financial assistance and thereby would likely be subject to a single audit. Circular A-133, *Audits of States, Local Governments and Non-Profit Organizations*, provides detailed guidance as to how audits of government organizations, including school districts, should be performed. The "Common Rule," *Administrative Requirements for Grants and Cooperative Agreements for State and Local Governments* details various OMB rules and regulations.

c. The auditors were correct in making inquiries as to both civil rights policies and political activities. As part of a single audit, the auditors must test for violations of general compliance requirements, two of which relate to civil rights and political activity.

d. A performance audit is conceptually different than a financial audit in that in a financial audit the auditors *attest* to the assertions of management as set forth in management-prepared financial statements. In performance audits, the auditors make, and report upon, their own, independent assessments of organizational performance.

e. The steps the auditors might undertake to discern the objectives of the program might include the following:
- review the legislative history of the program
- review the district's budgets, especially those related directly to the program
- examine school board minutes

- review internal memos
- interview school board members and district administrators and teachers

f. 1. By scheduling the disbursements, the auditors would have a starting point from which to determine whether the outlays were in compliance with the terms of the program and whether they were for purposes consistent with its objectives.

2. The auditors can gain an understanding of the internal controls by interviewing personnel involved in the program, preparing and administering internal control questionnaires, flowcharting relevant systems, and reviewing applicable policies.

3. If the program has been in existence only three years, then it would clearly be impossible to make definitive judgments as to its success in encouraging students to enter science-related fields. Nevertheless, the auditors can first determine the number of students participating in the program (i.e., taking extra science classes or engaging in science-related extracurricular activities). If this number is small, then it is unlikely that the program is achieving its objective. Similarly, they can identify any curriculum changes as a consequence of the program. The absence of significant improvements would suggest that the program is having only limited impact. Further, they can establish the percentage of students that are enrolled in university science-related programs and compare this percentage with those of past years or with those of control groups—students possessing similar characteristics (academic, economic, cultural) who have not participated in the program.

CHAPTER 16

Federal Government Accounting

LEARNING OBJECTIVES

After studying this chapter you should understand:

- the unique characteristics of the federal government that necessitate special accounting and reporting practices
- the roles of the main agencies responsible for federal accounting and reporting
- the key objectives of federal financial reporting
- the different types of federal budgets and their primary elements
- the types of accounts maintained by the federal government

- what constitutes a federal reporting entity
- the form and content of current government-wide financial reports
- the form and content of agency financial reports
- the main accounting issues being addressed by the Federal Accounting Standards Advisory Board (FASAB)
- the recent efforts by the federal government to improve its fiscal management

The federal government is unique among U.S. institutions—and so, also, are its accounting and reporting concerns. Although obviously distinguishable by its size (expenditures for fiscal year 2000 will exceed $1.9 trillion), it also is differentiated by:

- the range of its activities (e.g., defense, Social Security, and managing the money supply)
- the diversity of its resources (e.g., national parks and monuments, stores of gold bullion, and military hardware)
- the nature of its obligations (e.g., Social Security benefits, loan guarantees, and commitments to carry out social programs)
- the extent of its powers (e.g., to tax, to print currency, and to regulate commerce)

In this chapter we provide an overview of the federal accounting structure and the special accounting and reporting issues that it faces. First, we consider the roles played by the key agencies responsible for establishing and administering the federal accounting and reporting system. We follow by describing the federal budget and its relationship to federal accounts and reports. We then present the key features of a new accounting and reporting model being developed by the Federal Accounting Standards Advisory Board (FASAB). We set forth the main accounting issues addressed by the FASAB and indicate how they are being resolved. We conclude by describing recent federal initiatives to supplement the agency financial statements with reports on service efforts and accomplishments.

Thomas Jefferson believed that every American "should be able to comprehend [the nation's finances], to investigate abuses, and consequently to control them." Reflecting that view, the U.S. Constitution mandates that the federal government periodically issue financial reports. Article I, Section IX states:

> No money shall be drawn from the Treasury, but in consequence of appropriations made by law; and a regular statement and account of the receipts and expenditures of all public money shall be published from time to time.

The constitution left Congress and the executive branch to determine the form and content of the reports and to implement and administer the underlying accounting system. Had the founding fathers been able to foresee the nation's accounting and reporting system two hundred years after they ratified the Constitution, they might well have been more specific in establishing accounting and reporting requirements. As of 1997, the federal accounting and reporting system is clearly inadequate for an organization of the government's size and complexity. Owing to bookkeeping practices that it would never accept from the citizens and corporations that it taxes or regulates, the federal government is still unable to issue financial statements on which independent auditors can issue an unqualified opinion. According to the GAO, the financial systems of key agencies, such as the Defense Department and the Internal Revenue Service, are in such disarray that the amounts of unaccounted-for assets and improperly recorded transactions run into billions of dollars.

Fortunately, major improvements are underway. The Chief Financial Officers (CFO) Act of 1990 and the Government Performance and Results Act of 1993 are intended to modernize the government's planning, budgeting, and information systems and the FASAB's comprehensive model of accounting and reporting will facilitate the preparation of auditable, government-wide, financial statements.

WHICH AGENCIES ARE RESPONSIBLE FOR FEDERAL ACCOUNTING AND REPORTING?

Federal accounting historically has been decentralized among the government's various agencies and departments, with each agency and department having its own accounting system and preparing independent reports. Currently, however, the three federal agencies with oversight responsibility for financial management—the Department of the Treasury, the Office of Management and Budget, and the General Accounting Office—are taking major strides toward coordinating the accounting systems and reporting practices of the individual agencies.

Per the United States Code (31 USC 321), the Department of the Treasury is responsible for a broad range of financial functions. These include: managing the public debt; collecting receipts and making disbursements; minting coins and printing currency; managing the government's gold supply; and regulating the nation's banking system. The department's twelve bureaus include: the Internal Revenue Service; the U.S. Customs Service; the Bureau of Alcohol, Tobacco, and Firearms; the Secret Service; the U.S. Mint; and the Office of the Comptroller of the Currency.

DEPARTMENT OF THE TREASURY

Another of its bureaus, The Financial Management Service (FMS) is the government's central collection and disbursing agent. As such, it is responsible for taking in revenue from the IRS, Customs, and other agencies and writing most of the government's checks. It is also in charge of the government's main accounting functions, such as overseeing the central accounting and reporting systems, keeping track of monetary assets and liabilities, and issuing financial reports. The FMS also works with the individual federal agencies to bring greater uniformity to their accounting and reporting practices.

The **Office of Management and Budget (OMB)** assists the president in preparing the federal budget and supervises the executive branch agencies in implementing it. Because it has the authority to make budgetary recommendations to the president, the OMB is one of the most powerful agencies in the federal government. The OMB not only recommends overall funding priorities and assesses competing demands for resources, it also reviews each federal agency's spending plans and evaluates the effectiveness of its programs.

THE OFFICE OF MANAGEMENT AND BUDGET

In addition, the OMB oversees and coordinates the administration's procurement, financial management, information, and regulatory policies. It has the authority to prescribe the form and content of financial statements and other administrative reports pursuant to the CFO Act of 1990, a power that it exercises by issuing bulletins and circulars that establish reporting, cost accounting, auditing, and procurement standards.

The OMB has the further responsibility of *apportioning* federal appropriations. First, Congress (either with the approval of the president or by overriding his veto) appropriates the total amount that can be spent by each agency. Then, OMB grants the agency its apportionments. **Apportionments** are shares of the total appropriation that are available to be spent. The total appropriation is most commonly apportioned by specific time periods (such as quarters), but alternatively by programs, activities, or projects. The apportionment process helps to assure that an agency does not dissipate its resources prior to year-end and it gives the executive branch added control over its spending.

The OMB's responsibilities for fiscal management were substantially expanded by the Chief Financial Officers Act of 1990 (31 USC 501). Acknowledging that the loss of billions of dollars each year could be traced to fiscal ineptitude, the bill aimed to build a modern fiscal management structure. To this end, it established both a new position of **Chief Financial Officer (CFO) of the United States** and corresponding CFO positions within each federal agency and department. Officially designated as "Deputy Director for Management," and reporting to the head of the OMB, the CFO of the United States is responsible for:

- providing overall direction and leadership to the executive branch on financial management matters by monitoring the establishment and operation of financial policies and systems throughout the federal government
- reviewing agency budget requests for financial management systems
- monitoring the execution of the federal budget, including timely performance reports
- advising agency heads as to matters relating to the qualifications and selection of agency CFOs
- chairing the Chief Financial Officers' Council, another organization established by the new law

In addition, the act charged the agency CFOs with:

- developing and maintaining integrated accounting systems that comply with applicable accounting standards
- submitting annual reports to the OMB that describe and analyze the status of financial management in their agencies
- monitoring the financial execution of their agencies' budgets

The act also mandated that selected federal agencies submit their annual reports for independent audit either by their inspectors general or by independent external auditors selected by the agencies' heads (a requirement expected to be extended to all federal agencies). Further, it required the OMB to prepare an annual report setting forth its accomplishments in the area of fiscal management and, as appropriate, recommending improvements.

THE GENERAL ACCOUNTING OFFICE

The **General Accounting Office (GAO)** was created in 1921 (during the administration of President Harding) by the Budget and Accounting Act (31 USCS 702). Until then, all federal audit and accounting functions were within the domain of the Treasury Department. The act specified that the GAO was to be "independent of the executive departments and under the control and direction of the Comptroller General of the United States." Subsequently, the Reorganization Act of 1945 made clear that the GAO was part of the legislative branch.[1]

The GAO (the watchdog of Congress) is most closely identified with its role as the government's auditor, conducting both financial and performance examinations of federal organizations and programs. But it carries out other activities as well. For example, it handles legal services, including:

---

[1] For a comprehensive history of the GAO see Frederick C. Mosher, *The GAO: The Quest for Accountability in American Government* (Boulder, Colo.: Westview Press, 1979).

- providing advice to Congress on legal issues involving government programs and activities

- assisting in drafting legislation and reviewing legislative proposals before the Congress

- reviewing and reporting to the Congress on proposed rescissions and deferrals of government funds

- resolving bid protests that challenge government contract awards

- assisting government agencies in interpreting the laws governing the expenditure of public funds

- adjudicating claims for and against the government

- conducting special investigations into criminal and civil misconduct, referring the results of its investigations to the Department of Justice and other law enforcement authorities when warranted

The GAO also deals with *accounting and information management policy*. The GAO ensures that the Congress has available for its use current, accurate, and complete financial management data. To do this, the GAO:

- participates with OMB and Treasury in prescribing accounting principles and standards for the executive branch

- advises other federal agencies on fiscal and related policies and procedures

- prescribes standards for auditing and evaluating government programs

In addition, the Comptroller General, the Secretary of the Treasury, and the Director of the Office of Management and Budget develop standardized information and data processing systems. This includes standard terminology, definitions, classifications, and codes for fiscal, budgetary, and program-related data and information.[2]

FEDERAL ACCOUNTING STANDARDS ADVISORY BOARD (FASAB)

The **Federal Accounting Standards Advisory Board** is responsible for *recommending* federal accounting standards to the Treasury, the OMB, and the GAO—the three agencies through whose combined efforts the board was established by Congress. The three agencies have the authority to actually establish federal accounting standards; all have to concur with a proposed standard before it is adopted. This unusual arrangement of shared jurisdiction was agreed upon mainly to resolve conflicts as to whether standard setting should be within the purview of the legislative or the executive branches of government.

The FASAB is composed of nine members, six of whom must be drawn from the following federal agencies:

- GAO
- OMB
- Congressional Budget Office (the office responsible for calculating the budgetary impact of proposed legislation)
- Department of the Treasury
- Department of Defense
- One of the civilian federal agencies, such as the Department of Health and Human Services

---

[2] Primary Source: The GAO's worldwide web page, "http://www.gao.gov"

The remaining three members must come from outside the federal government.

The mission of the FASAB is "to recommend accounting standards . . . after considering the financial and budgetary information needs of congressional oversight groups, executive agencies, and the needs of other users of federal financial information."[3] Hence, its constituents encompass parties both within and outside of the federal government.

Standard setting for the federal government is especially challenging because key users have sharply contrasting information requirements. For example, economists request statistics on national income and product accounts so as to obtain a "macro" view of the economy. Budget analysts, however, need data on the various federal appropriation, apportionment and cash flow accounts so that they can monitor the budgetary process. Oversight agencies want information on financial position, results of operations and costs of services. Moreover, as shall be discussed in the following section, the federal budget takes several forms, depending on the purpose for which it is to be used.

Upon its establishment, the FASAB set out to develop, from the ground up, a fundamental model of federal accounting for both the federal government as a whole and its separate components. By mid-1996, it had largely accomplished that objective, having recommended standards that encompass the full range of federal resources, obligations, and transactions.

As one of its early projects (following the precedent of both the FASB and the GASB) the FASAB established a set of financial reporting objectives. These are summarized in Table 16–1. They were intended to lay the foundation for resolving specific accounting issues, the key ones of which are discussed in this chapter. In the remainder of this chapter we shall speak of the FASAB as establishing accounting objectives and standards, even though, as indicated, it has authority only to recommend them to the GAO, the OMB, and the Treasury.

WHAT CONSTITUTES THE FEDERAL BUDGET?

Upon seeing or hearing mention of the federal budget, a knowledgeable observer can—and must—rightfully ask, "Which budget do you have in mind?" Federal operations are accounted for in four types of funds: a general fund, special funds, trust funds, and revolving funds. Different forms of the budget encompass different combinations of funds and, as shall be noted, not all the funds are reported upon in the government's annual financial statements. The central objective of this section of the text is not to provide a comprehensive understanding of the intricacies of the various types of federal budgets. That is well beyond its scope and would require an additional several chapters. Instead, it is to put readers on notice that the different budgets can vary greatly in the surpluses or deficits that they project. More importantly, the budget that political figures choose to cite is often dictated more by self-interest rather than sound economic or fiscal considerations.

Like its counterpart in municipalities, the federal government's general fund accounts for the resources, mainly from income taxes, that are not restricted for specific purposes. These resources are used to pay for national defense, interest on the public debt, and most social programs. The federal government does not usually

---

[3] Mission statement as approved by the Board and the Secretary of the Treasury, the Director of the OMB and the Comptroller General of the United States.

TABLE 16–1
Summary of Objectives of Federal Financial Reporting

- *Budgetary Integrity.* Federal financial reporting should assist in fulfilling the government's duty to be publicly accountable for monies raised through taxes and other means and for their expenditure in accordance with the government's legally adopted budget and related laws and regulations. It should enable the reader to determine:

  - how budgetary resources have been obtained and used and whether the acquisition and use were in accordance with the enacted budget
  - the status of budgetary resources
  - how budgetary reporting relates to other information on the costs of programs

- *Operating Performance.* Federal reporting should assist report users in evaluating the service efforts, costs, and accomplishments of the reporting entity, the manner in which these efforts and accomplishments have been financed, and the management of the entity's assets and liabilities. It should enable the reader to determine:

  - the costs of providing specific programs and activities and the composition of, and changes in, these costs
  - the efforts and accomplishments associated with federal programs and the changes over time and in relation to costs
  - the efficiency and effectiveness of the government's management of its assets and liabilities

- *Stewardship.* Federal financial reporting should assist report users in assessing the impact on the country of the government's operations and investments for the period and show how, as a result, the government's and the nation's financial conditions have changed and may change in the future. It should enable the reader to determine:

  - whether the government's financial position improved or deteriorated over the period
  - whether future budgetary resources will likely be sufficient to sustain public services and to meet obligations as they come due
  - whether government operations have contributed to the nation's current and future well-being

- *Systems and Control.* Federal financial reporting should assist report users in understanding whether financial management systems and internal accounting and administrative controls are adequate to ensure that:

  - transactions are executed in accordance with budgetary and financial laws and the other requirements, are consistent with the purposes authorized, and are recorded in accordance with federal accounting standards
  - assets are properly safeguarded to deter fraud, waste, and abuse
  - performance measurement information is adequately supported.

Source: Statement of Federal Financial Accounting Concepts No. 1, *Objectives of Federal Financial Reporting* (September 1993).

budget capital expenditures separately from operating expenditures, and hence, disbursements for both general operations and capital acquisitions are made from the general fund.

Special funds, like the special revenue funds of municipalities, are maintained to account for resources that are designated for specific programs or activities. Typically financed by dedicated fees, these include the National Wildlife Refuge Fund and the Water Conservation Fund. Taken together the general fund and the special funds constitute **federal funds**. The federal funds budget therefore covers both general and special fund revenues and expenditures.

Trust funds are also used to account for resources restricted for specific purposes. Unlike special funds, however, they are not considered federal funds and their revenues and expenditures are excluded from the federal funds deficit, a widely used measure of the extent to which the government is covering its ongoing operating costs. The largest of the trust funds are the Old-Age and Survivors Insurance Fund (Social Security), the Supplementary Medical Insurance Fund (Medicare), and various government employee retirement funds.

Revolving funds, comparable to a municipality's enterprise funds, account for the federal government's business type activities. The most significant of these is the U.S. Postal Service. The activities accounted for in revolving funds generate their own receipts and therefore are authorized by law to expend their resources without annual Congressional appropriation.

In 1969 the government adopted the practice of preparing a **unified federal budget** that encompasses all four types of funds. The objective was to capture in a single document the impact of federal activities on the national economy. Yet ironically, Congress excluded Social Security receipts and disbursements from the unified budget, according them special "off-budget" standing. The aim of Congress was to prevent the surpluses that these activities generate from being used to reduce deficits in other funds. In recent years, cash receipts to the Social Security fund have exceeded cash disbursements, thereby producing a surplus. However, this relationship is certain to be reversed early in the twenty-first century as the baby boomers reach retirement age and turn from contributors to beneficiaries. Nevertheless, despite the special status of the Social Security trust fund, most references to federal surpluses or deficits incorporate the off-budget accounts. As one former member of the FASAB cogently explained, "The fact is that, in the document that everyone refers to as the budget, Social Security surpluses serve to reduce what everyone refers to as the budget deficit."

WHAT TYPES OF ACCOUNTS ARE MAINTAINED BY FEDERAL ENTITIES?

Federal departments, bureaus, agencies, and other types of units maintain dual systems of accounts:

- *Budgetary accounts* assure that the entity complies with budgetary mandates, does not overspend its appropriations, and is able to fulfill uniform budgetary reporting requirements
- *Proprietary accounts* provide the information for the financial statements based on FASAB standards and are intended to provide an economic, rather than a budgetary, measure of operations and resources. (The term *proprietary* does not, however, imply business activities as when used in a municipal context.)

The budgetary accounts are comparable to both the budgetary accounts and the encumbrance accounts established by municipalities. Entries are made to record apportionments, allotments (a part of an apportionment that an agency is permitted to expend during a specified time period), commitments (reservations of funds prior to an order), and obligations (encumbrances).

The proprietary accounts are similar to conventional revenue, expense, asset, liability, and equity accounts. The accounts that are unique to the federal government are mainly in the equity (referred to as "net position") section of the balance sheet.

Thus, for example, "unexpended appropriations" represents the portion of net assets made available by Congress, but not yet expended. "Cumulative results of operations" (the equivalent of retained earnings) indicates the net assets from operations in both the current and previous years.

WHICH ENTITIES SHOULD ISSUE FINANCIAL REPORTS?

One of the fundamental questions facing the FASAB when it was established was what types of federal entities should be required to issue financial reports. The issue exists because the federal government can be viewed from different perspectives. Reports drawn from each of the perspectives may be consistent with one or more objectives of reporting, but not others.[4]

The first perspective is that of organizations. At the top level, the federal government comprises mainly agencies and cabinet level departments. These are subdivided into thousands of smaller units, which bear titles such as bureaus, agencies, services, administrations, and corporations. Some of these units are too small, or lack sufficient independent authority, to be appropriate reporting entities. Moreover, the top-level organizations may administer thousands of programs, many of which may be only tangentially related. Financial statements of these organizations, if they aggregate all their subunits, would provide little information that is of value to users.

The second perspective is that of the budget accounts, with each account representing a specifically authorized expenditure. Congress is permitted wide discretion in appropriating resources. Depending on the degree of control it elects to exercise over a department or program, it may appropriate resources in many small amounts or a few large amounts. Budget accounts do not necessarily coincide with a department's or an agency's organizational structure and may cut across programmatic lines. Hence, reports on either individual budget accounts or aggregations of budget accounts may also provide information that is only of limited use.

One reason that budget accounts do not always correspond to organizational lines is that different Congressional committees have cross-cutting jurisdiction. Inasmuch as individual committees are generally reluctant to surrender responsibility and authority to other committees, these peculiarities have proven difficult to correct. A resultant adverse consequence is that program goals may be both vague and internally inconsistent.

The third perspective is that of programs and activities. As just noted, however, the budget accounts do not coincide with programs and activities. Some programs and activities are financed from more than one budget account, and conversely, some budget accounts finance more than one program or activity. As a consequence, reports formulated along the lines of programs or activities may not provide information on budgetary integrity.

Acknowledging the limitations of each of the perspectives, the FASAB established three criteria for a "component" to be considered a reporting entity:

- There is a management responsible for controlling and deploying the component's outputs and outcomes and for executing its budget. It is held accountable for its performance.

- The component is of sufficient size and significance that its financial statements would provide a meaningful representation of its operations and financial condition.

---

[4] This discussion is based on the Statement of Federal Accounting Concepts No. 2, *Entity and Display* (June 1995).

- Users are interested in the information to be reported in its financial statements and could use it to make resource allocation and related decisions.

These criteria allow the federal government considerable flexibility in constituting reporting entities. The board notes that most top-level departments and agencies would satisfy the three criteria and therefore should be considered primary reporting entities. However, because of the breadth of these organizations, subunit statements may be more useful than those of the primary entity. The board points out that many departments and agencies divide the budget accounts for which they are responsible into responsibility centers. These responsibility centers (the equivalent of cost centers, profit centers, or activity centers) may reflect the mission of the reporting entity, its organizational structure and budget accounts and funding authorities. Accordingly, they too may satisfy the three criteria, and thereby also constitute appropriate reporting entities.

WHAT ARE THE FORM AND CONTENT OF CURRENT GOVERNMENT-WIDE FEDERAL STATEMENTS?

The FASAB has not yet provided details as to the form and content of financial reports for the federal government at large—only those of the individual reporting entities. So far it has indicated merely that the government at large should prepare a balance sheet, statement of operations, a statement of program performance measures (which could consist mainly of nonfinancial data), various supplementary reports, and a management discussion and analysis.[5]

As of 1997 the Treasury produces two separate sets of government-wide financial statements—the "official" statements, incorporated into the *United States Government Annual Report* and the "prototype" (i.e., "unofficial") *Consolidated Financial Statements*.

The balance sheet and statement of operations that are part of the **annual report** are shown in Table 16–2. As is evident from the statements, their focus is on cash, other monetary assets, and monetary obligations. The statement of operations is budget-based; the account structure and basis of revenue and expenditure recognition are generally consistent with those of the unified federal budget. Note in particular that Social Security taxes and contributions (classified as "employment taxes and contributions"), though included in the statement, are explicitly marked "off-budget;" they are not a part of the unified federal budget.

The corresponding balance sheet and statement of operations that are part of the *Consolidated Financial Statements* are shown in Table 16–3. These reports are on a full accrual basis and accordingly encompass long-lived assets as well as accrued liabilities.

The differences between the two sets of statements are striking. Whereas for fiscal 1995, total liabilities per the *annual report* were $3.7 trillion, those per the *consolidated financial statements* were $5.8 trillion. As will be explained later, however, even the latter grossly understated the government's actual obligations, as it excludes the unfunded actuarial liabilities for both Social Security and Medicare—amounts that, while varying greatly according to assumptions, were well over $12 trillion. At the same time, the annual deficit as reported in the *consolidated financial statements* was $146 billion greater than in the *annual report*—$310 billion versus $164 billion.

---

[5] Statement of Federal Accounting Concepts No. 2, *Entity and Display* (June 1995), para. 79.

TABLE 16–2
U.S. Government Annual Report
Balance Sheet
as of September 30, 1995
(in Millions of Dollars)

Assets:

Cash and Monetary Assets
  U.S. Treasury Operating Cash:

Federal Reserve Account	$ 8,620
Tax and Loan Note Accounts	29,329
Special Drawing Rights:	
Total Holdings	11,035
Special Drawing Rights Certificates Issued to Federal Reserve Banks	(10,168)
Monetary Assets with International Monetary Fund (IMF)	14,682

Other Cash and Monetary Assets

U.S. Treasury Monetary Assets	356
Cash and Other Assets Held Outside the Treasury Account	29,697
U.S. Treasury Time Deposits	528
Total Cash and Monetary Assets	84,080

Loan Financing Accounts

Guaranteed Loans	(12,714)
Direct Loans	19,732
Miscellaneous Asset Accounts	(1,748)
Total Assets	$ 89,349

Excess of Liabilities Over Assets:

Excess of Liabilities Over Assets at Beginning of Fiscal Year	3,421,723
Add: Total Deficit for Fiscal Year	163,916
Subtotal	3,585,639
Deduct: Other Transactions Not Applied to Surplus or Deficit	(722)
Excess of Liabilities Over Assets at Close of Fiscal Year	3,584,917
Total Assets and Excess of Liabilities Over Assets	$ 3,674,266

Liabilities:

Borrowing from the Public

Public Debt Securities Outstanding	$ 4,973,985
Premium and Discount on Public Debt Securities	(79,996)
Total Public Debt Securities	4,893,989
Agency Securities Outstanding	26,955
Total Federal Securities	4,920,944
Deduct: Net Federal Securities Held as Investments by Government Accounts	(1,317,645)
Total Borrowing from the Public	3,603,299
Accrued Interest Payable	50,611
Special Drawing Rights Allocated by IMF	7,380
Deposit Fund Liabilities	8,186
Miscellaneous Liability Accounts (Checks Outstanding, Etc.)	4,790
Total Liabilities	$ 3,674,266

TABLE 16–2 (Continued)
U.S. Government Annual Report
Statement of Operations
as of September 30, 1995
(in Millions of Dollars)

Receipts:

Individual Income Taxes	590,243
Corporation Income Taxes	157,004
Social Insurance Taxes and Contributions:	
Employment Taxes and Contributions (Off-Budget)	351,080
Employment Taxes and Contributions (On-Budget)	99,966
Unemployment Insurance	28,878
Other Retirement Contributions	4,550
Excise Taxes	57,484
Estate and Gift Taxes	14,763
Custom Duties	19,300
Miscellaneous Receipts	28,226
Total Receipts	$ 1,351,495

Outlays:

Legislative Branch	2,621
The Judiciary	2,903
Executive Office of the President	213
Funds Appropriated to the President	11,164
Departments:	
Agriculture	56,667
Commerce	3,403
Defense-Military	259,565
Defense-Civil	31,664
Education	31,321
Energy	17,618
Health and Human Services	303,075
Housing and Urban Development	29,045
Interior	7,389
Justice	10,786
Labor	32,093
State	5,347
Transportation	38,776
Treasury	348,480
Veterans Affairs	37,769
Environmental Protection Agency	6,349
General Service Administration	709
National Aeronautics and Space Administration	13,377
Office of Personnel Management	41,279
Small Business Administration	678
Social Security Administration	362,226
Independent Agencies	(1,470)
Undistributed Offsetting Receipts	(137,635)
Total Outlays	$ 1,515,410
Surplus (+) or Deficit (–)	$ (163,916)

Details may not add to totals due to rounding.

TABLE 16-3

U.S. Government
Consolidated Statement of Financial Position
as of September 30, 1995
(in Billions of Dollars)

Assets:

Cash	$ 66.8
Other Monetary Assets	126.7
Accounts Receivable, Net of Allowances	87.2
Inventories and Related Properties	259.1
Loans Receivable, Net of Allowances	120.8
Advances and Prepayments	24.2
Property, Plant, and Equipment, Net of Accumulated Depreciation	503.4
Other Assets	109.4
Total Assets	$ 1,297.6

Liabilities:

Accounts Payable	$ 51.2
Interest Payable	51.3
Accrued Payroll and Benefits	17.3
Unearned Revenue	33.8
Federal Debt Held By the Public	3,603.3
Pensions and Other Actuarial Liabilities	1,628.2
Other Liabilities	425.5
Total Liabilities	$ 5,810.6
Accumulated Position	$(4,513.0)

TABLE 16-3 (Continued)

U.S. Government
Consolidated Statement of Operations
For Year Ending September 30, 1995
(in Billions of Dollars)

Revenues:

Levied Under the Government's Sovereign Power:

Individual Income Taxes	$ 590.2
Corporate Income Taxes	157.0
Social Insurance Taxes and Contributions	484.5
Excise Taxes	57.5
Estate and Gift Taxes	14.8
Customs Duties	19.3
Miscellaneous	27.3
	$ 1,350.6

Earned Through Government Business-Type Operations:

Sale of Goods and Services	83.0
Interest	11.4
Other	36.0
Total Revenues	$ 1,481.0

(continued)

TABLE 16–3 (Continued)
U.S. Government
Consolidated Statement of Operations
as of September 30, 1995
(in Billions of Dollars)

Expenses by Agency:

Legislative Branch	2.9
Judicial Branch	3.2
Executive Branch:	
Funds Appropriated to the President	1.8
Departments:	
Agriculture	60.1
Commerce	4.7
Defense (Military)	248.6
Defense (Civil)	30.2
Education	34.6
Energy	7.7
Health and Human Services	342.5
Housing and Urban Development	34.6
Interior	9.7
Justice	9.2
Labor	39.6
State	6.2
Transportation	40.2
Treasury:	
Interest on Debt Held By the Public	234.2
Other	33.5
Veterans Affairs	86.5
Independent:	
Social Security Administration	362.7
Other	198.3
Total Expenses	$ 1,791.0
Expenses in Excess of Revenues	$ 310.0

HOW DOES THE NEW FASAB MODEL APPLY TO INDIVIDUAL ENTITY FINANCIAL STATEMENTS?

The new FASAB model applies to the statements of the individual federal entities rather than to the statements of the federal government as a whole. It was designed primarily to provide decision makers, both internal and external to the entity, with the cost and related information that they need. The new model will not directly apply to the *consolidated financial statements* of the government at large as presented in Table 16–3. It will affect them indirectly, however, as it addresses the accounting principles on which the statements of the individual entities are to be based. The statements of each individual entity will be aggregated with those of the other entities to form the statements of federal government as a whole.

The FASAB has recommended that individual agencies prepare the following types of statements:

- *Balance sheet.* This statement shows the entity's assets liabilities and net position. The entity's assets would include its fund balance with the Treasury, which represents amounts that can be used only for the purposes for which they were appropriated. Net position is the residual difference between assets and liabilities. It is generally composed of unexpended appropriations (amounts not yet obligated or expended), plus the cumulative difference, over the years, between the entity's revenues and other financing sources and its expenses.

- *Statement of net cost.* This statement, in essence an operating statement, reports on operating costs and revenues. Unlike the typical income statement, it presents earned revenues (i.e., those from exchange transactions) as a deduction from costs, thereby highlighting the amount that must be paid from taxes and other financing sources.

- *Statement of custodial activities.* This statement is required only of entities, such as the Internal Revenue Service and the Customs Service, that collect funds to be turned over to the Treasury or other organizations. It shows the resources collected and disbursed.

- *Statement of changes in net position.* This statement summarizes all entity transactions other than those, such as earned revenues and expenses, reported in the statement of net cost. It explains how the entity financed its net costs. It includes amounts received from appropriations, dedicated taxes, borrowings, and other financing sources.

- *Statement of budgetary resources.* This statement, which is prepared on a budgetary, rather than an accrual basis, reports on the amounts available from both current and prior year appropriations and the year's cash outlays, newly incurred obligations (the federal equivalent of encumbrances) and obligations of prior years that have been liquidated. The amounts in this report would tie to the Treasury's annual report.

- *Statement of financing.* This statement reconciles the statement of budgetary resources to the statement of net cost.

These statements (with the exception of that of custodial activities) are illustrated in Table 16–4. The statements presented are those of a federal credit agency—one that provides financing to eligible borrowers—after its first year of operations. Note that the agency received appropriations of $1,500 (per the statement of budgetary resources). Of this amount it used only $515 (per the statement of changes in net position), leaving an unexpended balance (per the balance sheet) of $985. Further (as indicated in the statement of financing), the agency incurred obligations of $915, but reported net cost of operations (per the statement of financing, the statement of net cost, and the statement of changes in net position) of only $158. The obligations (encumbrances) are recognized only in the budgetary accounts. By contrast the net cost of operations represents the difference between the revenues and expenses as recorded in the proprietary accounts (and determined on the basis of FASAB rather than budgetary principles).

WHAT ARE THE MAIN ACCOUNTING ISSUES BEING ADDRESSED BY THE FASAB?

Not surprisingly, the issues being dealt with by the FASAB are similar to those being addressed by the GASB—and, in a broad sense—the FASB. They deal with the recognition of revenue and expenses and, correspondingly, with the valuation of assets and liabilities.

TABLE 16–4
Financial Statements as Recommended by the FASAB
in Millions of Dollars

One Credit Agency
Balance Sheet
For Year Ended September 30, 1998

Assets:

Fund Balance with Treasury		$1,425
Loans Receivable	$210	
Less: Allowance for Subsidy	(53)	157
Equipment	100	
Less: Accumulated Depreciation	(20)	80
Total Assets		$1,662

Liabilities and Net Position:

Liabilities		
Accounts Payable	$125	
Annual Leave Liability	30	
Principal Payment to Treasury	165	
Total Liabilities		$320
Net Position		
Unexpended Appropriations	$985	
Cumulative Results of Operations	357	
Total Net Position		1,342
Total Liabilities and Net Position		$1,662

One Credit Agency
Statement of Net Cost
For Year Ended September 30, 1998

Costs to Produce Exchange Revenue:

Interest Expense	$ 16	
Depreciation Expense	20	
Annual Leave Expense	30	
Subsidy Expense	58	
Other Expense	150	$ 274
Less Earned Revenue:		
Intragovernmental	100	
Interest Income	16	(116)
Net Cost of Operations		$ 158

One Credit Agency
Statement of Changes in Net Position
For Year Ended September 30, 1998

Financing Source—Appropriations Used	$ 515
Less: Net Cost of Operations	158
Net Result of Operations	357
Increase in Unexpended Appropriations	985

TABLE 16–4 (Continued)
Financial Statements as Recommended by the FASAB
in Millions of Dollars

Increase in Net Position	1,342
Net Position, October 1, 1997	0
Net Position, September 30, 1998	$1,342

One Credit Agency
Statement of Budgetary Resources
For Year Ended September 30, 1998

Budgetary Resources Made Available:

Current Appropriations	$1,500
Borrowing Authority	200
Collection of Loan Principal and Interest	50
Reimbursements for Services	100
Less: Principal Repaid to Treasury	(35)
Total, Budgetary Resources Made Available	$1,815

Status of Budgetary Resources:

Obligations Incurred (Gross)	915
Expired Authority	900
Total, Status of Budgetary Resources	$1,815

Outlays:

Obligations Incurred, Net	$ 765
Add: Obligated Fund Balance, October 1	0
Deduct: Obligated Fund Balance, September 30	(525)
Total Outlays	$ 240

One Credit Agency
Statement of Financing
For Year Ended September 30, 1998

Obligations and Nonbudgetary Resources:

Obligations Incurred (Gross)	$ 915
Less: Adjustments to Arrive at Net Obligations	(150)
Obligations Incurred, Net	765
Interest Income—Subsidy	5
Net Obligations and Nonbudgetary Resources	$ 770

Goods, Services, and Benefits Ordered But Not Yet Received or Provided

	(400)

Other Resources that Do Not Fund Net Cost of Operations:

Costs Capitalized on the Balance Sheet	(260)

Costs that Do Not Require Resources:

Depreciation	20

Financing Sources Yet to be Provided:

	28
Net Cost of Operations	$ 158

Source: Adapted from Implementation Guide to Statement of Federal Financial Accounting Standards No. 7, *Accounting for Revenue and Other Financing Sources* (June 1996).

MEASUREMENT FOCUS AND BASIS OF ACCOUNTING

The FASAB has not explicitly specified a measurement focus or basis of accounting for the federal government. However, its proposals as to specific revenue and expenses indicate that federal financial statements should focus on *all economic resources*. Revenues and expenses should be recognized on a full accrual basis (except when infeasible owing to measurement difficulties). Thus, agency balance sheets should report both fixed assets and long-term obligations, and statements of operations should include charges for depreciation. Nevertheless, owing to their unique characteristics, some types of long-lived assets, such as military hardware, should be expensed upon acquisition and not capitalized.

BASIS FOR RECOGNIZING REVENUES

The FASAB distinguishes between two types of revenues:

- *Exchange* (or earned) *revenues* arise from sales transactions in which each party receives benefits and incurs costs.

- *Nonexchange revenues* materialize when the government commands resources but gives nothing in exchange (at least not directly). Nonexchange revenues include taxes, duties, fines, and penalties.[6]

Exchange revenues, the FASAB recommends, should be recognized according to conventional business-type principles—that is, when goods or services are provided to the public or to another governmental entity. Thus, for example:

- Revenues from services should be recognized as an agency performs the services.

- Revenues from long-term contracts should be recognized on a percentage of completion basis. If a contract is expected to result in a loss, the loss should be spread over the contract in proportion to the share of estimated total costs incurred in each period. This provision is contrary to the principles of both the FASB and the GASB (as articulated in the FASB's Statement No. 5 and adopted by the GASB) that losses should be recognized when it is probable that an asset has been impaired or a liability incurred and the amount of the loss can be reasonably estimated.

- Revenues from goods sold should be recognized upon delivery of the goods to the customer.

Nonexchange revenues should be reported on *both* an accrual and a cash basis. This unusual approach is intended to fulfill conflicting reporting objectives—that of providing information on both the cost of services and the expenditure of budgetary resources. Under this approach, an entity would report the actual amount collected and add to (or subtract from) it an "accrual adjustment." Thus, for example, if an entity were entitled to $200 in taxes, but collected only $180, it would report its revenues as follows:

Cash Collections	$180
Accrual Adjustment	20
Total Revenues	$200

Correspondingly, the entity would recognize a receivable of $20 for the taxes "earned" but not yet collected.

---

[6] Statement of Federal Financial Accounting Standards No. 7, *Accounting for Revenues and Other Financing Sources*, (April 1996).

The accrual adjustment would be negative (subtracted from the cash collections) when the cash collections exceed the revenues earned. For example, if taxes applicable to a period were $300 but collections were $320, then the required accrual adjustment of $20 would be subtracted from the collections. At the same time, the entity would reduce its taxes receivable by $20.

According to the FASAB, a federal entity should accrue revenues "when a specifically identifiable, legally enforceable claim to resources arises, to the extent that collection is probable and the amount is measurable." Thus, for example:

- *Income taxes* should be recognized when assessed by the taxpayer (as indicated on a filed tax return) or by the result of audits, investigations, or litigation. The government should not recognize as revenues amounts that it estimates it will receive as the result of audits to be conducted in the future.

- *Fines and penalties* may be accrued (1) upon the expiration of the period during which the offender may contest a court summons, (2) when the offender pays the fine before a court date, or (3) when the court imposes a fine.

- *Donations* (as to a federal museum, presidential library, or memorial) should be recognized when the entity has a legally enforceable claim to the donated resources, collection is "more likely than not," and the amount is measurable.

ACCOUNTING FOR PLANT AND EQUIPMENT

The federal government controls more than a trillion dollars in long-lived assets, some of which are unlike assets owned by businesses or other levels of government. They include military weapons (acquired in the hope that they will never have to be used), national parks and monuments (that produce little or no revenue but are in constant need of maintenance and repair), and conventional assets, such as office buildings and equipment. Recognizing that their diversity necessitates different approaches to accounting and reporting, the FASAB groups the assets into four categories: general, stewardship, mission, and heritage.

General Assets

General assets are comparable to those of a business, so the FASAB recommends that they be accounted for similarly. That is, they should be capitalized and (with the exception of land) depreciated over their useful lives. This category consists of assets that:

- are used to produce goods or services or to support the mission of the entity and can be used for alternative purposes (i.e., by other government programs or nongovernmental entities)

- are used in business-type activities

- are used by entities in activities whose costs can be compared to those of other entities (e.g., costs of federal hospitals can be compared to costs of other hospitals)[7]

Stewardship Assets

This category encompasses lands other than those in the general category. It includes mainly national forests, national parks, and the federal government's vast holdings of undeveloped acreage.

---

[7] Statement of Federal Financial Accounting Standards No. 6, *Accounting for Property, Plant and Equipment* (June 1996).

In that it is neither used in government operations nor held for sale, stewardship land need not be capitalized, and therefore should not be reported on an entity's balance sheet. Instead, it should be expensed as acquired. In periods subsequent to acquisition, the entity should provide in a "stewardship report" salient information as to the amount of land owned, how it is being used, and its condition.[8]

Mission Assets

These assets are held for emergencies or have no alternative uses in the private sector or other government programs. Further, their useful lives are either indeterminate or unpredictable, and there is a high risk that they will be prematurely destroyed. They include primarily weapons systems and space exploration equipment. Inasmuch as mission assets do not have determinate economic lives, they should be expensed as acquired, and like stewardship land, described in the stewardship report.

Heritage Assets

These assets have value because of their historical, natural, cultural, educational, or artistic significance. They include museums, monuments, and historical sites.

Heritage assets may have the characteristics of both general assets and stewardship assets. The government holds some heritage assets, such as the Washington Monument, purely for their cultural, architectural, or aesthetic qualities. It holds others, such as the Old Executive Office Building in Washington D.C. (an operating administrative complex) for both its historical and functional attributes. Distinguishing between the two types, the Board directs that heritage assets being used in government operations should be accounted for as if they were general assets. They should be capitalized and depreciated over their productive lives. Heritage assets that have only historical, artistic, or cultural significance should be accounted for like stewardship assets. They should not be capitalized; they too should be reported upon in the supplementary stewardship report.

ACCOUNTING FOR "HUMAN CAPITAL"

One of the most intriguing questions facing the federal government is whether investments in **human capital** should be accorded the same accounting recognition as those in physical capital. As defined by the FASAB, investments in "human capital" are the outlays for the education and training of the public (excluding federal civilian and military employees) intended to increase the nation's productive capacity.

Government agencies undertake educational and training programs to benefit the future, not the present. Arguably, therefore, consistent with the concepts of both matching and interperiod equity, the costs of these programs should be capitalized as incurred and subsequently amortized over the periods to be benefited. Moreover, accounting principles permitting agencies to capitalize outlays for physical assets, but not human "assets," might bias allocation decisions in favor of the physical assets. The reported expenses for the physical assets would be reported over the life of the assets; those for the human assets would have to be recognized as the costs were incurred.

On the other hand, the long-term benefits of educational and training programs are far less identifiable and measurable than those of physical assets. Determinations of the length of the benefit period would necessarily require arbitrary assumptions.

Faced with obvious practical difficulties, the FASAB rejects the notion of capitalizing investments in human capital. Instead, however, it mandates supplemental

---

[8] Statement of Federal Financial Accounting Standards No. 8. *Supplementary Stewardship Reporting* (May 1996).

disclosure in the stewardship report. Minimal reporting, it says, should include the annual investment made for the past five years and a narrative description of the major human capital programs.[9]

In a statement that may appear more unconventional that it in fact is, the FASAB offers federal entities an option in accounting for inventories that are *held for sale*. They can value inventories held for sale at either of:

DETERMINATION OF INVENTORIES AND COST OF GOODS SOLD

- historical cost, as calculated by either the first-in, first-out (FIFO) or the weighted average methods
- latest acquisition cost, based on each item's last invoice price[10]

If an entity chooses the latter option, then it should show on its balance sheet both the latest acquisition cost and historical cost, with the difference between the two presented as an allowance for unrealized holding gains or losses. Thus, for example:

Inventory at Latest Acquisition Cost	$120,000
Allowance for Unrealized Holding Gains	(20,000)
Inventory at Historical Cost	$100,000

Similarly, cost of goods should be based on acquisition prices, but the operating statement should incorporate an adjustment equal to the change during the period in the allowance for unrealized holding gains. As a result, the "bottom line" of the operating statement would be the same as if the cost of goods sold were based on historical cost. Assume, for example, that at the beginning of a year inventory was as shown. At year-end it was as follows:

Inventory at Latest Acquisition Cost	$160,000
Allowance for Unrealized Holding Gains	(35,000)
Inventory at Historical Cost	$125,000

Thus, the allowance for unrealized holding gains increased by $15,000. If sales for the year were $950,000 and purchases $800,000 an operating statement would reflect the following:

Sales		$950,000
Cost of Goods Sold		
Beginning Inventory at Beginning-of-the-Period Latest Acquisition Cost	$120,000	
Less: Allowance for Unrealized Holding Gains at the Beginning of the Period	(20,000)	
Plus: Purchases	800,000	
Cost of Goods Available for Sale	900,000	
Less: Ending Inventory at End-of-the-Period Latest Acquisition Cost	(160,000)	
Plus: Allowance for Unrealized Holding Gains at the End of the Period	35,000	
Cost of Goods Sold		775,000
Net Results		$175,000

---

[9] Statement of Federal Financial Accounting Standards No. 8, *Supplementary Stewardship Reporting* (May 1996).

[10] Statement of Federal Financial Accounting Standards No. 3, *Accounting for Inventory and Related Property* (October 1993).

In contrast to the guidelines for inventories held for sale, those for other types of inventories, such as operating materials and supplies and stockpile materials (e.g., strategic materials held for national defense or national emergencies) call for conventional valuation—that is, at **historical cost**.

Although this approach to inventory valuation is seemingly quite progressive, it was adopted mainly to resolve a practical problem—the Department of Defense maintains its records on the basis of latest acquisition cost.

RECOGNIZING LIABILITIES AND RELATED EXPENSES

Of all the accounting and reporting issues facing the federal government, those pertaining to liabilities are probably the least tractable and the most controversial.[11]

As explained by the FASAB, government liabilities are attributable to *events.* "Events" encompass both "transactions" and other "happenings of consequence" involving the government.

Transactions can be of two types:

- *exchange transactions,* in which each party gives and receives something of value (e.g., when the government purchases goods or services).

- *nonexchange transactions,* in which the government provides something of value without directly receiving something of value in return—for example, when the government incurs an obligation under a grant or entitlement program. An entitlement program is one that provides benefits to parties if they satisfy certain conditions (such as being unemployed or having an income below a specified amount). Once the program is authorized, no further congressional action is needed to appropriate the funds to sustain it. Thus, the cost to the government is never certain; it depends on the number of parties satisfying the conditions.

Happenings of consequence can also be classified into two categories:

- *Government-related events* represent mainly accidents for which the government is responsible and required by law to reimburse the injured parties for damages.

- *Government-acknowledged events* are occurrences for which the government is not responsible but elects, as a matter of policy, to provide relief to the victims. They include primarily natural disasters, such as hurricanes and earthquakes.

Neither exchange transactions nor government-related events pose issues unique to governments. Therefore, consistent with the principles of accrual accounting, the FASAB prescribes that federal entities recognize both a liability and related expense resulting from an exchange transaction when an exchange takes place (e.g., when the government receives the contracted-for goods or services). They should recognize a liability and related expense for a government-related event as soon as the event occurs and the anticipated outflows of resources are both probable and measurable.

Nonexchange transactions and government-acknowledged events raise the difficult question of recognition because they stem from the government's use of its sovereign power and there may be no well-defined event or transaction that establishes the obligation. For example, Congress authorizes financial assistance to parties satisfying specified conditions. It thereby commits the federal government to a future outflow of resources. Yet until the parties demonstrate that they have met the specified conditions, the government does not yet have an obligation either of an established

---

[11] This discussion is based on Statement of Federal Financial Accounting Standards No. 5, *Accounting for Liabilities of the Federal Government* (September 1995).

amount or to identifiable parties. The commitment may extend over an unspecified number of years and the ultimate amount to be paid may depend on economic and social conditions well into the future. Further, the government can unilaterally cancel or change the program at any time.

To help assure consistency among a broad spectrum of events and transactions, the FASAB recommends that federal entities recognize liabilities for:

- *nonexchange transactions* when *due.* Thus, government agencies need recognize liabilities for grants and entitlements only as payments are due.

- *government-acknowledged events* when the government formally *acknowledges* financial responsibility for the event and an amount is *due and payable* as a result. Thus, the government need recognize liabilities for disaster relief only when it has authorized specific grants to specific individuals, or contractors have actually provided their goods or services.

The implications of these guidelines are most profound—and contentious—for social insurance programs in general and Social Security and Medicare in particular. The accounting controversy over social insurance programs stems largely from the different ways in which these programs can be interpreted. Social Security, for example, can be seen as either a government-sponsored pension plan (involving mainly exchange transactions) or as a government-managed income redistribution program (involving mainly nonexchange transactions). It is a pension program in that both employees and employers contribute to the fund over the course of the employees working lives in anticipation of the employees receiving a lifetime stipend upon retirement. It is an income redistribution program in that the government taxes both employees and employers, dedicating the tax to program beneficiaries. The tax rate is not calculated on an actuarial basis that is acceptable for funding under ERISA (the federal act regulating private pension plans) or for financial reporting under either GASB or FASB standards. Upon retirement, the beneficiaries, neither individually nor collectively, receive payments that are tied to the taxes that they or their employers paid.

Initially the FASAB determined that Social Security and Medicare were nonexchange transactions—and hence, the unfunded actuarial obligations need only be set forth in the stewardship report, not included as balance-sheet liabilities. However, owing to strong opposition, it backed away from that interpretation, electing instead to consider the issue as part of a separate agenda item. As of 1997, no applicable standard has been issued.

RECOGNIZING THE COST OF SUBSIDIZED DIRECT LOANS AND LOAN GUARANTEES

As part of their social, educational, and commercial programs, federal entities make low-interest direct loans and they guarantee loans made by banks and other institutions. The low-interest loans provide a direct benefit to the borrowers by providing funds at less than the rate they would otherwise have to pay. The guarantees virtually eliminate credit risks to the lenders and thereby enable them to provide funds to the borrowers at reduced interest rates. The targeted beneficiaries of these loan programs include farmers, veterans, students, and small businesses.

Prior to the Federal Credit Reform Act of 1990, agencies were not required to explicitly recognize the costs of making the low-interest loans. Instead, they simply reported less interest revenue than they would have had they charged prevailing interest rates. Correspondingly, they recognized the costs of the loan guarantees only as they reimbursed the lenders upon borrower defaults.

The Credit Reform Act of 1990 requires that the president's budget reflect the long-term costs in the year in which the direct loans and the guarantees are made.

Therefore, to enhance conformity between budgeting and accounting practices, the FASAB has directed that the same principles apply to annual financial reports.[12]

According to the FASAB, when a government makes a subsidized direct loan, it should recognize as an asset the **present value** of its estimated net cash receipts, including both interest and principal. It should report an expense equal to the difference between the face value of the loan and the present value of the estimated net cash receipts. Present value should be based on the average interest rate on Treasury securities of the same maturity as the loans.

EXAMPLE   *Subsidized Loan*

A government agency makes a three-year, 6 percent, direct loan of $1,000 at a time when prevailing Treasury rates on three-year securities are 10 percent. The loan is to be repaid in three annual installments of $374 (the amount required to amortize a $1,000, 6 percent loan over three years—$1,000 divided by 2.66730, the present value of an annuity of $1 for three periods).

Inasmuch as the present value of three payments of $374, discounted at 10 percent, is only $930 ($374 times 2.4869, the present value of an annuity of $1 for three periods) the agency should recognize an expense of $70 (the difference between the loan's $1,000 face value and the $930 present value of the payments). The following entry would therefore be appropriate when the loan is made:

Loan receivable	$930	
Loan subsidy (expense)	70	
Cash		$1,000
To record a direct loan		

In subsequent periods, the agency should recognize revenue of 10 percent of the balance of the loan receivable, and correspondingly reduce the balance of the loan receivable by the difference between the revenue recognized and the cash received. Thus, in the first year:

Cash	$374	
Loan receivable		$281
Interest revenue (10% of $930)		93
To record the first payment from the borrower		

The actual entries recommended by the FASAB are slightly more complex. Per the FASAB guidance, when recording the initial loan the agency should debit the face value of the loan ($1,000 in the example), offsetting it with a contra-account, "subsidy allowance" ($70). Thereafter, upon receipt of each payment, the agency should amortize the subsidy allowance until it is equal to zero after the final payment. The reported loan subsidy expense, interest revenue, and net loan receivable would be the same, however.

When a government guarantees loans, it should also recognize both an expense and an obligation in the amount of the present value of its anticipated payments to the lender. Then each year, the government should reassess the present value of the anticipated payments and recognize the change in value as either an increase or decrease in its loan guarantee liability, offset by either a debit or credit to loan guarantee expense.

---

[12] Statement of Federal Financial Accounting Standards No. 2, *Accounting for Direct Loans and Loan Guarantees* (July 1993).

EXAMPLE   *Loan Guarantees*

At the start of Year 1 an agency guarantees $100 million of student loans. The following schedule indicates the agency's estimates of the payments (all at year-end) that it will have to make to lenders owing to defaults and the present value of those payments. The agency applies a discount rate of 8 percent.

End of Year	Amount (in Millions)	Present Value of $1	Net Present Value
1	$2,100,000	.92593	$1,944,453
2	1,500,000	.85734	1,286,010
3	1,000,000	.79383	793,830
Total			$4,024,293

Upon guaranteeing the loans, the agency would make the following entry:

Loan guarantee expense	$4,024,293	
Liability for loan guarantees		$4,024,293
To record expense of guaranteeing loans		

Suppose that during the first year the agency pays lenders $2.1 million, as estimated, to fulfill its guarantees. Its new estimate of the present value of the anticipated payments, measured as of the end of Year 1, is now as follows:

End of Year	Amount (in Millions)	Present Value of $1	Net Present Value
2	$1,500,000	.92593	$1,388,895
3	1,000,000	.85734	857,340
Total			$2,246,235

The following entry would be appropriate to record the cash payment of $2.1 million and the adjustment of the liability:

Liability for loan guarantees	$1,778,058	
Loan guarantee expense	321,942	
Cash		$2,100,000
To record payment of $2,100,000 and adjust the balance on the remaining liability for the difference between $4,024,293 and $2,246,235. (The loan guarantee expense represents interest, at 8 percent, on the beginning of year balance of $4,024,293.)		

Insofar as the agency's estimate of the second- or third-year payments changes, then the loan guarantee expense would incorporate the net present value of the addition (or reduction) in expected payments. Thus, if the agency estimated that the Year 3 payment would now be $1.3 million, then it would substitute $1.3 million for $1 million in this computation.

WHAT ADDITIONAL STEPS HAS THE FEDERAL GOVERNMENT TAKEN TO IMPROVE ITS FISCAL MANAGEMENT?

Recognizing the limitations of traditional accounting systems that focus exclusively on financial metrics (as discussed in earlier chapters) Congress enacted *The Government Performance and Results Act of 1993*, which requires federal agencies to develop strategic plans, operational objectives, and measures of performance and to report on the extent to which it met its objectives.

As detailed in the Act, beginning in 1999, as part of its annual budget request to the OMB, each agency must prepare and submit a performance plan that includes:

- objective, quantifiable, and measurable goals that define the agency's anticipated level of performance
- a description of the operational processes, skills, technology, and "human capital" required to meet the performance goals
- a basis for comparing actual results to the goals
- the means of verifying and validating actual performance

Then, starting in 2000 it must also submit a report that:

- reviews success in achieving the performance goals of the previous fiscal year
- evaluates the performance plan for the current fiscal year relative to the previous year's results
- explains any deviations from its goals, indicating why a goal was not met, describing plans for achieving the goal, and, if the goals were impractical or infeasible, spelling out why and recommending corrective steps

In addition, the act requires agencies to develop "strategic plans" that cover five-year periods. The plans should set forth the agencies' missions, goals, and objectives and the means to achieve them.

SUMMARY

The U.S. Constitution left Congress and the executive branch to determine the form and content of financial reports and to implement and administer the underlying accounting systems of the government. The systems established over the years are now recognized to be inadequate for an organization of the size and complexity of the federal government.

The three federal agencies with oversight responsibility for financial management are making major strides in coordinating the accounting systems and reporting practices of individual agencies. The Department of the Treasury has a broad range of functions, including managing the public debt and being a central collecting and disbursing agent. The Office of Management and Budget, one of the most powerful agencies in the federal government, helps prepare and supervise the federal budget and reviews and evaluates agency programs. Although it performs an array of functions, the General Accounting Office is most closely identified with its role as the government's auditor—the watchdog of Congress.

The Federal Accounting Standards Advisory Board, which was established in 1990, *recommends* federal accounting standards to the Department of Treasury, the OMB, and the GAO. Since its inception, the FASAB has been

working toward developing a model of accounting for the government as a whole and its separate components.

The federal government prepares different budgets for different purposes. The unified budget, for example, is intended to show the impact of federal activities on the national economy. It encompasses four types of funds—the general fund, special funds, most trust funds, and revolving funds. Ironically, Social Security receipts and disbursements, despite their major impact on the fiscal welfare of both the government and the nation at large, are excluded from the unified budget. Nevertheless, they are included in the budget that is commonly at the center of most political and economic discussions.

Budget accounts ensure that a federal entity complies with budgetary mandates, does not overspend appropriations, and is able to fulfill budgetary reporting requirements. Proprietary accounts, which are based on FASAB standards, provide an economic rather than a budgetary, measure of the government's operations and resources.

The FASAB established three criteria for a component to be considered a reporting entity: there is a management responsible for controlling resources and accountable for performance; the entity's scope is such that its financial statements provide a meaningful representation of its operations and financial condition; users are interested in the information to be reported and could use it to make resource allocation and related decisions.

The FASAB has not yet established details for the financial reports of the government at large. Currently, the Department of the Treasury produces two sets of government-wide financial statements that differ significantly. The *annual report* is budget-based and focuses on cash and other monetary items. The *consolidated financial statements* are intended to provide a broader economic perspective and accordingly are on a full accrual basis.

The FASAB's comprehensive reporting model will help assure that the financial statements of the government at large as well as its component units focus on all economic resources and are on a full accrual basis. Key recommendations of the FASAB include the following:

- Exchange revenues should be recognized when goods or services are provided to the public or to another governmental agency. Nonexchange revenues should be recognized on both an accrual and a cash basis. That is, an entity should report the actual cash collections and add or subtract from them an "accrual adjustment" representing the difference between amounts accrued and amounts collected. Revenues should be accrued when the government has a legal claim upon the resources and collection of cash is both probable and measurable.

- General property plant and equipment should be capitalized and depreciated. By contrast, stewardship assets, heritage assets (assuming they have only historical, cultural or artistic significance) and mission assets, should be expensed as acquired and described in a stewardship report.

- Inventories held for sale may be valued at latest acquisition price; other types of inventories should be valued at historical cost.

- Investments in human capital should not be capitalized but should also be reported upon in a stewardship report.

- Liabilities for nonexchange transactions should be recognized when due; those for government-acknowledged events should be recognized when the government formally acknowledges financial responsibility and an amount is due and payable.

- Liabilities, and related expenses, for both loan guarantees and subsidized loans should be recognized at the time the loans are made.

The Government Performance and Results Act will further improve federal accounting and fiscal management. It requires that agencies establish specific goals and objectives and report annually on the extent to which they achieve them.

EXERCISE FOR REVIEW AND SELF-STUDY

Congress recently authorized the establishment of the Wilderness Lands Preservation Commission. The Commission satisfies the FASAB criteria as an independent reporting entity.

a. For its first year of operations, the Commission received an appropriation of $100 million. Of this amount, it spent only $80 million. Assuming that the appropriation does not lapse, how would the unspent $20 million be reported on the Commission's year-end balance sheet?

b. To educate the public as to the importance of wildlife preservation, the Commission received a legally binding pledge of $2 million from a private foundation. Of this amount only $0.5 million was received during the year. The balance is expected to be received in the following year. How much of the pledge should be recognized as revenue in the year it was made?

c. The Commission operates a gift shop in which it sells wildlife-related posters, books, and educational materials. In it first year, it had sales of $90,000. It purchased merchandise for $100,000, of which it sold $75,000. Based on the latest acquisition cost, the year-end inventory had a value of $30,000. Prepare a summary state-

ment of operations for the gift shop, assuming that the Commission shows the impact of changes in the inventory's latest acquisition cost.

d. One of the Commission's main functions is to encourage landowners to take specified conservation measures. To assist them in covering their costs, the Commission lends them the required funds at below-market rates. During its first year of operations, the Commission lent one landowner $400,000. The landowner was required to repay the loan in three annual payments of $144,139, an amount that reflects an interest rate of 4 percent. At the time of the loan the prevailing rate on three-year Treasury securities was 8 percent. How should the Commission account for the cost of the loan?

e. In the course of the year, the Commission acquired the following assets:

1. Buildings for $5 million (to provide office space)
2. Land for $1 million (on which to construct an office building)
3. Land for $40 million (acquired as a wildlife refuge)

How should each of these assets be accounted for?

f. Per regulations established by the Commission, landowners in specified areas near designated wildlife refuges are not permitted to kill or trap animals of prey. In return, the Commission promises to reimburse landowners for the value of any livestock killed by the animals. Toward the end of the year, one farmer sub-mitted a claim to the Commission for $12,000. As of year-end, the Commission verified that the claim was legitimate, but had not yet authorized payment. What journal entry, if any, should the Commission make to record the claim?

QUESTIONS FOR REVIEW AND DISCUSSION

1. What is the primary role of the Treasury Department's Financial Management Service?

2. The Office of Management and Budget is responsible for granting agencies *apportionments*. What are apportionments?

3. What is the authority of the Federal Accounting Standards Advisory Board with respect to establishing accounting standards?

4. What are the four main objectives of federal financial reporting, as established by the FASAB?

5. What is meant by the *unified* budget? How does it differ from the *federal funds* budget? Why are Social Security receipts and disbursements said to be "off budget"?

6. Why may it be unclear as to whether a particular program or sub-unit of an agency or department is an appropriate independent reporting entity?

7. What are the six basic statements that an agency may have to prepare (if they are appropriate) to be in compliance with FASAB standards?

8. In what significant way is the FASAB's approach to inventory accounting different from that of both the GASB and the FASB?

9. Into what four categories does the FASAB divide government assets? How are each of the four accounted for?

10. What is meant by investments in *human capital*? In what way are investments in human capital accounted for differently than investments in *physical capital*?

11. Why does it matter whether Social Security is considered a pension plan or an entitlement program?

12. If an agency makes a loan at a below-market rate, what would be the nature of any expense recognized at the time of the loan? If it guaranteed a loan made by others, what would be the nature of any expense recognized at the time of the guarantee?

EXERCISES

16-1

The financial statements of the federal government are unique.

The left-hand column of the following table describes each of six financial statements that the FASAB recommends agencies prepare. The right-hand column indicates the names of the six statements. Match the description in the left-hand column with the correct title in the right-hand column.

a. Summarizes all entity transactions other than those, such as earned revenues and expenses, reported in the statement of net cost; explains how the entity financed its net costs; includes amounts received from appropriations, dedicated taxes, borrowings and other financing sources.

1. Statement of budgetary resources

b. Shows the resources collected and disbursed; required only of entities, such as the Internal Revenue Service and the Customs Service, that collect funds to be turned over to the Treasury or other organizations.

2. Statement of custodial activities

c. Shows the entity's assets liabilities and net position, including fund balance with the Treasury.

3. Statement of financing

d. In essence an operating statement; shows operating costs and revenues.

4. Statement of changes in net position

e. Reconciles the statement of budgetary resources to the statement of net cost.

5. Statement of net cost

f. Prepared on a budget basis; shows amount available for appropriation, cash outlays and newly incurred obligations.

6. Balance sheet

16-2

Nonexchange, as opposed to exchange, revenues present the more difficult issues of accounting recognition.

In 1998 the federal government, through its various government agencies, engaged in the following transactions involving revenues.

1. It rented land to a tenant. It signed a three-year lease requiring monthly payments of $2,000. In 1998, the year in which the lease was signed, the tenant occupied the land for six months but paid an entire year's rent (i.e., $24,000).

2. It signed two contracts with a foreign government to provide engineering services. Each contract was for $50 million. During the year, the government completed 100 percent of one contract and 60 percent of the other. It collected the entire $100 million in cash.

3. It assessed fines of $100,000 each on two firms for polluting waterways. One offender paid the fine; the other notified the government that it would contest the fine in court.

4. It accepted from a private foundation a pledge of $120,000 to fund an exhibit in a government museum. During the year the foundation paid $40,000 of its pledge, promising to pay the balance in the following year. The pledge does not constitute an enforceable legal agreement.

5. As the result of an audit, it assessed a company $250,000 in income taxes for 1996. In their audit report, the auditors estimated that audits of subsequent years would yield an additional $150,000.

Prepare journal entries to record the transactions. Comment briefly on the amount of revenue recognized.

16-3

Low interest loans constitute a subsidy and hence an expense.

The Business Development Corporation (BDC), a federal agency, makes loans to high-tech companies that satisfy specified criteria. The loans are intended to encourage research and development and are made at rates substantially below market.

In 1998 the BDC made a loan of $100,000 to Interface Networks, Inc. The interest rate was 6 percent and the loan was payable over a three-year period in equal installments of $37,411. At the time of the loan, prevailing Treasury interest rates for loans of comparable maturities were 10 percent.

a. What was the amount of the loan subsidy?

b. How and when should the agency recognize the value of the subsidy? Explain.

c. Prepare a journal entry to record the loan and recognize the subsidy.

16-4

Different types of assets are accounted for in different ways.

The government purchased or constructed the following assets:

1. a monument to honor the sailors who served in the U.S. Coast Guard

2. land to be incorporated into a national forest

3. oil to be held in reserve to cover temporary shortages

4. an office building for the General Accounting Office

5. oil to be used in a government-owned utility that generates and sells electric power

6. operating room equipment for a Veterans Administration hospital

7. operating room equipment for a hospital ship

8. a historical building that is being used—and will continue to be used—to house federal offices

For each, indicate whether it should be:

a. capitalized and depreciated (or amortized) over its useful life

b. capitalized but not depreciated (or amortized)

c. expensed as acquired, and described in the supplementary stewardship statement

d. reported either at historical cost (based on either the FIFO or the weighted average methods) or at latest acquisition cost

e. reported only at historical cost

16-5

Certain types of government inventories may be accounted for at latest acquisition prices.

The statement of net cost of a federal agency included the following (in millions):

Sales		$405
Cost of Goods Sold		
Beginning Inventory at Beginning-of-the-Period Latest Acquisition Cost	$ 54	
Less: Allowance for Unrealized Holding Gains at the Beginning of the Period	(21)	
Plus: Purchases	360	
Cost of Goods Available for Sale	393	
Less: Ending Inventory at End-of-the-Period Latest Acquisition Cost	(72)	
Plus: Allowance for Unrealized Holding Gains at the End of the Period	35	
Cost of Goods Sold		356
Net Results		$ 49

a. What was the value of the beginning-of-year inventory stated at historical cost?

b. What was the value of the end-of-year inventory stated at historical cost?

c. What would be the cost of goods sold stated at latest acquisition cost?

d. Show how end-of-year inventory would be presented on the balance sheet.

PROBLEMS

16-1

Federal agency financial statements were illustrated but not discussed in detail in this chapter. Nevertheless, despite some unusual terminology, they are readily understandable.

Examine the following financial statements, which are condensed versions of those of a federal agency responsible for collecting taxes and duties and transferring them to the Treasury.

Statement of Custodial Activity for Year-Ended September 30 (in Millions)

Tax Revenues for Others:

Collections	$4,900
Increase in Taxes Receivable	200
Total Revenues for Others	$5,100

Disposition of Revenues:

Amounts Transferred to the Treasury	$4,800
Increase in Amounts to be Transferred	300
Total Disposition of Revenues	$5,100
Net Custodial Activity	$ 0

Statement of Net Cost for Year-Ended September 30 (in Millions)

Personnel Cost	$ 300
Other Costs	500
Net Cost of Operations	$ 800

Statement of Net Changes in Net Position for Year-Ended September 30 (in Millions)

Financing Sources—Appropriations Used	775
Less: Net Cost of Operations	800
Net Results of Operations	(25)
Increase in Unexpended Appropriations	125
Increase in Net Position	100
Net Position, Beginning of Year	450
Net Position, End of Year	$ 550

Balance Sheet as of September 30 (in Millions)

Assets:

Fund Balance with Treasury	$ 125
Taxes Receivable	615
Plant, Equipment and Other Assets (Net of Accumulated Depreciation)	285
Total Assets	$1,025

Liabilities:

Custodial Liability	$ 450
Other Liabilities	25
Total Liabilities	$ 475

Net position:

Unexpended Appropriations	$ 125
Cumulative Results of Operations	425
Total Net Position	$ 550
Total Liabilities and Net Position	$1,025

Statement of Budgetary Resources for Year-Ended September 30 (in Millions)

Budgetary Resources Made Available:

Current Appropriations	$ 900

Status of Budgetary Resource:

Obligations Incurred	$ 775
Unobligated Balance Not Available (Expired Allotments)	125
Total, Status of Budgetary Resources	$ 900

Outlays:

Obligations Incurred	$ 775
Add: Obligated Fund Balance and Accounts Payable, Beginning of Year	70
Deduct: Obligated Fund Balance and Accounts Payable, End of Year	(60)
Total Outlays	$ 785

Statement of Financing for Year-Ended September 30 (in Millions)	
Obligations and Nonbudgetary Resources	
Obligations Incurred	$ 775
Increase in Goods and Services Ordered But Not Yet Received	(5)
Costs Capitalized on the Balance Sheet and Not Expensed	
Acquisition of Fixed Assets	(10)
Expenses That Do Not Require Budgetary Resources	
Depreciation	40
Net Cost of Operations	$ 800

a. How much did the agency actually collect in taxes? How much did it submit to the Treasury? How much did it owe the Treasury at year-end, assuming that the amount owed includes both taxes collected and taxes receivable? How much did it owe at the beginning of the year?

b. How much did it cost the agency to carry out its activities during the year?

c. Of its operating costs, how much was financed by federally appropriated funds?

d. What was the total amount that the agency was appropriated during the year? What was the balance that was not used? Is this amount available for immediate use by the agency? If not, why not? Did the agency have a balance in unexpended appropriations at the start of the year? How can you tell?

e. What was the total amount of goods and services ordered by the agency during the year? How much of goods or services was received (including amounts ordered in the previous year but received in the current year)? How much was paid for?

f. Per the statement of financing, the agency ordered $775 of goods and services (obligations incurred), but the net cost of operations per both the statement of financing and the statement of net cost is $800. How can the net cost of operations exceed the amount of goods and services ordered? Explain and account for the differences.

16-2

Veterans benefits (not discussed in this chapter) present especially challenging issues of accounting.

The federal government's 1993 consolidated financial statements (issued before the FASAB recommended accounting principles pertaining to liabilities) contains the following excerpt from a note entitled "Veterans' compensation and pension"

> The Department of Veterans Affairs (VA) has a liability to veterans or their dependents for compensation benefits (if the veteran was disabled or died from military service-connected causes) or pension benefits for war veterans (if the veteran was disabled or died from non–service-connected causes).

The note also indicates that the actuarial value of the compensation benefits as of September 30, 1993, was $235.2 billion and that for pension and burial benefits was $44.3 billion.

In addition, the VA offers medical benefits to veterans. These are provided through VA hospitals, but only to the extent that required facilities are available (except for veterans with service-connected disabilities who are automatically entitled to medical services). The government makes no guarantees as to level of care and Congress decides annually how adequately the facilities will be funded.

Although this chapter did not address veterans benefits, it did raise the related question of whether the government should report a liability for the actuarial value of anticipated Social Security benefits and correspondingly recognize an expense for the benefits as they are "earned" by the beneficiaries.

Suppose that you were a member of the FASAB. Do you think that the VA should recognize a liability (and a corresponding expense) for each of the following benefits during the years in which the veterans perform their military service (or are injured or die)? Or alternatively, do you think that the liability (and related expense) for the benefits should be recognized only when the payments are actually due or the medical services are actually provided?

a. payments to be made to veterans or their families as a consequence of disability or death from service-connected causes

b. pension benefits attributable to non–service-connected causes (The actual amount of the benefits is tied mainly to need, rather than to length of service, compensation, or rank. These benefits are in addition to the traditional pension benefits available to career military personnel.)

c. medical benefits to be provided at VA facilities

Be sure to present your response in the context of FASAB recommended principles or issues under consideration as discussed in the text.

16-3

The primary statements of a federal agency can be constructed from the proprietary and budgetary accounts.

The following balances, in trial balance form, were drawn from the year-end ledgers of the Federal Lending Agency (a fictitious entity) following the agency's first year of operations. Some of the accounts are aggregations of those that would typically be maintained by a federal entity. Budgetary (as opposed to proprietary) accounts are marked with an asterisk.

	Debit	Credit
	(in millions)	
Various Expenses	$ 219	
Miscellaneous Revenues		$ 93
Appropriations Used		412
Fund Balance with the Treasury	1,140	
Loans Receivable	126	
Equipment	80	
Allowance for Depreciation		16
Accounts Payable and		
Other Liabilities		256
Unexpended Appropriations		788
Cumulative Results of Operation,		
Beginning of Year	0	
Current Appropriations	1,200*	
Borrowing Authority	160*	
Obligations Incurred		640*
Funds Available for Commitment		720*
	$2,925	$2,925

a. Following the formats illustrated in the text, prepare the following statements:

   1. a statement of net cost

   2. a statement of changes in net position

   3. a balance sheet

   4. a statement of budgetary resources (omitting the section on outlays)

b. Review the amounts on the financial statements.

   1. Do the cumulative results of operations per the balance sheet agree with the cumulative results of operations per the statement of changes in net position?

   2. Are the unexpended appropriations per the balance sheet equal to the appropriations received per the statement of budgetary resources less the appropriations used per the statement of changes in net position?

16-4

Federal revenues may be accounted for and reported in an unusual manner.

   A federal environmental agency engaged in the following transactions during a particular year.

1. It billed corporations for which it provided services $160 million. Of this it collected $140 million.

2. It levied $150 million in fines and penalties against corporations. Of this, $90 million was collected in cash. Of the balance, the protest period has expired on $35 million, which the agency expects to collect in the following year. The remaining $25 million is in dispute and court dates have not yet been set.

3. It collected an additional $20 million in fines and penalties that had been assessed by federal courts in the previous period.

4. It received cash donations of $3 million and pledges of an additional $2 million. The agency's counsel advises that the pledges are not legally enforceable.

a. Prepare journal entries to record the revenues and collections.

b. Show how the revenues and related receivables would be reported on the agency's balance sheet and statement of net cost (i.e. an operating statement).

16-5

Loan guarantee cost should be reported mainly in the year the guarantees are made.

   To help middle-income students finance the cost of their university educations, the Student Loan Authority guarantees student loans made by private banks. By guaranteeing the loans, the agency enables the banks to make the loans at rates far lower than they would without the guarantees.

   In 1998, the agency guaranteed $120 million of loans. It estimates that, owing to student defaults it will have to fulfill its guarantees as follows (in millions):

Year	Amount
1999	$0.5
2000	1.2
2001	2.0
2002	1.8

a. Prepare the entry that the agency should make in 1998, the year it guarantees the loans. The agency applies a discount rate of 6 percent. It assumes that all guarantee payments will be made at the end of the indicated years.

b. Prepare the entry that it should make at the end of 1999, assuming that it fulfills its guarantees, as estimated, of $0.5 million.

16-6

The reported value of inventory depends on its type.

   The Department of Agriculture maintains an educational division that sells publications to the general public.

   In a recent year the division reported publication sales of $3,850,000. At the start of the year it had inventory on hand that had cost $620,000. Based on latest invoice prices, however, the inventory would be valued at $650,000. During the year it purchased publications for $3,500,000 and sold publications that had cost $3,335,000. Its year-end inventory was $770,000 at cost and $830,000 at latest acquisition cost.

a. Show how the division would report its beginning and ending inventory on a comparative balance sheet, assuming that it values inventory at latest acquisition cost.

b. Prepare an operating statement for the year, assuming no operating costs other than cost of goods sold.

c. Suppose, instead, that the inventory maintained by the division was in agricultural commodities held for use in a natural disaster. Indicate the main difference in how it would be accounted for.

16-7

When should the costs of subsidized loan programs be recognized?

In 1998 Congress established a small business direct loan program. The program provides that qualifying businesses can obtain loans at a rate 5 percent below that prevailing on Treasury securities of comparable maturity. The program was to be in effect for a period of twelve years. Its total cost was estimated at $1.3 billion.

In 1999, the Small Business Administration, which administers the program, loaned the S & D Produce Company $100,000 for ten years at a rate of 5 percent. At the time, the prevailing Treasury rate was 10 percent. The loan was to be repaid in ten annual installments of $12,950.

a. What journal entry should the Small Business Administration make in 1998 when Congress authorized the program? Explain and justify your response.

b. What journal entry should it make in 1999 when it loaned the S & D Produce Company $100,000? Explain and justify your response.

c. What journal entries should it make in 2000 and 2001 upon collection of the first two loan repayments?

16-8

Federal expenditures raise unique issues of recognition

In 1998 the federal government was affected by the following transactions and events. For each, indicate the amount that it should recognize as an expense during 1998. Cite the FASAB principle upon which you rely.

a. The government ordered ten military aircraft from a manufacturer at a cost of $40 million each. During the year it received five and paid for two. Their expected useful life is ten years.

b. In response to extraordinary floods, Congress appropriated $2.4 billion in disaster relief. Some of the aid was targeted for infrastructure repair. During the year, the government contracted with a construction firm to repair a bridge at an agreed-upon price of $1.2 million. The contractor completed a portion of the job, billing the government for $600,000.

c. As part of the same program, the government authorized direct grants to individuals and businesses. During the year, it approved grants totaling $400 million, of which it actually paid $240 million. It expected to pay the balance in the following year.

d. To assist workers laid off as the result of a recently passed free-trade agreement, Congress approved an employee relief act. The act provides that eligible employees would receive direct payments of $500 per month for up to twelve months. The cost of the program over its lifetime is expected to be $380 million. During 1998, 25,000 laid-off workers applied, and were certified as eligible for benefits. They were paid a total of $50 million.

e. During the year the employees of one government agency earned pension benefits having an actuarial present value of $30 million. The government made actual payments of $23 million to employees who had previously retired from that agency.

16-9

Federal long-lived assets have unique characteristics justifying unique accounting practices.

During 1998 federal departments and agencies acquire the following assets. For each, indicate how the government should report the asset. If the asset is to be reported on the government's balance sheets, then state whether it should be amortized or depreciated. Justify your response by specifying the category into which the asset would fall.

1. The Department of Defense purchases for $3 million a mainframe computer to be used to maintain personnel files.

2. The Department of Defense purchases a mainframe computer for $6 million. The computer is specially designed to be used on board a guided-missile cruiser to target missiles.

3. The Department of Defense acquires for $20 million missiles to be used aboard the cruiser.

4. The Department of Interior constructs a monument, at a cost of $7 million, honoring the military personnel who served in the Gulf War.

5. The Department of Interior purchases land in Bethesda Maryland for $6 million. It expects to construct an office complex on the land.

6. The Department of the Interior purchases land in East Glacier, Montana, for $130 million. The land will be incorporated into Glacier National Park.

7. NASA incurs $24 million to improve facilities at its Johnson Space Center. The facilities are to be used both as a training center for astronauts and other personnel and as a museum for visitors.

16-10

The "official" government financial statements may understate both the deficit and the debt.

Review both the consolidated financial statements and the annual report of the federal government as presented in the text.

a. Both the public and the press often confuse the federal government's "deficit" and its "debt." What is the difference between the two?

b. By how much greater or less is the government's 1995 deficit as shown in the annual report than in the consolidated financial statements?

c. By how much greater or less are the assets of the federal government as stated in the 1995 annual report than as presented in the consolidated financial statements?

   1. What are the main reasons for the difference?

   2. Why might it be argued that even the Consolidated Financial Statements greatly understate the total assets of the federal government?

d. By how much greater or less are the liabilities of the federal government as stated in the annual report than as presented in the consolidated financial statements?

   1. What are the main reasons for the difference?

2. Why might it be argued that even the consolidated financial statements greatly understate the total liabilities of the federal government?

e. As best you can tell from the statements as presented, did the Social Security program increase or decrease the federal deficit, per the 1995 annual report? Explain.

f. Per the annual report, the outlays of the Treasury Department are even greater than those of the Defense Department. What is the main item of cost to the Treasury Department as indicated by information in the consolidated financial statements?

SOLUTION TO EXERCISE FOR REVIEW AND SELF-TESTING

a. The unexpended appropriation would be shown on the Commission's balance sheet as "Fund Balance with the Treasury." It would also be included in the equity (net position) account, "Unexpected Appropriations."

b. Donations should be recognized upon the receipt of a legally binding pledge. Hence, the entire $2 million should be recognized as revenue.

c. The sales and cost of goods sold would be reported as follows:

Sales		$90,000
Cost of Goods Sold		
Beginning Inventory at Beginning-of-the-Period Latest Acquisition Cost	$ 0	
Less: Allowance for Unrealized Holding Gains at the Beginning of the Period	(0)	
Plus: Purchases	100,000	
Cost of Goods Available for Sale	100,000	
Less: Ending Inventory at End-of-the-Period Latest Acquisition Cost	(30,000)	
Plus: Allowance for Unrealized Holding Gains at the End of the Period	5,000	
Cost of Goods Sold		75,000
Net Results		$15,000

d. The cost of subsidizing the loan is the difference between the loan's face value ($400,000) and the present value of the anticipated receipts (three payments of $144,139 discounted at 8 percent). The present value of the three payments is $371,461 ($144,139 times 2.5771, the present value of an annuity of $1 for three periods discounted at 8 percent); the difference is $28,539. The Commission should recognize this amount as an expense of the period in which it makes the loan.

e. The assets should be accounted for as follows:

   1. Buildings are general assets and should be capitalized and depreciated over their useful lives

   2. The land to be used for an office building is also a general asset and should therefore be capitalized

   3. The land to be used as a wildlife refuge is a stewardship asset. It should be expensed when acquired and in that year and subsequent years described in a supplementary stewardship report.

f. The Commission's obligation is the consequence of a "government-acknowledged event"—an occurrence for which the government is not responsible but elects, as a matter of policy, to provide relief to the victims. The government should recognize a liability and corresponding expense for such an event when it formally acknowledges financial responsibility and an amount is due and payable. Thus, the Commission need not recognize any liability or expense for the damages until an amount is due and payable.

GLOSSARY *

A

Account group - An accounting entity with a set of accounts that is self-balancing and is used to account for a government's general fixed assets or general long-term obligations. Account groups are distinguished from funds in that they are not used to account for sources, uses, and balances of expendable available financial resources.

ABC - See *Activity-Based Costing*.

Accrual basis - A method of accounting that recognizes revenues when earned and expenses when incurred regardless of when cash is received or paid.

Accrued expenses - Expenses that have been incurred and recorded, but have not yet been paid.

Accrued revenue - Revenue that has been earned and recorded, but not yet received.

Activity - A line of work contributing to a function or program.

Activity-based costing (ABC) - A method of costing where overhead costs are collected in cost pools and distributed to particular products or services using cost drivers. See *cost driver*.

Actuarial cost method - A means of allocating the total cost of expected pension benefits over the total years of employee service.

Advance refunding - Issuance of debt to retire outstanding bonds or other debt instruments prior to their maturity or call date.

Affiliated organization - A legally independent entity directly tied to a primary government. May be distinguished from both a component unit and a related organization (as defined in GASB Statement No. 14, *The Financial Reporting Entity*) in that the primary government does not appoint a majority of its governing board and it is not fiscally dependent upon the primary government.

Agency fund - A fund used to account for assets that a government holds temporarily for other parties (e.g., for taxes collected on their behalf).

Agent - A party that acts on behalf of another. For example, a government that collects taxes for another government.

Allocated costs - Costs that cannot be associated directly with specific products or services, but are assigned to them according to a predetermined formula or algorithm.

Allot - To divide a budgetary appropriation into amounts that may be encumbered or expended during an allotment period (e.g., a government may choose to allot its annual budget to twelve monthly periods), or for specified programs or activities.

Allotments - Periodic allocations of funds to departments or agencies to assure that an entire year's appropriation is not expended early in the period covered by the budget or expended for certain programs or activities to the detriment of others.

American Institute of Certified Public Accountants (AICPA) - A professional organization for certified public accountants (CPAs) that is responsible for establishing auditing and related professional standards.

Amortization - (1) The process of allocating the cost of an intangible asset over its useful life. (2) The reduction of debt by regular payments of principal and interest sufficient to retire the debt by maturity.

Annual report - The financial report of a business, government, or not-for-profit entity. Typically consists of a balance sheet, operating statement, statement of changes in equity, and a statement of cash flows and other supplementary information.

Annuity - A series of equal payments over a specified number of equal time periods.

Annuity fund - An endowment fund to account for gifts that provide fixed payments to the donor (or a person designated by the donor) for a specified term or for the remainder of his or her life. Thereafter, what remains of the gift will typically revert to the recipient organization.

Apportionment - The shares of a total federal appropriation that the Office of Management and Budget permits an agency to spend within a particular time period (such as a quarter) or for designated programs, activities, or projects.

Appropriation - An amount authorized by a legislative body for a department or to make expenditures and incur liabilities for a specified purpose.

Appropriations budget - The legislatively approved budget that grants expenditure authority to departments and other governmental units in accordance with applicable laws.

Arbitrage - The concurrent purchase and sale of the same or an equivalent security in order to profit from differences in interest rates. Generally, as it relates to state and local governments, the issuance of debt at relatively low, tax-exempt, rates of interest and the investment of the proceeds in taxable securities yielding a higher rate of return.

---

* Some of the definitions were taken directly, or adapted from, *Governmental Accounting, Auditing and Financial Reporting*, a publication of the Government Finance Officers Association. We appreciate the association's permission to use its material.

Attest - To affirm to be correct, true, or genuine; corroborate. The attest function (i.e. an audit) adds credibility to the assertions of others; in the case of an financial audit, to an entity's financial data as presented by management.

Audit - A systematic investigation or review to corroborate the assertions of others or to determine whether operations have conformed to prescribed criteria or standards. An examination of records to check their accuracy.

B

Basis of accounting - The means of determining the timing of revenue and expenditure recognition. See also *Cash Basis and Accrual Basis*.

Benefit–cost analysis - A generic term for any form of expenditure analysis that identifies and quantifies the benefits of a proposal and compares them to its costs.

Bequest - To give property by will.

Blending - One of two methods of reporting components units required by GASB Statement No. 14, *The Financial Reporting Entity* (see *discrete presentation* for a description of the other method). This method combines a component unit's transactions and balances with the data of the primary government as if the component unit were a part of that government.

Bond anticipation notes - (BANs) Short-term interest-bearing notes issued by a lender in the expectation that they will soon be replaced by long-term bonds.

Bond discount - The excess of a bond's stated value over the amount paid to acquire the bond. Bonds are issued at a discount so that the return to investors is equal to the prevailing market interest rate, even though the prevailing market interest rate is higher than the interest rate stated on the bond.

Bond premium - An amount paid to acquire a bond in excess of the bond's stated value. Bonds are issued at a premium so that the return to investors is equal to the prevailing market interest rate, even though the prevailing market interest rate is lower than the interest rate stated on the bond.

Bond rating agencies - Companies, the leading ones being Standard & Poor's (S&P), Moody's Investors Service, and Fitch's Investor Service, that evaluate bonds or other securities based on the likelihood that the issuer will not default on payments of principal or interest.

Bond refunding - The issuance of new bonds to replace bonds already outstanding, usually with the intent of reducing debt service costs.

Budget - A plan of financial operations embodying an estimate of proposed expenditures for a given period and the proposed means of financing them.

Budgetary accounts - Accounts used to enter a formally adopted annual operating budget into the general ledger so as to enhance management control over revenues and expenditures.

Budgetary control - The control or management of a government or enterprise in accordance with an approved budget to keep expenditures within the limitations of available appropriations and available revenues.

C

Call price - A predetermined price at which the issuer of bonds may redeem (call) the bonds irrespective of the current market price.

Callable bond - A bond that permits the issuer to redeem the obligation at a specified price before the stated maturity date.

Capital assets - Long-term assets, such as buildings, equipment, and infrastructure, intended to be held or used in operations.

Capital budget - A plan of proposed capital outlays, such as for infrastructure, buildings, equipment and other long-lived assets, and of the means of financing them.

Capital debt - Long-term debt issued to finance capital assets.

Capital expenditures - Expenditures to acquire or construct capital assets

Capital improvement program (CIP) - A plan for the acquisition of capital assets over several (typically five) years.

Capital lease - A lease which is essentially an installment purchase and meets the criteria of FASB Statement No. 13, *Accounting for Leases*. The lessee ("purchaser") records the acquired asset on its balance sheet as an asset and correspondingly recognizes the present value of the agreed upon lease payments as a liability.

Capital projects fund - A fund to account for financial resources set aside for the acquisition or construction of major capital facilities.

Cash basis - A method of accounting in which revenues and expenses are recognized and recorded when received, not necessarily when earned.

Cash flow statement - A financial statement that details the inflows and outflows of cash.

Chief Financial Officer of the United States - The Deputy Director for Management, a position created by the Chief Financial Officers Act of 1990. He or she is responsible for providing overall direction and leadership in the establishment of sound federal financial practices.

Codification the Government Accounting Standards Board - *Governmental Accounting and Financial Reporting Standards*, a compendium of GASB promulgated accounting principles, including those adopted from predecessor standard-setting organizations.

Collateral - Assets pledged to secure deposits, investments or loans.

Combined statements - The five basic statements that constitute General Purpose Financial Statements (GPFS). They include the (1) combined balance sheet—all fund types and account groups; (2) combined statement of revenues, expenditures, and changes in fund balances—all governmental fund types; (3) combined statement of revenues, expenditures, and changes in fund balances—budget and actual for general and special revenues funds (and other governmental fund types for which annual budgets have been legally adopted); (4) combined statement of revenues, expenses, and changes in retained earnings—all proprietary funds; and (5) combined statement of changes in financial position—all proprietary fund types.

Combining statements - A required component of the Comprehensive Annual Financial Report's financial section. The statements support the general purpose financial statements and provide the detail as to each of the individual fund types included in the columns of the general purpose financial statements.

Common Rule - See *Uniform Administrative Requirements for Grants and Cooperative Agreements to State and Local Governments.*

Compensated absences - Absences, such as vacations, illness, and holidays, for which it is expected employees will be paid. The term does not encompass severance or termination pay, postretirement benefits, deferred compensation, or other long-term fringe benefits, such as group insurance and long-term disability pay.

Component unit - Per GASB Statement No. 14, *The Financial Reporting Entity*, a legally separate government for which the elected officials of a primary government are financially accountable, can impose their will, or there is the potential for the organization to provide special financial benefits to, or impose specific financial burdens on, the primary government.

Comprehensive Annual Financial Report (CAFR) - The official annual report of a government. It includes (a) the five combined financial statements that constitute the general purpose financial statements; and (b) combining statements by fund type and individual fund and account group financial statements prepared in conformity with GAAP and organized into a financial reporting pyramid. It also includes supporting schedules necessary to demonstrate compliance with finance-related legal and contractual provisions, required supplementary information, extensive introductory material, and a detailed statistical section.

Comptroller General of the United States - The head of the General Accounting Office (GAO).

Conditional promise - A promise to donate an asset or provide a service in the future that is contingent on a specified future event.

Conduit debt - Obligations issued in the name of a government on behalf of a nongovernmental entity. The debt is expected to be serviced entirely by the nongovernmental unit.

Constant dollar cost - The cost of goods or services in dollars that have been adjusted to take into account changes in the general level of prices (i.e., inflation).

Contracting out - Engaging an outside, private-sector firm to provide services that have previously been performed in-house; also known as outsourcing or privatizing.

Control account - An account in the general ledger in which is recorded the aggregate of debit and credit postings to a number of related accounts called subsidiary accounts.

Consumption method - A method of accounting for inventories and prepaid costs, such as rent, in which goods or services are recorded as expenditures or expenses when used rather than when purchased; differentiated from the purchases method.

Contingent liability - An obligation that will become payable only if a specified future event occurs.

Contributed capital - The permanent capital of a proprietary fund, generally resulting from residual equity transfers from other funds, transfers-in of general fixed assets, or grants or customer fees restricted to capital acquisition or construction.

Cost accounting - The method of accounting that provides for the assembling and recording of all the elements of cost incurred to accomplish a purpose, to carry on an activity or operation, or to complete a unit of work or a specific job.

Cost driver - A basis for allocating overhead to particular products or services that is conceptually similar to an overhead charging rate. However, whereas in practice an overhead charging rate is based on broadly representative factors (such as direct labor dollars, direct labor hours, or direct materials) that influence the amount of overhead costs incurred, a cost driver is more specifically indicative of the factors affecting overhead. Examples include materials requisitions, machine hours, and maintenance costs.

Coupon rate - The stated interest rate on the face of a bond; a bond's nominal interest rate.

Current assets - Cash and other resources that are expected to be converted into cash during the normal operating cycle of the entity or within one year, whichever is longer.

Current fund - The general or main operating fund of a not-for-profit organization.

Current liabilities - Financial obligations that are reasonably expected to be paid using current assets or by creating other current liabilities within one year or the entity's operating cycle, whichever is longer.

D

Debt margin - The difference between the amount of debt outstanding computed according to applicable legal provisions and the maximum amount of debt that can legally be issued.

Debt service fund - A fund to account for financial resources set aside for the payment of interest and principal on long-term debt; a sinking fund.

Decision package - The key element of a zero-base budget in which the entity indicates the objectives of the activity for which funding is proposed, alternative means of accomplishing the same objectives; consequences of not performing the activity, and inputs, outputs, and outcomes at various levels of funding.

Deferred maintenance costs - The costs that an entity avoided in a current year or past years by failing to perform required routine maintenance and repairs, but that will have to be incurred in the future.

Deferred revenue - Receipts of cash or other assets for which asset recognition criteria have been met, but for which revenue recognition criteria have not been met. For example, taxes received in the period prior to that in which they are due.

Deficit - (1) The excess of liabilities and reserved equity of a fund over its assets. (2) The excess of expenditures over revenues during an accounting period; or in the case of proprietary funds, the excess of expenses over revenues.

Defined benefit pension plan - A pension plan that specifies the pension benefits to be paid to retirees, usually as a function of factors such as age, years of service, and compensation.

Defined contribution plan - A plan that specifies the amount of contributions to an individual's retirement account instead of the amount of benefits the individual is to receive. Under a defined contribution pension plan, the benefits a participant will receive depend on the amount contributed to the participant's account and the returns earned on investments of those contributions.

Demand bonds - Long-term debt instruments with demand ("put") provisions that require the issuer to repurchase the bonds upon notice from the bondholder at a specified price, usually equal to the principal plus accrued interest. To ensure their ability to redeem the bonds, issuers of demand bonds frequently enter into standby liquidity agreements ("takeout" agreements) with banks or other financial institutions.

Depreciation - The systematic and rational allocation of the cost of tangible noncurrent operating assets over the periods benefited by the use of the asset.

Derivative - A financial asset whose value is derived from the shift in the price of an underlying asset, such as a bond, or an index of asset values, such as the Standard & Poors' index of 500 stocks, or an index of interest rates.

Derived tax revenues - Tax revenues that are based on exchange transactions between parties other than the taxing government. Examples include sales taxes and income taxes.

Direct costs - Costs such as for labor and materials, directly associated with specific products or activities of an organization. Distinguished from indirect (overhead) costs.

Discrete presentation - One of two methods of reporting component units required by GASB Statement Number No. 14, *The Financial Reporting Entity* (See *blending* for description of other method). This method reports the component unit in a single column separate from the data of

the primary government (as if the unit were another fund or account group) on combined financial statements. For example, a state government might report its state colleges and universities in a single column.

Donated assets - Assets, other than cash, donated to an organization.

Donated services - Services provided for no charge to an organization by individual volunteers or businesses.

Due from (to) other funds - An asset (liability) account used to indicate amounts owed to (by) one fund by (to) another.

E

Economic cost - The full cost of goods or services, as opposed to that which might be recognized for financial accounting. For example, the full amount of compensation to be paid by a government, including that of pensions and compensated absences, rather than merely the amount paid to the employees in a current period.

Economic gain (loss) - In the context of an advance refunding, the difference between the present value of the old debt service requirements and the present value of the new debt service requirements, discounted at the effective interest rate and adjusted for additional cash paid.

Economy and efficiency audit - An audit carried out to assess whether an entity is acquiring, protecting, and using its resources economically and efficiently and whether it has complied with laws and regulations relating to economy and efficiency.

Encumbrances - Commitments to purchase goods or services.

Endowment fund - A nonexpendable trust fund used to account for contributions that the donor specifies are to be invested and that the income only from the investments may be expended.

Enterprise fund - A proprietary fund established to account for operations financed and operated in a manner similar to a private business (e.g., water, gas and electric utilities; airports; parking garages; and transit systems) and for which the governing body intends that costs (i.e., expenses, including depreciation) of providing goods or services to the general public on a continuing basis be financed or recovered primarily through user charges.

Entitlements - Payments, usually from a higher-level government, to which a state or local government or an individual is entitled as a matter of law in an amount determined by a specified formula.

Entity - (1) The combination of funds and account groups that constitutes the financial reporting unit. (2) The most basic accounting and reporting unit—i.e., a fund.

Exchange revenues - Revenues that arise from sales transactions in which each party receives benefits and incurs costs.

Exchange transaction - a sales-type transaction in which goods and services are exchanged for consideration of approximately equal value.

Expendable funds - Governmental funds whose resources are received from taxes, fees, or other sources and may be expended ("spent"); the governmental as opposed to the proprietary funds of a government.

Expenditures - Decreases in net financial resources under the modified accrual basis of accounting.

Expenses - Decreases in overall net assets from delivering services or producing goods under the full accrual basis.

Exposure draft - A preliminary version of a standard-setting authority's official pronouncement, issued as means of obtaining public comment.

External report - A report issued for use by parties outside the reporting entity, such as citizens, investors, and creditors, as opposed to inside parties, such as managers.

External subsidy - An amount of money, generally a grant, received by a governmental entity from a non-governmental source.

F

Face value - As applied to securities, the amount indicated on the face of a bond that will have to be paid at maturity.

FASAB - See *Federal Accounting Standards Advisory Board*.

FASB - See *Financial Accounting Standards Board*.

Federal Accounting Standards Advisory Board (FASAB) - The federal board charged with recommending federal accounting standards to the three agencies (GAO, OMB, and Department of the Treasury) responsible for setting them.

Federal funds - Resources of the federal government's general fund and special revenue funds.

Fiduciary funds - The trust and agency funds used to account for assets held by a government unit in a trustee capacity or as an agent for individuals, private organizations, other government units, or other funds.

Financial Accounting Standards Board (FASB) - The organization responsible for establishing external accounting and reporting standards for all nongovernmental entities, including not-for-profit organizations.

Financial audit - An examination or review made to determine whether financial statements or related financial reports conform to generally accepted accounting principles or other prescribed criteria.

Financial resources - Cash, investments and receivables, and other assets that can be expected to be transformed into cash in the normal course of operations. Financial resources minus the current claims against them equals net financial resources.

Financial related audits - In the context of federal auditing, these determine whether financial reports, including those on specific funds or accounts, are either fairly presented or presented in accordance with stated criteria, and whether the entity has complied with specific financial-related requirements, such as those set forth in laws and regulations, grants, and contracts.

Financial statement audits - Examinations that determine whether an entity's financial statements are presented fairly in accordance with generally accepted accounting principles and whether the entity has complied with laws and regulations that may have a material effect on the financial statements.

Fiscal capacity - the economic base that the government can draw upon for the resources necessary to provide the goods or services expected of it.

Fiscal effort - the extent to which a government is taking advantage of its fiscal capacity. Generally measured by comparing the revenues that the government generates from its own sources (i.e., total revenue excluding grants from other governments) with either the wealth or income of its taxpayers.

Fiscal funding clause - A clause in a lease agreement providing that the lease is cancelable if the legislature or other funding authority does not appropriate the funds necessary for the government unit to fulfill its obligations under the lease agreement.

Fiscal period (year) - Any period at the end of which a government determines its financial position and the results of its operations; also accounting period.

Fixed assets - Long-lived tangible assets, such as buildings, equipment, improvements other than buildings and land.

Fixed assets account group - See *General fixed assets account group*.

Fixed budget - A budget in which costs and revenues are fixed—i.e., not subject to change as a result of increases or decreases in the volume of goods or services to be provided.

Fixed costs - Costs of goods or services that do not vary with the volume of goods or services provided (e.g., rent, interest, executive salaries, and air-conditioning costs).

Flexible budget - A budget in which dollar amounts vary according to the volume of goods or services to be provided.

Full cost - The cost of goods or services that includes both direct and indirect (overhead) costs.

Functional classification - Expenditures that are grouped according to the purpose for which they are made, such as public safety, general administration, or recreation.

Fund - A fiscal and accounting entity with a self-balancing set of accounts used to account for resources, and claims against them, that are segregated in accord with legal or contractual restrictions or to carry out specific activities.

Fund accounting - An accounting system in which an entity's resources are divided among two or more accounting entities known as funds.

Funded pension plan - A pension plan in which contributions are made and assets are accumulated to pay benefits to potential recipients before cash payments to recipients actually are required.

Funding policy - In the context of pension plans, the policy that determines the amounts and timing of contributions to be made by plan employees, employers, and any other parties to accumulate the resources required to pay retirees their specified benefits.

Fund type - A fund category. In government accounting, any one of seven categories into which all funds are classified. The seven fund types are: general, special revenue, debt service, capital projects, enterprise, internal service, and trust and agency.

G

GASB - See *Governmental Accounting Standards Board*.

General Accounting Office (GAO) - The congressional agency responsible for conducting financial and performance audits of federal agencies, programs, and activities and for carrying out other accounting and finance-related actvities of the federal government.

General fixed assets - Capital assets that are not assets of any particular fund, but of the government unit as a whole. Most often these assets arise from the expenditure of the financial resources of governmental (as opposed to proprietary or fiduciary) funds.

General fixed assets account group (GFAAG) - A group or list of accounts in which the general fixed assets of a governmental unit are recorded.

General compliance requirements - A set of nine requirements that involve significant national policies with which all federal funds recipients must comply. Examples of policies addressed are those pertaining to civil rights, political activity, and drug-free workplaces.

General fund - A fund used to account for unrestricted resources. The fund that accounts for all resources that are not required to be accounted for in other funds.

General journal - A journal in which all entries are recorded, excluding those recorded in special journals.

General ledger - A record containing the accounts needed to reflect an entity's financial position and results of operations.

General long-term debt account group (GLTDAG) - A self-balancing group of accounts established to account for the unmatured general long-term debt of a government. The GLTDAG is also used to report the portion of liabilities, such as for claims, judgments, compensated absences,

and unfunded pension contributions of governmental funds and expendable trust funds, that is not expected to be liquidated through the use of expendable available financial resources.

General obligation debt - Debt that is secured by the full faith and credit of the issuing body.

Generally accepted accounting principles (GAAP) - Uniform minimum standards and guidelines for financial accounting and reporting that govern the form and content of financial statements. They encompass the conventions, rules, and procedures necessary to define accepted accounting practice at a particular time.

Generally accepted auditing standards (GAAS) - Standards established by the AICPA for the conduct and reporting of financial audits.

Generally accepted government auditing standards (GAGAS) - Standards established by the GAO in its publication *Standards for Audit of Governmental Organizations, Programs, Activities and Functions* (the Yellow Book) for the conduct and reporting of both financial and performance audits.

General purpose financial statements (GPFS) - The five combined financial statements that, together with accompanying notes, constitute the minimum level of financial reporting needed for fair presentation in conformity with GAAP. See *Combined statements*.

Government-assessed taxes - Taxes, such as property taxes, assessed by the government in which the government determines the amount owed. Distinguished from taxpayer-assessed taxes, such as income taxes, in which the parties other than the government determine the amount owed.

Governmental accounting - The composite activity of analyzing, recording, summarizing, reporting, and interpreting the financial transactions of governments.

Governmental Accounting Standards Board (GASB) - The authoritative accounting and financial reporting standard-setting body for government entities.

Government Accounting Standards (Standards for Audit of Government Organizations, Programs, Activities and Functions) - The auditing standards of the GAO; the Yellow Book.

Government Auditing Standards (GAS) - See *Generally accepted government auditing standards (GAGAS)*.

Government Finance Officers Association (GFOA) - An association of state and local governments and officials and other individuals interested in state and local government finance.

Governmental funds - Funds used to account for the acquisition, use, and balances of expendable financial resources and the related current liabilities, except those accounted for in proprietary funds and fiduciary funds; the four governmental fund types—general, special revenue, debt service, and capital projects.

Grant - A contribution from one party to another to be used or expended for a specified purpose, activity, or facility; ordinarily distinguished from an exchange transaction in that the grantor does not receive compensation in return for the resources contributed.

H–I–J

Heritage assets - As defined by the Federal Accounting Standards Advisory Board, assets that have values because of their historical, cultural, educational, or artistic significance.

Historical cost - The purchase price or construction cost plus any additional costs incurred in placing an asset in its intended location, condition, and purpose, less accumulated depreciation or amortization.

Human capital - As defined by the FASAB, outlays for education and training of the public intended to increase the nation's productive capacity.

Impact fees - Fees charged to developers by a governmental entity for costs of anticipated improvements, such as sidewalks and parks, that will be necessary as a result of a development.

Indirect costs - Costs that are related to an activity or object, but cannot be directly traced to that activity; overhead costs; distinguished from direct costs.

Industrial development bonds - Bonds issued by governmental units at low interest rates to encourage private development in their area. Repayment of the debt is expected to be the responsibility of the beneficiary of the bond.

Infrastructure assets - Public domain fixed assets such as roads, bridges, curbs, gutters, streets and sidewalks, drainage systems, lighting systems, and similar assets that are immovable and of value only to the government unit.

Inputs - The resources applied to a service, such as dollar cost, number of labor hours, and amount of material.

In-substance defeasance - An advance refunding (retirement of bonds) in which the government places sufficient resources in a trust account to cover all required principal and interest payments on the defeased debt. Although the government is not legally released from being the primary obligor on the refunded bonds, the possibility of it having to make additional payments is considered remote.

Intangible asset - An asset that has a future benefit, but cannot be physically seen—e.g., a patent or copyright.

Interfund transfers - All interfund transactions except loans, quasi-external transactions, and reimbursements. Transfers can be classified as belonging to one of two major categories: residual equity transfers or operating transfers.

Intergenerational equity - See *Interperiod equity*.

Internal service funds - Funds used to account for business-type activities in which the customers are other government departments or agencies.

Incremental receipts (disbursements) - Receipts (disbursements) that differ if one alternative course of action were chosen over another.

Interperiod equity - The extent to which current-year revenues are sufficient to pay for current-year services (as opposed to whether the costs of current-year services are being shifted to future years).

Insolvent - The condition of being unable to meet debts or discharge liabilities owing to a deficiency of available financial resources.

Issue costs - Costs incurred to issue bonds, such as amounts paid to underwriters, attorneys, accountants, and printers.

Investment in plant fund - A fund maintained mainly by colleges and universities and other not-for-profits to account for the entity's fixed assets and the liabilities incurred to acquire those assets; comparable to a government's general fixed assets and general long-term debt account groups.

Investment pools - Fiscal entities established to invest the resources of two or more funds or independent entities; comparable to a mutual fund.

Joint venture - A contractual arrangement whereby two or more participants agree to carry out a common activity, with each sharing in both risks and rewards.

Journal - A book of original entry.

K–L

Lessee - The entity that rents an asset from the asset's owner, the lessor.

Lessor - The owner of rental property who transfers the right to use the property to the user, the lessee.

Levy - To impose or collect a tax.

Life income fund - An endowment fund to account for gifts that provide a return to the donor (or a person designated by the donor) for the remainder of his or her life. Thereafter, what remains of the gift will typically revert to the recipient entity.

Liquidity - The ability of an entity to meet its financial obligations as they come due.

Loan fund - A fund used to account for resources that will provide loans to a designated class of beneficiaries, such as students or small businesses.

Long-term debt - In government, obligations that are not expected to be paid with currently available financial resources. In not-for-profits, obligations that are not expected to be paid in cash or other operating assets within one year or the entity's normal operating cycle.

Long-term debt account group - See *General long-term debt account group*.

M

Matching concept - The principle that expenses or expenditures should be recognized in the same accounting period as related revenues.

Measurement focus - The accounting convention that determines which assets and liabilities are included on an entity's balance sheet and which will thereby affect the determination of revenues and expenses (or expenditures) to be reported on the entity's operating statement. Measurement focus determines what is being measured—e.g., net profits or flows of financial resources.

Mission assets - As defined by the Federal Accounting Standards Advisory Board, assets, such as weapons systems or space exploration equipment, that are held for emergencies or have no alternative uses in the private sector or other government programs.

Modified accrual basis - The accrual basis of accounting adapted to the governmental fund-type measurement focus. Revenues are recognized in the period in which they become available and measurable. Some expenditures are recognized on a accrual basis; others on a cash basis.

Moral obligation debt - Bonds or notes issued by one entity (usually a state agency), but backed by the implied (not legally binding) promise of another entity (usually the state itself) to make up any debt service deficiencies.

Municipality - A city or town or other area incorporated for self-government. Also, in its broadest sense, any state or local government, including states, counties, cities, towns, and special districts.

Municipal bond - A bond issued by a municipality.

N

National Council on Governmental Accounting (NCGA) - The governmental accounting standard setting authority that preceded the GASB.

Natural classification - Expenditures that are grouped according to an object, such as salaries and wages.

Net assets - The residual of assets minus liabilities.

Nominal interest rate - The contractual interest rate shown on the face of a bond and used to compute the amount of interest to be paid; in contrast to the effective interest rate.

Nonappropriation budget - A financial plan for an organization, program, activity, or function approved in a manner authorized by constitution, charter, statute, or ordinance but not subject to appropriation and, therefore, outside the boundaries of an appropriated budget.

Nonappropriation clause - See *Fiscal funding clause*.

Nonexchange revenues - Revenues that materialize when a government commands resources but gives nothing in exchange (at least not directly). Examples include taxes, duties, fines and penalties.

Nonexchange transaction - A transaction in which one party provides resources to another without getting consideration of approximately equal value in return; includes voluntary nonexchange transactions, such as contributions and grants and imposed nonexchange transactions, such as taxes, duties, and fines.

Noncommitment debt - See *Conduit debt*.

Nonexpendable funds - Proprietary funds that "pay their own way" through customer charges. Contrasted with ex-

pendable funds, the resources of which are provided by taxes, fees, or other revenues and are expected to be spent each year.

Nonexpendable trust funds - Endowment funds, the principal of which must be maintained intact; only the income of which can be expended.

Nonreciprocal receipt - A contribution for which the recipient gives nothing in exchange. Per FASB 116, *Accounting for Contributions Received and Contributions Made*, contributions may be made in cash, marketable securities, property and equipment, utilities, supplies, intangible assets, and the services of professionals and craftsmen.

Not-for-profit organization - An entity that conducts operations for the benefit of its users without a profit motive.

Note disclosures - Information disclosed in the notes to the financial statements.

O–P

Object - An item in an expenditure classification that relates to the type of goods or services obtained rather than to the purpose of the expenditure or the nature of the activity that it supports. Examples include wages and salaries, supplies, and contractual services.

Object classification budget - A budget that details revenues and expenditures by object, rather than, for example, program or nature of activity.

Off-balance-sheet financing - Obligations, such as those from operating leases, that do not satisfy the accounting criteria of reportable liabilities and are therefore not disclosed on an entity's balance sheet.

Office of Management and Budget (OMB) - The executive branch agency of the federal government that assists the president in preparing the federal budget and supervises the executive branch agencies in implementing it. It also oversees and coordinates federal procurement, financial management, information and regulatory policies. It further has authority to prescribe the form and content of federal agency financial statements and related reports and to establish requirements pertaining to single audits.

On-behalf payments - Payments made by one government for the benefit of another. For example, pension contributions paid by a state for employees of a school district.

Operating debt - Debt issued to cover general operating, as opposed to capital, expenditures.

Operating lease - A rental agreement permitting an entity to use an asset for a specified period of time, but does not meet the criteria, set forth in FASB Statement No. 13, *Accounting for Leases*, of a capital lease.

Operating statement - A statement that shows an entity's revenues, expenditures/expenses and transfers over a specified period of time. See also, *Statement of activities*.

Operational audit - See *Performance auditing*.

Operational objectives - Specific sought-after results of a program or activity. The objectives should be quantifiable, measurable, and distinguishable from broad, nonspecific statements of purpose.

Opportunity cost - The economic gains that are forgone by choosing one course of action over an alternative.

Outcomes - The results (accomplishments) of a service, generally measured so as to take into account the quality of performance.

Outputs - The quantity, or units of service, provided by an activity.

Overhead - Indirect costs; those elements of cost necessary in the production of a good or service that are not directly traceable to the product or service, such as rent, heat, light, supplies, management and supervision.

Overlapping debt - The proportionate share that property within the reporting government must bear of the debts of all other governments located wholly or in part within its geographic boundaries.

Net pension obligation - The cumulative difference between an employer's annual pension costs (determined per the requirements of applicable accounting and actuarial standards) and the employer's contribution to the pension plan.

Pass-through grants - Grants that a government must transfer to, or spend on behalf of, a secondary recipient. For example, a federal education grant that a state must distribute to local school districts.

Pay-as-you-go-basis - In the context of pension accounting and risk management, the failure to finance retirement obligations or anticipated losses on a current basis using an acceptable actuarial funding method.

Payments in lieu of taxes - Amounts paid by one government in place of property taxes they are not required to pay. Generally occurs when a jurisdiction contains a substantial amount of facilities of other governments; for example, when the federal government makes payments to a local school district in lieu of property taxes it would be required to pay on a military base within the district if federal property were not tax-exempt.

Pension - Sums of money paid periodically (usually monthly) to a retired or disabled employee (or a surviving spouse) owing to his or her years of employment.

Pension contribution - The amount paid into a pension plan by an employer (or employee), pursuant to the terms of the plan, state law, actuarial calculations, or some other basis for determination.

Pension obligation - The portion of the actuarial present value of total projected benefits estimated to be payable in the future as a result of employee service to date.

Pension trust fund - A trust fund used to account for the assets accumulated by a pension plan. Pension trust funds, like nonexpendable trust funds, are accounted for on an accrual basis.

Per capita debt - The amount of a government's debt divided by its population.

Performance auditing - A systematic process of objectively obtaining and evaluating evidence regarding the performance of an organization, program, function, or activity in terms of its economy and efficiency of operations and its effectiveness in achieving desired results.

Performance budget - A budget that focuses on measurable units of efforts and accomplishments and associates dollar expenditures directly with anticipated units of outputs or outcomes.

Permanently restricted net assets - Endowments of which the principal must permanently remain intact. Only the income is available for expenditure. In the context of not-for-profit financial statements, one of the three main categories into which resources must be classified.

PERS - See *Public Employee Retirement System*.

Plant fund - A fund, generally maintained by colleges and universities and other not-for-profit organizations, to account for fixed assets and the resources set aside to acquire or replace fixed assets. As used by colleges and universities, plants funds may be of four types: unexpended plant fund, renewal and replacement fund, retirement of indebtedness fund, and investment in plant fund.

Pledge - A promise by a donor to make a donation of cash or assets in the future.

Present value - The amount that a buyer is willing to pay for one or a series of payments to be received in the future. Computed by discounting the future cash flows at an appropriate rate of interest and for an appropriate period of time.

Primary government - Per GASB Statement No. 14, *The Financial Reporting Entity*, a state government, a general purpose local government, such as a municipality or a county, or a special purpose government, such as a school district, that has a separately elected governing body, is legally separate from other primary governments, and is fiscally independent of other governments.

Privatization - See *Contracting out*.

Pro-forma statements - Projected financial statements of an organization for future periods.

Program - A series of related activities intended to fulfill a common objective.

Program audit - An audit to determine the extent to which an organization is achieving desired results or benefits and whether the entity has complied with significant laws and regulations applicable to its programs. See also *Performance auditing*.

Program budget - A budget in which resources and results are identified with programs rather than traditional organizational units. See also *Performance budget*.

Proprietary accounts - In the context of federal accounting, the accounts that provide the information necessary to prepare financial statements based on FASAB standards rather than to demonstrate budgetary compliance.

Propriety fund - An income determination fund that is used to account for a government's business-type activities; Enterprise, and internal service funds that are accounted for on a business-type basis.

Public Employee Retirement System (PERS) - A pension plan maintained for government employees.

Purchases method - A method of accounting for inventories and prepaid costs, such as rent, in which goods or services are recorded as expenses or expenditures when purchased, rather than when consumed. Differentiated from the consumption method.

Q–R

Qualified opinion - An audit opinion stating that "except for" the effect of the matter to which the qualification relates, the financial statements present fairly the financial position, results of operations and (when applicable), changes in financial position in conformity with GAAP. Generally expressed when auditors cannot obtain adequate information to express an unqualified opinion, there are significant uncertainties as to the value of assets or liabilities, or there are material departures from generally accepted accounting principles.

Quasi-endowment fund - A fund maintained to account for assets to be retained and invested as if they were contractually required endowments—for example, when an entity elects to set aside resources with the provision that the earnings (and only the earnings) from investments acquired with the resources are to be used for a specified purpose.

Quasi-external transactions - Interfund transactions that would be treated as revenues, expenditures, or expenses if they involved organizations external to the government unit (e.g., payments in lieu of taxes from an enterprise fund to the general fund; internal service fund billings to departments; routine employer contributions to a pension trust fund, and routine service charges for inspection, engineering, utilities or similar services). These transactions should be accounted for as revenues, expenditures, or expenses in the funds involved.

Redemption value - In the context of investment pools and mutual funds, the amount that the pool or fund will pay per share to an investor electing to withdraw its funds. Generally based on the current market value of the underlying securities.

Refinance - To replace existing debt with new debt, generally to take advantage of lower interest rates, or to shorten or lengthen the debt payout period.

Refundings - See *Bond refunding*.

Related organization - Per GASB Statement No. 14, *The Financial Reporting Entity*, an entity that satisfies the criteria of financial accountability, but not other necessary criteria and therefore does not qualify as a component unit.

Relevant range - The range of output that is relevant for the particular decision at hand. The span of output in which the behavior of fixed and variable costs is assumed to remain constant.

Renewal and replacement fund - A plant fund used to account for resources set aside to restore and replace existing buildings, equipment, and other fixed assets.

Replacement cost - The cost of acquiring or constructing an asset today that is identical to or has the same service potential as an asset already owned. An indicator of an asset's current value.

Reporting entity - The organizational unit covered by a set of financial statements. In government, the oversight unit and all of its component units, if any, that are combined in the financial statements per the requirements of GASB Statement No. 14, *The Financial Reporting Entity*, or FASAB Concepts Statement No. 2, *Entity and Display*.

Repurchase agreement ("Repo") - An investment instrument in which an investor (buyer-lender) transfers cash to a broker-dealer or financial institution (seller-borrower). The broker-dealer or financial institution transfers securities to the investor and promises to repay the cash plus interest in exchange for the same securities or for different securities. Contrast with a reverse repurchase agreement.

Required supplementary information - Statements, schedules, statistical data, or other information not included in, but required to supplement, the general purpose financial statements.

Reserved fund balance - That portion of fund balance that either represents resources that are not of a type that can be appropriated (e.g., reserves for inventory) or that are legally segregated for a specific future use (reserves for encumbrances).

Residual equity transfers - Nonrecurring or nonroutine transfers of equity between funds (e.g., the contribution of capital by the general fund to an enterprise fund or internal service fund, and the subsequent return of all or part of such contributions to the general fund).

Restricted grants - Payments intended for specified purposes, projects, or activities.

Retained earnings - An equity account reflecting the accumulated earnings of a government's enterprise or internal service fund or the accumulated excess of revenues over expenses of a not-for-profit organization.

Retirement of indebtedness fund - A fund maintained by colleges and universities and other not-for-profits that is comparable to a debt service fund and used to account for resources set aside for the retirement of indebtedness.

Revenue anticipation notes (RANS) - Short-term notes, issued in anticipation of the collection of revenues, that will not be converted into long-term instruments.

Revenue debt - Bonds and other obligations whose principal and interest are payable exclusively from earnings of a specific enterprise, such as an electric utility, toll road, or dormitory, and are thereby not backed by the full faith and credit of the issuer. Contrasted with general obligation debt.

Reverse repurchase agreement ("Reverse repo") - A borrowing instrument by which a borrower (seller) receives cash from a broker-dealer or financial institution (buyer-lender); in exchange the borrower (seller) transfers securities to the broker-dealer or financial institution and promises to repay the cash plus interest in exchange for the same or different securities. Contrast with a repurchase agreement.

Revolving funds - Funds used to account for business-type enterprises; See also *Expendable funds*.

S

Schedule of Expenditures of Federal Awards - A listing made by an organization of total expenditures under each federal program from which it receives funding.

SEA - See *Service efforts and accomplishments indicators*.

Self-insurance - The retention of a risk by an entity, as opposed to the transfer of the risk to an independent third party through the purchase of an insurance policy. It is sometimes, though not necessarily, accompanied by the designation of assets to fund possible losses.

Serial bonds - Bonds that mature in a series of installments at future dates—e.g., a portion of a bond issue matures in five years, a portion in six, a portion in seven, and so on.

Service assessments - Special assessments for operating activities, such as street cleaning or fire protection, as opposed to fixed assets and infrastructure

Service efforts and accomplishments (SEA) indicators - Measures of an entity's inputs, outputs, outcomes, and efficiency in carrying out its activities.

Shared revenues - Revenues levied by one government, such as a state, but shared on a predetermined basis with other governments, such as cities.

Short-term debt - Obligations that are expected to be paid within one year or the entity's operating cycle.

Single audit - An audit by a single audit organization intended to meet the needs of more than one regulatory agency or funds provider; an audit performed in accordance with the Single Audit Act and supporting Office of Management and Budget (OMB) circulars.

Sinking fund - See *Debt service fund*.

Special assessment - A compulsory levy on certain properties to defray all or part of the cost of a specific capital improvement or service deemed to benefit primarily those properties or their owners.

Special assessment bonds - Bonds payable from the proceeds of special assessments.

Special revenue fund - A fund used to account for the proceeds of specific revenue sources that are legally restricted to expenditure for specific purposes.

Statement of activities - An operating statement; a statement of revenues and expenditures (or expenses) and tranfers.

Statement of cash flows - The statement that provides information about the cash inflows (receipts) and outflows (payments) of an entity during a period of time.

Statement of changes in equity - The financial statement that reconciles the equity balances of an entity at the beginning and end of an accounting period and thereby links the operating statement to the balance sheet.

Statement of financial position - A balance sheet.

Statement of budgetary resources - In federal accounting, an operating statement prepared on a budgetary basis.

Statement of changes in net position - In federal accounting, a statement summarizing all agency transactions other than those reported in the statement of net cost.

Statement of custodial activities - In federal accounting, a statement showing resources collected and disbursed. Required only of agencies such as the Internal Revenue Service and Customs Service, that collect funds to be turned over to the Treasury or other agencies.

Statement of financing - In federal accounting, a statement that reconciles the statement of budgetary resources to the statement of net cost.

Statement of net cost - In federal accounting, an operating statement that shows an agency's operating costs and revenues and highlights the net costs that must be paid from taxes or other financing sources.

Statement of revenues and expenditures - The operating statement of a governmental fund that presents increases (revenues and other financing sources) and decreases (expenditures and other financing uses) in net current financial resources.

Stewardship land - In federal accounting, land that the federal government owns but does not use to produce goods or services. Includes mainly national parks and forests and undeveloped acreage.

Sunk costs - Costs that have already been incurred and cannot be recovered.

Suspense account - An account carrying charges or credits temporarily pending the determination of the proper account or accounts to which they are to be posted.

T–U–V

Tangible asset - An asset used in the normal operations of an organization that can be physically seen.

Tap fees - Fees charged by a governmental utility to new customers to hook up to its system.

Tax anticipation notes (TANs) - Short-term notes, not expected to be converted into long-term debts, issued in anticipation of future collection of taxes.

Taxpayer-assessed taxes - Taxes, such as sales and income taxes determined by parties other than the government. Distinguished from government-assessed taxes, such as property taxes.

Temporarily restricted net assets - Resources that must be used either for a specified purpose or when specified events have occurred. In the context of not-for-profit financial statements, one of the three main categories into which resources must be classified.

Term bonds - Bonds that mature in one lump sum at a specified future date.

Term endowment - An endowment (trust) in which the principal may be expended after a specified number of years.

Trustee - A party that administers property for a beneficiary.

Trust funds - Funds used to account for assets over which the entity acts as a trustee or that must be invested and the income only, not the principal, may be expended.

Unconditional promise - A pledge or promise to give an asset or provide a service in the future that is not dependent on a certain event occurring.

Unexpended plant fund - A plant fund used by colleges, universities, and other not-for-profits to account for resources set aside for the acquisition of plant and equipment.

Unified federal budget - The budget that encompasses all major types of federal funds and is intended to capture the impact of all federal activities on the national economy.

Uniform Administrative Requirements for Grants and Cooperative Agreements to State and Local Governments (the Common Rule,) - A detailed compendium of administrative rules and regulations that supplements the Single Audit Act and related circulars.

Unrestricted grants - Grants that are unrestricted as to purpose, project, or activity.

Unrestricted net assets - Assets that are not restricted as to when and how they can be used. In the context of not-

for-profit financial statements, one of the three main categories into which resources must be classified.

Unqualified opinion - An auditor's opinion stating that the financial statements present fairly the financial position, results of operations and (when applicable) changes in financial position in conformity with GAAP.

User charge - A charge for the use of a service, such as for parking or trash collections, as opposed to a tax that is unrelated to services received.

Variable costs - Costs that change in direct proportion to volume.

Vested benefit - A benefit for which an employer has an obligation to make payment even if an employee is terminated. Thus, the benefit is not contingent on an employee's future service.

Voluntary health and welfare organization - A not-for-profit organization formed to provide services to a community, rather than to its own members. Examples include the United Way, Boy and Girl Scouts, the American Heart Association, and most social service agencies.

W–X–Y–Z

Yellow Book - See *Government Accounting Standards (Standards for Audit of Government Organizations, Programs, Activities, and Functions)*

Yield rate - The actual (effective), as distinguished from the nominal (coupon or stated), rate of return on a bond or other investment.

Zero-base budgeting - A form of program budgeting characterized by its requirement that all activities, both existing and proposed, be evaluated and ranked.

Zero coupon bond - A bond with a stated annual interest rate of zero. It provides a return to investors in that it is issued at a price considerably less than the bond's face value and sufficiently low so that the difference between face value and issue price will equal a return comparable to that on conventional bonds.

VALUE TABLES

....

TABLE I
Future Value of 1 (Future Value of a Single Sum)
$\text{FVF}_{n,i} = (1 + i)^n$

(n) Periods	2%	2½%	3%	4%	5%	6%
1	1.02000	1.02500	1.03000	1.04000	1.05000	1.06000
2	1.04040	1.05063	1.06090	1.08160	1.10250	1.12360
3	1.06121	1.07689	1.09273	1.12486	1.15763	1.19102
4	1.08243	1.10381	1.12551	1.16986	1.21551	1.26248
5	1.10408	1.13141	1.15927	1.21665	1.27628	1.33823
6	1.12616	1.15969	1.19405	1.26532	1.34010	1.41852
7	1.14869	1.18869	1.22987	1.31593	1.40710	1.50363
8	1.17166	1.21840	1.26677	1.36857	1.47746	1.59385
9	1.19509	1.24886	1.30477	1.42331	1.55133	1.68948
10	1.21899	1.28008	1.34392	1.48024	1.62889	1.79085
11	1.24337	1.31209	1.38423	1.53945	1.71034	1.89830
12	1.26824	1.34489	1.42576	1.60103	1.79586	2.01220
13	1.29361	1.37851	1.46853	1.66507	1.88565	2.13293
14	1.31948	1.41297	1.51259	1.73168	1.97993	2.26090
15	1.34587	1.44830	1.55797	1.80094	2.07893	2.39656
16	1.37279	1.48451	1.60471	1.87298	2.18287	2.54035
17	1.40024	1.52162	1.65285	1.94790	2.29202	2.69277
18	1.42825	1.55966	1.70243	2.02582	2.40662	2.85434
19	1.45681	1.59865	1.75351	2.10685	2.52695	3.02560
20	1.48595	1.63862	1.80611	2.19112	2.65330	3.20714
21	1.51567	1.67958	1.86029	2.27877	2.78596	3.39956
22	1.54598	1.72157	1.91610	2.36992	2.92526	3.60354
23	1.57690	1.76461	1.97359	2.46472	3.07152	3.81975
24	1.60844	1.80873	2.03279	2.56330	3.22510	4.04893
25	1.64061	1.85394	2.09378	2.66584	3.38635	4.29187
26	1.67342	1.90029	2.15659	2.77247	3.55567	4.54938
27	1.70689	1.94780	2.22129	2.88337	3.73346	4.82235
28	1.74102	1.99650	2.28793	2.99870	3.92013	5.11169
29	1.77584	2.04641	2.35657	3.11865	4.11614	5.41839
30	1.81136	2.09757	2.42726	3.24340	4.32194	5.74349
31	1.84759	2.15001	2.50008	3.37313	4.53804	6.08810
32	1.88454	2.20376	2.57508	3.50806	4.76494	6.45339
33	1.92223	2.25885	2.65234	3.64838	5.00319	6.84059
34	1.96068	2.31532	2.73191	3.79432	5.25335	7.25103
35	1.99989	2.37321	2.81386	3.94609	5.51602	7.68609
36	2.03989	2.43254	2.89828	4.10393	5.79182	8.14725
37	2.08069	2.49335	2.98523	4.26809	6.08141	8.63609
38	2.12230	2.55568	3.07478	4.43881	6.38548	9.15425
39	2.16474	2.61957	3.16703	4.61637	6.70475	9.70351
40	2.20804	2.68506	3.26204	4.80102	7.03999	10.28572

TABLE I (Continued)
Future Value of 1 (Future Value of a Single Sum)

$$FVF_{n,i} = (1 + i)^n$$

8%	9%	10%	11%	12%	15%	(n) Periods
1.08000	1.09000	1.10000	1.11000	1.12000	1.15000	1
1.16640	1.18810	1.21000	1.23210	1.25440	1.32250	2
1.25971	1.29503	1.33100	1.36763	1.40493	1.52088	3
1.36049	1.41158	1.46410	1.51807	1.57352	1.74901	4
1.46933	1.53862	1.61051	1.68506	1.76234	2.01136	5
1.58687	1.67710	1.77156	1.87041	1.97382	2.31306	6
1.71382	1.82804	1.94872	2.07616	2.21068	2.66002	7
1.85093	1.99256	2.14359	2.30454	2.47596	3.05902	8
1.99900	2.17189	2.35795	2.55803	2.77308	3.51788	9
2.15892	2.36736	2.59374	2.83942	3.10585	4.04556	10
2.33164	2.58043	2.85312	3.15176	3.47855	4.65239	11
2.51817	2.81267	3.13843	3.49845	3.89598	5.35025	12
2.71962	3.06581	3.45227	3.88328	4.36349	6.15279	13
2.93719	3.34173	3.79750	4.31044	4.88711	7.07571	14
3.17217	3.64248	4.17725	4.78459	5.47357	8.13706	15
3.42594	3.97031	4.59497	5.31089	6.13039	9.35762	16
3.70002	4.32763	5.05447	5.89509	6.86604	10.76126	17
3.99602	4.71712	5.55992	6.54355	7.68997	12.37545	18
4.31570	5.14166	6.11591	7.26334	8.61276	14.23177	19
4.66096	5.60441	6.72750	8.06231	9.64629	16.36654	20
5.03383	6.10881	7.40025	8.94917	10.80385	18.82152	21
5.43654	6.65860	8.14028	9.93357	12.10031	21.64475	22
5.87146	7.25787	8.95430	11.02627	13.55235	24.89146	23
6.34118	7.91108	9.84973	12.23916	15.17863	28.62518	24
6.84847	8.62308	10.83471	13.58546	17.00000	32.91895	25
7.39635	9.39916	11.91818	15.07986	19.04007	37.85680	26
7.98806	10.24508	13.10999	16.73865	21.32488	43.53532	27
8.62711	11.16714	14.42099	18.57990	23.88387	50.06561	28
9.31727	12.17218	15.86309	20.62369	26.74993	57.57545	29
10.06266	13.26768	17.44940	22.89230	29.95992	66.21177	30
10.86767	14.46177	19.19434	25.41045	33.55511	76.14354	31
11.73708	15.76333	21.11378	28.20560	37.58173	87.56507	32
12.67605	17.18203	23.22515	31.30821	42.09153	100.69983	33
13.69013	18.72841	25.54767	34.75212	47.14252	115.80480	34
14.78534	20.41397	28.10244	38.57485	52.79962	133.17552	35
15.96817	22.25123	30.91268	42.81808	59.13557	153.15185	36
17.24563	24.25384	34.00395	47.52807	66.23184	176.12463	37
18.62528	26.43668	37.40434	52.75616	74.17966	202.54332	38
20.11530	28.81598	41.14479	58.55934	83.08122	232.92482	39
21.72452	31.40942	45.25926	65.00087	93.05097	267.86355	40

TABLE II
Present Value of 1 (Present Value of a Single Sum)

$$\text{PVF}_{n,i} = \frac{1}{(1 + i)^n} = (1 + i)^{-n}$$

(n) Periods	2%	2½%	3%	4%	5%	6%
1	.98039	.97561	.97087	.96154	.95238	.94340
2	.96117	.95181	.94260	.92456	.90703	.89000
3	.94232	.92860	.91514	.88900	.86384	.83962
4	.92385	.90595	.88849	.85480	.82270	.79209
5	.90573	.88385	.86261	.82193	.78353	.74726
6	.88797	.86230	.83748	.79031	.74622	.70496
7	.87056	.84127	.81309	.75992	.71068	.66506
8	.85349	.82075	.78941	.73069	.67684	.62741
9	.83676	.80073	.76642	.70259	.64461	.59190
10	.82035	.78120	.74409	.67556	.61391	.55839
11	.80426	.76214	.72242	.64958	.58468	.52679
12	.78849	.74356	.70138	.62460	.55684	.49697
13	.77303	.72542	.68095	.60057	.53032	.46884
14	.75788	.70773	.66112	.57748	.50507	.44230
15	.74301	.69047	.64186	.55526	.48102	.41727
16	.72845	.67362	.62317	.53391	.45811	.39365
17	.71416	.65720	.60502	.51337	.43630	.37136
18	.70016	.64117	.58739	.49363	.41552	.35034
19	.68643	.62553	.57029	.47464	.39573	.33051
20	.67297	.61027	.55368	.45639	.37689	.31180
21	.65978	.59539	.53755	.43883	.35894	.29416
22	.64684	.58086	.52189	.42196	.34185	.27751
23	.63416	.56670	.50669	.40573	.32557	.26180
24	.62172	.55288	.49193	.39012	.31007	.24698
25	.60953	.53939	.47761	.37512	.29530	.23300
26	.59758	.52623	.46369	.36069	.28124	.21981
27	.58586	.51340	.45019	.34682	.26785	.20737
28	.57437	.50088	.43708	.33348	.25509	.19563
29	.56311	.48866	.42435	.32065	.24295	.18456
30	.55207	.47674	.41199	.30832	.23138	.17411
31	.54125	.46511	.39999	.29646	.22036	.16425
32	.53063	.45377	.38834	.28506	.20987	.15496
33	.52023	.44270	.37703	.27409	.19987	.14619
34	.51003	.43191	.36604	.26355	.19035	.13791
35	.50003	.42137	.35538	.25342	.18129	.13011
36	.49022	.41109	.34503	.24367	.17266	.12274
37	.48061	.40107	.33498	.23430	.16444	.11579
38	.47119	.39128	.32523	.22529	.15661	.10924
39	.46195	.38174	.31575	.21662	.15661	.10306
40	.45289	.37243	.30656	.20829	.14205	.09722

TABLE II (Continued)
Present Value of 1 (Present Value of a Single Sum)

$$PVF_{n,i} = \frac{1}{(1 + i)^n} = (1 + i)^{-n}$$

8%	9%	10%	11%	12%	15%	(n) Periods
.92593	.91743	.90909	.90090	.89286	.86957	1
.85734	.84168	.82645	.81162	.79719	.75614	2
.79383	.77218	.75132	.73119	.71178	.65752	3
.73503	.70843	.68301	.65873	.63552	.57175	4
.68058	.64993	.62092	.59345	.56743	.49718	5
.63017	.59627	.56447	.53464	.50663	.43233	6
.58349	.54703	.51316	.48166	.45235	.37594	7
.54027	.50187	.46651	.43393	.40388	.32690	8
.50025	.46043	.42410	.39092	.36061	.28426	9
.46319	.42241	.38554	.35218	.32197	.24719	10
.42888	.38753	.35049	.31728	.28748	.21494	11
.39711	.35554	.31863	.28584	.25668	.18691	12
.36770	.32618	.28966	.25751	.22917	.16253	13
.34046	.29925	.26333	.23199	.20462	.14133	14
.31524	.27454	.23939	.20900	.18270	.12289	15
.29189	.25187	.21763	.18829	.16312	.10687	16
.27027	.23107	.19785	.16963	.14564	.09293	17
.25025	.21199	.17986	.15282	.13004	.08081	18
.23171	.19449	.16351	.13768	.11611	.07027	19
.21455	.17843	.14864	.12403	.10367	.06110	20
.19866	.16370	.13513	.11174	.09256	.05313	21
.18394	.15018	.12285	.10067	.08264	.04620	22
.17032	.13778	.11168	.09069	.07379	.04017	23
.15770	.12641	.10153	.08170	.06588	.03493	24
.14602	.11597	.09230	.07361	.05882	.03038	25
.13520	.10639	.08391	.06631	.05252	.02642	26
.12519	.09761	.07628	.05974	.04689	.02297	27
.11591	.08955	.06934	.05382	.04187	.01997	28
.10733	.08216	.06304	.04849	.03738	.01737	29
.09938	.07537	.05731	.04368	.03338	.01510	30
.09202	.06915	.05210	.03935	.02980	.01313	31
.08520	.06344	.04736	.03545	.02661	.01142	32
.07889	.05820	.04306	.03194	.02376	.00993	33
.07305	.05340	.03914	.02878	.02121	.00864	34
.06763	.04899	.03558	.02592	.01894	.00751	35
.06262	.04494	.03235	.02335	.01691	.00653	36
.05799	.04123	.02941	.02104	.01510	.00568	37
.05369	.03783	.02674	.01896	.01348	.00494	38
.04971	.03470	.02430	.01708	.01204	.00429	39
.04603	.03184	.02210	.01538	.01075	.00373	40

TABLE III
Future Value of an Ordinary Annuity of 1

$$FVF\text{-}OA_{n,i} = \frac{(1 + i)^n - 1}{i}$$

(n) Periods	2%	2½%	3%	4%	5%	6%
1	1.00000	1.00000	1.00000	1.00000	1.00000	1.00000
2	2.02000	2.02500	2.03000	2.04000	2.05000	2.06000
3	3.06040	3.07563	3.09090	3.12160	3.15250	3.18360
4	4.12161	4.15252	4.18363	4.24646	4.31013	4.37462
5	5.20404	5.25633	5.30914	5.41632	5.52563	5.63709
6	6.30812	6.38774	6.46841	6.63298	6.80191	6.97532
7	7.43428	7.54743	7.66246	7.89829	8.14201	8.39384
8	8.58297	8.73612	8.89234	9.21423	9.54911	9.89747
9	9.75463	9.95452	10.15911	10.58280	10.02656	11.49132
10	10.94972	11.20338	11.46338	12.00611	12.57789	13.18079
11	12.16872	12.48347	12.80780	13.48635	14.20679	14.97164
12	13.41209	13.79555	14.19203	15.02581	15.91713	16.86994
13	14.68033	15.14044	15.61779	16.62684	17.71298	18.88214
14	15.97394	16.51895	17.08632	18.29191	19.59863	21.01507
15	17.29342	17.93193	18.59891	20.02359	21.57856	23.27597
16	18.63929	19.38022	20.15688	21.82453	23.65749	25.67253
17	20.01207	20.86473	21.76159	23.69751	25.84037	28.21288
18	21.41231	22.38635	23.41444	25.64541	28.13238	30.90565
19	22.84056	23.94601	25.11687	27.67123	30.53900	33.75999
20	24.29737	25.54466	26.87037	29.77808	33.06595	36.78559
21	25.78332	27.18327	28.67649	31.96920	35.71925	39.99273
22	27.29898	28.86286	30.53678	34.24797	38.50521	43.39229
23	28.84496	30.58443	32.45288	36.61789	41.43048	46.99583
24	30.42186	32.34904	34.42647	39.08260	44.50200	50.81558
25	32.03030	34.15776	36.45926	41.64591	47.72710	54.86451
26	33.67091	36.01171	38.55304	44.31174	51.11345	59.15638
27	35.34432	37.91200	40.70963	47.08421	54.66913	63.70577
28	37.05121	39.85980	42.93092	49.96758	58.40258	68.52811
29	38.79223	41.85630	45.21885	52.96629	62.32271	73.63980
30	40.56808	43.90270	47.57542	56.08494	66.43885	79.05819
31	42.37944	46.00027	50.00268	59.32834	70.76079	84.80168
32	44.22703	48.15028	52.50276	62.70147	75.29883	90.88978
33	46.11157	50.35403	55.07784	66.20953	80.06377	97.34316
34	48.03380	52.61289	57.73018	69.85791	85.06696	104.18376
35	49.99448	54.92821	60.46208	73.65222	90.32031	111.43478
36	51.99437	57.30141	63.27594	77.59831	95.53632	119.12087
37	54.03425	59.73395	66.17422	81.70225	101.62814	127.26812
38	56.11494	62.22730	69.15945	85.97034	107.70955	135.90421
39	58.23724	64.78298	72.23423	90.40915	114.09502	145.05846
40	60.40198	67.40255	75.40126	95.02552	120.79977	154.76197

TABLE III (Continued)
Future Value of an Ordinary Annuity of 1

$$\text{FVF-OA}_{n,i} = \frac{(1 + i)^n - 1}{i}$$

8%	9%	10%	11%	12%	15%	(n) Periods
1.00000	1.00000	1.00000	1.00000	1.00000	1.00000	1
2.08000	2.09000	2.10000	2.11000	2.12000	2.15000	2
3.24640	3.27810	3.31000	3.34210	3.37440	3.47250	3
4.50611	4.57313	4.64100	4.70973	4.77933	4.99338	4
5.86660	5.98471	6.10510	6.22780	6.35285	6.74238	5
7.33592	7.52334	7.71561	7.91286	8.11519	8.75374	6
8.92280	9.20044	9.48717	9.78327	10.08901	11.06680	7
10.63663	11.02847	11.43589	11.85943	12.29969	13.72682	8
12.48756	13.02104	13.57948	14.16397	14.77566	16.78584	9
14.48656	15.19293	15.93743	16.72201	17.54874	20.30372	10
16.64549	17.56029	18.53117	19.56143	20.65458	24.34928	11
18.97713	20.14072	21.38428	22.71319	24.13313	29.00167	12
21.49530	22.95339	24.52271	26.21164	28.02911	34.35192	13
24.21492	26.01919	27.97498	30.09492	32.39260	40.50471	14
27.15211	29.36092	31.77248	34.40536	37.27972	47.58041	15
30.32428	33.00340	35.94973	39.18995	42.75328	55.71747	16
33.75023	36.97371	40.54470	44.50084	48.88367	65.07509	17
37.45024	41.30134	45.59917	50.39593	55.74972	75.83636	18
41.44026	46.01846	51.15909	56.93949	63.43968	88.21181	19
45.76196	51.16012	57.27500	64.20283	72.05244	102.44358	20
50.42292	56.76453	64.00250	72.26514	81.69874	118.81012	21
55.45676	62.87334	71.40275	81.21431	92.50258	137.63164	22
60.89330	69.53194	79.54302	91.14788	104.60289	159.27638	23
66.76476	76.78981	88.49733	102.17415	118.15524	184.16784	24
73.10594	84.70090	98.34706	114.41331	133.33387	212.79302	25
79.95442	93.32398	109.18177	127.99877	150.33393	245.71197	26
87.35077	102.72314	121.09994	143.07864	169.37401	283.56877	27
95.33883	112.96822	134.20994	159.81729	190.37401	327.10408	28
103.96594	124.13536	148.63093	178.39719	214.58275	377.16969	29
113.28321	136.30754	164.49402	199.02088	241.33268	434.74515	30
123.34587	149.57522	181.94343	221.9137	271.29261	500.95692	31
134.21354	164.03699	201.13777	247.32362	304.84772	577.10046	32
145.95062	179.80032	222.25154	275.52922	342.42945	644.66553	33
158.62667	196.98234	245.47670	306.83744	384.52098	765.36535	34
172.31680	215.71076	271.02437	341.58955	431.66350	881.17016	35
187.10215	236.12472	299.12681	380.16441	484.46312	1014.34568	36
203.07032	258.37595	330.03949	422.98249	543.59869	1167.49753	37
220.31595	282.62978	364.04343	470.51056	609.83053	1343.62216	38
238.94122	309.06646	401.44778	523.26673	684.01020	1546.16549	39
259.05652	337.88245	442.59256	581.82607	767.09142	1779.09031	40

TABLE IV
Present Value of an Ordinary Annuity of 1

$$\text{PVF-OA}_{n,i} = \frac{1 - \dfrac{1}{(1 + i)^n}}{i}$$

(n) Periods	2%	2½%	3%	4%	5%	6%
1	.98039	.97561	.97087	.96154	.95238	.94340
2	1.94156	1.92742	1.91347	1.88609	1.85941	1.83339
3	2.88388	2.85602	2.82861	2.77509	2.72325	2.67301
4	3.80773	3.76197	3.71710	3.62990	3.54595	3.46511
5	4.71346	4.64583	4.57971	4.45182	4.32948	4.21236
6	5.60143	5.50813	5.41719	5.24214	5.07569	4.91732
7	6.47199	6.34939	6.23028	6.00205	5.78637	5.58238
8	7.32548	7.17014	7.01969	6.73274	6.46321	6.20979
9	8.16224	7.97087	7.78611	7.43533	7.10782	6.80169
10	8.98259	8.75206	8.53020	8.11090	7.72173	7.36009
11	9.78685	9.51421	9.25262	8.76048	8.30641	7.88687
12	10.57534	10.25776	9.95400	9.38507	8.86325	8.38384
13	11.34837	10.98319	10.63496	9.98565	9.39357	8.85268
14	12.10625	11.69091	11.29607	10.56312	9.89864	9.29498
15	12.84926	12.38138	11.93794	11.11839	10.379966	9.71225
16	13.57771	13.05500	12.56110	11.65230	10.83777	10.10590
17	14.29187	13.71220	13.16612	12.16567	11.27407	10.47726
18	14.99203	14.35336	13.75351	12.65930	11.68959	10.82760
19	15.67846	14.97889	14.32380	13.13394	12.08532	11.15812
20	16.35143	15.58916	14.87747	13.59033	12.46221	11.46992
21	17.01121	16.18455	15.41502	14.02916	12.82115	11.76408
22	17.65805	16.76541	15.93692	14.45112	13.16300	12.04158
23	18.29220	17.33211	16.44361	14.85684	13.48857	12.30338
24	18.91393	17.88499	16.93554	15.24696	13.79864	12.55036
25	19.52346	18.42438	17.41315	15.62208	14.09394	12.78336
26	20.12104	18.95061	17.87684	15.98277	14.37519	13.00317
27	20.70690	19.46401	18.32703	16.32959	14.64303	13.21053
28	21.28127	19.96489	18.76411	16.66306	14.89813	13.40618
29	21.84438	20.45355	19.18845	16.98371	15.14107	13.59072
30	22.39646	20.93029	19.60044	17.29203	15.37245	13.76483
31	22.93770	21.39541	20.00043	17.58849	15.59281	13.92909
32	23.46833	21.84918	20.38877	17.87355	15.80268	14.08404
33	23.98856	22.29188	20.76579	18.14765	16.00255	14.23023
34	24.49859	22.72379	21.13184	18.41120	16.19290	14.36814
35	24.99862	23.14516	21.48722	18.66461	16.37419	14.49825
36	25.48884	23.55625	21.83225	18.90828	16.54685	14.62099
37	25.96945	23.95732	22.16724	19.14258	16.71129	14.73678
38	26.44064	24.34860	22.49246	19.36786	16.86789	14.84602
39	26.90259	24.73034	22.80822	19.58448	17.01704	14.94907
40	27.35548	25.10278	23.11477	19.79277	17.15909	15.04630

TABLE IV (Continued)
Present Value of an Ordinary Annuity of 1

$$PVF\text{-}OA_{n,i} = \frac{1 - \dfrac{1}{(1 + i)^n}}{i}$$

8%	9%	10%	11%	12%	15%	(n) Periods
.92593	.91743	.90909	.90090	.89286	.86957	1
1.78326	1.75911	1.73554	1.71252	1.69005	1.62571	2
2.57710	2.53130	2.48685	2.44371	2.40183	2.28323	3
3.31213	3.23972	3.16986	3.10245	3.03735	2.85498	4
3.99271	3.88965	3.79079	3.69590	3.60478	3.35216	5
4.62288	4.48592	4.35526	4.23054	4.11141	3.78448	6
5.20637	5.03295	4.86842	4.71220	4.56376	4.16042	7
5.74664	5.53482	5.33493	5.14612	4.96764	4.48732	8
6.24689	5.99525	5.75902	5.53705	5.32825	4.77158	9
6.71008	6.41766	6.14457	5.88923	5.65022	5.01877	10
7.13896	6.80519	6.49506	6.20652	5.93770	5.23371	11
7.53608	7.16073	6.81369	6.49236	6.19437	5.42962	12
7.90378	7.48690	7.10336	6.74987	6.42355	5.58315	13
8.24424	7.78615	7.36669	6.98187	6.62817	5.72448	14
8.55948	8.06069	7.60608	7.19087	6.81086	5.84737	15
8.85137	8.31256	7.82371	7.37916	6.97399	5.95424	16
9.12164	8.54363	8.02155	7.54879	7.11963	6.04716	17
9.37189	8.75563	8.20141	7.70162	7.24967	6.12797	18
9.60360	8.95012	8.36492	7.83929	7.36578	6.19823	19
9.81815	9.12855	8.51356	7.96333	7.46944	6.25933	20
10.01680	9.29224	8.64869	8.07507	7.56200	6.31246	21
10.20074	9.44243	8.77154	8.17574	7.64465	6.35866	22
10.37106	9.58021	8.88322	8.26643	7.71843	6.39884	23
10.52876	9.70661	8.98474	8.34814	7.78432	6.43377	24
10.67478	9.82258	9.07704	8.42174	7.84314	6.46415	25
10.80998	9.92897	9.16095	8.48806	7.89566	6.49056	26
10.93516	10.02658	9.23722	8.54780	7.94255	6.51353	27
11.05108	10.11613	9.30657	8.60162	7.98442	6.53351	28
11.15841	10.19828	9.36961	8.65011	8.02181	6.55088	29
11.25778	10.27365	9.42691	8.69379	8.05518	6.56598	30
11.34980	10.34280	9.47901	8.73315	8.08499	6.57911	31
11.43500	10.40624	9.52638	8.76860	8.11159	6.59053	32
11.51389	10.46444	9.56943	8.80054	8.13535	6.60046	33
11.58693	10.51784	9.60858	8.82932	8.15656	6.60910	34
11.65457	10.56682	9.64416	8.85524	8.17550	6.61661	35
11.71719	10.61176	9.67651	8.87859	8.19241	6.62314	36
11.75518	10.65299	9.70592	8.89963	8.20751	6.62882	37
11.82887	10.69082	9.73265	8.91859	8.22099	6.63375	38
11.87858	10.72552	9.75697	8.93567	8.23303	6.63805	39
11.92461	10.75736	9.77905	8.95105	8.24378	6.64178	40

INDEX

PHOTO CREDITS